Collins

M000014977

# Collins
# Spanish
# Dictionary

**HarperCollins Publishers**
Westerhill Road
Bishopbriggs
Glasgow
G64 2QT
Great Britain

First Edition 2006

© HarperCollins Publishers 2006

ISBN-13   978-0-00-723142-3
ISBN-10   0-00-723142-3

www.collins.co.uk

A catalogue record for this book is
available from the British Library

Typeset by Wordcraft, Glasgow

Printed and bound in Italy by
Legoprint S.P.A.

**Acknowledgements**
We would like to thank those
authors and publishers who kindly
gave permission for copyright
material to be used in the Collins
Word Web. We would also like to
thank Times Newspapers Ltd for
providing valuable data.

GENERAL EDITOR
Michela Clari

CONTRIBUTORS
José Martín Galera
Wendy Lee
José María Ruiz Vaca
Cordelia Lilly

EDITORIAL COORDINATION
Joyce Littlejohn

SERIES EDITOR
Lorna Knight

# ÍNDICE

# CONTENTS

**MARCAS REGISTRADAS**
Las marcas que creemos que
constituyen marcas registradas
las denominamos como tales.
Sin embargo, no debe considerarse
que la presencia o la ausencia
de esta designación tenga que
ver con la situación legal de
ninguna marca.

**NOTE ON TRADEMARKS**
Words which we have reason
to believe constitute trademarks
have been designated as such.
However, neither the presence
nor the absence of such
designation should be regarded
as affecting the legal status of
any trademark.

William Collins' dream of knowledge for all began with the publication of his first book in 1819. A self-educated mill worker, he not only enriched millions of lives, but also founded a flourishing publishing house. Today, staying true to this spirit, Collins books are packed with inspiration, innovation, and practical expertise. They place you at the centre of a world of possibility and give you exactly what you need to explore it.

Language is the key to this exploration, and at the heart of Collins Dictionaries is language as it is really used. New words, phrases, and meanings spring up every day, and all of them are captured and analysed by the Collins Word Web. Constantly updated, and with over 2.5 billion entries, this living language resource is unique to our dictionaries.

Words are tools for life. And a Collins Dictionary makes them work for you.

**Collins. Do more.**

## INTRODUCCIÓN

Estamos muy satisfechos de que hayas decidido comprar este diccionario y esperamos que lo disfrutes y que te sirva de gran ayuda ya sea en el colegio, en el trabajo, en tus vacaciones o en casa.

## INTRODUCTION

We are delighted that you have decided to buy this Spanish dictionary and hope you will enjoy and benefit from using it at school, at home, on holiday or at work.

# ABREVIATURAS

# ABBREVIATIONS

| | | |
|---|---|---|
| abreviatura | *ab(b)r* | abbreviation |
| adjetivo, locución adjetiva | *adj* | adjective, adjectival phrase |
| administración | *Admin* | administration |
| adverbio, locución adverbial | *adv* | adverb, adverbial phrase |
| agricultura | *Agr* | agriculture |
| anatomía | *Anat* | anatomy |
| Argentina | *Arg* | Argentina |
| arquitectura | *Arq, Arch* | architecture |
| el automóvil | *Aut(o)* | the motor car and motoring |
| aviación, viajes aéreos | *Aviac, Aviat* | flying, air travel |
| biología | *Bio(l)* | biology |
| botánica, flores | *Bot* | botany |
| inglés británico | BRIT | British English |
| Centroamérica | CAM | Central America |
| química | *Chem* | chemistry |
| comercio, finanzas, banca | *Com(m)* | commerce, finance, banking |
| informática | *Comput* | computing |
| conjunción | *conj* | conjunction |
| construcción | *Constr* | building |
| compuesto | *cpd* | compound element |
| Cono Sur | CS | Southern Cone |
| cocina | *Culin* | cookery |
| economía | *Econ* | economics |
| eletricidad, electrónica | *Elec* | electricity, electronics |
| enseñanza, sistema escolar y universitario | *Escol* | schooling, schools and universities |
| España | ESP | Spain |
| especialmente | *esp* | especially |
| exclamación, interjección | *excl* | exclamation, interjection |
| femenino | *f* | feminine |
| lengua familiar (! vulgar) | *fam(!)* | colloquial usage (! particularly offensive) |
| ferrocarril | *Ferro* | railways |
| uso figurado | *fig* | figurative use |
| fotografía | *Foto* | photography |
| (verbo inglés) del cual la partícula es inseparable | *fus* | (phrasal verb) where the particle is inseparable |
| generalmente | *gen* | generally |
| geografía, geología | *Geo* | geography, geology |
| geometría | *Geom* | geometry |
| historia | *Hist* | history |
| uso familiar (! vulgar) | *inf(!)* | colloquial usage (! particularly offensive) |
| infinitivo | *infin* | infinitive |
| informática | *Inform* | computing |
| invariable | *inv* | invariable |
| irregular | *irreg* | irregular |
| lo jurídico | *Jur* | law |
| América Latina | LAM | Latin America |
| gramática, lingüística | *Ling* | grammar, linguistics |

| | | |
|---|---|---|
| masculino | *m* | masculine |
| matemáticas | *Mat(h)* | mathematics |
| masculino/femenino | *m/f* | masculine/feminine |
| medicina | *Med* | medicine |
| México | *MÉX, MEX* | Mexico |
| lo militar, ejército | *Mil* | military matters |
| música | *Mús, Mus* | music |
| substantivo, nombre | *n* | noun |
| navegación, náutica | *Náut, Naut* | sailing, navigation |
| sustantivo numérico | *num* | numeral noun |
| complemento | *obj* | (grammatical) object |
| | *o.s.* | oneself |
| peyorativo | *pey, pej* | derogatory, pejorative |
| fotografía | *Phot* | photography |
| fisiología | *Physiol* | physiology |
| plural | *pl* | plural |
| política | *Pol* | politics |
| participio de pasado | *pp* | past participle |
| preposición | *prep* | preposition |
| pronombre | *pron* | pronoun |
| psicología, psiquiatría | *Psico, Psych* | psychology, psychiatry |
| tiempo pasado | *pt* | past tense |
| química | *Quím* | chemistry |
| ferrocarril | *Rail* | railways |
| religión | *Rel* | religion |
| Río de la Plata | *RPL* | River Plate |
| | *sb* | somebody |
| Cono Sur | *SC* | Southern Cone |
| enseñanza, sistema escolar | *Scol* | schooling, schools |
| y universitario | | and universities |
| singular | *sg* | singular |
| España | *SP* | Spain |
| | *sth* | something |
| sujeto | *su(b)j* | (grammatical) subject |
| subjuntivo | *subjun* | subjunctive |
| tauromaquia | *Taur* | bullfighting |
| también | *tb* | also |
| técnica, tecnología | *Tec(h)* | technical term, technology |
| telecomunicaciones | *Telec, Tel* | telecommunications |
| imprenta, tipografía | *Tip, Typ* | typography, printing |
| televisión | *TV* | television |
| universidad | *Univ* | university |
| inglés norteamericano | *US* | American English |
| verbo | *vb* | verb |
| verbo intransitivo | *vi* | intransitive verb |
| verbo pronominal | *vr* | reflexive verb |
| verbo transitivo | *vt* | transitive verb |
| zoología | *Zool* | zoology |
| marca registrada | ® | registered trademark |
| indica un equivalente cultural | ≈ | introduces a cultural equivalent |

## SPANISH PRONUNCIATION

### VOWELS

| | | | |
|---|---|---|---|
| a | [ a ] | p**a**ta | not as long as *a* in f*a*r. When followed by a consonant in the same syllable (i.e. in a closed syllable), as in *a*mante, the *a* is short, as in b*a*t |
| e | [ e ] | m**e** | like *e* in th*ey*. In a closed syllable, as in g**e**nte, the *e* is short as in p**e**t |
| i | [ i ] | p**i**no | as in m**ea**n or mach**i**ne |
| o | [ o ] | l**o** | as in l**o**cal. In a closed syllable, as in c**o**ntrol, the *o* is short as in c**o**t |
| u | [ u ] | l**u**nes | as in r**u**le. It is silent after q, and in g**u**e, g**u**i, unless marked g**ü**e, g**ü**i e.g. antig**ü**edad, when it is pronounced like *w* in *w*olf |

### SEMIVOWELS

| | | | |
|---|---|---|---|
| i, y | [ j ] | b**i**en | pronounced like *y* in *y*es |
| | | h**i**elo | |
| | | **y**unta | |
| u | [ w ] | h**u**evo | unstressed *u* between consonant and vowel is pronounced like *w* in *w*ell. See notes on *u* above. |
| | | f**u**ento | |
| | | antig**ü**edad | |

### DIPHTHONGS

| | | | |
|---|---|---|---|
| ai, ay | [ ai ] | b**ai**le | as *i* in r*i*de |
| au | [ au ] | **au**to | as *ou* in sh*ou*t |
| ei, ey | [ ei ] | bu**ey** | as *ey* in gr*ey* |
| eu | [ eu ] | d**eu**da | both elements pronounced independently [e] + [u] |
| oi, oy | [ oi ] | h**oy** | as *oy* in t*oy* |

### CONSONANTS

| | | | |
|---|---|---|---|
| b | [b, β] | **b**oda | see notes on *v* below |
| | | **b**omba | |
| | | la**b**or | |
| c | [ k ] | **c**aja | *c* before *a, o, u* is pronounced as in *c*at |
| ce, ci | [θe, θi] | **c**ero | *c* before *e* or *i* is pronounced as in *th*in |
| | | **c**ielo | |
| ch | [ tʃ ] | **ch**iste | *ch* is pronounced as *ch* in *ch*air |
| d | [d, ð] | **d**anés | at the beginning of a phrase or after *l* or *n*, *d* is pronounced as in English. In any other position it is pronounced like *th* in *th*e |
| | | ciu**d**ad | |

| g | [g, ɣ] | gafas | g before a, o or u is pronounced as in |
| | | paga | gap, if at the beginning of a phrase |
| | | | or after n. In other positions the sound |
| | | | is softened |
| ge, gi | [xe, xi] | gente | g before e or i is pronounced similar |
| | | girar | to ch in Scottish loch |
| h | | haber | h is always silent in Spanish |
| j | [ x ] | jugar | j is pronounced similar to ch in |
| | | | Scottish loch |
| ll | [ ʎ ] | talle | ll is pronounced like the y in yet or the |
| | | | lli in million |
| ñ | [ ʃ ] | niño | ñ is pronounced like the ni in onion |
| q | [ k ] | que | q is pronounced as k in king |
| r, rr | [r, rr] | quitar | r is always pronounced in Spanish, |
| | | garra | unlike the silent r in dancer. rr is trilled, |
| | | | like a Scottish r |
| s | [ s ] | quizás | s is usually pronounced as in pass, |
| | | isla | but before b, d, g, l, m or n it is |
| | | | pronounced as in rose |
| v | [b, β] | vía | v is pronounced something like b. |
| | | | At the beginning of a phrase or after |
| | | | m or n it is pronounced as b in boy. |
| | | | In any other position the sound is |
| | | | softened |
| z | [ θ ] | tenaz | z is pronounced as th in thin |

f, k, l, m, n, p, t and x are pronounced as in English.


**STRESS**

The rules of stress in Spanish are as follows:

(a)  when a word ends in a vowel or in n or s, the second last syllable
     is stressed:
     patata, patatas; come, comen
(b)  when a word ends in a consonant other than n or s, the stress
     falls on the last syllable:
     pared, hablar
(c)  when the rules set out in (a) and (b) are not applied, an acute
     accent appears over the stressed vowel:
     común, geografía, inglés

In the phonetic transcription, the symbol [ ˈ ] precedes the syllable
on which the stress falls.

# LA PRONUNCIACIÓN INGLESA

## VOCALES

| | Ejemplo inglés | Explicación |
|---|---|---|
| [ ɑː ] | father | Entre a de padre y o de noche |
| [ ʌ ] | but, come | a muy breve |
| [ æ ] | man, cat | Con los labios en la posición de e en pena y luego se pronuncia el sonido a parecido a la a de carro |
| [ ə ] | father, ago | Vocal neutra parecida a una e u o casi muda |
| [ əː ] | bird, heard | Entre e abierta y o cerrada, sonido alargado |
| [ ɛ ] | get, bed | Como en perro |
| [ ɪ ] | it, big | Más breve que en si |
| [ iː ] | tea, see | Como en fino |
| [ ɔ ] | hot, wash | Como en torre |
| [ ɔː ] | saw, all | Como en por |
| [ u ] | put, book | Sonido breve, más cerrado que burro |
| [ uː ] | too, you | Sonido largo, como en uno |

## DIPTONGOS

| | Ejemplo inglés | Explicación |
|---|---|---|
| [ aɪ ] | fly, high | Como en fraile |
| [ au ] | how, house | Como en pausa |
| [ ɛə ] | there, bear | Casi como en vea, pero el sonido a se mezcla con el indistinto [ə] |
| [ eɪ ] | day, obey | e cerrada seguida por una i débil |
| [ ɪə ] | here, hear | Como en manía, mezclándose el sonido a con el indistinto [ə] |
| [ əu ] | go, note | [ə] seguido por una breve u |
| [ əɪ ] | boy, oil | Como en voy |
| [ uə ] | poor, sure | u bastante larga más el sonido indistinto [ə] |

## CONSONANTES

| | Ejemplo inglés | Explicación |
|---|---|---|
| [ b ] | big, lobby | Como en tumban |
| [ d ] | mended | Como en conde, andar |
| [ g ] | go, get, big | Como en grande, gol |
| [ dʒ ] | gin, judge | Como en la ll andaluza y en Generalitat (catalán) |
| [ ŋ ] | sing | Como en vínculo |
| [ h ] | house, he | Como la jota hispanoamericana |
| [ j ] | young, yes | Como en ya |
| [ k ] | come, mock | Como en caña, Escocia |
| [ r ] | red, tread | Se pronuncia con la punta de la lengua hacia atrás y sin hacerla vibrar |
| [ s ] | sand, yes | Como en casa, sesión |
| [ z ] | rose, zebra | Como en desde, mismo |
| [ ʃ ] | she, machine | Como en chambre (francés), roxo (portugués) |
| [ tʃ ] | chin, rich | Como en chocolate |
| [ v ] | valley | Como f, pero se retiran los dientes superiores vibrándolos contra el labio inferior |
| [ w ] | water, which | Como la u de huevo, puede |
| [ ʒ ] | vision | Como en journal (francés) |
| [ θ ] | think, myth | Como en receta, zapato |
| [ ð ] | this, the | Como en hablado, verdad |

f, l, m, n, p, t y x iguales que en español.

El signo [ * ] indica que la r final escrita apenas se pronuncia en inglés británico cuando la palabra siguiente empieza con vocal.
El signo [ ' ] indica la sílaba acentuada.

# SPANISH VERB TABLES

1 Gerund 2 Imperative 3 Present 4 Preterite 5 Future 6 Present subjunctive 7 Imperfect subjunctive 8 Past participle 9 Imperfect

*Etc* indicates that the irregular root is used for all persons of the tense, e.g. **oír**: 6 oiga, oigas, oigamos, oigáis, oigan

**agradecer** 3 agradezco 6 agradezca *etc*

**aprobar** 2 aprueba 3 apruebo, apruebas, aprueba, aprueban 6 apruebe, apruebes, apruebe, aprueben

**atravesar** 2 atraviesa 3 atravieso, atraviesas, atraviesa, atraviesan 6 atraviese, atravieses, atraviese, atraviesen

**caber** 3 quepo 4 cupe, cupiste, cupo, cupimos, cupisteis, cupieron 5 cabré *etc* 6 quepa *etc* 7 cupiera *etc*

**caer** 1 cayendo 3 caigo 4 cayó, cayeron 6 caiga *etc* 7 cayera *etc*

**cerrar** 2 cierra 3 cierro, cierras, cierra, cierran 6 cierre, cierres, cierre, cierren

**COMER** 1 comiendo 2 come, comed 3 como, comes, come, comemos, coméis, comen 4 comí, comiste, comió, comimos, comisteis, comieron 5 comeré, comerás, comerá, comeremos, comeréis, comerán 6 coma, comas, coma, comamos, comáis, coman 7 comiera, comieras, comiera, comiéramos, comierais, comieran 8 comido 9 comía, comías, comía, comíamos, comíais, comían

**conocer** 3 conozco 6 conozca *etc*

**contar** 2 cuenta 3 cuento, cuentas, cuenta, cuentan 6 cuente, cuentes, cuente, cuenten

**dar** 3 doy 4 di, diste, dio, dimos, disteis, dieron 7 diera *etc*

**decir** 2 di 3 digo 4 dije, dijiste, dijo, dijimos, dijisteis, dijeron 5 diré *etc* 6 diga *etc* 7 dijera *etc* 8 dicho

**despertar** 2 despierta 3 despierto, despiertas, despierta, despiertan 6 despierte, despiertes, despierte, despierten

**divertir** 1 divirtiendo 2 divierte 3 divierto, diviertes, divierte, divierten 4 divirtió, divirtieron 6 divierta, diviertas, divierta, divirtamos, divirtáis, diviertan 7 divirtiera *etc*

**dormir** 1 durmiendo 2 duerme 3 duermo, duermes, duerme, duermen 4 durmió, durmieron 6 duerma, duermas, duerma, durmamos, durmáis, duerman 7 durmiera *etc*

**empezar** 2 empieza 3 empiezo, empiezas, empieza, empiezan 4 empecé 6 empiece, empieces, empiece, empecemos, empecéis, empiecen

**entender** 2 entiende 3 entiendo, entiendes, entiende, entienden 6 entienda, entiendas, entienda, entiendan

**ESTAR** 2 está 3 estoy, estás, está, están 4 estuve, estuviste, estuvo, estuvimos, estuvisteis, estuvieron 6 esté, estés, esté, estén 7 estuviera *etc*

**HABER** 3 he, has, ha, hemos, han 4 hube, hubiste, hubo, hubimos, hubisteis, hubieron 5 habré *etc* 6 haya *etc* 7 hubiera *etc*

**HABLAR** 1 hablando 2 habla, hablad 3 hablo, hablas, habla, hablamos, habláis, hablan 4 hablé, hablaste, habló, hablamos, hablasteis, hablaron 5 hablaré, hablarás, hablará, hablaremos, hablaréis, hablarán 6 hable, hables, hable, hablemos, habléis, hablen 7 hablara, hablaras, hablara, habláramos, hablarais, hablaran 8 hablado 9 hablaba, hablabas, hablaba, hablábamos, hablabais, hablaban

**hacer** 2 haz 3 hago 4 hice, hiciste, hizo, hicimos, hicisteis, hicieron 5 haré *etc* 6 haga *etc* 7 hiciera *etc* 8 hecho

**instruir** 1 instruyendo 2 instruye 3 instruyo, instruyes, instruye, instruyen 4 instruyó, instruyeron 6 instruya *etc* 7 instruyera *etc*

**ir** 1 yendo 2 ve 3 voy, vas, va, vamos, vais, van 4 fui, fuiste, fue, fuimos, fuisteis, fueron 6 vaya, vayas, vaya, vayamos, vayáis, vayan 7 fuera *etc* 9 iba, ibas, iba, íbamos, ibais, iban

**jugar** 2 juega 3 juego, juegas, juega, juegan 4 jugué 6 juegue *etc*

**leer** 1 leyendo 4 leyó, leyeron 7 leyera *etc*

**morir** 1 muriendo 2 muere 3 muero, mueres, muere, mueren 4 murió, murieron

6 muera, mueras, muera, muramos, muráis, mueran 7 muriera *etc* 8 muerto

**mover** 2 mueve 3 muevo, mueves, mueve, mueven 6 mueva, muevas, mueva, muevan

**negar** 2 niega 3 niego, niegas, niega, niegan 4 negué 6 niegue, niegues, niegue, neguemos, neguéis, nieguen

**ofrecer** 3 ofrezco 6 ofrezca *etc*

**oír** 1 oyendo 2 oye 3 oigo, oyes, oye, oyen 4 oyó, oyeron 6 oiga *etc* 7 oyera *etc*

**oler** 2 huele 3 huelo, hueles, huele, huelen 6 huela, huelas, huela, huelan

**parecer** 3 parezco 6 parezca *etc*

**pedir** 1 pidiendo 2 pide 3 pido, pides, pide, piden 4 pidió, pidieron 6 pida *etc* 7 pidiera *etc*

**pensar** 2 piensa 3 pienso, piensas, piensa, piensan 6 piense, pienses, piense, piensen

**perder** 2 pierde 3 pierdo, pierdes, pierde, pierden 6 pierda, pierdas, pierda, pierdan

**poder** 1 pudiendo 2 puede 3 puedo, puedes, puede, pueden 4 pude, pudiste, pudo, pudimos, pudisteis, pudieron 5 podré *etc* 6 pueda, puedas, pueda, puedan 7 pudiera *etc*

**poner** 2 pon 3 pongo 4 puse, pusiste, puso, pusimos, pusisteis, pusieron 5 pondré *etc* 6 ponga *etc* 7 pusiera *etc* 8 puesto

**preferir** 1 prefiriendo 2 prefiere 3 prefiero, prefieres, prefiere, prefieren 4 prefirió, prefirieron 6 prefiera, prefieras, prefiera, prefiramos, prefiráis, prefieran 7 prefiriera *etc*

**querer** 2 quiere 3 quiero, quieres, quiere, quieren 4 quise, quisiste, quiso, quisimos, quisisteis, quisieron 5 querré *etc* 6 quiera, quieras, quiera, quieran 7 quisiera *etc*

**reír** 2 ríe 3 río, ríes, ríe, ríen 4 reí, rieron 6 ría, rías, ría, riamos, riáis, rían 7 riera *etc*

**repetir** 1 repitiendo 2 repite 3 repito, repites, repite, repiten 4 repitió, repitieron 6 repita *etc* 7 repitiera *etc*

**rogar** 2 ruega 3 ruego, ruegas, ruega, ruegan 4 rogué 6 ruegue, ruegues, ruegue, roguemos, roguéis, rueguen

**saber** 3 sé 4 supe, supiste, supo, supimos, supisteis, supieron 5 sabré *etc* 6 sepa *etc* 7 supiera *etc*

**salir** 2 sal 3 salgo 5 saldré *etc* 6 salga *etc*

**seguir** 1 siguiendo 2 sigue 3 sigo, sigues, sigue, siguen 4 siguió, siguieron 6 siga *etc* 7 siguiera *etc*

**sentar** 2 sienta 3 siento, sientas, sienta, sientan 6 siente, sientes, siente, sienten

**sentir** 1 sintiendo 2 siente 3 siento, sientes, siente, sienten 4 sintió, sintieron 6 sienta, sientas, sienta, sintamos, sintáis, sientan 7 sintiera *etc*

**SER** 2 sé 3 soy, eres, es, somos, sois, son 4 fui, fuiste, fue, fuimos, fuisteis, fueron 6 sea *etc* 7 fuera *etc* 9 era, eras, era, éramos, erais, eran

**servir** 1 sirviendo 2 sirve 3 sirvo, sirves, sirve, sirven 4 sirvió, sirvieron 6 sirva *etc* 7 sirviera *etc*

**soñar** 2 sueña 3 sueño, sueñas, sueña, sueñan 6 sueñe, sueñes, sueñe, sueñen

**tener** 2 ten 3 tengo, tienes, tiene, tienen 4 tuve, tuviste, tuvo, tuvimos, tuvisteis, tuvieron 5 tendré *etc* 6 tenga *etc* 7 tuviera *etc*

**traer** 1 trayendo 3 traigo 4 traje, trajiste, trajo, trajimos, trajisteis, trajeron 6 traiga *etc* 7 trajera *etc*

**valer** 2 vale 3 valgo 5 valdré *etc* 6 valga *etc*

**venir** 2 ven 3 vengo, vienes, viene, vienen 4 vine, viniste, vino, vinimos, vinisteis, vinieron 5 vendré *etc* 6 venga *etc* 7 viniera *etc*

**ver** 3 veo 6 vea *etc* 8 visto 9 veía *etc*

**vestir** 1 vistiendo 2 viste 3 visto, vistes, viste, visten 4 vistió, vistieron 6 vista *etc* 7 vistiera *etc*

**VIVIR** 1 viviendo 2 vive, vivid 3 vivo, vives, vive, vivimos, vivís, viven 4 viví, viviste, vivió, vivimos, vivisteis, vivieron 5 viviré, vivirás, vivirá, viviremos, viviréis, vivirán 6 viva, vivas, viva, vivamos, viváis, vivan 7 viviera, vivieras, viviera, viviéramos, vivierais, vivieran 8 vivido 9 vivía, vivías, vivía, vivíamos, vivías, vivían

**volver** 2 vuelve 3 vuelvo, vuelves, vuelve, vuelven 6 vuelva, vuelvas, vuelva, vuelvan 8 vuelto

# VERBOS IRREGULARES EN INGLÉS

| PRESENTE | PASADO | PARTICIPIO | PRESENTE | PASADO | PARTICIPIO |
|---|---|---|---|---|---|
| arise | arose | arisen | fall | fell | fallen |
| awake | awoke | awoken | feed | fed | fed |
| be (am, is, are; being) | was, were | been | feel | felt | felt |
| | | | fight | fought | fought |
| bear | bore | born(e) | find | found | found |
| beat | beat | beaten | flee | fled | fled |
| become | became | become | fling | flung | flung |
| begin | began | begun | fly | flew | flown |
| bend | bent | bent | forbid | forbad(e) | forbidden |
| bet | bet, betted | bet, betted | forecast | forecast | forecast |
| | | | forget | forgot | forgotten |
| bid (at auction, cards) | bid | bid | forgive | forgave | forgiven |
| | | | forsake | forsook | forsaken |
| bid (say) | bade | bidden | freeze | froze | frozen |
| bind | bound | bound | get | got | got, (US) gotten |
| bite | bit | bitten | | | |
| bleed | bled | bled | give | gave | given |
| blow | blew | blown | go (goes) | went | gone |
| break | broke | broken | grind | ground | ground |
| breed | bred | bred | grow | grew | grown |
| bring | brought | brought | hang | hung | hung |
| build | built | built | hang (suspend) (execute) | hanged | hanged |
| burn | burnt, burned | burnt, burned | | | |
| | | | have | had | had |
| burst | burst | burst | hear | heard | heard |
| buy | bought | bought | hide | hid | hidden |
| can | could | (been able) | hit | hit | hit |
| cast | cast | cast | hold | held | held |
| catch | caught | caught | hurt | hurt | hurt |
| choose | chose | chosen | keep | kept | kept |
| cling | clung | clung | kneel | knelt, kneeled | knelt, kneeled |
| come | came | come | | | |
| cost (be valued at) | cost | cost | know | knew | known |
| | | | lay | laid | laid |
| cost (work out price of) | costed | costed | lead | led | led |
| | | | lean | leant, leaned | leant, leaned |
| creep | crept | crept | | | |
| cut | cut | cut | leap | leapt, leaped | leapt, leaped |
| deal | dealt | dealt | | | |
| dig | dug | dug | learn | learnt, learned | learnt, learned |
| do (does) | did | done | | | |
| draw | drew | drawn | leave | left | left |
| dream | dreamed, dreamt | dreamed, dreamt | lend | lent | lent |
| | | | let | let | let |
| drink | drank | drunk | lie (lying) | lay | lain |
| drive | drove | driven | light | lit, lighted | lit, lighted |
| dwell | dwelt | dwelt | | | |
| eat | ate | eaten | lose | lost | lost |

XV

| PRESENTE | PASADO | PARTICIPIO | PRESENTE | PASADO | PARTICIPIO |
|----------|--------|------------|----------|--------|------------|
| make | made | made | speed | sped, | sped, |
| may | might | – | | speeded | speeded |
| mean | meant | meant | spell | spelt, | spelt, |
| meet | met | met | | spelled | spelled |
| mistake | mistook | mistaken | spend | spent | spent |
| mow | mowed | mown, | spill | spilt, | spilt, |
| | | mowed | | spilled | spilled |
| must | (had to) | (had to) | spin | spun | spun |
| pay | paid | paid | spit | spat | spat |
| put | put | put | spoil | spoiled, | spoiled, |
| quit | quit, | quit, | | spoilt | spoilt |
| | quitted | quitted | spread | spread | spread |
| read | read | read | spring | sprang | sprung |
| rid | rid | rid | stand | stood | stood |
| ride | rode | ridden | steal | stole | stolen |
| ring | rang | rung | stick | stuck | stuck |
| rise | rose | risen | sting | stung | stung |
| run | ran | run | stink | stank | stunk |
| saw | sawed | sawed, | stride | strode | stridden |
| | | sawn | strike | struck | struck |
| say | said | said | strive | strove | striven |
| see | saw | seen | swear | swore | sworn |
| seek | sought | sought | sweep | swept | swept |
| sell | sold | sold | swell | swelled | swollen, |
| send | sent | sent | | | swelled |
| set | set | set | swim | swam | swum |
| sew | sewed | sewn | swing | swung | swung |
| shake | shook | shaken | take | took | taken |
| shear | sheared | shorn, | teach | taught | taught |
| | | sheared | tear | tore | torn |
| shed | shed | shed | tell | told | told |
| shine | shone | shone | think | thought | thought |
| shoot | shot | shot | throw | threw | thrown |
| show | showed | shown | thrust | thrust | thrust |
| shrink | shrank | shrunk | tread | trod | trodden |
| shut | shut | shut | wake | woke, | woken, |
| sing | sang | sung | | waked | waked |
| sink | sank | sunk | wear | wore | worn |
| sit | sat | sat | weave(on | wove | woven |
| slay | slew | slain | loom) | | |
| sleep | slept | slept | weave(wind) | weaved | weaved |
| slide | slid | slid | wed | wedded, | wedded, |
| sling | slung | slung | | wed | wed |
| slit | slit | slit | weep | wept | wept |
| smell | smelt, | smelt, | win | won | won |
| | smelled | smelled | wind | wound | wound |
| sow | sowed | sown, | wring | wrung | wrung |
| | | sowed | write | wrote | written |
| speak | spoke | spoken | | | |

# a

**○ PALABRA CLAVE**

**a** [a] (a + el = al) prep **1** (dirección) to; **fueron a Madrid/Grecia** they went to Madrid/Greece; **me voy a casa** I'm going home
**2** (distancia): **está a 15 km de aquí** it's 15 kms from here
**3** (posición): **estar a la mesa** to be at table; **al lado de** next to, beside; V tb **puerta**
**4** (tiempo): **a las 10/a medianoche** at 10/midnight; **a la mañana siguiente** the following morning; **a los pocos días** after a few days; **estamos a 9 de julio** it's the ninth of July; **a los 24 años** at the age of 24; **al año/la semana** a year/week later
**5** (manera): **a la francesa** the French way; **a caballo** on horseback; **a oscuras** in the dark
**6** (medio, instrumento): **a lápiz** in pencil; **a mano** by hand; **cocina a gas** gas stove
**7** (razón): **a 30 céntimos el kilo** at 30 cents a kilo; **a más de 50 km/h** at more than 50 kms per hour
**8** (dativo): **se lo di a él** I gave it to him; **vi al policía** I saw the policeman; **se lo compré a él** I bought it from him
**9** (tras ciertos verbos): **voy a verle** I'm going to see him; **empezó a trabajar** he started working o to work
**10** (+ infin): **al verlo, lo reconocí inmediatamente** when I saw him I recognized him at once; **el camino a recorrer** the distance we etc have to travel; **¡a callar!** keep quiet!; **¡a comer!** let's eat!

**abad, esa** [a'βað, 'ðesa] nm/f abbot/abbess; **abadía** nf abbey
**abajo** [a'βaxo] adv (situación) (down) below, underneath; (en edificio) downstairs; (dirección) down, downwards; **el piso de ~** the downstairs flat; **la parte de ~** the lower part; **¡~ el gobierno!** down with the government!; **cuesta/río ~** downhill/downstream; **de arriba ~** from top to bottom; **el ~ firmante** the undersigned; **más ~** lower o further down
**abalanzarse** [aβalan'θarse] vr: **~ sobre** o **contra** to throw o.s. at
**abanderado, -a** [aβande'raðo] nm/f (portaestandarte) standard bearer; (de un movimiento) champion, leader; (MÉX: linier) linesman, assistant referee
**abandonado, -a** [aβando'naðo, a] adj derelict; (desatendido) abandoned; (desierto) deserted; (descuidado) neglected
**abandonar** [aβando'nar] vt to leave; (persona) to abandon, desert; (cosa) to abandon, leave behind; (descuidar) to neglect; (renunciar a) to give up; (Inform) to quit; **abandonarse** vr: **~se a** to abandon o.s. to; **abandono** nm (acto) desertion, abandonment; (estado) abandon, neglect; (renuncia) withdrawal, retirement; **ganar por abandono** to win by default
**abanico** [aβa'niko] nm fan; (Náut) derrick
**abarcar** [aβar'kar] vt to include, embrace; (LAM: acaparar) to monopolize
**abarrotado, -a** [aβarro'taðo, a] adj packed
**abarrotar** [aβarro'tar] vt (local, estadio, teatro) to fill, pack
**abarrotero, -a** [aβarro'tero, a] (MÉX) nm/f grocer; **abarrotes** (MÉX) nmpl groceries; **tienda de abarrotes** (MÉX, CAM) grocery store
**abastecer** [aβaste'θer] vt: **~ (de)** to supply (with); **abastecimiento** nm supply
**abasto** [a'βasto] nm supply; **no dar ~ a** to be unable to cope with
**abatible** [aβa'tiβle] adj: **asiento ~** tip-up seat; (Auto) reclining seat
**abatido, -a** [aβa'tiðo, a] adj dejected, downcast
**abatir** [aβa'tir] vt (muro) to demolish; (pájaro) to shoot o bring down; (fig) to depress
**abdicar** [aβði'kar] vi to abdicate
**abdomen** [aβ'ðomen] nm abdomen; **abdominales** nmpl (tb: **ejercicios abdominales**) sit-ups
**abecedario** [aβeθe'ðarjo] nm alphabet
**abedul** [aβe'ðul] nm birch
**abeja** [a'βexa] nf bee
**abejorro** [aβe'xorro] nm bumblebee
**abertura** [aβer'tura] nf = **apertura**
**abeto** [a'βeto] nm fir
**abierto, -a** [a'βjerto, a] pp de **abrir** ▷ adj open
**abismal** [aβis'mal] adj (fig) vast, enormous

**abismo** [a'βismo] *nm* abyss

**ablandar** [aβlan'dar] *vt* to soften; **ablandarse** *vr* to get softer

**abocado, -a** [aβo'kaðo, a] *adj* (*vino*) smooth, pleasant

**abochornar** [aβotʃor'nar] *vt* to embarrass

**abofetear** [aβofete'ar] *vt* to slap (in the face)

**abogado, -a** [aβo'ɣaðo, a] *nm/f* lawyer; (*notario*) solicitor; (*en tribunal*) barrister (*BRIT*), attorney (*US*); **abogado defensor** defence lawyer *o* (*US*) attorney

**abogar** [aβo'ɣar] *vi*: ~ **por** to plead for; (*fig*) to advocate

**abolir** [aβo'lir] *vt* to abolish; (*cancelar*) to cancel

**abolladura** [aβoʎa'ðura] *nf* dent

**abollar** [aβo'ʎar] *vt* to dent

**abombarse** [aβom'barse] (*LAM*) *vr* to go bad

**abominable** [aβomi'naβle] *adj* abominable

**abonado, -a** [aβo'naðo, a] *adj* (*deuda*) paid(-up) ▷ *nm/f* subscriber

**abonar** [aβo'nar] *vt* (*deuda*) to settle; (*terreno*) to fertilize; (*idea*) to endorse; **abonarse** *vr* to subscribe; **abono** *nm* payment; fertilizer; subscription

**abordar** [aβor'ðar] *vt* (*barco*) to board; (*asunto*) to broach

**aborigen** [aβo'rixen] *nmf* aborigine

**aborrecer** [aβorre'θer] *vt* to hate, loathe

**abortar** [aβor'tar] *vi* (*malparir*) to have a miscarriage; (*deliberadamente*) to have an abortion; **aborto** *nm* miscarriage; abortion

**abovedado, -a** [aβoβe'ðaðo, a] *adj* vaulted, domed

**abrasar** [aβra'sar] *vt* to burn (up); (*Agr*) to dry up, parch

**abrazar** [aβra'θar] *vt* to embrace, hug

**abrazo** [a'βraθo] *nm* embrace, hug; **un ~** (*en carta*) with best wishes

**abrebotellas** [aβreβo'teʎas] *nm inv* bottle opener

**abrecartas** [aβre'kartas] *nm inv* letter opener

**abrelatas** [aβre'latas] *nm inv* tin (*BRIT*) *o* can opener

**abreviatura** [aβreβja'tura] *nf* abbreviation

**abridor** [aβri'ðor] *nm* bottle opener; (*de latas*) tin (*BRIT*) *o* can opener

**abrigador, a** [aβriɣa'ðor, a] (*MÉX*) *adj* warm

**abrigar** [aβri'ɣar] *vt* (*proteger*) to shelter; (*ropa*) to keep warm; (*fig*) to cherish

**abrigo** [a'βriɣo] *nm* (*prenda*) coat, overcoat; (*lugar protegido*) shelter

**abril** [a'βril] *nm* April

**abrillantador** [aβriʎanta'ðor] *nm* polish

**abrillantar** [aβriʎan'tar] *vt* to polish

**abrir** [a'βrir] *vt* to open (up) ▷ *vi* to open; **abrirse** *vr* to open (up); (*extenderse*) to open out; (*cielo*) to clear; **~se paso** to find *o* force a way through

**abrochar** [aβro'tʃar] *vt* (*con botones*) to button (up); (*zapato, con broche*) to do up

**abrupto, -a** [a'βrupto, a] *adj* abrupt; (*empinado*) steep

**absoluto, -a** [aβso'luto, a] *adj* absolute; **en ~** *adv* not at all

**absolver** [aβsol'βer] *vt* to absolve; (*Jur*) to pardon; (: *acusado*) to acquit

**absorbente** [aβsor'βente] *adj* absorbent; (*interesante*) absorbing

**absorber** [aβsor'βer] *vt* to absorb; (*embeber*) to soak up

**absorción** [aβsor'θjon] *nf* absorption; (*Com*) takeover

**abstemio, -a** [aβs'temjo, a] *adj* teetotal

**abstención** [aβsten'θjon] *nf* abstention

**abstenerse** [aβste'nerse] *vr*: ~ **(de)** to abstain *o* refrain (from)

**abstinencia** [aβsti'nenθja] *nf* abstinence; (*ayuno*) fasting

**abstracto, -a** [aβs'trakto, a] *adj* abstract

**abstraer** [aβstra'er] *vt* to abstract; **abstraerse** *vr* to be *o* become absorbed

**abstraído, -a** [aβstra'iðo, a] *adj* absent-minded

**absuelto** [aβ'swelto] *pp de* **absolver**

**absurdo, -a** [aβ'surðo, a] *adj* absurd

**abuchear** [aβutʃe'ar] *vt* to boo

**abuelo, -a** [a'βwelo, a] *nm/f* grandfather(-mother); **abuelos** *nmpl* grandparents

**abultado, -a** [aβul'taðo, a] *adj* bulky

**abultar** [aβul'tar] *vi* to be bulky

**abundancia** [aβun'danθja] *nf*: **una ~ de** plenty of; **abundante** *adj* abundant, plentiful

**abundar** [aβun'dar] *vi* to abound, be plentiful

**aburrido, -a** [aβu'rriðo, a] *adj* (*hastiado*) bored; (*que aburre*) boring; **aburrimiento** *nm* boredom, tedium

**aburrir** [aβu'rrir] *vt* to bore; **aburrirse** *vr* to be bored, get bored

**abusado, -a** [aβu'saðo, a] (*MÉX: fam*) *adj* (*astuto*) sharp, cunning ▷ *excl*: **¡~!** (*inv*) look out!, careful!

**abusar** [aβu'sar] *vi* to go too far; ~ **de** to abuse

**abusivo, -a** [aβu'siβo, a] *adj* (*precio*)

exorbitant

**abuso** [a'βuso] *nm* abuse

**acá** [a'ka] *adv (lugar)* here

**acabado, -a** [aka'βaðo, a] *adj* finished, complete; *(perfecto)* perfect; *(agotado)* worn out; *(fig)* masterly ▷ *nm* finish

**acabar** [aka'βar] *vt (llevar a su fin)* to finish, complete; *(consumir)* to use up; *(rematar)* to finish off ▷ *vi* to finish, end; **acabarse** *vr* to finish, stop; *(terminarse)* to be over; *(agotarse)* to run out; **~ con** to put an end to; **~ de llegar** to have just arrived; **~ por hacer** to end (up) by doing; **¡se acabó!** it's all over!; *(¡basta!)* that's enough!

**acabóse** [aka'βose] *nm:* **esto es el ~** this is the last straw

**academia** [aka'ðemja] *nf* academy; **academia de idiomas** language school; **académico, -a** *adj* academic

**acalorado, -a** [akalo'raðo, a] *adj (discusión)* heated

**acampar** [akam'par] *vi* to camp

**acantilado** [akanti'laðo] *nm* cliff

**acaparar** [akapa'rar] *vt* to monopolize; *(acumular)* to hoard

**acariciar** [akari'θjar] *vt* to caress; *(esperanza)* to cherish

**acarrear** [akarre'ar] *vt* to transport; *(fig)* to cause, result in

**acaso** [a'kaso] *adv* perhaps, maybe; **(por) si ~** (just) in case

**acatar** [aka'tar] *vt* to respect; *(ley)* obey

**acatarrarse** [akata'rrarse] *vr* to catch a cold

**acceder** [akθe'ðer] *vi:* **~ a** *(petición etc)* to agree to; *(tener acceso a)* to have access to; *(Inform)* to access

**accesible** [akθe'siβle] *adj* accessible

**acceso** [ak'θeso] *nm* access, entry; *(camino)* access, approach; *(Med)* attack, fit

**accesorio, -a** [akθe'sorjo, a] *adj, nm* accessory

**accidentado, -a** [akθiðen'taðo, a] *adj* uneven; *(montañoso)* hilly; *(azaroso)* eventful ▷ *nm/f* accident victim

**accidental** [akθiðen'tal] *adj* accidental

**accidente** [akθi'ðente] *nm* accident; **accidentes** *nmpl (de terreno)* unevenness *sg*; **accidente laboral** o **de trabajo/de tráfico** industrial/road o traffic accident

**acción** [ak'θjon] *nf* action; *(acto)* action, act; *(Com)* share; *(Jur)* action, lawsuit; **accionar** *vt* to work, operate; *(Inform)* to drive

**accionista** [akθjo'nista] *nmf* shareholder, stockholder

**acebo** [a'θeβo] *nm* holly; *(árbol)* holly tree

**acechar** [aθe'tʃar] *vt* to spy on; *(aguardar)* to lie in wait for; **acecho** *nm:* **estar al acecho (de)** to lie in wait (for)

**aceite** [a'θeite] *nm* oil; **aceite de girasol/ oliva** olive/sunflower oil; **aceitera** *nf* oilcan; **aceitoso, -a** *adj* oily

**aceituna** [aθei'tuna] *nf* olive; **aceituna rellena** stuffed olive

**acelerador** [aθelera'ðor] *nm* accelerator

**acelerar** [aθele'rar] *vt* to accelerate

**acelga** [a'θelxa] *nf* chard, beet

**acento** [a'θento] *nm* accent; *(acentuación)* stress

**acentuar** [aθen'twar] *vt* to accent; to stress; *(fig)* to accentuate

**acepción** [aθep'θjon] *nf* meaning

**aceptable** [aθep'taβle] *adj* acceptable

**aceptación** [aθepta'θjon] *nf* acceptance; *(aprobación)* approval

**aceptar** [aθep'tar] *vt* to accept; *(aprobar)* to approve; **~ hacer algo** to agree to do sth

**acequia** [a'θekja] *nf* irrigation ditch

**acera** [a'θera] *nf* pavement (BRIT), sidewalk (US)

**acerca** [a'θerka]: **~ de** *prep* about, concerning

**acercar** [aθer'kar] *vt* to bring o move nearer; **acercarse** *vr* to approach, come near

**acero** [a'θero] *nm* steel

**acérrimo, -a** [a'θerrimo, a] *adj (partidario)* staunch; *(enemigo)* bitter

**acertado, -a** [aθer'taðo, a] *adj* correct; *(apropiado)* apt; *(sensato)* sensible

**acertar** [aθer'tar] *vt (blanco)* to hit; *(solución)* to get right; *(adivinar)* to guess ▷ *vi* to get it right, be right; **~ a** to manage to; **~ con** to happen o hit on

**acertijo** [aθer'tixo] *nm* riddle, puzzle

**achacar** [atʃa'kar] *vt* to attribute

**achacoso, -a** [atʃa'koso, a] *adj* sickly

**achicar** [atʃi'kar] *vt* to reduce; *(Náut)* to bale out

**achicharrar** [atʃitʃa'rrar] *vt* to scorch, burn

**achichincle** [atʃi'tʃinkle] (MÉX: fam) *nmf* minion

**achicoria** [atʃi'korja] *nf* chicory

**achuras** [a'tʃuras] (RPL) *nfpl* offal *sg*

**acicate** [aθi'kate] *nm* spur

**acidez** [aθi'ðeθ] *nf* acidity

**ácido, -a** ['aθiðo, a] *adj* sour, acid ▷ *nm* acid

**acierto** *etc* [a'θjerto] *vb* V **acertar** ▷ *nm* success; *(buen paso)* wise move; *(solución)* solution; *(habilidad)* skill, ability

**acitronar** [aθitro'nar] (MÉX: fam) *vt* to brown

**aclamar** [akla'mar] *vt* to acclaim;

*(aplaudir)* to applaud

**aclaración** [aklara'θjon] *nf* clarification, explanation

**aclarar** [akla'rar] *vt* to clarify, explain; *(ropa)* to rinse ▷ *vi* to clear up; **aclararse** *vr (explicarse)* to understand; **~se la garganta** to clear one's throat

**aclimatación** [aklimata'θjon] *nf* acclimatization

**aclimatar** [aklima'tar] *vt* to acclimatize; **aclimatarse** *vr* to become acclimatized

**acné** [ak'ne] *nm* acne

**acobardar** [akoβar'ðar] *vt* to intimidate

**acogedor, a** [akoxe'ðor, a] *adj* welcoming; *(hospitalario)* hospitable

**acoger** [ako'xer] *vt* to welcome; *(abrigar)* to shelter

**acogida** [ako'xiða] *nf* reception; refuge

**acomedido, -a** [akome'ðiðo, a] *(MÉX) adj* helpful, obliging

**acometer** [akome'ter] *vt* to attack; *(emprender)* to undertake; **acometida** *nf* attack, assault

**acomodado, -a** [akomo'ðaðo, a] *adj (persona)* well-to-do

**acomodador, a** [akomoða'ðor, a] *nm/f* usher(ette)

**acomodar** [akomo'ðar] *vt* to adjust; *(alojar)* to accommodate; **acomodarse** *vr* to conform; *(instalarse)* to install o.s.; *(adaptarse)*: **~se (a)** to adapt (to)

**acompañar** [akompa'ɲar] *vt* to accompany; *(documentos)* to enclose

**acondicionar** [akondiθjo'nar] *vt* to arrange, prepare; *(pelo)* to condition

**aconsejar** [akonse'xar] *vt* to advise, counsel; **~ a algn hacer** *o* **que haga algo** to advise sb to do sth

**acontecer** [akonte'θer] *vi* to happen, occur; **acontecimiento** *nm* event

**acopio** [a'kopjo] *nm* store, stock

**acoplar** [ako'plar] *vt* to fit; *(Elec)* to connect; *(vagones)* to couple

**acorazado, -a** [akora'θaðo, a] *adj* armour-plated, armoured ▷ *nm* battleship

**acordar** [akor'ðar] *vt (resolver)* to agree, resolve; *(recordar)* to remind; **acordarse** *vr* to agree; **~ hacer algo** to agree to do sth; **~se (de algo)** to remember (sth); **acorde** *adj (Mús)* harmonious; **acorde con** *(medidas etc)* in keeping with ▷ *nm* chord

**acordeón** [akorðe'on] *nm* accordion

**acordonado, -a** [akorðo'naðo, a] *adj (calle)* cordoned-off

**acorralar** [akorra'lar] *vt* to round up, corral

**acortar** [akor'tar] *vt* to shorten; *(duración)* to cut short; *(cantidad)* to reduce; **acortarse** *vr* to become shorter

**acosar** [ako'sar] *vt* to pursue relentlessly; *(fig)* to hound, pester; **acoso** *nm* harassment; **acoso sexual** sexual harassment

**acostar** [akos'tar] *vt (en cama)* to put to bed; *(en suelo)* to lay down; **acostarse** *vr* to go to bed; to lie down; **~se con algn** to sleep with sb

**acostumbrado, -a** [akostum'braðo, a] *adj* usual; **~ a** used to

**acostumbrar** [akostum'brar] *vt*: **~ a algn a algo** to get sb used to sth ▷ *vi*: **~ (a) hacer** to be in the habit of doing; **acostumbrarse** *vr*: **~se a** to get used to

**acotación** [akota'θjon] *nf* marginal note; *(Geo)* elevation mark; *(de límite)* boundary mark; *(Teatro)* stage direction

**acotamiento** [akota'mjento] *(MÉX) nm* hard shoulder *(BRIT)*, berm *(US)*

**acre** ['akre] *adj (olor)* acrid; *(fig)* biting ▷ *nm* acre

**acreditar** [akreði'tar] *vt (garantizar)* to vouch for, guarantee; *(autorizar)* to authorize; *(dar prueba de)* to prove; *(Com: abonar)* to credit; *(embajador)* to accredit

**acreedor, a** [akree'ðor, a] *nm/f* creditor

**acribillar** [akriβi'ʎar] *vt*: **~ a balazos** to riddle with bullets

**acróbata** [a'kroβata] *nmf* acrobat

**acta** ['akta] *nf* certificate; *(de comisión)* minutes *pl*, record; **acta de matrimonio/ nacimiento** *(MÉX)* marriage/birth certificate; **acta notarial** affidavit

**actitud** [akti'tuð] *nf* attitude; *(postura)* posture

**activar** [akti'βar] *vt* to activate; *(acelerar)* to speed up

**actividad** [aktiβi'ðað] *nf* activity

**activo, -a** [ak'tiβo, a] *adj* active; *(vivo)* lively ▷ *nm (Com)* assets *pl*

**acto** ['akto] *nm* act, action; *(ceremonia)* ceremony; *(Teatro)* act; **en el ~** immediately

**actor** [ak'tor] *nm* actor; *(Jur)* plaintiff ▷ *adj*: **parte ~a** prosecution

**actriz** [ak'triθ] *nf* actress

**actuación** [aktwa'θjon] *nf* action; *(comportamiento)* conduct, behaviour; *(Jur)* proceedings *pl*; *(desempeño)* performance

**actual** [ak'twal] *adj* present(-day), current

No confundir **actual** con la palabra inglesa *actual*.

**actualidad** *nf* present; **actualidades** *nfpl (noticias)* news *sg*; **en la actualidad** at present; *(hoy día)* nowadays; **actualizar** [aktwali'θar] *vt* to update, modernize; **actualmente** [aktwal'mente] *adv* at

present; (*hoy día*) nowadays
  ▌ No confundir **actualmente** con la
  palabra inglesa *actually*.

**actuar** [ak'twar] *vi* (*obrar*) to work,
  operate; (*actor*) to act, perform ▷ *vt* to
  work, operate; **~ de** to act as

**acuarela** [akwa'rela] *nf* watercolour

**acuario** [a'kwarjo] *nm* aquarium;
  (*Astrología*): **A~** Aquarius

**acuático, -a** [a'kwatiko, a] *adj* aquatic

**acudir** [aku'ðir] *vi* (*asistir*) to attend; (*ir*) to
  go; **~ a** (*fig*) to turn to; **~ a una cita** to keep
  an appointment; **~ en ayuda de** to go to
  the aid of

**acuerdo** *etc* [a'kwerðo] *vb* V **acordar**
  ▷ *nm* agreement; **¡de ~!** agreed!; **de ~**
  **con** (*persona*) in agreement with; (*acción,
  documento*) in accordance with; **estar de ~**
  to be agreed, agree

**acumular** [akumu'lar] *vt* to accumulate,
  collect

**acuñar** [aku'ɲar] *vt* (*moneda*) to mint;
  (*frase*) to coin

**acupuntura** [akupun'tura] *nf*
  acupuncture

**acurrucarse** [akurru'karse] *vr* to crouch;
  (*ovillarse*) to curl up

**acusación** [akusa'θjon] *nf* accusation

**acusar** [aku'sar] *vt* to accuse; (*revelar*) to
  reveal; (*denunciar*) to denounce

**acuse** [a'kuse] *nm*: **~ de recibo**
  acknowledgement of receipt

**acústica** [a'kustika] *nf* acoustics *pl*

**acústico, -a** [a'kustiko, a] *adj* acoustic

**adaptación** [aðapta'θjon] *nf* adaptation

**adaptador** [aðapta'ðor] *nm* (*Elec*)
  adapter, adaptor; **adaptador universal**
  universal adapter *o* adaptor

**adaptar** [aðap'tar] *vt* to adapt; (*acomodar*)
  to fit

**adecuado, -a** [aðe'kwaðo, a] *adj* (*apto*)
  suitable; (*oportuno*) appropriate

**a. de J.C.** *abr* (= *antes de Jesucristo*) B.C.

**adelantado, -a** [aðelan'taðo, a] *adj*
  advanced; (*reloj*) fast; **pagar por ~** to pay in
  advance

**adelantamiento** [aðelanta'mjento] *nm*
  (*Auto*) overtaking

**adelantar** [aðelan'tar] *vt* to move
  forward; (*avanzar*) to advance; (*acelerar*)
  to speed up; (*Auto*) to overtake ▷ *vi* to go
  forward, advance; **adelantarse** *vr* to go
  forward, advance

**adelante** [aðe'lante] *adv* forward(s),
  ahead ▷ *excl* come in!; **de hoy en ~** from
  now on; **más ~** later on; (*más allá*) further on

**adelanto** [aðe'lanto] *nm* advance; (*mejora*)
  improvement; (*progreso*) progress

**adelgazar** [aðelɣa'θar] *vt* to thin (down)
  ▷ *vi* to get thin; (*con régimen*) to slim down,
  lose weight

**ademán** [aðe'man] *nm* gesture;
  **ademanes** *nmpl* manners

**además** [aðe'mas] *adv* besides; (*por otra
  parte*) moreover; (*también*) also; **~ de** besides,
  in addition to

**adentrarse** [aðen'trarse] *vr*: **~ en** to go
  into, get inside; (*penetrar*) to penetrate
  (into)

**adentro** [a'ðentro] *adv* inside, in; **mar ~**
  out at sea; **tierra ~** inland

**adepto, -a** [a'ðepto, a] *nm/f* supporter

**aderezar** [aðere'θar] *vt* (*ensalada*) to dress;
  (*comida*) to season; **aderezo** *nm* dressing;
  seasoning

**adeudar** [aðeu'ðar] *vt* to owe

**adherirse** [aðe'rirse] *vr*: **~ a** to adhere to;
  (*partido*) to join

**adhesión** [aðe'sjon] *nf* adhesion; (*fig*)
  adherence

**adicción** [aðik'θjon] *nf* addiction

**adición** [aði'θjon] *nf* addition

**adicto, -a** [a'ðikto, a] *adj*: **~ a** addicted
  to; (*dedicado*) devoted to ▷ *nm/f* supporter,
  follower; (*toxicómano*) addict

**adiestrar** [aðjes'trar] *vt* to train, teach;
  (*conducir*) to guide, lead

**adinerado, -a** [aðine'raðo, a] *adj*
  wealthy

**adiós** [a'ðjos] *excl* (*para despedirse*)
  goodbye!, cheerio!; (*al pasar*) hello!

**aditivo** [aði'tiβo] *nm* additive

**adivinanza** [aðiβi'nanθa] *nf* riddle

**adivinar** [aðiβi'nar] *vt* to prophesy;
  (*conjeturar*) to guess; **adivino, -a** *nm/f*
  fortune-teller

**adj** *abr* (= *adjunto*) encl

**adjetivo** [aðxe'tiβo] *nm* adjective

**adjudicar** [aðxuði'kar] *vt* to award;
  **adjudicarse** *vr*: **~se algo** to appropriate sth

**adjuntar** [aðxun'tar] *vt* to attach,
  enclose; **adjunto, -a** *adj* attached,
  enclosed ▷ *nm/f* assistant

**administración** [aðministra'θjon] *nf*
  administration; (*dirección*) management;
  **administrador, a** *nm/f* administrator,
  manager(ess)

**administrar** [aðminis'trar] *vt* to
  administer; **administrativo, -a** *adj*
  administrative

**admirable** [aðmi'raβle] *adj* admirable

**admiración** [aðmira'θjon] *nf* admiration;
  (*asombro*) wonder; (*Ling*) exclamation mark

**admirar** [aðmi'rar] *vt* to admire; (*extrañar*)
  to surprise

**admisible** [aðmi'siβle] *adj* admissible

**admisión** [aðmi'sjon] *nf* admission; (*reconocimiento*) acceptance

**admitir** [aðmi'tir] *vt* to admit; (*aceptar*) to accept

**adobar** [aðo'βar] *vt* (*Culin*) to season

**adobe** [a'ðoβe] *nm* adobe, sun-dried brick

**adolecer** [aðole'θer] *vi*: ~ **de** to suffer from

**adolescente** [aðoles'θente] *nmf* adolescent, teenager

**adonde** [a'ðonde] *conj* (to) where

**adónde** [a'ðonde] *adv* = **dónde**

**adopción** [aðop'θjon] *nf* adoption

**adoptar** [aðop'tar] *vt* to adopt

**adoptivo, -a** [aðop'tiβo, a] *adj* (*padres*) adoptive; (*hijo*) adopted

**adoquín** [aðo'kin] *nm* paving stone

**adorar** [aðo'rar] *vt* to adore

**adornar** [aðor'nar] *vt* to adorn

**adorno** [a'ðorno] *nm* ornament; (*decoración*) decoration

**adosado, -a** [aðo'saðo, a] *adj*: **casa adosada** semi-detached house

**adosar** [aðo'sar] (*MÉX*) *vt* (*adjuntar*) to attach, enclose (*with a letter*)

**adquiero** *etc vb* V **adquirir**

**adquirir** [aðki'rir] *vt* to acquire, obtain

**adquisición** [aðkisi'θjon] *nf* acquisition

**adrede** [a'ðreðe] *adv* on purpose

**ADSL** *nm abr* broadband

**aduana** [a'ðwana] *nf* customs *pl*

**aduanero, -a** [aðwa'nero, a] *adj* customs *cpd* ▷ *nm/f* customs officer

**adueñarse** [aðwe'narse] *vr*: ~ **de** to take possession of

**adular** [aðu'lar] *vt* to flatter

**adulterar** [aðulte'rar] *vt* to adulterate

**adulterio** [aðul'terjo] *nm* adultery

**adúltero, -a** [a'ðultero, a] *adj* adulterous ▷ *nm/f* adulterer/adulteress

**adulto, -a** [a'ðulto, a] *adj, nm/f* adult

**adverbio** [að'βerβjo] *nm* adverb

**adversario, -a** [aðβer'sarjo, a] *nm/f* adversary

**adversidad** [aðβersi'ðað] *nf* adversity; (*contratiempo*) setback

**adverso, -a** [að'βerso, a] *adj* adverse

**advertencia** [aðβer'tenθja] *nf* warning; (*prefacio*) preface, foreword

**advertir** [aðβer'tir] *vt* to notice; (*avisar*): ~ **a algn de** to warn sb about o of

**Adviento** [að'βjento] *nm* Advent

**advierto** *etc vb* V **advertir**

**aéreo, -a** [a'ereo, a] *adj* aerial

**aerobic** [ae'roβik] *nm* aerobics *sg*; **aerobics** (*MÉX*) *nmpl* aerobics *sg*

**aeromozo, -a** [aero'moθo, a] (*LAM*) *nm/f* air steward(ess)

**aeronáutica** [aero'nautika] *nf* aeronautics *sg*

**aeronave** [aero'naβe] *nm* spaceship

**aeroplano** [aero'plano] *nm* aeroplane

**aeropuerto** [aero'pwerto] *nm* airport

**aerosol** [aero'sol] *nm* aerosol

**afamado, -a** [afa'maðo, a] *adj* famous

**afán** [a'fan] *nm* hard work; (*deseo*) desire

**afanador, a** [afana'ðor, a] (*MÉX*) *nm/f* (*de limpieza*) cleaner

**afanar** [afa'nar] *vt* to harass; (*fam*) to pinch

**afear** [afe'ar] *vt* to disfigure

**afección** [afek'θjon] *nf* (*Med*) disease

**afectado, -a** [afek'taðo, a] *adj* affected

**afectar** [afek'tar] *vt* to affect

**afectísimo, -a** [afek'tisimo, a] *adj* affectionate; **suyo ~** yours truly

**afectivo, -a** [afek'tiβo, a] *adj* (*problema etc*) emotional

**afecto** [a'fekto] *nm* affection; **tenerle ~ a algn** to be fond of sb

**afectuoso, -a** [afek'twoso, a] *adj* affectionate

**afeitar** [afei'tar] *vt* to shave; **afeitarse** *vr* to shave

**afeminado, -a** [afemi'naðo, a] *adj* effeminate

**Afganistán** [afɣanis'tan] *nm* Afghanistan

**afianzar** [afjan'θar] *vt* to strengthen; to secure; **afianzarse** *vr* to become established

**afiche** [a'fitʃe] (*RPL*) *nm* poster

**afición** [afi'θjon] *nf* fondness, liking; **la ~** the fans *pl*; **pinto por ~** I paint as a hobby; **aficionado, -a** *adj* keen, enthusiastic; (*no profesional*) amateur ▷ *nm/f* enthusiast, fan; amateur; **ser aficionado a algo** to be very keen on o fond of sth

**aficionar** [afiθjo'nar] *vt*: ~ **a algn a algo** to make sb like sth; **aficionarse** *vr*: ~**se a algo** to grow fond of sth

**afilado, -a** [afi'laðo, a] *adj* sharp

**afilar** [afi'lar] *vt* to sharpen

**afiliarse** [afi'ljarse] *vr* to affiliate

**afín** [a'fin] *adj* (*parecido*) similar; (*conexo*) related

**afinar** [afi'nar] *vt* (*Tec*) to refine; (*Mús*) to tune ▷ *vi* (*tocar*) to play in tune; (*cantar*) to sing in tune

**afincarse** [afin'karse] *vr* to settle

**afinidad** [afini'ðað] *nf* affinity; (*parentesco*) relationship; **por ~** by marriage

**afirmación** [afirma'θjon] *nf* affirmation

**afirmar** [afir'mar] *vt* to affirm, state; **afirmativo, -a** *adj* affirmative

**afligir** [afli'xir] *vt* to afflict; (*apenar*) to distress

**aflojar** [aflo'xar] vt to slacken; (desatar) to loosen, undo; (relajar) to relax ▷ vi to drop; (bajar) to go down; **aflojarse** vr to relax

**afluente** [aflu'ente] adj flowing ▷ nm tributary

**afmo, -a** abr (= afectísimo(a) suyo(a)) Yours

**afónico, -a** [a'foniko, a] adj: **estar ~** to have a sore throat; to have lost one's voice

**aforo** [a'foro] nm (de teatro etc) capacity

**afortunado, -a** [afortu'naðo, a] adj fortunate, lucky

**África** ['afrika] nf Africa; **África del Sur** South Africa; **africano, -a** adj, nm/f African

**afrontar** [afron'tar] vt to confront; (poner cara a cara) to bring face to face

**afrutado, -a** [afru'taðo, a] adj fruity

**after** ['after] (pl **~s**) nm after-hours club; **afterhours** [after'aurs] nm inv = **after**

**afuera** [a'fwera] adv out, outside; **afueras** nfpl outskirts

**agachar** [aɣa'tʃar] vt to bend, bow; **agacharse** vr to stoop, bend

**agalla** [a'ɣaʎa] nf (Zool) gill; **tener ~s** (fam) to have guts

**agarradera** [aɣarra'ðera] (MÉX) nf handle

**agarrado, -a** [aɣa'rraðo, a] adj mean, stingy

**agarrar** [aɣa'rrar] vt to grasp, grab; (LAM: tomar) to take, catch; (recoger) to pick up ▷ vi (planta) to take root; **agarrarse** vr to hold on (tightly)

**agencia** [a'xenθja] nf agency; **agencia de viajes** travel agency; **agencia inmobiliaria** estate (BRIT) o real estate (US) agent's (office)

**agenciarse** [axen'θjarse] vr to obtain, procure

**agenda** [a'xenda] nf diary; **~ electronica** PDA

No confundir **agenda** con la palabra inglesa agenda.

**agente** [a'xente] nmf agent; (tb: **~ de policía**) policeman/policewoman; **agente de seguros** insurance agent; **agente de tránsito** (MÉX) traffic cop; **agente inmobiliario** estate agent (BRIT), realtor (US)

**ágil** ['axil] adj agile, nimble; **agilidad** nf agility, nimbleness

**agilizar** [axili'θar] vt (trámites) to speed up

**agiotista** [axjo'tista] (MÉX) nmf (usurero) usurer

**agitación** [axita'θjon] nf (de mano etc) shaking, waving; (de líquido etc) stirring; (fig) agitation

**agitado, -a** [axi'aðo, a] adj hectic; (viaje) bumpy

**agitar** [axi'tar] vt to wave, shake; (líquido) to stir; (fig) to stir up, excite; **agitarse** vr

to get excited; (inquietarse) to get worried o upset

**aglomeración** [aɣlomera'θjon] nf agglomeration; **aglomeración de gente/ tráfico** mass of people/traffic jam

**agnóstico, -a** [aɣ'nostiko, a] adj, nm/f agnostic

**agobiar** [aɣo'βjar] vt to weigh down; (oprimir) to oppress; (cargar) to burden

**agolparse** [aɣol'parse] vr to crowd together

**agonía** [aɣo'nia] nf death throes pl; (fig) agony, anguish

**agonizante** [aɣoni'θante] adj dying

**agonizar** [aɣoni'θar] vi to be dying

**agosto** [a'ɣosto] nm August

**agotado, -a** [aɣo'taðo, a] adj (persona) exhausted; (libros) out of print; (acabado) finished; (Com) sold out; **agotador, a** [aɣota'ðor, a] adj exhausting

**agotamiento** [aɣota'mjento] nm exhaustion

**agotar** [aɣo'tar] vt to exhaust; (consumir) to drain; (recursos) to use up, deplete; **agotarse** vr to be exhausted; (acabarse) to run out; (libro) to go out of print

**agraciado, -a** [aɣra'θjaðo, a] adj (atractivo) attractive; (en sorteo etc) lucky

**agradable** [aɣra'ðaβle] adj pleasant, nice

**agradar** [aɣra'ðar] vt: **él me agrada** I like him

**agradecer** [aɣraðe'θer] vt to thank; (favor etc) to be grateful for; **agradecido, -a** adj grateful; **¡muy agradecido!** thanks a lot!; **agradecimiento** nm thanks pl; gratitude

**agradezco** etc vb V **agradecer**

**agrado** [a'ɣraðo] nm: **ser de tu** etc **~** to be to your etc liking

**agrandar** [aɣran'dar] vt to enlarge; (fig) to exaggerate; **agrandarse** vr to get bigger

**agrario, -a** [a'ɣrarjo, a] adj agrarian, land cpd; (política) agricultural, farming

**agravante** [aɣra'βante] adj aggravating ▷ nm: **con el ~ de que ...** with the further difficulty that ...

**agravar** [aɣra'βar] vt (pesar sobre) to make heavier; (irritar) to aggravate; **agravarse** vr to worsen, get worse

**agraviar** [aɣra'βjar] vt to offend; (ser injusto con) to wrong

**agredir** [aɣre'ðir] vt to attack

**agregado, -a** [aɣre'ɣaðo, a] nm/f: **A~** ≈ teacher (who is not head of department) ▷ nm aggregate; (persona) attaché

**agregar** [aɣre'ɣar] vt to gather; (añadir) to add; (persona) to appoint

**agresión** [aɣre'sjon] nf aggression

**agresivo, -a** [aɣre'siβo, a] adj aggressive

**agriar** [a'xrjar] vt to (turn) sour

**agrícola** [a'xrikola] adj farming cpd, agricultural

**agricultor, a** [axrikul'tor, a] nm/f farmer

**agricultura** [axrikul'tura] nf agriculture, farming

**agridulce** [axri'ðulθe] adj bittersweet; (Culin) sweet and sour

**agrietarse** [axrje'tarse] vr to crack; (piel) to chap

**agrio, -a** ['axrjo, a] adj bitter

**agrupación** [axrupa'θjon] nf group; (acto) grouping

**agrupar** [axru'par] vt to group

**agua** ['axwa] nf water; (Náut) wake; (Arq) slope of a roof; **aguas** nfpl (de piedra) water sg, sparkle sg; (Med) water sg, urine sg; (Náut) waters; **agua bendita/destilada/potable** holy/distilled/drinking water; **agua caliente** hot water; **agua corriente** running water; **agua de colonia** eau de cologne; **agua mineral (con/sin gas)** (sparkling/still) mineral water; **agua oxigenada** hydrogen peroxide; **aguas abajo/arriba** downstream/upstream; **aguas jurisdiccionales** territorial waters

**aguacate** [axwa'kate] nm avocado (pear)

**aguacero** [axwa'θero] nm (heavy) shower, downpour

**aguado, -a** [a'xwaðo, a] adj watery, watered down

**aguafiestas** [axwa'fjestas] nmf inv spoilsport, killjoy

**aguamiel** [axwa'mjel] (Méx) nf fermented maguey o agave juice

**aguanieve** [axwa'njeβe] nf sleet

**aguantar** [axwan'tar] vt to bear, put up with; (sostener) to hold up ▷ vi to last; **aguantarse** vr to restrain o.s.; **aguante** nm (paciencia) patience; (resistencia) endurance

**aguar** [a'xwar] vt to water down

**aguardar** [axwar'ðar] vt to wait for

**aguardiente** [axwar'ðjente] nm brandy, liquor

**aguarrás** [axwa'rras] nm turpentine

**aguaviva** [axwa'βiβa] (RPL) nf jellyfish

**agudeza** [axu'ðeθa] nf sharpness; (ingenio) wit

**agudo, -a** [a'xuðo, a] adj sharp; (voz) high-pitched, piercing; (dolor, enfermedad) acute

**agüero** [a'xwero] nm: **buen/mal ~** good/bad omen

**aguijón** [axi'xon] nm sting; (fig) spur

**águila** ['axila] nf eagle; (fig) genius

**aguileño, -a** [axi'leɲo, a] adj (nariz) aquiline; (rostro) sharp-featured

**aguinaldo** [axi'naldo] nm Christmas box

**aguja** [a'xuxa] nf needle; (de reloj) hand; (Arq) spire; (Tec) firing-pin; **agujas** nfpl (Zool) ribs; (Ferro) points

**agujerear** [axuxere'ar] vt to make holes in

**agujero** [axu'xero] nm hole

**agujetas** [axu'xetas] nfpl stitch sg; (rigidez) stiffness sg

**ahí** [a'i] adv there; **de ~ que** so that, with the result that; **~ llega** here he comes; **por ~** that way; (allá) over there; **200 o por ~** 200 or so

**ahijado, -a** [ai'xaðo, a] nm/f godson/daughter

**ahogar** [ao'xar] vt to drown; (asfixiar) to suffocate, smother; (fuego) to put out; **ahogarse** vr (en el agua) to drown; (por asfixia) to suffocate

**ahogo** [a'oxo] nm breathlessness; (fig) financial difficulty

**ahondar** [aon'dar] vt to deepen, make deeper; (fig) to study thoroughly ▷ vi: **~ en** to study thoroughly

**ahora** [a'ora] adv now; (hace poco) a moment ago, just now; (dentro de poco) in a moment; **~ voy** I'm coming; **~ mismo** right now; **~ bien** now then; **por ~** for the present

**ahorcar** [aor'kar] vt to hang

**ahorita** [ao'rita] (fam) adv (LAM: en este momento) right now; (Méx: hace poco) just now; (: dentro de poco) in a minute

**ahorrar** [ao'rrar] vt (dinero) to save; (esfuerzos) to save, avoid; **ahorro** nm (acto) saving; **ahorros** nmpl (dinero) savings

**ahuecar** [awe'kar] vt to hollow (out); (voz) to deepen; **ahuecarse** vr to give o.s. airs

**ahumar** [au'mar] vt to smoke, cure; (llenar de humo) to fill with smoke ▷ vi to smoke; **ahumarse** vr to fill with smoke

**ahuyentar** [aujen'tar] vt to drive off, frighten off; (fig) to dispel

**aire** ['aire] nm air; (viento) wind; (corriente) draught; (Mús) tune; **al ~ libre** in the open air; **aire acondicionado** air conditioning; **airear** vt to air; **airearse** vr (persona) to go out for a breath of fresh air; **airoso, -a** adj windy; draughty; (fig) graceful

**aislado, -a** [ais'laðo, a] adj isolated; (incomunicado) cut-off; (Elec) insulated

**aislar** [ais'lar] vt to isolate; (Elec) to insulate

**ajardinado, -a** [axarði'naðo, a] adj landscaped

**ajedrez** [axe'ðreθ] nm chess

**ajeno, -a** [a'xeno, a] adj (que pertenece a otro) somebody else's; **~ a** foreign to

**ajetreado, -a** [axetre'aðo, a] adj busy

**ajetreo** [axe'treo] nm bustle

**ají** [a'xi] (cs) nm chil(l)i, red pepper; (salsa) chil(l)i sauce

**ajillo** [a'xiʎo] nm: **gambas al ~** garlic prawns

**ajo** ['axo] nm garlic

**ajuar** [a'xwar] nm household furnishings pl; (de novia) trousseau; (de niño) layette

**ajustado, -a** [axus'taðo, a] adj (tornillo) tight; (cálculo) right; (ropa) tight(-fitting); (resultado) close

**ajustar** [axus'tar] vt (adaptar) to adjust; (encajar) to fit; (Tec) to engage; (Imprenta) to make up; (apretar) to tighten; (concertar) to agree (on); (reconciliar) to reconcile; (cuentas, deudas) to settle ▷ vi to fit; **ajustarse** vr: **~se a** (precio etc) to be in keeping with, fit in with; **~ las cuentas a algn** to get even with sb

**ajuste** [a'xuste] nm adjustment; (Costura) fitting; (acuerdo) compromise; (de cuenta) settlement

**al** [al] = **a + el**; V **a**

**ala** ['ala] nf wing; (de sombrero) brim; winger; **ala delta** nf hang-glider

**alabanza** [ala'βanθa] nf praise

**alabar** [ala'βar] vt to praise

**alacena** [ala'θena] nf kitchen cupboard (BRIT) o closet (US)

**alacrán** [ala'kran] nm scorpion

**alambrada** [alam'braða] nf wire fence; (red) wire netting

**alambre** [a'lambre] nm wire; **alambre de púas** barbed wire

**alameda** [ala'meða] nf (plantío) poplar grove; (lugar de paseo) avenue, boulevard

**álamo** ['alamo] nm poplar

**alarde** [a'larðe] nm show, display; **hacer ~ de** to boast of

**alargador** [alarɣa'ðor] nm (Elec) extension lead

**alargar** [alar'ɣar] vt to lengthen, extend; (paso) to hasten; (brazo) to stretch out; (cuerda) to pay out; (conversación) to spin out; **alargarse** vr to get longer

**alarma** [a'larma] nf alarm; **alarma de incendios** fire alarm; **alarmar** vt to alarm; **alarmarse** to get alarmed; **alarmante** [alar'mante] adj alarming

**alba** ['alβa] nf dawn

**albahaca** [al'βaka] nf basil

**Albania** [al'βanja] nf Albania

**albañil** [alβa'ɲil] nm bricklayer; (cantero) mason

**albarán** [alβa'ran] nm (Com) delivery note, invoice

**albaricoque** [alβari'koke] nm apricot

**albedrío** [alβe'ðrio] nm: **libre ~** free will

**alberca** [al'βerka] nf reservoir; (MÉX: piscina) swimming pool

**albergar** [alβer'ɣar] vt to shelter

**albergue** etc [al'βerɣe] vb V **albergar** ▷ nm shelter, refuge; **albergue juvenil** youth hostel

**albóndiga** [al'βondixa] nf meatball

**albornoz** [alβor'noθ] nm (de los árabes) burnous; (para el baño) bathrobe

**alborotar** [alβoro'tar] vi to make a row ▷ vt to agitate, stir up; **alborotarse** vr to get excited; (mar) to get rough; **alboroto** nm row, uproar

**álbum** ['alβum] (pl **~s, ~es**) nm album; **álbum de recortes** scrapbook

**albur** [al'βur] (MÉX) nm (juego de palabras) pun; (doble sentido) double entendre

**alcachofa** [alka'tʃofa] nf artichoke

**alcalde, -esa** [al'kalde, esa] nm/f mayor(ess)

**alcaldía** [alkal'dia] nf mayoralty; (lugar) mayor's office

**alcance** etc [al'kanθe] vb V **alcanzar** ▷ nm reach; (Com) adverse balance; **al ~ de algn** available to sb

**alcancía** [alkan'θia] (LAM) nf (para ahorrar) money box; (para colectas) collection box

**alcantarilla** [alkanta'riʎa] nf (de aguas cloacales) sewer; (en la calle) gutter

**alcanzar** [alkan'θar] vt (algo: con la mano, el pie) to reach; (alguien: en el camino etc) to catch up (with); (autobús) to catch; (bala) to hit, strike ▷ vi (ser suficiente) to be enough; **~ a hacer** to manage to do

**alcaparra** [alka'parra] nf caper

**alcayata** [alka'jata] nf hook

**alcázar** [al'kaθar] nm fortress; (Náut) quarter-deck

**alcoba** [al'koβa] nf bedroom

**alcohol** [al'kol] nm alcohol; **alcohol metílico** methylated spirits pl (BRIT), wood alcohol (US); **alcohólico, -a** adj, nm/f alcoholic; **alcoholímetro** [alko'limetro] nm Breathalyser® (BRIT), drunkometer (US); **alcoholismo** [alko'lismo] nm alcoholism

**alcornoque** [alkor'noke] nm cork tree; (fam) idiot

**aldea** [al'dea] nf village; **aldeano, -a** adj village cpd ▷ nm/f villager

**aleación** [alea'θjon] nf alloy

**aleatorio, -a** [alea'torjo, a] adj random

**aleccionar** [alekθjo'nar] vt to instruct; (adiestrar) to train

**alegar** [ale'ɣar] vt to claim; (Jur) to plead ▷ vi (LAM: discutir) to argue

**alegoría** [aleɣo'ria] nf allegory

**alegrar** [ale'ɣrar] vt (causar alegría) to cheer (up); (fuego) to poke; (fiesta) to liven

up; **alegrarse** vr (fam) to get merry o tight;
**~se de** to be glad about

**alegre** [a'leɣre] adj happy, cheerful; (fam)
merry, tight; (chiste) risqué, blue; **alegría** nf
happiness; merriment

**alejar** [ale'xar] vt to remove; (fig) to
estrange; **alejarse** vr to move away

**alemán, -ana** [ale'man, ana] adj, nm/f
German ▷ nm (Ling) German

**Alemania** [ale'manja] nf Germany

**alentador, a** [alenta'ðor, a] adj
encouraging

**alentar** [alen'tar] vt to encourage

**alergia** [a'lerxja] nf allergy

**alero** [a'lero] nm (de tejado) eaves pl;
(guardabarros) mudguard

**alerta** [a'lerta] adj, nm alert

**aleta** [a'leta] nf (de pez) fin; (ala) wing; (de
foca, Deporte) flipper; (Auto) mudguard

**aletear** [alete'ar] vi to flutter

**alevín** [ale'βin] nm fry, young fish

**alevosía** [aleβo'sia] nf treachery

**alfabeto** [alfa'βeto] nm alphabet

**alfalfa** [al'falfa] nf alfalfa, lucerne

**alfarería** [alfare'ria] nf pottery; (tienda)
pottery shop; **alfarero, -a** nm/f potter

**alféizar** [al'feiθar] nm window-sill

**alférez** [al'fereθ] nm (Mil) second
lieutenant; (Náut) ensign

**alfil** [al'fil] nm (Ajedrez) bishop

**alfiler** [alfi'ler] nm pin; (broche) clip

**alfombra** [al'fombra] nf carpet; (más
pequeña) rug; **alfombrilla** nf rug, mat;
(Inform) mouse mat o pad

**alforja** [al'forxa] nf saddlebag

**algas** ['alɣas] nfpl seaweed

**álgebra** ['alxeβra] nf algebra

**algo** ['alɣo] pron something; anything
▷ adv somewhat, rather; **¿~ más?** anything
else?; (en tienda) is that all?; **por ~ será** there
must be some reason for it

**algodón** [alɣo'ðon] nm cotton; (planta)
cotton plant; **algodón de azúcar** candy
floss (BRIT), cotton candy (US); **algodón
hidrófilo** cotton wool (BRIT), absorbent
cotton (US)

**alguien** ['alɣjen] pron someone,
somebody; (en frases interrogativas) anyone,
anybody

**alguno, -a** [al'ɣuno, a] adj (delante de
nm): **algún** some; (después de n): **no tiene
talento ~** he has no talent, he doesn't
have any talent ▷ pron (alguien) someone,
somebody; **algún que otro libro** some book
or other; **algún día iré** I'll go one o some day;
**sin interés ~** without the slightest interest;
**~ que otro** an occasional one; **~s piensan**
some (people) think

**alhaja** [a'laxa] nf jewel; (tesoro) precious
object, treasure

**alhelí** [ale'li] nm wallflower, stock

**aliado, -a** [a'ljaðo, a] adj allied

**alianza** [a'ljanθa] nf alliance; (anillo)
wedding ring

**aliar** [a'ljar] vt to ally; **aliarse** vr to form
an alliance

**alias** ['aljas] adv alias

**alicatado** [alika'taðo] (ESP) nm tiling

**alicates** [ali'kates] nmpl pliers

**aliciente** [ali'θjente] nm incentive;
(atracción) attraction

**alienación** [aljena'θjon] nf alienation

**aliento** [a'ljento] nm breath; (respiración)
breathing; **sin ~** breathless

**aligerar** [alixe'rar] vt to lighten; (reducir)
to shorten; (aliviar) to alleviate; (mitigar) to
ease; (paso) to quicken

**alijo** [a'lixo] nm consignment

**alimaña** [ali'maɲa] nf pest

**alimentación** [alimenta'θjon] nf
(comida) food; (acción) feeding; (tienda)
grocer's (shop)

**alimentar** [alimen'tar] vt to feed; (nutrir)
to nourish; **alimentarse** vr to feed

**alimenticio, -a** [alimen'tiθjo, a] adj food
cpd; (nutritivo) nourishing, nutritious

**alimento** [ali'mento] nm food; (nutrición)
nourishment

**alineación** [alinea'θjon] nf alignment;
(Deporte) line-up

**alinear** [aline'ar] vt to align; (Deporte) to
select, pick

**aliñar** [ali'ɲar] vt (Culin) to season; **aliño**
nm (Culin) dressing

**alioli** [ali'oli] nm garlic mayonnaise

**alisar** [ali'sar] vt to smooth

**alistarse** [alis'tarse] vr to enlist;
(inscribirse) to enrol

**aliviar** [ali'βjar] vt (carga) to lighten;
(persona) to relieve; (dolor) to relieve,
alleviate

**alivio** [a'liβjo] nm alleviation, relief

**aljibe** [al'xiβe] nm cistern

**allá** [a'ʎa] adv (lugar) there; (por ahí) over
there; (tiempo) then; **~ abajo** down there;
**más ~** further on; **más ~ de** beyond; **¡~ tú!**
that's your problem!; **¡~ voy!** I'm coming!

**allanamiento** [aʎana'mjento] nm
(LAM: de policía) raid; **allanamiento de
morada** burglary

**allanar** [aʎa'nar] vt to flatten, level (out);
(igualar) to smooth (out); (fig) to subdue;
(Jur) to burgle, break into

**allegado, -a** [aʎe'ɣaðo, a] adj near, close
▷ nm/f relation

**allí** [a'ʎi] adv there; **~ mismo** right there;

**por ~** over there; (*por ese camino*) that way

**alma** ['alma] *nf* soul; (*persona*) person

**almacén** [alma'θen] *nm* (*depósito*) warehouse, store; (*Mil*) magazine; (cs: *de comestibles*) grocer's (shop); **grandes almacenes** department store *sg*; **almacenaje** *nm* storage

**almacenar** [almaθe'nar] *vt* to store, put in storage; (*proveerse*) to stock up with

**almanaque** [alma'nake] *nm* almanac

**almeja** [al'mexa] *nf* clam

**almendra** [al'mendra] *nf* almond; **almendro** *nm* almond tree

**almíbar** [al'miβar] *nm* syrup

**almidón** [almi'ðon] *nm* starch

**almirante** [almi'rante] *nm* admiral

**almohada** [almo'aða] *nf* pillow; (*funda*) pillowcase; **almohadilla** *nf* cushion; (*para alfileres*) pincushion; (*Tec*) pad

**almohadón** [almoa'ðon] *nm* large pillow; bolster

**almorranas** [almo'rranas] *nfpl* piles, haemorrhoids

**almorzar** [almor'θar] *vt*: **~ una tortilla** to have an omelette for lunch ▷ *vi* to (have) lunch

**almuerzo** *etc* [al'mwerθo] *vb* V **almorzar** ▷ *nm* lunch

**alocado, -a** [alo'kaðo, a] *adj* crazy

**alojamiento** [aloxa'mjento] *nm* lodging(s) *pl*; (*viviendas*) housing

**alojar** [alo'xar] *vt* to lodge; **alojarse** *vr* to lodge, stay

**alondra** [a'londra] *nf* lark, skylark

**alpargata** [alpar'ɣata] *nf* rope-soled sandal, espadrille

**Alpes** ['alpes] *nmpl*: **los ~** the Alps

**alpinismo** [alpi'nismo] *nm* mountaineering, climbing; **alpinista** *nmf* mountaineer, climber

**alpiste** [al'piste] *nm* birdseed

**alquilar** [alki'lar] *vt* (*propietario: inmuebles*) to let, rent (out); (: *coche*) to hire out; (: *TV*) to rent (out); (*alquilador: inmuebles, TV*) to rent; (: *coche*) to hire; **"se alquila casa"** "house to let (BRIT) o for rent (US)"

**alquiler** [alki'ler] *nm* renting; letting; hiring; (*arriendo*) rent; hire charge; **de ~** for hire; **alquiler de automóviles** o **coches** car hire

**alquimia** [al'kimja] *nf* alchemy

**alquitrán** [alki'tran] *nm* tar

**alrededor** [alreðe'ðor] *adv* around, about; **~ de** around, about; **mirar a su ~** to look (round) about one; **alrededores** *nmpl* surroundings

**alta** ['alta] *nf* (certificate of) discharge

**altar** [al'tar] *nm* altar

**altavoz** [alta'βoθ] *nm* loudspeaker; (*amplificador*) amplifier

**alteración** [altera'θjon] *nf* alteration; (*alboroto*) disturbance

**alterar** [alte'rar] *vt* to alter; to disturb; **alterarse** *vr* (*persona*) to get upset

**altercado** [alter'kaðo] *nm* argument

**alternar** [alter'nar] *vt* to alternate ▷ *vi* to alternate; (*turnar*) to take turns; **alternarse** *vr* to alternate; to take turns; **~ con** to mix with; **alternativa** *nf* alternative; (*elección*) choice; **alternativo, -a** *adj* alternative; (*alterno*) alternating; **alterno, -a** *adj* alternate; (*Elec*) alternating

**Alteza** [al'teθa] *nf* (*tratamiento*) Highness

**altibajos** [alti'βaxos] *nmpl* ups and downs

**altiplano** [alti'plano] *nm* = **altiplanicie**

**altisonante** [altiso'nante] *adj* high-flown, high-sounding

**altitud** [alti'tuð] *nf* height; (*Aviac, Geo*) altitude

**altivo, -a** [al'tiβo, a] *adj* haughty, arrogant

**alto, -a** ['alto, a] *adj* high; (*persona*) tall; (*sonido*) high, sharp; (*noble*) high, lofty ▷ *nm* halt; (*Mús*) alto; (*Geo*) hill ▷ *adv* (*de sitio*) high; (*de sonido*) loud, loudly ▷ *excl* halt!; **la pared tiene 2 metros de ~** the wall is 2 metres high; **en alta mar** on the high seas; **en voz alta** in a loud voice; **las altas horas de la noche** the small o wee hours; **en lo ~ de** at the top of; **pasar por ~** to overlook; **altoparlante** [altopar'lante] (LAM) *nm* loudspeaker

**altura** [al'tura] *nf* height; (*Náut*) depth; (*Geo*) latitude; **la pared tiene 1.80 de ~** the wall is 1 metre 80cm high; **a estas ~s** at this stage; **a estas ~s del año** at this time of the year

**alubia** [a'luβja] *nf* bean

**alucinación** [aluθina'θjon] *nf* hallucination

**alucinar** [aluθi'nar] *vi* to hallucinate ▷ *vt* to deceive; (*fascinar*) to fascinate

**alud** [a'luð] *nm* avalanche; (*fig*) flood

**aludir** [alu'ðir] *vi*: **~ a** to allude to; **darse por aludido** to take the hint

**alumbrado** [alum'braðo] *nm* lighting

**alumbrar** [alum'brar] *vt* to light (up) ▷ *vi* (*Med*) to give birth

**aluminio** [alu'minjo] *nm* aluminium (BRIT), aluminum (US)

**alumno, -a** [a'lumno, a] *nm/f* pupil, student

**alusión** [alu'sjon] *nf* allusion

**alusivo, -a** [alu'siβo, a] *adj* allusive

**aluvión** [alu'βjon] *nm* alluvium; (*fig*) flood

**alverja** [al'βerxa] (LAM) *nf* pea

**alza** ['alθa] *nf* rise; (*Mil*) sight
**alzamiento** [alθa'mjento] *nm* (*rebelión*) rising
**alzar** [al'θar] *vt* to lift (up); (*precio, muro*) to raise; (*cuello de abrigo*) to turn up; (*Agr*) to gather in; (*Imprenta*) to gather; **alzarse** *vr* to get up, rise; (*rebelarse*) to revolt; (*Com*) to go fraudulently bankrupt; (*Jur*) to appeal
**ama** ['ama] *nf* lady of the house; (*dueña*) owner; (*institutriz*) governess; (*madre adoptiva*) foster mother; **ama de casa** housewife; **ama de llaves** housekeeper
**amabilidad** [amaβili'ðað] *nf* kindness; (*simpatía*) niceness; **amable** *adj* kind; nice; **es usted muy amable** that's very kind of you
**amaestrado, -a** [amaes'traðo, a] *adj* (*animal: en circo etc*) performing
**amaestrar** [amaes'trar] *vt* to train
**amago** [a'maɣo] *nm* threat; (*gesto*) threatening gesture; (*Med*) symptom
**amainar** [amai'nar] *vi* (*viento*) to die down
**amamantar** [amaman'tar] *vt* to suckle, nurse
**amanecer** [amane'θer] *vi* to dawn ▷ *nm* dawn; **~ afiebrado** to wake up with a fever
**amanerado, -a** [amane'raðo, a] *adj* affected
**amante** [a'mante] *adj*: **~ de** fond of ▷ *nmf* lover
**amapola** [ama'pola] *nf* poppy
**amar** [a'mar] *vt* to love
**amargado, -a** [amar'ɣaðo, a] *adj* bitter
**amargar** [amar'ɣar] *vt* to make bitter; (*fig*) to embitter; **amargarse** *vr* to become embittered
**amargo, -a** [a'marɣo, a] *adj* bitter
**amarillento, -a** [amari'ʎento, a] *adj* yellowish; (*tez*) sallow; **amarillo, -a** *adj*, *nm* yellow
**amarrado, -a** [ama'rraðo, a] (*MÉx: fam*) *adj* mean, stingy
**amarrar** [ama'rrar] *vt* to moor; (*sujetar*) to tie up
**amarras** [a'marras] *nfpl*: **soltar ~** to set sail
**amasar** [ama'sar] *vt* (*masa*) to knead; (*mezclar*) to mix, prepare; (*confeccionar*) to concoct
**amateur** [ama'ter] *nmf* amateur
**amazona** [ama'θona] *nf* horsewoman; **Amazonas** *nm*: **el Amazonas** the Amazon
**ámbar** ['ambar] *nm* amber
**ambición** [ambi'θjon] *nf* ambition; **ambicionar** *vt* to aspire to; **ambicioso, -a** *adj* ambitious
**ambidextro, -a** [ambi'ðekstro, a] *adj* ambidextrous
**ambientación** [ambjenta'θjon] *nf* (*Cine, Teatro etc*) setting; (*Radio*) sound effects
**ambiente** [am'bjente] *nm* atmosphere; (*medio*) environment
**ambigüedad** [ambiɣwe'ðað] *nf* ambiguity; **ambiguo, -a** *adj* ambiguous
**ámbito** ['ambito] *nm* (*campo*) field; (*fig*) scope
**ambos, -as** ['ambos, as] *adj pl, pron pl* both
**ambulancia** [ambu'lanθja] *nf* ambulance
**ambulante** [ambu'lante] *adj* travelling *cpd*, itinerant
**ambulatorio** [ambula'torjo] *nm* state health-service clinic
**amén** [a'men] *excl* amen; **~ de** besides
**amenaza** [ame'naθa] *nf* threat; **amenazar** [amena'θar] *vt* to threaten ▷ *vi*: **amenazar con hacer** to threaten to do
**ameno, -a** [a'meno, a] *adj* pleasant
**América** [a'merika] *nf* America; **América Central/Latina** Central/Latin America; **América del Norte/del Sur** North/South America; **americana** *nf* coat, jacket; V *tb* **americano**; **americano, -a** *adj*, *nm/f* American
**ametralladora** [ametraʎa'ðora] *nf* machine gun
**amigable** [ami'ɣaβle] *adj* friendly
**amígdala** [a'miɣðala] *nf* tonsil; **amigdalitis** *nf* tonsillitis
**amigo, -a** [a'miɣo, a] *adj* friendly ▷ *nm/f* friend; (*amante*) lover; **ser ~ de algo** to be fond of sth; **ser muy ~s** to be close friends
**aminorar** [amino'rar] *vt* to diminish; (*reducir*) to reduce; **~ la marcha** to slow down
**amistad** [amis'tað] *nf* friendship; **amistades** *nfpl* (*amigos*) friends; **amistoso, -a** *adj* friendly
**amnesia** [am'nesja] *nf* amnesia
**amnistía** [amnis'tia] *nf* amnesty
**amo** ['amo] *nm* owner; (*jefe*) boss
**amolar** [amo'lar] (*MÉx: fam*) *vt* to ruin, damage
**amoldar** [amol'dar] *vt* to mould; (*adaptar*) to adapt
**amonestación** [amonesta'θjon] *nf* warning; **amonestaciones** *nfpl* (*Rel*) marriage banns
**amonestar** [amones'tar] *vt* to warn; (*Rel*) to publish the banns of
**amontonar** [amonto'nar] *vt* to collect, pile up; **amontonarse** *vr* to crowd together; (*acumularse*) to pile up
**amor** [a'mor] *nm* love; (*amante*) lover;

**hacer el ~** to make love; **amor propio** self-respect

**amoratado, -a** [amora'taðo, a] *adj* purple

**amordazar** [amorða'θar] *vt* to muzzle; *(fig)* to gag

**amorfo, -a** [a'morfo, a] *adj* amorphous, shapeless

**amoroso, -a** [amo'roso, a] *adj* affectionate, loving

**amortiguador** [amortigwa'ðor] *nm* shock absorber; *(parachoques)* bumper; **amortiguadores** *nmpl (Auto)* suspension *sg*

**amortiguar** [amorti'ɣwar] *vt* to deaden; *(ruido)* to muffle; *(color)* to soften

**amotinar** [amoti'nar] *vt* to stir up, incite (to riot); **amotinarse** *vr* to mutiny

**amparar** [ampa'rar] *vt* to protect; **ampararse** *vr* to seek protection; *(de la lluvia etc)* to shelter; **amparo** *nm* help, protection; **al amparo de** under the protection of

**amperio** [am'perjo] *nm* ampère, amp

**ampliación** [amplja'θjon] *nf* enlargement; *(extensión)* extension

**ampliar** [am'pljar] *vt* to enlarge; to extend

**amplificador** [amplifika'ðor] *nm* amplifier

**amplificar** [amplifi'kar] *vt* to amplify

**amplio, -a** ['ampljo, a] *adj* spacious; *(de falda etc)* full; *(extenso)* extensive; *(ancho)* wide; **amplitud** *nf* spaciousness; extent; *(fig)* amplitude

**ampolla** [am'poʎa] *nf* blister; *(Med)* ampoule

**amputar** [ampu'tar] *vt* to cut off, amputate

**amueblar** [amwe'βlar] *vt* to furnish

**anales** [a'nales] *nmpl* annals

**analfabetismo** [analfaβe'tismo] *nm* illiteracy; **analfabeto, -a** *adj, nm/f* illiterate

**analgésico** [anal'xesiko] *nm* painkiller, analgesic

**análisis** [a'nalisis] *nm inv* analysis

**analista** [ana'lista] *nmf (gen)* analyst

**analizar** [anali'θar] *vt* to analyse

**analógico, -a** [ana'loxiko, a] *adj (Inform)* analog; *(reloj)* analogue *(BRIT)*, analog *(US)*

**análogo, -a** [a'naloɣo, a] *adj* analogous, similar

**ananá** [ana'na] *(RPL) nm* pineapple

**anarquía** [anar'kia] *nf* anarchy; **anarquista** *nmf* anarchist

**anatomía** [anato'mia] *nf* anatomy

**anca** ['anka] *nf* rump, haunch; **ancas** *nfpl* *(fam)* behind *sg*

**ancho, -a** ['antʃo, a] *adj* wide; *(falda)* full; *(fig)* liberal ▷ *nm* width; *(Ferro)* gauge; **ponerse ~** to get conceited; **estar a sus anchas** to be at one's ease

**anchoa** [an'tʃoa] *nf* anchovy

**anchura** [an'tʃura] *nf* width; *(extensión)* wideness

**anciano, -a** [an'θjano, a] *adj* old, aged ▷ *nm/f* old man/woman; elder

**ancla** ['ankla] *nf* anchor

**Andalucía** [andalu'θia] *nf* Andalusia; **andaluz, -a** *adj, nm/f* Andalusian

**andamio** [an'damjo] *nm* scaffold(ing)

**andar** [an'dar] *vt* to go, cover, travel ▷ *vi* to go, walk, travel; *(funcionar)* to go, work; *(estar)* to be ▷ *nm* walk, gait, pace; **andarse** *vr* to go away; **~ a pie/a caballo/en bicicleta** to go on foot/on horseback/by bicycle; **~ haciendo algo** to be doing sth; **¡anda!** *(sorpresa)* go on!; **anda por** *o* **en los 40** he's about 40

**andén** [an'den] *nm (Ferro)* platform; *(Náut)* quayside; *(CAM: de la calle)* pavement *(BRIT)*, sidewalk *(US)*

**Andes** ['andes] *nmpl:* **los ~** the Andes

**andinismo** [andi'nismo] *(LAM) nm* mountaineering, climbing

**Andorra** [an'dorra] *nf* Andorra

**andrajoso, -a** [andra'xoso, a] *adj* ragged

**anduve** *etc vb* V **andar**

**anécdota** [a'nekðota] *nf* anecdote, story

**anegar** [ane'ɣar] *vt* to flood; *(ahogar)* to drown

**anemia** [a'nemja] *nf* anaemia

**anestesia** [anes'tesja] *nf (sustancia)* anaesthetic; *(proceso)* anaesthesia; **anestesia general/local** general/local anaesthetic

**anexar** [anek'sar] *vt* to annex; *(documento)* to attach; **anexión** *nf* annexation; **anexo, -a** *adj* attached ▷ *nm* annexe

**anfibio, -a** [an'fiβjo, a] *adj* amphibious ▷ *nm* amphibian

**anfiteatro** [anfite'atro] *nm* amphitheatre; *(Teatro)* dress circle

**anfitrión, -ona** [anfi'trjon, ona] *nm/f* host(ess)

**ánfora** ['anfora] *nf (cántaro)* amphora; *(MÉX Pol)* ballot box

**ángel** ['anxel] *nm* angel; **ángel de la guarda** guardian angel

**angina** [an'xina] *nf (Med)* inflammation of the throat; **tener ~s** to have tonsillitis; **angina de pecho** angina

**anglicano, -a** [angli'kano, a] *adj, nm/f* Anglican

**anglosajón, -ona** [anglosa'xon, ona] *adj*

Anglo-Saxon

**anguila** [an'gila] *nf* eel

**angula** [an'gula] *nf* elver, baby eel

**ángulo** ['angulo] *nm* angle; (*esquina*) corner; (*curva*) bend

**angustia** [an'gustja] *nf* anguish

**anhelar** [ane'lar] *vt* to be eager for; (*desear*) to long for, desire ▷ *vi* to pant, gasp; **anhelo** *nm* eagerness; desire

**anidar** [ani'ðar] *vi* to nest

**anillo** [a'niʎo] *nm* ring; **anillo de boda/compromiso** wedding/engagement ring

**animación** [anima'θjon] *nf* liveliness; (*vitalidad*) life; (*actividad*) activity; bustle

**animado, -a** [ani'maðo, a] *adj* lively; (*vivaz*) animated; **animador, a** *nm/f* (TV) host(ess), compère; (*Deporte*) cheerleader

**animal** [ani'mal] *adj* animal; (*fig*) stupid ▷ *nm* animal; (*fig*) fool; (*bestia*) brute

**animar** [ani'mar] *vt* (*Bio*) to animate, give life to; (*fig*) to liven up, brighten up, cheer up; (*estimular*) to stimulate; **animarse** *vr* to cheer up; to feel encouraged; (*decidirse*) to make up one's mind

**ánimo** ['animo] *nm* (*alma*) soul; (*mente*) mind; (*valentía*) courage ▷ *excl* cheer up!

**animoso, -a** [ani'moso, a] *adj* brave; (*vivo*) lively

**aniquilar** [aniki'lar] *vt* to annihilate, destroy

**anís** [a'nis] *nm* aniseed; (*licor*) anisette

**aniversario** [aniβer'sarjo] *nm* anniversary

**anoche** [a'notʃe] *adv* last night; **antes de ~** the night before last

**anochecer** [anotʃe'θer] *vi* to get dark ▷ *nm* nightfall, dark; **al ~** at nightfall

**anodino, -a** [ano'ðino, a] *adj* dull, anodyne

**anomalía** [anoma'lia] *nf* anomaly

**anonadado, -a** [anona'ðaðo, a] *adj*: **estar ~** to be overwhelmed *o* amazed

**anonimato** [anoni'mato] *nm* anonymity

**anónimo, -a** [a'nonimo, a] *adj* anonymous; (*Com*) limited ▷ *nm* (*carta anónima*) anonymous letter; (: *maliciosa*) poison-pen letter

**anormal** [anor'mal] *adj* abnormal

**anotación** [anota'θjon] *nf* note; annotation

**anotar** [ano'tar] *vt* to note down; (*comentar*) to annotate

**ansia** ['ansja] *nf* anxiety; (*añoranza*) yearning; **ansiar** *vt* to long for

**ansiedad** [ansje'ðað] *nf* anxiety

**ansioso, -a** [an'sjoso, a] *adj* anxious; (*anhelante*) eager; **~ de** *o* **por algo** greedy for sth

**antaño** [an'taɲo] *adv* long ago, formerly

**Antártico** [an'tartiko] *nm*: **el ~** the Antarctic

**ante** ['ante] *prep* before, in the presence of; (*problema etc*) faced with ▷ *nm* (*piel*) suede; **~ todo** above all

**anteanoche** [antea'notʃe] *adv* the night before last

**anteayer** [antea'jer] *adv* the day before yesterday

**antebrazo** [ante'βraθo] *nm* forearm

**antecedente** [anteθe'ðente] *adj* previous ▷ *nm* antecedent; **antecedentes** *nmpl* (*historial*) record *sg*; **antecedentes penales** criminal record

**anteceder** [anteθe'ðer] *vt* to precede, go before

**antecesor, a** [anteθe'sor, a] *nm/f* predecessor

**antelación** [antela'θjon] *nf*: **con ~** in advance

**antemano** [ante'mano]: **de ~** *adv* beforehand, in advance

**antena** [an'tena] *nf* antenna; (*de televisión etc*) aerial; **antena parabólica** satellite dish

**antenoche** [ante'notʃe] (LAM) *adv* the night before last

**anteojo** [ante'oxo] *nm* eyeglass; **anteojos** *nmpl* (LAM: *gafas*) glasses, spectacles

**antepasados** [antepa'saðos] *nmpl* ancestors

**anteponer** [antepo'ner] *vt* to place in front; (*fig*) to prefer

**anterior** [ante'rjor] *adj* preceding, previous; **anterioridad** *nf*: **con anterioridad a** prior to, before

**antes** ['antes] *adv* (*con prioridad*) before ▷ *prep*: **~ de** before ▷ *conj*: **~ de ir/de que te vayas** before going/before you go; **~ bien** (but) rather; **dos días ~** two days before *o* previously; **no quiso venir ~** she didn't want to come any earlier; **tomo el avión ~ que el barco** I take the plane rather than the boat; **~ de** *o* **que nada** (*en el tiempo*) first of all; (*indicando preferencia*) above all; **~ que yo** before me; **lo ~ posible** as soon as possible; **cuanto ~ mejor** the sooner the better

**antibalas** [anti'βalas] *adj inv*: **chaleco ~** bullet-proof jacket

**antibiótico** [anti'βjotiko] *nm* antibiotic

**anticaspa** [anti'kaspa] *adj inv* anti-dandruff *cpd*

**anticipación** [antiθipa'θjon] *nf* anticipation; **con 10 minutos de ~** 10 minutes early

**anticipado, -a** [antiθi'paðo, a] *adj* (*pago*) advance; **por ~** in advance

**anticipar** [antiθi'par] *vt* to anticipate;

(*adelantar*) to bring forward; (*Com*) to advance; **anticiparse** *vr*: **~se a su época** to be ahead of one's time

**anticipo** [anti'θipo] *nm* (*Com*) advance

**anticonceptivo, -a** [antikonθep'tiβo, a] *adj, nm* contraceptive

**anticongelante** [antikonxe'lante] *nm* antifreeze

**anticuado, -a** [anti'kwaðo, a] *adj* out-of-date, old-fashioned; (*desusado*) obsolete

**anticuario** [anti'kwarjo] *nm* antique dealer

**anticuerpo** [anti'kwerpo] *nm* (*Med*) antibody

**antidepresivo** [antiðepre'siβo] *nm* antidepressant

**antidóping** [anti'dopin] *adj inv*: **control ~** drugs test

**antídoto** [an'tiðoto] *nm* antidote

**antiestético, -a** [anties'tetiko, a] *adj* unsightly

**antifaz** [anti'faθ] *nm* mask; (*velo*) veil

**antiglobalización** [antigloβaliθa'θjon] *nf* anti-globalization; **antiglobalizador, a** *adj* anti-globalization *cpd*

**antiguamente** [antixwa'mente] *adv* formerly; (*hace mucho tiempo*) long ago

**antigüedad** [antixwe'ðað] *nf* antiquity; (*artículo*) antique; (*rango*) seniority

**antiguo, -a** [an'tixwo, a] *adj* old, ancient; (*que fue*) former

**Antillas** [an'tiʎas] *nfpl*: **las ~** the West Indies

**antílope** [an'tilope] *nm* antelope

**antinatural** [antinatu'ral] *adj* unnatural

**antipatía** [antipa'tia] *nf* antipathy, dislike; **antipático, -a** *adj* disagreeable, unpleasant

**antirrobo** [anti'rroβo] *adj inv* (*alarma etc*) anti-theft

**antisemita** [antise'mita] *adj* anti-Semitic ▷ *nmf* anti-Semite

**antiséptico, -a** [anti'septiko, a] *adj* antiseptic ▷ *nm* antiseptic

**antivirus** [anti'birus] *nm inv* (*Comput*) antivirus program

**antojarse** [anto'xarse] *vr* (*desear*): **se me antoja comprarlo** I have a mind to buy it; (*pensar*): **se me antoja que ...** I have a feeling that ...

**antojitos** [anto'xitos] (*MÉX*) *nmpl* snacks, nibbles

**antojo** [an'toxo] *nm* caprice, whim; (*rosa*) birthmark; (*lunar*) mole

**antología** [antolo'xia] *nf* anthology

**antorcha** [an'tortʃa] *nf* torch

**antro** ['antro] *nm* cavern

**antropología** [antropolo'xia] *nf* anthropology

**anual** [a'nwal] *adj* annual

**anuario** [a'nwarjo] *nm* yearbook

**anulación** [anula'θjon] *nf* annulment; (*cancelación*) cancellation

**anular** [anu'lar] *vt* (*contrato*) to annul, cancel; (*ley*) to revoke, repeal; (*suscripción*) to cancel ▷ *nm* ring finger

**anunciar** [anun'θjar] *vt* to announce; (*proclamar*) to proclaim; (*Com*) to advertise

**anuncio** [a'nunθjo] *nm* announcement; (*señal*) sign; (*Com*) advertisement; (*cartel*) poster

**anzuelo** [an'θwelo] *nm* hook; (*para pescar*) fish hook

**añadidura** [aɲaði'ðura] *nf* addition, extra; **por ~** besides, in addition

**añadir** [aɲa'ðir] *vt* to add

**añejo, -a** [a'ɲexo, a] *adj* old; (*vino*) mellow

**añicos** [a'ɲikos] *nmpl*: **hacer ~** to smash, shatter

**año** ['aɲo] *nm* year; **¡Feliz A~ Nuevo!** Happy New Year!; **tener 15 ~s** to be 15 (years old); **los ~s 90** the nineties; **el ~ que viene** next year; **año bisiesto/escolar/fiscal/sabático** leap/school/tax/sabbatical year

**añoranza** [aɲo'ranθa] *nf* nostalgia; (*anhelo*) longing

**apa** ['apa] (*MÉX*) *excl* goodness me!, good gracious!

**apabullar** [apaβu'ʎar] *vt* to crush, squash

**apacible** [apa'θiβle] *adj* gentle, mild

**apaciguar** [apaθi'ɣwar] *vt* to pacify, calm (down)

**apadrinar** [apaðri'nar] *vt* to sponsor, support; (*Rel*) to be godfather to

**apagado, -a** [apa'ɣaðo, a] *adj* (*volcán*) extinct; (*color*) dull; (*voz*) quiet; (*sonido*) muted, muffled; (*persona: apático*) listless; **estar ~** (*fuego, luz*) to be out; (*Radio, TV etc*) to be off

**apagar** [apa'ɣar] *vt* to put out; (*Elec, Radio, TV*) to turn off; (*sonido*) to silence, muffle; (*sed*) to quench

**apagón** [apa'ɣon] *nm* blackout; power cut

**apalabrar** [apala'βrar] *vt* to agree to; (*contratar*) to engage

**apalear** [apale'ar] *vt* to beat, thrash

**apantallar** [apanta'ʎar] (*MÉX*) *vt* to impress

**apañar** [apa'nar] *vt* to pick up; (*asir*) to take hold of, grasp; (*reparar*) to mend, patch up; **apañarse** *vr* to manage, get along

**apapachar** [apapa'tʃar] (*MÉX: fam*) *vt* to cuddle, hug

**aparador** [apara'ðor] *nm* sideboard; (*MÉX: escaparate*) shop window

**aparato** [apa'rato] *nm* apparatus;

(*máquina*) machine; (*doméstico*) appliance; (*boato*) ostentation; **aparato digestivo** (*Anat*) digestive system; **aparatoso, -a** *adj* showy, ostentatious

**aparcamiento** [aparka'mjento] *nm* car park (BRIT), parking lot (US)

**aparcar** [apar'kar] *vt, vi* to park

**aparear** [apare'ar] *vt* (*objetos*) to pair, match; (*animales*) to mate; **aparearse** *vr* to make a pair; to mate

**aparecer** [apare'θer] *vi* to appear; **aparecerse** *vr* to appear

**aparejador, a** [aparexa'ðor, a] *nm/f* (*Arq*) master builder

**aparejo** [apa'rexo] *nm* harness; rigging; (*de poleas*) block and tackle

**aparentar** [aparen'tar] *vt* (*edad*) to look; (*fingir*): **~ tristeza** to pretend to be sad

**aparente** [apa'rente] *adj* apparent; (*adecuado*) suitable

**aparezco** *etc vb* V **aparecer**

**aparición** [apari'θjon] *nf* appearance; (*de libro*) publication; (*espectro*) apparition

**apariencia** [apa'rjenθja] *nf* (outward) appearance; **en ~** outwardly, seemingly

**apartado, -a** [apar'taðo, a] *adj* separate; (*lejano*) remote ▷ *nm* (*tipográfico*) paragraph; **apartado de correos** (ESP) post office box; **apartado postal** (LAM) post office box

**apartamento** [aparta'mento] *nm* apartment, flat (BRIT)

**apartar** [apar'tar] *vt* to separate; (*quitar*) to remove; **apartarse** *vr* to separate, part; (*irse*) to move away; to keep away

**aparte** [a'parte] *adv* (*separadamente*) separately; (*además*) besides ▷ *nm* aside; (*tipográfico*) new paragraph

**aparthotel** [aparto'tel] *nm* serviced apartments

**apasionado, -a** [apasjo'naðo, a] *adj* passionate

**apasionar** [apasjo'nar] *vt* to excite; **le apasiona el fútbol** she's crazy about football; **apasionarse** *vr* to get excited

**apatía** [apa'tia] *nf* apathy

**apático, -a** [a'patiko, a] *adj* apathetic

**Apdo** *abr* (= *Apartado (de Correos)*) PO Box

**apeadero** [apea'ðero] *nm* halt, stop, stopping place

**apearse** [ape'arse] *vr* (*jinete*) to dismount; (*bajarse*) to get down o out; (*Auto, Ferro*) to get off o out

**apechugar** [apetʃu'xar] *vr*: **~ con algo** to face up to sth

**apegarse** [ape'xarse] *vr*: **~ a** to become attached to; **apego** *nm* attachment, devotion

**apelar** [ape'lar] *vi* to appeal; **~ a** (*fig*) to resort to

**apellidar** [apeʎi'ðar] *vt* to call, name; **apellidarse** *vr*: **se apellida Pérez** her (sur)name's Pérez

**apellido** [ape'ʎiðo] *nm* surname

**apenar** [ape'nar] *vt* to grieve, trouble; (LAM: *avergonzar*) to embarrass; **apenarse** *vr* to grieve; (LAM: *avergonzarse*) to be embarrassed

**apenas** [a'penas] *adv* scarcely, hardly ▷ *conj* as soon as, no sooner

**apéndice** [a'pendiθe] *nm* appendix; **apendicitis** *nf* appendicitis

**aperitivo** [aperi'tiβo] *nm* (*bebida*) aperitif; (*comida*) appetizer

**apertura** [aper'tura] *nf* opening; (*Pol*) liberalization

**apestar** [apes'tar] *vt* to infect ▷ *vi*: **~ (a)** to stink (of)

**apetecer** [apete'θer] *vt*: **¿te apetece un café?** do you fancy a (cup of) coffee?; **apetecible** *adj* desirable; (*comida*) appetizing

**apetito** [ape'tito] *nm* appetite; **apetitoso, -a** *adj* appetizing; (*fig*) tempting

**apiadarse** [apja'ðarse] *vr*: **~ de** to take pity on

**ápice** ['apiθe] *nm* whit, iota

**apilar** [api'lar] *vt* to pile o heap up

**apiñarse** [api'ɲarse] *vr* to crowd o press together

**apio** ['apjo] *nm* celery

**apisonadora** [apisona'ðora] *nf* steamroller

**aplacar** [apla'kar] *vt* to placate

**aplastante** [aplas'tante] *adj* overwhelming; (*lógica*) compelling

**aplastar** [aplas'tar] *vt* to squash (flat); (*fig*) to crush

**aplaudir** [aplau'ðir] *vt* to applaud

**aplauso** [a'plauso] *nm* applause; (*fig*) approval, acclaim

**aplazamiento** [aplaθa'mjento] *nm* postponement

**aplazar** [apla'θar] *vt* to postpone, defer

**aplicación** [aplika'θjon] *nf* application; (*esfuerzo*) effort

**aplicado, -a** [apli'kaðo, a] *adj* diligent, hard-working

**aplicar** [apli'kar] *vt* (*ejecutar*) to apply; **aplicarse** *vr* to apply o.s.

**aplique** *etc* [a'plike] *vb* V **aplicar** ▷ *nm* wall light

**aplomo** [a'plomo] *nm* aplomb, self-assurance

**apodar** [apo'ðar] *vt* to nickname

**apoderado** [apoðe'raðo] *nm* agent,

representative

**apoderarse** [apoðe'rarse] *vr*: **~ de** to take possession of

**apodo** [a'poðo] *nm* nickname

**apogeo** [apo'xeo] *nm* peak, summit

**apoquinar** [apoki'nar] *(fam)* *vt* to fork out, cough up

**aporrear** [aporre'ar] *vt* to beat (up)

**aportar** [apor'tar] *vt* to contribute ▷ *vi* to reach port; **aportarse** *vr* (LAM: *llegar*) to arrive, come

**aposta** [a'posta] *adv* deliberately, on purpose

**apostar** [apos'tar] *vt* to bet, stake; *(tropas etc)* to station, post ▷ *vi* to bet

**apóstol** [a'postol] *nm* apostle

**apóstrofo** [a'postrofo] *nm* apostrophe

**apoyar** [apo'jar] *vt* to lean, rest; *(fig)* to support, back; **apoyarse** *vr*: **~se en** to lean on; **apoyo** *nm* (gen) support; backing, help

**apreciable** [apre'θjaβle] *adj* considerable; *(fig)* esteemed

**apreciar** [apre'θjar] *vt* to evaluate, assess; *(Com)* to appreciate, value; *(persona)* to respect; *(tamaño)* to gauge, assess; *(detalles)* to notice

**aprecio** [a'preθjo] *nm* valuation, estimate; *(fig)* appreciation

**aprehender** [apreen'der] *vt* to apprehend, detain

**apremio** [a'premjo] *nm* urgency

**aprender** [apren'der] *vt, vi* to learn; **~ algo de memoria** to learn sth (off) by heart

**aprendiz, a** [apren'diθ, a] *nm/f* apprentice; *(principiante)* learner; **aprendizaje** *nm* apprenticeship

**aprensión** [apren'sjon] *nm* apprehension, fear; **aprensivo, -a** *adj* apprehensive

**apresar** [apre'sar] *vt* to seize; *(capturar)* to capture

**apresurado, -a** [apresu'raðo, a] *adj* hurried, hasty

**apresurar** [apresu'rar] *vt* to hurry, accelerate; **apresurarse** *vr* to hurry, make haste

**apretado, -a** [apre'taðo, a] *adj* tight; *(escritura)* cramped

**apretar** [apre'tar] *vt* to squeeze; *(Tec)* to tighten; *(presionar)* to press together, pack ▷ *vi* to be too tight

**apretón** [apre'ton] *nm* squeeze; **apretón de manos** handshake

**aprieto** [a'prjeto] *nm* squeeze; *(dificultad)* difficulty; **estar en un ~** to be in a fix

**aprisa** [a'prisa] *adv* quickly, hurriedly

**aprisionar** [aprisjo'nar] *vt* to imprison

**aprobación** [aproβa'θjon] *nf* approval

**aprobar** [apro'βar] *vt* to approve (of); *(examen, materia)* to pass ▷ *vi* to pass

**apropiado, -a** [apro'pjaðo, a] *adj* suitable

**apropiarse** [apro'pjarse] *vr*: **~ de** to appropriate

**aprovechado, -a** [aproβe't∫aðo, a] *adj* industrious, hard-working; *(económico)* thrifty; *(pey)* unscrupulous

**aprovechar** [aproβe't∫ar] *vt* to use; *(explotar)* to exploit; *(experiencia)* to profit from; *(oferta, oportunidad)* to take advantage of ▷ *vi* to progress, improve; **aprovecharse** *vr*: **~se de** to make use of; to take advantage of; **¡que aproveche!** enjoy your meal!

**aproximación** [aproksima'θjon] *nf* approximation; *(de lotería)* consolation prize

**aproximar** [aproksi'mar] *vt* to bring nearer; **aproximarse** *vr* to come near, approach

**apruebo** *etc vb* V **aprobar**

**aptitud** [apti'tuð] *nf* aptitude

**apto, -a** ['apto, a] *adj* suitable

**apuesta** [a'pwesta] *nf* bet, wager

**apuesto, -a** [a'pwesto, a] *adj* neat, elegant

**apuntar** [apun'tar] *vt* (con arma) to aim at; *(con dedo)* to point at o to; *(anotar)* to note (down); *(Teatro)* to prompt; **apuntarse** *vr* (Deporte: tanto, victoria) to score; *(Escol)* to enrol

▌ No confundir **apuntar** con la palabra
▌ inglesa *appoint*.

**apunte** [a'punte] *nm* note

**apuñalar** [apuɲa'lar] *vt* to stab

**apurado, -a** [apu'raðo, a] *adj* needy; *(difícil)* difficult; *(peligroso)* dangerous; *(LAM: con prisa)* hurried, rushed

**apurar** [apu'rar] *vt* (agotar) to drain; *(recursos)* to use up; *(molestar)* to annoy; **apurarse** *vr* (preocuparse) to worry; *(LAM: darse prisa)* to hurry

**apuro** [a'puro] *nm* (aprieto) fix, jam; *(escasez)* want, hardship; *(vergüenza)* embarrassment; *(LAM: prisa)* haste, urgency

**aquejado, -a** [ake'xaðo, a] *adj*: **~ de** (Med) afflicted by

**aquel, aquella** [a'kel, a'keʎa] *adj* that; **~los(as)** those

**aquél, aquélla** [a'kel, a'keʎa] *pron* that (one); **~los(as)** those (ones)

**aquello** [a'keʎo] *pron* that, that business

**aquí** [a'ki] *adv* (lugar) here; *(tiempo)* now; **~ arriba** up here; **~ mismo** right here; **~ yace** here lies; **de ~ a siete días** a week from now

**ara** ['ara] *nf*: **en ~s de** for the sake of

**árabe** ['araβe] *adj, nmf* Arab ▷ *nm* (Ling) Arabic

**Arabia** [a'raβja] nf Arabia; **Arabia Saudí** o **Saudita** Saudi Arabia

**arado** [a'raðo] nm plough

**Aragón** [ara'ɣon] nm Aragon; **aragonés, -esa** adj, nm/f Aragonese

**arancel** [aran'θel] nm tariff, duty

**arandela** [aran'dela] nf (Tec) washer

**araña** [a'raɲa] nf (Zool) spider; (lámpara) chandelier

**arañar** [ara'ɲar] vt to scratch

**arañazo** [ara'ɲaθo] nm scratch

**arbitrar** [arβi'trar] vt to arbitrate in; (Deporte) to referee ▷ vi to arbitrate

**arbitrario, -a** [arβi'trarjo, a] adj arbitrary

**árbitro** ['arβitro] nm arbitrator; (Deporte) referee; (Tenis) umpire

**árbol** ['arβol] nm (Bot) tree; (Náut) mast; (Tec) axle, shaft; **árbol de Navidad** Christmas tree

**arboleda** [arβo'leða] nf grove, plantation

**arbusto** [ar'βusto] nm bush, shrub

**arca** ['arka] nf chest, box

**arcada** [ar'kaða] nf arcade; (de puente) arch, span; **arcadas** nfpl (náuseas) retching sg

**arcaico, -a** [ar'kaiko, a] adj archaic

**arce** ['arθe] nm maple tree

**arcén** [ar'θen] nm (de autopista) hard shoulder; (de carretera) verge

**archipiélago** [artʃi'pjelaɣo] nm archipelago

**archivador** [artʃiβa'ðor] nm filing cabinet

**archivar** [artʃi'βar] vt to file (away); **archivo** nm file, archive(s) pl; **archivo adjunto** (Inform) attachment; **archivo de seguridad** (Inform) backup file

**arcilla** [ar'θiʎa] nf clay

**arco** ['arko] nm arch; (Mat) arc; (Mil, Mús) bow; **arco iris** rainbow

**arder** [ar'ðer] vi to burn; **estar que arde** (persona) to fume

**ardid** [ar'ðið] nm ploy, trick

**ardiente** [ar'ðjente] adj burning, ardent

**ardilla** [ar'ðiʎa] nf squirrel

**ardor** [ar'ðor] nm (calor) heat; (fig) ardour; **ardor de estómago** heartburn

**arduo, -a** ['arðwo, a] adj arduous

**área** ['area] nf area; (Deporte) penalty area

**arena** [a'rena] nf sand; (de una lucha) arena; **arenas movedizas** quicksand sg; **arenal** [are'nal] nm (terreno arenoso) sandy spot

**arenisca** [are'niska] nf sandstone; (cascajo) grit

**arenoso, -a** [are'noso, a] adj sandy

**arenque** [a'renke] nm herring

**arete** [a'rete] (MÉX) nm earring

**Argel** [ar'xel] n Algiers; **Argelia** nf Algeria; **argelino, -a** adj, nm/f Algerian

**Argentina** [arxen'tina] nf (tb: **la ~**) Argentina

**argentino, -a** [arxen'tino, a] adj Argentinian; (de plata) silvery ▷ nm/f Argentinian

**argolla** [ar'ɣoʎa] nf (large) ring

**argot** [ar'ɣo] (pl **-s**) nm slang

**argucia** [ar'ɣuθja] nf subtlety, sophistry

**argumentar** [arxumen'tar] vt, vi to argue

**argumento** [arxu'mento] nm argument; (razonamiento) reasoning; (de novela etc) plot; (Cine, TV) storyline

**aria** ['arja] nf aria

**aridez** [ari'ðeθ] nf aridity, dryness

**árido, -a** ['ariðo, a] adj arid, dry

**Aries** ['arjes] nm Aries

**arisco, -a** [a'risko, a] adj surly; (insociable) unsociable

**aristócrata** [aris'tokrata] nmf aristocrat

**arma** ['arma] nf arm; **armas** nfpl arms; **arma blanca** blade, knife; **arma de doble filo** double-edged sword; **arma de fuego** firearm; **armas de destrucción masiva** weapons of mass destruction

**armada** [ar'maða] nf armada; (flota) fleet

**armadillo** [arma'ðiʎo] nm armadillo

**armado, -a** [ar'maðo, a] adj armed; (Tec) reinforced

**armadura** [arma'ðura] nf (Mil) armour; (Tec) framework; (Zool) skeleton; (Física) armature

**armamento** [arma'mento] nm armament; (Náut) fitting-out

**armar** [ar'mar] vt (soldado) to arm; (máquina) to assemble; (navío) to fit out; **~la, ~ un lío** to start a row, kick up a fuss

**armario** [ar'marjo] nm wardrobe; (de cocina, baño) cupboard; **armario empotrado** built-in cupboard

**armatoste** [arma'toste] nm (mueble) monstrosity; (máquina) contraption

**armazón** [arma'θon] nf o m body, chassis; (de mueble etc) frame; (Arq) skeleton

**armiño** [ar'miɲo] nm stoat; (piel) ermine

**armisticio** [armis'tiθjo] nm armistice

**armonía** [armo'nia] nf harmony

**armónica** [ar'monika] nf harmonica

**armonizar** [armoni'θar] vt to harmonize; (diferencias) to reconcile

**aro** ['aro] nm ring; (tejo) quoit; (cs: pendiente) earring

**aroma** [a'roma] nm aroma, scent; **aromaterapia** n aromatherapy; **aromático, -a** [aro'matiko, a] adj aromatic

**arpa** ['arpa] nf harp

**arpía** [ar'pia] nf shrew

**arpón** [ar'pon] nm harpoon

**arqueología** [arkeolo'xia] nf
archaeology; **arqueólogo, -a** nm/f
archaeologist

**arquetipo** [arke'tipo] nm archetype

**arquitecto** [arki'tekto] nm architect;
**arquitectura** nf architecture

**arrabal** [arra'βal] nm poor suburb, slum;
**arrabales** nmpl (afueras) outskirts

**arraigar** [arrai'xar] vt to establish ▷ vi to
take root

**arrancar** [arran'kar] vt (sacar) to extract,
pull out; (arrebatar) to snatch (away);
(Inform) to boot; (fig) to extract ▷ vi (Auto,
máquina) to start; (ponerse en marcha) to get
going; **~ de** to stem from

**arranque** etc [a'rranke] vb V **arrancar**
▷ nm sudden start; (Auto) start; (fig) fit,
outburst

**arrasar** [arra'sar] vt (aplanar) to level,
flatten; (destruir) to demolish

**arrastrar** [arras'trar] vt to drag (along);
(fig) to drag down, degrade; (agua, viento) to
carry away ▷ vi to drag, trail on the ground;
**arrastrarse** vr to crawl; (fig) to grovel;
**llevar algo arrastrado** to drag sth along

**arrear** [arre'ar] vt to drive on, urge on ▷ vi
to hurry along

**arrebatar** [arreβa'tar] vt to snatch
(away), seize; (fig) to captivate

**arrebato** [arre'βato] nm fit of rage, fury;
(éxtasis) rapture

**arrecife** [arre'θife] nm reef

**arreglado, -a** [arre'xlaðo, a] adj
(ordenado) neat, orderly; (moderado)
moderate, reasonable

**arreglar** [arre'xlar] vt (poner orden) to
tidy up; (algo roto) to fix, repair; (problema)
to solve; **arreglarse** vr to reach an
understanding; **arreglárselas** (fam) to get
by, manage

**arreglo** [a'rrexlo] nm settlement;
(orden) order; (acuerdo) agreement; (Mús)
arrangement, setting

**arremangar** [arreman'gar] vt to roll up,
turn up; **arremangarse** vr to roll up one's
sleeves

**arremeter** [arreme'ter] vi: **~ contra** to
attack, rush at

**arrendamiento** [arrenda'mjento] nm
letting; (alquilar) hiring; (contrato) lease;
(alquiler) rent; **arrendar** vt to let, lease; to
rent; **arrendatario, -a** nm/f tenant

**arreos** [a'rreos] nmpl (de caballo) harness
sg, trappings

**arrepentimiento** [arrepenti'mjento] nm
regret, repentance

**arrepentirse** [arrepen'tirse] vr to repent;
**~ de** to regret

**arresto** [a'rresto] nm arrest; (Mil)
detention; (audacia) boldness, daring;
**arresto domiciliario** house arrest

**arriar** [a'rrjar] vt (velas) to haul down;
(bandera) to lower, strike; (cable) to pay out

○ **PALABRA CLAVE**

**arriba** [a'rriβa] adv **1** (posición) above;
**desde arriba** from above; **arriba de todo** at
the very top, right on top; **Juan está arriba**
Juan is upstairs; **lo arriba mencionado** the
aforementioned

**2** (dirección): **calle arriba** up the street

**3** **de arriba abajo** from top to bottom;
**mirar a algn de arriba abajo** to look sb up
and down

**4** **para arriba: de 5000 euros para arriba**
from 5000 euros up(wards)

▷ adj: **de arriba: el piso de arriba** the
upstairs (BRIT) flat o apartment; **la parte de
arriba** the top o upper part

▷ prep: **arriba de** (LAM: por encima de) above;
**arriba de 200 dólares** more than 200
dollars

▷ excl: **¡arriba!** up!; **¡manos arriba!** hands
up!; **¡arriba España!** long live Spain!

**arribar** [arri'βar] vi to put into port;
(llegar) to arrive

**arriendo** etc [a'rrjendo] vb V **arrendar**
▷ nm = **arrendamiento**

**arriesgado, -a** [arrjes'xaðo, a] adj
(peligroso) risky; (audaz) bold, daring

**arriesgar** [arrjes'xar] vt to risk; (poner
en peligro) to endanger; **arriesgarse** vr to
take a risk

**arrimar** [arri'mar] vt (acercar) to bring
close; (poner de lado) to set aside; **arrimarse**
vr to come close o closer; **~se a** to lean on

**arrinconar** [arrinko'nar] vt (colocar) to
put in a corner; (enemigo) to corner; (fig) to
put on one side; (abandonar) to push aside

**arroba** [a'rroβa] nf (Internet) at (sign)

**arrodillarse** [arroði'ʎarse] vr to kneel
(down)

**arrogante** [arro'xante] adj arrogant

**arrojar** [arro'xar] vt to throw, hurl; (humo)
to emit, give out; (Com) to yield, produce;
**arrojarse** vr to throw o hurl o.s.

**arrojo** [a'rroxo] nm daring

**arrollador, a** [arroʎa'ðor, a] adj
overwhelming

**arrollar** [arro'ʎar] vt (Auto etc) to run over,
knock down; (Deporte) to crush

**arropar** [arro'par] vt to cover, wrap up;

**arroparse** vr to wrap o.s. up

**arroyo** [a'rrojo] nm stream; (de la calle) gutter

**arroz** [a'rroθ] nm rice; **arroz con leche** rice pudding

**arruga** [a'rruxa] nf (de cara) wrinkle; (de vestido) crease; **arrugar** [arru'ɣar] vt to wrinkle; to crease; **arrugarse** vr to get creased

**arruinar** [arrwi'nar] vt to ruin, wreck; **arruinarse** vr to be ruined, go bankrupt

**arsenal** [arse'nal] nm naval dockyard; (Mil) arsenal

**arte** ['arte] (gen m en sg y siempre f en pl) nm art; (maña) skill, guile; **artes** nfpl (bellas artes) arts

**artefacto** [arte'fakto] nm appliance

**arteria** [ar'terja] nf artery

**artesanía** [artesa'nia] nf craftsmanship; (artículos) handicrafts pl; **artesano, -a** nm/f artisan, craftsman(-woman)

**ártico, -a** ['artiko, a] adj Arctic ▷ nm: **el Á~** the Arctic

**articulación** [artikula'θjon] nf articulation; (Med, Tec) joint

**artículo** [ar'tikulo] nm article; (cosa) thing, article; **artículos** nmpl (Com) goods; **artículos de escritorio** stationery

**artífice** [ar'tifiθe] nmf (fig) architect

**artificial** [artifi'θjal] adj artificial

**artillería** [artiʎe'ria] nf artillery

**artilugio** [arti'luxjo] nm gadget

**artimaña** [arti'maɲa] nf trap, snare; (astucia) cunning

**artista** [ar'tista] nmf (pintor) artist, painter; (Teatro) artist, artiste; **artista de cine** film actor/actress; **artístico, -a** adj artistic

**artritis** [ar'tritis] nf arthritis

**arveja** [ar'βexa] (LAM) nf pea

**arzobispo** [arθo'βispo] nm archbishop

**as** [as] nm ace

**asa** ['asa] nf handle; (fig) lever

**asado** [a'saðo] nm roast (meat); (LAM: barbacoa) barbecue

**asador** [asa'ðor] nm spit

**asadura** [asa'ðura] nf entrails pl, offal

**asalariado, -a** [asala'rjaðo, a] adj paid, salaried ▷ nm/f wage earner

**asaltar** [asal'tar] vt to attack, assault; (fig) to assail; **asalto** nm attack, assault; (Deporte) round

**asamblea** [asam'blea] nf assembly; (reunión) meeting

**asar** [a'sar] vt to roast

**ascendencia** [asθen'denθja] nf ancestry; (LAM: influencia) ascendancy; **de ~ francesa** of French origin

**ascender** [asθen'der] vi (subir) to ascend, rise; (ser promovido) to gain promotion ▷ vt to promote; **~ a** to amount to; **ascendiente** nm influence ▷ nmf ancestor

**ascensión** [asθen'sjon] nf ascent; (Rel): **la A~** the Ascension

**ascenso** [as'θenso] nm ascent; (promoción) promotion

**ascensor** [asθen'sor] nm lift (BRIT), elevator (US)

**asco** ['asko] nm: **¡qué ~!** how revolting o disgusting; **el ajo me da ~** I hate o loathe garlic; **estar hecho un ~** to be filthy

**ascua** ['askwa] nf ember

**aseado, -a** [ase'aðo, a] adj clean; (arreglado) tidy; (pulcro) smart

**asear** [ase'ar] vt to clean, wash; to tidy (up)

**asediar** [ase'ðjar] vt (Mil) to besiege, lay siege to; (fig) to chase, pester; **asedio** nm siege; (Com) run

**asegurado, -a** [aseɣu'raðo, a] adj insured

**asegurador, a** [aseɣura'ðor, a] nm/f insurer

**asegurar** [aseɣu'rar] vt (consolidar) to secure, fasten; (dar garantía de) to guarantee; (preservar) to safeguard; (afirmar, dar por cierto) to assure, affirm; (tranquilizar) to reassure; (tomar un seguro) to insure; **asegurarse** vr to assure o.s., make sure

**asemejarse** [aseme'xarse] vr to be alike; **~ a** to be like, resemble

**asentado, -a** [asen'taðo, a] adj established, settled

**asentar** [asen'tar] vt (sentar) to seat, sit down; (poner) to place, establish; (alisar) to level, smooth down o out; (anotar) to note down ▷ vi to settle, suit

**asentir** [asen'tir] vi to assent, agree; **~ con la cabeza** to nod (one's head)

**aseo** [a'seo] nm cleanliness; **aseos** nmpl (servicios) toilet sg (BRIT), cloakroom sg (BRIT), restroom sg (US)

**aséptico, -a** [a'septiko, a] adj germ-free,

free from infection

**asequible** [ase'kiβle] adj (precio) reasonable; (meta) attainable; (persona) approachable

**asesinar** [asesi'nar] vt to murder; (Pol) to assassinate; **asesinato** nm murder; assassination

**asesino, -a** [ase'sino, a] nm/f murderer, killer; (Pol) assassin

**asesor, a** [ase'sor, a] nm/f adviser, consultant; **asesorar** [aseso'rar] vt (Jur) to advise, give legal advice to; (Com) to act as consultant to; **asesorarse** vr: **asesorarse con o de** to take advice from, consult; **asesoría** nf (cargo) consultancy; (oficina) consultant's office

**asestar** [ases'tar] vt (golpe) to deal, strike

**asfalto** [as'falto] nm asphalt

**asfixia** [as'fiksja] nf asphyxia, suffocation; **asfixiar** [asfik'sjar] vt to asphyxiate, suffocate; **asfixiarse** vr to be asphyxiated, suffocate

**así** [a'si] adv (de esta manera) in this way, like this, thus; (aunque) although; (tan pronto como) as soon as; **~ que** so; **~ como** as well as; **~ y todo** even so; **¿no es ~?** isn't it?, didn't you? etc; **~ de grande** this big

**Asia** ['asja] nf Asia; **asiático, -a** adj, nm/f Asian, Asiatic

**asiduo, -a** [a'siðwo, a] adj assiduous; (frecuente) frequent ▷ nm/f regular (customer)

**asiento** [a'sjento] nm (mueble) seat, chair; (de coche, en tribunal etc) seat; (localidad) seat, place; (fundamento) site; **asiento delantero/ trasero** front/back seat

**asignación** [asiɣna'θjon] nf (atribución) assignment; (reparto) allocation; (sueldo) salary; **asignación (semanal)** pocket money

**asignar** [asiɣ'nar] vt to assign, allocate

**asignatura** [asiɣna'tura] nf subject; course

**asilo** [a'silo] nm (refugio) asylum, refuge; (establecimiento) home, institution; **asilo político** political asylum

**asimilar** [asimi'lar] vt to assimilate

**asimismo** [asi'mismo] adv in the same way, likewise

**asistencia** [asis'tenθja] nf audience; (Med) attendance; (ayuda) assistance; **asistencia en carretera** roadside assistance; **asistente** nmf assistant; **los asistentes** those present; **asistente social** social worker

**asistido, -a** [asis'tiðo, a] adj: **~ por ordenador** computer-assisted

**asistir** [asis'tir] vt to assist, help ▷ vi: **~ a** to attend, be present at

**asma** ['asma] nf asthma

**asno** ['asno] nm donkey; (fig) ass

**asociación** [asoθja'θjon] nf association; (Com) partnership; **asociado, -a** adj associate ▷ nm/f associate; (Com) partner

**asociar** [aso'θjar] vt to associate

**asomar** [aso'mar] vt to show, stick out ▷ vi to appear; **asomarse** vr to appear, show up; **~ la cabeza por la ventana** to put one's head out of the window

**asombrar** [asom'brar] vt to amaze, astonish; **asombrarse** vr (sorprenderse) to be amazed; (asustarse) to get a fright; **asombro** nm amazement, astonishment; (susto) fright; **asombroso, -a** adj astonishing, amazing

**asomo** [a'somo] nm hint, sign

**aspa** ['aspa] nf (cruz) cross; (de molino) sail; **en ~** X-shaped

**aspaviento** [aspa'βjento] nm exaggerated display of feeling; (fam) fuss

**aspecto** [as'pekto] nm (apariencia) look, appearance; (fig) aspect

**áspero, -a** ['aspero, a] adj rough; bitter; sour; harsh

**aspersión** [asper'sjon] nf sprinkling

**aspiración** [aspira'θjon] nf breath, inhalation; (Mús) short pause; **aspiraciones** nfpl (ambiciones) aspirations

**aspirador** [aspira'ðor] nm = **aspiradora**

**aspiradora** [aspira'ðora] nf vacuum cleaner, Hoover®

**aspirante** [aspi'rante] nmf (candidato) candidate; (Deporte) contender

**aspirar** [aspi'rar] vt to breathe in ▷ vi: **~ a** to aspire to

**aspirina** [aspi'rina] nf aspirin

**asqueroso, -a** [aske'roso, a] adj disgusting, sickening

**asta** ['asta] nf lance; (arpón) spear; (mango) shaft, handle; (Zool) horn; **a media ~** at half mast

**asterisco** [aste'risko] nm asterisk

**astilla** [as'tiʎa] nf splinter; (pedacito) chip; **astillas** nfpl (leña) firewood sg

**astillero** [asti'ʎero] nm shipyard

**astro** ['astro] nm star

**astrología** [astrolo'xia] nf astrology; **astrólogo, -a** nm/f astrologer

**astronauta** [astro'nauta] nmf astronaut

**astronomía** [astrono'mia] nf astronomy

**astucia** [as'tuθja] nf astuteness; (ardid) clever trick

**asturiano, -a** [astu'rjano, a] adj, nm/f Asturian

**astuto, -a** [as'tuto, a] adj astute; (taimado) cunning

**asumir** [asu'mir] vt to assume
**asunción** [asun'θjon] nf assumption;
(Rel): **A~** Assumption
**asunto** [a'sunto] nm (tema) matter,
subject; (negocio) business
**asustar** [asus'tar] vt to frighten;
**asustarse** vr to be (o become) frightened
**atacar** [ata'kar] vt to attack
**atadura** [ata'ðura] nf bond, tie
**atajar** [ata'xar] vt (enfermedad, mal) to stop
▷vi (persona) to take a short cut
**atajo** [a'taxo] nm short cut
**atañer** [ata'ɲer] vi: **~ a** to concern
**ataque** etc [a'take] vb V **atacar** ▷nm
attack; **ataque cardíaco** heart attack
**atar** [a'tar] vt to tie, tie up
**atarantado, -a** [ataran'taðo, a] (MÉX)
adj (aturdido) dazed
**atardecer** [atarðe'θer] vi to get dark ▷nm
evening; (crepúsculo) dusk
**atareado, -a** [atare'aðo, a] adj busy
**atascar** [atas'kar] vt to clog up; (obstruir)
to jam; (fig) to hinder; **atascarse** vr to
stall; (cañería) to get blocked up; **atasco** nm
obstruction; (Auto) traffic jam
**ataúd** [ata'uð] nm coffin
**ataviar** [ata'βjar] vt to deck, array
**atemorizar** [atemori'θar] vt to frighten,
scare
**Atenas** [a'tenas] n Athens
**atención** [aten'θjon] nf attention;
(bondad) kindness ▷excl (be) careful!, look
out!
**atender** [aten'der] vt to attend to, look
after; (Tel) to answer ▷vi to pay attention
**atenerse** [ate'nerse] vr: **~ a** to abide by,
adhere to
**atentado** [aten'taðo] nm crime, illegal
act; (asalto) assault; (tb: **~ terrorista**)
terrorist attack; **~ contra la vida de algn**
attempt on sb's life; **atentado suicida**
suicide bombing
**atentamente** [atenta'mente] adv: **Le
saluda ~** Yours faithfully
**atentar** [aten'tar] vi: **~ a o contra** to
commit an outrage against
**atento, -a** [a'tento, a] adj attentive,
observant; (cortés) polite, thoughtful; **estar
~ a** (explicación) to pay attention to
**atenuar** [ate'nwar] vt (disminuir) to
lessen, minimize
**ateo, -a** [a'teo, a] adj atheistic ▷nm/f
atheist
**aterrador, a** [aterra'ðor, a] adj
frightening
**aterrizaje** [aterri'θaxe] nm landing;
**aterrizaje forzoso** emergency o forced
landing

**aterrizar** [aterri'θar] vi to land
**aterrorizar** [aterrori'θar] vt to terrify
**atesorar** [ateso'rar] vt to hoard
**atestar** [ates'tar] vt to pack, stuff; (Jur) to
attest, testify to
**atestiguar** [atesti'ɣwar] vt to testify to,
bear witness to
**atiborrar** [atiβo'rrar] vt to fill, stuff;
**atiborrarse** vr to stuff o.s.
**ático** ['atiko] nm (desván) attic;
(apartamento) penthouse
**atinado, -a** [ati'naðo, a] adj (sensato)
wise; (correcto) right, correct
**atinar** [ati'nar] vi (al disparar): **~ al blanco**
to hit the target; (fig) to be right
**atizar** [ati'θar] vt to poke; (horno etc) to
stoke; (fig) to stir up, rouse
**atlántico, -a** [at'lantiko, a] adj Atlantic
▷nm: **el (océano) A~** the Atlantic (Ocean)
**atlas** ['atlas] nm inv atlas
**atleta** [at'leta] nm athlete; **atlético, -a** adj
athletic; **atletismo** nm athletics sg
**atmósfera** [at'mosfera] nf atmosphere
**atolladero** [atoʎa'ðero] nm (fig) jam, fix
**atómico, -a** [a'tomiko, a] adj atomic
**átomo** ['atomo] nm atom
**atónito, -a** [a'tonito, a] adj astonished,
amazed
**atontado, -a** [aton'taðo, a] adj stunned;
(bobo) silly, daft
**atormentar** [atormen'tar] vt to torture;
(molestar) to torment; (acosar) to plague,
harass
**atornillar** [atorni'ʎar] vt to screw on o
down
**atosigar** [atosi'ɣar] vt to harass, pester
**atracador, a** [ataka'ðor, a] nm/f robber
**atracar** [atra'kar] vt (Náut) to moor;
(robar) to hold up, rob ▷vi to moor;
**atracarse** vr: **~se (de)** to stuff o.s. (with)
**atracción** [atrak'θjon] nf attraction
**atraco** [a'trako] nm holdup, robbery
**atracón** [atra'kon] nm: **darse o pegarse
un ~ (de)** (fam) to stuff o.s. (with)
**atractivo, -a** [atrak'tiβo, a] adj
attractive ▷nm appeal
**atraer** [atra'er] vt to attract
**atragantarse** [atraɣan'tarse] vr: **~ (con)**
to choke (on); **se me ha atragantado el
chico** I can't stand the boy
**atrancar** [atran'kar] vt (puerta) to bar, bolt
**atrapar** [atra'par] vt to trap; (resfriado etc)
to catch
**atrás** [a'tras] adv (movimiento) back(-
wards); (lugar) behind; (tiempo) previously; **ir
hacia ~** to go back(wards), to go to the rear;
**estar ~** to be behind o at the back
**atrasado, -a** [atra'saðo, a] adj slow;

(*pago*) overdue, late; (*país*) backward
**atrasar** [atra'sar] *vi* to be slow; **atrasarse**
*vr* to remain behind; (*tren*) to be o run late;
**atraso** *nm* slowness; lateness, delay; (*de país*) backwardness; **atrasos** *nmpl* (*Com*)
arrears
**atravesar** [atraβe'sar] *vt* (*cruzar*) to
cross (over); (*traspasar*) to pierce; to go
through; (*poner al través*) to lay o put across;
**atravesarse** *vr* to come in between;
(*intervenir*) to interfere
**atravieso** *etc vb* V **atravesar**
**atreverse** [atre'βerse] *vr* to dare;
(*insolentarse*) to be insolent; **atrevido, -a** *adj*
daring; insolent; **atrevimiento** *nm* daring;
insolence
**atribución** [atriβu'θjon] *nf* attribution;
**atribuciones** *nfpl* (*Pol*) powers; (*Admin*)
responsibilities
**atribuir** [atriβu'ir] *vt* to attribute;
(*funciones*) to confer
**atributo** [atri'βuto] *nm* attribute
**atril** [a'tril] *nm* (*para libro*) lectern; (*Mús*)
music stand
**atropellar** [atrope'ʎar] *vt* (*derribar*)
to knock over o down; (*empujar*) to push
(aside); (*Auto*) to run over, run down;
(*agraviar*) to insult; **atropello** *nm* (*Auto*)
accident; (*empujón*) push; (*agravio*) wrong;
(*atrocidad*) outrage
**atroz** [a'troθ] *adj* atrocious, awful
**ATS** *nmf abr* (= *Ayudante Técnico Sanitario*)
nurse
**atuendo** [a'twendo] *nm* attire
**atún** [a'tun] *nm* tuna
**aturdir** [atur'ðir] *vt* to stun; (*de ruido*) to
deafen; (*fig*) to dumbfound, bewilder
**audacia** [au'ðaθja] *nf* boldness, audacity;
**audaz** *adj* bold, audacious
**audición** [auði'θjon] *nf* hearing; (*Teatro*)
audition
**audiencia** [au'ðjenθja] *nf* audience;
(*Jur: tribunal*) court
**audífono** [au'ðifono] *nm* (*para sordos*)
hearing aid
**auditor** [auði'tor] *nm* (*Jur*) judge advocate;
(*Com*) auditor
**auditorio** [auði'torjo] *nm* audience; (*sala*)
auditorium
**auge** ['auxe] *nm* boom; (*clímax*) climax
**augurar** [auɣu'rar] *vt* to predict;
(*presagiar*) to portend
**augurio** [au'ɣurjo] *nm* omen
**aula** ['aula] *nf* classroom; (*en universidad etc*) lecture room
**aullar** [au'ʎar] *vi* to howl, yell
**aullido** [au'ʎiðo] *nm* howl, yell
**aumentar** [aumen'tar] *vt* to increase;

(*precios*) to put up; (*producción*) to step up;
(*con microscopio, anteojos*) to magnify ▷ *vi* to
increase, be on the increase; **aumentarse**
*vr* to increase, be on the increase; **aumento**
*nm* increase; rise
**aun** [a'un] *adv* even; ~ **así** even so; ~ **más**
even o yet more
**aún** [a'un] *adv*: ~ **está aquí** he's still here; ~
**no lo sabemos** we don't know yet; **¿no ha
venido ~?** hasn't she come yet?
**aunque** [a'unke] *conj* though, although,
even though
**aúpa** [a'upa] *excl* come on!
**auricular** [auriku'lar] *nm* (*Tel*) receiver;
**auriculares** *nmpl* (*cascos*) headphones
**aurora** [au'rora] *nf* dawn
**ausencia** [au'senθja] *nf* absence
**ausentarse** [ausen'tarse] *vr* to go away;
(*por poco tiempo*) to go out
**ausente** [au'sente] *adj* absent
**austero, -a** [aus'tero, a] *adj* austere
**austral** [aus'tral] *adj* southern ▷ *nm*
monetary unit of Argentina
**Australia** [aus'tralja] *nf* Australia;
**australiano, -a** *adj, nm/f* Australian
**Austria** ['austrja] *nf* Austria; **austríaco,
-a** *adj, nm/f* Austrian
**auténtico, -a** [au'tentiko, a] *adj*
authentic
**auto** ['auto] *nm* (*Jur*) edict, decree;
(: *orden*) writ; (*Auto*) car; **autos** *nmpl* (*Jur*)
proceedings; (: *acta*) court record *sg*
**autoadhesivo** [autoaðe'siβo] *adj* self-
adhesive; (*sobre*) self-sealing
**autobiografía** [autoβjoɣra'fia] *nf*
autobiography
**autobomba** [auto'bomba] (*RPL*) *nm* fire
engine
**autobronceador** [autoβronθea'ðor] *adj*
self-tanning
**autobús** [auto'βus] *nm* bus; **autobús de
línea** long-distance coach
**autocar** [auto'kar] *nm* coach (*BRIT*),
(passenger) bus (*US*)
**autóctono, -a** [au'toktono, a] *adj* native,
indigenous
**autodefensa** [autoðe'fensa] *nf* self-
defence
**autodidacta** [autoði'ðakta] *adj* self-
taught
**autoescuela** [autoes'kwela] (*ESP*) *nf*
driving school
**autógrafo** [au'toɣrafo] *nm* autograph
**autómata** [au'tomata] *nm* automaton
**automático, -a** [auto'matiko, a] *adj*
automatic ▷ *nm* press stud
**automóvil** [auto'moβil] *nm* (motor) car
(*BRIT*), automobile (*US*); **automovilismo** *nm*

(*actividad*) motoring; (*Deporte*) motor racing;
**automovilista** *nmf* motorist, driver

**autonomía** [autono'mia] *nf* autonomy;
**autónomo, -a** (ESP), **autonómico, -a** (ESP)
*adj* (*Pol*) autonomous

**autopista** [auto'pista] *nf* motorway
(BRIT), freeway (US); **autopista de cuota**
(ESP) o **peaje** (MÉX) toll (BRIT) o turnpike
(US) road

**autopsia** [au'topsja] *nf* autopsy,
postmortem

**autor, a** [au'tor, a] *nm/f* author

**autoridad** [autori'ðað] *nf* authority;
**autoritario, -a** *adj* authoritarian

**autorización** [autoriθa'θjon] *nf*
authorization; **autorizado, -a** *adj*
authorized; (*aprobado*) approved

**autorizar** [autori'θar] *vt* to authorize;
(*aprobar*) to approve

**autoservicio** [autoser'βjeθjo] *nm* (*tienda*)
self-service shop (BRIT) o store (US);
(*restaurante*) self-service restaurant

**autostop** [auto'stop] *nm* hitch-hiking;
**hacer ~** to hitch-hike; **autostopista** *nmf*
hitch-hiker

**autovía** [auto'βia] *nf* ≈ A-road (BRIT), dual
carriageway (BRIT), ≈ state highway (US)

**auxiliar** [auksi'ljar] *vt* to help ▷ *nmf*
assistant; **auxilio** *nm* assistance, help;
**primeros auxilios** first aid *sg*

**Av** *abr* (=*Avenida*) Av(e)

**aval** [a'βal] *nm* guarantee; (*persona*)
guarantor

**avalancha** [aβa'lantʃa] *nf* avalanche

**avance** [a'βanθe] *nm* advance; (*pago*)
advance payment; (*Cine*) trailer

**avanzar** [aβan'θar] *vt*, *vi* to advance

**avaricia** [aβa'riθja] *nf* avarice, greed;
**avaricioso, -a** *adj* avaricious, greedy

**avaro, -a** [a'βaro, a] *adj* miserly, mean
▷ *nm/f* miser

**Avda** *abr* (=*Avenida*) Av(e)

**AVE** ['aβe] *nm abr* (=*Alta Velocidad Española*)
≈ bullet train

**ave** ['aβe] *nf* bird; **ave de rapiña** bird of
prey

**avecinarse** [aβeθi'narse] *vr* (*tormenta*: *fig*)
to be on the way

**avellana** [aβe'ʎana] *nf* hazelnut;
**avellano** *nm* hazel tree

**avemaría** [aβema'ria] *nm* Hail Mary,
Ave Maria

**avena** [a'βena] *nf* oats *pl*

**avenida** [aβe'niða] *nf* (*calle*) avenue

**aventajar** [aβenta'xar] *vt* (*sobrepasar*) to
surpass, outstrip

**aventón** [aβen'ton] (MÉX: *fam*) *nm* ride;
**dar ~ a algn** to give sb a ride

**aventura** [aβen'tura] *nf* adventure;
**aventurero, -a** *adj* adventurous

**avergonzar** [aβerɤon'θar] *vt* to shame;
(*desconcertar*) to embarrass; **avergonzarse**
*vr* to be ashamed; to be embarrassed

**avería** [aβe'ria] *nf* (*Tec*) breakdown, fault

**averiado, -a** [aβe'rjaðo, a] *adj* broken
down; **"~"** "out of order"

**averiguar** [aβeri'xwar] *vt* to investigate;
(*descubrir*) to find out, ascertain

**avestruz** [aβes'truθ] *nm* ostrich

**aviación** [aβja'θjon] *nf* aviation; (*fuerzas
aéreas*) air force

**aviador, a** [aβja'ðor, a] *nm/f* aviator,
airman(-woman)

**ávido, -a** ['aβiðo, a] *adj* avid, eager

**avinagrado, -a** [aβina'xraðo, a] *adj*
sour, acid

**avión** [a'βjon] *nm* aeroplane; (*ave*) martin;
**avión de reacción** jet (plane)

**avioneta** [aβjo'neta] *nf* light aircraft

**avisar** [aβi'sar] *vt* (*advertir*) to warn,
notify; (*informar*) to tell; (*aconsejar*) to advise,
counsel; **aviso** *nm* warning; (*noticia*) notice

**avispa** [a'βispa] *nf* wasp

**avispado, -a** [aβis'paðo, a] *adj* sharp,
clever

**avivar** [aβi'βar] *vt* to strengthen, intensify

**axila** [ak'sila] *nf* armpit

**ay** [ai] *excl* (*dolor*) ow!, ouch!; (*aflicción*) oh!,
oh dear!; **¡~ de mí!** poor me!

**ayer** [a'jer] *adv*, *nm* yesterday; **antes de
~** the day before yesterday; **~ mismo** only
yesterday

**ayote** [a'jote] (CAM) *nm* pumpkin

**ayuda** [a'juða] *nf* help, assistance ▷ *nm*
page; **ayudante** *nmf* assistant, helper;
(*Escol*) assistant; (*Mil*) adjutant

**ayudar** [aju'ðar] *vt* to help, assist

**ayunar** [aju'nar] *vi* to fast; **ayunas**
*nfpl*: **estar en ayunas** to be fasting; **ayuno**
*nm* fast; fasting

**ayuntamiento** [ajunta'mjento] *nm*
(*consejo*) town (o city) council; (*edificio*) town
(o city) hall

**azafata** [aθa'fata] *nf* air stewardess

**azafrán** [aθa'fran] *nm* saffron

**azahar** [aθa'ar] *nm* orange/lemon
blossom

**azar** [a'θar] *nm* (*casualidad*) chance, fate;
(*desgracia*) misfortune, accident; **por ~** by
chance; **al ~** at random

**Azores** [a'θores] *nfpl*: **las ~** the Azores

**azotar** [aθo'tar] *vt* to whip, beat; (*pegar*)
to spank; **azote** *nm* (*látigo*) whip; (*latigazo*)
lash, stroke; (*en las nalgas*) spank; (*calamidad*)
calamity

**azotea** [aθo'tea] *nf* (flat) roof

**azteca** [aθ'teka] *adj, nmf* Aztec
**azúcar** [a'θukar] *nm* sugar; **azucarado, -a**
*adj* sugary, sweet
**azucarero, -a** [aθuka'rero, a] *adj* sugar
*cpd* ▷ *nm* sugar bowl
**azucena** [aθu'θena] *nf* white lily
**azufre** [a'θufre] *nm* sulphur
**azul** [a'θul] *adj, nm* blue; **azul celeste/
marino**sky/navy blue
**azulejo** [aθu'lexo] *nm* tile
**azuzar** [aθu'θar] *vt* to incite, egg on

**B.A.** *abr* (= *Buenos Aires*) B.A.
**baba** ['baβa] *nf* spittle, saliva; **babear** *vi*
to drool, slaver
**babero** [ba'βero] *nm* bib
**babor** [ba'βor] *nm* port (side)
**babosada** [baβo'saða] (*MÉX, CAM: fam*) *nf*
drivel; **baboso, -a** [ba'βoso, a] (*LAM: fam*)
*adj* silly
**baca** ['baka] *nf* (*Auto*) luggage o roof rack
**bacalao** [baka'lao] *nm* cod(fish)
**bache** ['batʃe] *nm* pothole, rut; (*fig*) bad
patch
**bachillerato** [batʃiʎe'rato] *nm* higher
*secondary school course*
**bacinica** [baθi'nika] (*LAM*) *nf* potty
**bacteria** [bak'terja] *nf* bacterium, germ
**Bahama** [ba'ama]: **las (Islas) ~** *nfpl* the
Bahamas
**bahía** [ba'ia] *nf* bay
**bailar** [bai'lar] *vt, vi* to dance; **bailarín,
-ina** *nm/f* (ballet) dancer; **baile** *nm* dance;
(*formal*) ball
**baja** ['baxa] *nf* drop, fall; (*Mil*) casualty;
**dar de ~** (*soldado*) to discharge; (*empleado*)
to dismiss
**bajada** [ba'xaða] *nf* descent; (*camino*)
slope; (*de aguas*) ebb
**bajar** [ba'xar] *vi* to go down, come down;
(*temperatura, precios*) to drop, fall ▷ *vt*
(*cabeza*) to bow; (*escalera*) to go down, come
down; (*precio, voz*) to lower; (*llevar abajo*) to
take down; **bajarse** *vr* (*de coche*) to get out;
(*de autobús, tren*) to get off; **~ de** (*coche*) to get
out of; (*autobús, tren*) to get off; **~se algo de
Internet** to download sth from the Internet
**bajío** [ba'xio] (*LAM*) *nm* lowlands *pl*
**bajo, -a** ['baxo] *adj* (*mueble, número, precio*)
low; (*piso*) ground; (*de estatura*) small, short;
(*color*) pale; (*sonido*) faint, soft, low; (*voz: en
tono*) deep; (*metal*) base; (*humilde*) low,
humble ▷ *adv* (*hablar*) softly, quietly; (*volar*)

low ▷ *prep* under, below, underneath ▷ *nm* (*Mús*) bass; **~ la lluvia** in the rain

**bajón** [ba'xon] *nm* fall, drop

**bakalao** [baka'lao] (*ESP: fam*) *nm* rave (music)

**bala** ['bala] *nf* bullet

**balacear** [balaθe'ar] (*MÉX, CAM*) *vt* to shoot

**balance** [ba'lanθe] *nm* (*Com*) balance; (*: libro*) balance sheet; (*: cuenta general*) stocktaking

**balancear** [balanθe'ar] *vt* to balance ▷ *vi* to swing (to and fro); (*vacilar*) to hesitate; **balancearse** *vr* to swing (to and fro), to hesitate

**balanza** [ba'lanθa] *nf* scales *pl*, balance; **balanza comercial** balance of trade; **balanza de pagos** balance of payments

**balaustrada** [balaus'traða] *nf* balustrade; (*pasamanos*) banisters *pl*

**balazo** [ba'laθo] *nm* (*golpe*) shot; (*herida*) bullet wound

**balbucear** [balβuθe'ar] *vi, vt* to stammer, stutter

**balcón** [bal'kon] *nm* balcony

**balde** ['balde] *nm* bucket, pail; **de ~** (for) free, for nothing; **en ~** in vain

**baldosa** [bal'dosa] *nf* (*azulejo*) floor tile; (*grande*) flagstone; **baldosín** *nm* (small) tile

**Baleares** [bale'ares] *nfpl*: **las (Islas) ~** the Balearic Islands

**balero** [ba'lero] (*LAM*) *nm* (*juguete*) cup-and-ball toy

**baliza** [ba'liθa] *nf* (*Aviac*) beacon; (*Náut*) buoy

**ballena** [ba'ʎena] *nf* whale

**ballet** [ba'le] (*pl* **~s**) *nm* ballet

**balneario** [balne'arjo] *nm* spa; (*cs: en la costa*) seaside resort

**balón** [ba'lon] *nm* ball

**baloncesto** [balon'θesto] *nm* basketball

**balonmano** [balon'mano] *nm* handball

**balsa** ['balsa] *nf* raft; (*Bot*) balsa wood

**bálsamo** ['balsamo] *nm* balsam, balm

**baluarte** [ba'lwarte] *nm* bastion, bulwark

**bambú** [bam'bu] *nm* bamboo

**banana** [ba'nana] (*LAM*) *nf* banana; **banano** *nm* (*LAM: árbol*) banana tree; (*CAM: fruta*) banana

**banca** ['banka] *nf* (*Com*) banking

**bancario, -a** [ban'karjo, a] *adj* banking *cpd*, bank *cpd*

**bancarrota** [banka'rrota] *nf* bankruptcy; **hacer ~** to go bankrupt

**banco** ['banko] *nm* bench; (*Escol*) desk; (*Com*) bank; (*Geo*) stratum; **banco de arena** sandbank; **banco de crédito** credit bank; **banco de datos** databank

**banda** ['banda] *nf* band; (*pandilla*) gang; (*Náut*) side, edge; **banda ancha** broadband; **banda sonora** soundtrack

**bandada** [ban'daða] *nf* (*de pájaros*) flock; (*de peces*) shoal

**bandazo** [ban'daθo] *nm*: **dar ~s** to sway from side to side

**bandeja** [ban'dexa] *nf* tray

**bandera** [ban'dera] *nf* flag

**banderilla** [bande'riʎa] *nf* banderilla

**bandido** [ban'diðo] *nm* bandit

**bando** ['bando] *nm* (*edicto*) edict, proclamation; (*facción*) faction; **bandos** *nmpl* (*Rel*) banns

**bandolera** [bando'lera] *nf*: **llevar en ~** to wear across one's chest

**banquero** [ban'kero] *nm* banker

**banqueta** [ban'keta] *nf* stool; (*MÉX: en calle*) pavement (*BRIT*), sidewalk (*US*)

**banquete** [ban'kete] *nm* banquet; (*para convidados*) formal dinner; **banquete de boda(s)** wedding reception

**banquillo** [ban'kiʎo] *nm* (*Jur*) dock, prisoner's bench; (*banco*) bench; (*para los pies*) footstool

**banquina** [ban'kina] (*RPL*) *nf* hard shoulder (*BRIT*), berm (*US*)

**bañadera** [baɲa'ðera] (*RPL*) *nf* bathtub

**bañador** [baɲa'ðor] (*ESP*) *nm* swimming costume (*BRIT*), bathing suit (*US*)

**bañar** [ba'ɲar] *vt* to bath, bathe; (*objeto*) to dip; (*de barniz*) to coat; **bañarse** *vr* (*en el mar*) to bathe, swim; (*en la bañera*) to have a bath

**bañera** [ba'ɲera] (*ESP*) *nf* bath(tub)

**bañero, -a** [ba'ɲero, a] (*cs*) *nm/f* lifeguard

**bañista** [ba'ɲista] *nmf* bather

**baño** ['baɲo] *nm* (*en bañera*) bath; (*en río*) dip, swim; (*cuarto*) bathroom; (*bañera*) bath(tub); (*capa*) coating; **darse** *o* **tomar un ~** (*en bañera*) to have *o* take a bath; (*en mar, piscina*) to have a swim; **baño María** bain-marie

**bar** [bar] *nm* bar

**barahúnda** [bara'unda] *nf* uproar, hubbub

**baraja** [ba'raxa] *nf* pack (of cards); **barajar** *vt* (*naipes*) to shuffle; (*fig*) to jumble up

**baranda** [ba'randa] *nf* = **barandilla**

**barandilla** [baran'diʎa] *nf* rail, railing

**barata** [ba'rata] (*MÉX*) *nf* (*bargain*) sale

**baratillo** [bara'tiʎo] *nm* (*tienda*) junkshop; (*subasta*) bargain sale; (*conjunto de cosas*) secondhand goods *pl*

**barato, -a** [ba'rato, a] *adj* cheap ▷ *adv* cheap, cheaply

**barba** ['barβa] *nf* (*mentón*) chin; (*pelo*) beard

**barbacoa** [barβa'koa] nf (parrilla) barbecue; (carne) barbecued meat

**barbaridad** [barβari'ðað] nf barbarity; (acto) barbarism; (atrocidad) outrage; **una ~** (fam) loads; **¡qué ~!** (fam) how awful!

**barbarie** [bar'βarje] nf barbarism, savagery; (crueldad) barbarity

**bárbaro, -a** ['barβaro, a] adj barbarous, cruel; (grosero) rough, uncouth ▷ nm/f barbarian ▷ adv: **lo pasamos ~** (fam) we had a great time; **¡qué ~!** (fam) how marvellous!; **un éxito ~** (fam) a terrific success; **es un tipo ~** (fam) he's a great bloke

**barbero** [bar'βero] nm barber, hairdresser

**barbilla** [bar'βiʎa] nf chin, tip of the chin

**barbudo, -a** [bar'βuðo, a] adj bearded

**barca** ['barka] nf (small) boat; **barcaza** nf barge

**Barcelona** [barθe'lona] n Barcelona

**barco** ['barko] nm boat; (grande) ship; **barco de carga/pesca** cargo/fishing boat; **barco de vela** sailing ship

**barda** ['barða] (MÉX) nf (de madera) fence

**baremo** [ba'remo] nm (Mat: fig) scale

**barítono** [ba'ritono] nm baritone

**barman** ['barman] nm barman

**barniz** [bar'niθ] nm varnish; (en loza) glaze; (fig) veneer; **barnizar** vt to varnish; (loza) to glaze

**barómetro** [ba'rometro] nm barometer

**barquillo** [bar'kiʎo] nm cone, cornet

**barra** ['barra] nf bar, rod; (de un bar, café) bar; (de pan) French stick; (palanca) lever; **barra de labios** lipstick; **barra libre** free bar

**barraca** [ba'rraka] nf hut, cabin

**barranco** [ba'rranko] nm ravine; (fig) difficulty

**barrena** [ba'rrena] nf drill

**barrer** [ba'rrer] vt to sweep; (quitar) to sweep away

**barrera** [ba'rrera] nf barrier

**barriada** [ba'rrjaða] nf quarter, district

**barricada** [barri'kaða] nf barricade

**barrida** [ba'rriða] nf sweep, sweeping

**barriga** [ba'rriɣa] nf belly; (panza) paunch; **barrigón, -ona** adj potbellied; **barrigudo, -a** adj potbellied

**barril** [ba'rril] nm barrel, cask

**barrio** ['barrjo] nm (vecindad) area, neighborhood (US); (en afueras) suburb; **barrio chino** (ESP) red-light district

**barro** ['barro] nm (lodo) mud; (objetos) earthenware; (Med) pimple

**barroco, -a** [ba'rroko, a] adj, nm baroque

**barrote** [ba'rrote] nm (de ventana) bar

**bartola** [bar'tola] nf: **tirarse o tumbarse a la ~** to take it easy, be lazy

**bártulos** ['bartulos] nmpl things, belongings

**barullo** [ba'ruʎo] nm row, uproar

**basar** [ba'sar] vt to base; **basarse** vr: **~ en** to be based on

**báscula** ['baskula] nf (platform) scales

**base** ['base] nf base; **a ~ de** on the basis of; (mediante) by means of; **base de datos** (Inform) database

**básico, -a** ['basiko, a] adj basic

**basílica** [ba'silika] nf basilica

**básquetbol** ['basketbol] (LAM) nm basketball

○ **PALABRA CLAVE**

**bastante** [bas'tante] adj 1 (suficiente) enough; **bastante dinero** enough o sufficient money; **bastantes libros** enough books

2 (valor intensivo): **bastante gente** quite a lot of people; **tener bastante calor** to be rather hot

▷ adv: **bastante bueno/malo** quite good/ rather bad; **bastante rico** pretty rich; **(lo) bastante inteligente (como) para hacer algo** clever enough o sufficiently clever to do sth

**bastar** [bas'tar] vi to be enough o sufficient; **bastarse** vr to be self-sufficient; **~ para** to be enough to; **¡basta!** (that's) enough!

**bastardo, -a** [bas'tarðo, a] adj, nm/f bastard

**bastidor** [basti'ðor] nm frame; (de coche) chassis; (Teatro) wing; **entre ~es** (fig) behind the scenes

**basto, -a** ['basto, a] adj coarse, rough; **bastos** nmpl (Naipes) ≈ clubs

**bastón** [bas'ton] nm stick, staff; (para pasear) walking stick

**bastoncillo** [baston'θiʎo] nm cotton bud

**basura** [ba'sura] nf rubbish (BRIT), garbage (US) ▷ adj: **comida/televisión ~** junk food/TV

**basurero** [basu'rero] nm (hombre) dustman (BRIT), garbage man (US); (lugar) dump; (cubo) (rubbish) bin (BRIT), trash can (US)

**bata** ['bata] nf (gen) dressing gown; (cubretodo) smock, overall; (Med, Tec etc) lab(oratory) coat

**batalla** [ba'taʎa] nf battle; **de ~** (fig) for everyday use; **batalla campal** pitched battle

**batallón** [bata'ʎon] nm battalion

**batata** [ba'tata] nf sweet potato

**batería** [bate'ria] nf battery; (Mús) drums;

**batería de cocina** kitchen utensils

**batido, -a** [ba'tiðo, a] adj (camino) beaten, well-trodden ▷ nm (Culin: de leche) milk shake

**batidora** [bati'ðora] nf beater, mixer; **batidora eléctrica** food mixer, blender

**batir** [ba'tir] vt to beat, strike; (vencer) to beat, defeat; (revolver) to beat, mix; **batirse** vr to fight; **~ palmas** to applaud

**batuta** [ba'tuta] nf baton; **llevar la ~** (fig) to be the boss, be in charge

**baúl** [ba'ul] nm trunk; (Auto) boot (BRIT), trunk (US)

**bautismo** [bau'tismo] nm baptism, christening

**bautizar** [bauti'θar] vt to baptize, christen; (fam: diluir) to water down; **bautizo** nm baptism, christening

**bayeta** [ba'jeta] nf floorcloth

**baza** ['baθa] nf trick; **meter ~** to butt in

**bazar** [ba'θar] nm bazaar

**bazofia** [ba'θofja] nf trash

**be** [be] nf name of the letter B; **be chica/ grande** (MÉX) V/B; **be larga** (LAM) B

**beato, -a** [be'ato, a] adj blessed; (piadoso) pious

**bebé** [be'βe] (pl ~s) nm baby

**bebedero, a** [beβe'ðero, a] (MÉX, CS) nm drinking fountain

**bebedor, a** [beβe'ðor, a] adj hard-drinking

**beber** [be'βer] vt, vi to drink

**bebida** [be'βiða] nf drink; **bebido, -a** adj drunk

**beca** ['beka] nf grant, scholarship; **becario, -a** [be'karjo, a] nm/f scholarship holder, grant holder

**bedel** [be'ðel] nm (Escol) janitor; (Univ) porter

**béisbol** ['beisβol] nm baseball

**Belén** [be'len] nm Bethlehem; **belén** nm (de Navidad) nativity scene, crib

**belga** ['belɣa] adj, nmf Belgian

**Bélgica** ['belxika] nf Belgium

**bélico, -a** ['beliko, a] adj (actitud) warlike

**belleza** [be'ʎeθa] nf beauty

**bello, -a** ['beʎo, a] adj beautiful, lovely; **Bellas Artes** Fine Art

**bellota** [be'ʎota] nf acorn

**bemol** [be'mol] nm (Mús) flat; **esto tiene ~es** (fam) this is a tough one

**bencina** [ben'θina] nf (Quím) benzine

**bendecir** [bende'θir] vt to bless

**bendición** [bendi'θjon] nf blessing

**bendito, -a** [ben'dito, a] pp de **bendecir** ▷ adj holy; (afortunado) lucky; (feliz) happy; (sencillo) simple ▷ nm/f simple soul

**beneficencia** [benefi'θenθja] nf charity

**beneficiario, -a** [benefi'θjarjo, a] nm/f beneficiary

**beneficio** [bene'fiθjo] nm (bien) benefit, advantage; (ganancia) profit, gain; **a ~ de algn** in aid of sb; **beneficioso, -a** adj beneficial

**benéfico, -a** [be'nefiko, a] adj charitable

**beneplácito** [bene'plaθito] nm approval, consent

**benévolo, -a** [be'neβolo, a] adj benevolent, kind

**benigno, -a** [be'niɣno, a] adj kind; (suave) mild; (Med: tumor) benign, non-malignant

**berberecho** [berβe'retʃo] nm (Zool, Culin) cockle

**berenjena** [beren'xena] nf aubergine (BRIT), eggplant (US)

**Berlín** [ber'lin] n Berlin

**berlinesa** [berli'nesa] (RPL) nf doughnut, donut (US)

**bermudas** [ber'muðas] nfpl Bermuda shorts

**berrido** [be'rriðo] nm bellow(ing)

**berrinche** [be'rrintʃe] (fam) nm temper, tantrum

**berro** ['berro] nm watercress

**berza** ['berθa] nf cabbage

**besamel** [besa'mel] nf (Culin) white sauce, bechamel sauce

**besar** [be'sar] vt to kiss; (fig: tocar) to graze; **besarse** vr to kiss (one another); **beso** nm kiss

**bestia** ['bestja] nf beast, animal; (fig) idiot; **bestia de carga** beast of burden; **bestial** [bes'tjal] adj bestial; (fam) terrific; **bestialidad** nf bestiality; (fam) stupidity

**besugo** [be'suɣo] nm sea bream; (fam) idiot

**besuquear** [besuke'ar] vt to cover with kisses; **besuquearse** vr to kiss and cuddle

**betabel** [beta'bel] (MÉX) nm beetroot (BRIT), beet (US)

**betún** [be'tun] nm shoe polish; (Quím) bitumen

**biberón** [biβe'ron] nm feeding bottle

**Biblia** ['biβlja] nf Bible

**bibliografía** [biβljoɣra'fia] nf bibliography

**biblioteca** [biβljo'teka] nf library; (mueble) bookshelves; **biblioteca de consulta** reference library; **bibliotecario, -a** nm/f librarian

**bicarbonato** [bikarβo'nato] nm bicarbonate

**bicho** ['bitʃo] nm (animal) small animal; (sabandija) bug, insect; (Taur) bull

**bici** ['biθi] (fam) nf bike

**bicicleta** [biθi'kleta] nf bicycle, cycle; **ir**

**en ~** to cycle
**bidé** [bi'ðe] (*pl* **~s**) *nm* bidet
**bidón** [bi'ðon] *nm* (*de aceite*) drum; (*de gasolina*) can

○ **PALABRA CLAVE**

**bien** [bjen] *nm* **1**(*bienestar*) good; **te lo digo por tu bien** I'm telling you for your own good; **el bien y el mal** good and evil
**2** (*posesión*): **bienes** goods; **bienes de consumo** consumer goods; **bienes inmuebles** *o* **raíces/bienes muebles** real estate *sg*/personal property *sg* ▷ *adv*
**1** (*de manera satisfactoria, correcta etc*) well; **trabaja/come bien** she works/eats well; **contestó bien** he answered correctly; **me siento bien** I feel fine; **no me siento bien** I don't feel very well; **se está bien aquí** it's nice here
**2** (*frases*): **hiciste bien en llamarme** you were right to call me
**3** (*valor intensivo*) very; **un cuarto bien caliente** a nice warm room; **bien se ve que ...** it's quite clear that ...
**4 estar bien: estoy muy bien aquí** I feel very happy here; **está bien que vengan** it's all right for them to come; **¡está bien! lo haré** oh all right, I'll do it
**5** (*de buena gana*): **yo bien que iría pero ...** I'd gladly go but ... ▷ *excl*: **¡bien!** (*aprobación*) O.K.!; **¡muy bien!** well done! ▷ *adj inv* (*matiz despectivo*): **gente bien** posh people ▷ *conj*
**1 bien ... bien: bien en coche bien en tren** either by car or by train
**2** (*LAM*): **no bien: no bien llegue te llamaré** as soon as I arrive I'll call you
**3 si bien** even though; V *tb* **más**

**bienal** [bje'nal] *adj* biennial
**bienestar** [bjenes'tar] *nm* well-being, welfare
**bienvenida** [bjembe'niða] *nf* welcome; **dar la ~ a algn** to welcome sb
**bienvenido** [bjembe'niðo] *excl* welcome!
**bife** ['bife] (*cs*) *nm* steak
**bifurcación** [bifurka'θjon] *nf* fork
**bígamo, -a** ['biɣamo, a] *adj* bigamous ▷ *nm/f* bigamist
**bigote** [bi'ɣote] *nm* moustache; **bigotudo, -a** *adj* with a big moustache
**bikini** [bi'kini] *nm* bikini; (*Culin*) toasted ham and cheese sandwich
**bilingüe** [bi'lingwe] *adj* bilingual
**billar** [bi'ʎar] *nm* billiards *sg*; **billares** *nmpl* (*lugar*) billiard hall; (*sala de juegos*) amusement arcade; **billar americano** pool
**billete** [bi'ʎete] *nm* ticket; (*de banco*)

(bank)note (*BRIT*), bill (*US*); (*carta*) note; **~ de 20 libras** £20 note; **billete de ida y vuelta** return (*BRIT*) *o* round-trip (*US*) ticket; **billete sencillo** *o* **de ida** single (*BRIT*) *o* one-way (*US*) ticket; **billete electrónico** e-ticket
**billetera** [biʎe'tera] *nf* wallet
**billón** [bi'ʎon] *nm* billion
**bimensual** [bimen'swal] *adj* twice monthly
**bingo** ['bingo] *nm* bingo
**biodegradable** [bioðeɣra'ðaβle] *adj* biodegradable
**biografía** [bjoɣra'fia] *nf* biography
**biología** [bjolo'xia] *nf* biology; **biológico, -a** *adj* biological; (*cultivo, producto*) organic; **biólogo, -a** *nm/f* biologist
**biombo** ['bjombo] *nm* (folding) screen
**bioterrorismo** [bjoterro'rismo] *nm* bioterrorism
**biquini** [bi'kini] *nm o* (*RPL*) *f* bikini
**birlar** [bir'lar] (*fam*) *vt* to pinch
**Birmania** [bir'manja] *nf* Burma
**birome** [bi'rome] (*RPL*) *nf* ballpoint (pen)
**birria** ['birrja] *nf*: **ser una ~** (*película, libro*) to be rubbish
**bis** [bis] *excl* encore!
**bisabuelo, -a** [bisa'βwelo, a] *nm/f* great-grandfather(-mother)
**bisagra** [bi'saɣra] *nf* hinge
**bisiesto** [bi'sjesto] *adj*: **año ~** leap year
**bisnieto, -a** [bis'njeto, a] *nm/f* great-grandson/daughter
**bisonte** [bi'sonte] *nm* bison
**bisté** [bis'te] *nm* = **bistec**
**bistec** [bis'tek] *nm* steak
**bisturí** [bistu'ri] *nm* scalpel
**bisutería** [bisute'ria] *nf* imitation *o* costume jewellery
**bit** [bit] *nm* (*Inform*) bit
**bizco, -a** ['biθko, a] *adj* cross-eyed
**bizcocho** [biθ'kotʃo] *nm* (*Culin*) sponge cake
**blanca** ['blanka] *nf* (*Mús*) minim; **estar sin ~** (*ESP: fam*) to be broke; V *tb* **blanco**
**blanco, -a** ['blanko, a] *adj* white ▷ *nm/f* white man/woman, white ▷ *nm* (*color*) white; (*en texto*) blank; (*Mil, fig*) target; **en ~** blank; **noche en ~** sleepless night
**blandir** [blan'dir] *vt* to brandish
**blando, -a** ['blando, a] *adj* soft; (*tierno*) tender, gentle; (*carácter*) mild; (*fam*) cowardly
**blanqueador** [blankea'ðor] (*MÉX*) *nm* bleach
**blanquear** [blanke'ar] *vt* to whiten; (*fachada*) to whitewash; (*paño*) to bleach ▷ *vi* to turn white
**blanquillo** [blan'kiʎo] (*MÉX, CAM*) *nm* egg

**blasfemar** [blasfe'mar] *vi* to blaspheme, curse

**bledo** ['bleðo] *nm*: **me importa un ~** I couldn't care less

**blindado, -a** [blin'daðo, a] *adj* (*Mil*) armour-plated; (*antibala*) bullet-proof; **coche** (*ESP*) o **carro** (*LAM*) **~** armoured car

**bloc** [blok] (*pl* **~s**) *nm* writing pad

**blof** [blof] (*MÉX*) *nm* bluff; **blofear** (*MÉX*) *vi* to bluff

**blog** [bloɣ] (*pl* **~s**) *nm* blog

**bloque** ['bloke] *nm* block; (*Pol*) bloc

**bloquear** [bloke'ar] *vt* to blockade; **bloqueo** *nm* blockade; (*Com*) freezing, blocking; **bloqueo mental** mental block

**blusa** ['blusa] *nf* blouse

**bobada** [bo'βaða] *nf* foolish action; foolish statement; **decir ~s** to talk nonsense

**bobina** [bo'βina] *nf* (*Tec*) bobbin; (*Foto*) spool; (*Elec*) coil

**bobo, -a** ['boβo, a] *adj* (*tonto*) daft, silly; (*cándido*) naôve ▷ *nm/f* fool, idiot ▷ *nm* (*Teatro*) clown, funny man

**boca** ['boka] *nf* mouth; (*de crustáceo*) pincer; (*de cañón*) muzzle; (*entrada*) mouth, entrance; **bocas** *nfpl* (*de río*) mouth *sg*; **~ abajo/arriba** face down/up; **se me hace la ~ agua** my mouth is watering; **boca de incendios** hydrant; **boca del estómago** pit of the stomach; **boca de metro** underground (*BRIT*) o subway (*US*) entrance

**bocacalle** [boka'kaʎe] *nf* (*entrance to a*) street; **la primera ~** the first turning o street

**bocadillo** [boka'ðiʎo] *nm* sandwich

**bocado** [bo'kaðo] *nm* mouthful, bite; (*de caballo*) bridle

**bocajarro** [boka'xarro]: **a ~** *adv* (*disparar*) point-blank

**bocanada** [boka'naða] *nf* (*de vino*) mouthful, swallow; (*de aire*) gust, puff

**bocata** [bo'kata] (*fam*) *nm* sandwich

**bocazas** [bo'kaθas] (*fam*) *nm inv* bigmouth

**boceto** [bo'θeto] *nm* sketch, outline

**bochorno** [bo'tʃorno] *nm* (*vergüenza*) embarrassment; (*calor*) **hace ~** it's very muggy

**bocina** [bo'θina] *nf* (*Mús*) trumpet; (*Auto*) horn; (*para hablar*) megaphone

**boda** ['boða] *nf* (*tb*: **~s**) wedding, marriage; (*fiesta*) wedding reception; **bodas de oro/ plata** golden/silver wedding *sg*

**bodega** [bo'ðeɣa] *nf* (*de vino*) (wine) cellar; (*depósito*) storeroom; (*de barco*) hold

**bodegón** [boðe'ɣon] *nm* (*Arte*) still life

**bofetada** [bofe'taða] *nf* slap (in the face)

**boga** ['boɣa] *nf*: **en ~** (*fig*) in vogue

**Bogotá** [boɣo'ta] *n* Bogotá

**bohemio, -a** [bo'emjo, a] *adj*, *nm/f* Bohemian

**bohío** [bo'io] (*CAM*) *nm* shack, hut

**boicot** [boi'kot] (*pl* **~s**) *nm* boycott; **boicotear** *vt* to boycott

**bóiler** ['boiler] (*MÉX*) *nm* boiler

**boina** ['boina] *nf* beret

**bola** ['bola] *nf* ball; (*canica*) marble; (*Naipes*) (grand) slam; (*betún*) shoe polish; (*mentira*) tale, story; **bolas** *nfpl* (*LAM: caza*) bolas *sg*; **bola de billar** billiard ball; **bola de nieve** snowball

**boleadoras** [bolea'ðoras] *nfpl* bolas *sg*

**bolear** [bole'ar] (*MÉX*) *vt* (*zapatos*) to polish, shine

**bolera** [bo'lera] *nf* skittle o bowling alley

**bolero, -a** (*MÉX*) [bo'lero] *nm/f* (*limpiabotas*) shoeshine boy/girl

**boleta** [bo'leta] (*LAM*) *nf* (*de rifa*) ticket; (*CS: recibo*) receipt; **boleta de calificaciones** (*MÉX*) report card

**boletería** [bolete'ria] (*LAM*) *nf* ticket office

**boletín** [bole'tin] *nm* bulletin; (*periódico*) journal, review; **boletín de noticias** news bulletin

**boleto** [bo'leto] *nm* (*LAM*) ticket; **boleto de ida y vuelta** (*LAM*) round trip ticket; **boleto electrónico** (*LAM*) e-ticket; **boleto redondo** (*MÉX*) round trip ticket

**boli** ['boli] (*fam*) *nm* Biro®

**bolígrafo** [bo'liɣrafo] *nm* ball-point pen, Biro®

**bolilla** [bo'liʎa] (*RPL*) *nf* topic

**bolillo** [bo'liʎo] (*MÉX*) *nm* (*bread*) roll

**bolita** [bo'lita] (*CS*) *nf* marble

**bolívar** [bo'liβar] *nm* monetary unit of Venezuela

**Bolivia** [bo'liβja] *nf* Bolivia; **boliviano, -a** *adj*, *nm/f* Bolivian

**bollería** [boʎe'ria] *nf* cakes *pl* and pastries *pl*

**bollo** ['boʎo] *nm* (*pan*) roll; (*bulto*) bump, lump; (*abolladura*) dent

**bolo** ['bolo] *nm* skittle; (*píldora*) (large) pill; **(juego de) bolos** *nmpl* skittles *sg*

**bolsa** ['bolsa] *nf* (*para llevar algo*) bag; (*MÉX, CAM: bolsillo*) pocket; (*MÉX: de mujer*) handbag; (*Anat*) cavity, sac; (*Com*) stock exchange; (*Minería*) pocket; **de ~** pocket *cpd*; **bolsa de agua caliente** hot water bottle; **bolsa de aire** air pocket; **bolsa de dormir** (*MÉX, RPL*) sleeping bag; **bolsa de la compra** shopping bag; **bolsa de papel/plástico** paper/plastic bag

**bolsear** [bolse'ar] (*MÉX, CAM*) *vt*: **~ a algn** to pick sb's pocket

**bolsillo** [bol'siʎo] *nm* pocket; (*cartera*) purse; **de ~** pocket(-size)

**bolso** ['bolso] *nm* (*bolsa*) bag; (*de mujer*)

handbag

**bomba** ['bomba] nf (Mil) bomb; (Tec) pump ▷ adj (fam): **noticia ~** bombshell ▷ adv (fam): **pasarlo ~** to have a great time; **bomba atómica/de efecto retardado/de humo** atomic/time/smoke bomb

**bombacha** [bom'batʃa] (RPL) nf panties pl

**bombardear** [bombarðe'ar] vt to bombard; (Mil) to bomb; **bombardeo** nm bombardment; bombing

**bombazo** [bom'baθo] (MÉX) nm (explosión) explosion; (fam: notición) bombshell; (: éxito) smash hit

**bombear** [bombe'ar] vt (agua) to pump (out o up)

**bombero** [bom'bero] nm fireman

**bombilla** [bom'biʎa] (ESP) nf (light) bulb

**bombita** [bom'bita] (RPL) nf (light) bulb

**bombo** ['bombo] nm (Mús) bass drum; (Tec) drum

**bombón** [bom'bon] nm chocolate; (MÉX: de caramelo) marshmallow

**bombona** [bom'bona] (ESP) nf (de butano, oxígeno) cylinder

**bonachón, -ona** [bona'tʃon, ona] adj good-natured, easy-going

**bonanza** [bo'nanθa] nf (Náut) fair weather; (fig) bonanza; (Minería) rich pocket o vein

**bondad** [bon'dað] nf goodness, kindness; **tenga la ~ de** (please) be good enough to

**bonito, -a** [bo'nito, a] adj pretty; (agradable) nice ▷ nm (atún) tuna (fish)

**bono** ['bono] nm voucher; (Finanzas) bond

**bonobús** [bono'βus] (ESP) nm bus pass

**bonoloto** [bono'loto] nf state-run weekly lottery

**boquerón** [boke'ron] nm (pez) (kind of) anchovy; (agujero) large hole

**boquete** [bo'kete] nm gap, hole

**boquiabierto, -a** [bokia'βjerto, a] adj: **quedarse ~** to be amazed o flabbergasted

**boquilla** [bo'kiʎa] nf (para riego) nozzle; (para cigarro) cigarette holder; (Mús) mouthpiece

**borbotón** [borβo'ton] nm: **salir a borbotones** to gush out

**borda** ['borða] nf (Náut) (ship's) rail; **tirar algo/caerse por la ~** to throw sth/fall overboard

**bordado** [bor'ðaðo] nm embroidery

**bordar** [bor'ðar] vt to embroider

**borde** ['borðe] nm edge, border; (de camino etc) side; (en la costura) hem; **al ~ de** (fig) on the verge of; **ser ~** (ESP: fam) to be rude; **bordear** vt to border

**bordillo** [bor'ðiʎo] nm kerb (BRIT), curb (US)

**bordo** ['borðo] nm (Náut) side; **a ~** on board

**borlote** [bor'lote] (MÉX) nm row, uproar

**borrachera** [borra'tʃera] nf (ebriedad) drunkenness; (orgía) spree, binge

**borracho, -a** [bo'rratʃo, a] adj drunk ▷ nm/f (habitual) drunkard, drunk; (temporal) drunk, drunk man/woman

**borrador** [borra'ðor] nm (escritura) first draft, rough sketch; (goma) rubber (BRIT), eraser

**borrar** [bo'rrar] vt to erase, rub out

**borrasca** [bo'rraska] nf storm

**borrego, -a** [bo'rreɣo, a] nm/f (Zool: joven) (yearling) lamb; (adulto) sheep ▷ nm (MÉX: fam) false rumour

**borrico, -a** [bo'rriko, a] nm/f donkey/she-donkey; (fig) stupid man/woman

**borrón** [bo'rron] nm (mancha) stain

**borroso, -a** [bo'rroso, a] adj vague, unclear; (escritura) illegible

**bosque** ['boske] nm wood; (grande) forest

**bostezar** [boste'θar] vi to yawn; **bostezo** nm yawn

**bota** ['bota] nf (calzado) boot; (para vino) leather wine bottle; **botas de agua** o **goma** Wellingtons

**botana** [bo'tana] (MÉX) nf snack, appetizer

**botánica** [bo'tanika] nf (ciencia) botany; V tb **botánico**

**botánico, -a** [bo'taniko, a] adj botanical ▷ nm/f botanist

**botar** [bo'tar] vt to throw, hurl; (Náut) to launch; (LAM: echar) to throw out ▷ vi (ESP: saltar) to bounce

**bote** ['bote] nm (salto) bounce; (golpe) thrust; (ESP: envase) tin, can; (embarcación) boat; (MÉX, CAM: pey: cárcel) jail; **de ~ en ~** packed, jammed full; **bote de la basura** (MÉX) dustbin (BRIT), trashcan (US); **bote salvavidas** lifeboat

**botella** [bo'teʎa] nf bottle; **botellín** nm small bottle; **botellón** nm (ESP: fam) outdoor drinking session

**botijo** [bo'tixo] nm (earthenware) jug

**botín** [bo'tin] nm (calzado) half boot; (polaina) spat; (Mil) booty

**botiquín** [boti'kin] nm (armario) medicine cabinet; (portátil) first-aid kit

**botón** [bo'ton] nm button; (Bot) bud

**botones** [bo'tones] nm inv bellboy (BRIT), bellhop (US)

**bóveda** ['boβeða] nf (Arq) vault

**boxeador** [boksea'ðor] nm boxer

**boxeo** [bok'seo] nm boxing

**boya** ['boja] nf (Náut) buoy; (de caña) float

**boyante** [bo'jante] adj prosperous

**bozal** [bo'θal] nm (para caballos) halter; (de

*perro*) muzzle

**bragas** ['braɣas] *nfpl* (*de mujer*) panties, knickers (BRIT)

**bragueta** [bra'ɣeta] *nf* fly, flies *pl*

**braille** [breil] *nm* braille

**brasa** ['brasa] *nf* live o hot coal

**brasero** [bra'sero] *nm* brazier

**brasier** [bra'sjer] (MÉX) *nm* bra

**Brasil** [bra'sil] *nm* (*tb*: **el ~**) Brazil; **brasileño, -a** *adj, nm/f* Brazilian

**brassier** [bra'sjer] (MÉX) *nm* V **brasier**

**bravo, -a** ['braβo, a] *adj* (*valiente*) brave; (*feroz*) ferocious; (*salvaje*) wild; (*mar etc*) rough, stormy ▷ *excl* bravo!; **bravura** *nf* bravery; ferocity

**braza** ['braθa] *nf* fathom; **nadar a ~** to swim breast-stroke

**brazalete** [braθa'lete] *nm* (*pulsera*) bracelet; (*banda*) armband

**brazo** ['braθo] *nm* arm; (*Zool*) foreleg; (*Bot*) limb, branch; **luchar a ~ partido** to fight hand-to-hand; **ir cogidos del ~** to walk arm in arm

**brebaje** [bre'βaxe] *nm* potion

**brecha** ['bretʃa] *nf* (*hoyo, vacío*) gap, opening; (*Mil, fig*) breach

**brega** ['breɣa] *nf* (*lucha*) struggle; (*trabajo*) hard work

**breva** ['breβa] *nf* early fig

**breve** ['breβe] *adj* short, brief ▷ *nf* (*Mús*) breve; **en ~** (*pronto*) shortly, before long; **brevedad** *nf* brevity, shortness

**bribón, -ona** [bri'βon, ona] *adj* idle, lazy ▷ *nm/f* (*pícaro*) rascal, rogue

**bricolaje** [briko'laxe] *nm* do-it-yourself, DIY

**brida** ['briða] *nf* bridle, rein; (*Tec*) clamp

**bridge** [britʃ] *nm* bridge

**brigada** [bri'ɣaða] *nf* (*unidad*) brigade; (*de trabajadores*) squad, gang ▷ *nm* ≈ staff-sergeant, sergeant-major

**brillante** [bri'ʎante] *adj* brilliant ▷ *nm* diamond

**brillar** [bri'ʎar] *vi* to shine; (*joyas*) to sparkle

**brillo** ['briʎo] *nm* shine; (*brillantez*) brilliance; (*fig*) splendour; **sacar ~ a** to polish

**brincar** [brin'kar] *vi* to skip about, hop about, jump about

**brinco** ['brinko] *nm* jump, leap

**brindar** [brin'dar] *vi*: **~ a** o **por** to drink (a toast) to ▷ *vt* to offer, present

**brindis** ['brindis] *nm inv* toast

**brío** ['brio] *nm* spirit, dash

**brisa** ['brisa] *nf* breeze

**británico, -a** [bri'taniko, a] *adj* British

▷ *nm/f* Briton, British person

**brizna** ['briθna] *nf* (*de hierba, paja*) blade; (*de tabaco*) leaf

**broca** ['broka] *nf* (*Tec*) drill, bit

**brocha** ['brotʃa] *nf* (*large*) paintbrush; **brocha de afeitar** shaving brush

**broche** ['brotʃe] *nm* brooch

**broma** ['broma] *nf* joke; **de** o **en ~** in fun, as a joke; **broma pesada** practical joke; **bromear** *vi* to joke

**bromista** [bro'mista] *adj* fond of joking ▷ *nmf* joker, wag

**bronca** ['bronka] *nf* row; **echar una ~ a algn** to tick sb off

**bronce** ['bronθe] *nm* bronze; **bronceado, -a** *adj* bronze; (*por el sol*) tanned ▷ *nm* (*sun*)tan; (*Tec*) bronzing

**bronceador** [bronθea'ðor] *nm* suntan lotion

**broncearse** [bronθe'arse] *vr* to get a suntan

**bronquio** ['bronkjo] *nm* (*Anat*) bronchial tube

**bronquitis** [bron'kitis] *nf inv* bronchitis

**brotar** [bro'tar] *vi* (*Bot*) to sprout; (*aguas*) to gush (forth); (*Med*) to break out

**brote** ['brote] *nm* (*Bot*) shoot; (*Med, fig*) outbreak

**bruces** ['bruθes]: **de bruces** *adv*: **caer** o **dar de ~** to fall headlong, fall flat

**bruja** ['bruxa] *nf* witch; **brujería** *nf* witchcraft

**brujo** ['bruxo] *nm* wizard, magician

**brújula** ['bruxula] *nf* compass

**bruma** ['bruma] *nf* mist

**brusco, -a** ['brusko, a] *adj* (*súbito*) sudden; (*áspero*) brusque

**Bruselas** [bru'selas] *n* Brussels

**brutal** [bru'tal] *adj* brutal; **brutalidad** [brutali'ðað] *nf* brutality

**bruto, -a** ['bruto, a] *adj* (*idiota*) stupid; (*bestial*) brutish; (*peso*) gross; **en ~** raw, unworked

**Bs.As.** *abr* (= *Buenos Aires*) B.A.

**bucal** [bu'kal] *adj* oral; **por vía ~** orally

**bucear** [buθe'ar] *vi* to dive ▷ *vt* to explore; **buceo** *nm* diving

**bucle** ['bukle] *nm* curl

**budismo** [bu'ðismo] *nm* Buddhism

**buen** [bwen] *adj m* V **bueno**

**buenamente** [bwena'mente] *adv* (*fácilmente*) easily; (*voluntariamente*) willingly

**buenaventura** [bwenaβen'tura] *nf* (*suerte*) good luck; (*adivinación*) fortune

**buenmozo** [bwen'moθo] (MÉX) *adj* handsome

○ PALABRA CLAVE

**bueno, -a** ['bweno, a] (antes de nmsg: **buen**) adj **1** (excelente etc) good; **es un libro bueno, es un buen libro** it's a good book; **hace bueno, hace buen tiempo** the weather is fine, it is fine; **el bueno de Paco** good old Paco; **fue muy bueno conmigo** he was very nice o kind to me

**2** (apropiado): **ser bueno para** to be good for; **creo que vamos por buen camino** I think we're on the right track

**3** (irónico): **le di un buen rapapolvo** I gave him a good o real ticking off; **¡buen conductor estás hecho!** some o a fine driver you are!; **¡estaría bueno que ...!** a fine thing it would be if ...!

**4** (atractivo, sabroso): **está bueno este bizcocho** this sponge is delicious; **Carmen está muy buena** Carmen is gorgeous

**5** (saludos): **¡buen día!, ¡buenos días!** (good) morning!; **¡buenas (tardes)!** (good) afternoon!; (más tarde) (good) evening!; **¡buenas noches!** good night!

**6** (otras locuciones): **estar de buenas** to be in a good mood; **por las buenas o por las malas** by hook or by crook; **de buenas a primeras** all of a sudden ▷ excl: **¡bueno!** all right!; **bueno, ¿y qué?** well, so what?

**Buenos Aires** [bweno'saires] nm Buenos Aires
**buey** [bwei] nm ox
**búfalo** ['bufalo] nm buffalo
**bufanda** [bu'fanda] nf scarf
**bufete** [bu'fete] nm (despacho de abogado) lawyer's office
**bufón** [bu'fon] nm clown
**buhardilla** [buar'ðiʎa] nf attic
**búho** ['buo] nm owl; (fig) hermit, recluse
**buitre** ['bwitre] nm vulture
**bujía** [bu'xia] nf (vela) candle; (Elec) candle (power); (Auto) spark plug
**bula** ['bula] nf (papal) bull
**bulbo** ['bulβo] nm bulb
**bulevar** [bule'βar] nm boulevard
**Bulgaria** [bul'ɣarja] nf Bulgaria; **búlgaro, -a** adj, nm/f Bulgarian
**bulla** ['buʎa] nf (ruido) uproar; (de gente) crowd
**bullicio** [bu'ʎiθjo] nm (ruido) uproar; (movimiento) bustle
**bulto** ['bulto] nm (paquete) package; (fardo) bundle; (tamaño) size, bulkiness; (Med) swelling, lump; (silueta) vague shape
**buñuelo** [bu'ɲwelo] nm ≈ doughnut (BRIT), ≈ donut (US); (fruta de sartén) fritter
**buque** ['buke] nm ship, vessel; **buque de**

**guerra** warship
**burbuja** [bur'βuxa] nf bubble
**burdel** [bur'ðel] nm brothel
**burgués, -esa** [bur'ɣes, esa] adj middle-class, bourgeois; **burguesía** nf middle class, bourgeoisie
**burla** ['burla] nf (mofa) gibe; (broma) joke; (engaño) trick; **burlar** [bur'lar] vt (engañar) to deceive ▷ vi to joke; **burlarse** vr to joke; **burlarse de** to make fun of
**burlón, -ona** [bur'lon, ona] adj mocking
**buró** [bu'ro] (MÉX) nm bedside table
**burocracia** [buro'kraθja] nf civil service
**burrada** [bu'rraða] nf: **decir o soltar ~s** to talk nonsense; **hacer ~s** to act stupid; **una ~** (ESP: mucho) (a hell of a) lot
**burro, -a** ['burro, a] nm/f donkey/she-donkey; (fig) ass, idiot
**bursátil** [bur'satil] adj stock-exchange cpd
**bus** [bus] nm bus
**busca** ['buska] nf search, hunt ▷ nm (Tel) bleeper; **en ~ de** in search of
**buscador** [buska'ðor] nm (Internet) search engine
**buscar** [bus'kar] vt to look for, search for, seek ▷ vi to look, search, seek; **se busca secretaria** secretary wanted
**busque** etc vb V **buscar**
**búsqueda** ['buskeða] nf = **busca**
**busto** ['busto] nm (Anat, Arte) bust
**butaca** [bu'taka] nf armchair; (de cine, teatro) stall, seat
**butano** [bu'tano] nm butane (gas)
**buzo** ['buθo] nm diver
**buzón** [bu'θon] nm (en puerta) letter box; (en calle) pillar box

# C

**C.** *abr* (= *centígrado*) C; (*compañía*) Co.

**C/** *abr* (= *calle*) St

**cabal** [ka'βal] *adj* (*exacto*) exact; (*correcto*) right, proper; (*acabado*) finished, complete; **cabales** *nmpl*: **no está en sus cabales** she isn't in her right mind

**cábalas** ['kaβalas] *nfpl*: **hacer ~** to guess

**cabalgar** [kaβal'ɣar] *vt, vi* to ride

**cabalgata** [kaβal'ɣata] *nf* procession

**caballa** [ka'βaʎa] *nf* mackerel

**caballería** [kaβaʎe'ria] *nf* mount; (*Mil*) cavalry

**caballero** [kaβa'ʎero] *nm* gentleman; (*de la orden de caballería*) knight; (*trato directo*) sir

**caballete** [kaβa'ʎete] *nm* (*Arte*) easel; (*Tec*) trestle

**caballito** [kaβa'ʎito] *nm* (*caballo pequeño*) small horse, pony; **caballitos** *nmpl* (*en verbena*) roundabout, merry-go-round

**caballo** [ka'βaʎo] *nm* horse; (*Ajedrez*) knight; (*Naipes*) queen; **ir en ~** to ride; **caballo de carreras** racehorse; **caballo de fuerza** o **vapor** horsepower

**cabaña** [ka'βaɲa] *nf* (*casita*) hut, cabin

**cabecear** [kaβeθe'ar] *vt, vi* to nod

**cabecera** [kaβe'θera] *nf* head; (*Imprenta*) headline

**cabecilla** [kaβe'θiʎa] *nm* ringleader

**cabellera** [kaβe'ʎera] *nf* (head of) hair; (*de cometa*) tail

**cabello** [ka'βeʎo] *nm* (*tb*: **~s**) hair; **cabello de ángel** confectionery and pastry filling made of pumpkin and syrup

**caber** [ka'βer] *vi* (*entrar*) to fit, go; **caben 3 más** there's room for 3 more

**cabestrillo** [kaβes'triʎo] *nm* sling

**cabeza** [ka'βeθa] *nf* head; (*Pol*) chief, leader; **cabeza de ajo** bulb of garlic; **cabeza de familia** head of the household; **cabeza rapada** skinhead; **cabezada** *nf* (*golpe*) butt; **dar cabezadas** to nod off; **cabezón, -ona**

*adj* (*vino*) heady; (*fam: persona*) pig-headed

**cabida** [ka'βiða] *nf* space

**cabina** [ka'βina] *nf* cabin; (*de avión*) cockpit; (*de camión*) cab; **cabina telefónica** telephone (BRIT) box o booth

**cabizbajo, -a** [kaβiθ'βaxo, a] *adj* crestfallen, dejected

**cable** ['kaβle] *nm* cable

**cabo** ['kaβo] *nm* (*de objeto*) end, extremity; (*Mil*) corporal; (*Náut*) rope, cable; (*Geo*) cape; **al ~ de 3 días** after 3 days; **llevar a ~** to carry out

**cabra** ['kaβra] *nf* goat

**cabré** *etc vb* V **caber**

**cabrear** [kaβre'ar] (*fam*) *vt* to bug; **cabrearse** *vr* (*enfadarse*) to fly off the handle

**cabrito** [ka'βrito] *nm* kid

**cabrón** [ka'βron] *nm* cuckold; (*fam!*) bastard (!)

**caca** ['kaka] (*fam*) *nf* pooh

**cacahuete** [kaka'wete] (*ESP*) *nm* peanut

**cacao** [ka'kao] *nm* cocoa; (*Bot*) cacao

**cacarear** [kakare'ar] *vi* (*persona*) to boast; (*gallina*) to crow

**cacería** [kaθe'ria] *nf* hunt

**cacarizo, -a** [kaka'riθo, a] (*MÉX*) *adj* pockmarked

**cacerola** [kaθe'rola] *nf* pan, saucepan

**cachalote** [katʃa'lote] *nm* (*Zool*) sperm whale

**cacharro** [ka'tʃarro] *nm* earthenware pot; **cacharros** *nmpl* pots and pans

**cachear** [katʃe'ar] *vt* to search, frisk

**cachemir** [katʃe'mir] *nm* cashmere

**cachetada** [katʃe'taða] (*LAM: fam*) *nf* (*bofetada*) slap

**cachete** [ka'tʃete] *nm* (*Anat*) cheek; (*ESP: bofetada*) slap (in the face)

**cachivache** [katʃi'βatʃe] *nm* (*trasto*) piece of junk; **cachivaches** *nmpl* junk *sg*

**cacho** ['katʃo] *nm* (small) bit; (*LAM: cuerno*) horn

**cachondeo** [katʃon'deo] (*ESP: fam*) *nm* farce, joke

**cachondo, -a** [ka'tʃondo, a] *adj* (*Zool*) on heat; (*fam: sexualmente*) randy; (: *gracioso*) funny

**cachorro, -a** [ka'tʃorro, a] *nm/f* (*perro*) pup, puppy; (*león*) cub

**cachucha** [ka'tʃutʃa] (*MÉX: fam*) *nf* cap

**cacique** [ka'θike] *nm* chief, local ruler; (*Pol*) local party boss

**cactus** ['kaktus] *nm inv* cactus

**cada** ['kaða] *adj inv* each; (*antes de número*) every; **~ día** each day, every day; **~ dos días** every other day; **~ uno/a** each one, every one; **~ vez más/menos** more and more/less and less; **~ vez que ...** whenever, every time (that) ...; **uno de ~ diez** one out of every ten

**cadáver** [ka'ðaβer] nm (dead) body, corpse

**cadena** [ka'ðena] nf chain; (TV) channel; **trabajo en ~** assembly line work; **cadena montañosa** mountain range; **cadena perpetua** (Jur) life imprisonment

**cadera** [ka'ðera] nf hip

**cadete** [ka'ðete] nm cadet

**caducar** [kaðu'kar] vi to expire; **caduco, -a** adj expired; (persona) very old

**caer** [ka'er] vi to fall (down); **caerse** vr to fall (down); **me cae bien/mal** I get on well with him/I can't stand him; **~ en la cuenta** to realize; **dejar ~** to drop; **su cumpleaños cae en viernes** her birthday falls on a Friday

**café** [ka'fe] (pl **~s**) nm (bebida, planta) coffee; (lugar) café ⊳ adj (MÉX: color) brown, tan; **café con leche** white coffee; **café negro** (LAM) black coffee; **café solo** (ESP) black coffee

**cafetera** [kafe'tera] nf coffee pot

**cafetería** [kafete'ria] nf (gen) café

**cafetero, -a** [kafe'tero, a] adj coffee cpd; **ser muy ~** to be a coffee addict

**cafishio** [ka'fiʃjo] (CS) nm pimp

**cagar** [ka'ɣar] (fam!) vt to bungle, mess up ⊳ vi to have a shit (!)

**caída** [ka'iða] nf fall; (declive) slope; (disminución) fall, drop

**caído, -a** [ka'iðo, a] adj drooping

**caiga** etc vb V **caer**

**caimán** [kai'man] nm alligator

**caja** ['kaxa] nf box; (para reloj) case; (de ascensor) shaft; (Com) cashbox; (donde se hacen los pagos) cashdesk; (: en supermercado) checkout, till; **caja de ahorros** savings bank; **caja de cambios** gearbox; **caja de fusibles** fuse box; **caja fuerte** o **de caudales** safe, strongbox

**cajero, -a** [ka'xero, a] nm/f cashier; **cajero automático** cash dispenser

**cajetilla** [kaxe'tiʎa] nf (de cigarrillos) packet

**cajón** [ka'xon] nm big box; (de mueble) drawer

**cajuela** (MÉX) nf (Auto) boot (BRIT), trunk (US)

**cal** [kal] nf lime

**cala** ['kala] nf (Geo) cove, inlet; (de barco) hold

**calabacín** [kalaβa'θin] nm (Bot) baby marrow; (: más pequeño) courgette (BRIT), zucchini (US)

**calabacita** [kalaβa'θita] (MÉX) nf courgette (BRIT), zucchini (US)

**calabaza** [kala'βaθa] nf (Bot) pumpkin

**calabozo** [kala'βoθo] nm (cárcel) prison; (celda) cell

**calada** [ka'laða] (ESP) nf (de cigarrillo) puff

**calado, -a** [ka'laðo, a] adj (prenda) lace cpd ⊳ nm (Náut) draught

**calamar** [kala'mar] nm squid no pl

**calambre** [ka'lambre] nm (Elec) shock

**calar** [ka'lar] vt to soak, drench; (penetrar) to pierce, penetrate; (comprender) to see through; (vela) to lower; **calarse** vr (Auto) to stall; **~se las gafas** to stick one's glasses on

**calavera** [kala'βera] nf skull

**calcar** [kal'kar] vt (reproducir) to trace; (imitar) to copy

**calcetín** [kalθe'tin] nm sock

**calcio** ['kalθjo] nm calcium

**calcomanía** [kalkoma'nia] nf transfer

**calculador, a** [kalkula'ðor, a] adj (persona) calculating; **calculadora** [kalkula'ðora] nf calculator

**calcular** [kalku'lar] vt (Mat) to calculate, compute; **~ que ...** to reckon that ...

**caldera** [kal'dera] nf boiler

**calderilla** [kalde'riʎa] nf (moneda) small change

**caldo** ['kaldo] nm stock; (consomé) consommé

**calefacción** [kalefak'θjon] nf heating; **calefacción central** central heating

**calefón** [kale'fon] (RPL) nm boiler

**calendario** [kalen'darjo] nm calendar

**calentador** [kalenta'ðor] nm heater

**calentamiento** [kalenta'mjento] nm (Deporte) warm-up; **calentamiento global** global warming

**calentar** [kalen'tar] vt to heat (up); **calentarse** vr to heat up, warm up; (fig: discusión etc) to get heated

**calentón** [kalen'ton] (RPL: fam) adj (sexualmente) horny, randy (BRIT)

**calentura** [kalen'tura] nf (Med) fever, (high) temperature

**calesita** [kale'sita] (RPL) nf merry-go-round, carousel

**calibre** [ka'liβre] nm (de cañón) calibre, bore; (diámetro) diameter; (fig) calibre

**calidad** [kali'ðað] nf quality; **de ~** quality cpd; **en ~ de** in the capacity of, as

**cálido, -a** [ka'liðo, a] adj (Med); (fig) warm

**caliente** etc [ka'ljente] vb V **calentar** ⊳ adj hot; (fig) fiery; (disputa) heated; (fam: cachondo) randy

**calificación** [kalifika'θjon] nf qualification; (de alumno) grade, mark

**calificado, -a** [kalifi'kaðo, a] (LAM) adj (competente) qualified; (obrero) skilled

**calificar** [kalifi'kar] vt to qualify; (alumno) to grade, mark; **~ de** to describe as

**calima** [ka'lima] nf (cerca del mar) mist

**cáliz** ['kaliθ] nm chalice

**caliza** [ka'liθa] nf limestone

**callado, -a** [ka'ʎaðo, a] adj quiet

**callar** [ka'ʎar] vt (asunto delicado) to keep quiet about, say nothing about; (persona, opinión) to silence ▷ vi to keep quiet, be silent; **callarse** vr to keep quiet, be silent; **¡cállate!** be quiet!, shut up!

**calle** ['kaʎe] nf street; (Deporte) lane; **~ arriba/abajo** up/down the street; **calle de sentido único** one-way street; **calle mayor** (ESP) high (BRIT) o main (US) street; **calle peatonal** pedestrianized o pedestrian street; **calle principal** (LAM) high (BRIT) o main (US) street; **callejear** vi to wander (about) the streets; **callejero, -a** adj street cpd ▷ nm street map; **callejón** nm alley, passage; **callejón sin salida** cul-de-sac; **callejuela** nf side-street, alley

**callista** [ka'ʎista] nmf chiropodist

**callo** ['kaʎo] nm callus; (en el pie) corn; **callos** nmpl (Culin) tripe sg

**calma** ['kalma] nf calm

**calmante** [kal'mante] nm sedative, tranquillizer

**calmar** [kal'mar] vt to calm, calm down ▷ vi (tempestad) to abate; (mente etc) to become calm

**calor** [ka'lor] nm heat; (agradable) warmth; **hace ~** it's hot; **tener ~** to be hot

**caloría** [kalo'ria] nf calorie

**calumnia** [ka'lumnja] nf calumny, slander

**caluroso, -a** [kalu'roso, a] adj hot; (sin exceso) warm; (fig) enthusiastic

**calva** ['kalβa] nf bald patch; (en bosque) clearing

**calvario** [kal'βarjo] nm stations pl of the cross

**calvicie** [kal'βiθje] nf baldness

**calvo, -a** ['kalβo, a] adj bald; (terreno) bare, barren; (tejido) threadbare

**calza** ['kalθa] nf wedge, chock

**calzada** [kal'θaða] nf roadway, highway

**calzado, -a** [kal'θaðo, a] adj shod ▷ nm footwear

**calzador** [kalθa'ðor] nm shoehorn

**calzar** [kal'θar] vt (zapatos etc) to wear; (mueble) to put a wedge under; **calzarse** vr: **~se los zapatos** to put on one's shoes; **¿qué (número) calza?** what size do you take?

**calzón** [kal'θon] nm (ESP: pantalón corto) shorts; (LAM: ropa interior: de hombre) underpants, pants (BRIT), shorts (US); (: de mujer) panties, knickers (BRIT)

**calzoncillos** [kalθon'θiʎos] nmpl underpants

**cama** ['kama] nf bed; **hacer la ~** to make the bed; **cama individual/de matrimonio** single/double bed

**camaleón** [kamale'on] nm chameleon

**cámara** ['kamara] nf chamber; (habitación) room; (sala) hall; (Cine) cine camera; (fotográfica) camera; **cámara de aire** (ESP) inner tube; **cámara de comercio** chamber of commerce; **cámara de gas** gas chamber; **cámara digital** digital camera; **cámara frigorífica** cold-storage room

**camarada** [kama'raða] nmf comrade, companion

**camarera** [kama'rera] nf (en restaurante) waitress; (en casa, hotel) maid

**camarero** [kama'rero] nm waiter

**camarógrafo, -a** [kama'rografo, a] (LAM) nm/f cameraman/camerawoman

**camarón** [kama'ron] nm shrimp

**camarote** [kama'rote] nm cabin

**cambiable** [kam'bjaβle] adj (variable) changeable, variable; (intercambiable) interchangeable

**cambiante** [kam'bjante] adj variable

**cambiar** [kam'bjar] vt to change; (dinero) to exchange ▷ vi to change; **cambiarse** vr (mudarse) to move; (de ropa) to change; **~ de idea** u **opinión** to change one's mind; **~se de ropa** to change (one's clothes)

**cambio** ['kambjo] nm change; (trueque) exchange; (Com) rate of exchange; (oficina) bureau de change; (dinero menudo) small change; **a ~ de** in return o exchange for; **en ~** on the other hand; (en lugar de) instead; **cambio climático** climate change; **cambio de divisas** foreign exchange; **cambio de marchas** o **velocidades** gear lever

**camelar** [kame'lar] vt to sweet-talk

**camello** [ka'meʎo] nm camel; (fam: traficante) pusher

**camerino** [kame'rino] nm dressing room

**camilla** [ka'miʎa] nf (Med) stretcher

**caminar** [kami'nar] vi (marchar) to walk, go ▷ vt (recorrer) to cover, travel

**caminata** [kami'nata] nf long walk; (por el campo) hike

**camino** [ka'mino] nm way, road; (sendero) track; **a medio ~** halfway (there); **en el ~** on the way, en route; **~ de** on the way to; **Camino de Santiago** Way of St James; **camino particular** private road

● **CAMINO DE SANTIAGO**
●
● The **Camino de Santiago** is a medieval
● pilgrim route stretching from the
● Pyrenees to Santiago de Compostela

- in north-west Spain, where tradition
- has it the body of the Apostle James is
- buried. Nowadays it is a popular tourist
- route as well as a religious one.

**camión** [ka'mjon] *nm* lorry (BRIT), truck (US); (*MÉX: autobús*) bus; **camión cisterna** tanker; **camión de la basura** dustcart, refuse lorry; **camión de mudanzas** removal (BRIT) o moving (US) van; **camionero, -a** *nm/f* lorry o truck driver

**camioneta** [kamjo'neta] *nf* van, light truck

**camisa** [ka'misa] *nf* shirt; (*Bot*) skin; **camisa de fuerza** straitjacket

**camiseta** [kami'seta] *nf* (*prenda*) tee-shirt; (*ropa interior*) vest; (*de deportista*) top

**camisón** [kami'son] *nm* nightdress, nightgown

**camorra** [ka'morra] *nf*: **buscar ~** to look for trouble

**camote** [ka'mote] *nm* (*MÉX, CS: batata*) sweet potato, yam; (*MÉX: bulbo*) tuber, bulb; (*CS: fam: enamoramiento*) crush

**campamento** [kampa'mento] *nm* camp

**campana** [kam'pana] *nf* bell; **campanada** *nf* peal; **campanario** *nm* belfry

**campanilla** [kampa'niʎa] *nf* small bell

**campaña** [kam'paɲa] *nf* (*Mil, Pol*) campaign; **campaña electoral** election campaign

**campechano, -a** [kampe'tʃano, a] *adj* (*franco*) open

**campeón, -ona** [kampe'on, ona] *nm/f* champion; **campeonato** *nm* championship

**cámper** ['kamper] (*LAM*) *nm* o *f* caravan (BRIT), trailer (US)

**campera** [kam'pera] (*RPL*) *nf* anorak

**campesino, -a** [kampe'sino, a] *adj* country cpd, rural; (*gente*) peasant cpd ⊳ *nm/f* countryman/woman; (*agricultor*) farmer

**campestre** [kam'pestre] *adj* country cpd, rural

**camping** ['kampin] (*pl* **~s**) *nm* camping; (*lugar*) campsite; **ir** o **estar de ~** to go camping

**campo** ['kampo] *nm* (*fuera de la ciudad*) country, countryside; (*Agr, Elec*) field; (*de fútbol*) pitch; (*de golf*) course; (*Mil*) camp; **campo de batalla** battlefield; **campo de concentración** concentration camp; **campo de deportes** sports ground, playing field; **campo visual** field of vision, visual field

**camuflaje** [kamu'flaxe] *nm* camouflage

**cana** ['kana] *nf* white o grey hair; **tener ~s** to be going grey

**Canadá** [kana'ða] *nm* Canada; **canadiense** *adj, nmf* Canadian ⊳ *nf* fur-lined jacket

**canal** [ka'nal] *nm* canal; (*Geo*) channel, strait; (*de televisión*) channel; (*de tejado*) gutter; **canal de Panamá** Panama Canal

**canaleta** [kana'leta] (*LAM*) *nf* (*de tejado*) gutter

**canalizar** [kanali'θar] *vt* to channel

**canalla** [ka'naʎa] *nf* rabble, mob ⊳ *nm* swine

**canapé** [kana'pe] (*pl* **~s**) *nm* sofa, settee; (*Culin*) canapé

**Canarias** [ka'narjas] *nfpl* (*tb*: **las Islas ~**) the Canary Islands, the Canaries

**canario, -a** [ka'narjo, a] *adj, nm/f* (*native*) of the Canary Isles ⊳ *nm* (*Zool*) canary

**canasta** [ka'nasta] *nf* (*round*) basket

**canasto** [ka'nasto] *nm* large basket

**cancela** [kan'θela] *nf* gate

**cancelación** [kanθela'θjon] *nf* cancellation

**cancelar** [kanθe'lar] *vt* to cancel; (*una deuda*) to write off

**cáncer** ['kanθer] *nm* (*Med*) cancer; **C~** (*Astrología*) Cancer

**cancha** ['kantʃa] *nf* (*de baloncesto*) court; (*LAM: campo*) pitch; **cancha de tenis** (*LAM*) tennis court

**canciller** [kanθi'ʎer] *nm* chancellor

**canción** [kan'θjon] *nf* song; **canción de cuna** lullaby

**candado** [kan'daðo] *nm* padlock

**candente** [kan'dente] *adj* red-hot; (*fig: tema*) burning

**candidato, -a** [kandi'ðato, a] *nm/f* candidate

**cándido, -a** ['kandiðo, a] *adj* simple; naive

> No confundir **cándido** con la palabra inglesa *candid*.

**candil** [kan'dil] *nm* oil lamp; **candilejas** *nfpl* (*Teatro*) footlights

**canela** [ka'nela] *nf* cinnamon

**canelones** [kane'lones] *nmpl* cannelloni

**cangrejo** [kan'grexo] *nm* crab

**canguro** [kan'guro] *nm* kangaroo; **hacer de ~** to babysit

**caníbal** [ka'niβal] *adj, nmf* cannibal

**canica** [ka'nika] *nf* marble

**canijo, -a** [ka'nixo, a] *adj* frail, sickly

**canilla** [ka'niʎa] (*RPL*) *nf* tap (BRIT), faucet (US)

**canjear** [kanxe'ar] *vt* to exchange

**canoa** [ka'noa] *nf* canoe

**canon** ['kanon] *nm* canon; (*pensión*) rent;

(*Com*) tax

**canonizar** [kanoni'θar] *vt* to canonize

**canoso, -a** [ka'noso, a] *adj* grey-haired

**cansado, -a** [kan'saðo, a] *adj* tired, weary; (*tedioso*) tedious, boring

**cansancio** [kan'sanθjo] *nm* tiredness, fatigue

**cansar** [kan'sar] *vt* (*fatigar*) to tire, tire out; (*aburrir*) to bore; (*fastidiar*) to bother; **cansarse** *vr* to tire, get tired; (*aburrirse*) to get bored

**cantábrico, -a** [kan'taβriko, a] *adj* Cantabrian

**cantante** [kan'tante] *adj* singing ▷ *nmf* singer

**cantar** [kan'tar] *vt* to sing ▷ *vi* to sing; (*insecto*) to chirp ▷ *nm* (*acción*) singing; (*canción*) song; (*poema*) poem

**cántaro** ['kantaro] *nm* pitcher, jug; **llover a ~s** to rain cats and dogs

**cante** ['kante] *nm* (*Mús*) Andalusian folk song; **cante jondo** flamenco singing

**cantera** [kan'tera] *nf* quarry

**cantero** [kan'tero] (RPL) *nm* (*arriate*) border

**cantidad** [kanti'ðað] *nf* quantity, amount; **~ de** lots of

**cantimplora** [kantim'plora] *nf* (*frasco*) water bottle, canteen

**cantina** [kan'tina] *nf* canteen; (*de estación*) buffet; (LAM: *bar*) bar

**cantinero, -a** [kanti'nero, a] (MÉX) *nm/f* barman/barmaid, bartender (US)

**canto** ['kanto] *nm* singing; (*canción*) song; (*borde*) edge, rim; (*de cuchillo*) back; **canto rodado** boulder

**cantor, a** [kan'tor, a] *nm/f* singer

**canturrear** [kanturre'ar] *vi* to sing softly

**canuto** [ka'nuto] *nm* (*tubo*) small tube; (*fam: droga*) joint

**caña** ['kaɲa] *nf* (*Bot: tallo*) stem, stalk; (*carrizo*) reed; (*vaso*) tumbler; (*de cerveza*) glass of beer; (*Anat*) shinbone; **caña de azúcar** sugar cane; **caña de pescar** fishing rod

**cañada** [ka'ɲaða] *nf* (*entre dos montañas*) gully, ravine; (*camino*) cattle track

**cáñamo** ['kaɲamo] *nm* hemp

**cañería** [kaɲe'ria] *nf* (*tubo*) pipe

**caño** ['kaɲo] *nm* (*tubo*) tube, pipe; (*de albañal*) sewer; (*Mús*) pipe; (*de fuente*) jet

**cañón** [ka'ɲon] *nm* (*Mil*) cannon; (*de fusil*) barrel; (*Geo*) canyon, gorge

**caoba** [ka'oβa] *nf* mahogany

**caos** ['kaos] *nm* chaos

**capa** ['kapa] *nf* cloak, cape; (*Geo*) layer, stratum; **capa de ozono** ozone layer

**capacidad** [kapaθi'ðað] *nf* (*medida*)

capacity; (*aptitud*) capacity, ability

**caparazón** [kapara'θon] *nm* shell

**capataz** [kapa'taθ] *nm* foreman

**capaz** [ka'paθ] *adj* able, capable; (*amplio*) capacious, roomy

**capellán** [kape'ʎan] *nm* chaplain; (*sacerdote*) priest

**capicúa** [kapi'kua] *adj inv* (*número, fecha*) reversible

**capilla** [ka'piʎa] *nf* chapel

**capital** [kapi'tal] *adj* capital ▷ *nm* (*Com*) capital ▷ *nf* (*ciudad*) capital; **capital social** share o authorized capital

**capitalismo** [kapita'lismo] *nm* capitalism; **capitalista** *adj, nmf* capitalist

**capitán** [kapi'tan] *nm* captain

**capítulo** [ka'pitulo] *nm* chapter

**capó** [ka'po] *nm* (*Auto*) bonnet

**capón** [ka'pon] *nm* (*gallo*) capon

**capota** [ka'pota] *nf* (*de mujer*) bonnet; (*Auto*) hood (BRIT), top (US)

**capote** [ka'pote] *nm* (*abrigo: de militar*) greatcoat; (*de torero*) cloak

**capricho** [ka'pritʃo] *nm* whim, caprice; **caprichoso, -a** *adj* capricious

**Capricornio** [kapri'kornjo] *nm* Capricorn

**cápsula** ['kapsula] *nf* capsule

**captar** [kap'tar] *vt* (*comprender*) to understand; (*Radio*) to pick up; (*atención, apoyo*) to attract

**captura** [kap'tura] *nf* capture; (*Jur*) arrest; **capturar** *vt* to capture; to arrest

**capucha** [ka'putʃa] *nf* hood, cowl

**capuchón** [kapu'tʃon] (ESP) *nm* (*de bolígrafo*) cap

**capullo** [ka'puʎo] *nm* (*Bot*) bud; (*Zool*) cocoon; (*fam*) idiot

**caqui** ['kaki] *nm* khaki

**cara** ['kara] *nf* (*Anat: de moneda*) face; (*de disco*) side; (*descaro*) boldness; **~ a** facing; **de ~** opposite, facing; **dar la ~** to face the consequences; **¿~ o cruz?** heads or tails?; **¡qué ~ (más dura)!** what a nerve!

**Caracas** [ka'rakas] *n* Caracas

**caracol** [kara'kol] *nm* (*Zool*) snail; (*concha*) (sea) shell

**carácter** [ka'rakter] (*pl* **caracteres**) *nm* character; **tener buen/mal ~** to be good natured/bad tempered

**característica** [karakte'ristika] *nf* characteristic

**característico, -a** [karakte'ristiko, a] *adj* characteristic

**caracterizar** [karakteri'θar] *vt* to characterize, typify

**caradura** [kara'ðura] *nmf*: **es un ~** he's got a nerve

**carajillo** [kara'xiʎo] *nm* *coffee with a dash*

*of brandy*

**carajo** [ka'raxo] *(fam!) nm*: **¡~!** shit! (!)

**caramba** [ka'ramba] *excl* good gracious!

**caramelo** [kara'melo] *nm (dulce)* sweet; *(azúcar fundida)* caramel

**caravana** [kara'βana] *nf* caravan; *(fig)* group; *(Auto)* tailback

**carbón** [kar'βon] *nm* coal; **papel ~** carbon paper

**carbono** [kar'βono] *nm* carbon

**carburador** [karβura'ðor] *nm* carburettor

**carburante** [karβu'rante] *nm (para motor)* fuel

**carcajada** [karka'xaða] *nf (loud)* laugh, guffaw

**cárcel** ['karθel] *nf* prison, jail; *(Tec)* clamp

**carcoma** [kar'koma] *nf* woodworm

**cardar** [kar'ðar] *vt (pelo)* to backcomb

**cardenal** [karðe'nal] *nm (Rel)* cardinal; *(Med)* bruise

**cardíaco, -a** [kar'ðiako, a] *adj* cardiac, heart *cpd*

**cardinal** [karði'nal] *adj* cardinal

**cardo** ['karðo] *nm* thistle

**carecer** [kare'θer] *vi*: **~ de** to lack, be in need of

**carencia** [ka'renθja] *nf* lack; *(escasez)* shortage; *(Med)* deficiency

**careta** [ka'reta] *nf* mask

**carga** ['karɣa] *nf (peso, Elec)* load; *(de barco)* cargo, freight; *(Mil)* charge; *(responsabilidad)* duty, obligation

**cargado, -a** [kar'ɣaðo, a] *adj* loaded; *(Elec)* live; *(café, té)* strong; *(cielo)* overcast

**cargamento** [karɣa'mento] *nm (acción)* loading; *(mercancías)* load, cargo

**cargar** [kar'ɣar] *vt (barco, arma)* to load; *(Elec)* to charge; *(Com: algo en cuenta)* to charge; *(Inform)* to load ▷ *vi (Mil)* to charge; *(Auto)* to load (up); **~ con** to pick up, carry away; *(peso: fig)* to shoulder, bear; **cargarse** *vr (fam: estropear)* to break; (: *matar)* to bump off

**cargo** ['karɣo] *nm (puesto)* post, office; *(responsabilidad)* duty, obligation; *(Jur)* charge; **hacerse ~ de** to take charge of *o* responsibility for

**carguero** [kar'ɣero] *nm* freighter, cargo boat; *(avión)* freight plane

**Caribe** [ka'riβe] *nm*: **el ~** the Caribbean; **del ~** Caribbean; **caribeño, -a** [kari'βeɲo, a] *adj* Caribbean

**caricatura** [karika'tura] *nf* caricature

**caricia** [ka'riθja] *nf* caress

**caridad** [kari'ðað] *nf* charity

**caries** ['karjes] *nf inv* tooth decay

**cariño** [ka'riɲo] *nm* affection, love; *(caricia)* caress; *(en carta)* love ...; **tener ~ a** to be fond

of; **cariñoso, -a** *adj* affectionate

**carisma** [ka'risma] *nm* charisma

**caritativo, -a** [karita'tiβo, a] *adj* charitable

**cariz** [ka'riθ] *nm*: **tener** *o* **tomar buen/mal ~** to look good/bad

**carmín** [kar'min] *nm* lipstick

**carnal** [kar'nal] *adj* carnal; **primo ~** first cousin

**carnaval** [karna'βal] *nm* carnival

**carne** ['karne] *nf* flesh; *(Culin)* meat; **se me pone la ~ de gallina sólo verlo** I get the creeps just seeing it; **carne de cerdo/cordero/ternera/vaca** pork/lamb/veal/beef; **carne de gallina** *(fig)* gooseflesh; **carne molida** (LAM) mince (BRIT), ground meat (US); **carne picada** (ESP, RPL) mince (BRIT), ground meat (US)

**carné** [kar'ne] (ESP) *(pl ~s) nm*: **~ de conducir** driving licence (BRIT), driver's license (US); **~ de identidad** identity card; **~ de socio** membership card

**carnero** [kar'nero] *nm* sheep, ram; *(carne)* mutton

**carnet** [kar'ne] (ESP) *(pl ~s) nm* = **carné**

**carnicería** [karniθe'ria] *nf* butcher's (shop); *(fig: matanza)* carnage, slaughter

**carnicero, -a** [karni'θero, a] *adj* carnivorous ▷ *nm/f* butcher; *(carnívoro)* carnivore

**carnívoro, -a** [kar'niβoro, a] *adj* carnivorous

**caro, -a** ['karo, a] *adj* dear; *(Com)* dear, expensive ▷ *adv* dear, dearly

**carpa** ['karpa] *nf (pez)* carp; *(de circo)* big top; *(LAM: tienda de campaña)* tent

**carpeta** [kar'peta] *nf* folder, file; **carpeta de anillas** ring binder

**carpintería** [karpinte'ria] *nf* carpentry, joinery; **carpintero** *nm* carpenter

**carraspear** [karraspe'ar] *vi* to clear one's throat

**carraspera** [karras'pera] *nf* hoarseness

**carrera** [ka'rrera] nf (acción) run(ning); (espacio recorrido) run; (competición) race; (trayecto) course; (profesión) career; (licenciatura) degree; **a la ~** at (full) speed; **carrera de obstáculos** (Deporte) steeplechase

**carrete** [ka'rrete] nm reel, spool; (Tec) coil

**carretera** [karre'tera] nf (main) road, highway; **carretera de circunvalación** ring road; **carretera nacional** ≈ A road (BRIT), ≈ state highway (US)

**carretilla** [karre'tiʎa] nf trolley; (Agr) (wheel)barrow

**carril** [ka'rril] nm furrow; (de autopista) lane; (Ferro) rail; **carril-bici** cycle lane

**carrito** [ka'rrito] nm trolley

**carro** ['karro] nm cart, wagon; (Mil) tank; (LAM: coche) car; **carro patrulla** (LAM) patrol o panda (BRIT) car

**carrocería** [karroθe'ria] nf bodywork, coachwork

**carroña** [ka'rroɲa] nf carrion no pl

**carroza** [ka'rroθa] nf (carruaje) coach

**carrusel** [karru'sel] nm merry-go-round, roundabout

**carta** ['karta] nf letter; (Culin) menu; (naipe) card; (mapa) map; (Jur) document; **carta certificada/urgente** registered/ special-delivery letter

**cartabón** [karta'βon] nm set square

**cartel** [kar'tel] nm (anuncio) poster, placard; (Escol) wall chart; (Com) cartel; **cartelera** nf hoarding, billboard; (en periódico etc) entertainments guide; **"en cartelera"** "showing"

**cartera** [kar'tera] nf (de bolsillo) wallet; (de colegial, cobrador) satchel; (de señora) handbag; (para documentos) briefcase; (Com) portfolio; **ocupa la ~ de Agricultura** she is Minister of Agriculture

**carterista** [karte'rista] nmf pickpocket

**cartero** [kar'tero] nm postman

**cartilla** [kar'tiʎa] nf primer, first reading book; **cartilla de ahorros** savings book

**cartón** [kar'ton] nm cardboard; **cartón piedra** papier-mâché

**cartucho** [kar'tutʃo] nm (Mil) cartridge

**cartulina** [kartu'lina] nf card

**casa** ['kasa] nf house; (hogar) home; (Com) firm, company; **en ~** at home; **casa consistorial** town hall; **casa de campo** country house; **casa de huéspedes** boarding house; **casa de socorro** first aid post; **casa rodante** (cs) caravan (BRIT), trailer (US)

**casado, -a** [ka'saðo, a] adj married ▷ nm/f married man/woman

**casar** [ka'sar] vt to marry; (Jur) to quash, annul; **casarse** vr to marry, get married

**cascabel** [kaska'βel] nm (small) bell

**cascada** [kas'kaða] nf waterfall

**cascanueces** [kaska'nweθes] nm inv nutcrackers pl

**cascar** [kas'kar] vt to crack, split, break (open); **cascarse** vr to crack, split, break (open)

**cáscara** ['kaskara] nf (de huevo, fruta seca) shell; (de fruta) skin; (de limón) peel

**casco** ['kasko] nm (de bombero, soldado) helmet; (Náut: de barco) hull; (Zool: de caballo) hoof; (botella) empty bottle; (de ciudad): **el ~ antiguo** the old part; **el ~ urbano** the town centre; **los ~s azules** the UN peace-keeping force, the blue berets

**cascote** [kas'kote] nm rubble

**caserío** [kase'rio] (ESP) nm farmhouse; (casa) country mansion

**casero, -a** [ka'sero, a] adj (pan etc) home-made ▷ nm/f (propietario) landlord/lady; **ser muy ~** to be home-loving; **"comida casera"** "home cooking"

**caseta** [ka'seta] nf hut; (para bañista) cubicle; (de feria) stall

**casete** [ka'sete] nm o f cassette

**casi** ['kasi] adv almost, nearly; **~ nada** hardly anything; **~ nunca** hardly ever, almost never; **~ te caes** you almost fell

**casilla** [ka'siʎa] nf (casita) hut, cabin; (Ajedrez) square; (para cartas) pigeonhole; **casilla de correo** (cs) P.O. Box; **casillero** nm (para cartas) pigeonholes pl

**casino** [ka'sino] nm club; (de juego) casino

**caso** ['kaso] nm case; **en ~ de** in case of; **en ~ de que ...** in case ...; **el ~ es que ...** the fact is that ...; **en ese/todo ~** in that/any case; **hacer ~ a** to pay attention to; **venir al ~** to be relevant

**caspa** ['kaspa] nf dandruff

**cassette** [ka'sete] nm o f = **casete**

**castaña** [kas'taɲa] nf chestnut

**castaño, -a** [kas'taɲo, a] adj chestnut(-coloured), brown ▷ nm chestnut tree

**castañuelas** [kasta'ɲwelas] nfpl castanets

**castellano, -a** [kaste'ʎano, a] adj, nm/f Castilian ▷ nm (Ling) Castilian, Spanish

**castigar** [kasti'ɣar] vt to punish; (Deporte) to penalize; **castigo** nm punishment; (Deporte) penalty

**Castilla** [kas'tiʎa] nf Castille

**castillo** [kas'tiʎo] nm castle

**castizo, -a** [kas'tiθo, a] adj (Ling) pure

**casto, -a** ['kasto, a] adj chaste, pure

**castor** [kas'tor] nm beaver

**castrar** [kas'trar] vt to castrate

**casual** [ka'swal] *adj* chance, accidental
No confundir **casual** con la palabra inglesa *casual*.

**casualidad** *nf* chance, accident; *(combinación de circunstancias)* coincidence; **da la casualidad de que ...** it (just) so happens that ...; **¡qué casualidad!** what a coincidence!

**cataclismo** [kata'klismo] *nm* cataclysm

**catador, a** [kata'ðor, a] *nm/f* wine taster

**catalán, -ana** [kata'lan, ana] *adj, nm/f* Catalan ⊳ *nm (Ling)* Catalan

**catalizador** [kataliθa'ðor] *nm* catalyst; *(Auto)* catalytic convertor

**catalogar** [katalo'ɣar] *vt* to catalogue; **~ a algn (de)** *(fig)* to categorize sb (as)

**catálogo** [ka'taloɣo] *nm* catalogue

**Cataluña** [kata'luɲa] *nf* Catalonia

**catar** [ka'tar] *vt* to taste, sample

**catarata** [kata'rata] *nf (Geo)* waterfall; *(Med)* cataract

**catarro** [ka'tarro] *nm* catarrh; *(constipado)* cold

**catástrofe** [ka'tastrofe] *nf* catastrophe

**catear** [kate'ar] *(fam) vt (examen, alumno)* to fail

**cátedra** ['kateðra] *nf (Univ)* chair, professorship

**catedral** [kate'ðral] *nf* cathedral

**catedrático, -a** [kate'ðratiko, a] *nm/f* professor

**categoría** [kateɣo'ria] *nf* category; *(rango)* rank, standing; *(calidad)* quality; **de ~** *(hotel)* top-class

**cateto, -a** ['kateto, a] *(ESP: pey) nm/f* peasant

**catolicismo** [katoli'θismo] *nm* Catholicism

**católico, -a** [ka'toliko, a] *adj, nm/f* Catholic

**catorce** [ka'torθe] *num* fourteen

**cauce** ['kauθe] *nm (de río)* riverbed; *(fig)* channel

**caucho** ['kautʃo] *(ESP) nm* rubber

**caudal** [kau'ðal] *nm (de río)* volume, flow; *(fortuna)* wealth; *(abundancia)* abundance

**caudillo** [kau'ðiʎo] *nm* leader, chief

**causa** ['kausa] *nf* cause; *(razón)* reason; *(Jur)* lawsuit, case; **a ~ de** because of; **causar** [kau'sar] *vt* to cause

**cautela** [kau'tela] *nf* caution, cautiousness; **cauteloso, -a** *adj* cautious, wary

**cautivar** [kauti'βar] *vt* to capture; *(atraer)* to captivate

**cautiverio** [kauti'βerjo] *nm* captivity

**cautividad** [kautiβi'ðað] *nf* = **cautiverio**

**cautivo, -a** [kau'tiβo, a] *adj, nm/f* captive

**cauto, -a** ['kauto, a] *adj* cautious, careful

**cava** ['kaβa] *nm* champagne-type wine

**cavar** [ka'βar] *vt* to dig

**caverna** [ka'βerna] *nf* cave, cavern

**cavidad** [kaβi'ðað] *nf* cavity

**cavilar** [kaβi'lar] *vt* to ponder

**cayendo** *etc vb* V **caer**

**caza** ['kaθa] *nf (acción: gen)* hunting; *(: con fusil)* shooting; *(una caza)* hunt, chase; *(de animales)* game ⊳ *nm (Aviac)* fighter; **ir de ~** to go hunting; **caza mayor** game hunting; **cazador, a** [kaθa'ðor, a] *nm/f* hunter; **cazadora** *nf* jacket; **cazar** [ka'θar] *vt* to hunt; *(perseguir)* to chase; *(prender)* to catch

**cazo** ['kaθo] *nm* saucepan

**cazuela** [ka'θwela] *nf (vasija)* pan; *(guisado)* casserole

**CD** *nm abr (= compact disc)* CD

**CD-ROM** [θeðe'rom] *nm abr* CD-ROM

**CE** *nf abr (= Comunidad Europea)* EC

**cebada** [θe'βaða] *nf* barley

**cebar** [θe'βar] *vt (animal)* to fatten (up); *(anzuelo)* to bait; *(Mil, Tec)* to prime

**cebo** ['θeβo] *nm (para animales)* feed, food; *(para peces, fig)* bait; *(de arma)* charge

**cebolla** [θe'βoʎa] *nf* onion; **cebolleta** *nf* spring onion

**cebra** ['θeβra] *nf* zebra

**cecear** [θeθe'ar] *vi* to lisp

**ceder** [θe'ðer] *vt* to hand over, give up, part with ⊳ *vi (renunciar)* to give in, yield; *(disminuir)* to diminish, decline; *(romperse)* to give way

**cedro** ['θeðro] *nm* cedar

**cédula** ['θeðula] *nf* certificate, document; **cédula de identidad** *(LAM)* identity card; **cédula electoral** *(LAM)* ballot

**cegar** [θe'ɣar] *vt* to blind; *(tubería etc)* to block up, stop up ⊳ *vi* to go blind; **cegarse** *vr:* **~se (de)** to be blinded (by)

**ceguera** [θe'ɣera] *nf* blindness

**ceja** ['θexa] *nf* eyebrow

**cejar** [θe'xar] *vi (fig)* to back down

**celador, a** [θela'ðor, a] *nm/f (de edificio)* watchman; *(de museo etc)* attendant

**celda** ['θelda] *nf* cell

**celebración** [θeleβra'θjon] *nf* celebration

**celebrar** [θele'βrar] *vt* to celebrate; *(alabar)* to praise ⊳ *vi* to be glad; **celebrarse** *vr* to occur, take place

**célebre** ['θeleβre] *adj* famous

**celebridad** [θeleβri'ðað] *nf* fame; *(persona)* celebrity

**celeste** [θe'leste] *adj (azul)* sky-blue

**celestial** [θeles'tjal] *adj* celestial, heavenly

**celo¹** ['θelo] *nm* zeal; *(Rel)* fervour; *(Zool):* **en ~** on heat; **celos** *nmpl* jealousy *sg*; **dar ~s a algn** to make sb jealous; **tener ~s** to be jealous

**celo²®** ['θelo] nm Sellotape®

**celofán** [θelo'fan] nm cellophane

**celoso, -a** [θe'loso, a] adj jealous; (trabajador) zealous

**celta** ['θelta] adj Celtic ▷ nmf Celt

**célula** [θe'lula] nf cell

**celulitis** [θelu'litis] nf cellulite

**cementerio** [θemen'terjo] nm cemetery, graveyard

**cemento** [θe'mento] nm cement; (hormigón) concrete; (LAM: cola) glue

**cena** ['θena] nf evening meal, dinner; **cenar** [θe'nar] vt to have for dinner ▷ vi to have dinner

**cenicero** [θeni'θero] nm ashtray

**ceniza** [θe'niθa] nf ash, ashes pl

**censo** ['θenso] nm census; **censo electoral** electoral roll

**censura** [θen'sura] nf (Pol) censorship; **censurar** [θensu'rar] vt (idea) to censure; (cortar: película) to censor

**centella** [θen'teʎa] nf spark

**centenar** [θente'nar] nm hundred

**centenario, -a** [θente'narjo, a] adj centenary; hundred-year-old ▷ nm centenary

**centeno** [θen'teno] nm (Bot) rye

**centésimo, -a** [θen'tesimo, a] adj hundredth

**centígrado** [θen'tixraðo] adj centigrade

**centímetro** [θen'timetro] nm centimetre (BRIT), centimeter (US)

**céntimo** ['θentimo] nm cent

**centinela** [θenti'nela] nm sentry, guard

**centollo** [θen'toʎo] nm spider crab

**central** [θen'tral] adj central ▷ nf head office; (Tec) plant; (Tel) exchange; **central eléctrica** power station; **central nuclear** nuclear power station; **central telefónica** telephone exchange

**centralita** [θentra'lita] nf switchboard

**centralizar** [θentrali'θar] vt to centralize

**centrar** [θen'trar] vt to centre

**céntrico, -a** ['θentriko, a] adj central

**centrifugar** [θentrifu'ɣar] vt to spin-dry

**centro** ['θentro] nm centre; **centro comercial** shopping centre; **centro de atención al cliente** call centre; **centro de salud** health centre; **centro escolar** school; **centro juvenil** youth club; **centro turístico** (lugar muy visitado) tourist centre; **centro urbano** urban area, city

**centroamericano, -a** [θentroameri'kano, a] adj, nm/f Central American

**ceñido, -a** [θe'niðo, a] adj (chaqueta, pantalón) tight(-fitting)

**ceñir** [θe'nir] vt (rodear) to encircle, surround; (ajustar) to fit (tightly)

**ceño** ['θeno] nm frown, scowl; **fruncir el ~** to frown, knit one's brow

**cepillar** [θepi'ʎar] vt to brush; (madera) to plane (down)

**cepillo** [θe'piʎo] nm brush; (para madera) plane; **cepillo de dientes** toothbrush

**cera** ['θera] nf wax

**cerámica** [θe'ramika] nf pottery; (arte) ceramics

**cerca** ['θerka] nf fence ▷ adv near, nearby, close; **~ de** near, close to

**cercanías** [θerka'nias] nfpl (afueras) outskirts, suburbs

**cercano, -a** [θer'kano, a] adj close, near

**cercar** [θer'kar] vt to fence in; (rodear) to surround

**cerco** ['θerko] nm (Agr) enclosure; (LAM: valla) fence; (Mil) siege

**cerdo, -a** ['θerðo, a] nm/f pig/sow

**cereal** [θere'al] nm cereal; **cereales** nmpl cereals, grain sg

**cerebro** [θe'reβro] nm brain; (fig) brains pl

**ceremonia** [θere'monja] nf ceremony; **ceremonioso, -a** adj ceremonious

**cereza** [θe'reθa] nf cherry

**cerilla** [θe'riʎa] nf (fósforo) match

**cerillo** [θe'riʎo] nm (MÉX) match

**cero** ['θero] nm nothing, zero

**cerquillo** [θer'kiʎo] nm (CAM, RPL) fringe (BRIT), bangs pl (US)

**cerrado, -a** [θe'rraðo, a] adj closed, shut; (con llave) locked; (tiempo) cloudy, overcast; (curva) sharp; (acento) thick, broad

**cerradura** [θerra'ðura] nf (acción) closing; (mecanismo) lock

**cerrajero** [θerra'xero] nm locksmith

**cerrar** [θe'rrar] vt to close, shut; (paso, carretera) to close; (grifo) to turn off; (cuenta, negocio) to close ▷ vi to close, shut; (noche) to come down; **cerrarse** vr to close, shut; **~ con llave** to lock; **~ un trato** to strike a bargain

**cerro** ['θerro] nm hill

**cerrojo** [θe'rroxo] nm (herramienta) bolt; (de puerta) latch

**certamen** [θer'tamen] nm competition, contest

**certero, -a** [θer'tero, a] adj (gen) accurate

**certeza** [θer'teθa] nf certainty

**certidumbre** [θerti'ðumbre] nf = **certeza**

**certificado, -a** [θertifi'kaðo, a] adj (carta, paquete) registered; (aprobado) certified ▷ nm certificate; **certificado médico** medical certificate

**certificar** [θertifi'kar] vt (asegurar, atestar) to certify

**cervatillo** [θerβa'tiʎo] nm fawn
**cervecería** [θerβeθe'ria] nf (fábrica) brewery; (bar) public house, pub
**cerveza** [θer'βeθa] nf beer
**cesar** [θe'sar] vi to cease, stop ▷ vt (funcionario) to remove from office
**cesárea** [θe'sarea] nf (Med) Caesarean operation o section
**cese** ['θese] nm (de trabajo) dismissal; (de pago) suspension
**césped** ['θespeð] nm grass, lawn
**cesta** ['θesta] nf basket
**cesto** ['θesto] nm (large) basket, hamper
**cfr** abr (= confróntese) cf.
**chabacano, -a** [tʃaβa'kano, a] adj vulgar, coarse
**chabola** [tʃa'βola] (ESP) nf shack; **barrio de chabolas** shanty town
**chacal** [tʃa'kal] nm jackal
**chacha** ['tʃatʃa] (fam) nf maid
**cháchara** ['tʃatʃara] nf chatter; **estar de ~** to chatter away
**chacra** ['tʃakra] (CS) nf smallholding
**chafa** ['tʃafa] (MÉX: fam) adj useless, dud
**chafar** [tʃa'far] vt (aplastar) to crush; (plan etc) to ruin
**chal** [tʃal] nm shawl
**chalado, -a** [tʃa'lado, a] (fam) adj crazy
**chalé** [tʃa'le] (pl ~s) nm villa, ≈ detached house
**chaleco** [tʃa'leko] nm waistcoat, vest (US); **chaleco de seguridad** (Aut) reflective safety vest; **chaleco salvavidas** life jacket
**chalet** [tʃa'le] (pl ~s) nm = **chalé**
**chamaco, -a** (MÉX) [tʃa'mako, a] nm/f (niño) kid
**chambear** [tʃambe'ar] (MÉX: fam) vi to earn one's living
**champán** [tʃam'pan] nm champagne
**champiñón** [tʃampi'non] nm mushroom
**champú** [tʃam'pu] (pl ~es, ~s) nm shampoo
**chamuscar** [tʃamus'kar] vt to scorch, sear, singe
**chance** ['tʃanθe] (LAM) nm chance
**chancho, -a** ['tʃantʃo, a] (LAM) nm/f pig
**chanchullo** [tʃan'tʃuʎo] (fam) nm fiddle
**chandal** [tʃan'dal] nm tracksuit
**chantaje** [tʃan'taxe] nm blackmail
**chapa** ['tʃapa] nf (de metal) plate, sheet; (de madera) board, panel; (RPL Auto) number (BRIT) o license (US) plate; **chapado, -a** adj: **chapado en oro** gold-plated
**chaparrón** [tʃapa'rron] nm downpour, cloudburst
**chaperón** [tʃape'ron] (MÉX) nm: **hacer de ~** to play gooseberry; **chaperona** (LAM) nf: **hacer de chaperona** to play gooseberry

**chapopote** [tʃapo'pote] (MÉX) nm tar
**chapulín** [tʃapu'lin] (MÉX, CAM) nm grasshopper
**chapurrear** [tʃapurre'ar] vt (idioma) to speak badly
**chapuza** [tʃa'puθa] nf botched job
**chapuzón** [tʃapu'θon] nm: **darse un ~** to go for a dip
**chaqueta** [tʃa'keta] nf jacket
**chaquetón** [tʃake'ton] nm long jacket
**charca** ['tʃarka] nf pond, pool
**charco** ['tʃarko] nm pool, puddle
**charcutería** [tʃarkute'ria] nf (tienda) shop selling chiefly pork meat products; (productos) cooked pork meats pl
**charla** ['tʃarla] nf talk, chat; (conferencia) lecture; **charlar** [tʃar'lar] vi to talk, chat; **charlatán, -ana** [tʃarla'tan, ana] nm/f (hablador) chatterbox; (estafador) trickster
**charol** [tʃa'rol] nm varnish; (cuero) patent leather
**charola** [tʃa'rola] (MÉX) nf tray
**charro, -a** ['tʃarro, a] (MÉX) nm typical Mexican
**chasco** ['tʃasko] nm (desengaño) disappointment
**chasis** ['tʃasis] nm inv chassis
**chasquido** [tʃas'kiðo] nm crack; click
**chat** [tʃat] nm (Internet) chat room
**chatarra** [tʃa'tarra] nf scrap (metal)
**chatear** [tʃate'ar] vi (Internet) to chat
**chato, -a** ['tʃato, a] adj flat; (nariz) snub
**chaucha** ['tʃautʃa] (RPL) nf runner (BRIT) o pole (US) bean
**chaval, a** [tʃa'βal, a] (ESP) nm/f kid, lad/lass
**chavo, -a** ['tʃaβo] (MÉX: fam) nm/f guy/girl
**checar** [tʃe'kar] (MÉX) vt: **~ tarjeta** (al entrar) to clock in o on; (: al salir) to clock off o out
**checo, -a** ['tʃeko, a] adj, nm/f Czech ▷ nm (Ling) Czech
**checoslovaco, -a** [tʃekoslo'βako, a] adj, nm/f Czech, Czechoslovak
**Checoslovaquia** [tʃekoslo'βakja] nf (Hist) Czechoslovakia
**cheque** ['tʃeke] nm cheque (BRIT), check (US); **cobrar un ~** to cash a cheque; **cheque al portador** cheque payable to bearer; **cheque de viaje** traveller's cheque (BRIT), traveler's check (US); **cheque en blanco** blank cheque
**chequeo** [tʃe'keo] nm (Med) check-up; (Auto) service
**chequera** [tʃe'kera] (LAM) nf chequebook (BRIT), checkbook (US)
**chévere** ['tʃeβere] (LAM: fam) adj great
**chícharo** ['tʃitʃaro] (MÉX, CAM) nm pea

**chichón** [tʃi'tʃon] nm bump, lump

**chicle** ['tʃikle] nm chewing gum

**chico, -a** ['tʃiko, a] adj small, little ▷ nm/f (niño) child; (muchacho) boy/girl

**chiflado, -a** [tʃi'flaðo, a] adj crazy

**chiflar** [tʃi'flar] vt to hiss, boo

**chilango, -a** [tʃi'laŋgo, a] (MÉX) adj of o from Mexico City

**Chile** ['tʃile] nm Chile; **chileno, -a** adj, nm/f Chilean

**chile** ['tʃile] nm chilli pepper

**chillar** [tʃi'ʎar] vi (persona) to yell, scream; (animal salvaje) to howl; (cerdo) to squeal

**chillido** [tʃi'ʎiðo] nm (de persona) yell, scream; (de animal) howl

**chimenea** [tʃime'nea] nf chimney; (hogar) fireplace

**China** ['tʃina] nf (tb: **la ~**) China

**chinche** ['tʃintʃe] nf (insecto) (bed)bug; (Tec) drawing pin (BRIT), thumbtack (US) ▷ nmf nuisance, pest

**chincheta** [tʃin'tʃeta] nf drawing pin (BRIT), thumbtack (US)

**chingada** [tʃin'gaða] (MÉX: fam!) nf: **hijo de la ~** bastard

**chino, -a** ['tʃino, a] adj, nm/f Chinese ▷ nm (Ling) Chinese

**chipirón** [tʃipi'ron] nm (Zool, Culin) squid

**Chipre** ['tʃipre] nf Cyprus; **chipriota** adj, nmf Cypriot

**chiquillo, -a** [tʃi'kiʎo, a] nm/f (fam) kid

**chirimoya** [tʃiri'moja] nf custard apple

**chiringuito** [tʃirin'xito] nm small open-air bar

**chiripa** [tʃi'ripa] nf fluke

**chirriar** [tʃi'rrjar] vi to creak, squeak

**chirrido** [tʃi'rriðo] nm creak(ing), squeak(ing)

**chisme** ['tʃisme] nm (habladurías) piece of gossip; (fam: objeto) thingummyjig

**chismoso, -a** [tʃis'moso, a] adj gossiping ▷ nm/f gossip

**chispa** ['tʃispa] nf spark; (fig) sparkle; (ingenio) wit; (fam) drunkenness

**chispear** [tʃispe'ar] vi (lloviznar) to drizzle

**chiste** ['tʃiste] nm joke, funny story

**chistoso, -a** [tʃis'toso, a] adj funny, amusing

**chivo, -a** ['tʃiβo, a] nm/f (billy-/nanny-)goat; **chivo expiatorio** scapegoat

**chocante** [tʃo'kante] adj startling; (extraño) odd; (ofensivo) shocking

**chocar** [tʃo'kar] vi (coches etc) to collide, crash ▷ vt to shock; (sorprender) to startle; **~ con** to collide with; (fig) to run into, run up against; **¡chócala!** (fam) put it there!

**chochear** [tʃotʃe'ar] vi to be senile

**chocho, -a** ['tʃotʃo, a] adj doddering,

senile; (fig) soft, doting

**choclo** ['tʃoklo] (CS) nm (grano) sweet corn; (mazorca) corn on the cob

**chocolate** [tʃoko'late] adj, nm chocolate; **chocolatina** nf chocolate

**chofer** [tʃo'fer] nm = **chófer**

**chófer** ['tʃofer] nm driver

**chollo** ['tʃoʎo] (ESP: fam) nm bargain, snip

**choque** etc ['tʃoke] vb V **chocar** ▷ nm (impacto) impact; (golpe) jolt; (Auto) crash; (fig) conflict; **choque frontal** head-on collision

**chorizo** [tʃo'riθo] nm hard pork sausage, (type of) salami

**chorrada** [tʃo'rraða] (ESP: fam) nf: **¡es una ~!** that's crap! (!); **decir ~s** to talk crap (!)

**chorrear** [tʃorre'ar] vi to gush (out), spout (out); (gotear) to drip, trickle

**chorro** ['tʃorro] nm jet; (fig) stream

**choza** ['tʃoθa] nf hut, shack

**chubasco** [tʃu'βasko] nm squall

**chubasquero** [tʃuβas'kero] nm lightweight raincoat

**chuchería** [tʃutʃe'ria] nf trinket

**chuleta** [tʃu'leta] nf chop, cutlet

**chulo** ['tʃulo] nm (de prostituta) pimp

**chupaleta** [tʃupa'leta] (MÉX) nf lollipop

**chupar** [tʃu'par] vt to suck; (absorber) to absorb; **chuparse** vr to grow thin

**chupete** [tʃu'pete] (ESP, CS) nm dummy (BRIT), pacifier (US)

**chupetín** [tʃupe'tin] (RPL) nf lollipop

**chupito** [tʃu'pito] (fam) nm shot

**chupón** [tʃu'pon] nm (piruleta) lollipop; (LAM: chupete) dummy (BRIT), pacifier (US)

**churro** ['tʃurro] nm (type of) fritter

**chusma** ['tʃusma] nf rabble, mob

**chutar** [tʃu'tar] vi to shoot (at goal)

**Cía** abr (= compañía) Co.

**cianuro** [θja'nuro] nm cyanide

**cibercafé** [θiβerka'fe] nm cybercafé

**cibernauta** [θiβer'nauta] nmf web surfer, Internet user

**ciberterrorista** [θiβerterro'rista] nmf cyberterrorist

**cicatriz** [θika'triθ] nf scar; **cicatrizarse** vr to heal (up), form a scar

**ciclismo** [θi'klismo] nm cycling

**ciclista** [θi'klista] adj cycle cpd ▷ nmf cyclist

**ciclo** ['θiklo] nm cycle; **cicloturismo** nm touring by bicycle

**ciclón** [θi'klon] nm cyclone

**ciego, -a** ['θjexo, a] adj blind ▷ nm/f blind man/woman

**cielo** ['θjelo] nm sky; (Rel) heaven; **¡~s!** good heavens!

**ciempiés** [θjem'pjes] nm inv centipede

**cien** [θjen] *num* V **ciento**

**ciencia** ['θjenθja] *nf* science; **ciencias** *nfpl* (*Escol*) science *sg*; **ciencia-ficción** *nf* science fiction

**científico, -a** [θjen'tifiko, a] *adj* scientific ▷ *nm/f* scientist

**ciento** ['θjento] *num* hundred; **pagar al 10 por ~** to pay at 10 per cent; V *tb* **cien**

**cierre** *etc* [θjerre] *vb* V **cerrar** ▷ *nm* closing, shutting; (*con llave*) locking; (*LAM: cremallera*) zip (fastener)

**cierro** *etc vb* V **cerrar**

**cierto, -a** ['θjerto, a] *adj* sure, certain; (*un tal*) a certain; (*correcto*) right, correct; **por ~** by the way; **~ hombre** a certain man; **ciertas personas** certain *o* some people; **sí, es ~** yes, that's correct

**ciervo** ['θjerβo] *nm* deer; (*macho*) stag

**cifra** ['θifra] *nf* number; (*secreta*) code; **cifrar** [θi'frar] *vt* to code, write in code

**cigala** [θi'xala] *nf* Norway lobster

**cigarra** [θi'xarra] *nf* cicada

**cigarrillo** [θixa'rriλo] *nm* cigarette

**cigarro** [θi'xarro] *nm* cigarette; (*puro*) cigar

**cigüeña** [θi'xweɲa] *nf* stork

**cilíndrico, -a** [θi'lindriko, a] *adj* cylindrical

**cilindro** [θi'lindro] *nm* cylinder

**cima** ['θima] *nf* (*de montaña*) top, peak; (*de árbol*) top; (*fig*) height

**cimentar** [θimen'tar] *vt* to lay the foundations of; (*fig: fundar*) to found

**cimiento** [θi'mjento] *nm* foundation

**cincel** [θin'θel] *nm* chisel

**cinco** ['θinko] *num* five

**cincuenta** [θin'kwenta] *num* fifty

**cine** ['θine] *nm* cinema; **cinematográfico, -a** [θinemato'ɣrafiko, a] *adj* cine-, film *cpd*

**cínico, -a** ['θiniko, a] *adj* cynical ▷ *nm/f* cynic

**cinismo** [θi'nismo] *nm* cynicism

**cinta** ['θinta] *nf* band, strip; (*de tela*) ribbon; (*película*) reel; (*de máquina de escribir*) ribbon; **cinta adhesiva/aislante** sticky/insulating tape; **cinta de vídeo** videotape; **cinta magnetofónica** tape; **cinta métrica** tape measure

**cintura** [θin'tura] *nf* waist

**cinturón** [θintu'ron] *nm* belt; **cinturón de seguridad** safety belt

**ciprés** [θi'pres] *nm* cypress (tree)

**circo** ['θirko] *nm* circus

**circuito** [θir'kwito] *nm* circuit

**circulación** [θirkula'θjon] *nf* circulation; (*Auto*) traffic

**circular** [θirku'lar] *adj, nf* circular ▷ *vi, vt* to circulate ▷ *vi* (*Auto*) to drive; **"circule por la derecha"** "keep (to the) right"

**círculo** ['θirkulo] *nm* circle; **círculo vicioso** vicious circle

**circunferencia** [θirkunfe'renθja] *nf* circumference

**circunstancia** [θirkuns'tanθja] *nf* circumstance

**cirio** ['θirjo] *nm* (wax) candle

**ciruela** [θi'rwela] *nf* plum; **ciruela pasa** prune

**cirugía** [θiru'xia] *nf* surgery; **cirugía estética** *o* **plástica** plastic surgery

**cirujano** [θiru'xano] *nm* surgeon

**cisne** ['θisne] *nm* swan

**cisterna** [θis'terna] *nf* cistern, tank

**cita** ['θita] *nf* appointment, meeting; (*de novios*) date; (*referencia*) quotation

**citación** [θita'θjon] *nf* (*Jur*) summons *sg*

**citar** [θi'tar] *vt* (*gen*) to make an appointment with; (*Jur*) to summons; (*un autor, texto*) to quote; **citarse** *vr*: **se ~on en el cine** they arranged to meet at the cinema

**cítricos** ['θitrikos] *nmpl* citrus fruit(s)

**ciudad** [θju'ðað] *nf* town; (*más grande*) city; **ciudadano, -a** *nm/f* citizen

**cívico, -a** ['θiβiko, a] *adj* civic

**civil** [θi'βil] *adj* civil ▷ *nm* (*guardia*) policeman; **civilización** [θiβiliθa'θjon] *nf* civilization; **civilizar** [θiβili'θar] *vt* to civilize

**cizaña** [θi'θaɲa] *nf* (*fig*) discord

**cl.** *abr* (= *centilitro*) cl.

**clamor** [kla'mor] *nm* clamour, protest

**clandestino, -a** [klandes'tino, a] *adj* clandestine; (*Pol*) underground

**clara** ['klara] *nf* (*de huevo*) egg white

**claraboya** [klara'βoja] *nf* skylight

**clarear** [klare'ar] *vi* (*el día*) to dawn; (*el cielo*) to clear up, brighten up; **clarearse** *vr* to be transparent

**claridad** [klari'ðað] *nf* (*de día*) brightness; (*de estilo*) clarity

**clarificar** [klarifi'kar] *vt* to clarify

**clarinete** [klari'nete] *nm* clarinet

**claro, -a** ['klaro, a] *adj* clear; (*luminoso*) bright; (*color*) light; (*evidente*) clear, evident; (*poco espeso*) thin ▷ *nm* (*en bosque*) clearing ▷ *adv* clearly ▷ *excl*: **¡~ que sí!** of course!; **¡~ que no!** of course not!

**clase** ['klase] *nf* class; **dar ~(s)** to teach; **clase alta/media/obrera** upper/middle/working class; **clases particulares** private lessons *o* tuition *sg*

**clásico, -a** ['klasiko, a] *adj* classical

**clasificación** [klasifika'θjon] *nf* classification; (*Deporte*) league (table)

**clasificar** [klasifi'kar] *vt* to classify

**claustro** ['klaustro] *nm* cloister

**cláusula** ['klausula] nf clause
**clausura** [klau'sura] nf closing, closure
**clavar** [kla'βar] vt (clavo) to hammer in; (cuchillo) to stick, thrust
**clave** ['klaβe] nf key; (Mús) clef; **clave de acceso** password; **clave lada** (MÉX) dialling (BRIT) o area (US) code
**clavel** [kla'βel] nm carnation
**clavícula** [kla'βikula] nf collar bone
**clavija** [kla'βixa] nf peg, dowel, pin; (Elec) plug
**clavo** ['klaβo] nm (de metal) nail; (Bot) clove
**claxon** ['klakson] (pl **-s**) nm horn
**clérigo** ['klerixo] nm priest
**clero** ['klero] nm clergy
**clicar** [kli'kar] vi (Internet) to click; **~ en el icono** to click on an icon; **~ dos veces** to double-click
**cliché** [kli'tʃe] nm cliché; (Foto) negative
**cliente, -a** ['kljente, a] nm/f client, customer; **clientela** [kljen'tela] nf clientele, customers pl
**clima** ['klima] nm climate; **climatizado, -a** [klimati'θaðo, a] adj air-conditioned
**clímax** ['klimaks] nm inv climax
**clínica** ['klinika] nf clinic; (particular) private hospital
**clip** [klip] (pl **-s**) nm paper clip
**clítoris** ['klitoris] nm inv (Anat) clitoris
**cloaca** [klo'aka] nf sewer
**clonar** [klo'nar] vt to clone
**cloro** ['kloro] nm chlorine
**clóset** ['kloset] (MÉX) nm cupboard
**club** [klub] (pl **-s** o **-es**) nm club; **club nocturno** night club
**cm** abr (= centímetro, centímetros) cm
**coágulo** [ko'aɣulo] nm clot
**coalición** [koali'θjon] nf coalition
**coartada** [koar'taða] nf alibi
**coartar** [koar'tar] vt to limit, restrict
**coba** ['koβa] nf: **dar ~ a algn** (adular) to suck up to sb
**cobarde** [ko'βarðe] adj cowardly ▷ nm coward; **cobardía** nf cowardice
**cobaya** [ko'βaja] nf guinea pig
**cobertizo** [koβer'tiθo] nm shelter
**cobertura** [koβer'tura] nf cover; **aquí no hay ~** (Tel) I can't get a signal
**cobija** [ko'βixa] (LAM) nf blanket; **cobijar** [koβi'xar] vt (cubrir) to cover; (proteger) to shelter; **cobijo** nm shelter
**cobra** ['koβra] nf cobra
**cobrador, a** [koβra'ðor, a] nm/f (de autobús) conductor/conductress; (de impuestos, gas) collector
**cobrar** [ko'βrar] vt (cheque) to cash; (sueldo) to collect, draw; (objeto) to recover; (precio) to charge; (deuda) to collect ▷ vi to be paid;

**cóbrese al entregar** cash on delivery; **¿me cobra, por favor?** how much do I owe you?, can I have the bill, please?
**cobre** ['koβre] nm copper; **cobres** nmpl (Mús) brass instruments
**cobro** ['koβro] nm (de cheque) cashing; **presentar al ~** to cash
**cocaína** [koka'ina] nf cocaine
**cocción** [kok'θjon] nf (Culin) cooking; (en agua) boiling
**cocer** [ko'θer] vt, vi to cook; (en agua) to boil; (en horno) to bake
**coche** ['kotʃe] nm (Auto) car (BRIT), automobile (US); (de tren, de caballos) coach, carriage; (para niños) pram (BRIT), baby carriage (US); **ir en ~** to drive; **coche celular** police van; **coche de bomberos** fire engine; **coche de carreras** racing car; **coche fúnebre** hearse; **coche-cama** (pl **coches-cama**) nm (Ferro) sleeping car, sleeper
**cochera** [ko'tʃera] nf garage; (de autobuses, trenes) depot
**coche restaurante** (pl **coches restaurante**) nm (Ferro) dining car, diner
**cochinillo** [kotʃi'niʎo] nm (Culin) suckling pig, sucking pig
**cochino, -a** [ko'tʃino, a] adj filthy, dirty ▷ nm/f pig
**cocido** [ko'θiðo] nm stew
**cocina** [ko'θina] nf kitchen; (aparato) cooker, stove; (acto) cookery; **cocina eléctrica/de gas** electric/gas cooker; **cocina francesa** French cuisine; **cocinar** vt, vi to cook
**cocinero, -a** [koθi'nero, a] nm/f cook
**coco** ['koko] nm coconut
**cocodrilo** [koko'ðrilo] nm crocodile
**cocotero** [koko'tero] nm coconut palm
**cóctel** ['koktel] nm cocktail; **cóctel molotov** petrol bomb, Molotov cocktail
**codazo** [ko'ðaθo] nm: **dar un ~ a algn** to nudge sb
**codicia** [ko'ðiθja] nf greed; **codiciar** vt to covet
**código** ['koðixo] nm code; **código civil** common law; **código de barras** bar code; **código de circulación** highway code; **código de la zona** (LAM) dialling (BRIT) o area (US) code; **código postal** postcode
**codillo** [ko'ðiʎo] nm (Zool) knee; (Tec) elbow (joint)
**codo** ['koðo] nm (Anat, de tubo) elbow; (Zool) knee
**codorniz** [koðor'niθ] nf quail
**coexistir** [koe(k)sis'tir] vi to coexist
**cofradía** [kofra'ðia] nf brotherhood, fraternity
**cofre** ['kofre] nm (de joyas) case; (de dinero)

chest

**coger** [ko'xer] (*ESP*) *vt* to take (hold of); (*objeto caído*) to pick up; (*frutas*) to pick, harvest; (*resfriado, ladrón, pelota*) to catch ▷ *vi*: ~ **por el buen camino** to take the right road; **cogerse** *vr* (*el dedo*) to catch; **~se a algo** to get hold of sth

**cogollo** [ko'xoʎo] *nm* (*de lechuga*) heart

**cogote** [ko'xote] *nm* back o nape of the neck

**cohabitar** [koaβi'tar] *vi* to live together, cohabit

**coherente** [koe'rente] *adj* coherent

**cohesión** [koe'sjon] *nm* cohesion

**cohete** [ko'ete] *nm* rocket

**cohibido, -a** [koi'βiðo, a] *adj* (*Psico*) inhibited; (*tímido*) shy

**coincidencia** [koinθi'ðenθja] *nf* coincidence

**coincidir** [koinθi'ðir] *vi* (*en idea*) to coincide, agree; (*en lugar*) to coincide

**coito** ['koito] *nm* intercourse, coitus

**coja** *etc* *vb* V **coger**

**cojear** [koxe'ar] *vi* (*persona*) to limp, hobble; (*mueble*) to wobble, rock

**cojera** [ko'xera] *nf* limp

**cojín** [ko'xin] *nm* cushion

**cojo, -a** *etc* ['koxo, a] *vb* V **coger** ▷ *adj* (*que no puede andar*) lame, crippled; (*mueble*) wobbly ▷ *nm/f* lame person, cripple

**cojón** [ko'xon] (*fam!*) *nm*: **¡cojones!** shit! (*!*); **cojonudo, -a** (*fam*) *adj* great, fantastic

**col** [kol] *nf* cabbage; **coles de Bruselas** Brussels sprouts

**cola** ['kola] *nf* tail; (*de gente*) queue; (*lugar*) end, last place; (*para pegar*) glue, gum; **hacer ~** to queue (up)

**colaborador, a** [kolaβora'ðor, a] *nm/f* collaborator

**colaborar** [kolaβo'rar] *vi* to collaborate

**colada** [ko'laða] (*ESP*) *nf*: **hacer la ~** to do the washing

**colador** [kola'ðor] *nm* (*para líquidos*) strainer; (*para verduras etc*) colander

**colapso** [ko'lapso] *nm* collapse

**colar** [ko'lar] *vt* (*líquido*) to strain off; (*metal*) to cast ▷ *vi* to ooze, seep (through); **colarse** *vr* to jump the queue; **~se en** to get into without paying; (*fiesta*) to gatecrash

**colcha** ['koltʃa] *nf* bedspread

**colchón** [kol'tʃon] *nm* mattress; **colchón inflable** air bed o mattress

**colchoneta** [koltʃo'neta] *nf* (*en gimnasio*) mat; (*de playa*) air bed

**colección** [kolek'θjon] *nf* collection; **coleccionar** *vt* to collect; **coleccionista** *nmf* collector

**colecta** [ko'lekta] *nf* collection

**colectivo, -a** [kolek'tiβo, a] *adj* collective, joint ▷ *nm* (*ARG: autobús*) (small) bus

**colega** [ko'lexa] *nmf* colleague; (*ESP: amigo*) mate

**colegial, a** [kole'xjal, a] *nm/f* schoolboy(-girl)

**colegio** [ko'lexjo] *nm* college; (*escuela*) school; (*de abogados etc*) association; **colegio electoral** polling station; **colegio mayor** (*ESP*) hall of residence

● **COLEGIO**
●
● A **colegio** is normally a private primary
● or secondary school. In the state system
● it means a primary school although
● these are also called **escuelas**. State
● secondary schools are called **institutos**.

**cólera** ['kolera] *nf* (*ira*) anger; (*Med*) cholera

**colesterol** [koleste'rol] *nm* cholesterol

**coleta** [ko'leta] *nf* pigtail

**colgante** [kol'xante] *adj* hanging ▷ *nm* (*joya*) pendant

**colgar** [kol'xar] *vt* to hang (up); (*ropa*) to hang out ▷ *vi* to hang; (*Tel*) to hang up

**cólico** ['koliko] *nm* colic

**coliflor** [koli'flor] *nf* cauliflower

**colilla** [ko'liʎa] *nf* cigarette end, butt

**colina** [ko'lina] *nf* hill

**colisión** [koli'sjon] *nf* collision; **colisión frontal** head-on crash

**collar** [ko'ʎar] *nm* necklace; (*de perro*) collar

**colmar** [kol'mar] *vt* to fill to the brim; (*fig*) to fulfil, realize

**colmena** [kol'mena] *nf* beehive

**colmillo** [kol'miʎo] *nm* (*diente*) eye tooth; (*de elefante*) tusk; (*de perro*) fang

**colmo** ['kolmo] *nm*: **¡es el ~!** it's the limit!

**colocación** [koloka'θjon] *nf* (*acto*) placing; (*empleo*) job, position

**colocar** [kolo'kar] *vt* to place, put, position; (*dinero*) to invest; (*poner en empleo*) to find a job for; **colocarse** *vr* to get a job

**Colombia** [ko'lombja] *nf* Colombia; **colombiano, -a** *adj, nm/f* Colombian

**colonia** [ko'lonja] *nf* colony; (*agua de colonia*) cologne; (*MÉX: de casas*) residential area; **colonia proletaria** (*MÉX*) shantytown

**colonización** [koloniθa'θjon] *nf* colonization; **colonizador, a** [koloniθa'ðor, a] *adj* colonizing ▷ *nm/f* colonist, settler

**colonizar** [koloni'θar] *vt* to colonize

**coloquio** [ko'lokjo] *nm* conversation; (*congreso*) conference

**color** [ko'lor] nm colour
**colorado, -a** [kolo'raðo, a] adj (rojo) red; (MÉX: chiste) smutty, rude
**colorante** [kolo'rante] nm colouring
**colorear** [kolore'ar] vt to colour
**colorete** [kolo'rete] nm blusher
**colorido** [kolo'riðo] nm colouring
**columna** [ko'lumna] nf column; (pilar) pillar; (apoyo) support; (tb: **~ vertebral**) spine, spinal column; (fig) backbone
**columpiar** [kolum'pjar] vt to swing; **columpiarse** vr to swing; **columpio** nm swing
**coma** ['koma] nf comma ▷ nm (Med) coma
**comadre** [ko'maðre] nf (madrina) godmother; (chismosa) gossip; **comadrona** nf midwife
**comal** [ko'mal] (MÉX, CAM) nm griddle
**comandante** [koman'dante] nm commandant
**comarca** [ko'marka] nf region
**comba** ['komba] (ESP) nf (cuerda) skipping rope; **saltar a la ~** to skip
**combate** [kom'bate] nm fight
**combatir** [komba'tir] vt to fight, combat
**combinación** [kombina'θjon] nf combination; (Quím) compound; (prenda) slip
**combinar** [kombi'nar] vt to combine
**combustible** [kombus'tiβle] nm fuel
**comedia** [ko'meðja] nf comedy; (Teatro) play, drama; **comediante** [kome'ðjante] nmf (comic) actor/actress
**comedido, -a** [kome'ðiðo, a] adj moderate
**comedor, a** [kome'ðor, a] nm (habitación) dining room; (cantina) canteen
**comensal** [komen'sal] nmf fellow guest (o diner)
**comentar** [komen'tar] vt to comment on; **comentario** [komen'tarjo] nm comment, remark; (literario) commentary; **comentarios** nmpl (chismes) gossip sg; **comentarista** [komenta'rista] nmf commentator
**comenzar** [komen'θar] vt, vi to begin, start; **~ a hacer algo** to begin o start doing sth
**comer** [ko'mer] vt to eat; (Damas, Ajedrez) to take, capture ▷ vi to eat; (ESP, MÉX: almorzar) to have lunch; **comerse** vr to eat up
**comercial** [komer'θjal] adj commercial; (relativo al negocio) business cpd; **comercializar** vt (producto) to market; (pey) to commercialize
**comerciante** [komer'θjante] nmf trader,

merchant
**comerciar** [komer'θjar] vi to trade, do business
**comercio** [ko'merθjo] nm commerce, trade; (tienda) shop, store; (negocio) business; (fig) dealings pl; **comercio electrónico** e-commerce; **comercio exterior/interior** foreign/domestic trade
**comestible** [komes'tiβle] adj eatable, edible; **comestibles** nmpl food sg, foodstuffs
**cometa** [ko'meta] nm comet ▷ nf kite
**cometer** [kome'ter] vt to commit
**cometido** [kome'tiðo] nm task, assignment
**cómic** ['komik] nm comic
**comicios** [ko'miθjos] nmpl elections
**cómico, -a** ['komiko, a] adj comic(al) ▷ nm/f comedian
**comida** [ko'miða] nf (alimento) food; (almuerzo, cena) meal; (de mediodía) lunch; **comida basura** junk food; **comida chatarra** (MÉX) junk food
**comidilla** [komi'ðiʎa] nf: **ser la ~ del barrio** o **pueblo** to be the talk of the town
**comienzo** etc [ko'mjenθo] vb V **comenzar** ▷ nm beginning, start
**comillas** [ko'miʎas] nfpl quotation marks
**comilona** [komi'lona] (fam) nf blow-out
**comino** [ko'mino] nm: **(no) me importa un ~** I don't give a damn
**comisaría** [komisa'ria] nf (de policía) police station; (Mil) commissariat
**comisario** [komi'sarjo] nm (Mil etc) commissary; (Pol) commissar
**comisión** [komi'sjon] nf commission; **Comisiones Obreras** (ESP) Communist trade union
**comité** [komi'te] (pl **~s**) nm committee
**comitiva** [komi'tiβa] nf retinue
**como** ['komo] adv as; (tal **~**) like; (aproximadamente) about, approximately ▷ conj (ya que, puesto que) as, since; **¡~ no!** of course!; **~ no lo haga hoy** unless he does it today; **~ si** as if; **es tan alto ~ ancho** it is as high as it is wide
**cómo** ['komo] adv how?, why? ▷ excl what?, I beg your pardon? ▷ nm: **el ~ y el porqué** the whys and wherefores
**cómoda** ['komoða] nf chest of drawers
**comodidad** [komoði'ðað] nf comfort
**comodín** [komo'ðin] nm joker
**cómodo, -a** ['komoðo, a] adj comfortable; (práctico, de fácil uso) convenient
**compact** [kom'pakt] (pl **~s**) nm (tb: **~ disc**) compact disk player
**compacto, -a** [kom'pakto, a] adj

compact

**compadecer** [kompaðe'θer] vt to pity, be sorry for; **compadecerse** vr: **~se de** to pity, be o feel sorry for

**compadre** [kom'paðre] nm (padrino) godfather; (amigo) friend, pal

**compañero, -a** [kompa'ɲero, a] nm/f companion; (novio) boy/girlfriend; **compañero de clase** classmate

**compañía** [kompa'ɲia] nf company; **hacer ~ a algn** to keep sb company

**comparación** [kompara'θjon] nf comparison; **en ~ con** in comparison with

**comparar** [kompa'rar] vt to compare

**comparecer** [kompare'θer] vi to appear (in court)

**comparsa** [kom'parsa] nmf (Teatro) extra

**compartimiento** [komparti'mjento] nm (Ferro) compartment

**compartir** [kompar'tir] vt to share; (dinero, comida etc) to divide (up), share (out)

**compás** [kom'pas] nm (Mús) beat, rhythm; (Mat) compasses pl; (Náut etc) compass

**compasión** [kompa'sjon] nf compassion, pity

**compasivo, -a** [kompa'siβo, a] adj compassionate

**compatible** [kompa'tiβle] adj compatible

**compatriota** [kompa'trjota] nmf compatriot, fellow countryman/woman

**compenetrarse** [kompene'trarse] vr to be in tune

**compensación** [kompensa'θjon] nf compensation

**compensar** [kompen'sar] vt to compensate

**competencia** [kompe'tenθja] nf (incumbencia) domain, field; (Jur, habilidad) competence; (rivalidad) competition

**competente** [kompe'tente] adj competent

**competición** [kompeti'θjon] nf competition

**competir** [kompe'tir] vi to compete

**compinche** [kom'pintʃe] (LAM) nmf mate, buddy (US)

**complacer** [kompla'θer] vt to please; **complacerse** vr to be pleased

**complaciente** [kompla'θjente] adj kind, obliging, helpful

**complejo, -a** [kom'plexo, a] adj, nm complex

**complementario, -a** [komplemen'tarjo, a] adj complementary

**completar** [komple'tar] vt to complete

**completo, -a** [kom'pleto, a] adj complete; (perfecto) perfect; (lleno) full ▷ nm full complement

**complicado, -a** [kompli'kaðo, a] adj complicated; **estar ~ en** to be mixed up in

**cómplice** ['kompliθe] nmf accomplice

**complot** [kom'plo(t)] (pl **~s**) nm plot

**componer** [kompo'ner] vt (Mús, Literatura, Imprenta) to compose; (algo roto) to mend, repair; (arreglar) to arrange; **componerse** vr: **~se de** to consist of

**comportamiento** [komporta'mjento] nm behaviour, conduct

**comportarse** [kompor'tarse] vr to behave

**composición** [komposi'θjon] nf composition

**compositor, a** [komposi'tor, a] nm/f composer

**compostura** [kompos'tura] nf (actitud) composure

**compra** ['kompra] nf purchase; **hacer la ~** to do the shopping; **ir de ~s** to go shopping; **comprador, a** nm/f buyer, purchaser; **comprar** vt to buy, purchase

**comprender** [kompren'der] vt to understand; (incluir) to comprise, include

**comprensión** [kompren'sjon] nf understanding; **comprensivo, -a** adj (actitud) understanding

**compresa** [kom'presa] nf (para mujer) sanitary towel (BRIT) o napkin (US)

**comprimido, -a** [kompri'miðo, a] adj compressed ▷ nm (Med) pill, tablet

**comprimir** [kompri'mir] vt to compress; (Internet) to zip

**comprobante** [kompro'βante] nm proof; (Com) voucher; **comprobante de compra** proof of purchase

**comprobar** [kompro'βar] vt to check; (probar) to prove; (Tec) to check, test

**comprometer** [komprome'ter] vt to compromise; (poner en peligro) to endanger; **comprometerse** vr (involucrarse) to get involved

**compromiso** [kompro'miso] nm (obligación) obligation; (cometido) commitment; (convenio) agreement; (apuro) awkward situation

**compuesto, -a** [kom'pwesto, a] adj: **~ de** composed of, made up of ▷ nm compound

**computadora** [komputa'ðora] (LAM) nf computer; **computadora central** mainframe (computer); **computadora personal** personal computer

**cómputo** ['komputo] nm calculation

**comulgar** [komul'ɣar] vi to receive communion

**común** [ko'mun] adj common ▷ nm: **el ~** the community

**comunicación** [komunika'θjon] *nf* communication; (*informe*) report

**comunicado** [komuni'kado] *nm* announcement; **comunicado de prensa** press release

**comunicar** [komuni'kar] *vt, vi* to communicate; **comunicarse** *vr* to communicate; **está comunicando** (*Tel*) the line's engaged (*BRIT*) o busy (*US*); **comunicativo, -a** *adj* communicative

**comunidad** [komuni'ðað] *nf* community; **comunidad autónoma** (*ESP*) autonomous region; **Comunidad (Económica) Europea** European (Economic) Community; **comunidad de vecinos** residents' association

**comunión** [komu'njon] *nf* communion

**comunismo** [komu'nismo] *nm* communism; **comunista** *adj, nmf* communist

○ **PALABRA CLAVE**

**con** [kon] *prep* **1** (*medio, compañía*) with; **comer con cuchara** to eat with a spoon; **pasear con algn** to go for a walk with sb
**2** (*a pesar de*): **con todo, merece nuestros respetos** all the same, he deserves our respect
**3** (*para con*): **es muy bueno para con los niños** he's very good with (the) children
**4** (+ *infin*): **con llegar a las seis estará bien** if you come by six it will be fine ▷ *conj*: **con que: será suficiente con que le escribas** it will be sufficient if you write to her

**concebir** [konθe'βir] *vt, vi* to conceive

**conceder** [konθe'ðer] *vt* to concede

**concejal, a** [konθe'xal, a] *nm/f* town councillor

**concentración** [konθentra'θjon] *nf* concentration

**concentrar** [konθen'trar] *vt* to concentrate; **concentrarse** *vr* to concentrate

**concepto** [kon'θepto] *nm* concept

**concernir** [konθer'nir] *vi* to concern; **en lo que concierne a ...** as far as ... is concerned; **en lo que a mí concierne** as far as I'm concerned

**concertar** [konθer'tar] *vt* (*Mús*) to harmonize; (*acordar: precio*) to agree; (: *tratado*) to conclude; (*trato*) to arrange, fix up; (*combinar: esfuerzos*) to coordinate ▷ *vi* to harmonize, be in tune

**concesión** [konθe'sjon] *nf* concession

**concesionario** [konθesjo'narjo] *nm* (licensed) dealer, agent

**concha** ['kontʃa] *nf* shell

**conciencia** [kon'θjenθja] *nf* conscience; **tomar ~ de** to become aware of; **tener la ~ tranquila** to have a clear conscience

**concienciar** [konθjen'θjar] *vt* to make aware; **concienciarse** *vr* to become aware

**concienzudo, -a** [konθjen'θuðo, a] *adj* conscientious

**concierto** *etc* [kon'θjerto] *vb* V **concertar** ▷ *nm* concert; (*obra*) concerto

**conciliar** [konθi'ljar] *vt* to reconcile; **~ el sueño** to get to sleep

**concilio** [kon'θiljo] *nm* council

**conciso, -a** [kon'θiso, a] *adj* concise

**concluir** [konklu'ir] *vt, vi* to conclude; **concluirse** *vr* to conclude

**conclusión** [konklu'sjon] *nf* conclusion

**concordar** [konkor'ðar] *vt* to reconcile ▷ *vi* to agree, tally

**concordia** [kon'korðja] *nf* harmony

**concretar** [konkre'tar] *vt* to make concrete, make more specific; **concretarse** *vr* to become more definite

**concreto, -a** [kon'kreto, a] *adj, nm* (*LAM: hormigón*) concrete; **en ~** (*en resumen*) to sum up; (*específicamente*) specifically; **no hay nada en ~** there's nothing definite

**concurrido, -a** [konku'rriðo, a] *adj* (*calle*) busy; (*local, reunión*) crowded

**concursante** [konkur'sante] *nmf* competitor

**concurso** [kon'kurso] *nm* (*de público*) crowd; (*Escol, Deporte, competencia*) competition; (*ayuda*) help, cooperation

**condal** [kon'dal] *adj*: **la Ciudad C~** Barcelona

**conde** ['konde] *nm* count

**condecoración** [kondekora'θjon] *nf* (*Mil*) medal

**condena** [kon'dena] *nf* sentence; **condenación** [kondena'θjon] *nf* condemnation; (*Rel*) damnation; **condenar** [konde'nar] *vt* to condemn; (*Jur*) to convict; **condenarse** *vr* (*Rel*) to be damned

**condesa** [kon'desa] *nf* countess

**condición** [kondi'θjon] *nf* condition; **a ~ de que ...** on condition that ...; **condicional** *adj* conditional

**condimento** [kondi'mento] *nm* seasoning

**condominio** [kondo'minjo] (*LAM*) *nm* condominium

**condón** [kon'don] *nm* condom

**conducir** [kondu'θir] *vt* to take, convey; (*Auto*) to drive ▷ *vi* to drive; (*fig*) to lead; **conducirse** *vr* to behave

**conducta** [kon'dukta] *nf* conduct,

behaviour

**conducto** [kon'dukto] nm pipe, tube; (fig) channel

**conductor, a** [konduk'tor, a] adj leading, guiding ▷ nm (Física) conductor; (de vehículo) driver

**conduje** etc vb V **conducir**

**conduzco** etc vb V **conducir**

**conectado, -a** [konek'taðo, a] adj (Inform) on-line

**conectar** [konek'tar] vt to connect (up); (enchufar) plug in

**conejillo** [kone'xiʎo] nm: ~ **de Indias** guinea pig

**conejo** [ko'nexo] nm rabbit

**conexión** [konek'sjon] nf connection

**confección** [confe(k)'θjon] nf preparation; (industria) clothing industry

**confeccionar** [konfekθjo'nar] vt to make (up)

**conferencia** [konfe'renθja] nf conference; (lección) lecture; (ESP Tel) call; **conferencia de prensa** press conference

**conferir** [konfe'rir] vt to award

**confesar** [konfe'sar] vt to confess, admit

**confesión** [konfe'sjon] nf confession

**confesionario** [konfesjo'narjo] nm confessional

**confeti** [kon'feti] nm confetti

**confiado, -a** [kon'fjaðo, a] adj (crédulo) trusting; (seguro) confident

**confianza** [kon'fjanθa] nf trust; (seguridad) confidence; (familiaridad) intimacy, familiarity

**confiar** [kon'fjar] vt to entrust ▷ vi to trust; ~ **en algn** to trust sb; ~ **en que ...** to hope that ...

**confidencial** [konfiðen'θjal] adj confidential

**confidente** [konfi'ðente] nmf confidant/e; (policial) informer

**configurar** [konfixu'rar] vt to shape, form

**confín** [kon'fin] nm limit; **confines** nmpl confines, limits

**confirmar** [konfir'mar] vt to confirm

**confiscar** [konfis'kar] vt to confiscate

**confite** [kon'fite] nm sweet (BRIT), candy (US); **confitería** [konfite'ria] nf (tienda) confectioner's (shop)

**confitura** [konfi'tura] nf jam

**conflictivo, -a** [konflik'tiβo, a] adj (asunto, propuesta) controversial; (país, situación) troubled

**conflicto** [kon'flikto] nm conflict; (fig) clash

**confluir** [kon'flwir] vi (ríos) to meet; (gente) to gather

**conformar** [konfor'mar] vt to shape, fashion ▷ vi to agree; **conformarse** vr to conform; (resignarse) to resign o.s.; ~**se con algo** to be happy with sth

**conforme** [kon'forme] adj (correspondiente): ~ **con** in line with; (de acuerdo): **estar ~s (con algo)** to be in agreement (with sth) ▷ adv as ▷ excl agreed! ▷ prep: ~ **a** in accordance with; **quedarse ~ (con algo)** to be satisfied (with sth)

**confortable** [konfor'taβle] adj comfortable

**confortar** [konfor'tar] vt to comfort

**confrontar** [konfron'tar] vt to confront; (dos personas) to bring face to face; (cotejar) to compare

**confundir** [konfun'dir] vt (equivocar) to mistake, confuse; (turbar) to confuse; **confundirse** vr (turbarse) to get confused; (equivocarse) to make a mistake; (mezclarse) to mix

**confusión** [konfu'sjon] nf confusion

**confuso, -a** [kon'fuso, a] adj confused

**congelado, -a** [konxe'laðo, a] adj frozen; **congelados** nmpl frozen food(s); **congelador** nm (aparato) freezer, deep freeze

**congelar** [konxe'lar] vt to freeze; **congelarse** vr (sangre, grasa) to congeal

**congeniar** [konxe'njar] vi to get on (BRIT) o along (US) well

**congestión** [konxes'tjon] nf congestion

**congestionar** [konxestjo'nar] vt to congest

**congraciarse** [kongra'θjarse] vr to ingratiate o.s.

**congratular** [kongratu'lar] vt to congratulate

**congregar** [kongre'ɣar] vt to gather together; **congregarse** vr to gather together

**congresista** [kongre'sista] nmf delegate, congressman/woman

**congreso** [kon'greso] nm congress

**conjetura** [konxe'tura] nf guess; **conjeturar** vt to guess

**conjugar** [konxu'ɣar] vt to combine, fit together; (Ling) to conjugate

**conjunción** [konxun'θjon] nf conjunction

**conjunto, -a** [kon'xunto, a] adj joint, united ▷ nm whole; (Mús) band; **en ~** as a whole

**conmemoración** [konmemora'θjon] nf commemoration

**conmemorar** [konmemo'rar] vt to commemorate

**conmigo** [kon'miɣo] *pron* with me

**conmoción** [konmo'θjon] *nf* shock; (*fig*) upheaval; **conmoción cerebral** (*Med*) concussion

**conmovedor, a** [konmoβe'ðor, a] *adj* touching, moving; (*emocionante*) exciting

**conmover** [konmo'βer] *vt* to shake, disturb; (*fig*) to move

**conmutador** [konmuta'ðor] *nm* switch; (*LAM: centralita*) switchboard; (: *central*) telephone exchange

**cono** ['kono] *nm* cone; **Cono Sur** Southern Cone

**conocedor, a** [konoθe'ðor, a] *adj* expert, knowledgeable ▷ *nm/f* expert

**conocer** [kono'θer] *vt* to know; (*por primera vez*) to meet, get to know; (*entender*) to know about; (*reconocer*) to recognize; **conocerse** *vr* (*una persona*) to know o.s.; (*dos personas*) to (get to) know each other; ~ **a algn de vista** to know sb by sight

**conocido, -a** [kono'θiðo, a] *adj* (well-)known ▷ *nm/f* acquaintance

**conocimiento** [konoθi'mjento] *nm* knowledge; (*Med*) consciousness; **conocimientos** *nmpl* (*saber*) knowledge *sg*

**conozco** *etc vb* V **conocer**

**conque** ['konke] *conj* and so, so then

**conquista** [kon'kista] *nf* conquest; **conquistador, a** *adj* conquering ▷ *nm* conqueror; **conquistar** [konkis'tar] *vt* to conquer

**consagrar** [konsa'ɣrar] *vt* (*Rel*) to consecrate; (*fig*) to devote

**consciente** [kons'θjente] *adj* conscious

**consecución** [konseku'θjon] *nf* acquisition; (*de fin*) attainment

**consecuencia** [konse'kwenθja] *nf* consequence, outcome; (*coherencia*) consistency

**consecuente** [konse'kwente] *adj* consistent

**consecutivo, -a** [konseku'tiβo, a] *adj* consecutive

**conseguir** [konse'ɣir] *vt* to get, obtain; (*objetivo*) to attain

**consejero, -a** [konse'xero, a] *nm/f* adviser, consultant; (*Pol*) councillor

**consejo** [kon'sexo] *nm* advice; (*Pol*) council; **consejo de administración** (*Com*) board of directors; **consejo de guerra** court martial; **consejo de ministros** cabinet meeting

**consenso** [kon'senso] *nm* consensus

**consentimiento** [konsenti'mjento] *nm* consent

**consentir** [konsen'tir] *vt* (*permitir, tolerar*) to consent to; (*mimar*) to pamper, spoil;

(*aguantar*) to put up with ▷ *vi* to agree, consent; ~ **que algn haga algo** to allow sb to do sth

**conserje** [kon'serxe] *nm* caretaker; (*portero*) porter

**conservación** [konserβa'θjon] *nf* conservation; (*de alimentos, vida*) preservation

**conservador, a** [konserβa'ðor, a] *adj* (*Pol*) conservative ▷ *nm/f* conservative

**conservante** [konser'βante] *nm* preservative

**conservar** [konser'βar] *vt* to conserve, keep; (*alimentos, vida*) to preserve; **conservarse** *vr* to survive

**conservas** [kon'serβas] *nfpl* canned food(s) *pl*

**conservatorio** [konserβa'torjo] *nm* (*Mús*) conservatoire, conservatory

**considerable** [konsiðe'raβle] *adj* considerable

**consideración** [konsiðera'θjon] *nf* consideration; (*estimación*) respect

**considerado, -a** [konsiðe'raðo, a] *adj* (*atento*) considerate; (*respetado*) respected

**considerar** [konsiðe'rar] *vt* to consider

**consigna** [kon'siɣna] *nf* (*orden*) order, instruction; (*para equipajes*) left-luggage office

**consigo** *etc* [kon'siɣo] *vb* V **conseguir** ▷ *pron* (*m*) with him; (*f*) with her; (*Vd*) with you; (*reflexivo*) with o.s.

**consiguiendo** *etc vb* V **conseguir**

**consiguiente** [konsi'ɣjente] *adj* consequent; **por** ~ and so, therefore, consequently

**consistente** [konsis'tente] *adj* consistent; (*sólido*) solid, firm; (*válido*) sound

**consistir** [konsis'tir] *vi*: ~ **en** (*componerse de*) to consist of

**consola** [kon'sola] *nf* (*mueble*) console table; (*de videojuegos*) console

**consolación** [konsola'θjon] *nf* consolation

**consolar** [konso'lar] *vt* to console

**consolidar** [konsoli'ðar] *vt* to consolidate

**consomé** [konso'me] (*pl* ~**s**) *nm* consommé, clear soup

**consonante** [konso'nante] *adj* consonant, harmonious ▷ *nf* consonant

**consorcio** [kon'sorθjo] *nm* consortium

**conspiración** [konspira'θjon] *nf* conspiracy

**conspirar** [konspi'rar] *vi* to conspire

**constancia** [kon'stanθja] *nf* constancy; **dejar** ~ **de** to put on record

**constante** [kons'tante] *adj, nf* constant

**constar** [kons'tar] *vi* (*evidenciarse*) to be

clear o evident; **~ de** to consist of

**constipado, -a** [konsti'paðo, a] *adj*: **estar ~** to have a cold ▷ *nm* cold

▌ No confundir **constipado** con la palabra inglesa *constipated*.

**constitución** [konstitu'θjon] *nf* constitution

**constituir** [konstitu'ir] *vt* (*formar, componer*) to constitute, make up; (*fundar, erigir, ordenar*) to constitute, establish

**construcción** [konstruk'θjon] *nf* construction, building

**constructor, a** [konstruk'tor, a] *nm/f* builder

**construir** [konstru'ir] *vt* to build, construct

**construyendo** *etc vb* V **construir**

**consuelo** [kon'swelo] *nm* consolation, solace

**cónsul** ['konsul] *nm* consul; **consulado** *nm* consulate

**consulta** [kon'sulta] *nf* consultation; (*Med*): **horas de ~** surgery hours; **consultar** [konsul'tar] *vt* to consult; **consultar algo con algn** to discuss sth with sb; **consultorio** [konsul'torjo] *nm* (*Med*) surgery

**consumición** [konsumi'θjon] *nf* consumption; (*bebida*) drink; (*comida*) food; **consumición mínima** cover charge

**consumidor, a** [konsumi'ðor, a] *nm/f* consumer

**consumir** [konsu'mir] *vt* to consume; **consumirse** *vr* to be consumed; (*persona*) to waste away

**consumismo** [konsu'mismo] *nm* consumerism

**consumo** [kon'sumo] *nm* consumption

**contabilidad** [kontaβili'ðað] *nf* accounting, book-keeping; (*profesión*) accountancy; **contable** *nmf* accountant

**contacto** [kon'takto] *nm* contact; (*Auto*) ignition; **estar/ponerse en ~ con algn** to be/to get in touch with sb

**contado, -a** [kon'taðo, a] *adj*: **~s** (*escasos*) numbered, scarce, few ▷ *nm*: **pagar al ~** to pay (in) cash

**contador** [konta'ðor] *nm* (*ESP: aparato*) meter ▷ *nmf* (*LAM Com*) accountant

**contagiar** [konta'xjar] *vt* (*enfermedad*) to pass on, transmit; (*persona*) to infect; **contagiarse** *vr* to become infected

**contagio** [kon'taxjo] *nm* infection; **contagioso, -a** *adj* infectious; (*fig*) catching

**contaminación** [kontamina'θjon] *nf* contamination; (*polución*) pollution

**contaminar** [kontami'nar] *vt* to contaminate; (*aire, agua*) to pollute

**contante** [kon'tante] *adj*: **dinero ~ (y sonante)** cash

**contar** [kon'tar] *vt* (*páginas, dinero*) to count; (*anécdota, chiste etc*) to tell ▷ *vi* to count; **~ con** to rely on, count on

**contemplar** [kontem'plar] *vt* to contemplate; (*mirar*) to look at

**contemporáneo, -a** [kontempo'raneo, a] *adj, nm/f* contemporary

**contenedor** [kontene'ðor] *nm* container

**contener** [konte'ner] *vt* to contain, hold; (*retener*) to hold back, contain; **contenerse** *vr* to control o restrain o.s.

**contenido, -a** [konte'niðo, a] *adj* (*moderado*) restrained; (*risa etc*) suppressed ▷ *nm* contents *pl*, content

**contentar** [konten'tar] *vt* (*satisfacer*) to satisfy; (*complacer*) to please; **contentarse** *vr* to be satisfied

**contento, -a** [kon'tento, a] *adj* (*alegre*) pleased; (*feliz*) happy

**contestación** [kontesta'θjon] *nf* answer, reply

**contestador** [kontesta'ðor] *nm* (*tb: ~ automático*) answering machine

**contestar** [kontes'tar] *vt* to answer, reply; (*Jur*) to corroborate, confirm

▌ No confundir **contestar** con la palabra inglesa *contest*.

**contexto** [kon'te(k)sto] *nm* context

**contigo** [kon'tiɣo] *pron* with you

**contiguo, -a** [kon'tiɣwo, a] *adj* adjacent, adjoining

**continente** [konti'nente] *adj, nm* continent

**continuación** [kontinwa'θjon] *nf* continuation; **a ~** then, next

**continuar** [konti'nwar] *vt* to continue, go on with ▷ *vi* to continue, go on; **~ hablando** to continue talking o to talk

**continuidad** [kontinwi'ðað] *nf* continuity

**continuo, -a** [kon'tinwo, a] *adj* (*sin interrupción*) continuous; (*acción perseverante*) continual

**contorno** [kon'torno] *nm* outline; (*Geo*) contour; **contornos** *nmpl* neighbourhood *sg*, surrounding area *sg*

**contra** ['kontra] *prep, adv* against ▷ *nm inv* con ▷ *nf*: **la C~** (*de Nicaragua*) the Contras *pl*

**contraataque** [kontraa'take] *nm* counter-attack

**contrabajo** [kontra'βaxo] *nm* double bass

**contrabandista** [kontraβan'dista] *nmf* smuggler

**contrabando** [kontra'βando] *nm* (*acción*)

smuggling; (*mercancías*) contraband

**contracción** [kontrak'θjon] *nf*
contraction

**contracorriente** [kontrako'rrjente] *nf*
cross-current

**contradecir** [kontraðe'θir] *vt* to
contradict

**contradicción** [kontraðik'θjon] *nf*
contradiction

**contradictorio, -a** [kontraðik'torjo, a]
*adj* contradictory

**contraer** [kontra'er] *vt* to contract;
(*limitar*) to restrict; **contraerse** *vr* to
contract; (*limitarse*) to limit o.s.

**contraluz** [kontra'luθ] *nm* view against
the light

**contrapartida** [kontrapar'tiða] *nf*: **como
~ (de)** in return (for)

**contrapelo** [kontra'pelo]: **a ~** *adv* the
wrong way

**contrapeso** [kontra'peso] *nm*
counterweight

**contraportada** [kontrapor'taða] *nf* (*de
revista*) back cover

**contraproducente** [kontraproðu'θente]
*adj* counterproductive

**contrario, -a** [kon'trarjo, a] *adj* contrary;
(*persona*) opposed; (*sentido, lado*) opposite
▷ *nm/f* enemy, adversary; (*Deporte*)
opponent; **al o por el ~** on the contrary; **de
lo ~** otherwise

**contrarreloj** [kontrarre'lo] *nf* (*tb*: **prueba
~**) time trial

**contrarrestar** [kontrarres'tar] *vt* to
counteract

**contrasentido** [kontrasen'tiðo] *nm*
(*contradicción*) contradiction

**contraseña** [kontra'seɲa] *nf* (*Inform*)
password

**contrastar** [kontras'tar] *vt, vi* to contrast

**contraste** [kon'traste] *nm* contrast

**contratar** [kontra'tar] *vt firmar un acuerdo
para*, to contract for; (*empleados, obreros*) to
hire, engage

**contratiempo** [kontra'tjempo] *nm*
setback

**contratista** [kontra'tista] *nmf* contractor

**contrato** [kon'trato] *nm* contract

**contraventana** [kontraβen'tana] *nf*
shutter

**contribución** [kontriβu'θjon] *nf*
(*municipal etc*) tax; (*ayuda*) contribution

**contribuir** [kontriβu'ir] *vt, vi* to
contribute; (*Com*) to pay (in taxes)

**contribuyente** [kontriβu'jente] *nmf*
(*Com*) taxpayer; (*que ayuda*) contributor

**contrincante** [kontrin'kante] *nmf*
opponent

**control** [kon'trol] *nm* control; (*inspección*)
inspection, check; **control de pasaportes**
passport inspection; **controlador, a** *nm/f*
controller; **controlador aéreo** air-traffic
controller; **controlar** [kontro'lar] *vt* to
control; (*inspeccionar*) to inspect, check

**contundente** [kontun'dente] *adj*
(*instrumento*) blunt; (*argumento, derrota*)
overwhelming

**contusión** [kontu'sjon] *nf* bruise

**convalecencia** [kombale'θenθja] *nf*
convalescence

**convalecer** [kombale'θer] *vi* to
convalesce, get better

**convalidar** [kombali'ðar] *vt* (*título*) to
recognize

**convencer** [komben'θer] *vt* to convince;
**~ a algn (de** o **para hacer algo)** to persuade
sb (to do sth)

**convención** [komben'θjon] *nf*
convention

**conveniente** [kombe'njente] *adj*
suitable; (*útil*) useful

**convenio** [kom'benjo] *nm* agreement,
treaty

**convenir** [kombe'nir] *vi* (*estar de acuerdo*)
to agree; (*venir bien*) to suit, be suitable
| No confundir **convenir** con la palabra
inglesa *convene*.

**convento** [kom'bento] *nm* convent

**conversa** *etc vb* V **convencer**

**convergir** [komber'xir] *vi* = **converger**

**conversación** [kombersa'θjon] *nf*
conversation

**conversar** [komber'sar] *vi* to talk,
converse

**conversión** [komber'sjon] *nf* conversion

**convertir** [komber'tir] *vt* to convert

**convidar** [kombi'ðar] *vt* to invite; **~ a
algn a una cerveza** to buy sb a beer

**convincente** [kombin'θente] *adj*
convincing

**convite** [kom'bite] *nm* invitation;
(*banquete*) banquet

**convivencia** [kombi'βenθja] *nf*
coexistence, living together

**convivir** [kombi'βir] *vi* to live together

**convocar** [kombo'kar] *vt* to summon, call
(together)

**convocatoria** [komboka'torja] *nf* (*de
oposiciones, elecciones*) notice; (*de huelga*) call

**cónyuge** ['koɲxuxe] *nmf* spouse

**coñac** [ko'na(k)] (*pl* **~s**) *nm* cognac, brandy

**coño** ['koɲo] (*fam!*) *excl* (*enfado*) shit! (*!*);
(*sorpresa*) bloody hell! (*!*)

**cool** [kul] *adj* (*fam*) cool

**cooperación** [koopera'θjon] *nf*
cooperation

**cooperar** [koope'rar] *vi* to cooperate
**cooperativa** [koopera'tiβa] *nf* cooperative
**coordinadora** [koorðina'ðora] *nf (comité)* coordinating committee
**coordinar** [koorði'nar] *vt* to coordinate
**copa** ['kopa] *nf* cup; *(vaso)* glass; *(bebida)*: **tomar una ~** (to have a) drink; *(de árbol)* top; *(de sombrero)* crown; **copas** *nfpl (Naipes)* ≈ hearts
**copia** ['kopja] *nf* copy; **copia de respaldo** o **seguridad** *(Inform)* back-up copy; **copiar** *vt* to copy
**copla** ['kopla] *nf* verse; *(canción)* (popular) song
**copo** ['kopo] *nm*: **~ de nieve** snowflake; **~s de maíz** cornflakes
**coqueta** [ko'keta] *adj* flirtatious, coquettish; **coquetear** *vi* to flirt
**coraje** [ko'raxe] *nm* courage; *(ánimo)* spirit; *(ira)* anger
**coral** [ko'ral] *adj* choral ▷ *nf (Mús)* choir ▷ *nm (Zool)* coral
**coraza** [ko'raθa] *nf (armadura)* armour; *(blindaje)* armour-plating
**corazón** [kora'θon] *nm* heart
**corazonada** [koraθo'naða] *nf* impulse; *(presentimiento)* hunch
**corbata** [kor'βata] *nf* tie
**corchete** [kor'tʃete] *nm* catch, clasp
**corcho** ['kortʃo] *nm* cork; *(Pesca)* float
**cordel** [kor'ðel] *nm* cord, line
**cordero** [kor'ðero] *nm* lamb
**cordial** [kor'ðjal] *adj* cordial
**cordillera** [korði'ʎera] *nf* range (of mountains)
**Córdoba** ['korðoβa] *n* Cordova
**cordón** [kor'ðon] *nm (cuerda)* cord, string; *(de zapatos)* lace; *(Mil etc)* cordon; **cordón umbilical** umbilical cord
**cordura** [kor'ðura] *nf*: **con ~** *(obrar, hablar)* sensibly
**corneta** [kor'neta] *nf* bugle
**cornisa** [kor'nisa] *nf (Arq)* cornice
**coro** ['koro] *nm* chorus; *(conjunto de cantores)* choir
**corona** [ko'rona] *nf* crown; *(de flores)* garland
**coronel** [koro'nel] *nm* colonel
**coronilla** [koro'niʎa] *nf (Anat)* crown (of the head)
**corporal** [korpo'ral] *adj* corporal, bodily
**corpulento, -a** [korpu'lento, a] *adj (persona)* heavily-built
**corral** [ko'rral] *nm* farmyard
**correa** [ko'rrea] *nf* strap; *(cinturón)* belt; *(de perro)* lead, leash; **correa del ventilador** *(Auto)* fan belt

**corrección** [korrek'θjon] *nf* correction; *(reprensión)* rebuke; **correccional** *nm* reformatory
**correcto, -a** [ko'rrekto, a] *adj* correct; *(persona)* well-mannered
**corredizo, -a** [korre'ðiθo, a] *adj (puerta etc)* sliding
**corredor, a** [korre'ðor, a] *nm (pasillo)* corridor; *(balcón corrido)* gallery; *(Com)* agent, broker ▷ *nm/f (Deporte)* runner
**corregir** [korre'xir] *vt (error)* to correct; **corregirse** *vr* to reform
**correo** [ko'rreo] *nm* post, mail; *(persona)* courier; **Correos** *nmpl (ESP)* Post Office *sg*; **correo aéreo** airmail; **correo basura** *(Inform)* spam; **correo electrónico** e-mail, electronic mail; **correo web** webmail
**correr** [ko'rrer] *vt* to run; *(cortinas)* to draw; *(cerrojo)* to shoot ▷ *vi* to run; *(líquido)* to run, flow; **correrse** *vr* to slide, move; *(colores)* to run
**correspondencia** [korrespon'denθja] *nf* correspondence; *(Ferro)* connection
**corresponder** [korrespon'der] *vi* to correspond; *(convenir)* to be suitable; *(pertenecer)* to belong; *(concernir)* to concern; **corresponderse** *vr (por escrito)* to correspond; *(amarse)* to love one another
**correspondiente** [korrespon'djente] *adj* corresponding
**corresponsal** [korrespon'sal] *nmf* correspondent
**corrida** [ko'rriða] *nf (de toros)* bullfight
**corrido, -a** [ko'rriðo, a] *adj (avergonzado)* abashed; **un kilo ~** a good kilo
**corriente** [ko'rrjente] *adj (agua)* running; *(dinero etc)* current; *(común)* ordinary, normal ▷ *nf* current ▷ *nm* current month; **estar al ~ de** to be informed about; **corriente eléctrica** electric current
**corrija** *etc vb* V **corregir**
**corro** ['korro] *nm* ring, circle (of people)
**corromper** [korrom'per] *vt (madera)* to rot; *(fig)* to corrupt
**corrosivo, -a** [korro'siβo, a] *adj* corrosive
**corrupción** [korrup'θjon] *nf* rot, decay; *(fig)* corruption
**corsé** [kor'se] *nm* corset
**cortacésped** [korta'θespeð] *nm* lawn mower
**cortado, -a** [kor'taðo, a] *adj (gen)* cut; *(leche)* sour; *(tímido)* shy; *(avergonzado)* embarrassed ▷ *nm* coffee (with a little milk)
**cortafuegos** [korta'fweɣos] *nm inv (en el bosque)* firebreak, fire lane *(us)*; *(Internet)* firewall
**cortar** [kor'tar] *vt* to cut; *(suministro)* to

cut off; (un pasaje) to cut out ▷ vi to cut;
**cortarse** vr (avergonzarse) to become
embarrassed; (leche) to turn, curdle; **~se el
pelo** to have one's hair cut
**cortauñas** [korta'uɲas] nm inv nail
clippers pl
**corte** ['korte] nm cut, cutting; (de tela)
piece, length ▷ nf: **las C~s** the Spanish
Parliament; **corte de luz** power cut; **corte y
confección** dressmaking
**cortejo** [kor'texo] nm entourage; **cortejo
fúnebre** funeral procession
**cortés** [kor'tes] adj courteous, polite
**cortesía** [korte'sia] nf courtesy
**corteza** [kor'teθa] nf (de árbol) bark; (de
pan) crust
**cortijo** [kor'tixo] (ESP) nm farm,
farmhouse
**cortina** [kor'tina] nf curtain
**corto, -a** ['korto, a] adj (breve) short;
(tímido) bashful; **~ de luces** not very bright;
**~ de vista** short-sighted; **estar ~ de fondos**
to be short of funds; **cortocircuito** nm
short circuit; **cortometraje** nm (Cine) short
**cosa** ['kosa] nf thing; **~ de** about; **eso es ~
mía** that's my business
**coscorrón** [kosko'rron] nm bump on
the head
**cosecha** [ko'setʃa] nf (Agr) harvest; (de
vino) vintage; **cosechar** [kose'tʃar] vt to
harvest, gather (in)
**coser** [ko'ser] vt to sew
**cosmético, -a** [kos'metiko, a] adj, nm
cosmetic
**cosquillas** [kos'kiʎas] nfpl: **hacer ~** to
tickle; **tener ~** to be ticklish
**costa** ['kosta] nf (Geo) coast; **a toda ~** at
all costs; **Costa Brava** Costa Brava; **Costa
Cantábrica** Cantabrian Coast; **Costa del
Sol** Costa del Sol
**costado** [kos'taðo] nm side
**costanera** [kosta'nera] (CS) nf
promenade, sea front
**costar** [kos'tar] vt (valer) to cost; **me
cuesta hablarle** I find it hard to talk to him
**Costa Rica** [kosta'rika] nf Costa Rica;
**costarricense** adj, nmf Costa Rican;
**costarriqueño, -a** adj, nm/f Costa Rican
**coste** ['koste] nm = **costo**
**costear** [koste'ar] vt to pay for
**costero, -a** [kos'tero, a] adj (pueblecito,
camino) coastal
**costilla** [kos'tiʎa] nf rib; (Culin) cutlet
**costo** ['kosto] nm cost, price; **costo de (la)
vida** cost of living; **costoso, -a** adj costly,
expensive
**costra** ['kostra] nf (corteza) crust; (Med)
scab

**costumbre** [kos'tumbre] nf custom,
habit
**costura** [kos'tura] nf sewing, needlework;
(zurcido) seam
**costurera** [kostu'rera] nf dressmaker
**costurero** [kostu'rero] nm sewing box
o case
**cotidiano, -a** [koti'ðjano, a] adj daily,
day to day
**cotilla** [ko'tiʎa] (ESP: fam) nmf gossip;
**cotillear** (ESP) vi to gossip; **cotilleo** (ESP)
nm gossip(ing)
**cotizar** [koti'θar] vt (Com) to quote, price;
**cotizarse** vr: **~se a** to sell at, fetch; (Bolsa) to
stand at, be quoted at
**coto** ['koto] nm (terreno cercado) enclosure;
(de caza) reserve
**cotorra** [ko'torra] nf parrot
**coyote** [ko'jote] nm coyote, prairie wolf
**coz** [koθ] nf kick
**crack** [krak] nm (droga) crack
**cráneo** ['kraneo] nm skull, cranium
**cráter** ['krater] nm crater
**crayón** [kra'jon] (MÉX, RPL) nm crayon,
chalk
**creación** [krea'θjon] nf creation
**creador, a** [krea'ðor, a] adj creative
▷ nm/f creator
**crear** [kre'ar] vt to create, make
**crecer** [kre'θer] vi to grow; (precio) to rise
**creces** ['kreθes]: **con ~** adv amply, fully
**crecido, -a** [kre'θiðo, a] adj (persona,
planta) full-grown; (cantidad) large
**crecimiento** [kreθi'mjento] nm growth;
(aumento) increase
**credencial** [kreðen'θjal] nf (LAM: tarjeta)
card; **credenciales** nfpl credentials;
**credencial de socio** (LAM) membership card
**crédito** ['kreðito] nm credit
**credo** ['kreðo] nm creed
**creencia** [kre'enθja] nf belief
**creer** [kre'er] vt, vi to think, believe;
**creerse** vr to believe o.s. (to be); **~ en** to
believe in; **creo que sí/no** I think/don't
think so; **¡ya lo creo!** I should think so!
**creído, -a** [kre'iðo, a] adj (engreído)
conceited
**crema** ['krema] nf cream; **crema batida**
(LAM) whipped cream; **crema pastelera**
(confectioner's) custard
**cremallera** [krema'ʎera] nf zip (fastener)
**crepe** ['krepe] (ESP) nf pancake
**cresta** ['kresta] nf (Geo, Zool) crest
**creyendo** etc vb V **creer**
**creyente** [kre'jente] nmf believer
**creyó** etc vb V **creer**
**crezco** etc vb V **crecer**
**cría** etc ['kria] vb V **criar** ▷ nf (de animales)

rearing, breeding; (*animal*) young; V *tb* **crío**

**criadero** [kria'ðero] *nm* (*Zool*) breeding place

**criado, -a** [kri'aðo, a] *nm* servant ▷ *nf* servant, maid

**criador** [kria'ðor] *nm* breeder

**crianza** [kri'anθa] *nf* rearing, breeding; (*fig*) breeding

**criar** [kri'ar] *vt* (*educar*) to bring up; (*producir*) to grow, produce; (*animales*) to breed

**criatura** [kria'tura] *nf* creature; (*niño*) baby, (*small*) child

**cribar** [kri'βar] *vt* to sieve

**crimen** ['krimen] *nm* crime

**criminal** [krimi'nal] *adj*, *nmf* criminal

**crines** ['krines] *nfpl* mane

**crío, -a** ['krio, a] (*fam*) *nm/f* (*niño*) kid

**crisis** ['krisis] *nf inv* crisis; **crisis nerviosa** nervous breakdown

**crismas** ['krismas] (*ESP*) *nm inv* Christmas card

**cristal** [kris'tal] *nm* crystal; (*de ventana*) glass, pane; (*lente*) lens; **cristalino, -a** *adj* crystalline; (*fig*) clear ▷ *nm* lens (of the eye)

**cristianismo** [kristja'nismo] *nm* Christianity

**cristiano, -a** [kris'tjano, a] *adj*, *nm/f* Christian

**Cristo** ['kristo] *nm* Christ; (*crucifijo*) crucifix

**criterio** [kri'terjo] *nm* criterion; (*juicio*) judgement

**crítica** ['kritika] *nf* criticism; V *tb* **crítico**

**criticar** [kriti'kar] *vt* to criticize

**crítico, -a** ['kritiko, a] *adj* critical ▷ *nm/f* critic

**Croacia** [kro'aθja] *nf* Croatia

**cromo** ['kromo] *nm* chrome

**crónica** ['kronika] *nf* chronicle, account

**crónico, -a** ['kroniko, a] *adj* chronic

**cronómetro** [kro'nometro] *nm* stopwatch

**croqueta** [kro'keta] *nf* croquette

**cruce** *etc* ['kruθe] *vb* V **cruzar** ▷ *nm* (*para peatones*) crossing; (*de carreteras*) crossroads

**crucero** [kru'θero] *nm* (*viaje*) cruise

**crucificar** [kruθifi'kar] *vt* to crucify

**crucifijo** [kruθi'fixo] *nm* crucifix

**crucigrama** [kruθi'ɣrama] *nm* crossword (puzzle)

**cruda** ['kruða] (*MÉX*, *CAM*: *fam*) *nf* hangover

**crudo, -a** ['kruðo, a] *adj* raw; (*no maduro*) unripe; (*petróleo*) crude; (*rudo, cruel*) cruel ▷ *nm* crude (oil)

**cruel** [krwel] *adj* cruel; **crueldad** *nf* cruelty

**crujiente** [kru'xjente] *adj* (*galleta etc*) crunchy

**crujir** [kru'xir] *vi* (*madera etc*) to creak; (*dedos*) to crack; (*dientes*) to grind; (*nieve, arena*) to crunch

**cruz** [kruθ] *nf* cross; (*de moneda*) tails *sg*; **cruz gamada** swastika

**cruzada** [kru'θaða] *nf* crusade

**cruzado, -a** [kru'θaðo, a] *adj* crossed ▷ *nm* crusader

**cruzar** [kru'θar] *vt* to cross; **cruzarse** *vr* (*líneas etc*) to cross; (*personas*) to pass each other

**Cruz Roja** *nf* Red Cross

**cuaderno** [kwa'ðerno] *nm* notebook; (*de escuela*) exercise book; (*Náut*) logbook

**cuadra** ['kwaðra] *nf* (*caballeriza*) stable; (*LAM*: *entre calles*) block

**cuadrado, -a** [kwa'ðraðo, a] *adj* square ▷ *nm* (*Mat*) square

**cuadrar** [kwa'ðrar] *vt* to square ▷ *vi*: ~ **con** to square with, tally with; **cuadrarse** *vr* (*soldado*) to stand to attention

**cuadrilátero** [kwaðri'latero] *nm* (*Deporte*) boxing ring; (*Geom*) quadrilateral

**cuadrilla** [kwa'ðriʎa] *nf* party, group

**cuadro** ['kwaðro] *nm* square; (*Arte*) painting; (*Teatro*) scene; (*diagrama*) chart; (*Deporte, Med*) team; **tela a ~s** checked (*BRIT*) *o* chequered (*US*) material

**cuajar** [kwa'xar] *vt* (*leche*) to curdle; (*sangre*) to congeal; (*Culin*) to set; **cuajarse** *vr* to curdle; to congeal; to set; (*llenarse*) to fill up

**cuajo** ['kwaxo] *nm*: **de ~** (*arrancar*) by the roots; (*cortar*) completely

**cual** [kwal] *adv* like, as ▷ *pron*: **el** *etc* ~ which; (*persona sujeto*) who; (: *objeto*) whom ▷ *adj* such as; **cada ~** each one; **déjalo tal ~** leave it just as it is

**cuál** [kwal] *pron interr* which (one)

**cualesquier, a** [kwales'kjer(a)] *pl de* **cualquier(a)**

**cualidad** [kwali'ðað] *nf* quality

**cualquier** [kwal'kjer] *adj* V **cualquiera**

**cualquiera** [kwal'kjera] (*pl* **cualesquiera**) *adj* (*delante de nm y f* **cualquier**) any ▷ *pron* anybody; **un coche ~ servirá** any car will do; **no es un hombre ~** he isn't just anybody; **cualquier día/libro** any day/book; **eso ~ lo sabe hacer** anybody can do that; **es un ~** he's a nobody

**cuando** ['kwando] *adv* when; (*aún si*) if, even if ▷ *conj* (*puesto que*) since ▷ *prep*: **yo**, **~ niño ...** when I was a child ...; **~ no sea así** even if it is not so; **~ más** at (the) most; **~ menos** at least; **~ no** if not, otherwise; **de ~ en ~** from time to time

**cuándo** ['kwando] *adv* when; **¿desde ~?**

since when?

**cuantía** [kwan'tia] *nf* extent

○ **PALABRA CLAVE**

**cuanto, -a** ['kwanto, a] *adj* **1** (*todo*): **tiene todo cuanto desea** he's got everything he wants; **le daremos cuantos ejemplares necesite** we'll give him as many copies as o all the copies he needs; **cuantos hombres la ven** all the men who see her
**2 unos cuantos: había unos cuantos periodistas** there were a few journalists
**3** (+ *más*): **cuanto más vino bebes peor te sentirás** the more wine you drink the worse you'll feel
▷ *pron*: **tiene cuanto desea** he has everything he wants; **tome cuanto/ cuantos quiera** take as much/many as you want
▷ *adv*: **en cuanto: en cuanto profesor** as a teacher; **en cuanto a mí** as for me; *V tb* **antes**
▷ *conj* **1** **cuanto más gana menos gasta** the more he earns the less he spends; **cuanto más joven más confiado** the younger you are the more trusting you are
**2 en cuanto: en cuanto llegue/llegué** as soon as I arrive/arrived

**cuánto, -a** ['kwanto, a] *adj* (*exclamación*) what a lot of; (*interr: sg*) how much?; (: *pl*) how many? ▷ *pron, adv* how; (: *interr: sg*) how much?; (: *pl*) how many?; **¡cuánta gente!** what a lot of people!; **¿~ cuesta?** how much does it cost?; **¿a ~s estamos?** what's the date?

**cuarenta** [kwa'renta] *num* forty
**cuarentena** [kwaren'tena] *nf* quarantine
**cuaresma** [kwa'resma] *nf* Lent
**cuarta** ['kwarta] *nf* (*Mat*) quarter, fourth; (*palmo*) span
**cuartel** [kwar'tel] *nm* (*Mil*) barracks *pl*; **cuartel de bomberos** (*RPL*) fire station; **cuartel general** headquarters *pl*
**cuarteto** [kwar'teto] *nm* quartet
**cuarto, -a** ['kwarto, a] *adj* fourth ▷ *nm* (*Mat*) quarter, fourth; (*habitación*) room; **cuarto de baño** bathroom; **cuarto de estar** living room; **cuarto de hora** quarter (of an) hour; **cuarto de kilo** quarter kilo; **cuartos de final** quarter finals
**cuatro** ['kwatro] *num* four
**Cuba** ['kuβa] *nf* Cuba
**cuba** ['kuβa] *nf* cask, barrel
**cubano, -a** [ku'βano, a] *adj, nm/f* Cuban
**cubata** [ku'βata] *nm* (*fam*) large drink (*of rum and coke etc*)

**cubeta** [ku'βeta] (*ESP, MÉX*) *nf* (*balde*) bucket, tub
**cúbico, -a** ['kuβiko, a] *adj* cubic
**cubierta** [ku'βjerta] *nf* cover, covering; (*neumático*) tyre; (*Náut*) deck
**cubierto, -a** [ku'βjerto, a] *pp de* **cubrir** ▷ *adj* covered ▷ *nm* cover; (*lugar en la mesa*) place; **cubiertos** *nmpl* cutlery *sg*; **a ~** under cover
**cubilete** [kuβi'lete] *nm* (*en juegos*) cup
**cubito** [ku'βito] *nm* (*tb*: **~ de hielo**) ice-cube
**cubo** ['kuβo] *nm* (*Mat*) cube; (*ESP: balde*) bucket, tub; (*Tec*) drum; **cubo de (la) basura** dustbin (*BRIT*), trash can (*US*)
**cubrir** [ku'βrir] *vt* to cover; **cubrirse** *vr* (*cielo*) to become overcast
**cucaracha** [kuka'ratʃa] *nf* cockroach
**cuchara** [ku'tʃara] *nf* spoon; (*Tec*) scoop; **cucharada** *nf* spoonful; **cucharadita** *nf* teaspoonful
**cucharilla** [kutʃa'riʎa] *nf* teaspoon
**cucharón** [kutʃa'ron] *nm* ladle
**cuchilla** [ku'tʃiʎa] *nf* (*large*) knife; (*de arma blanca*) blade; **cuchilla de afeitar** razor blade
**cuchillo** [ku'tʃiʎo] *nm* knife
**cuchitril** [kutʃi'tril] *nm* hovel
**cuclillas** [ku'kliʎas] *nfpl*: **en ~** squatting
**cuco, -a** ['kuko, a] *adj* pretty; (*astuto*) sharp ▷ *nm* cuckoo
**cucurucho** [kuku'rutʃo] *nm* cornet
**cueca** ['kweka] *nf* Chilean national dance
**cuello** ['kweʎo] *nm* (*Anat*) neck; (*de vestido, camisa*) collar
**cuenca** ['kwenka] *nf* (*Anat*) eye socket; (*Geo*) bowl, deep valley
**cuenco** ['kwenko] *nm* bowl
**cuenta** *etc* ['kwenta] *vb V* **contar** ▷ *nf* (*cálculo*) count, counting; (*en café, restaurante*) bill (*BRIT*), check (*US*); (*Com*) account; (*de collar*) bead; **a fin de ~s** in the end; **caer en la ~** to catch on; **darse ~ de** to realize; **tener en ~** to bear in mind; **echar ~s** to take stock; **cuenta atrás** countdown; **cuenta corriente/de ahorros** current/savings account; **cuenta de correo (electrónica)** (*Inform*) email account; **cuentakilómetros** *nm inv* = milometer; (*de velocidad*) speedometer
**cuento** *etc* ['kwento] *vb V* **contar** ▷ *nm* story; **cuento chino** tall story; **cuento de hadas** a fairy tale
**cuerda** ['kwerða] *nf* rope; (*fina*) string; (*de reloj*) spring; **dar ~ a un reloj** to wind up a clock; **cuerda floja** tightrope; **cuerdas vocales** vocal cords
**cuerdo, -a** ['kwerðo, a] *adj* sane;

(*prudente*) wise, sensible

**cuerno** ['kwerno] *nm* horn

**cuero** ['kwero] *nm* leather; **en ~s** stark naked; **cuero cabelludo** scalp

**cuerpo** ['kwerpo] *nm* body

**cuervo** ['kwerβo] *nm* crow

**cuesta** *etc* ['kwesta] *vb* V **costar** ▷ *nf* slope; (*en camino etc*) hill; **~ arriba/abajo** uphill/downhill; **a ~s** on one's back

**cueste** *etc vb* V **costar**

**cuestión** [kwes'tjon] *nf* matter, question

**cuete** ['kwete] *adj* (*MÉX: fam*) drunk ▷ *nm* (*LAM: cohete*) rocket; (*MÉX,RPL: fam: embriaguez*) drunkenness; (*MÉX: Culin*) steak

**cueva** ['kweβa] *nf* cave

**cuidado** [kwi'ðaðo] *nm* care, carefulness; (*preocupación*) care, worry ▷ *excl* careful!, look out!; **eso me tiene sin ~** I'm not worried about that

**cuidadoso, -a** [kwiða'ðoso, a] *adj* careful; (*preocupado*) anxious

**cuidar** [kwi'ðar] *vt* (*Med*) to care for; (*ocuparse de*) to take care of, look after ▷ *vi*: **~ de** to take care of, look after; **cuidarse** *vr* to look after o.s.; **~se de hacer algo** to take care to do sth

**culata** [ku'lata] *nf* (*de fusil*) butt

**culebra** [ku'leβra] *nf* snake

**culebrón** [kule'βron] (*fam*) *nm* (*TV*) soap(-opera)

**culo** ['kulo] *nm* bottom, backside; (*de vaso, botella*) bottom

**culpa** ['kulpa] *nf* fault; (*Jur*) guilt; **por ~ de** because of; **echar la ~ a algn** to blame sb for sth; **tener la ~ (de)** to be to blame (for); **culpable** *adj* guilty ▷ *nmf* culprit; **culpar** [kul'par] *vt* to blame; (*acusar*) to accuse

**cultivar** [kulti'βar] *vt* to cultivate

**cultivo** [kul'tiβo] *nm* (*acto*) cultivation; (*plantas*) crop

**culto, -a** ['kulto, a] *adj* (*que tiene cultura*) cultured, educated ▷ *nm* (*homenaje*) worship; (*religión*) cult

**cultura** [kul'tura] *nf* culture

**culturismo** [kultu'rismo] *nm* bodybuilding

**cumbia** ['kumbja] *nf* popular Colombian dance

**cumbre** ['kumbre] *nf* summit, top

**cumpleaños** [kumple'aɲos] *nm inv* birthday

**cumplido, -a** [kum'pliðo, a] *adj* (*abundante*) plentiful; (*cortés*) courteous ▷ *nm* compliment; **visita de ~** courtesy call

**cumplidor, a** [kumpli'ðor, a] *adj* reliable

**cumplimiento** [kumpli'mjento] *nm* (*de un deber*) fulfilment; (*acabamiento*) completion

**cumplir** [kum'plir] *vt* (*orden*) to carry out, obey; (*promesa*) to carry out, fulfil; (*condena*) to serve ▷ *vi*: **~ con** (*deber*) to carry out, fulfil; **cumplirse** *vr* (*plazo*) to expire; **hoy cumple dieciocho años** he is eighteen today

**cuna** ['kuna] *nf* cradle, cot

**cundir** [kun'dir] *vi* (*noticia, rumor, pánico*) to spread; (*rendir*) to go a long way

**cuneta** [ku'neta] *nf* ditch

**cuña** ['kuɲa] *nf* wedge

**cuñado, -a** [ku'ɲaðo, a] *nm/f* brother-/sister-in-law

**cuota** ['kwota] *nf* (*parte proporcional*) share; (*cotización*) fee, dues *pl*

**cupe** *etc vb* V **caber**

**cupiera** *etc vb* V **caber**

**cupo** ['kupo] *vb* V **caber** ▷ *nm* quota

**cupón** [ku'pon] *nm* coupon

**cúpula** ['kupula] *nf* dome

**cura** ['kura] *nf* (*curación*) cure; (*método curativo*) treatment ▷ *nm* priest

**curación** [kura'θjon] *nf* cure

**curandero, -a** [kuran'dero, a] *nm/f* quack

**curar** [ku'rar] *vt* (*Med: herida*) to treat, dress; (: *enfermo*) to cure; (*Culin*) to cure, salt; (*cuero*) to tan; **curarse** *vr* to get well, recover

**curiosear** [kurjose'ar] *vt* to glance at, look over ▷ *vi* to look round, wander round; (*explorar*) to poke about

**curiosidad** [kurjosi'ðað] *nf* curiosity

**curioso, -a** [ku'rjoso, a] *adj* curious ▷ *nm/f* bystander, onlooker

**curita** [ku'rita] (*LAM*) *nf* (sticking) plaster (*BRIT*), Bandaid® (*US*)

**currante** [ku'rrante] (*ESP: fam*) *nmf* worker

**currar** [ku'rrar] (*ESP: fam*) *vi* to work

**currículo** [ku'rrikulo] = **curriculum**

**curriculum** [ku'rrikulum] *nm* curriculum vitae

**cursi** ['kursi] (*fam*) *adj* affected

**cursillo** [kur'siʎo] *nm* short course

**cursiva** [kur'siβa] *nf* italics *pl*

**curso** ['kurso] *nm* course; **en ~** (*año*) current; (*proceso*) going on, under way

**cursor** [kur'sor] *nm* (*Inform*) cursor

**curul** [ku'rul] (*MÉX*) *nm* (*escaño*) seat

**curva** ['kurβa] *nf* curve, bend

**custodia** [kus'toðja] *nf* safekeeping; custody

**cutis** ['kutis] *nm inv* skin, complexion

**cutre** ['kutre] (*ESP: fam*) *adj* (*lugar*) grotty

**cuyo, -a** ['kujo, a] *pron* (*de quien*) whose; (*de que*) whose, of which; **en ~ caso** in which case

**C.V.** *abr* (= *caballos de vapor*) H.P.

# d

**más tarde** we came across him two hours later; **al final di con la solución** I eventually came up with the answer
**2: dar en** (*blanco, suelo*) to hit; **el sol me da en la cara** the sun is shining (right) on my face
**3: dar de sí** (*zapatos etc*) to stretch; **darse** *vr* **1: darse por vencido** to give up
**2** (*ocurrir*): **se han dado muchos casos** there have been a lot of cases
**3: darse a: se ha dado a la bebida** he's taken to drinking
**4: se me dan bien/mal las ciencias** I'm good/bad at science
**5: dárselas de: se las da de experto** he fancies himself *o* poses as an expert

**D.** *abr* (= *Don*) Esq
**dado, -a** ['daðo, a] *pp de* **dar** ▷ *nm* die;
  **dados** *nmpl* dice; **~ que** given that
**daltónico, -a** [dal'toniko, a] *adj* colour-blind
**dama** ['dama] *nf* (*gen*) lady; (*Ajedrez*)
  queen; **damas** *nfpl* (*juego*) draughts *sg*;
  **dama de honor** bridesmaid
**damasco** [da'masko] (*RPL*) *nm* apricot
**danés, -esa** [da'nes, esa] *adj* Danish
  ▷ *nm/f* Dane
**dañar** [da'ɲar] *vt* (*objeto*) to damage;
  (*persona*) to hurt; **dañarse** *vr* (*objeto*) to get
  damaged
**dañino, -a** [da'ɲino, a] *adj* harmful
**daño** ['daɲo] *nm* (*objeto*) damage; (*persona*)
  harm, injury; **~s y perjuicios** (*Jur*) damages;
  **hacer ~ a** to damage; (*persona*) to hurt,
  injure; **hacerse ~** to hurt o.s.

### ○ PALABRA CLAVE

**dar** [dar] *vt* **1** (*gen*) to give; (*obra de teatro*)
  to put on; (*film*) to show; (*fiesta*) to hold; **dar
  algo a algn** to give sb sth *o* sth to sb; **dar de
  beber a algn** to give sb a drink
**2** (*producir: intereses*) to yield; (*fruta*) to
  produce
**3** (*locuciones + n*): **da gusto escucharle** it's a
  pleasure to listen to him; *V tb* **paseo**
**4** (*+ n. = perífrasis de verbo*): **me da asco** it
  sickens me
**5** (*considerar*): **dar algo por descontado/
  entendido** to take sth for granted/as read;
  **dar algo por concluido** to consider sth
  finished
**6** (*hora*): **el reloj dio las 6** the clock struck
  6 (o'clock)
**7: me da lo mismo** it's all the same to me; *V
  tb* **igual, más**
▷ *vi* **1 dar con: dimos con él dos horas**

**más tarde** we came across him two hours
later; **al final di con la solución** I eventually
came up with the answer
**2: dar en** (*blanco, suelo*) to hit; **el sol me
da en la cara** the sun is shining (right) on
my face
**3: dar de sí** (*zapatos etc*) to stretch
**darse** *vr* **1: darse por vencido** to give up
**2** (*ocurrir*): **se han dado muchos casos** there
have been a lot of cases
**3: darse a: se ha dado a la bebida** he's
taken to drinking
**4: se me dan bien/mal las ciencias** I'm
good/bad at science
**5: dárselas de: se las da de experto** he
fancies himself *o* poses as an expert

**dardo** ['darðo] *nm* dart
**dátil** ['datil] *nm* date
**dato** ['dato] *nm* fact, piece of information;
  **datos personales** personal details
**dcha.** *abr* (= *derecha*) r.h.
**d. de C.** *abr* (= *después de Cristo*) A.D.

### ○ PALABRA CLAVE

**de** [de] (*de + el = del*) *prep* **1** (*posesión*) of; **la
  casa de Isabel/mis padres** Isabel's/my
  parents' house; **es de ellos** it's theirs
**2** (*origen, distancia, con números*) from; **soy
  de Gijón** I'm from Gijón; **de 8 a 20** from 8
  to 20; **salir del cine** to go out of *o* leave the
  cinema; **de 2 en 2** 2 by 2, 2 at a time
**3** (*valor descriptivo*): **una copa de vino** a glass
  of wine; **la mesa de la cocina** the kitchen
  table; **un billete de 10 euros** a 10 euro note;
  **un niño de tres años** a three-year-old
  (child); **una máquina de coser** a sewing
  machine; **ir vestido de gris** to be dressed
  in grey; **la niña del vestido azul** the girl in
  the blue dress; **trabaja de profesora** she
  works as a teacher; **de lado** sideways; **de
  atrás/delante** rear/front
**4** (*hora, tiempo*): **a las 8 de la mañana** at 8
  o'clock in the morning; **de día/noche** by
  day/night; **de hoy en ocho días** a week
  from now; **de niño era gordo** as a child he
  was fat
**5** (*comparaciones*): **más/menos de cien
  personas** more/less than a hundred
  people; **el más caro de la tienda** the most
  expensive in the shop; **menos/más de lo
  pensado** less/more than expected
**6** (*causa*): **del calor** from the heat
**7** (*tema*) about; **clases de inglés** English
  classes; **¿sabes algo de él?** do you know
  anything about him?; **un libro de física** a
  physics book

**8** (*adj + de + infin*): **fácil de entender** easy to understand
**9** (*oraciones pasivas*): **fue respetado de todos** he was loved by all
**10** (*condicional + infin*) if; **de ser posible** if possible; **de no terminarlo hoy** if I *etc* don't finish it today

**dé** [de] *vb* V **dar**
**debajo** [de'βaxo] *adv* underneath; **~ de** below, under; **por ~ de** beneath
**debate** [de'βate] *nm* debate; **debatir** *vt* to debate
**deber** [de'βer] *nm* duty ▷ *vt* to owe ▷ *vi*: **debe (de)** it must, it should; **deberes** *nmpl* (*Escol*) homework; **deberse** *vr*: **~se a** to be owing *o* due to; **debo hacerlo** I must do it; **debe de ir** he should go
**debido, -a** [de'βiðo, a] *adj* proper, just; **~ a** due to, because of
**débil** ['deβil] *adj* (*persona, carácter*) weak; (*luz*) dim; **debilidad** *nf* weakness; dimness
**debilitar** [deβili'tar] *vt* to weaken; **debilitarse** *vr* to grow weak
**débito** ['deβito] *nm* debit; **débito bancario** (*LAM*) direct debit (*BRIT*) *o* billing (*US*)
**debutar** [deβu'tar] *vi* to make one's debut
**década** ['dekaða] *nf* decade
**decadencia** [deka'ðenθja] *nf* (*estado*) decadence; (*proceso*) decline, decay
**decaído, -a** [deka'iðo, a] *adj*: **estar ~** (*abatido*) to be down
**decano, -a** [de'kano, a] *nm/f* (*de universidad etc*) dean
**decena** [de'θena] *nf*: **una ~** ten (*or so*)
**decente** [de'θente] *adj* decent
**decepción** [deθep'θjon] *nf* disappointment

> No confundir **decepción** con la palabra inglesa *deception*.

**decepcionar** [deθepθjo'nar] *vt* to disappoint
**decidir** [deθi'ðir] *vt, vi* to decide; **decidirse** *vr*: **~se a** to make up one's mind to
**décimo, -a** ['deθimo, a] *adj* tenth ▷ *nm* tenth
**decir** [de'θir] *vt* to say; (*contar*) to tell; (*hablar*) to speak ▷ *nm* saying; **decirse** *vr*: **se dice que** it is said that; **es ~** that is (to say); **~ para sí** to say to o.s.; **querer ~** to mean; **¡dígame!** (*Tel*) hello!; (*en tienda*) can I help you?
**decisión** [deθi'sjon] *nf* (*resolución*) decision; (*firmeza*) decisiveness
**decisivo, -a** [deθi'siβo, a] *adj* decisive
**declaración** [deklara'θjon] *nf* (*manifestación*) statement; (*de amor*) declaration; **declaración fiscal** *o* **de la**

**renta** income-tax return
**declarar** [dekla'rar] *vt* to declare ▷ *vi* to declare; (*Jur*) to testify; **declararse** *vr* to propose
**decoración** [dekora'θjon] *nf* decoration
**decorado** [deko'raðo] *nm* (*Cine, Teatro*) scenery, set
**decorar** [deko'rar] *vt* to decorate; **decorativo, -a** *adj* ornamental, decorative
**decreto** [de'kreto] *nm* decree
**dedal** [de'ðal] *nm* thimble
**dedicación** [deðika'θjon] *nf* dedication
**dedicar** [deði'kar] *vt* (*libro*) to dedicate; (*tiempo, dinero*) to devote; (*palabras: decir, consagrar*) to dedicate, devote; **dedicatoria** *nf* (*de libro*) dedication
**dedo** ['deðo] *nm* finger; **hacer ~** (*fam*) to hitch (a lift); **dedo anular** ring finger; **dedo corazón** middle finger; **dedo (del pie)** toe; **dedo gordo** (*de la mano*) thumb; (*del pie*) big toe; **dedo índice** index finger; **dedo meñique** little finger; **dedo pulgar** thumb
**deducción** [deðuk'θjon] *nf* deduction
**deducir** [deðu'θir] *vt* (*concluir*) to deduce, infer; (*Com*) to deduct
**defecto** [de'fekto] *nm* defect, flaw; **defectuoso, -a** *adj* defective, faulty
**defender** [defen'der] *vt* to defend; **defenderse** *vr* (*desenvolverse*) to get by
**defensa** [de'fensa] *nf* defence ▷ *nm* (*Deporte*) defender, back; **defensivo, -a** *adj* defensive; **a la defensiva** on the defensive
**defensor, a** [defen'sor, a] *adj* defending ▷ *nm/f* (*abogado defensor*) defending counsel; (*protector*) protector
**deficiencia** [defi'θjenθja] *nf* deficiency
**deficiente** [defi'θjente] *adj* (*defectuoso*) defective; **~ en** lacking *o* deficient in; **ser un ~ mental** to be mentally handicapped
**déficit** ['defiθit] (*pl* **~s**) *nm* deficit
**definición** [defini'θjon] *nf* definition
**definir** [defi'nir] *vt* (*determinar*) to determine, establish; (*decidir*) to define; (*aclarar*) to clarify; **definitivo, -a** *adj* definitive; **en definitiva** definitively; (*en resumen*) in short
**deformación** [deforma'θjon] *nf* (*alteración*) deformation; (*Radio etc*) distortion
**deformar** [defor'mar] *vt* (*gen*) to deform; **deformarse** *vr* to become deformed; **deforme** *adj* (*informe*) deformed; (*feo*) ugly; (*malhecho*) misshapen
**defraudar** [defrau'ðar] *vt* (*decepcionar*) to disappoint; (*estafar*) to defraud
**defunción** [defun'θjon] *nf* death, demise
**degenerar** [dexene'rar] *vi* to degenerate
**degradar** [dexra'ðar] *vt* to debase,

degrade; **degradarse** vr to demean o.s.

**degustación** [deɣusta'θjon] nf sampling, tasting

**dejar** [de'xar] vt to leave; (permitir) to allow, let; (abandonar) to abandon, forsake; (beneficios) to produce, yield ▷ vi: ~ **de** (parar) to stop; (no hacer) to fail to; ~ **a un lado** to leave o set aside; ~ **entrar/salir** to let in/out; ~ **pasar** to let through

**del** [del] (= **de** + **el**) ∨ **de**

**delantal** [delan'tal] nm apron

**delante** [de'lante] adv in front; (enfrente) opposite; (adelante) ahead; ~ **de** in front of, before

**delantera** [delan'tera] nf (de vestido, casa etc) front part; (Deporte) forward line; **llevar la ~ (a algn)** to be ahead (of sb)

**delantero, -a** [delan'tero, a] adj front ▷ nm (Deporte) forward, striker

**delatar** [dela'tar] vt to inform on o against, betray; **delator, a** nm/f informer

**delegación** [deleɣa'θjon] nf (acción, delegados) delegation; (Com: oficina) office, branch; **delegación de policía** (MÉX) police station

**delegado, -a** [dele'ɣaðo, a] nm/f delegate; (Com) agent

**delegar** [dele'ɣar] vt to delegate

**deletrear** [deletre'ar] vt to spell (out)

**delfín** [del'fin] nm dolphin

**delgado, -a** [del'ɣaðo, a] adj thin; (persona) slim, thin; (tela etc) light, delicate

**deliberar** [deliβe'rar] vt to debate, discuss

**delicadeza** [delika'ðeθa] nf (gen) delicacy; (refinamiento, sutileza) refinement

**delicado, -a** [deli'kaðo, a] adj (gen) delicate; (sensible) sensitive; (quisquilloso) touchy

**delicia** [de'liθja] nf delight

**delicioso, -a** [deli'θjoso, a] adj (gracioso) delightful; (exquisito) delicious

**delimitar** [delimi'tar] vt (función, responsabilidades) to define

**delincuencia** [delin'kwenθja] nf delinquency; **delincuente** nmf delinquent; (criminal) criminal

**delineante** [deline'ante] nmf draughtsman/woman

**delirante** [deli'rante] adj delirious

**delirar** [deli'rar] vi to be delirious, rave

**delirio** [de'lirjo] nm (Med) delirium; (palabras insensatas) ravings pl

**delito** [de'lito] nm (gen) crime; (infracción) offence

**delta** ['delta] nm delta

**demacrado, -a** [dema'krado, a] adj: **estar ~** to look pale and drawn, be wasted away

**demanda** [de'manda] nf (pedido, Com) demand; (petición) request; (Jur) action, lawsuit; **demandar** [deman'dar] vt (gen) to demand; (Jur) to sue, file a lawsuit against

**demás** [de'mas] adj: **los ~ niños** the other o remaining children ▷ pron: **los/las ~** the others, the rest (of them); **lo ~** the rest (of it)

**demasía** [dema'sia] nf (exceso) excess, surplus; **comer en ~** to eat to excess

**demasiado, -a** [dema'sjaðo, a] adj: ~ **vino** too much wine ▷ adv (antes de adj, adv) too; **~s libros** too many books; **¡esto es ~!** that's the limit!; **hace ~ calor** it's too hot; ~ **despacio** too slowly; **~s** too many

**demencia** [de'menθja] nf (locura) madness

**democracia** [demo'kraθja] nf democracy

**demócrata** [de'mokrata] nmf democrat; **democrático, -a** adj democratic

**demoler** [demo'ler] vt to demolish; **demolición** nf demolition

**demonio** [de'monjo] nm devil, demon; **¡~s!** hell!, damn!; **¿cómo ~s?** how the hell?

**demora** [de'mora] nf delay

**demos** ['demos] vb ∨ **damos**

**demostración** [demostra'θjon] nf (Mat) proof; (de afecto) show, display

**demostrar** [demos'trar] vt (probar) to prove; (mostrar) to show; (manifestar) to demonstrate

**den** [den] vb ∨ **dar**

**denegar** [dene'ɣar] vt (rechazar) to refuse; (Jur) to reject

**denominación** [denomina'θjon] nf (acto) naming; **Denominación de Origen** see below

● **DENOMINACIÓN DE ORIGEN**
●
● The **Denominación de Origen**,
● abbreviated to **D.O.**, is a prestigious
● classification awarded to food products
● such as wines, cheeses, sausages
● and hams which meet the stringent
● quality and production standards of the
● designated region. **D.O.** labels serve as a
● guarantee of quality.

**densidad** [densi'ðað] nf density; (fig) thickness

**denso, -a** ['denso, a] adj dense; (espeso, pastoso) thick; (fig) heavy

**dentadura** [denta'ðura] nf (set of) teeth pl; **dentadura postiza** false teeth pl

**dentera** [den'tera] nf (grima): **dar ~ a algn** to set sb's teeth on edge

**dentífrico, -a** [den'tifriko, a] adj dental ▷ nm toothpaste

**dentista** [den'tista] *nmf* dentist

**dentro** ['dentro] *adv* inside ▷ *prep:* ~ **de** in, inside, within; **por** ~ (on the) inside; **mirar por** ~ to look inside; ~ **de tres meses** within three months

**denuncia** [de'nunθja] *nf* (*delación*) denunciation; (*acusación*) accusation; (*de accidente*) report; **denunciar** *vt* to report; (*delatar*) to inform on *o* against

**departamento** [departa'mento] *nm* *sección administrativa*, department, section; (LAM: *apartamento*) flat (BRIT), apartment

**depender** [depen'der] *vi:* ~ **de** to depend on; **depende** it (all) depends

**dependienta** [depen'djenta] *nf* saleswoman, shop assistant

**dependiente** [depen'djente] *adj* dependent ▷ *nm* salesman, shop assistant

**depilar** [depi'lar] *vt* (*con cera*) to wax; (*cejas*) to pluck

**deportar** [depor'tar] *vt* to deport

**deporte** [de'porte] *nm* sport; **hacer** ~ to play sports; **deportista** *adj* sports *cpd* ▷ *nmf* sportsman/woman; **deportivo, -a** *adj* (*club, periódico*) sports *cpd* ▷ *nm* sports car

**depositar** [deposi'tar] *vt* (*dinero*) to deposit; (*mercancías*) to put away, store; **depositarse** *vr* to settle

**depósito** [de'posito] *nm* (*gen*) deposit; (*almacén*) warehouse, store; (*de agua, gasolina etc*) tank; **depósito de cadáveres** mortuary

**depredador, a** [depreða'ðor, a] *adj* predatory ▷ *nm* predator

**depresión** [depre'sjon] *nf* depression; **depresión nerviosa** nervous breakdown

**deprimido, -a** [depri'miðo, a] *adj* depressed

**deprimir** [depri'mir] *vt* to depress; **deprimirse** *vr* (*persona*) to become depressed

**deprisa** [de'prisa] *adv* quickly, hurriedly

**depurar** [depu'rar] *vt* to purify; (*purgar*) to purge

**derecha** [de'retʃa] *nf* right(-hand) side; (*Pol*) right; **a la** ~ (*estar*) on the right; (*torcer etc*) (to the) right

**derecho, -a** [de'retʃo, a] *adj* right, right-hand ▷ *nm* (*privilegio*) right; (*lado*) right(-hand) side; (*leyes*) law ▷ *adv* straight, directly; **derechos** *nmpl* (*de aduana*) duty *sg*; (*de autor*) royalties; **tener** ~ **a** to have a right to; **derechos de autor** royalties

**deriva** [de'riβa] *nf:* **ir** *o* **estar a la** ~ to drift, be adrift

**derivado** [deri'βaðo] *nm* (*Com*) by-product

**derivar** [deri'βar] *vt* to derive; (*desviar*) to

direct ▷ *vi* to derive, be derived; (*Náut*) to drift; **derivarse** *vr* to derive, be derived; to drift

**derramamiento** [derrama'mjento] *nm* (*dispersión*) spilling; **derramamiento de sangre** bloodshed

**derramar** [derra'mar] *vt* to spill; (*verter*) to pour out; (*esparcir*) to scatter; **derramarse** *vr* to pour out

**derrame** [de'rrame] *nm* (*de líquido*) spilling; (*de sangre*) shedding; (*de tubo etc*) overflow; (*pérdida*) leakage; **derrame cerebral** brain haemorrhage

**derredor** [derre'ðor] *adv:* **al** *o* **en** ~ **de** around, about

**derretir** [derre'tir] *vt* (*gen*) to melt; (*nieve*) to thaw; **derretirse** *vr* to melt

**derribar** [derri'βar] *vt* to knock down; (*construcción*) to demolish; (*persona, gobierno, político*) to bring down

**derrocar** [derro'kar] *vt* (*gobierno*) to bring down, overthrow

**derrochar** [derro'tʃar] *vt* to squander; **derroche** *nm* (*despilfarro*) waste, squandering

**derrota** [de'rrota] *nf* (*Náut*) course; (*Mil, Deporte etc*) defeat, rout; **derrotar** *vt* (*gen*) to defeat; **derrotero** *nm* (*rumbo*) course

**derrumbar** [derrum'bar] *vt* (*edificio*) to knock down; **derrumbarse** *vr* to collapse

**des** *etc vb* V **dar**

**desabrochar** [desaβro'tʃar] *vt* (*botones, broches*) to undo, unfasten; **desabrocharse** *vr* (*ropa etc*) to come undone

**desacato** [desa'kato] *nm* (*falta de respeto*) disrespect; (*Jur*) contempt

**desacertado, -a** [desaθer'taðo, a] *adj* (*equivocado*) mistaken; (*inoportuno*) unwise

**desacierto** [desa'θjerto] *nm* mistake, error

**desaconsejar** [desakonse'xar] *vt* to advise against

**desacreditar** [desakreði'tar] *vt* (*desprestigiar*) to discredit, bring into disrepute; (*denigrar*) to run down

**desacuerdo** [desa'kwerðo] *nm* disagreement, discord

**desafiar** [desa'fjar] *vt* (*retar*) to challenge; (*enfrentarse a*) to defy

**desafilado, -a** [desafi'laðo, a] *adj* blunt

**desafinado, -a** [desafi'naðo, a] *adj:* **estar** ~ to be out of tune

**desafinar** [desafi'nar] *vi* (*al cantar*) to be *o* go out of tune

**desafío** *etc* [desa'fio] *vb* V **desafiar** ▷ *nm* (*reto*) challenge; (*combate*) duel; (*resistencia*) defiance

**desafortunado, -a** [desafortu'naðo, a]

*adj (desgraciado)* unfortunate, unlucky

**desagradable** [desaɣra'ðaβle] *adj (fastidioso, enojoso)* unpleasant; *(irritante)* disagreeable

**desagradar** [desaɣra'ðar] *vi (disgustar)* to displease; *(molestar)* to bother

**desagradecido, -a** [desaɣraðe'θiðo, a] *adj* ungrateful

**desagrado** [desa'ɣraðo] *nm (disgusto)* displeasure; *(contrariedad)* dissatisfaction

**desagüe** [des'aɣwe] *nm (de un líquido)* drainage; *(cañería)* drainpipe; *(salida)* outlet, drain

**desahogar** [desao'xar] *vt (aliviar)* to ease, relieve; *(ira)* to vent; **desahogarse** *vr (relajarse)* to relax; *(desfogarse)* to let off steam

**desahogo** [desa'oxo] *nm (alivio)* relief; *(comodidad)* comfort, ease

**desahuciar** [desau'θjar] *vt (enfermo)* to give up hope for; *(inquilino)* to evict

**desairar** [desai'rar] *vt (menospreciar)* to slight, snub

**desalentador, a** [desalenta'ðor, a] *adj* discouraging

**desaliño** [desa'liɲo] *nm* slovenliness

**desalmado, -a** [desal'maðo, a] *adj (cruel)* cruel, heartless

**desalojar** [desalo'xar] *vt (expulsar, echar)* to eject; *(abandonar)* to move out of ▷ *vi* to move out

**desamor** [desa'mor] *nm (frialdad)* indifference; *(odio)* dislike

**desamparado, -a** [desampa'raðo, a] *adj (persona)* helpless; *(lugar: expuesto)* exposed; *(desierto)* deserted

**desangrar** [desaŋ'grar] *vt* to bleed; *(fig: persona)* to bleed dry; **desangrarse** *vr* to lose a lot of blood

**desanimado, -a** [desani'maðo, a] *adj (persona)* downhearted; *(espectáculo, fiesta)* dull

**desanimar** [desani'mar] *vt (desalentar)* to discourage; *(deprimir)* to depress; **desanimarse** *vr* to lose heart

**desapacible** [desapa'θiβle] *adj (gen)* unpleasant

**desaparecer** [desapare'θer] *vi (gen)* to disappear; *(el sol, el luz)* to vanish; **desaparecido, -a** *adj* missing; **desaparición** *nf* disappearance

**desapercibido, -a** [desaperθi'βiðo, a] *adj (desprevenido)* unprepared; **pasar ~** to go unnoticed

**desaprensivo, -a** [desapren'siβo, a] *adj* unscrupulous

**desaprobar** [desapro'βar] *vt (reprobar)* to disapprove of; *(condenar)* to condemn; *(no*

*consentir)* to reject

**desaprovechado, -a** [desaproβe'tʃaðo, a] *adj (oportunidad, tiempo)* wasted; *(estudiante)* slack

**desaprovechar** [desaproβe'tʃar] *vt* to waste

**desarmador** [desarma'ðor] *(Méx) nm* screwdriver

**desarmar** [desar'mar] *vt (Mil, fig)* to disarm; *(Tec)* to take apart, dismantle; **desarme** *nm* disarmament

**desarraigar** [desarrai'xar] *vt* to uproot; **desarraigo** *nm* uprooting

**desarreglar** [desarre'ɣlar] *vt (desordenar)* to disarrange; *(trastocar)* to upset, disturb

**desarrollar** [desarro'ʎar] *vt (gen)* to develop; **desarrollarse** *vr* to develop; *(ocurrir)* to take place; *(Foto)* to develop; **desarrollo** *nm* development

**desarticular** [desartiku'lar] *vt (hueso)* to dislocate; *(objeto)* to take apart; *(fig)* to break up

**desasosegar** [desasose'xar] *vt (inquietar)* to disturb, make uneasy

**desasosiego** etc [desaso'sjexo] *vb* V **desasosegar** ▷ *nm (intranquilidad)* uneasiness, restlessness; *(ansiedad)* anxiety

**desastre** [de'sastre] *nm* disaster; **desastroso, -a** *adj* disastrous

**desatar** [desa'tar] *vt (nudo)* to untie; *(paquete)* to undo; *(separar)* to detach; **desatarse** *vr (zapatos)* to come untied; *(tormenta)* to break

**desatascar** [desatas'kar] *vt (cañería)* to unblock, clear

**desatender** [desaten'der] *vt* no prestar atención a, to disregard; *(abandonar)* to neglect

**desatino** [desa'tino] *nm (idiotez)* foolishness, folly; *(error)* blunder

**desatornillar** [desatorni'ʎar] *vt* to unscrew

**desatrancar** [desatran'kar] *vt (puerta)* to unbolt; *(cañería)* to clear, unblock

**desautorizado, -a** [desautori'θaðo, a] *adj* unauthorized

**desautorizar** [desautori'θar] *vt (oficial)* to deprive of authority; *(informe)* to deny

**desayunar** [desaju'nar] *vi* to have breakfast ▷ *vt* to have for breakfast; **desayuno** *nm* breakfast

**desazón** [desa'θon] *nf* anxiety

**desbarajuste** [desβara'xuste] *nm* confusion, disorder

**desbaratar** [desβara'tar] *vt (deshacer, destruir)* to ruin

**desbloquear** [desβloke'ar] *vt (negociaciónes, tráfico)* to get going again;

*(Com: cuenta)* to unfreeze

**desbordar** [desβor'ðar] *vt (sobrepasar)* to go beyond; *(exceder)* to exceed; **desbordarse** *vr (río)* to overflow; *(entusiasmo)* to erupt

**descabellado, -a** [deskaβe'ʎaðo, a] *adj (disparatado)* wild, crazy

**descafeinado, -a** [deskafei'naðo, a] *adj* decaffeinated ▷ *nm* decaffeinated coffee

**descalabro** [deska'laβro] *nm* blow; *(desgracia)* misfortune

**descalificar** [deskalifi'kar] *vt* to disqualify; *(desacreditar)* to discredit

**descalzar** [deskal'θar] *vt (zapato)* to take off; **descalzo, -a** *adj* barefoot(ed)

**descambiar** [deskam'bjar] *vt* to exchange

**descaminado, -a** [deskami'naðo, a] *adj (equivocado)* on the wrong road; *(fig)* misguided

**descampado** [deskam'paðo] *nm* open space

**descansado, -a** [deskan'saðo, a] *adj (gen)* rested; *(que tranquiliza)* restful

**descansar** [deskan'sar] *vt (gen)* to rest ▷ *vi* to rest, have a rest; *(echarse)* to lie down

**descansillo** [deskan'siʎo] *nm (de escalera)* landing

**descanso** [des'kanso] *nm (reposo)* rest; *(alivio)* relief; *(pausa)* break; *(Deporte)* interval, half time

**descapotable** [deskapo'taβle] *nm (tb: coche ~)* convertible

**descarado, -a** [deska'raðo, a] *adj* shameless; *(insolente)* cheeky

**descarga** [des'karɣa] *nf (Arq, Elec, Mil)* discharge; *(Náut)* unloading; **descargar** [deskar'ɣar] *vt* to unload; *(golpe)* to let fly; **descargarse** *vr* to unburden o.s.; **descargarse algo de Internet** to download sth from the Internet

**descaro** [des'karo] *nm* nerve

**descarriar** [deska'rrjar] *vt (descaminar)* to misdirect; *(fig)* to lead astray; **descarriarse** *vr (perderse)* to lose one's way; *(separarse)* to stray; *(pervertirse)* to err, go astray

**descarrilamiento** [deskarrila'mjento] *nm (de tren)* derailment

**descarrilar** [deskarri'lar] *vi* to be derailed

**descartar** [deskar'tar] *vt (rechazar)* to reject; *(eliminar)* to rule out; **descartarse** *vr (Naipes)* to discard; **~se de** to shirk

**descendencia** [desθen'denθja] *nf (origen)* origin, descent; *(hijos)* offspring

**descender** [desθen'der] *vt (bajar: escalera)* to go down ▷ *vi* to descend; *(temperatura, nivel)* to fall, drop; **~ de** to be descended from

**descendiente** [desθen'djente] *nmf* descendant

**descenso** [des'θenso] *nm* descent; *(de temperatura)* drop

**descifrar** [desθi'frar] *vt* to decipher; *(mensaje)* to decode

**descolgar** [deskol'ɣar] *vt (bajar)* to take down; *(teléfono)* to pick up; **descolgarse** *vr* to let o.s. down

**descolorido, -a** [deskolo'riðo, a] *adj* faded; *(pálido)* pale

**descompasado, -a** [deskompa'saðo, a] *adj (sin proporción)* out of all proportion; *(excesivo)* excessive

**descomponer** [deskompo'ner] *vt (desordenar)* to disarrange, disturb; *(Tec)* to put out of order; *(dividir)* to break down (into parts); *(fig)* to provoke; **descomponerse** *vr (corromperse)* to rot, decompose; *(LAM Tec)* to break down

**descomposición** [deskomposi'θjon] *nf (de un objeto)* breakdown; *(de fruta etc)* decomposition; **descomposición de vientre** *(ESP)* stomach upset, diarrhoea

**descompostura** [deskompos'tura] *nf (MÉX: avería)* breakdown, fault; *(LAM: diarrea)* diarrhoea

**descomprimir** [deskompri'mir] *(Internet)* to unzip

**descompuesto, -a** [deskom'pwesto, a] *adj (corrompido)* decomposed; *(roto)* broken

**desconcertado, -a** [deskonθer'taðo, a] *adj* disconcerted, bewildered

**desconcertar** [deskonθer'tar] *vt (confundir)* to baffle; *(incomodar)* to upset, put out; **desconcertarse** *vr (turbarse)* to be upset

**desconchado, -a** [deskon'tʃaðo, a] *adj (pintura)* peeling

**desconcierto** *etc* [deskon'θjerto] *vb* V **desconcertar** ▷ *nm (gen)* disorder; *(desorientación)* uncertainty; *(inquietud)* uneasiness

**desconectar** [deskonek'tar] *vt* to disconnect

**desconfianza** [deskon'fjanθa] *nf* distrust

**desconfiar** [deskon'fjar] *vi* to be distrustful; **~ de** to distrust, suspect

**descongelar** [deskonxe'lar] *vt* to defrost; *(Com, Pol)* to unfreeze

**descongestionar** [deskonxestjo'nar] *vt (cabeza, tráfico)* to clear

**desconocer** [deskono'θer] *vt (ignorar)* not to know, be ignorant of

**desconocido, -a** [deskono'θiðo, a] *adj* unknown ▷ *nm/f* stranger

**desconocimiento** [deskonoθi'mjento]

*nm falta de conocimientos*, ignorance

**desconsiderado, -a** [deskonsiðe'raðo, a] *adj* inconsiderate; *(insensible)* thoughtless

**desconsuelo** *etc* [deskon'swelo] *vb* V **desconsolar** ▷ *nm (tristeza)* distress; *(desesperación)* despair

**descontado, -a** [deskon'taðo, a] *adj*: **dar por ~ (que)** to take (it) for granted (that)

**descontar** [deskon'tar] *vt (deducir)* to take away, deduct; *(rebajar)* to discount

**descontento, -a** [deskon'tento, a] *adj* dissatisfied ▷ *nm* dissatisfaction, discontent

**descorchar** [deskor't∫ar] *vt* to uncork

**descorrer** [desko'rrer] *vt (cortinas, cerrojo)* to draw back

**descortés** [deskor'tes] *adj (mal educado)* discourteous; *(grosero)* rude

**descoser** [desko'ser] *vt* to unstitch; **descoserse** *vr* to come apart (at the seams)

**descosido, -a** [desko'siðo, a] *adj (Costura)* unstitched

**descreído, -a** [deskre'iðo, a] *adj (incrédulo)* incredulous; *(falto de fe)* unbelieving

**descremado, -a** [deskre'maðo, a] *adj* skimmed

**describir** [deskri'βir] *vt* to describe; **descripción** [deskrip'θjon] *nf* description

**descrito** [des'krito] *pp de* **describir**

**descuartizar** [deskwarti'θar] *vt (animal)* to cut up

**descubierto, -a** [desku'βjerto, a] *pp de* **descubrir** ▷ *adj* uncovered, bare; *(persona)* bareheaded ▷ *nm (bancario)* overdraft; **al ~** in the open

**descubrimiento** [deskuβri'mjento] *nm (hallazgo)* discovery; *(revelación)* revelation

**descubrir** [desku'βrir] *vt* to discover, find; *(inaugurar)* to unveil; *(vislumbrar)* to detect; *(revelar)* to reveal, show; *(destapar)* to uncover; **descubrirse** *vr* to reveal o.s.; *(quitarse sombrero)* to take off one's hat; *(confesar)* to confess

**descuento** *etc* [des'kwento] *vb* V **descontar** ▷ *nm* discount

**descuidado, -a** [deskwi'ðaðo, a] *adj (sin cuidado)* careless; *(desordenado)* untidy; *(olvidadizo)* forgetful; *(dejado)* neglected; *(desprevenido)* unprepared

**descuidar** [deskwi'ðar] *vt (dejar)* to neglect; *(olvidar)* to overlook; **descuidarse** *vr (distraerse)* to be careless; *(abandonarse)* to let o.s. go; *(desprevenirse)* to drop one's guard; **¡descuida!** don't worry!; **descuido** *nm*

*(dejadez)* carelessness; *(olvido)* negligence

---

○ **PALABRA CLAVE**

**desde** ['desðe] *prep* **1** *(lugar)* from; **desde Burgos hasta mi casa hay 30 km** it's 30 km from Burgos to my house
**2** *(posición)*: **hablaba desde el balcón** she was speaking from the balcony
**3** *(tiempo: + adv, n)*: **desde ahora** from now on; **desde la boda** since the wedding; **desde niño** since I *etc* was a child; **desde 3 años atrás** since 3 years ago
**4** *(tiempo: + vb, fecha)* since; for; **nos conocemos desde 1992/desde hace 20 años** we've known each other since 1992/for 20 years; **no le veo desde 1997/desde hace 5 años** I haven't seen him since 1997/for 5 years
**5** *(gama)*: **desde los más lujosos hasta los más económicos** from the most luxurious to the most reasonably priced
**6**: **desde luego (que no)** of course (not)
▷ *conj*: **desde que**: **desde que recuerdo** for as long as I can remember; **desde que llegó no ha salido** he hasn't been out since he arrived

---

**desdén** [des'ðen] *nm* scorn

**desdeñar** [desðe'nar] *vt (despreciar)* to scorn

**desdicha** [des'ðit∫a] *nf (desgracia)* misfortune; *(infelicidad)* unhappiness; **desdichado, -a** *adj (sin suerte)* unlucky; *(infeliz)* unhappy

**desear** [dese'ar] *vt* to want, desire, wish for

**desechar** [dese't∫ar] *vt (basura)* to throw out o away; *(ideas)* to reject, discard; **desechos** *nmpl* rubbish *sg*, waste *sg*

**desembalar** [desemba'lar] *vt* to unpack

**desembarazar** [desembara'θar] *vt (desocupar)* to clear; *(desenredar)* to free; **desembarazarse** *vr*: **~se de** to free o.s. of, get rid of

**desembarcar** [desembar'kar] *vt (mercancías etc)* to unload ▷ *vi* to disembark

**desembocadura** [desemboka'ðura] *nf (de río)* mouth; *(de calle)* opening

**desembocar** [desembo'kar] *vi (río)* to flow into; *(fig)* to result in

**desembolso** [desem'bolso] *nm* payment

**desembrollar** [desembro'λar] *vt (madeja)* to unravel; *(asunto, malentendido)* to sort out

**desemejanza** [deseme'xanθa] *nf* dissimilarity

**desempaquetar** [desempake'tar] *vt (regalo)* to unwrap; *(mercancía)* to unpack

**desempate** [desem'pate] nm (Fútbol) replay, play-off; (Tenis) tie-break(er)

**desempeñar** [desempe'ɲar] vt (cargo) to hold; (papel) to perform; (lo empeñado) to redeem; **~ un papel** (fig) to play (a role)

**desempleado, -a** [desemple'aðo, a] nm/f unemployed person; **desempleo** nm unemployment

**desencadenar** [desenkaðe'nar] vt to unchain; (ira) to unleash; **desencadenarse** vr to break loose; (tormenta) to burst; (guerra) to break out

**desencajar** [desenka'xar] vt (hueso) to dislocate; (mecanismo, pieza) to disconnect, disengage

**desencanto** [desen'kanto] nm disillusionment

**desenchufar** [desentʃu'far] vt to unplug

**desenfadado, -a** [desenfa'ðaðo, a] adj (desenvuelto) uninhibited; (descarado) forward; **desenfado** nm (libertad) freedom; (comportamiento) free and easy manner; (descaro) forwardness

**desenfocado, -a** [desenfo'kaðo, a] adj (Foto) out of focus

**desenfreno** [desen'freno] nm wildness; (de las pasiones) lack of self-control

**desenganchar** [desengan'tʃar] vt (gen) to unhook; (Ferro) to uncouple

**desengañar** [desenga'ɲar] vt to disillusion; **desengañarse** vr to become disillusioned; **desengaño** nm disillusionment; (decepción) disappointment

**desenlace** [desen'laθe] nm outcome

**desenmascarar** [desenmaska'rar] vt to unmask

**desenredar** [desenre'ðar] vt (pelo) to untangle; (problema) to sort out

**desenroscar** [desenros'kar] vt to unscrew

**desentenderse** [desenten'derse] vr: **~ de** to pretend not to know about; (apartarse) to have nothing to do with

**desenterrar** [desente'rrar] vt to exhume; (tesoro, fig) to unearth, dig up

**desentonar** [desento'nar] vi (Mús) to sing (o play) out of tune; (color) to clash

**desentrañar** [desentra'ɲar] vt (misterio) to unravel

**desenvoltura** [desenβol'tura] nf ease

**desenvolver** [desenβol'βer] vt (paquete) to unwrap; (fig) to develop; **desenvolverse** vr (desarrollarse) to unfold, develop; (arreglárselas) to cope

**deseo** [de'seo] nm desire, wish; **deseoso, -a** adj: **estar deseoso de** to be anxious to

**desequilibrado, -a** [desekili'βraðo, a] adj unbalanced

**desertar** [deser'tar] vi to desert

**desértico, -a** [de'sertiko, a] adj desert cpd

**desesperación** [desespera'θjon] nf (impaciencia) desperation, despair; (irritación) fury

**desesperar** [desespe'rar] vt to drive to despair; (exasperar) to drive to distraction ▷ vi: **~ de** to despair of; **desesperarse** vr to despair, lose hope

**desestabilizar** [desestaβili'θar] vt to destabilize

**desestimar** [desesti'mar] vt (menospreciar) to have a low opinion of; (rechazar) to reject

**desfachatez** [desfatʃa'teθ] nf (insolencia) impudence; (descaro) rudeness

**desfalco** [des'falko] nm embezzlement

**desfallecer** [desfaʎe'θer] vi (perder las fuerzas) to become weak; (desvanecerse) to faint

**desfasado, -a** [desfa'saðo, a] adj (anticuado) old-fashioned; **desfase** nm (diferencia) gap

**desfavorable** [desfaβo'raβle] adj unfavourable

**desfigurar** [desfixu'rar] vt (cara) to disfigure; (cuerpo) to deform

**desfiladero** [desfila'ðero] nm gorge

**desfilar** [desfi'lar] vi to parade; **desfile** nm procession; **desfile de modelos** fashion show

**desgana** [des'xana] nf (falta de apetito) loss of appetite; (apatía) unwillingness; **desganado, -a** adj: **estar desganado** (sin apetito) to have no appetite; (sin entusiasmo) to have lost interest

**desgarrar** [desxa'rrar] vt to tear (up); (fig) to shatter; **desgarro** nm (en tela) tear; (aflicción) grief

**desgastar** [desxas'tar] vt (deteriorar) to wear away o down; (estropear) to spoil; **desgastarse** vr to get worn out; **desgaste** nm wear (and tear)

**desglosar** [desxlo'sar] vt (factura) to break down

**desgracia** [des'xraθja] nf misfortune; (accidente) accident; (vergüenza) disgrace; (contratiempo) setback; **por ~** unfortunately; **desgraciado, -a** [desxra'θjaðo, a] adj (sin suerte) unlucky, unfortunate; (miserable) wretched; (infeliz) miserable

**desgravar** [desxra'βar] vt (impuestos) to reduce the tax o duty on

**desguace** [des'xwaθe] (ESP) nm junkyard

**deshabitado, -a** [desaβi'taðo, a] adj uninhabited

**deshacer** [desa'θer] vt (casa) to break up; (Tec) to take apart; (enemigo) to defeat; (diluir) to melt; (contrato) to break; (intriga) to solve; **deshacerse** vr (disolverse) to melt; (despedazarse) to come apart o undone; **~se de** to get rid of; **~se en lágrimas** to burst into tears

**deshecho, -a** [des'etʃo, a] adj undone; (roto) smashed; (persona): **estar ~** to be shattered

**desheredar** [desere'ðar] vt to disinherit

**deshidratar** [desiðra'tar] vt to dehydrate

**deshielo** [des'jelo] nm thaw

**deshonesto, -a** [deso'nesto, a] adj indecent

**deshonra** [des'onra] nf (deshonor) dishonour; (vergüenza) shame

**deshora** [des'ora]: **a ~** adv at the wrong time

**deshuesadero** [deswesa'ðero] (MÉX) nm junkyard

**deshuesar** [deswe'sar] vt (carne) to bone; (fruta) to stone

**desierto, -a** [de'sjerto, a] adj (casa, calle, negocio) deserted ▷ nm desert

**designar** [desix'nar] vt (nombrar) to designate; (indicar) to fix

**desigual** [desi'ɣwal] adj (terreno) uneven; (lucha etc) unequal

**desilusión** [desilu'sjon] nf disillusionment; (decepción) disappointment; **desilusionar** vt to disillusion; to disappoint; **desilusionarse** vr to become disillusioned

**desinfectar** [desinfek'tar] vt to disinfect

**desinflar** [desin'flar] vt to deflate

**desintegración** [desinteɣra'θjon] nf disintegration

**desinterés** [desinte'res] nm (desgana) lack of interest; (altruismo) unselfishness

**desintoxicarse** [desintoksi'karse] vr (drogadicto) to undergo detoxification

**desistir** [desis'tir] vi (renunciar) to stop, desist

**desleal** [desle'al] adj (infiel) disloyal; (Com: competencia) unfair; **deslealtad** nf disloyalty

**desligar** [desli'ɣar] vt (desatar) to untie, undo; (separar) to separate; **desligarse** vr (de un compromiso) to extricate o.s.

**desliz** [des'liθ] nm (fig) lapse; **deslizar** vt to slip, slide

**deslumbrar** [deslum'brar] vt to dazzle

**desmadrarse** [desma'ðrarse] (fam) vr (descontrolarse) to run wild; (divertirse) to let one's hair down; **desmadre** (fam) nm (desorganización) chaos; (jaleo) commotion

**desmán** [des'man] nm (exceso) outrage; (abuso de poder) abuse

**desmantelar** [desmante'lar] vt (deshacer) to dismantle; (casa) to strip

**desmaquillador** [desmakiʎa'ðor] nm make-up remover

**desmayar** [desma'jar] vi to lose heart; **desmayarse** vr (Med) to faint; **desmayo** nm (Med: acto) faint; (: estado) unconsciousness

**desmemoriado, -a** [desmemo'rjaðo, a] adj forgetful

**desmentir** [desmen'tir] vt (contradecir) to contradict; (refutar) to deny

**desmenuzar** [desmenu'θar] vt (deshacer) to crumble; (carne) to chop; (examinar) to examine closely

**desmesurado, -a** [desmesu'raðo, a] adj disproportionate

**desmontable** [desmon'taβle] adj (que se quita: pieza) detachable; (plegable) collapsible, folding

**desmontar** [desmon'tar] vt (deshacer) to dismantle; (tierra) to level ▷ vi to dismount

**desmoralizar** [desmorali'θar] vt to demoralize

**desmoronar** [desmoro'nar] vt to wear away, erode; **desmoronarse** vr (edificio, dique) to collapse; (economía) to decline

**desnatado, -a** [desna'taðo, a] adj skimmed

**desnivel** [desni'βel] nm (de terreno) unevenness

**desnudar** [desnu'ðar] vt (desvestir) to undress; (despojar) to strip; **desnudarse** vr (desvestirse) to get undressed; **desnudo, -a** adj naked ▷ nm/f nude; **desnudo de** devoid o bereft of

**desnutrición** [desnutri'θjon] nf malnutrition; **desnutrido, -a** adj undernourished

**desobedecer** [desoβeðe'θer] vt, vi to disobey; **desobediencia** nf disobedience

**desocupado, -a** [desoku'paðo, a] adj at leisure; (desempleado) unemployed; (deshabitado) empty, vacant

**desodorante** [desoðo'rante] nm deodorant

**desolación** [desola'θjon] nf (de lugar) desolation; (fig) grief

**desolar** [deso'lar] vt to ruin, lay waste

**desorbitado, -a** [desorβi'taðo, a] adj (excesivo: ambición) boundless; (deseos) excessive; (: precio) exorbitant

**desorden** [des'orðen] nm confusion; (político) disorder, unrest

**desorganización** [desorɣaniθa'θjon] nf (de persona) disorganization; (en empresa, oficina) disorder, chaos

**desorientar** [desorjen'tar] vt (extraviar) to mislead; (confundir, desconcertar) to confuse; **desorientarse** vr (perderse) to lose one's way

**despabilado, -a** [despaβi'laðo, a] adj (despierto) wide-awake; (fig) alert, sharp

**despachar** [despa'tʃar] vt (negocio) to do, complete; (enviar) to send, dispatch; (vender) to sell, deal in; (billete) to issue; (mandar ir) to send away

**despacho** [des'patʃo] nm (oficina) office; (de paquetes) dispatch; (venta) sale; (comunicación) message

**despacio** [des'paθjo] adv slowly

**desparpajo** [despar'paxo] nm self-confidence; (pey) nerve

**desparramar** [desparra'mar] vt (esparcir) to scatter; (líquido) to spill

**despecho** [des'petʃo] nm spite

**despectivo, -a** [despek'tiβo, a] adj (despreciativo) derogatory; (Ling) pejorative

**despedida** [despe'ðiða] nf (adiós) farewell; (de obrero) sacking

**despedir** [despe'ðir] vt (visita) to see off, show out; (empleado) to dismiss; (inquilino) to evict; (objeto) to hurl; (olor etc) to give out o off; **despedirse** vr: ~**se de** to say goodbye to

**despegar** [despe'ɣar] vt to unstick ▷vi (avión) to take off; **despegarse** vr to come loose, come unstuck; **despego** nm detachment

**despegue** etc [des'peɣe] vb V **despegar** ▷nm takeoff

**despeinado, -a** [despei'naðo, a] adj dishevelled, unkempt

**despejado, -a** [despe'xaðo, a] adj (lugar) clear, free; (cielo) clear; (persona) wide-awake, bright

**despejar** [despe'xar] vt (gen) to clear; (misterio) to clear up ▷vi (el tiempo) to clear; **despejarse** vr (tiempo, cielo) to clear (up); (misterio) to become clearer; (cabeza) to clear

**despensa** [des'pensa] nf larder

**despeñarse** [despe'ɲarse] vr to hurl o.s. down; (coche) to tumble over

**desperdicio** [desper'ðiθjo] nm (despilfarro) squandering; **desperdicios** nmpl (basura) rubbish sg (BRIT), garbage sg (US); (residuos) waste sg

**desperezarse** [despere'θarse] vr to stretch

**desperfecto** [desper'fekto] nm (deterioro) slight damage; (defecto) flaw, imperfection

**despertador** [desperta'ðor] nm alarm clock

**despertar** [desper'tar] nm awakening ▷vt (persona) to wake up; (recuerdos) to revive; (sentimiento) to arouse ▷vi to awaken, wake up; **despertarse** vr to awaken, wake up

**despido** etc [des'piðo] vb V **despedir** ▷nm dismissal, sacking

**despierto, -a** etc [des'pjerto, a] vb V **despertar** ▷adj awake; (fig) sharp, alert

**despilfarro** [despil'farro] nm (derroche) squandering; (lujo desmedido) extravagance

**despistar** [despis'tar] vt to throw off the track o scent; (confundir) to mislead, confuse; **despistarse** vr to take the wrong road; (confundirse) to become confused

**despiste** [des'piste] nm absent-mindedness; **un ~** a mistake o slip

**desplazamiento** [desplaθa'mjento] nm displacement

**desplazar** [despla'θar] vt to move; (Náut) to displace; (Inform) to scroll; (fig) to oust; **desplazarse** vr (persona) to travel

**desplegar** [desple'ɣar] vt (tela, papel) to unfold, open out; (bandera) to unfurl; **despliegue** etc [des'pleɣe] vb V **desplegar** ▷nm display

**desplomarse** [desplo'marse] vr (edificio, gobierno, persona) to collapse

**desplumar** [desplu'mar] vt (ave) to pluck; (fam: estafar) to fleece

**despoblado, -a** [despo'βlaðo, a] adj (sin habitantes) uninhabited

**despojar** [despo'xar] vt (alguien: de sus bienes) to divest of, deprive of; (casa) to strip, leave bare; (alguien: de su cargo) to strip of

**despojo** [des'poxo] nm (acto) plundering; (objetos) plunder, loot; **despojos** nmpl (de ave, res) offal sg

**desposado, -a** [despo'saðo, a] adj, nm/f newly-wed

**despreciar** [despre'θjar] vt (desdeñar) to despise, scorn; (afrentar) to slight; **desprecio** nm scorn, contempt; slight

**desprender** [despren'der] vt (broche) to unfasten; (olor) to give off; **desprenderse** vr (botón: caerse) to fall off; (broche) to come unfastened; (olor, perfume) to be given off; ~**se de algo que ...** to draw from sth that ...

**desprendimiento** [desprendi'mjento] nm (gen) loosening; (generosidad) disinterestedness; (de tierra, rocas) landslide; **desprendimiento de retina** detachment of the retina

**despreocupado, -a** [despreoku'paðo, a] adj (sin preocupación) unworried, nonchalant; (negligente) careless

**despreocuparse** [despreoku'parse] vr not to worry; ~ **de** to have no interest in

**desprestigiar** [despresti'xjar] vt (criticar) to run down; (desacreditar) to discredit

**desprevenido, -a** [despreβe'niðo, a] *adj*
(*no preparado*) unprepared, unready

**desproporcionado, -a**
[desproporθjo'naðo, a] *adj*
disproportionate, out of proportion

**desprovisto, -a** [despro'βisto, a] *adj*: ~
**de** devoid of

**después** [des'pwes] *adv* afterwards,
later; (*próximo paso*) next; ~ **de comer** after
lunch; **un año** ~ a year later; ~ **se debatió el
tema** next the matter was discussed; ~ **de
corregido el texto** after the text had been
corrected; ~ **de todo** after all

**desquiciado, -a** [deski'θjaðo, a] *adj*
deranged

**destacar** [desta'kar] *vt* to emphasize,
point up; (*Mil*) to detach, detail ▷ *vi*
(*resaltarse*) to stand out; (*persona*) to be
outstanding o exceptional; **destacarse**
*vr* to stand out; to be outstanding o
exceptional

**destajo** [des'taxo] *nm*: **trabajar a** ~ to do
piecework

**destapar** [desta'par] *vt* (*botella*) to open;
(*cacerola*) to take the lid off; (*descubrir*) to
uncover; **destaparse** *vr* (*revelarse*) to reveal
one's true character

**destartalado, -a** [destarta'laðo, a] *adj*
(*desordenado*) untidy; (*ruinoso*) tumbledown

**destello** [des'teʎo] *nm* (*de estrella*) twinkle;
(*de faro*) signal light

**destemplado, -a** [destem'plaðo, a] *adj*
(*Mús*) out of tune; (*voz*) harsh; (*Med*) out of
sorts; (*tiempo*) unpleasant, nasty

**desteñir** [deste'ɲir] *vt* to fade ▷ *vi* to
fade; **desteñirse** *vr* to fade; **esta tela no
destiñe** this fabric will not run

**desternillarse** [desterni'ʎarse] *vr*: ~ **de
risa** to split one's sides laughing

**desterrar** [deste'rrar] *vt* (*exiliar*) to exile;
(*fig*) to banish, dismiss

**destiempo** [des'tjempo]: **a** ~ *adv* out of
turn

**destierro** *etc* [des'tjerro] *vb* V **desterrar**
▷ *nm* exile

**destilar** [desti'lar] *vt* to distil; **destilería**
*nf* distillery

**destinar** [desti'nar] *vt* (*funcionario*) to
appoint, assign; (*fondos*) ~ **(a)** to set aside
(for)

**destinatario, -a** [destina'tarjo, a] *nm/f*
addressee

**destino** [des'tino] *nm* (*suerte*) destiny; (*de
avión, viajero*) destination; **con ~ a Londres**
(*barco*) (bound) for London; (*avión, carta*) to
London

**destituir** [destitu'ir] *vt* to dismiss

**destornillador** [destorniʎa'ðor] *nm*
screwdriver

**destornillar** [destorni'ʎar] *vt* (*tornillo*) to
unscrew; **destornillarse** *vr* to unscrew

**destreza** [des'treθa] *nf* (*habilidad*) skill;
(*maña*) dexterity

**destrozar** [destro'θar] *vt* (*romper*) to
smash, break (up); (*estropear*) to ruin;
(*nervios*) to shatter

**destrozo** [des'troθo] *nm* (*acción*)
destruction; (*desastre*) smashing; **destrozos**
*nmpl* (*pedazos*) pieces; (*daños*) havoc *sg*

**destrucción** [destruk'θjon] *nf*
destruction

**destruir** [destru'ir] *vt* to destroy

**desuso** [des'uso] *nm* disuse; **caer en** ~ to
become obsolete

**desvalijar** [desvali'xar] *vt* (*persona*) to rob;
(*casa, tienda*) to burgle; (*coche*) to break into

**desván** [des'βan] *nm* attic

**desvanecer** [desβane'θer] *vt* (*disipar*) to
dispel; (*borrar*) to blur; **desvanecerse** *vr*
(*humo etc*) to vanish, disappear; (*color*) to
fade; (*recuerdo, sonido*) to fade away; (*Med*) to
pass out; (*duda*) to be dispelled

**desvariar** [desβa'rjar] *vt* (*enfermo*) to be
delirious

**desvelar** [desβe'lar] *vt* to keep awake;
**desvelarse** *vr* (*no poder dormir*) to stay
awake; (*preocuparse*) to be vigilant o
watchful

**desventaja** [desβen'taxa] *nf*
disadvantage

**desvergonzado, -a** [desβerɣon'θaðo, a]
*adj* shameless

**desvestir** [desβes'tir] *vt* to undress;
**desvestirse** *vr* to undress

**desviación** [desβja'θjon] *nf* deviation;
(*Auto*) diversion, detour

**desviar** [des'βjar] *vt* to turn aside; (*río*)
to alter the course of; (*navío*) to divert, re-
route; (*conversación*) to sidetrack; **desviarse**
*vr* (*apartarse del camino*) to turn aside;
(: *barco*) to go off course

**desvío** *etc* [des'βio] *vb* V **desviar**
▷ *nm* (*desviación*) detour, diversion; (*fig*)
indifference

**desvivirse** [desβi'βirse] *vr*: ~ **por** (*anhelar*)
to long for, crave for; (*hacer lo posible por*) to
do one's utmost for

**detallar** [deta'ʎar] *vt* to detail

**detalle** [de'taʎe] *nm* detail; (*gesto*) gesture,
token; **al** ~ in detail; (*Com*) retail

**detallista** [deta'ʎista] *nmf* (*Com*) retailer

**detective** [detek'tiβe] *nmf* detective;
**detective privado** private detective

**detener** [dete'ner] *vt* (*gen*) to stop; (*Jur*)
to arrest; (*objeto*) to keep; **detenerse** *vr*
to stop; (*demorarse*): ~**se en** to delay over,

linger over

**detenidamente** [deteniða'mente] adv (minuciosamente) carefully; (extensamente) at great length

**detenido, -a** [dete'niðo, a] adj (arrestado) under arrest ▷ nm/f person under arrest, prisoner

**detenimiento** [deteni'mjento] nm: **con ~** thoroughly; (observar, considerar) carefully

**detergente** [deter'xente] nm detergent

**deteriorar** [deterjo'rar] vt to spoil, damage; **deteriorarse** vr to deteriorate; **deterioro** nm deterioration

**determinación** [determina'θjon] nf (empeño) determination; (decisión) decision; **determinado, -a** adj specific

**determinar** [determi'nar] vt (plazo) to fix; (precio) to settle; **determinarse** vr to decide

**detestar** [detes'tar] vt to detest

**detractor, a** [detrak'tor, a] nm/f slanderer, libeller

**detrás** [de'tras] adv (tb: **por ~**) behind; (atrás) at the back; **~ de** behind

**detrimento** [detri'mento] nm: **en ~ de** to the detriment of

**deuda** ['deuða] nf debt; **deuda exterior/ pública** foreign/national debt

**devaluación** [deßalwa'θjon] nf devaluation

**devastar** [deßas'tar] vt (destruir) to devastate

**deveras** [de'ßeras] (MÉX) nf inv: **un amigo de (a) ~** a true o real friend

**devoción** [deßo'θjon] nf devotion

**devolución** [deßolu'θjon] nf (reenvío) return, sending back; (reembolso) repayment; (Jur) devolution

**devolver** [deßol'ßer] vt to return; (lo extraviado, lo prestado) to give back; (carta al correo) to send back; (Com) to repay, refund ▷ vi (vomitar) to be sick

**devorar** [deßo'rar] vt to devour

**devoto, -a** [de'ßoto, a] adj devout ▷ nm/f admirer

**devuelto** pp de **devolver**

**devuelva** etc vb V **devolver**

**di** etc vb V **dar**; **decir**

**día** ['dia] nm day; **¿qué ~ es?** what's the date?; **estar/poner al ~** to be/keep up to date; **el ~ de hoy/de mañana** today/tomorrow; **al ~ siguiente** (on) the following day; **vivir al ~** to live from hand to mouth; **de ~** by day, in daylight; **en pleno ~** in full daylight; **Día de la Independencia** Independence Day; **Día de los Muertos** (MÉX) All Souls' Day; **Día de Reyes** Epiphany; **día feriado** (LAM) holiday; **día festivo** (ESP)

holiday; **día lectivo** teaching day; **día libre** day off

**diabetes** [dja'ßetes] nf diabetes

**diablo** ['djaßlo] nm devil; **diablura** nf prank

**diadema** [dja'ðema] nf tiara

**diafragma** [dja'fraɣma] nm diaphragm

**diagnóstico** [djaɣ'nostiko] nm = **diagnosis**

**diagonal** [djaɣo'nal] adj diagonal

**diagrama** [dja'ɣrama] nm diagram

**dial** [djal] nm dial

**dialecto** [dja'lekto] nm dialect

**dialogar** [djalo'ɣar] vi: **~ con** (Pol) to hold talks with

**diálogo** ['djaloɣo] nm dialogue

**diamante** [dja'mante] nm diamond

**diana** ['djana] nf (Mil) reveille; (de blanco) centre, bull's-eye

**diapositiva** [djaposi'tißa] nf (Foto) slide, transparency

**diario, -a** ['djarjo, a] adj daily ▷ nm newspaper; **a ~** daily; **de ~** everyday

**diarrea** [dja'rrea] nf diarrhoea

**dibujar** [dißu'xar] vt to draw, sketch; **dibujo** nm drawing; **dibujos animados** cartoons

**diccionario** [dikθjo'narjo] nm dictionary

**dice** etc vb V **decir**

**dicho, -a** ['ditʃo, a] pp de **decir** ▷ adj: **en ~s países** in the aforementioned countries ▷ nm saying

**dichoso, -a** [di'tʃoso, a] adj happy

**diciembre** [di'θjembre] nm December

**dictado** [dik'taðo] nm dictation

**dictador** [dikta'ðor] nm dictator; **dictadura** nf dictatorship

**dictar** [dik'tar] vt (carta) to dictate; (Jur: sentencia) to pronounce; (decreto) to issue; (LAM: clase) to give

**didáctico, -a** [di'ðaktiko, a] adj educational

**diecinueve** [djeθi'nweße] num nineteen

**dieciocho** [djeθi'otʃo] num eighteen

**dieciséis** [djeθi'seis] num sixteen

**diecisiete** [djeθi'sjete] num seventeen

**diente** ['djente] nm (Anat, Tec) tooth; (Zool) fang; (: de elefante) tusk; (de ajo) clove

**diera** etc vb V **dar**

**diesel** ['disel] adj: **motor ~** diesel engine

**diestro, -a** ['djestro, a] adj (derecho) right; (hábil) skilful

**dieta** ['djeta] nf diet; **estar a ~** to be on a diet

**diez** [djeθ] num ten

**diferencia** [dife'renθja] nf difference; **a ~ de** unlike; **diferenciar** vt to differentiate between ▷ vi to differ; **diferenciarse**

*vr* to differ, be different; (*distinguirse*) to distinguish o.s.

**diferente** [dife'rente] *adj* different

**diferido** [dife'riðo] *nm*: **en ~** (*TV etc*) recorded

**difícil** [di'fiθil] *adj* difficult

**dificultad** [difikul'tað] *nf* difficulty; (*problema*) trouble

**dificultar** [difikul'tar] *vt* (*complicar*) to complicate, make difficult; (*estorbar*) to obstruct

**difundir** [difun'dir] *vt* (*calor, luz*) to diffuse; (*Radio, TV*) to broadcast; **~ una noticia** to spread a piece of news; **difundirse** *vr* to spread (out)

**difunto, -a** [di'funto, a] *adj* dead, deceased ▷ *nm/f* deceased (person)

**difusión** [difu'sjon] *nf* (*Radio, TV*) broadcasting

**diga** *etc vb* V **decir**

**digerir** [dixe'rir] *vt* to digest; (*fig*) to absorb; **digestión** *nf* digestion; **digestivo, -a** *adj* digestive

**digital** [dixi'tal] *adj* digital

**dignarse** [diɣ'narse] *vr* to deign to

**dignidad** [diɣni'ðað] *nf* dignity

**digno, -a** ['diɣno, a] *adj* worthy

**digo** *etc vb* V **decir**

**dije** *etc vb* V **decir**

**dilatar** [dila'tar] *vt* (*cuerpo*) to dilate; (*prolongar*) to prolong

**dilema** [di'lema] *nm* dilemma

**diluir** [dilu'ir] *vt* to dilute

**diluvio** [di'luβjo] *nm* deluge, flood

**dimensión** [dimen'sjon] *nf* dimension

**diminuto, -a** [dimi'nuto, a] *adj* tiny, diminutive

**dimitir** [dimi'tir] *vi* to resign

**dimos** *vb* V **dar**

**Dinamarca** [dina'marka] *nf* Denmark

**dinámico, -a** [di'namiko, a] *adj* dynamic

**dinamita** [dina'mita] *nf* dynamite

**dínamo** ['dinamo] *nf* dynamo

**dineral** [dine'ral] *nm* large sum of money, fortune

**dinero** [di'nero] *nm* money; **dinero en efectivo** o **metálico** cash; **dinero suelto** (loose) change

**dio** *vb* V **dar**

**dios** [djos] *nm* god; **¡D~ mío!** (oh,) my God!; **¡por D~!** for heaven's sake!; **diosa** ['djosa] *nf* goddess

**diploma** [di'ploma] *nm* diploma

**diplomacia** [diplo'maθja] *nf* diplomacy; (*fig*) tact

**diplomado, -a** [diplo'maðo, a] *adj* qualified

**diplomático, -a** [diplo'matiko, a] *adj* diplomatic ▷ *nm/f* diplomat

**diputación** [diputa'θjon] *nf* (*tb*: **~ provincial**) ≈ county council

**diputado, -a** [dipu'taðo, a] *nm/f* delegate; (*Pol*) ≈ member of parliament (*BRIT*) ≈ representative (*US*)

**dique** ['dike] *nm* dyke

**diré** *etc vb* V **decir**

**dirección** [direk'θjon] *nf* direction; (*señas*) address; (*Auto*) steering; (*gerencia*) management; (*Pol*) leadership; **dirección única/prohibida** one-way street/no entry

**direccional** [direkθjo'nal] (*MÉX*) *nf* (*Auto*) indicator

**directa** [di'rekta] *nf* (*Auto*) top gear

**directiva** [direk'tiβa] *nf* (*tb*: **junta ~**) board of directors

**directo, -a** [di'rekto, a] *adj* direct; (*Radio, TV*) live; **transmitir en ~** to broadcast live

**director, a** [direk'tor, a] *adj* leading ▷ *nm/f* director; (*Escol*) head(teacher) (*BRIT*), principal (*US*); (*gerente*) manager/ ess; (*Prensa*) editor; **director de cine** film director; **director general** managing director

**directorio** [direk'torjo] (*MÉX*) *nm* (*telefónico*) phone book

**dirigente** [diri'xente] *nmf* (*Pol*) leader

**dirigir** [diri'xir] *vt* to direct; (*carta*) to address; (*obra de teatro, film*) to direct; (*Mús*) to conduct; (*negocio*) to manage; **dirigirse** *vr*: **~se a** to go towards, make one's way towards; (*hablar con*) to speak to

**dirija** *etc vb* V **dirigir**

**disciplina** [disθi'plina] *nf* discipline

**discípulo, -a** [dis'θipulo, a] *nm/f* disciple

**Discman®** ['diskman] *nm* Discman®

**disco** ['disko] *nm* disc; (*Deporte*) discus; (*Tel*) dial; (*Auto: semáforo*) light; (*Mús*) record; **disco compacto/de larga duración** compact disc/long-playing record; **disco de freno** brake disc; **disco flexible/duro** o **rígido** (*Inform*) floppy/hard disk

**disconforme** [diskon'forme] *adj* differing; **estar ~ (con)** to be in disagreement (with)

**discordia** [dis'korðja] *nf* discord

**discoteca** [disko'teka] *nf* disco(theque)

**discreción** [diskre'θjon] *nf* discretion; (*reserva*) prudence; **comer a ~** to eat as much as one wishes

**discreto, -a** [dis'kreto, a] *adj* discreet

**discriminación** [diskrimina'θjon] *nf* discrimination

**disculpa** [dis'kulpa] *nf* excuse; (*pedir perdón*) apology; **pedir ~s a/por** to apologize to/for; **disculpar** *vt* to excuse, pardon; **disculparse** *vr* to excuse o.s.; to apologize

**discurso** [disˈkurso] nm speech

**discusión** [diskuˈsjon] nf (diálogo) discussion; (riña) argument

**discutir** [diskuˈtir] vt (debatir) to discuss; (pelear) to argue about; (contradecir) to argue against ▷ vi (debatir) to discuss; (pelearse) to argue

**disecar** [diseˈkar] vt (conservar: animal) to stuff; (: planta) to dry

**diseñar** [diseˈɲar] vt, vi to design

**diseño** [diˈseɲo] nm design

**disfraz** [disˈfraθ] nm (máscara) disguise; (excusa) pretext; **disfrazar** vt to disguise; **disfrazarse** vr: **disfrazarse de** to disguise o.s. as

**disfrutar** [disfruˈtar] vt to enjoy ▷ vi to enjoy o.s.; **~ de** to enjoy, possess

**disgustar** [disɣusˈtar] vt (no gustar) to displease; (contrariar, enojar) to annoy, upset; **disgustarse** vr (enfadarse) to get upset; (dos personas) to fall out

No confundir **disgustar** con la palabra inglesa disgust.

**disgusto** [disˈɣusto] nm (contrariedad) annoyance; (tristeza) grief; (riña) quarrel

**disimular** [disimuˈlar] vt (ocultar) to hide, conceal ▷ vi to dissemble

**dislocarse** [disloˈkarse] vr (articulación) to sprain, dislocate

**disminución** [disminuˈθjon] nf decrease, reduction

**disminuido, -a** [disminuˈiðo, a] nm/f: **~ mental/físico** mentally/physically handicapped person

**disminuir** [disminuˈir] vt to decrease, diminish

**disolver** [disolˈβer] vt (gen) to dissolve; **disolverse** vr to dissolve; (Com) to go into liquidation

**dispar** [disˈpar] adj different

**disparar** [dispaˈrar] vt, vi to shoot, fire

**disparate** [dispaˈrate] nm (tontería) foolish remark; (error) blunder; **decir ~s** to talk nonsense

**disparo** [disˈparo] nm shot

**dispersar** [disperˈsar] vt to disperse; **dispersarse** vr to scatter

**disponer** [dispoˈner] vt (arreglar) to arrange; (ordenar) to put in order; (preparar) to prepare, get ready ▷ vi: **~ de** to have, own; **disponerse** vr: **~se a o para hacer** to prepare to do

**disponible** [dispoˈniβle] adj available

**disposición** [disposiˈθjon] nf arrangement, disposition; (voluntad) willingness; (Inform) layout; **a su ~** at your service

**dispositivo** [disposiˈtiβo] nm device, mechanism

**dispuesto, -a** [disˈpwesto, a] pp de **disponer** ▷ adj (arreglado) arranged; (preparado) disposed

**disputar** [dispuˈtar] vt (carrera) to compete in

**disquete** [disˈkete] nm floppy disk, diskette

**distancia** [disˈtanθja] nf distance; **distanciar** [distanˈθjar] vt to space out; **distanciarse** vr to become estranged; **distante** [disˈtante] adj distant

**diste** vb V **dar**

**disteis** vb V **dar**

**distinción** [distinˈθjon] nf distinction; (elegancia) elegance; (honor) honour

**distinguido, -a** [distinˈɡiðo, a] adj distinguished

**distinguir** [distinˈɡir] vt to distinguish; (escoger) to single out; **distinguirse** vr to be distinguished

**distintivo** [distinˈtiβo] nm badge; (fig) characteristic

**distinto, -a** [disˈtinto, a] adj different; (claro) clear

**distracción** [distrakˈθjon] nf distraction; (pasatiempo) hobby, pastime; (olvido) absent-mindedness, distraction

**distraer** [distraˈer] vt (atención) to distract; (divertir) to amuse; (fondos) to embezzle; **distraerse** vr (entretenerse) to amuse o.s.; (perder la concentración) to allow one's attention to wander

**distraído, -a** [distraˈiðo, a] adj (gen) absent-minded; (entretenido) amusing

**distribuidor, a** [distriβuiˈðor, a] nm/f distributor; **distribuidora** nf (Com) dealer, agent; (Cine) distributor

**distribuir** [distriβuˈir] vt to distribute

**distrito** [disˈtrito] nm (sector, territorio) region; (barrio) district; **Distrito Federal** (MÉX) Federal District; **distrito postal** postal district

**disturbio** [disˈturβjo] nm disturbance; (desorden) riot

**disuadir** [diswaˈðir] vt to dissuade

**disuelto** [diˈswelto] pp de **disolver**

**DIU** nm abr (= dispositivo intrauterino) IUD

**diurno, -a** [ˈdjurno, a] adj day cpd

**divagar** [diβaˈɣar] vi (desviarse) to digress

**diván** [diˈβan] nm divan

**diversidad** [diβersiˈðað] nf diversity, variety

**diversión** [diβerˈsjon] nf (gen) entertainment; (actividad) hobby, pastime

**diverso, -a** [diˈβerso, a] adj diverse; **~s libros** several books; **diversos** nmpl sundries

**divertido, -a** [diβer'tiðo, a] *adj* (*chiste*) amusing; (*fiesta etc*) enjoyable

**divertir** [diβer'tir] *vt* (*entretener, recrear*) to amuse; **divertirse** *vr* (*pasarlo bien*) to have a good time; (*distraerse*) to amuse o.s.

**dividendos** [diβi'ðendos] *nmpl* (*Com*) dividends

**dividir** [diβi'ðir] *vt* (*gen*) to divide; (*distribuir*) to distribute, share out

**divierta** *etc vb* V **divertir**

**divino, -a** [di'βino, a] *adj* divine

**divirtiendo** *etc vb* V **divertir**

**divisa** [di'βisa] *nf* (*emblema*) emblem, badge; **divisas** *nfpl* foreign exchange *sg*

**divisar** [diβi'sar] *vt* to make out, distinguish

**división** [diβi'sjon] *nf* (*gen*) division; (*de partido*) split; (*de país*) partition

**divorciar** [diβor'θjar] *vt* to divorce; **divorciarse** *vr* to get divorced; **divorcio** *nm* divorce

**divulgar** [diβul'ɣar] *vt* (*ideas*) to spread; (*secreto*) to divulge

**DNI** (*ESP*) *nm abr* (= *Documento Nacional de Identidad*) national identity card

- **DNI**
- The **Documento Nacional de Identidad** is a Spanish ID card which must be carried at all times and produced on request for the police. It contains the holder's photo, fingerprints and personal details. It is also known as the **DNI** or "carnet de identidad".

**Dña.** *abr* (= *doña*) Mrs

**do** [do] *nm* (*Mús*) do, C

**dobladillo** [doβla'ðiʎo] *nm* (*de vestido*) hem; (*de pantalón: vuelta*) turn-up (*BRIT*), cuff (*US*)

**doblar** [do'βlar] *vt* to double; (*papel*) to fold; (*caño*) to bend; (*la esquina*) to turn, go round; (*film*) to dub ▷ *vi* to turn; (*campana*) to toll; **doblarse** *vr* (*plegarse*) to fold (up), crease; (*encorvarse*) to bend; **~ a la derecha/ izquierda** to turn right/left

**doble** ['doβle] *adj* double; (*de dos aspectos*) dual; (*fig*) two-faced ▷ *nm* double ▷ *nmf* (*Teatro*) double, stand-in; **dobles** *nmpl* (*Deporte*) doubles *sg*; **con ~ sentido** with a double meaning

**doce** ['doθe] *num* twelve; **docena** *nf* dozen

**docente** [do'θente] *adj*: **centro/personal ~** teaching establishment/staff

**dócil** ['doθil] *adj* (*pasivo*) docile; (*obediente*) obedient

**doctor, a** [dok'tor, a] *nm/f* doctor

**doctorado** [dokto'raðo] *nm* doctorate

**doctrina** [dok'trina] *nf* doctrine, teaching

**documentación** [dokumenta'θjon] *nf* documentation, papers *pl*

**documental** [dokumen'tal] *adj, nm* documentary

**documento** [doku'mento] *nm* (*certificado*) document; **documento adjunto** (*Inform*) attachment; **documento nacional de identidad** identity card

**dólar** ['dolar] *nm* dollar

**doler** [do'ler] *vt, vi* to hurt; (*fig*) to grieve; **dolerse** *vr* (*de su situación*) to grieve, feel sorry; (*de las desgracias ajenas*) to sympathize; **me duele el brazo** my arm hurts

**dolor** [do'lor] *nm* pain; (*fig*) grief, sorrow; **dolor de cabeza/estómago/ muelas** headache/stomachache/ toothache

**domar** [do'mar] *vt* to tame

**domesticar** [domesti'kar] *vt* = **domar**

**doméstico, -a** [do'mestiko, a] *adj* (*vida, servicio*) home; (*tareas*) household; (*animal*) tame, pet

**domicilio** [domi'θiljo] *nm* home; **servicio a ~** home delivery service; **sin ~ fijo** of no fixed abode; **domicilio particular** private residence

**dominante** [domi'nante] *adj* dominant; (*persona*) domineering

**dominar** [domi'nar] *vt* (*gen*) to dominate; (*idiomas*) to be fluent in ▷ *vi* to dominate, prevail

**domingo** [do'mingo] *nm* Sunday; **Domingo de Ramos/Resurrección** Palm/ Easter Sunday

**dominio** [do'minjo] *nm* (*tierras*) domain; (*autoridad*) power, authority; (*de las pasiones*) grip, hold; (*de idiomas*) command

**don** [don] *nm* (*talento*) gift; **~ Juan Gómez** Mr Juan Gómez, Juan Gómez Esq (*BRIT*)

- **DON/DOÑA**
- The term **don/doña** often abbreviated to **D./Dña** is placed before the first name as a mark of respect to an older or more senior person – eg Don Diego, Doña Inés. Although becoming rarer in Spain it is still used with names and surnames on official documents and formal correspondence – eg "Sr. D. Pedro Rodríguez Hernández", "Sra. Dña. Inés Rodríguez Hernández".

**dona** ['dona] (*MÉX*) *nf* doughnut, donut (*US*)

**donar** [do'nar] *vt* to donate

**donativo** [dona'tiβo] *nm* donation

**donde** ['donde] *adv* where ▷ *prep*: **el coche está allí ~ el farol** the car is over there by the lamppost *o* where the lamppost is; **en ~** where, in which

**dónde** ['donde] *adv* where?; **¿a ~ vas?** where are you going (to)?; **¿de ~ vienes?** where have you been?; **¿por ~?** where?, whereabouts?

**dondequiera** [donde'kjera] *adv* anywhere; **por ~** everywhere, all over the place ▷ *conj*: **~ que** wherever

**donut**® [do'nut] (*ESP*) *nm* doughnut, donut (*US*)

**doña** ['dona] *nf*: **~ Alicia** Alicia; **~ Victoria Benito** Mrs Victoria Benito

**dorado, -a** [do'raðo, a] *adj* (*color*) golden; (*Tec*) gilt

**dormir** [dor'mir] *vt*: **~ la siesta** to have an afternoon nap ▷ *vi* to sleep; **dormirse** *vr* to fall asleep

**dormitorio** [dormi'torjo] *nm* bedroom

**dorsal** [dor'sal] *nm* (*Deporte*) number

**dorso** ['dorso] *nm* (*de mano*) back; (*de hoja*) other side

**dos** [dos] *num* two

**dosis** ['dosis] *nf inv* dose, dosage

**dotado, -a** [do'taðo, a] *adj* gifted; **~ de** endowed with

**dotar** [do'tar] *vt* to endow; **dote** *nf* dowry; **dotes** *nfpl* (*talentos*) gifts

**doy** [doj] *vb* V **dar**

**drama** ['drama] *nm* drama; **dramaturgo** [drama'turɣo] *nm* dramatist, playwright

**drástico, -a** ['drastiko, a] *adj* drastic

**drenaje** [dre'naxe] *nm* drainage

**droga** ['droɣa] *nf* drug; **drogadicto, -a** [droɣa'ðikto, a] *nm/f* drug addict

**droguería** [droɣe'ria] *nf* hardware shop (*BRIT*) *o* store (*US*)

**ducha** ['dutʃa] *nf* (*baño*) shower; (*Med*) douche; **ducharse** *vr* to take a shower

**duda** ['duða] *nf* doubt; **no cabe ~** there is no doubt about it; **dudar** *vt, vi* to doubt; **dudoso, -a** [du'ðoso, a] *adj* (*incierto*) hesitant; (*sospechoso*) doubtful

**duela** *etc vb* V **doler**

**duelo** ['dwelo] *vb* V **doler** ▷ *nm* (*combate*) duel; (*luto*) mourning

**duende** ['dwende] *nm* imp, goblin

**dueño, -a** ['dweno, a] *nm/f* (*propietario*) owner; (*de pensión, taberna*) landlord/lady; (*empresario*) employer

**duermo** *etc vb* V **dormir**

**dulce** ['dulθe] *adj* sweet ▷ *adv* gently, softly ▷ *nm* sweet

**dulcería** [dulθe'ria] (*LAM*) *nf* confectioner's (shop)

**dulzura** [dul'θura] *nf* sweetness; (*ternura*) gentleness

**dúo** ['duo] *nm* duet

**duplicar** [dupli'kar] *vt* (*hacer el doble de*) to duplicate

**duque** ['duke] *nm* duke; **duquesa** *nf* duchess

**duración** [dura'θjon] *nf* (*de película, disco etc*) length; (*de pila etc*) life; (*curso: de acontecimientos etc*) duration

**duradero, -a** [dura'ðero, a] *adj* (*tela etc*) hard-wearing; (*fe, paz*) lasting

**durante** [du'rante] *prep* during

**durar** [du'rar] *vi* to last; (*recuerdo*) to remain

**durazno** [du'raθno] (*LAM*) *nm* (*fruta*) peach; (*árbol*) peach tree

**durex** ['dureks] (*MÉX, ARG*) *nm* (*tira adhesiva*) Sellotape® (*BRIT*), Scotch tape® (*US*)

**dureza** [du'reθa] *nf* (*calidad*) hardness

**duro, -a** ['duro, a] *adj* hard; (*carácter*) tough ▷ *adv* hard ▷ *nm* (*moneda*) five-peseta coin o piece

**DVD** *nm abr* (= *disco de vídeo digital*) DVD

**E** *abr* (=*este*) E

**e** [e] *conj* and

**ébano** ['eβano] *nm* ebony

**ebrio, -a** ['eβrjo, a] *adj* drunk

**ebullición** [eβuλi'θjon] *nf* boiling

**echar** [e'tʃar] *vt* to throw; (*agua, vino*) to pour (out); (*empleado: despedir*) to fire, sack; (*hojas*) to sprout; (*cartas*) to post; (*humo*) to emit, give out ▷ *vi*: **~ a correr** to run off; **echarse** *vr* to lie down; **~ llave a** to lock (up); **~ abajo** (*gobierno*) to overthrow; (*edificio*) to demolish; **~ mano a** to lay hands on; **~ una mano a algn** (*ayudar*) to give sb a hand; **~ de menos** to miss; **~se atrás** (*fig*) to back out

**eclesiástico, -a** [ekle'sjastiko, a] *adj* ecclesiastical

**eco** ['eko] *nm* echo; **tener ~** to catch on

**ecología** [ekolo'xia] *nf* ecology; **ecológico, -a** *adj* (*producto, método*) environmentally-friendly; (*agricultura*) organic; **ecologista** *adj* ecological, environmental ▷ *nmf* environmentalist

**economía** [ekono'mia] *nf* (*sistema*) economy; (*carrera*) economics

**económico, -a** [eko'nomiko, a] *adj* (*barato*) cheap, economical; (*ahorrativo*) thrifty; (*Com: año etc*) financial; (*: situación*) economic

**economista** [ekono'mista] *nmf* economist

**Ecuador** [ekwa'ðor] *nm* Ecuador; **ecuador** *nm* (*Geo*) equator

**ecuatoriano, -a** [ekwato'rjano, a] *adj, nm/f* Ecuadorian

**ecuestre** [e'kwestre] *adj* equestrian

**edad** [e'ðað] *nf* age; **¿qué ~ tienes?** how old are you?; **tiene ocho años de ~** he's eight (years old); **de ~ mediana/avanzada** middle-aged/advanced in years; **la E~ Media** the Middle Ages

**edición** [eði'θjon] *nf* (*acto*) publication; (*ejemplar*) edition

**edificar** [eðifi'kar] *vt, vi* to build

**edificio** [eði'fiθjo] *nm* building; (*fig*) edifice, structure

**Edimburgo** [eðim'burxo] *nm* Edinburgh

**editar** [eði'tar] *vt* (*publicar*) to publish; (*preparar textos*) to edit

**editor, a** [eði'tor, a] *nm/f* (*que publica*) publisher; (*redactor*) editor ▷ *adj* publishing *cpd*; **editorial** *adj* editorial ▷ *nm* leading article, editorial; **casa editorial** publisher

**edredón** [eðre'ðon] *nm* duvet

**educación** [eðuka'θjon] *nf* education; (*crianza*) upbringing; (*modales*) (good) manners *pl*

**educado, -a** [eðu'kaðo, a] *adj*: **bien/mal ~** well/badly behaved

**educar** [eðu'kar] *vt* to educate; (*criar*) to bring up; (*voz*) to train

**EE. UU.** *nmpl abr* (= *Estados Unidos*) US(A)

**efectivamente** [efektiβa'mente] *adv* (*como respuesta*) exactly, precisely; (*verdaderamente*) really; (*de hecho*) in fact

**efectivo, -a** [efek'tiβo, a] *adj* effective; (*real*) actual, real ▷ *nm*: **pagar en ~** to pay (in) cash; **hacer ~ un cheque** to cash a cheque

**efecto** [e'fekto] *nm* effect, result; **efectos** *nmpl* (*efectos personales*) effects; (*bienes*) goods; (*Com*) assets; **en ~** in fact; (*respuesta*) exactly, indeed; **efecto invernadero** greenhouse effect; **efectos especiales/ secundarios/sonoros** special/side/sound effects

**efectuar** [efek'twar] *vt* to carry out; (*viaje*) to make

**eficacia** [efi'kaθja] *nf* (*de persona*) efficiency; (*de medicamento etc*) effectiveness

**eficaz** [efi'kaθ] *adj* (*persona*) efficient; (*acción*) effective

**eficiente** [efi'θjente] *adj* efficient

**egipcio, -a** [e'xipθjo, a] *adj, nm/f* Egyptian

**Egipto** [e'xipto] *nm* Egypt

**egoísmo** [exo'ismo] *nm* egoism

**egoísta** [exo'ista] *adj* egoistical, selfish ▷ *nmf* egoist

**Eire** ['eire] *nm* Eire

**ej.** *abr* (=*ejemplo*) eg

**eje** ['exe] *nm* (*Geo, Mat*) axis; (*de rueda*) axle; (*de máquina*) shaft, spindle

**ejecución** [exeku'θjon] *nf* execution; (*cumplimiento*) fulfilment; (*Mús*) performance; (*Jur: embargo de deudor*) attachment

**ejecutar** [exeku'tar] *vt* to execute, carry out; (*matar*) to execute; (*cumplir*) to fulfil;

(*Mús*) to perform; (*Jur: embargar*) to attach, distrain (on)

**ejecutivo, -a** [exeku'tiβo, a] *adj* executive; **el (poder) ~** the executive (power)

**ejemplar** [exem'plar] *adj* exemplary ▷ *nm* example; (*Zool*) specimen; (*de libro*) copy; (*de periódico*) number, issue

**ejemplo** [e'xemplo] *nm* example; **por ~** for example

**ejercer** [exer'θer] *vt* to exercise; (*influencia*) to exert; (*un oficio*) to practise ▷ *vi* (*practicar*): **~ (de)** to practise (as)

**ejercicio** [exer'θiθjo] *nm* exercise; (*período*) tenure; **hacer ~** to take exercise; **ejercicio comercial** financial year

**ejército** [e'xerθito] *nm* army; **entrar en el ~** to join the army, join up; **ejército del aire/de tierra** Air Force/Army

**ejote** [e'xote] (*MÉX*) *nm* green bean

○ PALABRA CLAVE

**el** [el] (*f* **la**, *pl* **los, las**, *neutro* **lo**) *art def* **1** the; **el libro/la mesa/los estudiantes** the book/table/students

**2** (*con n abstracto: no se traduce*): **el amor/la juventud** love/youth

**3** (*posesión: se traduce a menudo por adj posesivo*): **romperse el brazo** to break one's arm; **levantó la mano** he put his hand up; **se puso el sombrero** he put her hat on

**4** (*valor descriptivo*): **tener la boca grande/los ojos azules** to have a big mouth/blue eyes

**5** (*con días*): on; **me iré el viernes** I'll leave on Friday; **los domingos suelo ir a nadar** on Sundays I generally go swimming

**6** (*lo +adj*): **lo difícil/caro** what is difficult/expensive; (*cuán*): **no se da cuenta de lo pesado que es** he doesn't realise how boring he is

▷ *pron demos* **1**: **mi libro y el de usted** my book and yours; **las de Pepe son mejores** Pepe's are better; **no la(s) blanca(s) sino la(s) gris(es)** not the white one(s) but the grey one(s)

**2**: **lo de: lo de ayer** what happened yesterday; **lo de las facturas** that business about the invoices

▷ *pron relativo* **1** (*indef*): **el que: el (los) que quiera(n) que se vaya(n)** anyone who wants to can leave; **llévese el que más le guste** take the one you like best

**2** (*def*): **el que: el que compré ayer** the one I bought yesterday; **los que se van** those who leave

**3**: **lo que: lo que pienso yo/más me gusta** what I think/like most

▷ *conj*: **el que: el que lo diga** the fact that he says so; **el que sea tan vago me molesta** his being so lazy bothers me

▷ *excl*: **¡el susto que me diste!** what a fright you gave me!

▷ *pron personal* **1** (*persona: m*) him; (: *f*) her; (: *pl*) them; **lo/las veo** I can see him/them

**2** (*animal, cosa: sg*) it; (: *pl*) them; **lo (o la) veo** I can see it; **los (o las) veo** I can see them

**3** (*como sustituto de frase*): **lo: no lo sabía** I didn't know; **ya lo entiendo** I understand now

**él** [el] *pron* (*persona*) he; (*cosa*) it; (*después de prep: persona*) him; (: *cosa*) it; **de ~** his

**elaborar** [elaβo'rar] *vt* (*producto*) to make, manufacture; (*preparar*) to prepare; (*madera, metal etc*) to work; (*proyecto etc*) to work on o out

**elástico, -a** [e'lastiko, a] *adj* elastic; (*flexible*) flexible ▷ *nm* elastic; (*un elástico*) elastic band

**elección** [elek'θjon] *nf* election; (*selección*) choice, selection; **elecciones generales** general election *sg*

**electorado** [elekto'raðo] *nm* electorate, voters *pl*

**electricidad** [elektriθi'ðað] *nf* electricity

**electricista** [elektri'θista] *nmf* electrician

**eléctrico, -a** [e'lektriko, a] *adj* electric

**electro...** [elektro] *prefijo* electro...; **electrocardiograma** *nm* electrocardiogram; **electrocutar** *vt* to electrocute; **electrodo** *nm* electrode; **electrodomésticos** *nmpl* (electrical) household appliances

**electrónica** [elek'tronika] *nf* electronics *sg*

**electrónico, -a** [elek'troniko, a] *adj* electronic

**elefante** [ele'fante] *nm* elephant

**elegancia** [ele'ɣanθja] *nf* elegance, grace; (*estilo*) stylishness

**elegante** [ele'ɣante] *adj* elegant, graceful; (*estiloso*) stylish, fashionable

**elegir** [ele'xir] *vt* (*escoger*) to choose, select; (*optar*) to opt for; (*presidente*) to elect

**elemental** [elemen'tal] *adj* (*claro, obvio*) elementary; (*fundamental*) elemental, fundamental

**elemento** [ele'mento] *nm* element; (*fig*) ingredient; **elementos** *nmpl* elements, rudiments

**elevación** [eleβa'θjon] *nf* elevation; (*acto*) raising, lifting; (*de precios*) rise; (*Geo etc*) height, altitude

**elevar** [ele'βar] *vt* to raise, lift (up); (*precio*)

to put up; **elevarse** vr (edificio) to rise; (precios) to go up

**eligiendo** etc vb V **elegir**

**elija** etc vb V **elegir**

**eliminar** [elimi'nar] vt to eliminate, remove

**eliminatoria** [elimina'torja] nf heat, preliminary (round)

**élite** ['elite] nf elite

**ella** ['eʎa] pron (persona) she; (cosa) it; (después de prep: persona) her; (: cosa) it; **de ~** hers

**ellas** ['eʎas] pron (personas y cosas) they; (después de prep) them; **de ~** theirs

**ello** ['eʎo] pron it

**ellos** ['eʎos] pron they; (después de prep) them; **de ~** theirs

**elogiar** [elo'xjar] vt to praise; **elogio** nm praise

**elote** [e'lote] (MÉX) nm corn on the cob

**eludir** [elu'ðir] vt to avoid

**email** [i'mel] nm email; (dirección) email address; **mandar un ~ a** algn to email sb, send sb an email

**embajada** [emba'xaða] nf embassy

**embajador, a** [embaxa'ðor, a] nm/f ambassador/ambassadress

**embalar** [emba'lar] vt to parcel, wrap (up); **embalarse** vr to go fast

**embalse** [em'balse] nm (presa) dam; (lago) reservoir

**embarazada** [embara'θaða] adj pregnant ▷ nf pregnant woman

▌No confundir **embarazada** con la palabra inglesa embarrassed.

**embarazo** [emba'raθo] nm (de mujer) pregnancy; (impedimento) obstacle, obstruction; (timidez) embarrassment; **embarazoso, -a** adj awkward, embarrassing

**embarcación** [embarka'θjon] nf (barco) boat, craft; (acto) embarkation, boarding

**embarcadero** [embarka'ðero] nm pier, landing stage

**embarcar** [embar'kar] vt (cargamento) to ship, stow; (persona) to embark, put on board; **embarcarse** vr to embark, go on board

**embargar** [embar'xar] vt (Jur) to seize, impound

**embargo** [em'barxo] nm (Jur) seizure; (Com, Pol) embargo

**embargue** etc vb V **embargar**

**embarque** etc [em'barke] vb V **embarcar** ▷ nm shipment, loading

**embellecer** [embeʎe'θer] vt to embellish, beautify

**embestida** [embes'tiða] nf attack, onslaught; (carga) charge

**embestir** [embes'tir] vt to attack, assault; to charge, attack ▷ vi to attack

**emblema** [em'blema] nm emblem

**embobado, -a** [embo'βaðo, a] adj (atontado) stunned, bewildered

**embolia** [em'bolja] nf (Med) clot

**émbolo** ['embolo] nm (Auto) piston

**emborrachar** [emborra'tʃar] vt to make drunk, intoxicate; **emborracharse** vr to get drunk

**emboscada** [embos'kaða] nf ambush

**embotar** [embo'tar] vt to blunt, dull

**embotellamiento** [emboteʎa'mjento] nm (Auto) traffic jam

**embotellar** [embote'ʎar] vt to bottle

**embrague** [em'braxe] nm (tb: **pedal de ~**) clutch

**embrión** [em'brjon] nm embryo

**embrollo** [em'broʎo] nm (enredo) muddle, confusion; (aprieto) fix, jam

**embrujado, -a** [embru'xado, a] adj bewitched; **casa embrujada** haunted house

**embrutecer** [embrute'θer] vt (atontar) to stupefy

**embudo** [em'buðo] nm funnel

**embuste** [em'buste] nm (mentira) lie; **embustero, -a** adj lying, deceitful ▷ nm/f (mentiroso) liar

**embutido** [embu'tiðo] nm (Culin) sausage; (Tec) inlay

**emergencia** [emer'xenθja] nf emergency; (surgimiento) emergence

**emerger** [emer'xer] vi to emerge, appear

**emigración** [emixra'θjon] nf emigration; (de pájaros) migration

**emigrar** [emi'xrar] vi (personas) to emigrate; (pájaros) to migrate

**eminente** [emi'nente] adj eminent, distinguished; (elevado) high

**emisión** [emi'sjon] nf (acto) emission; (Com etc) issue; (Radio, TV: acto) broadcasting; (: programa) broadcast, programme (BRIT), program (US)

**emisora** [emi'sora] nf radio o broadcasting station

**emitir** [emi'tir] vt (olor etc) to emit, give off; (moneda etc) to issue; (opinión) to express; (Radio) to broadcast

**emoción** [emo'θjon] nf emotion; (excitación) excitement; (sentimiento) feeling

**emocionante** [emoθjo'nante] adj (excitante) exciting, thrilling

**emocionar** [emoθjo'nar] vt (excitar) to excite, thrill; (conmover) to move, touch; (impresionar) to impress

**emoticón** [emoti'kon], **emoticono**

[emoti'kono] *nm* smiley

**emotivo, -a** [emo'tiβo, a] *adj* emotional

**empacho** [em'patʃo] *nm* (*Med*) indigestion; (*fig*) embarrassment

**empalagoso, -a** [empala'ɤoso, a] *adj* cloying; (*fig*) tiresome

**empalmar** [empal'mar] *vt* to join, connect ▷ *vi* (*dos caminos*) to meet, join; **empalme** *nm* joint, connection; junction; (*de trenes*) connection

**empanada** [empa'naða] *nf* pie, pasty

**empañarse** [empa'ɲarse] *vr* (*cristales etc*) to steam up

**empapar** [empa'par] *vt* (*mojar*) to soak, saturate; (*absorber*) to soak up, absorb; **empaparse** *vr*: **~se de** to soak up

**empapelar** [empape'lar] *vt* (*paredes*) to paper

**empaquetar** [empake'tar] *vt* to pack, parcel up

**empastar** [empas'tar] *vt* (*embadurnar*) to paste; (*diente*) to fill

**empaste** [em'paste] *nm* (*de diente*) filling

**empatar** [empa'tar] *vi* to draw, tie; **~on a dos** they drew two-all; **empate** *nm* draw, tie

**empecé** *etc vb* V **empezar**

**empedernido, -a** [empeðer'niðo, a] *adj* hard, heartless; (*fumador*) inveterate

**empeine** [em'peine] *nm* (*de pie, zapato*) instep

**empeñado, -a** [empe'ɲaðo, a] *adj* (*persona*) determined; (*objeto*) pawned

**empeñar** [empe'ɲar] *vt* (*objeto*) to pawn, pledge; (*persona*) to compel; **empeñarse** *vr* (*endeudarse*) to get into debt; **~se en** to be set on, be determined to

**empeño** [em'peɲo] *nm* (*determinación, insistencia*) determination, insistence; **casa de ~s** pawnshop

**empeorar** [empeo'rar] *vt* to make worse, worsen ▷ *vi* to get worse, deteriorate

**empezar** [empe'θar] *vt, vi* to begin, start

**empiece** *etc vb* V **empezar**

**empiezo** *etc vb* V **empezar**

**emplasto** [em'plasto] *nm* (*Med*) plaster

**emplazar** [empla'θar] *vt* (*ubicar*) to site, place, locate; (*Jur*) to summons; (*convocar*) to summon

**empleado, -a** [emple'aðo, a] *nm/f* (*gen*) employee; (*de banco etc*) clerk

**emplear** [emple'ar] *vt* (*usar*) to use, employ; (*dar trabajo a*) to employ; **emplearse** *vr* (*conseguir trabajo*) to be employed; (*ocuparse*) to occupy o.s.

**empleo** [em'pleo] *nm* (*puesto*) job; (*puestos: colectivamente*) employment; (*uso*) use, employment

**empollar** [empo'ʎar] (*ESP: fam*) *vt, vi* to swot (up); **empollón, -ona** (*ESP: fam*) *nm/f* swot

**emporio** [em'porjo] (*LAM*) *nm* (*gran almacén*) department store

**empotrado, -a** [empo'traðo, a] *adj* (*armario etc*) built-in

**emprender** [empren'der] *vt* (*empezar*) to begin, embark on; (*acometer*) to tackle, take on

**empresa** [em'presa] *nf* (*de espíritu etc*) enterprise; (*Com*) company, firm; **empresariales** *nfpl* business studies; **empresario, -a** *nm/f* (*Com*) businessman(-woman)

**empujar** [empu'xar] *vt* to push, shove

**empujón** [empu'xon] *nm* push, shove

**empuñar** [empu'ɲar] *vt* (*asir*) to grasp, take (firm) hold of

○ **PALABRA CLAVE**

**en** [en] *prep* **1**(*posición*) in; (: *sobre*) on; **está en el cajón** it's in the drawer; **en Argentina/La Paz** in Argentina/La Paz; **en la oficina/el colegio** at the office/school; **está en el suelo/quinto piso** it's on the floor/the fifth floor

**2** (*dirección*) into; **entró en el aula** she went into the classroom; **meter algo en el bolso** to put sth into one's bag

**3** (*tiempo*) in; on; **en 1605/3 semanas/invierno** in 1605/3 weeks/winter; **en (el mes de) enero** in (the month of) January; **en aquella ocasión/época** on that occasion/at that time

**4** (*precio*) for; **lo vendió en 20 dólares** he sold it for 20 dollars

**5** (*diferencia*) by; **reducir/aumentar en una tercera parte/un 20 por ciento** to reduce/increase by a third/20 per cent

**6** (*manera*): **en avión/autobús** by plane/bus; **escrito en inglés** written in English

**7** (*después de vb que indica gastar etc*) on; **han cobrado demasiado en dietas** they've charged too much to expenses; **se le va la mitad del sueldo en comida** he spends half his salary on food

**8** (*tema, ocupación*): **experto en la materia** expert on the subject; **trabaja en la construcción** he works in the building industry

**9** (*adj + en + infin*): **lento en reaccionar** slow to react

**enaguas** [e'naɤwas] *nfpl* petticoat *sg*, underskirt *sg*

**enajenación** [enaxena'θjon] *nf* (*Psico: tb:*

**~ mental**) mental derangement

**enamorado, -a** [enamo'raðo, a] *adj* in love ▷ *nm/f* lover; **estar ~ (de)** to be in love (with)

**enamorar** [enamo'rar] *vt* to win the love of; **enamorarse** *vr:* **~se de algn** to fall in love with sb

**enano, -a** [e'nano, a] *adj* tiny ▷ *nm/f* dwarf

**encabezamiento** [enkaβeθa'mjento] *nm* (*de carta*) heading; (*de periódico*) headline

**encabezar** [enkaβe'θar] *vt* (*movimiento, revolución*) to lead, head; (*lista*) to head, be at the top of; (*carta*) to put a heading to

**encadenar** [enkaðe'nar] *vt* to chain (together); (*poner grilletes a*) to shackle

**encajar** [enka'xar] *vt* (*ajustar*): **~ (en)** to fit (into); (*fam: golpe*) to take ▷ *vi* to fit (well); (*fig: corresponder a*) to match

**encaje** [en'kaxe] *nm* (*labor*) lace

**encallar** [enka'ʎar] *vi* (*Náut*) to run aground

**encaminar** [enkami'nar] *vt* to direct, send

**encantado, -a** [enkan'taðo, a] *adj* (*hechizado*) bewitched; (*muy contento*) delighted; **¡~!** how do you do, pleased to meet you

**encantador, a** [enkanta'ðor, a] *adj* charming, lovely ▷ *nm/f* magician, enchanter/enchantress

**encantar** [enkan'tar] *vt* (*agradar*) to charm, delight; (*hechizar*) to bewitch, cast a spell on; **me encanta eso** I love that; **encanto** *nm* (*hechizo*) spell, charm; (*fig*) charm, delight

**encarcelar** [enkarθe'lar] *vt* to imprison, jail

**encarecer** [enkare'θer] *vt* to put up the price of; **encarecerse** *vr* to get dearer

**encargado, -a** [enkar'xaðo, a] *adj* in charge ▷ *nm/f* agent, representative; (*responsable*) person in charge

**encargar** [enkar'xar] *vt* to entrust; (*recomendar*) to urge, recommend; **encargarse** *vr:* **~se de** to look after, take charge of; **~ algo a algn** to put sb in charge of sth; **~ a algn que haga algo** to ask sb to do sth

**encargo** [en'karxo] *nm* (*tarea*) assignment, job; (*responsabilidad*) responsibility; (*Com*) order

**encariñarse** [enkari'narse] *vr:* **~ con** to grow fond of, get attached to

**encarnación** [enkarna'θjon] *nf* incarnation, embodiment

**encarrilar** [enkarri'lar] *vt* (*tren*) to put back on the rails; (*fig*) to correct, put on the right track

**encasillar** [enkasi'ʎar] *vt* (*fig*) to pigeonhole; (*actor*) to typecast

**encendedor** [enθende'ðor] *nm* lighter

**encender** [enθen'der] *vt* (*con fuego*) to light; (*luz, radio*) to put on, switch on; (*avivar: pasión*) to inflame; **encenderse** *vr* to catch fire; (*excitarse*) to get excited; (*de cólera*) to flare up; (*el rostro*) to blush

**encendido** [enθen'diðo] *nm* (*Auto*) ignition

**encerado** [enθe'raðo] *nm* (*Escol*) blackboard

**encerrar** [enθe'rrar] *vt* (*confinar*) to shut in, shut up; (*comprender, incluir*) to include, contain

**encharcado, -a** [entʃar'kaðo, a] *adj* (*terreno*) flooded

**encharcarse** [entʃar'karse] *vr* to get flooded

**enchufado, -a** [entʃu'faðo, a] (*fam*) *nm/f* well-connected person

**enchufar** [entʃu'far] *vt* (*Elec*) to plug in; (*Tec*) to connect, fit together; **enchufe** *nm* (*Elec: clavija*) plug; (: *toma*) socket; (*do dos tubos*) joint, connection; (*fam: influencia*) contact, connection; (: *puesto*) cushy job

**encía** [en'θia] *nf* gum

**encienda** *etc vb* V **encender**

**encierro** *etc* [en'θjerro] *vb* V **encerrar** ▷ *nm* shutting in, shutting up; (*calabozo*) prison

**encima** [en'θima] *adv* (*sobre*) above, over; (*además*) besides; **~ de** (*en*) on, on top of; (*sobre*) above, over; (*además de*) besides, on top of; **por ~ de** over; **¿llevas dinero ~?** have you (got) any money on you?; **se me vino ~** it took me by surprise

**encina** [en'θina] *nf* holm oak

**encinta** [en'θinta] *adj* pregnant

**enclenque** [en'klenke] *adj* weak, sickly

**encoger** [enko'xer] *vt* to shrink, contract; **encogerse** *vr* to shrink, contract; (*fig*) to cringe; **~se de hombros** to shrug one's shoulders

**encomendar** [enkomen'dar] *vt* to entrust, commend; **encomendarse** *vr:* **~se a** to put one's trust in

**encomienda** *etc* [enko'mjenda] *vb* V **encomendar** ▷ *nf* (*encargo*) charge, commission; (*elogio*) tribute; **encomienda postal** (*LAM*) package

**encontrar** [enkon'trar] *vt* (*hallar*) to find; (*inesperadamente*) to meet, run into; **encontrarse** *vr* to meet (each other); (*situarse*) to be (situated); **~se con** to meet; **~se bien (de salud)** to feel well

**encrucijada** [enkruθi'xaða] *nf*

crossroads *sg*

**encuadernación** [enkwaðerna'θjon] *nf*
binding

**encuadrar** [enkwa'ðrar] *vt (retrato)* to
frame; *(ajustar)* to fit, insert; *(contener)* to
contain

**encubrir** [enku'βrir] *vt (ocultar)* to hide,
conceal; *(criminal)* to harbour, shelter

**encontrar** *etc* [en'kwentro] *vb* V
**encontrar** ⊳ *nm (de personas)* meeting;
*(Auto etc)* collision, crash; *(Deporte)* match,
game; *(Mil)* encounter

**encuerado, -a** *(MÉX)* [enkwe'raðo, a] *adj*
nude, naked

**encuesta** [en'kwesta] *nf* inquiry,
investigation; *(sondeo)* (public) opinion poll

**encumbrar** [enkum'brar] *vt (persona)*
to exalt

**endeble** [en'deβle] *adj (persona)* weak;
*(argumento, excusa, persona)* weak

**endemoniado, -a** [endemo'njaðo, a] *adj*
possessed (of the devil); *(travieso)* devilish

**enderezar** [endere'θar] *vt (poner derecho)*
to straighten (out); *( : verticalmente)* to set
upright; *(situación)* to straighten o sort out;
*(dirigir)* to direct; **enderezarse** *vr (persona
sentada)* to straighten up

**endeudarse** [endeu'ðarse] *vr* to get
into debt

**endiablado, -a** [endja'βlaðo, a] *adj*
devilish, diabolical; *(travieso)* mischievous

**endilgar** [endil'ɣar] *(fam)* *vt:* ~**le algo a
algn** to lumber sb with sth

**endiñar** [endi'ɲar] *(ESP: fam)* *vt (bofetón)*
to land, belt

**endosar** [endo'sar] *vt (cheque etc)* to
endorse

**endulzar** [endul'θar] *vt* to sweeten;
*(suavizar)* to soften

**endurecer** [endure'θer] *vt* to harden;
**endurecerse** *vr* to harden, grow hard

**enema** [e'nema] *nm (Med)* enema

**enemigo, -a** [ene'miɣo, a] *adj* enemy,
hostile ⊳ *nm/f* enemy

**enemistad** [enemis'tað] *nf* enmity

**enemistar** [enemis'tar] *vt* to make
enemies of, cause a rift between;
**enemistarse** *vr* to become enemies;
*(amigos)* to fall out

**energía** [ener'xia] *nf (vigor)* energy, drive;
*(empuje)* push; *(Tec, Elec)* energy, power;
**energía eólica** wind power; **energía solar**
solar energy o power

**enérgico, -a** [e'nerxiko, a] *adj (gen)*
energetic; *(voz, modales)* forceful

**energúmeno, -a** [ener'ɣumeno, a] *(fam)*
*nm/f (fig)* madman(-woman)

**enero** [e'nero] *nm* January

**enfadado, -a** [enfa'ðaðo, a] *adj* angry,
annoyed

**enfadar** [enfa'ðar] *vt* to anger, annoy;
**enfadarse** *vr* to get angry o annoyed

**enfado** [en'faðo] *nm (enojo)* anger,
annoyance; *(disgusto)* trouble, bother

**énfasis** ['enfasis] *nm (emphasis, stress)*

**enfático, -a** [en'fatiko, a] *adj* emphatic

**enfermar** [enfer'mar] *vt* to make ill ⊳ *vi*
to fall ill, be taken ill

**enfermedad** [enferme'ðað] *nf* illness;
**enfermedad venérea** venereal disease

**enfermera** [enfer'mera] *nf* nurse

**enfermería** [enferme'ria] *nf* infirmary;
*(de colegio etc)* sick bay

**enfermero** [enfer'mero] *nm* (male) nurse

**enfermizo, -a** [enfer'miθo, a] *adj*
*(persona)* sickly, unhealthy; *(fig)* unhealthy

**enfermo, -a** [en'fermo, a] *adj* ill, sick
⊳ *nm/f* invalid, sick person; *(en hospital)*
patient; **caer** o **ponerse** ~ to fall ill

**enfocar** [enfo'kar] *vt (foto etc)* to focus;
*(problema etc)* to approach

**enfoque** *etc* [en'foke] *vb* V **enfocar** ⊳ *nm*
focus

**enfrentar** [enfren'tar] *vt (peligro)* to face
(up to), confront; *(oponer)* to bring face to
face; **enfrentarse** *vr (dos personas)* to face o
confront each other; *(Deporte: dos equipos)* to
meet; ~**se a** o **con** to face up to, confront

**enfrente** [en'frente] *adv* opposite; **la casa
de** ~ the house opposite, the house across
the street; ~ **de** opposite, facing

**enfriamiento** [enfria'mjento] *nm*
chilling, refrigeration; *(Med)* cold, chill

**enfriar** [enfri'ar] *vt (alimentos)* to cool,
chill; *(algo caliente)* to cool down; **enfriarse**
*vr* to cool down; *(Med)* to catch a chill;
*(amistad)* to cool

**enfurecer** [enfure'θer] *vt* to enrage,
madden; **enfurecerse** *vr* to become
furious, fly into a rage; *(mar)* to get rough

**enganchar** [engan'tʃar] *vt* to hook;
*(dos vagones)* to hitch up; *(Tec)* to couple,
connect; *(Mil)* to recruit; **engancharse** *vr*
*(Mil)* to enlist, join up

**enganche** [en'gantʃe] *nm* hook; *(ESP
Tec)* coupling, connection; *(acto)* hooking
(up); *(Mil)* recruitment, enlistment;
*(MÉX: depósito)* deposit

**engañar** [enga'ɲar] *vt* to deceive;
*(estafar)* to cheat, swindle; **engañarse** *vr*
*(equivocarse)* to be wrong; *(disimular la verdad)*
to deceive o.s.

**engaño** [en'gaɲo] *nm* deceit; *(estafa)* trick,
swindle; *(error)* mistake, misunderstanding;
*(ilusión)* delusion; **engañoso, -a** *adj*
*(tramposo)* crooked; *(mentiroso)* dishonest,

deceitful; (*aspecto*) deceptive; (*consejo*) misleading

**engatusar** [engatu'sar] (*fam*) *vt* to coax

**engendro** [en'xendro] *nm* (*Bio*) foetus; (*fig*) monstrosity

**englobar** [englo'βar] *vt* to include, comprise

**engordar** [engor'ðar] *vt* to fatten ▷ *vi* to get fat, put on weight

**engorroso, -a** [engo'rroso, a] *adj* bothersome, trying

**engranaje** [engra'naxe] *nm* (*Auto*) gear

**engrasar** [engra'sar] *vt* (*Tec: poner grasa*) to grease; (: *lubricar*) to lubricate, oil; (*manchar*) to make greasy

**engreído, -a** [engre'iðo, a] *adj* vain, conceited

**enhebrar** [ene'βrar] *vt* to thread

**enhorabuena** [enora'βwena] *excl* **¡~!** congratulations! ▷ *nf:* **dar la ~ a** to congratulate

**enigma** [e'niɣma] *nm* enigma; (*problema*) puzzle; (*misterio*) mystery

**enjambre** [en'xambre] *nm* swarm

**enjaular** [enxau'lar] *vt* to (put in a) cage; (*fam*) to jail, lock up

**enjuagar** [enxwa'ɣar] *vt* (*ropa*) to rinse (out)

**enjuague** *etc* [en'xwaɣe] *vb* V **enjuagar** ▷ *nm* (*Med*) mouthwash; (*de ropa*) rinse, rinsing

**enlace** [en'laθe] *nm* link, connection; (*relación*) relationship; (*tb:* **~ matrimonial**) marriage; (*de carretera, trenes*) connection; **enlace sindical** shop steward

**enlatado, -a** [enla'taðo, a] *adj* (*alimentos, productos*) tinned, canned

**enlazar** [enla'θar] *vt* (*unir con lazos*) to bind together; (*atar*) to tie; (*conectar*) to link, connect; (*LAM: caballo*) to lasso

**enloquecer** [enloke'θer] *vt* to drive mad ▷ *vi* to go mad

**enmarañar** [enmara'ɲar] *vt* (*enredar*) to tangle (up), entangle; (*complicar*) to complicate; (*confundir*) to confuse

**enmarcar** [enmar'kar] *vt* (*cuadro*) to frame

**enmascarar** [enmaska'rar] *vt* to mask; **enmascararse** *vr* to put on a mask

**enmendar** [enmen'dar] *vt* to emend, correct; (*constitución etc*) to amend; (*comportamiento*) to reform; **enmendarse** *vr* to reform, mend one's ways; **enmienda** *nf* correction; amendment; reform

**enmudecer** [enmuðe'θer] *vi* (*perder el habla*) to fall silent; (*guardar silencio*) to remain silent

**ennoblecer** [ennoβle'θer] *vt* to ennoble

**enojado, -a** [eno'xaðo, a] (*LAM*) *adj* angry

**enojar** [eno'xar] *vt* (*encolerizar*) to anger; (*disgustar*) to annoy, upset; **enojarse** *vr* to get angry; to get annoyed

**enojo** [e'noxo] *nm* (*cólera*) anger; (*irritación*) annoyance

**enorme** [e'norme] *adj* enormous, huge; (*fig*) monstrous

**enredadera** [enreða'ðera] *nf* (*Bot*) creeper, climbing plant

**enredar** [enre'ðar] *vt* (*cables, hilos etc*) to tangle (up), entangle; (*situación*) to complicate, confuse; (*meter cizaña*) to sow discord among o between; (*implicar*) to embroil, implicate; **enredarse** *vr* to get entangled, get tangled (up); (*situación*) to get complicated; (*persona*) to get embroiled; (*LAM: fam*) to meddle

**enredo** [en'reðo] *nm* (*maraña*) tangle; (*confusión*) mix-up, confusion; (*intriga*) intrigue

**enriquecer** [enrike'θer] *vt* to make rich, enrich; **enriquecerse** *vr* to get rich

**enrojecer** [enroxe'θer] *vt* to redden ▷ *vi* (*persona*) to blush; **enrojecerse** *vr* to blush

**enrollar** [enro'ʎar] *vt* to roll (up), wind (up)

**ensalada** [ensa'laða] *nf* salad; **ensaladilla (rusa)** *nf* Russian salad

**ensanchar** [ensan'tʃar] *vt* (*hacer más ancho*) to widen; (*agrandar*) to enlarge, expand; (*Costura*) to let out; **ensancharse** *vr* to get wider, expand

**ensayar** [ensa'jar] *vt* to test, try (out); (*Teatro*) to rehearse

**ensayo** [en'sajo] *nm* test, trial; (*Quím*) experiment; (*Teatro*) rehearsal; (*Deporte*) try; (*Escol, Literatura*) essay

**enseguida** [ense'ɣiða] *adv* at once, right away

**ensenada** [ense'naða] *nf* inlet, cove

**enseñanza** [ense'ɲanθa] *nf* (*educación*) education; (*acción*) teaching; (*doctrina*) teaching, doctrine; **enseñanza (de) primaria/secundaria** elementary/secondary education

**enseñar** [ense'ɲar] *vt* (*educar*) to teach; (*mostrar, señalar*) to show

**enseres** [en'seres] *nmpl* belongings

**ensuciar** [ensu'θjar] *vt* (*manchar*) to dirty, soil; (*fig*) to defile; **ensuciarse** *vr* to get dirty; (*bebé*) to dirty one's nappy

**entablar** [enta'βlar] *vt* (*recubrir*) to board (up); (*Ajedrez, Damas*) to set up; (*conversación*) to strike up; (*Jur*) to file ▷ *vi* to draw

**ente** ['ente] *nm* (*organización*) body, organization; (*fam: persona*) odd character

**entender** [enten'der] *vt* (*comprender*) to

understand; (*darse cuenta*) to realize ▷ *vi* to understand; (*creer*) to think, believe; **entenderse** *vr* (*comprenderse*) to be understood; (*ponerse de acuerdo*) to agree, reach an agreement; **~ de** to know all about; **~ algo de** to know a little about; **~ en** to deal with, have to do with; **~ mal** to misunderstand; **~se con algn** (*llevarse bien*) to get on *o* along with sb; **~se mal** (*dos personas*) to get on badly

**entendido, -a** [enten'diðo, a] *adj* (*comprendido*) understood; (*hábil*) skilled; (*inteligente*) knowledgeable ▷ *nm/f* (*experto*) expert ▷ *excl* agreed!; **entendimiento** *nm* (*comprensión*) understanding; (*inteligencia*) mind, intellect; (*juicio*) judgement

**enterado, -a** [ente'raðo, a] *adj* well-informed; **estar ~ de** to know about, be aware of

**enteramente** [entera'mente] *adv* entirely, completely

**enterar** [ente'rar] *vt* (*informar*) to inform, tell; **enterarse** *vr* to find out, get to know

**enterito** [ente'rito] (RPL) *nm* boiler suit (BRIT), overalls (US)

**entero, -a** [en'tero, a] *adj* (*total*) whole, entire; (*fig: honesto*) honest; (: *firme*) firm, resolute ▷ *nm* (Com: *punto*) point

**enterrar** [ente'rrar] *vt* to bury

**entidad** [enti'ðað] *nf* (*empresa*) firm, company; (*organismo*) body; (*sociedad*) society; (*Filosofía*) entity

**entiendo** *etc vb* V **entender**

**entierro** [en'tjerro] *nm* (*acción*) burial; (*funeral*) funeral

**entonación** [entona'θjon] *nf* (Ling) intonation

**entonar** [ento'nar] *vt* (*canción*) to intone; (*colores*) to tone; (*Med*) to tone up ▷ *vi* to be in tune

**entonces** [en'tonθes] *adv* then, at that time; **desde ~** since then; **en aquel ~** at that time; **(pues) ~** and so

**entornar** [entor'nar] *vt* (*puerta, ventana*) to half-close, leave ajar; (*los ojos*) to screw up

**entorpecer** [entorpe'θer] *vt* (*entendimiento*) to dull; (*impedir*) to obstruct, hinder; (: *tránsito*) to slow down, delay

**entrada** [en'traða] *nf* (*acción*) entry, access; (*sitio*) entrance, way in; (*Inform*) input; (Com) receipts *pl*, takings *pl*; (*Culin*) starter; (*Deporte*) innings *sg*; (*Teatro*) house, audience; (*billete*) ticket; **~s y salidas** (Com) income and expenditure; **de ~** from the outset; **entrada de aire** (Tec) air intake *o* inlet

**entrado, -a** [en'traðo, a] *adj*: **~ en años** elderly; **una vez ~ el verano** in the

summer(time), when summer comes

**entramparse** [entram'parse] *vr* to get into debt

**entrante** [en'trante] *adj* next, coming; **mes/año ~** next month/year; **entrantes** *nmpl* starters

**entraña** [en'traɲa] *nf* (*fig: centro*) heart, core; (*raíz*) root; **entrañas** *nfpl* (Anat) entrails; (*fig*) heart *sg*; **entrañable** *adj* close, intimate; **entrañar** *vt* to entail

**entrar** [en'trar] *vt* (*introducir*) to bring in; (*Inform*) to input ▷ *vi* (*meterse*) to go in, come in, enter; (*comenzar*): **~ diciendo** to begin by saying; **me entró sed/sueño** I started to feel thirsty/sleepy; **no me entra** I can't get the hang of it

**entre** ['entre] *prep* (*dos*) between; (*más de dos*) among(st)

**entreabrir** [entrea'βrir] *vt* to half-open, open halfway

**entrecejo** [entre'θexo] *nm*: **fruncir el ~** to frown

**entredicho** [entre'ðitʃo] *nm* (Jur) injunction; **poner en ~** to cast doubt on; **estar en ~** to be in doubt

**entrega** [en'trexa] *nf* (*de mercancías*) delivery; (*de novela etc*) instalment; **entregar** [entre'xar] *vt* (*dar*) to hand (over), deliver; **entregarse** *vr* (*rendirse*) to surrender, give in, submit; (*dedicarse*) to devote o.s.

**entremeses** [entre'meses] *nmpl* hors d'œuvres

**entremeter** [entreme'ter] *vt* to insert, put in; **entremeterse** *vr* to meddle, interfere; **entremetido, -a** *adj* meddling, interfering

**entremezclar** [entremeθ'klar] *vt* to intermingle; **entremezclarse** *vr* to intermingle

**entrenador, a** [entrena'ðor, a] *nm/f* trainer, coach

**entrenarse** [entre'narse] *vr* to train

**entrepierna** [entre'pjerna] *nf* crotch

**entresuelo** [entre'swelo] *nm* mezzanine

**entretanto** [entre'tanto] *adv* meanwhile, meantime

**entretecho** [entre'tetʃo] (cs) *nm* attic

**entretejer** [entrete'xer] *vt* to interweave

**entretener** [entrete'ner] *vt* (*divertir*) to entertain, amuse; (*detener*) to hold up, delay; **entretenerse** *vr* (*divertirse*) to amuse o.s.; (*retrasarse*) to delay, linger; **entretenido, -a** *adj* entertaining, amusing; **entretenimiento** *nm* entertainment, amusement

**entrever** [entre'βer] *vt* to glimpse, catch a glimpse of

**entrevista** [entre'βista] *nf* interview;

**entrevistar** *vt* to interview; **entrevistarse** *vr* to have an interview

**entristecer** [entriste'θer] *vt* to sadden, grieve; **entristecerse** *vr* to grow sad

**entrometerse** [entrome'terse] *vr*: **~ (en)** to interfere (in o with)

**entumecer** [entume'θer] *vt* to numb, benumb; **entumecerse** *vr* (*por el frío*) to go o become numb

**enturbiar** [entur'βjar] *vt* (*el agua*) to make cloudy; (*fig*) to confuse; **enturbiarse** *vr* (*oscurecerse*) to become cloudy; (*fig*) to get confused, become obscure

**entusiasmar** [entusjas'mar] *vt* to excite, fill with enthusiasm; (*gustar mucho*) to delight; **entusiasmarse** *vr*: **~se con** o **por** to get enthusiastic o excited about

**entusiasmo** [entu'sjasmo] *nm* enthusiasm; (*excitación*) excitement

**entusiasta** [entu'sjasta] *adj* enthusiastic ⊳ *nmf* enthusiast

**enumerar** [enume'rar] *vt* to enumerate

**envainar** [embai'nar] *vt* to sheathe

**envalentonar** [embalento'nar] *vt* to give courage to; **envalentonarse** *vr* (*pey: jactarse*) to boast, brag

**envasar** [emba'sar] *vt* (*empaquetar*) to pack, wrap; (*enfrascar*) to bottle; (*enlatar*) to can; (*embolsar*) to pocket

**envase** [em'base] *nm* (*en paquete*) packing, wrapping; (*en botella*) bottling; (*en lata*) canning; (*recipiente*) container; (*paquete*) package; (*botella*) bottle; (*lata*) tin (BRIT), can

**envejecer** [embexe'θer] *vt* to make old, age ⊳ *vi* (*volverse viejo*) to grow old; (*parecer viejo*) to age

**envenenar** [embene'nar] *vt* to poison; (*fig*) to embitter

**envergadura** [emberɣa'ðura] *nf* (*fig*) scope, compass

**enviar** [em'bjar] *vt* to send; **~ un mensaje a algn** (*por movil*) to text sb, to send sb a text message

**enviciarse** [embi'θjarse] *vr*: **~ (con)** to get addicted (to)

**envidia** [em'biðja] *nf* envy; **tener ~ a** to envy, be jealous of; **envidiar** *vt* to envy

**envío** [em'bio] *nm* (*acción*) sending; (*de mercancías*) consignment; (*de dinero*) remittance

**enviudar** [embju'ðar] *vi* to be widowed

**envoltura** [embol'tura] *nf* (*cobertura*) cover; (*embalaje*) wrapper, wrapping; **envoltorio** *nm* package

**envolver** [embol'βer] *vt* to wrap (up); (*cubrir*) to cover; (*enemigo*) to surround; (*implicar*) to involve, implicate

**envuelto** [em'bwelto] *pp de* **envolver**

**enyesar** [enje'sar] *vt* (*pared*) to plaster; (*Med*) to put in plaster

**enzarzarse** [enθar'θarse] *vr*: **~ en** (*pelea*) to get mixed up in; (*disputa*) to get involved in

**épica** ['epika] *nf* epic

**epidemia** [epi'ðemja] *nf* epidemic

**epilepsia** [epi'lepsja] *nf* epilepsy

**episodio** [epi'soðjo] *nm* episode

**época** ['epoka] *nf* period, time; (*Hist*) age, epoch; **hacer ~** to be epoch-making

**equilibrar** [ekili'βrar] *vt* to balance; **equilibrio** *nm* balance, equilibrium; **mantener/perder el equilibrio** to keep/lose one's balance; **equilibrista** *nmf* (*funámbulo*) tightrope walker; (*acróbata*) acrobat

**equipaje** [eki'paxe] *nm* luggage; (*avíos*): **hacer el ~** to pack; **equipaje de mano** hand luggage

**equipar** [eki'par] *vt* (*proveer*) to equip

**equipararse** [ekipa'rarse] *vr*: **~ con** to be on a level with

**equipo** [e'kipo] *nm* (*conjunto de cosas*) equipment; (*Deporte*) team; (*de obreros*) shift

**equis** ['ekis] *nf inv* (the letter) X

**equitación** [ekita'θjon] *nf* horse riding

**equivalente** [ekiβa'lente] *adj, nm* equivalent

**equivaler** [ekiβa'ler] *vi* to be equivalent o equal

**equivocación** [ekiβoka'θjon] *nf* mistake, error

**equivocado, -a** [ekiβo'kaðo, a] *adj* wrong, mistaken

**equivocarse** [ekiβo'karse] *vr* to be wrong, make a mistake; **~ de camino** to take the wrong road

**era** ['era] *vb* V **ser** ⊳ *nf* era, age

**erais** *vb* V **ser**

**éramos** *vb* V **ser**

**eran** *vb* V **ser**

**eras** *vb* V **ser**

**erección** [erek'θjon] *nf* erection

**eres** *vb* V **ser**

**erigir** [eri'xir] *vt* to erect, build; **erigirse** *vr*: **~se en** to set o.s. up as

**erizo** [e'riθo] *nm* (*Zool*) hedgehog; **erizo de mar** sea-urchin

**ermita** [er'mita] *nf* hermitage; **ermitaño, -a** [ermi'taɲo, a] *nm/f* hermit

**erosión** [ero'sjon] *nf* erosion

**erosionar** [erosjo'nar] *vt* to erode

**erótico, -a** [e'rotiko, a] *adj* erotic; **erotismo** *nm* eroticism

**errante** [e'rrante] *adj* wandering, errant

**erróneo, -a** [e'rroneo, a] *adj* (*equivocado*) wrong, mistaken

**error** [e'rror] *nm* error, mistake; (*Inform*)

bug; **error de imprenta** misprint

**eructar** [eruk'tar] vt to belch, burp

**erudito, -a** [eru'ðito, a] adj erudite, learned

**erupción** [erup'θjon] nf eruption; (Med) rash

**es** vb V **ser**

**esa** ['esa] (pl ~**s**) adj demos V **ese**

**ésa** ['esa] (pl ~**s**) pron V **ése**

**esbelto, -a** [es'βelto, a] adj slim, slender

**esbozo** [es'βoθo] nm sketch, outline

**escabeche** [eska'βetʃe] nm brine; (de aceitunas etc) pickle; **en ~** pickled

**escabullirse** [eskaβu'ʎirse] vr to slip away, to clear out

**escafandra** [eska'fandra] nf (buzo) diving suit; (escafandra espacial) space suit

**escala** [es'kala] nf (proporción, Mús) scale; (de mano) ladder; (Aviac) stopover; **hacer ~ en** to stop o call in at

**escalafón** [eskala'fon] nm (escala de salarios) salary scale, wage scale

**escalar** [eska'lar] vt to climb, scale

**escalera** [eska'lera] nf stairs pl, staircase; (escala) ladder; (Naipes) run; **escalera de caracol** spiral staircase; **escalera de incendios** fire escape; **escalera mecánica** escalator

**escalfar** [eskal'far] vt (huevos) to poach

**escalinata** [eskali'nata] nf staircase

**escalofriante** [eskalo'frjante] adj chilling

**escalofrío** [eskalo'frio] nm (Med) chill; **escalofríos** nmpl (fig) shivers

**escalón** [eska'lon] nm step, stair; (de escalera) rung

**escalope** [eska'lope] nm (Culin) escalope

**escama** [es'kama] nf (de pez, serpiente) scale; (de jabón) flake; (fig) resentment

**escampar** [eskam'par] vb impers to stop raining

**escandalizar** [eskandali'θar] vt to scandalize, shock; **escandalizarse** vr to be shocked; (ofenderse) to be offended

**escándalo** [es'kandalo] nm scandal; (alboroto, tumulto) row, uproar; **escandaloso, -a** adj scandalous, shocking

**escandinavo, -a** [eskandi'naβo, a] adj, nm/f Scandinavian

**escanear** [eskane'ar] vt to scan

**escaño** [es'kaɲo] nm bench; (Pol) seat

**escapar** [eska'par] vi (gen) to escape, run away; (Deporte) to break away; **escaparse** vr to escape, get away; (agua, gas) to leak (out)

**escaparate** [eskapa'rate] nm shop window

**escape** [es'kape] nm (de agua, gas) leak; (de motor) exhaust

**escarabajo** [eskara'βaxo] nm beetle

**escaramuza** [eskara'muθa] nf skirmish

**escarbar** [eskar'βar] vt (tierra) to scratch

**escarceos** [eskar'θeos] nmpl: **en mis ~ con la política ...** in my dealings with politics ...; **escarceos amorosos** love affairs

**escarcha** [es'kartʃa] nf frost; **escarchado, -a** [eskar'tʃaðo, a] adj (Culin: fruta) crystallized

**escarlatina** [eskarla'tina] nf scarlet fever

**escarmentar** [eskarmen'tar] vt to punish severely ▷ vi to learn one's lesson

**escarmiento** etc [eskar'mjento] vb V **escarmentar** ▷ nm (ejemplo) lesson; (castigo) punishment

**escarola** [eska'rola] nf endive

**escarpado, -a** [eskar'paðo, a] adj (pendiente) sheer, steep; (rocas) craggy

**escasear** [eskase'ar] vi to be scarce

**escasez** [eska'seθ] nf (falta) shortage, scarcity; (pobreza) poverty

**escaso, -a** [es'kaso, a] adj (poco) scarce; (raro) rare; (ralo) thin, sparse; (limitado) limited

**escatimar** [eskati'mar] vt to skimp (on), be sparing with

**escayola** [eska'jola] nf plaster

**escena** [es'θena] nf scene; **escenario** [esθe'narjo] nm (Teatro) stage; (Cine) set; (fig) scene

No confundir **escenario** con la palabra inglesa scenery.

**escenografía** nf set design

**escéptico, -a** [es'θeptiko, a] adj sceptical ▷ nm/f sceptic

**esclarecer** [esklare'θer] vt (misterio, problema) to shed light on

**esclavitud** [esklaβi'tuð] nf slavery

**esclavizar** [esklaβi'θar] vt to enslave

**esclavo, -a** [es'klaβo, a] nm/f slave

**escoba** [es'koβa] nf broom; **escobilla** nf brush

**escocer** [esko'θer] vi to burn, sting; **escocerse** vr to chafe, get chafed

**escocés, -esa** [esko'θes, esa] adj Scottish ▷ nm/f Scotsman(-woman), Scot

**Escocia** [es'koθja] nf Scotland

**escoger** [esko'xer] vt to choose, pick, select; **escogido, -a** adj chosen, selected

**escolar** [esko'lar] adj school cpd ▷ nmf schoolboy(-girl), pupil

**escollo** [es'koʎo] nm (obstáculo) pitfall

**escolta** [es'kolta] nf escort; **escoltar** vt to escort

**escombros** [es'kombros] nmpl (basura) rubbish sg; (restos) debris sg

**esconder** [eskon'der] vt to hide, conceal; **esconderse** vr to hide; **escondidas** (LAM) *nfpl*: **a escondidas** secretly; **escondite** *nm* hiding place; (*ESP: juego*) hide-and-seek; **escondrijo** *nm* hiding place, hideout

**escopeta** [esko'peta] *nf* shotgun

**escoria** [es'korja] *nf* (*de alto horno*) slag; (*fig*) scum, dregs *pl*

**Escorpio** [es'korpjo] *nm* Scorpio

**escorpión** [eskor'pjon] *nm* scorpion

**escotado, -a** [esko'taðo, a] *adj* low-cut

**escote** [es'kote] *nm* (*de vestido*) low neck; **pagar a ~** to share the expenses

**escotilla** [esko'tiʎa] *nf* (*Náut*) hatch(way)

**escozor** [esko'θor] *nm* (*dolor*) sting(ing)

**escribible** [eskri'βiβle] *adj* writable

**escribir** [eskri'βir] *vt, vi* to write; **~ a máquina** to type; **¿cómo se escribe?** how do you spell it?

**escrito, -a** [es'krito, a] *pp de* **escribir** ▷ *nm* (*documento*) document; (*manuscrito*) text, manuscript; **por ~** in writing

**escritor, a** [eskri'tor, a] *nm/f* writer

**escritorio** [eskri'torjo] *nm* desk

**escritura** [eskri'tura] *nf* (*acción*) writing; (*caligrafía*) (hand)writing; (*Jur: documento*) deed

**escrúpulo** [es'krupulo] *nm* scruple; (*minuciosidad*) scrupulousness; **escrupuloso, -a** *adj* scrupulous

**escrutinio** [eskru'tinjo] *nm* (*examen atento*) scrutiny; (*Pol: recuento de votos*) count(ing)

**escuadra** [es'kwaðra] *nf* (*Mil etc*) squad; (*Náut*) squadron; (*flota: de coches etc*) fleet; **escuadrilla** *nf* (*de aviones*) squadron; (*LAM: de obreros*) gang

**escuadrón** [eskwa'ðron] *nm* squadron

**escuálido, -a** [es'kwaliðo, a] *adj* skinny, scraggy; (*sucio*) squalid

**escuchar** [esku'tʃar] *vt* to listen to ▷ *vi* to listen

**escudo** [es'kuðo] *nm* shield

**escuela** [es'kwela] *nf* school; **escuela de artes y oficios** (*ESP*) ≈ technical college; **escuela de choferes** (*LAM*) driving school; **escuela de manejo** (*MÉX*) driving school

**escueto, -a** [es'kweto, a] *adj* plain; (*estilo*) simple

**escuincle, -a** [es'kwinkle, a] (*MÉX: fam*) *nm/f* kid

**esculpir** [eskul'pir] *vt* to sculpt; (*grabar*) to engrave; (*tallar*) to carve; **escultor, a** *nm/f* sculptor(-tress); **escultura** *nf* sculpture

**escupidera** [eskupi'ðera] *nf* spittoon

**escupir** [esku'pir] *vt, vi* to spit (out)

**escurreplatos** [eskurre'platos] (*ESP*) *nm inv* draining board, drainboard (*US*)

**escurridero** [eskurri'ðero] (*LAM*) *nm* draining board (*BRIT*), drainboard (*US*)

**escurridizo, -a** [eskurri'ðiθo, a] *adj* slippery

**escurridor** [eskurri'ðor] *nm* colander

**escurrir** [esku'rrir] *vt* (*ropa*) to wring out; (*verduras, platos*) to drain ▷ *vi* (*líquidos*) to drip; **escurrirse** *vr* (*secarse*) to drain; (*resbalarse*) to slip, slide; (*escaparse*) to slip away

**ese** ['ese] (*f* **esa**, *pl* **esos, esas**) *adj demos* (*sg*) that; (*pl*) those

**ése** ['ese] (*f* **ésa**, *pl* **ésos, ésas**) *pron* (*sg*) that (one); (*pl*) those (ones); **~ ... éste ...** the former ... the latter ...; **no me vengas con ésas** don't give me any more of that nonsense

**esencia** [e'senθja] *nf* essence; **esencial** *adj* essential

**esfera** [es'fera] *nf* sphere; (*de reloj*) face; **esférico, -a** *adj* spherical

**esforzarse** [esfor'θarse] *vr* to exert o.s., make an effort

**esfuerzo** *etc* [es'fwerθo] *vb* V **esforzarse** ▷ *nm* effort

**esfumarse** [esfu'marse] *vr* (*apoyo, esperanzas*) to fade away

**esgrima** [es'xrima] *nf* fencing

**esguince** [es'xinθe] *nm* (*Med*) sprain

**eslabón** [esla'βon] *nm* link

**eslip** [ez'lip] *nm* pants *pl* (*BRIT*), briefs *pl*

**eslovaco, -a** [eslo'βako, a] *adj, nm/f* Slovak, Slovakian ▷ *nm* (*Ling*) Slovak, Slovakian

**Eslovaquia** [eslo'βakja] *nf* Slovakia

**esmalte** [es'malte] *nm* enamel; **esmalte de uñas** nail varnish o polish

**esmeralda** [esme'ralda] *nf* emerald

**esmerarse** [esme'rarse] *vr* (*aplicarse*) to take great pains, exercise great care; (*afanarse*) to work hard

**esmero** [es'mero] *nm* (great) care

**esnob** [es'nob] (*pl* **~s**) *adj* (*persona*) snobbish ▷ *nmf* snob

**eso** ['eso] *pron* that, that thing o matter; **~ de su coche** that business about his car; **~ de ir al cine** that about going to the cinema; **a ~ de las cinco** at about five o'clock; **en ~** thereupon, at that point; **~ es** that's it; **¡~ sí que es vida!** now that is really living!; **por ~ te lo dije** that's why I told you; **y ~ que llovía** in spite of the fact it was raining

**esos** *adj demos* V **ese**

**ésos** *pron* V **ése**

**espabilar** *etc* [espaβi'lar] = **despabilar** *etc*

**espacial** [espa'θjal] *adj* (*del espacio*) space *cpd*

**espaciar** [espa'θjar] *vt* to space (out)

**espacio** [es'paθjo] *nm* space; (*Mús*)

interval; (*Radio, TV*) programme (*BRIT*), program (*US*); **el ~** space; **espacio aéreo/ exterior** air/outer space; **espacioso, -a** *adj* spacious, roomy

**espada** [es'paða] *nf* sword; **espadas** *nfpl* (*Naipes*) spades

**espaguetis** [espa'ɣetis] *nmpl* spaghetti *sg*

**espalda** [es'palda] *nf* (*gen*) back; **espaldas** *nfpl* (*hombros*) shoulders; **a ~s de algn** behind sb's back; **estar de ~s** to have one's back turned; **tenderse de ~s** to lie (down) on one's back; **volver la ~ a algn** to cold-shoulder sb

**espantajo** [espan'taxo] *nm* = **espantapájaros**

**espantapájaros** [espanta'paxaros] *nm inv* scarecrow

**espantar** [espan'tar] *vt* (*asustar*) to frighten, scare; (*ahuyentar*) to frighten off; (*asombrar*) to horrify, appal; **espantarse** *vr* to get frightened o scared; to be appalled

**espanto** [es'panto] *nm* (*susto*) fright; (*terror*) terror; (*asombro*) astonishment; **espantoso, -a** *adj* frightening; terrifying; astonishing

**España** [es'paɲa] *nf* Spain; **español, a** *adj* Spanish ▷ *nm/f* Spaniard ▷ *nm* (*Ling*) Spanish

**esparadrapo** [espara'ðrapo] *nm* (sticking) plaster (*BRIT*), adhesive tape (*US*)

**esparcir** [espar'θir] *vt* to spread; (*diseminar*) to scatter; **esparcirse** *vr* to spread (out), to scatter; (*divertirse*) to enjoy o.s.

**espárrago** [es'parraxo] *nm* asparagus

**esparto** [es'parto] *nm* esparto (grass)

**espasmo** [es'pasmo] *nm* spasm

**espátula** [es'patula] *nf* spatula

**especia** [es'peθja] *nf* spice

**especial** [espe'θjal] *adj* special; **especialidad** *nf* speciality (*BRIT*), specialty (*US*)

**especie** [es'peθje] *nf* (*Bio*) species; (*clase*) kind, sort; **en ~** in kind

**especificar** [espeθifi'kar] *vt* to specify; **específico, -a** *adj* specific

**espécimen** [es'peθimen] (*pl* **especímenes**) *nm* specimen

**espectáculo** [espek'takulo] *nm* (*gen*) spectacle; (*Teatro etc*) show

**espectador, a** [espekta'ðor, a] *nm/f* spectator

**especular** [espeku'lar] *vt, vi* to speculate

**espejismo** [espe'xismo] *nm* mirage

**espejo** [es'pexo] *nm* mirror; **(espejo) retrovisor** rear-view mirror

**espeluznante** [espeluθ'nante] *adj* horrifying, hair-raising

**espera** [es'pera] *nf* (*pausa, intervalo*) wait; (*Jur: plazo*) respite; **en ~ de** waiting for; (*con expectativa*) expecting

**esperanza** [espe'ranθa] *nf* (*confianza*) hope; (*expectativa*) expectation; **hay pocas ~s de que venga** there is little prospect of his coming; **esperanza de vida** life expectancy

**esperar** [espe'rar] *vt* (*aguardar*) to wait for; (*tener expectativa de*) to expect; (*desear*) to hope for ▷ *vi* to wait; to expect; to hope; **hacer ~ a algn** to keep sb waiting; **~ un bebé** to be expecting (a baby)

**esperma** [es'perma] *nf* sperm

**espeso, -a** [es'peso, a] *adj* thick; **espesor** *nm* thickness

**espía** [es'pia] *nmf* spy; **espiar** *vt* (*observar*) to spy on

**espiga** [es'piɣa] *nf* (*Bot: de trigo etc*) ear

**espigón** [espi'ɣon] *nm* (*Bot*) ear; (*Náut*) breakwater

**espina** [es'pina] *nf* thorn; (*de pez*) bone; **espina dorsal** (*Anat*) spine

**espinaca** [espi'naka] *nf* spinach

**espinazo** [espi'naθo] *nm* spine, backbone

**espinilla** [espi'niʎa] *nf* (*Anat: tibia*) shin(bone); (*grano*) blackhead

**espinoso, -a** [espi'noso, a] *adj* (*planta*) thorny, prickly; (*asunto*) difficult

**espionaje** [espjo'naxe] *nm* spying, espionage

**espiral** [espi'ral] *adj, nf* spiral

**espirar** [espi'rar] *vt* to breathe out, exhale

**espiritista** [espiri'tista] *adj, nmf* spiritualist

**espíritu** [es'piritu] *nm* spirit; **Espíritu Santo** Holy Ghost o Spirit; **espiritual** *adj* spiritual

**espléndido, -a** [es'plendiðo, a] *adj* (*magnífico*) magnificent, splendid; (*generoso*) generous

**esplendor** [esplen'dor] *nm* splendour

**espolvorear** [espolβore'ar] *vt* to dust, sprinkle

**esponja** [es'ponxa] *nf* sponge; (*fig*) sponger; **esponjoso, -a** *adj* spongy

**espontaneidad** [espontanei'ðað] *nf* spontaneity; **espontáneo, -a** *adj* spontaneous

**esposa** [es'posa] *nf* wife; **esposas** *nfpl* handcuffs; **esposar** *vt* to handcuff

**esposo** [es'poso] *nm* husband

**espray** [es'prai] *nm* spray

**espuela** [es'pwela] *nf* spur

**espuma** [es'puma] *nf* foam; (*de cerveza*) froth, head; (*de jabón*) lather; **espuma de afeitar** shaving foam; **espumadera** *nf* (*utensilio*) skimmer; **espumoso, -a** *adj* frothy, foamy; (*vino*) sparkling

**esqueleto** [eske'leto] *nm* skeleton

**esquema** [es'kema] *nm* (*diagrama*) diagram; (*dibujo*) plan; (*Filosofía*) schema

**esquí** [es'ki] (*pl* **~s**) *nm* (*objeto*) ski; (*Deporte*) skiing; **esquí acuático** water-skiing; **esquiar** *vi* to ski

**esquilar** [eski'lar] *vt* to shear

**esquimal** [eski'mal] *adj, nmf* Eskimo

**esquina** [es'kina] *nf* corner; **esquinazo** [eski'naθo] *nm*: **dar esquinazo a algn** to give sb the slip

**esquirol** [eski'rol] (*ESP*) *nm* strikebreaker, scab

**esquivar** [eski'βar] *vt* to avoid

**esta** ['esta] *adj demos* V **este²**

**está** *vb* V **estar**

**ésta** *pron* V **éste**

**estabilidad** [estaβili'ðað] *nf* stability; **estable** *adj* stable

**establecer** [estaβle'θer] *vt* to establish; **establecerse** *vr* to establish o.s.; (*echar raíces*) to settle (down); **establecimiento** *nm* establishment

**establo** [es'taβlo] *nm* (*Agr*) stable

**estaca** [es'taka] *nf* stake, post; (*de tienda de campaña*) peg

**estacada** [esta'kaða] *nf* (*cerca*) fence, fencing; (*palenque*) stockade

**estación** [esta'θjon] *nf* station; (*del año*) season; **estación balnearia** seaside resort; **estación de autobuses** bus station; **estación de servicio** service station

**estacionamiento** [estaθjona'mjento] *nm* (*Auto*) parking; (*Mil*) stationing

**estacionar** [estaθjo'nar] *vt* (*Auto*) to park; (*Mil*) to station

**estadía** [esta'ðia] (*LAM*) *nf* stay

**estadio** [es'taðjo] *nm* (*fase*) stage, phase; (*Deporte*) stadium

**estadista** [esta'ðista] *nm* (*Pol*) statesman; (*Mat*) statistician

**estadística** [esta'ðistika] *nf* figure, statistic; (*ciencia*) statistics *sg*

**estado** [es'taðo] *nm* (*Pol: condición*) state; **estar en ~** to be pregnant; **estado civil** marital status; **estado de ánimo** state of mind; **estado de cuenta** bank statement; **estado de sitio** state of siege; **estado mayor** staff; **Estados Unidos** United States (of America)

**estadounidense** [estaðouni'ðense] *adj* United States *cpd*, American ▷ *nmf* American

**estafa** [es'tafa] *nf* swindle, trick; **estafar** *vt* to swindle, defraud

**estáis** *vb* V **estar**

**estallar** [esta'ʎar] *vi* to burst; (*bomba*) to explode, go off; (*epidemia, guerra, rebelión*) to break out; **~ en llanto** to burst into tears; **estallido** *nm* explosion; (*fig*) outbreak

**estampa** [es'tampa] *nf* print, engraving; **estampado, -a** [estam'paðo, a] *adj* printed ▷ *nm* (*impresión: acción*) printing; (*: efecto*) print; (*marca*) stamping

**estampar** [estam'par] *vt* (*imprimir*) to print; (*marcar*) to stamp; (*metal*) to engrave; (*poner sello en*) to stamp; (*fig*) to stamp, imprint

**estampida** [estam'piða] *nf* stampede

**estampido** [estam'piðo] *nm* bang, report

**estampilla** [estam'piʎa] (*LAM*) *nf* (postage) stamp

**están** *vb* V **estar**

**estancado, -a** [estan'kaðo, a] *adj* stagnant

**estancar** [estan'kar] *vt* (*aguas*) to hold up, hold back; (*Com*) to monopolize; (*fig*) to block, hold up; **estancarse** *vr* to stagnate

**estancia** [es'tanθja] *nf* (*ESP, MÉX: permanencia*) stay; (*sala*) room; (*RPL: de ganado*) farm, ranch; **estanciero** (*RPL*) *nm* farmer, rancher

**estanco, -a** [es'tanko, a] *adj* watertight ▷ *nm* tobacconist's (shop), cigar store (*US*)

**ESTANCO**

Cigarettes, tobacco, postage stamps and official forms are all sold under state monopoly in shops called **estancos**. Although tobacco products can also be bought in bars and quioscos they are generally more expensive.

**estándar** [es'tandar] *adj, nm* standard

**estandarte** [estan'darte] *nm* banner, standard

**estanque** [es'tanke] *nm* (*lago*) pool, pond; (*Agr*) reservoir

**estanquero, -a** [estan'kero, a] *nm/f* tobacconist

**estante** [es'tante] *nm* (*armario*) rack, stand; (*biblioteca*) bookcase; (*anaquel*) shelf; **estantería** *nf* shelving, shelves *pl*

○ **PALABRA CLAVE**

**estar** [es'tar] *vi* **1** (*posición*) to be; **está en la plaza** it's in the square; **¿está Juan?** is Juan in?; **estamos a 30 km de Junín** we're 30 kms from Junín

**2** (+ *adj: estado*) to be; **estar enfermo** to be ill; **está muy elegante** he's looking very smart; **¿cómo estás?** how are you keeping?

**3** (+ *gerundio*) to be; **estoy leyendo** I'm

reading

**4** (*uso pasivo*): **está condenado a muerte** he's been condemned to death; **está envasado en ...** it's packed in ...

**5** (*con fechas*): **¿a cuántos estamos?** what's the date today?; **estamos a 5 de mayo** it's the 5th of May

**6** (*locuciones*): **¿estamos?** (*¿de acuerdo?*) okay?; (*¿listo?*) ready?

**7**: **estar de: estar de vacaciones/viaje** to be on holiday/away *o* on a trip; **está de camarero** he's working as a waiter

**8**: **estar para: está para salir** he's about to leave; **no estoy para bromas** I'm not in the mood for jokes

**9**: **estar por** (*propuesta etc*) to be in favour of; (*persona etc*) to support, side with; **está por limpiar** it still has to be cleaned

**10**: **estar sin: estar sin dinero** to have no money; **está sin terminar** it isn't finished yet

**estarse** *vr*: **se estuvo en la cama toda la tarde** he stayed in bed all afternoon

**estas** ['estas] *adj demos* V **este²**

**éstas** *pron* V **éste**

**estatal** [esta'tal] *adj* state *cpd*

**estático, -a** [es'tatiko, a] *adj* static

**estatua** [es'tatwa] *nf* statue

**estatura** [esta'tura] *nf* stature, height

**este¹** ['este] *nm* east

**este²** ['este] (*f* **esta**, *pl* **estos, estas**) *adj demos* (*sg*) this; (*pl*) these

**esté** *etc vb* V **estar**

**éste** ['este] (*f* **ésta**, *pl* **éstos, éstas**) *pron* (*sg*) this (one); (*pl*) these (ones); **ése ... ~ ...** the former ... the latter ...

**estén** *etc vb* V **estar**

**estepa** [es'tepa] *nf* (*Geo*) steppe

**estera** [es'tera] *nf* mat(ting)

**estéreo** [es'tereo] *adj inv*, *nm* stereo; **estereotipo** *nm* stereotype

**estéril** [es'teril] *adj* sterile, barren; (*fig*) vain, futile; **esterilizar** *vt* to sterilize

**esterlina** [ester'lina] *adj*: **libra ~** pound sterling

**estés** *etc vb* V **estar**

**estética** [es'tetika] *nf* aesthetics *sg*

**estético, -a** [es'tetiko, a] *adj* aesthetic

**estiércol** [es'tjerkol] *nm* dung, manure

**estigma** [es'tiɣma] *nm* stigma

**estilo** [es'tilo] *nm* style; (*Tec*) stylus; (*Natación*) stroke; **algo por el ~** something along those lines

**estima** [es'tima] *nf* esteem, respect; **estimación** [estima'θjon] *nf* (*evaluación*) estimation; (*aprecio, afecto*) esteem, regard; **estimado, a** *adj* esteemed; **E~ señor** Dear

Sir

**estimar** [esti'mar] *vt* (*evaluar*) to estimate; (*valorar*) to value; (*apreciar*) to esteem, respect; (*pensar, considerar*) to think, reckon

**estimulante** [estimu'lante] *adj* stimulating ▷ *nm* stimulant

**estimular** [estimu'lar] *vt* to stimulate; (*excitar*) to excite

**estímulo** [es'timulo] *nm* stimulus; (*ánimo*) encouragement

**estirar** [esti'rar] *vt* to stretch; (*dinero, suma etc*) to stretch out; **estirarse** *vr* to stretch

**estirón** [esti'ron] *nm* pull, tug; (*crecimiento*) spurt, sudden growth; **dar** *o* **pegar un ~** (*fam: niño*) to shoot up (*inf*)

**estirpe** [es'tirpe] *nf* stock, lineage

**estival** [esti'βal] *adj* summer *cpd*

**esto** ['esto] *pron* this, this thing *o* matter; **~ de la boda** this business about the wedding

**Estocolmo** [esto'kolmo] *nm* Stockholm

**estofado** [esto'faðo] *nm* stew

**estómago** [es'tomaxo] *nm* stomach; **tener ~** to be thick-skinned

**estorbar** [estor'βar] *vt* to hinder, obstruct; (*molestar*) to bother, disturb ▷ *vi* to be in the way; **estorbo** *nm* (*molestia*) bother, nuisance; (*obstáculo*) hindrance, obstacle

**estornudar** [estornu'ðar] *vi* to sneeze

**estos** ['estos] *adj demos* V **este²**

**éstos** *pron* V **éste**

**estoy** *vb* V **estar**

**estrado** [es'traðo] *nm* platform

**estrafalario, -a** [estrafa'larjo, a] *adj* odd, eccentric

**estrago** [es'traxo] *nm* ruin, destruction; **hacer ~s en** to wreak havoc among

**estragón** [estra'xon] *nm* tarragon

**estrambótico, -a** [estram'botiko, a] *adj* (*persona*) eccentric; (*peinado, ropa*) outlandish

**estrangular** [estrangu'lar] *vt* (*persona*) to strangle; (*Med*) to strangulate

**estratagema** [estrata'xema] *nf* (*Mil*) stratagem; (*astucia*) cunning

**estrategia** [estra'texja] *nf* strategy; **estratégico, -a** *adj* strategic

**estrato** [es'trato] *nm* stratum, layer

**estrechar** [estre'tʃar] *vt* (*reducir*) to narrow; (*Costura*) to take in; (*abrazar*) to hug, embrace; **estrecharse** *vr* (*reducirse*) to narrow, grow narrow; (*abrazarse*) to embrace; **~ la mano** to shake hands

**estrechez** [estre'tʃeθ] *nf* narrowness; (*de ropa*) tightness; **estrecheces** *nfpl* (*dificultades económicas*) financial difficulties

**estrecho, -a** [es'tretʃo, a] *adj* narrow; (*apretado*) tight; (*íntimo*) close, intimate; (*miserable*) mean ▷ *nm* strait; **~ de miras**

narrow-minded

**estrella** [es'treʎa] *nf* star; **estrella de mar** (*Zool*) starfish; **estrella fugaz** shooting star

**estrellar** [estre'ʎar] *vt* (*hacer añicos*) to smash (to pieces); (*huevos*) to fry; **estrellarse** *vr* to smash; (*chocarse*) to crash; (*fracasar*) to fail

**estremecer** [estreme'θer] *vt* to shake; **estremecerse** *vr* to shake, tremble

**estrenar** [estre'nar] *vt* (*vestido*) to wear for the first time; (*casa*) to move into; (*película*, *obra de teatro*) to première; **estrenarse** *vr* (*persona*) to make one's début; **estreno** *nm* (*Cine etc*) première

**estreñido, -a** [estre'ɲiðo, a] *adj* constipated

**estreñimiento** [estreɲi'mjento] *nm* constipation

**estrepitoso, -a** [estrepi'toso, a] *adj* noisy; (*fiesta*) rowdy

**estría** [es'tria] *nf* groove

**estribar** [estri'βar] *vi*: ~ **en** to lie on

**estribillo** [estri'βiʎo] *nm* (*Literatura*) refrain; (*Mús*) chorus

**estribo** [es'triβo] *nm* (*de jinete*) stirrup; (*de coche, tren*) step; (*de puente*) support; (*Geo*) spur; **perder los ~s** to fly off the handle

**estribor** [estri'βor] *nm* (*Náut*) starboard

**estricto, -a** [es'trikto, a] *adj* (*riguroso*) strict; (*severo*) severe

**estridente** [estri'ðente] *adj* (*color*) loud; (*voz*) raucous

**estropajo** [estro'paxo] *nm* scourer

**estropear** [estrope'ar] *vt* to spoil; (*dañar*) to damage; **estropearse** *vr* (*objeto*) to get damaged; (*persona, piel*) to be ruined

**estructura** [estruk'tura] *nf* structure

**estrujar** [estru'xar] *vt* (*apretar*) to squeeze; (*aplastar*) to crush; (*fig*) to drain, bleed

**estuario** [es'twarjo] *nm* estuary

**estuche** [es'tutʃe] *nm* box, case

**estudiante** [estu'ðjante] *nmf* student; **estudiantil** *adj* student *cpd*

**estudiar** [estu'ðjar] *vt* to study

**estudio** [es'tuðjo] *nm* study; (*Cine, Arte, Radio*) studio; **estudios** *nmpl* studies; (*erudición*) learning *sg*; **estudioso, -a** *adj* studious

**estufa** [es'tufa] *nf* heater, fire

**estupefaciente** [estupefa'θjente] *nm* drug, narcotic

**estupefacto, -a** [estupe'fakto, a] *adj* speechless, thunderstruck

**estupendo, -a** [estu'pendo, a] *adj* wonderful, terrific; (*fam*) great; **¡~!** that's great!, fantastic!

**estupidez** [estupi'ðeθ] *nf* (*torpeza*) stupidity; (*acto*) stupid thing (to do)

**estúpido, -a** [es'tupiðo, a] *adj* stupid, silly

**estuve** *etc vb* V **estar**

**ETA** ['eta] (*ESP*) *nf abr* (= *Euskadi ta Askatasuna*) ETA

**etapa** [e'tapa] *nf* (*de viaje*) stage; (*Deporte*) leg; (*parada*) stopping place; (*fase*) stage, phase

**etarra** [e'tarra] *nmf* member of ETA

**etc.** *abr* (= *etcétera*) etc

**etcétera** [et'θetera] *adv* etcetera

**eternidad** [eterni'ðað] *nf* eternity; **eterno, -a** *adj* eternal, everlasting

**ética** ['etika] *nf* ethics *pl*

**ético, -a** ['etiko, a] *adj* ethical

**etiqueta** [eti'keta] *nf* (*modales*) etiquette; (*rótulo*) label, tag

**Eucaristía** [eukaris'tia] *nf* Eucharist

**euforia** [eu'forja] *nf* euphoria

**euro** ['euro] *nm* (*moneda*) euro

**eurodiputado, -a** [eurodipu'taðo, a] *nm/f* Euro MP, MEP

**Europa** [eu'ropa] *nf* Europe; **europeo, -a** *adj, nm/f* European

**Euskadi** [eus'kaði] *nm* the Basque Country o Provinces *pl*

**euskera** [eus'kera] *nm* (*Ling*) Basque

**evacuación** [eβakwa'θjon] *nf* evacuation

**evacuar** [eβa'kwar] *vt* to evacuate

**evadir** [eβa'ðir] *vt* to evade, avoid; **evadirse** *vr* to escape

**evaluar** [eβa'lwar] *vt* to evaluate

**evangelio** [eβan'xeljo] *nm* gospel

**evaporar** [eβapo'rar] *vt* to evaporate; **evaporarse** *vr* to vanish

**evasión** [eβa'sjon] *nf* escape, flight; (*fig*) evasion; **evasión de capitales** flight of capital

**evasiva** [eβa'siβa] *nf* (*pretexto*) excuse

**evento** [e'βento] *nm* event

**eventual** [eβen'twal] *adj* possible, conditional (upon circumstances); (*trabajador*) casual, temporary

> No confundir **eventual** con la palabra inglesa *eventual*.

**evidencia** [eβi'ðenθja] *nf* evidence, proof

**evidente** [eβi'ðente] *adj* obvious, clear, evident

**evitar** [eβi'tar] *vt* (*evadir*) to avoid; (*impedir*) to prevent; **~ hacer algo** to avoid doing sth

**evocar** [eβo'kar] *vt* to evoke, call forth

**evolución** [eβolu'θjon] *nf* (*desarrollo*) evolution, development; (*cambio*) change; (*Mil*) manoeuvre; **evolucionar** *vi* to evolve; to manoeuvre

**ex** [eks] *adj* ex-; **el ~ ministro** the former minister, the ex-minister

**exactitud** [eksakti'tuð] *nf* exactness;

(*precisión*) accuracy; (*puntualidad*) punctuality; **exacto, -a** *adj* exact; accurate; punctual; **¡exacto!** exactly!

**exageración** [eksaxera'θjon] *nf* exaggeration

**exagerar** [eksaxe'rar] *vt, vi* to exaggerate

**exaltar** [eksal'tar] *vt* to exalt, glorify; **exaltarse** *vr* (*excitarse*) to get excited o worked up

**examen** [ek'samen] *nm* examination; **examen de conducir** driving test; **examen de ingreso** entrance examination

**examinar** [eksami'nar] *vt* to examine; **examinarse** *vr* to be examined, take an examination

**excavadora** [ekskaβa'ðora] *nf* excavator

**excavar** [ekska'βar] *vt* to excavate

**excedencia** [eksθe'ðenθja] *nf*: **estar en ~** to be on leave; **pedir** o **solicitar la ~** to ask for leave

**excedente** [eksθe'ðente] *adj, nm* excess, surplus

**exceder** [eksθe'ðer] *vt* to exceed, surpass; **excederse** *vr* (*extralimitarse*) to go too far

**excelencia** [eksθe'lenθja] *nf* excellence; **su E~** his Excellency; **excelente** *adj* excellent

**excéntrico, -a** [eks'θentriko, a] *adj, nm/f* eccentric

**excepción** [eksθep'θjon] *nf* exception; **a ~ de** with the exception of, except for; **excepcional** *adj* exceptional

**excepto** [eks'θepto] *adv* excepting, except (for)

**exceptuar** [eksθep'twar] *vt* to except, exclude

**excesivo, -a** [eksθe'siβo, a] *adj* excessive

**exceso** [eks'θeso] *nm* (*gen*) excess; (*Com*) surplus; **exceso de equipaje/peso** excess luggage/weight; **exceso de velocidad** speeding

**excitado, -a** [eksθi'taðo, a] *adj* excited; (*emociónes*) aroused

**excitar** [eksθi'tar] *vt* to excite; (*incitar*) to urge; **excitarse** *vr* to get excited

**exclamación** [eksklama'θjon] *nf* exclamation

**exclamar** [ekskla'mar] *vi* to exclaim

**excluir** [eksklu'ir] *vt* to exclude; (*dejar fuera*) to shut out; (*descartar*) to reject

**exclusiva** [eksklu'siβa] *nf* (*Prensa*) exclusive, scoop; (*Com*) sole right

**exclusivo, -a** [eksklu'siβo, a] *adj* exclusive; **derecho ~** sole o exclusive right

**Excmo.** *abr* = **excelentísmo**

**excomulgar** [ekskomul'ɣar] *vt* (*Rel*) to excommunicate

**excomunión** [ekskomu'njon] *nf* excommunication

**excursión** [ekskur'sjon] *nf* excursion, outing; **excursionista** *nmf* (*turista*) sightseer

**excusa** [eks'kusa] *nf* excuse; (*disculpa*) apology; **excusar** [eksku'sar] *vt* to excuse

**exhaustivo, -a** [eksaus'tiβo, a] *adj* (*análisis*) thorough; (*estudio*) exhaustive

**exhausto, -a** [ek'sausto, a] *adj* exhausted

**exhibición** [eksiβi'θjon] *nf* exhibition, display, show

**exhibir** [eksi'βir] *vt* to exhibit, display, show

**exigencia** [eksi'xenθja] *nf* demand, requirement; **exigente** *adj* demanding

**exigir** [eksi'xir] *vt* (*gen*) to demand, require; **~ el pago** to demand payment

**exiliado, -a** [eksi'ljaðo, a] *adj* exiled ▷ *nm/f* exile

**exilio** [ek'siljo] *nm* exile

**eximir** [eksi'mir] *vt* to exempt

**existencia** [eksis'tenθja] *nf* existence; **existencias** *nfpl* stock(s) *pl*

**existir** [eksis'tir] *vi* to exist, be

**éxito** ['eksito] *nm* (*triunfo*) success; (*Mús etc*) hit; **tener ~** to be successful

▌ No confundir **éxito** con la palabra inglesa *exit*.

**exorbitante** [eksorβi'tante] *adj* (*precio*) exorbitant; (*cantidad*) excessive

**exótico, -a** [ek'sotiko, a] *adj* exotic

**expandir** [ekspan'dir] *vt* to expand

**expansión** [ekspan'sjon] *nf* expansion

**expansivo, -a** [ekspan'siβo, a] *adj*: **onda expansiva** shock wave

**expatriarse** [ekspa'trjarse] *vr* to emigrate; (*Pol*) to go into exile

**expectativa** [ekspekta'tiβa] *nf* (*espera*) expectation; (*perspectiva*) prospect

**expedición** [ekspeði'θjon] *nf* (*excursión*) expedition

**expediente** [ekspe'ðjente] *nm* expedient; (*Jur: procedimento*) action, proceedings *pl*; (*: papeles*) dossier, file, record

**expedir** [ekspe'ðir] *vt* (*despachar*) to send, forward; (*pasaporte*) to issue

**expensas** [eks'pensas] *nfpl*: **a ~ de** at the expense of

**experiencia** [ekspe'rjenθja] *nf* experience

**experimentado, -a** [eksperimen'taðo, a] *adj* experienced

**experimentar** [eksperimen'tar] *vt* (*en laboratorio*) to experiment with; (*probar*) to test, try out; (*notar, observar*) to experience; (*deterioro, pérdida*) to suffer; **experimento** *nm* experiment

**experto, -a** [eks'perto, a] *adj* expert,
skilled ▷ *nm/f* expert

**expirar** [ekspi'rar] *vi* to expire

**explanada** [ekspla'naða] *nf* (*llano*) plain

**explayarse** [ekspla'jarse] *vr* (*en discurso*)
to speak at length; **~ con algn** to confide
in sb

**explicación** [eksplika'θjon] *nf*
explanation

**explicar** [ekspli'kar] *vt* to explain;
**explicarse** *vr* to explain (o.s.)

**explícito, -a** [eks'pliθito, a] *adj* explicit

**explique** *etc vb* V **explicar**

**explorador, a** [eksplora'ðor, a] *nm/f*
(*pionero*) explorer; (*Mil*) scout ▷ *nm* (*Med*)
probe; (*Tec*) (*radar*) scanner

**explorar** [eksplo'rar] *vt* to explore; (*Med*)
to probe; (*radar*) to scan

**explosión** [eksplo'sjon] *nf* explosion;
**explosivo, -a** *adj* explosive

**explotación** [eksplota'θjon] *nf*
exploitation; (*de planta etc*) running

**explotar** [eksplo'tar] *vt* to exploit to run,
operate ▷ *vi* to explode

**exponer** [ekspo'ner] *vt* to expose; (*cuadro*)
to display; (*vida*) to risk; (*idea*) to explain;
**exponerse** *vr*: **~se a (hacer) algo** to run the
risk of (doing) sth

**exportación** [eksporta'θjon] *nf* (*acción*)
export; (*mercancías*) exports *pl*

**exportar** [ekspor'tar] *vt* to export

**exposición** [eksposi'θjon] *nf* (*gen*)
exposure; (*de arte*) show, exhibition;
(*explicación*) explanation; (*declaración*)
account, statement

**expresamente** [ekspresa'mente] *adv*
(*decir*) clearly; (*a propósito*) expressly

**expresar** [ekspre'sar] *vt* to express;
**expresión** *nf* expression

**expresivo, -a** [ekspre'siβo, a] *adj*
(*persona, gesto, palabras*) expressive;
(*cariñoso*) affectionate

**expreso, -a** [eks'preso, a] *pp de* **expresar**
▷ *adj* (*explícito*) express; (*claro*) specific, clear;
(*tren*) fast ▷ *adv*: **enviar ~** to send by express
(delivery)

**express** [eks'pres] (LAM) *adv*: **enviar algo ~**
to send sth special delivery

**exprimidor** [eksprimi'ðor] *nm* squeezer

**exprimir** [ekspri'mir] *vt* (*fruta*) to
squeeze; (*zumo*) to squeeze out

**expuesto, -a** [eks'pwesto, a] *pp de*
**exponer** ▷ *adj* exposed; (*cuadro etc*) on
show, on display

**expulsar** [ekspul'sar] *vt* (*echar*) to eject,
throw out; (*alumno*) to expel; (*despedir*) to
sack, fire; (*Deporte*) to send off; **expulsión** *nf*
expulsion; sending-off

**exquisito, -a** [ekski'sito, a] *adj* exquisite;
(*comida*) delicious

**éxtasis** ['ekstasis] *nm* ecstasy

**extender** [eksten'der] *vt* to extend; (*los
brazos*) to stretch out, hold out; (*mapa, tela*)
to spread (out), open (out); (*mantequilla*)
to spread; (*certificado*) to issue; (*cheque,
recibo*) to make out; (*documento*) to draw up;
**extenderse** *vr* (*gen*) to extend; (*persona: en
el suelo*) to stretch out; (*epidemia*) to spread;
**extendido, -a** *adj* (*abierto*) spread out,
open; (*brazos*) outstretched; (*costumbre*)
widespread

**extensión** [eksten'sjon] *nf* (*de terreno,
mar*) expanse, stretch; (*de tiempo*) length,
duration; (*Tel*) extension; **en toda la ~ de la
palabra** in every sense of the word

**extenso, -a** [eks'tenso, a] *adj* extensive

**exterior** [ekste'rjor] *adj* (*de fuera*) external;
(*afuera*) outside, exterior; (*apariencia*)
outward; (*deuda, relaciones*) foreign ▷ *nm*
(*gen*) exterior, outside; (*aspecto*) outward
appearance; (*Deporte*) wing(er); (*países
extranjeros*) abroad; **en el ~** abroad; **al ~**
outwardly, on the surface

**exterminar** [ekstermi'nar] *vt* to
exterminate

**externo, -a** [eks'terno, a] *adj* (*exterior*)
external, outside; (*superficial*) outward
▷ *nm/f* day pupil

**extinguir** [ekstin'gir] *vt* (*fuego*) to
extinguish, put out; (*raza, población*) to wipe
out; **extinguirse** *vr* (*fuego*) to go out; (*Bio*)
to die out, become extinct

**extintor** [ekstin'tor] *nm* (*fire*)
extinguisher

**extirpar** [ekstir'par] *vt* (*Med*) to remove
(surgically)

**extra** ['ekstra] *adj inv* (*tiempo*) extra;
(*chocolate, vino*) good-quality ▷ *nmf* extra
▷ *nm* extra; (*bono*) bonus

**extracción** [ekstrak'θjon] *nf* extraction;
(*en lotería*) draw

**extracto** [eks'trakto] *nm* extract

**extradición** [ekstraði'θjon] *nf*
extradition

**extraer** [ekstra'er] *vt* to extract, take out

**extraescolar** [ekstraesko'lar]
*adj*: **actividad ~** extracurricular activity

**extranjero, -a** [ekstran'xero, a] *adj*
foreign ▷ *nm/f* foreigner ▷ *nm* foreign
countries *pl*; **en el ~** abroad

▌ No confundir **extranjero** con la palabra
inglesa *stranger*.

**extrañar** [ekstra'ɲar] *vt* (*sorprender*) to
find strange *o* odd; (*echar de menos*) to miss;
**extrañarse** *vr* (*sorprenderse*) to be amazed,
be surprised; **me extraña** I'm surprised

**extraño, -a** [eks'traɲo, a] *adj (extranjero)* foreign; *(raro, sorprendente)* strange, odd

**extraordinario, -a** [ekstraorði'narjo, a] *adj* extraordinary; *(edición, número)* special ▷ *nm (de periódico)* special edition; **horas extraordinarias** overtime *sg*

**extrarradio** [ekstra'rraðjo] *nm* suburbs

**extravagante** [ekstraβa'ɣante] *adj (excéntrico)* eccentric; *(estrafalario)* outlandish

**extraviado, -a** [ekstra'βjaðo, a] *adj* lost, missing

**extraviar** [ekstra'βjar] *vt (persona: desorientar)* to mislead, misdirect; *(perder)* to lose, misplace; **extraviarse** *vr* to lose one's way, get lost

**extremar** [ekstre'mar] *vt* to carry to extremes

**extremaunción** [ekstremaun'θjon] *nf* extreme unction

**extremidad** [ekstremi'ðað] *nf (punta)* extremity; **extremidades** *nfpl (Anat)* extremities

**extremo, -a** [eks'tremo, a] *adj* extreme; *(último)* last ▷ *nm* end; *(límite, grado sumo)* extreme; **en último ~** as a last resort

**extrovertido, -a** [ekstroβer'tiðo, a] *adj, nm/f* extrovert

**exuberante** [eksuβe'rante] *adj* exuberant; *(fig)* luxuriant, lush

**eyacular** [ejaku'lar] *vt, vi* to ejaculate

**fa** [fa] *nm (Mús)* fa, F

**fabada** [fa'βaða] *nf* bean and sausage stew

**fábrica** ['faβrika] *nf* factory; **marca de ~** trademark; **precio de ~** factory price
⏐ No confundir **fábrica** con la palabra inglesa *fabric*.

**fabricación** [faβrika'θjon] *nf (manufactura)* manufacture; *(producción)* production; **de ~ casera** home-made; **fabricación en serie** mass production

**fabricante** [faβri'kante] *nmf* manufacturer

**fabricar** [faβri'kar] *vt (manufacturar)* to manufacture, make; *(construir)* to build; *(cuento)* to fabricate, devise

**fábula** ['faβula] *nf (cuento)* fable; *(chisme)* rumour; *(mentira)* fib

**fabuloso, -a** [faβu'loso, a] *adj (oportunidad, tiempo)* fabulous, great

**facción** [fak'θjon] *nf (Pol)* faction; **facciones** *nfpl (de rostro)* features

**faceta** [fa'θeta] *nf* facet

**facha** ['fatʃa] *(fam) nf (aspecto)* look; *(cara)* face

**fachada** [fa'tʃaða] *nf (Arq)* façade, front

**fácil** ['faθil] *adj (simple)* easy; *(probable)* likely

**facilidad** [faθili'ðað] *nf (capacidad)* ease; *(sencillez)* simplicity; *(de palabra)* fluency; **facilidades** *nfpl* facilities; **facilidades de pago** credit facilities

**facilitar** [faθili'tar] *vt (hacer fácil)* to make easy; *(proporcionar)* to provide

**factor** [fak'tor] *nm* factor

**factura** [fak'tura] *nf (cuenta)* bill; **facturación** *nf (de equipaje)* check-in; **facturar** *vt (Com)* to invoice, charge for; *(equipaje)* to check in

**facultad** [fakul'tað] *nf (aptitud, Escol etc)* faculty; *(poder)* power

**faena** [fa'ena] nf (trabajo) work; (quehacer) task, job

**faisán** [fai'san] nm pheasant

**faja** ['faxa] nf (para la cintura) sash; (de mujer) corset; (de tierra) strip

**fajo** ['faxo] nm (de papeles) bundle; (de billetes) wad

**falda** ['falda] nf (prenda de vestir) skirt; **falda pantalón** culottes pl, split skirt

**falla** ['faʎa] nf (defecto) fault, flaw; **falla humana** (LAM) human error

**fallar** [fa'ʎar] vt (Jur) to pronounce sentence on ▷ vi (memoria) to fail; (motor) to miss

**Fallas** ['faʎas] nfpl Valencian celebration of the feast of St Joseph

⚬ **FALLAS**
⚬
⚬ In the week of 19 March (the feast
⚬ of San José), Valencia honours its
⚬ patron saint with a spectacular fiesta
⚬ called **Las Fallas**. The **Fallas** are huge
⚬ papier-mâché, cardboard and wooden
⚬ sculptures which are built by competing
⚬ teams throughout the year. They depict
⚬ politicians and well-known public
⚬ figures and are thrown onto bonfires
⚬ and set alight once a jury has judged
⚬ them – only the best sculpture escapes
⚬ the flames.

**fallecer** [faʎe'θer] vi to pass away, die; **fallecimiento** nm decease, demise

**fallido, -a** [fa'ʎido, a] adj (gen) frustrated, unsuccessful

**fallo** ['faʎo] nm (Jur) verdict, ruling; (fracaso) failure; **fallo cardíaco** heart failure; **fallo humano** (ESP) human error

**falsificar** [falsifi'kar] vt (firma etc) to forge; (moneda) to counterfeit

**falso, -a** ['falso, a] adj false; (documento, moneda etc) fake; **en ~** falsely

**falta** ['falta] nf (defecto) fault, flaw; (privación) lack, want; (ausencia) absence; (carencia) shortage; (equivocación) mistake; (Deporte) foul; **echar en ~** to miss; **hacer ~ hacer algo** to be necessary to do sth; **me hace ~ una pluma** I need a pen; **falta de educación** bad manners pl; **falta de ortografía** spelling mistake

**faltar** [fal'tar] vi (escasear) to be lacking, be wanting; (ausentarse) to be absent, be missing; **faltan 2 horas para llegar** there are 2 hours to go till arrival; **~ al respeto a algn** to be disrespectful to sb; **¡no faltaba más!** (no hay de qué) don't mention it

**fama** ['fama] nf (renombre) fame; (reputación) reputation

**familia** [fa'milja] nf family; **familia numerosa** large family; **familia política** in-laws pl

**familiar** [fami'ljar] adj (relativo a la familia) family cpd; (conocido, informal) familiar ▷ nm relative, relation

**famoso, -a** [fa'moso, a] adj (renombrado) famous

**fan** [fan] (pl ~s) nmf fan

**fanático, -a** [fa'natiko, a] adj fanatical ▷ nm/f fanatic; (Cine, Deporte) fan

**fanfarrón, -ona** [fanfa'rron, ona] adj boastful

**fango** ['fango] nm mud

**fantasía** [fanta'sia] nf fantasy, imagination; **joyas de ~** imitation jewellery sg

**fantasma** [fan'tasma] nm (espectro) ghost, apparition; (fanfarrón) show-off

**fantástico, -a** [fan'tastiko, a] adj fantastic

**farmacéutico, -a** [farma'θeutiko, a] adj pharmaceutical ▷ nm/f chemist (BRIT), pharmacist

**farmacia** [far'maθja] nf chemist's (shop) (BRIT), pharmacy; **farmacia de guardia** all-night chemist

**fármaco** ['farmako] nm drug

**faro** ['faro] nm (Náut: torre) lighthouse; (Auto) headlamp; **faros antiniebla** fog lamps; **faros delanteros/traseros** headlights/rear lights

**farol** [fa'rol] nm lantern, lamp

**farola** [fa'rola] nf street lamp (BRIT) o light (US)

**farra** ['farra] (LAM: fam) nf party; **ir de ~** to go on a binge

**farsa** ['farsa] nf (gen) farce

**farsante** [far'sante] nmf fraud, fake

**fascículo** [fas'θikulo] nm (de revista) part, instalment

**fascinar** [fasθi'nar] vt (gen) to fascinate

**fascismo** [fas'θismo] nm fascism; **fascista** adj, nmf fascist

**fase** ['fase] nf phase

**fashion** ['faʃon] adj (fam) trendy

**fastidiar** [fasti'ðjar] vt (molestar) to annoy, bother; (estropear) to spoil; **fastidiarse** vr: **¡que se fastidie!** (fam) he'll just have to put up with it!

**fastidio** [fas'tiðjo] nm (molestia) annoyance; **fastidioso, -a** adj (molesto) annoying

**fatal** [fa'tal] adj (gen) fatal; (desgraciado) ill-fated; (fam: malo, pésimo) awful; **fatalidad** nf (destino) fate; (mala suerte) misfortune

**fatiga** [fa'tixa] nf (cansancio) fatigue,

weariness

**fatigar** [fati'xar] vt to tire, weary

**fatigoso, -a** [fati'yoso, a] adj (cansador) tiring

**fauna** ['fauna] nf fauna

**favor** [fa'βor] nm favour; **estar a ~ de** to be in favour of; **haga el ~ de ...** would you be so good as to ..., kindly ...; **por ~** please; **favorable** adj favourable

**favorecer** [faβore'θer] vt to favour; (vestido etc) to become, flatter; **este peinado le favorece** this hairstyle suits him

**favorito, -a** [faβo'rito, a] adj, nm/f favourite

**fax** [faks] nm inv fax; **mandar por ~** to fax

**fe** [fe] nf (Rel) faith; (documento) certificate; **actuar con buena/mala ~** to act in good/ bad faith

**febrero** [fe'βrero] nm February

**fecha** ['fetʃa] nf date; **con ~ adelantada** postdated; **en ~ próxima** soon; **hasta la ~** to date, so far; **poner ~** to date; **fecha de caducidad** (de producto alimenticio) sell-by date; (de contrato etc) expiry date; **fecha de nacimiento** date of birth; **fecha límite** o **tope** deadline

**fecundo, -a** [fe'kundo, a] adj (fértil) fertile; (fig) prolific; (productivo) productive

**federación** [feðera'θjon] nf federation

**felicidad** [feliθi'ðað] nf happiness; **¡~es!** (deseos) best wishes, congratulations!; (en cumpleaños) happy birthday!

**felicitación** [feliθita'θjon] nf (tarjeta) greeting(s) card

**felicitar** [feliθi'tar] vt to congratulate

**feliz** [fe'liθ] adj happy

**felpudo** [fel'puðo] nm doormat

**femenino, -a** [feme'nino, a] adj, nm feminine

**feminista** [femi'nista] adj, nmf feminist

**fenómeno** [fe'nomeno] nm phenomenon; (fig) freak, accident ▷ adj great ▷ excl great!, marvellous!; **fenomenal** adj = **fenómeno**

**feo, -a** ['feo, a] adj (gen) ugly; (desagradable) bad, nasty

**féretro** ['feretro] nm (ataúd) coffin; (sarcófago) bier

**feria** ['ferja] nf (gen) fair; (descanso) holiday, rest day; (MÉX: cambio) small o loose change; (cs: mercado) village market

**feriado** [fe'rjaðo] (LAM) nm holiday

**fermentar** [fermen'tar] vi to ferment

**feroz** [fe'roθ] adj (cruel) cruel; (salvaje) fierce

**férreo, -a** ['ferreo, a] adj iron

**ferretería** [ferrete'ria] nf (tienda) ironmonger's (shop) (BRIT), hardware

store (US)

**ferrocarril** [ferroka'rril] nm railway

**ferroviario, -a** [ferro'βjarjo, a] adj rail cpd

**ferry** ['ferri] (pl **~s** o **ferries**) nm ferry

**fértil** ['fertil] adj (productivo) fertile; (rico) rich; **fertilidad** nf (gen) fertility; (productividad) fruitfulness

**fervor** [fer'βor] nm fervour

**festejar** [feste'xar] vt (celebrar) to celebrate

**festejo** [fes'texo] nm celebration; **festejos** nmpl (fiestas) festivals

**festín** [fes'tin] nm feast, banquet

**festival** [festi'βal] nm festival

**festividad** [festiβi'ðað] nf festivity

**festivo, -a** [fes'tiβo, a] adj (de fiesta) festive; (Cine, Literatura) humorous; **día ~** holiday

**feto** ['feto] nm foetus

**fiable** ['fjaβle] adj (persona) trustworthy; (máquina) reliable

**fiambre** ['fjambre] nm cold meat

**fiambrera** [fjam'brera] nf (para almuerzo) lunch box

**fianza** ['fjanθa] nf surety; (Jur): **libertad bajo ~** release on bail

**fiar** [fi'ar] vt (salir garante de) to guarantee; (vender a crédito) to sell on credit ▷ vi to trust; **fiarse** vr to trust (in), rely on; **~ a** (secreto) to confide (to); **~se de algn** to rely on sb

**fibra** ['fiβra] nf fibre; **fibra óptica** optical fibre

**ficción** [fik'θjon] nf fiction

**ficha** ['fitʃa] nf (Tel) token; (en juegos) counter, marker; (tarjeta) (index) card; **fichaje** nm (Deporte) signing; **fichar** vt (archivar) to file, index; (Deporte) to sign; **estar fichado** to have a record; **fichero** nm box file; (Inform) file

**ficticio, -a** [fik'tiθjo, a] adj (imaginario) fictitious; (falso) fabricated

**fidelidad** [fiðeli'ðað] nf (lealtad) fidelity, loyalty; **alta ~** high fidelity, hi-fi

**fideos** [fi'ðeos] nmpl noodles

**fiebre** ['fjeβre] nf (Med) fever; (fig) fever, excitement; **tener ~** to have a temperature; **fiebre aftosa** foot-and-mouth disease

**fiel** [fjel] adj (leal) faithful, loyal; (fiable) reliable; (exacto) accurate, faithful ▷ nm: **los ~es** the faithful

**fieltro** ['fjeltro] nm felt

**fiera** ['fjera] nf (animal feroz) wild animal o beast; (fig) dragon; V tb **fiero**

**fiero, -a** ['fjero, a] adj (cruel) cruel; (feroz) fierce; (duro) harsh

**fierro** ['fjerro] (LAM) nm (hierro) iron

**fiesta** ['fjesta] nf party; (de pueblo) festival; (vacaciones: tb: **~s**) holiday sg; **fiesta mayor** annual festival; **fiesta patria** (LAM) independence day

○ **FIESTAS**
○
○ **Fiestas** can be official public holidays
○ or holidays set by each autonomous
○ region, many of which coincide with
○ religious festivals. There are also
○ many **fiestas** all over Spain for a local
○ patron saint or the Virgin Mary. These
○ often last several days and can include
○ religious processions, carnival parades,
○ bullfights and dancing.

**figura** [fi'ɣura] nf (gen) figure; (forma, imagen) shape, form; (Naipes) face card
**figurar** [fiɣu'rar] vt (representar) to represent; (fingir) to figure ▷ vi to figure; **figurarse** vr (imaginarse) to imagine; (suponer) to suppose
**fijador** [fixa'ðor] nm (Foto etc) fixative; (de pelo) gel
**fijar** [fi'xar] vt (gen) to fix; (estampilla) to affix, stick (on); **fijarse** vr: **~se en** to notice
**fijo, -a** ['fixo, a] adj (gen) fixed; (firme) firm; (permanente) permanent ▷ adv: **mirar ~** to stare
**fila** ['fila] nf row; (Mil) rank; **ponerse en ~** to line up, get into line; **fila india** single file
**filatelia** [fila'telja] nf philately, stamp collecting
**filete** [fi'lete] nm (de carne) fillet steak; (de pescado) fillet
**filiación** [filja'θjon] nf (Pol) affiliation
**filial** [fi'ljal] adj filial ▷ nf subsidiary
**Filipinas** [fili'pinas] nfpl: **las (Islas) ~** the Philippines; **filipino, -a** adj, nm/f Philippine
**filmar** [fil'mar] vt to film, shoot
**filo** ['filo] nm (gen) edge; **sacar ~ a** to sharpen; **al ~ del mediodía** at about midday; **de doble ~** double-edged
**filología** [filolo'ɣia] nf philology; **filología inglesa** (Univ) English Studies
**filón** [fi'lon] nm (Minería) vein, lode; (fig) goldmine
**filosofía** [filoso'fia] nf philosophy; **filósofo, -a** nm/f philosopher
**filtrar** [fil'trar] vt, vi to filter, strain; **filtrarse** vr to filter; **filtro** nm (Tec, utensilio) filter
**fin** [fin] nm end; (objetivo) aim, purpose; **al ~ y al cabo** when all's said and done; **a ~ de** in order to; **por ~** finally; **en ~** in short; **fin de semana** weekend

**final** [fi'nal] adj final ▷ nm end, conclusion ▷ nf final; **al ~** in the end; **a ~es de** at the end of; **finalidad** nf (propósito) purpose, intention; **finalista** nmf finalist; **finalizar** vt to end, finish; (Inform) to log out o off ▷ vi to end, come to an end
**financiar** [finan'θjar] vt to finance; **financiero, -a** adj financial ▷ nm/f financier
**finca** ['finka] nf (casa de campo) country house; (ESP: bien inmueble) property, land; (LAM: granja) farm
**finde** ['finde] nm abr (fam: fin de semana) weekend
**fingir** [fin'xir] vt (simular) to simulate, feign ▷ vi (aparentar) to pretend
**finlandés, -esa** [finlan'des, esa] adj Finnish ▷ nm/f Finn ▷ nm (Ling) Finnish
**Finlandia** [fin'landja] nf Finland
**fino, -a** ['fino, a] adj fine; (delgado) slender; (de buenas maneras) polite, refined; (jerez) fino, dry
**firma** ['firma] nf signature; (Com) firm, company
**firmamento** [firma'mento] nm firmament
**firmar** [fir'mar] vt to sign
**firme** ['firme] adj firm; (estable) stable; (sólido) solid; (constante) steady; (decidido) resolute ▷ nm road (surface); **firmeza** nf firmness; (constancia) steadiness; (solidez) solidity
**fiscal** [fis'kal] adj fiscal ▷ nmf public prosecutor; **año ~** tax o fiscal year
**fisgonear** [fisɣone'ar] vt to poke one's nose into ▷ vi to pry, spy
**física** ['fisika] nf physics sg; V tb **físico**
**físico, -a** ['fisiko, a] adj physical ▷ nm physique ▷ nm/f physicist
**fisura** [fi'sura] nf crack; (Med) fracture
**flác(c)ido, -a** ['fla(k)θiðo, a] adj flabby
**flaco, -a** ['flako, a] adj (muy delgado) skinny, thin; (débil) weak, feeble
**flagrante** [fla'ɣrante] adj flagrant
**flama** ['flama] (MÉX) nf flame; **flamable** (MÉX) adj flammable
**flamante** [fla'mante] (fam) adj brilliant; (nuevo) brand-new
**flamenco, -a** [fla'menko, a] adj (de Flandes) Flemish; (baile, música) flamenco ▷ nm (baile, música) flamenco; (Zool) flamingo
**flamingo** [fla'mingo] (MÉX) nm flamingo
**flan** [flan] nm creme caramel

▎No confundir **flan** con la palabra inglesa flan.

**flash** [flaʃ] (pl ~ o -es) nm (Foto) flash
**flauta** ['flauta] nf (Mús) flute

**flecha** ['fletʃa] nf arrow
**flechazo** [fle'tʃaθo] nm love at first sight
**fleco** ['fleko] nm fringe
**flema** ['flema] nm phlegm
**flequillo** [fle'kiʎo] nm (pelo) fringe
**flexible** [flek'siβle] adj flexible
**flexión** [flek'sjon] nf press-up
**flexo** ['flekso] nm adjustable table-lamp
**flirtear** [flirte'ar] vi to flirt
**flojera** [flo'xera] (LAM: fam) nf: **me da ~** I can't be bothered
**flojo, -a** ['floxo, a] adj (gen) loose; (sin fuerzas) limp; (débil) weak
**flor** [flor] nf flower; **a ~ de** on the surface of; **flora** nf flora; **florecer** vi (Bot) to flower, bloom; (fig) to flourish; **florería** (LAM) nf florist's (shop); **florero** nm vase; **floristería** nf florist's (shop)
**flota** ['flota] nf fleet
**flotador** [flota'ðor] nm (gen) float; (para nadar) rubber ring
**flotar** [flo'tar] vi (gen) to float; **flote** nm: **a flote** afloat; **salir a flote** (fig) to get back on one's feet
**fluidez** [flui'ðeθ] nf fluidity; (fig) fluency
**fluido, -a** ['fluiðo, a] adj, nm fluid
**fluir** [flu'ir] vi to flow
**flujo** ['fluxo] nm flow; **flujo y reflujo** ebb and flow
**flúor** ['fluor] nm fluoride
**fluorescente** [flwores'θente] adj fluorescent ▷ nm fluorescent light
**fluvial** [fluβi'al] adj (navegación, cuenca) fluvial, river cpd
**fobia** ['foβja] nf phobia; **fobia a las alturas** fear of heights
**foca** ['foka] nf seal
**foco** ['foko] nm focus; (Elec) floodlight; (MÉX: bombilla) (light) bulb
**fofo, -a** ['fofo, a] adj soft, spongy; (carnes) flabby
**fogata** [fo'xata] nf bonfire
**fogón** [fo'xon] nm (de cocina) ring, burner
**folio** ['foljo] nm folio, page
**foliaje** [fo'ʎaxe] nm foliage
**folleto** [fo'ʎeto] nm (Pol) pamphlet
**follón** [fo'ʎon] (ESP: fam) nm (lío) mess; (conmoción) fuss; **armar un ~** to kick up a row
**fomentar** [fomen'tar] vt (Med) to foment
**fonda** ['fonda] nf inn
**fondo** ['fondo] nm (de mar) bottom; (de coche, sala) back; (Arte etc) background; (reserva) fund; **fondos** nmpl (Com) funds, resources; **una investigación a ~** a thorough investigation; **en el ~** at bottom, deep down
**fonobuzón** [fonoβu'θon] nm voice mail

**fontanería** [fontane'ria] nf plumbing; **fontanero, -a** nm/f plumber
**footing** ['futiŋ] nm jogging; **hacer ~** to jog, go jogging
**forastero, -a** [foras'tero, a] nm/f stranger
**forcejear** [forθexe'ar] vi (luchar) to struggle
**forense** [fo'rense] nmf pathologist
**forma** ['forma] nf (figura) form, shape; (Med) fitness; (método) way, means; **las ~s** the conventions; **estar en ~** to be fit; **de ~ que ...** so that ...; **de todas ~s** in any case
**formación** [forma'θjon] nf (gen) formation; (educación) education; **formación profesional** vocational training
**formal** [for'mal] adj (gen) formal; (fig: serio) serious; (: de fiar) reliable; **formalidad** nf formality; seriousness; **formalizar** vt (Jur) to formalize; (situación) to put in order, regularize; **formalizarse** vr (situación) to be put in order, be regularized
**formar** [for'mar] vt (componer) to form, shape; (constituir) to make up, constitute; (Escol) to train, educate; **formarse** vr (Escol) to be trained, educated; (cobrar forma) to form, take form; (desarrollarse) to develop
**formatear** [formate'ar] vt to format
**formato** [for'mato] nm format
**formidable** [formi'ðaβle] adj (temible) formidable; (estupendo) tremendous
**fórmula** ['formula] nf formula
**formulario** [formu'larjo] nm form
**fornido, -a** [for'niðo, a] adj well-built
**foro** ['foro] nm (Pol, Inform etc) forum
**forrar** [fo'rrar] vt (abrigo) to line; (libro) to cover; **forro** nm (de cuaderno) cover; (Costura) lining; (de sillón) upholstery; **forro polar** fleece
**fortalecer** [fortale'θer] vt to strengthen
**fortaleza** [forta'leθa] nf (Mil) fortress, stronghold; (fuerza) strength; (determinación) resolution
**fortuito, -a** [for'twito, a] adj accidental
**fortuna** [for'tuna] nf (suerte) fortune, (good) luck; (riqueza) fortune, wealth
**forzar** [for'θar] vt (puerta) to force (open); (compeler) to compel
**forzoso, -a** [for'θoso, a] adj necessary
**fosa** ['fosa] nf (sepultura) grave; (en tierra) pit; **fosas nasales** nostrils
**fósforo** ['fosforo] nm (Quím) phosphorus; (cerilla) match
**fósil** ['fosil] nm fossil
**foso** ['foso] nm ditch; (Teatro) pit; (Auto) inspection pit
**foto** ['foto] nf photo, snap(shot); **sacar una ~** to take a photo o picture; **foto (de)**

**carné** passport(-size) photo

**fotocopia** [foto'kopja] *nf* photocopy; **fotocopiadora** *nf* photocopier; **fotocopiar** *vt* to photocopy

**fotografía** [fotoɣra'fia] *nf* (*Arte*) photography; (*una fotografía*) photograph; **fotografiar** *vt* to photograph

**fotógrafo, -a** [fo'toɣrafo, a] *nm/f* photographer

**fotomatón** [fotoma'ton] *nm* photo booth

**FP** (ESP) *nf abr* (= *Formación Profesional*) *vocational courses for 14- to 18-year-olds*

**fracasar** [fraka'sar] *vi* (*gen*) to fail

**fracaso** [fra'kaso] *nm* failure

**fracción** [frak'θjon] *nf* fraction

**fractura** [frak'tura] *nf* fracture, break

**fragancia** [fra'ɣanθja] *nf* (*olor*) fragrance, perfume

**frágil** ['fraxil] *adj* (*débil*) fragile; (*Com*) breakable

**fragmento** [fraɣ'mento] *nm* (*pedazo*) fragment

**fraile** ['fraile] *nm* (*Rel*) friar; (: *monje*) monk

**frambuesa** [fram'bwesa] *nf* raspberry

**francés, -esa** [fran'θes, esa] *adj* French ▷ *nm/f* Frenchman(-woman) ▷ *nm* (*Ling*) French

**Francia** ['franθja] *nf* France

**franco, -a** ['franko, a] *adj* (*cándido*) frank, open; (*Com: exento*) free ▷ *nm* (*moneda*) franc

**francotirador, a** [frankotira'ðor, a] *nm/f* sniper

**franela** [fra'nela] *nf* flannel

**franja** ['franxa] *nf* fringe

**franquear** [franke'ar] *vt* (*camino*) to clear; (*carta, paquete postal*) to frank, stamp; (*obstáculo*) to overcome

**franqueo** [fran'keo] *nm* postage

**franqueza** [fran'keθa] *nf* (*candor*) frankness

**frasco** ['frasko] *nm* bottle, flask

**frase** ['frase] *nf* sentence; **frase hecha** set phrase; (*pey*) stock phrase

**fraterno, -a** [fra'terno, a] *adj* brotherly, fraternal

**fraude** ['frauðe] *nm* (*cualidad*) dishonesty; (*acto*) fraud

**frazada** [fra'saða] (LAM) *nf* blanket

**frecuencia** [fre'kwenθja] *nf* frequency; **con ~** frequently, often

**frecuentar** [frekwen'tar] *vt* to frequent

**frecuente** [fre'kwente] *adj* (*gen*) frequent

**fregadero** [freɣa'ðero] *nm* (kitchen) sink

**fregar** [fre'ɣar] *vt* (*frotar*) to scrub; (*platos*) to wash (up); (LAM: *fam: fastidiar*) to annoy; (: *malograr*) to screw up

**fregona** [fre'ɣona] *nf* mop

**freír** [fre'ir] *vt* to fry

**frenar** [fre'nar] *vt* to brake; (*fig*) to check

**frenazo** [fre'naθo] *nm*: **dar un ~** to brake sharply

**frenesí** [frene'si] *nm* frenzy

**freno** ['freno] *nm* (*Tec, Auto*) brake; (*de cabalgadura*) bit; (*fig*) check; **freno de mano** handbrake

**frente** ['frente] *nm* (*Arq, Pol*) front; (*de objeto*) front part ▷ *nf* forehead, brow; **~ a** in front of; (*en situación opuesta de*) opposite; **al ~ de** (*fig*) at the head of; **chocar de ~** to crash head-on; **hacer ~ a** to face up to

**fresa** ['fresa] (ESP) *nf* strawberry

**fresco, -a** ['fresko, a] *adj* (*nuevo*) fresh; (*frío*) cool; (*descarado*) cheeky ▷ *nm* (*aire*) fresh air; (*Arte*) fresco; (LAM: *jugo*) fruit drink ▷ *nm/f* (*fam*): **ser un ~** to have a nerve; **tomar el ~** to get some fresh air; **frescura** *nf* freshness; (*descaro*) cheek, nerve

**frialdad** [frial'daθ] *nf* (*gen*) coldness; (*indiferencia*) indifference

**frigidez** [frixi'ðeθ] *nf* frigidity

**frigorífico** [friɣo'rifiko] *nm* refrigerator

**frijol** [fri'xol] *nm* kidney bean

**frío, -a** *etc* ['frio, a] *vb* V **freír** ▷ *adj* cold; (*indiferente*) indifferent ▷ *nm* cold; indifference; **hace ~** it's cold; **tener ~** to be cold

**frito, -a** ['frito, a] *adj* fried; **me trae ~ ese hombre** I'm sick and tired of that man; **fritos** *nmpl* fried food

**frívolo, -a** ['friβolo, a] *adj* frivolous

**frontal** [fron'tal] *adj* frontal; **choque ~** head-on collision

**frontera** [fron'tera] *nf* frontier; **fronterizo, -a** *adj* frontier *cpd*; (*contiguo*) bordering

**frontón** [fron'ton] *nm* (*Deporte: cancha*) pelota court; (: *juego*) pelota

**frotar** [fro'tar] *vt* to rub; **frotarse** *vr*: **~se las manos** to rub one's hands

**fructífero, -a** [fruk'tifero, a] *adj* fruitful

**fruncir** [frun'θir] *vt* to pucker; (*Costura*) to pleat; **~ el ceño** to knit one's brow

**frustrar** [frus'trar] *vt* to frustrate

**fruta** ['fruta] *nf* fruit; **frutería** *nf* fruit shop; **frutero, -a** *adj* fruit *cpd* ▷ *nm/f* fruiterer ▷ *nm* fruit bowl

**frutilla** [fru'tiʎa] (CS) *nf* strawberry

**fruto** ['fruto] *nm* fruit; (*fig: resultado*) result; (: *beneficio*) benefit; **frutos secos** nuts and dried fruit *pl*

**fucsia** ['fuksja] *nf* fuchsia

**fue** [fwe] *vb* V **ser; ir**

**fuego** ['fweɣo] *nm* (*gen*) fire; **a ~ lento** on a low heat; **¿tienes ~?** have you (got) a light?; **fuego amigo** friendly fire; **fuegos artificiales** fireworks

**fuente** ['fwente] *nf* fountain; (*manantial: fig*) spring; (*origen*) source; (*plato*) large dish

**fuera** *etc* ['fwera] *vb* V **ser; ir** ▷ *adv* out(side); (*en otra parte*) away; (*excepto, salvo*) except, save ▷ *prep*: **~ de** outside; (*fig*) besides; **~ de sí** beside o.s.; **por ~** (on the) outside

**fuera-borda** [fwera'βorða] *nm* speedboat

**fuerte** ['fwerte] *adj* strong; (*golpe*) hard; (*ruido*) loud; (*comida*) rich; (*lluvia*) heavy; (*dolor*) intense ▷ *adv* strongly; hard; loud(ly)

**fuerza** *etc* ['fwerθa] *vb* V **forzar** ▷ *nf* (*fortaleza*) strength; (*Tec, Elec*) power; (*coacción*) force; (*Mil, Pol*) force; **a ~ de** by dint of; **cobrar ~s** to recover one's strength; **tener ~s para** to have the strength to; **a la ~** forcibly, by force; **por ~** of necessity; **fuerza de voluntad** willpower; **fuerzas aéreas** air force *sg*; **fuerzas armadas** armed forces

**fuga** ['fuxa] *nf* (*huida*) flight, escape; (*de gas etc*) leak

**fugarse** [fu'xarse] *vr* to flee, escape

**fugaz** [fu'xaθ] *adj* fleeting

**fugitivo, a** [fuxi'tiβo, a] *adj, nm/f* fugitive

**fui** [fwi] *vb* V **ser; ir**

**fulano, -a** [fu'lano, a] *nm/f* so-and-so, what's-his-name/what's-her-name

**fulminante** [fulmi'nante] *adj* (*fig: mirada*) fierce; (*Med: enfermedad, ataque*) sudden; (*fam: éxito, golpe*) sudden

**fumador, a** [fuma'ðor, a] *nm/f* smoker

**fumar** [fu'mar] *vt, vi* to smoke; **~ en pipa** to smoke a pipe

**función** [fun'θjon] *nf* function; (*en trabajo*) duties *pl*; (*espectáculo*) show; **entrar en funciones** to take up one's duties

**funcionar** [funθjo'nar] *vi* (*gen*) to function; (*máquina*) to work; **"no funciona"** "out of order"

**funcionario, -a** [funθjo'narjo, a] *nm/f* civil servant

**funda** ['funda] *nf* (*gen*) cover; (*de almohada*) pillowcase

**fundación** [funda'θjon] *nf* foundation

**fundamental** [fundamen'tal] *adj* fundamental, basic

**fundamento** [funda'mento] *nm* (*base*) foundation

**fundar** [fun'dar] *vt* to found; **fundarse** *vr*: **~se en** to be founded on

**fundición** [fundi'θjon] *nf* fusing; (*fábrica*) foundry

**fundir** [fun'dir] *vt* (*gen*) to fuse; (*metal*) to smelt, melt down; (*nieve etc*) to melt; (*Com*) to merge; (*estatua*) to cast; **fundirse** *vr* (*colores etc*) to merge, blend; (*unirse*) to fuse together; (*Elec: fusible, lámpara etc*) to fuse, blow; (*nieve etc*) to melt

**fúnebre** ['funeβre] *adj* funeral *cpd*, funereal

**funeral** [fune'ral] *nm* funeral; **funeraria** *nf* undertaker's

**funicular** [funiku'lar] *nm* (*tren*) funicular; (*teleférico*) cable car

**furgón** [fur'ɣon] *nm* wagon; **furgoneta** *nf* (*Auto, Com*) (transit) van (BRIT), pick-up (truck) (US)

**furia** ['furja] *nf* (*ira*) fury; (*violencia*) violence; **furioso, -a** (*iracundo*) furious; (*violento*) violent

**furtivo, -a** [fur'tiβo, a] *adj* furtive ▷ *nm* poacher

**fusible** [fu'siβle] *nm* fuse

**fusil** [fu'sil] *nm* rifle; **fusilar** *vt* to shoot

**fusión** [fu'sjon] *nf* (*gen*) melting; (*unión*) fusion; (*Com*) merger

**fútbol** ['futβol] *nm* football (BRIT), soccer (US); **fútbol americano** American football (BRIT), football (US); **fútbol sala** indoor football (BRIT) o soccer (US); **futbolín** *nm* table football; **futbolista** *nmf* footballer

**futuro, -a** [fu'turo, a] *adj, nm* future

# g

**gabardina** [gaβarˈðina] nf raincoat, gabardine

**gabinete** [gaβiˈnete] nm (Pol) cabinet; (estudio) study; (de abogados etc) office

**gachas** [ˈgatʃas] nfpl porridge sg

**gafas** [ˈgafas] nfpl glasses; **gafas de sol** sunglasses

**gafe** [ˈgafe] (ESP) nmf jinx

**gaita** [ˈgaita] nf bagpipes pl

**gajes** [ˈgaxes] nmpl: **~ del oficio** occupational hazards

**gajo** [ˈgaxo] nm (de naranja) segment

**gala** [ˈgala] nf (traje de etiqueta) full dress; **galas** nfpl (ropa) finery sg; **estar de ~** to be in one's best clothes; **hacer ~ de** to display

**galápago** [gaˈlapaɣo] nm (Zool) turtle

**galardón** [galarˈðon] nm award, prize

**galaxia** [gaˈlaksja] nf galaxy

**galera** [gaˈlera] nf (nave) galley; (carro) wagon; (Imprenta) galley

**galería** [galeˈria] nf (gen) gallery; (balcón) veranda(h); (pasillo) corridor; **galería comercial** shopping mall

**Gales** [ˈgales] nm (tb: **País de ~**) Wales; **galés, -esa** adj Welsh ▷ nm/f Welshman(-woman) ▷ nm (Ling) Welsh

**galgo, -a** [ˈgalɣo, a] nm/f greyhound

**gallego, -a** [gaˈʎeɣo, a] adj, nm/f Galician

**galleta** [gaˈʎeta] nf biscuit (BRIT), cookie (US)

**gallina** [gaˈʎina] nf hen ▷ nmf (fam: cobarde) chicken; **gallinero** nm henhouse; (Teatro) top gallery

**gallo** [ˈgaʎo] nm cock, rooster

**galopar** [galoˈpar] vi to gallop

**gama** [ˈgama] nf (fig) range

**gamba** [ˈgamba] nf prawn (BRIT), shrimp (US)

**gamberro, -a** [gamˈberro, a] (ESP) nm/f hooligan, lout

**gamuza** [gaˈmuθa] nf chamois

**gana** [ˈgana] nf (deseo) desire, wish; (apetito) appetite; (voluntad) will; (añoranza) longing; **de buena ~** willingly; **de mala ~** reluctantly; **me da ~s de** I feel like, I want to; **no me da la ~** I don't feel like it; **tener ~s de** to feel like

**ganadería** [ganaðeˈria] nf (ganado) livestock; (ganado vacuno) cattle pl; (cría, comercio) cattle raising

**ganadero, -a** [ganaˈðero, a] (ESP) nm/f (hacendado) rancher

**ganado** [gaˈnaðo] nm livestock; **ganado porcino** pigs pl

**ganador, a** [ganaˈðor, a] adj winning ▷ nm/f winner

**ganancia** [gaˈnanθja] nf (lo ganado) gain; (aumento) increase; (beneficio) profit; **ganancias** nfpl (ingresos) earnings; (beneficios) profit sg, winnings

**ganar** [gaˈnar] vt (obtener) to get, obtain; (sacar ventaja) to gain; (salario etc) to earn; (Deporte, premio) to win; (derrotar a) to beat; (alcanzar) to reach ▷ vi (Deporte) to win; **ganarse** vr: **~se la vida** to earn one's living

**ganchillo** [ganˈtʃiʎo] nm crochet

**gancho** [ˈgantʃo] nm (gen) hook; (colgador) hanger

**gandul, a** [ganˈdul, a] adj, nm/f good-for-nothing, layabout

**ganga** [ˈganga] nf bargain

**gangrena** [ganˈgrena] nf gangrene

**ganso, -a** [ˈganso, a] nm/f (Zool) goose; (fam) idiot

**ganzúa** [ganˈθua] nf skeleton key

**garabato** [garaˈβato] nm (escritura) scrawl, scribble

**garaje** [gaˈraxe] nm garage

**garantía** [garanˈtia] nf guarantee

**garantizar** [garantiˈθar] vt to guarantee

**garbanzo** [garˈβanθo] nm chickpea (BRIT), garbanzo (US)

**garfio** [ˈgarfjo] nm grappling iron

**garganta** [garˈɣanta] nf (Anat) throat; (de botella) neck; **gargantilla** nf necklace

**gárgaras** [ˈgarɣaras] nfpl: **hacer ~** to gargle

**gargarear** [garɣareˈar] (LAM) vi to gargle

**garita** [gaˈrita] nf cabin, hut; (Mil) sentry box

**garra** [ˈgarra] nf (de gato, Tec) claw; (de ave) talon; (fam: mano) hand, paw

**garrafa** [gaˈrrafa] nf carafe, decanter

**garrapata** [garraˈpata] nf tick

**gas** [gas] nm gas; **gases lacrimógenos** tear gas sg

**gasa** [ˈgasa] nf gauze

**gaseosa** [gaseˈosa] nf lemonade

**gaseoso, -a** [gaseˈoso, a] adj gassy, fizzy

**gasoil** [ga'soil] *nm* diesel (oil)

**gasóleo** [ga'soleo] *nm* = **gasoil**

**gasolina** [gaso'lina] *nf* petrol (BRIT), gas(oline) (US); **gasolinera** *nf* petrol (BRIT) o gas (US) station

**gastado, -a** [gas'taðo, a] *adj* (*dinero*) spent; (*ropa*) worn out; (*usado: frase etc*) trite

**gastar** [gas'tar] *vt* (*dinero, tiempo*) to spend; (*fuerzas*) to use up; (*desperdiciar*) to waste; (*llevar*) to wear; **gastarse** *vr* to wear out; (*estropearse*) to waste; **~ en** to spend on; **~ bromas** to crack jokes; **¿qué número gastas?** what size (shoe) do you take?

**gasto** ['gasto] *nm* (*desembolso*) expenditure, spending; (*consumo, uso*) use; **gastos** *nmpl* (*desembolsos*) expenses; (*cargos*) charges, costs

**gastronomía** [gastrono'mia] *nf* gastronomy

**gatear** [gate'ar] *vi* (*andar a gatas*) to go on all fours

**gatillo** [ga'tiʎo] *nm* (*de arma de fuego*) trigger; (*de dentista*) forceps

**gato, -a** ['gato, a] *nm/f* cat ▷ *nm* (Tec) jack; **andar a gatas** to go on all fours

**gaucho** ['gautʃo] *nm* gaucho

● **GAUCHO**

● **Gauchos** are the herdsmen or riders of
● the Southern Cone plains. Although
● popularly associated with Argentine
● folklore, **gauchos** belong equally to the
● cattle-raising areas of Southern Brazil
● and Uruguay. **Gauchos'** traditions and
● clothing reflect their mixed ancestry
● and cultural roots. Their baggy trousers
● are Arabic in origin, while the horse and
● guitar are inherited from the Spanish
● conquistadors; the poncho, maté and
● **boleadoras** (strips of leather weighted
● at either end with stones) form part of
● the Indian tradition.

**gaviota** [ga'βjota] *nf* seagull

**gay** [ge] *adj inv, nm* gay, homosexual

**gazpacho** [gaθ'patʃo] *nm* gazpacho

**gel** [xel] *nm:* **~ de baño/ducha** bath/shower gel

**gelatina** [xela'tina] *nf* jelly; (*polvos etc*) gelatine

**gema** ['xema] *nf* gem

**gemelo, -a** [xe'melo, a] *adj, nm/f* twin; **gemelos** *nmpl* (*de camisa*) cufflinks; (*prismáticos*) field glasses, binoculars

**gemido** [xe'miðo] *nm* (*quejido*) moan, groan; (*aullido*) howl

**Géminis** ['xeminis] *nm* Gemini

**gemir** [xe'mir] *vi* (*quejarse*) to moan, groan; (*aullar*) to howl

**generación** [xenera'θjon] *nf* generation

**general** [xene'ral] *adj* general ▷ *nm* general; **por lo** o **en ~** in general; **Generalitat** *nf* Catalan parliament; **generalizar** *vt* to generalize; **generalizarse** *vr* to become generalized, spread

**generar** [xene'rar] *vt* to generate

**género** ['xenero] *nm* (*clase*) kind, sort; (*tipo*) type; (Bio) genus; (Ling) gender; (Com) material; **género humano** human race

**generosidad** [xenerosi'ðað] *nf* generosity; **generoso, -a** *adj* generous

**genial** [xe'njal] *adj* inspired; (*idea*) brilliant; (*estupendo*) wonderful

**genio** ['xenjo] *nm* (*carácter*) nature, disposition; (*humor*) temper; (*facultad creadora*) genius; **de mal ~** bad-tempered

**genital** [xeni'tal] *adj* genital; **genitales** *nmpl* genitals

**genoma** [xe'noma] *nm* genome

**gente** ['xente] *nf* (*personas*) people *pl*; (*parientes*) relatives *pl*

**gentil** [xen'til] *adj* (*elegante*) graceful; (*encantador*) charming

▌ No confundir **gentil** con la palabra inglesa *gentle*.

**genuino, -a** [xe'nwino, a] *adj* genuine

**geografía** [xeoɣra'fia] *nf* geography

**geología** [xeolo'xia] *nf* geology

**geometría** [xeome'tria] *nf* geometry

**gerente** [xe'rente] *nmf* (*supervisor*) manager; (*jefe*) director

**geriatría** [xeria'tria] *nf* (Med) geriatrics *sg*

**germen** ['xermen] *nm* germ

**gesticular** [xestiku'lar] *vi* to gesticulate; (*hacer muecas*) to grimace; **gesticulación** *nf* gesticulation; (*mueca*) grimace

**gestión** [xes'tjon] *nf* management; (*diligencia, acción*) negotiation

**gesto** ['xesto] *nm* (*mueca*) grimace; (*ademán*) gesture

**Gibraltar** [xiβral'tar] *nm* Gibraltar; **gibraltareño, -a** *adj, nm/f* Gibraltarian

**gigante** [xi'ɣante] *adj, nmf* giant; **gigantesco, -a** *adj* gigantic

**gilipollas** [xili'poʎas] (*fam*) *adj inv* daft ▷ *nmf inv* wally

**gimnasia** [xim'nasja] *nf* gymnastics *pl*; **gimnasio** *nm* gymnasium; **gimnasta** *nmf* gymnast

**ginebra** [xi'neβra] *nf* gin

**ginecólogo, -a** [xine'koloɣo, a] *nm/f* gynaecologist

**gira** ['xira] *nf* tour, trip

**girar** [xi'rar] *vt* (*dar la vuelta*) to turn

(around); (: *rápidamente*) to spin; (*Com: giro postal*) to draw; (: *letra de cambio*) to issue ▷ *vi* to turn (round); (*rápido*) to spin

**girasol** [xira'sol] *nm* sunflower

**giratorio, -a** [xira'torjo, a] *adj* revolving

**giro** ['xiro] *nm* (*movimiento*) turn, revolution; (*Ling*) expression; (*Com*) draft; **giro bancario/postal** bank draft/money order

**gis** [xis] (*MÉX*) *nm* chalk

**gitano, -a** [xi'tano, a] *adj, nm/f* gypsy

**glacial** [gla'θjal] *adj* icy, freezing

**glaciar** [gla'θjar] *nm* glacier

**glándula** ['glandula] *nf* gland

**global** [glo'βal] *adj* global; **globalización** *nf* globalization

**globo** ['gloβo] *nm* (*esfera*) globe, sphere; (*aerostato, juguete*) balloon

**glóbulo** ['gloβulo] *nm* globule; (*Anat*) corpuscle

**gloria** ['glorja] *nf* glory

**glorieta** [glo'rjeta] *nf* (*de jardín*) bower, arbour; (*plazoleta*) roundabout (BRIT), traffic circle (US)

**glorioso, -a** [glo'rjoso, a] *adj* glorious

**glotón, -ona** [glo'ton, ona] *adj* gluttonous, greedy ▷ *nm/f* glutton

**glucosa** [glu'kosa] *nf* glucose

**gobernador, a** [goβerna'ðor, a] *adj* governing ▷ *nm/f* governor; **gobernante** *adj* governing

**gobernar** [goβer'nar] *vt* (*dirigir*) to guide, direct; (*Pol*) to rule, govern ▷ *vi* to govern; (*Náut*) to steer

**gobierno** etc [go'βjerno] *vb* V **gobernar** ▷ *nm* (*Pol*) government; (*dirección*) guidance, direction; (*Náut*) steering

**goce** etc ['goθe] *vb* V **gozar** ▷ *nm* enjoyment

**gol** [gol] *nm* goal

**golf** [golf] *nm* golf

**golfa** ['golfa] (*fam!*) *nf* (*mujer*) slut, whore

**golfo, -a** ['golfo, a] *nm* (*Geo*) gulf ▷ *nm/f* (*fam: niño*) urchin; (*gamberro*) lout

**golondrina** [golon'drina] *nf* swallow

**golosina** [golo'sina] *nf* (*dulce*) sweet; **goloso, -a** *adj* sweet-toothed

**golpe** ['golpe] *nm* blow; (*de puño*) punch; (*de mano*) smack; (*de remo*) stroke; (*fig: choque*) clash; **no dar ~** to be bone idle; **de un ~** with one blow; **de ~** suddenly; **golpe (de estado)** coup (d'état); **golpear** *vt, vi* to strike, knock; (*asestar*) to beat; (*de puño*) to punch; (*golpetear*) to tap

**goma** ['goma] *nf* (*caucho*) rubber; (*elástico*) elastic; (*una goma*) elastic band; **goma de borrar** eraser, rubber (BRIT); **goma espuma** foam rubber

**gomina** [go'mina] *nf* hair gel

**gomita** [go'mita] (RPL) *nf* rubber band

**gordo, -a** ['gorðo, a] *adj* (*gen*) fat; (*fam*) enormous; **el (premio) ~** (*en lotería*) first prize

**gorila** [go'rila] *nm* gorilla

**gorra** ['gorra] *nf* cap; (*de bebé*) bonnet; (*militar*) bearskin; **entrar de ~** (*fam*) to gatecrash; **ir de ~** to sponge

**gorrión** [go'rrjon] *nm* sparrow

**gorro** ['gorro] *nm* (*gen*) cap; (*de bebé, mujer*) bonnet

**gorrón, -ona** [go'rron, ona] *nm/f* scrounger; **gorronear** (*fam*) *vi* to scrounge

**gota** ['gota] *nf* (*gen*) drop; (*de sudor*) bead; (*Med*) gout; **gotear** *vi* to drip; (*lloviznar*) to drizzle; **gotera** *nf* leak

**gozar** [go'θar] *vi* to enjoy o.s.; **~ de** (*disfrutar*) to enjoy; (*poseer*) to possess

**gr.** *abr* (= *gramo, gramos*) g

**grabación** [graβa'θjon] *nf* recording

**grabado** [gra'βaðo] *nm* print, engraving

**grabadora** [graβa'ðora] *nf* tape-recorder; **grabadora de CD/DVD** CD/DVD writer

**grabar** [gra'βar] *vt* to engrave; (*discos, cintas*) to record

**gracia** ['graθja] *nf* (*encanto*) grace, gracefulness; (*humor*) humour, wit; **¡(muchas) ~s!** thanks (very much)!; **~s a** thanks to; **dar las ~s a algn por algo** to thank sb for sth; **tener ~** (*chiste etc*) to be funny; **no me hace ~** I am not keen; **gracioso, -a** *adj* (*divertido*) funny, amusing; (*cómico*) comical ▷ *nm/f* (*Teatro*) comic character

**grada** ['graða] *nf* (*de escalera*) step; (*de anfiteatro*) tier, row; **gradas** *nfpl* (*Deporte: de estadio*) terraces

**grado** ['graðo] *nm* degree; (*de aceite, vino*) grade; (*grada*) step; (*Mil*) rank; **de buen ~** willingly; **grado centígrado/Fahrenheit** degree centigrade/Fahrenheit

**graduación** [graðwa'θjon] *nf* (*del alcohol*) proof, strength; (*Escol*) graduation; (*Mil*) rank

**gradual** [gra'ðwal] *adj* gradual

**graduar** [gra'ðwar] *vt* (*gen*) to graduate; (*Mil*) to commission; **graduarse** *vr* to graduate; **~se la vista** to have one's eyes tested

**gráfica** ['grafika] *nf* graph

**gráfico, -a** ['grafiko, a] *adj* graphic ▷ *nm* diagram; **gráficos** *nmpl* (*Inform*) graphics

**grajo** ['graxo] *nm* rook

**gramática** [gra'matika] *nf* grammar

**gramo** ['gramo] *nm* gramme (BRIT), gram (US)

**gran** [gran] *adj* V **grande**

**grana** ['grana] nf (color, tela) scarlet

**granada** [gra'naða] nf pomegranate; (Mil) grenade

**granate** [gra'nate] adj deep red

**Gran Bretaña** [-bre'taɲa] nf Great Britain

**grande** ['grande] (antes de nmsg **gran**) adj (de tamaño) big, large; (alto) tall; (distinguido) great; (impresionante) grand ▷ nm grandee

**granel** [gra'nel]: **a ~** adv (Com) in bulk

**granero** [gra'nero] nm granary, barn

**granito** [gra'nito] nm (Agr) small grain; (roca) granite

**granizado** [grani'θaðo] nm iced drink

**granizar** [grani'θar] vi to hail; **granizo** nm hail

**granja** ['granxa] nf (gen) farm; **granjero, -a** nm/f farmer

**grano** ['grano] nm grain; (semilla) seed; (de café) bean; (Med) pimple, spot

**granuja** [gra'nuxa] nmf rogue; (golfillo) urchin

**grapa** ['grapa] nf staple; (Tec) clamp; **grapadora** nf stapler

**grasa** ['grasa] nf (gen) grease; (de cocinar) fat, lard; (sebo) suet; (mugre) filth; **grasiento, -a** adj greasy; (de aceite) oily; **graso, -a** adj (leche, queso, carne) fatty; (pelo, piel) greasy

**gratinar** [grati'nar] vt to cook au gratin

**gratis** ['gratis] adv free

**grato, -a** ['grato, a] adj (agradable) pleasant, agreeable

**gratuito, -a** [gra'twito, a] adj (gratis) free; (sin razón) gratuitous

**grave** ['graβe] adj heavy; (serio) grave, serious; **gravedad** nf gravity

**Grecia** ['greθja] nf Greece

**gremio** ['gremjo] nm trade, industry

**griego, -a** ['grjeɣo, a] adj, nm/f Greek

**grieta** ['grjeta] nf crack

**grifo** ['grifo] (ESP) nm tap (BRIT), faucet (US)

**grillo** ['griʎo] nm (Zool) cricket

**gripa** ['gripa] (MÉX) nf flu, influenza

**gripe** ['gripe] nf flu, influenza; **gripe aviar** bird flu

**gris** [gris] adj (color) grey

**gritar** [gri'tar] vt, vi to shout, yell; **grito** nm shout, yell; (de horror) scream

**grosella** [gro'seʎa] nf (red)currant

**grosero, -a** [gro'sero, a] adj (poco cortés) rude, bad-mannered; (ordinario) vulgar, crude

**grosor** [gro'sor] nm thickness

**grúa** ['grua] nf (Tec) crane; (de petróleo) derrick

**grueso, -a** ['grweso, a] adj thick; (persona) stout ▷ nm bulk; **el ~ de** the bulk of

**grulla** ['gruʎa] nf crane

**grumo** ['grumo] nm clot, lump

**gruñido** [gru'ɲiðo] nm grunt; (de persona) grumble

**gruñir** [gru'ɲir] vi (animal) to growl; (persona) to grumble

**grupo** ['grupo] nm group; (Tec) unit, set; **grupo de presión** pressure group; **grupo sanguíneo** blood group

**gruta** ['gruta] nf grotto

**guacho, -a** ['gwatʃo, a] (CS) nm/f homeless child

**guajolote** [gwaxo'lote] (MÉX) nm turkey

**guante** ['gwante] nm glove; **guantes de goma** rubber gloves; **guantera** nf glove compartment

**guapo, -a** ['gwapo, a] adj good-looking, attractive; (elegante) smart

**guarda** ['gwarða] nmf (persona) guard, keeper ▷ nf (acto) guarding; (custodia) custody; **guarda jurado** (armed) security guard; **guardabarros** nm inv mudguard (BRIT), fender (US); **guardabosques** nm inv gamekeeper; **guardacostas** nm inv coastguard vessel ▷ nmf guardian, protector; **guardaespaldas** nmf inv bodyguard; **guardameta** nmf goalkeeper; **guardar** vt (gen) to keep; (vigilar) to guard, watch over; (dinero: ahorrar) to save; **guardarse** vr (preservarse) to protect o.s.; (evitar) to avoid; **guardar cama** to stay in bed; **guardarropa** nm (armario) wardrobe; (en establecimiento público) cloakroom

**guardería** [gwarðe'ria] nf nursery

**guardia** ['gwarðja] nf (Mil) guard; (cuidado) care, custody ▷ nmf guard; (policía) policeman(-woman); **estar de ~** to be on guard; **montar ~** to mount guard; **Guardia Civil** Civil Guard

**guardián, -ana** [gwar'ðjan, ana] nm/f (gen) guardian, keeper

**guarida** [gwa'riða] nf (de animal) den, lair; (refugio) refuge

**guarnición** [gwarni'θjon] nf (de vestimenta) trimming; (de piedra) mount; (Culin) garnish; (arneses) harness; (Mil) garrison

**guarro, -a** ['gwarro, a] nm/f pig

**guasa** ['gwasa] nf joke; **guasón, -ona** adj (bromista) joking ▷ nm/f wit; joker

**Guatemala** [gwate'mala] nf Guatemala

**guay** [gwai] (fam) adj super, great

**güero, -a** ['gwero, a] (MÉX) adj blond(e)

**guerra** ['gerra] nf war; **dar ~** to annoy; **guerra civil** civil war; **guerra fría** cold war; **guerrero, -a** adj fighting; (carácter) warlike ▷ nm/f warrior

**guerrilla** [ge'rriʎa] nf guerrilla warfare; (tropas) guerrilla band o group

**guía** etc ['gia] vb V **guiar** ▷ nmf (persona)

guide; (nf: libro) guidebook; **guía telefónica** telephone directory; **guía turística** tourist guide

**guiar** [gi'ar] vt to guide, direct; (Auto) to steer; **guiarse** vr: **~se por** to be guided by

**guinda** ['ginda] nf morello cherry

**guindilla** [gin'diʎa] nf chilli pepper

**guiñar** [gi'ɲar] vt to wink

**guión** [gi'on] nm (Ling) hyphen, dash; (Cine) script; **guionista** nmf scriptwriter

**guiri** ['giri] (ESP: fam, pey) nmf foreigner

**guirnalda** [gir'nalda] nf garland

**guisado** [gi'saðo] nm stew

**guisante** [gi'sante] nm pea

**guisar** [gi'sar] vt, vi to cook; **guiso** nm cooked dish

**guitarra** [gi'tarra] nf guitar

**gula** ['gula] nf gluttony, greed

**gusano** [gu'sano] nm worm; (lombriz) earthworm

**gustar** [gus'tar] vt to taste, sample ▷ vi to please, be pleasing; **~ de algo** to like o enjoy sth; **me gustan las uvas** I like grapes; **le gusta nadar** she likes o enjoys swimming

**gusto** ['gusto] nm (sentido, sabor) taste; (placer) pleasure; **tiene ~ a menta** it tastes of mint; **tener buen ~** to have good taste; **coger el o tomar ~ a algo** to take a liking to sth; **sentirse a ~** to feel at ease; **mucho ~ (en conocerle)** pleased to meet you; **el ~ es mío** the pleasure is mine; **con ~** willingly, gladly

**ha** vb V **haber**

**haba** ['aβa] nf bean

**Habana** [a'βana] nf: **la ~** Havana

**habano** [a'βano] nm Havana cigar

**habéis** vb V **haber**

○ **PALABRA CLAVE**

**haber** [a'βer] vb aux **1**(tiempos compuestos) to have; **había comido** I had eaten; **antes/después de haberlo visto** before seeing/after seeing o having seen it

**2**: **¡haberlo dicho antes!** you should have said so before!

**3**: **haber de: he de hacerlo** I have to do it; **ha de llegar mañana** it should arrive tomorrow

▷ vb impers **1**(existencia: sg) there is; (: pl) there are; **hay un hermano/dos hermanos** there is one brother/there are two brothers; **¿cuánto hay de aquí a Sucre?** how far is it from here to Sucre?

**2**(obligación): **hay que hacer algo** something must be done; **hay que apuntarlo para acordarse** you have to write it down to remember

**3**: **¡hay que ver!** well I never!

**4**: **¡no hay de o por (LAM) qué!** don't mention it!, not at all!

**5**: **¿qué hay?** (¿qué pasa?) what's up?, what's the matter?; (¿qué tal?) how's it going?

▷ vt: **he aquí unas sugerencias** here are some suggestions; **no hay cintas blancas pero sí las hay rojas** there aren't any white ribbons but there are some red ones

▷ nm (en cuenta) credit side; **haberes** nmpl assets; **¿cuánto tengo en el haber?** how much do I have in my account?; **tiene varias novelas en su haber** he has several novels to his credit

**haberse** vr: **habérselas con algn** to have

it out with sb

**habichuela** [aβi'tʃwela] *nf* kidney bean
**hábil** ['aβil] *adj* (*listo*) clever, smart; (*capaz*)
fit, capable; (*experto*) expert; **día ~** working
day; **habilidad** *nf* skill, ability
**habitación** [aβita'θjon] *nf* (*cuarto*) room;
(*Bio: morada*) habitat; **habitación doble** *o*
**de matrimonio** double room; **habitación**
**individual** *o* **sencilla** single room
**habitante** [aβi'tante] *nmf* inhabitant
**habitar** [aβi'tar] *vt* (*residir en*) to inhabit;
(*ocupar*) to occupy ▷ *vi* to live
**hábito** ['aβito] *nm* habit
**habitual** [aβi'twal] *adj* usual
**habituar** [aβi'twar] *vt* to accustom;
**habituarse** *vr*: **~se a** to get used to
**habla** ['aβla] *nf* (*capacidad de hablar*)
speech; (*idioma*) language; (*dialecto*) dialect;
**perder el ~** to become speechless; **de ~**
**francesa** French-speaking; **estar al ~** to be
in contact; (*Tel*) to be on the line; **¡González**
**al ~!** (*Tel*) González speaking!
**hablador, a** [aβla'ðor, a] *adj* talkative
▷ *nm/f* chatterbox
**habladuría** [aβlaðu'ria] *nf* rumour;
**habladurías** *nfpl* gossip *sg*
**hablante** [a'βlante] *adj* speaking ▷ *nmf*
speaker
**hablar** [a'βlar] *vt* to speak, talk ▷ *vi* to
speak; **hablarse** *vr* to speak to each other;
**~ con** to speak to; **~ de** to speak of *o* about;
**¡ni ~!** it's out of the question!; **"se habla**
**inglés"** "English spoken here"
**habré** *etc* [a'βre] *vb* V **haber**
**hacendado** [aθen'daðo] (*LAM*) *nm*
rancher, farmer
**hacendoso, -a** [aθen'doso, a] *adj*
industrious

○ **PALABRA CLAVE**

**hacer** [a'θer] *vt* 1 (*fabricar, producir*) to
make; (*construir*) to build; **hacer una**
**película/un ruido** to make a film/noise;
**el guisado lo hice yo** I made *o* cooked the
stew
2 (*ejecutar: trabajo etc*) to do; **hacer la colada**
to do the washing; **hacer la comida** to do
the cooking; **¿qué haces?** what are you
doing?; **hacer el malo** *o* **el papel del malo**
(*Teatro*) to play the villain
3 (*estudios, algunos deportes*) to do; **hacer**
**español/económicas** to do *o* study
Spanish/economics; **hacer yoga/**
**gimnasia** to do yoga/go to gym
4 (*transformar, incidir en*): **esto lo hará más**
**difícil** this will make it more difficult; **salir**

**te hará sentir mejor** going out will make
you feel better
5 (*cálculo*): **2 y 2 hacen 4** 2 and 2 make 4; **éste**
**hace 100** this one makes 100
6 (+ *sub*): **esto hará que ganemos** this will
make us win; **harás que no quiera venir**
you'll stop him wanting to come
7 (*como sustituto de vb*) to do; **él bebió y yo**
**hice lo mismo** he drank and I did likewise
8 **no hace más que criticar** all he does is
criticize
▷ *vb semi-aux* (*directo*): **hacer +infin**: **les**
**hice venir** I made *o* had them come; **hacer**
**trabajar a los demás** to get others to work
▷ *vi* 1 **haz como que no lo sabes** act as if
you don't know
2 (*ser apropiado*): **si os hace** if it's alright
with you
3 **hacer de: hacer de Otelo** to play Othello
▷ *vb impers* 1 **hace calor/frío** it's hot/cold;
V *tb* **bueno, sol, tiempo**
2 (*tiempo*): **hace 3 años** 3 years ago; **hace**
**un mes que voy/no voy** I've been going/I
haven't been for a month
3 **¿cómo has hecho para llegar tan**
**rápido?** how did you manage to get here
so quickly?
**hacerse** *vr* 1 (*volverse*) to become; **se**
**hicieron amigos** they became friends
2 (*acostumbrarse*): **hacerse a** to get used to
3 **se hace con huevos y leche** it's made
out of eggs and milk; **eso no se hace** that's
not done
4 (*obtener*): **hacerse de** *o* **con algo** to get
hold of sth
5 (*fingirse*): **hacerse el sueco** to turn a deaf
ear

**hacha** ['atʃa] *nf* axe; (*antorcha*) torch
**hachís** [a'tʃis] *nm* hashish
**hacia** ['aθja] *prep* (*en dirección de*)
towards; (*cerca de*) near; (*actitud*) towards;
**~ adelante/atrás** forwards/backwards; **~**
**arriba/abajo** up(wards)/down(wards); **~**
**mediodía/las cinco** about noon/five
**hacienda** [a'θjenda] *nf* (*propiedad*)
property; (*finca*) farm; (*LAM: rancho*) ranch;
**(Ministerio de) H~** Exchequer (*BRIT*),
Treasury Department (*US*); **hacienda**
**pública** public finance
**hada** ['aða] *nf* fairy
**hago** *etc* *vb* V **hacer**
**Haití** [ai'ti] *nm* Haiti
**halagar** [ala'ɣar] *vt* to flatter
**halago** [a'laɣo] *nm* flattery
**halcón** [al'kon] *nm* falcon, hawk
**hallar** [a'ʎar] *vt* (*gen*) to find; (*descubrir*) to
discover; (*toparse con*) to run into; **hallarse**

vr to be (situated)

**halterofilia** [altero'filja] nf weightlifting

**hamaca** [a'maka] nf hammock

**hambre** ['ambre] nf hunger; (plaga) famine; (deseo) longing; **tener ~** to be hungry; **¡me muero de ~!** I'm starving!; **hambriento, -a** adj hungry, starving

**hamburguesa** [ambur'ɣesa] nf hamburger; **hamburguesería** nf burger bar

**han** vb V **haber**

**harapos** [a'rapos] nmpl rags

**haré** vb V **hacer**

**harina** [a'rina] nf flour; **harina de maíz** cornflour (BRIT), cornstarch (US); **harina de trigo** wheat flour

**hartar** [ar'tar] vt to satiate, glut; (fig) to tire, sicken; **hartarse** vr (de comida) to fill o.s., gorge o.s.; (cansarse): **~se (de)** to get fed up (with); **harto, -a** adj (lleno) full; (cansado) fed up ▷ adv (bastante) enough; (muy) very; **estar harto de hacer algo/de algn** to be fed up of doing sth/with sb

**has** vb V **haber**

**hasta** ['asta] adv even ▷ prep (alcanzando a) as far as; up to; down to; (de tiempo: a tal hora) till, until; (antes de) before ▷ conj: **~ que** ... until; **~ luego/el sábado** see you soon/ on Saturday; **~ ahora** (al despedirse) see you in a minute; **~ pronto** see you soon

**hay** vb V **haber**

**Haya** ['aja] nf: **la ~** The Hague

**haya** etc ['aja] vb V **haber** ▷ nf beech tree

**haz** [aθ] vb V **hacer** ▷ nm (de luz) beam

**hazaña** [a'θaɲa] nf feat, exploit

**hazmerreír** [aθmerre'ir] nm inv laughing stock

**he** vb V **haber**

**hebilla** [e'βiʎa] nf buckle, clasp

**hebra** ['eβra] nf thread; (Bot: fibra) fibre, grain

**hebreo, -a** [e'βreo, a] adj, nm/f Hebrew ▷ nm (Ling) Hebrew

**hechizar** [etʃi'θar] vt to cast a spell on, bewitch

**hechizo** [e'tʃiθo] nm witchcraft, magic; (acto de magía) spell, charm

**hecho, -a** ['etʃo, a] pp de **hacer** ▷ adj (carne) done; (Costura) ready-to-wear ▷ nm deed, act; (dato) fact; (cuestión) matter; (suceso) event ▷ excl agreed!, done!; **de ~** in fact, as a matter of fact; **el ~ es que** ... the fact is that ...; **¡bien ~!** well done!

**hechura** [e'tʃura] nf (forma) form, shape; (de persona) build

**hectárea** [ek'tarea] nf hectare

**helada** [e'laða] nf frost

**heladera** [ela'ðera] (LAM) nf (refrigerador) refrigerator

**helado, -a** [e'laðo, a] adj frozen; (glacial) icy; (fig) chilly, cold ▷ nm ice cream

**helar** [e'lar] vt to freeze, ice (up); (dejar atónito) to amaze; (desalentar) to discourage ▷ vi to freeze; **helarse** vr to freeze

**helecho** [e'letʃo] nm fern

**hélice** ['eliθe] nf (Tec) propeller

**helicóptero** [eli'koptero] nm helicopter

**hembra** ['embra] nf (Bot, Zool) female; (mujer) woman; (Tec) nut

**hemorragia** [emo'rraxja] nf haemorrhage

**hemorroides** [emo'rroiðes] nfpl haemorrhoids, piles

**hemos** vb V **haber**

**heno** ['eno] nm hay

**heredar** [ere'ðar] vt to inherit; **heredero, -a** nm/f heir(ess)

**hereje** [e'rexe] nmf heretic

**herencia** [e'renθja] nf inheritance

**herida** [e'riða] nf wound, injury; V tb **herido**

**herido, -a** [e'riðo, a] adj injured, wounded ▷ nm/f casualty

**herir** [e'rir] vt to wound, injure; (fig) to offend

**hermanastro, -a** [erma'nastro, a] nm/f stepbrother/sister

**hermandad** [erman'dað] nf brotherhood

**hermano, -a** [er'mano, a] nm/f brother/ sister; **hermano(-a) gemelo(-a)**, twin brother/sister; **hermano(-a) político(-a)**, brother-in-law/sister-in-law

**hermético, -a** [er'metiko, a] adj hermetic; (fig) watertight

**hermoso, -a** [er'moso, a] adj beautiful, lovely; (estupendo) splendid; (guapo) handsome; **hermosura** nf beauty

**hernia** ['ernja] nf hernia; **hernia discal** slipped disc

**héroe** ['eroe] nm hero

**heroína** [ero'ina] nf (mujer) heroine; (droga) heroin

**herradura** [erra'ðura] nf horseshoe

**herramienta** [erra'mjenta] nf tool

**herrero** [e'rrero] nm blacksmith

**hervidero** [erβi'ðero] nm (fig) swarm; (Pol etc) hotbed

**hervir** [er'βir] vi to boil; (burbujear) to bubble; **~ a fuego lento** to simmer; **hervor** nm boiling; (fig) ardour, fervour

**heterosexual** [eterosek'swal] adj heterosexual

**hice** etc vb V **hacer**

**hidratante** [iðra'tante] adj: **crema ~** moisturizing cream, moisturizer; **hidratar** vt (piel) to moisturize; **hidrato** nm hydrate;

**hidratos de carbono** carbohydrates
**hidráulico, -a** [i'ðrauliko, a] adj hydraulic
**hidro...** [iðro] prefijo hydro..., water-...;
**hidroeléctrico, -a** adj hydroelectric;
**hidrógeno** nm hydrogen
**hiedra** ['jeðra] nf ivy
**hiel** [jel] nf gall, bile; (fig) bitterness
**hiela** etc vb V **helar**
**hielo** ['jelo] nm (gen) ice; (escarcha) frost; (fig) coldness, reserve
**hiena** ['jena] nf hyena
**hierba** ['jerβa] nf (pasto) grass; (Culin, Med: planta) herb; **mala ~** weed; (fig) evil influence; **hierbabuena** nf mint
**hierro** ['jerro] nm (metal) iron; (objeto) iron object
**hígado** ['iɣaðo] nm liver
**higiene** [i'xjene] nf hygiene; **higiénico, -a** adj hygienic
**higo** ['iɣo] nm fig; **higo seco** dried fig; **higuera** nf fig tree
**hijastro, -a** [i'xastro, a] nm/f stepson/daughter
**hijo, -a** ['ixo, a] nm/f son/daughter, child; **hijos** nmpl children, sons and daughters; **hijo adoptivo** adopted child; **hijo de papá/mamá** daddy's/mummy's boy; **hijo de puta** (fam!) bastard (!), son of a bitch (!); **hijo/a político/a** son-/daughter-in-law
**hilera** [i'lera] nf row, file
**hilo** ['ilo] nm thread; (Bot) fibre; (metal) wire; (de agua) trickle, thin stream
**hilvanar** [ilβa'nar] vt (Costura) to tack (BRIT), baste (US); (fig) to do hurriedly
**himno** ['imno] nm hymn; **himno nacional** national anthem
**hincapié** [inka'pje] nm: **hacer ~ en** to emphasize
**hincar** [in'kar] vt to drive (in), thrust (in)
**hincha** ['intʃa] (fam) nmf fan
**hinchado, -a** [in'tʃaðo, a] adj (gen) swollen; (persona) pompous
**hinchar** [in'tʃar] vt (gen) to swell; (inflar) to blow up, inflate; (fig) to exaggerate; **hincharse** vr (inflarse) to swell up; (fam: de comer) to stuff o.s.; **hinchazón** nf (Med) swelling; (altivez) arrogance
**hinojo** [i'noxo] nm fennel
**hipermercado** [ipermer'kaðo] nm hypermarket, superstore
**hípico, -a** ['ipiko, a] adj horse cpd
**hipnotismo** [ipno'tismo] nm hypnotism; **hipnotizar** vt to hypnotize
**hipo** ['ipo] nm hiccups pl
**hipocresía** [ipokre'sia] nf hypocrisy; **hipócrita** adj hypocritical ▷ nmf hypocrite
**hipódromo** [i'poðromo] nm racetrack

**hipopótamo** [ipo'potamo] nm hippopotamus
**hipoteca** [ipo'teka] nf mortgage
**hipótesis** [i'potesis] nf inv hypothesis
**hispánico, -a** [is'paniko, a] adj Hispanic
**hispano, -a** [is'pano, a] adj Hispanic, Spanish, Hispano- ▷ nm/f Spaniard; **Hispanoamérica** nf Latin America; **hispanoamericano, -a** adj, nm/f Latin American
**histeria** [is'terja] nf hysteria
**historia** [is'torja] nf history; (cuento) story, tale; **historias** nfpl (chismes) gossip sg; **dejarse de ~s** to come to the point; **pasar a la ~** to go down in history; **historiador, a** nm/f historian; **historial** nm (profesional) curriculum vitae, C.V.; (Med) case history; **histórico, -a** adj historical; (memorable) historic
**historieta** [isto'rjeta] nf tale, anecdote; (dibujos) comic strip
**hito** ['ito] nm (fig) landmark
**hizo** vb V **hacer**
**hocico** [o'θiko] nm snout
**hockey** ['xokei] nm hockey; **hockey sobre hielo/patines** ice/roller hockey
**hogar** [o'ɣar] nm fireplace, hearth; (casa) home; (vida familiar) home life; **hogareño, -a** adj home cpd; (persona) home-loving
**hoguera** [o'ɣera] nf (gen) bonfire
**hoja** ['oxa] nf (gen) leaf; (de flor) petal; (de papel) sheet; (página) page; **hoja de afeitar** (LAM) razor blade; **hoja electrónica** o **de cálculo** spreadsheet; **hoja informativa** leaflet, handout
**hojalata** [oxa'lata] nf tin(plate)
**hojaldre** [o'xaldre] nm (Culin) puff pastry
**hojear** [oxe'ar] vt to leaf through, turn the pages of
**hojuela** [o'xwela] (MÉX) nf flake
**hola** ['ola] excl hello!
**holá** [o'la] (RPL) excl hello!
**Holanda** [o'landa] nf Holland; **holandés, -esa** adj Dutch ▷ nm/f Dutchman(-woman) ▷ nm (Ling) Dutch
**holgado, -a** [ol'ɣaðo, a] adj (ropa) loose, baggy; (rico) comfortable
**holgar** [ol'ɣar] vi (descansar) to rest; (sobrar) to be superfluous
**holgazán, -ana** [olɣa'θan, ana] adj idle, lazy ▷ nm/f loafer
**hollín** [o'ʎin] nm soot
**hombre** ['ombre] nm (gen) man; (raza humana): **el ~** man(kind) ▷ excl: **¡sí ~!** (claro) of course!; (para énfasis) man, old boy; **hombre de negocios** businessman; **hombre de pro** honest man; **hombre-rana** frogman

**hombrera** [om'brera] nf shoulder strap

**hombro** ['ombro] nm shoulder

**homenaje** [ome'naxe] nm (gen) homage; (tributo) tribute

**homicida** [omi'θiða] adj homicidal ⊳ nmf murderer; **homicidio** nm murder, homicide

**homologar** [omolo'ðar] vt (Com: productos, tamaños) to standardize

**homólogo, -a** [o'moloxo, a] nm/f: **su ~** his etc counterpart o opposite number

**homosexual** [omosek'swal] adj, nmf homosexual

**honda** ['onda] (cs) nf catapult

**hondo, -a** ['ondo, a] adj deep; **lo ~ the** depth(s) pl, the bottom; **hondonada** nf hollow, depression; (cañón) ravine

**Honduras** [on'duras] nf Honduras

**hondureño, -a** [ondu'reɲo, a] adj, nm/f Honduran

**honestidad** [onesti'ðað] nf purity, chastity; (decencia) decency; **honesto, -a** adj chaste; decent; honest; (justo) just

**hongo** ['ongo] nm (Bot: gen) fungus; (: comestible) mushroom; (: venenoso) toadstool

**honor** [o'nor] nm (gen) honour; **en ~ a la verdad** to be fair; **honorable** adj honourable

**honorario, -a** [ono'rarjo, a] adj honorary; **honorarios** nmpl fees

**honra** ['onra] nf (gen) honour; (renombre) good name; **honradez** nf honesty; (de persona) integrity; **honrado, -a** adj honest, upright; **honrar** [on'rar] vt to honour

**hora** ['ora] nf (una hora) (tiempo) time; **¿qué ~ es?** what time is it?; **¿a qué ~?** at what time?; **media ~** half an hour; **a la ~ de recreo** at playtime; **a primera ~** first thing (in the morning); **a última ~** at the last moment; **a altas ~s** in the small hours; **¡a buena ~!** about time too!; **pedir ~** to make an appointment; **dar la ~** to strike the hour; **horas de oficina/trabajo** office/working hours; **horas de visita** visiting times; **horas extras** o **extraordinarias** overtime sg; **horas pico** (LAM) rush o peak hours; **horas punta** (ESP) rush hours

**horario, -a** [o'rarjo, a] adj hourly, hour cpd ⊳ nm timetable; **horario comercial** business hours pl

**horca** ['orka] nf gallows sg

**horcajadas** [orka'xaðas]: **a ~** adv astride

**horchata** [or'tʃata] nf cold drink made from tiger nuts and water, tiger nut milk

**horizontal** [oriθon'tal] adj horizontal

**horizonte** [ori'θonte] nm horizon

**horma** ['orma] nf mould

**hormiga** [or'miɣa] nf ant; **hormigas** nfpl (Med) pins and needles

**hormigón** [ormi'ɣon] nm concrete; **hormigón armado/pretensado** reinforced/prestressed concrete; **hormigonera** nf cement mixer

**hormigueo** [ormi'ɣeo] nm (comezón) itch

**hormona** [or'mona] nf hormone

**hornillo** [or'niʎo] nm (cocina) portable stove; **hornillo de gas** gas ring

**horno** ['orno] nm (Culin) oven; (Tec) furnace; **alto ~** blast furnace

**horóscopo** [o'roskopo] nm horoscope

**horquilla** [or'kiʎa] nf hairpin; (Agr) pitchfork

**horrendo, -a** [o'rrendo, a] adj horrendous, frightful

**horrible** [o'rriβle] adj horrible, dreadful

**horripilante** [orripi'lante] adj hair-raising, horrifying

**horror** [o'rror] nm horror, dread; (atrocidad) atrocity; **¡qué ~!** (fam) how awful!; **horrorizar** vt to horrify, frighten; **horrorizarse** vr to be horrified; **horroroso, -a** adj horrifying, ghastly

**hortaliza** [orta'liθa] nf vegetable

**hortelano, -a** [orte'lano, a] nm/f (market) gardener

**hortera** [or'tera] (fam) adj tacky

**hospedar** [ospe'ðar] vt to put up; **hospedarse** vr to stay, lodge

**hospital** [ospi'tal] nm hospital

**hospitalario, -a** [ospita'larjo, a] adj (acogedor) hospitable; **hospitalidad** nf hospitality

**hostal** [os'tal] nm small hotel

**hostelería** [ostele'ria] nf hotel business o trade

**hostia** ['ostja] nf (Rel) host, consecrated wafer; (fam!: golpe) whack, punch ⊳ excl (fam!): **¡~(s)!** damn!

**hostil** [os'til] adj hostile

**hotdog** [ot'dog] (LAM) nm hot dog

**hotel** [o'tel] nm hotel; **hotelero, -a** adj hotel cpd ⊳ nm/f hotelier

### HOTEL

In Spain you can choose from the following categories of accommodation, in descending order of quality and price: **hotel** (from 5 stars to 1), **hostal**, **pensión**, **casa de huéspedes**, **fonda**. The State also runs luxury hotels called **paradores**, which are usually sited in places of particular historical interest and are often historic buildings themselves.

**hoy** [oi] *adv* (*este día*) today; (*la actualidad*)
now(adays) ▷ *nm* present time; **~ (en) día**
now(adays)

**hoyo** ['ojo] *nm* hole, pit

**hoz** [oθ] *nf* sickle

**hube** *etc vb* V **haber**

**hucha** ['utʃa] *nf* money box

**hueco, -a** ['weko, a] *adj* (*vacío*) hollow,
empty; (*resonante*) booming ▷ *nm* hollow,
cavity

**huelga** *etc* ['welɣa] *vb* V **holgar** ▷ *nf*
strike; **declararse en ~** to go on strike,
come out on strike; **huelga de hambre**
hunger strike; **huelga general** general
strike

**huelguista** [wel'ɣista] *nmf* striker

**huella** ['weʎa] *nf* (*pisada*) tread; (*marca
del paso*) footprint, footstep; (: *de animal,
máquina*) track; **huella dactilar** fingerprint

**huelo** *etc vb* V **oler**

**huérfano, -a** ['werfano, a] *adj*
orphan(ed) ▷ *nm/f* orphan

**huerta** ['werta] *nf* market garden; (*en
Murcia y Valencia*) irrigated region

**huerto** ['werto] *nm* kitchen garden; (*de
árboles frutales*) orchard

**hueso** ['weso] *nm* (*Anat*) bone; (*de fruta*)
stone

**huésped** ['wespeð] *nmf* guest

**hueva** ['weβa] *nf* roe

**huevera** [we'βera] *nf* eggcup

**huevo** ['weβo] *nm* egg; **huevo a la copa**
(cs) soft-boiled egg; **huevo duro/escalfado**
hard-boiled/poached egg; **huevo
estrellado** (*LAM*) fried egg; **huevo frito** (*ESP*)
fried egg; **huevo pasado por agua** soft-
boiled egg; **huevos revueltos** scrambled
eggs; **huevo tibio** (*MÉX*) soft-boiled egg

**huida** [u'iða] *nf* escape, flight

**huir** [u'ir] *vi* (*escapar*) to flee, escape; (*evitar*)
to avoid

**hule** ['ule] *nm* oilskin; (*MÉX: goma*) rubber

**hulera** [u'lera] (*MÉX*) *nf* catapult

**humanidad** [umani'ðað] *nf* (*género
humano*) man(kind); (*cualidad*) humanity

**humanitario, -a** [umani'tarjo, a] *adj*
humanitarian

**humano, -a** [u'mano, a] *adj* (*gen*) human;
(*humanitario*) humane ▷ *nm* human; **ser ~**
human being

**humareda** [uma'reða] *nf* cloud of smoke

**humedad** [ume'ðað] *nf* (*de clima*)
humidity; (*de pared etc*) dampness; **a prueba
de ~** damp-proof; **humedecer** *vt* to
moisten, wet; **humedecerse** *vr* to get wet

**húmedo, -a** ['umeðo, a] *adj* (*mojado*)
damp, wet; (*tiempo etc*) humid

**humilde** [u'milde] *adj* humble, modest

**humillación** [umiʎa'θjon] *nf*
humiliation; **humillante** *adj* humiliating

**humillar** [umi'ʎar] *vt* to humiliate

**humo** ['umo] *nm* (*de fuego*) smoke; (*gas
nocivo*) fumes *pl*; (*vapor*) steam, vapour;
**humos** *nmpl* (*fig*) conceit *sg*

**humor** [u'mor] *nm* (*disposición*) mood,
temper; (*lo que divierte*) humour; **de buen/
mal ~** in a good/bad mood; **humorista**
*nmf* comic; **humorístico, -a** *adj* funny,
humorous

**hundimiento** [undi'mjento] *nm* (*gen*)
sinking; (*colapso*) collapse

**hundir** [un'dir] *vt* to sink; (*edificio, plan*) to
ruin, destroy; **hundirse** *vr* to sink, collapse

**húngaro, -a** ['ungaro, a] *adj, nm/f*
Hungarian

**Hungría** [un'gria] *nf* Hungary

**huracán** [ura'kan] *nm* hurricane

**huraño, -a** [u'raɲo, a] *adj* (*antisocial*)
unsociable

**hurgar** [ur'ɣar] *vt* to poke, jab; (*remover*) to
stir (up); **hurgarse** *vr*: **~se (las narices)** to
pick one's nose

**hurón, -ona** [u'ron, ona] *nm* (*Zool*) ferret

**hurtadillas** [urta'ðiʎas]: **a ~** *adv* stealthily,
on the sly

**hurtar** [ur'tar] *vt* to steal; **hurto** *nm*
theft, stealing

**husmear** [usme'ar] *vt* (*oler*) to sniff out,
scent; (*fam*) to pry into

**huyo** *etc vb* V **huir**

**iba** etc vb V **ir**

**ibérico, -a** [i'βeriko, a] adj Iberian

**iberoamericano, -a** [iβeroameri'kano, a] adj, nm/f Latin American

**Ibiza** [i'βiθa] nf Ibiza

**iceberg** [iθe'βer] nm iceberg

**icono** [i'kono] nm ikon, icon

**ida** ['iða] nf going, departure; **~ y vuelta** round trip, return

**idea** [i'ðea] nf idea; **no tengo la menor ~** I haven't a clue

**ideal** [iðe'al] adj, nm ideal; **idealista** nmf idealist; **idealizar** vt to idealize

**ídem** ['iðem] pron ditto

**idéntico, -a** [i'ðentiko, a] adj identical

**identidad** [iðenti'ðað] nf identity

**identificación** [iðentifika'θjon] nf identification

**identificar** [iðentifi'kar] vt to identify; **identificarse** vr: **~se con** to identify with

**ideología** [iðeolo'xia] nf ideology

**idilio** [i'ðiljo] nm love-affair

**idioma** [i'ðjoma] nm (gen) language

> No confundir **idioma** con la palabra inglesa *idiom*.

**idiota** [i'ðjota] adj idiotic ▷ nmf idiot

**ídolo** ['iðolo] nm (tb fig) idol

**idóneo, -a** [i'ðoneo, a] adj suitable

**iglesia** [i'ɣlesja] nf church

**ignorante** [iɣno'rante] adj ignorant, uninformed ▷ nmf ignoramus

**ignorar** [iɣno'rar] vt not to know, be ignorant of; (no hacer caso a) to ignore

**igual** [i'ɣwal] adj (gen) equal; (similar) like, similar; (mismo) the same; (constante) constant; (temperatura) even ▷ nmf equal; **~ que** like, the same as; **me da o es ~** I don't care; **son ~es** they're the same; **al ~ que** (prep, conj) like, just like

**igualar** [iɣwa'lar] vt (gen) to equalize, make equal; (allanar, nivelar) to level (off),

even (out); **igualarse** vr (platos de balanza) to balance out

**igualdad** [iɣwal'dað] nf equality; (similaridad) sameness; (uniformidad) uniformity

**igualmente** [iɣwal'mente] adv equally; (también) also, likewise ▷ excl the same to you!

**ilegal** [ile'ɣal] adj illegal

**ilegítimo, -a** [ile'xitimo, a] adj illegitimate

**ileso, -a** [i'leso, a] adj unhurt

**ilimitado, -a** [ilimi'taðo, a] adj unlimited

**iluminación** [ilumina'θjon] nf illumination; (alumbrado) lighting

**iluminar** [ilumi'nar] vt to illuminate, light (up); (fig) to enlighten

**ilusión** [ilu'sjon] nf illusion; (quimera) delusion; (esperanza) hope; **hacerse ilusiones** to build up one's hopes; **ilusionado, -a** adj excited; **ilusionar: le ilusiona ir de vacaciones** he's looking forward to going on holiday; **ilusionarse** vr: **ilusionarse (con)** to get excited (about)

**iluso, -a** [i'luso, a] adj easily deceived ▷ nm/f dreamer

**ilustración** [ilustra'θjon] nf illustration; (saber) learning, erudition; **la I~** the Enlightenment; **ilustrado, -a** adj illustrated; learned

**ilustrar** [ilus'trar] vt to illustrate; (instruir) to instruct; (explicar) to explain, make clear

**ilustre** [i'lustre] adj famous, illustrious

**imagen** [i'maxen] nf (gen) image; (dibujo) picture

**imaginación** [imaxina'θjon] nf imagination

**imaginar** [imaxi'nar] vt (gen) to imagine; (idear) to think up; (suponer) to suppose; **imaginarse** vr to imagine; **imaginario, -a** adj imaginary; **imaginativo, -a** adj imaginative

**imán** [i'man] nm magnet

**imbécil** [im'beθil] nmf imbecile, idiot

**imitación** [imita'θjon] nf imitation; **de ~** imitation cpd

**imitar** [imi'tar] vt to imitate; (parodiar, remedar) to mimic, ape

**impaciente** [impa'θjente] adj impatient; (nervioso) anxious

**impacto** [im'pakto] nm impact

**impar** [im'par] adj odd

**imparcial** [impar'θjal] adj impartial, fair

**impecable** [impe'kaβle] adj impeccable

**impedimento** [impeði'mento] nm impediment, obstacle

**impedir** [impe'ðir] vt (obstruir) to impede, obstruct; (estorbar) to prevent; **~ a algn**

**hacer** o **que algn haga algo** to prevent sb (from) doing sth, stop sb doing sth

**imperativo, -a** [impera'tiβo, a] adj (urgente, Ling) imperative

**imperdible** [imper'ðiβle] nm safety pin

**imperdonable** [imperðo'naβle] adj unforgivable, inexcusable

**imperfecto, -a** [imper'fekto, a] adj imperfect

**imperio** [im'perjo] nm empire; (autoridad) rule, authority; (fig) pride, haughtiness

**impermeable** [imperme'aβle] adj waterproof ▷ nm raincoat, mac (BRIT)

**impersonal** [imperso'nal] adj impersonal

**impertinente** [imperti'nente] adj impertinent

**ímpetu** ['impetu] nm (impulso) impetus, impulse; (impetuosidad) impetuosity; (violencia) violence

**implantar** [implan'tar] vt to introduce

**implemento** [imple'mento] (LAM) nm tool, implement

**implicar** [impli'kar] vt to involve; (entrañar) to imply

**implícito, -a** [im'pliθito, a] adj (tácito) implicit; (sobreentendido) implied

**imponente** [impo'nente] adj (impresionante) impressive, imposing; (solemne) grand

**imponer** [impo'ner] vt (gen) to impose; (exigir) to exact; **imponerse** vr to assert o.s.; (prevalecer) to prevail; **imponible** adj (Com) taxable

**impopular** [impopu'lar] adj unpopular

**importación** [importa'θjon] nf (acto) importing; (mercancías) imports pl

**importancia** [impor'tanθja] nf importance; (valor) value, significance; (extensión) size, magnitude; **no tiene ~** it's nothing; **importante** adj important; valuable, significant

**importar** [impor'tar] vt (del extranjero) to import; (costar) to amount to ▷ vi to be important, matter; **me importa un rábano** I couldn't care less; **no importa** it doesn't matter; **¿le importa que fume?** do you mind if I smoke?

**importe** [im'porte] nm (total) amount; (valor) value

**imposible** [impo'siβle] adj (gen) impossible; (insoportable) unbearable, intolerable

**imposición** [imposi'θjon] nf imposition; (Com: impuesto) tax; (: inversión) deposit

**impostor, a** [impos'tor, a] nm/f impostor

**impotencia** [impo'tenθja] nf impotence; **impotente** adj impotent

**impreciso, -a** [impre'θiso, a] adj imprecise, vague

**impregnar** [impreɣ'nar] vt to impregnate; **impregnarse** vr to become impregnated

**imprenta** [im'prenta] nf (acto) printing; (aparato) press; (casa) printer's; (letra) print

**imprescindible** [impresθin'diβle] adj essential, vital

**impresión** [impre'sjon] nf (gen) impression; (Imprenta) printing; (edición) edition; (Foto) print; (marca) imprint; **impresión digital** fingerprint

**impresionante** [impresjo'nante] adj impressive; (tremendo) tremendous; (maravilloso) great, marvellous

**impresionar** [impresjo'nar] vt (conmover) to move; (afectar) to impress, strike; (película fotográfica) to expose; **impresionarse** vr to be impressed; (conmoverse) to be moved

**impreso, -a** [im'preso, a] pp de **imprimir** ▷ adj printed; **impresos** nmpl printed matter; **impresora** nf printer

**imprevisto, -a** [impre'βisto, a] adj (gen) unforeseen; (inesperado) unexpected

**imprimir** [impri'mir] vt to imprint, impress, stamp; (textos) to print; (Inform) to output, print out

**improbable** [impro'βaβle] adj improbable; (inverosímil) unlikely

**impropio, -a** [im'propjo, a] adj improper

**improvisado, -a** [improβi'saðo, a] adj improvised

**improvisar** [improβi'sar] vt to improvise

**improviso, -a** [impro'βiso, a] adj: **de ~** unexpectedly, suddenly

**imprudencia** [impru'ðenθja] nf imprudence; (indiscreción) indiscretion; (descuido) carelessness; **imprudente** adj unwise, imprudent; (indiscreto) indiscreet

**impuesto, -a** [im'pwesto, a] adj imposed ▷ nm tax; **impuesto al valor agregado** o **añadido** (LAM) value added tax (BRIT) ≈ sales tax (US); **impuesto sobre el valor añadido** (ESP) value added tax (BRIT) ≈ sales tax (US)

**impulsar** [impul'sar] vt to drive; (promover) to promote, stimulate

**impulsivo, -a** [impul'siβo, a] adj impulsive; **impulso** nm impulse; (fuerza, empuje) thrust, drive; (fig: sentimiento) urge, impulse

**impureza** [impu'reθa] nf impurity; **impuro, -a** adj impure

**inaccesible** [inakθe'siβle] adj inaccessible

**inaceptable** [inaθep'taβle] adj unacceptable

**inactivo, -a** [inak'tiβo, a] adj inactive

**inadecuado, -a** [inaðe'kwaðo, a] adj

(*insuficiente*) inadequate; (*inapto*) unsuitable

**inadvertido, -a** [inað̞βer'tið̞o, a] *adj* (*no visto*) unnoticed

**inaguantable** [inaɣwan'taβle] *adj* unbearable

**inanimado, -a** [inani'mað̞o, a] *adj* inanimate

**inaudito, -a** [inau'ð̞ito, a] *adj* unheard-of

**inauguración** [inauɣura'θjon] *nf* inauguration; opening

**inaugurar** [inauɣu'rar] *vt* to inaugurate; (*exposición*) to open

**inca** ['inka] *nmf* Inca

**incalculable** [inkalku'laβle] *adj* incalculable

**incandescente** [inkandes'θente] *adj* incandescent

**incansable** [inkan'saβle] *adj* tireless, untiring

**incapacidad** [inkapaθi'ð̞að̞] *nf* incapacity; (*incompetencia*) incompetence; **incapacidad física/mental** physical/mental disability

**incapacitar** [inkapaθi'tar] *vt* (*inhabilitar*) to incapacitate, render unfit; (*descalificar*) to disqualify

**incapaz** [inka'paθ] *adj* incapable

**incautarse** [inkau'tarse] *vr*: **~ de** to seize, confiscate

**incauto, -a** [in'kauto, a] *adj* (*imprudente*) incautious, unwary

**incendiar** [inθen'djar] *vt* to set fire to; (*fig*) to inflame; **incendiarse** *vr* to catch fire; **incendiario, -a** *adj* incendiary

**incendio** [in'θendjo] *nm* fire

**incentivo** [inθen'tiβo] *nm* incentive

**incertidumbre** [inθerti'ð̞umbre] *nf* (*inseguridad*) uncertainty; (*duda*) doubt

**incesante** [inθe'sante] *adj* incessant

**incesto** [in'θesto] *nm* incest

**incidencia** [inθi'ð̞enθja] *nf* (*Mat*) incidence

**incidente** [inθi'ð̞ente] *nm* incident

**incidir** [inθi'ð̞ir] *vi* (*influir*) to influence; (*afectar*) to affect

**incienso** [in'θjenso] *nm* incense

**incierto, -a** [in'θjerto, a] *adj* uncertain

**incineración** [inθinera'θjon] *nf* incineration; (*de cadáveres*) cremation

**incinerar** [inθine'rar] *vt* to burn; (*cadáveres*) to cremate

**incisión** [inθi'sjon] *nf* incision

**incisivo, -a** [inθi'siβo, a] *adj* sharp, cutting; (*fig*) incisive

**incitar** [inθi'tar] *vt* to incite, rouse

**inclemencia** [inkle'menθja] *nf* (*severidad*) harshness, severity; (*del tiempo*) inclemency

**inclinación** [inklina'θjon] *nf* (*gen*)

inclination; (*de tierras*) slope, incline; (*de cabeza*) nod, bow; (*fig*) leaning, bent

**inclinar** [inkli'nar] *vt* to incline; (*cabeza*) to nod, bow ▷ *vi* to lean, slope; **inclinarse** *vr* to bow; (*encorvarse*) to stoop; **~se a** (*parecerse a*) to take after, resemble; **~se ante** to bow down to; **me inclino a pensar que ...** I'm inclined to think that ...

**incluir** [inklu'ir] *vt* to include; (*incorporar*) to incorporate; (*meter*) to enclose

**inclusive** [inklu'siβe] *adv* inclusive ▷ *prep* including

**incluso** [in'kluso] *adv* even

**incógnita** [in'koɣnita] *nf* (*Mat*) unknown quantity

**incógnito** [in'koɣnito] *nm*: **de ~** incognito

**incoherente** [inkoe'rente] *adj* incoherent

**incoloro, -a** [inko'loro, a] *adj* colourless

**incomodar** [inkomo'ð̞ar] *vt* to inconvenience; (*molestar*) to bother, trouble; (*fastidiar*) to annoy

**incomodidad** [inkomoð̞i'ð̞að̞] *nf* inconvenience; (*fastidio, enojo*) annoyance; (*de vivienda*) discomfort

**incómodo, -a** [in'komoð̞o, a] *adj* (*inconfortable*) uncomfortable; (*molesto*) annoying; (*inconveniente*) inconvenient

**incomparable** [inkompa'raβle] *adj* incomparable

**incompatible** [inkompa'tiβle] *adj* incompatible

**incompetente** [inkompe'tente] *adj* incompetent

**incompleto, -a** [inkom'pleto, a] *adj* incomplete, unfinished

**incomprensible** [inkompren'siβle] *adj* incomprehensible

**incomunicado, -a** [inkomuni'kað̞o, a] *adj* (*aislado*) cut off, isolated; (*confinado*) in solitary confinement

**incondicional** [inkondiθjo'nal] *adj* unconditional; (*apoyo*) wholehearted; (*partidario*) staunch

**inconfundible** [inkonfun'diβle] *adj* unmistakable

**incongruente** [inkon'grwente] *adj* incongruous

**inconsciente** [inkons'θjente] *adj* unconscious; thoughtless

**inconsecuente** [inkonse'kwente] *adj* inconsistent

**inconstante** [inkons'tante] *adj* inconstant

**incontable** [inkon'taβle] *adj* countless, innumerable

**inconveniencia** [inkombe'njenθja] *nf* unsuitability, inappropriateness;

(*descortesía*) impoliteness; **inconveniente** *adj* unsuitable; impolite ▷ *nm* obstacle; (*desventaja*) disadvantage; **el inconveniente es que ...** the trouble is that ...

**incordiar** [inkor'ðjar] (*fam*) *vt* to bug, annoy

**incorporar** [inkorpo'rar] *vt* to incorporate; **incorporarse** *vr* to sit up; **~se a** to join

**incorrecto, -a** [inko'rrekto, a] *adj* (*gen*) incorrect, wrong; (*comportamiento*) bad-mannered

**incorregible** [inkorre'xiβle] *adj* incorrigible

**incrédulo, -a** [in'kreðulo, a] *adj* incredulous, unbelieving; sceptical

**increíble** [inkre'iβle] *adj* incredible

**incremento** [inkre'mento] *nm* increment; (*aumento*) rise, increase

**increpar** [inkre'par] *vt* to reprimand

**incruento, -a** [in'krwento, a] *adj* bloodless

**incrustar** [inkrus'tar] *vt* to incrust; (*piedras: en joya*) to inlay

**incubar** [inku'βar] *vt* to incubate

**inculcar** [inkul'kar] *vt* to inculcate

**inculto, -a** [in'kulto, a] *adj* (*persona*) uneducated; (*grosero*) uncouth ▷ *nm/f* ignoramus

**incumplimiento** [inkumpli'mjento] *nm* non-fulfilment; **incumplimiento de contrato** breach of contract

**incurrir** [inku'rrir] *vi*: **~ en** to incur; (*crimen*) to commit

**indagar** [inda'xar] *vt* to investigate; to search; (*averiguar*) to ascertain

**indecente** [inde'θente] *adj* indecent, improper; (*lascivo*) obscene

**indeciso, -a** [inde'θiso, a] *adj* (*por decidir*) undecided; (*vacilante*) hesitant

**indefenso, -a** [inde'fenso, a] *adj* defenceless

**indefinido, -a** [indefi'niðo, a] *adj* indefinite; (*vago*) vague, undefined

**indemne** [in'demne] *adj* (*objeto*) undamaged; (*persona*) unharmed, unhurt

**indemnizar** [indemni'θar] *vt* to indemnify; (*compensar*) to compensate

**independencia** [indepen'denθja] *nf* independence

**independiente** [indepen'djente] *adj* (*libre*) independent; (*autónomo*) self-sufficient

**indeterminado, -a** [indetermi'naðo, a] *adj* indefinite; (*desconocido*) indeterminate

**India** ['indja] *nf*: **la ~** India

**indicación** [indika'θjon] *nf* indication;

(*señal*) sign; (*sugerencia*) suggestion, hint

**indicado, -a** [indi'kaðo, a] *adj* (*momento, método*) right; (*tratamiento*) appropriate; (*solución*) likely

**indicador** [indika'ðor] *nm* indicator; (*Tec*) gauge, meter

**indicar** [indi'kar] *vt* (*mostrar*) to indicate, show; (*termómetro etc*) to read, register; (*señalar*) to point to

**índice** ['indiθe] *nm* index; (*catálogo*) catalogue; (*Anat*) index finger, forefinger; **índice de materias** table of contents

**indicio** [in'diθjo] *nm* indication, sign; (*en pesquisa etc*) clue

**indiferencia** [indife'renθja] *nf* indifference; (*apatía*) apathy; **indiferente** *adj* indifferent

**indígena** [in'dixena] *adj* indigenous, native ▷ *nmf* native

**indigestión** [indixes'tjon] *nf* indigestion

**indigesto, -a** [indi'xesto, a] *adj* (*alimento*) indigestible; (*fig*) turgid

**indignación** [indixna'θjon] *nf* indignation

**indignar** [indix'nar] *vt* to anger, make indignant; **indignarse** *vr*: **~se por** to get indignant about

**indigno, -a** [in'dixno, a] *adj* (*despreciable*) low, contemptible; (*inmerecido*) unworthy

**indio, -a** ['indjo, a] *adj, nm/f* Indian

**indirecta** [indi'rekta] *nf* insinuation, innuendo; (*sugerencia*) hint

**indirecto, -a** [indi'rekto, a] *adj* indirect

**indiscreción** [indiskre'θjon] *nf* (*imprudencia*) indiscretion; (*irreflexión*) tactlessness; (*acto*) gaffe, faux pas

**indiscreto, -a** [indis'kreto, a] *adj* indiscreet

**indiscutible** [indisku'tiβle] *adj* indisputable, unquestionable

**indispensable** [indispen'saβle] *adj* indispensable, essential

**indispuesto, -a** [indis'pwesto, a] *adj* (*enfermo*) unwell, indisposed

**indistinto, -a** [indis'tinto, a] *adj* indistinct; (*vago*) vague

**individual** [indiβi'ðwal] *adj* individual; (*habitación*) single ▷ *nm* (*Deporte*) singles *sg*

**individuo, -a** [indi'βiðwo, a] *adj, nm* individual

**índole** ['indole] *nf* (*naturaleza*) nature; (*clase*) sort, kind

**inducir** [indu'θir] *vt* to induce; (*inferir*) to infer; (*persuadir*) to persuade

**indudable** [indu'ðaβle] *adj* undoubted; (*incuestionable*) unquestionable

**indultar** [indul'tar] *vt* (*perdonar*) to pardon, reprieve; (*librar de pago*) to exempt;

**indulto** nm pardon; exemption

**industria** [in'dustrja] nf industry; (habilidad) skill; **industrial** adj industrial ▷ nm industrialist

**inédito, -a** [in'eðito, a] adj (texto) unpublished; (nuevo) new

**ineficaz** [inefi'kaθ] adj (inútil) ineffective; (ineficiente) inefficient

**ineludible** [inelu'ðiβle] adj inescapable, unavoidable

**ineptitud** [inepti'tuð] nf ineptitude, incompetence; **inepto, -a** adj inept, incompetent

**inequívoco, -a** [ine'kiβoko, a] adj unequivocal; (inconfundible) unmistakable

**inercia** [in'erθja] nf inertia; (pasividad) passivity

**inerte** [in'erte] adj inert; (inmóvil) motionless

**inesperado, -a** [inespe'raðo, a] adj unexpected, unforeseen

**inestable** [ines'taβle] adj unstable

**inevitable** [ineβi'taβle] adj inevitable

**inexacto, -a** [inek'sakto, a] adj inaccurate; (falso) untrue

**inexperto, -a** [inek'sperto, a] adj (novato) inexperienced

**infalible** [infa'liβle] adj infallible; (plan) foolproof

**infame** [in'fame] adj infamous; (horrible) dreadful; **infamia** nf infamy; (deshonra) disgrace

**infancia** [in'fanθja] nf infancy, childhood

**infantería** [infante'ria] nf infantry

**infantil** [infan'til] adj (pueril, aniñado) infantile; (cándido) childlike; (literatura, ropa etc) children's

**infarto** [in'farto] nm (tb: ~ de miocardio) heart attack

**infatigable** [infati'xaβle] adj tireless, untiring

**infección** [infek'θjon] nf infection; **infeccioso, -a** adj infectious

**infectar** [infek'tar] vt to infect; **infectarse** vr to become infected

**infeliz** [infe'liθ] adj unhappy, wretched ▷ nmf wretch

**inferior** [infe'rjor] adj inferior; (situación) lower ▷ nmf inferior, subordinate

**inferir** [infe'rir] vt (deducir) to infer, deduce; (causar) to cause

**infidelidad** [infiðeli'ðað] nf (gen) infidelity, unfaithfulness

**infiel** [in'fjel] adj unfaithful, disloyal; (erróneo) inaccurate ▷ nmf infidel, unbeliever

**infierno** [in'fjerno] nm hell

**infiltrarse** [infil'trarse] vr: ~ **en** to infiltrate in(to); (persona) to work one's way in(to)

**ínfimo, -a** ['infimo, a] adj (más bajo) lowest; (despreciable) vile, mean

**infinidad** [infini'ðað] nf infinity; (abundancia) great quantity

**infinito, -a** [infi'nito, a] adj, nm infinite

**inflación** [infla'θjon] nf (hinchazón) swelling; (monetaria) inflation; (fig) conceit

**inflamable** [infl'maβle] adj flammable

**inflamar** [infla'mar] vt (Med: fig) to inflame; **inflamarse** vr to catch fire; to become inflamed

**inflar** [in'flar] vt (hinchar) to inflate, blow up; (fig) to exaggerate; **inflarse** vr to swell (up); (fig) to get conceited

**inflexible** [inflek'siβle] adj inflexible; (fig) unbending

**influencia** [influ'enθja] nf influence

**influir** [influ'ir] vt to influence

**influjo** [in'fluxo] nm influence

**influya** etc vb V **influir**

**influyente** [influ'jente] adj influential

**información** [informa'θjon] nf information; (noticias) news sg; (Jur) inquiry; **I~** (oficina) Information Office; (mostrador) Information Desk; (Tel) Directory Enquiries

**informal** [infor'mal] adj (gen) informal

**informar** [infor'mar] vt (gen) to inform; (revelar) to reveal, make known ▷ vi (Jur) to plead; (denunciar) to inform; (dar cuenta de) to report on; **informarse** vr to find out; **~se de** to inquire into

**informática** [infor'matika] nf computer science, information technology

**informe** [in'forme] adj shapeless ▷ nm report

**infracción** [infrak'θjon] nf infraction, infringement

**infravalorar** [infrabalo'rar] vt to undervalue, underestimate

**infringir** [infrin'xir] vt to infringe, contravene

**infundado, -a** [infun'daðo, a] adj groundless, unfounded

**infundir** [infun'dir] vt to infuse, instil

**infusión** [infu'sjon] nf infusion; **infusión de manzanilla** camomile tea

**ingeniería** [inxenje'ria] nf engineering; **ingeniería genética** genetic engineering; **ingeniero, -a** nm/f engineer; **ingeniero civil o de caminos** civil engineer

**ingenio** [in'xenjo] nm (talento) talent; (agudeza) wit; (habilidad) ingenuity, inventiveness; **ingenio azucarero** (LAM) sugar refinery; **ingenioso, -a** [inxe'njoso, a] adj ingenious, clever; (divertido) witty; **ingenuo, -a** adj ingenuous

**ingerir** [inxe'rir] vt to ingest; (tragar) to swallow; (consumir) to consume

**Inglaterra** [ingla'terra] nf England

**ingle** ['ingle] nf groin

**inglés, -esa** [in'gles, esa] adj English ▷ nm/f Englishman(-woman) ▷ nm (Ling) English

**ingrato, -a** [in'grato, a] adj (gen) ungrateful

**ingrediente** [ingre'ðjente] nm ingredient

**ingresar** [ingre'sar] vt (dinero) to deposit ▷ vi to come in; **~ en el hospital** to go into hospital

**ingreso** [in'greso] nm (entrada) entry; (en hospital etc) admission; **ingresos** nmpl (dinero) income sg; (Com) takings pl

**inhabitable** [inaβi'taβle] adj uninhabitable

**inhalar** [ina'lar] vt to inhale

**inhibir** [ini'βir] vt to inhibit

**inhóspito, -a** [i'nospito, a] adj (región, paisaje) inhospitable

**inhumano, -a** [inu'mano, a] adj inhuman

**inicial** [ini'θjal] adj, nf initial

**iniciar** [ini'θjar] vt (persona) to initiate; (empezar) to begin, commence; (conversación) to start up

**iniciativa** [iniθja'tiβa] nf initiative; **iniciativa privada** private enterprise

**ininterrumpido, -a** [ininterrum'piðo, a] adj uninterrupted

**injertar** [inxer'tar] vt to graft; **injerto** nm graft

**injuria** [in'xurja] nf (agravio, ofensa) offence; (insulto) insult

▌ No confundir **injuria** con la palabra inglesa *injury*.

**injusticia** [inxus'tiθja] nf injustice

**injusto, -a** [in'xusto, a] adj unjust, unfair

**inmadurez** [inmaðu're θ] nf immaturity

**inmediaciones** [inmeðja'θjones] nfpl neighbourhood sg, environs

**inmediato, -a** [inme'ðjato, a] adj immediate; (contiguo) adjoining; (rápido) prompt; (próximo) neighbouring, next; **de ~** immediately

**inmejorable** [inmexo'raβle] adj unsurpassable; (precio) unbeatable

**inmenso, -a** [in'menso, a] adj immense, huge

**inmigración** [inmixra'θjon] nf immigration

**inmobiliaria** [inmoβi'ljarja] nf estate agency

**inmolar** [inmo'lar] vt to immolate, sacrifice

**inmoral** [inmo'ral] adj immoral

**inmortal** [inmor'tal] adj immortal; **inmortalizar** vt to immortalize

**inmóvil** [in'moβil] adj immobile

**inmueble** [in'mweβle] adj: **bienes ~s** real estate, landed property ▷ nm property

**inmundo, -a** [in'mundo, a] adj filthy

**inmune** [in'mune] adj: **~ (a)** (Med) immune (to)

**inmunidad** [inmuni'ðað] nf immunity

**inmutarse** [inmu'tarse] vr to turn pale; **no se inmutó** he didn't turn a hair

**innato, -a** [in'nato, a] adj innate

**innecesario, -a** [inneθe'sarjo, a] adj unnecessary

**innovación** [innoβa'θjon] nf innovation

**innovar** [inno'βar] vt to introduce

**inocencia** [ino'θenθja] nf innocence

**inocentada** [inoθen'taða] nf practical joke

**inocente** [ino'θente] adj (ingenuo) naive, innocent; (inculpable) innocent; (sin malicia) harmless ▷ nmf simpleton; **el día de los (Santos) I~s** ≈ April Fools' Day

● **DÍA DE LOS (SANTOS)**
● **INOCENTES**
●
● The 28th December, el **día de los**
● **(Santos) Inocentes**, is when the
● Church commemorates the story of
● Herod's slaughter of the innocent
● children of Judaea. On this day
● Spaniards play **inocentadas** (practical
● jokes) on each other, much like our April
● Fool's Day pranks.

**inodoro** [ino'ðoro] nm toilet, lavatory (BRIT)

**inofensivo, -a** [inofen'siβo, a] adj inoffensive, harmless

**inolvidable** [inolβi'ðaβle] adj unforgettable

**inoportuno, -a** [inopor'tuno, a] adj untimely; (molesto) inconvenient

**inoxidable** [inoksi'ðaβle] adj: **acero ~** stainless steel

**inquietar** [inkje'tar] vt to worry, trouble; **inquietarse** vr to worry, get upset; **inquieto, -a** adj anxious, worried; **inquietud** nf anxiety, worry

**inquilino, -a** [inki'lino, a] nm/f tenant

**insaciable** [insa'θjaβle] adj insatiable

**inscribir** [inskri'βir] vt to inscribe; **~ a algn en** (lista) to put sb on; (censo) to register sb on

**inscripción** [inskrip'θjon] nf inscription; (Escol etc) enrolment; (en censo) registration

**insecticida** [insekti'θiða] nm insecticide

**insecto** [in'sekto] nm insect
**inseguridad** [insexuri'ðað] nf insecurity; **inseguridad ciudadana** lack of safety in the streets
**inseguro, -a** [inse'xuro, a] adj insecure; (inconstante) unsteady; (incierto) uncertain
**insensato, -a** [insen'sato, a] adj foolish, stupid
**insensible** [insen'siβle] adj (gen) insensitive; (movimiento) imperceptible; (sin sentido) numb
**insertar** [inser'tar] vt to insert
**inservible** [inser'βiβle] adj useless
**insignia** [in'sixnja] nf (señal distintiva) badge; (estandarte) flag
**insignificante** [insixnifi'kante] adj insignificant
**insinuar** [insi'nwar] vt to insinuate, imply
**insípido, -a** [in'sipiðo, a] adj insipid
**insistir** [insis'tir] vi to insist; **~ en algo** to insist on sth; (enfatizar) to stress sth
**insolación** [insola'θjon] nf (Med) sunstroke
**insolente** [inso'lente] adj insolent
**insólito, -a** [in'solito, a] adj unusual
**insoluble** [inso'luβle] adj insoluble
**insomnio** [in'somnjo] nm insomnia
**insonorizado, -a** [insonori'θaðo, a] adj (cuarto etc) soundproof
**insoportable** [insopor'taβle] adj unbearable
**inspección** [inspek'θjon] nf inspection, check; **inspeccionar** vt (examinar) to inspect, examine; (controlar) to check
**inspector, a** [inspek'tor, a] nm/f inspector
**inspiración** [inspira'θjon] nf inspiration
**inspirar** [inspi'rar] vt to inspire; (Med) to inhale; **inspirarse** vr: **~se en** to be inspired by
**instalación** [instala'θjon] nf (equipo) fittings pl, equipment; **instalación eléctrica** wiring
**instalar** [insta'lar] vt (establecer) to instal; (erguir) to set up, erect; **instalarse** vr to establish o.s.; (en una vivienda) to move into
**instancia** [ins'tanθja] nf (Jur) petition; (ruego) request; **en última ~** as a last resort
**instantáneo, -a** [instan'taneo, a] adj instantaneous; **café ~** instant coffee
**instante** [ins'tante] nm instant, moment; **al ~** right now
**instar** [ins'tar] vt to press, urge
**instaurar** [instau'rar] vt (costumbre) to establish; (normas, sistema) to bring in, introduce; (gobierno) to instal
**instigar** [insti'xar] vt to instigate

**instinto** [ins'tinto] nm instinct; **por ~** instinctively
**institución** [institu'θjon] nf institution, establishment
**instituir** [institu'ir] vt to establish; (fundar) to found; **instituto** nm (gen) institute; (ESP Escol) ≈ comprehensive (BRIT) o high (US) school
**institutriz** [institu'triθ] nf governess
**instrucción** [instruk'θjon] nf instruction
**instruir** [instru'ir] vt (gen) to instruct; (enseñar) to teach, educate
**instrumento** [instru'mento] nm (gen) instrument; (herramienta) tool, implement
**insubordinarse** [insuβorði'narse] vr to rebel
**insuficiente** [insufi'θjente] adj (gen) insufficient; (Escol: calificación) unsatisfactory
**insular** [insu'lar] adj insular
**insultar** [insul'tar] vt to insult; **insulto** nm insult
**insuperable** [insupe'raβle] adj (excelente) unsurpassable; (problema etc) insurmountable
**insurrección** [insurrek'θjon] nf insurrection, rebellion
**intachable** [inta'tʃaβle] adj irreproachable
**intacto, -a** [in'takto, a] adj intact
**integral** [inte'xral] adj integral; (completo) complete; **pan ~** wholemeal (BRIT) o wholewheat (US) bread
**integrar** [inte'xrar] vt to make up, compose; (Mat: fig) to integrate
**integridad** [intexri'ðað] nf wholeness; (carácter) integrity; **íntegro, -a** adj whole, entire; (honrado) honest
**intelectual** [intelek'twal] adj, nmf intellectual
**inteligencia** [inteli'xenθja] nf intelligence; (ingenio) ability; **inteligente** adj intelligent
**intemperie** [intem'perje] nf: **a la ~** out in the open, exposed to the elements
**intención** [inten'θjon] nf (gen) intention, purpose; **con segundas intenciones** maliciously; **con ~** deliberately
**intencionado, -a** [intenθjo'naðo, a] adj deliberate; **mal ~** ill-disposed, hostile
**intensidad** [intensi'ðað] nf (gen) intensity; (Elec, Tec) strength; **llover con ~** to rain hard
**intenso, -a** [in'tenso, a] adj intense; (sentimiento) profound, deep
**intentar** [inten'tar] vt (tratar) to try, attempt; **intento** nm attempt
**interactivo, -a** [interak'tiβo, a] adj

(*Inform*) interactive

**intercalar** [interka'lar] *vt* to insert

**intercambio** [inter'kambjo] *nm* exchange, swap

**interceder** [interθe'ðer] *vi* to intercede

**interceptar** [interθep'tar] *vt* to intercept

**interés** [inte'res] *nm* (*gen*) interest; (*parte*) share, part; (*pey*) self-interest; **intereses creados** vested interests

**interesado, -a** [intere'saðo, a] *adj* interested; (*prejuiciado*) prejudiced; (*pey*) mercenary, self-seeking

**interesante** [intere'sante] *adj* interesting

**interesar** [intere'sar] *vt, vi* to interest, be of interest to; **interesarse** *vr*: **~se en** *o* **por** to take an interest in

**interferir** [interfe'rir] *vt* to interfere with; (*Tel*) to jam ▷ *vi* to interfere

**interfón** [inter'fon] (*MÉX*) *nm* entry phone

**interino, -a** [inte'rino, a] *adj* temporary ▷ *nm/f* temporary holder of a post; (*Med*) locum; (*Escol*) supply teacher

**interior** [inte'rjor] *adj* inner, inside; (*Com*) domestic, internal ▷ *nm* interior, inside; (*fig*) soul, mind; **Ministerio del I~** ≈ Home Office (*BRIT*), ≈ Department of the Interior (*US*); **interiorista** (*ESP*) *nmf* interior designer

**interjección** [interxek'θjon] *nf* interjection

**interlocutor, a** [interloku'tor, a] *nm/f* speaker

**intermedio, -a** [inter'meðjo, a] *adj* intermediate ▷ *nm* interval

**interminable** [intermi'naβle] *adj* endless

**intermitente** [intermi'tente] *adj* intermittent ▷ *nm* (*Auto*) indicator

**internacional** [internaθjo'nal] *adj* international

**internado** [inter'naðo] *nm* boarding school

**internar** [inter'nar] *vt* to intern; (*en un manicomio*) to commit; **internarse** *vr* (*penetrar*) to penetrate

**internauta** [inter'nauta] *nmf* web surfer, Internet user

**Internet, internet** [inter'net] *nm o f* Internet

**interno, -a** [in'terno, a] *adj* internal, interior; (*Pol etc*) domestic ▷ *nm/f* (*alumno*) boarder

**interponer** [interpo'ner] *vt* to interpose, put in; **interponerse** *vr* to intervene

**interpretación** [interpreta'θjon] *nf* interpretation

**interpretar** [interpre'tar] *vt* to interpret; (*Teatro, Mús*) to perform, play; **intérprete** *nmf* (*Ling*) interpreter, translator; (*Mús, Teatro*) performer, artist(e)

**interrogación** [interroxa'θjon] *nf* interrogation; (*Ling: tb:* **signo de ~**) question mark

**interrogar** [interro'xar] *vt* to interrogate, question

**interrumpir** [interrum'pir] *vt* to interrupt

**interrupción** [interrup'θjon] *nf* interruption

**interruptor** [interrup'tor] *nm* (*Elec*) switch

**intersección** [intersek'θjon] *nf* intersection

**interurbano, -a** [interur'βano, a] *adj*: **llamada interurbana** long-distance call

**intervalo** [inter'βalo] *nm* interval; (*descanso*) break

**intervenir** [interβe'nir] *vt* (*controlar*) to control, supervise; (*Med*) to operate on ▷ *vi* (*participar*) to take part, participate; (*mediar*) to intervene

**interventor, a** [interβen'tor, a] *nm/f* inspector; (*Com*) auditor

**intestino** [intes'tino] *nm* (*Med*) intestine

**intimar** [inti'mar] *vi* to become friendly

**intimidad** [intimi'ðað] *nf* intimacy; (*familiaridad*) familiarity; (*vida privada*) private life; (*Jur*) privacy

**íntimo, -a** ['intimo, a] *adj* intimate

**intolerable** [intole'raβle] *adj* intolerable, unbearable

**intoxicación** [intoksika'θjon] *nf* poisoning; **intoxicación alimenticia** food poisoning

**intranet** [intra'net] *nf* intranet

**intranquilo, -a** [intran'kilo, a] *adj* worried

**intransitable** [intransi'taβle] *adj* impassable

**intrépido, -a** [in'trepiðo, a] *adj* intrepid

**intriga** [in'trixa] *nf* intrigue; (*plan*) plot; **intrigar** *vt, vi* to intrigue

**intrínseco, -a** [in'trinseko, a] *adj* intrinsic

**introducción** [introðuk'θjon] *nf* introduction

**introducir** [introðu'θir] *vt* (*gen*) to introduce; (*moneda etc*) to insert; (*Inform*) to input, enter

**intromisión** [intromi'sjon] *nf* interference, meddling

**introvertido, -a** [introβer'tiðo, a] *adj, nm/f* introvert

**intruso, -a** [in'truso, a] *adj* intrusive
▷ *nm/f* intruder
**intuición** [intwi'θjon] *nf* intuition
**inundación** [inunda'θjon] *nf* flood(ing);
**inundar** *vt* to flood; (*fig*) to swamp,
inundate
**inusitado, -a** [inusi'taðo, a] *adj* unusual,
rare
**inútil** [in'util] *adj* useless; (*esfuerzo*) vain,
fruitless
**inutilizar** [inutili'θar] *vt* to make o render
useless
**invadir** [imba'ðir] *vt* to invade
**inválido, -a** [im'baliðo, a] *adj* invalid
▷ *nm/f* invalid
**invasión** [imba'sjon] *nf* invasion
**invasor, a** [imba'sor, a] *adj* invading
▷ *nm/f* invader
**invención** [imben'θjon] *nf* invention
**inventar** [imben'tar] *vt* to invent
**inventario** [imben'tarjo] *nm* inventory
**invento** [im'bento] *nm* invention
**inventor, a** [imben'tor, a] *nm/f* inventor
**invernadero** [imberna'ðero] *nm*
greenhouse
**inverosímil** [imbero'simil] *adj*
implausible
**inversión** [imber'sjon] *nf* (*Com*)
investment
**inverso, -a** [im'berso, a] *adj* inverse,
opposite; **en el orden ~** in reverse order; **a la
inversa** inversely, the other way round
**inversor, a** [imber'sor, a] *nm/f* (*Com*)
investor
**invertir** [imber'tir] *vt* (*Com*) to invest;
(*volcar*) to turn upside down; (*tiempo etc*)
to spend
**investigación** [imbestixa'θjon]
*nf* investigation; (*Escol*) research;
**investigación y desarrollo** research and
development
**investigar** [imbesti'xar] *vt* to investigate;
(*Escol*) to do research into
**invierno** [im'bjerno] *nm* winter
**invisible** [imbi'siβle] *adj* invisible
**invitado, -a** [imbi'taðo, a] *nm/f* guest
**invitar** [imbi'tar] *vt* to invite; (*incitar*) to
entice; (*pagar*) to buy, pay for
**invocar** [imbo'kar] *vt* to invoke, call on
**involucrar** [imbolu'krar] *vt*: **~ en** to
involve in; **involucrarse** *vr* (*persona*): **~se
en** to get mixed up in
**involuntario, -a** [imbolun'tarjo, a]
*adj* (*movimiento, gesto*) involuntary; (*error*)
unintentional
**inyección** [injek'θjon] *nf* injection
**inyectar** [injek'tar] *vt* to inject
**iPod®** ['ipoð] (*pl* **~s**) *nm* iPod®

○ **PALABRA CLAVE**

**ir** [ir] *vi* **1** to go; (*a pie*) to walk; (*viajar*) to
travel; **ir caminando** to walk; **fui en tren** I
went o travelled by train; **¡(ahora) voy!** (I'm
just) coming!
**2**: **ir (a) por: ir (a) por el médico** to fetch
the doctor
**3** (*progresar: persona, cosa*) to go; **el trabajo
va muy bien** work is going very well; **¿cómo
te va?** how are things going?; **me va muy
bien** I'm getting on very well; **le fue fatal** it
went awfully badly for him
**4** (*funcionar*): **el coche no va muy bien** the
car isn't running very well
**5**: **te va estupendamente ese color** that
colour suits you fantastically well
**6** (*locuciones*): **¿vino? – ¡que va!** did he come?
– of course not!; **vamos, no llores** come on,
don't cry; **¡vaya coche!** what a car!, that's
some car!
**7**: **no vaya a ser: tienes que correr, no
vaya a ser que pierdas el tren** you'll have
to run so as not to miss the train
**8** (+ *pp*): **iba vestido muy bien** he was very
well dressed
**9**: **ni me** *etc* **va ni me** *etc* **viene** I *etc* don't
care
▷ *vb aux* **1** **ir a**: **voy/iba a hacerlo hoy** I
am/was going to do it today
**2** (+ *gerundio*): **iba anocheciendo** it was
getting dark; **todo se me iba aclarando**
everything was gradually becoming clearer
to me
**3** (+ *pp* = *pasivo*): **van vendidos 300
ejemplares** 300 copies have been sold so far
**irse** *vr* **1**: **¿por dónde se va al zoológico?**
which is the way to the zoo?
**2** (*marcharse*) to leave; **ya se habrán ido** they
must already have left o gone

**ira** ['ira] *nf* anger, rage
**Irak** [i'rak] *nm* = **Iraq**
**Irán** [i'ran] *nm* Iran; **iraní** *adj, nmf* Iranian
**Iraq** [i'rak] *nm* Iraq; **iraquí** *adj, nmf* Iraqi
**iris** ['iris] *nm inv* (*tb*: **arco ~**) rainbow;
(*Anat*) iris
**Irlanda** [ir'landa] *nf* Ireland; **irlandés,
-esa** *adj* Irish ▷ *nm/f* Irishman(-woman);
**los irlandeses** the Irish
**ironía** [iro'nia] *nf* irony; **irónico, -a** *adj*
ironic(al)
**IRPF** *nm abr* (= *Impuesto sobre la Renta de las
Personas Físicas*) (personal) income tax
**irreal** [irre'al] *adj* unreal
**irregular** [irreɣu'lar] *adj* (*gen*) irregular;
(*situación*) abnormal
**irremediable** [irreme'ðjaβle] *adj*

irremediable; (*vicio*) incurable

**irreparable** [irrepa'raβle] *adj* (*daños*)
irreparable; (*pérdida*) irrecoverable

**irrespetuoso, -a** [irrespe'twoso, a] *adj*
disrespectful

**irresponsable** [irrespon'saβle] *adj*
irresponsible

**irreversible** [irreβer'sible] *adj* irreversible

**irrigar** [irri'xar] *vt* to irrigate

**irrisorio, -a** [irri'sorjo, a] *adj* derisory,
ridiculous

**irritar** [irri'tar] *vt* to irritate, annoy

**irrupción** [irrup'θjon] *nf* irruption;
(*invasión*) invasion

**isla** ['isla] *nf* island

**Islam** [is'lam] *nm* Islam; **las enseñanzas
del ~** the teachings of Islam; **islámico, -a**
*adj* Islamic

**islandés, -esa** [islan'des, esa] *adj*
Icelandic ▷ *nm/f* Icelander

**Islandia** [is'landja] *nf* Iceland

**isleño, -a** [is'leɲo, a] *adj* island *cpd* ▷ *nm/f*
islander

**Israel** [isra'el] *nm* Israel; **israelí** *adj*, *nmf*
Israeli

**istmo** ['istmo] *nm* isthmus

**Italia** [i'talja] *nf* Italy; **italiano, -a** *adj*,
*nm/f* Italian

**itinerario** [itine'rarjo] *nm* itinerary, route

**ITV** (*ESP*) *nf abr* (= *inspección técnica de
vehículos*) roadworthiness test, ≈ MOT (*BRIT*)

**IVA** ['iβa] *nm abr* (= *impuesto sobre el valor
añadido*) VAT

**izar** [i'θar] *vt* to hoist

**izdo, -a** *abr* (= *izquierdo, a*) l

**izquierda** [iθ'kjerda] *nf* left; (*Pol*) left
(wing); **a la ~** (*estar*) on the left; (*torcer etc*)
(to the) left

**izquierdo, -a** [iθ'kjerðo, a] *adj* left

**jabalí** [xaβa'li] *nm* wild boar

**jabalina** [xaβa'lina] *nf* javelin

**jabón** [xa'βon] *nm* soap

**jaca** ['xaka] *nf* pony

**jacal** [xa'kal] (*MÉX*) *nm* shack

**jacinto** [xa'θinto] *nm* hyacinth

**jactarse** [xak'tarse] *vr* to boast, brag

**jadear** [xaðe'ar] *vi* to pant, gasp for breath

**jaguar** [xa'ɣwar] *nm* jaguar

**jaiba** ['xaiβa] (*LAM*) *nf* crab

**jalar** [xa'lar] (*LAM*) *vt* to pull

**jalea** [xa'lea] *nf* jelly

**jaleo** [xa'leo] *nm* racket, uproar; **armar un
~** to kick up a racket

**jalón** [xa'lon] (*LAM*) *nm* tug

**jamás** [xa'mas] *adv* never

**jamón** [xa'mon] *nm* ham; **jamón dulce**
*o* **de York** cooked ham; **jamón serrano**
cured ham

**Japón** [xa'pon] *nm* Japan; **japonés, -esa**
*adj*, *nm/f* Japanese ▷ *nm* (*Ling*) Japanese

**jaque** ['xake] *nm* (*Ajedrez*) check; **jaque
mate** checkmate

**jaqueca** [xa'keka] *nf* (very bad) headache,
migraine

**jarabe** [xa'raβe] *nm* syrup

**jardín** [xar'ðin] *nm* garden; **jardín infantil**
*o* **de infancia** nursery (school); **jardinería**
*nf* gardening; **jardinero, -a** *nm/f* gardener

**jarra** ['xarra] *nf* jar; (*jarro*) jug

**jarro** ['xarro] *nm* jug

**jarrón** [xa'rron] *nm* vase

**jaula** ['xaula] *nf* cage

**jauría** [xau'ria] *nf* pack of hounds

**jazmín** [xaθ'min] *nm* jasmine

**J.C.** *abr* (= *Jesucristo*) J.C.

**jeans** [jins, dʒins] (*LAM*) *nmpl* jeans,
denims; **unos ~** a pair of jeans

**jefatura** [xefa'tura] *nf* (*tb*: **~ de policía**)
police headquarters *sg*

**jefe, -a** ['xefe, a] *nm/f* (*gen*) chief, head;

(*patrón*) boss; **jefe de cocina** chef; **jefe de estación** stationmaster; **jefe de Estado** head of state; **jefe de estudios** (*Escol*) director of studies; **jefe de gobierno** head of government

**jengibre** [xen'xiβre] *nm* ginger

**jeque** ['xeke] *nm* sheik

**jerárquico, -a** [xe'rarkiko, a] *adj* hierarchic(al)

**jerez** [xe're0] *nm* sherry

**jerga** ['xerɣa] *nf* jargon

**jeringa** [xe'riŋɡa] *nf* syringe; (*LAM: molestia*) annoyance, bother; **jeringuilla** *nf* syringe

**jeroglífico** [xero'ɣlifiko] *nm* hieroglyphic

**jersey** [xer'sei] (*pl* **~s**) *nm* jersey, pullover, jumper

**Jerusalén** [xerusa'len] *n* Jerusalem

**Jesucristo** [xesu'kristo] *nm* Jesus Christ

**jesuita** [xe'swita] *adj, nm* Jesuit

**Jesús** [xe'sus] *nm* Jesus; **¡~!** good heavens!; (*al estornudar*) bless you!

**jinete** [xi'nete] *nmf* horseman(-woman), rider

**jipijapa** [xipi'xapa] (*LAM*) *nm* straw hat

**jirafa** [xi'rafa] *nf* giraffe

**jirón** [xi'ron] *nm* rag, shred

**jitomate** [xito'mate] (*MÉX*) *nm* tomato

**joder** [xo'ðer] (*fam!*) *vt, vi* to fuck (!)

**jogging** ['joɣin] (*RPL*) *nm* tracksuit (*BRIT*), sweat suit (*US*)

**jornada** [xor'naða] *nf* (*viaje de un día*) day's journey; (*camino o viaje entero*) journey; (*día de trabajo*) working day

**jornal** [xor'nal] *nm* (day's) wage; **jornalero** *nm* (day) labourer

**joroba** [xo'roβa] *nf* hump, hunched back; **jorobado, -a** *adj* hunchbacked ▷ *nm/f* hunchback

**jota** ['xota] *nf* (the letter) J; (*danza*) Aragonese dance; **no saber ni ~** to have no idea

**joven** ['xoβen] (*pl* **jóvenes**) *adj* young ▷ *nm* young man, youth ▷ *nf* young woman, girl

**joya** ['xoja] *nf* jewel, gem; (*fig: persona*) gem; **joyas de fantasía** costume o imitation jewellery; **joyería** *nf* (*joyas*) jewellery; (*tienda*) jeweller's (shop); **joyero** *nm* (*persona*) jeweller; (*caja*) jewel case

**juanete** [xwa'nete] *nm* (*del pie*) bunion

**jubilación** [xuβila'θjon] *nf* (*retiro*) retirement

**jubilado, -a** [xuβi'laðo, a] *adj* retired ▷ *nm/f* pensioner (*BRIT*), senior citizen

**jubilar** [xuβi'lar] *vt* to pension off, retire; (*fam*) to discard; **jubilarse** *vr* to retire

**júbilo** ['xuβilo] *nm* joy, rejoicing; **jubiloso,**

**-a** *adj* jubilant

**judía** [xu'ðia] (*ESP*) *nf* (*Culin*) bean; **judía blanca/verde** haricot/French bean; V *tb* **judío**

**judicial** [xuði'θjal] *adj* judicial

**judío, -a** [xu'ðio, a] *adj* Jewish ▷ *nm/f* Jew(ess)

**judo** ['juðo] *nm* judo

**juego** *etc* ['xweɣo] *vb* V **jugar** ▷ *nm* (*gen*) play; (*pasatiempo, partido*) game; (*en casino*) gambling; (*conjunto*) set; **fuera de ~** (*Deporte: persona*) offside; (*: pelota*) out of play; **juego de palabras** pun, play on words; **Juegos Olímpicos** Olympic Games

**juerga** ['xwerɣa] (*ESP: fam*) *nf* binge; (*fiesta*) party; **ir de ~** to go out on a binge

**jueves** ['xweβes] *nm inv* Thursday

**juez** [xweθ] *nmf* judge; **juez de instrucción** examining magistrate; **juez de línea** linesman; **juez de salida** starter

**jugada** [xu'ɣaða] *nf* play; **buena ~** good move o shot o stroke *etc*

**jugador, a** [xuɣa'ðor, a] *nm/f* player; (*en casino*) gambler

**jugar** [xu'ɣar] *vt, vi* to play; (*en casino*) to gamble; (*apostar*) to bet; **~ al fútbol** to play football

**juglar** [xu'ɣlar] *nm* minstrel

**jugo** ['xuɣo] *nm* (*Bot*) juice; (*fig*) essence, substance; **jugo de naranja** (*LAM*) orange juice; **jugoso, -a** *adj* juicy; (*fig*) substantial, important

**juguete** [xu'ɣete] *nm* toy; **juguetear** *vi* to play; **juguetería** *nf* toyshop

**juguetón, -ona** [xuɣe'ton, ona] *adj* playful

**juicio** ['xwiθjo] *nm* judgement; (*razón*) sanity, reason; (*opinión*) opinion

**julio** ['xuljo] *nm* July

**jumper** ['dʒumper] (*LAM*) *nm* pinafore dress (*BRIT*), jumper (*US*)

**junco** ['xunko] *nm* rush, reed

**jungla** ['xuŋɡla] *nf* jungle

**junio** ['xunjo] *nm* June

**junta** ['xunta] *nf* (*asamblea*) meeting, assembly; (*comité, consejo*) council, committee; (*Com, Finanzas*) board; (*Tec*) joint; **junta directiva** board of directors

**juntar** [xun'tar] *vt* to join, unite; (*maquinaria*) to assemble, put together; (*dinero*) to collect; **juntarse** *vr* to join, meet; (*reunirse: personas*) to meet, assemble; (*arrimarse*) to approach, draw closer; **~se con algn** to join sb

**junto, -a** ['xunto, a] *adj* joined; (*unido*) united; (*anexo*) near, close; (*contiguo, próximo*) next, adjacent ▷ *adv*: **todo ~** all at once; **~s** together; **~ a** near (to), next to; **~**

**con** (together) with

**jurado** [xu'raðo] *nm* (*Jur: individuo*) juror; (: *grupo*) jury; (*de concurso: grupo*) panel (of judges); (: *individuo*) member of a panel

**juramento** [xura'mento] *nm* oath; (*maldición*) oath, curse; **prestar ~** to take the oath; **tomar ~ a** to swear in, administer the oath to

**jurar** [xu'rar] *vt, vi* to swear; **~ en falso** to commit perjury; **tenérsela jurada a algn** to have it in for sb

**jurídico, -a** [xu'riðiko, a] *adj* legal

**jurisdicción** [xurisðik'θjon] *nf* (*poder, autoridad*) jurisdiction; (*territorio*) district

**justamente** [xusta'mente] *adv* justly, fairly; (*precisamente*) just, exactly

**justicia** [xus'tiθja] *nf* justice; (*equidad*) fairness, justice

**justificación** [xustifika'θjon] *nf* justification; **justificar** *vt* to justify

**justo, -a** ['xusto, a] *adj* (*equitativo*) just, fair, right; (*preciso*) exact, correct; (*ajustado*) tight ▷ *adv* (*precisamente*) exactly, precisely; (*LAM: apenas a tiempo*) just in time

**juvenil** [xuβe'nil] *adj* youthful

**juventud** [xuβen'tuð] *nf* (*adolescencia*) youth; (*jóvenes*) young people *pl*

**juzgado** [xuθ'xaðo] *nm* tribunal; (*Jur*) court

**juzgar** [xuθ'xar] *vt* to judge; **a ~ por ...** to judge by ..., judging by ...

**kárate** ['karate] *nm* karate

**kg** *abr* (= *kilogramo*) kg

**kilo** ['kilo] *nm* kilo; **kilogramo** *nm* kilogramme; **kilometraje** *nm* distance in kilometres ≈ mileage; **kilómetro** *nm* kilometre; **kilovatio** *nm* kilowatt

**kiosco** ['kjosko] *nm* = **quiosco**

**kleenex**® [kli'neks] *nm* paper handkerchief, tissue

**Kosovo** [ko'soβo] *nm* Kosovo

**km** *abr* (= *kilómetro*) km

**kv** *abr* (= *kilovatio*) kw

**l** *abr* (= *litro*) l

**la** [la] *art def* the ▷ *pron* her; (*Ud.*) you; (*cosa*) it ▷ *nm* (*Mús*) la; **~ del sombrero rojo** the girl in the red hat; V tb **el**

**laberinto** [laβe'rinto] *nm* labyrinth

**labio** ['laβjo] *nm* lip

**labor** [la'βor] *nf* labour; (*Agr*) farm work; (*tarea*) job, task; (*Costura*) needlework; **labores domésticas** o **del hogar** household chores; **laborable** *adj* (*Agr*) workable; **día laborable** working day; **laboral** *adj* (*accidente*) at work; (*jornada*) working

**laboratorio** [laβora'torjo] *nm* laboratory

**laborista** [laβo'rista] *adj*: **Partido L~** Labour Party

**labrador, a** [laβra'ðor, a] *adj* farming *cpd* ▷ *nm/f* farmer

**labranza** [la'βranθa] *nf* (*Agr*) cultivation

**labrar** [la'βrar] *vt* (*gen*) to work; (*madera etc*) to carve; (*fig*) to cause, bring about

**laca** ['laka] *nf* lacquer

**lacio, -a** ['laθjo, a] *adj* (*pelo*) straight

**lacón** [la'kon] *nm* shoulder of pork

**lactancia** [lak'tanθja] *nf* lactation

**lácteo, -a** ['lakteo, a] *adj*: **productos ~s** dairy products

**ladear** [laðe'ar] *vt* to tip, tilt ▷ *vi* to tilt; **ladearse** *vr* to lean

**ladera** [la'ðera] *nf* slope

**lado** ['laðo] *nm* (*gen*) side; (*fig*) protection; (*Mil*) flank; **al ~** beside; **poner de ~** to put on its side; **poner a un ~** to put aside; **por todos ~s** on all sides, all round (BRIT)

**ladrar** [la'ðrar] *vi* to bark; **ladrido** *nm* bark, barking

**ladrillo** [la'ðriʎo] *nm* (*gen*) brick; (*azulejo*) tile

**ladrón, -ona** [la'ðron, ona] *nm/f* thief

**lagartija** [laɣar'tixa] *nf* (*Zool*) (small) lizard

**lagarto** [la'ɣarto] *nm* (*Zool*) lizard

**lago** ['laɣo] *nm* lake

**lágrima** ['laɣrima] *nf* tear

**laguna** [la'ɣuna] *nf* (*lago*) lagoon; (*hueco*) gap

**lamentable** [lamen'taβle] *adj* lamentable, regrettable; (*miserable*) pitiful

**lamentar** [lamen'tar] *vt* (*sentir*) to regret; (*deplorar*) to lament; **lamentarse** *vr* to lament; **lo lamento mucho** I'm very sorry

**lamer** [la'mer] *vt* to lick

**lámina** ['lamina] *nf* (*plancha delgada*) sheet; (*para estampar, estampa*) plate

**lámpara** ['lampara] *nf* lamp; **lámpara de alcohol/gas** spirit/gas lamp; **lámpara de pie** standard lamp

**lana** ['lana] *nf* wool

**lancha** ['lantʃa] *nf* launch; **lancha motora** motorboat, speedboat

**langosta** [lan'gosta] *nf* (*crustáceo*) lobster; (: *de río*) crayfish; **langostino** *nm* Dublin Bay prawn

**lanza** ['lanθa] *nf* (*arma*) lance, spear

**lanzamiento** [lanθa'mjento] *nm* (*gen*) throwing; (*Náut, Com*) launch, launching; **lanzamiento de peso** putting the shot

**lanzar** [lan'θar] *vt* (*gen*) to throw; (*Deporte: pelota*) to bowl; (*Náut, Com*) to launch; (*Jur*) to evict; **lanzarse** *vr* to throw o.s.

**lapa** ['lapa] *nf* limpet

**lapicero** [lapi'θero] (CAM) *nm* (*bolígrafo*) ballpoint pen, Biro®

**lápida** ['lapiða] *nf* stone; **lápida mortuoria** headstone

**lápiz** ['lapiθ] *nm* pencil; **lápiz de color** coloured pencil; **lápiz de labios** lipstick; **lápiz de ojos** eyebrow pencil

**largar** [lar'ɣar] *vt* (*soltar*) to release; (*aflojar*) to loosen; (*lanzar*) to launch; (*fam*) to let fly; (*velas*) to unfurl; (LAM: *lanzar*) to throw; **largarse** *vr* (*fam*) to beat it; **~se a** (cs: *empezar*) to start to

**largo, -a** ['larɣo, a] *adj* (*longitud*) long; (*tiempo*) lengthy; (*fig*) generous ▷ *nm* length; (*Mús*) largo; **dos años ~s** two long years; **tiene 9 metros de ~** it is 9 metres long; **a la larga** in the long run; **a lo ~ de** along; (*tiempo*) all through, throughout

No confundir **largo** con la palabra inglesa *large*.

**largometraje** *nm* feature film

**laringe** [la'rinxe] *nf* larynx; **laringitis** *nf* laryngitis

**las** [las] *art def* the ▷ *pron* them; **~ que cantan** the ones o women o girls who sing; V tb **el**

**lasaña** [la'saɲa] *nf* lasagne, lasagna

**láser** ['laser] *nm* laser

**lástima** ['lastima] *nf (pena)* pity; **dar ~** to be pitiful; **es una ~ que ...** it's a pity that ...; **¡qué ~!** what a pity!; **está hecha una ~** she looks pitiful

**lastimar** [lasti'mar] *vt (herir)* to wound; *(ofender)* to offend; **lastimarse** *vr* to hurt o.s.

**lata** ['lata] *nf (metal)* tin; *(caja)* tin *(BRIT)*, can; *(fam)* nuisance; **en ~** tinned *(BRIT)*, canned; **dar la ~** to be a nuisance

**latente** [la'tente] *adj* latent

**lateral** [late'ral] *adj* side *cpd*, lateral ⊳ *nm (Teatro)* wings

**latido** [la'tiðo] *nm (de corazón)* beat

**latifundio** [lati'fundjo] *nm* large estate

**latigazo** [lati'xaθo] *nm (golpe)* lash; *(sonido)* crack

**látigo** ['latixo] *nm* whip

**latín** [la'tin] *nm* Latin

**latino, -a** [la'tino, a] *adj* Latin; **latinoamericano, -a** *adj, nm/f* Latin-American

**latir** [la'tir] *vi (corazón, pulso)* to beat

**latitud** [lati'tuð] *nf (Geo)* latitude

**latón** [la'ton] *nm* brass

**laurel** [lau'rel] *nm (Bot)* laurel; *(Culin)* bay

**lava** ['laβa] *nf* lava

**lavabo** [la'βaβo] *nm (pila)* washbasin; *(tb: ~s)* toilet

**lavado** [la'βaðo] *nm* washing; *(de ropa)* laundry; *(Arte)* wash; **lavado de cerebro** brainwashing; **lavado en seco** dry-cleaning

**lavadora** [laβa'ðora] *nf* washing machine

**lavanda** [la'βanda] *nf* lavender

**lavandería** [laβande'ria] *nf* laundry; *(automática)* launderette

**lavaplatos** [laβa'platos] *nm inv* dishwasher

**lavar** [la'βar] *vt* to wash; *(borrar)* to wipe away; **lavarse** *vr* to wash o.s.; **~se las manos** to wash one's hands; **~se los dientes** to brush one's teeth; **~ y marcar** *(pelo)* to shampoo and set; **~ en seco** to dry-clean; **~ los platos** to wash the dishes

**lavarropas** [laβa'rropas] *(RPL) nm inv* washing machine

**lavavajillas** [laβaβa'xiʎas] *nm inv* dishwasher

**laxante** [lak'sante] *nm* laxative

**lazarillo** [laθa'riʎo] *nm (tb: perro ~)* guide dog

**lazo** ['laθo] *nm* knot; *(lazada)* bow; *(para animales)* lasso; *(trampa)* snare; *(vínculo)* tie

**le** [le] *pron (directo)* him *(o* her*)*; *(: usted)* you; *(indirecto)* to him *(o* her *o* it*)*; *(: usted)* to you

**leal** [le'al] *adj* loyal; **lealtad** *nf* loyalty

**lección** [lek'θjon] *nf* lesson

**leche** ['letʃe] *nf* milk; **tiene mala ~** *(fam!)* he's a swine *(!)*; **leche condensada** condensed milk; **leche desnatada** skimmed milk

**lecho** ['letʃo] *nm (cama: de río)* bed; *(Geo)* layer

**lechón** [le'tʃon] *nm* sucking *(BRIT) o* suckling *(us)* pig

**lechoso, -a** [le'tʃoso, a] *adj* milky

**lechuga** [le'tʃuxa] *nf* lettuce

**lechuza** [le'tʃuθa] *nf* owl

**lector, a** [lek'tor, a] *nm/f* reader ⊳ *nm:* **~ de discos compactos** CD player

**lectura** [lek'tura] *nf* reading

**leer** [le'er] *vt* to read

**legado** [le'xaðo] *nm (don)* bequest; *(herencia)* legacy; *(enviado)* legate

**legajo** [le'xaxo] *nm* file

**legal** [le'xal] *adj (gen)* legal; *(persona)* trustworthy; **legalizar** [lexali'θar] *vt* to legalize; *(documento)* to authenticate

**legaña** [le'xaɲa] *nf* sleep *(in eyes)*

**legión** [le'xjon] *nf* legion; **legionario, -a** *adj* legionary ⊳ *nm* legionnaire

**legislación** [lexisla'θjon] *nf* legislation

**legislar** [lexis'lar] *vi* to legislate

**legislatura** [lexisla'tura] *nf (Pol)* period of office

**legítimo, -a** [le'xitimo, a] *adj (genuino)* authentic; *(legal)* legitimate

**legua** ['lexwa] *nf* league

**legumbres** [le'xumbres] *nfpl* pulses

**leído, -a** [le'iðo, a] *adj* well-read

**lejanía** [lexa'nia] *nf* distance; **lejano, -a** *adj* far-off; *(en el tiempo)* distant; *(fig)* remote

**lejía** [le'xia] *nf* bleach

**lejos** ['lexos] *adv* far, far away; **a lo ~** in the distance; **de o desde ~** from afar; **~ de** far from

**lema** ['lema] *nm* motto; *(Pol)* slogan

**lencería** [lenθe'ria] *nf* linen, drapery

**lengua** ['lengwa] *nf* tongue; *(Ling)* language; **morderse la ~** to hold one's tongue

**lenguado** [len'gwaðo] *nm* sole

**lenguaje** [len'gwaxe] *nm* language; **lenguaje de programación** program(m)ing language

**lengüeta** [len'gweta] *nf (Anat)* epiglottis; *(zapatos)* tongue; *(Mús)* reed

**lente** ['lente] *nf* lens; *(lupa)* magnifying glass; **lentes** *nfpl* lenses ⊳ *nmpl (LAM: gafas)* glasses; **lentes bifocales/de sol** *(LAM)* bifocals/sunglasses; **lentes de contacto** contact lenses

**lenteja** [len'texa] *nf* lentil; **lentejuela** *nf* sequin

**lentilla** [len'tiʎa] *nf* contact lens

**lentitud** [lenti'tuð] *nf* slowness; **con ~**

slowly

**lento, -a** ['lento, a] *adj* slow

**leña** ['leɲa] *nf* firewood; **leñador, a** *nm/f* woodcutter

**leño** ['leɲo] *nm* (*trozo de árbol*) log; (*madero*) timber; (*fig*) blockhead

**Leo** ['leo] *nm* Leo

**león** [le'on] *nm* lion; **león marino** sea lion

**leopardo** [leo'parðo] *nm* leopard

**leotardos** [leo'tarðos] *nmpl* tights

**lepra** ['lepra] *nf* leprosy; **leproso, -a** *nm/f* leper

**les** [les] *pron* (*directo*) them; (: *ustedes*) you; (*indirecto*) to them; (: *ustedes*) to you

**lesbiana** [les'βjana] *adj, nf* lesbian

**lesión** [le'sjon] *nf* wound, lesion; (*Deporte*) injury; **lesionado, -a** *adj* injured ⊳ *nm/f* injured person

**letal** [le'tal] *adj* lethal

**letanía** [leta'nia] *nf* litany

**letra** ['letra] *nf* letter; (*escritura*) handwriting; (*Mús*) lyrics *pl*; **letra de cambio** bill of exchange; **letra de imprenta** print; **letrado, -a** *adj* learned ⊳ *nm/f* lawyer; **letrero** *nm* (*cartel*) sign; (*etiqueta*) label

**letrina** [le'trina] *nf* latrine

**leucemia** [leu'θemja] *nf* leukaemia

**levadura** [leβa'ðura] *nf* (*para el pan*) yeast; (*de cerveza*) brewer's yeast

**levantar** [leβan'tar] *vt* (*gen*) to raise; (*del suelo*) to pick up; (*hacia arriba*) to lift (up); (*plan*) to make, draw up; (*mesa*) to clear; (*campamento*) to strike; (*fig*) to cheer up, hearten; **levantarse** *vr* to get up; (*enderezarse*) to straighten up; (*rebelarse*) to rebel; **~ el ánimo** to cheer up

**levante** [le'βante] *nm* east coast; **el L~** *region of Spain extending from Castellón to Murcia*

**levar** [le'βar] *vt* to weigh

**leve** ['leβe] *adj* light; (*fig*) trivial

**levita** [le'βita] *nf* frock coat

**léxico** ['leksiko] *nm* (*vocabulario*) vocabulary

**ley** [lei] *nf* (*gen*) law; (*metal*) standard

**leyenda** [le'jenda] *nf* legend

**leyó** *etc vb* V **leer**

**liar** [li'ar] *vt* to tie (up); (*unir*) to bind; (*envolver*) to wrap (up); (*enredar*) to confuse; (*cigarrillo*) to roll; **liarse** *vr* (*fam*) to get involved; **~se a palos** to get involved in a fight

**Líbano** ['liβano] *nm*: **el ~** the Lebanon

**libélula** [li'βelula] *nf* dragonfly

**liberación** [liβera'θjon] *nf* liberation; (*de la cárcel*) release

**liberal** [liβe'ral] *adj, nmf* liberal

**liberar** [liβe'rar] *vt* to liberate

**libertad** [liβer'tað] *nf* liberty, freedom; **libertad bajo fianza** bail; **libertad bajo palabra** parole; **libertad condicional** probation; **libertad de culto/de prensa/de comercio** freedom of worship/of the press/of trade

**libertar** [liβer'tar] *vt* (*preso*) to set free; (*de una obligación*) to release; (*eximir*) to exempt

**libertino, -a** [liβer'tino, a] *adj* permissive ⊳ *nm/f* permissive person

**libra** ['liβra] *nf* pound; **L~** (*Astrología*) Libra; **libra esterlina** pound sterling

**libramiento** [liβra'mjento] (*MÉX*) *nm* ring road (*BRIT*), beltway (*US*)

**librar** [li'βrar] *vt* (*de peligro*) to save; (*batalla*) to wage, fight; (*de impuestos*) to exempt; (*cheque*) to make out; (*Jur*) to exempt; **librarse** *vr*: **~se de** to escape from, free o.s. from

**libre** ['liβre] *adj* free; (*lugar*) unoccupied; (*asiento*) vacant; (*de deudas*) free of debts; **~ de impuestos** free of tax; **tiro ~** free kick; **los 100 metros ~s** the 100 metres free-style (race); **al aire ~** in the open air

**librería** [liβre'ria] *nf* (*tienda*) bookshop

▌ No confundir **librería** con la palabra inglesa *library*.

**librero, -a** *nm/f* bookseller

**libreta** [li'βreta] *nf* notebook

**libro** ['liβro] *nm* book; **libro de bolsillo** paperback; **libro de texto** textbook; **libro electrónico** e-book

**Lic.** *abr* = **licenciado, a**

**licencia** [li'θenθja] *nf* (*gen*) licence; (*permiso*) permission; **licencia de caza** game licence; **licencia por enfermedad** (*MÉX, RPL*) sick leave; **licenciado, -a** *adj* licensed ⊳ *nm/f* graduate; **licenciar** *vt* (*empleado*) to dismiss; (*permitir*) to permit, allow; (*soldado*) to discharge; (*estudiante*) to confer a degree upon; **licenciarse** *vr*: **licenciarse en Derecho** to graduate in law

**lícito, -a** ['liθito, a] *adj* (*legal*) lawful; (*justo*) fair, just; (*permisible*) permissible

**licor** [li'kor] *nm* spirits *pl* (*BRIT*), liquor (*US*); (*de frutas etc*) liqueur

**licuadora** [likwa'ðora] *nf* blender

**líder** ['liðer] *nmf* leader; **liderato** *nm* leadership; **liderazgo** *nm* leadership

**lidia** ['liðja] *nf* bullfighting; (*una lidia*) bullfight; **toros de ~** fighting bulls; **lidiar** *vt, vi* to fight

**liebre** ['ljeβre] *nf* hare

**lienzo** ['ljenθo] *nm* linen; (*Arte*) canvas; (*Arq*) wall

**liga** ['liɣa] *nf* (*de medias*) garter, suspender; (*LAM: goma*) rubber band; (*confederación*)

league
**ligadura** [liɣa'ðura] *nf* bond, tie; (*Med*, *Mús*) ligature
**ligamento** [liɣa'mento] *nm* ligament
**ligar** [li'ɣar] *vt* (*atar*) to tie; (*unir*) to join; (*Med*) to bind up; (*Mús*) to slur ▷ *vi* to mix, blend; (*fam*): **(él) liga mucho** he pulls a lot of women; **ligarse** *vr* to commit o.s.
**ligero, -a** [li'xero, a] *adj* (*de peso*) light; (*tela*) thin; (*rápido*) swift, quick; (*ágil*) agile, nimble; (*de importancia*) slight; (*de carácter*) flippant, superficial ▷ *adv*: **a la ligera** superficially
**liguero** [li'ɣero] *nm* suspender (*BRIT*) o garter (*US*) belt
**lija** ['lixa] *nf* (*Zool*) dogfish; (*tb*: **papel de ~**) sandpaper
**lila** ['lila] *nf* lilac
**lima** ['lima] *nf* file; (*Bot*) lime; **lima de uñas** nailfile; **limar** *vt* to file
**limitación** [limita'θjon] *nf* limitation, limit
**limitar** [limi'tar] *vt* to limit; (*reducir*) to reduce, cut down ▷ *vi*: **~ con** to border on; **limitarse** *vr*: **~se a** to limit o.s. to
**límite** ['limite] *nm* (*gen*) limit; (*fin*) end; (*frontera*) border; **límite de velocidad** speed limit
**limítrofe** [li'mitrofe] *adj* neighbouring
**limón** [li'mon] *nm* lemon ▷ *adj*: **amarillo ~** lemon-yellow; **limonada** *nf* lemonade
**limosna** [li'mosna] *nf* alms *pl*; **vivir de ~** to live on charity
**limpiador** [limpja'ðor] (*MÉX*) *nm* = **limpiaparabrisas**
**limpiaparabrisas** [limpjapara'βrisas] *nm inv* windscreen (*BRIT*) o windshield (*US*) wiper
**limpiar** [lim'pjar] *vt* to clean; (*con trapo*) to wipe; (*quitar*) to wipe away; (*zapatos*) to shine, polish; (*fig*) to clean up
**limpieza** [lim'pjeθa] *nf* (*estado*) cleanliness; (*acto*) cleaning; (: *de las calles*) cleansing; (: *de zapatos*) polishing; (*habilidad*) skill; (*fig: Policía*) clean-up; (*pureza*) purity; (*Mil*): **operación de ~** mopping-up operation; **limpieza en seco** dry cleaning
**limpio, -a** ['limpjo, a] *adj* clean; (*moralmente*) pure; (*Com*) clear, net; (*fam*) honest ▷ *adv*: **jugar ~** to play fair; **pasar a** (*ESP*) o **en** (*LAM*) **~** to make a clean copy of
**lince** ['linθe] *nm* lynx
**linchar** [lin'tʃar] *vt* to lynch
**lindar** [lin'dar] *vi* to adjoin; **~ con** to border on
**lindo, -a** ['lindo, a] *adj* pretty, lovely ▷ *adv*: **nos divertimos de lo ~** we had a marvellous time; **canta muy ~** (*LAM*) he

sings beautifully
**línea** ['linea] *nf* (*gen*) line; **en ~** (*Inform*) on line; **línea aérea** airline; **línea de meta** goal line; (*en carrera*) finishing line; **línea discontinua** (*Auto*) broken line; **línea recta** straight line
**lingote** [lin'gote] *nm* ingot
**lingüista** [lin'gwista] *nmf* linguist; **lingüística** *nf* linguistics *sg*
**lino** ['lino] *nm* linen; (*Bot*) flax
**linterna** [lin'terna] *nf* torch (*BRIT*), flashlight (*US*)
**lío** ['lio] *nm* bundle; (*fam*) fuss; (*desorden*) muddle, mess; **armar un ~** to make a fuss
**liquen** ['liken] *nm* lichen
**liquidación** [likiða'θjon] *nf* liquidation; **venta de ~** clearance sale
**liquidar** [liki'ðar] *vt* (*mercancías*) to liquidate; (*deudas*) to pay off; (*empresa*) to wind up
**líquido, -a** ['likiðo, a] *adj* liquid; (*ganancia*) net ▷ *nm* liquid; **líquido imponible** net taxable income
**lira** ['lira] *nf* (*Mús*) lyre; (*moneda*) lira
**lírico, -a** ['liriko, a] *adj* lyrical
**lirio** ['lirjo] *nm* (*Bot*) iris
**lirón** [li'ron] *nm* (*Zool*) dormouse; (*fig*) sleepyhead
**Lisboa** [lis'βoa] *n* Lisbon
**lisiar** [li'sjar] *vt* to maim
**liso, -a** ['liso, a] *adj* (*terreno*) flat; (*cabello*) straight; (*superficie*) even; (*tela*) plain
**lista** ['lista] *nf* list; (*de alumnos*) school register; (*de libros*) catalogue; (*de platos*) menu; (*de precios*) price list; **pasar ~** to call the roll; **tela de ~s** striped material; **lista de espera** waiting list; **lista de precios** price list; **listín** *nm* (*tb*: **listín telefónico** o **de teléfonos**) telephone directory
**listo, -a** ['listo, a] *adj* (*perspicaz*) smart, clever; (*preparado*) ready
**listón** [lis'ton] *nm* (*de madera, metal*) strip
**litera** [li'tera] *nf* (*en barco, tren*) berth; (*en dormitorio*) bunk, bunk bed
**literal** [lite'ral] *adj* literal
**literario, -a** [lite'rarjo, a] *adj* literary
**literato, -a** [lite'rato, a] *adj* literary ▷ *nm/f* writer
**literatura** [litera'tura] *nf* literature
**litigio** [li'tixjo] *nm* (*Jur*) lawsuit; (*fig*): **en ~ con** in dispute with
**litografía** [litoɣra'fia] *nf* lithography; (*una litografía*) lithograph
**litoral** [lito'ral] *adj* coastal ▷ *nm* coast, seaboard
**litro** ['litro] *nm* litre
**lívido, -a** ['liβiðo, a] *adj* livid
**llaga** ['ʎaɣa] *nf* wound

**llama** ['ʎama] nf flame; (Zool) llama
**llamada** [ʎa'maða] nf call; **llamada a
cobro revertido** reverse-charge (BRIT)
o collect (US) call; **llamada al orden** call
to order; **llamada de atención** warning;
**llamada local** (LAM) local call; **llamada
metropolitana** (ESP) local call; **llamada por
cobrar** (MÉX) reverse-charge (BRIT) o collect
(US) call
**llamamiento** [ʎama'mjento] nm call
**llamar** [ʎa'mar] vt to call; (atención) to
attract ▷ vi (por teléfono) to telephone; (a
la puerta) to knock (o ring); (por señas) to
beckon; (Mil) to call up; **llamarse** vr to be
called, be named; **¿cómo se llama (usted)?**
what's your name?
**llamativo, -a** [ʎama'tiβo, a] adj showy;
(color) loud
**llano, -a** ['ʎano, a] adj (superficie) flat;
(persona) straightforward; (estilo) clear ▷ nm
plain, flat ground
**llanta** ['ʎanta] nf (ESP) (wheel) rim; **llanta
(de goma)** (LAM: neumático) tyre; (: cámara)
inner (tube); **llanta de repuesto** (LAM)
spare tyre
**llanto** ['ʎanto] nm weeping
**llanura** [ʎa'nura] nf plain
**llave** ['ʎaβe] nf key; (del agua) tap;
(Mecánica) spanner; (de la luz) switch;
(Mús) key; **echar la ~ a** to lock up; **llave de
contacto** (ESP Auto) ignition key; **llave de
encendido** (LAM Auto) ignition key; **llave
de paso** stopcock; **llave inglesa** monkey
wrench; **llave maestra** master key; **llavero**
nm keyring
**llegada** [ʎe'ɣaða] nf arrival
**llegar** [ʎe'ɣar] vi to arrive; (alcanzar) to
reach; (bastar) to be enough; **llegarse**
vr: **~se a** to approach; **~ a** to manage to,
succeed in; **~ a saber** to find out; **~ a ser** to
become; **~ a las manos de** to come into the
hands of
**llenar** [ʎe'nar] vt to fill; (espacio) to cover;
(formulario) to fill in o up; (fig) to heap
**lleno, -a** ['ʎeno, a] adj full, filled; (repleto)
full up ▷ nm (Teatro) full house; **dar de ~
contra un muro** to hit a wall head-on
**llevadero, -a** [ʎeβa'ðero, a] adj bearable,
tolerable
**llevar** [ʎe'βar] vt to take; (ropa) to wear;
(cargar) to carry; (quitar) to take away; (en
coche) to drive; (transportar) to transport;
(traer: dinero) to carry; (conducir) to lead;
(Mat) to carry ▷ vi (suj: camino etc): **~ a** to
lead to; **llevarse** vr to carry off, take away;
**llevamos dos días aquí** we have been here
for two days; **él me lleva 2 años** he's 2 years
older than me; **~ los libros** (Com) to keep the

books; **~se bien** to get on well (together)
**llorar** [ʎo'rar] vt, vi to cry, weep; **~ de risa**
to cry with laughter
**llorón, -ona** [ʎo'ron, ona] adj tearful
▷ nm/f cry-baby
**lloroso, -a** [ʎo'roso, a] adj (gen) weeping,
tearful; (triste) sad, sorrowful
**llover** [ʎo'βer] vi to rain
**llovizna** [ʎo'βiθna] nf drizzle; **lloviznar**
vi to drizzle
**llueve** etc vb V **llover**
**lluvia** ['ʎuβja] nf rain; **lluvia radioactiva**
(radioactive) fallout; **lluvioso, -a** adj rainy
**lo** [lo] art def: **~ bel~** the beautiful, what is
beautiful, that which is beautiful ▷ pron
(persona) him; (cosa) it; **~ que sea** whatever;
V tb **el**
**loable** [lo'aβle] adj praiseworthy
**lobo** ['loβo] nm wolf; **lobo de mar** (fig)
sea dog
**lóbulo** ['loβulo] nm lobe
**local** [lo'kal] adj local ▷ nm place, site;
(oficinas) premises pl; **localidad** nf (barrio)
locality; (lugar) location; (Teatro) seat,
ticket; **localizar** vt (ubicar) to locate, find;
(restringir) to localize; (situar) to place
**loción** [lo'θjon] nf lotion
**loco, -a** ['loko, a] adj mad ▷ nm/f lunatic,
mad person; **estar ~ con** o **por algo/por
algn** to be mad about sth/sb
**locomotora** [lokomo'tora] nf engine,
locomotive
**locuaz** [lo'kwaθ] adj loquacious
**locución** [loku'θjon] nf expression
**locura** [lo'kura] nf madness; (acto) crazy
act
**locutor, a** [loku'tor, a] nm/f (Radio)
announcer; (comentarista) commentator;
(TV) newsreader
**locutorio** [loku'torjo] nm (en telefónica)
telephone booth
**lodo** ['loðo] nm mud
**lógica** [loxika] nf logic
**lógico, -a** ['loxiko, a] adj logical
**login** ['loxin] nm login
**logística** [lo'xistika] nf logistics sg
**logotipo** [loðo'tipo] nm logo
**logrado, -a** [lo'ðraðo, a] adj
(interpretación, reproducción) polished,
excellent
**lograr** [lo'rar] vt to achieve; (obtener) to
get, obtain; **~ hacer** to manage to do; **~ que
algn venga** to manage to get sb to come
**logro** ['loxro] nm achievement, success
**lóker** ['loker] (LAM) nm locker
**loma** ['loma] nf hillock (BRIT), small hill
**lombriz** [lom'briθ] nf worm
**lomo** ['lomo] nm (de animal) back; (Culin: de

*cerdo*) pork loin; (: *de vaca*) rib steak; (*de libro*) spine

**lona** ['lona] *nf* canvas

**loncha** ['lontʃa] *nf* = **lonja**

**lonchería** [lontʃe'ria] (LAM) *nf* snack bar, diner (US)

**Londres** ['londres] *n* London

**longaniza** [longa'niθa] *nf* pork sausage

**longitud** [lonxi'tuð] *nf* length; (*Geo*) longitude; **tener 3 metros de ~** to be 3 metres long; **longitud de onda** wavelength

**lonja** ['lonxa] *nf* slice; (*de tocino*) rasher; **lonja de pescado** fish market

**loro** ['loro] *nm* parrot

**los** [los] *art def* the ▷ *pron* them; (*ustedes*) you; **mis libros y ~ tuyos** my books and yours; *V tb* **el**

**losa** ['losa] *nf* stone

**lote** ['lote] *nm* portion; (*Com*) lot

**lotería** [lote'ria] *nf* lottery; (*juego*) lotto

> ● **LOTERÍA**
> ●
> ● Millions of pounds are spent on lotteries
> ● each year in Spain, two of which are
> ● state-run: the **Lotería Primitiva** and
> ● the **Lotería Nacional**, with money
> ● raised going directly to the government.
> ● One of the most famous lotteries is run
> ● by the wealthy and influential society
> ● for the blind, "la ONCE".

**loza** ['loθa] *nf* crockery

**lubina** [lu'βina] *nf* sea bass

**lubricante** [luβri'kante] *nm* lubricant

**lubricar** [luβri'kar] *vt* to lubricate

**lucha** ['lutʃa] *nf* fight, struggle; **lucha de clases** class struggle; **lucha libre** wrestling; **luchar** *vi* to fight

**lúcido, -a** ['luθiðo, a] *adj* (*persona*) lucid; (*mente*) logical; (*idea*) crystal-clear

**luciérnaga** [lu'θjernaɣa] *nf* glow-worm

**lucir** [lu'θir] *vt* to illuminate, light (up); (*ostentar*) to show off ▷ *vi* (*brillar*) to shine; **lucirse** *vr* (*irónico*) to make a fool of o.s.

**lucro** ['lukro] *nm* profit, gain

**lúdico, -a** ['ludiko, a] *adj* (*aspecto, actividad*) play *cpd*

**luego** ['lweɣo] *adv* (*después*) next; (*más tarde*) later, afterwards

**lugar** [lu'ɣar] *nm* place; (*sitio*) spot; **en primer ~** in the first place, firstly; **en ~ de** instead of; **hacer ~** to make room; **fuera de ~** out of place; **sin ~ a dudas** without doubt, undoubtedly; **dar ~ a** to give rise to; **tener ~** to take place; **yo en su ~** if I were him; **lugar común** commonplace

**lúgubre** ['luɣuβre] *adj* mournful

**lujo** ['luxo] *nm* luxury; (*fig*) profusion, abundance; **de ~** luxury *cpd*, de luxe; **lujoso, -a** *adj* luxurious

**lujuria** [lu'xurja] *nf* lust

**lumbre** ['lumbre] *nf* fire; (*para cigarrillo*) light

**luminoso, -a** [lumi'noso, a] *adj* luminous, shining

**luna** ['luna] *nf* moon; (*de un espejo*) glass; (*de gafas*) lens; (*fig*) crescent; **estar en la ~** to have one's head in the clouds; **luna de miel** honeymoon; **luna llena/nueva** full/new moon

**lunar** [lu'nar] *adj* lunar ▷ *nm* (*Anat*) mole; **tela de ~es** spotted material

**lunes** ['lunes] *nm inv* Monday

**lupa** ['lupa] *nf* magnifying glass

**lustre** ['lustre] *nm* polish; (*fig*) lustre; **dar ~ a** to polish

**luto** ['luto] *nm* mourning; **llevar el o vestirse de ~** to be in mourning

**Luxemburgo** [luksem'burɣo] *nm* Luxembourg

**luz** [luθ] (*pl* **luces**) *nf* light; **dar a ~ un niño** to give birth to a child; **sacar a la ~** to bring to light; **dar o encender** (ESP) *o* **prender** (LAM)/**apagar la ~** to switch the light on/off; **tener pocas luces** to be dim *o* stupid; **traje de luces** bullfighter's costume; **luces de tráfico** traffic lights; **luz de freno** brake light; **luz roja/verde** red/green light

# m

**m** *abr* (= *metro*) m; (= *minuto*) m

**macana** [ma'kana] (*MÉX*) *nf* truncheon (*BRIT*), billy club (*US*)

**macarrones** [maka'rrones] *nmpl* macaroni *sg*

**macedonia** [maθe'ðonja] *nf* (*tb*: **~ de frutas**) fruit salad

**maceta** [ma'θeta] *nf* (*de flores*) pot of flowers; (*para plantas*) flowerpot

**machacar** [matʃa'kar] *vt* to crush, pound ▷ *vi* (*insistir*) to go on, keep on

**machete** [ma'tʃete] *nm* machete, (large) knife

**machetear** [matʃete'ar] (*MÉX*) *vt* to swot (*BRIT*), grind away (*US*)

**machismo** [ma'tʃismo] *nm* male chauvinism; **machista** *adj*, *nm* sexist

**macho** ['matʃo] *adj* male; (*fig*) virile ▷ *nm* male; (*fig*) he-man

**macizo, -a** [ma'θiθo, a] *adj* (*grande*) massive; (*fuerte, sólido*) solid ▷ *nm* mass, chunk

**madeja** [ma'ðexa] *nf* (*de lana*) skein, hank; (*de pelo*) mass, mop

**madera** [ma'ðera] *nf* wood; (*fig*) nature, character; **una ~** a piece of wood

**madrastra** [ma'ðrastra] *nf* stepmother

**madre** ['maðre] *adj* mother *cpd* ▷ *nf* mother; (*de vino etc*) dregs *pl*; **madre política/soltera** mother-in-law/unmarried mother

**Madrid** [ma'ðrið] *n* Madrid

**madriguera** [maðri'ɣera] *nf* burrow

**madrileño, -a** [maðri'leɲo, a] *adj* of o from Madrid ▷ *nm/f* native of Madrid

**madrina** [ma'ðrina] *nf* godmother; (*Arq*) prop, shore; (*Tec*) brace; (*de boda*) bridesmaid

**madrugada** [maðru'ɣaða] *nf* early morning; (*alba*) dawn, daybreak

**madrugador, a** [maðruxa'ðor, a] *adj* early-rising

**madrugar** [maðru'ɣar] *vi* to get up early; (*fig*) to get ahead

**madurar** [maðu'rar] *vt, vi* (*fruta*) to ripen; (*fig*) to mature; **madurez** *nf* ripeness; maturity; **maduro, -a** *adj* ripe; mature

**maestra** *nf* V **maestro**

**maestría** [maes'tria] *nf* mastery; (*habilidad*) skill, expertise

**maestro, -a** [ma'estro, a] *adj* masterly; (*principal*) main ▷ *nm/f* master/mistress; (*profesor*) teacher ▷ *nm* (*autoridad*) authority; (*Mús*) maestro; (*experto*) master; **maestro albañil** master mason

**magdalena** [maɣða'lena] *nf* fairy cake

**magia** ['maxja] *nf* magic; **mágico, -a** *adj* magic(al) ▷ *nm/f* magician

**magisterio** [maxis'terjo] *nm* (*enseñanza*) teaching; (*profesión*) teaching profession; (*maestros*) teachers *pl*

**magistrado** [maxis'traðo] *nm* magistrate

**magistral** [maxis'tral] *adj* magisterial; (*fig*) masterly

**magnate** [maɣ'nate] *nm* magnate, tycoon

**magnético, -a** [maɣ'netiko, a] *adj* magnetic

**magnetofón** [maɣneto'fon] *nm* tape recorder

**magnetófono** [maɣne'tofono] *nm* = **magnetofón**

**magnífico, -a** [maɣ'nifiko, a] *adj* splendid, magnificent

**magnitud** [maɣni'tuð] *nf* magnitude

**mago, -a** ['maɣo, a] *nm/f* magician; **los Reyes M~s** the Three Wise Men

**magro, -a** ['maɣro, a] *adj* (*carne*) lean

**mahonesa** [mao'nesa] *nf* mayonnaise

**maître** ['metre] *nm* head waiter

**maíz** [ma'iθ] *nm* maize (*BRIT*), corn (*US*); sweet corn

**majestad** [maxes'tað] *nf* majesty

**majo, -a** ['maxo, a] *adj* nice; (*guapo*) attractive, good-looking; (*elegante*) smart

**mal** [mal] *adv* badly; (*equivocadamente*) wrongly ▷ *adj* = **malo** ▷ *nm* evil; (*desgracia*) misfortune; (*daño*) harm, damage; (*Med*) illness; **~ que bien** rightly or wrongly; **ir de ~ en peor** to get worse and worse

**malabarista** [malaβa'rista] *nmf* juggler

**malaria** [ma'larja] *nf* malaria

**malcriado, -a** [mal'krjaðo, a] *adj* spoiled

**maldad** [mal'dað] *nf* evil, wickedness

**maldecir** [malde'θir] *vt* to curse

**maldición** [maldi'θjon] *nf* curse

**maldito, -a** [mal'dito, a] *adj* (*condenado*) damned; (*perverso*) wicked; **¡~ sea!** damn it!

**malecón** [male'kon] (*LAM*) *nm* sea front,

promenade

**maleducado, -a** [maleðuˈkaðo, a] *adj* bad-mannered, rude

**malentendido** [malentenˈdiðo] *nm* misunderstanding

**malestar** [malesˈtar] *nm* (*gen*) discomfort; (*fig: inquietud*) uneasiness; (*Pol*) unrest

**maleta** [maˈleta] *nf* case, suitcase; (*Auto*) boot (*BRIT*), trunk (*US*); **hacer las ~s** to pack; **maletero** *nm* (*Auto*) boot (*BRIT*), trunk (*US*); **maletín** *nm* small case, bag

**maleza** [maˈleθa] *nf* (*malas hierbas*) weeds *pl*; (*arbustos*) thicket

**malgastar** [malɣasˈtar] *vt* (*tiempo, dinero*) to waste; (*salud*) to ruin

**malhechor, a** [maleˈtʃor, a] *nm/f* delinquent

**malhumorado, -a** [malumoˈraðo, a] *adj* bad-tempered

**malicia** [maˈliθja] *nf* (*maldad*) wickedness; (*astucia*) slyness, guile; (*mala intención*) malice, spite; (*carácter travieso*) mischievousness

**maligno, -a** [maˈliɣno, a] *adj* evil; (*malévolo*) malicious; (*Med*) malignant

**malla** [ˈmaʎa] *nf* mesh; (*de baño*) swimsuit; (*de ballet, gimnasia*) leotard; **mallas** *nfpl* tights; **malla de alambre** wire mesh

**Mallorca** [maˈʎorka] *nf* Majorca

**malo, -a** [ˈmalo, a] *adj* bad, false ▷ *nm/f* villain; **estar ~** to be ill

**malograr** [maloˈɣrar] *vt* to spoil; (*plan*) to upset; (*ocasión*) to waste

**malparado, -a** [malpaˈraðo, a] *adj*: **salir ~** to come off badly

**malpensado, -a** [malpenˈsaðo, a] *adj* nasty

**malteada** [malteˈaða] (*LAM*) *nf* milkshake

**maltratar** [maltraˈtar] *vt* to ill-treat, mistreat

**malvado, -a** [malˈβaðo, a] *adj* evil, villainous

**Malvinas** [malˈβinas] *nfpl* (*tb*: **Islas ~**) Falklands, Falkland Islands

**mama** [ˈmama] *nf* (*de animal*) teat; (*de mujer*) breast

**mamá** [maˈma] (*pl* **~s**) (*fam*) *nf* mum, mummy

**mamar** [maˈmar] *vt, vi* to suck

**mamarracho** [mamaˈrratʃo] *nm* sight, mess

**mameluco** [mameˈluko] (*RPL*) *nm* dungarees *pl* (*BRIT*), overalls *pl* (*US*)

**mamífero** [maˈmifero] *nm* mammal

**mampara** [mamˈpara] *nf* (*entre habitaciones*) partition; (*biombo*) screen

**mampostería** [mamposteˈria] *nf* masonry

**manada** [maˈnaða] *nf* (*Zool*) herd; (*: de leones*) pride; (*: de lobos*) pack

**manantial** [mananˈtjal] *nm* spring

**mancha** [ˈmantʃa] *nf* stain, mark; (*Zool*) patch; **manchar** *vt* (*gen*) to stain, mark; (*ensuciar*) to soil, dirty

**manchego, -a** [manˈtʃeɣo, a] *adj* of o from La Mancha

**manco, -a** [ˈmanko, a] *adj* (*de un brazo*) one-armed; (*de una mano*) one-handed; (*fig*) defective, faulty

**mancuernas** [manˈkwernas] (*MÉX*) *nfpl* cufflinks

**mandado** [manˈdaðo] (*LAM*) *nm* errand

**mandamiento** [mandaˈmjento] *nm* (*orden*) order, command; (*Rel*) commandment

**mandar** [manˈdar] *vt* (*ordenar*) to order; (*dirigir*) to lead, command; (*enviar*) to send; (*pedir*) to order, ask for ▷ *vi* to be in charge; (*pey*) to be bossy; **¿mande?** (*MÉX: ¿cómo dice?*) pardon?, excuse me?; **~ hacer un traje** to have a suit made

**mandarina** [mandaˈrina] (*ESP*) *nf* tangerine, mandarin (*orange*)

**mandato** [manˈdato] *nm* (*orden*) order; (*Pol: período*) term of office; (*: territorio*) mandate

**mandíbula** [manˈdiβula] *nf* jaw

**mandil** [manˈdil] *nm* apron

**mando** [ˈmando] *nm* (*Mil*) command; (*de país*) rule; (*el primer lugar*) lead; (*Pol*) term of office; (*Tec*) control; **~ a la izquierda** left-hand drive; **mando a distancia** remote control

**mandón, -ona** [manˈdon, ona] *adj* bossy, domineering

**manejar** [maneˈxar] *vt* to manage; (*máquina*) to work, operate; (*caballo etc*) to handle; (*casa*) to run, manage; (*LAM: coche*) to drive; **manejarse** *vr* (*comportarse*) to act, behave; (*arreglárselas*) to manage; **manejo** *nm* (*de bicicleta*) handling; (*de negocio*) management, running; (*LAM Auto*) driving; (*facilidad de trato*) ease, confidence; **manejos** *nmpl* (*intrigas*) intrigues

**manera** [maˈnera] *nf* way, manner, fashion; **maneras** *nfpl* (*modales*) manners; **su ~ de ser** the way he is; (*aire*) his manner; **de ninguna ~** no way, by no means; **de otra ~** otherwise; **de todas ~s** at any rate; **no hay ~ de persuadirle** there's no way of convincing him

**manga** [ˈmanga] *nf* (*de camisa*) sleeve; (*de riego*) hose

**mango** [ˈmango] *nm* handle; (*Bot*) mango

**manguera** [manˈgera] *nf* hose

**maní** [maˈni] (*LAM*) *nm* peanut

**manía** [ma'nia] nf (Med) mania; (fig: moda) rage, craze; (disgusto) dislike; (malicia) spite; **coger ~ a algn** to take a dislike to sb; **tener ~ a algn** to dislike sb; **maníaco, -a** adj maniac(al) ▷ nm/f maniac

**maniático, -a** [ma'njatiko, a] adj maniac(al) ▷ nm/f maniac

**manicomio** [mani'komjo] nm mental hospital (BRIT), insane asylum (US)

**manifestación** [manifesta'θjon] nf (declaración) statement, declaration; (de emoción) show, display; (Pol: desfile) demonstration; (: concentración) mass meeting

**manifestar** [manifes'tar] vt to show, manifest; (declarar) to state, declare; **manifiesto, -a** adj clear, manifest ▷ nm manifesto

**manillar** [mani'ʎar] nm handlebars pl

**maniobra** [ma'njoβra] nf manoeuvre; **maniobras** nfpl (Mil) manoeuvres; **maniobrar** vt to manoeuvre

**manipulación** [manipula'θjon] nf manipulation

**manipular** [manipu'lar] vt to manipulate; (manejar) to handle

**maniquí** [mani'ki] nm dummy ▷ nmf model

**manivela** [mani'βela] nf crank

**manjar** [man'xar] nm (tasty) dish

**mano** ['mano] nf hand; (Zool) foot, paw; (de pintura) coat; (serie) lot, series; **a ~** by hand; **a ~ derecha/izquierda** on the right(-hand side)/left(-hand side); **de primera ~** (at) first hand; **de segunda ~** (at) second hand; **robo a ~ armada** armed robbery; **estrechar la ~ a algn** to shake sb's hand; **mano de obra** labour, manpower; **manos libres** adj inv (teléfono, dispositivo) hands-free ▷ nm inv hands-free kit

**manojo** [ma'noxo] nm handful, bunch; (de llaves) bunch

**manopla** [ma'nopla] nf mitten

**manosear** [manose'ar] vt (tocar) to handle, touch; (desordenar) to mess up, rumple; (insistir en) to overwork; (LAM: acariciar) to caress, fondle

**manotazo** [mano'taθo] nm slap, smack

**mansalva** [man'salβa]: **a ~** adv indiscriminately

**mansión** [man'sjon] nf mansion

**manso, -a** ['manso, a] adj gentle, mild; (animal) tame

**manta** ['manta] (ESP) nf blanket

**manteca** [man'teka] nf fat; (cs: mantequilla) butter; **manteca de cerdo** lard

**mantecado** [mante'kaðo] (ESP) nm Christmas sweet made from flour, almonds and lard

**mantel** [man'tel] nm tablecloth

**mantendré** etc vb V **mantener**

**mantener** [mante'ner] vt to support, maintain; (alimentar) to sustain; (conservar) to keep; (Tec) to maintain, service; **mantenerse** vr (seguir de pie) to be still standing; (no ceder) to hold one's ground; (subsistir) to sustain o.s., keep going; **mantenimiento** nm maintenance; sustenance; (sustento) support

**mantequilla** [mante'kiʎa] nf butter

**mantilla** [man'tiʎa] nf mantilla; **mantillas** nfpl (de bebé) baby clothes

**manto** ['manto] nm (capa) cloak; (de ceremonia) robe, gown

**mantuve** etc vb V **mantener**

**manual** [ma'nwal] adj manual ▷ nm manual, handbook

**manuscrito, -a** [manus'krito, a] adj handwritten ▷ nm manuscript

**manutención** [manuten'θjon] nf maintenance; (sustento) support

**manzana** [man'θana] nf apple; (Arq) block (of houses)

**manzanilla** [manθa'niʎa] nf (planta) camomile; (infusión) camomile tea

**manzano** [man'θano] nm apple tree

**maña** ['maɲa] nf (gen) skill, dexterity; (pey) guile; (destreza) trick, knack

**mañana** [ma'ɲana] adv tomorrow ▷ nm future ▷ nf morning; **de o por la ~** in the morning; **¡hasta ~!** see you tomorrow!; **~ por la ~** tomorrow morning

**mapa** ['mapa] nm map

**maple** ['maple] (LAM) nm maple

**maqueta** [ma'keta] nf (scale) model

**maquiladora** [makila'ðora] (MÉX) nf (Com) bonded assembly plant

**maquillaje** [maki'ʎaxe] nm make-up; (acto) making up

**maquillar** [maki'ʎar] vt to make up; **maquillarse** vr to put on (some) make-up

**máquina** ['makina] nf machine; (de tren) locomotive, engine; (Foto) camera; (fig) machinery; **escrito a ~** typewritten; **máquina de coser** sewing machine; **máquina de escribir** typewriter; **máquina fotográfica** camera

**maquinaria** [maki'narja] nf (máquinas) machinery; (mecanismo) mechanism, works pl

**maquinilla** [maki'niʎa] (ESP) nf (tb: ~ de afeitar) razor

**maquinista** [maki'nista] nmf (de tren) engine driver; (Tec) operator; (Náut) engineer

**mar** [mar] *nm o f* sea; **~ adentro** out at sea; **en alta ~** on the high seas; **la ~ de** *(fam)* lots of; **el Mar Negro/Báltico** the Black/Baltic Sea

**maraña** [ma'raɲa] *nf (maleza)* thicket; *(confusión)* tangle

**maravilla** [mara'βiʎa] *nf* marvel, wonder; *(Bot)* marigold; **maravillar** *vt* to astonish, amaze; **maravillarse** *vr* to be astonished, be amazed; **maravilloso, -a** *adj* wonderful, marvellous

**marca** ['marka] *nf (gen)* mark; *(sello)* stamp; *(Com)* make, brand; **de ~** excellent, outstanding; **marca de fábrica** trademark; **marca registrada** registered trademark

**marcado, -a** [mar'kaðo, a] *adj* marked, strong

**marcador** [marka'ðor] *nm (Deporte)* scoreboard; (: *persona)* scorer

**marcapasos** [marka'pasos] *nm inv* pacemaker

**marcar** [mar'kar] *vt (gen)* to mark; *(número de teléfono)* to dial; *(gol)* to score; *(números)* to record, keep a tally of; *(pelo)* to set ▷ *vi (Deporte)* to score; *(Tel)* to dial

**marcha** ['martʃa] *nf* march; *(Tec)* running, working; *(Auto)* gear; *(velocidad)* speed; *(fig)* progress; *(dirección)* course; **poner en ~** to put into gear; *(fig)* to set in motion, get going; **dar ~ atrás** to reverse, put into reverse; **estar en ~** to be under way, be in motion

**marchar** [mar'tʃar] *vi (ir)* to go; *(funcionar)* to work, go; **marcharse** *vr* to go (away), leave

**marchitar** [martʃi'tar] *vt* to wither, dry up; **marchitarse** *vr (Bot)* to wither; *(fig)* to fade away; **marchito, -a** *adj* withered, faded; *(fig)* in decline

**marciano, -a** [mar'θjano, a] *adj, nm/f* Martian

**marco** ['marko] *nm* frame; *(moneda)* mark; *(fig)* framework

**marea** [ma'rea] *nf* tide; **marea negra** oil slick

**marear** [mare'ar] *vt (fig)* to annoy, upset; *(Med)*: **~ a algn** to make sb feel sick; **marearse** *vr (tener náuseas)* to feel sick; *(desvanecerse)* to feel faint; *(aturdirse)* to feel dizzy; *(fam: emborracharse)* to get tipsy

**maremoto** [mare'moto] *nm* tidal wave

**mareo** [ma'reo] *nm (náusea)* sick feeling; *(en viaje)* travel sickness; *(aturdimiento)* dizziness; *(fam: lata)* nuisance

**marfil** [mar'fil] *nm* ivory

**margarina** [marɣa'rina] *nf* margarine

**margarita** [marɣa'rita] *nf (Bot)* daisy; *(Tip)* daisywheel

**margen** ['marxen] *nm (borde)* edge, border; *(fig)* margin, space ▷ *nf (de río etc)* bank; **dar ~ para** to give an opportunity for; **mantenerse al ~** to keep out (of things)

**marginar** [marxi'nar] *vt (socialmente)* to marginalize, ostracize

**mariachi** [ma'rjatʃi] *nm (persona)* mariachi musician; *(grupo)* mariachi band

**marica** [ma'rika] *(fam) nm* sissy

**maricón** [mari'kon] *(fam) nm* queer

**marido** [ma'riðo] *nm* husband

**marihuana** [mari'wana] *nf* marijuana, cannabis

**marina** [ma'rina] *nf* navy; **marina mercante** merchant navy

**marinero, -a** [mari'nero, a] *adj* sea *cpd* ▷ *nm* sailor, seaman

**marino, -a** [ma'rino, a] *adj* sea *cpd*, marine ▷ *nm* sailor

**marioneta** [marjo'neta] *nf* puppet

**mariposa** [mari'posa] *nf* butterfly

**mariquita** [mari'kita] *nf* ladybird (BRIT), ladybug (US)

**marisco** [ma'risko] *(ESP) nm* shellfish *inv*, seafood; **mariscos** (LAM) *nmpl* = **marisco**

**marítimo, -a** [ma'ritimo, a] *adj* sea *cpd*, maritime

**mármol** ['marmol] *nm* marble

**marqués, -esa** [mar'kes, esa] *nm/f* marquis/marchioness

**marrón** [ma'rron] *adj* brown

**marroquí** [marro'ki] *adj, nmf* Moroccan ▷ *nm* Morocco (leather)

**Marruecos** [ma'rrwekos] *nm* Morocco

**martes** ['martes] *nm inv* Tuesday; **~ y trece** ≈ Friday 13th

**martillo** [mar'tiʎo] nm hammer
**mártir** ['martir] nmf martyr; **martirio** nm
martyrdom; (fig) torture, torment
**marxismo** [mark'sismo] nm Marxism
**marzo** ['marθo] nm March

○ **PALABRA CLAVE**

**más** [mas] adj, adv 1: **más (que** o **de)**
(compar) more (than), ...+er (than);
**más grande/inteligente** bigger/more
intelligent; **trabaja más (que yo)** he works
more (than me); V tb **cada**
2 (superl): **el más** the most, ...+est; **el más
grande/inteligente (de)** the biggest/most
intelligent (in)
3 (negativo): **no tengo más dinero** I haven't
got any more money; **no viene más por
aquí** he doesn't come round here any more
4 (adicional): **no le veo más solución que
...** I see no other solution than to ...; **¿quién
más?** anybody else?
5 (+ adj: valor intensivo): **¡qué perro más
sucio!** what a filthy dog!; **¡es más tonto!**
he's so stupid!
6 (locuciones): **más o menos** more or less;
**los más** most people; **es más** furthermore;
**más bien** rather; **¡qué más da!** what does it
matter!; V tb **no**
7: **por más: por más que te esfuerces** no
matter how hard you try; **por más que
quisiera** ... much as I should like to ...
8: **de más: veo que aquí estoy de más** I can
see I'm not needed here; **tenemos uno de
más** we've got one extra ▷ prep: **2 más 2 son
4** 2 and o plus 2 are 4
▷ nm inv: **este trabajo tiene sus más y sus
menos** this job's got its good points and its
bad points

**mas** [mas] conj but
**masa** ['masa] nf (mezcla) dough; (volumen)
volume, mass; (Física) mass; **en ~** en masse;
**las ~s** (Pol) the masses
**masacre** [ma'sakre] nf massacre
**masaje** [ma'saxe] nm massage
**máscara** ['maskara] nf mask; **máscara
antigás/de oxígeno** gas/oxygen mask;
**mascarilla** nf (de belleza, Med) mask
**masculino, -a** [masku'lino, a] adj
masculine; (Bio) male
**masía** [ma'sia] nf farmhouse
**masivo, -a** [ma'siβo, a] adj mass cpd
**masoquista** [maso'kista] nmf masochist
**máster** ['master] (ESP) nm master
**masticar** [masti'kar] vt to chew
**mástil** ['mastil] nm (de navío) mast; (de
guitarra) neck

**mastín** [mas'tin] nm mastiff
**masturbarse** [mastur'βarse] vr to
masturbate
**mata** ['mata] nf (arbusto) bush, shrub; (de
hierba) tuft
**matadero** [mata'ðero] nm
slaughterhouse, abattoir
**matamoscas** [mata'moskas] nm inv
(pala) fly swat
**matanza** [ma'tanθa] nf slaughter
**matar** [ma'tar] vt, vi to kill; **matarse**
vr (suicidarse) to kill o.s., commit suicide;
(morir) to be o get killed; **~ el hambre** to
stave off hunger
**matasellos** [mata'seʎos] nm inv
postmark
**mate** ['mate] adj matt ▷ nm (en ajedrez)
(check)mate; (LAM: hierba) maté; (: vasija)
gourd
**matemáticas** [mate'matikas] nfpl
mathematics; **matemático, -a** adj
mathematical ▷ nm/f mathematician
**materia** [ma'terja] nf (gen) matter;
(Tec) material; (Escol) subject; **en ~ de**
on the subject of; **materia prima** raw
material; **material** adj material ▷ nm
material; (Tec) equipment; **materialista**
adj materialist(ic); **materialmente** adv
materially; (fig) absolutely
**maternal** [mater'nal] adj motherly,
maternal
**maternidad** [materni'ðað] nf
motherhood, maternity; **materno, -a** adj
maternal; (lengua) mother cpd
**matinal** [mati'nal] adj morning cpd
**matiz** [ma'tiθ] nm shade; **matizar** vt
(variar) to vary; (Arte) to blend; **matizar de**
to tinge with
**matón** [ma'ton] nm bully
**matorral** [mato'rral] nm thicket
**matrícula** [ma'trikula] nf (registro)
register; (Auto) registration number; (: placa)
number plate; **matrícula de honor** (Univ)
top marks in a subject at university with the
right to free registration the following year;
**matricular** vt to register, enrol
**matrimonio** [matri'monjo] nm (pareja)
(married) couple; (unión) marriage
**matriz** [ma'triθ] nf (Anat) womb; (Tec)
mould
**matrona** [ma'trona] nf (persona de edad)
matron; (comadrona) midwife
**matufia** [ma'tufja] (RPL: fam) nf put-up
job
**maullar** [mau'ʎar] vi to mew, miaow
**maxilar** [maksi'lar] nm jaw(bone)
**máxima** ['maksima] nf maxim
**máximo, -a** ['maksimo, a] adj

maximum; (*más alto*) highest; (*más grande*)
greatest ▷ *nm* maximum; **como ~** at most
**mayo** ['majo] *nm* May
**mayonesa** [majo'nesa] *nf* mayonnaise
**mayor** [ma'jor] *adj* main, chief; (*adulto*)
adult; (*de edad avanzada*) elderly; (*Mús*)
major; (*compar: de tamaño*) bigger; (: *de edad*)
older; (*superl: de tamaño*) biggest; (: *de edad*)
oldest ▷ *nm* (*adulto*) adult; **mayores** *nmpl*
(*antepasados*) ancestors; **al por ~** wholesale;
**mayor de edad** adult
**mayoral** [majo'ral] *nm* foreman
**mayordomo** [major'ðomo] *nm* butler
**mayoría** [majo'ria] *nf* majority, greater
part
**mayorista** [majo'rista] *nmf* wholesaler
**mayoritario, -a** [majori'tarjo, a] *adj*
majority *cpd*
**mayúscula** [ma'juskula] *nf* capital letter
**mazapán** [maθa'pan] *nm* marzipan
**mazo** ['maθo] *nm* (*martillo*) mallet; (*de
flores*) bunch; (*Deporte*) bat
**me** [me] *pron* (*directo*) me; (*indirecto*) (to)
me; (*reflexivo*) (to) myself; **¡dá~lo!** give it
to me!
**mear** [me'ar] (*fam*) *vi* to pee, piss (!)
**mecánica** [me'kanika] *nf* (*Escol*)
mechanics *sg*; (*mecanismo*) mechanism; *V tb*
**mecánico**
**mecánico, -a** [me'kaniko, a] *adj*
mechanical ▷ *nm/f* mechanic
**mecanismo** [meka'nismo] *nm*
mechanism; (*marcha*) gear
**mecanografía** [mekanoɣra'fia] *nf*
typewriting; **mecanógrafo, -a** *nm/f* typist
**mecate** [me'kate] (*MÉX, CAM*) *nm* rope
**mecedora** [meθe'ðora] *nf* rocking chair
**mecer** [me'θer] *vt* (*cuna*) to rock; **mecerse**
*vr* to rock; (*rama*) to sway
**mecha** ['metʃa] *nf* (*de vela*) wick; (*de bomba*)
fuse
**mechero** [me'tʃero] *nm* (cigarette) lighter
**mechón** [me'tʃon] *nm* (*gen*) tuft; (*de pelo*)
lock
**medalla** [me'ðaʎa] *nf* medal
**media** ['meðja] *nf* stocking; (*LAM: calcetín*)
sock; (*promedio*) average
**mediado, -a** [me'ðjaðo, a] *adj* half-full;
(*trabajo*) half-completed; **a ~s de** in the
middle of, halfway through
**mediano, -a** [me'ðjano, a] *adj* (*regular*)
medium, average; (*mediocre*) mediocre
**medianoche** [meðja'notʃe] *nf* midnight
**mediante** [me'ðjante] *adv* by (means of),
through
**mediar** [me'ðjar] *vi* (*interceder*) to mediate,
intervene
**medicamento** [meðika'mento] *nm*

medicine, drug
**medicina** [meði'θina] *nf* medicine
**médico, -a** ['meðiko, a] *adj* medical
▷ *nm/f* doctor
**medida** [me'ðiða] *nf* measure; (*medición*)
measurement; (*prudencia*) moderation,
prudence; **en cierta/gran ~** up to a point/
to a great extent; **un traje a la ~** a made-to-
measure suit; **~ de cuello** collar size; **a ~ de**
in proportion to; (*de acuerdo con*) in keeping
with; **a ~ que** (*conforme*) as; **medidor** (*LAM*)
*nm* meter
**medio, -a** ['meðjo, a] *adj* half (a); (*punto*)
mid, middle; (*promedio*) average ▷ *adv* half
▷ *nm* (*centro*) middle, centre; (*promedio*)
average; (*método*) means, way; (*ambiente*)
environment; **medios** *nmpl* means,
resources; **~ litro** half a litre; **las tres y**
**media** half past three; **a ~ terminar** half
finished; **pagar a medias** to share the
cost; **medio ambiente** environment;
**medio de transporte** means of transport;
**Medio Oriente** Middle East; **medios de**
**comunicación** media; **medioambiental**
*adj* (*política, efectos*) environmental
**mediocre** [me'ðjokre] *adj* mediocre
**mediodía** [meðjo'ðia] *nm* midday, noon
**medir** [me'ðir] *vt, vi* (*gen*) to measure
**meditar** [meði'tar] *vt* to ponder, think
over, meditate on; (*planear*) to think out
**mediterráneo, -a** [meðite'rraneo,
a] *adj* Mediterranean ▷ *nm:* **el M~** the
Mediterranean
**médula** ['meðula] *nf* (*Anat*) marrow;
**médula espinal** spinal cord
**medusa** [me'ðusa] (*ESP*) *nf* jellyfish
**megáfono** [me'ɣafono] *nm* megaphone
**megapíxel** [meɣa'piksel] (*pl* **megapixels**
*or* **~es**) *nm* megapixel
**mejilla** [me'xiʎa] *nf* cheek
**mejillón** [mexi'ʎon] *nm* mussel
**mejor** [me'xor] *adj, adv* (*compar*) better;
(*superl*) best; **a lo ~** probably; (*quizá*) maybe;
**~ dicho** rather; **tanto ~** so much the better
**mejora** [me'xora] *nf* improvement;
**mejorar** *vt* to improve, make better ▷ *vi*
to improve, get better; **mejorarse** *vr* to
improve, get better
**melancólico, -a** [melan'koliko, a] *adj*
(*triste*) sad, melancholy; (*soñador*) dreamy
**melena** [me'lena] *nf* (*de persona*) long hair;
(*Zool*) mane
**mellizo, -a** [me'ʎiθo, a] *adj, nm/f* twin
**melocotón** [meloko'ton] (*ESP*) *nm* peach
**melodía** [melo'ðia] *nf* melody, tune
**melodrama** [melo'ðrama] *nm*
melodrama; **melodramático, -a** *adj*
melodramatic

**melón** [me'lon] nm melon

**membrete** [mem'brete] nm letterhead

**membrillo** [mem'briλo] nm quince;
**(carne de) ~** quince jelly

**memoria** [me'morja] nf (gen) memory;
**memorias** nfpl (de autor) memoirs;
**memorizar** vt to memorize

**menaje** [me'naxe] nm (tb: **artículos de ~**)
household items

**mencionar** [menθjo'nar] vt to mention

**mendigo, -a** [men'diɤo, a] nm/f beggar

**menear** [mene'ar] vt to move; **menearse**
vr to shake; (balancearse) to sway; (moverse)
to move; (fig) to get a move on

**menestra** [me'nestra] nf (tb: **~ de
verduras**) vegetable stew

**menopausia** [meno'pausja] nf
menopause

**menor** [me'nor] adj (más pequeño: compar)
smaller; (: superl) smallest; (más
joven: compar) younger; (: superl) youngest;
(Mús) minor ▷ nmf (joven) young person,
juvenile; **no tengo la ~ idea** I haven't the
faintest idea; **al por ~** retail; **menor de edad**
person under age

**Menorca** [me'norka] nf Minorca

○ **PALABRA CLAVE**

**menos** [menos] adj 1: **menos (que o de)**
(compar: cantidad) less (than); (: número)
fewer (than); **con menos entusiasmo**
with less enthusiasm; **menos gente** fewer
people; V tb **cada**
2 (superl): **es el que menos culpa tiene** he is
the least to blame
▷ adv 1 (compar): **menos (que o de)** less
(than); **me gusta menos que el otro** I like it
less than the other one
2 (superl): **es el menos listo (de su clase)**
he's the least bright in his class; **de todas
ellas es la que menos me agrada** out of all
of them she's the one I like least
3 (locuciones): **no quiero verle y menos
visitarle** I don't want to see him, let alone
visit him; **tenemos siete de menos** we're
seven short; **(por) lo menos** at (the very)
least; **¡menos mal!** thank goodness!
▷ prep except; (cifras) minus; **todos menos
él** everyone except (for) him; **5 menos 2** 5
minus 2
▷ conj: **a menos que: a menos que venga
mañana** unless he comes tomorrow

**menospreciar** [menospre'θjar] vt to
underrate, undervalue; (despreciar) to scorn,
despise

**mensaje** [men'saxe] nm message; **enviar**

**un ~ a algn** (por móvil) to text sb, send sb
a text message; **mensaje de texto** text
message; **mensajero, -a** nm/f messenger

**menso, -a** ['menso, a] (MÉX: fam) adj
stupid

**menstruación** [menstrua'θjon] nf
menstruation

**mensual** [men'swal] adj monthly; **100
euros ~es** 100 euros a month; **mensualidad**
nf (salario) monthly salary; (Com) monthly
payment, monthly instalment

**menta** ['menta] nf mint

**mental** [men'tal] adj mental; **mentalidad**
nf mentality; **mentalizar** vt (sensibilizar) to
make aware; (convencer) to convince; (padres)
to prepare (mentally); **mentalizarse**
vr (concienciarse) to become aware;
**mentalizarse (de)** to get used to the idea
(of); **mentalizarse de que ...** (convencerse)
to get it into one's head that ...

**mente** ['mente] nf mind

**mentir** [men'tir] vi to lie

**mentira** [men'tira] nf (una mentira) lie;
(acto) lying; (invención) fiction; **parece
mentira que ...** it seems incredible that
..., I can't believe that ...; **mentiroso, -a**
[menti'roso, a] adj lying ▷ nm/f liar

**menú** [me'nu] (pl **~s**) nm menu; **menú del
día** set menu; **menú turístico** tourist menu

**menudencias** [menu'ðenθjas] (LAM)
nfpl giblets

**menudo, -a** [me'nuðo, a] adj (pequeño)
small, tiny; (sin importancia) petty,
insignificant; **¡~ negocio!** (fam) some deal!;
**a ~** often, frequently

**meñique** [me'ɲike] nm little finger

**mercadillo** [merka'ðiλo] (ESP) nm flea
market

**mercado** [mer'kaðo] nm market;
**mercado de pulgas** (LAM) flea market

**mercancía** [merkan'θia] nf commodity;
**mercancías** nfpl goods, merchandise sg

**mercenario, -a** [merθe'narjo, a] adj, nm
mercenary

**mercería** [merθe'ria] nf haberdashery
(BRIT), notions pl (US); (tienda) haberdasher's
(BRIT), notions store (US)

**mercurio** [mer'kurjo] nm mercury

**merecer** [mere'θer] vt to deserve, merit
▷ vi to be deserving, be worthy; **merece
la pena** it's worthwhile; **merecido, -a** adj
(well) deserved; **llevar su merecido** to get
one's deserts

**merendar** [meren'dar] vt to have for
tea ▷ vi to have tea; (en el campo) to have a
picnic; **merendero** nm open-air cafe

**merengue** [me'renge] nm meringue

**meridiano** [meri'ðjano] nm (Geo)

meridian

**merienda** [me'rjenda] *nf* (light) tea, afternoon snack; (*de campo*) picnic

**mérito** ['merito] *nm* merit; (*valor*) worth, value

**merluza** [mer'luθa] *nf* hake

**mermelada** [merme'laða] *nf* jam

**mero, -a** ['mero, a] *adj* mere; (*MÉX, CAM: fam*) very

**merodear** [meroðe'ar] *vi*: **~ por** to prowl about

**mes** [mes] *nm* month

**mesa** ['mesa] *nf* table; (*de trabajo*) desk; (*Geo*) plateau; **poner/quitar la ~** to lay/clear the table; **mesa electoral** *officials in charge of a polling station*; **mesa redonda** (*reunión*) round table; **mesero, -a** (*LAM*) *nm/f* waiter/waitress

**meseta** [me'seta] *nf* (*Geo*) plateau, tableland

**mesilla** [me'siʎa] *nf* (*tb*: **~ de noche**) bedside table

**mesón** [me'son] *nm* inn

**mestizo, -a** [mes'tiθo, a] *adj* half-caste, of mixed race ▷ *nm/f* half-caste

**meta** ['meta] *nf* goal; (*de carrera*) finish

**metabolismo** [metaβo'lismo] *nm* metabolism

**metáfora** [me'tafora] *nf* metaphor

**metal** [me'tal] *nm* (*materia*) metal; (*Mús*) brass; **metálico, -a** *adj* metallic; (*de metal*) metal ▷ *nm* (*dinero contante*) cash

**meteorología** [meteorolo'xia] *nf* meteorology

**meter** [me'ter] *vt* (*colocar*) to put, place; (*introducir*) to put in, insert; (*involucrar*) to involve; (*causar*) to make, cause; **meterse** *vr*: **~se en** to go into, enter; (*fig*) to interfere in, meddle in; **~se a** to start; **~se a escritor** to become a writer; **~se con uno** to provoke sb, pick a quarrel with sb

**meticuloso, -a** [metiku'loso, a] *adj* meticulous, thorough

**metódico, -a** [me'toðiko, a] *adj* methodical

**método** ['metoðo] *nm* method

**metralleta** [metra'ʎeta] *nf* sub-machine-gun

**métrico, -a** ['metriko, a] *adj* metric

**metro** ['metro] *nm* metre; (*tren*) underground (*BRIT*), subway (*US*)

**metrosexual** [metrosek'swal] *adj, nm* metrosexual

**mexicano, -a** [mexi'kano, a] *adj, nm/f* Mexican

**México** ['mexiko] *nm* Mexico; **Ciudad de ~** Mexico City

**mezcla** ['meθkla] *nf* mixture; **mezcladora**

(*MÉX*) *nf* (*tb*: **mezcladora de cemento**) cement mixer; **mezclar** *vt* to mix (up); **mezclarse** *vr* to mix, mingle; **mezclarse en** to get mixed up in, get involved in

**mezquino, -a** [meθ'kino, a] *adj* mean

**mezquita** [meθ'kita] *nf* mosque

**mg.** *abr* (= *miligramo*) mg

**mi** [mi] *adj pos* my ▷ *nm* (*Mús*) E

**mí** [mi] *pron* me; myself

**mía** *pron* V **mío**

**michelín** [mitʃe'lin] (*fam*) *nm* (*de grasa*) spare tyre

**microbio** [mi'kroβjo] *nm* microbe

**micrófono** [mi'krofono] *nm* microphone

**microondas** [mikro'ondas] *nm inv* (*tb*: **horno ~**) microwave (oven)

**microscopio** [mikro'skopjo] *nm* microscope

**miedo** ['mjeðo] *nm* fear; (*nerviosismo*) apprehension, nervousness; **tener ~** to be afraid; **de ~** wonderful, marvellous; **hace un frío de ~** (*fam*) it's terribly cold; **miedoso, -a** *adj* fearful, timid

**miel** [mjel] *nf* honey

**miembro** ['mjembro] *nm* limb; (*socio*) member; **miembro viril** penis

**mientras** ['mjentras] *conj* while; (*duración*) as long as ▷ *adv* meanwhile; **~ tanto** meanwhile

**miércoles** ['mjerkoles] *nm inv* Wednesday

**mierda** ['mjerða] (*fam!*) *nf* shit (!)

**miga** ['miɣa] *nf* crumb; (*fig: meollo*) essence; **hacer buenas ~s** (*fam*) to get on well

**mil** [mil] *num* thousand; **dos ~ libras** two thousand pounds

**milagro** [mi'laɣro] *nm* miracle; **milagroso, -a** *adj* miraculous

**milésima** [mi'lesima] *nf* (*de segundo*) thousandth

**mili** ['mili] (*ESP: fam*) *nf*: **hacer la ~** to do one's military service

**milímetro** [mi'limetro] *nm* millimetre

**militante** [mili'tante] *adj* militant

**militar** [mili'tar] *adj* military ▷ *nmf* soldier ▷ *vi* (*Mil*) to serve; (*en un partido*) to be a member

**milla** ['miʎa] *nf* mile

**millar** [mi'ʎar] *nm* thousand

**millón** [mi'ʎon] *num* million; **millonario, -a** *nm/f* millionaire

**milusos** [mi'lusos] (*MÉX*) *nm inv* odd-job man

**mimar** [mi'mar] *vt* to spoil, pamper

**mimbre** ['mimbre] *nm* wicker

**mímica** ['mimika] *nf* (*para comunicarse*) sign language; (*imitación*) mimicry

**mimo** ['mimo] *nm* (*caricia*) caress; (*de niño*)

spoiling; (*Teatro*) mime; (: *actor*) mime artist
**mina** ['mina] *nf* mine
**mineral** [mine'ral] *adj* mineral ▷ *nm*
(*Geo*) mineral; (*mena*) ore
**minero, -a** [mi'nero, a] *adj* mining *cpd*
▷ *nm/f* miner
**miniatura** [minja'tura] *adj inv*, *nf*
miniature
**minidisco** [mini'disko] *nm* MiniDisc®
**minifalda** [mini'falda] *nf* miniskirt
**mínimo, -a** ['minimo, a] *adj*, *nm*
minimum
**minino, -a** [mi'nino, a] (*fam*) *nm/f* puss,
pussy
**ministerio** [minis'terjo] *nm* Ministry;
**Ministerio de Hacienda/de Asuntos
Exteriores** Treasury (BRIT), Treasury
Department (US)/Foreign Office (BRIT),
State Department (US)
**ministro, -a** [mi'nistro, a] *nm/f* minister
**minoría** [mino'ria] *nf* minority
**minúscula** [mi'nuskula] *nf* small letter
**minúsculo, -a** [mi'nuskulo, a] *adj* tiny,
minute
**minusválido, -a** [minus'βaliðo, a]
*adj* (physically) handicapped ▷ *nm/f*
(physically) handicapped person
**minuta** [mi'nuta] *nf* (*de comida*) menu
**minutero** [minu'tero] *nm* minute hand
**minuto** [mi'nuto] *nm* minute
**mío, -a** ['mio, a] *pron*: **el ~/la mía** mine; **un
amigo ~** a friend of mine; **lo ~** what is mine
**miope** [mi'ope] *adj* short-sighted
**mira** ['mira] *nf* (*de arma*) sight(s) (*pl*); (*fig*)
aim, intention
**mirada** [mi'raða] *nf* look, glance;
(*expresión*) look, expression; **clavar la ~ en** to
stare at; **echar una ~ a** to glance at
**mirado, -a** [mi'raðo, a] *adj* (*sensato*)
sensible; (*considerado*) considerate; **bien/
mal ~** (*estimado*) well/not well thought of;
**bien ~ ...** all things considered ...
**mirador** [mira'ðor] *nm* viewpoint,
vantage point
**mirar** [mi'rar] *vt* to look at; (*observar*) to
watch; (*considerar*) to consider, think over;
(*vigilar, cuidar*) to watch, look after ▷ *vi* to
look; (*Arq*) to face; **mirarse** *vr* (*dos personas*)
to look at each other; **~ bien/mal** to think
highly of/have a poor opinion of; **~se al
espejo** to look at o.s. in the mirror
**mirilla** [mi'riʎa] *nf* spyhole, peephole
**mirlo** ['mirlo] *nm* blackbird
**misa** ['misa] *nf* mass
**miserable** [mise'raβle] *adj* (*avaro*)
mean, stingy; (*nimio*) miserable, paltry;
(*lugar*) squalid; (*fam*) vile, despicable ▷ *nmf*
(*malvado*) rogue

**miseria** [mi'serja] *nf* (*pobreza*) poverty;
(*tacañería*) meanness, stinginess;
(*condiciones*) squalor; **una ~** a pittance
**misericordia** [miseri'korðja] *nf*
(*compasión*) compassion, pity; (*piedad*) mercy
**misil** [mi'sil] *nm* missile
**misión** [mi'sjon] *nf* mission; **misionero,
-a** *nm/f* missionary
**mismo, -a** ['mismo, a] *adj* (*semejante*)
same; (*después de pron*) -self; (*para énfasis*)
very ▷ *adv*: **aquí/hoy ~** right here/this very
day; **ahora ~** right now ▷ *conj*: **lo ~ que** just
like o as; **el ~ traje** the same suit; **en ese ~
momento** at that very moment; **vino el ~
ministro** the minister himself came; **yo ~
lo vi** I saw it myself; **lo ~ the same** (thing);
**da lo ~** it's all the same; **quedamos en las
mismas** we're no further forward; **por lo ~**
for the same reason
**misterio** [mis'terjo] *nm* mystery;
**misterioso, -a** *adj* mysterious
**mitad** [mi'tað] *nf* (*medio*) half; (*centro*)
middle; **a ~ de precio** (at) half-price; **en o a ~
del camino** halfway along the road; **cortar
por la ~** to cut through the middle
**mitin** ['mitin] (*pl* **mítines**) *nm* meeting
**mito** ['mito] *nm* myth
**mixto, -a** ['miksto, a] *adj* mixed
**ml.** *abr* (= *mililitro*) ml
**mm.** *abr* (= *milímetro*) mm
**mobiliario** [moβi'ljarjo] *nm* furniture
**mochila** [mo'tʃila] *nf* rucksack (BRIT),
back-pack
**moco** ['moko] *nm* mucus; **mocos** *nmpl*
(*fam*) snot; **limpiarse los ~s de la nariz** (*fam*)
to wipe one's nose
**moda** ['moða] *nf* fashion; (*estilo*) style; **a la
o de ~** in fashion, fashionable; **pasado de ~**
out of fashion
**modales** [mo'ðales] *nmpl* manners
**modelar** [moðe'lar] *vt* to model
**modelo** [mo'ðelo] *adj inv*, *nmf* model
**módem** ['moðem] *nm* (*Inform*) modem
**moderado, -a** [moðe'raðo, a] *adj*
moderate
**moderar** [moðe'rar] *vt* to moderate;
(*violencia*) to restrain, control; (*velocidad*)
to reduce; **moderarse** *vr* to restrain o.s.,
control o.s.
**modernizar** [moðerni'θar] *vt* to
modernize
**moderno, -a** [mo'ðerno, a] *adj* modern;
(*actual*) present-day
**modestia** [mo'ðestja] *nf* modesty;
**modesto, -a** *adj* modest
**modificar** [moðifi'kar] *vt* to modify
**modisto, -a** [mo'ðisto, a] *nm/f* (*diseñador*)
couturier, designer; (*que confecciona*)

dressmaker

**modo** ['moðo] *nm* way, manner; (*Mús*) mode; **modos** *nmpl* manners; **de ningún ~** in no way; **de todos ~s** at any rate; **modo de empleo** directions *pl* (for use)

**mofarse** [mo'farse] *vr:* **~ de** to mock, scoff at

**mofle** ['mofle] (*MÉX, CAM*) *nm* silencer (*BRIT*), muffler (*US*)

**mogollón** [moɣo'ʎon] (*ESP: fam*) *adv* a hell of a lot

**moho** ['moo] *nm* mould, mildew; (*en metal*) rust

**mojar** [mo'xar] *vt* to wet; (*humedecer*) to damp(en), moisten; (*calar*) to soak; **mojarse** *vr* to get wet

**molcajete** [molka'xete] (*MÉX*) *nm* mortar

**molde** ['molde] *nm* mould; (*Costura*) pattern; (*fig*) model; **moldeado** *nm* soft perm; **moldear** *vt* to mould

**mole** ['mole] *nf* mass, bulk; (*edificio*) pile

**moler** [mo'ler] *vt* to grind, crush

**molestar** [moles'tar] *vt* to bother; (*fastidiar*) to annoy; (*incomodar*) to inconvenience, put out ▷ *vi* to be a nuisance; **molestarse** *vr* to bother; (*incomodarse*) to go to trouble; (*ofenderse*) to take offence; **¿(no) te molesta si ...?** do you mind if ...?

▌No confundir **molestar** con la palabra inglesa *molest*.

**molestia** [mo'lestja] *nf* bother, trouble; (*incomodidad*) inconvenience; (*Med*) discomfort; **es una ~** it's a nuisance; **molesto, -a** *adj* (*que fastidia*) annoying; (*incómodo*) inconvenient; (*inquieto*) uncomfortable, ill at ease; (*enfadado*) annoyed

**molido, -a** [mo'liðo, a] *adj:* **estar ~** (*fig*) to be exhausted o dead beat

**molinillo** [moli'niʎo] *nm* hand mill; **molinillo de café** coffee grinder

**molino** [mo'lino] *nm* (*edificio*) mill; (*máquina*) grinder

**momentáneo, -a** [momen'taneo, a] *adj* momentary

**momento** [mo'mento] *nm* moment; **de ~** at o for the moment

**momia** ['momja] *nf* mummy

**monarca** [mo'narka] *nmf* monarch, ruler; **monarquía** *nf* monarchy

**monasterio** [monas'terjo] *nm* monastery

**mondar** [mon'dar] *vt* to peel; **mondarse** *vr* (*ESP*): **~se de risa** (*fam*) to split one's sides laughing

**mondongo** [mon'dongo] (*LAM*) *nm* tripe

**moneda** [mo'neða] *nf* (*tipo de dinero*) currency, money; (*pieza*) coin; **una ~ de 2**

**euros** a 2 euro piece; **monedero** *nm* purse

**monitor, a** [moni'tor, a] *nm/f* instructor, coach ▷ *nm* (*TV*) set; (*Inform*) monitor

**monja** ['monxa] *nf* nun

**monje** ['monxe] *nm* monk

**mono, -a** ['mono, a] *adj* (*bonito*) lovely, pretty; (*gracioso*) nice, charming ▷ *nm/f* monkey, ape ▷ *nm* dungarees *pl*; (*overoles*) overalls *pl*

**monopatín** [monopa'tin] *nm* skateboard

**monopolio** [mono'poljo] *nm* monopoly; **monopolizar** *vt* to monopolize

**monótono, -a** [mo'notono, a] *adj* monotonous

**monstruo** ['monstrwo] *nm* monster ▷ *adj inv* fantastic; **monstruoso, -a** *adj* monstrous

**montaje** [mon'taxe] *nm* assembly; (*Teatro*) décor; (*Cine*) montage

**montaña** [mon'taɲa] *nf* (*monte*) mountain; (*sierra*) mountains *pl*, mountainous area; **montaña rusa** roller coaster; **montañero, -a** *nm/f* mountaineer; **montañismo** *nm* mountaineering

**montar** [mon'tar] *vt* (*subir a*) to mount, get on; (*Tec*) to assemble, put together; (*negocio*) to set up; (*arma*) to cock; (*colocar*) to lift on to; (*Culin*) to beat ▷ *vi* to mount, get on; (*sobresalir*) to overlap; **~ en bicicleta** to ride a bicycle; **~ en cólera** to get angry; **~ a caballo** to ride, go horseriding

**monte** ['monte] *nm* (*montaña*) mountain; (*bosque*) woodland; (*área sin cultivar*) wild area, wild country; **monte de piedad** pawnshop

**montón** [mon'ton] *nm* heap, pile; (*fig*): **un ~ de** heaps o lots of

**monumento** [monu'mento] *nm* monument

**moño** ['moɲo] *nm* bun

**moqueta** [mo'keta] *nf* fitted carpet

**mora** ['mora] *nf* blackberry; V *tb* **moro**

**morado, -a** [mo'raðo, a] *adj* purple, violet ▷ *nm* bruise

**moral** [mo'ral] *adj* moral ▷ *nf* (*ética*) ethics *pl*; (*moralidad*) morals *pl*, morality; (*ánimo*) morale

**moraleja** [mora'lexa] *nf* moral

**morboso, -a** [mor'βoso, a] *adj* morbid

**morcilla** [mor'θiʎa] *nf* blood sausage ≈ black pudding (*BRIT*)

**mordaza** [mor'ðaθa] *nf* (*para la boca*) gag; (*Tec*) clamp

**morder** [mor'ðer] *vt* to bite; (*fig: consumir*) to eat away, eat into; **mordisco** *nm* bite

**moreno, -a** [mo'reno, a] *adj* (*color*) (dark) brown; (*de tez*) dark; (*de pelo moreno*) dark-haired; (*negro*) black

**morfina** [mor'fina] *nf* morphine

**moribundo, -a** [mori'βundo, a] *adj* dying

**morir** [mo'rir] *vi* to die; (*fuego*) to die down; (*luz*) to go out; **morirse** *vr* to die; (*fig*) to be dying; **murió en un accidente** he was killed in an accident; **~se por algo** to be dying for sth

**moro, -a** ['moro, a] *adj* Moorish ▷ *nm/f* Moor

**moroso, -a** [mo'roso, a] *nm/f* bad debtor, defaulter

**morraña** [mo'rraɲa] (*MÉX*) *nf* (*cambio*) small *o* loose change

**morro** ['morro] *nm* (*Zool*) snout, nose; (*Auto, Aviac*) nose

**morsa** ['morsa] *nf* walrus

**mortadela** [morta'ðela] *nf* mortadella

**mortal** [mor'tal] *adj* mortal; (*golpe*) deadly; **mortalidad** *nf* mortality

**mortero** [mor'tero] *nm* mortar

**mosca** ['moska] *nf* fly

**Moscú** [mos'ku] *n* Moscow

**mosquearse** [moske'arse] (*fam*) *vr* (*enojarse*) to get cross; (*ofenderse*) to take offence

**mosquitero** [moski'tero] *nm* mosquito net

**mosquito** [mos'kito] *nm* mosquito

**mostaza** [mos'taθa] *nf* mustard

**mosto** ['mosto] *nm* (unfermented) grape juice

**mostrador** [mostra'ðor] *nm* (*de tienda*) counter; (*de café*) bar

**mostrar** [mos'trar] *vt* to show; (*exhibir*) to display, exhibit; (*explicar*) to explain; **mostrarse** *vr*: **~se amable** to be kind; to prove to be kind; **no se muestra muy inteligente** he doesn't seem (to be) very intelligent

**mota** ['mota] *nf* speck, tiny piece; (*en diseño*) dot

**mote** ['mote] *nm* nickname

**motín** [mo'tin] *nm* (*del pueblo*) revolt, rising; (*del ejército*) mutiny

**motivar** [moti'βar] *vt* (*causar*) to cause, motivate; (*explicar*) to explain, justify; **motivo** *nm* motive, reason

**moto** ['moto] (*fam*) *nf* = **motocicleta**

**motocicleta** [motoθi'kleta] *nf* motorbike (*BRIT*), motorcycle

**motoneta** [moto'neta] (*cs*) *nf* scooter

**motor** [mo'tor] *nm* motor, engine; **motor a chorro** *o* **de reacción/de explosión** jet engine/internal combustion engine

**motora** [mo'tora] *nf* motorboat

**movedizo, -a** *adj* V **arena**

**mover** [mo'βer] *vt* to move; (*cabeza*) to shake; (*accionar*) to drive; (*fig*) to cause, provoke; **moverse** *vr* to move; (*fig*) to get a move on

**móvil** ['moβil] *adj* mobile; (*pieza de máquina*) moving; (*mueble*) movable ▷ *nm* (*motivo*) motive; (*teléfono*) mobile

**movimiento** [moβi'mjento] *nm* movement; (*Tec*) motion; (*actividad*) activity

**mozo, -a** ['moθo, a] *adj* (*joven*) young ▷ *nm/f* youth, young man/girl; (*cs: mesero*) waiter/waitress

**MP3** *nm* MP3; **reproductor (de) ~** MP3 player

**mucama** [mu'kama] (*RPL*) *nf* maid

**muchacho, -a** [mu'tʃatʃo, a] *nm/f* (*niño*) boy/girl; (*criado*) servant; (*criada*) maid

**muchedumbre** [mutʃe'ðumbre] *nf* crowd

○ **PALABRA CLAVE**

**mucho, -a** ['mutʃo, a] *adj* **1** (*cantidad*) a lot of, much; (*número*) lots of, a lot of, many; **mucho dinero** a lot of money; **hace mucho calor** it's very hot; **muchas amigas** lots *o* a lot of friends

**2** (*sg: grande*): **ésta es mucha casa para él** this house is much too big for him

▷ *pron*: **tengo mucho que hacer** I've got a lot to do; **muchos dicen que …** a lot of people say that …; V *tb* **tener**

▷ *adv* **1** **me gusta mucho** I like it a lot; **lo siento mucho** I'm very sorry; **come mucho** he eats a lot; **¿te vas a quedar mucho?** are you going to stay long?

**2** (*respuesta*) very; **¿estás cansado? – ¡mucho!** are you tired? – very!

**3** (*locuciones*): **como mucho** at (the) most; **con mucho: el mejor con mucho** by far the best; **ni mucho menos: no es rico ni mucho menos** he's far from being rich

**4**: **por mucho que: por mucho que le creas** no matter how *o* however much you believe her

**muda** ['muða] *nf* change of clothes

**mudanza** [mu'ðanθa] *nf* (*de casa*) move

**mudar** [mu'ðar] *vt* to change; (*Zool*) to shed ▷ *vi* to change; **mudarse** *vr* (*ropa*) to change; **~se de casa** to move house

**mudo, -a** ['muðo, a] *adj* dumb; (*callado, Cine*) silent

**mueble** ['mweβle] *nm* piece of furniture; **muebles** *nmpl* furniture *sg*

**mueca** ['mweka] *nf* face, grimace; **hacer ~s a** to make faces at

**muela** ['mwela] *nf* back tooth; **muela del**

**juicio** wisdom tooth

**muelle** ['mweʎe] *nm* spring; (*Náut*) wharf; (*malecón*) pier

**muero** *etc vb* V **morir**

**muerte** ['mwerte] *nf* death; (*homicidio*) murder; **dar ~ a** to kill

**muerto, -a** ['mwerto, a] *pp de* **morir**
▷ *adj* dead ▷ *nm/f* dead man/woman; (*difunto*) deceased; (*cadáver*) corpse; **estar ~ de cansancio** to be dead tired; **Día de los Muertos** (*MÉX*) All Souls' Day

● **DÍA DE LOS MUERTOS**
●
● All Souls' Day (or "Day of the Dead")
● in Mexico coincides with All Saints'
● Day, which is celebrated in the
● Catholic countries of Latin America on
● November 1st and 2nd. All Souls' Day
● is actually a celebration which begins
● in the evening of October 31st and
● continues until November 2nd. It is a
● combination of the Catholic tradition
● of honouring the Christian saints and
● martyrs, and the ancient Mexican or
● Aztec traditions, in which death was
● not something sinister. For this reason
● all the dead are honoured by bringing
● offerings of food, flowers and candles to
● the cemetery.

**muestra** ['mwestra] *nf* (*señal*) indication, sign; (*demostración*) demonstration; (*prueba*) proof; (*estadística*) sample; (*modelo*) model, pattern; (*testimonio*) token

**muestro** *etc vb* V **mostrar**

**muevo** *etc vb* V **mover**

**mugir** [mu'xir] *vi* (*vaca*) to moo

**mugre** ['muɣre] *nf* dirt, filth

**mujer** [mu'xer] *nf* woman; (*esposa*) wife; **mujeriego** *nm* womanizer

**mula** ['mula] *nf* mule

**muleta** [mu'leta] *nf* (*para andar*) crutch; (*Taur*) stick with red cape attached

**multa** ['multa] *nf* fine; **poner una ~ a** to fine; **multar** *vt* to fine

**multicines** [multi'θines] *nmpl* multiscreen cinema *sg*

**multinacional** [multinaθjo'nal] *nf* multinational

**múltiple** ['multiple] *adj* multiple; (*pl*) many, numerous

**multiplicar** [multipli'kar] *vt* (*Mat*) to multiply; (*fig*) to increase; **multiplicarse** *vr* (*Bio*) to multiply; (*fig*) to be everywhere at once

**multitud** [multi'tuð] *nf* (*muchedumbre*) crowd; **~ de** lots of

**mundial** [mun'djal] *adj* world-wide, universal; (*guerra, récord*) world *cpd*

**mundo** ['mundo] *nm* world; **todo el ~** everybody; **tener ~** to be experienced, know one's way around

**munición** [muni'θjon] *nf* ammunition

**municipal** [muniθi'pal] *adj* municipal, local

**municipio** [muni'θipjo] *nm* (*ayuntamiento*) town council, corporation; (*territorio administrativo*) town, municipality

**muñeca** [mu'ɲeka] *nf* (*Anat*) wrist; (*juguete*) doll

**muñeco** [mu'ɲeko] *nm* (*figura*) figure; (*marioneta*) puppet; (*fig*) puppet, pawn

**mural** [mu'ral] *adj* mural, wall *cpd* ▷ *nm* mural

**muralla** [mu'raʎa] *nf* (*city*) wall(s) (*pl*)

**murciélago** [mur'θjelaɣo] *nm* bat

**murmullo** [mur'muʎo] *nm* murmur(ing); (*cuchicheo*) whispering

**murmurar** [murmu'rar] *vi* to murmur, whisper; (*cotillear*) to gossip

**muro** ['muro] *nm* wall

**muscular** [musku'lar] *adj* muscular

**músculo** ['muskulo] *nm* muscle

**museo** [mu'seo] *nm* museum; **museo de arte** art gallery

**musgo** ['musɣo] *nm* moss

**música** ['musika] *nf* music; V *tb* **músico**

**músico, -a** ['musiko, a] *adj* musical ▷ *nm/f* musician

**muslo** ['muslo] *nm* thigh

**musulmán, -ana** [musul'man, ana] *nm/f* Moslem

**mutación** [muta'θjon] *nf* (*Bio*) mutation; (*cambio*) (sudden) change

**mutilar** [muti'lar] *vt* to mutilate; (*a una persona*) to maim

**mutuo, -a** ['mutwo, a] *adj* mutual

**muy** [mwi] *adv* very; (*demasiado*) too; **M~ Señor mío** Dear Sir; **~ de noche** very late at night; **eso es ~ de él** that's just like him

# n

**N** *abr* (=*norte*) N
**nabo** ['naβo] *nm* turnip
**nacer** [na'θer] *vi* to be born; (*de huevo*) to hatch; (*vegetal*) to sprout; (*río*) to rise; **nací en Barcelona** I was born in Barcelona; **nacido, -a** *adj* born; **recién nacido** newborn; **nacimiento** *nm* birth; (*de Navidad*) Nativity; (*de río*) source
**nación** [na'θjon] *nf* nation; **nacional** *adj* national; **nacionalismo** *nm* nationalism
**nada** ['naða] *pron* nothing ▷ *adv* not at all, in no way; **no decir ~** to say nothing, not to say anything; **~ más** nothing else; **de ~** don't mention it
**nadador, a** [naða'ðor, a] *nm/f* swimmer
**nadar** [na'ðar] *vi* to swim
**nadie** ['naðje] *pron* nobody, no-one; **~ habló** nobody spoke; **no había ~** there was nobody there, there wasn't anybody there
**nado** ['naðo] **a nado**: *adv*: **pasar a ~** to swim across
**nafta** ['nafta] (RPL) *nf* petrol (BRIT), gas (US)
**naipe** ['naipe] *nm* (playing) card; **naipes** *nmpl* cards
**nalgas** ['nalɣas] *nfpl* buttocks
**nalguear** [nalɣe'ar] (MÉX, CAM) *vt* to spank
**nana** ['nana] (ESP) *nf* lullaby
**naranja** [na'ranxa] *adj inv, nf* orange; **media ~** (*fam*) better half; **naranjada** *nf* orangeade; **naranjo** *nm* orange tree
**narciso** [nar'θiso] *nm* narcissus
**narcótico, -a** [nar'kotiko, a] *adj, nm* narcotic; **narcotizar** *vt* to drug; **narcotráfico** *nm* drug trafficking *o* running
**nariz** [na'riθ] *nf* nose; **nariz chata/respingona** snub/turned-up nose
**narración** [narra'θjon] *nf* narration
**narrar** [na'rrar] *vt* to narrate, recount; **narrativa** *nf* narrative

**nata** ['nata] *nf* cream; **nata montada** whipped cream
**natación** [nata'θjon] *nf* swimming
**natal** [na'tal] *adj*: **ciudad ~** home town; **natalidad** *nf* birth rate
**natillas** [na'tiʎas] *nfpl* custard *sg*
**nativo, -a** [na'tiβo, a] *adj, nm/f* native
**natural** [natu'ral] *adj* natural; (*fruta etc*) fresh ▷ *nmf* native ▷ *nm* (*disposición*) nature
**naturaleza** [natura'leθa] *nf* nature; (*género*) nature, kind; **naturaleza muerta** still life
**naturalmente** [natural'mente] *adv* (*de modo natural*) in a natural way; **¡~!** of course!
**naufragar** [naufra'ɣar] *vi* to sink; **naufragio** *nm* shipwreck
**nauseabundo, -a** [nausea'βundo, a] *adj* nauseating, sickening
**náuseas** ['nauseas] *nfpl* nausea *sg*; **me da ~** it makes me feel sick
**náutico, -a** ['nautiko, a] *adj* nautical
**navaja** [na'βaxa] *nf* knife; (*de barbero, peluquero*) razor
**naval** [na'βal] *adj* naval
**Navarra** [na'βarra] *n* Navarre
**nave** ['naβe] *nf* (*barco*) ship, vessel; (*Arq*) nave; **nave espacial** spaceship; **nave industrial** factory premises *pl*
**navegador** [naβeɣa'ðor] *nm* (*Inform*) browser
**navegante** [naβe'ɣante] *nmf* navigator
**navegar** [naβe'ɣar] *vi* (*barco*) to sail; (*avión*) to fly; **~ por Internet** to surf the Net
**Navidad** [naβi'ðað] *nf* Christmas; **Navidades** *nfpl* Christmas time; **¡Feliz ~!** Merry Christmas!; **navideño, -a** *adj* Christmas *cpd*
**nazca** *etc vb V* **nacer**
**nazi** ['naθi] *adj, nmf* Nazi
**NE** *abr* (=*nor(d)este*) NE
**neblina** [ne'βlina] *nf* mist
**necesario, -a** [neθe'sarjo, a] *adj* necessary
**neceser** [neθe'ser] *nm* toilet bag; (*bolsa grande*) holdall
**necesidad** [neθesi'ðað] *nf* need; (*lo inevitable*) necessity; (*miseria*) poverty; **en caso de ~** in case of need o emergency; **hacer sus ~es** to relieve o.s.
**necesitado, -a** [neθesi'taðo, a] *adj* needy, poor; **~ de** in need of
**necesitar** [neθesi'tar] *vt* to need, require
**necio, -a** ['neθjo, a] *adj* foolish
**nectarina** [nekta'rina] *nf* nectarine
**nefasto, -a** [ne'fasto, a] *adj* ill-fated, unlucky
**negación** [neɣa'θjon] *nf* negation;

(*rechazo*) refusal, denial
**negar** [ne'xar] vt (*renegar, rechazar*) to refuse; (*prohibir*) to refuse, deny; (*desmentir*) to deny; **negarse** vr: **~se a** to refuse to
**negativa** [nexa'tiβa] nf negative; (*rechazo*) refusal, denial
**negativo, -a** [nexa'tiβo, a] adj, nm negative
**negociante** [nexo'θjante] nmf businessman/woman
**negociar** [nexo'θjar] vt, vi to negotiate; **~ en** to deal o trade in
**negocio** [ne'xoθjo] nm (Com) business; (*asunto*) affair, business; (*operación comercial*) deal, transaction; (*lugar*) place of business; **los ~s** business sg; **hacer ~** to do business
**negra** ['nexra] nf (Mús) crotchet; V tb **negro**
**negro, -a** ['nexro, a] adj black; (*suerte*) awful ▷ nm black ▷ nm/f black man/woman
**nene, -a** ['nene, a] nm/f baby, small child
**neón** [ne'on] nm: **luces/lámpara de ~** neon lights/lamp
**neoyorquino, -a** [neojor'kino, a] adj (of) New York
**nervio** ['nerβjo] nm nerve; **nerviosismo** nm nervousness, nerves pl; **nervioso, -a** adj nervous
**neto, -a** ['neto, a] adj net
**neumático, -a** [neu'matiko, a] adj pneumatic ▷ nm (ESP) tyre (BRIT), tire (US); **neumático de recambio** spare tyre
**neurólogo, -a** [neu'roloxo, a] nm/f neurologist
**neurona** [neu'rona] nf nerve cell
**neutral** [neu'tral] adj neutral; **neutralizar** vt to neutralize; (*contrarrestar*) to counteract
**neutro, -a** ['neutro, a] adj (Bio, Ling) neuter
**neutrón** [neu'tron] nm neutron
**nevada** [ne'βaða] nf snowstorm; (*caída de nieve*) snowfall
**nevar** [ne'βar] vi to snow
**nevera** [ne'βera] (ESP) nf refrigerator (BRIT), icebox (US)
**nevería** [neβe'ria] (MÉX) nf ice-cream parlour
**nexo** ['nekso] nm link, connection
**ni** [ni] conj nor, neither; (tb: **~ siquiera**) not ... even; **~ aunque que** not even if; **~ blanco ~ negro** neither white nor black
**Nicaragua** [nika'raxwa] nf Nicaragua; **nicaragüense** adj, nmf Nicaraguan
**nicho** ['nitʃo] nm niche
**nicotina** [niko'tina] nf nicotine
**nido** ['niðo] nm nest
**niebla** ['njeβla] nf fog; (*neblina*) mist

**niego** etc vb V **negar**
**nieto, -a** ['njeto, a] nm/f grandson/daughter; **nietos** nmpl grandchildren
**nieve** etc ['njeβe] vb V **nevar** ▷ nf snow; (MÉX: *helado*) ice cream
**NIF** nm abr (= Número de Identificación Fiscal) personal identification number used for financial and tax purposes
**ninfa** ['ninfa] nf nymph
**ningún** adj V **ninguno**
**ninguno, -a** [nin'guno, a] (adj **ningún**) no pron (*nadie*) nobody; (*ni uno*) none, not one; (*ni uno ni otro*) neither; **de ninguna manera** by no means, not at all
**niña** ['nina] nf (Anat) pupil; V tb **niño**
**niñera** [ni'nera] nf nursemaid, nanny
**niñez** [ni'neθ] nf childhood; (*infancia*) infancy
**niño, -a** ['nino, a] adj (*joven*) young; (*inmaduro*) immature ▷ nm/f child, boy/girl
**nipón, -ona** [ni'pon, ona] adj, nm/f Japanese
**níquel** ['nikel] nm nickel
**níspero** ['nispero] nm medlar
**nítido, -a** ['nitiðo, a] adj clear; sharp
**nitrato** [ni'trato] nm nitrate
**nitrógeno** [ni'troxeno] nm nitrogen
**nivel** [ni'βel] nm (Geo) level; (*norma*) level, standard; (*altura*) height; **nivel de aceite** oil level; **nivel de aire** spirit level; **nivel de vida** standard of living; **nivelar** vt to level out; (*fig*) to even up; (Com) to balance
**no** [no] adv no; not; (*con verbo*) not ▷ excl no!; **~ tengo nada** I don't have anything, I have nothing; **~ es el mío** it's not mine; **ahora ~** not now; **¿~ lo sabes?** don't you know?; **~ mucho** not much; **~ bien termine, lo entregaré** as soon as I finish, I'll hand it over; **~ más: ayer ~ más** just yesterday; **¡pase ~ más!** come in!; **¡a que ~ lo sabes!** I bet you don't know!; **¡cómo ~!** of course!; **la ~ intervención** non-intervention
**noble** ['noβle] adj, nmf noble; **nobleza** nf nobility
**noche** ['notʃe] nf night, night-time; (*la tarde*) evening; **de ~, por la ~** at night; **es de ~** it's dark; **Noche de San Juan** see below

○ **NOCHE DE SAN JUAN**

● The **Noche de San Juan** on the 24th June
● is a **fiesta** coinciding with the summer
● solstice and which has taken the
● place of other ancient pagan festivals.
● Traditionally fire plays a major part in
● these festivities with celebrations and
● dancing taking place around bonfires
● in towns and villages across the country.

**nochebuena** [notʃe'βwena] *nf* Christmas Eve

**nochevieja** [notʃe'βjexa] *nf* New Year's Eve

**nocivo, -a** [no'θiβo, a] *adj* harmful

**noctámbulo, -a** [nok'tambulo, a] *nm/f* sleepwalker

**nocturno, -a** [nok'turno, a] *adj (de la noche)* nocturnal, night *cpd; (de la tarde)* evening *cpd* ⊳ *nm* nocturne

**nogal** [no'ɣal] *nm* walnut tree

**nómada** ['nomaða] *adj* nomadic ⊳ *nmf* nomad

**nombrar** [nom'brar] *vt (designar)* to name; *(mencionar)* to mention; *(dar puesto a)* to appoint

**nombre** ['nombre] *nm* name; *(sustantivo)* noun; **~ y apellidos** name in full; **poner ~ a** to call, name; **nombre común/propio** common/proper noun; **nombre de pila/de soltera** Christian/maiden name

**nómina** ['nomina] *nf (lista)* payroll; *(hoja)* payslip

**nominal** [nomi'nal] *adj* nominal

**nominar** [nomi'nar] *vt* to nominate

**nominativo, -a** [nomina'tiβo, a] *adj (Com)*: **cheque ~ a X** cheque made out to X

**nordeste** [nor'ðeste] *adj* north-east, north-eastern, north-easterly ⊳ *nm* north-east

**nórdico, -a** ['norðiko, a] *adj* Nordic

**noreste** [no'reste] *adj, nm* = **nordeste**

**noria** ['norja] *nf (Agr)* waterwheel; *(de carnaval)* big (BRIT) o Ferris (US) wheel

**norma** ['norma] *nf* rule (of thumb)

**normal** [nor'mal] *adj (corriente)* normal; *(habitual)* usual, natural; **normalizarse** *vr* to return to normal; **normalmente** *adv* normally

**normativa** [norma'tiβa] *nf* (set of) rules *pl*, regulations *pl*

**noroeste** [noro'este] *adj* north-west, north-western, north-westerly ⊳ *nm* north-west

**norte** ['norte] *adj* north, northern, northerly ⊳ *nm* north; *(fig)* guide

**norteamericano, -a** [norteameri'kano, a] *adj, nm/f* (North) American

**Noruega** [no'rweɣa] *nf* Norway

**noruego, -a** [no'rweɣo, a] *adj, nm/f* Norwegian

**nos** [nos] *pron (directo)* us; *(indirecto)* us; to us; for us; from us; *(reflexivo)* (to) ourselves; *(recíproco)* (to) each other; **~ levantamos a las 7** we get up at 7

**nosotros, -as** [no'sotros, as] *pron (sujeto)* we; *(después de prep)* us

**nostalgia** [nos'talxja] *nf* nostalgia

**nota** ['nota] *nf* note; *(Escol)* mark

**notable** [no'taβle] *adj* notable; *(Escol)* outstanding

**notar** [no'tar] *vt* to notice, note; **notarse** *vr* to be obvious; **se nota que ...** one observes that ...

**notario** [no'tarjo] *nm* notary

**noticia** [no'tiθja] *nf (información)* piece of news; **las ~s** the news *sg*; **tener ~s de algn** to hear from sb

> No confundir **noticia** con la palabra inglesa *notice*.

**noticiero** [noti'θjero] (LAM) *nm* news bulletin

**notificar** [notifi'kar] *vt* to notify, inform

**notorio, -a** [no'torjo, a] *adj (público)* well-known; *(evidente)* obvious

**novato, -a** [no'βato, a] *adj* inexperienced ⊳ *nm/f* beginner, novice

**novecientos, -as** [noβe'θjentos, as] *num* nine hundred

**novedad** [noβe'ðað] *nf (calidad de nuevo)* newness; *(noticia)* piece of news; *(cambio)* change, (new) development

**novel** [no'βel] *adj* new; *(inexperto)* inexperienced ⊳ *nmf* beginner

**novela** [no'βela] *nf* novel

**noveno, -a** [no'βeno, a] *adj* ninth

**noventa** [no'βenta] *num* ninety

**novia** *nf* V **novio**

**novicio, -a** [no'βiθjo, a] *nm/f* novice

**noviembre** [no'βjembre] *nm* November

**novillada** [noβi'ʎaða] *nf (Taur)* bullfight with young bulls; **novillero** *nm* novice bullfighter; **novillo** *nm* young bull, bullock; **hacer novillos** *(fam)* to play truant

**novio, -a** ['noβjo, a] *nm/f* boyfriend/girlfriend; *(prometido)* fiancé/fiancée; *(recién casado)* bridegroom/bride; **los ~s** the newly-weds

**nube** ['nuβe] *nf* cloud

**nublado, -a** [nu'βlaðo, a] *adj* cloudy; **nublarse** *vr* to grow dark

**nubosidad** [nuβosi'ðað] *nf* cloudiness;

**había mucha ~** it was very cloudy

**nuca** ['nuka] *nf* nape of the neck

**nuclear** [nukle'ar] *adj* nuclear

**núcleo** ['nukleo] *nm* (*centro*) core; (*Física*) nucleus; **núcleo urbano** city centre

**nudillo** [nu'ðiʎo] *nm* knuckle

**nudista** [nu'ðista] *adj* nudist

**nudo** ['nuðo] *nm* knot; (*de carreteras*) junction

**nuera** ['nwera] *nf* daughter-in-law

**nuestro, -a** ['nwestro, a] *adj pos* our ▷ *pron* ours; **~ padre** our father; **un amigo ~** a friend of ours; **es el ~** it's ours

**Nueva York** [-jɔrk] *n* New York

**Nueva Zelanda** [-θe'landa] *nf* New Zealand

**nueve** ['nweβe] *num* nine

**nuevo, -a** ['nweβo, a] *adj* (*gen*) new; **de ~** again

**nuez** [nweθ] *nf* walnut; (*Anat*) Adam's apple; **nuez moscada** nutmeg

**nulo, -a** ['nulo, a] *adj* (*inepto, torpe*) useless; (*inválido*) (null and) void; (*Deporte*) drawn, tied

**núm.** *abr* (= *número*) no.

**numerar** [nume'rar] *vt* to number

**número** ['numero] *nm* (*gen*) number; (*tamaño: de zapato*) size; (*ejemplar: de diario*) number, issue; **sin ~** numberless, unnumbered; **número atrasado** back number; **número de matrícula/teléfono** registration/telephone number; **número impar/par** odd/even number; **número romano** Roman numeral

**numeroso, -a** [nume'roso, a] *adj* numerous

**nunca** ['nunka] *adv* (*jamás*) never; **~ lo pensé** I never thought it; **no viene ~** he never comes; **~ más** never again; **más que ~** more than ever

**nupcias** ['nupθjas] *nfpl* wedding *sg*, nuptials

**nutria** ['nutrja] *nf* otter

**nutrición** [nutri'θjon] *nf* nutrition

**nutrir** [nu'trir] *vt* (*alimentar*) to nourish; (*dar de comer*) to feed; (*fig*) to strengthen; **nutritivo, -a** *adj* nourishing, nutritious

**nylon** [ni'lon] *nm* nylon

**ñango, -a** ['ɲango, a] (*MÉX*) *adj* puny

**ñapa** ['ɲapa] (*LAM*) *nf* extra

**ñata** ['ɲata] (*LAM: fam*) *nf* nose; V *tb* **ñato**

**ñato, -a** ['ɲato, a] (*LAM*) *adj* snub-nosed

**ñoñería** [ɲoɲe'ria] *nf* insipidness

**ñoño, -a** ['ɲoɲo, a] *adj* (*fam: tonto*) silly, stupid; (*soso*) insipid; (*persona*) spineless; (*ESP: película, novela*) sentimental

# O

**O** *abr* (= *oeste*) W

**o** [o] *conj* or

**oasis** [o'asis] *nm inv* oasis

**obcecarse** [oβθe'karse] *vr* to get o become stubborn

**obedecer** [oβeðe'θer] *vt* to obey; **obediente** *adj* obedient

**obertura** [oβer'tura] *nf* overture

**obeso, -a** [o'βeso, a] *adj* obese

**obispo** [o'βispo] *nm* bishop

**obituario** [oβi'twarjo] (*LAM*) *nm* obituary

**objetar** [oβxe'tar] *vt, vi* to object

**objetivo, -a** [oβxe'tiβo, a] *adj, nm* objective

**objeto** [oβ'xeto] *nm* (*cosa*) object; (*fin*) aim

**objetor, a** [oβxe'tor, a] *nm/f* objector

**obligación** [oβliɣa'θjon] *nf* obligation; (*Com*) bond

**obligar** [oβli'ɣar] *vt* to force; **obligarse** *vr* to bind o.s.; **obligatorio, -a** *adj* compulsory, obligatory

**oboe** [o'βoe] *nm* oboe

**obra** [o'βra] *nf* work; (*Arq*) construction, building; (*Teatro*) play; **por ~ de** thanks to (the efforts of); **obra maestra** masterpiece; **obras públicas** public works; **obrar** *vt* to work; (*tener efecto*) to have an effect on ▷ *vi* to act, behave; (*tener efecto*) to have an effect; **la carta obra en su poder** the letter is in his/her possession

**obrero, -a** [o'βrero, a] *adj* (*clase*) working; (*movimiento*) labour *cpd* ▷ *nm/f* (*gen*) worker; (*sin oficio*) labourer

**obsceno, -a** [oβs'θeno, a] *adj* obscene

**obscu...** = **oscu...**

**obsequiar** [oβse'kjar] *vt* (*ofrecer*) to present with; (*agasajar*) to make a fuss of, lavish attention on; **obsequio** *nm* (*regalo*) gift; (*cortesía*) courtesy, attention

**observación** [oβserβa'θjon] *nf* observation; (*reflexión*) remark

**observador, a** [oβserβa'ðor, a] *nm/f* observer

**observar** [oβser'βar] *vt* to observe; (*anotar*) to notice; **observarse** *vr* to keep to, observe

**obsesión** [oβse'sjon] *nf* obsession; **obsesivo, -a** *adj* obsessive

**obstáculo** [oβs'takulo] *nm* obstacle; (*impedimento*) hindrance, drawback

**obstante** [oβs'tante]: **no ~** *adv* nevertheless

**obstinado, -a** [oβsti'naðo, a] *adj* obstinate, stubborn

**obstinarse** [oβsti'narse] *vr* to be obstinate; **~ en** to persist in

**obstruir** [oβstru'ir] *vt* to obstruct

**obtener** [oβte'ner] *vt* (*gen*) to obtain; (*premio*) to win

**obturador** [oβtura'ðor] *nm* (*Foto*) shutter

**obvio, -a** ['oββjo, a] *adj* obvious

**oca** ['oka] *nf* (*animal*) goose; (*juego*) ≈ snakes and ladders

**ocasión** [oka'sjon] *nf* (*oportunidad*) opportunity, chance; (*momento*) occasion, time; (*causa*) cause; **de ~** secondhand; **ocasionar** *vt* to cause

**ocaso** [o'kaso] *nm* (*fig*) decline

**occidente** [okθi'ðente] *nm* west

**OCDE** *nf abr* (= *Organización de Cooperación y Desarrollo Económico*) OECD

**océano** [o'θeano] *nm* ocean; **Océano índico** Indian Ocean

**ochenta** [o'tʃenta] *num* eighty

**ocho** ['otʃo] *num* eight; **dentro de ~ días** within a week

**ocio** ['oθjo] *nm* (*tiempo*) leisure; (*pey*) idleness

**octavilla** [okta'βiʎa] *nf* leaflet, pamphlet

**octavo, -a** [ok'taβo, a] *adj* eighth

**octubre** [ok'tuβre] *nm* October

**oculista** [oku'lista] *nmf* oculist

**ocultar** [okul'tar] *vt* (*esconder*) to hide; (*callar*) to conceal; **oculto, -a** *adj* hidden; (*fig*) secret

**ocupación** [okupa'θjon] *nf* occupation

**ocupado, -a** [oku'paðo, a] *adj* (*persona*) busy; (*plaza*) occupied, taken; (*teléfono*) engaged; **ocupar** *vt* (*gen*) to occupy; **ocuparse** *vr*: **ocuparse de o en** (*gen*) to concern o.s. with; (*cuidar*) to look after

**ocurrencia** [oku'rrenθja] *nf* (*idea*) bright idea

**ocurrir** [oku'rrir] *vi* to happen; **ocurrirse** *vr*: **se me ocurrió que ...** it occurred to me that ...

**odiar** [o'ðjar] *vt* to hate; **odio** *nm* hate, hatred; **odioso, -a** *adj* (*gen*) hateful; (*malo*) nasty

**odontólogo, -a** [oðon'toloɣo, a] nm/f dentist, dental surgeon

**oeste** [o'este] nm west; **una película del ~** a western

**ofender** [ofen'der] vt (agraviar) to offend; (insultar) to insult; **ofenderse** vr to take offence; **ofensa** nf offence; **ofensiva** nf offensive; **ofensivo, -a** adj offensive

**oferta** [o'ferta] nf offer; (propuesta) proposal; **la ~ y la demanda** supply and demand; **artículos en ~** goods on offer

**oficial** [ofi'θjal] adj official ⊳ nm (Mil) officer

**oficina** [ofi'θina] nf office; **oficina de correos** post office; **oficina de información** information bureau; **oficina de turismo** tourist office; **oficinista** nmf clerk

**oficio** [o'fiθjo] nm (profesión) profession; (puesto) post; (Rel) service; **ser del ~** to be an old hand; **tener mucho ~** to have a lot of experience; **oficio de difuntos** funeral service

**ofimática** [ofi'matika] nf office automation

**ofrecer** [ofre'θer] vt (dar) to offer; (proponer) to propose; **ofrecerse** vr (persona) to offer o.s., volunteer; (situación) to present itself; **¿qué se le ofrece?, ¿se le ofrece algo?** what can I do for you?, can I get you anything?

**ofrecimiento** [ofreθi'mjento] nm offer

**oftalmólogo, -a** [oftal'moloɣo, a] nm/f ophthalmologist

**oída** [o'iða] nf: **de ~s** by hearsay

**oído** [o'iðo] nm (Anat) ear; (sentido) hearing

**oigo** etc vb V **oír**

**oír** [o'ir] vt (gen) to hear; (atender a) to listen to; **¡oiga!** listen!; **~ misa** to attend mass

**OIT** nf abr (= Organización Internacional del Trabajo) ILO

**ojal** [o'xal] nm buttonhole

**ojalá** [oxa'la] excl if only (it were so)!, some hope! ⊳ conj if only …!, would that …!; **~ (que) venga hoy** I hope he comes today

**ojeada** [oxe'aða] nf glance

**ojera** [o'xera] nf: **tener ~s** to have bags under one's eyes

**ojo** ['oxo] nm eye; (de puente) span; (de cerradura) keyhole ⊳ excl careful!; **tener ~ para** to have an eye for; **ojo de buey** porthole

**okey** ['okei] (LAM) excl O.K.

**okupa** [o'kupa] (ESP: fam) nmf squatter

**ola** ['ola] nf wave

**olé** [o'le] excl bravo!, olé!

**oleada** [ole'aða] nf big wave, swell; (fig) wave

**oleaje** [ole'axe] nm swell

**óleo** ['oleo] nm oil; **oleoducto** nm (oil) pipeline

**oler** [o'ler] vt (gen) to smell; (inquirir) to pry into; (fig: sospechar) to sniff out ⊳ vi to smell; **~ a** to smell of

**olfatear** [olfate'ar] vt to smell; (inquirir) to pry into; **olfato** nm sense of smell

**olimpiada** [olim'piaða] nf: **las O~s** the Olympics; **olímpico, -a** [o'limpiko, a] adj Olympic

**oliva** [o'liβa] nf (aceituna) olive; **aceite de ~** olive oil; **olivo** nm olive tree

**olla** ['oʎa] nf pan; (comida) stew; **olla exprés** o **a presión** pressure cooker; **olla podrida** type of Spanish stew

**olmo** ['olmo] nm elm (tree)

**olor** [o'lor] nm smell; **oloroso, -a** adj scented

**olvidar** [olβi'ðar] vt to forget; (omitir) to omit; **olvidarse** vr (fig) to forget o.s.; **se me olvidó** I forgot

**olvido** [ol'βiðo] nm oblivion; (despiste) forgetfulness

**ombligo** [om'bliɣo] nm navel

**omelette** [ome'lete] (LAM) nf omelet(te)

**omisión** [omi'sjon] nf (abstención) omission; (descuido) neglect

**omiso, -a** [o'miso, a] adj: **hacer caso ~ de** to ignore, pass over

**omitir** [omi'tir] vt to omit

**omnipotente** [omnipo'tente] adj omnipotent

**omóplato** [o'moplato] nm shoulder blade

**OMS** nf abr (= Organización Mundial de la Salud) WHO

**once** ['onθe] num eleven; **onces** (CS) nfpl tea break sg

**onda** ['onda] nf wave; **onda corta/larga/media** short/long/medium wave; **ondear** vt, vi to wave; (tener ondas) to be wavy; (agua) to ripple

**ondulación** [ondula'θjon] nf undulation; **ondulado, -a** adj wavy

**ONG** nf abr (= organización no gubernamental) NGO

**ONU** ['onu] nf abr (= Organización de las Naciones Unidas) UNO

**opaco, -a** [o'pako, a] adj opaque

**opción** [op'θjon] nf (gen) option; (derecho) right, option

**OPEP** ['opep] nf abr (= Organización de Países Exportadores de Petróleo) OPEC

**ópera** ['opera] nf opera; **ópera bufa** o **cómica** comic opera

**operación** [opera'θjon] nf (gen) operation; (Com) transaction, deal

**operador, a** [opera'ðor, a] nm/f operator; (Cine: de proyección) projectionist; (: de rodaje) cameraman

**operar** [ope'rar] vt (*producir*) to produce, bring about; (*Med*) to operate on ▷ vi (*Com*) to operate, deal; **operarse** vr to occur; (*Med*) to have an operation

**opereta** [ope'reta] nf operetta

**opinar** [opi'nar] vt to think ▷ vi to give one's opinion; **opinión** nf (*creencia*) belief; (*criterio*) opinion

**opio** ['opjo] nm opium

**oponer** [opo'ner] vt (*resistencia*) to put up, offer; **oponerse** vr (*objetar*) to object; (*estar frente a frente*) to be opposed; (*dos personas*) to oppose each other; **~ A a B** to set A against B; **me opongo a pensar que ...** I refuse to believe o think that ...

**oportunidad** [oportuni'ðað] nf (*ocasión*) opportunity; (*posibilidad*) chance

**oportuno, -a** [opor'tuno, a] adj (*en su tiempo*) opportune, timely; (*respuesta*) suitable; **en el momento ~** at the right moment

**oposición** [oposi'θjon] nf opposition; **oposiciones** nfpl (*Escol*) public examinations

**opositor, a** [oposi'tor, a] nm/f (*adversario*) opponent; (*candidato*): **~ (a)** candidate (for)

**opresión** [opre'sjon] nf oppression; **opresor, a** nm/f oppressor

**oprimir** [opri'mir] vt to squeeze; (*fig*) to oppress

**optar** [op'tar] vi (*elegir*) to choose; **~ por** to opt for; **optativo, -a** adj optional

**óptico, -a** ['optiko, a] adj optic(al) ▷ nm/f optician; **óptica** nf optician's (shop); **desde esta óptica** from this point of view

**optimismo** [opti'mismo] nm optimism; **optimista** nmf optimist

**opuesto, -a** [o'pwesto, a] adj (*contrario*) opposite; (*antagónico*) opposing

**oración** [ora'θjon] nf (*Rel*) prayer; (*Ling*) sentence

**orador, a** [ora'ðor, a] nm/f (*conferenciante*) speaker, orator

**oral** [o'ral] adj oral

**orangután** [orangu'tan] nm orangutan

**orar** [o'rar] vi to pray

**oratoria** [ora'torja] nf oratory

**órbita** ['orβita] nf orbit

**orden** ['orðen] nm (*gen*) order ▷ nf (*gen*) order; (*Inform*) command; **en ~ de prioridad** in order of priority; **orden del día** agenda

**ordenado, -a** [orðe'naðo, a] adj (*metódico*) methodical; (*arreglado*) orderly

**ordenador** [orðena'ðor] nm computer; **ordenador central** mainframe computer

**ordenar** [orðe'nar] vt (*mandar*) to order; (*poner orden*) to put in order, arrange;

**ordenarse** vr (*Rel*) to be ordained

**ordeñar** [orðe'nar] vt to milk

**ordinario, -a** [orði'narjo, a] adj (*común*) ordinary, usual; (*vulgar*) vulgar, common

**orégano** [o'reɣano] nm oregano

**oreja** [o'rexa] nf ear; (*Mecánica*) lug, flange

**orfanato** [orfa'nato] nm orphanage

**orfebrería** [orfeβre'ria] nf gold/silver work

**orgánico, -a** [or'ɣaniko, a] adj organic

**organismo** [orɣa'nismo] nm (*Bio*) organism; (*Pol*) organization

**organización** [orɣaniθa'θjon] nf organization; **organizar** vt to organize

**órgano** ['orɣano] nm organ

**orgasmo** [or'ɣasmo] nm orgasm

**orgía** [or'xia] nf orgy

**orgullo** [or'ɣuʎo] nm pride; **orgulloso, -a** adj (*gen*) proud; (*altanero*) haughty

**orientación** [orjenta'θjon] nf (*posición*) position; (*dirección*) direction

**oriental** [orjen'tal] adj eastern; (*del Extremo Oriente*) oriental

**orientar** [orjen'tar] vt (*situar*) to orientate; (*señalar*) to point; (*dirigir*) to direct; (*guiar*) to guide; **orientarse** vr to get one's bearings

**oriente** [o'rjente] nm east; **el O~ Medio** the Middle East; **el Próximo/Extremo O~** the Near/Far East

**origen** [o'rixen] nm origin

**original** [orixi'nal] adj (*nuevo*) original; (*extraño*) odd, strange; **originalidad** nf originality

**originar** [orixi'nar] vt to start, cause; **originarse** vr to originate; **originario, -a** adj original; **originario de** native of

**orilla** [o'riʎa] nf (*borde*) border; (*de río*) bank; (*de bosque, tela*) edge; (*de mar*) shore

**orina** [o'rina] nf urine; **orinal** nm (chamber) pot; **orinar** vi to urinate; **orinarse** vr to wet o.s.

**oro** ['oro] nm gold; **oros** nmpl (*Naipes*) hearts

**orquesta** [or'kesta] nf orchestra; **orquesta sinfónica** symphony orchestra

**orquídea** [or'kiðea] nf orchid

**ortiga** [or'tiɣa] nf nettle

**ortodoxo, -a** [orto'ðokso, a] adj orthodox

**ortografía** [ortoɣra'fia] nf spelling

**ortopedia** [orto'peðja] nf orthopaedics sg; **ortopédico, -a** adj orthopaedic

**oruga** [o'ruɣa] nf caterpillar

**orzuelo** [or'θwelo] nm stye

**os** [os] pron (*gen*) you; (*a vosotros*) to you

**osa** ['osa] nf (she-)bear; **Osa Mayor/Menor** Great/Little Bear

**osadía** [osa'ðia] nf daring
**osar** [o'sar] vi to dare
**oscilación** [osθila'θjon] nf (movimiento) oscillation; (fluctuación) fluctuation
**oscilar** [osθi'lar] vi to oscillate; to fluctuate
**oscurecer** [oskure'θer] vt to darken ▷ vi to grow dark; **oscurecerse** vr to grow o get dark
**oscuridad** [oskuri'ðað] nf obscurity; (tinieblas) darkness
**oscuro, -a** [os'kuro, a] adj dark; (fig) obscure; **a oscuras** in the dark
**óseo, -a** ['oseo, a] adj bone cpd
**oso** ['oso] nm bear; **oso de peluche** teddy bear; **oso hormiguero** anteater
**ostentar** [osten'tar] vt (gen) to show; (pey) to flaunt, show off; (poseer) to have, possess
**ostión** [os'tjon] (MÉX) nm = **ostra**
**ostra** ['ostra] nf oyster
**OTAN** ['otan] nf abr (= Organización del Tratado del Atlántico Norte) NATO
**otitis** [o'titis] nf earache
**otoñal** [oto'ɲal] adj autumnal
**otoño** [o'toɲo] nm autumn
**otorgar** [otor'ɣar] vt (conceder) to concede; (dar) to grant
**otorrino, -a** [oto'rrino, a], **otorrinolaringólogo, -a** [otorrinolarin'ɣoloɣo, a] nm/f ear, nose and throat specialist

○ PALABRA CLAVE

**otro, -a** ['otro, a] adj 1 (distinto: sg) another; (: pl) other; **con otros amigos** with other o different friends
2 (adicional): **tráigame otro café (más), por favor** can I have another coffee please; **otros diez días más** another ten days
▷ pron 1 **el otro** the other one; **(los) otros** (the) others; **de otro** somebody else's; **que lo haga otro** let somebody else do it
2 (recíproco): **se odian (la) una a (la) otra** they hate one another o each other
3: **otro tanto: comer otro tanto** to eat the same o as much again; **recibió una decena de telegramas y otras tantas llamadas** he got about ten telegrams and as many calls

**ovación** [oβa'θjon] nf ovation
**oval** [o'βal] adj oval; **ovalado, -a** adj oval; **óvalo** nm oval
**ovario** [o'βario] nm ovary
**oveja** [o'βexa] nf sheep
**overol** [oβe'rol] (LAM) nm overalls pl
**ovillo** [o'βiʎo] nm (de lana) ball of wool
**OVNI** ['oβni] nm abr (= objeto volante no identificado) UFO
**ovulación** [oβula'θjon] nf ovulation; **óvulo** nm ovum
**oxidación** [oksiða'θjon] nf rusting
**oxidar** [oksi'ðar] vt to rust; **oxidarse** vr to go rusty
**óxido** ['oksiðo] nm oxide
**oxigenado, -a** [oksixe'naðo, a] adj (Quím) oxygenated; (pelo) bleached
**oxígeno** [ok'sixeno] nm oxygen
**oyente** [o'jente] nmf listener
**oyes** etc vb V **oír**
**ozono** [o'θono] nm ozone

# P

**pabellón** [paβe'ʎon] nm bell tent; (Arq) pavilion; (de hospital etc) block, section; (bandera) flag

**pacer** [pa'θer] vi to graze

**paciencia** [pa'θjenθja] nf patience

**paciente** [pa'θjente] adj, nmf patient

**pacificación** [paθifika'θjon] nf pacification

**pacífico, -a** [pa'θifiko, a] adj (persona) peaceable; (existencia) peaceful; **el (Océano) P~** the Pacific (Ocean)

**pacifista** [paθi'fista] nmf pacifist

**pacotilla** [pako'tiʎa] nf: **de ~** (actor, escritor) third-rate

**pactar** [pak'tar] vt to agree to o on ▷ vi to come to an agreement

**pacto** ['pakto] nm (tratado) pact; (acuerdo) agreement

**padecer** [paðe'θer] vt (sufrir) to suffer; (soportar) to endure, put up with; **padecimiento** nm suffering

**padrastro** [pa'ðrastro] nm stepfather

**padre** ['paðre] nm father ▷ adj (fam): **un éxito ~** a tremendous success; **padres** nmpl parents; **padre político** father-in-law

**padrino** [pa'ðrino] nm (Rel) godfather; (tb: **~ de boda**) best man; (fig) sponsor, patron; **padrinos** nmpl godparents

**padrón** [pa'ðron] nm (censo) census, roll

**padrote** [pa'ðrote] (MÉX: fam) nm pimp

**paella** [pa'eʎa] nf paella, dish of rice with meat, shellfish etc

**paga** ['paɣa] nf (pago) payment; (sueldo) pay, wages pl

**pagano, -a** [pa'ɣano, a] adj, nm/f pagan, heathen

**pagar** [pa'ɣar] vt to pay; (las compras, crimen) to pay for; (fig: favor) to repay ▷ vi to pay; **~ al contado/a plazos** to pay (in) cash/in instalments

**pagaré** [paɣa're] nm I.O.U.

**página** ['paxina] nf page; **página de inicio** (Inform) home page; **página web** (Inform) web page

**pago** ['paɣo] nm (dinero) payment; **en ~ de** in return for; **pago anticipado/a cuenta/ contra reembolso/en especie** advance payment/payment on account/cash on delivery/payment in kind

**pág(s).** abr (= página(s)) p(p).

**pague** etc vb V **pagar**

**país** [pa'is] nm (gen) country; (región) land; **los P~es Bajos** the Low Countries; **el P~ Vasco** the Basque Country

**paisaje** [pai'saxe] nm landscape, scenery

**paisano, -a** [pai'sano, a] adj of the same country ▷ nm/f (compatriota) fellow countryman/woman; **vestir de ~** (soldado) to be in civvies; (guardia) to be in plain clothes

**paja** ['paxa] nf straw; (fig) rubbish (BRIT), trash (US)

**pajarita** [paxa'rita] nf (corbata) bow tie

**pájaro** ['paxaro] nm bird; **pájaro carpintero** woodpecker

**pajita** [pa'xita] nf (drinking) straw

**pala** ['pala] nf spade, shovel; (raqueta etc) bat; (: de tenis) racquet; (Culin) slice; **pala mecánica** power shovel

**palabra** [pa'laβra] nf word; (facultad) (power of) speech; (derecho de hablar) right to speak; **tomar la ~** (en mitin) to take the floor

**palabrota** [pala'βrota] nf swearword

**palacio** [pa'laθjo] nm palace; (mansión) mansion, large house; **palacio de justicia** courthouse; **palacio municipal** town o city hall

**paladar** [pala'ðar] nm palate; **paladear** vt to taste

**palanca** [pa'lanka] nf lever; (fig) pull, influence

**palangana** [palan'gana] nf washbasin

**palco** ['palko] nm box

**Palestina** [pales'tina] nf Palestine; **palestino, -a** nm/f Palestinian

**paleta** [pa'leta] nf (de pintor) palette; (de albañil) trowel; (de ping-pong) bat; (MÉX, CAM: helado) ice lolly (BRIT), Popsicle® (US)

**palidecer** [paliðe'θer] vi to turn pale; **palidez** nf paleness; **pálido, -a** adj pale

**palillo** [pa'liʎo] nm (mondadientes) toothpick; (para comer) chopstick

**palito** [pa'lito] (RPL) nm (helado) ice lolly (BRIT), Popsicle® (US)

**paliza** [pa'liθa] nf beating, thrashing

**palma** ['palma] nf (Anat) palm; (árbol) palm tree; **batir o dar ~s** to clap, applaud; **palmada** nf slap; **palmadas** nfpl clapping *sg*, applause *sg*

**palmar** [pal'mar] (*fam*) *vi* (*tb*: **~la**) to die, kick the bucket

**palmear** [palme'ar] *vi* to clap

**palmera** [pal'mera] *nf* (*Bot*) palm tree

**palmo** ['palmo] *nm* (*medida*) span; (*fig*) small amount; **~ a ~** inch by inch

**palo** ['palo] *nm* stick; (*poste*) post; (*de tienda de campaña*) pole; (*mango*) handle, shaft; (*golpe*) blow, hit; (*de golf*) club; (*de béisbol*) bat; (*Náut*) mast; (*Naipes*) suit

**paloma** [pa'loma] *nf* dove, pigeon

**palomitas** [palo'mitas] *nfpl* popcorn *sg*

**palpar** [pal'par] *vt* to touch, feel

**palpitar** [palpi'tar] *vi* to palpitate; (*latir*) to beat

**palta** ['palta] (*CS*) *nf* avocado

**paludismo** [palu'ðismo] *nm* malaria

**pamela** [pa'mela] *nf* picture hat, sun hat

**pampa** ['pampa] *nf* pampas, prairie

**pan** [pan] *nm* bread; (*una barra*) loaf; **pan integral** wholemeal (*BRIT*) o wholewheat (*US*) bread; **pan rallado** breadcrumbs *pl*; **pan tostado** (*MÉX: tostada*) toast

**pana** ['pana] *nf* corduroy

**panadería** [panaðe'ria] *nf* baker's (shop); **panadero, -a** *nm/f* baker

**Panamá** [pana'ma] *nm* Panama; **panameño, -a** *adj* Panamanian

**pancarta** [pan'karta] *nf* placard, banner

**panceta** [pan'θeta] (*ESP, RPL*) *nf* bacon

**pancho** ['pantʃo] (*RPL*) *nm* hot dog

**pancito** [pan'θito] *nm* (bread) roll

**panda** ['panda] *nm* (*Zool*) panda

**pandereta** [pande'reta] *nf* tambourine

**pandilla** [pan'diʎa] *nf* set, group; (*de criminales*) gang; (*pey: camarilla*) clique

**panecillo** [pane'θiʎo] (*ESP*) *nm* (bread) roll

**panel** [pa'nel] *nm* panel; **panel solar** solar panel

**panfleto** [pan'fleto] *nm* pamphlet

**pánico** ['paniko] *nm* panic

**panorama** [pano'rama] *nm* panorama; (*vista*) view

**panqueque** [pan'keke] (*LAM*) *nm* pancake

**pantalla** [pan'taʎa] *nf* (*de cine*) screen; (*de lámpara*) lampshade

**pantalón** [panta'lon] *nm* trousers; **pantalones** *nmpl* trousers; **pantalones cortes** shorts

**pantano** [pan'tano] *nm* (*ciénaga*) marsh, swamp; (*depósito: de agua*) reservoir; (*fig*) jam, difficulty

**panteón** [pante'on] *nm* (*monumento*) pantheon

**pantera** [pan'tera] *nf* panther

**pantimedias** [panti'meðjas] (*MÉX*) *nfpl*

= **pantis**

**pantis** ['pantis] *nmpl* tights (*BRIT*), pantyhose (*US*)

**pantomima** [panto'mima] *nf* pantomime

**pantorrilla** [panto'rriʎa] *nf* calf (of the leg)

**pants** [pants] (*MÉX*) *nmpl* tracksuit (*BRIT*), sweat suit (*US*)

**pantufla** [pan'tufla] *nf* slipper

**panty(s)** ['panti(s)] *nm(pl)* tights (*BRIT*), pantyhose (*US*)

**panza** ['panθa] *nf* belly, paunch

**pañal** [pa'ɲal] *nm* nappy (*BRIT*), diaper (*US*); **pañales** *nmpl* (*fig*) early stages, infancy *sg*

**paño** ['paɲo] *nm* (*tela*) cloth; (*pedazo de tela*) (piece of) cloth; (*trapo*) duster, rag; **paños menores** underclothes

**pañuelo** [pa'ɲwelo] *nm* handkerchief, hanky; (*fam: para la cabeza*) (head)scarf

**papa** ['papa] *nm*: **el P~** the Pope ▷ *nf* (*LAM: patata*) potato; **papas fritas** (*LAM*) French fries, chips (*BRIT*); (*de bolsa*) crisps (*BRIT*), potato chips (*US*)

**papá** [pa'pa] (*fam*) *nm* dad(dy), pa (*US*)

**papada** [pa'paða] *nf* double chin

**papagayo** [papa'xajo] *nm* parrot

**papalote** [papa'lote] (*MÉX, CAM*) *nm* kite

**papanatas** [papa'natas] (*fam*) *nm inv* simpleton

**papaya** [pa'paja] *nf* papaya

**papear** [pape'ar] (*fam*) *vt, vi* to scoff

**papel** [pa'pel] *nm* paper; (*hoja de papel*) sheet of paper; (*Teatro: fig*) role; **papel de aluminio** aluminium (*BRIT*) o aluminum (*US*) foil; **papel de arroz/envolver/fumar** rice/wrapping/cigarette paper; **papel de estaño** o **plata** tinfoil; **papel de lija** sandpaper; **papel higiénico** toilet paper; **papel moneda** paper money; **papel secante** blotting paper

**papeleo** [pape'leo] *nm* red tape

**papelera** [pape'lera] *nf* wastepaper basket; (*en la calle*) litter bin; **papelera (de reciclaje)** (*Inform*) wastebasket

**papelería** [papele'ria] *nf* stationer's (shop)

**papeleta** [pape'leta] (*ESP*) *nf* (*Pol*) ballot paper

**paperas** [pa'peras] *nfpl* mumps *sg*

**papilla** [pa'piʎa] *nf* (*de bebé*) baby food

**paquete** [pa'kete] *nm* (*de cigarrillos etc*) packet; (*Correos etc*) parcel

**par** [par] *adj* (*igual*) like, equal; (*Mat*) even ▷ *nm* equal; (*de guantes*) pair; (*de veces*) couple; (*Pol*) peer; (*Golf, Com*) par; **abrir de ~ en ~** to open wide

**para** ['para] prep for; **no es ~ comer** it's not for eating; **decir ~ sí** to say to o.s.; **¿~ qué lo quieres?** what do you want it for?; **se casaron ~ separarse otra vez** they married only to separate again; **lo tendré ~ mañana** I'll have it (for) tomorrow; **ir ~ casa** to go home, head for home; **~ profesor es muy estúpido** he's very stupid for a teacher; **¿quién es usted ~ gritar así?** who are you to shout like that?; **tengo bastante ~ vivir** I have enough to live on; V tb **con**

**parabién** [para'βjen] nm congratulations pl

**parábola** [pa'raβola] nf parable; (Mat) parabola; **parabólica** nf (tb: **antena parabólica**) satellite dish

**parabrisas** [para'βrisas] nm inv windscreen (BRIT), windshield (US)

**paracaídas** [paraka'iðas] nm inv parachute; **paracaidista** nmf parachutist; (Mil) paratrooper

**parachoques** [para'tʃokes] nm inv (Auto) bumper; (Mecánica etc) shock absorber

**parada** [pa'raða] nf stop; (acto) stopping; (de industria) shutdown, stoppage; (lugar) stopping place; **parada de autobús** bus stop; **parada de taxis** taxi stand o rank (BRIT)

**paradero** [para'ðero] nm stopping-place; (situación) whereabouts

**parado, -a** [pa'raðo, a] adj (persona) motionless, standing still; (fábrica) closed, at a standstill; (coche) stopped; (LAM: de pie) standing (up); (ESP: sin empleo) unemployed, idle

**paradoja** [para'ðoxa] nf paradox

**parador** [para'ðor] nm parador, state-run hotel

**paragolpes** [para'golpes] (RPL) nm inv (Auto) bumper, fender (US)

**paraguas** [pa'raɣwas] nm inv umbrella

**Paraguay** [paraɣ'wai] nm Paraguay; **paraguayo, -a** adj, nm/f Paraguayan

**paraíso** [para'iso] nm paradise, heaven

**paraje** [pa'raxe] nm place, spot

**paralelo, -a** [para'lelo, a] adj parallel

**parálisis** [pa'ralisis] nf inv paralysis; **paralítico, -a** adj, nm/f paralytic

**paralizar** [parali'θar] vt to paralyse; **paralizarse** vr to become paralysed; (fig) to come to a standstill

**páramo** ['paramo] nm bleak plateau

**paranoico, -a** [para'noiko, a] nm/f paranoiac

**parapente** [para'pente] nm (deporte) paragliding; (aparato) paraglider

**parapléjico, -a** [para'plexiko, a] adj, nm/f paraplegic

**parar** [pa'rar] vt to stop; (golpe) to ward off ▷ vi to stop; **pararse** vr to stop; (LAM: ponerse de pie) to stand up; **ha parado de llover** it has stopped raining; **van a ir a ~ a comisaría** they're going to end up in the police station; **~se en** to pay attention to

**pararrayos** [para'rrajos] nm inv lightning conductor

**parásito, -a** [pa'rasito, a] nm/f parasite

**parcela** [par'θela] nf plot, piece of ground

**parche** ['partʃe] nm (gen) patch

**parchís** [par'tʃis] nm ludo

**parcial** [par'θjal] adj (pago) part-; (eclipse) partial; (Jur) prejudiced, biased; (Pol) partisan

**parecer** [pare'θer] nm (opinión) opinion, view; (aspecto) looks pl ▷ vi (tener apariencia) to seem, look; (asemejarse) to look o seem like; (aparecer, llegar) to appear; **parecerse** vr to look alike, resemble each other; **al ~** apparently; **según parece** evidently, apparently; **~se a** to look like, resemble; **me parece que** I think (that), it seems to me that

**parecido, -a** [pare'θiðo, a] adj similar ▷ nm similarity, likeness, resemblance; **bien ~** good-looking, nice-looking

**pared** [pa'reð] nf wall

**pareja** [pa'rexa] nf (par) pair; (dos personas) couple; (otro: de un par) other one (of a pair); (persona) partner

**parentesco** [paren'tesko] nm relationship

**paréntesis** [pa'rentesis] nm inv parenthesis; (en escrito) bracket

**parezco** etc vb V **parecer**

**pariente** [pa'rjente] nmf relative, relation
▌ No confundir **pariente** con la palabra inglesa parent.

**parir** [pa'rir] vt to give birth to ▷ vi (mujer) to give birth, have a baby

**París** [pa'ris] n Paris

**parka** ['parka] (LAM) nf anorak

**parking** ['parkin] nm car park (BRIT), parking lot (US)

**parlamentar** [parlamen'tar] vi to parley

**parlamentario, -a** [parlamen'tarjo, a] adj parliamentary ▷ nm/f member of parliament

**parlamento** [parla'mento] nm parliament

**parlanchín, -ina** [parlan'tʃin, ina] adj indiscreet ▷ nm/f chatterbox

**parlar** [par'lar] vi to chatter (away)

**paro** ['paro] nm (huelga) stoppage (of work), strike; (ESP: desempleo) unemployment; (: subsidio) unemployment benefit; **estar en ~** (ESP) to be unemployed;

**paro cardíaco** cardiac arrest
**parodia** [pa'roðja] nf parody; **parodiar**
vt to parody
**parpadear** [parpaðe'ar] vi (ojos) to blink;
(luz) to flicker
**párpado** ['parpaðo] nm eyelid
**parque** ['parke] nm (lugar verde) park;
(MÉX: munición) ammunition; **parque
de atracciones** fairground; **parque de
bomberos** (ESP) fire station; **parque
infantil/temático/zoológico** playground/
theme park/zoo
**parqué** [par'ke] nm parquet (flooring)
**parquímetro** [par'kimetro] nm parking
meter
**parra** ['parra] nf (grape)vine
**párrafo** ['parrafo] nm paragraph; **echar
un ~** (fam) to have a chat
**parranda** [pa'rranda] (fam) nf spree,
binge
**parrilla** [pa'rriʎa] nf (Culin) grill; (de coche)
grille; **(carne a la) ~** barbecue; **parrillada**
nf barbecue
**párroco** ['parroko] nm parish priest
**parroquia** [pa'rrokja] nf parish; (iglesia)
parish church; (Com) clientele, customers pl;
**parroquiano, -a** nm/f parishioner; (Com)
client, customer
**parte** ['parte] nm message; (informe)
report ▷ nf part; (lado, cara) side; (de reparto)
share; (Jur) party; **en alguna ~ de Europa**
somewhere in Europe; **en o por todas ~s**
everywhere; **en gran ~** to a large extent; **la
mayor ~ de los españoles** most Spaniards;
**de un tiempo a esta ~** for some time past;
**de ~ de algn** on sb's behalf; **¿de ~ de quién?**
(Tel) who is speaking?; **por ~ de** on the part
of; **yo por mi ~** I for my part; **por otra ~** on
the other hand; **dar ~** to inform; **tomar ~** to
take part; **parte meteorológico** weather
forecast o report
**participación** [partiθipa'θjon] nf (acto)
participation, taking part; (parte, Com)
share; (de lotería) shared prize; (aviso) notice,
notification
**participante** [partiθi'pante] nmf
participant
**participar** [partiθi'par] vt to notify,
inform ▷ vi to take part, participate
**partícipe** [par'tiθipe] nmf participant
**particular** [partiku'lar] adj (especial)
particular, special; (individual, personal)
private, personal ▷ nm (punto, asunto)
particular, point; (individuo) individual;
**tiene coche ~** he has a car of his own
**partida** [par'tiða] nf (salida) departure;
(Com) entry, item; (juego) game; (grupo de
personas) band, group; **mala ~** dirty trick;

**partida de nacimiento/matrimonio/
defunción** (ESP) birth/marriage/death
certificate
**partidario, -a** [parti'ðarjo, a] adj
partisan ▷ nm/f supporter, follower
**partido** [par'tiðo] nm (Pol) party; (Deporte)
game, match; **sacar ~ de** to profit o benefit
from; **tomar ~** to take sides
**partir** [par'tir] vt (dividir) to split, divide;
(compartir, distribuir) to share (out),
distribute; (romper) to break open, split
open; (rebanada) to cut (off) ▷ vi (ponerse en
camino) to set off o out; (comenzar) to start
(off o out); **partirse** vr to crack o split o
break (in two etc); **a ~ de** (starting) from
**partitura** [parti'tura] nf (Mús) score
**parto** ['parto] nm birth; (fig) product,
creation; **estar de ~** to be in labour
**parvulario** [parβu'larjo] (ESP) nm
nursery school, kindergarten
**pasa** ['pasa] nf raisin; **pasa de Corinto**
currant
**pasacintas** [pasa'θintas] (LAM) nm
cassette player
**pasada** [pa'saða] nf passing, passage;
**de ~** in passing, incidentally; **una mala ~** a
dirty trick
**pasadizo** [pasa'ðiθo] nm (pasillo) passage,
corridor; (callejuela) alley
**pasado, -a** [pa'saðo, a] adj past;
(malo: comida, fruta) bad; (muy cocido)
overdone; (anticuado) out of date ▷ nm past;
**~ mañana** the day after tomorrow; **el mes
~** last month
**pasador** [pasa'ðor] nm (cerrojo) bolt; (de
pelo) hair slide; (horquilla) grip
**pasaje** [pa'saxe] nm passage; (pago de
viaje) fare; (los pasajeros) passengers pl;
(pasillo) passageway
**pasajero, -a** [pasa'xero, a] adj passing;
(situación, estado) temporary; (amor,
enfermedad) brief ▷ nm/f passenger
**pasamontañas** [pasamon'taɲas] nm inv
balaclava helmet
**pasaporte** [pasa'porte] nm passport
**pasar** [pa'sar] vt to pass; (tiempo) to spend;
(desgracias) to suffer, endure; (noticia) to
give, pass on; (río) to cross; (barrera) to
pass through; (falta) to overlook, tolerate;
(contrincante) to surpass, do better than;
(coche) to overtake; (Cine) to show;
(enfermedad) to give, infect with ▷ vi (gen)
to pass; (terminarse) to be over; (ocurrir) to
happen; **pasarse** vr (flores) to fade; (comida)
to go bad o off; (fig) to overdo it, go too far;
**~ de** to go beyond, exceed; **~ por** (LAM) to
fetch; **~lo bien/mal** to have a good/bad
time; **¡pase!** come in!; **hacer ~** to show in;

**lo que pasa es que ...** the thing is ...; **~se al enemigo** to go over to the enemy; **se me pasó** I forgot; **no se le pasa nada** he misses nothing; **pase lo que pase** come what may; **¿qué pasa?** what's going on?, what's up?; **¿qué te pasa?** what's wrong?

**pasarela** [pasa'rela] nf footbridge; (en barco) gangway

**pasatiempo** [pasa'tjempo] nm pastime, hobby

**Pascua** ['paskwa] nf (en Semana Santa) Easter; **Pascuas** nfpl Christmas (time); **¡felices ~s!** Merry Christmas!

**pase** ['pase] nm pass; (Cine) performance, showing

**pasear** [pase'ar] vt to take for a walk; (exhibir) to parade, show off ▷ vi to walk, go for a walk; **pasearse** vr to walk, go for a walk; **~ en coche** to go for a drive; **paseo** nm (avenida) avenue; (distancia corta) walk, stroll; **dar un** o **ir de paseo** to go for a walk; **paseo marítimo** (ESP) promenade

**pasillo** [pa'siʎo] nm passage, corridor

**pasión** [pa'sjon] nf passion

**pasivo, -a** [pa'siβo, a] adj passive; (inactivo) inactive ▷ nm (Com) liabilities pl, debts pl

**pasmoso, -a** [pas'moso, a] adj amazing, astonishing

**paso, -a** ['paso, a] adj dried ▷ nm step; (modo de andar) walk; (huella) footprint; (rapidez) speed, pace, rate; (camino accesible) way through, passage; (cruce) crossing; (pasaje) passing, passage; (Geo) pass; (estrecho) strait; (fig) at that rate; **salir al ~ de** o **a** to waylay; **estar de ~** to be passing through; **prohibido el ~** no entry; **ceda el ~** give way; **paso a nivel** (Ferro) level-crossing; **paso (de) cebra** (ESP) zebra crossing; **paso de peatones** pedestrian crossing; **paso elevado** flyover

**pasota** [pa'sota] (ESP: fam) adj, nmf = dropout; **ser un ~** to be a bit of a dropout; (ser indiferente) not to care about anything

**pasta** ['pasta] nf paste; (Culin: masa) dough; (: de bizcochos etc) pastry; (fam) dough; **pastas** nfpl (bizcochos) pastries, small cakes; (fideos, espaguetis etc) pasta; **pasta dentífrica** o **de dientes** toothpaste

**pastar** [pas'tar] vt, vi to graze

**pastel** [pas'tel] nm (dulce) cake; (Arte) pastel; **pastel de carne** meat pie; **pastelería** nf cake shop

**pastilla** [pas'tiʎa] nf (de jabón, chocolate) bar; (píldora) tablet, pill

**pasto** ['pasto] nm (hierba) grass; (lugar) pasture, field; **pastor, a** [pas'tor, a] nm/f shepherd/ess ▷ nm (Rel) clergyman, pastor;

**pastor alemán** Alsatian

**pata** ['pata] nf (pierna) leg; (pie) foot; (de muebles) leg; **~s arriba** upside down; **metedura de ~** (fam) gaffe; **meter la ~** (fam) to put one's foot in it; **tener buena/mala ~** to be lucky/unlucky; **pata de cabra** (Tec) crowbar; **patada** nf kick; (en el suelo) stamp

**patata** [pa'tata] nf potato; **patatas fritas** chips, French fries; (de bolsa) crisps

**paté** [pa'te] nm pâté

**patente** [pa'tente] adj obvious, evident; (Com) patent ▷ nf patent

**paternal** [pater'nal] adj fatherly, paternal; **paterno, -a** adj paternal

**patético, -a** [pa'tetiko, a] adj pathetic, moving

**patilla** [pa'tiʎa] nf (de gafas) side(piece); **patillas** nfpl sideburns

**patín** [pa'tin] nm skate; (de trineo) runner; **patín de ruedas** roller skate; **patinaje** nm skating; **patinar** vi to skate; (resbalarse) to skid, slip; (fam) to slip up, blunder

**patineta** [pati'neta] nf (MÉX: patinete) scooter; (cs: monopatín) skateboard

**patinete** [pati'nete] nm scooter

**patio** ['patjo] nm (de casa) patio, courtyard; **patio de recreo** playground

**pato** ['pato] nm duck; **pagar el ~** (fam) to take the blame, carry the can

**patoso, -a** [pa'toso, a] (fam) adj clumsy

**patotero** [pato'tero] (cs) nm hooligan, lout

**patraña** [pa'traɲa] nf story, fib

**patria** ['patrja] nf native land, mother country

**patrimonio** [patri'monjo] nm inheritance; (fig) heritage

**patriota** [pa'trjota] nmf patriot

**patrocinar** [patroθi'nar] vt to sponsor

**patrón, -ona** [pa'tron, ona] nm/f (jefe) boss, chief, master(mistress); (propietario) landlord/lady; (Rel) patron saint ▷ nm (Tec, Costura) pattern

**patronato** [patro'nato] nm sponsorship; (acto) patronage; (fundación benéfica) trust, foundation

**patrulla** [pa'truʎa] nf patrol

**pausa** ['pausa] nf pause, break

**pauta** ['pauta] nf line, guide line

**pava** ['paβa] (RPL) nf kettle

**pavimento** [paβi'mento] nm (de losa) pavement, paving

**pavo** ['paβo] nm turkey; **pavo real** peacock

**payaso, -a** [pa'jaso, a] nm/f clown

**payo, -a** ['pajo, a] nm/f non-gipsy

**paz** [paθ] nf peace; (tranquilidad) peacefulness, tranquillity; **hacer las paces** to make peace; (fig) to make up; **¡déjame en**

**~!** leave me alone!

**PC** nm PC, personal computer

**P.D.** abr (= posdata) P.S., p.s.

**peaje** [pe'axe] nm toll

**peatón** [pea'ton] nm pedestrian; **peatonal** adj pedestrian

**peca** ['peka] nf freckle

**pecado** [pe'kaðo] nm sin; **pecador, a** adj sinful ▷ nm/f sinner

**pecaminoso, -a** [pekami'noso, a] adj sinful

**pecar** [pe'kar] vi (Rel) to sin; **peca de generoso** he is generous to a fault

**pecera** [pe'θera] nf fish tank; (redonda) goldfish bowl

**pecho** ['petʃo] nm (Anat) chest; (de mujer) breast; **dar el ~ a** to breast-feed; **tomar algo a ~** to take sth to heart

**pechuga** [pe'tʃuxa] nf breast

**peculiar** [peku'ljar] adj special, peculiar; (característico) typical, characteristic

**pedal** [pe'ðal] nm pedal; **pedalear** vi to pedal

**pedante** [pe'ðante] adj pedantic ▷ nmf pedant

**pedazo** [pe'ðaθo] nm piece, bit; **hacerse ~s** to smash, shatter

**pediatra** [pe'ðjatra] nmf paediatrician

**pedido** [pe'ðiðo] nm (Com) order; (petición) request

**pedir** [pe'ðir] vt to ask for, request; (comida, Com: mandar) to order; (necesitar) to need, demand, require ▷ vi to ask; **me pidió que cerrara la puerta** he asked me to shut the door; **¿cuánto piden por el coche?** how much are they asking for the car?

**pedo** ['peðo] (fam!) nm fart

**pega** ['pexa] nf snag; **poner ~s (a)** to complain (about)

**pegadizo, -a** [pexa'ðiθo, a] adj (Mús) catchy

**pegajoso, -a** [pexa'xoso, a] adj sticky, adhesive

**pegamento** [pexa'mento] nm gum, glue

**pegar** [pe'xar] vt (papel, sellos) to stick (on); (cartel) to stick up; (coser) to sew (on); (unir: partes) to join, fix together; (Comput) to paste; (Med) to give, infect with; (dar: golpe) to give, deal ▷ vi (adherirse) to stick, adhere; (ir juntos: colores) to match, go together; (golpear) to hit; (quemar: el sol) to strike hot, burn; **pegarse** vr (gen) to stick; (dos personas) to hit each other, fight; (fam): **~ un grito** to let out a yell; **~ un salto** to jump (with fright); **~ en** to touch; **~se un tiro** to shoot o.s.

**pegatina** [pexa'tina] nf sticker

**pegote** [pe'xote] (fam) nm eyesore, sight

**peinado** [pei'naðo] nm hairstyle

**peinar** [pei'nar] vt to comb; (hacer estilo) to style; **peinarse** vr to comb one's hair

**peine** ['peine] nm comb; **peineta** nf ornamental comb

**p.ej.** abr (= por ejemplo) e.g.

**Pekín** [pe'kin] n Pekin(g)

**pelado, -a** [pe'laðo, a] adj (fruta, patata etc) peeled; (cabeza) shorn; (campo, fig) bare; (fam: sin dinero) broke

**pelar** [pe'lar] vt (fruta, patatas etc) to peel; (cortar el pelo a) to cut the hair of; (quitar la piel: animal) to skin; **pelarse** vr (la piel) to peel off; **voy a ~me** I'm going to get my hair cut

**peldaño** [pel'daɲo] nm step

**pelea** [pe'lea] nf (lucha) fight; (discusión) quarrel, row; **peleado, -a** [pele'aðo, a] adj: **estar peleado (con algn)** to have fallen out (with sb); **pelear** [pele'ar] vi to fight; **pelearse** vr to fight; (reñirse) to fall out, quarrel

**pelela** [pe'lela] (cs) nf potty

**peletería** [pelete'ria] nf furrier's, fur shop

**pelícano** [pe'likano] nm pelican

**película** [pe'likula] nf film; (cobertura ligera) thin covering; (Foto: rollo) roll o reel of film; **película de dibujos (animados)/del oeste** cartoon/western

**peligro** [pe'lixro] nm danger; (riesgo) risk; **correr ~ de** to run the risk of; **peligroso, -a** adj dangerous; risky

**pelirrojo, -a** [peli'rroxo, a] adj red-haired, red-headed ▷ nm/f redhead

**pellejo** [pe'ʎexo] nm (de animal) skin, hide

**pellizcar** [peʎiθ'kar] vt to pinch, nip

**pelma** ['pelma] (ESP: fam) nmf pain (in the neck)

**pelmazo** [pel'maθo] (fam) nm = **pelma**

**pelo** ['pelo] nm (cabellos) hair; (de barba, bigote) whisker; (de animal: pellejo) hair, fur, coat; **venir al ~** to be exactly what one needs; **un hombre de ~ en pecho** a brave man; **por los ~s** by the skin of one's teeth; **no tener ~s en la lengua** to be outspoken, not to mince one's words; **con ~s y señales** in minute detail; **tomar el ~ a algn** to pull sb's leg

**pelota** [pe'lota] nf ball; **en ~** stark naked; **hacer la ~ (a algn)** (ESP: fam) to creep (to sb); **pelota vasca** pelota

**pelotón** [pelo'ton] nm (Mil) squad, detachment

**peluca** [pe'luka] nf wig

**peluche** [pe'lutʃe] nm: **oso/muñeco de ~** teddy bear/soft toy

**peludo, -a** [pe'luðo, a] adj hairy, shaggy

**peluquería** [peluke'ria] nf hairdresser's;

**peluquero, -a** *nm/f* hairdresser
**pelusa** [pe'lusa] *nf* (*Bot*) down; (*en tela*) fluff
**pena** ['pena] *nf* (*congoja*) grief, sadness; (*remordimiento*) regret; (*dificultad*) trouble; (*dolor*) pain; (*Jur*) sentence; **merecer** o **valer la ~** to be worthwhile; **a duras ~s** with great difficulty; **¡qué ~!** what a shame!; **pena capital** capital punishment; **pena de muerte** death penalty
**penal** [pe'nal] *adj* penal ▷ *nm* (*cárcel*) prison
**penalidad** [penali'ðað] *nf* (*problema, dificultad*) trouble, hardship; (*Jur*) penalty, punishment; **penalidades** *nfpl* trouble *sg*, hardship *sg*
**penalti** [pe'nalti] *nm* = **penalty**
**penalty** [pe'nalti] (*pl* **~s** o **penalties**) *nm* penalty (kick)
**pendiente** [pen'djente] *adj* pending, unsettled ▷ *nm* earring ▷ *nf* hill, slope
**pene** ['pene] *nm* penis
**penetrante** [pene'trante] *adj* (*herida*) deep; (*persona, arma*) sharp; (*sonido*) penetrating, piercing; (*mirada*) searching; (*viento, ironía*) biting
**penetrar** [pene'trar] *vt* to penetrate, pierce; (*entender*) to grasp ▷ *vi* to penetrate, go in; (*entrar*) to enter, go in; (*líquido*) to soak in; (*fig*) to pierce
**penicilina** [peniθi'lina] *nf* penicillin
**península** [pe'ninsula] *nf* peninsula; **peninsular** *adj* peninsular
**penique** [pe'nike] *nm* penny
**penitencia** [peni'tenθja] *nf* penance
**penoso, -a** [pe'noso, a] *adj* (*lamentable*) distressing; (*difícil*) arduous, difficult
**pensador, a** [pensa'ðor, a] *nm/f* thinker
**pensamiento** [pensa'mjento] *nm* thought; (*mente*) mind; (*idea*) idea
**pensar** [pen'sar] *vt* to think; (*considerar*) to think over, think out; (*proponerse*) to intend, plan; (*imaginarse*) to think up, invent ▷ *vi* to think; **~ en** to aim at, aspire to; **pensativo, -a** *adj* thoughtful, pensive
**pensión** [pen'sjon] *nf* (*casa*) boarding o guest house; (*dinero*) pension; (*cama y comida*) board and lodging; **media ~** half-board; **pensión completa** full board; **pensionista** *nmf* (*jubilado*) (old-age) pensioner; (*huésped*) lodger
**penúltimo, -a** [pe'nultimo, a] *adj* penultimate, last but one
**penumbra** [pe'numbra] *nf* half-light
**peña** ['pena] *nf* (*roca*) rock; (*cuesta*) cliff, crag; (*grupo*) group, circle; (*LAM: club*) folk club
**peñasco** [pe'nasko] *nm* large rock, boulder

**peñón** [pe'non] *nm* wall of rock; **el P~** the Rock (of Gibraltar)
**peón** [pe'on] *nm* labourer; (*LAM Agr*) farm labourer, farmhand; (*Ajedrez*) pawn
**peonza** [pe'onθa] *nf* spinning top
**peor** [pe'or] *adj* (*comparativo*) worse; (*superlativo*) worst ▷ *adv* worse; worst; **de mal en ~** from bad to worse
**pepinillo** [pepi'niʎo] *nm* gherkin
**pepino** [pe'pino] *nm* cucumber; **(no) me importa un ~** I don't care one bit
**pepita** [pe'pita] *nf* (*Bot*) pip; (*Minería*) nugget
**pepito** [pe'pito] (*ESP*) *nm* (*tb:* **~ de ternera**) steak sandwich
**pequeño, -a** [pe'keno, a] *adj* small, little
**pera** ['pera] *nf* pear; **peral** *nm* pear tree
**percance** [per'kanθe] *nm* setback, misfortune
**percatarse** [perka'tarse] *vr:* **~ de** to notice, take note of
**percebe** [per'θeβe] *nm* barnacle
**percepción** [perθep'θjon] *nf* (*vista*) perception; (*idea*) notion, idea
**percha** ['pertʃa] *nf* (*coat*)hanger; (*ganchos*) coat hooks *pl*; (*de ave*) perch
**percibir** [perθi'βir] *vt* to perceive, notice; (*Com*) to earn, get
**percusión** [perku'sjon] *nf* percussion
**perdedor, a** [perðe'ðor, a] *adj* losing ▷ *nm/f* loser
**perder** [per'ðer] *vt* to lose; (*tiempo, palabras*) to waste; (*oportunidad*) to lose, miss; (*tren*) to miss ▷ *vi* to lose; **perderse** *vr* (*extraviarse*) to get lost; (*desaparecer*) to disappear, be lost to view; (*arruinarse*) to be ruined; **echar a ~** (*comida*) to spoil, ruin; (*oportunidad*) to waste
**pérdida** ['perðiða] *nf* loss; (*de tiempo*) waste; **pérdidas** *nfpl* (*Com*) losses
**perdido, -a** [per'ðiðo, a] *adj* lost
**perdiz** [per'ðiθ] *nf* partridge
**perdón** [per'ðon] *nm* (*disculpa*) pardon, forgiveness; (*clemencia*) mercy; **¡~!** sorry!, I beg your pardon!; **perdonar** *vt* to pardon, forgive; (*la vida*) to spare; (*excusar*) to exempt, excuse; **¡perdone (usted)!** sorry!, I beg your pardon!
**perecedero, -a** [pereθe'ðero, a] *adj* perishable
**perecer** [pere'θer] *vi* to perish, die
**peregrinación** [perexrina'θjon] *nf* (*Rel*) pilgrimage
**peregrino, -a** [pere'xrino, a] *adj* (*idea*) strange, absurd ▷ *nm/f* pilgrim
**perejil** [pere'xil] *nm* parsley
**perenne** [pe'renne] *adj* everlasting, perennial

**pereza** [pe'reθa] *nf* laziness, idleness; **perezoso, -a** *adj* lazy, idle
**perfección** [perfek'θjon] *nf* perfection; **perfeccionar** *vt* to perfect; *(mejorar)* to improve; *(acabar)* to complete, finish
**perfecto, -a** [per'fekto, a] *adj* perfect; *(total)* complete
**perfil** [per'fil] *nm* profile; *(contorno)* silhouette, outline; *(Arq)* (cross) section; **perfiles** *nmpl* features
**perforación** [perfora'θjon] *nf* perforation; *(con taladro)* drilling; **perforadora** *nf* punch
**perforar** [perfo'rar] *vt* to perforate; *(agujero)* to drill, bore; *(papel)* to punch a hole in ▷ *vi* to drill, bore
**perfume** [per'fume] *nm* perfume, scent
**periferia** [peri'ferja] *nf* periphery; *(de ciudad)* outskirts *pl*
**periférico** [peri'feriko] *(LAM)* *nm* ring road *(BRIT)*, beltway *(US)*
**perilla** [pe'riʎa] *nf* *(barba)* goatee; *(LAM: de puerta)* doorknob, door handle
**perímetro** [pe'rimetro] *nm* perimeter
**periódico, -a** [pe'rjoðiko, a] *adj* periodic(al) ▷ *nm* newspaper
**periodismo** [perjo'ðismo] *nm* journalism; **periodista** *nmf* journalist
**periodo** [pe'rjoðo] *nm* period
**período** [pe'rioðo] *nm* = **periodo**
**periquito** [peri'kito] *nm* budgerigar, budgie
**perito, -a** [pe'rito, a] *adj* *(experto)* expert; *(diestro)* skilled, skilful ▷ *nm/f* expert; skilled worker; *(técnico)* technician
**perjudicar** [perxuði'kar] *vt* *(gen)* to damage, harm; **perjudicial** *adj* damaging, harmful; *(en detrimento)* detrimental; **perjuicio** *nm* damage, harm
**perjurar** [perxu'rar] *vi* to commit perjury
**perla** ['perla] *nf* pearl; **me viene de ~s** it suits me fine
**permanecer** [permane'θer] *vi* *(quedarse)* to stay, remain; *(seguir)* to continue to be
**permanente** [perma'nente] *adj* permanent, constant ▷ *nf* perm
**permiso** [per'miso] *nm* permission; *(licencia)* permit, licence; **con ~** excuse me; **estar de ~** *(Mil)* to be on leave; **permiso de conducir** driving licence *(BRIT)*, driver's license *(US)*; **permiso por enfermedad** *(LAM)* sick leave
**permitir** [permi'tir] *vt* to permit, allow
**pernera** [per'nera] *nf* trouser leg
**pero** ['pero] *conj* but; *(aún)* yet ▷ *nm* *(defecto)* flaw, defect; *(reparo)* objection
**perpendicular** [perpendiku'lar] *adj* perpendicular

**perpetuo, -a** [per'petwo, a] *adj* perpetual
**perplejo, -a** [per'plexo, a] *adj* perplexed, bewildered
**perra** ['perra] *nf* *(Zool)* bitch; **estar sin una ~** *(ESP: fam)* to be flat broke
**perrera** [pe'rrera] *nf* kennel
**perrito** [pe'rrito] *nm* *(tb: ~ caliente)* hot dog
**perro** ['perro] *nm* dog
**persa** ['persa] *adj, nmf* Persian
**persecución** [perseku'θjon] *nf* pursuit, chase; *(Rel, Pol)* persecution
**perseguir** [perse'ɣir] *vt* to pursue, hunt; *(cortejar)* to chase after; *(molestar)* to pester, annoy; *(Rel, Pol)* to persecute
**persiana** [per'sjana] *nf* *(Venetian)* blind
**persistente** [persis'tente] *adj* persistent
**persistir** [persis'tir] *vi* to persist
**persona** [per'sona] *nf* person; **persona mayor** elderly person
**personaje** [perso'naxe] *nm* important person, celebrity; *(Teatro etc)* character
**personal** [perso'nal] *adj* *(particular)* personal; *(para una persona)* single, for one person ▷ *nm* personnel, staff; **personalidad** *nf* personality
**personarse** [perso'narse] *vr* to appear in person
**personificar** [personifi'kar] *vt* to personify
**perspectiva** [perspek'tiβa] *nf* perspective; *(vista, panorama)* view, panorama; *(posibilidad futura)* outlook, prospect
**persuadir** [perswa'ðir] *vt* *(gen)* to persuade; *(convencer)* to convince; **persuadirse** *vr* to become convinced; **persuasión** *nf* persuasion
**pertenecer** [pertene'θer] *vi* to belong; *(fig)* to concern; **perteneciente** *adj*: **perteneciente a** belonging to; **pertenencia** *nf* ownership; **pertenencias** *nfpl* *(bienes)* possessions, property *sg*
**pertenezca** *etc vb* V **pertenecer**
**pértiga** ['pertixa] *nf*: **salto de ~** pole vault
**pertinente** [perti'nente] *adj* relevant, pertinent; *(apropiado)* appropriate; **~ a** concerning, relevant to
**perturbación** [perturβa'θjon] *nf* *(Pol)* disturbance; *(Med)* upset, disturbance
**Perú** [pe'ru] *nm* Peru; **peruano, -a** *adj, nm/f* Peruvian
**perversión** [perβer'sjon] *nf* perversion; **perverso, -a** *adj* perverse; *(depravado)* depraved
**pervertido, -a** [perβer'tiðo, a] *adj* perverted ▷ *nm/f* pervert
**pervertir** [perβer'tir] *vt* to pervert,

corrupt

**pesa** ['pesa] nf weight; (Deporte) shot

**pesadez** [pesa'ðeθ] nf (peso) heaviness; (lentitud) slowness; (aburrimiento) tediousness

**pesadilla** [pesa'ðiʎa] nf nightmare, bad dream

**pesado, -a** [pe'saðo, a] adj heavy; (lento) slow; (difícil, duro) tough, hard; (aburrido) boring, tedious; (tiempo) sultry

**pésame** ['pesame] nm expression of condolence, message of sympathy; **dar el ~** to express one's condolences

**pesar** [pe'sar] vt to weigh ▷ vi to weigh; (ser pesado) to weigh a lot, be heavy; (fig: opinión) to carry weight; **no pesa mucho** it's not very heavy ▷ nm (arrepentimiento) regret; (pena) grief, sorrow; **a ~ de** o **pese a (que)** in spite of, despite

**pesca** ['peska] nf (acto) fishing; (lo pescado) catch; **ir de ~** to go fishing

**pescadería** [peskaðe'ria] nf fish shop, fishmonger's (BRIT)

**pescadilla** [peska'ðiʎa] nf whiting

**pescado** [pes'kaðo] nm fish

**pescador, a** [peska'ðor, a] nm/f fisherman/woman

**pescar** [pes'kar] vt (tomar) to catch; (intentar tomar) to fish for; (conseguir: trabajo) to manage to get ▷ vi to fish, go fishing

**pesebre** [pe'seβre] nm manger

**peseta** [pe'seta] nf (Hist) peseta

**pesimista** [pesi'mista] adj pessimistic ▷ nmf pessimist

**pésimo, -a** ['pesimo, a] adj awful, dreadful

**peso** ['peso] nm weight; (balanza) scales pl; (moneda) peso; **vender al ~** to sell by weight; **peso bruto/neto** gross/net weight; **peso pesado/pluma** heavyweight/featherweight

**pesquero, -a** [pes'kero, a] adj fishing cpd

**pestaña** [pes'taɲa] nf (Anat) eyelash; (borde) rim

**peste** ['peste] nf plague; (mal olor) stink, stench

**pesticida** [pesti'θiða] nm pesticide

**pestillo** [pes'tiʎo] nm (cerrojo) bolt; (picaporte) door handle

**petaca** [pe'taka] nf (de cigarros) cigarette case; (de pipa) tobacco pouch; (MÉX: maleta) suitcase

**pétalo** ['petalo] nm petal

**petardo** [pe'tardo] nm firework, firecracker

**petición** [peti'θjon] nf (pedido) request, plea; (memorial) petition; (Jur) plea

**peto** ['peto] nm (ESP) dungarees pl,

overalls pl (US)

**petróleo** [pe'troleo] nm oil, petroleum; **petrolero, -a** adj petroleum cpd ▷ nm (oil) tanker

**peyorativo, -a** [pejora'tiβo, a] adj pejorative

**pez** [peθ] nm fish; **pez espada** swordfish

**pezón** [pe'θon] nm teat, nipple

**pezuña** [pe'θuɲa] nf hoof

**pianista** [pja'nista] nmf pianist

**piano** ['pjano] nm piano

**piar** [pjar] vi to cheep

**pibe, -a** ['piβe, a] (RPL) nm/f boy/girl

**picadero** [pika'ðero] nm riding school

**picadillo** [pika'ðiʎo] nm mince, minced meat

**picado, -a** [pi'kaðo, a] adj pricked, punctured; (Culin) minced, chopped; (mar) choppy; (diente) bad; (tabaco) cut; (enfadado) cross

**picador** [pika'ðor] nm (Taur) picador; (minero) faceworker

**picadura** [pika'ðura] nf (pinchazo) puncture; (de abeja) sting; (de mosquito) bite; (tabaco picado) cut tobacco

**picante** [pi'kante] adj hot; (comentario) racy, spicy

**picaporte** [pika'porte] nm (manija) doorhandle; (pestillo) latch

**picar** [pi'kar] vt (agujerear, perforar) to prick, puncture; (abeja) to sting; (mosquito, serpiente) to bite; (Culin) to mince, chop; (incitar) to incite, goad; (dañar, irritar) to annoy, bother; (quemar: lengua) to burn, sting ▷ vi (pez) to bite, take the bait; (sol) to burn, scorch; (abeja, Med) to sting; (mosquito) to bite; **picarse** vr (agriarse) to turn sour, go off; (ofenderse) to take offence

**picardía** [pikar'ðia] nf villainy; (astucia) slyness, craftiness; (una picardía) dirty trick; (palabra) rude/bad word o expression

**pícaro, -a** ['pikaro, a] adj (malicioso) villainous; (travieso) mischievous ▷ nm (astuto) crafty sort; (sinvergüenza) rascal, scoundrel

**pichi** ['pitʃi] (ESP) nm pinafore dress (BRIT), jumper (US)

**pichón** [pi'tʃon] nm young pigeon

**pico** ['piko] nm (de ave) beak; (punta) sharp point; (Tec) pick, pickaxe; (Geo) peak, summit; **y ~** and a bit; **las seis y ~** six and a bit

**picor** [pi'kor] nm itch

**picoso, -a** [pi'koso, a] (MÉX) adj (comida) hot

**picudo, -a** [pi'kuðo, a] adj pointed, with a point

**pidió** etc vb V **pedir**

**pido** etc vb V **pedir**

**pie** [pje] (pl **~s**) nm foot; (fig: motivo) motive, basis; (: fundamento) foothold; **ir a ~** to go on foot, walk; **estar de ~** to be standing (up); **ponerse de ~** to stand up; **de ~s a cabeza** from top to bottom; **al ~ de la letra** (citar) literally, verbatim; (copiar) exactly, word for word; **en ~ de guerra** on a war footing; **dar ~ a** to give cause for; **hacer ~** (en el agua) to touch (the) bottom

**piedad** [pje'ðað] nf (lástima) pity, compassion; (clemencia) mercy; (devoción) piety, devotion

**piedra** ['pjeðra] nf stone; (roca) rock; (de mechero) flint; (Meteorología) hailstone; **piedra preciosa** precious stone

**piel** [pjel] nf (Anat) skin; (Zool) skin, hide, fur; (cuero) leather; (Bot) skin, peel

**pienso** etc vb V **pensar**

**pierdo** etc vb V **perder**

**pierna** ['pjerna] nf leg

**pieza** ['pjeθa] nf piece; (habitación) room; **pieza de recambio** o **repuesto** spare (part)

**pigmeo, -a** [pix'meo, a] adj, nm/f pigmy

**pijama** [pi'xama] nm pyjamas pl (BRIT), pajamas pl (US)

**pila** ['pila] nf (Elec) battery; (montón) heap, pile; (lavabo) sink

**píldora** ['pildora] nf pill; **la ~ (anticonceptiva)** the (contraceptive) pill

**pileta** [pi'leta] (RPL) nf (fregadero) (kitchen) sink; (piscina) swimming pool

**pillar** [pi'ʎar] vt (saquear) to pillage, plunder; (fam: coger) to catch; (: agarrar) to grasp, seize; (: entender) to grasp, catch on to; **pillarse** vr: **~se un dedo con la puerta** to catch one's finger in the door

**pillo, -a** ['piʎo, a] adj villainous; (astuto) sly, crafty ▷ nm/f rascal, rogue, scoundrel

**piloto** [pi'loto] nm pilot; (de aparato) (pilot) light; (Auto: luz) tail o rear light; (: conductor) driver; **piloto automático** automatic pilot

**pimentón** [pimen'ton] nm paprika

**pimienta** [pi'mjenta] nf pepper

**pimiento** [pi'mjento] nm pepper, pimiento

**pin** [pin] (pl **~s**) nm badge

**pinacoteca** [pinako'teka] nf art gallery

**pinar** [pi'nar] nm pine forest (BRIT), pine grove (US)

**pincel** [pin'θel] nm paintbrush

**pinchadiscos** [pintʃa'ðiskos] (ESP) nmf inv disc-jockey, DJ

**pinchar** [pin'tʃar] vt (perforar) to prick, pierce; (neumático) to puncture; (fig) to prod; (Inform) to click

**pinchazo** [pin'tʃaθo] nm (perforación) prick; (de neumático) puncture; (fig) prod

**pincho** ['pintʃo] nm savoury (snack); **pincho de tortilla** small slice of omelette; **pincho moruno** shish kebab

**ping-pong** ['pin'pon] nm table tennis

**pingüino** [pin'gwino] nm penguin

**pino** ['pino] nm pine (tree)

**pinta** ['pinta] nf spot; (de líquidos) spot, drop; (aspecto) appearance, look(s) (pl); **pintado, -a** adj spotted; (de colores) colourful; **pintadas** nfpl graffiti sg

**pintalabios** [pinta'laβjos] (ESP) nm inv lipstick

**pintar** [pin'tar] vt to paint ▷ vi to paint; (fam) to count, be important; **pintarse** vr to put on make-up

**pintor, a** [pin'tor, a] nm/f painter

**pintoresco, -a** [pinto'resko, a] adj picturesque

**pintura** [pin'tura] nf painting; **pintura al óleo** oil painting

**pinza** ['pinθa] nf (Zool) claw; (para colgar ropa) clothes peg; (Tec) pincers pl; **pinzas** nfpl (para depilar etc) tweezers pl

**piña** ['pina] nf (de pino) pine cone; (fruta) pineapple; (fig) group

**piñata** [pi'nata] nf container hung up at parties to be beaten with sticks until sweets or presents fall out

⬤ **PIÑATA**

**Piñata** is a very popular party game in Mexico. The **piñata** itself is a hollow figure made of papier maché or, traditionally, from adobe, in the shape of an object, a star, a person or an animal. It is filled with either sweets and toys, or fruit and yam beans. The game consists of hanging the **piñata** from the ceiling, and beating it with a stick, blindfolded, until it breaks and the presents fall out.

**piñón** [pi'non] nm (fruto) pine nut; (Tec) pinion

**pío, -a** ['pio, a] adj (devoto) pious, devout; (misericordioso) merciful

**piojo** ['pjoxo] nm louse

**pipa** ['pipa] nf pipe; **pipas** nfpl (Bot) (edible) sunflower seeds

**pipí** [pi'pi] (fam) nm: **hacer ~** to have a wee(-wee) (BRIT), have to go (wee-wee) (US)

**pique** ['pike] nm (resentimiento) pique, resentment; (rivalidad) rivalry, competition; **irse a ~** to sink; (esperanza, familia) to be ruined

**piqueta** [pi'keta] nf pick(axe)

**piquete** [pi'kete] nm (Mil) squad, party;

(de obreros) picket; (MÉX: de insecto) bite;
**piquetear** (LAM) vt to picket
**pirado, -a** [pi'raðo, a] (fam) adj round the
bend ▷ nm/f nutter
**piragua** [pi'raɣwa] nf canoe; **piragüismo**
nm canoeing
**pirámide** [pi'ramiðe] nf pyramid
**pirata** [pi'rata] adj, nmf pirate; **pirata
informático** hacker
**Pirineo(s)** [piri'neo(s)] nm(pl) Pyrenees pl
**pirómano, -a** [pi'romano, a] nm/f (Med,
Jur) arsonist
**piropo** [pi'ropo] nm compliment, (piece
of) flattery
**pirueta** [pi'rweta] nf pirouette
**piruleta** [piru'leta] (ESP) nf lollipop
**pis** [pis] (fam) nm pee, piss; **hacer ~** to have
a pee; (para niños) to wee-wee
**pisada** [pi'saða] nf (paso) footstep; (huella)
footprint
**pisar** [pi'sar] vt (caminar sobre) to walk on,
tread on; (apretar con el pie) to press; (fig)
to trample on, walk all over ▷ vi to tread,
step, walk
**piscina** [pis'θina] nf swimming pool
**Piscis** [pis'θis] nm Pisces
**piso** ['piso] nm (suelo, planta) floor;
(ESP: apartamento) flat (BRIT), apartment;
**primer ~** (ESP) first floor; (LAM: planta baja)
ground floor
**pisotear** [pisote'ar] vt to trample (on o
underfoot)
**pista** ['pista] nf track, trail; (indicio) clue;
**pista de aterrizaje** runway; **pista de baile**
dance floor; **pista de hielo** ice rink; **pista de
tenis** (ESP) tennis court
**pistola** [pis'tola] nf pistol; (Tec) spray-gun
**pistón** [pis'ton] nm (Tec) piston; (Mús) key
**pitar** [pi'tar] vt (silbato) to blow; (rechiflar)
to whistle at, boo ▷ vi to whistle; (Auto)
to sound o toot one's horn; (LAM: fumar) to
smoke
**pitillo** [pi'tiʎo] nm cigarette
**pito** ['pito] nm whistle; (de coche) horn
**pitón** [pi'ton] nm (Zool) python
**pitonisa** [pito'nisa] nf fortune-teller
**pitorreo** [pito'rreo] nm joke; **estar de ~**
to be joking
**píxel** ['piksel] (pl **pixels** or **~es**) nm pixel
**piyama** [pi'jama] (LAM) nm pyjamas pl
(BRIT), pajamas pl (US)
**pizarra** [pi'θarra] nf (piedra) slate;
(ESP: encerado) blackboard; **pizarra
blanca** whiteboard; **pizarra interactiva**
interactive whiteboard
**pizarrón** [piθa'rron] (LAM) nm blackboard
**pizca** ['piθka] nf pinch, spot; (fig) spot,
speck; **ni ~** not a bit

**placa** ['plaka] nf plate; (distintivo) badge,
insignia; **placa de matrícula** (LAM) number
plate
**placard** [pla'kar] (RPL) nm cupboard
**placer** [pla'θer] nm pleasure ▷ vt to please
**plaga** ['plaɣa] nf pest; (Med) plague;
(abundancia) abundance
**plagio** ['plaxjo] nm plagiarism
**plan** [plan] nm (esquema, proyecto) plan;
(idea, intento) idea, intention; **tener ~** (fam)
to have a date; **tener un ~** (fam) to have an
affair; **en ~ económico** (fam) on the cheap;
**vamos en ~ de turismo** we're going as
tourists; **si te pones en ese ~ ...** if that's
your attitude ...
**plana** ['plana] nf sheet (of paper), page;
(Tec) trowel; **en primera ~** on the front page
**plancha** ['plantʃa] nf (para planchar) iron;
(rótulo) plate, sheet; (Náut) gangway; **a la ~**
(Culin) grilled; **planchar** vt to iron ▷ vi to
do the ironing
**planear** [plane'ar] vt to plan ▷ vi to glide
**planeta** [pla'neta] nm planet
**plano, -a** ['plano, a] adj flat, level, even
▷ nm (Mat, Tec) plane; (Foto) shot; (Arq) plan;
(Geo) map; (de ciudad) map, street plan;
**primer ~** close-up
**planta** ['planta] nf (Bot, Tec) plant;
(Anat) sole of the foot, foot; (piso) floor;
(LAM: personal) staff; **planta baja** ground
floor
**plantar** [plan'tar] vt (Bot) to plant;
(levantar) to erect, set up; **plantarse** vr to
stand firm; **~ a algn en la calle** to throw sb
out; **dejar plantado a algn** (fam) to stand
sb up
**plantear** [plante'ar] vt (problema) to pose;
(dificultad) to raise
**plantilla** [plan'tiʎa] nf (de zapato) insole;
(ESP: personal) personnel; **ser de ~** (ESP) to be
on the staff
**plantón** [plan'ton] nm (Mil) guard, sentry;
(fam) long wait; **dar (un) ~ a algn** to stand
sb up
**plasta** ['plasta] (ESP: fam) adj inv boring
▷ nmf bore
**plástico, -a** ['plastiko, a] adj plastic ▷ nm
plastic
**Plastilina®** [plasti'lina] nf Plasticine®
**plata** ['plata] nf (metal) silver; (cosas hechas
de plata) silverware; (cs: dinero) cash, dough
**plataforma** [plata'forma] nf platform;
**plataforma de lanzamiento/perforación**
launch(ing) pad/drilling rig
**plátano** ['platano] nm (fruta) banana;
(árbol) plane tree; banana tree
**platea** [pla'tea] nf (Teatro) pit
**plática** ['platika] nf talk, chat; **platicar** vi

to talk, chat

**platillo** [pla'tiʎo] nm saucer; **platillos**
nmpl (Mús) cymbals; **platillo volante**flying
saucer

**platino** [pla'tino] nm platinum; **platinos**
nmpl (Auto) contact points

**plato** ['plato] nm plate, dish; (parte de
comida) course; (comida) dish; **primer ~**first
course; **plato combinado**set main course
(served on one plate); **plato fuerte**main
course

**playa** ['plaja] nf beach; (costa) seaside;
**playa de estacionamiento**(cs) car park
(BRIT), parking lot (US)

**playera** [pla'jera] nf (MÉX: camiseta) T-
shirt; **playeras** nfpl (zapatos) canvas shoes

**plaza** [pla'θa] nf square; (mercado)
market(place); (sitio) room, space; (de
vehículo) seat, place; (colocación) post, job;
**plaza de toros**bullring

**plazo** ['plaθo] nm (lapso de tiempo) time,
period; (fecha de vencimiento) expiry date;
(pago parcial) instalment; **a corto/largo ~**
short-/long-term; **comprar algo a ~s** to
buy sth on hire purchase (BRIT) o on time
(US)

**plazoleta** [plaθo'leta] nf small square

**plebeyo, -a** [ple'βejo, a] adj plebeian;
(pey) coarse, common

**plegable** [ple'ɣaβle] adj collapsible; (silla)
folding

**pleito** ['pleito] nm (Jur) lawsuit, case; (fig)
dispute, feud

**plenitud** [pleni'tuð] nf plenitude,
fullness; (abundancia) abundance

**pleno, -a** ['pleno, a] adj full; (completo)
complete ⊳nm plenum; **en ~ día** in broad
daylight; **en ~ verano**at the height of
summer; **en plena cara** full in the face

**pliego** etc ['pljeɣo] vb V **plegar** ⊳nm (hoja)
sheet (of paper); (carta) sealed letter/
document; **pliego de condiciones**details
pl, specifications pl

**pliegue** etc ['pljeɣe] vb V **plegar** ⊳nm
fold, crease; (de vestido) pleat

**plomería** [plome'ria] (LAM) nf plumbing;
**plomero**(LAM) nm plumber

**plomo** ['plomo] nm (metal) lead; (Elec) fuse;
**sin ~**unleaded

**pluma** ['pluma] nf feather; (para escribir): **~
(estilográfica)** ink pen; **~ fuente** (LAM)
fountain pen

**plumero** [plu'mero] nm (para el polvo)
feather duster

**plumón** [plu'mon] nm (de ave) down

**plural** [plu'ral] adj plural

**pluriempleo** [pluriem'pleo] nm having
more than one job

**plus** [plus] nm bonus

**población** [poβla'θjon] nf population;
(pueblo, ciudad) town, city

**poblado, -a** [po'βlaðo, a] adj inhabited
⊳nm (aldea) village; (pueblo) (small) town;
**densamente ~** densely populated

**poblador, a** [poβla'ðor, a] nm/f settler,
colonist

**pobre** ['poβre] adj poor ⊳nmf poor
person; **pobreza** nf poverty

**pocilga** [po'θilɣa] nf pigsty

**poco, -a** ['poko, a] adj **1**(sg) little, not
much; **poco tiempo** little o not much time;
**de poco interés** of little interest, not very
interesting; **poca cosa**not much

**2**(pl) few, not many; **unos pocos** a few,
some; **pocos niños comen lo que les
conviene** few children eat what they should
⊳adv **1**little, not much; **cuesta poco** it
doesn't cost much

**2**(+ adj: negativo, antónimo): **poco amable/
inteligente** not very nice/intelligent

**3**: **por poco me caigo** I almost fell

**4**: **a poco: a poco de haberse casado**
shortly after getting married

**5**: **poco a poco** little by little
⊳nm a little, a bit; **un poco triste/de
dinero**a little sad/money

**podar** [po'ðar] vt to prune

**poder** [po'ðer] vi **1**(tener capacidad) can, be
able to; **no puedo hacerlo** I can't do it, I'm
unable to do it

**2**(tener permiso) can, may, be allowed to; **¿se
puede?** may I (o we)?; **puedes irte ahora**
you may go now; **no se puede fumar en
este hospital** smoking is not allowed in
this hospital

**3**(tener posibilidad) may, might, could;
**puede llegar mañana** he may o might
arrive tomorrow; **pudiste haberte hecho
daño** you might o could have hurt yourself;
**¡podías habérmelo dicho antes!** you
might have told me before!

**4**: **puede ser** perhaps; **puede ser que lo
sepa Tomás** Tomás may o might know

**5**: **¡no puedo más!** I've had enough!; **es
tonto a más no poder** he's as stupid as
they come

**6**: **poder con: no puedo con este crío** this
kid's too much for me
⊳nm power; **detentar** o **ocupar** o

estar en el poder to be in power; **poder adquisitivo/ejecutivo/legislativo** purchasing/executive/legislative power; **poder judicial** judiciary

**poderoso, -a** [poðe'roso, a] *adj* (*político, país*) powerful

**podio** ['poðjo] *nm* (*Deporte*) podium

**podium** ['poðjum] = **podio**

**podrido, -a** [po'ðriðo, a] *adj* rotten, bad; (*fig*) rotten, corrupt

**podrir** [po'ðrir] = **pudrir**

**poema** [po'ema] *nm* poem

**poesía** [poe'sia] *nf* poetry

**poeta** [po'eta] *nmf* poet; **poético, -a** *adj* poetic(al)

**poetisa** [poe'tisa] *nf* (woman) poet

**póker** ['poker] *nm* poker

**polaco, -a** [po'lako, a] *adj* Polish ▷ *nm/f* Pole

**polar** [po'lar] *adj* polar

**polea** [po'lea] *nf* pulley

**polémica** [po'lemika] *nf* polemics *sg*; (*una polémica*) controversy, polemic

**polen** ['polen] *nm* pollen

**policía** [poli'θia] *nmf* policeman/woman ▷ *nf* police; **policíaco, -a** *adj* police *cpd*; **novela policíaca** detective story; **policial** *adj* police *cpd*

**polideportivo** [poliðepor'tiβo] *nm* sports centre o complex

**polígono** [po'liɣono] *nm* (*Mat*) polygon; **polígono industrial** (*ESP*) industrial estate

**polilla** [po'liʎa] *nf* moth

**polio** ['poljo] *nf* polio

**política** [po'litika] *nf* politics *sg*; (*económica, agraria etc*) policy; *V tb* **político**

**político, -a** [po'litiko, a] *adj* political; (*discreto*) tactful; (*de familia*) ...-in-law ▷ *nm/f* politician; **padre ~** father-in-law

**póliza** ['poliθa] *nf* certificate, voucher; (*impuesto*) tax stamp; **póliza de seguro(s)** insurance policy

**polizón** [poli'θon] *nm* stowaway

**pollera** [po'ʎera] (*cs*) *nf* skirt

**pollo** ['poʎo] *nm* chicken

**polo** ['polo] *nm* (*Geo, Elec*) pole; (*helado*) ice lolly (*BRIT*), Popsicle® (*US*); (*Deporte*) polo; (*suéter*) polo-neck; **polo Norte/Sur** North/South Pole

**Polonia** [po'lonja] *nf* Poland

**poltrona** [pol'trona] *nf* easy chair

**polución** [polu'θjon] *nf* pollution

**polvera** [pol'βera] *nf* powder compact

**polvo** ['polβo] *nm* dust; (*Quím, Culin, Med*) powder; **polvos** *nmpl* (*maquillaje*) powder *sg*; **en ~** powdered; **quitar el ~** to dust; **estar hecho ~** (*fam*) to be worn out o exhausted;

polvos de talco talcum powder *sg*

**pólvora** ['polβora] *nf* gunpowder

**polvoriento, -a** [polβo'rjento, a] *adj* (*superficie*) dusty; (*sustancia*) powdery

**pomada** [po'maða] *nf* cream, ointment

**pomelo** [po'melo] *nm* grapefruit

**pómez** ['pomeθ] *nf*: **piedra ~** pumice stone

**pomo** ['pomo] *nm* doorknob

**pompa** ['pompa] *nf* (*burbuja*) bubble; (*bomba*) pump; (*esplendor*) pomp, splendour

**pómulo** ['pomulo] *nm* cheekbone

**pon** [pon] *vb* V **poner**

**ponchadura** [pontʃa'dura] (*MÉX*) *nf* puncture (*BRIT*), flat (*US*); **ponchar** (*MÉX*) *vt* (*llanta*) to puncture

**ponche** ['pontʃe] *nm* punch

**poncho** ['pontʃo] *nm* poncho

**pondré** *etc vb* V **poner**

○ **PALABRA CLAVE**

**poner** [po'ner] *vt* **1** (*colocar*) to put; (*telegrama*) to send; (*obra de teatro*) to put on; (*película*) to show; **ponlo más fuerte** turn it up; **¿qué ponen en el Excelsior?** what's on at the Excelsior?

**2** (*tienda*) to open; (*instalar: gas etc*) to put in; (*radio, TV*) to switch o turn on

**3** (*suponer*): **pongamos que ...** let's suppose that ...

**4** (*contribuir*): **el gobierno ha puesto otro millón** the government has contributed another million

**5** (*Tel*): **póngame con el Sr. López** can you put me through to Mr. López?

**6**: **poner de: le han puesto de director general** they've appointed him general manager

**7** (+ *adj*) to make; **me estás poniendo nerviosa** you're making me nervous

**8** (*dar nombre*): **al hijo le pusieron Diego** they called their son Diego
▷ *vi* (*gallina*) to lay

**ponerse** *vr* **1** (*colocarse*): **se puso a mi lado** he came and stood beside me; **tú ponte en esa silla** you go and sit on that chair

**2** (*vestido, cosméticos*) to put on; **¿por qué no te pones el vestido nuevo?** why don't you put on o wear your new dress?

**3** (+ *adj*) to turn; to get, become; **se puso muy serio** he got very serious; **después de lavarla la tela se puso azul** after washing it the material turned blue

**4**: **ponerse a: se puso a llorar** he started to cry; **tienes que ponerte a estudiar** you must get down to studying

**pongo** *etc vb* V **poner**

**poniente** [po'njente] *nm* (*occidente*) west; (*viento*) west wind

**pontífice** [pon'tifiθe] *nm* pope, pontiff

**popa** ['popa] *nf* stern

**popote** [po'pote] (*MÉX*) *nm* straw

**popular** [popu'lar] *adj* popular; (*cultura*) of the people, folk *cpd*; **popularidad** *nf* popularity

○ **PALABRA CLAVE**

**por** [por] *prep* **1** (*objetivo*) for; **luchar por la patria** to fight for one's country

**2** (+ *infin*): **por no llegar tarde** so as not to arrive late; **por citar unos ejemplos** to give a few examples

**3** (*causa*) out of, because of; **por escasez de fondos** through *o* for lack of funds

**4** (*tiempo*): **por la mañana/noche** in the morning/at night; **se queda por una semana** she's staying (for) a week

**5** (*lugar*): **pasar por Madrid** to pass through Madrid; **ir a Guayaquil por Quito** to go to Guayaquil via Quito; **caminar por la calle** to walk along the street; V *tb* **todo**

**6** (*cambio, precio*): **te doy uno nuevo por el que tienes** I'll give you a new one (in return) for the one you've got

**7** (*valor distributivo*): **6 euros por hora/cabeza** 6 euros an *o* per hour/a *o* per head

**8** (*modo, medio*) by; **por correo/avión** by post/air; **entrar por la entrada principal** to go in through the main entrance

**9**: **10 por 10 son 100** 10 times 10 is 100

**10** (*en lugar de*): **vino él por su jefe** he came instead of his boss

**11**: **por mí que revienten** as far as I'm concerned they can drop dead

**12**: **¿por qué?** why?; **¿por qué no?** why not?

**porcelana** [porθe'lana] *nf* porcelain; (*china*) china

**porcentaje** [porθen'taxe] *nm* percentage

**porción** [por'θjon] *nf* (*parte*) portion, share; (*cantidad*) quantity, amount

**porfiar** [por'fjar] *vi* to persist, insist; (*disputar*) to argue stubbornly

**pormenor** [porme'nor] *nm* detail, particular

**pornografía** [pornoɣra'fia] *nf* pornography

**poro** ['poro] *nm* pore

**pororó** [poro'ro] (*RPL*) *nm* popcorn

**poroso, -a** [po'roso, a] *adj* porous

**poroto** [po'roto] (*CS*) *nm* bean

**porque** ['porke] *conj* (*a causa de*) because; (*ya que*) since; (*con el fin de*) so that, in order that

**porqué** [por'ke] *nm* reason, cause

**porquería** [porke'ria] *nf* (*suciedad*) filth, dirt; (*acción*) dirty trick; (*objeto*) small thing, trifle; (*fig*) rubbish

**porra** ['porra] (*ESP*) *nf* (*arma*) stick, club

**porrazo** [po'rraθo] *nm* blow, bump

**porro** ['porro] (*fam*) *nm* (*droga*) joint (*fam*)

**porrón** [po'rron] *nm* glass wine jar with a long spout

**portaaviones** [porta'(a)βjones] *nm inv* aircraft carrier

**portada** [por'taða] *nf* (*de revista*) cover

**portador, a** [porta'ðor, a] *nm/f* carrier, bearer; (*Com*) bearer, payee

**portaequipajes** [portaeki'paxes] *nm inv* (*Auto: maletero*) boot; (: *baca*) luggage rack

**portafolio** [porta'foljo] (*LAM*) *nm* briefcase

**portal** [por'tal] *nm* (*entrada*) vestibule, hall; (*portada*) porch, doorway; (*puerta de entrada*) main door; (*Internet*) portal; **portales** *nmpl* (*LAM*) arcade *sg*

**portamaletas** [portama'letas] *nm inv* (*Auto: maletero*) boot; (: *baca*) roof rack

**portarse** [por'tarse] *vr* to behave, conduct o.s.

**portátil** [por'tatil] *adj* portable

**portavoz** [porta'βoθ] *nmf* spokesman/ woman

**portazo** [por'taθo] *nm*: **dar un ~** to slam the door

**porte** ['porte] *nm* (*Com*) transport; (*precio*) transport charges *pl*

**portentoso, -a** [porten'toso, a] *adj* marvellous, extraordinary

**porteño, -a** [por'teɲo, a] *adj* of *o* from Buenos Aires

**portería** [porte'ria] *nf* (*oficina*) porter's office; (*Deporte*) goal

**portero, -a** [por'tero, a] *nm/f* porter; (*conserje*) caretaker; (*ujier*) doorman; (*Deporte*) goalkeeper; **portero automático** (*ESP*) entry phone

**pórtico** ['portiko] *nm* (*patio*) portico, porch; (*fig*) gateway; (*arcada*) arcade

**portorriqueño, -a** [portorri'keɲo, a] *adj* Puerto Rican

**Portugal** [portu'ɣal] *nm* Portugal; **portugués, -esa** *adj, nm/f* Portuguese ▷ *nm* (*Ling*) Portuguese

**porvenir** [porβe'nir] *nm* future

**pos** [pos] *prep*: **en ~ de** after, in pursuit of

**posaderas** [posa'ðeras] *nfpl* backside *sg*, buttocks

**posar** [po'sar] *vt* (*en el suelo*) to lay down, put down; (*la mano*) to place, put gently ▷ *vi* (*modelo*) to sit, pose; **posarse** *vr* to settle; (*pájaro*) to perch; (*avión*) to land, come down

**posavasos** [posa'basos] nm inv coaster;
(para cerveza) beermat

**posdata** [pos'ðata] nf postscript

**pose** ['pose] nf pose

**poseedor, a** [posee'ðor, a] nm/f owner,
possessor; (de récord, puesto) holder

**poseer** [pose'er] vt to possess, own;
(ventaja) to enjoy; (récord, puesto) to hold

**posesivo, -a** [pose'siβo, a] adj possessive

**posibilidad** [posiβili'ðað] nf possibility;
(oportunidad) chance; **posibilitar** vt to
make possible; (hacer realizable) to make
feasible

**posible** [po'siβle] adj possible; (realizable)
feasible; **de ser ~** if possible; **en lo ~** as far
as possible

**posición** [posi'θjon] nf position; (rango
social) status

**positivo, -a** [posi'tiβo, a] adj positive

**poso** ['poso] nm sediment; (heces) dregs pl

**posponer** [pospo'ner] vt (relegar) to put
behind/below; (aplazar) to postpone

**posta** ['posta] nf: **a ~** deliberately, on
purpose

**postal** [pos'tal] adj postal ▷ nf postcard

**poste** ['poste] nm (de telégrafos etc) post,
pole; (columna) pillar

**póster** ['poster] (pl **~es, ~s**) nm poster

**posterior** [poste'rjor] adj back, rear;
(siguiente) following, subsequent; (más
tarde) later

**postgrado** [post'graðo] nm = **posgrado**

**postizo, -a** [pos'tiθo, a] adj false,
artificial ▷ nm hairpiece

**postre** ['postre] nm sweet, dessert

**póstumo, -a** ['postumo, a] adj
posthumous

**postura** [pos'tura] nf (del cuerpo) posture,
position; (fig) attitude, position

**potable** [po'taβle] adj drinkable; **agua ~**
drinking water

**potaje** [po'taxe] nm thick vegetable soup

**potencia** [po'tenθja] nf power; **potencial**
[poten'θjal] adj, nm potential

**potente** [po'tente] adj powerful

**potro, -a** ['potro, a] nm/f (Zool) colt/filly
▷ nm (de gimnasia) vaulting horse

**pozo** ['poθo] nm well; (de río) deep pool; (de
mina) shaft

**PP** (ESP) nm abr = **Partido Popular**

**práctica** ['praktika] nf practice; (método)
method; (arte, capacidad) skill; **en la ~** in
practice

**practicable** [prakti'kaβle] adj
practicable; (camino) passable

**practicante** [prakti'kante] nmf
(Med: ayudante de doctor) medical assistant;
(: enfermero) nurse; (quien practica algo)

practitioner ▷ adj practising

**practicar** [prakti'kar] vt to practise;
(Deporte) to play; (realizar) to carry out,
perform

**práctico, -a** ['praktiko, a] adj practical;
(instruido: persona) skilled, expert

**practique** etc vb V **practicar**

**pradera** [pra'ðera] nf meadow; (US etc)
prairie

**prado** ['praðo] nm (campo) meadow, field;
(pastizal) pasture

**Praga** ['praɣa] n Prague

**pragmático, -a** [praɣ'matiko, a] adj
pragmatic

**precario, -a** [pre'karjo, a] adj precarious

**precaución** [prekau'θjon] nf (medida
preventiva) preventive measure, precaution;
(prudencia) caution, wariness

**precedente** [preθe'ðente] adj preceding;
(anterior) former ▷ nm precedent

**preceder** [preθe'ðer] vt, vi to precede, go
before, come before

**precepto** [pre'θepto] nm precept

**precinto** [pre'θinto] nm (tb: **~ de
garantía**) seal

**precio** ['preθjo] nm price; (costo) cost;
(valor) value, worth; (de viaje) fare; **precio
al contado/de coste/de oportunidad**
cash/cost/bargain price; **precio al por
menor** retail price; **precio de ocasión**
bargain price; **precio de venta al público**
retail price; **precio tope** top price

**preciosidad** [preθjosi'ðað] nf (valor)
(high) value, (great) worth; (encanto) charm;
(cosa bonita) beautiful thing; **es una ~** it's
lovely, it's really beautiful

**precioso, -a** [pre'θjoso, a] adj precious;
(de mucho valor) valuable; (fam) lovely,
beautiful

**precipicio** [preθi'piθjo] nm cliff, precipice;
(fig) abyss

**precipitación** [preθipita'θjon] nf haste;
(lluvia) rainfall

**precipitado, -a** [preθipi'taðo, a] adj
(conducta) hasty, rash; (salida) hasty, sudden

**precipitar** [preθipi'tar] vt (arrojar) to hurl
down, throw; (apresurar) to hasten; (acelerar)
to speed up, accelerate; **precipitarse** vr to
throw o.s.; (apresurarse) to rush; (actuar sin
pensar) to act rashly

**precisamente** [preθisa'mente] adv
precisely; (exactamente) precisely, exactly

**precisar** [preθi'sar] vt (necesitar) to need,
require; (fijar) to determine exactly, fix;
(especificar) to specify

**precisión** [preθi'sjon] nf (exactitud)
precision

**preciso, -a** [pre'θiso, a] adj (exacto)

precise; (*necesario*) necessary, essential

**preconcebido, -a** [prekonθe'βiðo, a] *adj* preconceived

**precoz** [pre'koθ] *adj* (*persona*) precocious; (*calvicie etc*) premature

**predecir** [preðe'θir] *vt* to predict, forecast

**predestinado, -a** [preðesti'naðo, a] *adj* predestined

**predicar** [preði'kar] *vt, vi* to preach

**predicción** [preðik'θjon] *nf* prediction

**predilecto, -a** [preði'lekto, a] *adj* favourite

**predisposición** [preðisposi'θjon] *nf* inclination; prejudice, bias

**predominar** [preðomi'nar] *vt* to dominate ⊳ *vi* to predominate; (*prevalecer*) to prevail; **predominio** *nm* predominance; prevalence

**preescolar** [pre(e)sko'lar] *adj* preschool

**prefabricado, -a** [prefaβri'kaðo, a] *adj* prefabricated

**prefacio** [pre'faθjo] *nm* preface

**preferencia** [prefe'renθja] *nf* preference; **de ~** preferably, for preference

**preferible** [prefe'riβle] *adj* preferable

**preferir** [prefe'rir] *vt* to prefer

**prefiero** *etc vb* V **preferir**

**prefijo** [pre'fixo] *nm* (*Tel*) (dialling) code

**pregunta** [pre'ɣunta] *nf* question; **hacer una ~** to ask a question; **preguntas frecuentes** FAQs, frequently asked questions

**preguntar** [preɣun'tar] *vt* to ask; (*cuestionar*) to question ⊳ *vi* to ask; **preguntarse** *vr* to wonder; **preguntar por algn** to ask for sb; **preguntón, -ona** [preɣun'ton, ona] *adj* inquisitive

**prehistórico, -a** [preis'toriko, a] *adj* prehistoric

**prejuicio** [pre'xwiθjo] *nm* (*acto*) prejudgement; (*idea preconcebida*) preconception; (*parcialidad*) prejudice, bias

**preludio** [pre'luðjo] *nm* prelude

**prematuro, -a** [prema'turo, a] *adj* premature

**premeditar** [premeði'tar] *vt* to premeditate

**premiar** [pre'mjar] *vt* to reward; (*en un concurso*) to give a prize to

**premio** ['premjo] *nm* reward; prize; (*Com*) premium

**prenatal** [prena'tal] *adj* antenatal, prenatal

**prenda** ['prenda] *nf* (*ropa*) garment, article of clothing; (*garantía*) pledge; **prendas** *nfpl* (*talentos*) talents, gifts

**prender** [pren'der] *vt* (*captar*) to catch, capture; (*detener*) to arrest; (*Costura*) to

pin, attach; (*sujetar*) to fasten ⊳ *vi* to catch; (*arraigar*) to take root; **prenderse** *vr* (*encenderse*) to catch fire

**prendido, -a** [pren'diðo, a] (*LAM*) *adj* (*luz etc*) on

**prensa** ['prensa] *nf* press; **la ~** the press

**preñado, -a** [pre'ɲaðo, a] *adj* pregnant; **~ de** pregnant with, full of

**preocupación** [preokupa'θjon] *nf* worry, concern; (*ansiedad*) anxiety

**preocupado, -a** [preoku'paðo, a] *adj* worried, concerned; (*ansioso*) anxious

**preocupar** [preoku'par] *vt* to worry; **preocuparse** *vr* to worry; **~se de algo** (*hacerse cargo*) to take care of sth

**preparación** [prepara'θjon] *nf* (*acto*) preparation; (*estado*) readiness; (*entrenamiento*) training

**preparado, -a** [prepa'raðo, a] *adj* (*dispuesto*) prepared; (*Culin*) ready (to serve) ⊳ *nm* preparation

**preparar** [prepa'rar] *vt* (*disponer*) to prepare, get ready; (*Tec: tratar*) to prepare, process; (*entrenar*) to teach, train; **prepararse** *vr*: **~se a o para** to prepare to o for, get ready to o for; **preparativo, -a** *adj* preparatory, preliminary; **preparativos** *nmpl* preparations; **preparatoria** (*MÉX*) *nf* sixth-form college (*BRIT*), senior high school (*US*)

**presa** ['presa] *nf* (*cosa apresada*) catch; (*víctima*) victim; (*de animal*) prey; (*de agua*) dam

**presagiar** [presa'xjar] *vt* to presage, forebode; **presagio** *nm* omen

**prescindir** [presθin'dir] *vi*: **~ de** (*privarse de*) to do o go without; (*descartar*) to dispense with

**prescribir** [preskri'βir] *vt* to prescribe

**presencia** [pre'senθja] *nf* presence; **presenciar** *vt* to be present at; (*asistir a*) to attend; (*ver*) to see, witness

**presentación** [presenta'θjon] *nf* presentation; (*introducción*) introduction

**presentador, a** [presenta'ðor, a] *nm/f* presenter, compère

**presentar** [presen'tar] *vt* to present; (*ofrecer*) to offer; (*mostrar*) to show, display; (*a una persona*) to introduce; **presentarse** *vr* (*llegar inesperadamente*) to appear, turn up; (*ofrecerse: como candidato*) to run, stand; (*aparecer*) to show, appear; (*solicitar empleo*) to apply

**presente** [pre'sente] *adj* present ⊳ *nm* present; **hacer ~** to state, declare; **tener ~** to remember, bear in mind

**presentimiento** [presenti'mjento] *nm* premonition, presentiment

**presentir** [presen'tir] *vt* to have a premonition of

**preservación** [preserβa'θjon] *nf* protection, preservation

**preservar** [preser'βar] *vt* to protect, preserve; **preservativo** *nm* sheath, condom

**presidencia** [presi'ðenθja] *nf* presidency; *(de comité)* chairmanship

**presidente** [presi'ðente] *nmf* president; *(de comité)* chairman/woman

**presidir** [presi'ðir] *vt (dirigir)* to preside at, preside over; *(: comité)* to take the chair at; *(dominar)* to dominate, rule ▷ *vi* to preside; to take the chair

**presión** [pre'sjon] *nf* pressure; **presión atmosférica** atmospheric o air pressure; **presionar** *vt* to press; *(fig)* to press, put pressure on ▷ *vi*: **presionar para** to press for

**preso, -a** ['preso, a] *nm/f* prisoner; **tomar** o **llevar ~ a algn** to arrest sb, take sb prisoner

**prestación** [presta'θjon] *nf* service; *(subsidio)* benefit; **prestaciones** *nfpl (Tec, Auto)* performance features

**prestado, -a** [pres'taðo, a] *adj* on loan; **pedir ~** to borrow

**prestamista** [presta'mista] *nmf* moneylender

**préstamo** ['prestamo] *nm* loan; **préstamo hipotecario** mortgage

**prestar** [pres'tar] *vt* to lend, loan; *(atención)* to pay; *(ayuda)* to give

**prestigio** [pres'tixjo] *nm* prestige; **prestigioso, -a** *adj (honorable)* prestigious; *(famoso, renombrado)* renowned, famous

**presumido, -a** [presu'miðo, a] *adj (persona)* vain

**presumir** [presu'mir] *vt* to presume ▷ *vi (tener aires)* to be conceited; **presunto, -a** *adj (supuesto)* supposed, presumed; *(así llamado)* so-called; **presuntuoso, -a** *adj* conceited, presumptuous

**presupuesto** [presu'pwesto] *pp de* **presuponer** ▷ *nm (Finanzas)* budget; *(estimación: de costo)* estimate

**pretencioso, -a** [preten'θjoso, a] *adj* pretentious

**pretender** [preten'der] *vt (intentar)* to try to, seek to; *(reivindicar)* to claim; *(buscar)* to seek, try for; *(cortejar)* to woo, court; **~ que** to expect that

▎No confundir **pretender** con la palabra inglesa *pretend*.

**pretendiente** *nmf (amante)* suitor; *(al trono)* pretender; **pretensión** *nf (aspiración)* aspiration; *(reivindicación)* claim; *(orgullo)* pretension

**pretexto** [pre'teksto] *nm* pretext; *(excusa)* excuse

**prevención** [preβen'θjon] *nf* prevention; *(precaución)* precaution

**prevenido, -a** [preβe'niðo, a] *adj* prepared, ready; *(cauteloso)* cautious

**prevenir** [preβe'nir] *vt (impedir)* to prevent; *(predisponer)* to prejudice, bias; *(avisar)* to warn; *(preparar)* to prepare, get ready; **prevenirse** *vr* to get ready, prepare; **~se contra** to take precautions against; **preventivo, -a** *adj* preventive, precautionary

**prever** [pre'βer] *vt* to foresee

**previo, -a** ['preβjo, a] *adj (anterior)* previous; *(preliminar)* preliminary ▷ *prep*: **~ acuerdo de los otros** subject to the agreement of the others

**previsión** [preβi'sjon] *nf (perspicacia)* foresight; *(predicción)* forecast; **previsto, -a** *adj* anticipated, forecast

**prima** ['prima] *nf (Com)* bonus; *(de seguro)* premium; *V tb* **primo**

**primario, -a** [pri'marjo, a] *adj* primary

**primavera** [prima'βera] *nf* spring(-time)

**primera** [pri'mera] *nf (Auto)* first gear; *(Ferro: tb:* **~ clase***)* first class; **de ~** *(fam)* first-class, first-rate

**primero, -a** [pri'mero, a] *adj (adj* **primer***)* first; *(principal)* prime *adv* first; *(más bien)* sooner, rather; **primera plana** front page

**primitivo, -a** [primi'tiβo, a] *adj* primitive; *(original)* original

**primo, -a** ['primo, a] *adj* prime ▷ *nm/f* cousin; *(fam)* fool, idiot; **materias primas** raw materials; **primo hermano** first cousin

**primogénito, -a** [primo'xenito, a] *adj* first-born

**primoroso, -a** [primo'roso, a] *adj* exquisite, delicate

**princesa** [prin'θesa] *nf* princess

**principal** [prinθi'pal] *adj* principal, main ▷ *nm (jefe)* chief, principal

**príncipe** ['prinθipe] *nm* prince

**principiante** [prinθi'pjante] *nmf* beginner

**principio** [prin'θipjo] *nm (comienzo)* beginning, start; *(origen)* origin; *(primera etapa)* rudiment, basic idea; *(moral)* principle; **desde el ~** from the first; **en un ~** at first; **a ~s de** at the beginning of

**pringue** ['pringe] *nm (grasa)* grease, fat, dripping

**prioridad** [priori'ðað] *nf* priority

**prisa** ['prisa] *nf (apresuramiento)* hurry, haste; *(rapidez)* speed; *(urgencia)* (sense of) urgency; **a** o **de ~** quickly; **correr ~** to be urgent; **darse ~** to hurry up; **tener ~** to be in a hurry

**prisión** [pri'sjon] *nf (cárcel)* prison; *(período de cárcel)* imprisonment; **prisionero, -a** *nm/f* prisoner

**prismáticos** [pris'matikos] *nmpl* binoculars

**privado, -a** [pri'βaðo, a] *adj* private

**privar** [pri'βar] *vt* to deprive; **privativo, -a** *adj* exclusive

**privilegiar** [priβile'xjar] *vt* to grant a privilege to; *(favorecer)* to favour

**privilegio** [priβi'lexjo] *nm* privilege; *(concesión)* concession

**pro** [pro] *nm o f* profit, advantage
▷ *prep:* **asociación ~ ciegos** association for the blind ▷ *prefijo:* **~ americano** pro-American; **en ~ de** on behalf of, for; **los ~s y los contras** the pros and cons

**proa** ['proa] *nf* bow, prow; **de ~** bow *cpd*, fore

**probabilidad** [proβaβili'ðað] *nf* probability, likelihood; *(oportunidad, posibilidad)* chance, prospect; **probable** *adj* probable, likely

**probador** [proβa'ðor] *nm (en tienda)* fitting room

**probar** [pro'βar] *vt (demostrar)* to prove; *(someter a prueba)* to test, try out; *(ropa)* to try on; *(comida)* to taste ▷ *vi* to try; **~se un traje** to try on a suit

**probeta** [pro'βeta] *nf* test tube

**problema** [pro'βlema] *nm* problem

**procedente** [proθe'ðente] *adj (razonable)* reasonable; *(conforme a derecho)* proper, fitting; **~ de** coming from, originating in

**proceder** [proθe'ðer] *vi (avanzar)* to proceed; *(actuar)* to act; *(ser correcto)* to be right (and proper), be fitting ▷ *nm (comportamiento)* behaviour, conduct; **~ de** to come from, originate in; **procedimiento** *nm* procedure; *(proceso)* process; *(método)* means *pl*, method

**procesador** [proθesa'ðor] *nm* processor; **procesador de textos** word processor

**procesar** [proθe'sar] *vt* to try, put on trial

**procesión** [proθe'sjon] *nf* procession

**proceso** [pro'θeso] *nm* process; *(Jur)* trial

**proclamar** [prokla'mar] *vt* to proclaim

**procrear** [prokre'ar] *vt, vi* to procreate

**procurador, a** [prokura'ðor, a] *nm/f* attorney

**procurar** [proku'rar] *vt (intentar)* to try, endeavour; *(conseguir)* to get, obtain; *(asegurar)* to secure; *(producir)* to produce

**prodigio** [pro'ðixjo] *nm* prodigy; *(milagro)* wonder, marvel; **prodigioso, -a** *adj* prodigious, marvellous

**pródigo, -a** ['proðixo, a] *adj:* **hijo ~**

prodigal son

**producción** [proðuk'θjon] *nf (gen)* production; *(producto)* output; **producción en serie** mass production

**producir** [proðu'θir] *vt* to produce; *(causar)* to cause, bring about; **producirse** *vr (cambio)* to come about; *(accidente)* to take place; *(problema etc)* to arise; *(hacerse)* to be produced, be made; *(estallar)* to break out

**productividad** [proðuktiβi'ðað] *nf* productivity; **productivo, -a** *adj* productive; *(provechoso)* profitable

**producto** [pro'ðukto] *nm* product

**productor, a** [proðuk'tor, a] *adj* productive, producing ▷ *nm/f* producer

**proeza** [pro'eθa] *nf* exploit, feat

**profano, -a** [pro'fano, a] *adj* profane ▷ *nm/f* layman/woman

**profecía** [profe'θia] *nf* prophecy

**profesión** [profe'sjon] *nf* profession; *(en formulario)* occupation; **profesional** *adj* professional

**profesor, a** [profe'sor, a] *nm/f* teacher; **profesorado** *nm* teaching profession

**profeta** [pro'feta] *nmf* prophet

**prófugo, -a** ['profuxo, a] *nm/f* fugitive; *(Mil: desertor)* deserter

**profundidad** [profundi'ðað] *nf* depth; **profundizar** *vi:* **profundizar en** to go deeply into; **profundo, -a** *adj* deep; *(misterio, pensador)* profound

**progenitor** [proxeni'tor] *nm* ancestor; **progenitores** *nmpl (padres)* parents

**programa** [pro'ɣrama] *nm* programme *(BRIT),* program *(US);* **programa de estudios** curriculum, syllabus; **programación** *nf* programming; **programador, a** *nm/f* programmer; **programar** *vt* to program

**progresar** [proɣre'sar] *vi* to progress, make progress; **progresista** *adj, nmf* progressive; **progresivo, -a** *adj* progressive; *(gradual)* gradual; *(continuo)* continuous; **progreso** *nm* progress

**prohibición** [proiβi'θjon] *nf* prohibition, ban

**prohibir** [proi'βir] *vt* to prohibit, ban, forbid; **prohibido o se prohibe fumar** no smoking; **"prohibido el paso"** "no entry"

**prójimo, -a** ['proximo, a] *nm/f* fellow man; *(vecino)* neighbour

**prólogo** ['proloɣo] *nm* prologue

**prolongar** [prolon'ɣar] *vt* to extend; *(reunión etc)* to prolong; *(calle, tubo)* to extend

**promedio** [pro'meðjo] *nm* average; *(de distancia)* middle, mid-point

**promesa** [pro'mesa] *nf* promise

**prometer** [prome'ter] *vt* to promise ▷ *vi* to show promise; **prometerse** *vr (novios)* to get engaged; **prometido, -a** *adj* promised; engaged ▷ *nm/f* fiancé/fiancée

**prominente** [promi'nente] *adj* prominent

**promoción** [promo'θjon] *nf* promotion

**promotor** [promo'tor] *nm* promoter; (*instigador*) instigator

**promover** [promo'βer] *vt* to promote; (*causar*) to cause; (*instigar*) to instigate, stir up

**promulgar** [promul'xar] *vt* to promulgate; (*anunciar*) to proclaim

**pronombre** [pro'nombre] *nm* pronoun

**pronosticar** [pronosti'kar] *vt* to predict, foretell, forecast; **pronóstico** *nm* prediction, forecast; **pronóstico del tiempo** weather forecast

**pronto, -a** ['pronto, a] *adj* (*rápido*) prompt, quick; (*preparado*) ready ▷ *adv* quickly, promptly; (*en seguida*) at once, right away; (*dentro de poco*) soon; (*temprano*) early ▷ *nm*: **tiene unos ~s muy malos** he gets ratty all of a sudden (*inf*); **de ~** suddenly; **por lo ~** meanwhile, for the present

**pronunciación** [pronunθja'θjon] *nf* pronunciation

**pronunciar** [pronun'θjar] *vt* to pronounce; (*discurso*) to make, deliver; **pronunciarse** *vr* to revolt, rebel; (*declararse*) to declare o.s.

**propagación** [propaxa'θjon] *nf* propagation

**propaganda** [propa'xanda] *nf* (*Pol*) propaganda; (*Com*) advertising

**propenso, -a** [pro'penso, a] *adj* inclined to; **ser ~ a** to be inclined to, have a tendency to

**propicio, -a** [pro'piθjo, a] *adj* favourable, propitious

**propiedad** [propje'ðað] *nf* property; (*posesión*) possession, ownership; **propiedad particular** private property

**propietario, -a** [propje'tarjo, a] *nm/f* owner, proprietor

**propina** [pro'pina] *nf* tip

**propio, -a** ['propjo, a] *adj* own, of one's own; (*característico*) characteristic, typical; (*debido*) proper; (*mismo*) selfsame, very; **el ~ ministro** the minister himself; **¿tienes casa propia?** have you a house of your own?

**proponer** [propo'ner] *vt* to propose, put forward; (*problema*) to pose; **proponerse** *vr* to propose, intend

**proporción** [propor'θjon] *nf* proportion; (*Mat*) ratio; **proporciones** *nfpl* (*dimensiones*) dimensions; (*fig*) size *sg*; **proporcionado, -a** *adj* proportionate; (*regular*) medium, middling; (*justo*) just right; **proporcionar** *vt*

(*dar*) to give, supply, provide

**proposición** [proposi'θjon] *nf* proposition; (*propuesta*) proposal

**propósito** [pro'posito] *nm* purpose; (*intento*) aim, intention ▷ *adv*: **a ~** by the way, incidentally; (*a posta*) on purpose, deliberately; **a ~ de** about, with regard to

**propuesta** [pro'pwesta] *vb* V **proponer** ▷ *nf* proposal

**propulsar** [propul'sar] *vt* to drive, propel; (*fig*) to promote, encourage; **propulsión** *nf* propulsion; **propulsión a chorro** o **por reacción** jet propulsion

**prórroga** ['prorroxa] *nf* extension; (*Jur*) stay; (*Com*) deferment; (*Deporte*) extra time; **prorrogar** *vt* (*período*) to extend; (*decisión*) to defer, postpone

**prosa** ['prosa] *nf* prose

**proseguir** [prose'xir] *vt* to continue, carry on ▷ *vi* to continue, go on

**prospecto** [pros'pekto] *nm* prospectus

**prosperar** [prospe'rar] *vi* to prosper, thrive, flourish; **prosperidad** *nf* prosperity; (*éxito*) success; **próspero, -a** *adj* prosperous, flourishing; (*que tiene éxito*) successful

**prostíbulo** [pros'tiβulo] *nm* brothel (BRIT), house of prostitution (US)

**prostitución** [prostitu'θjon] *nf* prostitution

**prostituir** [prosti'twir] *vt* to prostitute; **prostituirse** *vr* to prostitute o.s., become a prostitute

**prostituta** [prosti'tuta] *nf* prostitute

**protagonista** [protaxo'nista] *nmf* protagonist

**protección** [protek'θjon] *nf* protection

**protector, a** [protek'tor, a] *adj* protective, protecting ▷ *nm/f* protector

**proteger** [prote'xer] *vt* to protect; **protegido, -a** *nm/f* protégé/protégée

**proteína** [prote'ina] *nf* protein

**protesta** [pro'testa] *nf* protest; (*declaración*) protestation

**protestante** [protes'tante] *adj* Protestant

**protestar** [protes'tar] *vt* to protest, declare ▷ *vi* to protest

**protocolo** [proto'kolo] *nm* protocol

**prototipo** [proto'tipo] *nm* prototype

**provecho** [pro'βetʃo] *nm* advantage, benefit; (*Finanzas*) profit; **¡buen ~!** bon appétit!; **en ~ de** to the benefit of; **sacar ~ de** to benefit from, profit by

**provenir** [proβe'nir] *vi*: **~ de** to come o stem from

**proverbio** [pro'βerβjo] *nm* proverb

**providencia** [proβi'ðenθja] *nf* providence

**provincia** [proˈβinθja] nf province

**provisión** [proβiˈsjon] nf provision; (abastecimiento) provision, supply; (medida) measure, step

**provisional** [proβisjoˈnal] adj provisional

**provocar** [proβoˈkar] vt to provoke; (alentar) to tempt, invite; (causar) to bring about, lead to; (promover) to promote; (estimular) to rouse, stimulate; ¿te provoca un café? (CAM) would you like a coffee?; **provocativo, -a** adj provocative

**proxeneta** [prokseˈneta] nm pimp

**próximamente** [proksimaˈmente] adv shortly, soon

**proximidad** [proksimiˈðað] nf closeness, proximity; **próximo, -a** adj near, close; (vecino) neighbouring; (siguiente) next

**proyectar** [projekˈtar] vt (objeto) to hurl, throw; (luz) to cast, shed; (Cine) to screen, show; (planear) to plan

**proyectil** [projekˈtil] nm projectile, missile

**proyecto** [proˈjekto] nm plan; (estimación de costo) detailed estimate

**proyector** [projekˈtor] nm (Cine) projector

**prudencia** [pruˈðenθja] nf (sabiduría) wisdom; (cuidado) care; **prudente** adj sensible, wise; (conductor) careful

**prueba** etc ['prweβa] vb V **probar** ▷ nf proof; (ensayo) test, trial; (degustación) tasting, sampling; (de ropa) fitting; **a ~** on trial; **a ~ de** proof against; **a ~ de agua/fuego** waterproof/fireproof; **someter a ~** to put to the test

**psico...** [siko] prefijo psycho...; **psicología** nf psychology; **psicológico, -a** adj psychological; **psicólogo, -a** nm/f psychologist; **psicópata** nmf psychopath; **psicosis** nf inv psychosis

**psiquiatra** [siˈkjatra] nmf psychiatrist; **psiquiátrico, -a** adj psychiatric

**PSOE** [peˈsoe] (ESP) nm abr = **Partido Socialista Obrero Español**

**púa** ['pua] nf (Bot, Zool) prickle, spine; (para guitarra) plectrum (BRIT), pick (US); **alambre de ~** barbed wire

**pubertad** [puβerˈtað] nf puberty

**publicación** [puβlikaˈθjon] nf publication

**publicar** [puβliˈkar] vt (editar) to publish; (hacer público) to publicize; (divulgar) to make public, divulge

**publicidad** [puβliθiˈðað] nf publicity; (Com: propaganda) advertising; **publicitario, -a** adj publicity cpd; advertising cpd

**público, -a** ['puβliko, a] adj public ▷ nm public; (Teatro etc) audience

**puchero** [puˈtʃero] nm (Culin: guiso) stew; (: olla) cooking pot; **hacer ~s** to pout

**pucho** ['putʃo] (CS: fam) nm cigarette, fag (BRIT)

**pude** etc vb V **poder**

**pudiente** [puˈðjente] adj (rico) wealthy, well-to-do

**pudiera** etc vb V **poder**

**pudor** [puˈðor] nm modesty

**pudrir** [puˈðrir] vt to rot; **pudrirse** vr to rot, decay

**pueblo** ['pweβlo] nm people; (nación) nation; (aldea) village

**puedo** etc vb V **poder**

**puente** ['pwente] nm bridge; **hacer ~** (fam) to take extra days off work between 2 public holidays; to take a long weekend; **puente aéreo** shuttle service; **puente colgante** suspension bridge; **puente levadizo** drawbridge

○ **HACER PUENTE**
○
○ When a public holiday in Spain falls on
○ a Tuesday or Thursday it is common
○ practice for employers to make the
○ Monday or Friday a holiday as well and
○ to give everyone a four-day weekend.
○ This is known as **hacer puente**. When
○ a named public holiday such as the **Día
○ de la Constitución** falls on a Tuesday
○ or Thursday, people refer to the whole
○ holiday period as e.g. the **puente de la
○ Constitución**.

**puerco, -a** ['pwerko, a] nm/f pig/sow ▷ adj (sucio) dirty, filthy; (obsceno) disgusting; **puerco espín** porcupine

**pueril** [pweˈril] adj childish

**puerro** ['pwerro] nm leek

**puerta** ['pwerta] nf door; (de jardín) gate; (portal) doorway; (fig) gateway; (portería) goal; **a la ~** at the door; **a ~ cerrada** behind closed doors; **puerta giratoria** revolving door

**puerto** ['pwerto] nm port; (paso) pass; (fig) haven, refuge

**Puerto Rico** [pwertoˈriko] nm Puerto Rico; **puertorriqueño, -a** adj, nm/f Puerto Rican

**pues** [pwes] adv (entonces) then; (bueno) well, well then; (así que) so ▷ conj (ya que) since; ¡~ sí! yes!, certainly!

**puesta** ['pwesta] nf (apuesta) bet, stake; **puesta al día** updating; **puesta a punto** fine tuning; **puesta de sol** sunset; **puesta en marcha** starting

**puesto, -a** ['pwesto, a] pp de **poner** ▷ adj: **tener algo ~** to have sth on, be wearing sth ▷ *nm* (*lugar, posición*) place; (*trabajo*) post, job; (*Com*) stall ▷ *conj*: **~ que** since, as

**púgil** ['puxil] *nm* boxer

**pulga** ['pulɣa] *nf* flea

**pulgada** [pul'ɣaða] *nf* inch

**pulgar** [pul'ɣar] *nm* thumb

**pulir** [pu'lir] *vt* to polish; (*alisar*) to smooth; (*fig*) to polish up, touch up

**pulmón** [pul'mon] *nm* lung; **pulmonía** *nf* pneumonia

**pulpa** ['pulpa] *nf* pulp; (*de fruta*) flesh, soft part

**pulpería** [pulpe'ria] (*LAM*) *nf* (*tienda*) small grocery store

**púlpito** ['pulpito] *nm* pulpit

**pulpo** ['pulpo] *nm* octopus

**pulque** ['pulke] *nm* pulque

○ **PULQUE**
○
○
○ **Pulque** is a thick, white, alcoholic
○ drink which is very popular in Mexico.
○ In ancient times it was considered
○ sacred by the Aztecs. It is produced by
○ fermenting the juice of the **maguey**,
○ a Mexican cactus similar to the agave.
○ It can be drunk by itself or mixed with
○ fruit or vegetable juice.

**pulsación** [pulsa'θjon] *nf* beat; **pulsaciones** pulse rate

**pulsar** [pul'sar] *vt* (*tecla*) to touch, tap; (*Mús*) to play; (*botón*) to press, push ▷ *vi* to pulsate; (*latir*) to beat, throb

**pulsera** [pul'sera] *nf* bracelet

**pulso** ['pulso] *nm* (*Anat*) pulse; (*fuerza*) strength; (*firmeza*) steadiness, steady hand

**pulverizador** [pulβeriθa'ðor] *nm* spray, spray gun

**pulverizar** [pulβeri'θar] *vt* to pulverize; (*líquido*) to spray

**puna** ['puna] (*CAM*) *nf* mountain sickness

**punta** ['punta] *nf* point, tip; (*extremo*) end; (*fig*) touch, trace; **horas ~** peak o rush hours; **sacar ~ a** to sharpen

**puntada** [pun'taða] *nf* (*Costura*) stitch

**puntal** [pun'tal] *nm* prop, support

**puntapié** [punta'pje] *nm* kick

**puntería** [punte'ria] *nf* (*de arma*) aim, aiming; (*destreza*) marksmanship

**puntero, -a** [pun'tero, a] *adj* leading ▷ *nm* (*palo*) pointer

**puntiagudo, -a** [puntja'ɣuðo, a] *adj* sharp, pointed

**puntilla** [pun'tiʎa] *nf* (*encaje*) lace edging o trim; **(andar) de ~s** (to walk) on tiptoe

**punto** ['punto] *nm* (*gen*) point; (*señal* diminuta*) spot, dot; (*Costura, Med*) stitch; (*lugar*) spot, place; (*momento*) moment; **a ~** ready; **estar a ~ de** to be on the point of o about to; **en ~** on the dot; **hasta cierto ~** to some extent; **hacer ~** (*ESP: tejer*) to knit; **dos ~s** (*Ling*) colon; **punto de interrogación** question mark; **punto de vista** point of view, viewpoint; **punto final** full stop (*BRIT*), period (*US*); **punto muerto** dead center; (*Auto*) neutral (gear); **punto y aparte** (*en dictado*) full stop, new paragraph; **punto y coma** semicolon

**puntocom** [punto'kom] *adj inv, nf inv* dotcom

**puntuación** [puntwa'θjon] *nf* punctuation; (*puntos: en examen*) mark(s) (*pl*); (*Deporte*) score

**puntual** [pun'twal] *adj* (*a tiempo*) punctual; (*exacto*) exact, accurate; **puntualidad** *nf* punctuality; exactness, accuracy

**puntuar** [pun'twar] *vi* (*Deporte*) to score, count

**punzante** [pun'θante] *adj* (*dolor*) shooting, sharp; (*herramienta*) sharp

**puñado** [pu'ɲaðo] *nm* handful

**puñal** [pu'ɲal] *nm* dagger; **puñalada** *nf* stab

**puñetazo** [puɲe'taθo] *nm* punch

**puño** ['puɲo] *nm* (*Anat*) fist; (*cantidad*) fistful, handful; (*Costura*) cuff; (*de herramienta*) handle

**pupila** [pu'pila] *nf* pupil

**pupitre** [pu'pitre] *nm* desk

**puré** [pu're] *nm* purée; (*sopa*) (thick) soup; **puré de papas** (*LAM*) mashed potatoes; **puré de patatas** (*ESP*) mashed potatoes

**purga** ['purɣa] *nf* purge; **purgante** *adj, nm* purgative

**purgatorio** [purɣa'torjo] *nm* purgatory

**purificar** [purifi'kar] *vt* to purify; (*refinar*) to refine

**puritano, -a** [puri'tano, a] *adj* (*actitud*) puritanical; (*iglesia, tradición*) puritan ▷ *nm/f* puritan

**puro, -a** ['puro, a] *adj* pure; (*verdad*) simple, plain ▷ *nm* cigar

**púrpura** ['purpura] *nf* purple

**pus** [pus] *nm* pus

**puse** etc *vb* V **poder**

**pusiera** etc *vb* V **poder**

**puta** ['puta] (*fam!*) *nf* whore, prostitute

**putrefacción** [putrefak'θjon] *nf* rotting, putrefaction

**PVP** *nm abr* (= *precio de venta al público*) RRP

**pyme, PYME** ['pime] *nf abr* (= *Pequeña y Mediana Empresa*) SME

# q

**que** [ke] *conj* **1**(*con oración subordinada: muchas veces no se traduce*) that; **dijo que vendría** he said (that) he would come; **espero que lo encuentres** I hope (that) you find it; V *tb* **el**

**2** (*en oración independiente*): **¡que entre!** send him in; **¡que aproveche!** enjoy your meal!; **¡que se mejore tu padre!** I hope your father gets better

**3** (*enfático*): **¿me quieres? – ¡que sí!** do you love me? – of course!

**4** (*consecutivo: muchas veces no se traduce*) that; **es tan grande que no lo puedo levantar** it's so big (that) I can't lift it

**5** (*comparaciones*) than; **yo que tú/él** if I were you/him; V *tb* **más, menos, mismo**

**6** (*valor disyuntivo*): **que le guste o no** whether he likes it or not; **que venga o que no venga** whether he comes or not

**7** (*porque*): **no puedo, que tengo que quedarme en casa** I can't, I've got to stay in ▷ *pron* **1**(*cosa*) that, which; (*+ prep*) which; **el sombrero que te compraste** the hat (that o which) you bought; **la cama en que dormí** the bed (that o which) I slept in

**2** (*persona: suj*) that, who; (*: objeto*) that, whom; **el amigo que me acompañó al museo** the friend that o who went to the museum with me; **la chica que invité** the girl (that o whom) I invited

○ PALABRA CLAVE

**qué** [ke] *adj* what?, which? ▷ *pron* what?; **¡~ divertido!** how funny!; **¿~ edad tienes?** how old are you?; **¿de ~ me hablas?** what are you saying to me?; **¿~ tal?** how are you?, how are things?; **¿~ hay (de nuevo)?** what's new?

**quebrado, -a** [ke'βraðo, a] *adj* (*roto*) broken ▷ *nm/f* bankrupt ▷ *nm* (*Mat*) fraction

**quebrantar** [keβran'tar] *vt* (*infringir*) to violate, transgress

**quebrar** [ke'βrar] *vt* to break, smash ▷ *vi* to go bankrupt

**quedar** [ke'ðar] *vi* to stay, remain; (*encontrarse: sitio*) to be; (*haber aún*) to remain, be left; **quedarse** *vr* to remain, stay (behind); **~se (con) algo** to keep sth; **~ en** (*acordar*) to agree on/to; **~ en nada** to come to nothing; **~ por hacer** to be still to be done; **~ ciego/mudo** to be left blind/dumb; **no te queda bien ese vestido** that dress doesn't suit you; **eso queda muy lejos** that's a long way (away); **quedamos a las seis** we agreed to meet at six

**quedo, -a** ['keðo, a] *adj* still ▷ *adv* softly, gently

**quehacer** [kea'θer] *nm* task, job; **quehaceres (domésticos)** *nmpl* household chores

**queja** ['kexa] *nf* complaint; **quejarse** *vr* (*enfermo*) to moan, groan; (*protestar*) to complain; **quejarse de que** to complain that; **quejido** *nm* moan

**quemado, -a** [ke'maðo, a] *adj* burnt

**quemadura** [kema'ðura] *nf* burn, scald

**quemar** [ke'mar] *vt* to burn; (*fig: malgastar*) to burn up, squander ▷ *vi* to be burning hot; **quemarse** *vr* (*consumirse*) to burn (up); (*del sol*) to get sunburnt

**quemarropa** [kema'rropa]: **a ~** *adv* point-blank

**quepo** *etc vb* V **caber**

**querella** [ke'reʎa] *nf* (*Jur*) charge; (*disputa*) dispute

○ PALABRA CLAVE

**querer** [ke'rer] *vt* **1**(*desear*) to want; **quiero más dinero** I want more money; **quisiera** *o* **querría un té** I'd like a tea; **sin querer** unintentionally; **quiero ayudar/que vayas** I want to help/you to go

**2** (*preguntas: para pedir algo*) **¿quiere abrir la ventana?** could you open the window?; **¿quieres echarme una mano?** can you give me a hand?

**3** (*amar*) to love; (*tener cariño a*) to be fond of; **te quiero** I love you; **quiere mucho a sus hijos** he's very fond of his children

**4** **le pedí que me dejara ir pero no quiso** I asked him to let me go but he refused

**querido, -a** [ke'riðo, a] *adj* dear ▷ *nm/f* darling; (*amante*) lover

**queso** ['keso] *nm* cheese; **queso crema** (*LAM*) cream cheese; **queso de untar** (*ESP*) cream cheese; **queso manchego** *sheep's milk cheese made in La Mancha*

**quicio** ['kiθjo] *nm* hinge; **sacar a algn de ~** to get on sb's nerves

**quiebra** ['kjeβra] *nf* break, split; (*Com*) bankruptcy; (*Econ*) slump

**quiebro** ['kjeβro] *nm* (*del cuerpo*) swerve

**quien** [kjen] *pron* who; **hay ~ piensa que** there are those who think that; **no hay ~ lo haga** no-one will do it

**quién** [kjen] *pron* who, whom; **¿~ es?** who's there?

**quienquiera** [kjen'kjera] (*pl* **quienesquiera**) *pron* whoever

**quiero** *etc vb* V **querer**

**quieto, -a** ['kjeto, a] *adj* still; (*carácter*) placid

▌ No confundir **quieto** con la palabra inglesa *quiet*.

**quietud** *nf* stillness

**químico, -a** ['kimiko, a] *adj* chemical ▷ *nm/f* chemist ▷ *nf* chemistry

**quincalla** [kin'kaʎa] *nf* hardware, ironmongery (*BRIT*)

**quince** ['kinθe] *num* fifteen; **~ días** a fortnight; **quinceañero, -a** *nm/f* teenager; **quincena** *nf* fortnight; (*pago*) fortnightly pay; **quincenal** *adj* fortnightly

**quiniela** [ki'njela] *nf* football pools *pl*; **quinielas** *nfpl* (*impreso*) pools coupon *sg*

**quinientos, -as** [ki'njentos, as] *adj*, *num* five hundred

**quinto, -a** ['kinto, a] *adj* fifth ▷ *nf* country house; (*Mil*) call-up, draft

**quiosco** ['kjosko] *nm* (*de música*) bandstand; (*de periódicos*) news stand

**quirófano** [ki'rofano] *nm* operating theatre

**quirúrgico, -a** [ki'rurxiko, a] *adj* surgical

**quise** *etc vb* V **querer**

**quisiera** *etc vb* V **querer**

**quisquilloso, -a** [kiski'ʎoso, a] *adj* (*susceptible*) touchy; (*meticuloso*) pernickety

**quiste** ['kiste] *nm* cyst

**quitaesmalte** [kitaes'malte] *nm* nail-polish remover

**quitamanchas** [kita'mantʃas] *nm inv* stain remover

**quitanieves** [kita'njeβes] *nm inv* snowplough (*BRIT*), snowplow (*US*)

**quitar** [ki'tar] *vt* to remove, take away; (*ropa*) to take off; (*dolor*) to relieve; **¡quita de ahí!** get away!; **quitarse** *vr* to withdraw; (*ropa*) to take off; **se quitó el sombrero** he took off his hat

**Quito** ['kito] *n* Quito

**quizá(s)** [ki'θa(s)] *adv* perhaps, maybe

# r

**rábano** ['raβano] *nm* radish; **me importa un ~** I don't give a damn

**rabia** ['raβja] *nf* (*Med*) rabies *sg*; (*ira*) fury, rage; **rabiar** *vi* to have rabies; to rage, be furious; **rabiar por algo** to long for sth

**rabieta** [ra'βjeta] *nf* tantrum, fit of temper

**rabino** [ra'βino] *nm* rabbi

**rabioso, -a** [ra'βjoso, a] *adj* rabid; (*fig*) furious

**rabo** ['raβo] *nm* tail

**racha** ['ratʃa] *nf* gust of wind; **buena/mala ~** spell of good/bad luck

**racial** [ra'θjal] *adj* racial, race *cpd*

**racimo** [ra'θimo] *nm* bunch

**ración** [ra'θjon] *nf* portion; **raciones** *nfpl* rations

**racional** [raθjo'nal] *adj* (*razonable*) reasonable; (*lógico*) rational

**racionar** [raθjo'nar] *vt* to ration (out)

**racismo** [ra'θismo] *nm* racism; **racista** *adj*, *nm* racist

**radar** [ra'ðar] *nm* radar

**radiador** [raðja'ðor] *nm* radiator

**radiante** [ra'ðjante] *adj* radiant

**radical** [raði'kal] *adj*, *nmf* radical

**radicar** [raði'kar] *vi*: **~ en** (*dificultad, problema*) to lie in; (*solución*) to consist in

**radio** ['raðjo] *nf* radio; (*aparato*) radio (set) ▷ *nm* (*Mat*) radius; (*Quím*) radium; **radioactividad** *nf* radioactivity; **radioactivo, -a** *adj* radioactive; **radiografía** *nf* X-ray; **radioterapia** *nf* radiotherapy; **radioyente** *nmf* listener

**ráfaga** ['rafaxa] *nf* gust; (*de luz*) flash; (*de tiros*) burst

**raíz** [ra'iθ] *nf* root; **a ~ de** as a result of; **raíz cuadrada** square root

**raja** ['raxa] *nf* (*de melón etc*) slice; (*grieta*) crack; **rajar** *vt* to split; (*fam*) to slash; **rajarse** *vr* to split, crack; **rajarse de** to back out of

**rajatabla** [raxa'taβla]: **a ~** adv (estrictamente) strictly, to the letter

**rallador** [raʎa'ðor] nm grater

**rallar** [ra'ʎar] vt to grate

**rama** ['rama] nf branch; **ramaje** nm branches pl, foliage; **ramal** nm (de cuerda) strand; (Ferro) branch line (BRIT); (Auto) branch (road) (BRIT)

**rambla** ['rambla] nf (avenida) avenue

**ramo** ['ramo] nm branch; (sección) department, section

**rampa** ['rampa] nf ramp; **rampa de acceso** entrance ramp

**rana** ['rana] nf frog; **salto de ~** leapfrog

**ranchero** [ran'tʃero] (MÉX) nm (hacendado) rancher; smallholder

**rancho** ['rantʃo] nm (grande) ranch; (pequeño) small farm

**rancio, -a** ['ranθjo, a] adj (comestibles) rancid; (vino) aged, mellow; (fig) ancient

**rango** ['rango] nm rank, standing

**ranura** [ra'nura] nf groove; (de teléfono etc) slot

**rapar** [ra'par] vt to shave; (los cabellos) to crop

**rapaz** [ra'paθ] (nf **~a**) nmf young boy/girl ⊳ adj (Zool) predatory

**rape** ['rape] nm (pez) monkfish; **al ~** cropped

**rapé** [ra'pe] nm snuff

**rapidez** [rapi'ðeθ] nf speed, rapidity; **rápido, -a** adj fast, quick ⊳ adv quickly ⊳ nm (Ferro) express; **rápidos** nmpl rapids

**rapiña** [ra'piɲa] nm robbery; **ave de ~** bird of prey

**raptar** [rap'tar] vt to kidnap; **rapto** nm kidnapping; (impulso) sudden impulse; (éxtasis) ecstasy, rapture

**raqueta** [ra'keta] nf racquet

**raquítico, -a** [ra'kitiko, a] adj stunted; (fig) poor, inadequate

**rareza** [ra'reθa] nf rarity; (fig) eccentricity

**raro, -a** ['raro, a] adj (poco común) rare; (extraño) odd, strange; (excepcional) remarkable

**ras** [ras] nm: **a ~ de** level with; **a ~ de tierra** at ground level

**rasar** [ra'sar] vt (igualar) to level

**rascacielos** [raska'θjelos] nm inv skyscraper

**rascar** [ras'kar] vt (con las uñas etc) to scratch; (raspar) to scrape; **rascarse** vr to scratch (o.s.)

**rasgar** [ras'xar] vt to tear, rip (up)

**rasgo** ['rasxo] nm (con pluma) stroke; **rasgos** nmpl (facciones) features, characteristics; **a grandes ~s** in outline, broadly

**rasguño** [ras'xuɲo] nm scratch

**raso, -a** ['raso, a] adj (liso) flat, level; (a baja altura) very low ⊳ nm satin; **cielo ~** clear sky

**raspadura** [raspa'ðura] nf (acto) scrape, scraping; (marca) scratch; **raspaduras** nfpl (de papel etc) scrapings

**raspar** [ras'par] vt to scrape; (arañar) to scratch; (limar) to file

**rastra** ['rastra] nf (Agr) rake; **a ~s** by dragging; (fig) unwillingly

**rastrear** [rastre'ar] vt (seguir) to track

**rastrero, -a** [ras'trero, a] adj (Bot, Zool) creeping; (fig) despicable, mean

**rastrillo** [ras'triʎo] nm rake

**rastro** ['rastro] nm (Agr) rake; (pista) track, trail; (vestigio) trace; **el R~** (ESP) the Madrid fleamarket

**rasurado** [rasu'raðo] (MÉX) nm shaving; **rasuradora** [rasura'ðora] (MÉX) nf electric shaver; **rasurar** [rasu'rar] (MÉX) vt to shave; **rasurarse** vr to shave

**rata** ['rata] nf rat

**ratear** [rate'ar] vt (robar) to steal

**ratero, -a** [ra'tero, a] adj light-fingered ⊳ nm/f (carterista) pickpocket; (ladrón) petty thief

**rato** ['rato] nm while, short time; **a ~s** from time to time; **hay para ~** there's still a long way to go; **al poco ~** soon afterwards; **pasar el ~** to kill time; **pasar un buen/mal ~** to have a good/rough time; **en mis ~s libres** in my spare time

**ratón** [ra'ton] nm mouse; **ratonera** nf mousetrap

**raudal** [rau'ðal] nm torrent; **a ~es** in abundance

**raya** ['raja] nf line; (marca) scratch; (en tela) stripe; (de pelo) parting; (límite) boundary; (pez) ray; (puntuación) dash; **a ~s** striped; **pasarse de la ~** to go too far; **tener a ~** to keep in check; **rayar** vt to line; to scratch; (subrayar) to underline ⊳ vi: **rayar en** o **con** to border on

**rayo** ['rajo] nm (del sol) ray, beam; (de luz) shaft; (en una tormenta) (flash of) lightning; **rayos X** X-rays

**raza** ['raθa] nf race; **raza humana** human race

**razón** [ra'θon] nf reason; (justicia) right, justice; (razonamiento) reasoning; (motivo) reason, motive; (Mat) ratio; **a ~ de 10 cada día** at the rate of 10 a day; **en ~ de** with regard to; **dar ~ a algn** to agree that sb is right; **tener ~** to be right; **razón de ser** raison d'être; **razón directa/inversa** direct/inverse proportion; **razonable** adj reasonable; (justo, moderado) fair; **razonamiento** nm (juicio) judg(e)ment;

(*argumento*) reasoning; **razonar** *vt, vi* to reason, argue

**re** [re] *nm* (*Mús*) D

**reacción** [reak'θjon] *nf* reaction; **avión a ~** jet plane; **reacción en cadena** chain reaction; **reaccionar** *vi* to react

**reacio, -a** [re'aθjo, a] *adj* stubborn

**reactivar** [reakti'βar] *vt* to revitalize

**reactor** [reak'tor] *nm* reactor

**real** [re'al] *adj* real; (*del rey, fig*) royal

**realidad** [reali'ðað] *nf* reality, fact; (*verdad*) truth

**realista** [rea'lista] *nmf* realist

**realización** [realiθa'θjon] *nf* fulfilment

**realizador, a** [realiθa'ðor, a] *nm/f* film-maker

**realizar** [reali'θar] *vt* (*objetivo*) to achieve; (*plan*) to carry out; (*viaje*) to make, undertake; **realizarse** *vr* to come about, come true

**realmente** [real'mente] *adv* really, actually

**realzar** [real'θar] *vt* to enhance; (*acentuar*) to highlight

**reanimar** [reani'mar] *vt* to revive; (*alentar*) to encourage; **reanimarse** *vr* to revive

**reanudar** [reanu'ðar] *vt* (*renovar*) to renew; (*historia, viaje*) to resume

**reaparición** [reapari'θjon] *nf* reappearance

**rearme** [re'arme] *nm* rearmament

**rebaja** [re'βaxa] *nf* (*Com*) reduction; (*: descuento*) discount; **rebajas** *nfpl* (*Com*) sale; **rebajar** *vt* (*bajar*) to lower; (*reducir*) to reduce; (*disminuir*) to lessen; (*humillar*) to humble

**rebanada** [reβa'naða] *nf* slice

**rebañar** [reβa'ɲar] *vt* (*comida*) to scrape up; (*plato*) to scrape clean

**rebaño** [re'βaɲo] *nm* herd; (*de ovejas*) flock

**rebatir** [reβa'tir] *vt* to refute

**rebeca** [re'βeka] *nf* cardigan

**rebelarse** [reβe'larse] *vr* to rebel, revolt

**rebelde** [re'βelde] *adj* rebellious; (*niño*) unruly ▷ *nmf* rebel; **rebeldía** *nf* rebelliousness; (*desobediencia*) disobedience

**rebelión** [reβe'ljon] *nf* rebellion

**reblandecer** [reβlande'θer] *vt* to soften

**rebobinar** [reβoβi'nar] *vt* (*cinta, película de video*) to rewind

**rebosante** [reβo'sante] *adj* overflowing

**rebosar** [reβo'sar] *vi* (*líquido, recipiente*) to overflow; (*abundar*) to abound, be plentiful

**rebotar** [reβo'tar] *vt* to bounce; (*rechazar*) to repel ▷ *vi* (*pelota*) to bounce; (*bala*) to ricochet; **rebote** *nm* rebound; **de rebote** on the rebound

**rebozado, -a** [reβo'θaðo, a] *adj* fried in batter *o* breadcrumbs

**rebozar** [reβo'θar] *vt* to wrap up; (*Culin*) to fry in batter *o* breadcrumbs

**rebuscado, -a** [reβus'kaðo, a] *adj* (*amanerado*) affected; (*palabra*) recherché; (*idea*) far-fetched

**rebuscar** [reβus'kar] *vi:* **~ (en/por)** to search carefully (in/for)

**recado** [re'kaðo] *nm* (*mensaje*) message; (*encargo*) errand; **tomar un ~** (*Tel*) to take a message

**recaer** [reka'er] *vi* to relapse; **~ en** to fall to *o* on; (*criminal etc*) to fall back into, relapse into; **recaída** *nf* relapse

**recalcar** [rekal'kar] *vt* (*fig*) to stress, emphasize

**recalentar** [rekalen'tar] *vt* (*volver a calentar*) to reheat; (*calentar demasiado*) to overheat

**recámara** [re'kamara] (*MÉX*) *nf* bedroom

**recambio** [re'kambjo] *nm* spare; (*de pluma*) refill

**recapacitar** [rekapaθi'tar] *vi* to reflect

**recargado, -a** [rekar'ɣaðo, a] *adj* overloaded

**recargar** [rekar'ɣar] *vt* to overload; (*batería*) to recharge; **~ el saldo de** (*Tel*) to top up; **recargo** *nm* surcharge; (*aumento*) increase

**recatado, -a** [reka'taðo, a] *adj* (*modesto*) modest, demure; (*prudente*) cautious

**recaudación** [rekauða'θjon] *nf* (*acción*) collection; (*cantidad*) takings pl; (*en deporte*) gate; **recaudador, a** *nm/f* tax collector

**recelar** [reθe'lar] *vt:* **~ que ...** (*sospechar*) to suspect that ...; (*temer*) to fear that ... ▷ *vi:* **~ de** to distrust; **recelo** *nm* distrust, suspicion

**recepción** [reθep'θjon] *nf* reception; **recepcionista** *nmf* receptionist

**receptor, a** [reθep'tor, a] *nm/f* recipient ▷ *nm* (*Tel*) receiver

**recesión** [reθe'sjon] *nf* (*Com*) recession

**receta** [re'θeta] *nf* (*Culin*) recipe; (*Med*) prescription

▎ No confundir **receta** con la palabra inglesa *receipt*.

**rechazar** [retʃa'θar] *vt* to reject; (*oferta*) to turn down; (*ataque*) to repel

**rechazo** [re'tʃaθo] *nm* rejection

**rechinar** [retʃi'nar] *vi* to creak; (*dientes*) to grind

**rechistar** [retʃis'tar] *vi:* **sin ~** without a murmur

**rechoncho, -a** [re'tʃontʃo, a] (*fam*) *adj* thickset (*BRIT*), heavy-set (*US*)

**rechupete** [retʃu'pete]: **de ~** *adj* (*comida*)

delicious, scrumptious

**recibidor** [reθiβi'ðor] nm entrance hall

**recibimiento** [reθiβi'mjento] nm reception, welcome

**recibir** [reθi'βir] vt to receive; (dar la bienvenida) to welcome ▷ vi to entertain; **recibo** nm receipt

**reciclable** [reθi'klaβle] adj recyclable

**reciclar** [reθi'klar] vt to recycle

**recién** [re'θjen] adv recently, newly; **los ~ casados** the newly-weds; **el ~ llegado** the newcomer; **el ~ nacido** the newborn child

**reciente** [re'θjente] adj recent; (fresco) fresh

**recinto** [re'θinto] nm enclosure; (área) area, place

**recio, -a** ['reθjo, a] adj strong, tough; (voz) loud ▷ adv hard, loud(ly)

**recipiente** [reθi'pjente] nm receptacle

**recíproco, -a** [re'θiproco, a] adj reciprocal

**recital** [reθi'tal] nm (Mús) recital; (Literatura) reading

**recitar** [reθi'tar] vt to recite

**reclamación** [reklama'θjon] nf claim, demand; (queja) complaint

**reclamar** [rekla'mar] vt to claim, demand ▷ vi: **~ contra** to complain about; **reclamo** nm (anuncio) advertisement; (tentación) attraction

**reclinar** [rekli'nar] vt to recline, lean; **reclinarse** vr to lean back

**reclusión** [reklu'sjon] nf (prisión) prison; (refugio) seclusion

**recluta** [re'kluta] nmf recruit ▷ nf recruitment; **reclutar** vt (datos) to collect; (dinero) to collect up; **reclutamiento** nm recruitment

**recobrar** [reko'βrar] vt (salud) to recover; (rescatar) to get back; **recobrarse** vr to recover

**recodo** [re'koðo] nm (de río, camino) bend

**recogedor** [rekoxe'ðor] nm dustpan

**recoger** [reko'xer] vt to collect; (Agr) to harvest; (levantar) to pick up; (juntar) to gather; (pasar a buscar) to come for, get; (dar asilo) to give shelter to; (faldas) to gather up; (pelo) to put up; **recogerse** vr (retirarse) to retire; **recogido, -a** adj (lugar) quiet, secluded; (pequeño) small ▷ nf (Correos) collection; (Agr) harvest

**recolección** [rekolek'θjon] nf (Agr) harvesting; (colecta) collection

**recomendación** [rekomenda'θjon] nf (sugerencia) suggestion, recommendation; (referencia) reference

**recomendar** [rekomen'dar] vt to suggest, recommend; (confiar) to entrust

**recompensa** [rekom'pensa] nf reward, recompense; **recompensar** vt to reward, recompense

**reconciliación** [rekonθilja'θjon] nf reconciliation

**reconciliar** [rekonθi'ljar] vt to reconcile; **reconciliarse** vr to become reconciled

**recóndito, -a** [re'kondito, a] adj (lugar) hidden, secret

**reconocer** [rekono'θer] vt to recognize; (registrar) to search; (Med) to examine; **reconocido, -a** adj recognized; (agradecido) grateful; **reconocimiento** nm recognition; search; examination; gratitude; (confesión) admission

**reconquista** [rekon'kista] nf reconquest; **la R~** the Reconquest (of Spain)

**reconstituyente** [rekonstitu'jente] nm tonic

**reconstruir** [rekonstru'ir] vt to reconstruct

**reconversión** [rekonβer'sjon] nf (reestructuración) restructuring; **reconversión industrial** industrial rationalization

**recopilación** [rekopila'θjon] nf (resumen) summary; (compilación) compilation; **recopilar** vt to compile

**récord** ['rekorð] (pl **~s**) adj inv, nm record

**recordar** [rekor'ðar] vt (acordarse de) to remember; (acordar a otro) to remind ▷ vi to remember

> No confundir **recordar** con la palabra inglesa record.

**recorrer** [reko'rrer] vt (país) to cross, travel through; (distancia) to cover; (registrar) to search; (repasar) to look over; **recorrido** nm run, journey; **tren de largo recorrido** main-line train

**recortar** [rekor'tar] vt to cut out; **recorte** nm (acción, de prensa) cutting; (de telas, chapas) trimming; **recorte presupuestario** budget cut

**recostar** [rekos'tar] vt to lean; **recostarse** vr to lie down

**recoveco** [reko'βeko] nm (de camino, río etc) bend; (en casa) cubby hole

**recreación** [rekrea'θjon] nf recreation

**recrear** [rekre'ar] vt (entretener) to entertain; (volver a crear) to recreate; **recreativo, -a** adj recreational; **recreo** nm recreation; (Escol) break, playtime

**recriminar** [rekrimi'nar] vt to reproach ▷ vi to recriminate; **recriminarse** vr to reproach each other

**recrudecer** [rekruðe'θer] vt, vi to worsen; **recrudecerse** vr to worsen

**recta** ['rekta] nf straight line

**rectángulo, -a** [rek'tangulo, a] *adj* rectangular ▷ *nm* rectangle

**rectificar** [rektifi'kar] *vt* to rectify; (*volverse recto*) to straighten ▷ *vi* to correct o.s.

**rectitud** [rekti'tuð] *nf* straightness

**recto, -a** ['rekto, a] *adj* straight; (*persona*) honest, upright; **siga todo ~** go straight on ▷ *nm* rectum

**rector, a** [rek'tor, a] *adj* governing

**recuadro** [re'kwaðro] *nm* box; (*Tip*) inset

**recubrir** [reku'βrir] *vt*: **~ (con)** (*pintura*, *crema*) to cover (with)

**recuento** [re'kwento] *nm* inventory; **hacer el ~ de** to count o reckon up

**recuerdo** [re'kwerðo] *nm* souvenir; **recuerdos** *nmpl* (*memorias*) memories; **¡~s a tu madre!** give my regards to your mother!

**recular** [reku'lar] *vi* to back down

**recuperación** [rekupera'θjon] *nf* recovery

**recuperar** [rekupe'rar] *vt* to recover; (*tiempo*) to make up; **recuperarse** *vr* to recuperate

**recurrir** [reku'rrir] *vi* (*Jur*) to appeal; **~ a** to resort to; (*persona*) to turn to; **recurso** *nm* resort; (*medios*) means *pl*, resources *pl*; (*Jur*) appeal

**red** [reð] *nf* net, mesh; (*Ferro etc*) network; (*trampa*) trap; **la R~** (*Internet*) the Net

**redacción** [reðak'θjon] *nf* (*acción*) editing; (*personal*) editorial staff; (*Escol*) essay, composition

**redactar** [reðak'tar] *vt* to draw up, draft; (*periódico*) to edit

**redactor, a** [reðak'tor, a] *nm/f* editor

**redada** [re'ðaða] *nf* (*de policía*) raid, round-up

**rededor** [reðe'ðor] *nm*: **al** o **en ~** around, round about

**redoblar** [reðo'βlar] *vt* to redouble ▷ *vi* (*tambor*) to roll

**redonda** [re'ðonda] *nf*: **a la ~** around, round about

**redondear** [reðonde'ar] *vt* to round, round off

**redondel** [reðon'del] *nm* (*círculo*) circle; (*Taur*) bullring, arena

**redondo, -a** [re'ðondo, a] *adj* (*circular*) round; (*completo*) complete

**reducción** [reðuk'θjon] *nf* reduction

**reducido, -a** [reðu'θiðo, a] *adj* reduced; (*limitado*) limited; (*pequeño*) small

**reducir** [reðu'θir] *vt* to reduce; to limit; **reducirse** *vr* to diminish

**redundancia** [reðun'danθja] *nf* redundancy

**reembolsar** [re(e)mbol'sar] *vt* (*persona*) to reimburse; (*dinero*) to repay, pay back; (*depósito*) to refund; **reembolso** *nm* reimbursement; refund

**reemplazar** [re(e)mpla'θar] *vt* to replace; **reemplazo** *nm* replacement; **de reemplazo** (*Mil*) reserve

**reencuentro** [re(e)n'kwentro] *nm* reunion

**reescribible** [reeskri'βiβle] *adj* rewritable

**refacción** [refak'θjon] (*MÉX*) *nf* spare (part)

**referencia** [refe'renθja] *nf* reference; **con ~ a** with reference to

**referéndum** [refe'rendum] (*pl* **~s**) *nm* referendum

**referente** [refe'rente] *adj*: **~ a** concerning, relating to

**réferi** ['referi] (*LAM*) *nmf* referee

**referir** [refe'rir] *vt* (*contar*) to tell, recount; (*relacionar*) to refer, relate; **referirse** *vr*: **~se a** to refer to

**refilón** [refi'lon]: **de ~** *adv* obliquely

**refinado, -a** [refi'naðo, a] *adj* refined

**refinar** [refi'nar] *vt* to refine; **refinería** *nf* refinery

**reflejar** [refle'xar] *vt* to reflect; **reflejo, -a** *adj* reflected; (*movimiento*) reflex ▷ *nm* reflection; (*Anat*) reflex

**reflexión** [reflek'sjon] *nf* reflection; **reflexionar** *vt* to reflect on ▷ *vi* to reflect; (*detenerse*) to pause (to think)

**reflexivo, -a** [reflek'siβo, a] *adj* thoughtful; (*Ling*) reflexive

**reforma** [re'forma] *nf* reform; (*Arq etc*) repair; **reforma agraria** agrarian reform

**reformar** [refor'mar] *vt* to reform; (*modificar*) to change, alter; (*Arq*) to repair; **reformarse** *vr* to mend one's ways

**reformatorio** [reforma'torjo] *nm* reformatory

**reforzar** [refor'θar] *vt* to strengthen; (*Arq*) to reinforce; (*fig*) to encourage

**refractario, -a** [refrak'tarjo, a] *adj* (*Tec*) heat-resistant

**refrán** [re'fran] *nm* proverb, saying

**refregar** [refre'xar] *vt* to scrub

**refrescante** [refres'kante] *adj* refreshing, cooling

**refrescar** [refres'kar] *vt* to refresh ▷ *vi* to cool down; **refrescarse** *vr* to get cooler; (*tomar aire fresco*) to go out for a breath of fresh air; (*beber*) to have a drink

**refresco** [re'fresko] *nm* soft drink, cool drink; **"~s"** "refreshments"

**refriega** [re'frjexa] *nf* scuffle, brawl

**refrigeración** [refrixera'θjon] *nf* refrigeration; (*de sala*) air-conditioning

**refrigerador** [refrixera'ðor] nm refrigerator (BRIT), icebox (US)

**refrigerar** [refrixe'rar] vt to refrigerate; (sala) to air-condition

**refuerzo** [re'fwerθo] nm reinforcement; (Tec) support

**refugiado, -a** [refu'xjaðo, a] nm/f refugee

**refugiarse** [refu'xjarse] vr to take refuge, shelter

**refugio** [re'fuxjo] nm refuge; (protección) shelter

**refunfuñar** [refunfu'ɲar] vi to grunt, growl; (quejarse) to grumble

**regadera** [rexa'ðera] nf watering can

**regadío** [rexa'ðio] nm irrigated land

**regalado, -a** [rexa'laðo, a] adj comfortable, luxurious; (gratis) free, for nothing

**regalar** [rexa'lar] vt (dar) to give (as a present); (entregar) to give away; (mimar) to pamper, make a fuss of

**regaliz** [rexa'liθ] nm liquorice

**regalo** [re'xalo] nm (obsequio) gift, present; (gusto) pleasure

**regañadientes** [rexaɲa'ðjentes]: **a ~** adv reluctantly

**regañar** [rexa'ɲar] vt to scold ▷ vi to grumble; **regañón, -ona** adj nagging

**regar** [re'xar] vt to water, irrigate; (fig) to scatter, sprinkle

**regatear** [rexate'ar] vt (Com) to bargain over; (escatimar) to be mean with ▷ vi to bargain, haggle; (Deporte) to dribble; **regateo** nm bargaining; dribbling; (del cuerpo) swerve, dodge

**regazo** [re'xaθo] nm lap

**regenerar** [rexene'rar] vt to regenerate

**régimen** ['reximen] (pl **regímenes**) nm regime; (Med) diet

**regimiento** [rexi'mjento] nm regiment

**regio, -a** ['rexjo, a] adj royal, regal; (fig: suntuoso) splendid; (cs: fam) great, terrific

**región** [re'xjon] nf region

**regir** [re'xir] vt to govern, rule; (dirigir) to manage, run ▷ vi to apply, be in force

**registrar** [rexis'trar] vt (buscar) to search; (: en cajón) to look through; (inspeccionar) to inspect; (anotar) to register, record; (Inform) to log; **registrarse** vr to register; (ocurrir) to happen

**registro** [re'xistro] nm (acto) registration; (Mús, libro) register; (inspección) inspection, search; **registro civil** registry office

**regla** ['rexla] nf (ley) rule, regulation; (de medir) ruler, rule; (Med: período) period; **en ~** in order

**reglamentación** [rexlamenta'θjon] nf (acto) regulation; (lista) rules pl

**reglamentar** [rexlamen'tar] vt to regulate; **reglamentario, -a** adj statutory; **reglamento** nm rules pl, regulations pl

**regocijarse** [rexoθi'xarse] vr (alegrarse) to rejoice; **regocijo** nm joy, happiness

**regrabadora** [regraβa'ðora] nf rewriter; **regrabadora de DVD** DVD rewriter

**regresar** [rexre'sar] vi to come back, go back, return; **regreso** nm return

**reguero** [re'xero] nm (de sangre etc) trickle; (de humo) trail

**regulador** [rexula'ðor] nm regulator; (de radio etc) knob, control

**regular** [rexu'lar] adj regular; (normal) normal, usual; (común) ordinary; (organizado) regular, orderly; (mediano) average; (fam) not bad, so-so ▷ adv so-so, alright ▷ vt (controlar) to control, regulate; (Tec) to adjust; **por lo ~** as a rule; **regularidad** nf regularity; **regularizar** vt to regularize

**rehabilitación** [reaβilita'θjon] nf rehabilitation; (Arq) restoration

**rehabilitar** [reaβili'tar] vt to rehabilitate; (Arq) to restore; (reintegrar) to reinstate

**rehacer** [rea'θer] vt (reparar) to mend, repair; (volver a hacer) to redo, repeat; **rehacerse** vr (Med) to recover

**rehén** [re'en] nm hostage

**rehuir** [reu'ir] vt to avoid, shun

**rehusar** [reu'sar] vt, vi to refuse

**reina** ['reina] nf queen; **reinado** nm reign

**reinar** [rei'nar] vi to reign

**reincidir** [reinθi'ðir] vi to relapse

**reincorporarse** [reinkorpo'rarse] vr: **~ a** to rejoin

**reino** ['reino] nm kingdom; **reino animal/vegetal** animal/plant kingdom; **el Reino Unido** the United Kingdom

**reintegrar** [reinte'xrar] vt (reconstituir) to reconstruct; (persona) to reinstate; (dinero) to refund, pay back; **reintegrarse** vr: **~se a** to return to

**reír** [re'ir] vi to laugh; **reírse** vr to laugh; **~se de** to laugh at

**reiterar** [reite'rar] vt to reiterate

**reivindicación** [reiβindika'θjon] nf (demanda) claim, demand; (justificación) vindication

**reivindicar** [reiβindi'kar] vt to claim

**reja** ['rexa] nf (de ventana) grille, bars pl; (en la calle) grating

**rejilla** [re'xiʎa] nf grating, grille; (muebles) wickerwork; (de ventilación) vent; (de coche etc) luggage rack

**rejoneador** [rexonea'ðor] nm mounted bullfighter

**rejuvenecer** [rexuβene'θer] vt, vi to rejuvenate

**relación** [rela'θjon] nf relation, relationship; (Mat) ratio; (narración) report; **con ~ a, en ~ con** in relation to; **relaciones públicas** public relations; **relacionar** vt to relate, connect; **relacionarse** vr to be connected, be linked

**relajación** [relaxa'θjon] nf relaxation

**relajar** [rela'xar] vt to relax; **relajarse** vr to relax

**relamerse** [rela'merse] vr to lick one's lips

**relámpago** [re'lampaxo] nm flash of lightning; **visita ~** lightning visit

**relatar** [rela'tar] vt to tell, relate

**relativo, -a** [rela'tiβo, a] adj relative; **en lo ~ a** concerning

**relato** [re'lato] nm (narración) story, tale

**relegar** [rele'xar] vt to relegate

**relevante** [rele'βante] adj eminent, outstanding

**relevar** [rele'βar] vt (sustituir) to relieve; **relevarse** vr to relay; **~ a algn de un cargo** to relieve sb of his post

**relevo** [re'leβo] nm relief; **carrera de ~s** relay race

**relieve** [re'ljeβe] nm (Arte, Tec) relief; (fig) prominence, importance; **bajo ~** bas-relief

**religión** [reli'xjon] nf religion; **religioso, -a** adj religious ⊳ nm/f monk/nun

**relinchar** [relin'tʃar] vi to neigh

**reliquia** [re'likja] nf relic; **reliquia de familia** heirloom

**rellano** [re'ʎano] nm (Arq) landing

**rellenar** [reʎe'nar] vt (llenar) to fill up; (Culin) to stuff; (Costura) to pad; **relleno, -a** adj full up; stuffed ⊳ nm stuffing; (de tapicería) padding

**reloj** [re'lo(x)] nm clock; **poner el ~ (en hora)** to set one's watch (o the clock); **reloj (de pulsera)** wristwatch; **reloj despertador** alarm (clock); **reloj digital** digital watch; **relojero, -a** nm/f clockmaker; watchmaker

**reluciente** [relu'θjente] adj brilliant, shining

**relucir** [relu'θir] vi to shine; (fig) to excel

**remachar** [rema'tʃar] vt to rivet; (fig) to hammer home, drive home; **remache** nm rivet

**remangar** [reman'gar] vt to roll up

**remanso** [re'manso] nm pool

**remar** [re'mar] vi to row

**rematado, -a** [rema'taðo, a] adj complete, utter

**rematar** [rema'tar] vt to finish off; (Com) to sell off cheap ⊳ vi to end, finish off; (Deporte) to shoot

**remate** [re'mate] nm end, finish; (punta) tip; (Deporte) shot; (Arq) top; **de o para ~** to crown it all (BRIT), to top it off

**remedar** [reme'ðar] vt to imitate

**remediar** [reme'ðjar] vt to remedy; (subsanar) to make good, repair; (evitar) to avoid

**remedio** [re'meðjo] nm remedy; (alivio) relief, help; (Jur) recourse, remedy; **poner ~ a** to correct, stop; **no tener más ~** to have no alternative; **¡qué ~!** there's no choice!; **sin ~** hopeless

**remendar** [remen'dar] vt to repair; (con parche) to patch

**remiendo** [re'mjendo] nm mend; (con parche) patch; (cosido) darn

**remilgado, -a** [remil'xaðo, a] adj prim; (afectado) affected

**remiso, -a** [re'miso, a] adj slack, slow

**remite** [re'mite] nm (en sobre) name and address of sender

**remitir** [remi'tir] vt to remit, send ⊳ vi to slacken; (en carta): **remite: X** sender: X; **remitente** nmf sender

**remo** ['remo] nm (de barco) oar; (Deporte) rowing

**remojar** [remo'xar] vt to steep, soak; (galleta etc) to dip, dunk

**remojo** [re'moxo] nm: **dejar la ropa en ~** to leave clothes to soak

**remolacha** [remo'latʃa] nf beet, beetroot

**remolcador** [remolka'ðor] nm (Náut) tug; (Auto) breakdown lorry

**remolcar** [remol'kar] vt to tow

**remolino** [remo'lino] nm eddy; (de agua) whirlpool; (de viento) whirlwind; (de gente) crowd

**remolque** [re'molke] nm tow, towing; (cuerda) towrope; **llevar a ~** to tow

**remontar** [remon'tar] vt to mend; **remontarse** vr to soar; **~se a** (Com) to amount to; **~ el vuelo** to soar

**remorder** [remor'ðer] vt to distress, disturb; **~le la conciencia a algn** to have a guilty conscience; **remordimiento** nm remorse

**remoto, -a** [re'moto, a] adj remote

**remover** [remo'βer] vt to stir; (tierra) to turn over; (objetos) to move round

**remuneración** [remunera'θjon] nf remuneration

**remunerar** [remune'rar] vt to remunerate; (premiar) to reward

**renacer** [rena'θer] vi to be reborn; (fig) to revive; **renacimiento** nm rebirth; **el Renacimiento** the Renaissance

**renacuajo** [rena'kwaxo] nm (Zool) tadpole

**renal** [re'nal] *adj* renal, kidney *cpd*

**rencilla** [ren'θiʎa] *nf* quarrel

**rencor** [ren'kor] *nm* rancour, bitterness;
**rencoroso, -a** *adj* spiteful

**rendición** [rendi'θjon] *nf* surrender

**rendido, -a** [ren'diðo, a] *adj* (*sumiso*)
submissive; (*cansado*) worn-out, exhausted

**rendija** [ren'dixa] *nf* (*hendedura*) crack,
cleft

**rendimiento** [rendi'mjento] *nm*
(*producción*) output; (*Tec, Com*) efficiency

**rendir** [ren'dir] *vt* (*vencer*) to defeat;
(*producir*) to produce; (*dar beneficio*) to yield;
(*agotar*) to exhaust ▷ *vi* to pay; **rendirse**
*vr* (*someterse*) to surrender; (*cansarse*) to
wear o.s. out; **~ homenaje** *o* **culto a** to pay
homage to

**renegar** [rene'xar] *vi* (*renunciar*) to
renounce; (*blasfemar*) to blaspheme;
(*quejarse*) to complain

**RENFE** ['renfe] *nf abr* (= *Red Nacional de los
Ferrocarriles Españoles*)

**renglón** [ren'glon] *nm* (*línea*) line; (*Com*)
item, article; **a ~ seguido** immediately after

**renombre** [re'nombre] *nm* renown

**renovación** [renoβa'θjon] *nf* (*de contrato*)
renewal; (*Arq*) renovation

**renovar** [reno'βar] *vt* to renew; (*Arq*) to
renovate

**renta** ['renta] *nf* (*ingresos*) income;
(*beneficio*) profit; (*alquiler*) rent; **renta
vitalicia** annuity; **rentable** *adj* profitable

**renuncia** [re'nunθja] *nf* resignation;
**renunciar** [renun'θjar] *vt* to renounce;
(*tabaco, alcohol etc*): **renunciar a** to give up;
(*oferta, oportunidad*) to turn down; (*puesto*) to
resign ▷ *vi* to resign

**reñido, -a** [re'ɲiðo, a] *adj* (*batalla*) bitter,
hard-fought; **estar ~ con algn** to be on bad
terms with sb

**reñir** [re'ɲir] *vt* (*regañar*) to scold ▷ *vi*
(*estar peleado*) to quarrel, fall out; (*combatir*)
to fight

**reo** ['reo] *nmf* culprit, offender; (*acusado*)
accused, defendant

**reojo** [re'oxo]: **de ~** *adv* out of the corner
of one's eye

**reparación** [repara'θjon] *nf* (*acto*)
mending, repairing; (*Tec*) repair; (*fig*)
amends *pl*, reparation

**reparar** [repa'rar] *vt* to repair; (*fig*) to
make amends for; (*observar*) to observe
▷ *vi*: **~ en** (*darse cuenta de*) to notice; (*prestar
atención a*) to pay attention to

**reparo** [re'paro] *nm* (*advertencia*)
observation; (*duda*) doubt; (*dificultad*)
difficulty; **poner ~s (a)** to raise objections
(to)

**repartidor, a** [reparti'ðor, a] *nm/f*
distributor

**repartir** [repar'tir] *vt* to distribute,
share out; (*Correos*) to deliver; **reparto** *nm*
distribution; delivery; (*Teatro, Cine*) cast;
(*CAM: urbanización*) housing estate (*BRIT*),
real estate development (*US*)

**repasar** [repa'sar] *vt* (*Escol*) to revise;
(*Mecánica*) to check, overhaul; (*Costura*)
to mend; **repaso** *nm* revision; overhaul,
checkup; mending

**repecho** [re'petʃo] *nm* steep incline

**repelente** [repe'lente] *adj* repellent,
repulsive

**repeler** [repe'ler] *vt* to repel

**repente** [re'pente] *nm*: **de ~** suddenly

**repentino, -a** [repen'tino, a] *adj* sudden

**repercusión** [reperku'sjon] *nf*
repercussion

**repercutir** [reperku'tir] *vi* (*objeto*) to
rebound; (*sonido*) to echo; **~ en** (*fig*) to have
repercussions on

**repertorio** [reper'torjo] *nm* list; (*Teatro*)
repertoire

**repetición** [repeti'θjon] *nf* repetition

**repetir** [repe'tir] *vt* to repeat; (*plato*) to
have a second helping of ▷ *vi* to repeat;
(*sabor*) to come back; **repetirse** *vr* (*volver
sobre un tema*) to repeat o.s.

**repetitivo, -a** [repeti'tiβo, a] *adj*
repetitive, repetitious

**repique** [re'pike] *nm* pealing, ringing;
**repiqueteo** *nm* pealing; (*de tambor*)
drumming

**repisa** [re'pisa] *nf* ledge, shelf; (*de ventana*)
windowsill; **la ~ de la chimenea** the
mantelpiece

**repito** *etc vb V* **repetir**

**replantearse** [replante'arse] *vr*: **~ un
problema** to reconsider a problem

**repleto, -a** [re'pleto, a] *adj* replete, full up

**réplica** ['replika] *nf* answer; (*Arte*) replica

**replicar** [repli'kar] *vi* to answer; (*objetar*)
to argue, answer back

**repliegue** [re'pljexe] *nm* (*Mil*) withdrawal

**repoblación** [repoβla'θjon] *nf*
repopulation; (*de río*) restocking;
**repoblación forestal** reafforestation

**repoblar** [repo'βlar] *vt* to repopulate; (*con
árboles*) to reafforest

**repollito** [repo'ʎito] (*cs*) *nm*: **~s de
Bruselas** (Brussels) sprouts

**repollo** [re'poʎo] *nm* cabbage

**reponer** [repo'ner] *vt* to replace, put back;
(*Teatro*) to revive; **reponerse** *vr* to recover;
**~ que ...** to reply that ...

**reportaje** [repor'taxe] *nm* report, article

**reportero, -a** [repor'tero, a] *nm/f*

reporter

**reposacabezas** [reposaka'βeθas] *nm inv* headrest

**reposar** [repo'sar] *vi* to rest, repose

**reposera** [repo'sera] (*RPL*) *nf* deck chair

**reposición** [reposi'θjon] *nf* replacement; (*Cine*) remake

**reposo** [re'poso] *nm* rest

**repostar** [repos'tar] *vt* to replenish; (*Auto*) to fill up (with petrol (*BRIT*) o gasoline (*US*))

**repostería** [reposte'ria] *nf* confectioner's (shop)

**represa** [re'presa] *nf* dam; (*lago artificial*) lake, pool

**represalia** [repre'salja] *nf* reprisal

**representación** [representa'θjon] *nf* representation; (*Teatro*) performance; **representante** *nmf* representative; performer

**representar** [represen'tar] *vt* to represent; (*Teatro*) to perform; (*edad*) to look; **representarse** *vr* to imagine; **representativo, -a** *adj* representative

**represión** [repre'sjon] *nf* repression

**reprimenda** [repri'menda] *nf* reprimand, rebuke

**reprimir** [repri'mir] *vt* to repress

**reprobar** [repro'βar] *vt* to censure, reprove

**reprochar** [repro'tʃar] *vt* to reproach; **reproche** *nm* reproach

**reproducción** [reproðuk'θjon] *nf* reproduction

**reproducir** [reproðu'θir] *vt* to reproduce; **reproducirse** *vr* to breed; (*situación*) to recur

**reproductor, a** [reproðuk'tor, a] *adj* reproductive ▷ *nm* player; **reproductor de CD** CD player

**reptil** [rep'til] *nm* reptile

**república** [re'puβlika] *nf* republic; **República Dominicana** Dominican Republic; **republicano, -a** *adj, nm* republican

**repudiar** [repu'ðjar] *vt* to repudiate; (*fe*) to renounce

**repuesto** [re'pwesto] *nm* (*pieza de recambio*) spare (part); (*abastecimiento*) supply; **rueda de ~** spare wheel

**repugnancia** [repuɣ'nanθja] *nf* repugnance; **repugnante** *adj* repugnant, repulsive

**repugnar** [repuɣ'nar] *vt* to disgust

**repulsa** [re'pulsa] *nf* rebuff

**repulsión** [repul'sjon] *nf* repulsion, aversion; **repulsivo, -a** *adj* repulsive

**reputación** [reputa'θjon] *nf* reputation

**requerir** [reke'rir] *vt* (*pedir*) to ask, request; (*exigir*) to require; (*llamar*) to send for, summon

**requesón** [reke'son] *nm* cottage cheese

**requete...** [re'kete] *prefijo* extremely

**réquiem** ['rekjem] (*pl* **~s**) *nm* requiem

**requisito** [reki'sito] *nm* requirement, requisite

**res** [res] *nf* beast, animal

**resaca** [re'saka] *nf* (*de mar*) undertow, undercurrent; (*fam*) hangover

**resaltar** [resal'tar] *vi* to project, stick out; (*fig*) to stand out

**resarcir** [resar'θir] *vt* to compensate; **resarcirse** *vr* to make up for

**resbaladero** [resβala'ðero] (*MÉX*) *nm* slide

**resbaladizo, -a** [resβala'ðiθo, a] *adj* slippery

**resbalar** [resβa'lar] *vi* to slip, slide; (*fig*) to slip (up); **resbalarse** *vr* to slip, slide; to slip (up); **resbalón** *nm* (*acción*) slip

**rescatar** [reska'tar] *vt* (*salvar*) to save, rescue; (*objeto*) to get back, recover; (*cautivos*) to ransom

**rescate** [res'kate] *nm* rescue; (*de objeto*) recovery; **pagar un ~** to pay a ransom

**rescindir** [resθin'dir] *vt* to rescind

**rescisión** [resθi'sjon] *nf* cancellation

**resecar** [rese'kar] *vt* to dry thoroughly; (*Med*) to cut out, remove; **resecarse** *vr* to dry up

**reseco, -a** [re'seko, a] *adj* very dry; (*fig*) skinny

**resentido, -a** [resen'tiðo, a] *adj* resentful

**resentimiento** [resenti'mjento] *nm* resentment, bitterness

**resentirse** [resen'tirse] *vr* (*debilitarse: persona*) to suffer; **~ de** (*consecuencias*) to feel the effects of; **~ de (o por) algo** to resent sth, be bitter about sth

**reseña** [re'seɲa] *nf* (*cuenta*) account; (*informe*) report; (*Literatura*) review

**reseñar** [rese'ɲar] *vt* to describe; (*Literatura*) to review

**reserva** [re'serβa] *nf* reserve; (*reservación*) reservation

**reservado, -a** [reser'βaðo, a] *adj* reserved; (*retraído*) cold, distant ▷ *nm* private room

**reservar** [reser'βar] *vt* (*guardar*) to keep; (*habitación, entrada*) to reserve; **reservarse** *vr* to save o.s.; (*callar*) to keep to o.s.

**resfriado** [resfri'aðo] *nm* cold; **resfriarse** *vr* to cool; (*Med*) to catch a cold

**resguardar** [resɣwar'ðar] *vt* to protect, shield; **resguardarse** *vr*: **~se de** to guard against; **resguardo** *nm* defence; (*vale*) voucher; (*recibo*) receipt, slip

**residencia** [resi'ðenθja] *nf* residence; **residencia de ancianos** residential home, old people's home; **residencia universitaria** hall of residence; **residencial** *nf* (*urbanización*) housing estate

**residente** [resi'ðente] *adj, nmf* resident

**residir** [resi'ðir] *vi* to reside, live; **~ en** to reside in, lie in

**residuo** [re'siðwo] *nm* residue

**resignación** [resiɣna'θjon] *nf* resignation; **resignarse** *vr*: **resignarse a** *o* **con** to resign o.s. to, be resigned to

**resina** [re'sina] *nf* resin

**resistencia** [resis'tenθja] *nf* (*dureza*) endurance, strength; (*oposición, Elec*) resistance; **resistente** *adj* strong, hardy; resistant

**resistir** [resis'tir] *vt* (*soportar*) to bear; (*oponerse a*) to resist, oppose; (*aguantar*) to put up with ▷ *vi* to resist; (*aguantar*) to last, endure; **resistirse** *vr*: **~se a** to refuse to, resist

**resoluto, -a** [reso'luto, a] *adj* resolute

**resolver** [resol'βer] *vt* to resolve; (*solucionar*) to solve, resolve; (*decidir*) to decide, settle; **resolverse** *vr* to make up one's mind

**resonar** [reso'nar] *vi* to ring, echo

**resoplar** [reso'plar] *vi* to snort; **resoplido** *nm* heavy breathing

**resorte** [re'sorte] *nm* spring; (*fig*) lever

**resortera** [resor'tera] (*MÉX*) *nf* catapult

**respaldar** [respal'dar] *vt* to back (up), support; **respaldarse** *vr* to lean back; **~se con** *o* **en** (*fig*) to take one's stand on; **respaldo** *nm* (*de sillón*) back; (*fig*) support, backing

**respectivo, -a** [respek'tiβo, a] *adj* respective; **en lo ~ a** with regard to

**respecto** [res'pekto] *nm*: **al ~** on this matter; **con ~ a, ~ de** with regard to, in relation to

**respetable** [respe'taβle] *adj* respectable

**respetar** [respe'tar] *vt* to respect; **respeto** *nm* respect; (*acatamiento*) deference; **respetos** *nmpl* respects; **respetuoso, -a** *adj* respectful

**respingo** [res'pingo] *nm* start, jump

**respiración** [respira'θjon] *nf* breathing; (*Med*) respiration; (*ventilación*) ventilation; **respiración asistida** artificial respiration (*by machine*)

**respirar** [respi'rar] *vi* to breathe; **respiratorio, -a** *adj* respiratory; **respiro** *nm* breathing; (*fig: descanso*) respite

**resplandecer** [resplande'θer] *vi* to shine; **resplandeciente** *adj* resplendent, shining; **resplandor** *nm* brilliance, brightness; (*de luz, fuego*) blaze

**responder** [respon'der] *vt* to answer ▷ *vi* to answer; (*fig*) to respond; (*pey*) to answer back; **~ de** *o* **por** to answer for; **respondón, -ona** *adj* cheeky

**responsabilidad** [responsaβili'ðað] *nf* responsibility

**responsabilizarse** [responsaβili'θarse] *vr* to make o.s. responsible, take charge

**responsable** [respon'saβle] *adj* responsible

**respuesta** [res'pwesta] *nf* answer, reply

**resquebrajar** [reskeβra'xar] *vt* to crack, split; **resquebrajarse** *vr* to crack, split

**resquicio** [res'kiθjo] *nm* chink; (*hendedura*) crack

**resta** ['resta] *nf* (*Mat*) remainder

**restablecer** [restaβle'θer] *vt* to re-establish, restore; **restablecerse** *vr* to recover

**restante** [res'tante] *adj* remaining; **lo ~** the remainder

**restar** [res'tar] *vt* (*Mat*) to subtract; (*fig*) to take away ▷ *vi* to remain, be left

**restauración** [restaura'θjon] *nf* restoration

**restaurante** [restau'rante] *nm* restaurant

**restaurar** [restau'rar] *vt* to restore

**restituir** [restitu'ir] *vt* (*devolver*) to return, give back; (*rehabilitar*) to restore

**resto** ['resto] *nm* (*residuo*) rest, remainder; (*apuesta*) stake; **restos** *nmpl* remains

**restorán** [resto'ran] *nm* (*Lam*) restaurant

**restregar** [restre'xar] *vt* to scrub, rub

**restricción** [restrik'θjon] *nf* restriction

**restringir** [restrin'xir] *vt* to restrict, limit

**resucitar** [resuθi'tar] *vt, vi* to resuscitate, revive

**resuelto, -a** [re'swelto, a] *pp de* **resolver** ▷ *adj* resolute, determined

**resultado** [resul'taðo] *nm* result; (*conclusión*) outcome; **resultante** *adj* resulting, resultant

**resultar** [resul'tar] *vi* (*ser*) to be; (*llegar a ser*) to turn out to be; (*salir bien*) to turn out well; (*Com*) to amount to; **~ de** to stem from; **me resulta difícil hacerlo** it's difficult for me to do it

**resumen** [re'sumen] (*pl* **resúmenes**) *nm* summary, résumé; **en ~** in short

**resumir** [resu'mir] *vt* to sum up; (*cortar*) to abridge, cut down; (*condensar*) to summarize

▌ No confundir **resumir** con la palabra inglesa *resume*.

**resurgir** [resur'xir] *vi* (*reaparecer*) to reappear

**resurrección** [resurre(k)'θjon] nf resurrection

**retablo** [re'taβlo] nm altarpiece

**retaguardia** [reta'ɣwarðja] nf rearguard

**retahíla** [reta'ila] nf series, string

**retal** [re'tal] nm remnant

**retar** [re'tar] vt to challenge; (desafiar) to defy, dare

**retazo** [re'taθo] nm snippet (BRIT), fragment

**retención** [reten'θjon] nf (tráfico) hold-up; **retención fiscal** deduction for tax purposes

**retener** [rete'ner] vt (intereses) to withhold

**reticente** [reti'θente] adj (tono) insinuating; (postura) reluctant; **ser ~ a hacer algo** to be reluctant o unwilling to do sth

**retina** [re'tina] nf retina

**retintín** [retin'tin] nm jangle, jingle

**retirada** [reti'raða] nf (Mil, refugio) retreat; (de dinero) withdrawal; (de embajador) recall; **retirado, -a** adj (lugar) remote; (vida) quiet; (jubilado) retired

**retirar** [reti'rar] vt to withdraw; (quitar) to remove; (jubilar) to retire, pension off; **retirarse** vr to retreat, withdraw; to retire; (acostarse) to retire, go to bed; **retiro** nm retreat; retirement; (pago) pension

**reto** ['reto] nm dare, challenge

**retocar** [reto'kar] vt (fotografía) to touch up, retouch

**retoño** [re'toɲo] nm sprout, shoot; (fig) offspring, child

**retoque** [re'toke] nm retouching

**retorcer** [retor'θer] vt to twist; (manos, lavado) to wring; **retorcerse** vr to become twisted; (mover el cuerpo) to writhe

**retorcido, -a** [retor'θiðo, a] adj (persona) devious

**retorcijón** [retorθi'jon] (LAM) nm (tb: ~ de tripas) stomach cramp

**retórica** [re'torika] nf rhetoric; (pey) affectedness

**retorno** [re'torno] nm return

**retortijón** [retorti'xon] (ESP) nm (tb: ~ de tripas) stomach cramp

**retozar** [reto'θar] vi (juguetear) to frolic, romp; (saltar) to gambol

**retracción** [retrak'θjon] nf retraction

**retraerse** [retra'erse] vr to retreat, withdraw; **retraído, -a** adj shy, retiring; **retraimiento** nm retirement; (timidez) shyness

**retransmisión** [retransmi'sjon] nf repeat (broadcast)

**retransmitir** [retransmi'tir] vt (mensaje) to relay; (TV etc) to repeat, retransmit; (: en vivo) to broadcast live

**retrasado, -a** [retra'saðo, a] adj late; (Med) mentally retarded; (país etc) backward, underdeveloped

**retrasar** [retra'sar] vt (demorar) to postpone, put off; (retardar) to slow down ▷ vi (atrasarse) to be late; (reloj) to be slow; (producción) to fall (off); (quedarse atrás) to lag behind; **retrasarse** vr to be late; to be slow; to fall (off); to lag behind

**retraso** [re'traso] nm (demora) delay; (lentitud) slowness; (tardanza) lateness; (atraso) backwardness; **retrasos** nmpl (Finanzas) arrears; **llegar con ~** to arrive late; **retraso mental** mental deficiency

**retratar** [retra'tar] vt (Arte) to paint the portrait of; (fotografiar) to photograph; (fig) to depict, describe; **retrato** nm portrait; (fig) likeness; **retrato-robot** (ESP) nm Identikit®

**retrete** [re'trete] nm toilet

**retribuir** [retri'βwir] vt (recompensar) to reward; (pagar) to pay

**retro...** ['retro] prefijo retro...

**retroceder** [retroθe'ðer] vi (echarse atrás) to move back(wards); (fig) to back down

**retroceso** [retro'θeso] nm backward movement; (Med) relapse; (fig) backing down

**retrospectivo, -a** [retrospek'tiβo, a] adj retrospective

**retrovisor** [retroβi'sor] nm (tb: **espejo ~**) rear-view mirror

**retumbar** [retum'bar] vi to echo, resound

**reúma** [re'uma], **reuma** ['reuma] nm rheumatism

**reunión** [reu'njon] nf (asamblea) meeting; (fiesta) party

**reunir** [reu'nir] vt (juntar) to reunite, join (together); (recoger) to gather (together); (personas) to get together; (cualidades) to combine; **reunirse** vr (personas: en asamblea) to meet, gather

**revalidar** [reβali'ðar] vt (ratificar) to confirm, ratify

**revalorizar** [reβalori'θar] vt to revalue, reassess

**revancha** [re'βantʃa] nf revenge

**revelación** [reβela'θjon] nf revelation

**revelado** [reβe'laðo] nm developing

**revelar** [reβe'lar] vt to reveal; (Foto) to develop

**reventa** [re'βenta] nf (de entradas: para concierto) touting

**reventar** [reβen'tar] vt to burst, explode

**reventón** [reβen'ton] nm (Auto) blow-out (BRIT), flat (US)

**reverencia** [reβe'renθja] nf reverence; **reverenciar** vt to revere

**reverendo, -a** [reβe'rendo, a] *adj* reverend

**reverente** [reβe'rente] *adj* reverent

**reversa** [re'βersa] (*MÉX, CAM*) *nf* reverse (gear)

**reversible** [reβer'siβle] *adj* (*prenda*) reversible

**reverso** [re'βerso] *nm* back, other side; (*de moneda*) reverse

**revertir** [reβer'tir] *vi* to revert

**revés** [re'βes] *nm* back, wrong side; (*fig*) reverse, setback; (*Deporte*) backhand; **al ~** the wrong way round; (*de arriba abajo*) upside down; (*ropa*) inside out; **volver algo del ~** to turn sth round; (*ropa*) to turn sth inside out

**revisar** [reβi'sar] *vt* (*examinar*) to check; (*texto etc*) to revise; **revisión** *nf* revision; **revisión salarial** wage review

**revisor, a** [reβi'sor, a] *nm/f* inspector; (*Ferro*) ticket collector

**revista** [re'βista] *nf* magazine, review; (*Teatro*) revue; (*inspección*) inspection; **pasar ~ a** to review, inspect; **revista del corazón** *magazine featuring celebrity gossip and real-life romance stories*

**revivir** [reβi'βir] *vi* to revive

**revolcarse** [reβol'karse] *vr* to roll about

**revoltijo** [reβol'tixo] *nm* mess, jumble

**revoltoso, -a** [reβol'toso, a] *adj* (*travieso*) naughty, unruly

**revolución** [reβolu'θjon] *nf* revolution; **revolucionario, -a** *adj, nm/f* revolutionary

**revolver** [reβol'βer] *vt* (*desordenar*) to disturb, mess up; (*mover*) to move about ▷ *vi*: **~ en** to go through, rummage (about) in; **revolverse** *vr* (*volver contra*) to turn on o against

**revólver** [re'βolβer] *nm* revolver

**revuelo** [re'βwelo] *nm* fluttering; (*fig*) commotion

**revuelta** [re'βwelta] *nf* (*motín*) revolt; (*agitación*) commotion

**revuelto, -a** [re'βwelto, a] *pp de* **revolver** ▷ *adj* (*mezclado*) mixed-up, in disorder

**rey** [rei] *nm* king; **Día de R~es** Twelfth Night; **los R~es Magos** the Three Wise Men, the Magi

the town by land or sea to the delight of the children.

**reyerta** [re'jerta] *nf* quarrel, brawl

**rezagado, -a** [reθa'ɣaðo, a] *nm/f* straggler

**rezar** [re'θar] *vi* to pray; **~ con** (*fam*) to concern, have to do with; **rezo** *nm* prayer

**rezumar** [reθu'mar] *vt* to ooze

**ría** ['ria] *nf* estuary

**riada** [ri'aða] *nf* flood

**ribera** [ri'βera] *nf* (*de río*) bank; (: *área*) riverside

**ribete** [ri'βete] *nm* (*de vestido*) border; (*fig*) addition

**ricino** [ri'θino] *nm*: **aceite de ~** castor oil

**rico, -a** ['riko, a] *adj* rich; (*adinerado*) wealthy, rich; (*lujoso*) luxurious; (*comida*) delicious; (*niño*) lovely, cute ▷ *nm/f* rich person

**ridiculez** [riðiku'leθ] *nf* absurdity

**ridiculizar** [riðikuli'θar] *vt* to ridicule

**ridículo, -a** [ri'ðikulo, a] *adj* ridiculous; **hacer el ~** to make a fool of o.s.; **poner a algn en ~** to make a fool of sb

**riego** ['rjeɣo] *nm* (*aspersión*) watering; (*irrigación*) irrigation; **riego sanguíneo** blood flow o circulation

**riel** [rjel] *nm* rail

**rienda** ['rjenda] *nf* rein; **dar ~ suelta a** to give free rein to

**riesgo** ['rjesɣo] *nm* risk; **correr el ~ de** to run the risk of

**rifa** ['rifa] *nf* (*lotería*) raffle; **rifar** *vt* to raffle

**rifle** ['rifle] *nm* rifle

**rigidez** [rixi'ðeθ] *nf* rigidity, stiffness; (*fig*) strictness; **rígido, -a** *adj* rigid, stiff; strict, inflexible

**rigor** [ri'ɣor] *nm* strictness, rigour; (*inclemencia*) harshness; **de ~** de rigueur, essential; **riguroso, -a** *adj* rigorous; harsh; (*severo*) severe

**rimar** [ri'mar] *vi* to rhyme

**rimbombante** [rimbom'bante] *adj* pompous

**rímel** ['rimel] *nm* mascara

**rímmel** ['rimel] *nm* = **rímel**

**rin** [rin] (*MÉX*) *nm* (*wheel*) rim

**rincón** [rin'kon] *nm* corner (*inside*)

**rinoceronte** [rinoθe'ronte] *nm* rhinoceros

**riña** ['riɲa] *nf* (*disputa*) argument; (*pelea*) brawl

**riñón** [ri'ɲon] *nm* kidney

**río** *etc* ['rio] *vb* V **reír** ▷ *nm* river; (*fig*) torrent, stream; **río abajo/arriba** downstream/upstream; **Río de la Plata** River Plate

**rioja** [ri'oxa] *nm* (*vino*) rioja (wine)

**rioplatense** [riopla'tense] *adj* of o from the River Plate region

**riqueza** [ri'keθa] *nf* wealth, riches *pl*; (*cualidad*) richness

**risa** ['risa] *nf* laughter; (*una risa*) laugh; **¡qué ~!** what a laugh!

**risco** ['risko] *nm* crag, cliff

**ristra** ['ristra] *nf* string

**risueño, -a** [ri'sweɲo, a] *adj* (*sonriente*) smiling; (*contento*) cheerful

**ritmo** ['ritmo] *nm* rhythm; **a ~ lento** slowly; **trabajar a ~ lento** to go slow; **ritmo cardíaco** heart rate

**rito** ['rito] *nm* rite

**ritual** [ri'twal] *adj*, *nm* ritual

**rival** [ri'βal] *adj*, *nmf* rival; **rivalidad** *nf* rivalry; **rivalizar** *vi*: **rivalizar con** to rival, vie with

**rizado, -a** [ri'θaðo, a] *adj* curly ▷ *nm* curls *pl*

**rizar** [ri'θar] *vt* to curl; **rizarse** *vr* (*pelo*) to curl; (*agua*) to ripple; **rizo** *nm* curl; ripple

**RNE** *nf abr* = **Radio Nacional de España**

**robar** [ro'βar] *vt* to rob; (*objeto*) to steal; (*casa etc*) to break into; (*Naipes*) to draw

**roble** ['roβle] *nm* oak; **robledal** *nm* oakwood

**robo** ['roβo] *nm* robbery, theft

**robot** [ro'βot] *nm* robot; **robot (de cocina)** (ESP) food processor

**robustecer** [roβuste'θer] *vt* to strengthen

**robusto, -a** [ro'βusto, a] *adj* robust, strong

**roca** ['roka] *nf* rock

**roce** ['roθe] *nm* (*caricia*) brush; (*Tec*) friction; (*en la piel*) graze; **tener ~ con** to be in close contact with

**rociar** [ro'θjar] *vt* to spray

**rocín** [ro'θin] *nm* nag, hack

**rocío** [ro'θio] *nm* dew

**rocola** [ro'kola] (LAM) *nf* jukebox

**rocoso, -a** [ro'koso, a] *adj* rocky

**rodaballo** [roða'baʎo] *nm* turbot

**rodaja** [ro'ðaxa] *nf* slice

**rodaje** [ro'ðaxe] *nm* (*Cine*) shooting, filming; (*Auto*): **en ~** running in

**rodar** [ro'ðar] *vt* (*vehículo*) to wheel (along); (*escalera*) to roll down; (*viajar por*) to travel (over) ▷ *vi* to roll; (*coche*) to go, run; (*Cine*) to shoot, film

**rodear** [roðe'ar] *vt* to surround ▷ *vi* to go round; **rodearse** *vr*: **~se de amigos** to surround o.s. with friends

**rodeo** [ro'ðeo] *nm* (*ruta indirecta*) detour; (*evasión*) evasion; (*Deporte*) rodeo; **hablar sin ~s** to come to the point, speak plainly

**rodilla** [ro'ðiʎa] *nf* knee; **de ~s** kneeling;

**ponerse de ~s** to kneel (down)

**rodillo** [ro'ðiʎo] *nm* roller; (*Culin*) rolling-pin

**roedor, a** [roe'ðor, a] *adj* gnawing ▷ *nm* rodent

**roer** [ro'er] *vt* (*masticar*) to gnaw; (*corroer*, *fig*) to corrode

**rogar** [ro'ɣar] *vt*, *vi* (*pedir*) to ask for; (*suplicar*) to beg, plead; **se ruega no fumar** please do not smoke

**rojizo, -a** [ro'xiθo, a] *adj* reddish

**rojo, -a** ['roxo, a] *adj*, *nm* red; **al ~ vivo** red-hot

**rol** [rol] *nm* list, roll; (*papel*) role

**rollito** [ro'ʎito] *nm* (*tb*: **~ de primavera**) spring roll

**rollizo, -a** [ro'ʎiθo, a] *adj* (*objeto*) cylindrical; (*persona*) plump

**rollo** ['roʎo] *nm* roll; (*de cuerda*) coil; (*madera*) log; (ESP: *fam*) bore; **¡qué ~!** (ESP: *fam*) what a carry-on!

**Roma** ['roma] *n* Rome

**romance** [ro'manθe] *nm* (*amoroso*) romance; (*Literatura*) ballad

**romano, -a** [ro'mano, a] *adj*, *nm/f* Roman; **a la romana** in batter

**romanticismo** [romanti'θismo] *nm* romanticism

**romántico, -a** [ro'mantiko, a] *adj* romantic

**rombo** ['rombo] *nm* (*Geom*) rhombus

**romería** [rome'ria] *nf* (*Rel*) pilgrimage; (*excursión*) trip, outing

**romero, -a** [ro'mero, a] *nm/f* pilgrim ▷ *nm* rosemary

**romo, -a** ['romo, a] *adj* blunt; (*fig*) dull

**rompecabezas** [rompeka'βeθas] *nm inv* riddle, puzzle; (*juego*) jigsaw (puzzle)

**rompehuelgas** [rompe'welɣas] (LAM) *nm inv* strikebreaker, scab

**rompeolas** [rompe'olas] *nm inv* breakwater

**romper** [rom'per] *vt* to break; (*hacer pedazos*) to smash; (*papel, tela etc*) to tear, rip ▷ *vi* (*olas*) to break; (*sol, diente*) to break through; **romperse** *vr* to break; **~ un**

**contrato** to break a contract; **~ a** (*empezar a*) to start (suddenly) to; **~ a llorar** to burst into tears; **~ con algn** to fall out with sb
**ron** [ron] *nm* rum
**roncar** [ron'kar] *vi* to snore
**ronco, -a** ['ronko, a] *adj* (*afónico*) hoarse; (*áspero*) raucous
**ronda** ['ronda] *nf* (*gen*) round; (*patrulla*) patrol; **rondar** *vt* to patrol ▷ *vi* to patrol; (*fig*) to prowl round
**ronquido** [ron'kiðo] *nm* snore, snoring
**ronronear** [ronrone'ar] *vi* to purr
**roña** ['rona] *nf* (*Veterinaria*) mange; (*mugre*) dirt, grime; (*óxido*) rust
**roñoso, -a** [ro'noso, a] *adj* (*mugriento*) filthy; (*tacaño*) mean
**ropa** ['ropa] *nf* clothes *pl*, clothing; **ropa blanca** linen; **ropa de cama** bed linen; **ropa de color** coloureds *pl*; **ropa interior** underwear; **ropa sucia** dirty washing; **ropaje** *nm* gown, robes *pl*
**ropero** [ro'pero] *nm* linen cupboard; (*guardarropa*) wardrobe
**rosa** ['rosa] *adj* pink ▷ *nf* rose
**rosado, -a** [ro'saðo, a] *adj* pink ▷ *nm* rosé
**rosal** [ro'sal] *nm* rosebush
**rosario** [ro'sarjo] *nm* (*Rel*) rosary; **rezar el ~** to say the rosary
**rosca** ['roska] *nf* (*de tornillo*) thread; (*de humo*) coil, spiral; (*pan, postre*) ring-shaped roll/pastry
**rosetón** [rose'ton] *nm* rosette; (*Arq*) rose window
**rosquilla** [ros'kiʎa] *nf* doughnut-shaped fritter
**rostro** ['rostro] *nm* (*cara*) face
**rotativo, -a** [rota'tiβo, a] *adj* rotary
**roto, -a** ['roto, a] *pp de* **romper** ▷ *adj* broken
**rotonda** [ro'tonda] *nf* roundabout
**rótula** ['rotula] *nf* kneecap; (*Tec*) ball-and-socket joint
**rotulador** [rotula'ðor] *nm* felt-tip pen
**rótulo** ['rotulo] *nm* heading, title; label; (*letrero*) sign
**rotundamente** [rotunda'mente] *adv* (*negar*) flatly; (*responder, afirmar*) emphatically; **rotundo, -a** *adj* round; (*enfático*) emphatic
**rotura** [ro'tura] *nf* (*acto*) breaking; (*Med*) fracture
**rozadura** [roθa'ðura] *nf* abrasion, graze
**rozar** [ro'θar] *vt* (*frotar*) to rub; (*arañar*) to scratch; (*tocar ligeramente*) to shave, touch lightly; **rozarse** *vr* to rub (together); **~se con** (*fam*) to rub shoulders with
**rte.** *abr* (= *remite, remitente*) sender
**RTVE** *nf abr* = **Radiotelevisión Española**

**rubí** [ru'βi] *nm* ruby; (*de reloj*) jewel
**rubio, -a** ['ruβjo, a] *adj* fair-haired, blond(e) ▷ *nm/f* blond/blonde; **tabaco ~** Virginia tobacco
**rubor** [ru'βor] *nm* (*sonrojo*) blush; (*timidez*) bashfulness; **ruborizarse** *vr* to blush
**rúbrica** ['ruβrika] *nf* (*de la firma*) flourish; **rubricar** *vt* (*firmar*) to sign with a flourish; (*concluir*) to sign and seal
**rudimentario, -a** [ruðimen'tarjo, a] *adj* rudimentary
**rudo, -a** ['ruðo, a] *adj* (*sin pulir*) unpolished; (*grosero*) coarse; (*violento*) violent; (*sencillo*) simple
**rueda** ['rweða] *nf* wheel; (*círculo*) ring, circle; (*rodaja*) slice, round; **rueda de auxilio** (*RPL*) spare tyre; **rueda delantera/trasera/de repuesto** front/back/spare wheel; **rueda de prensa** press conference; **rueda gigante** (*LAM*) big (*BRIT*) o Ferris (*US*) wheel
**ruedo** ['rweðo] *nm* (*círculo*) circle; (*Taur*) arena, bullring
**ruego** *etc* ['rweɣo] *vb* V **rogar** ▷ *nm* request
**rugby** ['ruɣβi] *nm* rugby
**rugido** [ru'xiðo] *nm* roar
**rugir** [ru'xir] *vi* to roar
**rugoso, -a** [ru'ɣoso, a] *adj* (*arrugado*) wrinkled; (*áspero*) rough; (*desigual*) ridged
**ruido** ['rwiðo] *nm* noise; (*sonido*) sound; (*alboroto*) racket, row; (*escándalo*) commotion, rumpus; **ruidoso, -a** *adj* noisy, loud; (*fig*) sensational
**ruin** [rwin] *adj* contemptible, mean
**ruina** ['rwina] *nf* ruin; (*colapso*) collapse; (*de persona*) ruin, downfall
**ruinoso, -a** [rwi'noso, a] *adj* ruinous; (*destartalado*) dilapidated, tumbledown; (*Com*) disastrous
**ruiseñor** [rwise'nor] *nm* nightingale
**rulero** [ru'lero] (*RPL*) *nm* roller
**ruleta** [ru'leta] *nf* roulette
**rulo** ['rulo] *nm* (*para el pelo*) curler
**Rumanía** [ruma'nia] *nf* Rumania
**rumba** ['rumba] *nf* rumba
**rumbo** ['rumbo] *nm* (*ruta*) route, direction; (*ángulo de dirección*) course, bearing; (*fig*) course of events; **ir con ~ a** to be heading for
**rumiante** [ru'mjante] *nm* ruminant
**rumiar** [ru'mjar] *vt* to chew; (*fig*) to chew over ▷ *vi* to chew the cud
**rumor** [ru'mor] *nm* (*ruido sordo*) low sound; (*murmuración*) murmur, buzz; **rumorearse** *vr*: **se rumorea que ...** it is rumoured that ...
**rupestre** [ru'pestre] *adj* rock *cpd*
**ruptura** [rup'tura] *nf* rupture
**rural** [ru'ral] *adj* rural

**Rusia** ['rusja] nf Russia; **ruso, -a** adj, nm/f
Russian
**rústico, -a** ['rustiko, a] adj rustic;
(ordinario) coarse, uncouth ▷ nm/f yokel
**ruta** ['ruta] nf route
**rutina** [ru'tina] nf routine

# S

**S** abr (= santo, a) St; (= sur) S
**s.** abr (= siglo) C.; (= siguiente) foll
**S.A.** abr (= Sociedad Anónima) Ltd. (BRIT),
Inc. (US)
**sábado** ['saβaðo] nm Saturday
**sábana** ['saβana] nf sheet
**sabañón** [saβa'non] nm chilblain
**saber** [sa'βer] vt to know; (llegar a
conocer) to find out, learn; (tener capacidad
de) to know how to ▷ vi: **~ a** to taste of,
taste like ▷ nm knowledge, learning; **a ~**
namely; **¿sabes conducir/nadar?** can you
drive/swim?; **¿sabes francés?** do you speak
French?; **~ de memoria** to know by heart;
**hacer ~ algo a algn** to inform sb of sth, let
sb know sth
**sabiduría** [saβiðu'ria] nf (conocimientos)
wisdom; (instrucción) learning
**sabiendas** [sa'βjendas]: **a ~** adv knowingly
**sabio, -a** ['saβjo,a] adj (docto) learned;
(prudente) wise, sensible
**sabor** [sa'βor] nm taste, flavour; **saborear**
vt to taste, savour; (fig) to relish
**sabotaje** [saβo'taxe] nm sabotage
**sabré** etc vb V **saber**
**sabroso, -a** [sa'βroso, a] adj tasty;
(fig: fam) racy, salty
**sacacorchos** [saka'kortʃos] nm inv
corkscrew
**sacapuntas** [saka'puntas] nm inv pencil
sharpener
**sacar** [sa'kar] vt to take out; (fig: extraer)
to get (out); (quitar) to remove, get out;
(hacer salir) to bring out; (conclusión) to draw;
(novela etc) to publish, bring out; (ropa) to
take off; (obra) to make; (premio) to receive;
(entradas) to get; (Tenis) to serve; **~ adelante**
(niño) to bring up; (negocio) to carry on, go on
with; **~ a algn a bailar** to get sb up to dance;
**~ una foto** to take a photo; **~ la lengua** to
stick out one's tongue; **~ buenas/malas**

**notas** to get good/bad marks
**sacarina** [saka'rina] *nf* saccharin(e)
**sacerdote** [saθer'ðote] *nm* priest
**saciar** [sa'θjar] *vt* (*hambre, sed*) to satisfy;
**saciarse** *vr* (*de comida*) to get full up
**saco** ['sako] *nm* bag; (*grande*) sack; (*su contenido*) bagful; (LAM: *chaqueta*) jacket;
**saco de dormir** sleeping bag
**sacramento** [sakra'mento] *nm* sacrament
**sacrificar** [sakrifi'kar] *vt* to sacrifice;
**sacrificio** *nm* sacrifice
**sacristía** [sakris'tia] *nf* sacristy
**sacudida** [saku'ðiða] *nf* (*agitación*) shake, shaking; (*sacudimiento*) jolt, bump;
**sacudida eléctrica** electric shock
**sacudir** [saku'ðir] *vt* to shake; (*golpear*) to hit
**Sagitario** [saxi'tarjo] *nm* Sagittarius
**sagrado, -a** [sa'ɣraðo, a] *adj* sacred, holy
**Sáhara** ['saara] *nm*: **el ~** the Sahara (desert)
**sal** [sal] *vb* V **salir** ▷ *nf* salt; **sales de baño** bath salts
**sala** ['sala] *nf* room; (*tb*: **~ de estar**) living room; (*Teatro*) house, auditorium; (*de hospital*) ward; **sala de espera** waiting room; **sala de estar** living room; **sala de fiestas** dance hall
**salado, -a** [sa'laðo, a] *adj* salty; (*fig*) witty, amusing; **agua salada** salt water
**salar** [sa'lar] *vt* to salt, add salt to
**salario** [sa'larjo] *nm* wage, pay
**salchicha** [sal'tʃitʃa] *nf* (*pork*) sausage;
**salchichón** *nm* (salami-type) sausage
**saldo** ['saldo] *nm* (*pago*) settlement; (*de una cuenta*) balance; (*lo restante*) remnant(s) (*pl*), remainder; (*de móvil*) credit; **saldos** *nmpl* (*en tienda*) sale
**saldré** *etc vb* V **salir**
**salero** [sa'lero] *nm* salt cellar
**salgo** *etc vb* V **salir**
**salida** [sa'liða] *nf* (*puerta etc*) exit, way out; (*acto*) leaving, going out; (*de tren, Aviac*) departure; (*Tec*) output, production; (*fig*) way out; (*Com*) opening; (*Geo, válvula*) outlet; (*de gas*) leak; **calle sin ~** cul-de-sac; **salida de baño** (RPL) bathrobe; **salida de emergencia/incendios** emergency exit/fire escape

○ PALABRA CLAVE

**salir** [sa'lir] *vi* **1** (*partir: tb*: **salir de**) to leave; **Juan ha salido** Juan is out; **salió de la cocina** he came out of the kitchen
**2** (*aparecer*) to appear; (*disco, libro*) to come out; **anoche salió en la tele** she appeared *o* was on TV last night; **salió en todos los**

**periódicos** it was in all the papers
**3** (*resultar*): **la muchacha nos salió muy trabajadora** the girl turned out to be a very hard worker; **la comida te ha salido exquisita** the food was delicious; **sale muy caro** it's very expensive
**4** : **salirle a uno algo: la entrevista que hice me salió bien/mal** the interview I did went *o* turned out well/badly
**5** : **salir adelante: no sé como haré para salir adelante** I don't know how I'll get by
**salirse** *vr* (*líquido*) to spill; (*animal*) to escape

**saliva** [sa'liβa] *nf* saliva
**salmo** ['salmo] *nm* psalm
**salmón** [sal'mon] *nm* salmon
**salmonete** [salmo'nete] *nm* red mullet
**salón** [sa'lon] *nm* (*de casa*) living room, lounge; (*muebles*) lounge suite; **salón de baile** dance hall; **salón de belleza** beauty parlour
**salpicadera** [salpika'ðera] (MÉX) *nf* mudguard (BRIT), fender (US)
**salpicadero** [salpika'ðero] *nm* (*Auto*) dashboard
**salpicar** [salpi'kar] *vt* (*rociar*) to sprinkle, spatter; (*esparcir*) to scatter
**salpicón** [salpi'kon] *nm* (*tb*: **~ de marisco**) seafood salad
**salsa** ['salsa] *nf* sauce; (*con carne asada*) gravy; (*fig*) spice
**saltamontes** [salta'montes] *nm inv* grasshopper
**saltar** [sal'tar] *vt* to jump (over), leap (over); (*dejar de lado*) to skip, miss out ▷ *vi* to jump, leap; (*pelota*) to bounce; (*al aire*) to fly up; (*quebrarse*) to break; (*al agua*) to dive; (*fig*) to explode, blow up
**salto** ['salto] *nm* jump, leap; (*al agua*) dive;
**salto de agua** waterfall; **salto de altura/ longitud** high/long jump
**salud** [sa'luð] *nf* health; **¡(a su) ~!** cheers!, good health!; **saludable** *adj* (*de buena salud*) healthy; (*provechoso*) good, beneficial
**saludar** [salu'ðar] *vt* to greet; (*Mil*) to salute; **saludo** *nm* greeting; **"saludos"** (*en carta*) "best wishes", "regards"
**salvación** [salβa'θjon] *nf* salvation; (*rescate*) rescue
**salvado** [sal'βaðo] *nm* bran
**salvaje** [sal'βaxe] *adj* wild; (*tribu*) savage
**salvamanteles** [salβaman'teles] *nm inv* table mat
**salvamento** [salβa'mento] *nm* rescue
**salvapantallas** [salβapan'taʎas] *nm inv* screen saver
**salvar** [sal'βar] *vt* (*rescatar*) to save, rescue; (*resolver*) to overcome, resolve; (*cubrir*

*distancias)* to cover, travel; *(hacer excepción)* to except, exclude; *(barco)* to salvage
**salvavidas** [salβa'βiðas] *adj inv*: **bote/ chaleco ~** lifeboat/life jacket
**salvo, -a** ['salβo, a] *adj* safe ▷ *adv* except (for), save; **a ~** out of danger; **~ que** unless
**san** [san] *adj* saint; **S~ Juan** St John
**sanar** [sa'nar] *vt (herida)* to heal; *(persona)* to cure ▷ *vi (persona)* to get well, recover; *(herida)* to heal
**sanatorio** [sana'torjo] *nm* sanatorium
**sanción** [san'θjon] *nf* sanction
**sancochado, -a** [sanko'tʃado, a] *(MÉX) adj (Culin)* underdone, rare
**sandalia** [san'dalja] *nf* sandal
**sandía** [san'dia] *nf* watermelon
**sandwich** ['sandwitʃ] *(pl* **~s, ~es**) *nm* sandwich
**sanfermines** [sanfer'mines] *nmpl* festivities in celebration of San Fermín (Pamplona)

**sangrar** [san'grar] *vt, vi* to bleed; **sangre** *nf* blood
**sangría** [san'gria] *nf* sangria, *sweetened drink of red wine with fruit*
**sangriento, -a** [san'grjento, a] *adj* bloody
**sanguíneo, -a** [san'gineo, a] *adj* blood *cpd*
**sanidad** [sani'ðað] *nf (tb: ~ pública)* public health
**San Isidro** [sani'sidro] *nm patron saint of Madrid*

⬤ now include music, dance, a famous
⬤ **romería**, theatre and bullfighting.

**sanitario, -a** [sani'tarjo, a] *adj* health *cpd*; **sanitarios** *nmpl* toilets (BRIT), washroom (US)
**sano, -a** ['sano, a] *adj* healthy; *(sin daños)* sound; *(comida)* wholesome; *(entero)* whole, intact; **~ y salvo** safe and sound

▌ No confundir **sano** con la palabra inglesa ▌ *sane*.

**Santiago** [san'tjaxo] *nm*: **~ (de Chile)** Santiago
**santiamén** [santja'men] *nm*: **en un ~** in no time at all
**santidad** [santi'ðað] *nf* holiness, sanctity
**santiguarse** [santi'xwarse] *vr* to make the sign of the cross
**santo, -a** ['santo, a] *adj* holy; *(fig)* wonderful, miraculous ▷ *nm/f* saint ▷ *nm* saint's day; **~ y seña** password
**santuario** [san'twarjo] *nm* sanctuary, shrine
**sapo** ['sapo] *nm* toad
**saque** ['sake] *nm (Tenis)* service, serve; *(Fútbol)* throw-in; **saque de esquina** corner (kick)
**saquear** [sake'ar] *vt (Mil)* to sack; *(robar)* to loot, plunder; *(fig)* to ransack
**sarampión** [saram'pjon] *nm* measles *sg*
**sarcástico, -a** [sar'kastiko, a] *adj* sarcastic
**sardina** [sar'ðina] *nf* sardine
**sargento** [sar'xento] *nm* sergeant
**sarmiento** [sar'mjento] *nm (Bot)* vine shoot
**sarna** ['sarna] *nf* itch; *(Med)* scabies
**sarpullido** [sarpu'ʎiðo] *nm (Med)* rash
**sarro** ['sarro] *nm (en dientes)* tartar, plaque
**sartén** [sar'ten] *nf* frying pan
**sastre** ['sastre] *nm* tailor; **sastrería** *nf (arte)* tailoring; *(tienda)* tailor's (shop)
**Satanás** [sata'nas] *nm* Satan
**satélite** [sa'telite] *nm* satellite
**sátira** ['satira] *nf* satire
**satisfacción** [satisfak'θjon] *nf* satisfaction
**satisfacer** [satisfa'θer] *vt* to satisfy; *(gastos)* to meet; *(pérdida)* to make good; **satisfacerse** *vr* to satisfy o.s., be satisfied; *(vengarse)* to take revenge; **satisfecho, -a** *adj* satisfied; *(contento)* content(ed), happy; *(tb:* **satisfecho de sí mismo)** self-satisfied, smug
**saturar** [satu'rar] *vt* to saturate; **saturarse** *vr (mercado, aeropuerto)* to reach saturation point
**sauce** ['sauθe] *nm* willow; **sauce llorón**

weeping willow

**sauna** ['sauna] *nf* sauna

**savia** ['saβja] *nf* sap

**saxofón** [sakso'fon] *nm* saxophone

**sazonar** [saθo'nar] *vt* to ripen; (*Culin*) to flavour, season

**scooter** [e'skuter] (*ESP*) *nf* scooter

**Scotch®** [skotʃ] (*LAM*) *nm* Sellotape® (*BRIT*), Scotch tape® (*US*)

**SE** *abr* (= *sudeste*) SE

○ **PALABRA CLAVE**

**se** [se] *pron* **1** (*reflexivo: sg: m*) himself; (*: f*) herself; (*: pl*) themselves; (*: cosa*) itself; (*: de Vd*) yourself; (*: de Vds*) yourselves; **se está preparando** she's preparing herself
**2** (*con complemento indirecto*) to him; to her; to them; to it; to you; **a usted se lo dije ayer** I told you yesterday; **se compró un sombrero** he bought himself a hat; **se rompió la pierna** he broke his leg
**3** (*uso recíproco*) each other, one another; **se miraron (el uno al otro)** they looked at each other o one another
**4** (*en oraciones pasivas*): **se han vendido muchos libros** a lot of books have been sold
**5** (*impers*): **se dice que ...** people say that ..., it is said that ...; **allí se come muy bien** the food there is very good, you can eat very well there

**sé** *etc* [se] *vb* V **saber; ser**

**sea** *etc vb* V **ser**

**sebo** ['seβo] *nm* fat, grease

**secador** [seka'ðor] *nm*: **~ de pelo** hairdryer

**secadora** [seka'ðora] *nf* tumble dryer

**secar** [se'kar] *vt* to dry; **secarse** *vr* to dry (off); (*río, planta*) to dry up

**sección** [sek'θjon] *nf* section

**seco, -a** ['seko, a] *adj* dry; (*carácter*) cold; (*respuesta*) sharp, curt; **parar en ~** to stop dead; **decir algo a secas** to say sth curtly

**secretaría** [sekreta'ria] *nf* secretariat

**secretario, -a** [sekre'tarjo, a] *nm/f* secretary

**secreto, -a** [se'kreto, a] *adj* secret; (*persona*) secretive ▷ *nm* secret; (*calidad*) secrecy

**secta** ['sekta] *nf* sect

**sector** [sek'tor] *nm* sector

**secuela** [se'kwela] *nf* consequence

**secuencia** [se'kwenθja] *nf* sequence

**secuestrar** [sekwes'trar] *vt* to kidnap; (*bienes*) to seize, confiscate; **secuestro** *nm* kidnapping; seizure, confiscation

**secundario, -a** [sekun'darjo, a] *adj* secondary

**sed** [seð] *nf* thirst; **tener ~** to be thirsty

**seda** ['seða] *nf* silk

**sedal** [se'ðal] *nm* fishing line

**sedán** [se'ðan] (*LAM*) *nm* saloon (*BRIT*), sedan (*US*)

**sedante** [se'ðante] *nm* sedative

**sede** ['seðe] *nf* (*de gobierno*) seat; (*de compañía*) headquarters *pl*; **Santa S~** Holy See

**sedentario, -a** [seðen'tario, a] *adj* sedentary

**sediento, -a** [se'ðjento, a] *adj* thirsty

**sedimento** [seði'mento] *nm* sediment

**seducción** [seðuk'θjon] *nf* seduction

**seducir** [seðu'θir] *vt* to seduce; (*cautivar*) to charm, fascinate; (*atraer*) to attract; **seductor, a** *adj* seductive; charming, fascinating; attractive ▷ *nm/f* seducer

**segar** [se'ɣar] *vt* (*mies*) to reap, cut; (*hierba*) to mow, cut

**seglar** [se'ɣlar] *adj* secular, lay

**seguida** [se'ɣiða] *nf*: **en ~** at once, right away

**seguido, -a** [se'ɣiðo, a] *adj* (*continuo*) continuous, unbroken; (*recto*) straight ▷ *adv* (*directo*) straight (on); (*después*) after; (*LAM: a menudo*) often; **~s** consecutive, successive; **5 días ~s** 5 days running, 5 days in a row

**seguir** [se'ɣir] *vt* to follow; (*venir después*) to follow on, come after; (*proseguir*) to continue; (*perseguir*) to chase, pursue ▷ *vi* (*gen*) to follow; (*continuar*) to continue, carry o go on; **seguirse** *vr* to follow; **sigo sin comprender** I still don't understand; **sigue lloviendo** it's still raining

**según** [se'ɣun] *prep* according to ▷ *adv*: **¿irás? ~** are you going? – it all depends ▷ *conj* as; **~ caminamos** while we walk

**segundo, -a** [se'ɣundo, a] *adj* second ▷ *nm* second ▷ *nf* second meaning; **de segunda mano** second-hand; **segunda (clase)** second class; **segunda (marcha)** (*Auto*) second (gear)

**seguramente** [seɣura'mente] *adv* surely; (*con certeza*) for sure, with certainty

**seguridad** [seɣuri'ðað] *nf* safety; (*del estado, de casa etc*) security; (*certidumbre*) certainty; (*confianza*) confidence; (*estabilidad*) stability; **seguridad social** social security

**seguro, -a** [se'ɣuro, a] *adj* (*cierto*) sure, certain; (*fiel*) trustworthy; (*libre de peligro*) safe; (*bien defendido, firme*) secure ▷ *adv* for sure, certainly ▷ *nm* (*Com*) insurance; **seguro contra terceros/a todo riesgo** third party/comprehensive insurance;

**seguros sociales** social security *sg*
**seis** [seis] *num* six
**seísmo** [se'ismo] *nm* tremor, earthquake
**selección** [selek'θjon] *nf* selection;
  **seleccionar** *vt* to pick, choose, select
**selectividad** [selektiβi'ðað] (ESP) *nf*
  university entrance examination
**selecto, -a** [se'lekto, a] *adj* select, choice;
  *(escogido)* selected
**sellar** [se'ʎar] *vt (documento oficial)* to seal;
  *(pasaporte, visado)* to stamp
**sello** ['seʎo] *nm* stamp; *(precinto)* seal
**selva** ['selβa] *nf (bosque)* forest, woods *pl*;
  *(jungla)* jungle
**semáforo** [se'maforo] *nm (Auto)* traffic
  lights *pl*; *(Ferro)* signal
**semana** [se'mana] *nf* week; **entre ~**
  during the week; **Semana Santa** Holy
  Week; **semanal** *adj* weekly; **semanario** *nm*
  weekly magazine

○ **SEMANA SANTA**
○
○ In Spain celebrations for **Semana Santa**
○ (Holy Week) are often spectacular.
○ "Viernes Santo", "Sábado Santo" and
○ "Domingo de Resurrección" (Good
○ Friday, Holy Saturday, Easter Sunday)
○ are all national public holidays,
○ with additional days being given as
○ local holidays. There are fabulous
○ **procesiones** all over the country, with
○ members of "cofradías" (brotherhoods)
○ dressing in hooded robes and parading
○ their "pasos" (religious floats and
○ sculptures) through the streets. Seville
○ has the most famous Holy Week
○ processions.

**sembrar** [sem'brar] *vt* to sow; *(objetos)*
  to sprinkle, scatter about; *(noticias etc)* to
  spread
**semejante** [seme'xante] *adj (parecido)*
  similar ▷ *nm* fellow man, fellow creature;
  **~s** alike, similar; **nunca hizo cosa ~** he
  never did any such thing; **semejanza** *nf*
  similarity, resemblance
**semejar** [seme'xar] *vi* to seem like,
  resemble; **semejarse** *vr* to look alike, be
  similar
**semen** ['semen] *nm* semen
**semestral** [semes'tral] *adj* half-yearly,
  bi-annual
**semicírculo** [semi'θirkulo] *nm* semicircle
**semidesnatado, -a** [semiðesna'taðo, a]
  *adj* semi-skimmed
**semifinal** [semifi'nal] *nf* semifinal
**semilla** [se'miʎa] *nf* seed

**seminario** [semi'narjo] *nm (Rel)*
  seminary; *(Escol)* seminar
**sémola** ['semola] *nf* semolina
**senado** [se'naðo] *nm* senate; **senador, a**
  *nm/f* senator
**sencillez** [senθi'ʎeθ] *nf* simplicity; *(de
  persona)* naturalness; **sencillo, -a** *adj*
  simple; natural, unaffected
**senda** ['senda] *nf* path, track
**senderismo** [sende'rismo] *nm* hiking
**sendero** [sen'dero] *nm* path, track
**sendos, -as** ['sendos, as] *adj pl*: **les dio ~
  golpes** he hit both of them
**senil** [se'nil] *adj* senile
**seno** ['seno] *nm (Anat)* bosom, bust; *(fig)*
  bosom; **~s** breasts
**sensación** [sensa'θjon] *nf* sensation;
  *(sentido)* sense; *(sentimiento)* feeling;
  **sensacional** *adj* sensational
**sensato, -a** [sen'sato, a] *adj* sensible
**sensible** [sen'sible] *adj* sensitive;
  *(apreciable)* perceptible, appreciable;
  *(pérdida)* considerable

▌ No confundir **sensible** con la palabra
  inglesa *sensible*.

**sensiblero, -a** *adj* sentimental
**sensitivo, -a** [sensi'tiβo, a] *adj* sense *cpd*
**sensorial** [senso'rjal] *adj* sensory
**sensual** [sen'swal] *adj* sensual
**sentada** [sen'taða] *nf* sitting; *(protesta)*
  sit-in
**sentado, -a** [sen'taðo, a] *adj*: **estar ~** to
  sit, be sitting (down); **dar por ~** to take for
  granted, assume
**sentar** [sen'tar] *vt* to sit, seat; *(fig)* to
  establish ▷ *vi (vestido)* to suit; *(alimento)*: **~
  bien/mal a** to agree/disagree with;
  **sentarse** *vr (persona)* to sit, sit down; *(los
  depósitos)* to settle
**sentencia** [sen'tenθja] *nf (máxima)*
  maxim, saying; *(Jur)* sentence; **sentenciar**
  *vt* to sentence
**sentido, -a** [sen'tiðo, a] *adj (pérdida)*
  regrettable; *(carácter)* sensitive ▷ *nm* sense;
  *(sentimiento)* feeling; *(significado)* sense,
  meaning; *(dirección)* direction; **mi más ~
  pésame** my deepest sympathy; **tener ~**
  to make sense; **sentido común** common
  sense; **sentido del humor** sense of humour;
  **sentido único** one-way (street)
**sentimental** [sentimen'tal] *adj*
  sentimental; **vida ~** love life
**sentimiento** [senti'mjento] *nm* feeling
**sentir** [sen'tir] *vt* to feel; *(percibir)* to
  perceive, sense; *(lamentar)* to regret, be
  sorry for ▷ *vi (tener la sensación)* to feel;
  *(lamentarse)* to feel sorry ▷ *nm* opinion,
  judgement; **~se bien/mal** to feel well/ill; **lo**

**siento** I'm sorry

**seña** ['seɲa] nf sign; (Mil) password; **señas** nfpl (dirección) address sg; **señas personales** personal description sg

**señal** [se'ɲal] nf sign; (síntoma) symptom; (Ferro, Tel) signal; (marca) mark; (Com) deposit; **en ~ de** as a token o sign of; **señalar** vt to mark; (indicar) to point out, indicate

**señor** [se'ɲor] nm (hombre) man; (caballero) gentleman; (dueño) owner, master; (trato: antes de nombre propio) Mr; (: hablando directamente) sir; **muy ~ mío** Dear Sir; **el ~ alcalde/presidente** the mayor/president

**señora** [se'ɲora] nf (dama) lady; (trato: antes de nombre propio) Mrs; (: hablando directamente) madam; (esposa) wife; **Nuestra S~** Our Lady

**señorita** [seɲo'rita] nf (con nombre y/o apellido) Miss; (mujer joven) young lady

**señorito** [seɲo'rito] nm young gentleman; (pey) rich kid

**sepa** etc vb V **saber**

**separación** [separa'θjon] nf separation; (división) division; (hueco) gap

**separar** [sepa'rar] vt to separate; (dividir) to divide; **separarse** vr (parte) to come away; (partes) to come apart; (persona) to leave, go away; (matrimonio) to separate; **separatismo** nm separatism

**sepia** ['sepja] nf cuttlefish

**septentrional** [septentrjo'nal] adj northern

**septiembre** [sep'tjembre] nm September

**séptimo, -a** ['septimo, a] adj, nm seventh

**sepulcral** [sepul'kral] adj (fig: silencio, atmósfera) deadly; **sepulcro** nm tomb, grave

**sepultar** [sepul'tar] vt to bury; **sepultura** nf (acto) burial; (tumba) grave, tomb

**sequía** [se'kia] nf drought

**séquito** ['sekito] nm (de rey etc) retinue; (seguidores) followers pl

○ **PALABRA CLAVE**

**ser** [ser] vi **1** (descripción) to be; **es médica/muy alta** she's a doctor/very tall; **la familia es de Cuzco** his (o her etc) family is from Cuzco; **soy Ana** (Tel) Ana speaking o here

**2** (propiedad): **es de Joaquín** it's Joaquín's, it belongs to Joaquín

**3** (horas, fechas, números): **es la una** it's one o'clock; **son las seis y media** it's half-past six; **es el 1 de junio** it's the first of June; **somos/son seis** there are six of us/them

**4** (en oraciones pasivas): **ha sido descubierto ya** it's already been discovered

**5: es de esperar que ...** it is to be hoped o I etc hope that ...

**6** (locuciones con sub): **o sea** that is to say; **sea él sea su hermana** either him or his sister

**7: a no ser por él ...** but for him ...

**8: a no ser que: a no ser que tenga uno ya** unless he's got one already ▷ nm being; **ser humano** human being

**sereno, -a** [se'reno, a] adj (persona) calm, unruffled; (el tiempo) fine, settled; (ambiente) calm, peaceful ▷ nm night watchman

**serial** [se'rjal] nm serial

**serie** ['serje] nf series; (cadena) sequence, succession; **fuera de ~** out of order; (fig) special, out of the ordinary; **fabricación en ~** mass production

**seriedad** [serje'ðað] nf seriousness; (formalidad) reliability; **serio, -a** adj serious; reliable, dependable; grave, serious; **en serio** adv seriously

**serigrafía** [serixra'fia] nf silk-screen printing

**sermón** [ser'mon] nm (Rel) sermon

**seropositivo, -a** [seroposi'tiβo] adj HIV positive

**serpentear** [serpente'ar] vi to wriggle; (camino, río) to wind, snake

**serpentina** [serpen'tina] nf streamer

**serpiente** [ser'pjente] nf snake; **serpiente de cascabel** rattlesnake

**serranía** [serra'nia] nf mountainous area

**serrar** [se'rrar] vt = **aserrar**

**serrín** [se'rrin] nm sawdust

**serrucho** [se'rrutʃo] nm saw

**service** [ser'βis] (RPL) nm (Auto) service

**servicio** [ser'βiθjo] nm service; (LAM Auto) service; **servicios** nmpl (ESP) toilet(s); **servicio incluido** service charge included; **servicio militar** military service

**servidumbre** [serβi'ðumbre] nf (sujeción) servitude; (criados) servants pl, staff

**servil** [ser'βil] adj servile

**servilleta** [serβi'ʎeta] nf serviette, napkin

**servir** [ser'βir] vt to serve ▷ vi to serve; (tener utilidad) to be of use, be useful; **servirse** vr to serve o help o.s.; **~se de algo** to make use of sth, use sth; **sírvase pasar** please come in

**sesenta** [se'senta] num sixty

**sesión** [se'sjon] nf (Pol) session, sitting; (Cine) showing

**seso** ['seso] nm brain; **sesudo, -a** adj sensible, wise

**seta** ['seta] nf mushroom; **seta venenosa** toadstool

**setecientos, -as** [sete'θjentos, as] adj, num seven hundred

**setenta** [se'tenta] num seventy

**seto** ['seto] nm hedge

**severo, -a** [se'βero, a] *adj* severe

**Sevilla** [se'βiʎa] *n* Seville; **sevillano, -a** *adj* of o from Seville ▷ *nm/f* native o inhabitant of Seville

**sexo** ['sekso] *nm* sex

**sexto, -a** ['seksto, a] *adj*, *nm* sixth

**sexual** [sek'swal] *adj* sexual; **vida ~** sex life

**si** [si] *conj* if ▷ *nm* (*Mús*) B; **me pregunto ~ ...** I wonder if o whether ...

**sí** [si] *adv* yes ▷ *nm* consent ▷ *pron* (*uso impersonal*) oneself; (*sg*: *m*) himself; (: *f*) herself; (: *de cosa*) itself; (*de usted*) yourself; (*pl*) themselves; (*de ustedes*) yourselves; (*recíproco*) each other; **él no quiere pero yo ~** he doesn't want to but I do; **ella ~ vendrá** she will certainly come, she is sure to come; **claro que ~** of course; **creo que ~** I think so

**siamés, -esa** [sja'mes, esa] *adj*, *nm/f* Siamese

**SIDA** ['siða] *nm abr* (= *Síndrome de Inmunodeficiencia Adquirida*) AIDS

**siderúrgico, -a** [siðe'rurxiko, a] *adj* iron and steel *cpd*

**sidra** ['siðra] *nf* cider

**siembra** ['sjembra] *nf* sowing

**siempre** ['sjempre] *adv* always; (*todo el tiempo*) all the time; **~ que** (*cada vez*) whenever; (*dado que*) provided that; **como ~** as usual; **para ~** for ever

**sien** [sjen] *nf* temple

**siento** etc ['sjento] *vb* V **sentar; sentir**

**sierra** ['sjerra] *nf* (*Tec*) saw; (*cadena de montañas*) mountain range

**siervo, -a** ['sjerβo, a] *nm/f* slave

**siesta** ['sjesta] *nf* siesta, nap; **echar la ~** to have an afternoon nap o a siesta

**siete** ['sjete] *num* seven

**sifón** [si'fon] *nm* syphon

**sigla** ['siɣla] *nf* abbreviation; acronym

**siglo** ['siɣlo] *nm* century; (*fig*) age

**significado** [siɣnifi'kaðo] *nm* (*de palabra etc*) meaning

**significar** [siɣnifi'kar] *vt* to mean, signify; (*notificar*) to make known, express

**signo** ['siɣno] *nm* sign; **signo de admiración** o **exclamación** exclamation mark; **signo de interrogación** question mark

**sigo** etc *vb* V **seguir**

**siguiente** [si'ɣjente] *adj* next, following

**siguió** etc *vb* V **seguir**

**sílaba** ['silaβa] *nf* syllable

**silbar** [sil'βar] *vt*, *vi* to whistle; **silbato** *nm* whistle; **silbido** *nm* whistle, whistling

**silenciador** [silenθja'ðor] *nm* silencer

**silenciar** [silen'θjar] *vt* (*persona*) to silence; (*escándalo*) to hush up; **silencio** *nm* silence, quiet; **silencioso, -a** *adj* silent, quiet

**silla** ['siʎa] *nf* (*asiento*) chair; (*tb:* **~ de montar**) saddle; **silla de ruedas** wheelchair

**sillón** [si'ʎon] *nm* armchair, easy chair

**silueta** [si'lweta] *nf* silhouette; (*de edificio*) outline; (*figura*) figure

**silvestre** [sil'βestre] *adj* wild

**simbólico, -a** [sim'boliko, a] *adj* symbolic(al)

**simbolizar** [simboli'θar] *vt* to symbolize

**símbolo** ['simbolo] *nm* symbol

**similar** [simi'lar] *adj* similar

**simio** ['simjo] *nm* ape

**simpatía** [simpa'tia] *nf* liking; (*afecto*) affection; (*amabilidad*) kindness; **simpático, -a** *adj* nice, pleasant; kind

▌ No confundir **simpático** con la palabra inglesa *sympathetic*.

**simpatizante** [simpati'θante] *nmf* sympathizer

**simpatizar** [simpati'θar] *vi*: **~ con** to get on well with

**simple** ['simple] *adj* simple; (*elemental*) simple, easy; (*mero*) mere; (*puro*) pure, sheer ▷ *nmf* simpleton; **simpleza** *nf* simpleness; (*necedad*) silly thing; **simplificar** *vt* to simplify

**simposio** [sim'posjo] *nm* symposium

**simular** [simu'lar] *vt* to simulate

**simultáneo, -a** [simul'taneo, a] *adj* simultaneous

**sin** [sin] *prep* without; **la ropa está ~ lavar** the clothes are unwashed; **~ que** without; **~ embargo** however, still

**sinagoga** [sina'ɣoɣa] *nf* synagogue

**sinceridad** [sinθeri'ðað] *nf* sincerity; **sincero, -a** *adj* sincere

**sincronizar** [sinkroni'θar] *vt* to synchronize

**sindical** [sindi'kal] *adj* union *cpd*, trade-union *cpd*; **sindicalista** *adj*, *nmf* trade unionist

**sindicato** [sindi'kato] *nm* (*de trabajadores*) trade(s) union; (*de negociantes*) syndicate

**síndrome** ['sindrome] *nm* (*Med*) syndrome; **síndrome de abstinencia** (*Med*) withdrawal symptoms; **síndrome de la clase turista** (*Med*) economy-class syndrome

**sinfín** [sin'fin] *nm*: **un ~ de** a great many, no end of

**sinfonía** [sinfo'nia] *nf* symphony

**singular** [singu'lar] *adj* singular; (*fig*) outstanding, exceptional; (*raro*) peculiar, odd

**siniestro, -a** [si'njestro, a] *adj* sinister ▷ *nm* (*accidente*) accident

**sinnúmero** [sin'numero] *nm* = **sinfín**

**sino** ['sino] nm fate, destiny ▷ conj (pero) but; (salvo) except, save

**sinónimo, -a** [si'nonimo, a] adj synonymous ▷ nm synonym

**síntesis** ['sintesis] nf synthesis; **sintético, -a** adj synthetic

**sintió** vb V **sentir**

**síntoma** ['sintoma] nm symptom

**sintonía** [sinto'nia] nf (Radio, Mús: de programa) tuning; **sintonizar** vt (Radio: emisora) to tune (in)

**sinvergüenza** [simber'ɣwenθa] nmf rogue, scoundrel; **¡es un ~!** he's got a nerve!

**siquiera** [si'kjera] conj even if, even though ▷ adv at least; **ni ~** not even

**Siria** ['sirja] nf Syria

**sirviente, -a** [sir'βjente, a] nm/f servant

**sirvo** etc vb V **servir**

**sistema** [sis'tema] nm system; (método) method; **sistema educativo** education system; **sistemático, -a** adj systematic

● **SISTEMA EDUCATIVO**
●
●
● The reform of the Spanish **sistema**
● **educativo** (education system) begun
● in the early 90s has replaced the
● courses **EGB**, **BUP** and **COU** with the
● following: "Primaria" a compulsory 6
● years; "Secundaria" a compulsory 4 years
● and "Bachillerato" an optional 2-year
● secondary school course, essential
● for those wishing to go on to higher
● education.

**sitiar** [si'tjar] vt to besiege, lay siege to

**sitio** ['sitjo] nm (lugar) place; (espacio) room, space; (Mil) siege; **sitio de taxis** (MÉX: parada) taxi stand o rank (BRIT); **sitio web** (Inform) website

**situación** [sitwa'θjon] nf situation, position; (estatus) position, standing

**situado, -a** [situ'aðo] adj situated, placed

**situar** [si'twar] vt to place, put; (edificio) to locate, situate

**slip** [slip] nm pants pl, briefs pl

**smoking** ['smokin, es'mokin] (pl **~s**) nm dinner jacket (BRIT), tuxedo (US)

▌No confundir **smoking** con la palabra inglesa smoking.

**SMS** nm (mensaje) text message, SMS message

**snob** [es'nob] = **esnob**

**SO** abr (= suroeste) SW

**sobaco** [so'βako] nm armpit

**sobar** [so'βar] vt (ropa) to rumple; (comida) to play around with

**soberanía** [soβera'nia] nf sovereignty;

**soberano, -a** adj sovereign; (fig) supreme ▷ nm/f sovereign

**soberbia** [so'βerβja] nf pride; haughtiness, arrogance; magnificence

**soberbio, -a** [so'βerβjo, a] adj (orgulloso) proud; (altivo) arrogant; (estupendo) magnificent, superb

**sobornar** [soβor'nar] vt to bribe; **soborno** nm bribe

**sobra** ['soβra] nf excess, surplus; **sobras** nfpl left-overs, scraps; **de ~** surplus, extra; **tengo de ~** I've more than enough; **sobrado, -a** adj (más que suficiente) more than enough; (superfluo) excessive; **sobrante** adj remaining, extra ▷ nm surplus, remainder

**sobrar** [so'βrar] vt to exceed, surpass ▷ vi (tener de más) to be more than enough; (quedar) to remain, be left (over)

**sobrasada** [soβra'saða] nf pork sausage spread

**sobre** ['soβre] prep (gen) on; (encima) on (top of); (por encima de, arriba de) over, above; (más que) more than; (además) in addition to, besides; (alrededor de) about ▷ nm envelope; **~ todo** above all

**sobrecama** [soβre'kama] nf bedspread

**sobrecargar** [soβrekar'ɣar] vt (camión) to overload; (Com) to surcharge

**sobredosis** [soβre'ðosis] nf inv overdose

**sobreentender** [soβre(e)nten'der] vt to deduce, infer; **sobreentenderse** vr: **se sobreentiende que ...** it is implied that ...

**sobrehumano, -a** [soβreu'mano, a] adj superhuman

**sobrellevar** [soβreʎe'βar] vt to bear, endure

**sobremesa** [soβre'mesa] nf: **durante la ~** after dinner

**sobrenatural** [soβrenatu'ral] adj supernatural

**sobrenombre** [soβre'nombre] nm nickname

**sobrepasar** [soβrepa'sar] vt to exceed, surpass

**sobreponerse** [soβrepo'nerse] vr: **~ a** to overcome

**sobresaliente** [soβresa'ljente] adj outstanding, excellent

**sobresalir** [soβresa'lir] vi to project, jut out; (fig) to stand out, excel

**sobresaltar** [soβresal'tar] vt (asustar) to scare, frighten; (sobrecoger) to startle; **sobresalto** nm (movimiento) start; (susto) scare; (turbación) sudden shock

**sobretodo** [soβre'toðo] nm overcoat

**sobrevenir** [soβreβe'nir] vi (ocurrir) to happen (unexpectedly); (resultar) to follow, ensue

**sobrevivir** [soβreβi'βir] vi to survive

**sobrevolar** [soβreβo'lar] vt to fly over

**sobriedad** [soβrje'ðað] nf sobriety, soberness; (moderación) moderation, restraint

**sobrino, -a** [so'βrino, a] nm/f nephew/niece

**sobrio, -a** ['soβrjo, a] adj sober; (moderado) moderate, restrained

**socarrón, -ona** [soka'rron, ona] adj (sarcástico) sarcastic, ironic(al)

**socavón** [soka'βon] nm (hoyo) hole

**sociable** [so'θjaβle] adj (persona) sociable, friendly; (animal) social

**social** [so'θjal] adj social; (Com) company cpd

**socialdemócrata** [soθjalde'mokrata] nmf social democrat

**socialista** [soθja'lista] adj, nm socialist

**socializar** [soθjali'θar] vt to socialize

**sociedad** [soθje'ðað] nf society; (Com) company; **sociedad anónima** limited company; **sociedad de consumo** consumer society

**socio, -a** ['soθjo, a] nm/f (miembro) member; (Com) partner

**sociología** [soθjolo'xja] nf sociology; **sociólogo, -a** nm/f sociologist

**socorrer** [soko'rrer] vt to help; **socorrista** nmf first aider; (en piscina, playa) lifeguard; **socorro** nm (ayuda) help, aid; (Mil) relief; **¡socorro!** help!

**soda** ['soða] nf (sosa) soda; (bebida) soda (water)

**sofá** [so'fa] (pl ~s) nm sofa, settee; **sofá-cama** nm studio couch; sofa bed

**sofocar** [sofo'kar] vt to suffocate; (apagar) to smother, put out; **sofocarse** vr to suffocate; (fig) to blush, feel embarrassed; **sofoco** nm suffocation; embarrassment

**sofreír** [sofre'ir] vt (Culin) to fry lightly

**soga** ['soɣa] nf rope

**sois** etc vb V **ser**

**soja** ['soxa] nf soya

**sol** [sol] nm sun; (luz) sunshine, sunlight; (Mús) G; **hace ~** it's sunny

**solamente** [sola'mente] adv only, just

**solapa** [so'lapa] nf (de chaqueta) lapel; (de libro) jacket

**solapado, -a** [sola'paðo, a] adj (intenciónes) underhand; (gestos, movimiento) sly

**solar** [so'lar] adj solar, sun cpd

**soldado** [sol'daðo] nm soldier; **soldado raso** private

**soldador** [solda'ðor] nm soldering iron; (persona) welder

**soldar** [sol'dar] vt to solder, weld

**soleado, -a** [sole'aðo, a] adj sunny

**soledad** [sole'ðað] nf solitude; (estado infeliz) loneliness

**solemne** [so'lemne] adj solemn

**soler** [so'ler] vi to be in the habit of, be accustomed to; **suele salir a las ocho** she usually goes out at eight o'clock

**solfeo** [sol'feo] nm solfa

**solicitar** [soliθi'tar] vt (permiso) to ask for, seek; (puesto) to apply for; (votos) to canvass for; (atención) to attract

**solícito, -a** [so'liθito, a] adj (diligente) diligent; (cuidadoso) careful; **solicitud** nf (calidad) great care; (petición) request; (a un puesto) application

**solidaridad** [soliðari'ðað] nf solidarity; **solidario, -a** adj (participación) joint, common; (compromiso) mutually binding

**sólido, -a** ['soliðo, a] adj solid

**soliloquio** [soli'lokjo] nm soliloquy

**solista** [so'lista] nmf soloist

**solitario, -a** [soli'tarjo, a] adj (persona) lonely, solitary; (lugar) lonely, desolate ▷ nm/f (recluso) recluse; (en la sociedad) loner ▷ nm solitaire

**sollozar** [soʎo'θar] vi to sob; **sollozo** nm sob

**solo, -a** ['solo, a] adj (único) single, sole; (sin compañía) alone; (solitario) lonely; **hay una sola dificultad** there is just one difficulty; **a solas** alone, by oneself

**sólo** ['solo] adv only, just

**solomillo** [solo'miʎo] nm sirloin

**soltar** [sol'tar] vt (dejar ir) to let go of; (desprender) to unfasten, loosen; (librar) to release, set free; (risa etc) to let out

**soltero, -a** [sol'tero, a] adj single, unmarried ▷ nm/f bachelor/single woman; **solterón, -ona** nm/f old bachelor/spinster

**soltura** [sol'tura] nf looseness, slackness; (de los miembros) agility, ease of movement; (en el hablar) fluency, ease

**soluble** [so'luβle] adj (Quím) soluble; (problema) solvable; **~ en agua** soluble in water

**solución** [solu'θjon] nf solution; **solucionar** vt (problema) to solve; (asunto) to settle, resolve

**solventar** [solβen'tar] vt (pagar) to settle, pay; (resolver) to resolve; **solvente** adj (Econ: empresa, persona) solvent

**sombra** ['sombra] nf shadow; (como protección) shade; **sombras** nfpl (oscuridad) darkness sg, shadows; **tener buena/mala ~** to be lucky/unlucky

**sombrero** [som'brero] nm hat

**sombrilla** [som'briʎa] nf parasol,

sunshade

**sombrío, -a** [som'brio, a] *adj (oscuro)* dark; *(triste)* sombre, sad; *(persona)* gloomy

**someter** [some'ter] *vt (país)* to conquer; *(persona)* to subject to one's will; *(informe)* to present, submit; **someterse** *vr* to give in, yield, submit; **~ a** to subject to

**somier** [so'mjer] *(pl* **~s)** *n* spring mattress

**somnífero** [som'nifero] *nm* sleeping pill

**somos** *vb* V **ser**

**son** [son] *vb* V **ser** ▷ *nm* sound

**sonaja** [so'naxa] *(MÉX) nf* = **sonajero**

**sonajero** [sona'xero] *nm* (baby's) rattle

**sonambulismo** [sonambu'lismo] *nm* sleepwalking; **sonámbulo, -a** *nm/f* sleepwalker

**sonar** [so'nar] *vt* to ring ▷ *vi* to sound; *(hacer ruido)* to make a noise; *(pronunciarse)* to be sounded, be pronounced; *(ser conocido)* to sound familiar; *(campana)* to ring; *(reloj)* to strike, chime; **sonarse** *vr*: **~se (las narices)** to blow one's nose; **me suena ese nombre** that name rings a bell

**sonda** ['sonda] *nf (Náut)* sounding; *(Tec)* bore, drill; *(Med)* probe

**sondear** [sonde'ar] *vt* to sound; to bore (into), drill; to probe, sound; *(fig)* to sound out; **sondeo** *nm* sounding; boring, drilling; *(fig)* poll, enquiry

**sonido** [so'niðo] *nm* sound

**sonoro, -a** [so'noro, a] *adj* sonorous; *(resonante)* loud, resonant

**sonreír** [sonre'ir] *vi* to smile; **sonreírse** *vr* to smile; **sonriente** *adj* smiling; **sonrisa** *nf* smile

**sonrojarse** [sonro'xarse] *vr* to blush, go red; **sonrojo** *nm* blush

**soñador, a** [sopa'ðor, a] *nm/f* dreamer

**soñar** [so'par] *vt, vi* to dream; **~ con** to dream about o of

**soñoliento, -a** [sopo'ljento, a] *adj* sleepy, drowsy

**sopa** ['sopa] *nf* soup

**soplar** [so'plar] *vt (polvo)* to blow away, blow off; *(inflar)* to blow up; *(vela)* to blow out ▷ *vi* to blow; **soplo** *nm* blow, puff; *(de viento)* puff, gust

**soplón, -ona** [so'plon, ona] *(fam) nm/f (niño)* telltale; *(de policía)* grass *(fam)*

**soporífero** [sopo'rifero] *nm* sleeping pill

**soportable** [sopor'taβle] *adj* bearable

**soportar** [sopor'tar] *vt* to bear, carry; *(fig)* to bear, put up with

> No confundir **soportar** con la palabra inglesa *support*.

**soporte** *nm* support; *(fig)* pillar, support

**soprano** [so'prano] *nf* soprano

**sorber** [sor'βer] *vt (chupar)* to sip; *(absorber)* to soak up, absorb

**sorbete** [sor'βete] *nm* iced fruit drink

**sorbo** ['sorβo] *nm (trago: grande)* gulp, swallow; (: *pequeño)* sip

**sordera** [sor'ðera] *nf* deafness

**sórdido, -a** [sor'ðiðo, a] *adj* dirty, squalid

**sordo, -a** ['sorðo, a] *adj (persona)* deaf ▷ *nm/f* deaf person; **sordomudo, -a** *adj* deaf and dumb

**sorna** ['sorna] *nf* sarcastic tone

**soroche** [so'rotʃe] *(CAM) nm* mountain sickness

**sorprendente** [sorpren'dente] *adj* surprising

**sorprender** [sorpren'der] *vt* to surprise; **sorpresa** *nf* surprise

**sortear** [sorte'ar] *vt* to draw lots for; *(rifar)* to raffle; *(dificultad)* to avoid; **sorteo** *nm (en lotería)* draw; *(rifa)* raffle

**sortija** [sor'tixa] *nf* ring; *(rizo)* ringlet, curl

**sosegado, -a** [sose'ɣaðo, a] *adj* quiet, calm

**sosiego** [so'sjeɣo] *nm* quiet(ness), calm(ness)

**soso, -a** ['soso, a] *adj (Culin)* tasteless; *(aburrido)* dull, uninteresting

**sospecha** [sos'petʃa] *nf* suspicion; **sospechar** *vt* to suspect; **sospechoso, -a** *adj* suspicious; *(testimonio, opinión)* suspect ▷ *nm/f* suspect

**sostén** [sos'ten] *nm (apoyo)* support; *(sujetador)* bra; *(alimentación)* sustenance, food

**sostener** [soste'ner] *vt* to support; *(mantener)* to keep up, maintain; *(alimentar)* to sustain, keep going; **sostenerse** *vr* to support o.s.; *(seguir)* to continue, remain; **sostenido, -a** *adj* continuous, sustained; *(prolongado)* prolonged

**sotana** [so'tana] *nf (Rel)* cassock

**sótano** ['sotano] *nm* basement

**soy** [soi] *vb* V **ser**

**soya** ['soja] *(LAM) nf* soya *(BRIT)*, soy *(US)*

**Sr.** *abr* (= *Señor)* Mr

**Sra.** *abr* (= *Señora)* Mrs

**Sres.** *abr* (= *Señores)* Messrs

**Srta.** *abr* (= *Señorita)* Miss

**Sta.** *abr* (= *Santa)* St

**Sto.** *abr* (= *Santo)* St

**su** [su] *pron (de él)* his; *(de ella)* her; *(de una cosa)* its; *(de ellos, ellas)* their; *(de usted, ustedes)* your

**suave** ['swaβe] *adj* gentle; *(superficie)* smooth; *(trabajo)* easy; *(música, voz)* soft, sweet; **suavidad** *nf* gentleness; smoothness; softness, sweetness; **suavizante** *nm (de ropa)* softener; *(del pelo)* conditioner; **suavizar** *vt* to soften; *(quitar* *la aspereza*) to smooth (out)

**subasta** [su'βasta] *nf* auction; **subastar** *vt* to auction (off)

**subcampeón, -ona** [suβkampe'on, ona] *nm/f* runner-up

**subconsciente** [suβkon'sθjente] *adj, nm* subconscious

**subdesarrollado, -a** [suβðesarro'ʎaðo, a] *adj* underdeveloped

**subdesarrollo** [suβðesa'rroʎo] *nm* underdevelopment

**subdirector, a** [suβðirek'tor, a] *nm/f* assistant director

**súbdito, -a** ['suβðito, a] *nm/f* subject

**subestimar** [suβesti'mar] *vt* to underestimate, underrate

**subida** [su'βiða] *nf* (*de montaña etc*) ascent, climb; (*de precio*) rise, increase; (*pendiente*) slope, hill

**subir** [su'βir] *vt* (*objeto*) to raise, lift up; (*cuesta, calle*) to go up; (*colina, montaña*) to climb; (*precio*) to raise, put up ▷ *vi* to go up, come up; (*a un coche*) to get in; (*a un autobús, tren o avión*) to get on, board; (*precio*) to rise, go up; (*río, marea*) to rise; **subirse** *vr* to get up, climb

**súbito, -a** ['suβito, a] *adj* (*repentino*) sudden; (*imprevisto*) unexpected

**subjetivo, -a** [suβxe'tiβo, a] *adj* subjective

**sublevar** [suβle'βar] *vt* to rouse to revolt; **sublevarse** *vr* to revolt, rise

**sublime** [su'βlime] *adj* sublime

**submarinismo** [suβmari'nismo] *nm* scuba diving

**submarino, -a** [suβma'rino, a] *adj* underwater ▷ *nm* submarine

**subnormal** [suβnor'mal] *adj* subnormal ▷ *nmf* subnormal person

**subordinado, -a** [suβorði'naðo, a] *adj, nm/f* subordinate

**subrayar** [suβra'jar] *vt* to underline

**subsanar** [suβsa'nar] *vt* to rectify

**subsidio** [suβ'siðjo] *nm* (*ayuda*) aid, financial help; (*subvención*) subsidy, grant; (*de enfermedad, paro etc*) benefit, allowance

**subsistencia** [suβsis'tenθja] *nf* subsistence

**subsistir** [suβsis'tir] *vi* to subsist; (*sobrevivir*) to survive, endure

**subte** ['suβte] (*RPL*) *nm* underground (*BRIT*), subway (*US*)

**subterráneo, -a** [suβte'rraneo, a] *adj* underground, subterranean ▷ *nm* underpass, underground passage

**subtítulo** [suβ'titulo] *nm* (*Cine*) subtitle

**suburbio** [su'βurβjo] *nm* (*barrio*) slum quarter

**subvención** [suββen'θjon] *nf* (*Econ*) subsidy, grant; **subvencionar** *vt* to subsidize

**sucedáneo, -a** [suθe'ðaneo, a] *adj* substitute ▷ *nm* substitute (food)

**suceder** [suθe'ðer] *vt, vi* to happen; (*seguir*) to succeed, follow; **lo que sucede es que ...** the fact is that ...; **sucesión** *nf* succession; (*serie*) sequence, series

**sucesivamente** [suθesiβa'mente] *adv*: **y así ~** and so on

**sucesivo, -a** [suθe'siβo, a] *adj* successive, following; **en lo ~** in future, from now on

**suceso** [su'θeso] *nm* (*hecho*) event, happening; (*incidente*) incident

┃ No confundir **suceso** con la palabra inglesa *success*.

**suciedad** [suθje'ðað] *nf* (*estado*) dirtiness; (*mugre*) dirt, filth

**sucio, -a** ['suθjo, a] *adj* dirty

**suculento, -a** [suku'lento, a] *adj* succulent

**sucumbir** [sukum'bir] *vi* to succumb

**sucursal** [sukur'sal] *nf* branch (office)

**sudadera** [suða'ðera] *nf* sweatshirt

**Sudáfrica** [suð'afrika] *nf* South Africa

**Sudamérica** [suða'merika] *nf* South America; **sudamericano, -a** *adj, nm/f* South American

**sudar** [su'ðar] *vt, vi* to sweat

**sudeste** [su'ðeste] *nm* south-east

**sudoeste** [suðo'este] *nm* south-west

**sudor** [su'ðor] *nm* sweat; **sudoroso, -a** *adj* sweaty, sweating

**Suecia** ['sweθja] *nf* Sweden; **sueco, -a** *adj* Swedish ▷ *nm/f* Swede

**suegro, -a** ['sweɣro, a] *nm/f* father-/ mother-in-law

**suela** ['swela] *nf* sole

**sueldo** ['sweldo] *nm* pay, wage(s) (*pl*)

**suele** *etc vb* V **soler**

**suelo** ['swelo] *nm* (*tierra*) ground; (*de casa*) floor

**suelto, -a** ['swelto, a] *adj* loose; (*libre*) free; (*separado*) detached; (*ágil*) quick, agile ▷ *nm* (loose) change, small change

**sueñito** [swe'ɲito] (*LAM*) *nm* nap

**sueño** *etc* ['sweɲo] *vb* V **soñar** ▷ *nm* sleep; (*somnolencia*) sleepiness, drowsiness; (*lo soñado, fig*) dream; **tener ~** to be sleepy

**suero** ['swero] *nm* (*Med*) serum; (*de leche*) whey

**suerte** ['swerte] *nf* (*fortuna*) luck; (*azar*) chance; (*destino*) fate, destiny; (*especie*) sort, kind; **tener ~** to be lucky

**suéter** ['sweter] *nm* sweater

**suficiente** [sufi'θjente] *adj* enough, sufficient ▷ *nm* (*Escol*) pass

**sufragio** [su'fraxjo] *nm* (*voto*) vote; (*derecho de voto*) suffrage

**sufrido, -a** [su'friðo, a] *adj* (*persona*) tough; (*paciente*) long-suffering, patient

**sufrimiento** [sufri'mjento] *nm* (*dolor*) suffering

**sufrir** [su'frir] *vt* (*padecer*) to suffer; (*soportar*) to bear, put up with; (*apoyar*) to hold up, support ⊳ *vi* to suffer

**sugerencia** [suxe'renθja] *nf* suggestion

**sugerir** [suxe'rir] *vt* to suggest; (*sutilmente*) to hint

**sugestión** [suxes'tjon] *nf* suggestion; (*sutil*) hint; **sugestionar** *vt* to influence

**sugestivo, -a** [suxes'tiβo, a] *adj* stimulating; (*fascinante*) fascinating

**suicida** [sui'θiða] *adj* suicidal ⊳ *nmf* suicidal person; (*muerto*) suicide, person who has committed suicide; **suicidarse** *vr* to commit suicide, kill o.s.; **suicidio** *nm* suicide

**Suiza** ['swiθa] *nf* Switzerland; **suizo, -a** *adj, nm/f* Swiss

**sujeción** [suxe'θjon] *nf* subjection

**sujetador** [suxeta'ðor] *nm* (*sostén*) bra

**sujetar** [suxe'tar] *vt* (*fijar*) to fasten; (*detener*) to hold down; **sujetarse** *vr* to subject o.s.; **sujeto, -a** *adj* fastened, secure ⊳ *nm* subject; (*individuo*) individual; **sujeto a** subject to

**suma** ['suma] *nf* (*cantidad*) total, sum; (*de dinero*) sum; (*acto*) adding (up), addition; **en ~ short**

**sumamente** [suma'mente] *adv* extremely, exceedingly

**sumar** [su'mar] *vt* to add (up) ⊳ *vi* to add up

**sumergir** [sumer'xir] *vt* to submerge; (*hundir*) to sink

**suministrar** [sumini'strar] *vt* to supply, provide; **suministro** *nm* supply; (*acto*) supplying, providing

**sumir** [su'mir] *vt* to sink, submerge; (*fig*) to plunge

**sumiso, -a** [su'miso, a] *adj* submissive, docile

**sumo, -a** ['sumo, a] *adj* great, extreme; (*autoridad*) highest, supreme

**suntuoso, -a** [sun'twoso, a] *adj* sumptuous, magnificent

**supe** *etc vb* V **saber**

**super...** [super] *prefijo* super..., over...

**superbueno, -a** [super'bweno, a] *adj* great, fantastic

**súper** ['super] *nf* (*gasolina*) four-star (petrol)

**superar** [supe'rar] *vt* (*sobreponerse a*) to overcome; (*rebasar*) to surpass, do better

than; (*pasar*) to go beyond; **superarse** *vr* to excel o.s.

**superficial** [superfi'θjal] *adj* superficial; (*medida*) surface *cpd*, of the surface

**superficie** [super'fiθje] *nf* surface; (*área*) area

**superfluo, -a** [su'perflwo, a] *adj* superfluous

**superior** [supe'rjor] *adj* (*piso, clase*) upper; (*temperatura, número, nivel*) higher; (*mejor: calidad, producto*) superior, better ⊳ *nmf* superior; **superioridad** *nf* superiority

**supermercado** [supermer'kaðo] *nm* supermarket

**superponer** [superpo'ner] *vt* to superimpose

**superstición** [supersti'θjon] *nf* superstition; **supersticioso, -a** *adj* superstitious

**supervisar** [superβi'sar] *vt* to supervise

**supervivencia** [superβi'βenθja] *nf* survival

**superviviente** [superβi'βjente] *adj* surviving

**supiera** *etc vb* V **saber**

**suplantar** [suplan'tar] *vt* to supplant

**suplemento** [suple'mento] *nm* supplement

**suplente** [su'plente] *adj, nm* substitute

**supletorio, -a** [suple'torjo, a] *adj* supplementary ⊳ *nm* supplement; **teléfono ~** extension

**súplica** ['suplika] *nf* request; (*Jur*) petition

**suplicar** [supli'kar] *vt* (*cosa*) to beg (for), plead for; (*persona*) to beg, plead with

**suplicio** [su'pliθjo] *nm* torture

**suplir** [su'plir] *vt* (*compensar*) to make good, make up for; (*reemplazar*) to replace, substitute ⊳ *vi*: **~ a** to take the place of, substitute for

**supo** *etc vb* V **saber**

**suponer** [supo'ner] *vt* to suppose; **suposición** *nf* supposition

**suprimir** [supri'mir] *vt* to suppress; (*derecho, costumbre*) to abolish; (*palabra etc*) to delete; (*restricción*) to cancel, lift

**supuesto, -a** [su'pwesto, a] *pp de* **suponer** ⊳ *adj* (*hipotético*) supposed ⊳ *nm* assumption, hypothesis; **~ que** since; **por ~** of course

**sur** [sur] *nm* south

**surcar** [sur'kar] *vt* to plough; **surco** *nm* (*en metal, disco*) groove; (*Agr*) furrow

**surgir** [sur'xir] *vi* to arise, emerge; (*dificultad*) to come up, crop up

**suroeste** [suro'este] *nm* south-west

**surtido, -a** [sur'tiðo, a] *adj* mixed,

assorted ▷ *nm* (*selección*) selection, assortment; (*abastecimiento*) supply, stock; **surtidor** *nm* (*tb*: **surtidor de gasolina**) petrol pump (*BRIT*), gas pump (*US*)

**surtir** [sur'tir] *vt* to supply, provide ▷ *vi* to spout, spurt

**susceptible** [susθep'tiβle] *adj* susceptible; (*sensible*) sensitive; **~ de** capable of

**suscitar** [susθi'tar] *vt* to cause, provoke; (*interés, sospechas*) to arouse

**suscribir** [suskri'βir] *vt* (*firmar*) to sign; (*respaldar*) to subscribe to, endorse; **suscribirse** *vr* to subscribe; **suscripción** *nf* subscription

**susodicho, -a** [suso'ðitʃo, a] *adj* above-mentioned

**suspender** [suspen'der] *vt* (*objeto*) to hang (up), suspend; (*trabajo*) to stop, suspend; (*Escol*) to fail; (*interrumpir*) to adjourn; (*atrasar*) to postpone

**suspense** [sus'pense] (*ESP*) *nm* suspense; **película/novela de ~** thriller

**suspensión** [suspen'sjon] *nf* suspension; (*fig*) stoppage, suspension

**suspenso, -a** [sus'penso, a] *adj* hanging, suspended; (*ESP Escol*) failed ▷ *nm* (*ESP Escol*) fail; **película** o **novela de ~** (*LAM*) thriller; **quedar** o **estar en ~** to be pending

**suspicaz** [suspi'kaθ] *adj* suspicious, distrustful

**suspirar** [suspi'rar] *vi* to sigh; **suspiro** *nm* sigh

**sustancia** [sus'tanθja] *nf* substance

**sustento** [sus'tento] *nm* support; (*alimento*) sustenance, food

**sustituir** [sustitu'ir] *vt* to substitute, replace; **sustituto, -a** *nm/f* substitute, replacement

**susto** ['susto] *nm* fright, scare

**sustraer** [sustra'er] *vt* to remove, take away; (*Mat*) to subtract

**susurrar** [susu'rrar] *vi* to whisper; **susurro** *nm* whisper

**sutil** [su'til] *adj* (*aroma, diferencia*) subtle; (*tenue*) thin; (*inteligencia, persona*) sharp

**suyo, -a** ['sujo, a] (*con artículo* o *después del verbo* **ser**) *adj* (*de él*) his; (*de ella*) hers; (*de ellos, ellas*) theirs; (*de Ud, Uds*) yours; **un amigo ~** a friend of his (o hers o theirs o yours)

# t

**Tabacalera** [taβaka'lera] *nf Spanish state tobacco monopoly*

**tabaco** [ta'βako] *nm* tobacco; (*ESP: fam*) cigarettes *pl*

**tabaquería** [tabake'ria] (*LAM*) *nf* tobacconist's (shop) (*BRIT*), smoke shop (*US*); **tabaquero, -a** *nm/f* tobacconist

**taberna** [ta'βerna] *nf* bar, pub (*BRIT*)

**tabique** [ta'βike] *nm* partition (wall)

**tabla** ['taβla] *nf* (*de madera*) plank; (*estante*) shelf; (*de vestido*) pleat; (*Arte*) panel; **tablas** *nfpl*: **estar** o **quedar en ~s** to draw; **tablado** *nm* (*plataforma*) platform; (*Teatro*) stage

**tablao** [ta'βlao] *nm* (*tb*: **~ flamenco**) flamenco show

**tablero** [ta'βlero] *nm* (*de madera*) plank, board; (*de ajedrez, damas*) board; **tablero de mandos** (*LAM Auto*) dashboard

**tableta** [ta'βleta] *nf* (*Med*) tablet; (*de chocolate*) bar

**tablón** [ta'βlon] *nm* (*de suelo*) plank; (*de techo*) beam; **tablón de anuncios** notice (*BRIT*) o bulletin (*US*) board

**tabú** [ta'βu] *nm* taboo

**taburete** [taβu'rete] *nm* stool

**tacaño, -a** [ta'kaɲo, a] *adj* mean

**tacha** ['tatʃa] *nf* flaw; (*Tec*) stud; **tachar** *vt* (*borrar*) to cross out; **tachar de** to accuse of

**tacho** ['tatʃo] (*cs*) *nm* (*balde*) bucket; **tacho de la basura** rubbish bin (*BRIT*), trash can (*US*)

**taco** ['tako] *nm* (*Billar*) cue; (*de billetes*) book; (*cs: de zapato*) heel; (*tarugo*) peg; (*palabrota*) swear word

**tacón** [ta'kon] *nm* heel; **de ~ alto** high-heeled

**táctica** ['taktika] *nf* tactics *pl*

**táctico, -a** ['taktiko, a] *adj* tactical

**tacto** ['takto] *nm* touch; (*fig*) tact

**tajada** [ta'xaða] *nf* slice

**tajante** [ta'xante] *adj* sharp

**tajo** ['taxo] nm (corte) cut; (Geo) cleft

**tal** [tal] adj such ▷ pron (persona) someone, such a one; (cosa) something, such a thing ▷ adv: ~ **como** (igual) just as ▷ conj: **con ~ de que** provided that; ~ **cual** (como es) just as it is; ~ **vez** perhaps; ~ **como** such as; ~ **para cual** (dos iguales) two of a kind; **¿qué ~?** how are things?; **¿qué ~ te gusta?** how do you like it?

**taladrar** [tala'ðrar] vt to drill; **taladro** nm drill

**talante** [ta'lante] nm (humor) mood; (voluntad) will, willingness

**talar** [ta'lar] vt to fell, cut down; (devastar) to devastate

**talco** ['talko] nm (polvos) talcum powder

**talento** [ta'lento] nm talent; (capacidad) ability

**TALGO** ['talɣo] (ESP) nm abr (= tren articulado ligero Goicoechea-Oriol) ≈ HST (BRIT)

**talismán** [talis'man] nm talisman

**talla** ['taʎa] nf (estatura, fig, Med) height, stature; (palo) measuring rod; (Arte) carving; (medida) size

**tallar** [ta'ʎar] vt (madera) to carve; (metal etc) to engrave; (medir) to measure

**tallarines** [taʎa'rines] nmpl noodles

**talle** ['taʎe] nm (Anat) waist; (fig) appearance

**taller** [ta'ʎer] nm (Tec) workshop; (de artista) studio

**tallo** ['taʎo] nm (de planta) stem; (de hierba) blade; (brote) shoot

**talón** [ta'lon] nm (Anat) heel; (Com) counterfoil; (cheque) cheque (BRIT), check (US)

**talonario** [talo'narjo] nm (de cheques) chequebook (BRIT), checkbook (US); (de recibos) receipt book

**tamaño, -a** [ta'maɲo, a] adj (tan grande) such a big; (tan pequeño) such a small ▷ nm size; **de ~ natural** full-size

**tamarindo** [tama'rindo] nm tamarind

**tambalearse** [tambale'arse] vr (persona) to stagger; (vehículo) to sway

**también** [tam'bjen] adv (igualmente) also, too, as well; (además) besides

**tambor** [tam'bor] nm drum; (Anat) eardrum; **tambor del freno** brake drum

**tamizar** [tami'θar] vt to sieve

**tampoco** [tam'poko] adv nor, neither; **yo ~ lo compré** I didn't buy it either

**tampón** [tam'pon] nm tampon

**tan** [tan] adv so; ~ **es así que ...** so much so that ...

**tanda** ['tanda] nf (gen) series; (turno) shift

**tangente** [tan'xente] nf tangent

**tangerina** [tanxe'rina] (LAM) nf tangerine

**tangible** [tan'xiβle] adj tangible

**tanque** ['tanke] nm (cisterna, Mil) tank; (Auto) tanker

**tantear** [tante'ar] vt (calcular) to reckon (up); (medir) to take the measure of; (probar) to test, try out; (tomar la medida: persona) to take the measurements of; (situación) to weigh up; (persona: opinión) to sound out ▷ vi (Deporte) to score; **tanteo** nm (cálculo) (rough) calculation; (prueba) test, trial; (Deporte) scoring

**tanto, -a** ['tanto, a] adj (cantidad) so much, as much ▷ adv (cantidad) so much, as much; (tiempo) so long, as long ▷ conj: **en ~ que** while ▷ nm (suma) certain amount; (proporción) so much; (punto) point; (gol) goal; **un ~ perezoso** somewhat lazy ▷ pron: **cada uno paga ~** each one pays so much; ~**s** so many, as many; **20 y ~s** 20-odd; **hasta ~ (que)** until such time as; ~ **tú como yo** both you and I; ~ **como eso** as much as that; ~ **más ... cuanto que** all the more ... because; ~ **mejor/peor** so much the better/the worse; ~ **si viene como si va** whether he comes or whether he goes; ~ **es así que** so much so that; **por (lo)** ~ therefore; **entre** ~ meanwhile; **estar al** ~ to be up to date; **me he vuelto ronco de o con ~ hablar** I have become hoarse with so much talking; **a ~s de agosto** on such and such a day in August

**tapa** ['tapa] nf (de caja, olla) lid; (de botella) top; (de libro) cover; (comida) snack

**tapadera** [tapa'ðera] nf lid, cover

**tapar** [ta'par] vt (cubrir) to cover; (envolver) to wrap o cover up; (la vista) to obstruct; (persona, falta) to conceal; (MÉX, CAM: diente) to fill; **taparse** vr to wrap o.s. up

**taparrabo** [tapa'rraβo] nm loincloth

**tapete** [ta'pete] nm table cover

**tapia** ['tapja] nf (garden) wall

**tapicería** [tapiθe'ria] nf tapestry; (para muebles) upholstery; (tienda) upholsterer's (shop)

**tapiz** [ta'piθ] nm (alfombra) carpet; (tela tejida) tapestry; **tapizar** vt (muebles) to upholster

**tapón** [ta'pon] nm (de botella) top; (de lavabo) plug; **tapón de rosca** screw-top

**taquigrafía** [takixra'fia] nf shorthand; **taquígrafo, -a** nm/f shorthand writer, stenographer

**taquilla** [ta'kiʎa] nf (donde se compra) booking office; (suma recogida) takings pl

**tarántula** [ta'rantula] nf tarantula

**tararear** [tarare'ar] vi to hum

**tardar** [tar'ðar] vi (tomar tiempo) to take a

long time; (*llegar tarde*) to be late; (*demorar*) to delay; **¿tarda mucho el tren?** does the train take (very) long?; **a más ~** at the latest; **no tardes en venir** come soon

**tarde** ['tarðe] *adv* late ▷ *nf* (*de día*) afternoon; (*al anochecer*) evening; **de ~ en ~** from time to time; **¡buenas ~s!** good afternoon!; **a** *o* **por la ~** in the afternoon; in the evening

**tardío, -a** [tar'ðio, a] *adj* (*retrasado*) late; (*lento*) slow (to arrive)

**tarea** [ta'rea] *nf* task; (*faena*) chore; (*Escol*) homework

**tarifa** [ta'rifa] *nf* (*lista de precios*) price list; (*precio*) tariff

**tarima** [ta'rima] *nf* (*plataforma*) platform

**tarjeta** [tar'xeta] *nf* card; **tarjeta de crédito/de Navidad/postal/telefónica** credit card/Christmas card/postcard/phonecard; **tarjeta de embarque** boarding pass; **tarjeta de memoria** memory card; **tarjeta prepago** top-up card; **tarjeta SIM** SIM card

**tarro** ['tarro] *nm* jar, pot

**tarta** ['tarta] *nf* (*pastel*) cake; (*de base dura*) tart

**tartamudear** [tartamuðe'ar] *vi* to stammer; **tartamudo, -a** *adj* stammering ▷ *nm/f* stammerer

**tártaro, -a** ['tartaro, a] *adj*: **salsa tártara** tartar(e) sauce

**tasa** ['tasa] *nf* (*precio*) (fixed) price, rate; (*valoración*) valuation; (*medida, norma*) measure, standard; **tasa de cambio/interés** exchange/interest rate; **tasas de aeropuerto** airport tax; **tasas universitarias** university fees

**tasar** [ta'sar] *vt* (*arreglar el precio*) to fix a price for; (*valorar*) to value, assess

**tasca** ['taska] (*fam*) *nf* pub

**tatarabuelo, -a** [tatara'βwelo, a] *nm/f* great-great-grandfather/mother

**tatuaje** [ta'twaxe] *nm* (*dibujo*) tattoo; (*acto*) tattooing

**tatuar** [ta'twar] *vt* to tattoo

**taurino, -a** [tau'rino, a] *adj* bullfighting *cpd*

**Tauro** ['tauro] *nm* Taurus

**tauromaquia** [tauro'makja] *nf* tauromachy, (art of) bullfighting

**taxi** ['taksi] *nm* taxi; **taxista** [tak'sista] *nmf* taxi driver

**taza** ['taθa] *nf* cup; (*de retrete*) bowl; **~ para café** coffee cup; **taza de café** cup of coffee; **tazón** *nm* (*taza grande*) mug, large cup; (*de fuente*) basin

**te** [te] *pron* (*complemento de objeto*) you; (*complemento indirecto*) (to) you; (*reflexivo*)

(to) yourself; **¿~ duele mucho el brazo?** does your arm hurt a lot?; **~ equivocas** you're wrong; **¡cálma~!** calm down!

**té** [te] *nm* tea

**teatral** [tea'tral] *adj* theatre *cpd*; (*fig*) theatrical

**teatro** [te'atro] *nm* theatre; (*Literatura*) plays *pl*, drama

**tebeo** [te'βeo] *nm* comic

**techo** ['tetʃo] *nm* (*externo*) roof; (*interno*) ceiling; **techo corredizo** sunroof

**tecla** ['tekla] *nf* key; **teclado** *nm* keyboard; **teclear** *vi* (*Mús*) to strum; (*con los dedos*) to tap ▷ *vt* (*Inform*) to key in

**técnica** ['teknika] *nf* technique; (*tecnología*) technology; *V tb* **técnico**

**técnico, -a** ['tekniko, a] *adj* technical ▷ *nm/f* technician; (*experto*) expert

**tecnología** [teknolo'xia] *nf* technology; **tecnológico, -a** *adj* technological

**tecolote** [teko'lote] (*MÉX*) *nm* owl

**tedioso, -a** [te'ðjoso, a] *adj* boring, tedious

**teja** ['texa] *nf* tile; (*Bot*) lime (tree); **tejado** *nm* (tiled) roof

**tejemaneje** [texema'nexe] *nm* (*lío*) fuss; (*intriga*) intrigue

**tejer** [te'xer] *vt* to weave; (*hacer punto*) to knit; (*fig*) to fabricate; **tejido** *nm* (*tela*) material, fabric; (*telaraña*) web; (*Anat*) tissue

**tel** [tel] *abr* (= *teléfono*) tel

**tela** ['tela] *nf* (*tejido*) material; (*telaraña*) web; (*en líquido*) skin; **telar** *nm* (*máquina*) loom

**telaraña** [tela'raɲa] *nf* cobweb

**tele** ['tele] (*fam*) *nf* telly (BRIT), tube (US)

**tele...** ['tele] *prefijo* tele...; **telebasura** *nf* trash TV; **telecomunicación** *nf* telecommunication; **telediario** *nm* television news; **teledirigido, -a** *adj* remote-controlled

**teleférico** [tele'feriko] *nm* (*de esquí*) ski-lift

**telefonear** [telefone'ar] *vi* to telephone

**telefónico, -a** [tele'foniko, a] *adj* telephone *cpd*

**telefonillo** [telefo'niʎo] *nm* (*de puerta*) intercom

**telefonista** [telefo'nista] *nmf* telephonist

**teléfono** [te'lefono] *nm* (tele)phone; **estar hablando al ~** to be on the phone; **llamar a algn por ~** to ring sb (up) *o* phone sb (up); **teléfono celular** (LAM) mobile phone; **teléfono con cámara** camera phone; **teléfono inalámbrico** cordless phone; **teléfono móvil** (ESP) mobile phone

**telégrafo** [te'leɣrafo] *nm* telegraph

**telegrama** [tele'ɣrama] *nm* telegram

**tele: telenovela** nf soap (opera);
**teleobjetivo** nm telephoto lens; **telepatía**
nf telepathy; **telepático, -a** adj telepathic;
**telerrealidad** nf reality TV; **telescopio**
nm telescope; **telesilla** nf chairlift;
**telespectador, a** nm/f viewer; **telesquí**
nm ski-lift; **teletarjeta** nf phonecard;
**teletipo** nm teletype; **teletrabajador,
a** nm/f teleworker; **teletrabajo** nm
teleworking; **televentas** nfpl telesales
**televidente** [teleβi'ðente] nmf viewer
**televisar** [teleβi'sar] vt to televise
**televisión** [teleβi'sjon] nf television;
**televisión digital** digital television
**televisor** [teleβi'sor] nm television set
**télex** ['teleks] nm inv telex
**telón** [te'lon] nm curtain; **telón de acero**
(Pol) iron curtain; **telón de fondo** backcloth,
background
**tema** ['tema] nm (asunto) subject, topic;
(Mús) theme; **temático, -a** adj thematic
**temblar** [tem'blar] vi to shake, tremble;
(por frío) to shiver; **temblor** nm trembling;
(de tierra) earthquake; **tembloroso, -a** adj
trembling
**temer** [te'mer] vt to fear ▷ vi to be afraid;
**temo que llegue tarde** I am afraid he may
be late
**temible** [te'miβle] adj fearsome
**temor** [te'mor] nm (miedo) fear; (duda)
suspicion
**témpano** ['tempano] nm (tb: ~ de hielo)
ice-floe
**temperamento** [tempera'mento] nm
temperament
**temperatura** [tempera'tura] nf
temperature
**tempestad** [tempes'tað] nf storm
**templado, -a** [tem'plaðo, a] adj
(moderado) moderate; (frugal) frugal; (agua)
lukewarm; (clima) mild; (Mús) well-tuned;
**templanza** nf moderation; mildness
**templar** [tem'plar] vt (moderar) to
moderate; (furia) to restrain; (calor) to
reduce; (afinar) to tune (up); (acero) to
temper; (tuerca) to tighten up; **temple**
nm (ajuste) tempering; (afinación) tuning;
(pintura) tempera
**templo** ['templo] nm (iglesia) church;
(pagano etc) temple
**temporada** [tempo'raða] nf time, period;
(estación) season
**temporal** [tempo'ral] adj (no permanente)
temporary ▷ nm storm
**temprano, -a** [tem'prano, a] adj early;
(demasiado pronto) too soon, too early
**ten** vb V **tener**
**tenaces** [te'naθes] adj pl V **tenaz**

**tenaz** [te'naθ] adj (material) tough;
(persona) tenacious; (creencia, resistencia)
stubborn
**tenaza(s)** [te'naθa(s)] nf(pl) (Med) forceps;
(Tec) pliers; (Zool) pincers
**tendedero** [tende'ðero] nm (para ropa)
drying place; (cuerda) clothes line
**tendencia** [ten'denθja] nf tendency;
**tener ~ a** to tend to, have a tendency to
**tender** [ten'der] vt (extender) to spread out;
(colgar) to hang out; (vía férrea, cable) to lay;
(estirar) to stretch ▷ vi: **~ a** to tend to, have
a tendency towards; **tenderse** vr to lie
down; **~ la cama/mesa** (LAM) to make the
bed/lay (BRIT) o set (US) the table
**tenderete** [tende'rete] nm (puesto) stall;
(exposición) display of goods
**tendero, -a** [ten'dero, a] nm/f
shopkeeper
**tendón** [ten'don] nm tendon
**tendré** etc vb V **tener**
**tenebroso, -a** [tene'βroso, a] adj (oscuro)
dark; (fig) gloomy
**tenedor** [tene'ðor] nm (Culin) fork
**tenencia** [te'nenθja] nf (de casa) tenancy;
(de oficio) tenure; (de propiedad) possession

○ **PALABRA CLAVE**

**tener** [te'ner] vt **1** (poseer, gen) to have; (en
la mano) to hold; **¿tienes un boli?** have you
got a pen?; **va a tener un niño** she's going
to have a baby; **¡ten** (o **tenga**)!**, ¡aquí tienes**
(o **tiene**)! here you are!
**2** (edad, medidas) to be; **tiene 7 años** she's 7
(years old); **tiene 15 cm de largo** it's 15 cm
long; V **calor; hambre** etc
**3** (considerar): **lo tengo por brillante** I
consider him to be brilliant; **tener en
mucho a algn** to think very highly of sb
**4** (+ pp: = pretérito): **tengo terminada ya la
mitad del trabajo** I've done half the work
already
**5 tener que hacer algo** to have to do sth;
**tengo que acabar este trabajo hoy** I have
to finish this job today
**6 ¿qué tienes, estás enfermo?** what's the
matter with you, are you ill?
**tenerse** vr **1 tenerse en pie** to stand up
**2 tenerse por** to think o.s.

**tengo** etc vb V **tener**
**tenia** ['tenja] nf tapeworm
**teniente** [te'njente] nm (rango)
lieutenant; (ayudante) deputy
**tenis** ['tenis] nm tennis; **tenis de mesa**
table tennis; **tenista** nmf tennis player
**tenor** [te'nor] nm (sentido) meaning; (Mús)

tenor; **a ~ de** on the lines of

**tensar** [ten'sar] vt to tighten; (arco) to draw

**tensión** [ten'sjon] nf tension; (Tec) stress; **tener la ~ alta** to have high blood pressure; **tensión arterial** blood pressure

**tenso, -a** ['tenso, a] adj tense

**tentación** [tenta'θjon] nf temptation

**tentáculo** [ten'takulo] nm tentacle

**tentador, a** [tenta'ðor, a] adj tempting

**tentar** [ten'tar] vt (seducir) to tempt; (atraer) to attract

**tentempié** [tentem'pje] nm snack

**tenue** ['tenwe] adj (delgado) thin, slender; (neblina) light; (lazo, vínculo) slight

**teñir** [te'ɲir] vt to dye; (fig) to tinge; **teñirse** vr to dye; **~se el pelo** to dye one's hair

**teología** [teolo'xia] nf theology

**teoría** [teo'ria] nf theory; **en ~** in theory; **teórico, -a** adj theoretic(al) ▷ nm/f theoretician, theorist; **teorizar** vi to theorize

**terapéutico, -a** [tera'peutiko, a] adj therapeutic

**terapia** [te'rapja] nf therapy

**tercer** adj V **tercero**

**tercermundista** [terθermun'dista] adj Third World cpd

**tercero, -a** [ter'θero, a] (delante de nmsg: **tercer**) adj third ▷ nm (Jur) third party

**terceto** [ter'θeto] nm trio

**terciar** [ter'θjar] vi (participar) to take part; (hacer de árbitro) to mediate; **terciario, -a** adj tertiary

**tercio** ['terθjo] nm third

**terciopelo** [terθjo'pelo] nm velvet

**terco, -a** ['terko, a] adj obstinate

**tergal®** [ter'xal] nm type of polyester

**tergiversar** [terxiβer'sar] vt to distort

**termal** [ter'mal] adj thermal

**termas** ['termas] nfpl hot springs

**térmico, -a** ['termiko, a] adj thermal

**terminal** [termi'nal] adj, nm, nf terminal

**terminante** [termi'nante] adj (final) final, definitive; (tajante) categorical; **terminantemente** adv: **terminantemente prohibido** strictly forbidden

**terminar** [termi'nar] vt (completar) to complete, finish; (concluir) to end ▷ vi (llegar a su fin) to end; (parar) to stop; (acabar) to finish; **terminarse** vr to come to an end; **~ por hacer algo** to end up (by) doing sth

**término** ['termino] nm end, conclusion; (parada) terminus; (límite) boundary; **en último ~** (a fin de cuentas) in the last analysis; (como último recurso) as a last resort; **término medio** average; (fig) middle way

**termómetro** [ter'mometro] nm thermometer

**termo(s)®** ['termo(s)] nm Thermos®

**termostato** [termo'stato] nm thermostat

**ternero, -a** [ter'nero, a] nm/f (animal) calf ▷ nf (carne) veal

**ternura** [ter'nura] nf (trato) tenderness; (palabra) endearment; (cariño) fondness

**terrado** [te'rraðo] nm terrace

**terraplén** [terra'plen] nm embankment

**terrateniente** [terrate'njente] nmf landowner

**terraza** [te'rraθa] nf (balcón) balcony; (tejado) (flat) roof; (Agr) terrace

**terremoto** [terre'moto] nm earthquake

**terrenal** [terre'nal] adj earthly

**terreno** [te'rreno] nm (tierra) land; (parcela) plot; (suelo) soil; (fig) field; **un ~** a piece of land

**terrestre** [te'rrestre] adj terrestrial; (ruta) land cpd

**terrible** [te'rriβle] adj terrible, awful

**territorio** [terri'torjo] nm territory

**terrón** [te'rron] nm (de azúcar) lump; (de tierra) clod, lump

**terror** [te'rror] nm terror; **terrorífico, -a** adj terrifying; **terrorista** adj, nmf terrorist; **terrorista suicida** suicide bomber

**terso, -a** ['terso, a] adj (liso) smooth; (pulido) polished

**tertulia** [ter'tulja] nf (reunión informal) social gathering; (grupo) group, circle

**tesis** ['tesis] nf inv thesis

**tesón** [te'son] nm (firmeza) firmness; (tenacidad) tenacity

**tesorero, -a** [teso'rero, a] nm/f treasurer

**tesoro** [te'soro] nm treasure; (Com, Pol) treasury

**testamento** [testa'mento] nm will

**testarudo, -a** [testa'ruðo, a] adj stubborn

**testículo** [tes'tikulo] nm testicle

**testificar** [testifi'kar] vt to testify; (fig) to attest ▷ vi to give evidence

**testigo** [tes'tixo] nmf witness; **testigo de cargo/descargo** witness for the prosecution/defence; **testigo ocular** eye witness

**testimonio** [testi'monjo] nm testimony

**teta** ['teta] nf (de biberón) teat; (Anat: fam) breast

**tétanos** ['tetanos] nm tetanus

**tetera** [te'tera] nf teapot

**tétrico, -a** ['tetriko, a] adj gloomy, dismal

**textil** [teks'til] adj textile

**texto** ['teksto] nm text; **textual** adj textual

**textura** [teks'tura] nf (de tejido) texture

**tez** [teθ] nf (cutis) complexion

**ti** [ti] pron you; (reflexivo) yourself

**tía** ['tia] nf (pariente) aunt; (fam) chick, bird

**tibio, -a** ['tiβjo, a] adj lukewarm

**tiburón** [tiβu'ron] nm shark

**tic** [tik] nm (ruido) click; (de reloj) tick; (Med): ~ **nervioso** nervous tic

**tictac** [tik'tak] nm (de reloj) tick tock

**tiempo** ['tjempo] nm time; (época, período) age, period; (Meteorología) weather; (Ling) tense; (Deporte) half; **a ~** in time; **a un** o **al mismo ~** at the same time; **al poco ~** very soon (after); **se quedó poco ~** he didn't stay very long; **hace poco ~** not long ago; **mucho ~** a long time; **de ~ en ~** from time to time; **hace buen/mal ~** the weather is fine/bad; **estar a ~** to be in time; **hace ~** some time ago; **hacer ~** to while away the time; **motor de 2 ~s** two-stroke engine; **primer ~** first half

**tienda** ['tjenda] nf shop, store; **tienda de abarrotes** (MÉX, CAM) grocer's (BRIT), grocery store (US); **tienda de alimentación** o **comestibles** grocer's (BRIT), grocery store (US); **tienda de campaña** tent

**tienes** etc vb V **tener**

**tienta** etc ['tjenta] vb V **tentar** ▷ nf: **andar a ~s** to grope one's way along

**tiento** etc ['tjento] vb V **tentar** ▷ nm (tacto) touch; (precaución) wariness

**tierno, -a** ['tjerno, a] adj (blando) tender; (fresco) fresh; (amable) sweet

**tierra** ['tjerra] nf earth; (suelo) soil; (mundo) earth, world; (país) country, land; ~ **adentro** inland

**tieso, -a** ['tjeso, a] adj (rígido) rigid; (duro) stiff; (fam: orgulloso) conceited

**tiesto** ['tjesto] nm flowerpot

**tifón** [ti'fon] nm typhoon

**tifus** ['tifus] nm typhus

**tigre** ['tiɣre] nm tiger

**tijera** [ti'xera] nf scissors pl; (Zool) claw; **tijeras** nfpl scissors; (para plantas) shears

**tila** ['tila] nf lime blossom tea

**tildar** [til'dar] vt: ~ **de** to brand as

**tilde** ['tilde] nf (Tip) tilde

**tilín** [ti'lin] nm tinkle

**timar** [ti'mar] vt (estafar) to swindle

**timbal** [tim'bal] nm small drum

**timbre** ['timbre] nm (sello) stamp; (campanilla) bell; (tono) timbre; (Com) stamp duty

**timidez** [timi'ðeθ] nf shyness; **tímido, -a** adj shy

**timo** ['timo] nm swindle

**timón** [ti'mon] nm helm, rudder; **timonel** nm helmsman

**tímpano** ['timpano] nm (Anat) eardrum; (Mús) small drum

**tina** ['tina] nf tub; (baño) bath(tub); **tinaja** nf large jar

**tinieblas** [ti'njeβlas] nfpl darkness sg; (sombras) shadows

**tino** ['tino] nm (habilidad) skill; (juicio) insight

**tinta** ['tinta] nf ink; (Tec) dye; (Arte) colour

**tinte** ['tinte] nm dye

**tintero** [tin'tero] nm inkwell

**tinto** ['tinto] nm red wine

**tintorería** [tintore'ria] nf dry cleaner's

**tío** ['tio] nm (pariente) uncle; (fam: individuo) bloke (BRIT), guy

**tiovivo** [tio'βiβo] nm merry-go-round

**típico, -a** ['tipiko, a] adj typical

**tipo** ['tipo] nm (clase) type, kind; (hombre) fellow; (Anat: de hombre) build; (: de mujer) figure; (Imprenta) type; **tipo bancario/de descuento/de interés/de cambio** bank/ discount/interest/exchange rate

**tipografía** [tipoɣra'fia] nf printing cpd

**tíquet** ['tiket] (pl ~s) nm ticket; (en tienda) cash slip

**tiquismiquis** [tikis'mikis] nm inv fussy person ▷ nmpl (querellas) squabbling sg; (escrúpulos) silly scruples

**tira** ['tira] nf strip; (fig) abundance; **tira y afloja** give and take

**tirabuzón** [tiraβu'θon] nm (rizo) curl

**tirachinas** [tira'tʃinas] nm inv catapult

**tirada** [ti'raða] nf (acto) cast, throw; (serie) series; (Tip) printing, edition; **de una ~** at one go

**tirado, -a** [ti'raðo, a] adj (barato) dirt-cheap; (fam: fácil) very easy

**tirador** [tira'ðor] nm (mango) handle

**tirano, -a** [ti'rano, a] adj tyrannical ▷ nm/f tyrant

**tirante** [ti'rante] adj (cuerda etc) tight, taut; (relaciones) strained ▷ nm (Arq) brace; (Tec) stay; **tirantes** nmpl (de pantalón) braces (BRIT), suspenders (US); **tirantez** nf tightness; (fig) tension

**tirar** [ti'rar] vt to throw; (dejar caer) to drop; (volcar) to upset; (derribar) to knock down o over; (desechar) to throw out o away; (dinero) to squander; (imprimir) to print ▷ vi (disparar) to shoot; (de la puerta etc) to pull; (fam: andar) to go; (tender a, buscar realizar) to tend to; (Deporte) to shoot; **tirarse** vr to throw o.s.; ~ **abajo** to bring down, destroy; **tira más a su padre** he takes more after his father; **ir tirando** to manage

**tirita** [ti'rita] nf (sticking) plaster (BRIT), Bandaid® (US)

**tiritar** [tiri'tar] vi to shiver

**tiro** ['tiro] nm (lanzamiento) throw; (disparo) shot; (Deporte) shot; (Golf, Tenis) drive; (alcance) range; **caballo de ~** cart-horse; **tiro al blanco** target practice

**tirón** [ti'ron] nm (sacudida) pull, tug; **de un ~** in one go, all at once

**tiroteo** [tiro'teo] nm exchange of shots, shooting

**tisis** ['tisis] nf inv consumption, tuberculosis

**títere** ['titere] nm puppet

**titubear** [tituβe'ar] vi to stagger; to stammer; (fig) to hesitate; **titubeo** nm staggering; stammering; hesitation

**titulado, -a** [titu'laðo, a] adj (libro) entitled; (persona) titled

**titular** [titu'lar] adj titular ⊳ nmf holder ⊳ nm headline ⊳ vt to title; **titularse** vr to be entitled; **título** nm title; (de diario) headline; (certificado) professional qualification; (universitario) (university) degree; **a título de** in the capacity of

**tiza** ['tiθa] nf chalk

**toalla** [to'aʎa] nf towel

**tobillo** [to'βiʎo] nm ankle

**tobogán** [toβo'xan] nm (montaña rusa) roller-coaster; (de niños) chute, slide

**tocadiscos** [toka'ðiskos] nm inv record player

**tocado, -a** [to'kaðo, a] adj (fam) touched ⊳ nm headdress

**tocador** [toka'ðor] nm (mueble) dressing table; (cuarto) boudoir; (fam) ladies' toilet (BRIT) o room (US)

**tocar** [to'kar] vt to touch; (Mús) to play; (referirse a) to allude to; (timbre) to ring ⊳ vi (a la puerta) to knock (on o at the door); (ser de turno) to fall to, be the turn of; (ser hora) to be due; **tocarse** vr (cubrirse la cabeza) to cover one's head; (tener contacto) to touch (each other); **por lo que a mí me toca** as far as I am concerned; **te toca a ti** it's your turn

**tocayo, -a** [to'kajo, a] nm/f namesake

**tocino** [to'θino] nm bacon

**todavía** [toða'βia] adv (aun) even; (aún) still, yet; **~ más** yet more; **~ no** not yet

○ **PALABRA CLAVE**

**todo, -a** ['toðo, a] adj **1** (con artículo sg) all; **toda la carne** all the meat; **toda la noche** all night, the whole night; **todo el libro** the whole book; **toda una botella** a whole bottle; **todo lo contrario** quite the opposite; **está toda sucia** she's all dirty; **por todo el país** throughout the whole country

**2** (con artículo pl) all; every; **todos los libros** all the books; **todas las noches** every night; **todos los que quieran salir** all those who want to leave

⊳ pron **1** everything, all; **todos** everyone, everybody; **lo sabemos todo** we know everything; **todos querían más tiempo** everybody o everyone wanted more time; **nos marchamos todos** all of us left

**2**: **con todo: con todo él me sigue gustando** even so I still like him

⊳ adv all; **vaya todo seguido** keep straight on o ahead

⊳ nm: **como un todo** as a whole; **del todo: no me agrada del todo** I don't entirely like it

**todopoderoso, -a** [toðopoðe'roso, a] adj all powerful; (Rel) almighty

**todoterreno** [toðote'rreno] sm inv four-wheel drive, SUV (ESP US)

**toga** ['toxa] nf toga; (Escol) gown

**Tokio** ['tokjo] n Tokyo

**toldo** ['toldo] nm (para el sol) sunshade (BRIT), parasol; (tienda) marquee

**tolerancia** [tole'ranθja] nf tolerance; **tolerante** adj (sociedad) liberal; (persona) open-minded

**tolerar** [tole'rar] vt to tolerate; (resistir) to endure

**toma** ['toma] nf (acto) taking; (Med) dose; **toma de corriente** socket; **toma de tierra** earth (wire); **tomacorriente** (LAM) nm socket

**tomar** [to'mar] vt to take; (aspecto) to take on; (beber) to drink ⊳ vi to take; (LAM: beber) to drink; **tomarse** vr to take; **~se por** to consider o.s. to be; **~ a bien/mal** to take well/badly; **~ en serio** to take seriously; **~ el pelo a algn** to pull sb's leg; **~la con algn** to pick a quarrel with sb; **¡tome!** here you are!; **~ el sol** to sunbathe

**tomate** [to'mate] nm tomato

**tomillo** [to'miʎo] nm thyme

**tomo** ['tomo] nm (libro) volume

**ton** [ton] abr = **tonelada** ⊳ nm: **sin ~ ni son** without rhyme or reason

**tonalidad** [tonali'ðað] nf tone

**tonel** [to'nel] nm barrel

**tonelada** [tone'laða] nf ton; **tonelaje** nm tonnage

**tónica** ['tonika] nf (Mús) tonic; (fig) keynote

**tónico, -a** ['toniko, a] adj tonic ⊳ nm (Med) tonic

**tono** ['tono] nm tone; **fuera de ~** inappropriate

**tontería** [tonte'ria] nf (estupidez) foolishness; (cosa) stupid thing; (acto) foolish act; **tonterías** nfpl (disparates) rubbish sg, nonsense sg

**tonto, -a** ['tonto, a] adj stupid, silly ▷ nm/f fool

**topar** [to'par] vi: **~ contra** o **en** to run into; **~ con** to run up against

**tope** ['tope] adj maximum ▷ nm (fin) end; (límite) limit; (Ferro) buffer; (Auto) bumper; **al ~** end to end

**tópico, -a** ['topiko, a] adj topical ▷ nm platitude

**topo** ['topo] nm (Zool) mole; (fig) blunderer

**toque** etc vb V **tocar** ▷ nm touch; (Mús) beat; (de campana) peal; **dar un ~ a** to warn; **toque de queda** curfew

**toqué** etc vb V **tocar**

**toquetear** [tokete'ar] vt to finger

**toquilla** [to'kiʎa] nf (pañuelo) headscarf; (chal) shawl

**tórax** ['toraks] nm thorax

**torbellino** [torbe'ʎino] nm whirlwind; (fig) whirl

**torcedura** [torθe'ðura] nf twist; (Med) sprain

**torcer** [tor'θer] vt to twist; (la esquina) to turn; (Med) to sprain ▷ vi (desviar) to turn off; **torcerse** vr (ladearse) to bend; (desviarse) to go astray; (fracasar) to go wrong; **torcido, -a** adj twisted; (fig) crooked ▷ nm curl

**tordo, -a** ['torðo, a] adj dappled ▷ nm thrush

**torear** [tore'ar] vt (fig: evadir) to avoid; (jugar con) to tease ▷ vi to fight bulls; **toreo** nm bullfighting; **torero, -a** nm/f bullfighter

**tormenta** [tor'menta] nf storm; (fig: confusión) turmoil

**tormento** [tor'mento] nm torture; (fig) anguish

**tornar** [tor'nar] vt (devolver) to return, give back; (transformar) to transform ▷ vi to go back

**tornasolado, -a** [tornaso'laðo, a] adj (brillante) iridescent; (reluciente) shimmering

**torneo** [tor'neo] nm tournament

**tornillo** [tor'niʎo] nm screw

**torniquete** [torni'kete] nm (Med) tourniquet

**torno** ['torno] nm (Tec) winch; (tambor) drum; **en ~ (a)** round, about

**toro** ['toro] nm bull; (fam) he-man; **los ~s** bullfighting

**toronja** [to'ronxa] nf grapefruit

**torpe** ['torpe] adj (poco hábil) clumsy, awkward; (necio) dim; (lento) slow

**torpedo** [tor'peðo] nm torpedo

**torpeza** [tor'peθa] nf (falta de agilidad) clumsiness; (lentitud) slowness; (error) mistake

**torre** ['torre] nf tower; (de petróleo) derrick

**torrefacto, -a** [torre'facto, a] adj roasted

**torrente** [to'rrente] nm torrent

**torrija** [to'rrixa] nf French toast

**torsión** [tor'sjon] nf twisting

**torso** ['torso] nm torso

**torta** ['torta] nf cake; (fam) slap

**tortícolis** [tor'tikolis] nm inv stiff neck

**tortilla** [tor'tiʎa] nf omelette; (LAM: de maíz) maize pancake; **tortilla de papas** (LAM) potato omelette; **tortilla de patatas** (ESP) potato omelette; **tortilla francesa** (ESP) plain omelette

**tórtola** ['tortola] nf turtledove

**tortuga** [tor'tuɣa] nf tortoise

**tortuoso, -a** [tor'twoso, a] adj winding

**tortura** [tor'tura] nf torture; **torturar** vt to torture

**tos** [tos] nf cough; **tos ferina** whooping cough

**toser** [to'ser] vi to cough

**tostada** [tos'taða] nf piece of toast; **tostado, -a** adj toasted; (por el sol) dark brown; (piel) tanned

**tostador** [tosta'ðor] (ESP) nm toaster; **tostadora** (LAM) nf = **tostador**

**tostar** [tos'tar] vt to toast; (café) to roast; (persona) to tan; **tostarse** vr to get brown

**total** [to'tal] adj total ▷ adv in short; (al fin y al cabo) when all is said and done ▷ nm total; **en ~** in all; **~ que ...** to cut (BRIT) o make (US) a long story short ...

**totalidad** [totali'ðað] nf whole

**totalitario, -a** [totali'tarjo, a] adj totalitarian

**tóxico, -a** ['toksiko, a] adj toxic ▷ nm poison; **toxicómano, -a** nm/f drug addict

**toxina** [to'ksina] nf toxin

**tozudo, -a** [to'θuðo, a] adj obstinate

**trabajador, a** [traβaxa'ðor, a] adj hard-working ▷ nm/f worker; **trabajador autónomo** o **por cuenta propia** self-employed person

**trabajar** [traβa'xar] vt to work; (Agr) to till; (empeñarse en) to work at; (convencer) to persuade ▷ vi to work; (esforzarse) to strive; **trabajo** nm work; (tarea) task; (Pol) labour; (fig) effort; **tomarse el trabajo de** to take the trouble to; **trabajo a destajo** piecework; **trabajo en equipo** teamwork; **trabajo por turnos** shift work; **trabajos forzados** hard labour sg

**trabalenguas** [traβa'lengwas] nm inv tongue twister

**tracción** [trak'θjon] nf traction; **tracción delantera/trasera** front-wheel/rear-wheel drive

**tractor** [trak'tor] *nm* tractor
**tradición** [traði'θjon] *nf* tradition;
 **tradicional** *adj* traditional
**traducción** [traðuk'θjon] *nf* translation
**traducir** [traðu'θir] *vt* to translate;
 **traductor, a** *nm/f* translator
**traer** [tra'er] *vt* to bring; (*llevar*) to carry;
 (*llevar puesto*) to wear; (*incluir*) to carry;
 (*causar*) to cause; **traerse** *vr*: ~se algo to
 be up to sth
**traficar** [trafi'kar] *vi* to trade
**tráfico** ['trafiko] *nm* (*Com*) trade; (*Auto*)
 traffic
**tragaluz** [traɣa'luθ] *nm* skylight
**tragamonedas** [traɣamo'neðas] (*LAM*) *nf
 inv* slot machine
**tragaperras** [traɣa'perras] (*ESP*) *nf inv*
 slot machine
**tragar** [tra'ɣar] *vt* to swallow; (*devorar*) to
 devour, bolt down; **tragarse** *vr* to swallow
**tragedia** [tra'xeðja] *nf* tragedy; **trágico,
 -a** *adj* tragic
**trago** ['traɣo] *nm* (*líquido*) drink; (*bocado*)
 gulp; (*fam: de bebida*) swig; (*desgracia*) blow;
 **echar un ~** to have a drink
**traición** [trai'θjon] *nf* treachery; (*Jur*)
 treason; (*una traición*) act of treachery;
 **traicionar** *vt* to betray
**traidor, a** [trai'ðor, a] *adj* treacherous
 ▷ *nm/f* traitor
**traigo** *etc vb* V **traer**
**traje** ['traxe] *vb* V **traer** ▷ *nm* (*de hombre*)
 suit; (*de mujer*) dress; (*vestido típico*) costume;
 **traje de baño/chaqueta** swimsuit/suit;
 **traje de etiqueta** dress suit; **traje de luces**
 bullfighter's costume
**trajera** *etc vb* V **traer**
**trajín** [tra'xin] *nm* (*fam: movimiento*) bustle;
 **trajinar** *vi* (*moverse*) to bustle about
**trama** ['trama] *nf* (*intriga*) plot; (*de tejido*)
 weft (*BRIT*), woof (*US*); **tramar** *vt* to plot;
 (*Tec*) to weave
**tramitar** [trami'tar] *vt* (*asunto*) to
 transact; (*negociar*) to negotiate
**trámite** ['tramite] *nm* (*paso*) step; (*Jur*)
 transaction; **trámites** *nmpl* (*burocracia*)
 procedure *sg*; (*Jur*) proceedings
**tramo** ['tramo] *nm* (*de tierra*) plot; (*de
 escalera*) flight; (*de vía*) section
**trampa** ['trampa] *nf* trap; (*en el suelo*)
 trapdoor; (*truco*) trick; (*engaño*) fiddle;
 **trampear** *vt, vi* to cheat
**trampolín** [trampo'lin] *nm* (*de piscina etc*)
 diving board
**tramposo, -a** [tram'poso, a] *adj* crooked,
 cheating ▷ *nm/f* crook, cheat
**tranca** ['tranka] *nf* (*palo*) stick; (*de puerta,
 ventana*) bar; **trancar** *vt* to bar

**trance** ['tranθe] *nm* (*momento difícil*)
 difficult moment o juncture; (*estado
 hipnotizado*) trance
**tranquilidad** [trankili'ðað] *nf* (*calma*)
 calmness, stillness; (*paz*) peacefulness
**tranquilizar** [trankili'θar] *vt* (*calmar*)
 to calm (down); (*asegurar*) to reassure;
 **tranquilizarse** *vr* to calm down;
 **tranquilo, -a** *adj* (*calmado*) calm; (*apacible*)
 peaceful; (*mar*) calm; (*mente*) untroubled
**transacción** [transak'θjon] *nf*
 transaction
**transbordador** [transβorða'ðor] *nm*
 ferry
**transbordo** [trans'βorðo] *nm* transfer;
 **hacer ~** to change (*trains etc*)
**transcurrir** [transku'rrir] *vi* (*tiempo*) to
 pass; (*hecho*) to take place
**transcurso** [trans'kurso] *nm*: ~ **del
 tiempo** lapse (of time)
**transeúnte** [transe'unte] *nmf* passer-by
**transferencia** [transfe'renθja] *nf*
 transference; (*Com*) transfer
**transferir** [transfe'rir] *vt* to transfer
**transformador** [transforma'ðor] *nm*
 (*Elec*) transformer
**transformar** [transfor'mar] *vt* to
 transform; (*convertir*) to convert
**transfusión** [transfu'sjon] *nf* transfusion
**transgénico, -a** [trans'xeniko, a] *adj*
 genetically modified, GM
**transición** [transi'θjon] *nf* transition
**transigir** [transi'xir] *vi* to compromise,
 make concessions
**transitar** [transi'tar] *vi* to go (from place
 to place); **tránsito** *nm* transit; (*Auto*)
 traffic; **transitorio, -a** *adj* transitory
**transmisión** [transmi'sjon] *nf* (*Tec*)
 transmission; (*transferencia*) transfer;
 **transmisión exterior/en directo** outside/
 live broadcast
**transmitir** [transmi'tir] *vt* to transmit;
 (*Radio, TV*) to broadcast
**transparencia** [transpa'renθja] *nf*
 transparency; (*claridad*) clearness, clarity;
 (*foto*) slide
**transparentar** [transparen'tar] *vt* to
 reveal ▷ *vi* to be transparent; **transparente**
 *adj* transparent; (*claro*) clear
**transpirar** [transpi'rar] *vi* to perspire
**transportar** [transpor'tar] *vt* to
 transport; (*llevar*) to carry; **transporte** *nm*
 transport; (*Com*) haulage
**transversal** [transβer'sal] *adj* transverse,
 cross
**tranvía** [tram'bia] *nm* tram
**trapeador** [trapea'ðor] (*LAM*) *nm* mop;
 **trapear** (*LAM*) *vt* to mop

**trapecio** [tra'peθjo] nm trapeze;
 **trapecista** nmf trapeze artist
**trapero, -a** [tra'pero, a] nm/f ragman
**trapicheo** [trapi'tʃeo] (fam) nm scheme,
 fiddle
**trapo** ['trapo] nm (tela) rag; (de cocina) cloth
**tráquea** ['trakea] nf windpipe
**traqueteo** [trake'teo] nm rattling
**tras** [tras] prep (detrás) behind; (después)
 after
**trasatlántico** [trasat'lantiko] nm (barco)
 (cabin) cruiser
**trascendencia** [trasθen'denθja] nf
 (importancia) importance; (Filosofía)
 transcendence
**trascendental** [trasθenden'tal] adj
 important; (Filosofía) transcendental
**trasero, -a** [tra'sero, a] adj back, rear
 ▷ nm (Anat) bottom
**trasfondo** [tras'fondo] nm background
**trasgredir** [trasxre'ðir] vt to contravene
**trashumante** [trasu'mante] adj
 (animales) migrating
**trasladar** [trasla'ðar] vt to move;
 (persona) to transfer; (postergar) to postpone;
 (copiar) to copy; **trasladarse** vr (mudarse) to
 move; **traslado** nm move; (mudanza) move,
 removal
**traslucir** [traslu'θir] vt to show
**trasluz** [tras'luθ] nm reflected light; **al ~**
 against o up to the light
**trasnochador, a** [trasnotʃa'ðor, a] nm/f
 night owl
**trasnochar** [trasno'tʃar] vi (acostarse
 tarde) to stay up late
**traspapelar** [traspape'lar] vt (documento,
 carta) to mislay, misplace
**traspasar** [traspa'sar] vt (suj: bala etc)
 to pierce, go through; (propiedad) to sell,
 transfer; (calle) to cross over; (límites) to go
 beyond; (ley) to break; **traspaso** nm (venta)
 transfer, sale
**traspatio** [tras'patjo] (LAM) nm backyard
**traspié** [tras'pje] nm (tropezón) trip; (error)
 blunder
**trasplantar** [trasplan'tar] vt to
 transplant
**traste** ['traste] nm (Mús) fret; **dar al ~ con
 algo** to ruin sth
**trastero** [tras'tero] nm storage room
**trastienda** [tras'tjenda] nf back of shop
**trasto** ['trasto] (pey) nm (cosa) piece of
 junk; (persona) dead loss
**trastornado, -a** [trastor'naðo, a] adj
 (loco) mad, crazy
**trastornar** [trastor'nar] vt (fig: planes) to
 disrupt; (: nervios) to shatter; (: persona) to
 drive crazy; **trastornarse** vr (volverse loco)

to go mad o crazy; **trastorno** nm (acto)
 overturning; (confusión) confusion
**tratable** [tra'taβle] adj friendly
**tratado** [tra'taðo] nm (Pol) treaty; (Com)
 agreement
**tratamiento** [trata'mjento] nm
 treatment; **tratamiento de textos** (Inform)
 word processing cpd
**tratar** [tra'tar] vt (ocuparse de) to treat;
 (manejar, Tec) to handle; (Med) to treat;
 (dirigirse a: persona) to address ▷ vi: **~
 de** (hablar sobre) to deal with, be about;
 (intentar) to try to; **tratarse** vr to treat each
 other; **~ con** (Com) to trade in; (negociar) to
 negotiate with; (tener contactos) to have
 dealings with; **¿de qué se trata?** what's it
 about?; **trato** nm dealings pl; (relaciónes)
 relationship; (comportamiento) manner;
 (Com) agreement
**trauma** ['trauma] nm trauma
**través** [tra'βes] nm (fig) reverse; **al ~**
 across, crossways; **a ~ de** across; (sobre)
 over; (por) through
**travesaño** [traβe'saɲo] nm (Arq)
 crossbeam; (Deporte) crossbar
**travesía** [traβe'sia] nf (calle) cross-street;
 (Náut) crossing
**travesura** [traβe'sura] nf (broma) prank;
 (ingenio) wit
**travieso, -a** [tra'βjeso, a] adj (niño)
 naughty
**trayecto** [tra'jekto] nm (ruta) road, way;
 (viaje) journey; (tramo) stretch; **trayectoria**
 nf trajectory; (fig) path
**traza** ['traθa] nf (aspecto) looks pl; (señal)
 sign; **trazado, -a** adj: **bien trazado** shapely,
 well-formed ▷ nm (Arq) plan, design; (fig)
 outline
**trazar** [tra'θar] vt (Arq) to plan; (Arte) to
 sketch; (fig) to trace; (plan) to draw up; **trazo**
 nm (línea) line; (bosquejo) sketch
**trébol** ['treβol] nm (Bot) clover
**trece** ['treθe] num thirteen
**trecho** ['tretʃo] nm (distancia) distance;
 (tiempo) while
**tregua** ['trexwa] nf (Mil) truce; (fig) respite
**treinta** ['treinta] num thirty
**tremendo, -a** [tre'mendo, a] adj (terrible)
 terrible; (imponente: cosa) imposing;
 (fam: fabuloso) tremendous
**tren** [tren] nm train; **tren de aterrizaje**
 undercarriage; **tren de cercanías** suburban
 train
**trenca** ['trenka] nf duffel coat
**trenza** ['trenθa] nf (de pelo) plait (BRIT),
 braid (US)
**trepadora** [trepa'ðora] nf (Bot) climber
**trepar** [tre'par] vt, vi to climb

**tres** [tres] *num* three

**tresillo** [tre'siʎo] *nm* three-piece suite; (*Mús*) triplet

**treta** ['treta] *nf* trick

**triángulo** ['trjangulo] *nm* triangle

**tribu** ['triβu] *nf* tribe

**tribuna** [tri'βuna] *nf* (*plataforma*) platform; (*Deporte*) (grand)stand

**tribunal** [triβu'nal] *nm* (*Jur*) court; (*comisión, fig*) tribunal; ~ **popular** jury

**tributo** [tri'βuto] *nm* (*Com*) tax

**trigal** [tri'ɣal] *nm* wheat field

**trigo** ['triɣo] *nm* wheat

**trigueño, -a** [tri'ɣeɲo, a] *adj* (*pelo*) corn-coloured

**trillar** [tri'ʎar] *vt* (*Agr*) to thresh

**trimestral** [trimes'tral] *adj* quarterly; (*Escol*) termly

**trimestre** [tri'mestre] *nm* (*Escol*) term

**trinar** [tri'nar] *vi* (*pájaros*) to sing; (*rabiar*) to fume, be angry

**trinchar** [trin'tʃar] *vt* to carve

**trinchera** [trin'tʃera] *nf* (*fosa*) trench

**trineo** [tri'neo] *nm* sledge

**trinidad** [trini'ðað] *nf* trio; (*Rel*): **la T~** the Trinity

**tripa** ['tripa] *nf* (*Anat*) intestine; (*fam: tb:* ~**s**) insides *pl*

**triple** ['triple] *adj* triple

**triplicado, -a** [tripli'kaðo, a] *adj*: **por ~** in triplicate

**tripulación** [tripula'θjon] *nf* crew

**tripulante** [tripu'lante] *nmf* crewman/woman

**tripular** [tripu'lar] *vt* (*barco*) to man; (*Auto*) to drive

**triquiñuela** [triki'nwela] *nf* trick

**tris** [tris] *nm inv* crack

**triste** ['triste] *adj* sad; (*lamentable*) sorry, miserable; **tristeza** *nf* (*aflicción*) sadness; (*melancolía*) melancholy

**triturar** [tritu'rar] *vt* (*moler*) to grind; (*mascar*) to chew

**triunfar** [trjun'far] *vi* (*tener éxito*) to triumph; (*ganar*) to win; **triunfo** *nm* triumph

**trivial** [tri'βjal] *adj* trivial

**triza** ['triθa] *nf*: **hacer ~s** to smash to bits; (*papel*) to tear to shreds

**trocear** [troθe'ar] *vt* (*carne, manzana*) to cut up, cut into pieces

**trocha** ['trotʃa] *nf* short cut

**trofeo** [tro'feo] *nm* (*premio*) trophy; (*éxito*) success

**tromba** ['tromba] *nf* downpour

**trombón** [trom'bon] *nm* trombone

**trombosis** [trom'bosis] *nf inv* thrombosis

**trompa** ['trompa] *nf* horn; (*trompo*)

humming top; (*hocico*) snout; (*fam*): **cogerse una ~** to get tight

**trompazo** [trom'paθo] *nm* bump, bang

**trompeta** [trom'peta] *nf* trumpet; (*clarín*) bugle

**trompicón** [trompi'kon]: **a trompicones** *adv* in fits and starts

**trompo** ['trompo] *nm* spinning top

**trompón** [trom'pon] *nm* bump

**tronar** [tro'nar] *vt* (*MÉX, CAM: fusilar*) to shoot; (*MÉX: examen*) to flunk ▷ *vi* to thunder; (*fig*) to rage

**tronchar** [tron'tʃar] *vt* (*árbol*) to chop down; (*fig: vida*) to cut short; (*: esperanza*) to shatter; (*persona*) to tire out; **troncharse** *vr* to fall down

**tronco** ['tronko] *nm* (*de árbol, Anat*) trunk

**trono** ['trono] *nm* throne

**tropa** ['tropa] *nf* (*Mil*) troop; (*soldados*) soldiers *pl*

**tropezar** [trope'θar] *vi* to trip, stumble; (*errar*) to slip up; ~ **con** to run into; (*topar con*) to bump into; **tropezón** *nm* trip; (*fig*) blunder

**tropical** [tropi'kal] *adj* tropical

**trópico** ['tropiko] *nm* tropic

**tropiezo** [tro'pjeθo] *vb* V **tropezar** ▷ *nm* (*error*) slip, blunder; (*desgracia*) misfortune; (*obstáculo*) snag

**trotamundos** [trota'mundos] *nm inv* globetrotter

**trotar** [tro'tar] *vi* to trot; **trote** *nm* trot; (*fam*) travelling; **de mucho trote** hard-wearing

**trozar** [tro'θar] (*LAM*) *vt* to cut up, cut into pieces

**trozo** ['troθo] *nm* bit, piece

**trucha** ['trutʃa] *nf* trout

**truco** ['truko] *nm* (*habilidad*) knack; (*engaño*) trick

**trueno** ['trweno] *nm* thunder; (*estampido*) bang

**trueque** *etc* ['trweke] *vb* V **trocar** ▷ *nm* exchange; (*Com*) barter

**trufa** ['trufa] *nf* (*Bot*) truffle

**truhán, -ana** [tru'an, ana] *nm/f* rogue

**truncar** [trun'kar] *vt* (*cortar*) to truncate; (*fig: la vida etc*) to cut short; (*: el desarrollo*) to stunt

**tu** [tu] *adj* your

**tú** [tu] *pron* you

**tubérculo** [tu'βerkulo] *nm* (*Bot*) tuber

**tuberculosis** [tuβerku'losis] *nf inv* tuberculosis

**tubería** [tuβe'ria] *nf* pipes *pl*; (*conducto*) pipeline

**tubo** ['tuβo] *nm* tube, pipe; **tubo de ensayo** test tube; **tubo de escape** exhaust

(pipe)

**tuerca** ['twerka] *nf* nut

**tuerto, -a** ['twerto, a] *adj* blind in one eye
▷ *nm/f* one-eyed person

**tuerza** *etc vb* V **torcer**

**tuétano** ['twetano] *nm* marrow; (*Bot*) pith

**tufo** ['tufo] *nm* (*hedor*) stench

**tul** [tul] *nm* tulle

**tulipán** [tuli'pan] *nm* tulip

**tullido, -a** [tu'ʎiðo, a] *adj* crippled

**tumba** ['tumba] *nf* (*sepultura*) tomb

**tumbar** [tum'bar] *vt* to knock down;
**tumbarse** *vr* (*echarse*) to lie down;
(*extenderse*) to stretch out

**tumbo** ['tumbo] *nm*: **dar ~s** to stagger

**tumbona** [tum'bona] *nf* (*butaca*) easy
chair; (*de playa*) deckchair (BRIT), beach
chair (US)

**tumor** [tu'mor] *nm* tumour

**tumulto** [tu'multo] *nm* turmoil

**tuna** ['tuna] *nf* (*Mús*) student music group;
V *tb* **tuno**

---

● **TUNA**
●
● A **tuna** is a musical group made up of
● university students or former students
● who dress up in costumes from the
● "Edad de Oro", the Spanish Golden
● Age. These groups go through the
● town playing their guitars, lutes and
● tambourines and serenade the young
● ladies in the halls of residence or make
● impromptu appearances at weddings
● or parties singing traditional Spanish
● songs for a few coins.

---

**tunante** [tu'nante] *nmf* rascal

**tunear** [tune'ar] *vt* (*Auto*) to style, mod
(*inf*)

**túnel** ['tunel] *nm* tunnel

**tuning** ['tunin] *nm* (*Auto*) car styling,
modding (*inf*)

**tuno, -a** ['tuno, a] *nm/f* (*fam*) rogue ▷ *nm*
member of student music group

**tupido, -a** [tu'piðo, a] *adj* (*denso*) dense;
(*tela*) close-woven

**turbante** [tur'ßante] *nm* turban

**turbar** [tur'ßar] *vt* (*molestar*) to disturb;
(*incomodar*) to upset

**turbina** [tur'ßina] *nf* turbine

**turbio, -a** ['turßjo, a] *adj* cloudy; (*tema
etc*) confused

**turbulencia** [turßu'lenθja] *nf*
turbulence; (*fig*) restlessness; **turbulento,
-a** *adj* turbulent; (*fig*: *intranquilo*) restless;
(: *ruidoso*) noisy

**turco, -a** ['turko, a] *adj* Turkish ▷ *nm/f*
Turk

**turismo** [tu'rismo] *nm* tourism; (*coche*)
car; **turista** *nmf* tourist; **turístico, -a** *adj*
tourist *cpd*

**turnar** [tur'nar] *vi* to take (it in) turns;
**turnarse** *vr* to take (it in) turns; **turno** *nm*
(*de trabajo*) shift; (*en juegos etc*) turn

**turquesa** [tur'kesa] *nf* turquoise

**Turquía** [tur'kia] *nf* Turkey

**turrón** [tu'rron] *nm* (*dulce*) nougat

**tutear** [tute'ar] *vt* to address as familiar
"tú"; **tutearse** *vr* to be on familiar terms

**tutela** [tu'tela] *nf* (*legal*) guardianship;
**tutelar** *adj* tutelary ▷ *vt* to protect

**tutor, a** [tu'tor, a] *nm/f* (*legal*) guardian;
(*Escol*) tutor

**tuve** *etc vb* V **tener**

**tuviera** *etc vb* V **tener**

**tuyo, -a** ['tujo, a] *adj* yours, of yours
▷ *pron* yours; **un amigo ~** a friend of yours;
**los ~s** (*fam*) your relations o family

**TV** *nf abr* (= *televisión*) TV

**TVE** *nf abr* = **Televisión Española**

# u

**u** [u] *conj* or
**ubicar** [uβi'kar] *vt* to place, situate; (LAM: *encontrar*) to find; **ubicarse** *vr* (LAM: *encontrarse*) to lie, be located
**ubre** ['uβre] *nf* udder
**UCI** *nf abr* (= Unidad de Cuidados Intensivos) ICU
**Ud(s)** *abr* = **usted(es)**
**UE** *nf abr* (= Unión Europea) EU
**ufanarse** [ufa'narse] *vr* to boast; **ufano, -a** *adj* (*arrogante*) arrogant; (*presumido*) conceited
**UGT** (ESP) *nf abr* = **Unión General de Trabajadores**
**úlcera** ['ulθera] *nf* ulcer
**ulterior** [ulte'rjor] *adj* (*más allá*) farther, further; (*subsecuente, siguiente*) subsequent
**últimamente** ['ultimamente] *adv* (*recientemente*) lately, recently
**ultimar** [ulti'mar] *vt* to finish; (*finalizar*) to finalize; (LAM: *matar*) to kill
**ultimátum** [ulti'matum] (*pl* ~**s**) *nm* ultimatum
**último, -a** ['ultimo, a] *adj* last; (*más reciente*) latest, most recent; (*más bajo*) bottom; (*más alto*) top; **en las últimas** on one's last legs; **por ~** finally
**ultra** ['ultra] *adj* ultra ▷ *nmf* extreme right-winger
**ultraje** [ul'traxe] *nm* outrage; insult
**ultramar** [ultra'mar] *nm*: **de** *o* **en ~** abroad, overseas
**ultramarinos** [ultrama'rinos] *nmpl* groceries; **tienda de ~** grocer's (shop)
**ultranza** [ul'tranθa]: **a ~** *adv* (*a todo trance*) at all costs; (*completo*) outright
**umbral** [um'bral] *nm* (*gen*) threshold

**un, una** [un, 'una] *art indef* a; (*antes de vocal*) an; **una mujer/naranja** a woman/an orange
▷ *adj*: **unos** (*o* **unas**): **hay unos regalos para ti** there are some presents for you; **hay unas cervezas en la nevera** there are some beers in the fridge

**unánime** [u'nanime] *adj* unanimous; **unanimidad** *nf* unanimity
**undécimo, -a** [un'deθimo, a] *adj* eleventh
**ungir** [un'xir] *vt* to anoint
**ungüento** [un'gwento] *nm* ointment
**único, -a** ['uniko, a] *adj* only, sole; (*sin par*) unique
**unidad** [uni'ðað] *nf* unity; (Com, Tec *etc*) unit
**unido, -a** [u'niðo, a] *adj* joined, linked; (*fig*) united
**unificar** [unifi'kar] *vt* to unite, unify
**uniformar** [unifor'mar] *vt* to make uniform, level up; (*persona*) to put into uniform
**uniforme** [uni'forme] *adj* uniform, equal; (*superficie*) even ▷ *nm* uniform
**unilateral** [unilate'ral] *adj* unilateral
**unión** [u'njon] *nf* union; (*acto*) uniting, joining; (*unidad*) unity; (Tec) joint; **Unión Europea** European Union
**unir** [u'nir] *vt* (*juntar*) to join, unite; (*atar*) to tie, fasten; (*combinar*) to combine; **unirse** *vr* to join together, unite; (*empresas*) to merge
**unísono** [u'nisono] *nm*: **al ~** in unison
**universal** [uniβer'sal] *adj* universal; (*mundial*) world *cpd*
**universidad** [uniβersi'ðað] *nf* university
**universitario, -a** [uniβersi'tarjo, a] *adj* university *cpd* ▷ *nm/f* (*profesor*) lecturer; (*estudiante*) (university) student; (*graduado*) graduate
**universo** [uni'βerso] *nm* universe

**uno, -a** ['uno, a] *adj* one; **unos pocos** a few; **unos cien** about a hundred ▷ *pron*
**1** one; **quiero sólo uno** I only want one; **uno de ellos** one of them
**2** (*alguien*) somebody, someone; **conozco a uno que se te parece** I know somebody *o* someone who looks like you; **uno mismo** oneself; **unos querían quedarse** some (people) wanted to stay
**3** **(los) unos ... (los) otros ...** some ... others
▷ *nf* one; **es la una** it's one o'clock
▷ *nm* (*number*) one

**untar** [un'tar] vt (mantequilla) to spread; (engrasar) to grease, oil

**uña** ['uɲa] nf (Anat) nail; (garra) claw; (casco) hoof; (arrancaclavos) claw

**uranio** [u'ranjo] nm uranium

**urbanización** [urβaniθa'θjon] nf (barrio, colonia) housing estate

**urbanizar** [urβani'θar] vt (zona) to develop, urbanize

**urbano, -a** [ur'βano, a] adj (de ciudad) urban; (cortés) courteous, polite

**urbe** ['urβe] nf large city

**urdir** [ur'ðir] vt to warp; (complot) to plot, contrive

**urgencia** [ur'xenθja] nf urgency; (prisa) haste, rush; (emergencia) emergency; **servicios de ~** emergency services; **"U~s"** "Casualty"; **urgente** adj urgent

**urgir** [ur'xir] vi to be urgent; **me urge** I'm in a hurry for it

**urinario, -a** [uri'narjo, a] adj urinary ▷ nm urinal

**urna** ['urna] nf urn; (Pol) ballot box

**urraca** [u'rraka] nf magpie

**URSS** [urs] nf (Hist): **la URSS** the USSR

**Uruguay** [uru'ɣwai] nm (tb: **el ~**) Uruguay; **uruguayo, -a** adj, nm/f Uruguayan

**usado, -a** [u'saðo, a] adj used; (de segunda mano) secondhand

**usar** [u'sar] vt to use; (ropa) to wear; (tener costumbre) to be in the habit of; **usarse** vr to be used; **uso** nm use; wear; (costumbre) usage, custom; (moda) fashion; **al uso** in keeping with custom; **al uso de** in the style of; **de uso externo** (Med) for external use

**usted** [us'teð] pron (sg) you sg; (pl): **~es** you pl

**usual** [u'swal] adj usual

**usuario, -a** [usu'arjo, a] nm/f user

**usurpar** [usur'par] vt to usurp

**utensilio** [uten'siljo] nm tool; (Culin) utensil

**útero** ['utero] nm uterus, womb

**útil** ['util] adj useful ▷ nm tool; **utilidad** nf usefulness; (Com) profit; **utilizar** vt to use, utilize

**uva** ['uβa] nf grape

---

● **LAS UVAS**
●
● In Spain **Las uvas** play a big part on
● New Year's Eve (**Nochevieja**), when on
● the stroke of midnight people gather
● at home, in restaurants or in the **plaza**
● **mayor** and eat a grape for each stroke
● of the clock of the **Puerta del Sol** in
● Madrid. It is said to bring luck for the
● following year.

---

**v** abr (= voltio) v

**va** vb V **ir**

**vaca** ['baka] nf (animal) cow; **carne de ~** beef

**vacaciones** [baka'θjones] nfpl holidays

**vacante** [ba'kante] adj vacant, empty ▷ nf vacancy

**vaciar** [ba'θjar] vt to empty out; (ahuecar) to hollow out; (moldear) to cast; **vaciarse** vr to empty

**vacilar** [baθi'lar] vi to be unsteady; (al hablar) to falter; (dudar) to hesitate, waver; (memoria) to fail

**vacío, -a** [ba'θio, a] adj empty; (puesto) vacant; (desocupado) idle; (vano) vain ▷ nm emptiness; (Física) vacuum; (un vacío) (empty) space

**vacuna** [ba'kuna] nf vaccine; **vacunar** vt to vaccinate

**vacuno, -a** [ba'kuno, a] adj cow cpd; **ganado ~** cattle

**vadear** [baðe'ar] vt (río) to ford; **vado** nm ford

**vagabundo, -a** [baɣa'βundo, a] adj wandering ▷ nm tramp

**vagancia** [ba'ɣanθja] nf (pereza) idleness, laziness

**vagar** [ba'ɣar] vi to wander; (no hacer nada) to idle

**vagina** [ba'xina] nf vagina

**vago, -a** ['baɣo, a] adj vague; (perezoso) lazy ▷ nm/f (vagabundo) tramp; (flojo) lazybones sg, idler

**vagón** [ba'ɣon] nm (Ferro: de pasajeros) carriage; (: de mercancías) wagon

**vaho** ['bao] nm (vapor) vapour, steam; (respiración) breath

**vaina** ['baina] nf sheath

**vainilla** [bai'niʎa] nf vanilla

**vais** vb V **ir**

**vaivén** [bai'βen] nm to-and-fro

movement; (*de tránsito*) coming and going; **vaivenes** *nmpl* (*fig*) ups and downs

**vajilla** [ba'xiʎa] *nf* crockery, dishes *pl*; (*juego*) service, set

**valdré** *etc vb* V **valer**

**vale** ['bale] *nm* voucher; (*recibo*) receipt; (*pagaré*) IOU

**valedero, -a** [bale'ðero, a] *adj* valid

**valenciano, -a** [balen'θjano, a] *adj* Valencian

**valentía** [balen'tia] *nf* courage, bravery

**valer** [ba'ler] *vt* to be worth; (*Mat*) to equal; (*costar*) to cost ▷ *vi* (*ser útil*) to be useful; (*ser válido*) to be valid; **valerse** *vr* to take care of oneself; **~se de** to make use of, take advantage of; **~ la pena** to be worthwhile; **¿vale?** (*ESP*) OK?; **más vale que nos vayamos** we'd better go; **¡eso a mí no me vale!** (*MÉX: fam: no importar*) I couldn't care less about that

**valeroso, -a** [bale'roso, a] *adj* brave, valiant

**valgo** *etc vb* V **valer**

**valía** [ba'lia] *nf* worth, value

**validar** [bali'ðar] *vt* to validate; **validez** *nf* validity; **válido, -a** *adj* valid

**valiente** [ba'ljente] *adj* brave, valiant ▷ *nm* hero

**valija** [ba'lixa] (*cs*) *nf* (suit)case

**valioso, -a** [ba'ljoso, a] *adj* valuable

**valla** ['baʎa] *nf* fence; (*Deporte*) hurdle; **valla publicitaria** hoarding; **vallar** *vt* to fence in

**valle** ['baʎe] *nm* valley

**valor** [ba'lor] *nm* value, worth; (*precio*) price; (*valentía*) valour, courage; (*importancia*) importance; **valores** *nmpl* (*Com*) securities; **valorar** *vt* to value

**vals** [bals] *nm inv* waltz

**válvula** ['balβula] *nf* valve

**vamos** *vb* V **ir**

**vampiro, -resa** [bam'piro, 'resa] *nm/f* vampire

**van** *vb* V **ir**

**vanguardia** [ban'gwardja] *nf* vanguard; (*Arte etc*) avant-garde

**vanidad** [bani'ðað] *nf* vanity; **vanidoso, -a** *adj* vain, conceited

**vano, -a** ['bano, a] *adj* vain

**vapor** [ba'por] *nm* vapour; (*vaho*) steam; **al ~** (*Culin*) steamed; **vapor de agua** water vapour; **vaporizador** *nm* atomizer; **vaporizar** *vt* to vaporize; **vaporoso, -a** *adj* vaporous

**vaquero, -a** [ba'kero, a] *adj* cattle *cpd* ▷ *nm* cowboy; **vaqueros** *nmpl* (*pantalones*) jeans

**vaquilla** [ba'kiʎa] *nf* (*Zool*) heifer

**vara** ['bara] *nf* stick; (*Tec*) rod

**variable** [ba'rjaβle] *adj, nf* variable

**variación** [barja'θjon] *nf* variation

**variar** [bar'jar] *vt* to vary; (*modificar*) to modify; (*cambiar de posición*) to switch around ▷ *vi* to vary

**varicela** [bari'θela] *nf* chickenpox

**varices** [ba'riθes] *nfpl* varicose veins

**variedad** [barje'ðað] *nf* variety

**varilla** [ba'riʎa] *nf* stick; (*Bot*) twig; (*Tec*) rod; (*de rueda*) spoke

**vario, -a** ['barjo, a] *adj* varied; **~s** various, several

**varita** [ba'rita] *nf* (*tb: ~ mágica*) magic wand

**varón** [ba'ron] *nm* male, man; **varonil** *adj* manly, virile

**Varsovia** [bar'soβja] *n* Warsaw

**vas** *vb* V **ir**

**vasco, -a** ['basko, a] *adj, nm/f* Basque; **vascongado, -a** [baskon'gaðo, a] *adj* Basque; **las Vascongadas** the Basque Country

**vaselina** [base'lina] *nf* Vaseline®

**vasija** [ba'sixa] *nf* container, vessel

**vaso** ['baso] *nm* glass, tumbler; (*Anat*) vessel

> No confundir **vaso** con la palabra inglesa *vase*.

**vástago** ['bastaɣo] *nm* (*Bot*) shoot; (*Tec*) rod; (*fig*) offspring

**vasto, -a** ['basto, a] *adj* vast, huge

**Vaticano** [bati'kano] *nm*: **el ~** the Vatican

**vatio** ['batjo] *nm* (*Elec*) watt

**vaya** *etc vb* V **ir**

**Vd(s)** *abr* = **usted(es)**

**ve** [be] *vb* V **ir**; **ver**

**vecindad** [beθin'dað] *nf* neighbourhood; (*habitantes*) residents *pl*

**vecindario** [beθin'darjo] *nm* neighbourhood; residents *pl*

**vecino, -a** [be'θino, a] *adj* neighbouring ▷ *nm/f* neighbour; (*residente*) resident

**veda** ['beða] *nf* prohibition; **vedar** [be'ðar] *vt* (*prohibir*) to ban, prohibit; (*impedir*) to stop, prevent

**vegetación** [bexeta'θjon] *nf* vegetation

**vegetal** [bexe'tal] *adj, nm* vegetable

**vegetariano, -a** [bexeta'rjano, a] *adj, nm/f* vegetarian

**vehículo** [be'ikulo] *nm* vehicle; (*Med*) carrier

**veía** *etc vb* V **ver**

**veinte** ['beinte] *num* twenty

**vejar** [be'xar] *vt* (*irritar*) to annoy, vex; (*humillar*) to humiliate

**vejez** [be'xeθ] *nf* old age

**vejiga** [be'xiɣa] *nf* (*Anat*) bladder

**vela** ['bela] nf (de cera) candle; (Náut) sail; (insomnio) sleeplessness; (vigilia) vigil; (Mil) sentry duty; **estar a dos ~s** (fam: sin dinero) to be skint

**velado, -a** [be'laðo, a] adj veiled; (sonido) muffled; (Foto) blurred ▷ nf soirée

**velar** [be'lar] vt (vigilar) to keep watch over ▷ vi to stay awake; **~ por** to watch over, look after

**velatorio** [bela'torjo] nm (funeral) wake

**velero** [be'lero] nm (Náut) sailing ship; (Aviac) glider

**veleta** [be'leta] nf weather vane

**veliz** [be'lis] (MÉX) nm (suit)case

**vello** ['beʎo] nm down, fuzz

**velo** ['belo] nm veil

**velocidad** [beloθi'ðað] nf speed; (Tec, Auto) gear

**velocímetro** [belo'θimetro] nm speedometer

**velorio** [be'lorjo] (LAM) nm (funeral) wake

**veloz** [be'loθ] adj fast

**ven** vb V **venir**

**vena** ['bena] nf vein

**venado** [be'naðo] nm deer

**vencedor, a** [benθe'ðor, a] adj victorious ▷ nm/f victor, winner

**vencer** [ben'θer] vt (dominar) to defeat, beat; (derrotar) to vanquish; (superar, controlar) to overcome, master ▷ vi (triunfar) to win (through), triumph; (plazo) to expire; **vencido, -a** adj (derrotado) defeated, beaten; (Com) due ▷ adv: **pagar vencido** to pay in arrears

**venda** ['benda] nf bandage; **vendaje** nm bandage, dressing; **vendar** vt to bandage; **vendar los ojos** to blindfold

**vendaval** [benda'βal] nm (viento) gale

**vendedor, a** [bende'ðor, a] nm/f seller

**vender** [ben'der] vt to sell; **venderse** vr (estar a la venta) to be on sale; **~ al contado/al por mayor/al por menor** to sell for cash/wholesale/retail; **"se vende"** "for sale"

**vendimia** [ben'dimja] nf grape harvest

**vendré** etc vb V **venir**

**veneno** [be'neno] nm poison; (de serpiente) venom; **venenoso, -a** adj poisonous; venomous

**venerable** [bene'raβle] adj venerable; **venerar** vt (respetar) to revere; (adorar) to worship

**venéreo, -a** [be'nereo, a] adj: **enfermedad venérea** venereal disease

**venezolano, -a** [beneθo'lano, a] adj Venezuelan

**Venezuela** [bene'θwela] nf Venezuela

**venganza** [ben'ganθa] nf vengeance, revenge; **vengar** vt to avenge; **vengarse** vr to take revenge; **vengativo, -a** adj (persona) vindictive

**vengo** etc vb V **venir**

**venia** ['benja] nf (perdón) pardon; (permiso) consent

**venial** [be'njal] adj venial

**venida** [be'niða] nf (llegada) arrival; (regreso) return

**venidero, -a** [beni'ðero, a] adj coming, future

**venir** [be'nir] vi to come; (llegar) to arrive; (ocurrir) to happen; (fig): **~ de** to stem from; **~ bien/mal** to be suitable/unsuitable; **el año que viene** next year; **~se abajo** to collapse

**venta** ['benta] nf (Com) sale; **"en ~"** "for sale"; **estar a la** o **en ~** to be (up) for sale o on the market; **venta a domicilio** door-to-door selling; **venta a plazos** hire purchase; **venta al contado/al por mayor/al por menor** cash sale/wholesale/retail

**ventaja** [ben'taxa] nf advantage; **ventajoso, -a** adj advantageous

**ventana** [ben'tana] nf window; **ventanilla** nf (de taquilla) window (of booking office etc)

**ventilación** [bentila'θjon] nf ventilation; (corriente) draught

**ventilador** [bentila'ðor] nm fan

**ventilar** [benti'lar] vt to ventilate; (para secar) to put out to dry; (asunto) to air, discuss

**ventisca** [ben'tiska] nf blizzard

**ventrílocuo, -a** [ben'trilokwo, a] nm/f ventriloquist

**ventura** [ben'tura] nf (felicidad) happiness; (buena suerte) luck; (destino) fortune; **a la (buena)** ~ at random; **venturoso, -a** adj happy; (afortunado) lucky, fortunate

**veo** etc vb V **ver**

**ver** [ber] vt to see; (mirar) to look at, watch; (entender) to understand; (investigar) to look into ▷ vi to see; to understand; **verse** vr (encontrarse) to meet; (dejarse ver) to be seen; (hallarse: en un apuro) to find o.s., be; **(vamos) a ~** let's see; **no tener nada que ~ con** to have nothing to do with; **a mi modo de ~** as I see it; **ya ~emos** we'll see

**vera** ['bera] nf edge, verge; (de río) bank

**veranear** [berane'ar] vi to spend the summer; **veraneo** nm summer holiday; **veraniego, -a** adj summer cpd

**verano** [be'rano] nm summer

**veras** ['beras] nfpl truth sg; **de ~** really, truly

**verbal** [ber'βal] adj verbal

**verbena** [ber'βena] nf (baile) open-air dance

**verbo** ['berβo] nm verb

**verdad** [ber'ðað] nf truth; (fiabilidad) reliability; **de ~** real, proper; **a decir ~** to tell the truth; **verdadero, -a** adj (veraz) true, truthful; (fiable) reliable; (fig) real

**verde** ['berðe] adj green; (chiste) blue, dirty ▷ nm green; **viejo ~** dirty old man; **verdear** vi to turn green; **verdor** nm greenness

**verdugo** [ber'ðuxo] nm executioner

**verdulero, -a** [berðu'lero, a] nm/f greengrocer

**verduras** [ber'ðuras] nfpl (Culin) greens

**vereda** [be'reða] nf path; (cs: acera) pavement (BRIT), sidewalk (US)

**veredicto** [bere'ðikto] nm verdict

**vergonzoso, -a** [berxon'θoso, a] adj shameful; (tímido) timid, bashful

**vergüenza** [ber'xwenθa] nf shame, sense of shame; (timidez) bashfulness; (pudor) modesty; **me da ~** I'm ashamed

**verídico, -a** [be'riðiko, a] adj true, truthful

**verificar** [berifi'kar] vt to check; (corroborar) to verify; (llevar a cabo) to carry out; **verificarse** vr (predicción) to prove to be true

**verja** ['berxa] nf (cancela) iron gate; (valla) iron railings pl; (de ventana) grille

**vermut** [ber'mut] (pl ~s) nm vermouth

**verosímil** [bero'simil] adj likely, probable; (relato) credible

**verruga** [be'rruxa] nf wart

**versátil** [ber'satil] adj versatile

**versión** [ber'sjon] nf version

**verso** ['berso] nm verse; **un ~** a line of poetry

**vértebra** ['berteβra] nf vertebra

**verter** [ber'ter] vt (líquido: adrede) to empty, pour (out); (: sin querer) to spill; (basura) to dump ▷ vi to flow

**vertical** [berti'kal] adj vertical

**vértice** ['bertiθe] nm vertex, apex

**vertidos** [ber'tiðos] nmpl waste sg

**vertiente** [ber'tjente] nf slope; (fig) aspect

**vértigo** ['bertixo] nm vertigo; (mareo) dizziness

**vesícula** [be'sikula] nf blister

**vespino®** [bes'pino] nm o nf moped

**vestíbulo** [bes'tiβulo] nm hall; (de teatro) foyer

**vestido** [bes'tiðo] nm (ropa) clothes pl, clothing; (de mujer) dress, frock ▷ pp de **vestir**; **~ de azul/marinero** dressed in blue/as a sailor

**vestidor** [besti'ðor] (MÉX) nm (Deporte) changing (BRIT) o locker (US) room

**vestimenta** [besti'menta] nf clothing

**vestir** [bes'tir] vt (poner: ropa) to put on; (llevar: ropa) to wear; (proveer de ropa a) to clothe; (sastre) to make clothes for ▷ vi to dress; (verse bien) to look good; **vestirse** vr to get dressed, dress o.s.

**vestuario** [bes'twarjo] nm clothes pl, wardrobe; (Teatro: cuarto) dressing room; (Deporte) changing (BRIT) o locker (US) room

**vetar** [be'tar] vt to veto

**veterano, -a** [bete'rano, a] adj, nm veteran

**veterinaria** [beteri'narja] nf veterinary science; V tb **veterinario**

**veterinario, -a** [beteri'narjo, a] nm/f vet(erinary surgeon)

**veto** ['beto] nm veto

**vez** [beθ] nf time; (turno) turn; **a la ~ que** at the same time as; **a su ~** in its turn; **otra ~** again; **una ~** once; **de una ~** in one go; **de una ~ para siempre** once and for all; **en ~ de** instead of; **a o algunas veces** sometimes; **una y otra ~** repeatedly; **de ~ en cuando** from time to time; **7 veces 9** 7 times 9; **hacer las veces de** to stand in for; **tal ~** perhaps

**vía** ['bia] nf track, route; (Ferro) line; (fig) way; (Anat) passage, tube ▷ prep via, by way of; **por ~ judicial** by legal means; **en ~s de** in the process of; **vía aérea** airway; **Vía Láctea** Milky Way; **vía pública** public road o thoroughfare

**viable** ['bjaβle] adj (solución, plan, alternativa) feasible

**viaducto** [bja'ðukto] nm viaduct

**viajante** [bja'xante] nm commercial traveller

**viajar** [bja'xar] vi to travel; **viaje** nm journey; (gira) tour; (Náut) voyage; **estar de viaje** to be on a trip; **viaje de ida y vuelta** round trip; **viaje de novios** honeymoon; **viajero, -a** adj travelling; (Zool) migratory ▷ nm/f (quien viaja) traveller; (pasajero) passenger

**víbora** ['biβora] nf (Zool) viper; (: MÉX: venenoso) poisonous snake

**vibración** [biβra'θjon] nf vibration

**vibrar** [bi'βrar] vt, vi to vibrate

**vicepresidente** [biθepresi'ðente] nmf vice-president

**viceversa** [biθe'βersa] adv vice versa

**vicio** ['biθjo] nm vice; (mala costumbre) bad habit; **vicioso, -a** adj (muy malo) vicious; (corrompido) depraved ▷ nm/f depraved person

**víctima** ['biktima] nf victim

**victoria** [bik'torja] nf victory; **victorioso, -a** adj victorious

**vid** [bið] nf vine

**vida** ['biða] nf (gen) life; (duración) lifetime;

**de por ~** for life; **en la** *o* **mi ~** never; **estar con ~** to be still alive; **ganarse la ~** to earn one's living

**vídeo** ['biðeo] *nm* video ▷ *adj inv*: **película de ~** video film; **videocámara** *nf* camcorder; **videocasete** *nm* video cassette, videotape; **videoclub** *nm* video club; **videojuego** *nm* video game; **videollamada** *nf* video call; **videoteléfono** *nf* videophone

**vidrio** ['biðrjo] *nm* glass

**vieira** ['bjeira] *nf* scallop

**viejo, -a** ['bjexo, a] *adj* old ▷ *nm/f* old man/woman; **hacerse ~** to get old

**Viena** ['bjena] *n* Vienna

**vienes** *etc vb* V **venir**

**vienés, -esa** [bje'nes, esa] *adj* Viennese

**viento** ['bjento] *nm* wind; **hacer ~** to be windy

**vientre** ['bjentre] *nm* belly; *(matriz)* womb

**viernes** ['bjernes] *nm inv* Friday; **Viernes Santo** Good Friday

**Vietnam** [bjet'nam] *nm* Vietnam; **vietnamita** *adj* Vietnamese

**viga** ['bixa] *nf* beam, rafter; *(de metal)* girder

**vigencia** [bi'xenθja] *nf* validity; **estar en ~** to be in force; **vigente** *adj* valid, in force; *(imperante)* prevailing

**vigésimo, -a** [bi'xesimo, a] *adj* twentieth

**vigía** [bi'xia] *nm* look-out

**vigilancia** [bixi'lanθja] *nf*: **tener a algn bajo ~** to keep watch on sb

**vigilar** [bixi'lar] *vt* to watch over ▷ *vi* *(gen)* to be vigilant; *(hacer guardia)* to keep watch; **~ por** to take care of

**vigilia** [vi'xilja] *nf* wakefulness, being awake; *(Rel)* fast

**vigor** [bi'xor] *nm* vigour, vitality; **en ~** in force; **entrar/poner en ~** to come/put into effect; **vigoroso, -a** *adj* vigorous

**VIH** *nm abr* (= *virus de la inmunodeficiencia humana*) HIV; **VIH negativo/positivo** HIV-negative/-positive

**vil** [bil] *adj* vile, low

**villa** ['biʎa] *nf* (*casa*) villa; *(pueblo)* small town; *(municipalidad)* municipality

**villancico** [biʎan'θiko] *nm* (Christmas) carol

**vilo** ['bilo]: **en ~** *adv* in the air, suspended; *(fig)* on tenterhooks, in suspense

**vinagre** [bi'naxre] *nm* vinegar

**vinagreta** [bina'xreta] *nf* vinaigrette, French dressing

**vinculación** [binkula'θjon] *nf* (*lazo*) link, bond; *(acción)* linking

**vincular** [binku'lar] *vt* to link, bind;

**vínculo** *nm* link, bond

**vine** *etc vb* V **venir**

**vinicultura** [binikul'tura] *nf* wine growing

**viniera** *etc vb* V **venir**

**vino** ['bino] *vb* V **venir** ▷ *nm* wine; **vino blanco/tinto** white/red wine

**viña** ['bina] *nf* vineyard; **viñedo** *nm* vineyard

**viola** ['bjola] *nf* viola

**violación** [bjola'θjon] *nf* violation; *(sexual)* rape

**violar** [bjo'lar] *vt* to violate; *(sexualmente)* to rape

**violencia** [bjo'lenθja] *nf* violence, force; *(incomodidad)* embarrassment; *(acto injusto)* unjust act; **violentar** *vt* to force; *(casa)* to break into; *(agredir)* to assault; *(violar)* to violate; **violento, -a** *adj* violent; *(furioso)* furious; *(situación)* embarrassing; *(acto)* forced, unnatural

**violeta** [bjo'leta] *nf* violet

**violín** [bjo'lin] *nm* violin

**violón** [bjo'lon] *nm* double bass

**virar** [bi'rar] *vi* to change direction

**virgen** ['birxen] *adj, nf* virgin

**Virgo** ['birxo] *nm inv* Virgo

**viril** [bi'ril] *adj* virile; **virilidad** *nf* virility

**virtud** [bir'tuð] *nf* virtue; **en ~ de** by virtue of; **virtuoso, -a** *adj* virtuous ▷ *nm/f* virtuoso

**viruela** [bi'rwela] *nf* smallpox

**virulento, -a** [biru'lento, a] *adj* virulent

**virus** ['birus] *nm inv* virus

**visa** ['bisa] (*LAM*) *nf* = **visado**

**visado** [bi'saðo] (*ESP*) *nm* visa

**víscera** ['bisθera] *nf* (Anat, Zool) gut, bowel; **vísceras** *nfpl* entrails

**visceral** [bisθe'ral] *adj* (*odio*) intense; **reacción ~** gut reaction

**visera** [bi'sera] *nf* visor

**visibilidad** [bisiβili'ðað] *nf* visibility; **visible** *adj* visible; *(fig)* obvious

**visillos** [bi'siʎos] *nmpl* lace curtains

**visión** [bi'sjon] *nf* (Anat) vision, (eye)sight; *(fantasía)* vision, fantasy

**visita** [bi'sita] *nf* call, visit; *(persona)* visitor; **hacer una ~** to pay a visit; **visitar** [bisi'tar] *vt* to visit, call on

**visón** [bi'son] *nm* mink

**visor** [bi'sor] *nm* (Foto) viewfinder

**víspera** ['bispera] *nf*: **la ~ de ...** the day before ...

**vista** ['bista] *nf* sight, vision; *(capacidad de ver)* (eye)sight; *(mirada)* look(s) (*pl*); **a primera ~** at first glance; **hacer la ~ gorda** to turn a blind eye; **volver la ~** to look back; **está a la ~ que** it's obvious that; **en ~ de** in view of; **en ~ de que** in view of the fact that; **¡hasta la ~!** so long!, see you!; **con ~s a** with a view to; **vistazo** *nm* glance; **dar** *o* **echar un vistazo a** to glance at

**visto, -a** ['bisto, a] *pp de* **ver** ▷ *vb* ∨ *tb* **vestir** ▷ *adj* seen; (*considerado*) considered ▷ *nm:* **~ bueno** approval; **por lo ~** apparently; **está ~ que** it's clear that; **está bien/mal ~** it's acceptable/unacceptable; **~ que** since, considering that

**vistoso, -a** [bis'toso, a] *adj* colourful

**visual** [bi'swal] *adj* visual

**vital** [bi'tal] *adj* life *cpd*, living *cpd;* (*fig*) vital; (*persona*) lively, vivacious; **vitalicio, -a** *adj* for life; **vitalidad** *nf* (*de persona, negocio*) energy; (*de ciudad*) liveliness

**vitamina** [bita'mina] *nf* vitamin

**vitorear** [bitore'ar] *vt* to cheer, acclaim

**vitrina** [bi'trina] *nf* show case; (*LAM: escaparate*) shop window

**viudo, -a** ['bjuðo, a] *nm/f* widower/widow

**viva** ['biβa] *excl* hurrah!; **¡~ el rey!** long live the king!

**vivaracho, -a** [biβa'ratʃo, a] *adj* jaunty, lively; (*ojos*) bright, twinkling

**vivaz** [bi'βaθ] *adj* lively

**víveres** ['biβeres] *nmpl* provisions

**vivero** [bi'βero] *nm* (*para plantas*) nursery; (*para peces*) fish farm; (*fig*) hotbed

**viveza** [bi'βeθa] *nf* liveliness; (*agudeza: mental*) sharpness

**vivienda** [bi'βjenda] *nf* housing; (*una vivienda*) house; (*piso*) flat (*BRIT*), apartment (*US*)

**viviente** [bi'βjente] *adj* living

**vivir** [bi'βir] *vt, vi* to live ▷ *nm* life, living

**vivo, -a** ['biβo, a] *adj* living, alive; (*fig: descripción*) vivid; (*persona: astuto*) smart, clever; **en ~** (*transmisión etc*) live

**vocablo** [bo'kaβlo] *nm* (*palabra*) word; (*término*) term

**vocabulario** [bokaβu'larjo] *nm* vocabulary

**vocación** [boka'θjon] *nf* vocation; **vocacional** (*LAM*) *nf* ≈ technical college

**vocal** [bo'kal] *adj* vocal ▷ *nf* vowel; **vocalizar** *vt* to vocalize

**vocero** [bo'θero] (*LAM*) *nmf* spokesman/woman

**voces** ['boθes] *pl de* **voz**

**vodka** [boðka] *nm o f* vodka

**vol** *abr* = **volumen**

**volado** [bo'laðo] (*MÉX*) *adv* in a rush, hastily

**volador, a** [bola'ðor, a] *adj* flying

**volandas** [bo'landas]: **en ~** *adv* in the air

**volante** [bo'lante] *adj* flying ▷ *nm* (*de coche*) steering wheel; (*de reloj*) balance

**volar** [bo'lar] *vt* (*edificio*) to blow up ▷ *vi* to fly

**volátil** [bo'latil] *adj* volatile

**volcán** [bol'kan] *nm* volcano; **volcánico, -a** *adj* volcanic

**volcar** [bol'kar] *vt* to upset, overturn; (*tumbar, derribar*) to knock over; (*vaciar*) to empty out ▷ *vi* to overturn; **volcarse** *vr* to tip over

**voleibol** [bolei'βol] *nm* volleyball

**volqué** *etc vb* ∨ **volcar**

**voltaje** [bol'taxe] *nm* voltage

**voltear** [bolte'ar] *vt* to turn over; (*volcar*) to turn upside down

**voltereta** [bolte'reta] *nf* somersault

**voltio** ['boltjo] *nm* volt

**voluble** [bo'luβle] *adj* fickle

**volumen** [bo'lumen] (*pl* **volúmenes**) *nm* volume; **voluminoso, -a** *adj* voluminous; (*enorme*) massive

**voluntad** [bolun'tað] *nf* will; (*resolución*) willpower; (*deseo*) desire, wish

**voluntario, -a** [bolun'tarjo, a] *adj* voluntary ▷ *nm/f* volunteer

**volver** [bol'βer] *vt* (*gen*) to turn; (*dar vuelta a*) to turn (over); (*voltear*) to turn round, turn upside down; (*poner al revés*) to turn inside out; (*devolver*) to return ▷ *vi* to return, go back, come back; **volverse** *vr* to turn round; **~ la espalda** to turn one's back; **~ triste** *etc* **a algn** to make sb sad *etc*; **~ a hacer** to do again; **~ en sí** to come to; **~se insoportable/muy caro** to get *o* become unbearable/very expensive; **~se loco** to go mad

**vomitar** [bomi'tar] *vt, vi* to vomit; **vómito** *nm* vomit

**voraz** [bo'raθ] *adj* voracious

**vos** [bos] (*LAM*) *pron* you

**vosotros, -as** [bo'sotros, as] (*ESP*) *pron* you; (*reflexivo*): **entre/para ~** among/for yourselves

**votación** [bota'θjon] *nf* (*acto*) voting; (*voto*) vote

**votar** [bo'tar] *vi* to vote; **voto** *nm* vote; (*promesa*) vow; **votos** *nmpl* (good) wishes

**voy** *vb* ∨ **ir**

**voz** [boθ] *nf* voice; (*grito*) shout; (*rumor*) rumour; (*Ling*) word; **dar voces** to shout, yell; **de viva ~** verbally; **en ~ alta** aloud; **en ~ baja** in a low voice, in a whisper; **voz de mando** command

**vuelco** ['bwelko] *vb* ∨ **volcar** ▷ *nm* spill, overturning

**vuelo** ['bwelo] *vb* ∨ **volar** ▷ *nm* flight; (*encaje*) lace, frill; **coger al ~** to catch in flight; **vuelo chárter/regular** charter/

scheduled flight; **vuelo libre** (*Deporte*)
hang-gliding
**vuelque** *etc vb* V **volcar**
**vuelta** ['bwelta] *nf* (*gen*) turn; (*curva*)
bend, curve; (*regreso*) return; (*revolución*)
revolution; (*de circuito*) lap; (*de papel, tela*)
reverse; (*cambio*) change; **a la ~** on one's
return; **a la ~ (de la esquina)** round the
corner; **a ~ de correo** by return of post; **dar
~s** (*cabeza*) to spin; **dar(se) la ~** (*volverse*) to
turn round; **dar ~s a una idea** to turn over
an idea (in one's head); **estar de ~** to be
back; **dar una ~** to go for a walk; (*en coche*)
to go for a drive; **vuelta ciclista** (*Deporte*)
(cycle) tour
**vuelto** ['bwelto] *pp de* **volver**
**vuelvo** *etc vb* V **volver**
**vuestro, -a** ['bwestro, a] *adj pos* your;
**un amigo ~** a friend of yours ▷ *pron:* **el ~/la
vuestra, los ~s/las vuestras** yours
**vulgar** [bul'ɤar] *adj* (*ordinario*) vulgar;
(*común*) common; **vulgaridad** *nf*
commonness; (*acto*) vulgarity; (*expresión*)
coarse expression
**vulnerable** [bulne'raβle] *adj* vulnerable
**vulnerar** [bulne'rar] *vt* (*ley, acuerdo*) to
violate, breach; (*derechos, intimidad*) to
violate; (*reputación*) to damage

**walkie-talkie** [walki-'talki] (*pl* **~s**) *nm*
walkie-talkie
**Walkman**® ['walkman] *nm* Walkman®
**wáter** ['bater] *nm* (*taza*) toilet; (*LAM: lugar*)
toilet (*BRIT*), rest room (*US*)
**web** [web] *nm o f* (*página*) website; (*red*)
(World Wide) Web; **webcam** *nf* webcam;
**webmaster** *nmf* webmaster; **website** *nm*
website
**western** ['western] (*pl* **~s**) *nm* western
**whisky** ['wiski] *nm* whisky, whiskey
**windsurf** ['winsurf] *nm* windsurfing;
**hacer ~** to go windsurfing

# X Y

**xenofobia** [kseno'foβja] *nf* xenophobia
**xilófono** [ksi'lofono] *nm* xylophone
**xocoyote, -a** [ksoko'yote, a] (*MÉX*) *nm/f* baby of the family, youngest child

**y** [i] *conj* and
**ya** [ja] *adv* (*gen*) already; (*ahora*) now; (*en seguida*) at once; (*pronto*) soon ▷ *excl* all right! ▷ *conj* (*ahora que*) now that; **~ lo sé** I know; **~ que ...** since; **¡~ está bien!** that's (quite) enough!; **¡~ voy!** coming!
**yacaré** [jaka're] (*cs*) *nm* cayman
**yacer** [ja'θer] *vi* to lie
**yacimiento** [jaθi'mjento] *nm* (*de mineral*) deposit; (*arqueológico*) site
**yanqui** ['janki] *adj, nmf* Yankee
**yate** ['jate] *nm* yacht
**yazco** *etc vb* V **yacer**
**yedra** ['jeðra] *nf* ivy
**yegua** ['jeɣwa] *nf* mare
**yema** ['jema] *nf* (*del huevo*) yolk; (*Bot*) leaf bud; (*fig*) best part; **yema del dedo** fingertip
**yerno** ['jerno] *nm* son-in-law
**yeso** ['jeso] *nm* plaster
**yo** [jo] *pron* I; **soy ~** it's me
**yodo** ['joðo] *nm* iodine
**yoga** ['joɣa] *nm* yoga
**yogur(t)** [jo'ɣur(t)] *nm* yoghurt
**yuca** ['juka] *nf* (*alimento*) cassava, manioc root
**Yugoslavia** [juɣos'laβja] *nf* (*Hist*) Yugoslavia
**yugular** [juɣu'lar] *adj* jugular
**yunque** ['junke] *nm* anvil
**yuyo** ['jujo] (*RPL*) *nm* (*mala hierba*) weed

# Z

**zafar** [θa'far] vt (soltar) to untie; (superficie) to clear; **zafarse** vr (escaparse) to escape; (Tec) to slip off

**zafiro** [θa'firo] nm sapphire

**zaga** ['θaxa] nf: **a la ~** behind

**zaguán** [θa'ɣwan] nm hallway

**zalamero, -a** [θala'mero, a] adj flattering; (cobista) suave

**zamarra** [θa'marra] nf (chaqueta) sheepskin jacket

**zambullirse** [θambu'ʎirse] vr to dive

**zampar** [θam'par] vt to gobble down

**zanahoria** [θana'orja] nf carrot

**zancadilla** [θanka'ðiʎa] nf trip

**zanco** ['θanko] nm stilt

**zanja** ['θanxa] nf ditch; **zanjar** vt (resolver) to resolve

**zapata** [θa'pata] nf (Mecánica) shoe

**zapatería** [θapate'ria] nf (oficio) shoemaking; (tienda) shoe shop; (fábrica) shoe factory; **zapatero, -a** nm/f shoemaker

**zapatilla** [θapa'tiʎa] nf slipper; **zapatilla de deporte** training shoe

**zapato** [θa'pato] nm shoe

**zapping** ['θapin] nm channel-hopping; **hacer ~** to channel-hop

**zar** [θar] nm tsar, czar

**zarandear** [θarande'ar] (fam) vt to shake vigorously

**zarpa** ['θarpa] nf (garra) claw

**zarpar** [θar'par] vi to weigh anchor

**zarza** ['θarθa] nf (Bot) bramble; **zarzamora** nf blackberry

**zarzuela** [θar'θwela] nf Spanish light opera

**zigzag** [θiɣ'θaɣ] nm zigzag

**zinc** [θink] nm zinc

**zíper** ['θiper] (MÉX, CAM) nm zip (fastener) (BRIT), zipper (US)

**zócalo** ['θokalo] nm (Arq) plinth, base; (de pared) skirting board (BRIT), baseboard (US); (MÉX: plaza) main o public square

**zoclo** ['θoklo] (MÉX) nm skirting board (BRIT), baseboard (US)

**zodíaco** [θo'ðiako] nm zodiac

**zona** ['θona] nf zone; **zona fronteriza** border area; **zona roja** (LAM) red-light district

**zonzo, -a** (LAM: fam) ['θonθo, a] adj silly ▷ nm/f fool

**zoo** ['θoo] nm zoo

**zoología** [θoolo'xia] nf zoology; **zoológico, -a** adj zoological ▷ nm (tb: **parque zoológico**) zoo; **zoólogo, -a** nm/f zoologist

**zoom** [θum] nm zoom lens

**zopilote** [θopi'lote] (MÉX, CAM) nm buzzard

**zoquete** [θo'kete] nm (fam) blockhead

**zorro, -a** ['θorro, a] adj crafty ▷ nm/f fox/vixen

**zozobrar** [θoθo'βrar] vi (hundirse) to capsize; (fig) to fail

**zueco** ['θweko] nm clog

**zumbar** [θum'bar] vt (golpear) to hit ▷ vi to buzz; **zumbido** nm buzzing

**zumo** ['θumo] nm juice

**zurcir** [θur'θir] vt (coser) to darn

**zurdo, -a** ['θurðo, a] adj left-handed

**zurrar** [θu'rrar] (fam) vt to wallop

# a

**A** [eɪ] *n* (*Mus*) la *m*

**a** [ə] (*before vowel or silent h: an*) *indef art*
**1** un(a); **a book** un libro; **an apple** una manzana; **she's a doctor** (ella) es médica
**2** (*instead of the number "one"*) un(a); **a year ago** hace un año; **a hundred/thousand** *etc* **pounds** cien/mil *etc* libras
**3** (*in expressing ratios, prices etc*): **3 a day/week** 3 al día/a la semana; **10 km an hour** 10 km por hora; **£5 a person** £5 por persona; **30p a kilo** 30p el kilo

**A2** (*BRIT: Scol*) *n* segunda parte de los "A levels"
**A.A.** *n abbr* (*BRIT:* = *Automobile Association*) ≈ RACE *m* (*SP*); (= *Alcoholics Anonymous*) Alcohólicos Anónimos
**A.A.A.** (*US*) *n abbr* (= *American Automobile Association*) ≈ RACE *m* (*SP*)
**aback** [ə'bæk] *adv:* **to be taken ~** quedar desconcertado
**abandon** [ə'bændən] *vt* abandonar; (*give up*) renunciar a
**abattoir** ['æbətwɑː*] (*BRIT*) *n* matadero
**abbey** ['æbɪ] *n* abadía
**abbreviation** [ə'briːvɪ'eɪʃən] *n* (*short form*) abreviatura
**abdomen** ['æbdəmən] *n* abdomen *m*
**abduct** [æb'dʌkt] *vt* raptar, secuestrar
**abide** [ə'baɪd] *vt:* **I can't ~ it/him** no lo/le puedo ver; **abide by** *vt fus* atenerse a
**ability** [ə'bɪlɪtɪ] *n* habilidad *f*, capacidad *f*; (*talent*) talento
**able** ['eɪbl] *adj* capaz; (*skilled*) hábil; **to be ~ to do sth** poder hacer algo
**abnormal** [æb'nɔːməl] *adj* anormal
**aboard** [ə'bɔːd] *adv* a bordo ▷ *prep* a bordo de
**abolish** [ə'bɒlɪʃ] *vt* suprimir, abolir

**abolition** [æbəu'lɪʃən] *n* supresión *f*, abolición *f*
**abort** [ə'bɔːt] *vt, vi* abortar; **abortion** [ə'bɔːʃən] *n* aborto; **to have an abortion** abortar, hacerse abortar

**about** [ə'baut] *adv* **1** (*approximately*) más o menos, aproximadamente; **about a hundred/thousand** *etc* unos(unas) cien/mil *etc*; **it takes about 10 hours** se tarda unas or más o menos 10 horas; **at about 2 o'clock** sobre las dos; **I've just about finished** casi he terminado
**2** (*referring to place*) por todas partes; **to leave things lying about** dejar las cosas (tiradas) por ahí; **to run about** correr por todas partes; **to walk about** pasearse, ir y venir
**3**: **to be about to do sth** estar a punto de hacer algo
▷ *prep* **1** (*relating to*) de, sobre, acerca de; **a book about London** un libro sobre *or* acerca de Londres; **what is it about?** ¿de qué se trata?; **we talked about it** hablamos de eso *or* ello; **what** *or* **how about doing this?** ¿qué tal si hacemos esto?
**2** (*referring to place*) por; **to walk about the town** caminar por la ciudad

**above** [ə'bʌv] *adv* encima, por encima, arriba ▷ *prep* encima de; (*greater than: in number*) más de; (: *in rank*) superior a; **mentioned ~** susodicho; **~ all** sobre todo
**abroad** [ə'brɔːd] *adv* (*to be*) en el extranjero; (*to go*) al extranjero
**abrupt** [ə'brʌpt] *adj* (*sudden*) brusco; (*curt*) áspero
**abscess** ['æbsɪs] *n* absceso
**absence** ['æbsəns] *n* ausencia
**absent** ['æbsənt] *adj* ausente; **absent-minded** *adj* distraído
**absolute** ['æbsəluːt] *adj* absoluto; **absolutely** [-'luːtlɪ] *adv* (*totally*) totalmente; (*certainly!*) ¡por supuesto (que sí)!
**absorb** [əb'zɔːb] *vt* absorber; **to be ~ed in a book** estar absorto en un libro; **absorbent cotton** (*US*) *n* algodón *m* hidrófilo; **absorbing** *adj* absorbente
**abstain** [əb'steɪn] *vi:* **to ~ (from)** abstenerse (de)
**abstract** ['æbstrækt] *adj* abstracto
**absurd** [əb'səːd] *adj* absurdo
**abundance** [ə'bʌndəns] *n* abundancia
**abundant** [ə'bʌndənt] *adj* abundante
**abuse** [*n* ə'bjuːs, *vb* ə'bjuːz] *n* (*insults*)

insultos *mpl*, injurias *fpl*; (*ill-treatment*) malos tratos *mpl*; (*misuse*) abuso ▷ *vt* insultar; maltratar; abusar de; **abusive** *adj* ofensivo

**abysmal** [əˈbɪzməl] *adj* pésimo; (*failure*) garrafal; (*ignorance*) supino

**academic** [ækəˈdɛmɪk] *adj* académico, universitario; (*pej: issue*) puramente teórico ▷ *n* estudioso/a, profesor(a) *m/f* universitario/a; **academic year** *n* (*Univ*) año *m* académico; (*Scol*) año *m* escolar

**academy** [əˈkædəmɪ] *n* (*learned body*) academia; (*school*) instituto, colegio; **~ of music** conservatorio

**accelerate** [ækˈsɛləreɪt] *vt, vi* acelerar; **acceleration** [æksɛləˈreɪʃən] *n* aceleración *f*; **accelerator** (*BRIT*) *n* acelerador *m*

**accent** [ˈæksɛnt] *n* acento; (*fig*) énfasis *m*

**accept** [əkˈsɛpt] *vt* aceptar; (*responsibility, blame*) admitir; **acceptable** *adj* aceptable; **acceptance** *n* aceptación *f*

**access** [ˈæksɛs] *n* acceso; **to have ~ to** tener libre acceso a; **accessible** [-ˈsɛsəbl] *adj* (*place, person*) accesible; (*knowledge etc*) asequible

**accessory** [ækˈsɛsərɪ] *n* accesorio; (*Law*): **~ to** cómplice de

**accident** [ˈæksɪdənt] *n* accidente *m*; (*chance event*) casualidad *f*; **by ~** (*unintentionally*) sin querer; (*by chance*) por casualidad; **accidental** [-ˈdɛntl] *adj* accidental, fortuito; **accidentally** [-ˈdɛntəlɪ] *adv* sin querer; por casualidad; **Accident and Emergency Department** *n* (*BRIT*) Urgencias *fpl*; **accident insurance** *n* seguro contra accidentes

**acclaim** [əˈkleɪm] *vt* aclamar, aplaudir ▷ *n* aclamación *f*, aplausos *mpl*

**accommodate** [əˈkɒmədeɪt] *vt* (*person*) alojar, hospedar; (: *car, hotel etc*) tener cabida para; (*oblige, help*) complacer

**accommodation** [əkɒməˈdeɪʃən] (*US* **accommodations**) *n* alojamiento

**accompaniment** [əˈkʌmpənɪmənt] *n* acompañamiento

**accompany** [əˈkʌmpənɪ] *vt* acompañar

**accomplice** [əˈkʌmplɪs] *n* cómplice *mf*

**accomplish** [əˈkʌmplɪʃ] *vt* (*finish*) concluir; (*achieve*) lograr; **accomplishment** *n* (*skill: gen pl*) talento; (*completion*) realización *f*

**accord** [əˈkɔːd] *n* acuerdo ▷ *vt* conceder; **of his own ~** espontáneamente; **accordance** *n*: **in accordance with** de acuerdo con; **according** ▷ **according to** *prep* según; (*in accordance with*) conforme a; **accordingly** *adv* (*appropriately*) de acuerdo con esto; (*as a result*) en consecuencia

**account** [əˈkaunt] *n* (*Comm*) cuenta; (*report*) informe *m*; **accounts** *npl* (*Comm*) cuentas *fpl*; **of no ~** de ninguna importancia; **on ~** a cuenta; **on no ~** bajo ningún concepto; **on ~ of** a causa de, por motivo de; **to take into ~, take ~ of** tener en cuenta; **account for** *vt fus* (*explain*) explicar; (*represent*) representar; **accountable** *adj*: **accountable (to)** responsable (ante); **accountant** *n* contable *mf*, contador(a) *m/f*; **account number** *n* (*at bank etc*) número de cuenta

**accumulate** [əˈkjuːmjuleɪt] *vt* acumular ▷ *vi* acumularse

**accuracy** [ˈækjurəsɪ] *n* (*of total*) exactitud *f*; (*of description etc*) precisión *f*

**accurate** [ˈækjurɪt] *adj* (*total*) exacto; (*description*) preciso; (*person*) cuidadoso; (*device*) de precisión; **accurately** *adv* con precisión

**accusation** [ækjuˈzeɪʃən] *n* acusación *f*

**accuse** [əˈkjuːz] *vt*: **to ~ sb (of sth)** acusar a algn (de algo); **accused** *n* (*Law*) acusado/a

**accustomed** [əˈkʌstəmd] *adj*: **~ to** acostumbrado a

**ace** [eɪs] *n* as *m*

**ache** [eɪk] *n* dolor *m* ▷ *vi* doler; **my head ~s** me duele la cabeza

**achieve** [əˈtʃiːv] *vt* (*aim, result*) alcanzar; (*success*) lograr, conseguir; **achievement** *n* (*completion*) realización *f*; (*success*) éxito

**acid** [ˈæsɪd] *adj* ácido; (*taste*) agrio ▷ *n* (*Chem, inf: LSD*) ácido

**acknowledge** [əkˈnɒlɪdʒ] *vt* (*letter: also: ~ receipt of*) acusar recibo de; (*fact, situation, person*) reconocer; **acknowledgement** *n* acuse *m* de recibo

**acne** [ˈæknɪ] *n* acné *m*

**acorn** [ˈeɪkɔːn] *n* bellota

**acoustic** [əˈkuːstɪk] *adj* acústico

**acquaintance** [əˈkweɪntəns] *n* (*person*) conocido/a; (*with person, subject*) conocimiento

**acquire** [əˈkwaɪə*] *vt* adquirir; **acquisition** [ækwɪˈzɪʃən] *n* adquisición *f*

**acquit** [əˈkwɪt] *vt* absolver, exculpar; **to ~ o.s. well** salir con éxito

**acre** [ˈeɪkə*] *n* acre *m*

**acronym** [ˈækrənɪm] *n* siglas *fpl*

**across** [əˈkrɒs] *prep* (*on the other side of*) al otro lado de, del otro lado de; (*crosswise*) a través de ▷ *adv* de un lado a otro, de una parte a otra; a través, al través; (*measurement*): **the road is 10m ~** la carretera tiene 10m de ancho; **to run/swim ~** atravesar corriendo/nadando; **~ from** enfrente de

**acrylic** [əˈkrɪlɪk] *adj* acrílico ▷ *n* acrílica

**act** [ækt] n acto, acción f; (of play) acto; (in music hall etc) número; (Law) decreto, ley f ▷ vi (behave) comportarse; (have effect: drug, chemical) hacer efecto; (Theatre) actuar; (pretend) fingir; (take action) obrar ▷ vt (part) hacer el papel de; **in the ~ of: to catch sb in the ~ of ...** pillar a algn en el momento en que ...; **to ~ as** actuar or hacer de; **act up** (inf) vi (person) portarse mal; **acting** adj suplente ▷ n (activity) actuación f; (profession) profesión f de actor

**action** ['ækʃən] n acción f, acto; (Mil) acción f, batalla; (Law) proceso, demanda; **out of ~** (person) fuera de combate; (thing) estropeado; **to take ~** tomar medidas; **action replay** n (TV) repetición f

**activate** ['æktiveit] vt activar

**active** ['æktiv] adj activo, enérgico; (volcano) en actividad; **actively** adv (participate) activamente; (discourage, dislike) enérgicamente

**activist** ['æktivist] n activista m/f

**activity** [-'tiviti] n actividad f; **activity holiday** n vacaciones con actividades organizadas

**actor** ['æktə*] n actor m, actriz f

**actress** ['æktris] n actriz f

**actual** ['æktjuəl] adj verdadero, real; (emphatic use) propiamente dicho
▌ Be careful not to translate **actual** by the Spanish word *actual*.

**actually** ['æktjuəli] adv realmente, en realidad; (even) incluso
▌ Be careful not to translate **actually** by the Spanish word *actualmente*.

**acupuncture** ['ækjupʌŋktʃə*] n acupuntura

**acute** [ə'kju:t] adj agudo

**ad** [æd] n abbr = **advertisement**

**A.D.** adv abbr (= anno Domini) DC

**adamant** ['ædəmənt] adj firme, inflexible

**adapt** [ə'dæpt] vt adaptar ▷ vi: **to ~ (to)** adaptarse (a), ajustarse (a); **adapter** (us **adaptor**) n (Elec) adaptador m; (for several plugs) ladrón m

**add** [æd] vt añadir, agregar; **add up** vt (figures) sumar ▷ vi (fig): **it doesn't add up** no tiene sentido; **add up to** vt fus (Math) sumar, ascender a; (fig: mean) querer decir, venir a ser

**addict** ['ædikt] n adicto/a; (enthusiast) entusiasta mf; **addicted** [ə'diktid] adj: **to be addicted to** ser adicto a, ser fanático de; **addiction** [ə'dikʃən] n (to drugs etc) adicción f; **addictive** [ə'diktiv] adj que causa adicción

**addition** [ə'diʃən] n (adding up) adición f; (thing added) añadidura, añadido; **in ~** además, por añadidura; **in ~ to** además de; **additional** adj adicional

**additive** ['æditiv] n aditivo

**address** [ə'drɛs] n dirección f, señas fpl; (speech) discurso ▷ vt (letter) dirigir; (speak to) dirigirse a, dirigir la palabra a; (problem) tratar; **address book** n agenda (de direcciones)

**adequate** ['ædikwit] adj (satisfactory) adecuado; (enough) suficiente

**adhere** [əd'hiə*] vi: **to ~ to** (stick to) pegarse a; (fig: abide by) observar; (: belief etc) ser partidario de

**adhesive** [əd'hi:ziv] n adhesivo; **adhesive tape** n (BRIT) cinta adhesiva; (US Med) esparadrapo

**adjacent** [ə'dʒeisənt] adj: **~ to** contiguo a, inmediato a

**adjective** ['ædʒektiv] n adjetivo

**adjoining** [ə'dʒɔiniŋ] adj contiguo, vecino

**adjourn** [ə'dʒə:n] vt aplazar ▷ vi suspenderse

**adjust** [ə'dʒʌst] vt (change) modificar; (clothing) arreglar; (machine) ajustar ▷ vi: **to ~ (to)** adaptarse (a); **adjustable** adj ajustable; **adjustment** n adaptación f; (to machine, prices) ajuste m

**administer** [əd'ministə*] vt administrar; **administration** [-'treiʃən] n (management) administración f; (government) gobierno; **administrative** [-trətiv] adj administrativo

**administrator** [əd'ministreitə*] n administrador(a) m/f

**admiral** ['ædmərəl] n almirante m

**admiration** [ædmə'reiʃən] n admiración f

**admire** [əd'maiə*] vt admirar; **admirer** n (fan) admirador(a) m/f

**admission** [əd'miʃən] n (to university, club) ingreso; (entry fee) entrada; (confession) confesión f

**admit** [əd'mit] vt (confess) confesar; (permit to enter) dejar entrar, dar entrada a; (to club, organization) admitir; (accept: defeat) reconocer; **to be ~ted to hospital** ingresar en el hospital; **admit to** vt fus confesarse culpable de; **admittance** n entrada; **admittedly** adv es cierto or verdad que

**adolescent** [ædəu'lɛsnt] adj, n adolescente mf

**adopt** [ə'dɔpt] vt adoptar; **adopted** adj adoptivo; **adoption** [ə'dɔpʃən] n adopción f

**adore** [ə'dɔ:*] vt adorar

**adorn** [ə'dɔ:n] vt adornar

**Adriatic** [eidri'ætik] n: **the ~ (Sea)** el (Mar) Adriático

**adrift** [ə'drɪft] *adv* a la deriva
**adult** ['ædʌlt] *n* adulto/a ▷ *adj* (*grown-up*)
adulto; (*for adults*) para adultos; **adult
education** *n* educación *f* para adultos
**adultery** [ə'dʌltərɪ] *n* adulterio
**advance** [əd'vɑːns] *n* (*progress*) adelanto,
progreso; (*money*) anticipo, préstamo;
(*Mil*) avance *m* ▷ *adj*: **~ booking** venta
anticipada; **~ notice, ~ warning** previo
aviso ▷ *vt* (*money*) anticipar; (*theory, idea*)
proponer (para la discusión) ▷ *vi* avanzar,
adelantarse; **to make ~s (to sb)** hacer
proposiciones (a algn); **in ~** por adelantado;
**advanced** *adj* avanzado; (*Scol: studies*)
adelantado
**advantage** [əd'vɑːntɪdʒ] *n* (*also Tennis*)
ventaja; **to take ~ of** (*person*) aprovecharse
de; (*opportunity*) aprovechar
**advent** ['ædvənt] *n* advenimiento; **A~**
Adviento
**adventure** [əd'ventʃə*] *n* aventura;
**adventurous** [-tʃərəs] *adj* atrevido;
aventurero
**adverb** ['ædvɜːb] *n* adverbio
**adversary** ['ædvəsərɪ] *n* adversario,
contrario
**adverse** ['ædvɜːs] *adj* adverso, contrario
**advert** ['ædvɜːt] (*BRIT*) *n abbr* =
**advertisement**
**advertise** ['ædvətaɪz] *vi* (*in newspaper etc*)
anunciar, hacer publicidad; **to ~ for** (*staff,
accommodation etc*) buscar por medio de
anuncios ▷ *vt* anunciar; **advertisement**
[əd'vɜːtɪsmənt] *n* (*Comm*) anuncio;
**advertiser** *n* anunciante *mf*; **advertising**
*n* publicidad *f*, anuncios *mpl*; (*industry*)
industria publicitaria
**advice** [əd'vaɪs] *n* consejo, consejos *mpl*;
(*notification*) aviso; **a piece of ~** un consejo;
**to take legal ~** consultar con un abogado
**advisable** [əd'vaɪzəbl] *adj* aconsejable,
conveniente
**advise** [əd'vaɪz] *vt* aconsejar; (*inform*): **to
~ sb of sth** informar a algn de algo; **to ~
sb against sth/doing sth** desaconsejar
algo a algn/aconsejar a algn que no haga
algo; **adviser, advisor** *n* consejero/a;
(*lawyer*) asesor(a) *m/f*; **advisory** *adj*
consultivo
**advocate** [*vb* 'ædvəkeɪt, *n* -kɪt] *vt* abogar
por ▷ *n* (*lawyer*) abogado/a; (*supporter*): **~ of**
defensor(a) *m/f* de
**Aegean** [iː'dʒiːən] *n*: **the ~ (Sea)** el (Mar)
Egeo
**aerial** ['ɛərɪəl] *n* antena ▷ *adj* aéreo
**aerobics** [ɛə'rəʊbɪks] *n* aerobic *m*
**aeroplane** ['ɛərəpleɪn] (*BRIT*) *n* avión *m*
**aerosol** ['ɛərəsɒl] *n* aerosol *m*

**affair** [ə'fɛə*] *n* asunto; (*also*: **love ~**)
aventura (amorosa)
**affect** [ə'fɛkt] *vt* (*influence*) afectar,
influir en; (*afflict, concern*) afectar; (*move*)
conmover; **affected** *adj* afectado;
**affection** *n* afecto, cariño; **affectionate**
*adj* afectuoso, cariñoso
**afflict** [ə'flɪkt] *vt* afligir
**affluent** ['æfluənt] *adj* (*wealthy*)
acomodado; **the ~ society** la sociedad
opulenta
**afford** [ə'fɔːd] *vt* (*provide*) proporcionar;
**can we ~ (to buy) it?** ¿tenemos bastante
dinero para comprarlo?; **affordable** *adj*
asequible
**Afghanistan** [æf'gænɪstæn] *n*
Afganistán *m*
**afraid** [ə'freɪd] *adj*: **to be ~ of** (*person*) tener
miedo a; (*thing*) tener miedo de; **to be ~ to**
tener miedo de, temer; **I am ~ that** me temo
que; **I am ~ not/so** lo siento, pero no/es así
**Africa** ['æfrɪkə] *n* África; **African** *adj*, *n*
africano/a *m/f*; **African-American** *adj*, *n*
afroamericano/a
**after** ['ɑːftə*] *prep* (*time*) después de; (*place,
order*) detrás de, tras ▷ *adv* después ▷ *conj*
después (de) que; **what/who are you ~?**
¿qué/a quién busca usted?; **~ having done/
he left** después de haber hecho/después
de que se marchó; **to name sb ~ sb** llamar
a algn por algn; **it's twenty ~ eight** (*US*)
son las ocho y veinte; **to ask ~ sb** preguntar
por algn; **~ all** después de todo, al fin y al
cabo; **~ you!** ¡pase usted!; **after-effects** *npl*
consecuencias *fpl*, efectos *mpl*; **aftermath**
*n* consecuencias *fpl*, resultados *mpl*;
**afternoon** *n* tarde *f*; **after-shave (lotion)**
*n* aftershave *m*; **aftersun (lotion/cream)**
*n* loción *f*/crema para después del sol,
aftersun *m*; **afterwards** (*US* **afterward**) *adv*
después, más tarde
**again** [ə'gɛn] *adv* otra vez, de nuevo; **to
do sth ~** volver a hacer algo; **~ and ~** una y
otra vez
**against** [ə'gɛnst] *prep* (*in opposition to*)
en contra de; (*leaning on, touching*) contra,
junto a
**age** [eɪdʒ] *n* edad *f*; (*period*) época ▷ *vi*
envejecer(se) ▷ *vt* envejecer; **she is 20
years of ~** tiene 20 años; **to come of ~** llegar
a la mayoría de edad; **it's been ~s since I
saw you** hace siglos que no te veo; **~d 10** de
10 años de edad; **age group** *n*: **to be in the
same age group** tener la misma edad; **age
limit** *n* edad *f* mínima (*or* máxima)
**agency** ['eɪdʒənsɪ] *n* agencia
**agenda** [ə'dʒɛndə] *n* orden *m* del día
◼ Be careful not to translate **agenda** by the

Spanish word *agenda*.

**agent** ['eɪdʒənt] *n* agente *mf*; (*Comm: holding concession*) representante *mf*, delegado/a; (*Chem, fig*) agente *m*

**aggravate** ['ægrəveɪt] *vt* (*situation*) agravar; (*person*) irritar

**aggression** [ə'grɛʃən] *n* agresión *f*

**aggressive** [ə'grɛsɪv] *adj* (*belligerent*) agresivo; (*assertive*) enérgico

**agile** ['ædʒaɪl] *adj* ágil

**agitated** ['ædʒɪteɪtɪd] *adj* agitado

**AGM** *n abbr* (= *annual general meeting*) asamblea anual

**ago** [ə'gəu] *adv*: **2 days ~** hace 2 días; **not long ~** hace poco; **how long ~?** ¿hace cuánto tiempo?

**agony** ['ægənɪ] *n* (*pain*) dolor *m* agudo; (*distress*) angustia; **to be in ~** retorcerse de dolor

**agree** [ə'griː] *vt* (*price, date*) acordar, quedar en ▷ *vi* (*have same opinion*) **to ~ (with/that)** estar de acuerdo (con/que); (*correspond*) coincidir, concordar; (*consent*) acceder; **to ~ with** (*person*) estar de acuerdo con, ponerse de acuerdo con; (: *food*) sentar bien a; (*Ling*) concordar con; **to ~ to sth/to do sth** consentir en algo/aceptar hacer algo; **to ~ that** (*admit*) estar de acuerdo en que; **agreeable** *adj* (*sensation*) agradable; (*person*) simpático; (*willing*) de acuerdo, conforme; **agreed** *adj* (*time, place*) convenido; **agreement** *n* acuerdo; (*contract*) contrato; **in agreement** de acuerdo, conforme

**agricultural** [ægrɪ'kʌltʃərəl] *adj* agrícola

**agriculture** ['ægrɪkʌltʃə*] *n* agricultura

**ahead** [ə'hɛd] *adv* (*in front*) delante; (*into the future*): **she had no time to think ~** no tenía tiempo de hacer planes para el futuro; **~ of** delante de; (*in advance of*) antes de; **~ of time** antes de la hora; **go right** *or* **straight ~** (*direction*) siga adelante; (*permission*) hazlo (*or* hágalo)

**aid** [eɪd] *n* ayuda, auxilio; (*device*) aparato ▷ *vt* ayudar, auxiliar; **to ~** a beneficio de

**aide** [eɪd] *n* (*person, also Mil*) ayudante *mf*

**AIDS** [eɪdz] *n abbr* (= *acquired immune deficiency syndrome*) SIDA *m*

**ailing** ['eɪlɪŋ] *adj* (*person, economy*) enfermizo

**ailment** ['eɪlmənt] *n* enfermedad *f*, achaque *m*

**aim** [eɪm] *vt* (*gun, camera*) apuntar; (*missile, remark*) dirigir; (*blow*) asestar ▷ *vi* (*also*: **take ~**) apuntar ▷ *n* (*in shooting: skill*) puntería; (*objective*) propósito, meta; **to ~ at** (*with weapon*) apuntar a; (*objective*) aspirar a, pretender; **to ~ to do** tener la intención de hacer

**ain't** [eɪnt] (*inf*) = **am not; aren't; isn't**

**air** [ɛə*] *n* aire *m*; (*appearance*) aspecto ▷ *vt* (*room*) ventilar; (*clothes, ideas*) airear ▷ *cpd* aéreo; **to throw sth into the ~** (*ball etc*) lanzar algo al aire; **by ~** (*travel*) en avión; **to be on the ~** (*Radio, TV*) estar en antena; **airbag** *n* airbag *m inv*; **airbed** (BRIT) *n* colchón *m* neumático; **airborne** *adj* (*in the air*) en el aire; **as soon as the plane was airborne** tan pronto como el avión estuvo en el aire; **air-conditioned** *adj* climatizado; **air conditioning** *n* aire acondicionado; **aircraft** *n inv* avión *m*; **airfield** *n* campo de aviación; **Air Force** *n* fuerzas *fpl* aéreas, aviación *f*; **air hostess** (BRIT) *n* azafata; **airing cupboard** (BRIT) *n* armario *m* para oreo; **airlift** *n* puente *m* aéreo; **airline** *n* línea aérea; **airliner** *n* avión *m* de pasajeros; **airmail** *n*: **by airmail** por avión; **airplane** (US) *n* avión *m*; **airport** *n* aeropuerto; **air raid** *n* ataque *m* aéreo; **airsick** *adj*: **to be airsick** marearse (en avión); **airspace** *n* espacio aéreo; **airstrip** *n* pista de aterrizaje; **air terminal** *n* terminal *f*; **airtight** *adj* hermético; **air-traffic controller** *n* controlador(a) *m/f* aéreo/a; **airy** *adj* (*room*) bien ventilado; (*fig: manner*) desenfadado

**aisle** [aɪl] *n* (*of church*) nave *f*; (*of theatre, supermarket*) pasillo; **aisle seat** *n* (*on plane*) asiento de pasillo

**ajar** [ə'dʒɑː*] *adj* entreabierto

**à la carte** [ælæ'kɑːt] *adv* a la carta

**alarm** [ə'lɑːm] *n* (*in shop, bank*) alarma; (*anxiety*) inquietud *f* ▷ *vt* asustar, inquietar; **alarm call** *n* (*in hotel etc*) alarma; **alarm clock** *n* despertador *m*; **alarmed** *adj* (*person*) alarmado, asustado; (*house, car etc*) con alarma; **alarming** *adj* alarmante

**Albania** [æl'beɪnɪə] *n* Albania

**albeit** [ɔːl'biːɪt] *conj* aunque

**album** ['ælbəm] *n* álbum *m*; (L.P.) elepé *m*

**alcohol** ['ælkəhɔl] *n* alcohol *m*; **alcohol-free** *adj* sin alcohol; **alcoholic** [-'hɔlɪk] *adj*, *n* alcohólico/a *m/f*

**alcove** ['ælkəuv] *n* nicho, hueco

**ale** [eɪl] *n* cerveza

**alert** [ə'ləːt] *adj* (*attentive*) atento; (*to danger, opportunity*) alerta ▷ *n* alerta *m*, alarma ▷ *vt* poner sobre aviso; **to be on the ~** (*also Mil*) estar alerta *or* sobre aviso

**algebra** ['ældʒɪbrə] *n* álgebra

**Algeria** [æl'dʒɪərɪə] *n* Argelia

**alias** ['eɪlɪəs] *adv* alias, conocido por ▷ *n* (*of criminal*) apodo; (*of writer*) seudónimo

**alibi** ['ælɪbaɪ] *n* coartada

**alien** ['eɪlɪən] *n* (*foreigner*) extranjero/a;

(*extraterrestrial*) extraterrestre *mf* ▷ *adj:* **~ to** ajeno a; **alienate** *vt* enajenar, alejar

**alight** [əˈlaɪt] *adj* ardiendo; (*eyes*) brillante ▷ *vi* (*person*) apearse, bajar; (*bird*) posarse

**align** [əˈlaɪn] *vt* alinear

**alike** [əˈlaɪk] *adj* semejantes, iguales ▷ *adv* igualmente, del mismo modo; **to look ~** parecerse

**alive** [əˈlaɪv] *adj* vivo; (*lively*) alegre

○ **KEYWORD**

**all** [ɔːl] *adj* (*sg*) todo/a; (*pl*) todos/as; **all day** todo el día; **all night** toda la noche; **all men** todos los hombres; **all five came** vinieron los cinco; **all the books** todos los libros; **all his life** toda su vida
▷ *pron* 1 todo; **I ate it all, I ate all of it** me lo comí todo; **all of us went** fuimos todos; **all the boys went** fueron todos los chicos; **is that all?** ¿eso es todo?, ¿algo más?; (*in shop*) ¿algo más?, ¿alguna cosa más?
2 (*in phrases*): **above all** sobre todo; por encima de todo; **after all** después de todo; **at all: not at all** (*in answer to question*) en absoluto; (*in answer to thanks*) ¡de nada!, ¡no hay de qué!; **I'm not at all tired** no estoy nada cansado/a; **anything at all will do** cualquier cosa viene bien; **all in all** a fin de cuentas
▷ *adv:* **all alone** completamente solo/a; **it's not as hard as all that** no es tan difícil como lo pintas; **all the more/the better** tanto más/mejor; **all but** casi; **the score is 2 all** están empatados a 2

**Allah** [ˈælə] *n* Alá *m*

**allegation** [ælɪˈɡeɪʃən] *n* alegato

**alleged** [əˈlɛdʒd] *adj* supuesto, presunto; **allegedly** *adv* supuestamente, según se afirma

**allegiance** [əˈliːdʒəns] *n* lealtad *f*

**allergic** [əˈlɜːdʒɪk] *adj:* **~ to** alérgico a

**allergy** [ˈælədʒɪ] *n* alergia

**alleviate** [əˈliːvɪeɪt] *vt* aliviar

**alley** [ˈælɪ] *n* callejuela

**alliance** [əˈlaɪəns] *n* alianza

**allied** [ˈælaɪd] *adj* aliado

**alligator** [ˈælɪɡeɪtə*] *n* (*Zool*) caimán *m*

**all-in** (*BRIT*) [ˈɔːlɪn] *adj, adv* (*charge*) todo incluido

**allocate** [ˈæləkeɪt] *vt* (*money etc*) asignar

**allot** [əˈlɒt] *vt* asignar

**all-out** [ˈɔːlaʊt] *adj* (*effort etc*) supremo

**allow** [əˈlaʊ] *vt* permitir, dejar; (*a claim*) admitir; (*sum, time etc*) dar, conceder; (*concede*): **to ~ that** reconocer que; **to ~ sb to do** permitir a algn hacer; **he is ~ed to**

... se le permite ...; **allow for** *vt fus* tener en cuenta; **allowance** *n* subvención *f*; (*welfare payment*) subsidio, pensión *f*; (*pocket money*) dinero de bolsillo; (*tax allowance*) desgravación *f*; **to make allowances for** (*person*) disculpar a; (*thing*) tener en cuenta

**all right** *adv* bien; (*as answer*) ¡conforme!, ¡está bien!

**ally** [ˈælaɪ] *n* aliado/a ▷ *vt:* **to ~ o.s. with** aliarse con

**almighty** [ɔːlˈmaɪtɪ] *adj* todopoderoso; (*row etc*) imponente

**almond** [ˈɑːmənd] *n* almendra

**almost** [ˈɔːlməʊst] *adv* casi

**alone** [əˈləʊn] *adj, adv* solo; **to leave sb ~** dejar a algn en paz; **to leave sth ~** no tocar algo, dejar algo sin tocar; **let ~ ...** y mucho menos ...

**along** [əˈlɒŋ] *prep* a lo largo de, por ▷ *adv:* **is he coming ~ with us?** ¿viene con nosotros?; **he was limping ~** iba cojeando; **~ with** junto con; **all ~** (*all the time*) desde el principio; **alongside** *prep* al lado de ▷ *adv* al lado

**aloof** [əˈluːf] *adj* reservado ▷ *adv:* **to stand ~** mantenerse apartado

**aloud** [əˈlaʊd] *adv* en voz alta

**alphabet** [ˈælfəbɛt] *n* alfabeto

**Alps** [ælps] *npl:* **the ~** los Alpes

**already** [ɔːlˈrɛdɪ] *adv* ya

**alright** [ˈɔːlˈraɪt] (*BRIT*) *adv* = **all right**

**also** [ˈɔːlsəʊ] *adv* también, además

**altar** [ˈɔltə*] *n* altar *m*

**alter** [ˈɔltə*] *vt* cambiar, modificar ▷ *vi* cambiar; **alteration** [ɔltəˈreɪʃən] *n* cambio; (*to clothes*) arreglo; (*to building*) arreglos *mpl*

**alternate** [*adj* ɔlˈtəːnɪt, *vb* ˈɔltəneɪt] *adj* (*actions etc*) alternativo; (*events*) alterno; (*us*) = **alternative** ▷ *vi:* **to ~ (with)** alternar (con); **on ~ days** un día sí y otro no

**alternative** [ɔlˈtəːnətɪv] *adj* alternativo ▷ *n* alternativa; **~ medicine** medicina alternativa; **alternatively** *adv:* **alternatively one could ...** por otra parte se podría ...

**although** [ɔːlˈðəʊ] *conj* aunque

**altitude** [ˈæltɪtjuːd] *n* altura

**altogether** [ɔːltəˈɡɛðə*] *adv* completamente, del todo; (*on the whole*) en total, en conjunto

**aluminium** [æljuˈmɪnɪəm] (*BRIT*), **aluminum** [əˈluːmɪnəm] (*us*) *n* aluminio

**always** [ˈɔːlweɪz] *adv* siempre

**Alzheimer's (disease)** [ˈæltshaɪməz-] *n* enfermedad *f* de Alzheimer

**am** [æm] *vb see* **be**

**amalgamate** [əˈmælɡəmeɪt] *vi*

amalgamarse ▷ vt amalgamar, unir

**amass** [ə'mæs] vt amontonar, acumular

**amateur** ['æmətə*] n aficionado/a, amateur mf

**amaze** [ə'meɪz] vt asombrar, pasmar; **to be ~d (at)** quedar pasmado (de); **amazed** adj asombrado; **amazement** n asombro, sorpresa; **amazing** adj extraordinario; (fantastic) increíble

**Amazon** ['æməzən] n (Geo) Amazonas m

**ambassador** [æm'bæsədə*] n embajador(a) m/f

**amber** ['æmbə*] n ámbar m; **at ~** (BRIT Aut) en el amarillo

**ambiguous** [æm'bɪgjuəs] adj ambiguo

**ambition** [æm'bɪʃən] n ambición f; **ambitious** [-ʃəs] adj ambicioso

**ambulance** ['æmbjuləns] n ambulancia

**ambush** ['æmbuʃ] n emboscada ▷ vt tender una emboscada a

**amen** [ɑː'mɛn] excl amén

**amend** [ə'mɛnd] vt enmendar; **to make ~s** dar cumplida satisfacción; **amendment** n enmienda

**amenities** [ə'miːnɪtɪz] npl comodidades fpl

**America** [ə'mɛrɪkə] n (USA) Estados mpl Unidos; **American** adj, n norteamericano/a; estadounidense mf; **American football** n (BRIT) fútbol m americano

**amicable** ['æmɪkəbl] adj amistoso, amigable

**amid(st)** [ə'mɪd(st)] prep entre, en medio de

**ammunition** [æmju'nɪʃən] n municiones fpl

**amnesty** ['æmnɪstɪ] n amnistía

**among(st)** [ə'mʌŋ(st)] prep entre, en medio de

**amount** [ə'maunt] n (gen) cantidad f; (of bill etc) suma, importe m ▷ vi: **to ~ to** sumar; (be same as) equivaler a, significar

**amp(ère)** ['æmp(eə*)] n amperio

**ample** ['æmpl] adj (large) grande; (abundant) abundante; (enough) bastante, suficiente

**amplifier** ['æmplɪfaɪə*] n amplificador m

**amputate** ['æmpjuteɪt] vt amputar

**Amtrak** ['æmtræk] (US) n empresa nacional de ferrocarriles de los EEUU

**amuse** [ə'mjuːz] vt divertir; (distract) distraer, entretener; **amusement** n diversión f; (pastime) pasatiempo; (laughter) risa; **amusement arcade** n salón m de juegos; **amusement park** n parque m de atracciones

**amusing** [ə'mjuːzɪŋ] adj divertido

**an** [æn] indef art see **a**

**anaemia** [ə'niːmɪə] (US **anemia**) n anemia

**anaemic** [ə'niːmɪk] (US **anemic**) adj anémico; (fig) soso, insípido

**anaesthetic** [ænɪs'θɛtɪk] (US **anesthetic**) n anestesia

**analog(ue)** ['ænəlɔg] adj (computer, watch) analógico

**analogy** [ə'nælədʒɪ] n analogía

**analyse** ['ænəlaɪz] (US **analyze**) vt analizar; **analysis** [ə'næləsɪs] (pl **analyses**) n análisis m inv; **analyst** [-lɪst] n (political analyst, psychoanalyst) analista mf

**analyze** ['ænəlaɪz] (US) vt = **analyse**

**anarchy** ['ænəkɪ] n anarquía, desorden m

**anatomy** [ə'nætəmɪ] n anatomía

**ancestor** ['ænsɪstə*] n antepasado

**anchor** ['æŋkə*] n ancla, áncora ▷ vi (also: **to drop ~**) anclar ▷ vt anclar; **to weigh ~** levar anclas

**anchovy** ['æntʃəvɪ] n anchoa

**ancient** ['eɪnʃənt] adj antiguo

**and** [ænd] conj y; (before i-, hi- + consonant) e; **men ~ women** hombres y mujeres; **father ~ son** padre e hijo; **trees ~ grass** árboles y hierba; **~ so on** etcétera, y así sucesivamente; **try ~ come** procura venir; **he talked ~ talked** habló sin parar; **better ~ better** cada vez mejor

**Andes** ['ændiːz] npl: **the ~** los Andes

**Andorra** [æn'dɔːrə] n Andorra

**anemia** etc [ə'niːmɪə] (US) = **anaemia** etc

**anesthetic** [ænɪs'θɛtɪk] (US) = **anaesthetic**

**angel** ['eɪndʒəl] n ángel m

**anger** ['æŋgə*] n cólera

**angina** [æn'dʒaɪnə] n angina (del pecho)

**angle** ['æŋgl] n ángulo; **from their ~** desde su punto de vista

**angler** ['æŋglə*] n pescador(a) m/f (de caña)

**Anglican** ['æŋglɪkən] adj, n anglicano/a m/f

**angling** ['æŋglɪŋ] n pesca con caña

**angrily** ['æŋgrɪlɪ] adv coléricamente, airadamente

**angry** ['æŋgrɪ] adj enfadado, airado; (wound) inflamado; **to be ~ with sb/at sth** estar enfadado con algn/por algo; **to get ~** enfadarse, enojarse

**anguish** ['æŋgwɪʃ] n (physical) tormentos mpl; (mental) angustia

**animal** ['ænɪməl] n animal m; (pej: person) bestia ▷ adj animal

**animated** [-meɪtɪd] adj animado

**animation** [ænɪ'meɪʃən] n animación f

**aniseed** ['ænɪsiːd] n anís m

**ankle** ['æŋkl] n tobillo

**annex** [n 'æneks, vb æ'neks] n (BRIT: also: ~e: building) edificio anexo ▷ vt (territory) anexionar

**anniversary** [ænɪ'vəːsərɪ] n aniversario

**announce** [ə'nauns] vt anunciar; **announcement** n anuncio; (official) declaración f; **announcer** n (Radio) locutor(a) m/f; (TV) presentador(a) m/f

**annoy** [ə'nɔɪ] vt molestar, fastidiar; **don't get ~ed!** ¡no se enfade!; **annoying** adj molesto, fastidioso; (person) pesado

**annual** ['ænjuəl] adj anual ▷ n (Bot) anual m; (book) anuario; **annually** adv anualmente, cada año

**annum** ['ænəm] n see **per**

**anonymous** [ə'nɒnɪməs] adj anónimo

**anorak** ['ænəræk] n anorak m

**anorexia** [ænə'reksɪə] n (Med: also: ~ nervosa) anorexia

**anorexic** [ænə'reksɪk] adj, n anoréxico/a m/f

**another** [ə'nʌðə*] adj (one more, a different one) otro ▷ pron otro; see **one**

**answer** ['ɑ:nsə*] n contestación f, respuesta; (to problem) solución f ▷ vi contestar, responder ▷ vt (reply to) contestar a, responder a; (problem) resolver; (prayer) escuchar; **in ~ to your letter** contestando or en contestación a su carta; **to ~ the phone** contestar or coger el teléfono; **to ~ the bell** or **the door** acudir a la puerta; **answer back** vi replicar, ser respondón/ona; **answerphone** n (esp BRIT) contestador m (automático)

**ant** [ænt] n hormiga

**Antarctic** [ænt'ɑːktɪk] n: **the ~** el Antártico

**antelope** ['æntɪləup] n antílope m

**antenatal** ['æntɪ'neɪtl] adj antenatal, prenatal

**antenna** [æn'tɛnə, pl -niː] (pl **antennae**) n antena

**anthem** ['ænθəm] n: **national ~** himno nacional

**anthology** [æn'θɒlədʒɪ] n antología

**anthrax** ['ænθræks] n ántrax m

**anthropology** [ænθrə'pɒlədʒɪ] n antropología

**anti** [ænti] prefix anti; **antibiotic** [-baɪ'ɒtɪk] n antibiótico; **antibody** ['æntɪbɒdɪ] n anticuerpo

**anticipate** [æn'tɪsɪpeɪt] vt prever; (expect) esperar, contar con; (look forward to) esperar con ilusión; (do first) anticiparse a, adelantarse a; **anticipation** [-'peɪʃən] n (expectation) previsión f; (eagerness) ilusión f, expectación f

**anticlimax** [ænti'klaɪmæks] n

decepción f

**anticlockwise** [ænti'klɔkwaɪz] (BRIT) adv en dirección contraria a la de las agujas del reloj

**antics** ['æntɪks] npl gracias fpl

**anti: antidote** ['æntɪdəut] n antídoto; **antifreeze** ['æntɪfriːz] n anticongelante m; **antihistamine** [-'hɪstəmiːn] n antihistamínico; **antiperspirant** ['æntɪpəːspɪrənt] n antitranspirante m

**antique** [æn'tiːk] n antigüedad f ▷ adj antiguo; **antique shop** n tienda de antigüedades

**antiseptic** [ænti'septɪk] adj, n antiséptico

**antisocial** [ænti'səuʃəl] adj antisocial

**antivirus** [ænti'vaiərəs] adj (program, software) antivirus inv

**antlers** ['æntləz] npl cuernas fpl, cornamenta sg

**anxiety** [æŋ'zaɪətɪ] n inquietud f; (Med) ansiedad f; **~ to do** deseo de hacer

**anxious** ['æŋkʃəs] adj inquieto, preocupado; (worrying) preocupante; (keen): **to be ~ to do** tener muchas ganas de hacer

○ **KEYWORD**

**any** ['ɛnɪ] adj **1**(in questions etc) algún/ alguna; **have you any butter/children?** ¿tienes mantequilla/hijos?; **if there are any tickets left** si quedan billetes, si queda algún billete

**2**(with negative): **I haven't any money/ books** no tengo dinero/libros

**3**(no matter which) cualquier; **any excuse will do** valdrá or servirá cualquier excusa; **choose any book you like** escoge el libro que quieras

**4**(in phrases): **in any case** de todas formas, en cualquier caso; **any day now** cualquier día (de estos); **at any moment** en cualquier momento, de un momento a otro; **at any rate** en todo caso; **any time: come (at) any time** ven cuando quieras; **he might come (at) any time** podría llegar de un momento a otro

▷ pron **1**(in questions etc): **have you got any?** ¿tienes alguno(s)/a(s)?; **can any of you sing?** ¿sabe cantar alguno de vosotros/ ustedes?

**2**(with negative): **I haven't any (of them)** no tengo ninguno

**3**(no matter which one(s)): **take any of those books (you like)** toma el libro que quieras de ésos

▷ adv **1**(in questions etc): **do you want any**

**more soup/sandwiches?** ¿quieres más sopa/bocadillos?; **are you feeling any better?** ¿te sientes algo mejor?

**2** (with negative): **I can't hear him any more** ya no le oigo; **don't wait any longer** no esperes más

**any: anybody** pron cualquiera; (in interrogative sentences) alguien; (in negative sentences): **I don't see anybody** no veo a nadie; **if anybody should phone …** si llama alguien…; **anyhow** adv (at any rate) de todos modos, de todas formas; (haphazard): **do it anyhow you like** hazlo como quieras; **she leaves things just anyhow** deja las cosas como quiera or de cualquier modo; **I shall go anyhow** de todos modos iré; **anyone** pron = **anybody**; **anything** pron (in questions etc) algo, alguna cosa; (with negative) nada; **can you see anything?** ¿ves algo?; **if anything happens to me …** si algo me ocurre…; (no matter what): **you can say anything you like** puedes decir lo que quieras; **anything will do** vale todo or cualquier cosa; **he'll eat anything** come de todo or lo que sea; **anytime** adv (at any moment) en cualquier momento, de un momento a otro; (whenever) no importa cuándo, cuando quiera; **anyway** adv (at any rate) de todos modos, de todas formas; **I shall go anyway** iré de todos modos; (besides): **anyway, I couldn't come even if I wanted to** además, no podría venir aunque quisiera; **why are you phoning, anyway?** ¿entonces, por qué llamas? ¿por qué llamas, pues?; **anywhere** adv (in questions etc): **can you see him anywhere?** ¿le ves por algún lado?; **are you going anywhere?** ¿vas a algún sitio?; (with negative): **I can't see him anywhere** no le veo por ninguna parte; **anywhere in the world** (no matter where) en cualquier parte (del mundo); **put the books down anywhere** deja los libros donde quieras

**apart** [əˈpɑːt] adv (aside) aparte; (situation): **~ (from)** separado (de); (movement): **to pull ~** separar; **10 miles ~** separados por 10 millas; **to take ~** desmontar; **~ from** prep aparte de

**apartment** [əˈpɑːtmənt] n (US) piso (SP), departamento (LAM), apartamento; (room) cuarto; **apartment building** (US) n edificio de apartamentos

**apathy** [ˈæpəθɪ] n apatía, indiferencia

**ape** [eɪp] n mono ⊳ vt imitar, remedar

**aperitif** [əˈpɛrɪtɪf] n aperitivo

**aperture** [ˈæpətʃjʊə*] n rendija,

resquicio; (Phot) abertura

**APEX** [ˈeɪpɛks] n abbr (= Advanced Purchase Excursion Fare) tarifa f APEX

**apologize** [əˈpɒlədʒaɪz] vi: **to ~ (for sth to sb)** disculparse (con algn de algo)

**apology** [əˈpɒlədʒɪ] n disculpa, excusa

> ▌ Be careful not to translate **apology** by
> ▌ the Spanish word apología.

**apostrophe** [əˈpɒstrəfɪ] n apóstrofo

**appal** [əˈpɔːl] (US **appall**) vt horrorizar, espantar; **appalling** adj espantoso; (awful) pésimo

**apparatus** [æpəˈreɪtəs] n (equipment) equipo; (organization) aparato; (in gymnasium) aparatos mpl

**apparent** [əˈpærənt] adj aparente; (obvious) evidente; **apparently** adv por lo visto, al parecer

**appeal** [əˈpiːl] vi (Law) apelar ⊳ n (Law) apelación f; (request) llamamiento; (plea) petición f; (charm) atractivo; **to ~ for** reclamar; **to ~ to** (be attractive to) atraer; **it doesn't ~ to me** no me atrae, no me llama la atención; **appealing** adj (attractive) atractivo

**appear** [əˈpɪə*] vi aparecer, presentarse; (Law) comparecer; (publication) salir (a luz), publicarse; (seem) parecer; **to ~ on TV/in "Hamlet"** salir por la tele/hacer un papel en "Hamlet"; **it would ~ that** parecería que; **appearance** n aparición f; (look) apariencia, aspecto

**appendices** [əˈpɛndɪsiːz] npl of **appendix**

**appendicitis** [əpɛndɪˈsaɪtɪs] n apendicitis f

**appendix** [əˈpɛndɪks] (pl **appendices**) n apéndice m

**appetite** [ˈæpɪtaɪt] n apetito; (fig) deseo, anhelo

**appetizer** [ˈæpɪtaɪzə*] n (drink) aperitivo; (food) tapas fpl (SP)

**applaud** [əˈplɔːd] vt, vi aplaudir

**applause** [əˈplɔːz] n aplausos mpl

**apple** [ˈæpl] n manzana; **apple pie** n pastel m de manzana, pay m de manzana (LAM)

**appliance** [əˈplaɪəns] n aparato

**applicable** [əˈplɪkəbl] adj (relevant): **to be ~ (to)** referirse (a)

**applicant** [ˈæplɪkənt] n candidato/a; solicitante mf

**application** [æplɪˈkeɪʃən] n aplicación f; (for a job etc) solicitud f, petición f; **application form** n solicitud f

**apply** [əˈplaɪ] vt (paint etc) poner; (law etc: put into practice) poner en vigor ⊳ vi: **to ~ to** (ask) dirigirse a; (be applicable) ser aplicable a; **to ~ for** (permit, grant, job) solicitar; **to ~ o.s. to** aplicarse a, dedicarse a

**appoint** [ə'pɔɪnt] vt (to post) nombrar a

▌ Be careful not to translate **appoint** by the Spanish word *apuntar*.

**appointment** n (with client) cita; (act) nombramiento; (post) puesto; (at hairdresser etc): **to have an appointment** tener hora; **to make an appointment (with sb)** citarse (con algn)

**appraisal** [ə'preɪzl] n valoración f

**appreciate** [ə'pri:ʃɪeɪt] vt apreciar, tener en mucho; (be grateful for) agradecer; (be aware) comprender ▷ vi (Comm) aumentar(se) en valor; **appreciation** [-'eɪʃən] n apreciación f; (gratitude) reconocimiento, agradecimiento; (Comm) aumento en valor

**apprehension** [æprɪ'hɛnʃən] n (fear) aprensión f

**apprehensive** [æprɪ'hɛnsɪv] adj aprensivo

**apprentice** [ə'prɛntɪs] n aprendiz(a) m/f

**approach** [ə'prəʊtʃ] vi acercarse ▷ vt acercarse a; (ask, apply to) dirigirse a; (situation, problem) abordar ▷ n acercamiento; (access) acceso; (to problem, situation): **~ (to)** actitud f (ante)

**appropriate** [adj ə'prəʊprɪɪt, vb ə'prəʊprɪeɪt] adj apropiado, conveniente ▷ vt (take) apropiarse de

**approval** [ə'pru:vəl] n aprobación f, visto bueno; (permission) consentimiento; **on ~** (Comm) a prueba

**approve** [ə'pru:v] vt aprobar; **approve of** vt fus (thing) aprobar; (person): **they don't approve of her** (ella) no les parece bien

**approximate** [ə'prɔksɪmɪt] adj aproximado; **approximately** adv aproximadamente, más o menos

**Apr.** abbr (= April) abr

**apricot** ['eɪprɪkɔt] n albaricoque m, chabacano (MEX), damasco (RPL)

**April** ['eɪprəl] n abril m; **April Fools' Day** n el primero de abril, ≈ día m de los Inocentes (28 December)

**apron** ['eɪprən] n delantal m

**apt** [æpt] adj acertado, apropiado; (likely): **~ to do** propenso a hacer

**aquarium** [ə'kwɛərɪəm] n acuario

**Aquarius** [ə'kwɛərɪəs] n Acuario

**Arab** ['ærəb] adj, n árabe mf

**Arabia** [ə'reɪbɪə] n Arabia; **Arabian** adj árabe; **Arabic** ['ærəbɪk] adj árabe; (numerals) arábigo ▷ n árabe m

**arbitrary** ['ɑ:bɪtrərɪ] adj arbitrario

**arbitration** [ɑ:bɪ'treɪʃən] n arbitraje m

**arc** [ɑ:k] n arco

**arcade** [ɑ:'keɪd] n (round a square) soportales mpl; (shopping mall) galería comercial

**arch** [ɑ:tʃ] n arco; (of foot) arco del pie ▷ vt arquear

**archaeology** [ɑ:kɪ'ɔlədʒɪ] (US **archeology**) n arqueología

**archbishop** [ɑ:tʃ'bɪʃəp] n arzobispo

**archeology** [ɑ:kɪ'ɔlədʒɪ] (US) = **archaeology**

**architect** ['ɑ:kɪtɛkt] n arquitecto/a; **architectural** [ɑ:kɪ'tɛktʃərəl] adj arquitectónico; **architecture** n arquitectura

**archive** ['ɑ:kaɪv] n (often pl: also Comput) archivo

**Arctic** ['ɑ:ktɪk] adj ártico ▷ n: **the ~** el Ártico

**are** [ɑ:*] vb see **be**

**area** ['ɛərɪə] n área, región f; (part of place) zona; (Math etc) área, superficie f; (in room: e.g. dining area) parte f; (of knowledge, experience) campo; **area code** (US) n (Tel) prefijo

**arena** [ə'ri:nə] n estadio; (of circus) pista

**aren't** [ɑ:nt] = **are not**

**Argentina** [ɑ:dʒən'ti:nə] n Argentina; **Argentinian** [-'tɪnɪən] adj, n argentino/a m/f

**arguably** ['ɑ:gjʊəblɪ] adv posiblemente

**argue** ['ɑ:gju:] vi (quarrel) discutir, pelearse; (reason) razonar, argumentar; **to ~ that** sostener que

**argument** ['ɑ:gjʊmənt] n discusión f, pelea; (reasons) argumento

**Aries** ['ɛərɪz] n Aries m

**arise** [ə'raɪz] (pt **arose**, pp **arisen**) vi surgir, presentarse

**arithmetic** [ə'rɪθmətɪk] n aritmética

**arm** [ɑ:m] n brazo ▷ vt armar; **arms** npl armas fpl; **~ in ~** cogidos del brazo; **armchair** ['ɑ:mtʃɛə*] n sillón m, butaca

**armed** [ɑ:md] adj armado; **armed robbery** n robo a mano armada

**armour** ['ɑ:mə*] (US **armor**) n armadura; (Mil: tanks) blindaje m

**armpit** ['ɑ:mpɪt] n sobaco, axila

**armrest** ['ɑ:mrɛst] n apoyabrazos m inv

**army** ['ɑ:mɪ] n ejército; (fig) multitud f

**A road** n (BRIT) ≈ carretera f nacional

**aroma** [ə'rəʊmə] n aroma m, fragancia; **aromatherapy** n aromaterapia

**arose** [ə'rəʊz] pt of **arise**

**around** [ə'raʊnd] adv alrededor; (in the area): **there is no one else ~** no hay nadie más por aquí ▷ prep alrededor de

**arouse** [ə'raʊz] vt despertar; (anger) provocar

**arrange** [ə'reɪndʒ] vt arreglar, ordenar;

(*organize*) organizar; **to ~ to do sth** quedar en hacer algo; **arrangement** n arreglo; (*agreement*) acuerdo; **arrangements** npl (*preparations*) preparativos mpl

**array** [ə'reɪ] n: **~ of** (*things*) serie f de; (*people*) conjunto de

**arrears** [ə'rɪəz] npl atrasos mpl; **to be in ~ with one's rent** estar retrasado en el pago del alquiler

**arrest** [ə'rɛst] vt detener; (*sb's attention*) llamar ▷ n detención f; **under ~** detenido

**arrival** [ə'raɪvəl] n llegada; **new ~** recién llegado/a; (*baby*) recién nacido

**arrive** [ə'raɪv] vi llegar; (*baby*) nacer; **arrive at** vt fus (*decision, solution*) llegar a

**arrogance** ['ærəgəns] n arrogancia, prepotencia (LAM)

**arrogant** ['ærəgənt] adj arrogante

**arrow** ['ærəʊ] n flecha

**arse** [ɑːs] n (BRIT: inf!) n culo, trasero

**arson** ['ɑːsn] n incendio premeditado

**art** [ɑːt] n arte m; (*skill*) destreza; **art college** n escuela f de Bellas Artes

**artery** ['ɑːtərɪ] n arteria

**art gallery** n pinacoteca; (*saleroom*) galería de arte

**arthritis** [ɑː'θraɪtɪs] n artritis f

**artichoke** ['ɑːtɪtʃəʊk] n alcachofa; **Jerusalem ~** aguaturma

**article** ['ɑːtɪkl] n artículo

**articulate** [adj ɑː'tɪkjʊlɪt, vb ɑː'tɪkjʊleɪt] adj claro, bien expresado ▷ vt expresar

**artificial** [ɑːtɪ'fɪʃəl] adj artificial; (*affected*) afectado

**artist** ['ɑːtɪst] n artista mf; (*Mus*) intérprete mf; **artistic** [ɑː'tɪstɪk] adj artístico

**art school** n escuela de bellas artes

○ KEYWORD

**as** [æz] conj **1** (*referring to time*) cuando, mientras; a medida que; **as the years went by** con el paso de los años; **he came in as I was leaving** entró cuando me marchaba; **as from tomorrow** desde or a partir de mañana

**2** (*in comparisons*): **as big as** tan grande como; **twice as big as** el doble de grande que; **as much money/many books as** tanto dinero/tantos libros como; **as soon as** en cuanto

**3** (*since, because*) como, ya que; **he left early as he had to be home by 10** se fue temprano ya que tenía que estar en casa a las 10

**4** (*referring to manner, way*): **do as you wish** haz lo que quieras; **as she said** como dijo;

he gave it to me as a present me lo dio de regalo

**5** (*in the capacity of*): **he works as a barman** trabaja de barman; **as chairman of the company, he ...** como presidente de la compañía ...

**6** (*concerning*): **as for** or **to that** por or en lo que respecta a eso

**7**: **as if** or **though** como si; **he looked as if he was ill** parecía como si estuviera enfermo, tenía aspecto de enfermo; see also **long; such; well**

**a.s.a.p.** abbr (= as soon as possible) cuanto antes

**asbestos** [æz'bɛstəs] n asbesto, amianto

**ascent** [ə'sɛnt] n subida; (*slope*) cuesta, pendiente f

**ash** [æʃ] n ceniza; (*tree*) fresno

**ashamed** [ə'ʃeɪmd] adj avergonzado, apenado (LAM); **to be ~ of** avergonzarse de

**ashore** [ə'ʃɔː*] adv en tierra; (*swim etc*) a tierra

**ashtray** ['æʃtreɪ] n cenicero

**Ash Wednesday** n miércoles m de Ceniza

**Asia** ['eɪʃə] n Asia; **Asian** adj, n asiático/a m/f

**aside** [ə'saɪd] adv a un lado ▷ n aparte m

**ask** [ɑːsk] vt (*question*) preguntar; (*invite*) invitar; **to ~ sb sth/to do sth** preguntar algo a algn/pedir a algn que haga algo; **to ~ sb about sth** preguntar algo a algn; **to ~ (sb) a question** hacer una pregunta (a algn); **to ~ sb out to dinner** invitar a cenar a algn; **ask for** vt fus pedir; (*trouble*) buscar

**asleep** [ə'sliːp] adj dormido; **to fall ~** dormirse, quedarse dormido

**asparagus** [əs'pærəgəs] n (*plant*) espárrago; (*food*) espárragos mpl

**aspect** ['æspɛkt] n aspecto, apariencia; (*direction in which a building etc faces*) orientación f

**aspirations** [æspə'reɪʃənz] npl aspiraciones fpl; (*ambition*) ambición f

**aspire** [əs'paɪə*] vi: **to ~ to** aspirar a, ambicionar

**aspirin** ['æsprɪn] n aspirina

**ass** [æs] n asno, burro; (*inf: idiot*) imbécil mf; (*us: inf!*) culo, trasero

**assassin** [ə'sæsɪn] n asesino/a; **assassinate** vt asesinar

**assault** [ə'sɔːlt] n asalto; (*Law*) agresión f ▷ vt asaltar, atacar; (*sexually*) violar

**assemble** [ə'sɛmbl] vt reunir, juntar; (*Tech*) montar ▷ vi reunirse, juntarse

**assembly** [ə'sɛmblɪ] n reunión f, asamblea; (*parliament*) parlamento; (*construction*) montaje m

**assert** [əˈsəːt] vt afirmar; (authority) hacer valer; **assertion** [-ʃən] n afirmación f

**assess** [əˈses] vt valorar, calcular; (tax, damages) fijar; (for tax) gravar; **assessment** n valoración f; (for tax) gravamen m

**asset** [ˈæset] n ventaja; **assets** npl (Comm) activo; (property, funds) fondos mpl

**assign** [əˈsaɪn] vt: **to ~ (to)** (date) fijar (para); (task) asignar (a); (resources) destinar (a); **assignment** n tarea

**assist** [əˈsɪst] vt ayudar; **assistance** n ayuda, auxilio; **assistant** n ayudante mf; (BRIT: also: **shop assistant**) dependiente/a m/f

**associate** [adj, n əˈsəuʃɪɪt, vb əˈsəuʃɪeɪt] adj asociado ▷ n (at work) colega mf ▷ vt asociar; (ideas) relacionar ▷ vi: **to ~ with sb** tratar con algn

**association** [əsəusɪˈeɪʃən] n asociación f

**assorted** [əˈsɔːtɪd] adj surtido, variado

**assortment** [əˈsɔːtmənt] n (of shapes, colours) surtido; (of books) colección f; (of people) mezcla

**assume** [əˈsjuːm] vt suponer; (responsibilities) asumir; (attitude) adoptar, tomar

**assumption** [əˈsʌmpʃən] n suposición f, presunción f; (of power etc) toma

**assurance** [əˈʃuərəns] n garantía, promesa; (confidence) confianza, aplomo; (insurance) seguro

**assure** [əˈʃuə*] vt asegurar

**asterisk** [ˈæstərɪsk] n asterisco

**asthma** [ˈæsmə] n asma

**astonish** [əˈstɔnɪʃ] vt asombrar, pasmar; **astonished** adj estupefacto, pasmado; **to be astonished (at)** asombrarse (de); **astonishing** adj asombroso, pasmoso; I **find it astonishing that …** me asombra or pasma que …; **astonishment** n asombro, sorpresa

**astound** [əˈstaund] vt asombrar, pasmar

**astray** [əˈstreɪ] adv: **to go ~** extraviarse; **to lead ~** (morally) llevar por mal camino

**astrology** [æsˈtrɔlədʒɪ] n astrología

**astronaut** [ˈæstrənɔːt] n astronauta mf

**astronomer** [əsˈtrɔnəmə*] n astrónomo/a

**astronomical** [æstrəˈnɔmɪkəl] adj astronómico

**astronomy** [æsˈtrɔnəmɪ] n astronomía

**astute** [əsˈtjuːt] adj astuto

**asylum** [əˈsaɪləm] n (refuge) asilo; (mental hospital) manicomio

○ **KEYWORD**

**at** [æt] prep **1** (referring to position) en; (direction) a; **at the top** en lo alto; **at home/school** en casa/la escuela; **to look at sth/sb** mirar algo/a algn

**2** (referring to time): **at 4 o'clock** a las 4; **at night** por la noche; **at Christmas** en Navidad; **at times** a veces

**3** (referring to rates, speed etc): **at £1 a kilo** a una libra el kilo; **two at a time** de dos en dos; **at 50 km/h** a 50 km/h

**4** (referring to manner): **at a stroke** de un golpe; **at peace** en paz

**5** (referring to activity): **to be at work** estar trabajando; (in the office etc) estar en el trabajo; **to play at cowboys** jugar a los vaqueros; **to be good at sth** ser bueno en algo

**6** (referring to cause): **shocked/surprised/ annoyed at sth** asombrado/sorprendido/ fastidiado por algo; I **went at his suggestion** fui a instancias suyas

**7** (symbol) arroba

**ate** [eɪt] pt of **eat**

**atheist** [ˈeɪθɪɪst] n ateo/a

**Athens** [ˈæθɪnz] n Atenas

**athlete** [ˈæθliːt] n atleta mf

**athletic** [æθˈletɪk] adj atlético; **athletics** n atletismo

**Atlantic** [ətˈlæntɪk] adj atlántico ▷ n: **the ~ (Ocean)** el (Océano) Atlántico

**atlas** [ˈætləs] n atlas m inv

**A.T.M.** n abbr (= automated telling machine) cajero automático

**atmosphere** [ˈætməsfɪə*] n atmósfera; (of place) ambiente m

**atom** [ˈætəm] n átomo; **atomic** [əˈtɔmɪk] adj atómico; **atom(ic) bomb** n bomba atómica

**A to Z®** n (map) callejero

**atrocity** [əˈtrɔsɪtɪ] n atrocidad f

**attach** [əˈtætʃ] vt (fasten) atar; (join) unir, sujetar; (document, letter) adjuntar; (importance etc) dar, conceder; **to be ~ed to sb/sth** (to like) tener cariño a algn/algo; **attachment** n (tool) accesorio; (Comput) archivo, documento adjunto; (love): **attachment (to)** apego (a)

**attack** [əˈtæk] vt (Mil) atacar; (criminal) agredir, asaltar; (criticize) criticar; (task) emprender ▷ n ataque m, asalto; (on sb's life) atentado; (fig: criticism) crítica; (of illness) ataque m; **heart ~** infarto (de miocardio); **attacker** n agresor(a) m/f, asaltante mf

**attain** [əˈteɪn] vt (also: **~ to**) alcanzar; (achieve) lograr, conseguir

**attempt** [əˈtempt] n tentativa, intento; (attack) atentado ▷ vt intentar

**attend** [əˈtend] vt asistir a; (patient)

atender; **attend to** vt fus ocuparse de; (customer, patient) atender a; **attendance** n asistencia, presencia; (people present) concurrencia; **attendant** n ayudante mf; (in garage etc) encargado/a ▷ adj (dangers) concomitante

**attention** [ə'tɛnʃən] n atención f; (care) atenciones fpl ▷ excl (Mil) ¡firme(s)!; **for the ~ of ...** (Admin) atención ...

**attic** ['ætɪk] n desván m

**attitude** ['ætɪtjuːd] n actitud f; (disposition) disposición f

**attorney** [ə'təːnɪ] n (lawyer) abogado/a; **Attorney General** n (BRIT) ≈ Presidente m del Consejo del Poder Judicial (SP); (US) ≈ ministro de Justicia

**attract** [ə'trækt] vt atraer; (sb's attention) llamar; **attraction** [ə'trækʃən] n encanto; (gen pl: amusements) diversiones fpl; (Physics) atracción f; (fig: towards sb, sth) atractivo; **attractive** adj guapo; (interesting) atrayente

**attribute** [n 'ætrɪbjuːt, vb ə'trɪbjuːt] n atributo ▷ vt: **to ~ sth to** atribuir algo a

**aubergine** ['əubəʒiːn] (BRIT) n berenjena; (colour) morado

**auburn** ['ɔːbən] adj color castaño rojizo

**auction** ['ɔːkʃən] n (also: **sale by ~**) subasta ▷ vt subastar

**audible** ['ɔːdɪbl] adj audible, que se puede oír

**audience** ['ɔːdɪəns] n público; (Radio) radioescuchas mpl; (TV) telespectadores mpl; (interview) audiencia

**audit** ['ɔːdɪt] vt revisar, intervenir

**audition** [ɔː'dɪʃən] n audición f

**auditor** ['ɔːdɪtə*] n interventor(a) m/f, censor(a) m/f de cuentas

**auditorium** [ɔːdɪ'tɔːrɪəm] n auditorio

**Aug.** abbr (= August) ag

**August** ['ɔːgəst] n agosto

**aunt** [ɑːnt] n tía; **auntie** n diminutive of **aunt**; **aunty** n diminutive of **aunt**

**au pair** ['əu'pɛə*] n (also: **~ girl**) (chica) au pair f

**aura** ['ɔːrə] n aura; (atmosphere) ambiente m

**austerity** [ɔ'stɛrɪtɪ] n austeridad f

**Australia** [ɔs'treɪlɪə] n Australia; **Australian** adj, n australiano/a m/f

**Austria** ['ɒstrɪə] n Austria; **Austrian** adj, n austríaco/a m/f

**authentic** [ɔː'θɛntɪk] adj auténtico

**author** ['ɔːθə*] n autor(a) m/f

**authority** [ɔː'θɒrɪtɪ] n autoridad f; (official permission) autorización f; **the authorities** npl las autoridades

**authorize** ['ɔːθəraɪz] vt autorizar

**auto** ['ɔːtəu] (US) n coche m (SP), carro (LAM), automóvil m

**auto: autobiography** [ɔːtəbaɪ'ɒgrəfɪ] n autobiografía; **autograph** ['ɔːtəgrɑːf] n autógrafo ▷ vt (photo etc) dedicar; (programme) firmar; **automatic** [ɔːtə'mætɪk] adj automático ▷ n (gun) pistola automática; (car) coche m automático; **automatically** adv automáticamente; **automobile** ['ɔːtəməbiːl] (US) n coche m (SP), carro (LAM), automóvil m; **autonomous** [ɔː'tɒnəməs] adj autónomo; **autonomy** [ɔː'tɒnəmɪ] n autonomía

**autumn** ['ɔːtəm] n otoño

**auxiliary** [ɔːg'zɪlɪərɪ] adj, n auxiliar mf

**avail** [ə'veɪl] vt: **to ~ o.s. of** aprovechar(se) de ▷ n: **to no ~** en vano, sin resultado

**availability** [əveɪlə'bɪlɪtɪ] n disponibilidad f

**available** [ə'veɪləbl] adj disponible; (unoccupied) libre; (person: unattached) soltero y sin compromiso

**avalanche** ['ævəlɑːnʃ] n alud m, avalancha

**Ave.** abbr = **avenue**

**avenue** ['ævənjuː] n avenida; (fig) camino

**average** ['ævərɪdʒ] n promedio, término medio ▷ adj medio, de término medio; (ordinary) regular, corriente ▷ vt sacar un promedio de; **on ~** por regla general

**avert** [ə'vəːt] vt prevenir; (blow) desviar; (one's eyes) apartar

**avid** ['ævɪd] adj ávido

**avocado** [ævə'kɑːdəu] n (also BRIT: **~ pear**) aguacate m, palta (SC)

**avoid** [ə'vɔɪd] vt evitar, eludir

**await** [ə'weɪt] vt esperar, aguardar

**awake** [ə'weɪk] (pt **awoke**, pp **awoken** or **awaked**) adj despierto ▷ vt despertar ▷ vi despertarse; **to be ~** estar despierto

**award** [ə'wɔːd] n premio; (Law: damages) indemnización f ▷ vt otorgar, conceder; (Law: damages) adjudicar

**aware** [ə'wɛə*] adj: **~ (of)** consciente (de); **to become ~ (of/that)** (realize) darse cuenta de/de que; (learn) enterarse de/de que; **awareness** n conciencia; (knowledge) conocimiento

**away** [ə'weɪ] adv fuera; (movement): **she went ~** se marchó; **far ~** lejos; **two kilometres ~** a dos kilómetros de distancia; **two hours ~ by car** a dos horas en coche; **the holiday was two weeks ~** faltaban dos semanas para las vacaciones; **he's ~ for a week** estará ausente una semana; **to take ~ (from)** quitar (a); (subtract) substraer (de); **to work/pedal ~** seguir

trabajando/pedaleando; **to fade ~** (*colour*)
desvanecerse; (*sound*) apagarse
**awe** [ɔ:] *n* admiración *f* respetuosa;
**awesome** ['ɔ:səm] (*us*) *adj* (*excellent*)
formidable
**awful** ['ɔ:fəl] *adj* horroroso; (*quantity*): **an
~ lot (of)** cantidad (de); **awfully** *adv* (*very*)
terriblemente
**awkward** ['ɔ:kwəd] *adj* desmañado,
torpe; (*shape*) incómodo; (*embarrassing*)
delicado, difícil
**awoke** [ə'wəuk] *pt of* **awake**
**awoken** [ə'wəukən] *pp of* **awake**
**axe** [æks] (*us* **ax**) *n* hacha ▷ *vt* (*project*)
cortar; (*jobs*) reducir
**axle** ['æksl] *n* eje *m*, árbol *m*
**ay(e)** [aɪ] *excl* sí
**azalea** [ə'zeɪlɪə] *n* azalea

**B** [bi:] *n* (*Mus*) si *m*
**B.A.** *abbr* = **Bachelor of Arts**
**baby** ['beɪbɪ] *n* bebé *mf*; (*us: inf: darling*)
mi amor; **baby carriage** (*us*) *n* cochecito;
**baby-sit** *vi* hacer de canguro; **baby-sitter**
*n* canguro/a; **baby wipe** *n* toallita húmeda
(*para bebés*)
**bachelor** ['bætʃələ*] *n* soltero; **B~ of
Arts/Science** licenciado/a en Filosofía y
Letras/Ciencias
**back** [bæk] *n* (*of person*) espalda; (*of
animal*) lomo; (*of hand*) dorso; (*as opposed
to front*) parte *f* de atrás; (*of chair*) respaldo;
(*of page*) reverso; (*of book*) final *m*; (*Football*)
defensa *m*; (*of crowd*): **the ones at the ~**
los del fondo ▷ *vt* (*candidate: also: ~ **up**)
respaldar, apoyar; (*horse: at races*) apostar
a; (*car*) dar marcha atrás a *or* con ▷ *vi* (*car
etc*) ir (*or* salir *or* entrar) marcha atrás
▷ *adj* (*payment, rent*) atrasado; (*seats,
wheels*) de atrás ▷ *adv* (*not forward*) (hacia)
atrás; (*returned*): **he's ~** está de vuelta,
ha vuelto; **he ran ~** volvió corriendo;
(*restitution*): **throw the ball ~** devuelve la
pelota; **can I have it ~?** ¿me lo devuelve?;
(*again*): **he called ~** llamó de nuevo; **back
down** *vi* echarse atrás; **back out** *vi* (*of
promise*) volverse atrás; **back up** *vt* (*person*)
apoyar, respaldar; (*theory*) defender;
(*Comput*) hacer una copia preventiva
*or* de reserva; **backache** *n* dolor *m* de
espalda; **backbencher** (*BRIT*) *n* miembro del
parlamento sin cargo relevante; **backbone** *n*
columna vertebral; **back door** *n* puerta
*f* trasera; **backfire** *vi* (*Aut*) petardear;
(*plans*) fallar, salir mal; **backgammon** *n*
backgammon *m*; **background** *n* fondo; (*of
events*) antecedentes *mpl*; (*basic knowledge*)
bases *fpl*; (*experience*) conocimientos *mpl*,
educación *f*; **family background** origen *m*,
antecedentes *mpl*; **backing** *n* (*fig*) apoyo,

respaldo; **backlog** n: **backlog of work** trabajo atrasado; **backpack** n mochila; **backpacker** n mochilero/a; **backslash** n pleca, barra inversa; **backstage** adv entre bastidores; **backstroke** n espalda; **backup** adj suplementario; (Comput) de reserva ▷ n (support) apoyo; (also: **backup file**) copia preventiva or de reserva; **backward** adj (person, country) atrasado; **backwards** adv hacia atrás; (read a list) al revés; (fall) de espaldas; **backyard** n traspatio

**bacon** ['beɪkən] n tocino, beicon m

**bacteria** [bæk'tɪərɪə] npl bacterias fpl

**bad** [bæd] adj malo; (mistake, accident) grave; (food) podrido, pasado; **his ~ leg** su pierna lisiada; **to go ~** (food) pasarse

**badge** [bædʒ] n insignia; (policeman's) chapa, placa

**badger** ['bædʒə*] n tejón m

**badly** ['bædlɪ] adv mal; **to reflect ~ on sb** influir negativamente en la reputación de algn; **~ wounded** gravemente herido; **he needs it ~** le hace gran falta; **to be ~ off (for money)** andar mal de dinero

**bad-mannered** ['bæd'mænəd] adj mal educado

**badminton** ['bædmɪntən] n bádminton m

**bad-tempered** ['bæd'tempəd] adj de mal genio or carácter; (temporarily) de mal humor

**bag** [bæg] n bolsa; (handbag) bolso; (satchel) mochila; (case) maleta; **~s of** (inf) un montón de; **baggage** n equipaje m; **baggage allowance** n límite m de equipaje; **baggage reclaim** n recogida de equipajes; **baggy** adj amplio; **bagpipes** npl gaita

**bail** [beɪl] n fianza ▷ vt (prisoner: gen: **grant bail to**) poner en libertad bajo fianza; (boat: also: **~ out**) achicar; **on ~** (prisoner) bajo fianza; **to ~ sb out** obtener la libertad de algn bajo fianza

**bait** [beɪt] n cebo ▷ vt poner cebo en; (tease) tomar el pelo a

**bake** [beɪk] vt cocer (al horno) ▷ vi cocerse; **baked beans** npl judías fpl en salsa de tomate; **baked potato** n patata al horno; **baker** n panadero; **bakery** n panadería; (for cakes) pastelería; **baking** n (act) amasar m; (batch) hornada; **baking powder** n levadura (en polvo)

**balance** ['bæləns] n equilibrio; (Comm: sum) balance m; (remainder) resto; (scales) balanza ▷ vt equilibrar; (budget) nivelar; (account) saldar; (make equal) equilibrar; **~ of trade/payments** balanza de comercio/pagos; **balanced** adj (personality, diet) equilibrado; (report) objetivo; **balance sheet** n balance m

**balcony** ['bælkənɪ] n (open) balcón m; (closed) galería; (in theatre) anfiteatro

**bald** [bɔːld] adj calvo; (tyre) liso

**Balearics** [bælɪ'ærɪks] npl: **the ~** las Baleares

**ball** [bɔːl] n pelota; (football) balón m; (of wool, string) ovillo; (dance) baile m; **to play ~** (fig) cooperar

**ballerina** [bælə'riːnə] n bailarina

**ballet** ['bæleɪ] n ballet m; **ballet dancer** n bailarín/ina m/f

**balloon** [bə'luːn] n globo

**ballot** ['bælət] n votación f

**ballpoint (pen)** ['bɔːlpɔɪnt-] n bolígrafo

**ballroom** ['bɔːlrum] n salón m de baile

**Baltic** ['bɔːltɪk] n: **the ~ (Sea)** el (Mar) Báltico

**bamboo** [bæm'buː] n bambú m

**ban** [bæn] n prohibición f, proscripción f ▷ vt prohibir, proscribir

**banana** [bə'nɑːnə] n plátano, banana (LAM), banano (CAM)

**band** [bænd] n grupo; (strip) faja, tira; (stripe) lista; (Mus: jazz) orquesta; (: rock) grupo; (Mil) banda

**bandage** ['bændɪdʒ] n venda, vendaje m ▷ vt vendar

**Band-Aid®** ['bændeɪd] (US) n tirita

**bandit** ['bændɪt] n bandido

**bang** [bæŋ] n (of gun, exhaust) estallido, detonación f; (of door) portazo; (blow) golpe m ▷ vt (door) cerrar de golpe; (one's head) golpear ▷ vi estallar; (door) cerrar de golpe

**Bangladesh** [bɑːŋglə'deʃ] n Bangladesh m

**bangle** ['bæŋgl] n brazalete m, ajorca

**bangs** [bæŋz] (US) npl flequillo

**banish** ['bænɪʃ] vt desterrar

**banister(s)** ['bænɪstə(z)] n(pl) barandilla, pasamanos m inv

**banjo** ['bændʒəu] (pl **~es** or **~s**) n banjo

**bank** [bæŋk] n (Comm) banco; (of river, lake) ribera, orilla; (of earth) terraplén m ▷ vi (Aviat) ladearse; **bank on** vt fus contar con; **bank account** n cuenta de banco; **bank balance** n saldo; **bank card** n tarjeta bancaria; **bank charges** npl comisión fsg; **banker** n banquero; **bank holiday** n (BRIT) día m festivo or de fiesta; **banking** n banca; **bank manager** n director(a) m/f (de sucursal) de banco; **banknote** n billete m de banco

**BANK HOLIDAY**

El término **bank holiday** se aplica en el Reino Unido a todo día festivo oficial en el que cierran bancos y comercios.

- Los más importantes son en Navidad,
- Semana Santa, finales de mayo y
- finales de agosto y, al contrario que
- en los países de tradición católica, no
- coinciden necesariamente con una
- celebración religiosa.

**bankrupt** ['bæŋkrʌpt] adj quebrado, insolvente; **to go ~** hacer bancarrota; **to be ~** estar en quiebra; **bankruptcy** n quiebra
**bank statement** n balance m or detalle m de cuenta
**banner** ['bænə*] n pancarta
**bannister(s)** ['bænɪstə(z)] n(pl) = **banister(s)**
**banquet** ['bæŋkwɪt] n banquete m
**baptism** ['bæptɪzəm] n bautismo; (act) bautizo
**baptize** [bæp'taɪz] vt bautizar
**bar** [bɑ:*] n (pub) bar m; (counter) mostrador m; (rod) barra; (of window, cage) reja; (of soap) pastilla; (of chocolate) tableta; (fig: hindrance) obstáculo; (prohibition) proscripción f; (Mus) barra ▷ vt (road) obstruir; (person) excluir; (activity) prohibir; **the B~** (Law) la abogacía; **behind ~s** entre rejas; **~ none** sin excepción
**barbaric** [bɑ:'bærɪk] adj bárbaro
**barbecue** ['bɑ:bɪkju:] n barbacoa
**barbed wire** ['bɑ:bd-] n alambre m de púas
**barber** ['bɑ:bə*] n peluquero, barbero; **barber's (shop)** (US **barber (shop)**) n peluquería
**bar code** n código de barras
**bare** [bɛə*] adj desnudo; (trees) sin hojas; (necessities etc) básico ▷ vt desnudar; (teeth) enseñar; **barefoot** adj, adv descalzo; **barely** adv apenas
**bargain** ['bɑ:gɪn] n pacto, negocio; (good buy) ganga ▷ vi negociar; (haggle) regatear; **into the ~** además, por añadidura; **bargain for** vt fus: **he got more than he bargained for** le resultó peor de lo que esperaba
**barge** [bɑ:dʒ] n barcaza; **barge in** vi irrumpir; (interrupt: conversation) interrumpir
**bark** [bɑ:k] n (of tree) corteza; (of dog) ladrido ▷ vi ladrar
**barley** ['bɑ:lɪ] n cebada
**barmaid** ['bɑ:meɪd] n camarera
**barman** ['bɑ:mən] (irreg) n camarero, barman m
**barn** [bɑ:n] n granero
**barometer** [bə'rɒmɪtə*] n barómetro
**baron** ['bærən] n barón m; (press baron etc) magnate m; **baroness** n baronesa
**barracks** ['bærəks] npl cuartel m
**barrage** ['bærɑ:ʒ] n (Mil) descarga, bombardeo; (dam) presa; (of criticism) lluvia, aluvión m

**barrel** ['bærəl] n barril m; (of gun) cañón m
**barren** ['bærən] adj estéril
**barrette** [bə'rɛt] (US) n pasador m (LAM, SP), broche m (MEX)
**barricade** [bærɪ'keɪd] n barricada
**barrier** ['bærɪə*] n barrera
**barring** ['bɑ:rɪŋ] prep excepto, salvo
**barrister** ['bærɪstə*] (BRIT) n abogado/a
**barrow** ['bærəu] n (cart) carretilla (de mano)
**bartender** ['bɑ:tɛndə*] (US) n camarero, barman m
**base** [beɪs] n base f ▷ vt: **to ~ sth on** basar or fundar algo en ▷ adj bajo, infame
**baseball** ['beɪsbɔ:l] n béisbol m; **baseball cap** n gorra f de béisbol
**basement** ['beɪsmənt] n sótano
**bases¹** ['beɪsi:z] npl of **basis**
**bases²** ['beɪsɪz] npl of **base**
**bash** [bæʃ] (inf) vt golpear
**basic** ['beɪsɪk] adj básico; **basically** adv fundamentalmente, en el fondo; (simply) sencillamente; **basics** npl: **the basics** los fundamentos
**basil** ['bæzl] n albahaca
**basin** ['beɪsn] n cuenco, tazón m; (Geo) cuenca; (also: **wash~**) lavabo
**basis** ['beɪsɪs] (pl **bases**) n base f; **on a part-time/trial ~** a tiempo parcial/a prueba
**basket** ['bɑ:skɪt] n cesta, cesto; canasta; **basketball** n baloncesto
**bass** [beɪs] n (Mus: instrument) bajo; (double bass) contrabajo; (singer) bajo
**bastard** ['bɑ:stəd] n bastardo; (inf!) hijo de puta (!)
**bat** [bæt] n (Zool) murciélago; (for ball games) palo; (BRIT: for table tennis) pala ▷ vt: **he didn't ~ an eyelid** ni pestañeó
**batch** [bætʃ] n (of bread) hornada; (of letters etc) lote m
**bath** [bɑ:θ, pl bɑ:ðz] n (action) baño; (bathtub) bañera (SP), tina (LAM), bañadera (RPL) ▷ vt bañar; **to have a ~** bañarse, tomar un baño; see also **baths**
**bathe** [beɪð] vi bañarse ▷ vt (wound) lavar
**bathing** ['beɪðɪŋ] n el bañarse; **bathing costume** (US **bathing suit**) n traje m de baño
**bath: bathrobe** n (man's) batín m; (woman's) bata; **bathroom** n (cuarto de) baño; **baths** [bɑ:ðz] npl (also: **swimming baths**) piscina; **bath towel** n toalla de baño; **bathtub** n bañera
**baton** ['bætən] n (Mus) batuta; (Athletics) testigo; (weapon) porra

**batter** ['bætə*] vt maltratar; (rain etc) azotar ▷ n masa (para rebozar); **battered** adj (hat, pan) estropeado

**battery** ['bætərɪ] n (Aut) batería; (of torch) pila; **battery farming** n cría intensiva

**battle** ['bætl] n batalla; (fig) lucha ▷ vi luchar; **battlefield** n campo m de batalla

**bay** [beɪ] n (Geo) bahía; **B~ of Biscay** = mar Cantábrico; **to hold sb at ~** mantener a algn a raya

**bazaar** [bə'zɑ:*] n bazar m; (fete) venta con fines benéficos

**B. & B.** n abbr = **bed and breakfast**; (place) pensión f; (terms) cama y desayuno

**BBC** n abbr (= British Broadcasting Corporation) cadena de radio y televisión estatal británica

**B.C.** adv abbr (= before Christ) a. de C.

○ KEYWORD

**be** [bi:] (pt **was, were**, pp **been**) aux vb
1 (with present participle: forming continuous tenses): **what are you doing?** ¿qué estás haciendo?, ¿qué haces?; **they're coming tomorrow** vienen mañana; **I've been waiting for you for hours** llevo horas esperándote
2 (with pp: forming passives) ser (but often replaced by active or reflexive constructions); **to be murdered** ser asesinado; **the box had been opened** habían abierto la caja; **the thief was nowhere to be seen** no se veía al ladrón por ninguna parte
3 (in tag questions): **it was fun, wasn't it?** fue divertido, ¿no? or ¿verdad?; **he's good-looking, isn't he?** es guapo, ¿no te parece?; **she's back again, is she?** entonces, ¿ha vuelto?
4 (+to +infin): **the house is to be sold** (necessity) hay que vender la casa; (future) van a vender la casa; **he's not to open it** no tiene que abrirlo ▷ vb +complement
1 (with n or num complement, but see also 3, 4, 5 and impers vb below) ser; **he's a doctor** es médico; **2 and 2 are 4** 2 y 2 son 4
2 (with adj complement: expressing permanent or inherent quality) ser; (: expressing state seen as temporary or reversible) estar; **I'm English** soy inglés/esa; **she's tall/pretty** es alta/bonita; **he's young** es joven; **be careful/good/quiet** ten cuidado/pórtate bien/cállate; **I'm tired** estoy cansado/a; **it's dirty** está sucio/a
3 (of health) estar; **how are you?** ¿cómo estás?; **he's very ill** está muy enfermo; **I'm better now** ya estoy mejor
4 (of age) tener; **how old are you?** ¿cuántos

años tienes?; **I'm sixteen (years old)** tengo dieciséis años
5 (cost) costar; ser; **how much was the meal?** ¿cuánto fue or costó la comida?; **that'll be £5.75, please** son £5.75, por favor; **this shirt is £17** esta camisa cuesta £17 ▷ vi 1 (exist, occur etc) existir, haber; **the best singer that ever was** el mejor cantante que existió jamás; **is there a God?** ¿hay un Dios?, ¿existe Dios?; **be that as it may** sea como sea; **so be it** así sea
2 (referring to place) estar; **I won't be here tomorrow** no estaré aquí mañana
3 (referring to movement): **where have you been?** ¿dónde has estado?
▷ impers vb 1 (referring to time): **it's 5 o'clock** son las 5; **it's the 28th of April** estamos a 28 de abril
2 (referring to distance): **it's 10 km to the village** el pueblo está a 10 km
3 (referring to the weather): **it's too hot/cold** hace demasiado calor/frío; **it's windy today** hace viento hoy
4 (emphatic): **it's me** soy yo; **it was Maria who paid the bill** fue María la que pagó la cuenta

**beach** [bi:tʃ] n playa ▷ vt varar

**beacon** ['bi:kən] n (lighthouse) faro; (marker) guía

**bead** [bi:d] n cuenta; (of sweat etc) gota; **beads** npl (necklace) collar m

**beak** [bi:k] n pico

**beam** [bi:m] n (Arch) viga, travesaño; (of light) rayo, haz m de luz ▷ vi brillar; (smile) sonreír

**bean** [bi:n] n judía; **runner/broad ~** habichuela/haba; **coffee ~** grano de café; **beansprouts** npl brotes mpl de soja

**bear** [beə*] (pt **bore**, pp **borne**) n oso ▷ vt (weight etc) llevar; (cost) pagar; (responsibility) tener; (endure) soportar, aguantar; (children) parir, tener; (fruit) dar ▷ vi: **to ~ right/left** torcer a la derecha/izquierda

**beard** [bɪəd] n barba

**bearer** ['bεərə*] n portador(a) m/f

**bearing** ['bεərɪŋ] n porte m, comportamiento; (connection) relación f

**beast** [bi:st] n bestia; (inf) bruto, salvaje m

**beat** [bi:t] (pt **~**, pp **beaten**) n (of heart) latido; (Mus) ritmo, compás m; (of policeman) ronda ▷ vt pegar, golpear; (eggs) batir; (defeat: opponent) vencer, derrotar; (: record) sobrepasar ▷ vi (heart) latir; (drum) redoblar; (rain, wind) azotar; **off the ~en track** aislado; **to ~ it** (inf) largarse; **beat up** vt (attack) dar una paliza a; **beating** n paliza

**beautiful** ['bju:tɪful] adj precioso,

hermoso, bello; **beautifully** adv
maravillosamente

**beauty** ['bju:tɪ] n belleza; **beauty parlour**
(US **beauty parlor**) n salón m de belleza;
**beauty salon** n salón m de belleza; **beauty
spot** n (Tourism) lugar m pintoresco

**beaver** ['bi:və*] n castor m

**became** [bɪ'keɪm] pt of **become**

**because** [bɪ'kɒz] conj porque; **~ of** debido
a, a causa de

**beckon** ['bɛkən] vt (also: **~ to**) llamar con
señas

**become** (pt **became**, pp **~**)
vt (suit) favorecer, sentar bien a ▷ vi (+
n) hacerse, llegar a ser; (+ adj) ponerse,
volverse; **to ~ fat** engordar

**bed** [bɛd] n cama; (of flowers) macizo; (of
coal, clay) capa; (of river) lecho; (of sea) fondo;
**to go to ~** acostarse; **bed and breakfast** n
(place) pensión f; (terms) cama y desayuno;
**bedclothes** npl ropa de cama; **bedding**
n ropa de cama; **bed linen** n (BRIT) ropa f
de cama

● BED AND BREAKFAST
●
● Se llama **bed and breakfast** a una forma
● de alojamiento, en el campo o la ciudad,
● que ofrece cama y desayuno a precios
● inferiores a los de un hotel. El servicio
● se suele anunciar con carteles en los
● que a menudo se usa únicamente la
● abreviatura **B. & B.**

**bed: bedroom** n dormitorio; **bedside** n: **at
the bedside of** a la cabecera de; **bedside
lamp** n lámpara de noche; **bedside
table** n mesilla de noche; **bedsit(ter)**
(BRIT) n cuarto de alquiler; **bedspread** n
cubrecama m, colcha; **bedtime** n hora de
acostarse

**bee** [bi:] n abeja

**beech** [bi:tʃ] n haya

**beef** [bi:f] n carne f de vaca; **roast ~** rosbif
m; **beefburger** n hamburguesa; **Beefeater**
n alabardero de la Torre de Londres

**been** [bi:n] pp of **be**

**beer** [bɪə*] n cerveza; **beer garden** n
(BRIT) terraza f de verano, jardín m (de un
bar)

**beet** [bi:t] (US) n (also: **red ~**) remolacha

**beetle** ['bi:tl] n escarabajo

**beetroot** ['bi:tru:t] (BRIT) n remolacha

**before** [bɪ'fɔ:*] prep (of time) antes de;
(of space) delante de ▷ conj antes (de)
que ▷ adv antes, anteriormente; delante,
adelante; **~ going** antes de marcharse; **~
she goes** antes de que se vaya; **the week**

**~ la semana anterior; I've never seen it ~**
no lo he visto nunca; **beforehand** adv de
antemano, con anticipación

**beg** [bɛg] vi pedir limosna ▷ vt pedir,
rogar; (entreat) suplicar; **to ~ sb to do sth**
rogar a algn que haga algo; see also **pardon**

**began** [bɪ'gæn] pt of **begin**

**beggar** ['bɛgə*] n mendigo/a

**begin** [bɪ'gɪn] (pt **began**, pp **begun**) vt,
vi empezar, comenzar; **to ~ doing** or **to
do sth** empezar a hacer algo; **beginner** n
principiante mf; **beginning** n principio,
comienzo

**begun** [bɪ'gʌn] pp of **begin**

**behalf** [bɪ'hɑ:f] n: **on ~ of** en nombre
de, por; (for benefit of) en beneficio de; **on
my/his ~** por mí/él

**behave** [bɪ'heɪv] vi (person) portarse,
comportarse; (well: also: **~ o.s.**) portarse
bien; **behaviour** (US **behavior**) n
comportamiento, conducta

**behind** [bɪ'haɪnd] prep detrás de;
(supporting): **to be ~ sb** apoyar a algn ▷ adv
detrás, por detrás, atrás ▷ n trasero; **to be
~ (schedule)** ir retrasado; **~ the scenes** (fig)
entre bastidores

**beige** [beɪʒ] adj color beige

**Beijing** ['beɪ'dʒɪŋ] n Pekín m

**being** ['bi:ɪŋ] n ser m; (existence): **in ~**
existente; **to come into ~** aparecer

**belated** [bɪ'leɪtɪd] adj atrasado, tardío

**belch** [bɛltʃ] vi eructar ▷ vt (gen: belch
out: smoke etc) arrojar

**Belgian** ['bɛldʒən] adj, n belga mf

**Belgium** ['bɛldʒəm] n Bélgica

**belief** [bɪ'li:f] n opinión f; (faith) fe f

**believe** [bɪ'li:v] vt, vi creer; **to ~ in** creer
en; **believer** n partidario/a; (Rel) creyente
mf, fiel mf

**bell** [bɛl] n campana; (small) campanilla;
(on door) timbre m

**bellboy** ['bɛlbɔɪ] (BRIT) n botones m inv

**bellhop** ['bɛlhɒp] (US) n = **bellboy**

**bellow** ['bɛləʊ] vi bramar; (person) rugir

**bell pepper** n (esp US) pimiento, pimentón
m (LAM)

**belly** ['bɛlɪ] n barriga, panza; **belly button**
(inf) n ombligo

**belong** [bɪ'lɒŋ] vi: **to ~ to** pertenecer a;
(club etc) ser socio de; **this book ~s here** este
libro va aquí; **belongings** npl pertenencias
fpl

**beloved** [bɪ'lʌvɪd] adj querido/a

**below** [bɪ'ləʊ] prep bajo, debajo de; (less
than) inferior a ▷ adv abajo, (por) debajo;
**see ~** véase más abajo

**belt** [bɛlt] n cinturón m; (Tech) correa, cinta
▷ vt (thrash) pegar con correa; **beltway** (US)

*n (Aut)* carretera de circunvalación

**bemused** [bɪ'mjuːzd] *adj* perplejo

**bench** [bɛntʃ] *n* banco; (*BRIT Pol*): **the Government/Opposition ~es** (los asientos de) los miembros del Gobierno/ de la Oposición; **the B~** (*Law: judges*) magistratura

**bend** [bɛnd] (*pt, pp* **bent**) *vt* doblar ▷ *vi* inclinarse ▷ *n* (*BRIT: in road, river*) curva; (*in pipe*) codo; **bend down** *vi* inclinarse, doblarse; **bend over** *vi* inclinarse

**beneath** [bɪ'niːθ] *prep* bajo, debajo de; (*unworthy*) indigno de ▷ *adv* abajo, (por) debajo

**beneficial** [bɛnɪ'fɪʃəl] *adj* beneficioso

**benefit** ['bɛnɪfɪt] *n* beneficio; (*allowance of money*) subsidio ▷ *vt* beneficiar ▷ *vi*: **he'll ~ from it** le sacará provecho

**benign** [bɪ'naɪn] *adj* benigno; (*smile*) afable

**bent** [bɛnt] *pt, pp* of **bend** ▷ *n* inclinación *f* ▷ *adj*: **to be ~ on** estar empeñado en

**bereaved** [bɪ'riːvd] *npl*: **the ~** los íntimos de una persona afligidos por su muerte

**beret** ['bɛreɪ] *n* boina

**Berlin** [bəː'lɪn] *n* Berlín

**Bermuda** [bəː'mjuːdə] *n* las Bermudas

**berry** ['bɛrɪ] *n* baya

**berth** [bəːθ] *n* (*bed*) litera; (*cabin*) camarote *m*; (*for ship*) amarradero ▷ *vi* atracar, amarrar

**beside** [bɪ'saɪd] *prep* junto a, al lado de; **to be ~ o.s. with anger** estar fuera de sí; **that's ~ the point** eso no tiene nada que ver; **besides** *adv* además ▷ *prep* además de

**best** [bɛst] *adj* (el/la) mejor ▷ *adv* (lo) mejor; **the ~ part of** (*quantity*) la mayor parte de; **at ~** en el mejor de los casos; **to make the ~ of sth** sacar el mejor partido de algo; **to do one's ~** hacer todo lo posible; **to the ~ of my knowledge** que yo sepa; **to the ~ of my ability** como mejor puedo; **best-before date** *n* fecha de consumo preferente; **best man** (*irreg*) *n* padrino de boda; **bestseller** *n* éxito de librería, bestseller *m*

**bet** [bɛt] (*pt, pp* ~ *or* **~ted**) *n* apuesta ▷ *vt*: **to ~ money on** apostar dinero por ▷ *vi* apostar; **to ~ sb sth** apostar algo a algn

**betray** [bɪ'treɪ] *vt* traicionar; (*trust*) faltar a

**better** ['bɛtə*] *adj, adv* mejor ▷ *vt* superar ▷ *n*: **to get the ~ of sb** quedar por encima de algn; **you had ~ do it** más vale que lo hagas; **he thought ~ of it** cambió de parecer; **to get ~** (*Med*) mejorar(se)

**betting** ['bɛtɪŋ] *n* juego, el apostar; **betting shop** (*BRIT*) *n* agencia de apuestas

**between** [bɪ'twiːn] *prep* entre ▷ *adv*

(*time*) mientras tanto; (*place*) en medio

**beverage** ['bɛvərɪdʒ] *n* bebida

**beware** [bɪ'wɛə*] *vi*: **to ~ (of)** tener cuidado (con); **"~ of the dog"** "perro peligroso"

**bewildered** [bɪ'wɪldəd] *adj* aturdido, perplejo

**beyond** [bɪ'jɔnd] *prep* más allá de; (*past: understanding*) fuera de; (*after: date*) después de, más allá de; (*above*) superior a ▷ *adv* (*in space*) más allá; (*in time*) posteriormente; **~ doubt** fuera de toda duda; **~ repair** irreparable

**bias** ['baɪəs] *n* (*prejudice*) prejuicio, pasión *f*; (*preference*) predisposición *f*; **bias(s)ed** *adj* parcial

**bib** [bɪb] *n* babero

**Bible** ['baɪbl] *n* Biblia

**bicarbonate of soda** [baɪ'kɑːbənɪt-] *n* bicarbonato sódico

**biceps** ['baɪsɛps] *n* bíceps *m*

**bicycle** ['baɪsɪkl] *n* bicicleta; **bicycle pump** *n* bomba de bicicleta

**bid** [bɪd] (*pt* **bade** *or* ~, *pp* **bidden** *or* ~) *n* oferta, postura; (*in tender*) licitación *f*; (*attempt*) tentativa, conato ▷ *vi* hacer una oferta ▷ *vt* (*offer*) ofrecer; **to ~ sb good day** dar a algn los buenos días; **bidder** *n*: **the highest bidder** el mejor postor

**bidet** ['biːdeɪ] *n* bidet *m*

**big** [bɪg] *adj* grande; (*brother, sister*) mayor; **bigheaded** *adj* engreído; **big toe** *n* dedo gordo (del pie)

**bike** [baɪk] *n* bici *f*; **bike lane** *n* carril-bici *m*

**bikini** [bɪ'kiːnɪ] *n* bikini *m*

**bilateral** [baɪ'lætərl] *adj* (*agreement*) bilateral

**bilingual** [baɪ'lɪŋgwəl] *adj* bilingüe

**bill** [bɪl] *n* cuenta; (*invoice*) factura; (*Pol*) proyecto de ley; (*US: banknote*) billete *m*; (*of bird*) pico; (*of show*) programa *m*; **"post no ~s"** "prohibido fijar carteles"; **to fit** *or* **fill the ~** (*fig*) cumplir con los requisitos; **billboard** (*US*) *n* cartelera; **billfold** ['bɪlfəʊld] (*US*) *n* cartera

**billiards** ['bɪljədz] *n* billar *m*

**billion** ['bɪljən] *n* (*BRIT*) billón *m* (*millón de millones*); (*US*) mil millones *mpl*

**bin** [bɪn] *n* (*for rubbish*) cubo *or* bote *m* (*MEX*) *or* tacho (*SC*) de la basura; (*container*) recipiente *m*

**bind** [baɪnd] (*pt, pp* **bound**) *vt* atar; (*book*) encuadernar; (*oblige*) obligar ▷ *n* (*inf: nuisance*) lata

**binge** [bɪndʒ] (*inf*) *n*: **to go on a ~** ir de juerga

**bingo** ['bɪŋgəʊ] *n* bingo *m*

**binoculars** [bɪˈnɔkjuləz] npl prismáticos mpl

**bio...** [baɪə*] prefix: **biochemistry** n bioquímica; **biodegradable** [baɪə udrˈɡreɪdəbl] adj biodegradable; **biography** [baɪˈɔɡrəfɪ] n biografía; **biological** adj biológico; **biology** [baɪˈɔlədʒɪ] n biología; **biometric** [baɪəˈmɛtrɪk] adj biométrico

**birch** [bəːtʃ] n (tree) abedul m

**bird** [bəːd] n ave f, pájaro; (BRIT: inf: girl) chica; **bird flu** n gripe f aviar; **bird of prey** n ave f de presa; **birdwatching** n: **he likes to go birdwatching on Sundays** los domingos le gusta ir a ver pájaros

**Biro®** [ˈbaɪrəu] n boli

**birth** [bəːθ] n nacimiento; **to give ~ to** parir, dar a luz; **birth certificate** n partida de nacimiento; **birth control** n (policy) control m de natalidad; (methods) métodos mpl anticonceptivos; **birthday** n cumpleaños m inv ▷ cpd (cake, card etc) de cumpleaños; **birthmark** n antojo, marca de nacimiento; **birthplace** n lugar m de nacimiento

**biscuit** [ˈbɪskɪt] (BRIT) n galleta

**bishop** [ˈbɪʃəp] n obispo; (Chess) alfil m

**bistro** [ˈbiːstrəu] n café-bar m

**bit** [bɪt] pt of **bite** ▷ n trozo, pedazo, pedacito; (Comput) bit m, bitio; (for horse) freno, bocado; **a ~ of** un poco de; **a ~ mad** un poco loco; **~ by ~** poco a poco

**bitch** [bɪtʃ] n perra; (inf!: woman) zorra (!)

**bite** [baɪt] (pt **bit**, pp **bitten**) vt, vi morder; (insect etc) picar ▷ n (insect bite) picadura; (mouthful) bocado; **to ~ one's nails** comerse las uñas; **let's have a ~ (to eat)** (inf) vamos a comer algo

**bitten** [ˈbɪtn] pp of **bite**

**bitter** [ˈbɪtə*] adj amargo; (wind) cortante, penetrante; (battle) encarnizado ▷ n (BRIT: beer) cerveza típica británica a base de lúpulos

**bizarre** [bɪˈzɑː*] adj raro, extraño

**black** [blæk] adj negro; (tea, coffee) solo ▷ n color m negro; (person): **B~** negro/a ▷ vt (BRIT Industry) boicotear; **to give sb a ~ eye** ponerle a algn el ojo morado; **~ and blue** (bruised) amoratado; **to be in the ~** (bank account) estar en números negros; **black out** vi (faint) desmayarse; **blackberry** n zarzamora; **blackbird** n mirlo; **blackboard** n pizarra; **black coffee** n café m solo; **blackcurrant** n grosella negra; **black ice** n hielo invisible en la carretera; **blackmail** n chantaje m ▷ vt chantajear; **black market** n mercado negro; **blackout** n (Mil) oscurecimiento; (power cut) apagón

m; (TV, Radio) interrupción f de programas; (fainting) desvanecimiento; **black pepper** n pimienta f negra; **black pudding** n morcilla; **Black Sea** n: **the Black Sea** el Mar Negro

**bladder** [ˈblædə*] n vejiga

**blade** [bleɪd] n hoja; (of propeller) paleta; **a ~ of grass** una brizna de hierba

**blame** [bleɪm] n culpa ▷ vt: **to ~ sb for sth** echar a algn la culpa de algo; **to be to ~ (for)** tener la culpa (de)

**bland** [blænd] adj (music, taste) soso

**blank** [blæŋk] adj en blanco; (look) sin expresión ▷ n (of memory): **my mind is a ~** no puedo recordar nada; (on form) blanco, espacio en blanco; (cartridge) cartucho sin bala or de fogueo

**blanket** [ˈblæŋkɪt] n manta (sp), cobija (LAM); (of snow) capa; (of fog) manto

**blast** [blɑːst] n (of wind) ráfaga, soplo; (of explosive) explosión f ▷ vt (blow up) volar

**blatant** [ˈbleɪtənt] adj descarado

**blaze** [bleɪz] n (fire) fuego; (fig: of colour) despliegue m; (: of glory) esplendor m ▷ vi arder en llamas; (fig) brillar ▷ vt: **to ~ a trail** (fig) abrir (un) camino; **in a ~ of publicity** con gran publicidad

**blazer** [ˈbleɪzə*] n chaqueta de uniforme de colegial o de socio de club

**bleach** [bliːtʃ] n (also: **household ~**) lejía ▷ vt blanquear; **bleachers** (US) npl (Sport) gradas fpl al sol

**bleak** [bliːk] adj (countryside) desierto; (prospect) poco prometedor(a); (weather) crudo; (smile) triste

**bled** [blɛd] pt, pp of **bleed**

**bleed** [bliːd] (pt, pp **bled**) vt, vi sangrar; **my nose is ~ing** me está sangrando la nariz

**blemish** [ˈblɛmɪʃ] n marca, mancha; (on reputation) tacha

**blend** [blɛnd] n mezcla ▷ vt mezclar; (colours etc) combinar, mezclar ▷ vi (colours etc: also: **~ in**) combinarse, mezclarse; **blender** n (Culin) batidora

**bless** [blɛs] (pt, pp **~ed** or **blest**) vt bendecir; **~ you!** (after sneeze) ¡Jesús!; **blessing** n (approval) aprobación f; (godsend) don m del cielo, bendición f; (advantage) beneficio, ventaja

**blew** [bluː] pt of **blow**

**blight** [blaɪt] vt (hopes etc) frustrar, arruinar

**blind** [blaɪnd] adj ciego; (fig): **~ (to)** ciego (a) ▷ n (for window) persiana ▷ vt cegar; (dazzle) deslumbrar; (deceive): **to ~ sb to ...** cegar a algn a ...; **the blind** npl los ciegos; **blind alley** n callejón m sin salida; **blindfold** n venda ▷ adv con los ojos

vendados ▷ vt vendar los ojos a
**blink** [blɪŋk] vi parpadear, pestañear;
(light) oscilar
**bliss** [blɪs] n felicidad f
**blister** ['blɪstə*] n ampolla ▷ vi (paint)
ampollarse
**blizzard** ['blɪzəd] n ventisca
**bloated** ['bləʊtɪd] adj hinchado;
(person: full) ahíto
**blob** [blɔb] n (drop) gota; (indistinct object)
bulto
**block** [blɔk] n bloque m; (in pipes)
obstáculo; (of buildings) manzana (sp),
cuadra (lam) ▷ vt obstruir, cerrar; (progress)
estorbar; **~ of flats** (brit) bloque m de pisos;
**mental ~** bloqueo mental; **block up** vt
tapar, obstruir; (pipe) atascar; **blockade**
[-'keɪd] n bloqueo ▷ vt bloquear; **blockage**
n estorbo, obstrucción f; **blockbuster** n
(book) bestseller m; (film) éxito de público;
**block capitals** npl mayúsculas fpl; **block
letters** npl mayúsculas fpl
**blog** [blɔg] n blog m
**bloke** [bləʊk] (brit: inf) n tipo, tío
**blond(e)** [blɔnd] adj, n rubio/a m/f
**blood** [blʌd] n sangre f; **blood donor**
n donante mf de sangre; **blood group**
n grupo sanguíneo; **blood poisoning**
n envenenamiento de la sangre; **blood
pressure** n presión f sanguínea;
**bloodshed** n derramamiento de sangre;
**bloodshot** adj inyectado en sangre;
**bloodstream** n corriente f sanguínea;
**blood test** n análisis m inv de sangre;
**blood transfusion** n transfusión f de
sangre; **blood type** n grupo sanguíneo;
**blood vessel** n vaso sanguíneo; **bloody**
adj sangriento; (nose etc) lleno de sangre;
(brit: inf!) **this bloody ...** este condenado o
puñetero ... (!) ▷ adv: **bloody strong/good**
(brit: inf!) terriblemente fuerte/bueno
**bloom** [bluːm] n flor f ▷ vi florecer
**blossom** ['blɔsəm] n flor f ▷ vi florecer
**blot** [blɔt] n borrón m; (fig) mancha ▷ vt
(stain) manchar
**blouse** [blaʊz] n blusa
**blow** [bləʊ] (pt **blew**, pp **blown**) n golpe
m; (with sword) espadazo ▷ vi soplar; (dust,
sand etc) volar; (fuse) fundirse ▷ vt (wind)
llevarse; (fuse) quemar; (instrument) tocar;
**to ~ one's nose** sonarse; **blow away** vt
llevarse, arrancar; **blow out** vi apagarse;
**blow up** vi estallar ▷ vt volar; (tyre) inflar;
(Phot) ampliar; **blow-dry** n moldeado (con
secador)
**blown** [bləʊn] pp of **blow**
**blue** [bluː] adj azul; (depressed) deprimido;
**~ film/joke** película/chiste m verde;

**out of the ~** (fig) de repente; **bluebell** n
campanilla, campánula azul; **blueberry**
n arándano; **blue cheese** n queso azul;
**blues** npl: **the blues** (Mus) el blues; **to have
the blues** estar triste; **bluetit** n herrerillo
m (común)
**bluff** [blʌf] vi tirarse un farol, farolear ▷ n
farol m; **to call sb's ~** coger a algn la palabra
**blunder** ['blʌndə*] n patinazo, metedura
de pata ▷ vi cometer un error, meter la pata
**blunt** [blʌnt] adj (pencil) despuntado;
(knife) desafilado, romo; (person) franco,
directo
**blur** [bləː*] n (shape): **to become a ~**
hacerse borroso ▷ vt (vision) enturbiar;
(distinction) borrar; **blurred** adj borroso
**blush** [blʌʃ] vi ruborizarse, ponerse
colorado ▷ n rubor m; **blusher** n colorete
m

**board** [bɔːd] n (cardboard) cartón m;
(wooden) tabla, tablero; (on wall) tablón
m; (for chess etc) tablero; (committee)
junta, consejo; (in firm) mesa or junta
directiva; (Naut, Aviat): **on ~** a bordo ▷ vt
(ship) embarcarse en; (train) subir a; **full
~** (brit) pensión completa; **half ~** (brit)
media pensión; **to go by the ~** (fig) ser
abandonado or olvidado; **board game** n
juego de tablero; **boarding card** (brit) n
tarjeta de embarque; **boarding pass** (us)
n = **boarding card**; **boarding school** n
internado; **board room** n sala de juntas
**boast** [bəʊst] vi: **to ~ (about** or **of)** alardear
(de)
**boat** [bəʊt] n barco, buque m; (small)
barca, bote m
**bob** [bɔb] vi (also: **~ up and down**)
menearse, balancearse
**bobby pin** ['bɔbɪ-] (us) n horquilla
**body** ['bɔdɪ] n cuerpo; (corpse) cadáver m;
(of car) caja, carrocería; (fig: group) grupo;
(: organization) organismo; **body-building** n
culturismo; **bodyguard** n guardaespaldas
m inv; **bodywork** n carrocería
**bog** [bɔg] n pantano, ciénaga ▷ vt: **to get
~ged down** (fig) empantanarse, atascarse
**bogus** ['bəʊgəs] adj falso, fraudulento
**boil** [bɔɪl] vt (water) hervir; (eggs) pasar
por agua, cocer ▷ vi hervir; (fig: with anger)
estar furioso; (: with heat) asfixiarse ▷ n
(Med) furúnculo, divieso; **to come to the
~, to come to a ~** (us) comenzar a hervir;
**to ~ down to** (fig) reducirse a; **boil over** vi
salirse, rebosar; (anger etc) llegar al colmo;
**boiled egg** n (soft) huevo tibio (mex) or
pasado por agua or a la copa (sc); (hard)
huevo duro; **boiled potatoes** npl patatas
fpl (sp) or papas fpl (lam) cocidas; **boiler** n

caldera; **boiling** ['bɔɪlɪŋ] adj: **I'm boiling (hot)** (inf) estoy asado; **boiling point** n punto de ebullición

**bold** [bəuld] adj valiente, audaz; (pej) descarado; (colour) llamativo

**Bolivia** [bə'lɪvɪə] n Bolivia; **Bolivian** adj, n boliviano/a m/f

**bollard** ['bɔləd] (BRIT) n (Aut) poste m

**bolt** [bəult] n (lock) cerrojo; (with nut) perno, tornillo ▷ adv: **upright** rígido, erguido ▷ vt (door) echar el cerrojo a; (also: **~ together**) sujetar con tornillos; (food) engullir ▷ vi fugarse; (horse) desbocarse

**bomb** [bɔm] n bomba ▷ vt bombardear; **bombard** [bɔm'baːd] vt bombardear; (fig) asediar; **bomber** n (Aviat) bombardero; **bomb scare** n amenaza de bomba

**bond** [bɔnd] n (promise) fianza; (Finance) bono; (link) vínculo, lazo; (Comm): **in ~** en depósito bajo fianza; **bonds** npl (chains) cadenas fpl

**bone** [bəun] n hueso; (of fish) espina ▷ vt deshuesar; quitar las espinas a

**bonfire** ['bɔnfaɪə*] n hoguera, fogata

**bonnet** ['bɔnɪt] n gorra; (BRIT: of car) capó m

**bonus** ['bəunəs] n (payment) paga extraordinaria, plus m; (fig) bendición f

**boo** [buː] excl ¡uh! ▷ vt abuchear, rechiflar

**book** [buk] n libro; (of tickets) taco; (of stamps etc) librito ▷ vt (ticket) sacar; (seat, room) reservar; **books** npl (Comm) cuentas fpl, contabilidad f; **book in** vi (at hotel) registrarse; **book up** vt: **to be booked up** (hotel) estar completo; **bookcase** n librería, estante m para libros; **booking** n reserva; **booking office** n (BRIT Rail) despacho de billetes (SP) or boletos (LAM); (Theatre) taquilla (SP), boletería (LAM); **book-keeping** n contabilidad f; **booklet** n folleto; **bookmaker** n corredor m de apuestas; **bookmark** n (also Comput) marcador; **bookseller** n librero; **bookshelf** n estante m (para libros); **bookshop, book store** n librería

**boom** [buːm] n (noise) trueno, estampido; (in prices etc) alza rápida; (Econ, in population) boom m ▷ vi (cannon) hacer gran estruendo, retumbar; (Econ) estar en alza

**boost** [buːst] n estímulo, empuje m ▷ vt estimular, empujar

**boot** [buːt] n bota; (BRIT: of car) maleta, maletero ▷ vt (Comput) arrancar; **to ~** (in addition) además, por añadidura

**booth** [buːð] n (telephone booth, voting booth) cabina

**booze** [buːz] (inf) n bebida

**border** ['bɔːdə*] n borde m, margen m; (of a country) frontera; (for flowers) arriate m ▷ vt (road) bordear; (another country: also: **~ on**) lindar con; **borderline** n: **on the borderline** en el límite

**bore** [bɔː*] pt of **bear** ▷ vt (hole) hacer un agujero en; (well) perforar; (person) aburrir ▷ n (person) pelmazo, pesado; (of gun) calibre m; **bored** adj aburrido; **he's bored to tears** or **to death** or **stiff** está aburrido como una ostra, está muerto de aburrimiento; **boredom** n aburrimiento

**boring** ['bɔːrɪŋ] adj aburrido

**born** [bɔːn] adj: **to be ~** nacer; **I was ~ in 1960** nací en 1960

**borne** [bɔːn] pp of **bear**

**borough** ['bʌrə] n municipio

**borrow** ['bɔrəu] vt: **to ~ sth (from sb)** tomar algo prestado (a algn)

**Bosnia(-Herzegovina)** ['bɔːsnɪə(hɜrzə'gəuviːnə)] n Bosnia(-Herzegovina); **Bosnian** ['bɔznɪən] adj, n bosnio/a

**bosom** ['buzəm] n pecho

**boss** [bɔs] n jefe m ▷ vt (also: **~ about or around**) mangonear; **bossy** adj mandón/ona

**both** [bəuθ] adj, pron ambos/as, los dos(las dos); **~ of us went, we ~ went** fuimos los dos, ambos fuimos ▷ adv: **~ A and B** tanto A como B

**bother** ['bɔðə*] vt (worry) preocupar; (disturb) molestar, fastidiar ▷ vi (also: **~ o.s.**) molestarse ▷ n (trouble) dificultad f; (nuisance) molestia, lata; **to ~ doing** tomarse la molestia de hacer

**bottle** ['bɔtl] n botella; (small) frasco; (baby's) biberón m ▷ vt embotellar; **bottle bank** n contenedor de vidrio; **bottle-opener** n abrebotellas m inv

**bottom** ['bɔtəm] n (of box, sea) fondo; (buttocks) trasero, culo; (of page) pie m; (of list) final m; (of class) último/a ▷ adj (lowest) más bajo; (last) último

**bought** [bɔːt] pt, pp of **buy**

**boulder** ['bəuldə*] n canto rodado

**bounce** [bauns] vi (ball) (re)botar; (cheque) ser rechazado ▷ vt hacer (re)botar ▷ n (rebound) (re)bote m; **bouncer** (inf) n gorila m (que echa a los alborotadores de un bar, club etc)

**bound** [baund] pt, pp of **bind** ▷ n (leap) salto; (gen pl: limit) límite m ▷ vi (leap) saltar ▷ vt (border) rodear ▷ adj: **~ by** rodeado de; **to be ~ to do sth** (obliged) tener el deber de hacer algo; **he's ~ to come** es seguro que vendrá; **out of ~s** prohibido el paso; **~ for** con destino a

**boundary** ['baundrɪ] n límite m

**bouquet** ['bukeɪ] n (of flowers) ramo
**bourbon** ['buəbən] (us) n (also: **~ whiskey**) whisky m americano, bourbon m
**bout** [baut] n (of malaria etc) ataque m; (of activity) período; (Boxing etc) combate m, encuentro
**boutique** [buː'tiːk] n boutique f, tienda de ropa
**bow¹** [bəu] n (knot) lazo; (weapon, Mus) arco
**bow²** [bau] n (of the head) reverencia; (Naut: also: **~s**) proa ▷ vi inclinarse, hacer una reverencia
**bowels** [bauəlz] npl intestinos mpl, vientre m; (fig) entrañas fpl
**bowl** [bəul] n (for washing) tazón m, cuenco; (ball) bola ▷ vi (Cricket) arrojar la pelota; see also **bowls**; **bowler** n (Cricket) lanzador m (de la pelota); (BRIT: also: **bowler hat**) hongo, bombín m; **bowling** n (game) bolos mpl, bolos mpl; **bowling alley** n bolera; **bowling green** n pista para bochas; **bowls** n juego de las bochas, bolos mpl
**bow tie** ['bəu-] n corbata de lazo, pajarita
**box** [bɒks] n (also: **cardboard ~**) caja, cajón m; (Theatre) palco ▷ vt encajonar ▷ vi (Sport) boxear; **boxer** ['bɒksə'] n (person) boxeador m; **boxer shorts** ['bɒksəʃɔːts] pl n bóxers; **a pair of boxer shorts** unos bóxers; **boxing** ['bɒksɪŋ] n (Sport) boxeo; **Boxing Day** (BRIT) n día en que se dan los aguinaldos, 26 de diciembre; **boxing gloves** npl guantes mpl de boxeo; **boxing ring** n ring m, cuadrilátero; **box office** n taquilla (SP), boletería (LAM)
**boy** [bɔɪ] n (young) niño; (older) muchacho, chico; (son) hijo; **boy band** n boy band m (grupo musical de chicos)
**boycott** ['bɔɪkɒt] n boicot m ▷ vt boicotear
**boyfriend** ['bɔɪfrɛnd] n novio
**bra** [brɑː] n sostén m, sujetador m
**brace** [breɪs] n (BRIT: also: **~s: on teeth**) corrector m, aparato; (tool) berbiquí m ▷ vt (knees, shoulders) tensionar; **braces** npl (BRIT) tirantes mpl; **to ~ o.s.** (fig) prepararse
**bracelet** ['breɪslɪt] n pulsera, brazalete m
**bracket** ['brækɪt] n (Tech) soporte m, puntal m; (group) clase f, categoría; (also: **brace ~**) soporte m, abrazadera; (also: **round ~**) paréntesis m inv; (also: **square ~**) corchete m ▷ vt (word etc) poner entre paréntesis
**brag** [bræg] vi jactarse
**braid** [breɪd] n (trimming) galón m; (of hair) trenza
**brain** [breɪn] n cerebro; **brains** npl sesos mpl; **she's got ~s** es muy lista
**braise** [breɪz] vt cocer a fuego lento
**brake** [breɪk] n (on vehicle) freno ▷ vi frenar; **brake light** n luz f de frenado
**bran** [bræn] n salvado
**branch** [brɑːntʃ] n rama; (Comm) sucursal f; **branch off** vi: **a small road branches off to the right** hay una carretera pequeña que sale hacia la derecha; **branch out** vi (fig) extenderse
**brand** [brænd] n marca; (fig: type) tipo ▷ vt (cattle) marcar con hierro candente; **brand name** n marca; **brand-new** adj flamante, completamente nuevo
**brandy** ['brændɪ] n coñac m
**brash** [bræʃ] adj (forward) descarado
**brass** [brɑːs] n latón m; **the ~** (Mus) los cobres; **brass band** n banda de metal
**brat** [bræt] n (pej) mocoso/a
**brave** [breɪv] adj valiente, valeroso ▷ vt (face up to) desafiar; **bravery** n valor m, valentía
**brawl** [brɔːl] n pelea, reyerta
**Brazil** [brə'zɪl] n (el) Brasil; **Brazilian** adj, n brasileño/a m/f
**breach** [briːtʃ] vt abrir brecha en ▷ n (gap) brecha; (breaking): **~ of contract** f de contrato; **~ of the peace** perturbación f del órden público
**bread** [brɛd] n pan m; **breadbin** n panera; **breadbox** (us) n panera; **breadcrumbs** npl migajas fpl; (Culin) pan rallado
**breadth** [brɛtθ] n anchura; (fig) amplitud f
**break** [breɪk] (pt **broke**, pp **broken**) vt romper; (promise) faltar a; (law) violar, infringir; (record) batir ▷ vi romperse, quebrarse; (storm) estallar; (weather) cambiar; (dawn) despuntar; (news etc) darse a conocer ▷ n (gap) abertura; (fracture) fractura; (time) intervalo; (: at school) (período de) recreo; (chance) oportunidad f; **to ~ the news to sb** comunicar la noticia a algn; **break down** vt (figures, data) analizar, descomponer ▷ vi (machine) estropearse; (Aut) averiarse; (person) romper a llorar; (talks) fracasar; **break in** vt (horse etc) domar ▷ vi (burglar) forzar una entrada; (interrupt) interrumpir; **break into** vt fus (house) forzar; **break off** vi (speaker) pararse, detenerse; (branch) partir; **break out** vi estallar; (prisoner) escaparse; **to break out in spots** salirle a algn granos; **break up** vi (ship) hacerse pedazos; (crowd, meeting) disolverse; (marriage) deshacerse; (Scol) terminar (el curso); (line) cortarse ▷ vt (rocks etc) partir; (journey) partir; (fight etc) acabar con; **the line's** or **you're breaking up** se corta; **breakdown** n (Aut) avería; (in communications) interrupción f; (Med: also: **nervous breakdown**) colapso, crisis f nerviosa; (of marriage, talks) fracaso; (of

*statistics*) análisis *m inv*; **breakdown truck, breakdown van** *n* (camión *m*) grúa
**breakfast** ['brɛkfəst] *n* desayuno
**break: break-in** *n* robo con allanamiento de morada; **breakthrough** *n* (*also fig*) avance *m*
**breast** [brɛst] *n* (*of woman*) pecho, seno; (*chest*) pecho; (*of bird*) pechuga; **breast-feed** (*pt, pp* **breast-fed**) *vt, vi* amamantar, criar a los pechos; **breast-stroke** *n* braza (de pecho)
**breath** [brɛθ] *n* aliento, respiración *f*; **to take a deep ~** respirar hondo; **out of ~** sin aliento, sofocado
**Breathalyser**® ['brɛθəlaɪzə*] (BRIT) *n* alcoholímetro
**breathe** [briːð] *vt, vi* respirar; **breathe in** *vt, vi* aspirar; **breathe out** *vt, vi* espirar; **breathing** *n* respiración *f*
**breath: breathless** *adj* sin aliento, jadeante; **breathtaking** *adj* imponente, pasmoso; **breath test** *n* prueba de la alcoholemia
**bred** [brɛd] *pt, pp of* **breed**
**breed** [briːd] (*pt, pp* **bred**) *vt* criar ▷ *vi* reproducirse, procrear ▷ *n* (*Zool*) raza, casta; (*type*) tipo
**breeze** [briːz] *n* brisa
**breezy** ['briːzɪ] *adj* de mucho viento, ventoso; (*person*) despreocupado
**brew** [bruː] *vt* (*tea*) hacer; (*beer*) elaborar ▷ *vi* (*fig: trouble*) prepararse; (*storm*) amenazar; **brewery** *n* fábrica de cerveza, cervecería
**bribe** [braɪb] *n* soborno ▷ *vt* sobornar, cohechar; **bribery** *n* soborno, cohecho
**bric-a-brac** ['brɪkəbræk] *n inv* baratijas *fpl*
**brick** [brɪk] *n* ladrillo; **bricklayer** *n* albañil *m*
**bride** [braɪd] *n* novia; **bridegroom** *n* novio; **bridesmaid** *n* dama de honor
**bridge** [brɪdʒ] *n* puente *m*; (*Naut*) puente *m* de mando; (*of nose*) caballete *m*; (*Cards*) bridge *m* ▷ *vt* (*fig*): **to ~ a gap** llenar un vacío
**bridle** ['braɪdl] *n* brida, freno
**brief** [briːf] *adj* breve, corto ▷ *n* (*Law*) escrito; (*task*) cometido, encargo ▷ *vt* informar; **briefs** *npl* (*for men*) calzoncillos *mpl*; (*for women*) bragas *fpl*; **briefcase** *n* cartera (SP), portafolio (LAM); **briefing** *n* (*Press*) informe *m*; **briefly** *adv* (*glance*) fugazmente; (*say*) en pocas palabras
**brigadier** [brɪɡə'dɪə*] *n* general *m* de brigada
**bright** [braɪt] *adj* brillante; (*room*) luminoso; (*day*) de sol; (*person: clever*) listo,

inteligente; (*: lively*) alegre; (*colour*) vivo; (*future*) prometedor(a)
**brilliant** ['brɪljənt] *adj* brillante; (*inf*) fenomenal
**brim** [brɪm] *n* borde *m*; (*of hat*) ala
**brine** [braɪn] *n* (*Culin*) salmuera
**bring** [brɪŋ] (*pt, pp* **brought**) *vt* (*thing, person: with you*) traer; (*: to sb*) llevar, conducir; (*trouble, satisfaction*) causar; **bring about** *vt* ocasionar, producir; **bring back** *vt* volver a traer; (*return*) devolver; (*price*) rebajar; **bring in** *vt* (*harvest*) recoger; (*person*) hacer entrar or pasar; (*object*) traer; (*Pol: bill, law*) presentar; (*produce: income*) producir, rendir; **bring on** *vt* (*illness, attack*) producir, causar; (*player, substitute*) sacar (de la reserva), hacer salir; **bring out** *vt* sacar; (*book etc*) publicar; (*meaning*) subrayar; **bring up** *vt* subir; (*person*) educar, criar; (*question*) sacar a colación; (*food: vomit*) devolver, vomitar
**brink** [brɪŋk] *n* borde *m*
**brisk** [brɪsk] *adj* (*abrupt: tone*) brusco; (*person*) enérgico, vigoroso; (*pace*) rápido; (*trade*) activo
**bristle** ['brɪsl] *n* cerda ▷ *vi*: **to ~ in anger** temblar de rabia
**Brit** [brɪt] *n abbr* (*inf:* = *British person*) británico/a
**Britain** ['brɪtən] *n* (*also*: **Great ~**) Gran Bretaña
**British** ['brɪtɪʃ] *adj* británico ▷ *npl*: **the ~** los británicos; **British Isles** *npl*: **the British Isles** las Islas Británicas
**Briton** ['brɪtən] *n* británico/a
**brittle** ['brɪtl] *adj* quebradizo, frágil
**broad** [brɔːd] *adj* ancho, amplio; (*range*) amplio; (*smile*) abierto; (*general: outlines etc*) general; (*accent*) cerrado; **in ~ daylight** en pleno día; **broadband** *n* banda ancha; **broad bean** *n* haba; **broadcast** (*pt, pp* **~**) *n* emisión *f* ▷ *vt* (*Radio*) emitir; (*TV*) transmitir ▷ *vi* emitir; transmitir; **broaden** *vt* ampliar ▷ *vi* ensancharse; **to broaden one's mind** hacer más tolerante a algn; **broadly** *adv* en general; **broad-minded** *adj* tolerante, liberal
**broccoli** ['brɔkəlɪ] *n* brécol *m*
**brochure** ['brəʊʃjʊə*] *n* folleto
**broil** [brɔɪl] *vt* (*Culin*) asar a la parrilla
**broiler** ['brɔɪlə*] *n* (*grill*) parrilla
**broke** [brəʊk] *pt of* **break** ▷ *adj* (*inf*) pelado, sin blanca
**broken** ['brəʊkən] *pp of* **break** ▷ *adj* roto; (*machine: also*: **~ down**) averiado; **~ leg** pierna rota; **in ~ English** en un inglés imperfecto

**broker** ['brəukə*] n agente mf, bolsista mf; (insurance broker) agente de seguros

**bronchitis** [brɔŋ'kaɪtɪs] n bronquitis f

**bronze** [brɔnz] n bronce m

**brooch** [brəutʃ] n prendedor m, broche m

**brood** [bru:d] n camada, cría ▷ vi (person) dejarse obsesionar

**broom** [brum] n escoba; (Bot) retama

**Bros.** abbr (= Brothers) Hnos

**broth** [brɔθ] n caldo

**brothel** ['brɔθl] n burdel m

**brother** ['brʌðə*] n hermano; **brother-in-law** n cuñado

**brought** [brɔːt] pt, pp of **bring**

**brow** [brau] n (forehead) frente m; (eyebrow) ceja; (of hill) cumbre f

**brown** [braun] adj (colour) marrón; (hair) castaño; (tanned) bronceado, moreno ▷ n (colour) color m marrón or pardo ▷ vt (Culin) dorar; **brown bread** n pan integral

**Brownie** ['braunɪ] n niña exploradora

**brown rice** n arroz m integral

**brown sugar** n azúcar m terciado

**browse** [brauz] vi (through book) hojear; (in shop) mirar; **browser** n (Comput) navegador m

**bruise** [bru:z] n cardenal m (SP), moretón m ▷ vt magullar

**brunette** [bru:'net] n morena

**brush** [brʌʃ] n cepillo; (for painting, shaving etc) brocha; (artist's) pincel m; (with police etc) roce m ▷ vt (sweep) barrer; (groom) cepillar; (also: ~ against) rozar al pasar

**Brussels** ['brʌslz] n Bruselas

**Brussels sprout** n col f de Bruselas

**brutal** ['bru:tl] adj brutal

**B.Sc.** abbr (= Bachelor of Science) licenciado en Ciencias

**BSE** n abbr (= bovine spongiform encephalopathy) encefalopatía espongiforme bovina

**bubble** ['bʌbl] n burbuja ▷ vi burbujear, borbotar; **bubble bath** n espuma para el baño; **bubble gum** n chicle m de globo; **bubblejet printer** ['bʌbldʒet-] n impresora de inyección por burbujas

**buck** [bʌk] n (rabbit) conejo macho; (deer) gamo; (us: inf) dólar m ▷ vi corcovear; **to pass the ~ (to sb)** echar (a algn) el muerto

**bucket** ['bʌkɪt] n cubo, balde m

**buckle** ['bʌkl] n hebilla ▷ vt abrochar con hebilla ▷ vi combarse

**bud** [bʌd] n (of plant) brote m, yema; (of flower) capullo ▷ vi brotar, echar brotes

**Buddhism** ['budɪzm] n Budismo

**Buddhist** ['budɪst] adj, n budista m/f

**buddy** ['bʌdɪ] (us) n compañero, compinche m

**budge** [bʌdʒ] vt mover; (fig) hacer ceder ▷ vi moverse, ceder

**budgerigar** ['bʌdʒərɪgɑ:*] n periquito

**budget** ['bʌdʒɪt] n presupuesto ▷ vi: **to ~ for sth** presupuestar algo

**budgie** ['bʌdʒɪ] n = **budgerigar**

**buff** [bʌf] adj (colour) color de ante ▷ n (inf: enthusiast) entusiasta mf

**buffalo** ['bʌfələu] (pl ~ or **-es**) n (BRIT) búfalo; (US: bison) bisonte m

**buffer** ['bʌfə*] n (Comput) memoria intermedia; (Rail) tope m

**buffet[1]** ['bʌfɪt] vt golpear

**buffet[2]** ['bufeɪ] n (BRIT: in station) bar m, cafetería; (food) buffet m; **buffet car** (BRIT) n (Rail) coche-comedor m

**bug** [bʌg] n (esp us: insect) bicho, sabandija; (Comput) error m; (germ) microbio, bacilo; (spy device) micrófono oculto ▷ vt (inf: annoy) fastidiar; (room) poner micrófono oculto en

**buggy** ['bʌgɪ] n cochecito de niño

**build** [bɪld] (pt, pp **built**) n (of person) tipo ▷ vt construir, edificar; **build up** vt (morale, forces, production) acrecentar; (stocks) acumular; **builder** n (contractor) contratista mf; **building** n construcción f; (structure) edificio; **building site** n obra; **building society** (BRIT) n sociedad f inmobiliaria

**built** [bɪlt] pt, pp of **build**; **built-in** adj (cupboard) empotrado; (device) interior, incorporado; **built-up** adj (area) urbanizado

**bulb** [bʌlb] n (Bot) bulbo; (Elec) bombilla, foco (MEX), bujía (CAM), bombita (RPL)

**Bulgaria** [bʌl'geəriə] n Bulgaria; **Bulgarian** adj, n búgaro/a m/f

**bulge** [bʌldʒ] n bulto, protuberancia ▷ vi bombearse, pandearse; (pocket etc): **to ~ (with)** rebosar (de)

**bulimia** [bə'lɪmɪə] n bulimia

**bulimic** [bju:'lɪmɪk] adj, n bulímico/a m/f

**bulk** [bʌlk] n masa, mole f; **in ~** (Comm) a granel; **the ~ of** la mayor parte de; **bulky** adj voluminoso, abultado

**bull** [bul] n toro; (male elephant, whale) macho

**bulldozer** ['buldəuzə*] n bulldozer m

**bullet** ['bulɪt] n bala

**bulletin** ['bulɪtɪn] n anuncio, parte m; (journal) boletín m; **bulletin board** n (us) tablón m de anuncios; (Comput) tablero de noticias

**bullfight** ['bulfaɪt] n corrida de toros; **bullfighter** n torero; **bullfighting** n los toros, el toreo

**bully** ['bulɪ] n valentón m, matón m ▷ vt

intimidar, tiranizar

**bum** [bʌm] n (inf: backside) culo; (esp US: tramp) vagabundo

**bumblebee** ['bʌmblbi:] n abejorro

**bump** [bʌmp] n (blow) tope m, choque m; (jolt) sacudida; (on road etc) bache m; (on head etc) chichón m ▷ vt (strike) chocar contra; **bump into** vt fus chocar contra, tropezar con; (person) toparcon; **bumper** n (Aut) parachoques m inv ▷ adj: **bumper crop** or **harvest** cosecha abundante; **bumpy** adj (road) lleno de baches

**bun** [bʌn] n (BRIT: cake) pastel m; (US: bread) bollo; (of hair) moño

**bunch** [bʌntʃ] n (of flowers) ramo; (of keys) manojo; (of bananas) piña; (of people) grupo; **bunches** npl (in hair) coletas fpl

**bundle** ['bʌndl] n bulto, fardo; (of sticks) haz m; (of papers) legajo ▷ vt (also: ~ up) atar, envolver; **to ~ sth/sb into** meter algo/a algn precipitadamente en

**bungalow** ['bʌŋgələu] n bungalow m, chalé m

**bungee jumping** ['bʌndʒi:'dʒʌmpɪŋ] n puenting m, banyi m

**bunion** ['bʌnjən] n juanete m

**bunk** [bʌŋk] n litera; **bunk beds** npl literas fpl

**bunker** ['bʌŋkə*] n (coal store) carbonera; (Mil) refugio; (Golf) búnker m

**bunny** ['bʌnɪ] n (inf: also: ~ rabbit) conejito

**buoy** [bɔɪ] n boya; **buoyant** adj (ship) capaz de flotar; (economy) boyante; (person) optimista

**burden** ['bə:dn] n carga ▷ vt cargar

**bureau** [bjuə'rəu] (pl **-x**) n (BRIT: writing desk) escritorio, buró m; (US: chest of drawers) cómoda; (office) oficina, agencia

**bureaucracy** [bjuə'rɔkrəsɪ] n burocracia

**bureaucrat** ['bjuərəkræt] n burócrata m/f

**bureau de change** [-də'ʃãʒ] (pl **bureaux de change**) n caja f de cambio

**bureaux** ['bjuərəuz] npl of **bureau**

**burger** ['bə:gə*] n hamburguesa

**burglar** ['bə:glə*] n ladrón/ona m/f; **burglar alarm** n alarma f antirrobo; **burglary** n robo con allanamiento, robo de una casa

**burial** ['berɪəl] n entierro

**burn** [bə:n] (pt, pp **~ed** or **~t**) vt quemar; (house) incendiar ▷ vi quemarse, arder; incendiarse; (sting) escocer ▷ n quemadura; **burn down** vt incendiar; **burn out** vt (writer etc): **to burn o.s. out** agotarse; **burning** adj (building etc) en llamas; (hot: sand etc) abrasador(a); (ambition) ardiente

**Burns' Night** [bə:nz-] n ver abajo

**burnt** [bə:nt] pt, pp of **burn**

**burp** [bə:p] (inf) n eructo ▷ vi eructar

**burrow** ['bʌrəu] n madriguera ▷ vi hacer una madriguera; (rummage) hurgar

**burst** [bə:st] (pt, pp **~**) vt reventar; (river: banks etc) romper ▷ vi reventarse; (tyre) pincharse ▷ n (of gunfire) ráfaga; (also: ~ pipe) reventón m; **a ~ of energy/speed/ enthusiasm** una explosión de energía/ un ímpetu de velocidad/un arranque de entusiasmo; **to ~ into flames** estallar en llamas; **to ~ into tears** deshacerse en lágrimas; **to ~ out laughing** soltar la carcajada; **to ~ open** abrirse de golpe; **to be ~ing with** (container) estar lleno a rebosar de; (: person) reventar por or de; **burst into** vt fus (room etc) irrumpir en

**bury** ['berɪ] vt enterrar; (body) enterrar, sepultar

**bus** [bʌs] (pl **~es**) n autobús m

**bush** [buʃ] n arbusto; (scrub land) monte m; **to beat about the ~** andar(se) con rodeos

**business** ['bɪznɪs] n (matter) asunto; (trading) comercio, negocios mpl; (firm) empresa, casa; (occupation) oficio; **to be away on ~** estar en viaje de negocios; **it's my ~ to ...** me toca or corresponde ...; **it's none of my ~** yo no tengo nada que ver; **he means ~** habla en serio; **business class** n (Aer) clase f preferente; **businesslike** adj eficiente; **businessman** (irreg) n hombre m de negocios; **business trip** n viaje m de negocios; **businesswoman** (irreg) n mujer f de negocios

**busker** ['bʌskə*] (BRIT) n músico/a ambulante

**bus: bus pass** n bonobús m; **bus shelter** n parada cubierta; **bus station** n estación f de autobuses; **bus stop** n parada de autobús

**bust** [bʌst] n (Anat) pecho; (sculpture) busto

▷ *adj* (*inf: broken*) roto, estropeado; **to go ~** quebrar

**bustling** ['bʌslɪŋ] *adj* (*town*) animado, bullicioso

**busy** ['bɪzɪ] *adj* ocupado, atareado; (*shop, street*) concurrido, animado; (*Tel: line*) comunicando ▷ *vt*: **to ~ o.s. with** ocuparse en; **busy signal** (us) *n* (*Tel*) señal *f* de comunicando

○ **KEYWORD**

**but** [bʌt] *conj* **1** pero; **he's not very bright, but he's hard-working** no es muy inteligente, pero es trabajador
**2** (*in direct contradiction*) sino; **he's not English but French** no es inglés sino francés; **he didn't sing but he shouted** no cantó sino que gritó
**3** (*showing disagreement, surprise etc*): **but that's far too expensive!** ¡pero eso es carísimo!; **but it does work!** ¡(pero) sí que funciona!
▷ *prep* (*apart from, except*) menos, salvo; **we've had nothing but trouble** no hemos tenido más que problemas; **no-one but him can do it** nadie más que él puede hacerlo; **who but a lunatic would do such a thing** ¡sólo un loco haría una cosa así!; **but for you/your help** si no fuera por ti/tu ayuda; **anything but that** cualquier cosa menos eso
▷ *adv* (*just, only*): **she's but a child** no es más que una niña; **had I but known** si lo hubiera sabido; **I can but try** al menos lo puedo intentar; **it's all but finished** está casi acabado

**butcher** ['bʊtʃə*] *n* carnicero ▷ *vt* hacer una carnicería con; (*cattle etc*) matar; **butcher's (shop)** *n* carnicería

**butler** ['bʌtlə*] *n* mayordomo

**butt** [bʌt] *n* (*barrel*) tonel *m*; (*of gun*) culata; (*of cigarette*) colilla; (brit: *fig: target*) blanco ▷ *vt* dar cabezadas contra, top(et)ar

**butter** ['bʌtə*] *n* mantequilla ▷ *vt* untar con mantequilla; **buttercup** *n* botón *m* de oro

**butterfly** ['bʌtəflaɪ] *n* mariposa; (*Swimming: also*: **~ stroke**) braza de mariposa

**buttocks** ['bʌtəks] *npl* nalgas *fpl*

**button** ['bʌtn] *n* botón *m*; (us) placa, chapa ▷ *vt* (*also*: **~ up**) abotonar, abrochar ▷ *vi* abrocharse

**buy** [baɪ] (*pt, pp* **bought**) *vt* comprar ▷ *n* compra; **to ~ sb sth/sth from sb** comprarle algo a algn; **to ~ sb a drink** invitar a algn a tomar algo; **buy out** *vt* (*partner*) comprar la parte de; **buy up** *vt* (*property*) acaparar; (*stock*) comprar todas las existencias de; **buyer** *n* comprador(a) *m/f*

**buzz** [bʌz] *n* zumbido; (*inf: phone call*) llamada (por teléfono) ▷ *vi* zumbar; **buzzer** *n* timbre *m*

○ **KEYWORD**

**by** [baɪ] *prep* **1** (*referring to cause, agent*) por; de; **killed by lightning** muerto por un relámpago; **a painting by Picasso** un cuadro de Picasso
**2** (*referring to method, manner, means*): **by bus/car/train** en autobús/coche/tren; **to pay by cheque** pagar con un cheque; **by moonlight/candlelight** a la luz de la luna/ una vela; **by saving hard he ...** ahorrando ...
**3** (*via, through*) por; **we came by Dover** vinimos por Dover
**4** (*close to, past*): **the house by the river** la casa junto al río; **she rushed by me** pasó a mi lado como una exhalación; **I go by the post office every day** paso por delante de Correos todos los días
**5** (*time: not later than*) para; (: *during*): **by daylight** de día; **by 4 o'clock** para las cuatro; **by this time tomorrow** mañana a estas horas; **by the time I got here it was too late** cuando llegué ya era demasiado tarde
**6** (*amount*): **by the metre/kilo** por metro/ kilo; **paid by the hour** pagado por hora
**7** (*Math, measure*): **to divide/multiply by 3** dividir/multiplicar por 3; **a room 3 metres by 4** una habitación de 3 metros por 4; **it's broader by a metre** es un metro más ancho
**8** (*according to*) según, de acuerdo con; **it's 3 o'clock by my watch** según mi reloj, son las tres; **it's all right by me** por mí, está bien
**9**: **(all) by oneself** *etc* todo solo; **he did it (all) by himself** lo hizo él solo; **he was standing (all) by himself in a corner** estaba de pie solo en un rincón
**10**: **by the way** a propósito, por cierto; **this wasn't my idea, by the way** pues, no fue idea mía
▷ *adv* **1** *see* **go; pass** *etc*
**2**: **by and by** finalmente; **they'll come back by and by** acabarán volviendo; **by and large** en líneas generales, en general

**bye(-bye)** ['baɪ('baɪ)] *excl* adiós, hasta luego

**by-election** (brit) *n* elección *f* parcial

**bypass** ['baɪpɑːs] *n* carretera de circunvalación; (*Med*) (operación *f* de) by-pass *f* ▷ *vt* evitar

**byte** [baɪt] *n* (*Comput*) byte *m*, octeto

# C

**C** [siː] n (Mus) do m

**cab** [kæb] n taxi m; (of truck) cabina

**cabaret** ['kæbəreɪ] n cabaret m

**cabbage** ['kæbɪdʒ] n col f, berza

**cabin** ['kæbɪn] n cabaña; (on ship) camarote m; (on plane) cabina; **cabin crew** n tripulación f de cabina

**cabinet** ['kæbɪnɪt] n (Pol) consejo de ministros; (furniture) armario; (also: **display ~**) vitrina; **cabinet minister** n ministro/a (del gabinete)

**cable** ['keɪbl] n cable m ▷ vt cablegrafiar; **cable car** n teleférico; **cable television** n televisión f por cable

**cactus** ['kæktəs] (pl **cacti**) n cacto

**café** ['kæfeɪ] n café m

**cafeteria** [kæfɪ'tɪərɪə] n cafetería

**caffein(e)** ['kæfiːn] n cafeína

**cage** [keɪdʒ] n jaula

**cagoule** [kə'guːl] n chubasquero

**cake** [keɪk] n (Culin: large) tarta; (: small) pastel m; (of soap) pastilla

**calcium** ['kælsɪəm] n calcio

**calculate** ['kælkjuleɪt] vt calcular; **calculation** [-'leɪʃən] n cálculo, cómputo; **calculator** n calculadora

**calendar** ['kæləndə*] n calendario

**calf** [kɑːf] (pl **calves**) n (of cow) ternero, becerro; (of other animals) cría; (also: **~skin**) piel f de becerro; (Anat) pantorrilla

**calibre** ['kælɪbə*] (us **caliber**) n calibre m

**call** [kɔːl] vt llamar; (meeting) convocar ▷ vi (shout) llamar; (Tel) llamar (por teléfono); (visit: also: **~ in, ~ round**) hacer una visita ▷ n llamada; (of bird) canto; **to be ~ed** llamarse; **on ~** (on duty) de guardia; **call back** vi (return) volver; (Tel) volver a llamar; **call for** vt fus (demand) pedir, exigir; (fetch) pasar a recoger; **call in** vt (doctor, expert, police) llamar; **call off** vt (cancel: meeting, race) cancelar; (: deal) anular; (: strike)

desconvocar; **call on** vt fus (visit) visitar; (turn to) acudir a; **call out** vi gritar; **call up** vt (Mil) llamar al servicio militar; (Tel) llamar; **callbox** (BRIT) n cabina telefónica; **call centre** (us **call center**) n centro de atención al cliente; **caller** n visita; (Tel) usuario/a

**callous** ['kæləs] adj insensible, cruel

**calm** [kɑːm] adj tranquilo; (sea) liso, en calma ▷ n calma, tranquilidad f ▷ vt calmar, tranquilizar; **calm down** vi calmarse, tranquilizarse ▷ vt calmar, tranquilizar; **calmly** ['kɑːmlɪ] adv tranquilamente, con calma

**Calor gas®** ['kælə*-] n butano

**calorie** ['kælərɪ] n caloría

**calves** [kɑːvz] npl of **calf**

**camcorder** ['kæmkɔːdə*] n videocámara

**came** [keɪm] pt of **come**

**camel** ['kæməl] n camello

**camera** ['kæmərə] n máquina fotográfica; (Cinema, TV) cámara; **in ~** (Law) a puerta cerrada; **cameraman** (irreg) n cámara m; **camera phone** n teléfono con cámara

**camouflage** ['kæməflɑːʒ] n camuflaje m ▷ vt camuflar

**camp** [kæmp] n campamento, camping m; (Mil) campamento; (for prisoners) campo; (fig: faction) bando ▷ vi acampar ▷ adj afectado, afeminado

**campaign** [kæm'peɪn] n (Mil, Pol etc) campaña ▷ vi hacer campaña; **campaigner** n: **campaigner for** defensor(a) m/f de

**camp: camped** (BRIT) n cama de campaña; **camper** n campista mf; (vehicle) caravana; **campground** (us) n camping m, campamento; **camping** n camping m; **to go camping** hacer camping; **campsite** n camping m

**campus** ['kæmpəs] n ciudad f universitaria

**can¹** [kæn] n (of oil, water) bidón m; (tin) lata, bote m ▷ vt enlatar

○ **KEYWORD**

**can²** [kæn] (negative **cannot**, **can't**, conditional and pt **could**) aux vb **1** (be able to) poder; **you can do it if you try** puedes hacerlo si lo intentas; **I can't see you** no te veo

**2** (know how to) saber; **I can swim/play tennis/drive** sé nadar/jugar al tenis/conducir; **can you speak French?** ¿hablas or sabes hablar francés?

**3** (may) poder; **can I use your phone?** ¿me dejas or puedo usar tu teléfono?

**4** (expressing disbelief, puzzlement etc): **it can't**

**be true!** ¡no puede ser (verdad)!; **what CAN he want?** ¿qué querrá?
**5** (*expressing possibility, suggestion etc*): **he could be in the library** podría estar en la biblioteca; **she could have been delayed** pudo haberse retrasado

**Canada** ['kænədə] n (el) Canadá; **Canadian** [kə'neɪdɪən] adj, n canadiense mf

**canal** [kə'næl] n canal m

**canary** [kə'neərɪ] n canario

**Canary Islands** [kə'neərɪ'aɪləndz] npl: **the ~** las (Islas) Canarias

**cancel** ['kænsəl] vt cancelar; (*train*) suprimir; (*cross out*) tachar, borrar; **cancellation** [-'leɪʃən] n cancelación f; supresión f

**Cancer** ['kænsə*] n (*Astrology*) Cáncer m

**cancer** ['kænsə*] n cáncer m

**candidate** ['kændɪdeɪt] n candidato/a

**candle** ['kændl] n vela; (*in church*) cirio; **candlestick** n (*single*) candelero; (*low*) palmatoria; (*bigger, ornate*) candelabro

**candy** ['kændɪ] n azúcar m cande; (*us*) caramelo; **candy bar** (*us*) n barrita (*dulce*); **candyfloss** (*BRIT*) n algodón m (azucarado)

**cane** [keɪn] n (*Bot*) caña; (*stick*) vara, palmeta; (*for furniture*) mimbre f ▷ vt (*BRIT: Scol*) castigar (con vara)

**canister** ['kænɪstə*] n bote m, lata; (*of gas*) bombona

**cannabis** ['kænəbɪs] n marijuana

**canned** [kænd] adj en lata, de lata

**cannon** ['kænən] (pl ~ or ~s) n cañón m

**cannot** ['kænɔt] = **can not**

**canoe** [kə'nu:] n canoa; (*Sport*) piragua; **canoeing** n piragüismo

**canon** ['kænən] n (*clergyman*) canónigo; (*standard*) canon m

**can-opener** ['kænəupnə*] n abrelatas m inv

**can't** [kænt] = **can not**

**canteen** [kæn'ti:n] n (*eating place*) cantina; (*BRIT: of cutlery*) juego

**canter** ['kæntə*] vi ir a medio galope

**canvas** ['kænvəs] n (*material*) lona; (*painting*) lienzo; (*Naut*) velas fpl

**canvass** ['kænvəs] vi (*Pol*): **to ~ for** solicitar votos por ▷ vt (*Comm*) sondear

**canyon** ['kænjən] n cañón m

**cap** [kæp] n (*hat*) gorra; (*of pen*) capuchón m; (*of bottle*) tapa, tapón m; (*contraceptive*) diafragma m; (*for toy gun*) cápsula ▷ vt (*outdo*) superar; (*limit*) recortar

**capability** [keɪpə'bɪlɪtɪ] n capacidad f

**capable** ['keɪpəbl] adj capaz

**capacity** [kə'pæsɪtɪ] n capacidad f;

(*position*) calidad f

**cape** [keɪp] n capa; (*Geo*) cabo

**caper** ['keɪpə*] n (*Culin: gen pl*) alcaparra; (*prank*) broma

**capital** ['kæpɪtl] n (*also:* **~ city**) capital f; (*money*) capital m; (*also:* **~ letter**) mayúscula; **capitalism** n capitalismo; **capitalist** adj, n capitalista mf; **capital punishment** n pena de muerte

**Capitol** ['kæpɪtl] n *ver abajo*

● **CAPITOL**
●
● El Capitolio (**Capitol**) es el edificio del
● Congreso (**Congress**) de los Estados
● Unidos, situado en la ciudad de
● Washington. Por extensión, también
● se suele llamar así al edificio en el que
● tienen lugar las sesiones parlamentarias
● de la cámara de representantes de
● muchos de los estados.

**Capricorn** ['kæprɪkɔːn] n Capricornio

**capsize** [kæp'saɪz] vt volcar, hacer zozobrar ▷ vi volcarse, zozobrar

**capsule** ['kæpsjuːl] n cápsula

**captain** ['kæptɪn] n capitán m

**caption** ['kæpʃən] n (*heading*) título; (*to picture*) leyenda

**captivity** [kæp'tɪvɪtɪ] n cautiverio

**capture** ['kæptʃə*] vt prender, apresar; (*animal, Comput*) capturar; (*place*) tomar; (*attention*) captar, llamar ▷ n apresamiento; captura; toma; (*data capture*) formulación f de datos

**car** [kɑː*] n coche m, carro (*LAM*), automóvil m; (*us Rail*) vagón m

**carafe** [kə'ræf] n jarra

**caramel** ['kærəməl] n caramelo

**carat** ['kærət] n quilate m

**caravan** ['kærəvæn] n (*BRIT*) caravana, ruló f; (*in desert*) caravana; **caravan site** (*BRIT*) n camping m para caravanas

**carbohydrate** [kɑːbəu'haɪdreɪt] n hidrato de carbono; (*food*) fécula

**carbon** ['kɑːbən] n carbono; **carbon dioxide** n dióxido de carbono, anhídrido carbónico; **carbon monoxide** n monóxido de carbono

**car boot sale** n mercadillo organizado en un aparcamiento, en el que se exponen las mercancías en el maletero del coche

**carburettor** [kɑːbju'retə*] (*us* **carburetor**) n carburador m

**card** [kɑːd] n (*material*) cartulina; (*index card etc*) ficha; (*playing card*) carta, naipe m; (*visiting card, greetings card etc*) tarjeta; **cardboard** n cartón m; **card game** n

juego de naipes or cartas
**cardigan** ['kɑːdɪɡən] n rebeca
**cardinal** ['kɑːdɪnl] adj cardinal;
(importance, principal) esencial ▷ n cardenal
m
**cardphone** ['kɑːdfəun] n cabina que
funciona con tarjetas telefónicas
**care** [keə*] n cuidado; (worry) inquietud
f; (charge) cargo, custodia ▷ vi: **to ~ about**
(person, animal) tener cariño a; (thing, idea)
preocuparse por; **~ of** en casa de, al cuidado
de; **in sb's ~** a cargo de algn; **to take ~ to**
cuidarse de, tener cuidado de; **to take ~ of**
cuidar; (problem etc) ocuparse de; **I don't
~** no me importa; **I couldn't ~ less** eso me
trae sin cuidado; **care for** vt fus cuidar a;
(like) querer
**career** [kə'rɪə*] n profesión f; (in work,
school) carrera ▷ vi (also: **~ along**) correr a
toda velocidad
**care: carefree** adj despreocupado; **careful**
adj cuidadoso; (cautious) cauteloso; **(be)
careful!** ¡tenga cuidado!; **carefully** adv con
cuidado, cuidadosamente; con cautela;
**caregiver** (US) n (professional) enfermero/a
m/f; (unpaid) persona que cuida a un pariente o
vecino; **careless** adj descuidado; (heedless)
poco atento; **carelessness** n descuido,
falta de atención; **carer** ['kɛərə*] n
(professional) enfermero/a m/f; (unpaid)
persona que cuida a un pariente o vecino;
**caretaker** n portero/a, conserje mf
**car-ferry** ['kɑːfɛrɪ] n transbordador m
para coches
**cargo** ['kɑːɡəu] (pl **~es**) n cargamento,
carga
**car hire** n alquiler m de automóviles
**Caribbean** [kærɪ'biːən] n: **the ~ (Sea)** el
(Mar) Caribe
**caring** ['kɛərɪŋ] adj humanitario;
(behaviour) afectuoso
**carnation** [kɑː'neɪʃən] n clavel m
**carnival** ['kɑːnɪvəl] n carnaval m;
(US: funfair) parque m de atracciones
**carol** ['kærəl] n: **(Christmas) ~** villancico
**carousel** [kærə'sɛl] (US) n tiovivo,
caballitos mpl
**car park** (BRIT) n aparcamiento, parking m
**carpenter** ['kɑːpɪntə*] n carpintero/a
**carpet** ['kɑːpɪt] n alfombra; (fitted)
moqueta ▷ vt alfombrar
**car rental** (US) n alquiler m de coches
**carriage** ['kærɪdʒ] n (BRIT Rail) vagón m;
(horse-drawn) coche m; (of goods) transporte
m; (: cost) porte m, flete m; **carriageway**
(BRIT) n (part of road) calzada
**carrier** ['kærɪə*] n (transport company)
transportista, empresa de transportes;

(Med) portador(a) m/f; **carrier bag** (BRIT) n
bolsa de papel or plástico
**carrot** ['kærət] n zanahoria
**carry** ['kærɪ] vt (person) llevar; (transport)
transportar; (involve: responsibilities etc)
entrañar, implicar; (Med) ser portador de
▷ vi (sound) oírse; **to get carried away**
(fig) entusiasmarse; **carry on** vi (continue)
seguir (adelante), continuar ▷ vt proseguir,
continuar; **carry out** vt (orders) cumplir;
(investigation) llevar a cabo, realizar
**cart** [kɑːt] n carro, carreta ▷ vt
(inf: transport) acarrear
**carton** ['kɑːtən] n (box) caja (de cartón); (of
milk etc) bote m; (of yogurt) tarrina
**cartoon** [kɑː'tuːn] n (Press) caricatura;
(comic strip) tira cómica; (film) dibujos mpl
animados
**cartridge** ['kɑːtrɪdʒ] n cartucho; (of pen)
recambio
**carve** [kɑːv] vt (meat) trinchar; (wood,
stone) cincelar, esculpir; (initials etc) grabar;
**carving** n (object) escultura; (design) talla;
(art) tallado
**car wash** n lavado de coches
**case** [keɪs] n (container) caja; (Med) caso;
(for jewels etc) estuche m; (Law) causa,
proceso; (BRIT: also: **suit~**) maleta; **in ~ of**
en caso de; **in any ~** en todo caso; **just in ~**
por si acaso
**cash** [kæʃ] n dinero en efectivo, dinero
contante ▷ vt cobrar, hacer efectivo; **to
pay (in) ~** pagar al contado; **~ on delivery**
cóbrese al entregar; **cashback** n (discount)
devolución f; (at supermarket etc) retirada de
dinero en efectivo de un establecimiento donde se
ha pagado con tarjeta; también dinero retirado;
**cash card** n tarjeta f dinero; **cash desk**
(BRIT) n caja; **cash dispenser** n cajero
automático
**cashew** [kæ'ʃuː] n (also: **~ nut**) anacardo
**cashier** [kæ'ʃɪə*] n cajero/a
**cashmere** ['kæʃmɪə*] n cachemira
**cash point** n cajero automático
**cash register** n caja
**casino** [kə'siːnəu] n casino
**casket** ['kɑːskɪt] n cofre m, estuche m;
(US: coffin) ataúd m
**casserole** ['kæsərəul] n (food, pot) cazuela
**cassette** [kæ'sɛt] n casete f; **cassette
player, cassette recorder** n casete m
**cast** [kɑːst] (pt, pp **~**) vt (throw) echar,
arrojar, lanzar; (glance, eyes) dirigir;
(Theatre): **to ~ sb as Othello** dar a algn el
papel de Otelo ▷ vi (Fishing) lanzar ▷ n
(Theatre) reparto; (also: **plaster ~**) vaciado;
**to ~ one's vote** votar; **to ~ doubt on**
suscitar dudas acerca de; **cast off** vi (Naut)

desamarrar; *(Knitting)* cerrar (los puntos)

**castanets** [kæstə'nɛts] *npl* castañuelas *fpl*

**caster sugar** ['kɑːstə*-] *(BRIT)* n azúcar *m* extrafino

**Castile** [kæs'tiːl] n Castilla; **Castilian** *adj*, n castellano/a *m/f*

**cast-iron** ['kɑːstaɪən] *adj (lit)* (hecho) de hierro fundido; *(fig: case)* irrebatible

**castle** ['kɑːsl] n castillo; *(Chess)* torre *f*

**casual** ['kæʒjul] *adj* fortuito; *(irregular: work etc)* eventual, temporero; *(unconcerned)* despreocupado; *(clothes)* informal

⏐ Be careful not to translate **casual** by the Spanish word *casual*.

**casualty** ['kæʒjultɪ] n víctima, herido/a; *(dead)* muerto/a; *(Med: department)* urgencias *fpl*

**cat** [kæt] n gato; *(big cat)* felino

**Catalan** ['kætəlæn] *adj*, n catalán/ana *m/f*

**catalogue** ['kætələɡ] *(US* **catalog**) n catálogo ▷ *vt* catalogar

**Catalonia** [kætə'ləʊnɪə] n Cataluña

**catalytic converter** [kætə'lɪtɪkkən'vɜːtə*] n catalizador *m*

**cataract** ['kætərækt] n *(Med)* cataratas *fpl*

**catarrh** [kə'tɑː*] n catarro

**catastrophe** [kə'tæstrəfɪ] n catástrofe *f*

**catch** [kætʃ] *(pt, pp* **caught**) *vt* coger *(SP)*, agarrar *(LAM)*; *(arrest)* detener; *(grasp)* asir; *(breath)* contener; *(surprise: person)* sorprender; *(attract: attention)* captar; *(hear)* oír; *(Med)* contagiarse de, coger; *(also: ~ up)* alcanzar ▷ *vi (fire)* encenderse; *(in branches etc)* enredarse ▷ n *(fish etc)* pesca; *(act of catching)* cogida; *(hidden problem)* dificultad *f*; *(game)* pilla-pilla; *(of lock)* pestillo, cerradura; **to ~ fire** encenderse; **to ~ sight of** divisar; **catch up** *vi (fig)* ponerse al día; **catching** ['kætʃɪŋ] *adj (Med)* contagioso

**category** ['kætɪɡərɪ] n categoría, clase *f*

**cater** ['keɪtə*] *vi*: **to ~ for** *(BRIT)* abastecer a; *(needs)* atender a; *(Comm: parties etc)* proveer comida a

**caterpillar** ['kætəpɪlə*] n oruga, gusano

**cathedral** [kə'θiːdrəl] n catedral *f*

**Catholic** ['kæθəlɪk] *adj*, n *(Rel)* católico/a *m/f*

**Catseye®** ['kæts'aɪ] *(BRIT)* n *(Aut)* catafoto

**cattle** ['kætl] *npl* ganado

**catwalk** ['kætwɔːk] n pasarela

**caught** [kɔːt] *pt, pp* de **catch**

**cauliflower** ['kɒlɪflaʊə*] n coliflor *f*

**cause** [kɔːz] n causa, motivo, razón *f*; *(principle: also Pol)* causa ▷ *vt* causar

**caution** ['kɔːʃən] n cautela, prudencia; *(warning)* advertencia, amonestación *f*

▷ *vt* amonestar; **cautious** *adj* cauteloso, prudente, precavido

**cave** [keɪv] n cueva, caverna; **cave in** *vi (roof etc)* derrumbarse, hundirse

**caviar(e)** ['kævɪɑː*] n caviar *m*

**cavity** ['kævɪtɪ] n hueco, cavidad *f*

**cc** *abbr (= cubic centimetres)* c.c.; *(= carbon copy)* copia hecha con papel del carbón

**CCTV** n *abbr (= closed-circuit television)* circuito cerrado de televisión

**CD** n *abbr (= compact disc)* CD *m*; *(player)* (reproductor *m* de) CD; **CD player** n reproductor *m* de CD; **CD-ROM** [siːdiː'rɒm] n *abbr* CD-ROM *m*; **CD writer** n grabadora de CD

**cease** [siːs] *vt*, *vi* cesar; **ceasefire** n alto *m* el fuego

**cedar** ['siːdə*] n cedro

**ceilidh** ['keɪlɪ] n baile con música y danzas tradicionales escocesas o irlandesas

**ceiling** ['siːlɪŋ] n techo; *(fig)* límite *m*

**celebrate** ['sɛlɪbreɪt] *vt* celebrar ▷ *vi* divertirse; **celebration** [-'breɪʃən] n fiesta, celebración *f*

**celebrity** [sɪ'lɛbrɪtɪ] n celebridad *f*

**celery** ['sɛlərɪ] n apio

**cell** [sɛl] n celda; *(Biol)* célula; *(Elec)* elemento

**cellar** ['sɛlə*] n sótano; *(for wine)* bodega

**cello** ['tʃɛləʊ] n violoncelo

**Cellophane®** ['sɛləfeɪn] n celofán *m*

**cellphone** ['sɛlfəʊn] n teléfono celular

**Celsius** ['sɛlsɪəs] *adj* centígrado

**Celtic** ['kɛltɪk] *adj* celta

**cement** [sə'mɛnt] n cemento

**cemetery** ['sɛmɪtrɪ] n cementerio

**censor** ['sɛnsə*] n censor *m* ▷ *vt (cut)* censurar; **censorship** n censura

**census** ['sɛnsəs] n censo

**cent** [sɛnt] n *(unit of dollar)* centavo, céntimo; *(unit of euro)* céntimo; *see also* **per**

**centenary** [sɛn'tiːnərɪ] n centenario

**centennial** [sɛn'tɛnɪəl] *(US)* n centenario

**center** ['sɛntə*] *(US)* n = **centre**

**centi...** [sɛntɪ] *prefix*: **centigrade** *adj* centígrado; **centimetre** *(US* **centimeter**) n centímetro; **centipede** ['sɛntɪpiːd] n ciempiés *m inv*

**central** ['sɛntrəl] *adj* central; *(of house etc)* céntrico; **Central America** n Centroamérica; **central heating** n calefacción *f* central; **central reservation** n *(BRIT Aut)* mediana

**centre** ['sɛntə*] *(US* **center**) n centro; *(fig)* núcleo ▷ *vt* centrar; **centre-forward** n *(Sport)* delantero centro; **centre-half** n *(Sport)* medio centro

**century** ['sɛntjurɪ] n siglo; **20th ~** siglo

veinte

**CEO** n abbr = **chief executive officer**

**ceramic** [sɪˈræmɪk] adj cerámico

**cereal** [ˈsiːrɪəl] n cereal m

**ceremony** [ˈserɪmənɪ] n ceremonia; **to stand on ~** hacer ceremonias, estar de cumplido

**certain** [ˈsəːtən] adj seguro; (person): **a ~ Mr Smith** un tal Sr. Smith; (particular, some) cierto; **for ~** a ciencia cierta; **certainly** adv (undoubtedly) ciertamente; (of course) desde luego, por supuesto; **certainty** n certeza, certidumbre f, seguridad f; (inevitability) certeza

**certificate** [səˈtɪfɪkɪt] n certificado

**certify** [ˈsəːtɪfaɪ] vt certificar; (award diploma to) conceder un diploma a; (declare insane) declarar loco

**cf.** abbr (= compare) cfr

**CFC** n abbr (= chlorofluorocarbon) CFC m

**chain** [tʃeɪn] n cadena; (of mountains) cordillera; (of events) sucesión f ▷ vt (also: ~ up) encadenar; **chain-smoke** vi fumar un cigarrillo tras otro

**chair** [tʃeə*] n silla; (armchair) sillón m, butaca; (of university) cátedra; (of meeting etc) presidencia ▷ vt (meeting) presidir; **chairlift** n telesilla; **chairman** (irreg) n presidente m; **chairperson** n presidente/a m/f; **chairwoman** (irreg) n presidenta

**chalet** [ˈʃæleɪ] n chalet m (de madera)

**chalk** [tʃɔːk] n (Geo) creta; (for writing) tiza, gis m (MEX); **chalkboard** (US) n pizarrón (LAM), pizarra (SP)

**challenge** [ˈtʃælɪndʒ] n desafío, reto ▷ vt desafiar, retar; (statement, right) poner en duda; **to ~ sb to do sth** retar a algn a que haga algo; **challenging** adj exigente; (tone) de desafío

**chamber** [ˈtʃeɪmbə*] n cámara, sala; (Pol) cámara; (BRIT Law: gen pl) despacho; **~ of commerce** cámara de comercio; **chambermaid** n camarera

**champagne** [ʃæmˈpeɪn] n champaña m, champán m

**champion** [ˈtʃæmpɪən] n campeón/ona m/f; (of cause) defensor(a) m/f; **championship** n campeonato

**chance** [tʃɑːns] n (opportunity) ocasión f, oportunidad f; (likelihood) posibilidad f; (risk) riesgo ▷ vt arriesgar, probar ▷ adj fortuito, casual; **to ~ it** arriesgarse, intentarlo; **to take a ~** arriesgarse; **by ~** por casualidad

**chancellor** [ˈtʃɑːnsələ*] n canciller m; **Chancellor of the Exchequer** (BRIT) n Ministro de Hacienda

**chandelier** [ʃændəˈlɪə*] n araña (de luces)

**change** [tʃeɪndʒ] vt cambiar; (replace) cambiar, reemplazar; (gear, clothes, job) cambiar de; (transform) transformar ▷ vi cambiar(se); (change trains) hacer transbordo; (traffic lights) cambiar de color; (be transformed): **to ~ into** transformarse en ▷ n cambio; (alteration) modificación f; (transformation) transformación f; (of clothes) muda; (coins) suelto, sencillo; (money returned) vuelta; **to ~ gear** (Aut) cambiar de marcha; **to ~ one's mind** cambiar de opinión o idea; **for a ~** para variar; **change over** vi (from sth to sth) cambiar; (players etc) cambiar(se) ▷ vt cambiar; **changeable** adj (weather) cambiable; **change machine** n máquina de cambio; **changing room** (BRIT) n vestuario

**channel** [ˈtʃænl] n (TV) canal m; (of river) cauce m; (groove) conducto; (fig: medium) medio ▷ vt (river etc) encauzar; **the (English) C~** el Canal (de la Mancha); **the C~ Islands** las Islas Normandas; **Channel Tunnel** n: **the Channel Tunnel** el túnel del Canal de la Mancha, el Eurotúnel

**chant** [tʃɑːnt] n (of crowd) gritos mpl; (Rel) canto ▷ vt (slogan, word) repetir a gritos

**chaos** [ˈkeɪɔs] n caos m

**chaotic** [keɪˈɔtɪk] adj caótico

**chap** [tʃæp] (BRIT: inf) n (man) tío, tipo

**chapel** [ˈtʃæpəl] n capilla

**chapped** [tʃæpt] adj agrietado

**chapter** [ˈtʃæptə*] n capítulo

**character** [ˈkærɪktə*] n carácter m, naturaleza, índole f; (moral strength, personality) carácter; (in novel, film) personaje m; **characteristic** [-ˈrɪstɪk] adj característico ▷ n característica; **characterize** [ˈkærɪktəraɪz] vt caracterizar

**charcoal** [ˈtʃɑːkəʊl] n carbón m vegetal; (Art) carboncillo

**charge** [tʃɑːdʒ] n (Law) cargo, acusación f; (cost) precio, coste m; (responsibility) cargo ▷ vt (Law): **to ~ (with)** acusar (de); (battery) cargar; (price) pedir; (customer) cobrar ▷ vi precipitarse; (Mil) cargar, atacar; **charge card** n tarjeta de cuenta; **charger** n (also: **battery charger**) cargador m (de baterías)

**charismatic** [kærɪzˈmætɪk] adj carismático

**charity** [ˈtʃærɪtɪ] n caridad f; (organization) sociedad f benéfica; (money, gifts) limosnas fpl; **charity shop** n (BRIT) tienda de artículos de segunda mano que dedica su recaudación a causas benéficas

**charm** [tʃɑːm] n encanto, atractivo; (talisman) hechizo; (on bracelet) dije m ▷ vt encantar; **charming** adj encantador(a)

**chart** [tʃɑːt] n (diagram) cuadro; (graph) gráfica; (map) carta de navegación ▷ vt (course) trazar; (progress) seguir; **charts** npl (Top 40): **the ~s** = los 40 principales (SP)

**charter** ['tʃɑːtə*] vt (plane) alquilar; (ship) fletar ▷ n (document) carta; (of university, company) estatutos mpl; **chartered accountant** (BRIT) n contable m/f diplomado/a; **charter flight** n vuelo chárter

**chase** [tʃeɪs] vt (pursue) perseguir; (also: ~ away) ahuyentar ▷ n persecución f

**chat** [tʃæt] vi (also: **have a ~**) charlar; (on Internet) chatear ▷ n charla; **chat up** vt (inf: girl) ligar con, enrollarse con; **chat room** n (Internet) chat m, canal m de charla; **chat show** n (BRIT) programa m de entrevistas

**chatter** ['tʃætə*] vi (person) charlar; (teeth) castañetear ▷ n (of birds) parloteo; (of people) charla, cháchara

**chauffeur** ['ʃəʊfə*] n chófer m

**chauvinist** ['ʃəʊvɪnɪst] n (male chauvinist) machista m; (nationalist) chovinista mf

**cheap** [tʃiːp] adj barato; (joke) de mal gusto; (poor quality) de mala calidad ▷ adv barato; **cheap day return** n billete de ida y vuelta el mismo día; **cheaply** adv barato, a bajo precio

**cheat** [tʃiːt] vi hacer trampa ▷ vt: **to ~ sb (out of sth)** estafar (algo) a algn ▷ n (person) tramposo/a; **cheat on** vt fus engañar

**Chechnya** [tʃtʃnjɑː] n Chechenia

**check** [tʃek] vt (examine) controlar; (facts) comprobar; (halt) parar, detener; (restrain) refrenar, restringir ▷ n (inspection) control m, inspección f; (curb) freno; (US: bill) nota, cuenta; (US) = **cheque**; (pattern: gen pl) cuadro; **check in** vi (at hotel) firmar el registro; (at airport) facturar el equipaje ▷ vt (luggage) facturar; **check off** vt (esp US: check) comprobar; (cross off) tachar; **check out** vi (of hotel) marcharse; **check up** vi: **to check up on sth** comprobar algo; **to check up on sb** investigar a algn; **checkbook** (US) = **chequebook**; **checked** adj a cuadros; **checkers** (US) n juego de damas; **check-in** n (also: **check-in desk**: at airport) mostrador m de facturación; **checking account** (US) n cuenta corriente; **checklist** n lista (de control); **checkmate** n jaque m mate; **checkout** n caja; **checkpoint** n (punto de) control m; **checkroom** (US) n consigna; **checkup** n (Med) reconocimiento general

**cheddar** ['tʃedə*] n (also: **~ cheese**) queso m cheddar

**cheek** [tʃiːk] n mejilla; (impudence) descaro; **what a ~!** ¡qué cara!; **cheekbone** n pómulo; **cheeky** adj fresco, descarado

**cheer** [tʃɪə*] vt vitorear, aplaudir; (gladden) alegrar, animar ▷ vi dar vivas ▷ n viva m; **cheer up** vi animarse ▷ vt alegrar, animar; **cheerful** adj alegre

**cheerio** [tʃɪərɪˈəʊ] (BRIT) excl ¡hasta luego!

**cheerleader** ['tʃɪəliːdə*] n animador(a) m/f

**cheese** [tʃiːz] n queso; **cheeseburger** n hamburguesa con queso; **cheesecake** n pastel m de queso

**chef** [ʃef] n jefe/a m/f de cocina

**chemical** ['kemɪkəl] adj químico ▷ n producto químico

**chemist** ['kemɪst] n (BRIT: pharmacist) farmacéutico/a; (scientist) químico/a; **chemistry** n química; **chemist's (shop)** (BRIT) n farmacia

**cheque** [tʃek] (US **check**) n cheque m; **chequebook** n talonario de cheques (SP), chequera (LAM); **cheque card** n tarjeta de cheque

**cherry** ['tʃerɪ] n cereza; (also: **~ tree**) cerezo

**chess** [tʃes] n ajedrez m

**chest** [tʃest] n (Anat) pecho; (box) cofre m, cajón m

**chestnut** ['tʃesnʌt] n castaña; (also: **~ tree**) castaño

**chest of drawers** n cómoda

**chew** [tʃuː] vt mascar, masticar; **chewing gum** n chicle m

**chic** [ʃiːk] adj elegante

**chick** [tʃɪk] n pollito, polluelo; (inf: girl) chica

**chicken** ['tʃɪkɪn] n gallina, pollo; (food) pollo; (inf: coward) gallina mf; **chicken out** (inf) vi rajarse; **chickenpox** n varicela

**chickpea** ['tʃɪkpiː] n garbanzo

**chief** [tʃiːf] n jefe/a m/f ▷ adj principal; **chief executive (officer)** n director(a) m/f general; **chiefly** adv principalmente

**child** [tʃaɪld] (pl **~ren**) n niño/a; (offspring) hijo/a; **child abuse** n (with violence) malos tratos mpl a niños; (sexual) abuso m sexual de niños; **child benefit** n (BRIT) subsidio por cada hijo pequeño; **childbirth** n parto; **childcare** n cuidado de los niños; **childhood** n niñez f, infancia; **childish** adj pueril, aniñado; **child minder** (BRIT) n madre f de día; **children** ['tʃɪldrən] npl of **child**

**Chile** ['tʃɪlɪ] n Chile m; **Chilean** adj, n chileno/a m/f

**chill** [tʃɪl] n frío; (Med) resfriado ▷ vt enfriar; (Culin) congelar; **chill out** vi (esp US: inf) tranquilizarse

**chil(l)i** ['tʃɪlɪ] (BRIT) n chile m, ají m (SC)

**chilly** ['tʃɪlɪ] adj frío

**chimney** ['tʃɪmnɪ] n chimenea
**chimpanzee** [tʃɪmpæn'zi:] n chimpancé m
**chin** [tʃɪn] n mentón m, barbilla
**China** ['tʃaɪnə] n China
**china** ['tʃaɪnə] n porcelana; (crockery) loza
**Chinese** [tʃaɪ'ni:z] adj chino ▷ n inv chino/a m/f; (Ling) chino
**chip** [tʃɪp] n (gen pl: Culin: BRIT) patata (SP) or papa (LAM) frita; (: US: also: **potato ~**) patata or papa frita; (of wood) astilla; (of glass, stone) lasca; (at poker) ficha; (Comput) chip m ▷ vt (cup, plate) desconchar; **chip shop** pescadería (donde se vende principalmente pescado rebozado y patatas fritas)
**chiropodist** [kɪ'rɔpədɪst] (BRIT) n pedicuro/a, callista m/f
**chisel** ['tʃɪzl] n (for wood) escoplo; (for stone) cincel m
**chives** [tʃaɪvz] npl cebollinos mpl
**chlorine** ['klɔ:ri:n] n cloro
**choc-ice** ['tʃɔkaɪs] n (BRIT) helado m cubierto de chocolate
**chocolate** ['tʃɔklɪt] n chocolate m; (sweet) bombón m
**choice** [tʃɔɪs] n elección f, selección f; (option) opción f; (preference) preferencia ▷ adj escogido
**choir** ['kwaɪə*] n coro
**choke** [tʃəuk] vi ahogarse; (on food) atragantarse ▷ vt estrangular, ahogar; (block): **to be ~d with** estar atascado de ▷ n (Aut) estárter m
**cholesterol** [kə'lɛstərɔl] n colesterol m
**choose** [tʃu:z] (pt **chose**, pp **chosen**) vt escoger, elegir; (team) seleccionar; **to ~ to do sth** optar por hacer algo
**chop** [tʃɔp] vt (wood) cortar, tajar; (Culin: also: **~ up**) picar ▷ n (Culin) chuleta; **chop down** vt (tree) talar; **chop off** vt cortar (de un tajo); **chopsticks** ['tʃɔpstɪks] npl palillos mpl
**chord** [kɔ:d] n (Mus) acorde m
**chore** [tʃɔ:*] n faena, tarea; (routine task) trabajo rutinario
**chorus** ['kɔ:rəs] n coro; (repeated part of song) estribillo
**chose** [tʃəuz] pt of **choose**
**chosen** ['tʃəuzn] pp of **choose**
**Christ** [kraɪst] n Cristo
**christen** ['krɪsn] vt bautizar; **christening** n bautizo
**Christian** ['krɪstɪən] adj, n cristiano/a m/f; **Christianity** [-'ænɪtɪ] n cristianismo; **Christian name** n nombre m de pila
**Christmas** ['krɪsməs] n Navidad f; **Merry ~!** ¡Felices Pascuas!; **Christmas**

**card** n crismas m inv, tarjeta de Navidad; **Christmas carol** n villancico m; **Christmas Day** n día m de Navidad; **Christmas Eve** n Nochebuena; **Christmas pudding** n (esp BRIT) pudin m de Navidad; **Christmas tree** n árbol m de Navidad
**chrome** [krəum] n cromo
**chronic** ['krɔnɪk] adj crónico
**chrysanthemum** [krɪ'sænθəməm] n crisantemo
**chubby** ['tʃʌbɪ] adj regordete
**chuck** [tʃʌk] (inf) vt lanzar, arrojar; (BRIT: also: **~ up**) abandonar; **chuck out** vt (person) echar (fuera); (rubbish etc) tirar
**chuckle** ['tʃʌkl] vi reírse entre dientes
**chum** [tʃʌm] n compañero/a
**chunk** [tʃʌŋk] n pedazo, trozo
**church** [tʃə:tʃ] n iglesia; **churchyard** n cementerio
**churn** [tʃə:n] n (for butter) mantequera; (for milk) lechera
**chute** [ʃu:t] n (also: **rubbish ~**) vertedero; (for coal etc) rampa de caída
**chutney** ['tʃʌtnɪ] n condimento a base de frutas de la India
**CIA** (US) n abbr (= Central Intelligence Agency) CIA f
**CID** (BRIT) n abbr (= Criminal Investigation Department) ≈ B.I.C. f (SP)
**cider** ['saɪdə*] n sidra
**cigar** [sɪ'gɑ:*] n puro
**cigarette** [sɪgə'rɛt] n cigarrillo; **cigarette lighter** n mechero
**cinema** ['sɪnəmə] n cine m
**cinnamon** ['sɪnəmən] n canela
**circle** ['sə:kl] n círculo; (in theatre) anfiteatro ▷ vi dar vueltas ▷ vt (surround) rodear, cercar; (move round) dar la vuelta a
**circuit** ['sə:kɪt] n circuito; (tour) gira; (track) pista; (lap) vuelta
**circular** ['sə:kjulə*] adj circular ▷ n circular f
**circulate** ['sə:kjuleɪt] vi circular; (person: at party etc) hablar con los invitados ▷ vt poner en circulación; **circulation** [-'leɪʃən] n circulación f; (of newspaper) tirada
**circumstances** ['sə:kəmstənsɪz] npl circunstancias fpl; (financial condition) situación f económica
**circus** ['sə:kəs] n circo
**cite** [saɪt] vt citar
**citizen** ['sɪtɪzn] n (Pol) ciudadano/a; (of city) vecino/a, habitante mf; **citizenship** n ciudadanía; (BRIT: Scol) civismo
**citrus fruits** ['sɪtrəs-] npl agrios mpl
**city** ['sɪtɪ] n ciudad f; **the C~** centro financiero de Londres; **city centre** (BRIT)

*n* centro de la ciudad; **city technology college** *n* centro de formación profesional (*centro de enseñanza secundaria que da especial importancia a la ciencia y tecnología.*)

**civic** ['sɪvɪk] *adj* cívico; (*authorities*) municipal

**civil** ['sɪvɪl] *adj* civil; (*polite*) atento, cortés; **civilian** [sɪ'vɪlɪən] *adj* civil (*no militar*) ▷ *n* civil *mf*, paisano/a

**civilization** [sɪvɪlaɪ'zeɪʃən] *n* civilización *f*

**civilized** ['sɪvɪlaɪzd] *adj* civilizado

**civil: civil law** *n* derecho civil; **civil rights** *npl* derechos *mpl* civiles; **civil servant** *n* funcionario/a del Estado; **Civil Service** *n* administración *f* pública; **civil war** *n* guerra civil

**CJD** *n abbr* (= *Creutzfeldt-Jakob disease*) enfermedad de Creutzfeldt-Jakob

**claim** [kleɪm] *vt* exigir, reclamar; (*rights etc*) reivindicar; (*assert*) pretender ▷ *vi* (*for insurance*) reclamar ▷ *n* reclamación *f*; pretensión *f*; **claim form** *n* solicitud *f*

**clam** [klæm] *n* almeja

**clamp** [klæmp] *n* abrazadera, grapa ▷ *vt* (*two things together*) cerrar fuertemente; (*one thing on another*) afianzar (con abrazadera); (*Aut: wheel*) poner el cepo a

**clan** [klæn] *n* clan *m*

**clap** [klæp] *vi* aplaudir

**claret** ['klærət] *n* burdeos *m inv*

**clarify** ['klærɪfaɪ] *vt* aclarar

**clarinet** [klærɪ'nɛt] *n* clarinete *m*

**clarity** ['klærɪtɪ] *n* claridad *f*

**clash** [klæʃ] *n* enfrentamiento; choque *m*; desacuerdo; estruendo ▷ *vi* (*fight*) enfrentarse; (*beliefs*) chocar; (*disagree*) estar en desacuerdo; (*colours*) desentonar; (*two events*) coincidir

**clasp** [klɑːsp] *n* (*hold*) apretón *m*; (*of necklace, bag*) cierre *m* ▷ *vt* apretar; abrazar

**class** [klɑːs] *n* clase *f* ▷ *vt* clasificar

**classic** ['klæsɪk] *adj*, *n* clásico; **classical** *adj* clásico

**classification** [klæsɪfɪ'keɪʃən] *n* clasificación *f*

**classify** ['klæsɪfaɪ] *vt* clasificar

**classmate** ['klɑːsmeɪt] *n* compañero/a de clase

**classroom** ['klɑːsrum] *n* aula; **classroom assistant** *n* profesor(a) *m/f* de apoyo

**classy** ['klɑːsɪ] *adj* (*inf*) elegante, con estilo

**clatter** ['klætə*] *n* estrépito ▷ *vi* hacer ruido *or* estrépito

**clause** [klɔːz] *n* cláusula; (*Ling*) oración *f*

**claustrophobic** [klɔːstrə'fəubɪk] *adj* claustrofóbico; **I feel ~** me entra claustrofobia

**claw** [klɔː] *n* (*of cat*) uña; (*of bird of prey*)

garra; (*of lobster*) pinza

**clay** [kleɪ] *n* arcilla

**clean** [kliːn] *adj* limpio; (*record, reputation*) bueno, intachable; (*joke*) decente ▷ *vt* limpiar; (*hands etc*) lavar; **clean up** *vt* limpiar, asear; **cleaner** *n* (*person*) asistenta; (*substance*) producto para la limpieza; **cleaner's** *n* tintorería; **cleaning** *n* limpieza

**cleanser** ['klɛnzə*] *n* (*for face*) crema limpiadora

**clear** [klɪə*] *adj* claro; (*road, way*) libre; (*conscience*) limpio, tranquilo; (*skin*) terso; (*sky*) despejado ▷ *vt* (*space*) despejar, limpiar; (*Law: suspect*) absolver; (*obstacle*) salvar, saltar por encima de; (*cheque*) aceptar ▷ *vi* (*fog etc*) despejarse ▷ *adv*: **~ of** a distancia de; **to ~ the table** recoger *or* levantar la mesa; **clear away** *vt* (*things, clothes etc*) quitar (de en medio); (*dishes*) retirar; **clear up** *vt* limpiar; (*mystery*) aclarar, resolver; **clearance** *n* (*removal*) despeje *m*; (*permission*) acreditación *f*; **clear-cut** *adj* bien definido, nítido; **clearing** *n* (*in wood*) claro; **clearly** *adv* claramente; (*evidently*) sin duda; **clearway** (BRIT) *n* carretera donde no se puede parar

**clench** [klɛntʃ] *vt* apretar, cerrar

**clergy** ['klɜːdʒɪ] *n* clero

**clerk** [klɑːk, (US) klɑːrk] *n* (BRIT) oficinista *mf*; (US) dependiente/a *m/f*

**clever** ['klɛvə*] *adj* (*intelligent*) inteligente, listo; (*skilful*) hábil; (*device, arrangement*) ingenioso

**cliché** ['kliːʃeɪ] *n* cliché *m*, frase *f* hecha

**click** [klɪk] *vt* (*tongue*) chasquear; (*heels*) taconear ▷ *vi* (*Comput*) hacer clic; **to ~ on an icon** hacer clic en un icono

**client** ['klaɪənt] *n* cliente *m/f*

**cliff** [klɪf] *n* acantilado

**climate** ['klaɪmɪt] *n* clima *m*; **climate change** *n* cambio climático

**climax** ['klaɪmæks] *n* (*of battle, career*) apogeo; (*of film, book*) punto culminante; (*sexual*) orgasmo

**climb** [klaɪm] *vi* subir; (*plant*) trepar; (*move with effort*): **to ~ over a wall/into a car** trepar a una tapia/subir a un coche ▷ *vt* (*stairs*) subir; (*tree*) trepar a; (*mountain*) escalar ▷ *n* subida; **climb down** *vi* (*fig*) volverse atrás; **climber** *n* alpinista *mf* (SP, MEX), andinista *mf* (LAM); **climbing** *n* alpinismo (SP, MEX), andinismo (LAM)

**clinch** [klɪntʃ] *vt* (*deal*) cerrar; (*argument*) remachar

**cling** [klɪŋ] (*pt*, *pp* clung) *vi*: **to ~ to** agarrarse a; (*clothes*) pegarse a

**Clingfilm®** ['klɪŋfɪlm] *n* plástico

adherente
**clinic** ['klɪnɪk] n clínica
**clip** [klɪp] n (for hair) horquilla; (also: **paper ~**) sujetapapeles m inv, clip m; (TV, Cinema) fragmento ▷ vt (cut) cortar; (also: **~ together**) unir; **clipping** n (newspaper) recorte m
**cloak** [kləuk] n capa, manto ▷ vt (fig) encubrir, disimular; **cloakroom** n guardarropa; (BRIT: WC) lavabo (SP), aseos mpl (SP), baño (LAM)
**clock** [klɔk] n reloj m; **clock in or on** vi (with card) fichar, picar; (start work) entrar a trabajar; **clock off or out** vi (with card) fichar or picar la salida; (leave work) salir del trabajar; **clockwise** adv en el sentido de las agujas del reloj; **clockwork** n aparato de relojería ▷ adj (toy) de cuerda
**clog** [klɔg] n zueco, chanclo ▷ vt atascar ▷ vi (also: **~ up**) atascarse
**clone** [kləun] n clon m ▷ vt clonar
**close¹** [kləus] adj (near): **~ (to)** cerca (de); (friend) íntimo; (connection) estrecho; (examination) detallado, minucioso; (weather) bochornoso ▷ adv cerca; **~ by, ~ at hand** muy cerca; **to have a ~ shave** (fig) escaparse por un pelo
**close²** [kləuz] vt (shut) cerrar; (end) concluir, terminar ▷ vi (shop etc) cerrarse; (end) concluirse, terminarse ▷ n (end) fin m, final m, conclusión f; **close down** vi cerrarse definitivamente; **closed** adj (shop etc) cerrado
**closely** ['kləuslɪ] adv (study) con detalle; (watch) de cerca; (resemble) estrechamente
**closet** ['klɔzɪt] n armario
**close-up** ['kləusʌp] n primer plano
**closing time** n hora de cierre
**closure** ['kləuʒə*] n cierre m
**clot** [klɔt] n (gen) coágulo; (inf: idiot) imbécil m/f ▷ vi (blood) coagularse
**cloth** [klɔθ] n (material) tela, paño; (rag) trapo
**clothes** [kləuðz] npl ropa; **clothes line** n cuerda (para tender la ropa); **clothes peg** (US **clothes pin**) n pinza
**clothing** ['kləuðɪŋ] n = **clothes**
**cloud** [klaud] n nube f; **cloud over** vi (also fig) nublarse; **cloudy** adj nublado, nuboso; (liquid) turbio
**clove** [kləuv] n clavo; **~ of garlic** diente m de ajo
**clown** [klaun] n payaso ▷ vi (also: **~ about, ~ around**) hacer el payaso
**club** [klʌb] n (society) club m; (weapon) porra, cachiporra; (also: **golf ~**) palo ▷ vt aporrear ▷ vi: **to ~ together** (for gift) comprar entre todos; **clubs** npl (Cards)

tréboles mpl; **club class** n (Aviat) clase f preferente
**clue** [klu:] n pista; (in crosswords) indicación f; **I haven't a ~** no tengo ni idea
**clump** [klʌmp] n (of trees) grupo
**clumsy** ['klʌmzɪ] adj (person) torpe, desmañado; (tool) difícil de manejar; (movement) desgarbado
**clung** [klʌŋ] pt, pp of **cling**
**cluster** ['klʌstə*] n grupo ▷ vi agruparse, apiñarse
**clutch** [klʌtʃ] n (Aut) embrague m; (grasp): **~es** garras fpl ▷ vt asir; agarrar
**cm** abbr (= centimetre) cm
**Co.** abbr = **county; company**
**c/o** abbr (= care of) c/a, a/c
**coach** [kəutʃ] n autocar m (SP), coche de línea; (horse-drawn) coche m; (of train) vagón m, coche m; (Sport) entrenador(a) m/f, instructor(a) m/f; (tutor) profesor(a) m/f particular ▷ vt (Sport) entrenar; (student) preparar, enseñar; **coach station** n (BRIT) estación f de autobuses etc; **coach trip** n excursión f en autocar
**coal** [kəul] n carbón m
**coalition** [kəuə'lɪʃən] n coalición f
**coarse** [kɔːs] adj basto, burdo; (vulgar) grosero, ordinario
**coast** [kəust] n costa, litoral m ▷ vi (Aut) ir en punto muerto; **coastal** adj costero, costanero; **coastguard** n guardacostas m inv; **coastline** n litoral m
**coat** [kəut] n abrigo; (of animal) pelaje m, lana; (of paint) mano f, capa ▷ vt cubrir, revestir; **coat hanger** n percha (SP), gancho (LAM); **coating** n capa, baño
**coax** [kəuks] vt engatusar
**cob** [kɔb] n see **corn**
**cobbled** ['kɔbld] adj: **~ street** calle f empedrada, calle f adoquinada
**cobweb** ['kɔbweb] n telaraña
**cocaine** [kə'keɪn] n cocaína
**cock** [kɔk] n (rooster) gallo; (male bird) macho ▷ vt (gun) amartillar; **cockerel** n gallito
**cockney** ['kɔknɪ] n habitante de ciertos barrios de Londres
**cockpit** ['kɔkpɪt] n cabina
**cockroach** ['kɔkrəutʃ] n cucaracha
**cocktail** ['kɔkteɪl] n coctel m, cóctel m
**cocoa** ['kəukəu] n cacao; (drink) chocolate m
**coconut** ['kəukənʌt] n coco
**cod** [kɔd] n bacalao
**C.O.D.** abbr (= cash on delivery) C.A.E.
**code** [kəud] n código; (cipher) clave f; (dialling code) prefijo; (post code) código postal

**coeducational** [kəuɛdju'keɪʃənl] adj mixto

**coffee** ['kɒfɪ] n café m; **coffee bar** (BRIT) n cafetería; **coffee bean** n grano de café; **coffee break** n descanso (para tomar café); **coffee maker** n máquina de hacer café, cafetera; **coffeepot** n cafetera; **coffee shop** n café m; **coffee table** n mesita (para servir el café)

**coffin** ['kɒfɪn] n ataúd m

**cog** [kɔg] n (wheel) rueda dentada; (tooth) diente m

**cognac** ['kɒnjæk] n coñac m

**coherent** [kəu'hɪərənt] adj coherente

**coil** [kɔɪl] n rollo; (Elec) bobina, carrete m; (contraceptive) espiral f ▷ vt enrollar

**coin** [kɔɪn] n moneda ▷ vt (word) inventar, idear

**coincide** [kəuɪn'saɪd] vi coincidir; (agree) estar de acuerdo; **coincidence** [kəu'ɪnsɪdəns] n casualidad f

**Coke®** [kəuk] n Coca-Cola®

**coke** [kəuk] n (coal) coque m

**colander** ['kɒləndə*] n colador m, escurridor m

**cold** [kəuld] adj frío ▷ n frío; (Med) resfriado; **it's ~** hace frío; **to be ~** (person) tener frío; **to catch (a) ~** resfriarse; **in ~ blood** a sangre fría; **cold sore** n herpes mpl or fpl

**coleslaw** ['kəulslɔ:] n especie de ensalada de col

**colic** ['kɒlɪk] n cólico

**collaborate** [kə'læbəreɪt] vi colaborar

**collapse** [kə'læps] vi hundirse, derrumbarse; (Med) sufrir un colapso ▷ n hundimiento, derrumbamiento; (Med) colapso

**collar** ['kɒlə*] n (of coat, shirt) cuello; (of dog etc) collar; **collarbone** n clavícula

**colleague** ['kɒli:g] n colega mf; (at work) compañero/a

**collect** [kə'lɛkt] vt (litter, mail etc) recoger; (as a hobby) coleccionar; (BRIT: call and pick up) recoger; (debts, subscriptions etc) recaudar ▷ vi reunirse; (dust) acumularse; **to call ~** (us Tel) llamar a cobro revertido; **collection** [kə'lɛkʃən] n colección f; (of mail, for charity) recogida; **collective** [kə'lɛktɪv] adj colectivo; **collector** n coleccionista mf

**college** ['kɒlɪdʒ] n colegio mayor; (of agriculture, technology) escuela universitaria

**collide** [kə'laɪd] vi chocar

**collision** [kə'lɪʒən] n choque m

**cologne** [kə'ləun] n (also: **eau de ~**) (agua de) colonia

**Colombia** [kə'lɒmbɪə] n Colombia; **Colombian** adj, n colombiano/a

**colon** ['kəulən] n (sign) dos puntos; (Med) colon m

**colonel** ['kə:nl] n coronel m

**colonial** [kə'ləunɪəl] adj colonial

**colony** ['kɒlənɪ] n colonia

**colour** etc ['kʌlə*] (us **color** etc) n color m ▷ vt color(e)ar; (dye) teñir; (fig: account) adornar; (: judgement) distorsionar ▷ vi (blush) sonrojarse; **colour in** vt colorear; **colour-blind** adj daltónico; **coloured** adj de color; (photo) en color; **colour film** n película en color; **colourful** adj lleno de color; (story) fantástico; (person) excéntrico; **colouring** n (complexion) tez f; (in food) colorante m; **colour television** n televisión f en color

**column** ['kɒləm] n columna

**coma** ['kəumə] n coma m

**comb** [kəum] n peine m; (ornamental) peineta ▷ vt (hair) peinar; (area) registrar a fondo

**combat** ['kɒmbæt] n combate m ▷ vt combatir

**combination** [kɒmbɪ'neɪʃən] n combinación f

**combine** [vb kəm'baɪn, n 'kɒmbaɪn] vt combinar; (qualities) reunir ▷ vi combinarse ▷ n (Econ) cartel m

○ **KEYWORD**

**come** [kʌm] (pt **came**, pp **come**) vi
**1** (movement towards) venir; **to come running** venir corriendo
**2** (arrive) llegar; **he's come here to work** ha venido aquí para trabajar; **to come home** volver a casa
**3** (reach): **to come to** llegar a; **the bill came to £40** la cuenta ascendía a cuarenta libras
**4** (occur): **an idea came to me** se me ocurrió una idea
**5** (be, become): **to come loose/undone** etc aflojarse/desabrocharse/desatarse etc; **I've come to like him** por fin ha llegado a gustarme

**come across** vt fus (person) topar con; (thing) dar con

**come along** vi (BRIT: progress) ir

**come back** vi (return) volver

**come down** vi (price) bajar; (tree, building) ser derribado

**come from** vt fus (place, source) ser de

**come in** vi (visitor) entrar; (train, report) llegar; (fashion) ponerse de moda; (on deal etc) entrar

**come off** vi (button) soltarse, desprenderse; (attempt) salir bien

**come on** vi (pupil) progresar; (work, project)

desarrollarse; (*lights*) encenderse; (*electricity*) volver; **come on!** ¡vamos!

**come out** *vi* (*fact*) salir a la luz; (*book, sun*) salir; (*stain*) quitarse

**come round** *vi* (*after faint, operation*) volver en sí

**come to** *vi* (*wake*) volver en sí

**come up** *vi* (*sun*) salir; (*problem*) surgir; (*event*) aproximarse; (*in conversation*) mencionarse

**come up with** *vt fus* (*idea*) sugerir; (*money*) conseguir

**comeback** ['kʌmbæk] *n*: **to make a ~** (*Theatre*) volver a las tablas

**comedian** [kə'miːdɪən] *n* humorista *mf*

**comedy** ['kɒmɪdɪ] *n* comedia; (*humour*) comicidad *f*

**comet** ['kɒmɪt] *n* cometa *m*

**comfort** ['kʌmfət] *n* bienestar *m*; (*relief*) alivio ▷ *vt* consolar; **comfortable** *adj* cómodo; (*financially*) acomodado; (*easy*) fácil; **comfort station** (*US*) *n* servicios *mpl*

**comic** ['kɒmɪk] *adj* (*also*: **~al**) cómico ▷ *n* (*comedian*) cómico; (*BRIT: for children*) tebeo; (*BRIT: for adults*) comic *m*; **comic book** (*US*) *n* libro *m* de cómics; **comic strip** *n* tira cómica

**comma** ['kɒmə] *n* coma

**command** [kə'mɑːnd] *n* orden *f*, mandato; (*Mil: authority*) mando; (*mastery*) dominio ▷ *vt* (*troops*) mandar; (*give orders to*): **to ~ sb to do** mandar *or* ordenar a algn hacer; **commander** *n* (*Mil*) comandante *mf*, jefe/a *m/f*

**commemorate** [kə'mɛmərɛɪt] *vt* conmemorar

**commence** [kə'mɛns] *vt, vi* comenzar, empezar; **commencement** (*US*) *n* (*Univ*) (ceremonia de) graduación *f*

**commend** [kə'mɛnd] *vt* elogiar, alabar; (*recommend*) recomendar

**comment** ['kɒmɛnt] *n* comentario ▷ *vi*: **to ~ on** hacer comentarios sobre; **"no ~"** (*written*) "sin comentarios"; (*spoken*) "no tengo nada que decir"; **commentary** ['kɒməntərɪ] *n* comentario; **commentator** ['kɒmənteɪtə*] *n* comentarista *mf*

**commerce** ['kɒmɜːs] *n* comercio

**commercial** [kə'mɜːʃəl] *adj* comercial ▷ *n* (*TV, Radio*) anuncio; **commercial break** *n* intermedio para publicidad

**commission** [kə'mɪʃən] *n* (*committee, fee*) comisión *f* ▷ *vt* (*work of art*) encargar; **out of ~** fuera de servicio; **commissioner** *n* (*Police*) comisario de policía

**commit** [kə'mɪt] *vt* (*act*) cometer; (*resources*) dedicar; (*to sb's care*) entregar;

**to ~ o.s. (to do)** comprometerse (a hacer); **to ~ suicide** suicidarse; **commitment** *n* compromiso; (*to ideology etc*) entrega

**committee** [kə'mɪtɪ] *n* comité *m*

**commodity** [kə'mɒdɪtɪ] *n* mercancía

**common** ['kɒmən] *adj* común; (*pej*) ordinario ▷ *n* campo común; **commonly** *adv* comúnmente; **commonplace** *adj* de lo más común; **Commons** (*BRIT*) *npl* (*Pol*): **the Commons** (la Cámara de) los Comunes; **common sense** *n* sentido común; **Commonwealth** *n*: **the Commonwealth** la Commonwealth

**communal** ['kɒmjuːnl] *adj* (*property*) comunal; (*kitchen*) común

**commune** [*n* 'kɒmjuːn, *vb* kə'mjuːn] *n* (*group*) comuna ▷ *vi*: **to ~ with** comulgar *or* conversar con

**communicate** [kə'mjuːnɪkeɪt] *vt* comunicar ▷ *vi*: **to ~ (with)** comunicarse (con); (*in writing*) estar en contacto (con)

**communication** [kəmjuːnɪ'keɪʃən] *n* comunicación *f*

**communion** [kə'mjuːnɪən] *n* (*also*: **Holy ~**) comunión *f*

**communism** ['kɒmjunɪzəm] *n* comunismo; **communist** *adj, n* comunista *mf*

**community** [kə'mjuːnɪtɪ] *n* comunidad *f*; (*large group*) colectividad *f*; **community centre** (*US* **community center**) *n* centro social; **community service** *n* trabajo *m* comunitario (*prestado en lugar de cumplir una pena de prisión*)

**commute** [kə'mjuːt] *vi* viajar a diario de la casa al trabajo ▷ *vt* conmutar; **commuter** *n* persona que viaja a diario de la casa al trabajo

**compact** [*adj* kəm'pækt, *n* 'kɒmpækt] *adj* compacto ▷ *n* (*also*: **powder ~**) polvera; **compact disc** *n* compact disc *m*; **compact disc player** *n* reproductor *m* de disco compacto, compact disc *m*

**companion** [kəm'pænɪən] *n* compañero/a

**company** ['kʌmpənɪ] *n* compañía; (*Comm*) sociedad *f*, compañía; **to keep sb ~** acompañar a algn; **company car** *n* coche *m* de la empresa; **company director** *n* director(a) *m/f* de empresa

**comparable** ['kɒmpərəbl] *adj* comparable

**comparative** [kəm'pærətɪv] *adj* relativo; (*study*) comparativo; **comparatively** *adv* (*relatively*) relativamente

**compare** [kəm'pɛə*] *vt*: **to ~ sth/sb with** *or* **to** comparar algo/a algn con ▷ *vi*: **to ~ (with)** compararse (con); **comparison** [-'pærɪsn] *n* comparación *f*

**compartment** [kəm'pɑːtmənt] n
(also: Rail) compartim(i)ento
**compass** ['kʌmpəs] n brújula;
**compasses** npl (Math) compás m
**compassion** [kəm'pæʃən] n compasión f
**compatible** [kəm'pætɪbl] adj compatible
**compel** [kəm'pel] vt obligar; **compelling**
adj (fig: argument) convincente
**compensate** ['kɒmpənseɪt] vt
compensar ▷ vi: **to ~ for** compensar;
**compensation** [-'seɪʃən] n (for loss)
indemnización f
**compete** [kəm'piːt] vi (take part) tomar
parte, concurrir; (vie with): **to ~ with**
competir con, hacer competencia a
**competent** ['kɒmpɪtənt] adj
competente, capaz
**competition** [kɒmpɪ'tɪʃən] n (contest)
concurso; (rivalry) competencia
**competitive** [kəm'petɪtɪv] adj (Econ,
Sport) competitivo
**competitor** [kəm'petɪtə*] n (rival)
competidor(a) m/f; (participant) concursante
mf
**complacent** [kəm'pleɪsənt] adj
autocomplaciente
**complain** [kəm'pleɪn] vi quejarse; (Comm)
reclamar; **complaint** n queja; reclamación
f; (Med) enfermedad f
**complement** [n 'kɒmplɪmənt, vb
'kɒmplɪment] n complemento; (esp
of ship's crew) dotación f ▷ vt (enhance)
complementar; **complementary**
[kɒmplɪ'mentərɪ] adj complementario
**complete** [kəm'pliːt] adj (full) completo;
(finished) acabado ▷ vt (fulfil) completar;
(finish) acabar; (a form) llenar; **completely**
adv completamente; **completion**
[-'pliːʃən] n terminación f; (of contract)
realización f
**complex** ['kɒmpleks] adj, n complejo
**complexion** [kəm'plekʃən] n (of face) tez
f, cutis m
**compliance** [kəm'plaɪəns] n (submission)
sumisión f; (agreement) conformidad f; **in ~
with** de acuerdo con
**complicate** ['kɒmplɪkeɪt] vt complicar;
**complicated** adj complicado;
**complication** [-'keɪʃən] n complicación f
**compliment** ['kɒmplɪmənt] n (formal)
cumplido ▷ vt felicitar; **complimentary**
[-'mentərɪ] adj lisonjero; (free) de favor
**comply** [kəm'plaɪ] vi: **to ~ with** cumplir
con
**component** [kəm'pəunənt] adj
componente ▷ n (Tech) pieza
**compose** [kəm'pəuz] vt: **to be ~d of**
componerse de; (music etc) componer;

**to ~ o.s.** tranquilizarse; **composer** n
(Mus) compositor(a) m/f; **composition**
[kɒmpə'zɪʃən] n composición f
**composure** [kəm'pəuʒə*] n serenidad
f, calma
**compound** ['kɒmpaund] n (Chem)
compuesto; (Ling) palabra compuesta;
(enclosure) recinto ▷ adj compuesto;
(fracture) complicado
**comprehension** [-'henʃən] n
comprensión f
**comprehensive** [kɒmprɪ'hensɪv] adj
exhaustivo; (Insurance) contra todo riesgo;
**comprehensive (school)** n centro estatal de
enseñanza secundaria ≈ Instituto Nacional de
Bachillerato (SP)
**compress** [vb kəm'pres, n 'kɒmpres] vt
comprimir; (information) condensar ▷ n
(Med) compresa
**comprise** [kəm'praɪz] vt (also: **be ~d
of**) comprender, constar de; (constitute)
constituir
**compromise** ['kɒmprəmaɪz] n
(agreement) arreglo ▷ vt comprometer ▷ vi
transigir
**compulsive** [kəm'pʌlsɪv] adj compulsivo;
(viewing, reading) obligado
**compulsory** [kəm'pʌlsərɪ] adj
obligatorio
**computer** [kəm'pjuːtə*] n ordenador m,
computador m, computadora; **computer
game** n juego para ordenador; **computer-
generated** adj realizado por ordenador,
creado por ordenador; **computerize** vt
(data) computerizar; (system) informatizar;
**we're computerized now** ya nos hemos
informatizado; **computer programmer**
n programador(a) m/f; **computer
programming** n programación f;
**computer science** n informática;
**computer studies** npl informática fsg,
computación fsg (LAM); **computing** [kəm-
'pjuːtɪŋ] n (activity, science) informática
**con** [kɒn] vt (deceive) engañar; (cheat)
estafar ▷ n estafa
**conceal** [kən'siːl] vt ocultar
**concede** [kən'siːd] vt (point, argument)
reconocer; (territory) ceder; **to ~ (defeat)**
darse por vencido; **to ~ that** admitir que
**conceited** [kən'siːtɪd] adj presumido
**conceive** [kən'siːv] vt, vi concebir
**concentrate** ['kɒnsəntreɪt] vi
concentrarse ▷ vt concentrar
**concentration** [kɒnsən'treɪʃən] n
concentración f
**concept** ['kɒnsept] n concepto
**concern** [kən'sɜːn] n (matter) asunto;
(Comm) empresa; (anxiety) preocupación

f ▷ vt (worry) preocupar; (involve) afectar;
(relate to) tener que ver con; **to be ~ed
(about)** interesarse (por), preocuparse
(por); **concerning** prep sobre, acerca de
**concert** ['kɔnsət] n concierto; **concert
hall** n sala de conciertos
**concerto** [kən'tʃəːtəu] n concierto
**concession** [kən'sɛʃən] n concesión f; **tax
~** privilegio fiscal
**concise** [kən'saɪs] adj conciso
**conclude** [kən'kluːd] vt concluir; (treaty
etc) firmar; (agreement) llegar a; (decide) llegar
a la conclusión de; **conclusion** [-'kluːʒən] n
conclusión f; firma
**concrete** ['kɔnkriːt] n hormigón m ▷ adj
de hormigón; (fig) concreto
**concussion** [kən'kʌʃən] n conmoción f
cerebral
**condemn** [kən'dɛm] vt condenar;
(building) declarar en ruina
**condensation** [kɔndɛn'seɪʃən] n
condensación f
**condense** [kən'dɛns] vi condensarse ▷ vt
condensar, abreviar
**condition** [kən'dɪʃən] n condición f,
estado; (requirement) condición f ▷ vt
condicionar; **on ~ that** a condición (de) que;
**conditional** [kən'dɪʃənl] adj condicional;
**conditioner** n suavizante
**condo** ['kɔndəu] (US) n (inf) =
**condominium**
**condom** ['kɔndəm] n condón m
**condominium** [kɔndə'mɪnɪəm] (US) n
(building) bloque m de pisos or apartamentos
(propiedad de quienes lo habitan), condominio
(LAM); (apartment) piso or apartamento (en
propiedad), condominio (LAM)
**condone** [kən'dəun] vt condonar
**conduct** [n 'kɔndʌkt, vb kən'dʌkt] n
conducta, comportamiento ▷ vt (lead)
conducir; (manage) llevar a cabo, dirigir;
(Mus) dirigir; **to ~ o.s.** comportarse;
**conducted tour** (BRIT) n visita
acompañada; **conductor** n (of orchestra)
director m; (US: on train) revisor(a) m/f; (on
bus) cobrador m; (Elec) conductor m
**cone** [kəun] n cono; (pine cone) piña; (on
road) pivote m; (for ice-cream) cucurucho
**confectionery** [kən'fɛkʃənrɪ] n dulces
mpl
**confer** [kən'fəː*] vt: **to ~ sth on** otorgar
algo a ▷ vi conferenciar
**conference** ['kɔnfərns] n (meeting)
reunión f; (convention) congreso
**confess** [kən'fɛs] vt y confesar ▷ vi admitir;
**confession** [-'fɛʃən] n confesión f
**confide** [kən'faɪd] vi: **to ~ in** confiar en
**confidence** ['kɔnfɪdns] n (also: self-~)

confianza; (secret) confidencia; **in ~** (speak,
write) en confianza; **confident** adj seguro
de sí mismo; (certain) seguro; **confidential**
[kɔnfɪ'dɛnʃəl] adj confidencial
**confine** [kən'faɪn] vt (limit) limitar; (shut
up) encerrar; **confined** adj (space) reducido
**confirm** [kən'fəːm] vt confirmar;
**confirmation** [kɔnfə'meɪʃən] n
confirmación f
**confiscate** ['kɔnfɪskeɪt] vt confiscar
**conflict** [n 'kɔnflɪkt, vb kən'flɪkt] n
conflicto ▷ vi chocar
**conform** [kən'fɔːm] vi conformarse; **to ~
to** ajustarse a
**confront** [kən'frʌnt] vt (problems)
hacer frente a; (enemy, danger) enfrentarse
con; **confrontation** [kɔnfrən'teɪʃən] n
enfrentamiento
**confuse** [kən'fjuːz] vt (perplex) aturdir,
desconcertar; (mix up) confundir;
(complicate) complicar; **confused** adj
confuso; (person) perplejo; **confusing**
adj confuso; **confusion** [-'fjuːʒən] n
confusión f
**congestion** [kən'dʒɛstʃən] n congestión f
**congratulate** [kən'grætjuleɪt] vt: **to ~ sb
(on)** felicitar a algn (por); **congratulations**
[-'leɪʃənz] npl felicitaciones fpl;
**congratulations!** ¡enhorabuena!
**congregation** [-'geɪʃən] n (of a church)
feligreses mpl
**congress** ['kɔŋgrɛs] n congreso; (US): **C~**
Congreso; **congressman** (irreg: US) n
miembro del Congreso; **congresswoman**
(irreg: US) n diputada, miembro f del
Congreso
**conifer** ['kɔnɪfə*] n conífera
**conjugate** ['kɔndʒugeɪt] vt conjugar
**conjugation** [kɔndʒə'geɪʃən] n
conjugación f
**conjunction** [kən'dʒʌŋkʃən] n
conjunción f; **in ~ with** junto con
**conjure** ['kʌndʒə*] vi hacer juegos de
manos
**connect** [kə'nɛkt] vt juntar, unir; (Elec)
conectar; (Tel: subscriber) poner; (: caller)
poner al habla; (fig) relacionar, asociar
▷ vi: **to ~ with** (train) enlazar con; **to be ~ed
with** (associated) estar relacionado con;
**connecting flight** n vuelo m de enlace;
**connection** [-ʃən] n juntura, unión
f; (Elec) conexión f; (Rail) enlace m; (Tel)
comunicación f; (fig) relación f
**conquer** ['kɔŋkə*] vt (territory) conquistar;
(enemy, feelings) vencer
**conquest** ['kɔŋkwɛst] n conquista
**cons** [kɔnz] npl see **convenience; pro;
mod**

conscience ['kɔnʃəns] n conciencia
conscientious [kɔnʃɪ'enʃəs] adj concienzudo; (objection) de conciencia
conscious ['kɔnʃəs] adj (deliberate) deliberado; (awake, aware) consciente; consciousness n conciencia; (Med) conocimiento
consecutive [kən'sekjutɪv] adj consecutivo; on 3 ~ occasions en 3 ocasiones consecutivas
consensus [kən'sensəs] n consenso
consent [kən'sent] n consentimiento ▷ vi: to ~ (to) consentir (en)
consequence ['kɔnsɪkwəns] n consecuencia; (significance) importancia
consequently ['kɔnsɪkwəntlɪ] adv por consiguiente
conservation [kɔnsə'veɪʃən] n conservación f
conservative [kən'sə:vətɪv] adj conservador(a); (estimate etc) cauteloso; Conservative (BRIT) adj, n (Pol) conservador(a) m/f
conservatory [kən'sə:vətrɪ] n invernadero; (Mus) conservatorio
consider [kən'sɪdə*] vt considerar; (take into account) tener en cuenta; (study) estudiar, examinar; to ~ doing sth pensar en (la posibilidad de) hacer algo; considerable adj considerable; considerably adv notablemente; considerate adj considerado; consideration [-'reɪʃən] n consideración f; (factor) factor m; to give sth further consideration estudiar algo más a fondo; considering prep teniendo en cuenta
consignment [kən'saɪnmənt] n envío
consist [kən'sɪst] vi: to ~ of consistir en
consistency [kən'sɪstənsɪ] n (of argument etc) coherencia; consecuencia; (thickness) consistencia
consistent [kən'sɪstənt] adj (person) consecuente; (argument etc) coherente
consolation [kɔnsə'leɪʃən] n consuelo
console¹ [kən'səul] vt consolar
console² ['kɔnsəul] n consola
consonant ['kɔnsənənt] n consonante f
conspicuous [kən'spɪkjuəs] adj (visible) visible
conspiracy [kən'spɪrəsɪ] n conjura, complot m
constable ['kʌnstəbl] (BRIT) n policía mf; chief ~ ≈ jefe m de policía
constant ['kɔnstənt] adj constante; constantly adv constantemente
constipated ['kɔnstɪpeɪtəd] adj estreñido

Be careful not to translate **constipated** by the Spanish word constipado.

constipation [kɔnstɪ'peɪʃən] n estreñimiento
constituency [kən'stɪtjuənsɪ] n (Pol: area) distrito electoral; (: electors) electorado
constitute ['kɔnstɪtjuːt] vt constituir
constitution [kɔnstɪ'tjuːʃən] n constitución f
constraint [kən'streɪnt] n obligación f; (limit) restricción f
construct [kən'strʌkt] vt construir; construction [-ʃən] n construcción f; constructive adj constructivo
consul ['kɔnsl] n cónsul mf; consulate ['kɔnsjulɪt] n consulado
consult [kən'sʌlt] vt consultar; consultant n (BRIT Med) especialista mf; (other specialist) asesor(a) m/f; consultation [kɔnsəl'teɪʃən] n consulta; consulting room (BRIT) n consultorio
consume [kən'sjuːm] vt (eat) comerse; (drink) beberse; (fire etc, Comm) consumir; consumer n consumidor(a) m/f
consumption [kən'sʌmpʃən] n consumo
cont. abbr (=continued) sigue
contact ['kɔntækt] n contacto; (person) contacto; (: pej) enchufe m ▷ vt ponerse en contacto con; contact lenses npl lentes fpl de contacto
contagious [kən'teɪdʒəs] adj contagioso
contain [kən'teɪn] vt contener; to ~ o.s. contenerse; container n recipiente m; (for shipping etc) contenedor m
contaminate [kən'tæmɪneɪt] vt contaminar
cont'd abbr (=continued) sigue
contemplate ['kɔntəmpleɪt] vt contemplar; (reflect upon) considerar
contemporary [kən'tempərərɪ] adj, n contemporáneo/a m/f
contempt [kən'tempt] n desprecio; ~ of court (Law) desacato (a los tribunales)
contend [kən'tend] vt (argue) afirmar ▷ vi: to ~ with/for luchar contra/por
content [adj, vb kən'tent, n 'kɔntent] adj (happy) contento; (satisfied) satisfecho ▷ vt contentar; satisfacer ▷ n contenido; contents npl contenido; (table of) ~s índice m de materias; contented adj contento; satisfecho
contest [n 'kɔntest, vb kən'test] n lucha; (competition) concurso ▷ vt (dispute) impugnar; (Pol) presentarse como candidato/a en

Be careful not to translate **contest** by the Spanish word contestar.

contestant [kən'testənt] n concursante

*mf*; (*in fight*) contendiente *mf*

**context** ['kɒntekst] *n* contexto

**continent** ['kɒntɪnənt] *n* continente *m*; **the C~** (BRIT) el continente europeo; **continental** [-'nentl] *adj* continental; **continental breakfast** *n* desayuno estilo europeo; **continental quilt** (BRIT) *n* edredón *m*

**continual** [kən'tɪnjuəl] *adj* continuo; **continually** *adv* constantemente

**continue** [kən'tɪnju:] *vi, vt* seguir, continuar

**continuity** [kɒntɪ'nju:ɪtɪ] *n* (*also Cine*) continuidad *f*

**continuous** [kən'tɪnjuəs] *adj* continuo; **continuous assessment** (BRIT) evaluación *f* continua; **continuously** *adv* continuamente

**contour** ['kɒntuə*] *n* contorno; (*also:* ~ **line**) curva de nivel

**contraception** [kɒntrə'sepʃən] *n* contracepción *f*

**contraceptive** [kɒntrə'septɪv] *adj, n* anticonceptivo

**contract** [*n* 'kɒntrækt, *vb* kən'trækt] *n* contrato ▷ *vi*: **to ~ to do sth** comprometerse por contrato a hacer algo; (*become smaller*) contraerse, encogerse ▷ *vt* contraer; **contractor** *n* contratista *mf*

**contradict** [kɒntrə'dɪkt] *vt* contradecir; **contradiction** [-ʃən] *n* contradicción *f*

**contrary**[1] ['kɒntrərɪ] *adj* contrario ▷ *n* lo contrario; **on the ~** al contrario; **unless you hear to the ~** a no ser que le digan lo contrario

**contrary**[2] [kən'treərɪ] *adj* (*perverse*) terco

**contrast** [*n* 'kɒntrɑ:st, *vt* kən'trɑ:st] *n* contraste *m* ▷ *vt* comparar; **in ~ to** en contraste con

**contribute** [kən'trɪbju:t] *vi* contribuir ▷ *vt*: **to ~ £10/an article to** contribuir con 10 libras/un artículo a; **to ~ to** (*charity*) donar a; (*newspaper*) escribir para; (*discussion*) intervenir en; **contribution** [kɒntrɪ'bju:-ʃən] *n* (*donation*) donativo; (BRIT: *for social security*) cotización *f*; (*to debate*) intervención *f*; (*to journal*) colaboración *f*; **contributor** *n* contribuyente *mf*; (*to newspaper*) colaborador(a) *m/f*

**control** [kən'trəul] *vt* controlar; (*process etc*) dirigir; (*machinery*) manejar; (*temper*) dominar; (*disease*) contener ▷ *n* control *m*; **controls** *npl* (*of vehicle*) instrumentos *mpl* de mando; (*of radio*) controles *mpl*; (*governmental*) medidas *fpl* de control; **under ~** bajo control; **to be in ~ of** tener el mando de; **the car went out of ~** se perdió el control del coche; **control tower** *n* (*Aviat*)

torre *f* de control

**controversial** [kɒntrə'və:ʃl] *adj* polémico

**controversy** ['kɒntrəvə:sɪ] *n* polémica

**convenience** [kən'vi:nɪəns] *n* (*easiness*) comodidad *f*; (*suitability*) idoneidad *f*; (*advantage*) ventaja; **at your ~** cuando le sea conveniente; **all modern ~s, all mod cons** (BRIT) todo confort

**convenient** [kən'vi:nɪənt] *adj* (*useful*) útil; (*place, time*) conveniente

**convent** ['kɒnvənt] *n* convento

**convention** [kən'venʃən] *n* convención *f*; (*meeting*) asamblea; (*agreement*) convenio; **conventional** *adj* convencional

**conversation** [kɒnvə'seɪʃən] *n* conversación *f*

**conversely** [-'və:slɪ] *adv* a la inversa

**conversion** [kən'və:ʃən] *n* conversión *f*

**convert** [*vb* kən'və:t, *n* 'kɒnvə:t] *vt* (*Rel, Comm*) convertir; (*alter*): **to ~ sth into/to** transformar algo en/convertir algo a ▷ *n* converso/a; **convertible** *adj* convertible ▷ *n* descapotable *m*

**convey** [kən'veɪ] *vt* llevar; (*thanks*) comunicar; (*idea*) expresar; **conveyor belt** *n* cinta transportadora

**convict** [*vb* kən'vɪkt, *n* 'kɒnvɪkt] *vt* (*find guilty*) declarar culpable a ▷ *n* presidiario/a; **conviction** [-ʃən] *n* condena; (*belief, certainty*) convicción *f*

**convince** [kən'vɪns] *vt* convencer; **convinced** *adj*: **convinced of/that** convencido de/de que; **convincing** *adj* convincente

**convoy** ['kɒnvɔɪ] *n* convoy *m*

**cook** [kuk] *vt* (*stew etc*) guisar; (*meal*) preparar ▷ *vi* cocer; (*person*) cocinar ▷ *n* cocinero/a; **cook book** *n* libro de cocina; **cooker** *n* cocina; **cookery** *n* cocina; **cookery book** (BRIT) *n* = **cook book**; **cookie** (US) *n* galleta; **cooking** *n* cocina

**cool** [ku:l] *adj* fresco; (*not afraid*) tranquilo; (*unfriendly*) frío ▷ *vt* enfriar ▷ *vi* enfriarse; **cool down** *vi* enfriarse; (*fig: person, situation*) calmarse; **cool off** *vi* (*become calmer*) calmarse, apaciguarse; (*lose enthusiasm*) perder (el) interés, enfriarse

**cop** [kɒp] (*inf*) *n* poli *mf* (SP), tira *mf* (MEX)

**cope** [kəup] *vi*: **to ~ with** (*problem*) hacer frente a

**copper** ['kɒpə*] *n* (*metal*) cobre *m*; (BRIT: *inf*) poli *mf*, tira *mf* (MEX)

**copy** ['kɒpɪ] *n* copia; (*of book etc*) ejemplar *m* ▷ *vt* copiar; **copyright** *n* derechos *mpl* de autor

**coral** ['kɒrəl] *n* coral *m*

**cord** [kɔ:d] *n* cuerda; (*Elec*) cable *m*; (*fabric*) pana; **cords** *npl* (*trousers*) pantalones *mpl* de pana; **cordless** adj sin hilos

**corduroy** ['kɔ:dərɔɪ] n pana

**core** [kɔ:*] n centro, núcleo; (of fruit) corazón m; (of problem) meollo ▷ vt quitar el corazón de

**coriander** [kɒrɪˈændə*] n culantro

**cork** [kɔ:k] n corcho; (tree) alcornoque m; **corkscrew** n sacacorchos m inv

**corn** [kɔ:n] n (BRIT: cereal crop) trigo; (US: maize) maíz m; (on foot) callo; **~ on the cob** (Culin) mazorca, elote m (MEX), choclo (SC)

**corned beef** ['kɔ:nd-] n carne f acecinada (en lata)

**corner** ['kɔ:nə*] n (outside) esquina; (inside) rincón m; (in road) curva; (Football) córner m; (Boxing) esquina ▷ vt (trap) arrinconar; (Comm) acaparar ▷ vi (in car) tomar las curvas; **corner shop** (BRIT) tienda de la esquina

**cornflakes** ['kɔ:nfleɪks] npl copos mpl de maíz, cornflakes mpl

**cornflour** ['kɔ:nflauə*] (BRIT) n harina de maíz

**cornstarch** ['kɔ:nstɑ:tʃ] (US) n = **cornflour**

**Cornwall** ['kɔ:nwəl] n Cornualles m

**coronary** ['kɒrənərɪ] n (also: **~ thrombosis**) infarto

**coronation** [kɒrəˈneɪʃən] n coronación f

**coroner** ['kɒrənə*] n juez mf de instrucción

**corporal** ['kɔ:pərl] n cabo ▷ adj: **~ punishment** castigo corporal

**corporate** ['kɔ:pərɪt] adj (action, ownership) colectivo; (finance, image) corporativo

**corporation** [kɔ:pəˈreɪʃən] n (of town) ayuntamiento; (Comm) corporación f

**corps** [kɔ:*, pl kɔ:z] n inv cuerpo; **diplomatic ~** cuerpo diplomático; **press ~** gabinete m de prensa

**corpse** [kɔ:ps] n cadáver m

**correct** [kəˈrɛkt] adj justo, exacto; (proper) correcto ▷ vt corregir; (exam) corregir, calificar; **correction** [-ʃən] n (act) corrección f; (instance) rectificación f

**correspond** [kɒrɪsˈpɒnd] vi (write): to **~ (with)** escribirse (con); (be equivalent to): to **~ (to)** corresponder (a); (be in accordance): to **~ (with)** corresponder (con); **correspondence** n correspondencia; **correspondent** n corresponsal mf; **corresponding** adj correspondiente

**corridor** ['kɔ:rɪdɔ:*] n pasillo

**corrode** [kəˈrəud] vt corroer ▷ vi corroerse

**corrupt** [kəˈrʌpt] adj (person) corrupto; (Comput) corrompido ▷ vt corromper;

(Comput) degradar; **corruption** n corrupción f; (of data) alteración f

**Corsica** ['kɔ:sɪkə] n Córcega

**cosmetic** [kɒzˈmɛtɪk] adj, n cosmético; **cosmetic surgery** n cirugía f estética

**cosmopolitan** [kɒzməˈpɔlɪtn] adj cosmopolita

**cost** [kɒst] (pt, pp ~) n (price) precio ▷ vi costar, valer ▷ vt preparar el presupuesto de; **how much does it ~?** ¿cuánto cuesta?; **to ~ sb time/effort** costarle a algn tiempo/ esfuerzo; **it ~ him his life** le costó la vida; **at all ~s** cueste lo que cueste; **costs** npl (Comm) costes mpl; (Law) costas fpl

**co-star** ['kəustɑ:*] n coprotagonista mf

**Costa Rica** ['kɒstəˈri:kə] n Costa Rica; **Costa Rican** adj, n costarriqueño/a

**costly** ['kɒstlɪ] adj costoso

**cost of living** n costo or coste m (Sp) de la vida

**costume** ['kɒstju:m] n traje m; (BRIT: also: **swimming ~**) traje de baño

**cosy** ['kəuzɪ] (US **cozy**) adj (person) cómodo; (room) acogedor(a)

**cot** [kɒt] n (BRIT: child's) cuna; (US: campbed) cama de campaña

**cottage** ['kɒtɪdʒ] n casita de campo; (rustic) barraca; **cottage cheese** n requesón m

**cotton** ['kɒtn] n algodón m; (thread) hilo; **cotton on** vi (inf): **to cotton on (to sth)** caer en la cuenta (de algo); **cotton bud** n (BRIT) bastoncillo m de algodón; **cotton candy** (US) n algodón m (azucarado); **cotton wool** (BRIT) n algodón m (hidrófilo)

**couch** [kautʃ] n sofá m; (doctor's etc) diván m

**cough** [kɒf] vi toser ▷ n tos f; **cough mixture** n jarabe m para la tos

**could** [kud] pt of **can²**; **couldn't** = **could not**

**council** ['kaunsl] n consejo; **city** or **town ~** consejo municipal; **council estate** (BRIT) n urbanización de viviendas municipales de alquiler; **council house** (BRIT) n vivienda municipal de alquiler; **councillor** (US **councilor**) n concejal(a) m/f; **council tax** n (BRIT) contribución f municipal (dependiente del valor de la vivienda)

**counsel** ['kaunsl] n (advice) consejo; (lawyer) abogado/a ▷ vt aconsejar; **counselling** (US **counseling**) n (Psych) asistencia f psicológica; **counsellor** (US **counselor**) n consejero/a, abogado/a

**count** [kaunt] vt contar; (include) incluir ▷ vi contar ▷ n cuenta; (of votes) escrutinio; (level) nivel m; (nobleman) conde m; **count in** (inf) vt: **to count sb in on sth** contar con

algn para algo; **count on** *vt fus* contar con;
**countdown** *n* cuenta atrás

**counter** ['kauntə*] *n* (*in shop*) mostrador
*m*; (*in games*) ficha ▷ *vt* contrarrestar
▷ *adv*: **to run ~ to** ser contrario a, ir en
contra de; **counter clockwise** (*US*) *adv* en
sentido contrario al de las agujas del reloj

**counterfeit** ['kauntəfɪt] *n* falsificación
*f*, simulación *f* ▷ *vt* falsificar ▷ *adj* falso,
falsificado

**counterpart** ['kauntəpɑːt] *n* homólogo/
a

**countess** ['kauntɪs] *n* condesa

**countless** ['kauntlɪs] *adj* innumerable

**country** ['kʌntrɪ] *n* país *m*; (*native land*)
patria; (*as opposed to town*) campo; (*region*)
región *f*, tierra; **country and western
(music)** *n* música country; **country house**
*n* casa de campo; **countryside** *n* campo

**county** ['kauntɪ] *n* condado

**coup** [kuː] (*pl* **~s**) *n* (*also*: **~ d'état**) golpe *m*
(de estado); (*achievement*) éxito

**couple** ['kʌpl] *n* (*of things*) par *m*; (*of people*)
pareja; (*married couple*) matrimonio; **a ~ of**
un par de

**coupon** ['kuːpɔn] *n* cupón *m*; (*voucher*)
valé *m*

**courage** ['kʌrɪdʒ] *n* valor *m*, valentía;
**courageous** [kə'reɪdʒəs] *adj* valiente

**courgette** [kuə'ʒet] (*BRIT*) *n* calabacín *m*,
calabacita (*MEX*)

**courier** ['kurɪə*] *n* mensajero/a; (*for
tourists*) guía *mf* (de turismo)

**course** [kɔːs] *n* (*direction*) dirección *f*;
(*of river, Scol*) curso; (*process*) transcurso;
(*Med*): **~ of treatment** tratamiento; (*of ship*)
rumbo; (*part of meal*) plato; (*Golf*) campo; **of
~** desde luego, naturalmente; **of ~!** ¡claro!

**court** [kɔːt] *n* (*royal*) corte *f*; (*Law*) tribunal
*m*, juzgado; (*Tennis etc*) pista, cancha ▷ *vt*
(*woman*) cortejar a; **to take to ~** demandar

**courtesy** ['kɔːtəsɪ] *n* cortesía; **(by) ~ of**
por cortesía de; **courtesy bus, courtesy
coach** *n* autobús *m* gratuito

**court: court-house** ['kɔːthaus] (*US*) *n*
palacio de justicia; **courtroom** ['kɔːtrum]
*n* sala de justicia; **courtyard** ['kɔːtjɑːd]
*n* patio

**cousin** ['kʌzn] *n* primo/a; **first ~** primo/a
carnal, primo/a hermano/a

**cover** ['kʌvə*] *vt* cubrir; (*feelings, mistake*)
ocultar; (*with lid*) tapar; (*book etc*) forrar;
(*distance*) recorrer; (*include*) abarcar;
(*protect: also: Insurance*) cubrir; (*Press*)
investigar; (*discuss*) tratar ▷ *n* cubierta; (*lid*)
tapa; (*for chair etc*) funda; (*envelope*) sobre
*m*; (*for book*) forro; (*of magazine*) portada;
(*shelter*) abrigo; (*Insurance*) cobertura; (*of

spy*) cobertura; **covers** *npl* (*on bed*) sábanas;
mantas; **to take ~** (*shelter*) protegerse,
resguardarse; **under ~** (*indoors*) bajo techo;
**under ~ of darkness** al amparo de la
oscuridad; **under separate ~** (*Comm*) por
separado; **cover up** *vi*: **to cover up for sb**
encubrir a algn; **coverage** *n* (*TV, Press*)
cobertura; **cover charge** *n* precio del
cubierto; **cover-up** *n* encubrimiento

**cow** [kau] *n* vaca; (*inf!: woman*) bruja ▷ *vt*
intimidar

**coward** ['kauəd] *n* cobarde *mf*; **cowardly**
*adj* cobarde

**cowboy** ['kaubɔɪ] *n* vaquero

**cozy** ['kəuzɪ] (*US*) *adj* = **cosy**

**crab** [kræb] *n* cangrejo

**crack** [kræk] *n* grieta; (*noise*) crujido; (*drug*)
crack *m* ▷ *vt* agrietar, romper; (*nut*) cascar;
(*solve: problem*) resolver; (*: code*) descifrar;
(*whip etc*) chasquear; (*knuckles*) crujir; (*joke*)
contar ▷ *adj* (*expert*) de primera; **crack
down on** *vt fus* adoptar fuertes medidas
contra; **cracked** *adj* (*cup, window*) rajado;
(*wall*) resquebrajado; **cracker** *n* (*biscuit*)
cráquer *m*; (*Christmas cracker*) petardo
sorpresa

**crackle** ['krækl] *vi* crepitar

**cradle** ['kreɪdl] *n* cuna

**craft** [krɑːft] *n* (*skill*) arte *m*; (*trade*) oficio;
(*cunning*) astucia; (*boat: pl inv*) barco;
(*plane: pl inv*) avión *m*; **craftsman** (*irreg*)
*n* artesano; **craftsmanship** *n* (*quality*)
destreza

**cram** [kræm] *vt* (*fill*): **to ~ sth with** llenar
algo (a reventar) de; (*put*): **to ~ sth into**
meter algo a la fuerza en ▷ *vi* (*for exams*)
empollar

**cramp** [kræmp] *n* (*Med*) calambre *m*;
**cramped** *adj* apretado, estrecho

**cranberry** ['krænbərɪ] *n* arándano agrio

**crane** [kreɪn] *n* (*Tech*) grúa; (*bird*) grulla

**crap** [kræp] *n* (*inf!*) mierda (!)

**crash** [kræʃ] *n* (*noise*) estrépito; (*of cars
etc*) choque *m*; (*of plane*) accidente m de
aviación; (*Comm*) quiebra ▷ *vt* (*car, plane*)
estrellar ▷ *vi* (*car, plane*) estrellarse; (*two
cars*) chocar; (*Comm*) quebrar; **crash course**
*n* curso acelerado; **crash helmet** *n* casco
(protector)

**crate** [kreɪt] *n* cajón *m* de embalaje; (*for
bottles*) caja

**crave** [kreɪv] *vt, vi*: **to ~ (for)** ansiar,
anhelar

**crawl** [krɔːl] *vi* (*drag o.s.*) arrastrarse; (*child*)
andar a gatas, gatear; (*vehicle*) avanzar
(lentamente) ▷ *n* (*Swimming*) crol *m*

**crayfish** ['kreɪfɪʃ] *n inv* (*freshwater*)
cangrejo de río; (*saltwater*) cigala

**crayon** ['kreɪən] n lápiz m de color

**craze** [kreɪz] n (fashion) moda

**crazy** ['kreɪzɪ] adj (person) loco; (idea) disparatado; (inf: keen): **~ about sb/sth** loco por algn/algo

**creak** [kri:k] vi (floorboard) crujir; (hinge etc) chirriar, rechinar

**cream** [kri:m] n (of milk) nata, crema; (lotion) crema; (fig) flor f y nata ▷ adj (colour) color crema; **cream cheese** n queso blanco; **creamy** adj cremoso; (colour) color crema

**crease** [kri:s] n (fold) pliegue m; (in trousers) raya; (wrinkle) arruga ▷ vt (wrinkle) arrugar ▷ vi (wrinkle up) arrugarse

**create** [kri:'eɪt] vt crear; **creation** [-ʃən] n creación f; **creative** adj creativo; **creator** n creador(a) m/f

**creature** ['kri:tʃə*] n (animal) animal m, bicho; (person) criatura

**crèche** [krɛʃ] n guardería (infantil)

**credentials** [krɪ'dɛnʃlz] npl (references) referencias fpl; (identity papers) documentos mpl de identidad

**credibility** [krɛdɪ'bɪlɪtɪ] n credibilidad f

**credible** ['krɛdɪbl] adj creíble; (trustworthy) digno de confianza

**credit** ['krɛdɪt] n crédito; (merit) honor m, mérito ▷ vt (Comm) abonar; (believe: also: **give ~ to**) creer, prestar fe a ▷ adj crediticio; **credits** npl (Cinema) fichas fpl técnicas; **to be in ~** (person) tener saldo a favor; **to ~ sb with** (fig) reconocer a algn el mérito de; **credit card** n tarjeta de crédito

**creek** [kri:k] n cala, ensenada; (us) riachuelo

**creep** [kri:p] (pt, pp crept) vi arrastrarse

**cremate** [krɪ'meɪt] vt incinerar

**crematorium** [krɛmə'tɔ:rɪəm] (pl **crematoria**) n crematorio

**crept** [krɛpt] pt, pp of **creep**

**crescent** ['krɛsnt] n media luna; (street) calle f (en forma de semicírculo)

**cress** [krɛs] n berro

**crest** [krɛst] n (of bird) cresta; (of hill) cima, cumbre f; (of coat of arms) blasón m

**crew** [kru:] n (of ship etc) tripulación f; (TV, Cinema) equipo; **crew-neck** n cuello a la caja

**crib** [krɪb] n cuna ▷ vt (inf) plagiar

**cricket** ['krɪkɪt] n (insect) grillo; (game) críquet m; **cricketer** n jugador(a) m/f de críquet

**crime** [kraɪm] n (no pl: illegal activities) crimen m; (illegal action) delito; **criminal** ['krɪmɪnl] n criminal mf, delincuente mf ▷ adj criminal; (illegal) delictivo; (law) penal

**crimson** ['krɪmzn] adj carmesí

**cringe** [krɪndʒ] vi agacharse, encogerse

**cripple** ['krɪpl] n lisiado/a, cojo/a ▷ vt lisiar, mutilar

**crisis** ['kraɪsɪs] (pl **crises**) n crisis f inv

**crisp** [krɪsp] adj fresco; (vegetables etc) crujiente; (manner) seco; **crispy** adj crujiente

**criterion** [kraɪ'tɪərɪən] (pl **criteria**) n criterio

**critic** ['krɪtɪk] n crítico/a; **critical** adj crítico; (illness) grave; **criticism** ['krɪtɪsɪzm] n crítica; **criticize** ['krɪtɪsaɪz] vt criticar

**Croat** ['krəuæt] adj, n = **Croatian**

**Croatia** [krəu'eɪʃə] n Croacia; **Croatian** adj, n croata m/f ▷ n (Ling) croata m

**crockery** ['krɔkərɪ] n loza, vajilla

**crocodile** ['krɔkədaɪl] n cocodrilo

**crocus** ['krəukəs] n croco, crocus m

**croissant** ['krwasn] n croissant m, medialuna (esp LAM)

**crook** [kruk] n ladrón/ona m/f; (of shepherd) cayado; **crooked** ['krukɪd] adj torcido; (dishonest) nada honrado

**crop** [krɔp] n (produce) cultivo; (amount produced) cosecha; (riding crop) látigo de montar ▷ vt cortar, recortar; **crop up** vi surgir, presentarse

**cross** [krɔs] n cruz f; (hybrid) cruce m ▷ vt (street etc) cruzar, atravesar ▷ adj de mal humor, enojado; **cross off** vt tachar; **cross out** vt tachar; **cross over** vi cruzar; **cross-Channel ferry** ['krɔs'tʃænl-] n transbordador m que cruza el Canal de la Mancha; **crosscountry (race)** n carrera a campo traviesa, cross m; **crossing** n (sea passage) travesía; (also: **pedestrian crossing**) paso para peatones; **crossing guard** (us) n persona encargada de ayudar a los niños a cruzar la calle; **crossroads** n cruce m, encrucijada; **crosswalk** (us) n paso de peatones; **crossword** n crucigrama m

**crotch** [krɔtʃ] n (Anat, of garment) entrepierna

**crouch** [krautʃ] vi agacharse, acurrucarse

**crouton** ['kru:tɔn] n cubito de pan frito

**crow** [krəu] n (bird) cuervo; (of cock) canto, cacareo ▷ vi (cock) cantar

**crowd** [kraud] n muchedumbre f, multitud f ▷ vt (fill) llenar ▷ vi (gather): **to ~ round** reunirse en torno a; (cram): **to ~ in** entrar en tropel; **crowded** adj (full) atestado; (densely populated) superpoblado

**crown** [kraun] n corona; (of head) coronilla; (for tooth) funda; (of hill) cumbre f ▷ vt coronar; (fig) completar, rematar; **crown jewels** npl joyas fpl reales

**crucial** ['kru:ʃl] adj decisivo

**crucifix** ['kru:sɪfɪks] n crucifijo

**crude** [kru:d] *adj* (*materials*) bruto; (*fig: basic*) tosco; (: *vulgar*) ordinario; **crude (oil)** *n* (petróleo) crudo

**cruel** ['kruəl] *adj* cruel; **cruelty** *n* crueldad *f*

**cruise** [kru:z] *n* crucero ▷ *vi* (*ship*) hacer un crucero; (*car*) ir a velocidad de crucero

**crumb** [krʌm] *n* miga, migaja

**crumble** ['krʌmbl] *vt* desmenuzar ▷ *vi* (*building, also fig*) desmoronarse

**crumpet** ['krʌmpɪt] *n* ≈ bollo para tostar

**crumple** ['krʌmpl] *vt* (*paper*) estrujar; (*material*) arrugar

**crunch** [krʌntʃ] *vt* (*with teeth*) mascar; (*underfoot*) hacer crujir ▷ *n* (*fig*) hora or momento de la verdad; **crunchy** *adj* crujiente

**crush** [krʌʃ] *n* (*crowd*) aglomeración *f*; (*infatuation*): **to have a ~ on sb** estar loco por algn; (*drink*): **lemon ~** limonada ▷ *vt* aplastar; (*paper*) estrujar; (*cloth*) arrugar; (*fruit*) exprimir; (*opposition*) aplastar; (*hopes*) destruir

**crust** [krʌst] *n* corteza; (*of snow, ice*) costra; **crusty** *adj* (*bread*) crujiente; (*person*) de mal carácter

**crutch** [krʌtʃ] *n* muleta

**cry** [kraɪ] *vi* llorar ▷ *n* (*shriek*) chillido; (*shout*) grito; **cry out** *vi* (*call out, shout*) lanzar un grito, echar un grito ▷ *vt* gritar

**crystal** ['krɪstl] *n* cristal *m*

**cub** [kʌb] *n* cachorro; (*also*: **~ scout**) niño explorador

**Cuba** ['kju:bə] *n* Cuba; **Cuban** *adj, n* cubano/a *m/f*

**cube** [kju:b] *n* cubo ▷ *vt* (*Math*) cubicar

**cubicle** ['kju:bɪkl] *n* (*at pool*) caseta; (*for bed*) cubículo

**cuckoo** ['kuku:] *n* cuco

**cucumber** ['kju:kʌmbə*] *n* pepino

**cuddle** ['kʌdl] *vt* abrazar ▷ *vi* abrazarse

**cue** [kju:] *n* (*snooker cue*) taco; (*Theatre etc*) señal *f*

**cuff** [kʌf] *n* (*of sleeve*) puño; (*US: of trousers*) vuelta; (*blow*) bofetada ▷ **off the ~** *adv* de improviso; **cufflinks** *npl* gemelos *mpl*

**cuisine** [kwɪ'zi:n] *n* cocina

**cul-de-sac** ['kʌldəsæk] *n* callejón *m* sin salida

**cull** [kʌl] *vt* (*idea*) sacar ▷ *n* (*of animals*) matanza selectiva

**culminate** ['kʌlmɪneɪt] *vi*: **to ~ in** terminar en

**culprit** ['kʌlprɪt] *n* culpable *mf*

**cult** [kʌlt] *n* culto

**cultivate** ['kʌltɪveɪt] *vt* cultivar

**cultural** ['kʌltʃərəl] *adj* cultural

**culture** ['kʌltʃə*] *n* (*also fig*) cultura; (*Biol*) cultivo

**cumin** ['kʌmɪn] *n* (*spice*) comino

**cunning** ['kʌnɪŋ] *n* astucia ▷ *adj* astuto

**cup** [kʌp] *n* taza; (*as prize*) copa

**cupboard** ['kʌbəd] *n* armario; (*in kitchen*) alacena

**cup final** *n* (*Football*) final *f* de copa

**curator** [kjuə'reɪtə*] *n* director(a) *m/f*

**curb** [kə:b] *vt* refrenar; (*person*) reprimir ▷ *n* freno; (*US*) bordillo

**curdle** ['kə:dl] *vi* cuajarse

**cure** [kjuə*] *vt* curar ▷ *n* cura, curación *f*; (*fig: solution*) remedio

**curfew** ['kə:fju:] *n* toque *m* de queda

**curiosity** [kjuərɪ'ɔsɪtɪ] *n* curiosidad *f*

**curious** ['kjuərɪəs] *adj* curioso; (*person: interested*): **to be ~** sentir curiosidad

**curl** [kə:l] *n* rizo ▷ *vt* (*hair*) rizar ▷ *vi* rizarse; **curl up** *vi* (*person*) hacerse un ovillo; **curler** *n* rulo; **curly** *adj* rizado

**currant** ['kʌrnt] *n* pasa (de Corinto); (*blackcurrant, redcurrant*) grosella

**currency** ['kʌrnsɪ] *n* moneda; **to gain ~** (*fig*) difundirse

**current** ['kʌrnt] *n* corriente *f* ▷ *adj* (*accepted*) corriente; (*present*) actual; **current account** (*BRIT*) *n* cuenta corriente; **current affairs** *npl* noticias *fpl* de actualidad; **currently** *adv* actualmente

**curriculum** [kə'rɪkjuləm] (*pl* **~s** *or* **curricula**) *n* plan *m* de estudios; **curriculum vitae** *n* currículum *m*

**curry** ['kʌrɪ] *n* curry *m* ▷ *vt*: **to ~ favour with** buscar favores con; **curry powder** *n* curry *m* en polvo

**curse** [kə:s] *vi* soltar tacos ▷ *vt* maldecir ▷ *n* maldición *f*; (*swearword*) palabrota, taco

**cursor** ['kə:sə*] *n* (*Comput*) cursor *m*

**curt** [kə:t] *adj* corto, seco

**curtain** ['kə:tn] *n* cortina; (*Theatre*) telón *m*

**curve** [kə:v] *n* curva ▷ *vi* (*road*) hacer una curva; (*line etc*) curvarse; **curved** *adj* curvo

**cushion** ['kuʃən] *n* cojín *m*; (*of air*) colchón *m* ▷ *vt* (*shock*) amortiguar

**custard** ['kʌstəd] *n* natillas *fpl*

**custody** ['kʌstədɪ] *n* custodia; **to take into ~** detener

**custom** ['kʌstəm] *n* costumbre *f*; (*Comm*) clientela

**customer** ['kʌstəmə*] *n* cliente *m/f*

**customized** ['kʌstəmaɪzd] *adj* (*car etc*) hecho a encargo

**customs** ['kʌstəmz] *npl* aduana; **customs officer** *n* aduanero/a

**cut** [kʌt] (*pt, pp* **~**) *vt* cortar; (*price*) rebajar; (*text, programme*) acortar; (*reduce*) reducir ▷ *vi* cortar ▷ *n* (*of garment*) corte *m*; (*in skin*) cortadura; (*in salary etc*) rebaja; (*in spending*)

reducción f, recorte m; (slice of meat) tajada;
**to ~ a tooth** echar un diente; **to ~ and
paste** (Comput) cortar y pegar; **cut back**
vt (plants) podar; (production, expenditure)
reducir; **cut down** vt (tree) derribar; (reduce)
reducir; **cut off** vt cortar; (person, place)
aislar; (Tel) desconectar; **cut out** vt (shape)
recortar; (stop: activity etc) dejar; (remove)
quitar; **cut up** vt cortar (en pedazos);
**cutback** n reducción f
**cute** [kjuːt] adj mono
**cutlery** ['kʌtlərɪ] n cubiertos mpl
**cutlet** ['kʌtlɪt] n chuleta; (nut etc cutlet)
plato vegetariano hecho con nueces y verdura en
forma de chuleta
**cut-price** ['kʌt'praɪs] (BRIT) adj a precio
reducido
**cut-rate** ['kʌt'reɪt] (US) adj = **cut-price**
**cutting** ['kʌtɪŋ] adj (remark) mordaz ▷ n
(BRIT: from newspaper) recorte m; (from plant)
esqueje m
**CV** n abbr = **curriculum vitae**
**cwt** abbr = **hundredweight(s)**
**cybercafé** ['saɪbəkæfeɪ] n cibercafé m
**cyberspace** ['saɪbəspeɪs] n ciberespacio
**cycle** ['saɪkl] n ciclo; (bicycle) bicicleta ▷ vi
ir en bicicleta; **cycle hire** n alquiler m de
bicicletas; **cycle lane** n carril-bici m; **cycle
path** n carril-bici m; **cycling** n ciclismo;
**cyclist** n ciclista mf
**cyclone** ['saɪkləun] n ciclón m
**cylinder** ['sɪlɪndə*] n cilindro; (of gas)
bombona
**cymbal** ['sɪmbl] n címbalo, platillo
**cynical** ['sɪnɪkl] adj cínico
**Cypriot** ['sɪprɪət] adj, n chipriota m/f
**Cyprus** ['saɪprəs] n Chipre f
**cyst** [sɪst] n quiste m; **cystitis** [-'taɪtɪs]
n cistitis f
**czar** [zɑː*] n zar m
**Czech** [tʃɛk] adj, n checo/a m/f; **Czech
Republic** n: **the Czech Republic** la
República Checa

# d

**D** [diː] n (Mus) re m
**dab** [dæb] vt (eyes, wound) tocar
(ligeramente); (paint, cream) poner un
poco de
**dad** [dæd] n = **daddy**
**daddy** ['dædɪ] n papá m
**daffodil** ['dæfədɪl] n narciso
**daft** [dɑːft] adj tonto
**dagger** ['dægə*] n puñal m, daga
**daily** ['deɪlɪ] adj diario, cotidiano ▷ adv
todos los días, cada día
**dairy** ['dɛərɪ] n (shop) lechería; (on farm)
vaquería; **dairy produce** n productos mpl
lácteos
**daisy** ['deɪzɪ] n margarita
**dam** [dæm] n presa ▷ vt construir una
presa sobre, represar
**damage** ['dæmɪdʒ] n lesión f; daño; (dents
etc) desperfectos mpl; (fig) perjuicio ▷ vt
dañar, perjudicar; (spoil, break) estropear;
**damages** npl (Law) daños mpl y perjuicios
**damn** [dæm] vt condenar; (curse) maldecir
▷ n (inf): **I don't give a ~** me importa un
pito ▷ adj (inf: also: **~ed**) maldito; **~ (it)!**
¡maldito sea!
**damp** [dæmp] adj húmedo, mojado ▷ n
humedad f ▷ vt (also: **~en**: cloth, rag) mojar;
(: enthusiasm) enfriar
**dance** [dɑːns] n baile m ▷ vi bailar;
**dance floor** n pista f de baile; **dancer** n
bailador(a) m/f; (professional) bailarín/ina
m/f; **dancing** n baile m
**dandelion** ['dændɪlaɪən] n diente m de
león
**dandruff** ['dændrəf] n caspa
**Dane** [deɪn] n danés/esa m/f
**danger** ['deɪndʒə*] n peligro; (risk) riesgo;
**~!** (on sign) ¡peligro de muerte!; **to be in ~ of**
correr riesgo de; **dangerous** adj peligroso
**dangle** ['dæŋgl] vt colgar ▷ vi pender,
colgar

**Danish** ['deɪnɪʃ] *adj* danés/esa ▷*n* (*Ling*) danés *m*

**dare** [dɛə*] *vt*: **to ~ sb to do** desafiar a algn a hacer ▷*vi*: **to ~ (to) do sth** atreverse a hacer algo; **I ~ say** (*I suppose*) puede ser (que); **daring** *adj* atrevido, osado ▷*n* atrevimiento, osadía

**dark** [dɑːk] *adj* oscuro; (*hair, complexion*) moreno ▷*n*: **in the ~** a oscuras; **to be in the ~ about** (*fig*) no saber nada de; **after ~** después del anochecer; **darken** *vt* (*colour*) hacer más oscuro ▷*vi* oscurecerse; **darkness** *n* oscuridad *f*; **darkroom** *n* cuarto oscuro

**darling** ['dɑːlɪŋ] *adj, n* querido/a *m/f*

**dart** [dɑːt] *n* dardo; (*in sewing*) sisa ▷*vi* precipitarse; **dartboard** *n* diana; **darts** *n* (*game*) dardos *mpl*

**dash** [dæʃ] *n* (*small quantity: of liquid*) gota, chorrito; (*sign*) raya ▷*vt* (*throw*) tirar; (*hopes*) defraudar ▷*vi* precipitarse, ir de prisa

**dashboard** ['dæʃbɔːd] *n* (*Aut*) salpicadero

**data** ['deɪtə] *npl* datos *mpl*; **database** *n* base *f* de datos; **data processing** *n* proceso de datos

**date** [deɪt] *n* (*day*) fecha; (*with friend*) cita; (*fruit*) dátil *m* ▷*vt* fechar; (*person*) salir con; **~ of birth** fecha de nacimiento; **to ~** *adv* hasta la fecha; **dated** *adj* anticuado

**daughter** ['dɔːtə*] *n* hija; **daughter-in-law** *n* nuera, hija política

**daunting** ['dɔːntɪŋ] *adj* desalentador(a)

**dawn** [dɔːn] *n* alba, amanecer *m*; (*fig*) nacimiento ▷*vi* (*day*) amanecer; (*fig*): **it ~ed on him that ...** cayó en la cuenta de que ...

**day** [deɪ] *n* día *m*; (*working day*) jornada; (*heyday*) tiempos *mpl*, días *mpl*; **the ~ before/after** el día anterior/siguiente; **the ~ after tomorrow** pasado mañana; **the ~ before yesterday** anteayer; **the following ~** el día siguiente; **by ~** de día; **day-care centre** ['deɪkeə-] *n* centro de día; (*for children*) guardería infantil; **daydream** *vi* soñar despierto; **daylight** *n* luz *f* (del día); **day return** (*BRIT*) *n* billete *m* de ida y vuelta (en un día); **daytime** *n* día *m*; **day-to-day** *adj* cotidiano; **day trip** *n* excursión *f* (de un día)

**dazed** [deɪzd] *adj* aturdido

**dazzle** ['dæzl] *vt* deslumbrar; **dazzling** *adj* (*light, smile*) deslumbrante; (*colour*) fuerte

**DC** *abbr* (= *direct current*) corriente *f* continua

**dead** [dɛd] *adj* muerto; (*limb*) dormido; (*telephone*) cortado; (*battery*) agotado ▷*adv* (*completely*) totalmente; (*exactly*) exactamente; **to shoot sb ~** matar a algn a tiros; **~ tired** muerto (de cansancio); **to**

**stop ~** parar en seco; **dead end** *n* callejón *m* sin salida; **deadline** *n* fecha (*or* hora) tope; **deadly** *adj* mortal, fatal; **Dead Sea** *n*: **the Dead Sea** el Mar Muerto

**deaf** [dɛf] *adj* sordo; **deafen** *vt* ensordecer; **deafening** *adj* ensordecedor/a

**deal** [diːl] (*pt, pp* **~t**) *n* (*agreement*) pacto, convenio; (*business deal*) trato ▷*vt* dar; (*card*) repartir; **a great ~ (of)** bastante, mucho; **deal with** *vt fus* (*people*) tratar con; (*problem*) ocuparse de; (*subject*) tratar de; **dealer** *n* comerciante *m/f*; (*Cards*) mano *f*; **dealings** *npl* (*Comm*) transacciones *fpl*; (*relations*) relaciones *fpl*

**dealt** [dɛlt] *pt, pp of* **deal**

**dean** [diːn] *n* (*Rel*) deán *m*; (*Scol: BRIT*) decano; (: *US*) decano; rector *m*

**dear** [dɪə*] *adj* querido; (*expensive*) caro ▷*n*: **my ~** mi querido/a ▷*excl*: **~ me!** ¡Dios mío!; **D~ Sir/Madam** (*in letter*) Muy Señor Mío, Estimado Señor/Estimada Señora; **D~ Mr/Mrs X** Estimado/a Señor(a) X; **dearly** *adv* (*love*) mucho; (*pay*) caro

**death** [dɛθ] *n* muerte *f*; **death penalty** *n* pena de muerte; **death sentence** *n* condena a muerte

**debate** [dɪ'beɪt] *n* debate *m* ▷*vt* discutir

**debit** ['dɛbɪt] *n* debe *m* ▷*vt*: **to ~ a sum to sb** *or* **to sb's account** cargar una suma en cuenta a algn; **debit card** *n* tarjeta *f* de débito

**debris** ['dɛbriː] *n* escombros *mpl*

**debt** [dɛt] *n* deuda; **to be in ~** tener deudas

**debut** ['deɪbjuː] *n* presentación *f*

**Dec.** *abbr* (= *December*) dic

**decade** ['dɛkeɪd] *n* decenio, década

**decaffeinated** [dɪ'kæfɪneɪtɪd] *adj* descafeinado

**decay** [dɪ'keɪ] *n* (*of building*) desmoronamiento; (*of tooth*) caries *f inv* ▷*vi* (*rot*) pudrirse

**deceased** [dɪ'siːst] *n*: **the ~** el(la) difunto/a

**deceit** [dɪ'siːt] *n* engaño; **deceive** [dɪ'siːv] *vt* engañar

**December** [dɪ'sɛmbə*] *n* diciembre *m*

**decency** ['diːsənsɪ] *n* decencia

**decent** ['diːsənt] *adj* (*proper*) decente; (*person: kind*) amable, bueno

**deception** [dɪ'sɛpʃən] *n* engaño

**deceptive** [dɪ'sɛptɪv] *adj* engañoso

▌Be careful not to translate **deception** by
▌the Spanish word *decepción*.

**decide** [dɪ'saɪd] *vt* (*person*) decidir; (*question, argument*) resolver ▷*vi* decidir; **to ~ to do/that** decidir hacer/que; **to ~ on sth** decidirse por algo

**decimal** ['dɛsɪməl] *adj* decimal ▷*n* decimal *m*

**decision** [dɪ'sɪʒən] n decisión f
**decisive** [dɪ'saɪsɪv] adj decisivo; (person) decidido
**deck** [dɛk] n (Naut) cubierta; (of bus) piso; (record deck) platina; (of cards) baraja; **deckchair** n tumbona
**declaration** [dɛklə'reɪʃən] n declaración f
**declare** [dɪ'klɛə*] vt declarar
**decline** [dɪ'klaɪn] n disminución f, descenso ▷ vt rehusar ▷ vi (person, business) decaer; (strength) disminuir
**decorate** ['dɛkəreɪt] vt (adorn): **to ~ (with)** adornar (de), decorar (de); (paint) pintar; (paper) empapelar; **decoration** [-'reɪʃən] n adorno; (act) decoración f; (medal) condecoración f; **decorator** n (workman) pintor m (decorador)
**decrease** [n 'diːkriːs, vb dɪ'kriːs] n: **~ (in)** disminución f (de) ▷ vt disminuir, reducir ▷ vi reducirse
**decree** [dɪ'kriː] n decreto
**dedicate** ['dɛdɪkeɪt] vt dedicar; **dedicated** adj dedicado; (Comput) especializado; **dedicated word processor** procesador m de textos especializado or dedicado; **dedication** [-'keɪʃən] n (devotion) dedicación f; (in book) dedicatoria
**deduce** [dɪ'djuːs] vt deducir
**deduct** [dɪ'dʌkt] vt restar; descontar; **deduction** [dɪ'dʌkʃən] n (amount deducted) descuento; (conclusion) deducción f, conclusión f
**deed** [diːd] n hecho, acto; (feat) hazaña; (Law) escritura
**deem** [diːm] vt (formal) juzgar, considerar
**deep** [diːp] adj profundo; (expressing measurements) de profundidad; (voice) bajo; (breath) profundo; (colour) intenso ▷ adv: **the spectators stood 20 ~** los espectadores se formaron de 20 en fondo; **to be 4 metres ~** tener 4 metros de profundidad; **deep-fry** vt freír en aceite abundante; **deeply** adv (breathe) a pleno pulmón; (interested, moved, grateful) profundamente, hondamente
**deer** [dɪə*] n inv ciervo
**default** [dɪ'fɔːlt] n: **by ~** (win) por incomparecencia ▷ adj (Comput) por defecto
**defeat** [dɪ'fiːt] n derrota ▷ vt derrotar, vencer
**defect** [n 'diːfɛkt, vb dɪ'fɛkt] n defecto ▷ vi: **to ~ to the enemy** pasarse al enemigo; **defective** [dɪ'fɛktɪv] adj defectuoso
**defence** [dɪ'fɛns] (us **defense**) n defensa
**defend** [dɪ'fɛnd] vt defender; **defendant** n acusado/a; (in civil case) demandado/a; **defender** n defensor(a) m/f; (Sport) defensa mf

**defense** [dɪ'fɛns] (us) = **defence**
**defensive** [dɪ'fɛnsɪv] adj defensivo ▷ n: **on the ~** a la defensiva
**defer** [dɪ'fɜː*] vt aplazar
**defiance** [dɪ'faɪəns] n desafío; **in ~ of** en contra de; **defiant** [dɪ'faɪənt] adj (challenging) desafiante, retador(a)
**deficiency** [dɪ'fɪʃənsɪ] n (lack) falta; (defect) defecto; **deficient** [dɪ'fɪʃənt] adj deficiente
**deficit** ['dɛfɪsɪt] n déficit m
**define** [dɪ'faɪn] vt (word etc) definir; (limits etc) determinar
**definite** ['dɛfɪnɪt] adj (fixed) determinado; (obvious) claro; (certain) indudable; **he was ~ about it** no dejó lugar a dudas (sobre ello); **definitely** adv desde luego, por supuesto
**definition** [dɛfɪ'nɪʃən] n definición f; (clearness) nitidez f
**deflate** [diː'fleɪt] vt desinflar
**deflect** [dɪ'flɛkt] vt desviar
**defraud** [dɪ'frɔːd] vt: **to ~ sb of sth** estafar algo a algn
**defrost** [diː'frɔst] vt descongelar
**defuse** [diː'fjuːz] vt desactivar; (situation) calmar
**defy** [dɪ'faɪ] vt (resist) oponerse a; (challenge) desafiar; (fig): **it defies description** resulta imposible describirlo
**degree** [dɪ'griː] n grado; (Scol) título; **to have a ~ in maths** tener una licenciatura en matemáticas; **by ~s** (gradually) poco a poco, por etapas; **to some ~** hasta cierto punto
**dehydrated** [diːhaɪ'dreɪtɪd] adj deshidratado; (milk) en polvo
**de-icer** [diː'aɪsə*] n descongelador m
**delay** [dɪ'leɪ] vt demorar, aplazar; (person) entretener; (train) retrasar ▷ vi tardar ▷ n demora, retraso; **to be ~ed** retrasarse; **without ~** en seguida, sin tardar
**delegate** [n 'dɛlɪgɪt, vb 'dɛlɪgeɪt] n delegado/a ▷ vt (person) delegar en; (task) delegar
**delete** [dɪ'liːt] vt suprimir, tachar
**deli** ['dɛlɪ] n = **delicatessen**
**deliberate** [adj dɪ'lɪbərɪt, vb dɪ'lɪbəreɪt] adj (intentional) intencionado; (slow) pausado, lento ▷ vi deliberar; **deliberately** adv (on purpose) a propósito
**delicacy** ['dɛlɪkəsɪ] n delicadeza; (choice food) manjar m
**delicate** ['dɛlɪkɪt] adj delicado; (fragile) frágil
**delicatessen** [dɛlɪkə'tɛsn] n ultramarinos mpl finos
**delicious** [dɪ'lɪʃəs] adj delicioso
**delight** [dɪ'laɪt] n (feeling) placer m, deleite m; (person, experience etc) encanto,

delicia ▷ vt encantar, deleitar; **to take ~ in** deleitarse en; **delighted** adj: **delighted (at** or **with/to do)** encantado (con/de hacer); **delightful** adj encantador(a), delicioso

**delinquent** [dɪ'lɪŋkwənt] adj, n delincuente mf

**deliver** [dɪ'lɪvə*] vt (distribute) repartir; (hand over) entregar; (message) comunicar; (speech) pronunciar; (Med) asistir al parto de; **delivery** n reparto; entrega; (of speaker) modo de expresarse; (Med) parto, alumbramiento; **to take delivery of** recibir

**delusion** [dɪ'luːʒən] n ilusión f, engaño

**de luxe** [də'lʌks] adj de lujo

**delve** [dɛlv] vi: **to ~ into** hurgar en

**demand** [dɪ'mɑːnd] vt (gen) exigir; (rights) reclamar ▷ n exigencia; (claim) reclamación f; (Econ) demanda; **to be in ~** ser muy solicitado; **on ~** a solicitud; **demanding** adj (boss) exigente; (work) absorbente

**demise** [dɪ'maɪz] n (death) fallecimiento

**demo** ['dɛməu] (inf) n abbr (= demonstration) manifestación f

**democracy** [dɪ'mɔkrəsɪ] n democracia; **democrat** ['dɛməkræt] n demócrata mf; **democratic** [dɛmə'krætɪk] adj democrático; (us) demócrata

**demolish** [dɪ'mɔlɪʃ] vt derribar, demoler; (fig: argument) destruir

**demolition** [dɛmə'lɪʃən] n derribo, demolición f

**demon** ['diːmən] n (evil spirit) demonio

**demonstrate** ['dɛmənstreɪt] vt demostrar; (skill, appliance) mostrar ▷ vi manifestarse; **demonstration** [-'streɪʃən] n (Pol) manifestación f; (proof, exhibition) demostración f; **demonstrator** n (Pol) manifestante mf; (Comm) demostrador(a) m/f; vendedor(a) m/f

**demote** [dɪ'məut] vt degradar

**den** [dɛn] n (of animal) guarida; (room) habitación f

**denial** [dɪ'naɪəl] n (refusal) negativa; (of report etc) negación f

**denim** ['dɛnɪm] n tela vaquera; **denims** npl vaqueros mpl

**Denmark** ['dɛnmɑːk] n Dinamarca

**denomination** [dɪnɔmɪ'neɪʃən] n valor m; (Rel) confesión f

**denounce** [dɪ'nauns] vt denunciar

**dense** [dɛns] adj (crowd) denso; (thick) espeso; (: foliage etc) tupido; (inf: stupid) torpe

**density** ['dɛnsɪtɪ] n densidad f ▷ **single/double-~ disk** n (Comput) disco de densidad sencilla/de doble densidad

**dent** [dɛnt] n abolladura ▷ vt (also: **make a ~ in**) abollar

**dental** ['dɛntl] adj dental; **dental floss** [-flɔs] n seda dental; **dental surgery** n clínica f dental, consultorio m dental

**dentist** ['dɛntɪst] n dentista mf

**dentures** ['dɛntʃəz] npl dentadura (postiza)

**deny** [dɪ'naɪ] vt negar; (charge) rechazar

**deodorant** [diː'əudərənt] n desodorante m

**depart** [dɪ'pɑːt] vi irse, marcharse; (train) salir; **to ~ from** (fig: differ from) apartarse de

**department** [dɪ'pɑːtmənt] n (Comm) sección f; (Scol) departamento; (Pol) ministerio; **department store** n gran almacén m

**departure** [dɪ'pɑːtʃə*] n partida, ida; (of train) salida; (of employee) marcha; **a new ~** un nuevo rumbo; **departure lounge** n (at airport) sala de embarque

**depend** [dɪ'pɛnd] vi: **to ~ on** depender de; (rely on) contar con; **it ~s** depende, según; **~ing on the result** según el resultado; **dependant** n dependiente mf; **dependent** adj: **to be dependent on** depender de ▷ n = **dependant**

**depict** [dɪ'pɪkt] vt (in picture) pintar; (describe) representar

**deport** [dɪ'pɔːt] vt deportar

**deposit** [dɪ'pɔzɪt] n depósito; (Chem) sedimento; (of ore, oil) yacimiento f ▷ vt (gen) depositar; **deposit account** (BRIT) n cuenta de ahorros

**depot** ['dɛpəu] n (storehouse) depósito; (for vehicles) parque m; (us) estación f

**depreciate** [dɪ'priːʃɪeɪt] vi depreciarse, perder valor

**depress** [dɪ'prɛs] vt deprimir; (wages etc) hacer bajar; (press down) apretar; **depressed** adj deprimido; **depressing** adj deprimente; **depression** [dɪ'prɛʃən] n depresión f

**deprive** [dɪ'praɪv] vt: **to ~ sb of** privar a algn de; **deprived** adj necesitado

**dept.** abbr (= department) dto

**depth** [dɛpθ] n profundidad f; (of cupboard) fondo; **to be in the ~s of despair** sentir la mayor desesperación; **to be out of one's ~** (in water) no hacer pie; (fig) sentirse totalmente perdido

**deputy** ['dɛpjutɪ] adj: **~ head** subdirector(a) m/f ▷ n sustituto/a, suplente mf; (us Pol) diputado/a; (us: also: **~ sheriff**) agente m del sheriff

**derail** [dɪ'reɪl] vt: **to be ~ed** descarrilarse

**derelict** ['dɛrɪlɪkt] adj abandonado

**derive** [dɪ'raɪv] vt (benefit etc) obtener ▷ vi: **to ~ from** derivarse de

**descend** [dɪ'sɛnd] vt, vi descender, bajar;

**to ~ from** descender de; **to ~ to** rebajarse a; **descendant** n descendiente mf

**descent** [dɪˈsɛnt] n descenso; (origin) descendencia

**describe** [dɪsˈkraɪb] vt describir; **description** [-ˈkrɪpʃən] n descripción f; (sort) clase f, género

**desert** [n ˈdɛzət, vb dɪˈzəːt] n desierto ▷ vt abandonar ▷ vi (Mil) desertar; **deserted** [dɪˈzəːtɪd] adj desierto

**deserve** [dɪˈzəːv] vt merecer, ser digno de

**design** [dɪˈzaɪn] n (sketch) bosquejo; (layout, shape) diseño; (pattern) dibujo; (intention) intención f ▷ vt diseñar; **design and technology** (BRIT: Scol) n ≈ dibujo y tecnología

**designate** [vb ˈdɛzɪgneɪt, adj ˈdɛzɪgnɪt] vt (appoint) nombrar; (destine) designar ▷ adj designado

**designer** [dɪˈzaɪnə*] n diseñador(a) m/f; (fashion designer) modisto/a, diseñador(a) m/f de moda

**desirable** [dɪˈzaɪərəbl] adj (proper) deseable; (attractive) atractivo

**desire** [dɪˈzaɪə*] n deseo ▷ vt desear

**desk** [dɛsk] n (in office) escritorio; (for pupil) pupitre m; (in hotel, at airport) recepción f; (BRIT: in shop, restaurant) caja; **desk-top publishing** [ˈdɛsktɔp-] n autoedición f

**despair** [dɪsˈpɛə*] n desesperación f ▷ vi: **to ~ of** perder la esperanza de

**despatch** [dɪsˈpætʃ] n, vt = **dispatch**

**desperate** [ˈdɛspərɪt] adj desesperado; (fugitive) peligroso; **to be ~ for sth/to do** necesitar urgentemente algo/hacer; **desperately** adv desesperadamente; (very) terriblemente, gravemente

**desperation** [dɛspəˈreɪʃən] n desesperación f; **in (sheer) ~** (absolutamente) desesperado

**despise** [dɪsˈpaɪz] vt despreciar

**despite** [dɪsˈpaɪt] prep a pesar de, pese a

**dessert** [dɪˈzəːt] n postre m; **dessertspoon** n cuchara (de postre)

**destination** [dɛstɪˈneɪʃən] n destino

**destined** [ˈdɛstɪnd] adj: **~ for London** con destino a Londres

**destiny** [ˈdɛstɪnɪ] n destino

**destroy** [dɪsˈtrɔɪ] vt destruir; (animal) sacrificar

**destruction** [dɪsˈtrʌkʃən] n destrucción f

**destructive** [dɪsˈtrʌktɪv] adj destructivo, destructor(a)

**detach** [dɪˈtætʃ] vt separar; (unstick) despegar; **detached** adj (attitude) objetivo, imparcial; **detached house** n ≈ chalé m, ≈ chalet m

**detail** [ˈdiːteɪl] n detalle m; (no pl; (: in picture etc) detalles mpl; (trifle) pequeñez f ▷ vt detallar; (Mil) destacar; **in ~** detalladamente; **detailed** adj detallado

**detain** [dɪˈteɪn] vt retener; (in captivity) detener

**detect** [dɪˈtɛkt] vt descubrir; (Med, Police) identificar; (Mil, Radar, Tech) detectar; **detection** [dɪˈtɛkʃən] n descubrimiento; identificación f; **detective** n detective mf; **detective story** n novela policíaca

**detention** [dɪˈtɛnʃən] n detención f, arresto; (Scol) castigo

**deter** [dɪˈtəː*] vt (dissuade) disuadir

**detergent** [dɪˈtəːdʒənt] n detergente m

**deteriorate** [dɪˈtɪərɪəreɪt] vi deteriorarse

**determination** [dɪtəːmɪˈneɪʃən] n resolución f

**determine** [dɪˈtəːmɪn] vt determinar; **determined** adj (person) resuelto, decidido; **determined to do** resuelto a hacer

**deterrent** [dɪˈtɛrənt] n (Mil) fuerza de disuasión

**detest** [dɪˈtɛst] vt aborrecer

**detour** [ˈdiːtuə*] n (gen, US Aut) desviación f

**detract** [dɪˈtrækt] vt: **to ~ from** quitar mérito a, desvirtuar

**detrimental** [dɛtrɪˈmɛntl] adj: **~ (to)** perjudicial (a)

**devastating** [ˈdɛvəsteɪtɪŋ] adj devastador(a); (fig) arrollador(a)

**develop** [dɪˈvɛləp] vt desarrollar; (Phot) revelar; (disease) coger; (habit) adquirir; (fault) empezar a tener ▷ vi desarrollarse; (advance) progresar; (facts, symptoms) aparecer; **developing country** n país m en (vías de) desarrollo; **development** n desarrollo; (advance) progreso; (of affair, case) desenvolvimiento; (of land) urbanización f

**device** [dɪˈvaɪs] n (apparatus) aparato, mecanismo

**devil** [ˈdɛvl] n diablo, demonio

**devious** [ˈdiːvɪəs] adj taimado

**devise** [dɪˈvaɪz] vt idear, inventar

**devote** [dɪˈvəut] vt: **to ~ sth to** dedicar algo a; **devoted** adj (loyal) leal, fiel; **to be devoted to sb** querer con devoción a algn; **the book is devoted to politics** el libro trata de la política; **devotion** n dedicación f; (Rel) devoción f

**devour** [dɪˈvauə*] vt devorar

**devout** [dɪˈvaut] adj devoto

**dew** [djuː] n rocío

**diabetes** [daɪəˈbiːtiːz] n diabetes f

**diabetic** [daɪəˈbɛtɪk] adj, n diabético/a m/f

**diagnose** [ˈdaɪəgnəuz] vt diagnosticar

**diagnosis** [daɪəgˈnəusɪs] (pl **-ses**) n

diagnóstico

**diagonal** [daɪˈægənl] *adj, n* diagonal *f*

**diagram** [ˈdaɪəgræm] *n* diagrama *m*, esquema *m*

**dial** [ˈdaɪəl] *n* esfera (SP), cara (LAM); (*on radio etc*) dial *m*; (*of phone*) disco ▷ *vt* (*number*) marcar

**dialect** [ˈdaɪəlɛkt] *n* dialecto

**dialling code** [ˈdaɪəlɪŋ-] *n* prefijo

**dialling tone** (US **dial tone**) *n* (BRIT) señal *f* or tono de marcar

**dialogue** [ˈdaɪəlɔg] (US **dialog**) *n* diálogo

**diameter** [daɪˈæmɪtə*] *n* diámetro

**diamond** [ˈdaɪəmənd] *n* diamante *m*; (*shape*) rombo; **diamonds** *npl* (*Cards*) diamantes *mpl*

**diaper** [ˈdaɪəpə*] (US) *n* pañal *m*

**diarrhoea** [daɪəˈriːə] (US **diarrhea**) *n* diarrea

**diary** [ˈdaɪərɪ] *n* (*daily account*) diario; (*book*) agenda

**dice** [daɪs] *n inv* dados *mpl* ▷ *vt* (*Culin*) cortar en cuadritos

**dictate** [dɪkˈteɪt] *vt* dictar; (*conditions*) imponer; **dictation** [-ˈteɪʃən] *n* dictado; (*giving of orders*) órdenes *fpl*

**dictator** [dɪkˈteɪtə*] *n* dictador *m*

**dictionary** [ˈdɪkʃənrɪ] *n* diccionario

**did** [dɪd] *pt of* **do**

**didn't** [ˈdɪdənt] = **did not**

**die** [daɪ] *vi* morir; (*fig: fade*) desvanecerse, desaparecer; **to be dying for sth/to do sth** morirse por algo/de ganas de hacer algo; **die down** *vi* apagarse; (*wind*) amainar; **die out** *vi* desaparecer

**diesel** [ˈdiːzəl] *n* vehículo con motor Diesel

**diet** [ˈdaɪət] *n* dieta; (*restricted food*) régimen *m* ▷ *vi* (*also:* **be on a ~**) estar a dieta, hacer régimen

**differ** [ˈdɪfə*] *vi*: **to ~ (from)** (*be different*) ser distinto (a), diferenciarse (de); (*disagree*) discrepar (de); **difference** *n* diferencia; (*disagreement*) desacuerdo; **different** *adj* diferente, distinto; **differentiate** [-ˈrenʃɪeɪt] *vi*: **to differentiate (between)** distinguir (entre); **differently** *adv* de otro modo, en forma distinta

**difficult** [ˈdɪfɪkəlt] *adj* difícil; **difficulty** *n* dificultad *f*

**dig** [dɪg] (*pt, pp* **dug**) *vt* (*hole, ground*) cavar ▷ *n* (*prod*) empujón *m*; (*archaeological*) excavación *f*; (*remark*) indirecta; **to ~ one's nails into** clavar las uñas en; **dig up** *vt* (*information*) desenterrar; (*plant*) desarraigar

**digest** [*vb* daɪˈdʒɛst, *n* ˈdaɪdʒɛst] *vt* (*food*) digerir; (*facts*) asimilar ▷ *n* resumen *m*; **digestion** [dɪˈdʒɛstʃən] *n* digestión *f*

**digit** [ˈdɪdʒɪt] *n* (*number*) dígito; (*finger*)

dedo; **digital** *adj* digital; **digital camera** *n* cámara digital; **digital TV** *n* televisión *f* digital

**dignified** [ˈdɪgnɪfaɪd] *adj* grave, solemne

**dignity** [ˈdɪgnɪtɪ] *n* dignidad *f*

**digs** [dɪgz] (BRIT: *inf*) *npl* pensión *f*, alojamiento

**dilemma** [daɪˈlɛmə] *n* dilema *m*

**dill** [dɪl] *n* eneldo

**dilute** [daɪˈluːt] *vt* diluir

**dim** [dɪm] *adj* (*light*) débil; (*outline*) indistinto; (*room*) oscuro; (*inf: stupid*) lerdo ▷ *vt* (*light*) bajar

**dime** [daɪm] (US) *n* moneda de diez centavos

**dimension** [dɪˈmɛnʃən] *n* dimensión *f*

**diminish** [dɪˈmɪnɪʃ] *vt, vi* disminuir

**din** [dɪn] *n* estruendo, estrépito

**dine** [daɪn] *vi* cenar; **diner** *n* (*person*) comensal *mf*

**dinghy** [ˈdɪŋgɪ] *n* bote *m*; (*also:* **rubber ~**) lancha (neumática)

**dingy** [ˈdɪndʒɪ] *adj* (*room*) sombrío; (*colour*) sucio

**dining car** [ˈdaɪnɪŋ-] (BRIT) *n* (*Rail*) coche-comedor *m*

**dining room** [ˈdaɪnɪŋ-] *n* comedor *m*

**dining table** *n* mesa *f* de comedor

**dinner** [ˈdɪnə*] *n* (*evening meal*) cena; (*lunch*) comida; (*public*) cena, banquete *m*; **dinner jacket** *n* smoking *m*; **dinner party** *n* cena; **dinner time** *n* (*evening*) hora de cenar; (*midday*) hora de comer

**dinosaur** [ˈdaɪnəsɔː*] *n* dinosaurio

**dip** [dɪp] *n* (*slope*) pendiente *m*; (*in sea*) baño; (*Culin*) salsa ▷ *vt* (*in water*) mojar; (*ladle etc*) meter; (BRIT *Aut*): **to ~ one's lights** poner luces de cruce ▷ *vi* (*road etc*) descender, bajar

**diploma** [dɪˈpləumə] *n* diploma *m*

**diplomacy** [dɪˈpləuməsɪ] *n* diplomacia

**diplomat** [ˈdɪpləmæt] *n* diplomático/a; **diplomatic** [dɪpləˈmætɪk] *adj* diplomático

**dipstick** [ˈdɪpstɪk] (BRIT) *n* (*Aut*) varilla de nivel (del aceite)

**dire** [daɪə*] *adj* calamitoso

**direct** [daɪˈrɛkt] *adj* directo; (*challenge*) claro; (*person*) franco ▷ *vt* dirigir; (*order*): **to ~ sb to do sth** mandar a algn hacer algo ▷ *adv* derecho; **can you ~ me to ...?** ¿puede indicarme dónde está ...?; **direct debit** (BRIT) *n* domiciliación *f* bancaria de recibos

**direction** [dɪˈrɛkʃən] *n* dirección *f*; **sense of ~** sentido de la dirección; **directions** *npl* (*instructions*) instrucciones *fpl*; **~s for use** modo de empleo

**directly** [dɪˈrɛktlɪ] *adv* (*in straight line*) directamente; (*at once*) en seguida

**director** [dɪˈrɛktə*] *n* director(a) *m/f*

**directory** [dɪ'rɛktərɪ] n (Tel) guía
(telefónica); (Comput) directorio; **directory
enquiries** (us **directory assistance**) n
(servicio de) información f
**dirt** [dəːt] n suciedad f; (earth) tierra; **dirty**
adj sucio; (joke) verde, colorado (MEX) ▷ vt
ensuciar; (stain) manchar
**disability** [dɪsə'bɪlɪtɪ] n incapacidad f
**disabled** [dɪs'eɪbld] adj: **to be physically
~** ser minusválido/a; **to be mentally ~** ser
deficiente mental
**disadvantage** [dɪsəd'vɑːntɪdʒ] n
desventaja, inconveniente m
**disagree** [dɪsə'griː] vi (differ) discrepar;
**to ~ (with)** no estar de acuerdo (con);
**disagreeable** adj desagradable; (person)
antipático; **disagreement** n desacuerdo
**disappear** [dɪsə'pɪə*] vi desaparecer;
**disappearance** n desaparición f
**disappoint** [dɪsə'pɔɪnt] vt decepcionar,
defraudar; **disappointed** adj
decepcionado; **disappointing** adj
decepcionante; **disappointment** n
decepción f
**disapproval** [dɪsə'pruːvəl] n
desaprobación f
**disapprove** [dɪsə'pruːv] vi: **to ~ of** ver mal
**disarm** [dɪs'ɑːm] vt desarmar;
**disarmament** [dɪs'ɑːməmənt] n desarme
m
**disaster** [dɪ'zɑːstə*] n desastre m
**disastrous** [dɪ'zɑːstrəs] adj desastroso
**disbelief** [dɪsbə'liːf] n incredulidad f
**disc** [dɪsk] n disco; (Comput) = **disk**
**discard** [dɪs'kɑːd] vt (old things) tirar; (fig)
descartar
**discharge** [vb dɪs'tʃɑːdʒ, n 'dɪstʃɑːdʒ] vt
(task, duty) cumplir; (waste) verter; (patient)
dar de alta; (employee) despedir; (soldier)
licenciar; (defendant) poner en libertad
▷ n (Elec) descarga; (Med) supuración f;
(dismissal) despedida; (of duty) desempeño;
(of debt) pago, descargo
**discipline** ['dɪsɪplɪn] n disciplina ▷ vt
disciplinar; (punish) castigar
**disc jockey** n pinchadiscos mf inv
**disclose** [dɪs'kləuz] vt revelar
**disco** ['dɪskəu] n abbr discoteca
**discoloured** [dɪs'kʌləd] (us **discolored**)
adj descolorido
**discomfort** [dɪs'kʌmfət] n incomodidad
f; (unease) inquietud f; (physical) malestar m
**disconnect** [dɪskə'nɛkt] vt separar; (Elec
etc) desconectar
**discontent** [dɪskən'tɛnt] n descontento
**discontinue** [dɪskən'tɪnjuː] vt
interrumpir; (payments) suspender; **"~d"**
(Comm) "ya no se fabrica"

**discount** [n 'dɪskaunt, vb dɪs'kaunt] n
descuento ▷ vt descontar
**discourage** [dɪs'kʌrɪdʒ] vt desalentar;
(advise against): **to ~ sb from doing** disuadir
a algn de hacer
**discover** [dɪs'kʌvə*] vt descubrir;
(error) darse cuenta de; **discovery** n
descubrimiento
**discredit** [dɪs'krɛdɪt] vt desacreditar
**discreet** [dɪ'skriːt] adj (tactful) discreto;
(careful) prudente
**discrepancy** [dɪ'skrɛpənsɪ] n diferencia
**discretion** [dɪ'skrɛʃən] n (tact) discreción
f; **at the ~ of** a criterio de
**discriminate** [dɪ'skrɪmɪneɪt] vi: **to ~
between** distinguir entre; **to ~ against**
discriminar contra; **discrimination**
[-'neɪʃən] n (discernment) perspicacia; (bias)
discriminación f
**discuss** [dɪ'skʌs] vt discutir; (a theme)
tratar; **discussion** [dɪ'skʌʃən] n discusión f
**disease** [dɪ'ziːz] n enfermedad f
**disembark** [dɪsɪm'bɑːk] vt, vi
desembarcar
**disgrace** [dɪs'greɪs] n ignominia; (shame)
vergüenza, escándalo ▷ vt deshonrar;
**disgraceful** adj vergonzoso
**disgruntled** [dɪs'grʌntld] adj disgustado,
descontento
**disguise** [dɪs'gaɪz] n disfraz m ▷ vt
disfrazar; **in ~** disfrazado
**disgust** [dɪs'gʌst] n repugnancia ▷ vt
repugnar, dar asco a

   ■ Be careful not to translate **disgust** by the
Spanish word disgustar.

**disgusted** [dɪs'gʌstɪd] adj indignado

   ■ Be careful not to translate **disgusted** by
the Spanish word disgustado.

**disgusting** [dɪs'gʌstɪŋ] adj repugnante,
asqueroso; (behaviour etc) vergonzoso
**dish** [dɪʃ] n (gen) plato; **to do** or **wash the
~es** fregar los platos; **dishcloth** n estropajo
**dishonest** [dɪs'ɔnɪst] adj (person) poco
honrado, tramposo; (means) fraudulento
**dishtowel** ['dɪʃtauəl] (us) n estropajo
**dishwasher** ['dɪʃwɔʃə*] n lavaplatos m inv
**disillusion** [dɪsɪ'luːʒən] vt desilusionar
**disinfectant** [dɪsɪn'fɛktənt] n
desinfectante m
**disintegrate** [dɪs'ɪntɪgreɪt] vi
disgregarse, desintegrarse
**disk** [dɪsk] n (esp us) = **disc**; (Comput) disco,
disquete m; **single-/double-sided ~** disco
de una cara/dos caras; **disk drive** n disc
drive m; **diskette** n = **disk**
**dislike** [dɪs'laɪk] n antipatía, aversión f
▷ vt tener antipatía a
**dislocate** ['dɪsləkeɪt] vt dislocar

**disloyal** [dɪs'lɔɪəl] *adj* desleal

**dismal** ['dɪzml] *adj* (*gloomy*) deprimente, triste; (*very bad*) malísimo, fatal

**dismantle** [dɪs'mæntl] *vt* desmontar, desarmar

**dismay** [dɪs'meɪ] *n* consternación f ▷ *vt* consternar

**dismiss** [dɪs'mɪs] *vt* (*worker*) despedir; (*pupils*) dejar marchar; (*soldiers*) dar permiso para irse; (*idea, Law*) rechazar; (*possibility*) descartar; **dismissal** *n* despido

**disobedient** [dɪsə'biːdɪənt] *adj* desobediente

**disobey** [dɪsə'beɪ] *vt* desobedecer

**disorder** [dɪs'ɔːdə*] *n* desorden m; (*rioting*) disturbios mpl; (*Med*) trastorno

**disorganized** [dɪs'ɔːgənaɪzd] *adj* desorganizado

**disown** [dɪs'əʊn] *vt* (*action*) renegar de; (*person*) negar cualquier tipo de relación con

**dispatch** [dɪs'pætʃ] *vt* enviar ▷ *n* (*sending*) envío; (*Press*) informe m; (*Mil*) parte m

**dispel** [dɪs'pel] *vt* disipar

**dispense** [dɪs'pens] *vt* (*medicines*) preparar; **dispense with** *vt fus* prescindir de; **dispenser** *n* (*container*) distribuidor m automático

**disperse** [dɪs'pəːs] *vt* dispersar ▷ *vi* dispersarse

**display** [dɪs'pleɪ] *n* (*in shop window*) escaparate m; (*exhibition*) exposición f; (*Comput*) visualización f; (*of feeling*) manifestación f ▷ *vt* exponer; manifestar; (*ostentatiously*) lucir

**displease** [dɪs'pliːz] *vt* (*offend*) ofender; (*annoy*) fastidiar

**disposable** [dɪs'pəʊzəbl] *adj* desechable; (*income*) disponible

**disposal** [dɪs'pəʊzl] *n* (*of rubbish*) destrucción f; **at one's ~** a su disposición

**dispose** [dɪs'pəʊz] *vi*: **to ~ of** (*unwanted goods*) deshacerse de; (*problem etc*) resolver; **disposition** [dɪspə'zɪʃən] *n* (*nature*) temperamento; (*inclination*) propensión f

**disproportionate** [dɪsprə'pɔːʃənət] *adj* desproporcionado

**dispute** [dɪs'pjuːt] *n* disputa; (*also:* **industrial ~**) conflicto (laboral) ▷ *vt* (*argue*) disputar, discutir; (*question*) cuestionar

**disqualify** [dɪs'kwɔlɪfaɪ] *vt* (*Sport*) desclasificar; **to ~ sb for sth/from doing sth** incapacitar a algn para algo/hacer algo

**disregard** [dɪsrɪ'gaːd] *vt* (*ignore*) no hacer caso de

**disrupt** [dɪs'rʌpt] *vt* (*plans*) desbaratar, trastornar; (*conversation*) interrumpir; **disruption** [dɪs'rʌpʃən] *n* trastorno, desbaratamiento; interrupción f

**dissatisfaction** [dɪssætɪs'fækʃən] *n* disgusto, descontento

**dissatisfied** [dɪs'sætɪsfaɪd] *adj* insatisfecho

**dissect** [dɪ'sekt] *vt* disecar

**dissent** [dɪ'sent] *n* disensión f

**dissertation** [dɪsə'teɪʃən] *n* tesina

**dissolve** [dɪ'zɔlv] *vt* disolver ▷ *vi* disolverse; **to ~ in(to) tears** deshacerse en lágrimas

**distance** ['dɪstəns] *n* distancia; **in the ~** a lo lejos

**distant** ['dɪstənt] *adj* lejano; (*manner*) reservado, frío

**distil** [dɪs'tɪl] (*us* **distill**) *vt* destilar; **distillery** *n* destilería

**distinct** [dɪs'tɪŋkt] *adj* (*different*) distinto; (*clear*) claro; (*unmistakeable*) inequívoco; **as ~ from** a diferencia de; **distinction** [dɪs'tɪŋkʃən] *n* distinción f; (*honour*) honor m; (*in exam*) sobresaliente m; **distinctive** *adj* distintivo

**distinguish** [dɪs'tɪŋgwɪʃ] *vt* distinguir; **to ~ o.s.** destacarse; **distinguished** *adj* (*eminent*) distinguido

**distort** [dɪs'tɔːt] *vt* distorsionar; (*shape, image*) deformar

**distract** [dɪs'trækt] *vt* distraer; **distracted** *adj* distraído; **distraction** [dɪs'trækʃən] *n* distracción f; (*confusion*) aturdimiento

**distraught** [dɪs'trɔːt] *adj* loco de inquietud

**distress** [dɪs'tres] *n* (*anguish*) angustia, aflicción f ▷ *vt* afligir; **distressing** *adj* angustioso; doloroso

**distribute** [dɪs'trɪbjuːt] *vt* distribuir; (*share out*) repartir; **distribution** [-'bjuːʃən] *n* distribución f, reparto; **distributor** *n* (*Aut*) distribuidor m; (*Comm*) distribuidora

**district** ['dɪstrɪkt] *n* (*of country*) zona, región f; (*of town*) barrio; (*Admin*) distrito; **district attorney** (*us*) *n* fiscal mf

**distrust** [dɪs'trʌst] *n* desconfianza ▷ *vt* desconfiar de

**disturb** [dɪs'təːb] *vt* (*person: bother, interrupt*) molestar; (: *upset*) perturbar, inquietar; (*disorganize*) alterar; **disturbance** *n* (*upheaval*) perturbación f; (*political etc: gen pl*) disturbio; (*of mind*) trastorno; **disturbed** *adj* (*worried, upset*) preocupado, angustiado; **emotionally disturbed** trastornado; (*childhood*) inseguro; **disturbing** *adj* inquietante, perturbador(a)

**ditch** [dɪtʃ] *n* zanja; (*irrigation ditch*) acequia ▷ *vt* (*inf: partner*) deshacerse de; (: *plan, car etc*) abandonar

**ditto** ['dɪtəʊ] *adv* ídem, lo mismo

**dive** [daɪv] n (from board) salto; (underwater) buceo; (of submarine) sumersión f ▷ vi (swimmer: into water) saltar; (: under water) zambullirse, bucear; (fish, submarine) sumergirse; (bird) lanzarse en picado; **to ~ into** (bag etc) meter la mano en; (place) meterse de prisa en; **diver** n (underwater) buzo

**diverse** [daɪˈvəːs] adj diversos/as, varios/as

**diversion** [daɪˈvəːʃən] n (BRIT Aut) desviación f; (distraction, Mil) diversión f; (of funds) distracción f

**diversity** [daɪˈvəːsɪtɪ] n diversidad f

**divert** [daɪˈvəːt] vt (turn aside) desviar

**divide** [dɪˈvaɪd] vt dividir; (separate) separar ▷ vi dividirse; (road) bifurcarse; **divided highway** (US) n carretera de doble calzada

**divine** [dɪˈvaɪn] adj (also fig) divino

**diving** [ˈdaɪvɪŋ] n (Sport) salto; (underwater) buceo; **diving board** n trampolín m

**division** [dɪˈvɪʒən] n división f; (sharing out) reparto; (disagreement) diferencias fpl; (Comm) sección f

**divorce** [dɪˈvɔːs] n divorcio ▷ vt divorciarse de; **divorced** adj divorciado; **divorcee** [-ˈsiː] n divorciado/a

**D.I.Y.** (BRIT) adj, n abbr = **do-it-yourself**

**dizzy** [ˈdɪzɪ] adj (spell) de mareo; **to feel ~** marearse

**DJ** n abbr = **disc jockey**

**DNA** n abbr (= deoxyribonucleic acid) ADN m

○ **KEYWORD**

**do** [duː] (pt **did**, pp **done**) n (inf: party etc): **we're having a little do on Saturday** damos una fiestecita el sábado; **it was rather a grand do** fue un acontecimiento a lo grande

▷ aux vb **1** (in negative constructions: not translated): **I don't understand** no entiendo

**2** (to form questions: not translated): **didn't you know?** ¿no lo sabías?; **what do you think?** ¿qué opinas?

**3** (for emphasis, in polite expressions): **people do make mistakes sometimes** sí que se cometen errores a veces; **she does seem rather late** a mí también me parece que se ha retrasado; **do sit down/help yourself** siéntate/sírvete por favor; **do take care!** ¡ten cuidado(, te pido)!

**4** (used to avoid repeating vb): **she sings better than I do** canta mejor que yo; **do you agree? – yes, I do/no, I don't** ¿estás de acuerdo? – sí (lo estoy)/no (lo estoy); **she lives in Glasgow – so do I** vive en Glasgow

– yo también; **he didn't like it and neither did we** no le gustó y a nosotros tampoco; **who made this mess? – I did** ¿quién hizo esta chapuza? – yo; **he asked me to help him and I did** me pidió que le ayudara y lo hice

**5** (in question tags): **you like him, don't you?** te gusta, ¿verdad? or ¿no?; **I don't know him, do I?** creo que no le conozco

▷ vt **1** (gen, carry out, perform etc): **what are you doing tonight?** ¿qué haces esta noche?; **what can I do for you?** ¿en qué puedo servirle?; **to do the washing-up/cooking** fregar los platos/cocinar; **to do one's teeth/hair/nails** lavarse los dientes/arreglarse el pelo/arreglarse las uñas

**2** (Aut etc): **the car was doing 100** el coche iba a 100; **we've done 200 km already** ya hemos hecho 200 km; **he can do 100 in that car** puede ir a 100 en ese coche

▷ vi **1** (act, behave) hacer; **do as I do** haz como yo

**2** (get on, fare): **he's doing well/badly at school** va bien/mal en la escuela; **the firm is doing well** la empresa anda or va bien; **how do you do?** mucho gusto; (less formal) ¿qué tal?

**3** (suit): **will it do?** ¿sirve?, ¿está or va bien?

**4** (be sufficient) bastar; **will £10 do?** ¿será bastante con £10?; **that'll do** así está bien; **that'll do!** (in annoyance) ¡ya está bien!, ¡basta ya!; **to make do (with)** arreglárselas (con)

**do up** vt (laces) atar; (zip, dress, shirt) abrochar; (renovate: room, house) renovar

**do with** vt fus (need): **I could do with a drink/some help** no me vendría mal un trago/un poco de ayuda; (be connected) tener que ver con; **what has it got to do with you?** ¿qué tiene que ver contigo?

**do without** vi pasar sin; **if you're late for tea then you'll do without** si llegas tarde tendrás que quedarte sin cenar

▷ vt fus pasar sin; **I can do without a car** puedo pasar sin coche

**dock** [dɔk] n (Naut) muelle m; (Law) banquillo (de los acusados) ▷ vi (enter dock) atracar (la) muelle; (Space) acoplarse; **docks** npl (Naut) muelles mpl, puerto sg

**doctor** [ˈdɔktə*] n médico/a; (Ph.D. etc) doctor(a) m/f ▷ vt (drink etc) adulterar; **Doctor of Philosophy** n Doctor en Filosofía y Letras

**document** [ˈdɔkjumənt] n documento; **documentary** [-ˈmentərɪ] adj documental ▷ n documental m; **documentation** [-mɛnˈteɪʃən] n documentación f

**dodge** [dɔdʒ] n (fig) truco ▷ vt evadir; (blow) esquivar

**dodgy** ['dɔdʒɪ] adj (inf: uncertain) dudoso; (suspicious) sospechoso; (risky) arriesgado

**does** [dʌz] vb see **do**

**doesn't** ['dʌznt] = **does not**

**dog** [dɔg] n perro ▷ vt seguir los pasos de; (bad luck) perseguir; **doggy bag** ['dɔgɪ-] n bolsa para llevarse las sobras de la comida

**do-it-yourself** ['duːɪtjɔːˈsɛlf] n bricolaje m

**dole** [dəul] (BRIT) n (payment) subsidio de paro; **on the ~** parado

**doll** [dɔl] n muñeca; (US: inf: woman) muñeca, gachí f

**dollar** ['dɔlə*] n dólar m

**dolphin** ['dɔlfɪn] n delfín m

**dome** [dəum] n (Arch) cúpula

**domestic** [dəˈmɛstɪk] adj (animal, duty) doméstico; (flight, policy) nacional; **domestic appliance** n aparato m doméstico, aparato m de uso doméstico

**dominant** ['dɔmɪnənt] adj dominante

**dominate** ['dɔmɪneɪt] vt dominar

**domino** ['dɔmɪnəu] (pl **-es**) n ficha de dominó; **dominoes** n (game) dominó

**donate** [dəˈneɪt] vt donar; **donation** [dəˈneɪʃən] n donativo

**done** [dʌn] pp of **do**

**donkey** ['dɔŋkɪ] n burro

**donor** ['dəunə*] n donante mf; **donor card** n carnet m de donante

**don't** [dəunt] = **do not**

**donut** ['dəunʌt] (US) n = **doughnut**

**doodle** ['duːdl] vi hacer dibujitos or garabatos

**doom** [duːm] n (fate) suerte f ▷ vt: **to be ~ed to failure** estar condenado al fracaso

**door** [dɔː*] n puerta; **doorbell** n timbre m; **door handle** n tirador m; (of car) manija; **doorknob** n pomo m de la puerta, manilla f (LAM); **doorstep** n peldaño; **doorway** n entrada, puerta

**dope** [dəup] n (inf: illegal drug) droga; (: person) imbécil mf ▷ vt (horse etc) drogar

**dormitory** ['dɔːmɪtrɪ] n (BRIT) dormitorio; (US) colegio mayor

**DOS** n abbr (= disk operating system) DOS m

**dosage** ['dəusɪdʒ] n dosis f inv

**dose** [dəus] n dosis f inv

**dot** [dɔt] n punto ▷ vi: **~ted with** salpicado de; **on the ~** en punto; **dotcom** [dɔtˈkɔm] n puntocom f inv; **dotted line** ['dɔtɪd-] n: **to sign on the dotted line** firmar

**double** ['dʌbl] adj doble ▷ adv (twice): **to cost ~** costar el doble ▷ n doble m ▷ vt doblar ▷ vi doblarse; **on the ~, at the ~** (BRIT) corriendo; **double back** vi (person)

volver sobre sus pasos; **double bass** n contrabajo; **double bed** n cama de matrimonio; **double-check** vt volver a revisar ▷ vi: **I'll double-check** voy a revisarlo otra vez; **double-click** vi (Comput) hacer doble clic; **double-cross** vt (trick) engañar; (betray) traicionar; **doubledecker** n autobús m de dos pisos; **double glazing** (BRIT) n doble acristalamiento; **double room** n habitación f doble; **doubles** n (Tennis) juego de dobles; **double yellow lines** npl (BRIT: Aut) línea doble amarilla de prohibido aparcar, ≈ línea fsg amarilla continua

**doubt** [daut] n duda ▷ vt dudar; (suspect) dudar de; **to ~ that** dudar que; **doubtful** adj dudoso; (person): **to be doubtful about sth** tener dudas sobre algo; **doubtless** adv sin duda

**dough** [dəu] n masa, pasta; **doughnut** (US **donut**) n ≈ rosquilla

**dove** [dʌv] n paloma

**down** [daun] n (feathers) plumón m, flojel m ▷ adv (downwards) abajo, hacia abajo; (on the ground) por or en tierra ▷ prep abajo ▷ vt (inf: drink) beberse; **~ with X!** ¡abajo X!; **down-and-out** n vagabundo/a; **downfall** n caída, ruina; **downhill** adv: **to go downhill** (also fig) ir cuesta abajo

**Downing Street** ['daunɪŋ-] n (BRIT) Downing Street f

**download** vt (Comput) bajar; **downright** adj (nonsense, lie) manifiesto; (refusal) terminante

**Down's syndrome** ['daunz-] n síndrome m de Down

**downstairs** adv (below) (en el piso de) abajo; (downwards) escaleras abajo; **down-to-earth** adj práctico; **downtown** adv en el centro de la ciudad; **down under** adv en Australia (or Nueva Zelanda); **downward** [-wəd] adj, adv hacia abajo; **downwards** [-wədz] adv hacia abajo

**doz.** abbr = **dozen**

**doze** [dəuz] vi dormitar

**dozen** ['dʌzn] n docena; **a ~ books** una docena de libros; **~s of** cantidad de

**Dr.** abbr = **doctor; drive**

**drab** [dræb] adj gris, monótono

**draft** [drɑːft] n (first copy) borrador m; (Pol: of bill) anteproyecto; (US: call-up) quinta ▷ vt (plan) preparar; (write roughly) hacer un borrador de; see also **draught**

**drag** [dræg] vt arrastrar; (river) dragar, rastrear ▷ vi (time) pasar despacio; (play, film etc) hacerse pesado ▷ n (inf) lata; (women's clothing): **in ~** vestido de travesti; **to ~ and drop** (Comput) arrastrar y soltar

**dragon** ['drægən] n dragón m

**dragonfly** ['drægənflaɪ] n libélula

**drain** [dreɪn] n desaguadero; (in street) sumidero; (source of loss): **to be a ~ on** consumir, agotar ▷ vt (land, marshes) desaguar; (reservoir) desecar; (vegetables) escurrir ▷ vi escurrirse; **drainage** n (act) desagüe m; (Med, Agr) drenaje m; (sewage) alcantarillado; **drainpipe** n tubo de desagüe

**drama** ['drɑːmə] n (art) teatro; (play) drama m; (excitement) emoción f; **dramatic** [drə'mætɪk] adj dramático; (sudden, marked) espectacular

**drank** [dræŋk] pt of **drink**

**drape** [dreɪp] vt (cloth) colocar; (flag) colgar; **drapes** npl (us) cortinas fpl

**drastic** ['dræstɪk] adj (measure) severo; (change) radical, drástico

**draught** [drɑːft] (us **draft**) n (of air) corriente f de aire; (Naut) calado; **on ~** (beer) de barril; **draught beer** n cerveza de barril; **draughts** (BRIT) n (game) juego de damas

**draw** [drɔː] (pt **drew**, pp **drawn**) vt (picture) dibujar; (cart) tirar de; (curtain) correr; (take out) sacar; (attract) atraer; (money) retirar; (wages) cobrar ▷ vi (Sport) empatar ▷ n (Sport) empate m; (lottery) sorteo; **draw out** vi (lengthen) alargarse ▷ vt sacar; **draw up** vi (stop) pararse ▷ vt (chair) acercar; (document) redactar; **drawback** n inconveniente m, desventaja

**drawer** [drɔː*] n cajón m

**drawing** ['drɔːɪŋ] n dibujo; **drawing pin** (BRIT) n chincheta; **drawing room** n salón m

**drawn** [drɔːn] pp of **draw**

**dread** [dred] n pavor m, terror m ▷ vt temer, tener miedo or pavor a; **dreadful** adj horroroso

**dream** [driːm] (pt, pp **~ed** or **~t**) n sueño ▷ vt, vi soñar; **dreamer** n soñador(a) m/f

**dreamt** [dremt] pt, pp of **dream**

**dreary** ['drɪərɪ] adj monótono

**drench** [drentʃ] vt empapar

**dress** [dres] n vestido; (clothing) ropa ▷ vt vestir; (wound) vendar ▷ vi vestirse; **to get ~ed** vestirse; **dress up** vi vestirse de etiqueta; (in fancy dress) disfrazarse; **dress circle** (BRIT) n principal m; **dresser** n (furniture) aparador m; (: us) cómoda (con espejo); **dressing** n (Med) vendaje m; (Culin) aliño; **dressing gown** (BRIT) n bata; **dressing room** n (Theatre) camarín m; (Sport) vestuario; **dressing table** n tocador m; **dressmaker** n modista, costurera

**drew** [druː] pt of **draw**

**dribble** ['drɪbl] vi (baby) babear ▷ vt (ball) regatear

**dried** [draɪd] adj (fruit) seco; (milk) en polvo

**drier** ['draɪə*] n = **dryer**

**drift** [drɪft] n (of current etc) flujo; (of snow) ventisquero; (meaning) significado ▷ vi (boat) ir a la deriva; (sand, snow) amontonarse

**drill** [drɪl] n (drill bit) broca; (tool for DIY etc) taladro; (of dentist) fresa; (for mining etc) perforadora, barrena; (Mil) instrucción f ▷ vt perforar, taladrar; (troops) enseñar la instrucción a ▷ vi (for oil) perforar

**drink** [drɪŋk] (pt **drank**, pp **drunk**) n bebida; (sip) trago ▷ vt, vi beber; **to have a ~** tomar algo; tomar una copa or un trago; **a ~ of water** un trago de agua; **drink-driving** n: **to be charged with drink-driving** ser acusado de conducir borracho or en estado de embriaguez; **drinker** n bebedor(a) m/f; **drinking water** n agua potable

**drip** [drɪp] n (act) goteo; (one drip) gota; (Med) gota a gota m ▷ vi gotear

**drive** [draɪv] (pt **drove**, pp **driven**) n (journey) viaje m (en coche); (also: **~way**) entrada; (energy) energía, vigor m; (Comput: also: **disk ~**) drive m ▷ vt (car) conducir (SP), manejar (LAM); (nail) clavar; (push) empujar; (Tech: motor) impulsar ▷ vi (Aut: at controls) conducir; (: travel) pasearse en coche; **left-/right-hand ~** conducción f a la izquierda/derecha; **to ~ sb mad** volverle loco a algn; **drive out** vt (force out) expulsar, echar; **drive-in** adj (esp us): **drive-in cinema** autocine m

**driven** ['drɪvn] pp of **drive**

**driver** ['draɪvə*] n conductor(a) m/f (SP), chofer mf (LAM); (of taxi, bus) chófer mf (SP), chofer mf (LAM); **driver's license** (us) n carnet m de conducir

**driveway** ['draɪvweɪ] n entrada

**driving** ['draɪvɪŋ] n el conducir (SP), el manejar (LAM); **driving instructor** n profesor(a) m/f de autoescuela (SP), instructor(a) m/f de manejo (LAM); **driving lesson** n clase f de conducir (SP) or manejar (LAM); **driving licence** (BRIT) n licencia de manejo (LAM), carnet m de conducir (SP); **driving test** n examen m de conducir (SP) or manejar (LAM)

**drizzle** ['drɪzl] n llovizna

**droop** [druːp] vi (flower) marchitarse; (shoulders) encorvarse; (head) inclinarse

**drop** [drɔp] n (of water) gota; (lessening) baja; (fall) caída ▷ vt dejar caer; (voice, eyes, price) bajar; (passenger) dejar; (omit) omitir ▷ vi (object) caer; (wind) amainar; **drop in** vi (inf: visit): **to drop in (on)** pasar por casa (de); **drop off** vi (sleep) dormirse ▷ vt (*passenger*) dejar; **drop out** *vi* (*withdraw*) retirarse

**drought** [draut] *n* sequía

**drove** [drəuv] *pt of* **drive**

**drown** [draun] *vt* ahogar ▷ *vi* ahogarse

**drowsy** ['drauzɪ] *adj* soñoliento; **to be ~** tener sueño

**drug** [drʌg] *n* medicamento; (*narcotic*) droga ▷ *vt* drogar; **to be on ~s** drogarse; **drug addict** *n* drogadicto/a; **drug dealer** *n* traficante *mf* de drogas; **druggist** (*us*) *n* farmacéutico; **drugstore** (*us*) *n* farmacia

**drum** [drʌm] *n* tambor *m*; (*for oil, petrol*) bidón *m*; **drums** *npl* batería; **drummer** *n* tambor *m*

**drunk** [drʌŋk] *pp of* **drink** ▷ *adj* borracho ▷ *n* (*also:* **~ard**) borracho/a; **drunken** *adj* borracho; (*laughter, party*) de borrachos

**dry** [draɪ] *adj* seco; (*day*) sin lluvia; (*climate*) árido, seco ▷ *vt* secar; (*tears*) enjugarse ▷ *vi* secarse; **dry off** *vi* secarse ▷ *vt* secar; **dry up** *vi* (*river*) secarse; **dry-cleaner's** *n* tintorería; **dry-cleaning** *n* lavado en seco; **dryer** *n* (*for hair*) secador *m*; (*us: for clothes*) secadora

**DSS** *n abbr* = **Department of Social Security**

**D & T** (*BRIT: Scol*) *n abbr* (= *design and technology*) ≈ dibujo y tecnología

**DTP** *n abbr* (= *desk-top publishing*) autoedición *f*

**dual** ['djuəl] *adj* doble; **dual carriageway** (*BRIT*) *n* carretera de doble calzada

**dubious** ['dju:bɪəs] *adj* indeciso; (*reputation, company*) sospechoso

**duck** [dʌk] *n* pato ▷ *vi* agacharse

**due** [dju:] *adj* (*owed*): **he is ~ £10** se le deben 10 libras; (*expected: event*): **the meeting is ~ on Wednesday** la reunión tendrá lugar el miércoles; (: *arrival*): **the train is ~ at 8am** el tren tiene su llegada para las 8; (*proper*) debido ▷ *n*: **to give sb his** (*or* **her**) **~** ser justo con algn ▷ *adv*: **~ north** derecho al norte

**duel** ['djuəl] *n* duelo

**duet** [dju:'ɛt] *n* dúo

**dug** [dʌg] *pt, pp of* **dig**

**duke** [dju:k] *n* duque *m*

**dull** [dʌl] *adj* (*light*) débil; (*stupid*) torpe; (*boring*) pesado; (*sound, pain*) sordo; (*weather, day*) gris ▷ *vt* (*pain, grief*) aliviar; (*mind, senses*) entorpecer

**dumb** [dʌm] *adj* mudo; (*pej: stupid*) estúpido

**dummy** ['dʌmɪ] *n* (*tailor's dummy*) maniquí *m*; (*mock-up*) maqueta; (*BRIT: for baby*) chupete *m* ▷ *adj* falso, postizo

**dump** [dʌmp] *n* (*also:* **rubbish ~**) basurero,

vertedero; (*inf: place*) cuchitril *m* ▷ *vt* (*put down*) dejar; (*get rid of*) deshacerse de; (*Comput: data*) transferir

**dumpling** ['dʌmplɪŋ] *n* bola de masa hervida

**dune** [dju:n] *n* duna

**dungarees** [dʌŋgə'ri:z] *npl* mono

**dungeon** ['dʌndʒən] *n* calabozo

**duplex** ['dju:plɛks] *n* dúplex *m*

**duplicate** [*n* 'dju:plɪkət, *vb* 'dju:plɪkeɪt] *n* duplicado ▷ *vt* duplicar; (*photocopy*) fotocopiar; (*repeat*) repetir; **in ~** por duplicado

**durable** ['djuərəbl] *adj* duradero

**duration** [djuə'reɪʃən] *n* duración *f*

**during** ['djuərɪŋ] *prep* durante

**dusk** [dʌsk] *n* crepúsculo, anochecer *m*

**dust** [dʌst] *n* polvo ▷ *vt* quitar el polvo a, desempolvar; (*cake etc*): **to ~ with** espolvorear de; **dustbin** (*BRIT*) *n* cubo o bote *m* (*MEX*) or tacho (*sc*) de la basura; **duster** *n* paño, trapo; **dustman** (*BRIT: irreg*) *n* basurero; **dustpan** *n* cogedor *m*; **dusty** *adj* polvoriento

**Dutch** [dʌtʃ] *adj* holandés/esa ▷ *n* (*Ling*) holandés *m*; **the Dutch** *npl* los holandeses; **to go ~** (*inf*) pagar cada uno lo suyo; **Dutchman** (*irreg*) *n* holandés *m*; **Dutchwoman** (*irreg*) *n* holandésa

**duty** ['dju:tɪ] *n* deber *m*; (*tax*) derechos *mpl* de aduana; **on ~** de servicio; (*at night etc*) de guardia; **off ~** libre (de servicio); **duty-free** *adj* libre de impuestos

**duvet** ['du:veɪ] (*BRIT*) *n* edredón *m*

**DVD** *n abbr* (= *digital versatile or video disc*) DVD *m*; **DVD player** *n* lector *m* de DVD; **DVD writer** *n* grabadora de DVD

**dwarf** [dwɔ:f] (*pl* **dwarves**) *n* enano/a ▷ *vt* empequeñecer

**dwell** [dwɛl] (*pt, pp* **dwelt**) *vi* morar; **dwell on** *vt fus* explayarse en

**dwelt** [dwɛlt] *pt, pp of* **dwell**

**dwindle** ['dwɪndl] *vi* disminuir

**dye** [daɪ] *n* tinte *m* ▷ *vt* teñir

**dying** ['daɪɪŋ] *adj* moribundo

**dynamic** [daɪ'næmɪk] *adj* dinámico

**dynamite** ['daɪnəmaɪt] *n* dinamita

**dyslexia** [dɪs'lɛksɪə] *n* dislexia

**dyslexic** [dɪs'lɛksɪk] *adj, n* disléxico/a *m/f*

# e

**E** [i:] n (Mus) mi m

**E111** n abbr (= form E111) impreso E111

**each** [i:tʃ] adj cada inv ▷ pron cada uno; **~ other** el uno al otro; **they hate ~ other** se odian (entre ellos or mutuamente); **they have 2 books ~** tienen 2 libros por persona

**eager** ['i:gə*] adj (keen) entusiasmado; **to be ~ to do sth** tener muchas ganas de hacer algo, impacientarse por hacer algo; **to be ~ for** tener muchas ganas de

**eagle** ['i:gl] n águila

**ear** [ɪə*] n oreja; oído; (of corn) espiga; **earache** n dolor m de oídos; **eardrum** n tímpano

**earl** [ə:l] n conde m

**earlier** ['ə:lɪə*] adj anterior ▷ adv antes

**early** ['ə:lɪ] adv temprano; (before time) con tiempo, con anticipación ▷ adj temprano; (settlers etc) primitivo; (death, departure) prematuro; (reply) pronto; **to have an ~ night** acostarse temprano; **in the ~ or ~ in the spring/19th century** a principios de primavera/del siglo diecinueve; **early retirement** n jubilación f anticipada

**earmark** ['ɪəma:k] vt: **to ~ (for)** reservar (para), destinar (a)

**earn** [ə:n] vt (salary) percibir; (interest) devengar; (praise) merecerse

**earnest** ['ə:nɪst] adj (wish) fervoroso; (person) serio, formal; **in ~** en serio

**earnings** ['ə:nɪŋz] npl (personal) sueldo, ingresos mpl; (company) ganancias fpl

**ear: earphones** npl auriculares mpl; **earplugs** npl tapones mpl para los oídos; **earring** n pendiente m, arete m

**earth** [ə:θ] n tierra; (BRIT Elec) cable m de toma de tierra ▷ vt (BRIT Elec) conectar a tierra; **earthquake** n terremoto

**ease** [i:z] n facilidad f; (comfort) comodidad f ▷ vt (lessen: problem) mitigar; (: pain) aliviar; (: tension) reducir; **to ~ sth in/out** meter/sacar algo con cuidado; **at ~!** (Mil) ¡descansen!

**easily** ['i:zɪlɪ] adv fácilmente

**east** [i:st] n este m ▷ adj del este, oriental; (wind) este ▷ adv al este, hacia el este; **the E~** el Oriente; (Pol) los países del Este; **eastbound** adj en dirección este

**Easter** ['i:stə*] n Pascua (de Resurrección); **Easter egg** n huevo de Pascua

**eastern** ['i:stən] adj del este, oriental; (oriental) oriental

**Easter Sunday** n Domingo de Resurrección

**easy** ['i:zɪ] adj fácil; (simple) sencillo; (comfortable) holgado, cómodo; (relaxed) tranquilo ▷ adv: **to take it** or **things ~** (not worry) tomarlo con calma; (rest) descansar; **easy-going** adj acomodadizo

**eat** [i:t] (pt **ate**, pp **eaten**) vt comer; **eat out** vi comer fuera

**eavesdrop** ['i:vzdrɔp] vi: **to ~ (on)** escuchar a escondidas

**e-book** ['i:buk] n libro electrónico

**e-business** ['i:bɪznɪs] n (company) negocio electrónico; (commerce) comercio electrónico

**EC** n abbr (= European Community) CE f

**eccentric** [ɪk'sɛntrɪk] adj, n excéntrico/a m/f

**echo** ['ɛkəu] (pl **-es**) n eco ▷ vt (sound) repetir ▷ vi resonar, hacer eco

**eclipse** [ɪ'klɪps] n eclipse m

**eco-friendly** ['i:kəufrɛndlɪ] adj ecológico

**ecological** [i:kə'lɔdʒɪkl] adj ecológico

**ecology** [ɪ'kɔlədʒɪ] n ecología

**e-commerce** n abbr comercio electrónico

**economic** [i:kə'nɔmɪk] adj económico; (business etc) rentable; **economical** adj económico; **economics** n (Scol) economía ▷ npl (of project etc) rentabilidad f

**economist** [ɪ'kɔnəmɪst] n economista m/f

**economize** [ɪ'kɔnəmaɪz] vi economizar, ahorrar

**economy** [ɪ'kɔnəmɪ] n economía; **economy class** n (Aviat) clase f económica; **economy class syndrome** n síndrome m de la clase turista

**ecstasy** ['ɛkstəsɪ] n éxtasis m inv; (drug) éxtasis m inv; **ecstatic** [ɛks'tætɪk] adj extático

**eczema** ['ɛksɪmə] n eczema m

**edge** [ɛdʒ] n (of knife) filo; (of object) borde m; (of lake) orilla ▷ vt (Sewing) ribetear; **on ~ (fig)** = **edgy**; **to ~ away from** alejarse poco a poco de

**edgy** ['ɛdʒɪ] adj nervioso, inquieto

**edible** ['ɛdɪbl] adj comestible

**Edinburgh** ['ɛdɪnbərə] n Edimburgo
**edit** ['ɛdɪt] vt (be editor of) dirigir; (text, report) corregir, preparar; **edition** [ɪ'dɪʃən] n edición f; **editor** n (of newspaper) director(a) m/f; (of column): **foreign/political editor** encargado de la sección de extranjero/política; (of book) redactor(a) m/f; **editorial** [-'tɔːrɪəl] adj editorial ▷ n editorial m
**educate** ['ɛdjukeɪt] vt (gen) educar; (instruct) instruir; **educated** ['ɛdjukeɪtɪd] adj culto
**education** [ɛdju'keɪʃən] n educación f; (schooling) enseñanza; (Scol) pedagogía; **educational** adj (policy etc) educacional; (experience) docente; (toy) educativo
**eel** [iːl] n anguila
**eerie** ['ɪərɪ] adj misterioso
**effect** [ɪ'fɛkt] n efecto ▷ vt efectuar, llevar a cabo; **to take ~** (law) entrar en vigor or vigencia; (drug) surtir efecto; **in ~** en realidad; **effects** npl (property) efectos mpl; **effective** adj eficaz; (actual) verdadero; **effectively** adv eficazmente; (in reality) efectivamente
**efficiency** [ɪ'fɪʃənsɪ] n eficiencia; rendimiento
**efficient** [ɪ'fɪʃənt] adj eficiente; (machine) de buen rendimiento; **efficiently** adv eficientemente, de manera eficiente
**effort** ['ɛfət] n esfuerzo; **effortless** adj sin ningún esfuerzo; (style) natural
**e.g.** adv abbr (= exempli gratia) p. ej.
**egg** [ɛg] n huevo; **hard-boiled/soft-boiled ~** huevo duro/pasado por agua; **eggcup** n huevera; **eggplant** (esp US) n berenjena; **eggshell** n cáscara de huevo; **egg white** n clara de huevo; **egg yolk** n yema de huevo
**ego** ['iːgəu] n ego
**Egypt** ['iːdʒɪpt] n Egipto; **Egyptian** [ɪ'dʒɪpʃən] adj, n egipcio/a m/f
**eight** [eɪt] num ocho; **eighteen** num diez y ocho, dieciocho; **eighteenth** adj decimoctavo; **the eighteenth floor** la planta dieciocho; **the eighteenth of August** el dieciocho de agosto; **eighth** num octavo; **eightieth** ['eɪtɪɪθ] adj octogésimo
**eighty** ['eɪtɪ] num ochenta
**Eire** ['ɛərə] n Eire m
**either** ['aɪðə*] adj cualquiera de los dos; (both, each) cada ▷ pron: **~ (of them)** cualquiera (de los dos) ▷ adv tampoco ▷ conj: **~ yes or no** o sí o no; **on ~ side** en ambos lados; **I don't like ~** no me gusta ninguno/a de los(las) dos; **no, I don't ~** no, yo tampoco
**eject** [ɪ'dʒɛkt] vt echar, expulsar; (tenant) desahuciar
**elaborate** [adj ɪ'læbərɪt, vb ɪ'læbəreɪt] adj

(complex) complejo ▷ vt (expand) ampliar; (refine) refinar ▷ vi explicar con más detalles
**elastic** [ɪ'læstɪk] n elástico ▷ adj elástico; (fig) flexible; **elastic band** (BRIT) n gomita
**elbow** ['ɛlbəu] n codo
**elder** ['ɛldə*] adj mayor ▷ n (tree) saúco; (person) mayor; **elderly** adj de edad, mayor ▷ npl: **the elderly** los mayores
**eldest** ['ɛldɪst] adj, n el/la mayor
**elect** [ɪ'lɛkt] vt elegir ▷ adj: **the president ~** el presidente electo; **to ~ to do** optar por hacer; **election** n elección f; **electoral** adj electoral; **electorate** n electorado
**electric** [ɪ'lɛktrɪk] adj eléctrico; **electrical** adj eléctrico; **electric blanket** n manta eléctrica; **electric fire** n estufa eléctrica; **electrician** [ɪlɛk'trɪʃən] n electricista mf; **electricity** [ɪlɛk'trɪsɪtɪ] n electricidad f; **electric shock** n electrochoque m; **electrify** [ɪ'lɛktrɪfaɪ] vt (Rail) electrificar; (fig: audience) electrizar
**electronic** [ɪlɛk'trɔnɪk] adj electrónico; **electronic mail** n correo electrónico; **electronics** n electrónica
**elegance** ['ɛlɪgəns] n elegancia
**elegant** ['ɛlɪgənt] adj elegante
**element** ['ɛlɪmənt] n elemento; (of kettle etc) resistencia
**elementary** [ɛlɪ'mɛntərɪ] adj elemental; (primitive) rudimentario; **elementary school** (US) n escuela de enseñanza primaria
**elephant** ['ɛlɪfənt] n elefante m
**elevate** ['ɛlɪveɪt] vt (gen) elevar; (in rank) ascender
**elevator** ['ɛlɪveɪtə*] (US) n ascensor m; (in warehouse etc) montacargas m inv
**eleven** [ɪ'lɛvn] num once; **eleventh** adj undécimo
**eligible** ['ɛlɪdʒəbl] adj: **an ~ young man/ woman** un buen partido; **to be ~ for sth** llenar los requisitos para algo
**eliminate** [ɪ'lɪmɪneɪt] vt (suspect, possibility) descartar
**elm** [ɛlm] n olmo
**eloquent** ['ɛləkwənt] adj elocuente
**else** [ɛls] adv: **something ~** otra cosa; **somewhere ~** en otra parte; **everywhere ~** en todas partes menos aquí; **where ~?** ¿dónde más?, ¿en qué otra parte?; **there was little ~ to do** apenas quedaba otra cosa que hacer; **nobody ~ spoke** no habló nadie más; **elsewhere** adv (be) en otra parte; (go) a otra parte
**elusive** [ɪ'luːsɪv] adj esquivo; (quality) difícil de encontrar
**e-mail** ['iːmeɪl] n abbr (= electronic mail) correo electrónico, e-mail m; **e-mail**

**address** n dirección f electrónica, email m
**embankment** [ɪmˈbæŋkmənt] n
terraplén m
**embargo** [ɪmˈbɑːgəʊ] (pl **~es**) n (Comm,
Naut) embargo; (prohibition) prohibición f; **to
put an ~ on sth** poner un embargo en algo
**embark** [ɪmˈbɑːk] vi embarcarse ▷ vt
embarcar; **to ~ on** (journey) emprender;
(course of action) lanzarse a
**embarrass** [ɪmˈbærəs] vt avergonzar;
(government etc) dejar en mal lugar;
**embarrassed** adj (laugh, silence)
embarazoso

Be careful not to translate **embarrassed**
by the Spanish word embarazada.

**embarrassing** adj (situation) violento;
(question) embarazoso; **embarrassment**
n (shame) vergüenza; (problem): **to be an
embarrassment for sb** poner en un aprieto
a algn
**embassy** [ˈembəsɪ] n embajada
**embrace** [ɪmˈbreɪs] vt abrazar, dar un
abrazo a; (include) abarcar ▷ vi abrazarse
▷ n abrazo
**embroider** [ɪmˈbrɔɪdə*] vt bordar;
**embroidery** n bordado
**embryo** [ˈembrɪəʊ] n embrión m
**emerald** [ˈemərəld] n esmeralda
**emerge** [ɪˈmɜːdʒ] vi salir; (arise) surgir
**emergency** [ɪˈmɜːdʒənsɪ] n crisis f inv;
**in an ~** en caso de urgencia; **state of ~**
estado de emergencia; **emergency brake**
(US) n freno de mano; **emergency exit** n
salida de emergencia; **emergency landing**
n aterrizaje m forzoso; **emergency room**
(US: Med) n sala f de urgencias; **emergency
services** (fire, police, ambulance) n
servicios mpl de urgencia o emergencia
**emigrate** [ˈemɪgreɪt] vi emigrar;
**emigration** [emɪˈgreɪʃən] n emigración f
**eminent** [ˈemɪnənt] adj eminente
**emissions** [ɪˈmɪʃənz] npl emisión f
**emit** [ɪˈmɪt] vt emitir; (smoke) arrojar;
(smell) despedir; (sound) producir
**emotion** [ɪˈməʊʃən] n emoción f;
**emotional** adj (needs) emocional; (person)
sentimental; (scene) conmovedor(a),
emocionante; (speech) emocionado
**emperor** [ˈempərə*] n emperador m
**emphasis** [ˈemfəsɪs] (pl **-ses**) n énfasis
m inv
**emphasize** [ˈemfəsaɪz] vt (word, point)
subrayar, recalcar; (feature) hacer resaltar
**empire** [ˈempaɪə*] n imperio
**employ** [ɪmˈplɔɪ] vt emplear; **employee**
[-ˈiː] n empleado/a; **employer** n patrón
ona m/f; empresario; **employment** n
(work) trabajo; **employment agency** n

agencia de colocaciones
**empower** [ɪmˈpaʊə*] vt: **to ~ sb to do sth**
autorizar a algn para hacer algo
**empress** [ˈemprɪs] n emperatriz f
**emptiness** [ˈemptɪnɪs] n vacío; (of life etc)
vaciedad f
**empty** [ˈemptɪ] adj vacío; (place) desierto;
(house) desocupado; (threat) vano ▷ vt
vaciar; (place) dejar vacío ▷ vi vaciarse;
(house etc) quedar desocupado; **empty-
handed** adj con las manos vacías
**EMU** n abbr (= European Monetary Union)
UME f
**emulsion** [ɪˈmʌlʃən] n emulsión f; (also: ~
**paint**) pintura emulsión
**enable** [ɪˈneɪbl] vt: **to ~ sb to do sth**
permitir a algn hacer algo
**enamel** [ɪˈnæml] n esmalte m; (also: ~
**paint**) pintura esmaltada
**enchanting** [ɪnˈtʃɑːntɪŋ] adj
encantador(a)
**encl.** abbr (= enclosed) adj
**enclose** [ɪnˈkləʊz] vt (land) cercar; (letter
etc) adjuntar; **please find ~d** le mandamos
adjunto
**enclosure** [ɪnˈkləʊʒə*] n cercado, recinto
**encore** [ɒŋˈkɔː*] excl ¡otra!, ¡bis! ▷ n bis m
**encounter** [ɪnˈkaʊntə*] n encuentro
▷ vt encontrar, encontrarse con; (difficulty)
tropezar con
**encourage** [ɪnˈkʌrɪdʒ] vt alentar, animar;
(activity) fomentar; (growth) estimular;
**encouragement** n estímulo; (of industry)
fomento
**encouraging** [ɪnˈkʌrɪdʒɪŋ] adj
alentador(a)
**encyclop(a)edia** [ensaɪkləʊˈpiːdɪə] n
enciclopedia
**end** [end] n fin m; (of table) extremo; (of
street) final m; (Sport) lado ▷ vt terminar,
acabar; (also: **bring to an ~, put an ~ to**)
acabar con ▷ vi terminar, acabar; **in the
~** al fin; **on ~** (object) de punta, de cabeza;
**to stand on ~** (hair) erizarse; **for hours on
~** hora tras hora; **end up** vi: **to end up in**
terminar en; (place) ir a parar en
**endanger** [ɪnˈdeɪndʒə*] vt poner en
peligro; **an ~ed species** una especie en
peligro de extinción
**endearing** [ɪnˈdɪərɪŋ] adj simpático,
atractivo
**endeavour** [ɪnˈdevə*] (US **endeavor**) n
esfuerzo; (attempt) tentativa ▷ vi: **to ~ to do**
esforzarse por hacer; (try) procurar hacer
**ending** [ˈendɪŋ] n (of book) desenlace m;
(Ling) terminación f
**endless** [ˈendlɪs] adj interminable,
inacabable

**endorse** [ɪnˈdɔːs] vt (cheque) endosar; (approve) aprobar; **endorsement** n (on driving licence) nota de inhabilitación

**endurance** [ɪnˈdjuərəns] n resistencia

**endure** [ɪnˈdjuə*] vt (bear) aguantar, soportar ▷ vi (last) durar

**enemy** [ˈɛnəmɪ] adj, n enemigo/a m/f

**energetic** [ɛnəˈdʒɛtɪk] adj enérgico

**energy** [ˈɛnədʒɪ] n energía

**enforce** [ɪnˈfɔːs] vt (Law) hacer cumplir

**engaged** [ɪnˈgeɪdʒd] adj (BRIT: busy, in use) ocupado; (betrothed) prometido; **to get ~** prometerse; **engaged tone** (BRIT) n (Tel) señal f de comunicando

**engagement** [ɪnˈgeɪdʒmənt] n (appointment) compromiso, cita; (booking) contratación f; (to marry) compromiso; (period) noviazgo; **engagement ring** n anillo de prometida

**engaging** [ɪnˈgeɪdʒɪŋ] adj atractivo

**engine** [ˈɛndʒɪn] n (Aut) motor m; (Rail) locomotora

**engineer** [ɛndʒɪˈnɪə*] n ingeniero; (BRIT: for repairs) mecánico; (on ship, US Rail) maquinista m; **engineering** n ingeniería

**England** [ˈɪŋglənd] n Inglaterra

**English** [ˈɪŋglɪʃ] adj inglés/esa ▷ n (Ling) inglés m; **the English** npl los ingleses mpl; **English Channel** n: **the English Channel** (el Canal de) la Mancha; **Englishman** (irreg) n inglés m; **Englishwoman** (irreg) n inglésa

**engrave** [ɪnˈgreɪv] vt grabar

**engraving** [ɪnˈgreɪvɪŋ] n grabado

**enhance** [ɪnˈhɑːns] vt (gen) aumentar; (beauty) realzar

**enjoy** [ɪnˈdʒɔɪ] vt (health, fortune) disfrutar de, gozar de; (like) gustarle a algn; **to ~ o.s.** divertirse; **enjoyable** adj agradable; (amusing) divertido; **enjoyment** n (joy) placer m; (activity) diversión f

**enlarge** [ɪnˈlɑːdʒ] vt aumentar; (broaden) extender; (Phot) ampliar ▷ vi: **to ~ on** (subject) tratar con más detalles; **enlargement** n (Phot) ampliación f

**enlist** [ɪnˈlɪst] vt alistar; (support) conseguir ▷ vi alistarse

**enormous** [ɪˈnɔːməs] adj enorme

**enough** [ɪˈnʌf] adj: **~ time/books** bastante tiempo/bastantes libros ▷ pron bastante(s) ▷ adv: **big ~** bastante grande; **he has not worked ~** no ha trabajado bastante; **have you got ~?** ¿tiene usted bastante(s)?; **~ to eat** (lo) suficiente or (lo) bastante para comer; **~!** ¡basta ya!; **that's ~, thanks** con eso basta, gracias; **I've had ~ of him** estoy harto de él; **... which, funnily** or **oddly ~ ...** ... lo que, por extraño que parezca ...

**enquire** [ɪnˈkwaɪə*] vt, vi = **inquire**

**enquiry** [ɪnˈkwaɪərɪ] n (official investigation) investigación

**enrage** [ɪnˈreɪdʒ] vt enfurecer

**enrich** [ɪnˈrɪtʃ] vt enriquecer

**enrol** [ɪnˈrəul] (US **enroll**) vt (members) inscribir; (Scol) matricular ▷ vi inscribirse; matricularse; **enrolment** (US **enrollment**) n inscripción f; matriculación f

**en route** [ɒnˈruːt] adv durante el viaje

**en suite** [ɒnˈswiːt] adj: **with ~ bathroom** con baño

**ensure** [ɪnˈʃuə*] vt asegurar

**entail** [ɪnˈteɪl] vt suponer

**enter** [ˈɛntə*] vt (room) entrar en; (club) hacerse socio de; (army) alistarse en; (sb for a competition) inscribir; (write down) anotar, apuntar; (Comput) meter ▷ vi entrar

**enterprise** [ˈɛntəpraɪz] n empresa; (spirit) iniciativa; **free ~** la libre empresa; **private ~** la iniciativa privada; **enterprising** adj emprendedor/a

**entertain** [ɛntəˈteɪn] vt (amuse) divertir; (invite: guest) invitar (a casa); (idea) abrigar; **entertainer** n artista mf; **entertaining** adj divertido, entretenido; **entertainment** n (amusement) diversión f; (show) espectáculo

**enthusiasm** [ɪnˈθuːzɪæzəm] n entusiasmo

**enthusiast** [ɪnˈθuːzɪæst] n entusiasta mf; **enthusiastic** [-ˈæstɪk] adj entusiasta; **to be enthusiastic about** entusiasmarse por

**entire** [ɪnˈtaɪə*] adj entero; **entirely** adv totalmente

**entitle** [ɪnˈtaɪtl] vt: **to ~ sb to sth** dar a algn derecho a algo; **entitled** adj (book) titulado; **to be entitled to do** tener derecho a hacer

**entrance** [n ˈɛntrəns, vb ɪnˈtrɑːns] n entrada ▷ vt encantar, hechizar; **to gain ~ to** (university etc) ingresar en; **entrance examination** n examen m de ingreso; **entrance fee** n cuota; **entrance ramp** (US) n (Aut) rampa de acceso

**entrant** [ˈɛntrənt] n (in race, competition) participante mf; (in examination) candidato/a

**entrepreneur** [ɒntrəprəˈnəː] n empresario

**entrust** [ɪnˈtrʌst] vt: **to ~ sth to sb** confiar algo a algn

**entry** [ˈɛntrɪ] n entrada; (in competition) participación f; (in register) apunte m; (in account) partida; (in reference book) artículo; **"no ~"** "prohibido el paso"; (Aut) "dirección prohibida"; **entry phone** n portero automático

**envelope** [ˈɛnvələup] n sobre m

**envious** [ˈɛnvɪəs] adj envidioso; (look) de

envidia

**environment** [ɪn'vaɪərnmənt] n
(surroundings) entorno; (natural world):
**the ~** el medio ambiente; **environmental**
[-'mɛntl] adj ambiental; medioambiental;
**environmentally** [-'mɛntəlɪ]
adv: **environmentally sound/friendly**
ecológico

**envisage** [ɪn'vɪzɪdʒ] vt prever

**envoy** ['ɛnvɔɪ] n enviado

**envy** ['ɛnvɪ] n envidia ▷ vt tener envidia a;
**to ~ sb sth** envidiar algo a algn

**epic** ['ɛpɪk] n épica ▷ adj épico

**epidemic** [ɛpɪ'dɛmɪk] n epidemia

**epilepsy** ['ɛpɪlɛpsɪ] n epilepsia

**epileptic** [ɛpɪ'lɛptɪk] adj, n epiléptico/a
m/f; **epileptic fit** [ɛpɪ'lɛptɪk-] n ataque m
de epilepsia, acceso m epiléptico

**episode** ['ɛpɪsəud] n episodio

**equal** ['iːkwl] adj igual; (treatment)
equitativo ▷ n igual mf ▷ vt ser igual a;
(fig) igualar; **to be ~ to** (task) estar a la altura
de; **equality** [iː'kwɔlɪtɪ] n igualdad f;
**equalize** vi (Sport) empatar; **equally** adv
igualmente; (share etc) a partes iguales

**equation** [ɪ'kweɪʒən] n (Math) ecuación f

**equator** [ɪ'kweɪtə*] n ecuador m

**equip** [ɪ'kwɪp] vt equipar; (person) proveer;
**to be well ~ped** estar bien equipado;
**equipment** n equipo; (tools) avíos mpl

**equivalent** [ɪ'kwɪvələnt] adj: **~ (to)**
equivalente (a) ▷ n equivalente m

**ER** abbr (BRIT: = Elizabeth Regina) la reina
Isabel; (US: Med) = **emergency room**

**era** ['ɪərə] n era, época

**erase** [ɪ'reɪz] vt borrar; **eraser** n goma
de borrar

**erect** [ɪ'rɛkt] adj erguido ▷ vt erigir,
levantar; (assemble) montar; **erection** [-ʃən]
n construcción f; (assembly) montaje m;
(Physiol) erección f

**ERM** n abbr (= Exchange Rate Mechanism) tipo
de cambio europeo

**erode** [ɪ'rəud] vt (Geo) erosionar; (metal)
corroer, desgastar; (fig) desgastar

**erosion** [ɪ'rəuʒən] n erosión f; desgaste m

**erotic** [ɪ'rɔtɪk] adj erótico

**errand** ['ɛrnd] n recado (SP), mandado
(LAM)

**erratic** [ɪ'rætɪk] adj desigual, poco
uniforme

**error** ['ɛrə*] n error m, equivocación f

**erupt** [ɪ'rʌpt] vi entrar en erupción; (fig)
estallar; **eruption** [ɪ'rʌpʃən] n erupción f;
(of war) estallido

**escalate** ['ɛskəleɪt] vi extenderse,
intensificarse

**escalator** ['ɛskəleɪtə*] n escalera móvil

**escape** [ɪ'skeɪp] n fuga ▷ vi escaparse;
(flee) huir, evadirse; (leak) fugarse
▷ vt (responsibility etc) evitar, eludir;
(consequences) escapar a; (elude): **his name
~s me** no me sale su nombre; **to ~ from**
(place) escaparse de; (person) escaparse a

**escort** [n 'ɛskɔːt, vb ɪ'skɔːt] n
acompañante mf; (Mil) escolta mf ▷ vt
acompañar

**especially** [ɪ'spɛʃlɪ] adv (above all)
sobre todo; (particularly) en particular,
especialmente

**espionage** ['ɛspɪənɑːʒ] n espionaje m

**essay** ['ɛseɪ] n (Literature) ensayo;
(Scol: short) redacción f; (: long) trabajo

**essence** ['ɛsns] n esencia

**essential** [ɪ'sɛnʃl] adj (necessary)
imprescindible; (basic) esencial; **essentially**
adv esencialmente; **essentials** npl lo
imprescindible, lo esencial

**establish** [ɪ'stæblɪʃ] vt establecer;
(prove) demostrar; (relations) entablar;
(reputation) ganarse; **establishment** n
establecimiento; **the Establishment** la
clase dirigente

**estate** [ɪ'steɪt] n (land) finca, hacienda;
(inheritance) herencia; (BRIT: also: **housing
~**) urbanización f; **estate agent** (BRIT) n
agente mf inmobiliario/a; **estate car** (BRIT)
n furgoneta

**estimate** [n 'ɛstɪmət, vb 'ɛstɪmeɪt] n
estimación f, apreciación f; (assessment)
tasa, cálculo; (Comm) presupuesto ▷ vt
estimar, tasar; calcular

**etc** abbr (= et cetera) etc

**eternal** [ɪ'təːnl] adj eterno

**eternity** [ɪ'təːnɪtɪ] n eternidad f

**ethical** ['ɛθɪkl] adj ético; **ethics** ['ɛθɪks] n
ética ▷ npl moralidad f

**Ethiopia** [iːθɪ'əupɪə] n Etiopía

**ethnic** ['ɛθnɪk] adj étnico; **ethnic
minority** n minoría étnica

**e-ticket** ['iːtɪkɪt] n billete m electrónico
(SP), boleto electrónico (LAM)

**etiquette** ['ɛtɪkɛt] n etiqueta

**EU** n abbr (= European Union) UE f

**euro** n euro

**Europe** ['juərəp] n Europa; **European**
[-'piːən] adj, n europeo/a m/f; **European
Community** n Comunidad f Europea;
**European Union** n Unión f Europea

**Eurostar®** ['juərəustɑː*] n Eurostar® m

**evacuate** [ɪ'vækjueɪt] vt (people) evacuar;
(place) desocupar

**evade** [ɪ'veɪd] vt evadir, eludir

**evaluate** [ɪ'væljueɪt] vt evaluar; (value)
tasar; (evidence) interpretar

**evaporate** [ɪ'væpəreɪt] vi evaporarse; (fig)

desvanecerse

**eve** [i:v] *n*: **on the ~ of** en vísperas de

**even** ['i:vn] *adj* (*level*) llano; (*smooth*) liso; (*speed, temperature*) uniforme; (*number*) par ▷ *adv* hasta, incluso; (*introducing a comparison*) aún, todavía; **~ if, ~ though** aunque +*subjun*; **~ more** aun más; **~ so** aun así; **not ~** ni siquiera; **~ he was there** hasta él estuvo allí; **~ on Sundays** incluso los domingos; **to get ~ with sb** ajustar cuentas con algn

**evening** ['i:vnɪŋ] *n* tarde *f*; (*late*) noche *f*; **in the ~** por la tarde; **evening class** *n* clase *f* nocturna; **evening dress** *n* (*no pl: formal clothes*) traje *m* de etiqueta; (*woman's*) traje *m* de noche

**event** [ɪ'vɛnt] *n* suceso, acontecimiento; (*Sport*) prueba; **in the ~ of** en caso de; **eventful** *adj* (*life*) activo; (*day*) ajetreado

**eventual** [ɪ'vɛntʃuəl] *adj* final

> Be careful not to translate **eventual** by the Spanish word *eventual*.

**eventually** *adv* (*finally*) finalmente; (*in time*) con el tiempo

**ever** ['ɛvə*] *adv* (*at any time*) nunca, jamás; (*at all times*) siempre; (*in question*): **why ~ not?** ¿y por qué no?; **the best ~** lo nunca visto; **have you ~ seen it?** ¿lo ha visto usted alguna vez?; **better than ~** mejor que nunca; **~ since** *adv* desde entonces ▷ *conj* después de que; **evergreen** *n* árbol *m* de hoja perenne

○ **KEYWORD**

**every** ['ɛvrɪ] *adj* **1** (*each*) cada; **every one of them** (*persons*) todos ellos/as; (*objects*) cada uno de ellos/as; **every shop in the town was closed** todas
las tiendas de la ciudad estaban cerradas
**2** (*all possible*) todo/a; **I gave you every assistance** te di toda la ayuda posible; **I have every confidence in him** tiene toda mi confianza; **we wish you every success** te deseamos toda suerte de éxitos
**3** (*showing recurrence*) todo/a; **every day/week** todos los días/todas las semanas; **every other car had been broken into** habían forzado uno de cada dos coches; **she visits me every other/third day** me visita cada dos/tres días; **every now and then** de vez en cuando

**every:** **everybody** *pron* = **everyone**; **everyday** *adj* (*daily*) cotidiano, de todos los días; (*usual*) acostumbrado; **everyone** *pron* todos/as, todo el mundo; **everything** *pron* todo; **this shop sells everything**

esta tienda vende de todo; **everywhere** *adv*: **I've been looking for you everywhere** te he estado buscando por todas partes; **everywhere you go you meet ...** en todas partes encuentras ...

**evict** [ɪ'vɪkt] *vt* desahuciar

**evidence** ['ɛvɪdəns] *n* (*proof*) prueba; (*of witness*) testimonio; (*sign*) indicios *mpl*; **to give ~** prestar declaración, dar testimonio

**evident** ['ɛvɪdənt] *adj* evidente, manifiesto; **evidently** *adv* por lo visto

**evil** ['i:vl] *adj* malo; (*influence*) funesto ▷ *n* mal *m*

**evoke** [ɪ'vəuk] *vt* evocar

**evolution** [i:və'lu:ʃən] *n* evolución *f*

**evolve** [ɪ'vɔlv] *vt* desarrollar ▷ *vi* evolucionar, desarrollarse

**ewe** [ju:] *n* oveja

**ex** [ɛks] (*inf*) *n*: **my ~** mi ex

**ex-** [ɛks] *prefix* ex

**exact** [ɪg'zækt] *adj* exacto; (*person*) meticuloso ▷ *vt*: **to ~ sth (from)** exigir algo (de); **exactly** *adv* exactamente; (*indicating agreement*) exacto

**exaggerate** [ɪg'zædʒəreɪt] *vt*, *vi* exagerar; **exaggeration** [-'reɪʃən] *n* exageración *f*

**exam** [ɪg'zæm] *n abbr* (*Scol*) = **examination**

**examination** [ɪgzæmɪ'neɪʃən] *n* examen *m*; (*Med*) reconocimiento

**examine** [ɪg'zæmɪn] *vt* examinar; (*inspect*) inspeccionar, escudriñar; (*Med*) reconocer; **examiner** *n* examinador(a) *m/f*

**example** [ɪg'zɑ:mpl] *n* ejemplo; **for ~** por ejemplo

**exasperated** [ɪg'zɑ:spəreɪtɪd] *adj* exasperado

**excavate** ['ɛkskəveɪt] *vt* excavar

**exceed** [ɪk'si:d] *vt* (*amount*) exceder; (*number*) pasar de; (*speed limit*) sobrepasar; (*powers*) excederse en; (*hopes*) superar; **exceedingly** *adv* sumamente, sobremanera

**excel** [ɪk'sɛl] *vi* sobresalir; **to ~ o.s** lucirse

**excellence** ['ɛksələns] *n* excelencia

**excellent** ['ɛksələnt] *adj* excelente

**except** [ɪk'sɛpt] *prep* (*also*: **~ for, ~ing**) excepto, salvo ▷ *vt* exceptuar, excluir; **~ if/when** excepto si/cuando; **~ that** salvo que; **exception** [ɪk'sɛpʃən] *n* excepción *f*; **to take exception to** ofenderse por; **exceptional** [ɪk'sɛpʃənl] *adj* excepcional; **exceptionally** [ɪk'sɛpʃənəlɪ] *adv* excepcionalmente, extraordinariamente

**excerpt** ['ɛksə:pt] *n* extracto

**excess** [ɪk'sɛs] *n* exceso; **excess baggage** *n* exceso de equipaje; **excessive** *adj* excesivo

**exchange** [ɪks'tʃeɪndʒ] *n* intercambio; (*conversation*) diálogo; (*also*: **telephone ~**)

central f (telefónica); ▷ vt: **to ~ (for)** cambiar (por); **exchange rate** n tipo de cambio

**excite** [ɪkˈsaɪt] vt (stimulate) estimular; (arouse) excitar; **excited** adj: **to get excited** emocionarse; **excitement** n (agitation) excitación f; (exhilaration) emoción f; **exciting** adj emocionante

**exclaim** [ɪkˈskleɪm] vi exclamar; **exclamation** [ɛksklɔˈmeɪʃən] n exclamación f; **exclamation mark** n punto de admiración; **exclamation point** (us) = **exclamation mark**

**exclude** [ɪkˈskluːd] vt excluir; exceptuar

**excluding** [ɪksˈkluːdɪŋ] prep: **~ VAT** IVA no incluido

**exclusion** [ɪksˈkluːʒən] n exclusión f; **to the ~ of** con exclusión de

**exclusive** [ɪksˈkluːsɪv] adj exclusivo; (club, district) selecto; **~ of tax** excluyendo impuestos; **exclusively** adv únicamente

**excruciating** [ɪksˈkruːʃieitɪŋ] adj (pain) agudísimo, atroz; (noise, embarrassment) horrible

**excursion** [ɪksˈkəːʃən] n (tourist excursion) excursión f

**excuse** [n ɪkˈskjuːs, vb ɪkˈskjuːz] n disculpa, excusa; (pretext) pretexto ▷ vt (justify) justificar; (forgive) disculpar, perdonar; **to ~ sb from doing sth** dispensar a algn de hacer algo; **~ me!** (attracting attention) ¡por favor!; (apologizing) ¡perdón!; **if you will ~ me** con su permiso

**ex-directory** [ˈɛksdɪˈrɛktərɪ] (BRIT) adj que no consta en la guía

**execute** [ˈɛksɪkjuːt] vt (plan) realizar; (order) cumplir; (person) ajusticiar, ejecutar; **execution** [-ˈkjuːʃən] n realización f; cumplimiento; ejecución f

**executive** [ɪgˈzɛkjutɪv] n (person, committee) ejecutivo; (Pol: committee) poder m ejecutivo ▷ adj ejecutivo

**exempt** [ɪgˈzɛmpt] adj: **~ from** exento de ▷ vt: **to ~ sb from** eximir a algn de

**exercise** [ˈɛksəsaɪz] n ejercicio ▷ vt (patience) usar de; (right) valerse de; (dog) llevar de paseo; (mind) preocupar ▷ vi (also: **to take ~**) hacer ejercicio(s); **exercise book** n cuaderno

**exert** [ɪgˈzəːt] vt ejercer; **to ~ o.s.** esforzarse; **exertion** [-ʃən] n esfuerzo

**exhale** [eksˈheɪl] vt despedir ▷ vi exhalar

**exhaust** [ɪgˈzɔːst] n (Aut: also: **~ pipe**) escape m; (: fumes) gases mpl de escape ▷ vt agotar; **exhausted** adj agotado; **exhaustion** [ɪgˈzɔːstʃən] n agotamiento; **nervous exhaustion** postración f nerviosa

**exhibit** [ɪgˈzɪbɪt] n (Art) obra expuesta; (Law) objeto expuesto ▷ vt (show: emotions)

manifestar; (: courage, skill) demostrar; (paintings) exponer; **exhibition** [ɛksɪˈbɪʃən] n exposición f; (of talent etc) demostración f

**exhilarating** [ɪgˈzɪləreɪtɪŋ] adj estimulante, tónico

**exile** [ˈɛksaɪl] n exilio; (person) exiliado/a ▷ vt desterrar, exiliar

**exist** [ɪgˈzɪst] vi existir; (live) vivir; **existence** n existencia; **existing** adj existente, actual

**exit** [ˈɛksɪt] n salida ▷ vi (Theatre) hacer mutis; (Comput) salir (del sistema)

▌ Be careful not to translate **exit** by the Spanish word éxito.

**exit ramp** (us) n (Aut) vía de acceso

**exotic** [ɪgˈzɔtɪk] adj exótico

**expand** [ɪkˈspænd] vt ampliar; (number) aumentar ▷ vi (population) aumentar; (trade etc) expandirse; (gas, metal) dilatarse

**expansion** [ɪkˈspænʃən] n (of population) aumento; (of trade) expansión f

**expect** [ɪkˈspɛkt] vt esperar; (require) contar con; (suppose) suponer ▷ vi: **to be ~ing** (pregnant woman) estar embarazada; **expectation** [ɛkspɛkˈteɪʃən] n (hope) esperanza; (belief) expectativa

**expedition** [ɛkspəˈdɪʃən] n expedición f

**expel** [ɪkˈspɛl] vt arrojar; (from place) expulsar

**expenditure** [ɪksˈpɛndɪtʃə*] n gastos mpl, desembolso; consumo

**expense** [ɪkˈspɛns] n gasto, gastos mpl; (high cost) costa; **expenses** npl (Comm) gastos mpl; **at the ~ of** a costa de; **expense account** n cuenta de gastos

**expensive** [ɪkˈspɛnsɪv] adj caro, costoso

**experience** [ɪkˈspɪərɪəns] n experiencia ▷ vt experimentar; (suffer) sufrir; **experienced** adj experimentado

**experiment** [ɪkˈspɛrɪmənt] n experimento ▷ vi hacer experimentos; **experimental** [-ˈmɛntl] adj experimental; **the process is still at the experimental stage** el proceso está todavía en prueba

**expert** [ˈɛkspəːt] adj experto, perito ▷ n experto/a, perito/a; (specialist) especialista mf; **expertise** [-ˈtiːz] n pericia

**expire** [ɪkˈspaɪə*] vi caducar, vencer; **expiry** n vencimiento; **expiry date** n (of medicine, food item) fecha de caducidad

**explain** [ɪkˈspleɪn] vt explicar; **explanation** [ɛkspləˈneɪʃən] n explicación f

**explicit** [ɪkˈsplɪsɪt] adj explícito

**explode** [ɪkˈspləud] vi estallar, explotar; (population) crecer rápidamente; (with anger) reventar

**exploit** [n ˈɛksplɔɪt, vb ɪkˈsplɔɪt] n hazaña

▷ vt explotar; **exploitation** [-'teɪʃən] n explotación f

**explore** [ɪk'splɔ:*] vt explorar; (fig) examinar; investigar; **explorer** n explorador(a) m/f

**explosion** [ɪk'spləuʒən] n explosión f; **explosive** [ɪks'pləusɪv] adj, n explosivo

**export** [vb εk'spɔ:t, n, cpd 'εkspɔ:t] vt exportar ▷ n (process) exportación f; (product) producto de exportación ▷ cpd de exportación; **exporter** n exportador m

**expose** [ɪk'spəuz] vt exponer; (unmask) desenmascarar; **exposed** adj expuesto

**exposure** [ɪk'spəuʒə*] n exposición f; (publicity) publicidad f; (Phot: speed) velocidad f de obturación; (: shot) fotografía; **to die from ~** (Med) morir de frío

**express** [ɪk'sprεs] adj (definite) expreso, explícito; (BRIT: letter etc) urgente ▷ n (train) rápido ▷ vt expresar; **expression** [ɪk'sprεʃən] n expresión f; (of actor etc) sentimiento; **expressway** (US) n (urban motorway) autopista

**exquisite** [εk'skwɪzɪt] adj exquisito

**extend** [ɪk'stεnd] vt (visit, street) prolongar; (building) ampliar; (invitation) ofrecer ▷ vi (land) extenderse; (period of time) prolongarse

**extension** [ɪk'stεnʃən] n extensión f; (building) ampliación f; (of time) prolongación f; (Tel: in private house) línea derivada; (: in office) extensión f; **extension lead** n alargador m, alargadera f

**extensive** [ɪk'stεnsɪv] adj extenso; (damage) importante; (knowledge) amplio

**extent** [ɪk'stεnt] n (breadth) extensión f; (scope) alcance m; **to some ~** hasta cierto punto; **to the ~ of ...** hasta el punto de ...; **to such an ~ that ...** hasta tal punto que ...; **to what ~?** ¿hasta qué punto?

**exterior** [εk'stɪərɪə*] adj exterior, externo ▷ n exterior m

**external** [εk'stə:nl] adj externo

**extinct** [ɪk'stɪŋkt] adj (volcano) extinguido; (race) extinto; **extinction** n extinción f

**extinguish** [ɪk'stɪŋgwɪʃ] vt extinguir, apagar

**extra** ['εkstrə] adj adicional ▷ adv (in addition) de más ▷ n (luxury, addition) extra m; (Cinema, Theatre) extra mf, comparsa mf

**extract** [vb ɪk'strækt, n 'εkstrækt] vt sacar; (tooth) extraer; (money, promise) obtener ▷ n extracto

**extradite** ['εkstrədaɪt] vt extraditar

**extraordinary** [ɪk'strɔ:dnrɪ] adj extraordinario; (odd) raro

**extravagance** [ɪk'strævəgəns] n derroche m, despilfarro; (thing bought) extravagancia

**extravagant** [ɪk'strævəgənt] adj (lavish: person) pródigo; (: gift) (demasiado) caro; (wasteful) despilfarrador(a)

**extreme** [ɪk'stri:m] adj extremo, extremado ▷ n extremo; **extremely** adv sumamente, extremadamente

**extremist** [ɪk'stri:mɪst] adj, n extremista m/f

**extrovert** ['εkstrəvə:t] n extrovertido/a

**eye** [aɪ] n ojo ▷ vt mirar de soslayo, ojear; **to keep an ~ on** vigilar; **eyeball** n globo ocular; **eyebrow** n ceja; **eyedrops** npl gotas fpl para los ojos, colirio; **eyelash** n pestaña; **eyelid** n párpado; **eyeliner** n delineador m (de ojos); **eyeshadow** n sombreador m de ojos; **eyesight** n vista; **eye witness** n testigo mf presencial

**F** [ɛf] n (*Mus*) fa m

**fabric** ['fæbrɪk] n tejido, tela

> Be careful not to translate **fabric** by the Spanish word *fábrica*.

**fabulous** ['fæbjuləs] adj fabuloso

**face** [feɪs] n (*Anat*) cara, rostro; (*of clock*) esfera (*SP*), cara (*LAM*); (*of mountain*) cara, ladera; (*of building*) fachada ▷ vt (*direction*) estar de cara a; (*situation*) hacer frente a; (*facts*) aceptar; **~ down** (*person, card*) boca abajo; **to lose ~** desprestigiarse; **to make** *or* **pull a ~** hacer muecas; **in the ~ of** (*difficulties etc*) ante; **on the ~ of it** a primera vista; **~ to ~** cara a cara; **face up** vt fus hacer frente a, arrostrar; **face cloth** (*BRIT*) n manopla; **face pack** n (*BRIT*) mascarilla

**facial** ['feɪʃəl] adj de la cara ▷ n (*also:* **beauty ~**) tratamiento facial, limpieza

**facilitate** [fə'sɪlɪteɪt] vt facilitar

**facilities** [fə'sɪlɪtɪz] npl (*buildings*) instalaciones fpl; (*equipment*) servicios mpl; **credit ~** facilidades fpl de crédito

**fact** [fækt] n hecho; **in ~** en realidad

**faction** ['fækʃən] n facción f

**factor** ['fæktə*] n factor m

**factory** ['fæktərɪ] n fábrica

**factual** ['fæktjuəl] adj basado en los hechos

**faculty** ['fækəltɪ] n facultad f; (*US: teaching staff*) personal m docente

**fad** [fæd] n novedad f, moda

**fade** [feɪd] vi desteñirse; (*sound, smile*) desvanecerse; (*light*) apagarse; (*flower*) marchitarse; (*hope, memory*) perderse; **fade away** vi (*sound*) apagarse

**fag** [fæg] (*BRIT: inf*) n (*cigarette*) pitillo (*SP*), cigarro

**Fahrenheit** ['fɑːrənhaɪt] n Fahrenheit m

**fail** [feɪl] vt (*candidate, test*) suspender (*SP*), reprobar (*LAM*); (*memory etc*) fallar a ▷ vi suspender (*SP*), reprobar (*LAM*); (*be unsuccessful*) fracasar; (*strength, brakes*) fallar; (*light*) acabarse; **to ~ to do sth** (*neglect*) dejar de hacer algo; (*be unable*) no poder hacer algo; **without ~** sin falta; **failing** n falta, defecto ▷ prep a falta de; **failure** ['feɪljə*] n fracaso; (*person*) fracasado/a; (*mechanical etc*) fallo

**faint** [feɪnt] adj débil; (*recollection*) vago; (*mark*) apenas visible ▷ n desmayo ▷ vi desmayarse; **to feel ~** estar mareado, marearse; **faintest** adj: **I haven't the faintest idea** no tengo la más remota idea; **faintly** adv débilmente; (*vaguely*) vagamente

**fair** [fɛə*] adj justo; (*hair, person*) rubio; (*weather*) bueno; (*good enough*) regular; (*considerable*) considerable ▷ adv (*play*) limpio ▷ n feria; (*BRIT: funfair*) parque m de atracciones; **fairground** n recinto ferial; **fair-haired** adj (*person*) rubio; **fairly** adv (*justly*) con justicia; (*quite*) bastante; **fair trade** n comercio justo; **fairway** n (*Golf*) calle f

**fairy** ['fɛərɪ] n hada; **fairy tale** n cuento de hadas

**faith** [feɪθ] n fe f; (*trust*) confianza; (*sect*) religión f; **faithful** adj (*loyal: troops etc*) leal; (*spouse*) fiel; (*account*) exacto; **faithfully** adv fielmente; **yours faithfully** (*BRIT: in letters*) le saluda atentamente

**fake** [feɪk] n (*painting etc*) falsificación f; (*person*) impostor(a) m/f ▷ adj falso ▷ vt fingir; (*painting etc*) falsificar

**falcon** ['fɔːlkən] n halcón m

**fall** [fɔːl] (*pt* fell, *pp* fallen) n caída; (*in price etc*) descenso; (*US*) otoño ▷ vi caer(se); (*price*) bajar, descender; **falls** npl (*waterfall*) cascada, salto de agua; **to ~ flat** (*on one's face*) caerse (boca abajo); (*plan*) fracasar; (*joke, story*) no hacer gracia; **fall apart** vi deshacerse; **fall down** vi (*person*) caerse; (*building, hopes*) derrumbarse; **fall for** vt fus (*trick*) dejarse engañar por; (*person*) enamorarse de; **fall off** vi caerse; (*diminish*) disminuir; **fall out** vi (*friends etc*) reñir; (*hair, teeth*) caerse; **fall over** vi caer(se); **fall through** vi (*plan, project*) fracasar

**fallen** ['fɔːlən] *pp of* **fall**

**fallout** ['fɔːlaut] n lluvia radioactiva

**false** [fɔːls] adj falso; **under ~ pretences** con engaños; **false alarm** n falsa alarma; **false teeth** (*BRIT*) npl dentadura postiza

**fame** [feɪm] n fama

**familiar** [fə'mɪlɪə*] adj conocido, familiar; (*tone*) de confianza; **to be ~ with** (*subject*) conocer (bien); **familiarize** [fə'mɪlɪəraɪz] vt: **to familiarize o.s. with** familiarizarse con

**family** ['fæmɪlɪ] n familia; **family doctor** n médico/a de cabecera; **family planning** n planificación f familiar

**famine** ['fæmɪn] n hambre f, hambruna

**famous** ['feɪməs] adj famoso, célebre

**fan** [fæn] n abanico; (Elec) ventilador m; (of pop star) fan mf; (Sport) hincha mf ▷ vt abanicar; (fire, quarrel) atizar

**fanatic** [fə'nætɪk] n fanático/a

**fan belt** n correa del ventilador

**fan club** n club m de fans

**fancy** ['fænsɪ] n (whim) capricho, antojo; (imagination) imaginación f ▷ adj (luxury) lujoso, de lujo ▷ vt (feel like, want) tener ganas de; (imagine) imaginarse; (think) creer; **to take a ~ to sb** tomar cariño a algn; **he fancies her** (inf) le gusta (ella) mucho; **fancy dress** n disfraz m

**fan heater** n calefactor m de aire

**fantasize** ['fæntəsaɪz] vi fantasear, hacerse ilusiones

**fantastic** [fæn'tæstɪk] adj (enormous) enorme; (strange, wonderful) fantástico

**fantasy** ['fæntəzɪ] n (dream) sueño; (unreality) fantasía

**fanzine** ['fænziːn] n fanzine m

**FAQs** abbr (= frequently asked questions) preguntas frecuentes

**far** [fɑː*] adj (distant) lejano ▷ adv lejos; (much, greatly) mucho; **~ away, ~ off** (a lo) lejos; **~ better** mucho mejor; **~ from** lejos de; **by ~** con mucho; **go as ~ as the farm** vaya hasta la granja; **as ~ as I know** que yo sepa; **how ~?** ¿hasta dónde?; (fig) ¿hasta qué punto?

**farce** [fɑːs] n farsa

**fare** [fɛə*] n (on trains, buses) precio (del billete); (in taxi: cost) tarifa; (food) comida; **half ~** medio pasaje m; **full ~** pasaje completo

**Far East** n: **the ~** el Extremo Oriente

**farewell** [fɛə'wɛl] excl, n adiós m

**farm** [fɑːm] n cortijo (SP), hacienda (LAM), rancho (MEX), estancia (RPL) ▷ vt cultivar; **farmer** n granjero, hacendado (LAM), ranchero (MEX), estanciero (RPL); **farmhouse** n granja, casa del hacendado (LAM), rancho (MEX), casco de la estancia (RPL); **farming** n agricultura; (of crops) cultivo; (of animals) cría; **farmyard** n corral m

**far-reaching** [fɑː'riːtʃɪŋ] adj (reform, effect) de gran alcance

**fart** [fɑːt] (inf!) vi tirarse un pedo (!)

**farther** ['fɑːðə*] adv más lejos, más allá ▷ adj más lejano

**farthest** ['fɑːðɪst] superlative of **far**

**fascinate** ['fæsɪneɪt] vt fascinar; **fascinated** adj fascinado

**fascinating** ['fæsɪneɪtɪŋ] adj fascinante

**fascination** [-'neɪʃən] n fascinación f

**fascist** ['fæʃɪst] adj, n fascista m/f

**fashion** ['fæʃən] n moda; (fashion industry) industria de la moda; (manner) manera ▷ vt formar; **in ~** a la moda; **out of ~** pasado de moda; **fashionable** adj de moda; **fashion show** n desfile m de modelos

**fast** [fɑːst] adj rápido; (dye, colour) resistente; (clock): **to be ~** estar adelantado ▷ adv rápidamente, de prisa; (stuck, held) firmemente ▷ n ayuno ▷ vi ayunar; **~ asleep** profundamente dormido

**fasten** ['fɑːsn] vt atar, sujetar; (coat, belt) abrochar ▷ vi atarse; abrocharse

**fast food** n comida rápida, platos mpl preparados

**fat** [fæt] adj gordo; (book) grueso; (profit) grande, pingüe ▷ n grasa; (on person) carnes fpl; (lard) manteca

**fatal** ['feɪtl] adj (mistake) fatal; (injury) mortal; **fatality** [fə'tælɪtɪ] n (road death etc) víctima; **fatally** adv fatalmente; mortalmente

**fate** [feɪt] n destino; (of person) suerte f

**father** ['fɑːðə*] n padre m; **Father Christmas** n Papá m Noel; **father-in-law** n suegro

**fatigue** [fə'tiːg] n fatiga, cansancio

**fattening** ['fætnɪŋ] adj (food) que hace engordar

**fatty** ['fætɪ] adj (food) graso ▷ n (inf) gordito/a, gordinflón/ona m/f

**faucet** ['fɔːsɪt] (US) n grifo (SP), llave f, canilla (RPL)

**fault** [fɔːlt] n (blame) culpa; (defect: in person, machine) defecto; (Geo) falla ▷ vt criticar; **it's my ~** es culpa mía; **to find ~ with** criticar, poner peros a; **at ~** culpable; **faulty** adj defectuoso

**fauna** ['fɔːnə] n fauna

**favour etc** ['feɪvə*] (US **favor** etc) n favor m; (approval) aprobación f ▷ vt (proposition) estar a favor de, aprobar; (assist) ser propicio a; **to do sb a ~** hacer un favor a algn; **to find ~ with sb** caer en gracia a algn; **in ~ of** a favor de; **favourable** adj favorable; **favourite** ['feɪvrɪt] adj, n favorito, preferido

**fawn** [fɔːn] n cervato ▷ adj (also: **~-coloured**) color de cervato, leonado ▷ vi: **to ~ (up)on** adular

**fax** [fæks] n (document) fax m; (machine) telefax m ▷ vt mandar por telefax

**FBI** (US) n abbr (= Federal Bureau of Investigation) ≈ BIC f (SP)

**fear** [fɪə*] n miedo, temor m ▷ vt tener

miedo de, temer; **for ~ of** por si; **fearful**
*adj* temeroso, miedoso; (*awful*) terrible;
**fearless** *adj* audaz

**feasible** ['fiːzəbl] *adj* factible

**feast** [fiːst] *n* banquete *m*; (*Rel: also:* **~ day**)
fiesta ▷ *vi* festejar

**feat** [fiːt] *n* hazaña

**feather** ['fɛðə*] *n* pluma

**feature** ['fiːtʃə*] *n* característica; (*article*)
artículo de fondo ▷ *vt* (*film*) presentar
▷ *vi*: **to ~ in** tener un papel destacado en;
**features** *npl* (*of face*) facciones *fpl*; **feature
film** *n* largometraje *m*

**Feb.** *abbr* (= *February*) feb

**February** ['fɛbruərɪ] *n* febrero

**fed** [fɛd] *pt, pp of* **feed**

**federal** ['fɛdərəl] *adj* federal

**federation** [fɛdə'reɪʃən] *n* federación *f*

**fed up** [fɛd'ʌp] *adj*: **to be ~ (with)** estar
harto de

**fee** [fiː] *n* pago; (*professional*) derechos *mpl*,
honorarios *mpl*; (*of club*) cuota; **school ~s**
matrícula

**feeble** ['fiːbl] *adj* débil; (*joke*) flojo

**feed** [fiːd] (*pt, pp* **fed**) *n* comida; (*of
animal*) pienso; (*on printer*) dispositivo
de alimentación ▷ *vt* alimentar;
(*BRIT: baby: breastfeed*) dar el pecho a; (*animal*)
dar de comer a; (*data, information*): **to ~
into** meter en; **feedback** *n* reacción *f*,
feedback *m*

**feel** [fiːl] (*pt, pp* **felt**) *n* (*sensation*) sensación
*f*; (*sense of touch*) tacto; (*impression*): **to
have the ~ of** parecerse a ▷ *vt* tocar;
(*pain etc*) sentir; (*think, believe*) creer; **to
~ hungry/cold** tener hambre/frío; **to ~
lonely/better** sentirse solo/mejor; **I don't
~ well** no me siento bien; **it ~s soft** es suave
al tacto; **to ~ like** (*want*) tener ganas de;
**feeling** *n* (*physical*) sensación *f*; (*foreboding*)
presentimiento; (*emotion*) sentimiento

**feet** [fiːt] *npl of* **foot**

**fell** [fɛl] *pt of* **fall** ▷ *vt* (*tree*) talar

**fellow** ['fɛləu] *n* tipo, tío (*sp*); (*comrade*)
compañero; (*of learned society*) socio/a;
**fellow citizen** *n* conciudadano/a; **fellow
countryman** (*irreg*) *n* compatriota
*m*; **fellow men** *npl* semejantes *mpl*;
**fellowship** *n* compañerismo; (*grant*) beca

**felony** ['fɛlənɪ] *n* crimen *m*

**felt** [fɛlt] *pt, pp of* **feel** ▷ *n* fieltro; **felt-tip**
*n* (*also:* **felt-tip pen**) rotulador *m*

**female** ['fiːmeɪl] *n* (*pej: woman*) mujer *f*,
tía; (*Zool*) hembra ▷ *adj* femenino; hembra

**feminine** ['fɛmɪnɪn] *adj* femenino

**feminist** ['fɛmɪnɪst] *n* feminista

**fence** [fɛns] *n* valla, cerca ▷ *vt* (*also:* **~ in**)
cercar ▷ *vi* (*Sport*) hacer esgrima; **fencing**

*n* esgrima

**fend** [fɛnd] *vi*: **to ~ for o.s.** valerse por
sí mismo; **fend off** *vt* (*attack*) rechazar;
(*questions*) evadir

**fender** ['fɛndə*] (*US*) *n* guardafuego; (*Aut*)
parachoques *m inv*

**fennel** ['fɛnl] *n* hinojo

**ferment** [*vb* fə'mɛnt, *n* 'fəːmɛnt] *vi*
fermentar ▷ *n* (*fig*) agitación *f*

**fern** [fəːn] *n* helecho

**ferocious** [fə'rəuʃəs] *adj* feroz

**ferret** ['fɛrɪt] *n* hurón *m*

**ferry** ['fɛrɪ] *n* (*small*) barca (de pasaje),
balsa; (*large: also:* **~ boat**) transbordador *m*,
ferry *m* ▷ *vt* transportar

**fertile** ['fəːtaɪl] *adj* fértil; (*Biol*) fecundo;
**fertilize** ['fəːtɪlaɪz] *vt* (*Biol*) fecundar; (*Agr*)
abonar; **fertilizer** *n* abono

**festival** ['fɛstɪvəl] *n* (*Rel*) fiesta; (*Art, Mus*)
festival *m*

**festive** ['fɛstɪv] *adj* festivo; **the ~ season**
(*BRIT: Christmas*) las Navidades

**fetch** [fɛtʃ] *vt* ir a buscar; (*sell for*) venderse
por

**fête** [feɪt] *n* fiesta

**fetus** ['fiːtəs] (*US*) *n* = **foetus**

**feud** [fjuːd] *n* (*hostility*) enemistad *f*;
(*quarrel*) disputa

**fever** ['fiːvə*] *n* fiebre *f*; **feverish** *adj* febril

**few** [fjuː] *adj* (*not many*) pocos ▷ *pron*
pocos; algunos; **a ~** *adj* unos pocos,
algunos; **fewer** *adj* menos; **fewest** *adj*
los(las) menos

**fiancé** [fɪ'ãːŋseɪ] *n* novio, prometido;
**fiancée** *n* novia, prometida

**fiasco** [fɪ'æskəu] *n* fiasco

**fib** [fɪb] *n* mentirilla

**fibre** ['faɪbə*] (*US* **fiber**) *n* fibra; **fibreglass**
(*US* **Fiberglass**®) *n* fibra de vidrio

**fickle** ['fɪkl] *adj* inconstante

**fiction** ['fɪkʃən] *n* ficción *f*; **fictional** *adj*
novelesco

**fiddle** ['fɪdl] *n* (*Mus*) violín *m*; (*cheating*)
trampa ▷ *vt* (*BRIT: accounts*) falsificar; **fiddle
with** *vt fus* juguetear con

**fidelity** [fɪ'dɛlɪtɪ] *n* fidelidad *f*

**field** [fiːld] *n* campo; (*fig*) campo, esfera;
(*Sport*) campo (*sp*), cancha (*LAM*); **field
marshal** *n* mariscal *m*

**fierce** [fɪəs] *adj* feroz; (*wind, heat*) fuerte;
(*fighting, enemy*) encarnizado

**fifteen** [fɪf'tiːn] *num* quince; **fifteenth** *adj*
decimoquinto; **the fifteenth floor** la planta
quince; **the fifteenth of August** el quince
de agosto

**fifth** [fɪfθ] *num* quinto

**fiftieth** ['fɪftɪɪθ] *adj* quincuagésimo

**fifty** ['fɪftɪ] *num* cincuenta; **fifty-fifty** *adj*

**fig** | 288

(*deal*, *split*) a medias ▷ *adv* a medias, mitad por mitad

**fig** [fɪg] *n* higo

**fight** [faɪt] (*pt*, *pp* **fought**) *n* (*gen*) pelea; (*Mil*) combate *m*; (*struggle*) lucha ▷ *vt* luchar contra; (*cancer*, *alcoholism*) combatir; (*election*) intentar ganar; (*emotion*) resistir ▷ *vi* pelear, luchar; **fight back** *vi* defenderse; (*after illness*) recuperarse ▷ *vt* (*tears*) contener; **fight off** *vt* (*attack*, *attacker*) rechazar; (*disease*, *sleep*, *urge*) luchar contra; **fighting** *n* combate *m*, pelea

**figure** ['fɪgə*] *n* (*Drawing*, *Geom*) figura, dibujo; (*number*, *cipher*) cifra; (*body*, *outline*) tipo; (*personality*) figura ▷ *vt* (*esp US*) imaginar ▷ *vi* (*appear*) figurar; **figure out** *vt* (*work out*) resolver

**file** [faɪl] *n* (*tool*) lima; (*dossier*) expediente *m*; (*folder*) carpeta; (*Comput*) fichero; (*row*) fila ▷ *vt* limar; (*Law: claim*) presentar; (*store*) archivar; **filing cabinet** *n* fichero, archivador *m*

**Filipino** [fɪlɪ'piːnəʊ] *adj* filipino ▷ *n* (*person*) filipino/a *m/f*; (*Ling*) tagalo

**fill** [fɪl] *vt* (*space*): **to ~ (with)** llenar (de); (*vacancy*, *need*) cubrir ▷ *n*: **to eat one's ~** llenarse; **fill in** *vt* rellenar; **fill out** *vt* (*form*, *receipt*) rellenar; **fill up** *vt* llenar (hasta el borde) ▷ *vi* (*Aut*) poner gasolina

**fillet** ['fɪlɪt] *n* filete *m*; **fillet steak** *n* filete *m* de ternera

**filling** ['fɪlɪŋ] *n* (*Culin*) relleno; (*for tooth*) empaste *m*; **filling station** *n* estación *f* de servicio

**film** [fɪlm] *n* película ▷ *vt* (*scene*) filmar ▷ *vi* rodar (una película); **film star** *n* astro, estrella de cine

**filter** ['fɪltə*] *n* filtro ▷ *vt* filtrar; **filter lane** (*BRIT*) *n* carril *m* de selección

**filth** [fɪlθ] *n* suciedad *f*; **filthy** *adj* sucio; (*language*) obsceno

**fin** [fɪn] *n* (*gen*) aleta

**final** ['faɪnl] *adj* (*last*) final, último; (*definitive*) definitivo, terminante ▷ *n* (*BRIT Sport*) final *f*; **finals** *npl* (*Scol*) examen *m* final; (*US Sport*) final *f*

**finale** [fɪ'nɑːlɪ] *n* final *m*

**final: finalist** *n* (*Sport*) finalista *mf*; **finalize** *vt* concluir, completar; **finally** *adv* (*lastly*) por último, finalmente; (*eventually*) por fin

**finance** [faɪ'næns] *n* (*money*) fondos *mpl* ▷ *vt* financiar; **finances** *npl* finanzas *fpl*; (*personal finances*) situación *f* económica; **financial** [-'nænʃəl] *adj* financiero; **financial year** *n* ejercicio (financiero)

**find** [faɪnd] (*pt*, *pp* **found**) *vt* encontrar, hallar; (*come upon*) descubrir ▷ *n* hallazgo; descubrimiento; **to ~ sb guilty** (*Law*)

declarar culpable a algn; **find out** *vt* averiguar; (*truth*, *secret*) descubrir; **to find out about** (*subject*) informarse sobre; (*by chance*) enterarse de; **findings** *npl* (*Law*) veredicto, fallo; (*of report*) recomendaciones *fpl*

**fine** [faɪn] *adj* excelente; (*thin*) fino ▷ *adv* (*well*) bien ▷ *n* (*Law*) multa ▷ *vt* (*Law*) multar; **to be ~** (*person*) estar bien; (*weather*) hacer buen tiempo; **fine arts** *npl* bellas artes *fpl*

**finger** ['fɪŋgə*] *n* dedo ▷ *vt* (*touch*) manosear; **little/index ~** (*dedo*) meñique *m*/índice *m*; **fingernail** *n* uña; **fingerprint** *n* huella dactilar; **fingertip** *n* yema del dedo

**finish** ['fɪnɪʃ] *n* (*end*) fin *m*; (*Sport*) meta; (*polish etc*) acabado ▷ *vt*, *vi* terminar; **to ~ doing sth** acabar de hacer algo; **to ~ third** llegar el tercero; **finish off** *vt* acabar, terminar; (*kill*) acabar con; **finish up** *vt* acabar, terminar ▷ *vi* ir a parar, terminar

**Finland** ['fɪnlənd] *n* Finlandia

**Finn** [fɪn] *n* finlandés/esa *m/f*; **Finnish** *adj* finlandés/esa ▷ *n* (*Ling*) finlandés *m*

**fir** [fə:*] *n* abeto

**fire** ['faɪə*] *n* fuego; (*in hearth*) lumbre *f*; (*accidental*) incendio; (*heater*) estufa ▷ *vt* (*gun*) disparar; (*interest*) despertar; (*inf: dismiss*) despedir ▷ *vi* (*shoot*) disparar; **on ~** ardiendo, en llamas; **fire alarm** *n* alarma de incendios; **firearm** *n* arma de fuego; **fire brigade** (*US* **fire department**) *n* (cuerpo de) bomberos *mpl*; **fire engine** (*BRIT*) *n* coche *m* de bomberos; **fire escape** *n* escalera de incendios; **fire exit** *n* salida de incendios; **fire extinguisher** *n* extintor *m* (de incendios); **fireman** (*irreg*) *n* bombero; **fireplace** *n* chimenea; **fire station** *n* parque *m* de bomberos; **firetruck** (*US*) *n* = **fire engine**; **firewall** *n* (*Internet*) firewall *m*; **firewood** *n* leña; **fireworks** *npl* fuegos *mpl* artificiales

**firm** [fə:m] *adj* firme; (*look*, *voice*) resuelto ▷ *n* firma, empresa; **firmly** *adv* firmemente; resueltamente

**first** [fə:st] *adj* primero ▷ *adv* (*before others*) primero; (*when listing reasons etc*) en primer lugar, primeramente ▷ *n* (*person: in race*) primero/a; (*Aut*) primera; (*BRIT Scol*) título de licenciado con calificación de sobresaliente; **at ~** al principio; **~ of all** ante todo; **first aid** *n* primera ayuda, primeros auxilios *mpl*; **first-aid kit** *n* botiquín *m*; **first-class** *adj* (*excellent*) de primera (categoría); (*ticket etc*) de primera clase; **first-hand** *adj* de primera mano; **first lady** *n* (*esp US*) primera dama; **firstly** *adv* en primer lugar; **first**

**name** n nombre m (de pila); **first-rate** adj estupendo

**fiscal** ['fɪskəl] adj fiscal; **fiscal year** n año fiscal, ejercicio

**fish** [fɪʃ] n inv pez m; (food) pescado ▷ vt, vi pescar; **to go ~ing** ir de pesca; **~ and chips** pescado frito con patatas fritas; **fisherman** (irreg) n pescador m; **fish fingers** (BRIT) npl croquetas fpl de pescado; **fishing** n pesca; **fishing boat** n barca de pesca; **fishing line** n sedal m; **fishmonger** n (BRIT) pescadero/a; **fishmonger's (shop)** (BRIT) n pescadería; **fish sticks** (US) npl = **fish fingers**; **fishy** (inf) adj sospechoso

**fist** [fɪst] n puño

**fit** [fɪt] adj (healthy) en (buena) forma; (proper) adecuado, apropiado ▷ vt (clothes) estar or sentar bien a; (instal) poner; (equip) proveer, dotar; (facts) cuadrar or corresponder con ▷ vi (clothes) sentar bien; (in space, gap) caber; (facts) coincidir ▷ n (Med) ataque m; **~ to** (ready) a punto de; **~ for** apropiado para; **a ~ of anger/pride** un arranque de cólera/orgullo; **this dress is a good ~** este vestido me sienta bien; **by ~s and starts** a rachas; **fit in** vi (fig: person) llevarse bien (con todos); **fitness** n (Med) salud f; **fitted** adj (jacket, shirt) entallado; (sheet) de cuatro picos; **fitted carpet** n moqueta; **fitted kitchen** n cocina amueblada; **fitting** adj apropiado ▷ n (of dress) prueba; (of piece of equipment) instalación f; **fitting room** n probador m; **fittings** npl instalaciones fpl

**five** [faɪv] num cinco; **fiver** (inf) n (BRIT) billete m de cinco libras; (US) billete m de cinco dólares

**fix** [fɪks] vt (secure) fijar, asegurar; (mend) arreglar; (prepare) preparar ▷ n: **to be in a ~** estar en un aprieto; **fix up** vt (meeting) arreglar; **to fix sb up with sth** proveer a algn de algo; **fixed** adj (prices etc) fijo; **fixture** n (Sport) encuentro

**fizzy** ['fɪzɪ] adj (drink) gaseoso

**flag** [flæg] n bandera; (stone) losa ▷ vi decaer ▷ vt: **to ~ sb down** hacer señas a algn para que se pare; **flagpole** n asta de bandera

**flair** [fleə*] n aptitud f especial

**flak** [flæk] n (Mil) fuego antiaéreo; (inf: criticism) lluvia de críticas

**flake** [fleɪk] n (of rust, paint) escama; (of snow, soap powder) copo ▷ vi (also: **~ off**) desconcharse

**flamboyant** [flæm'bɔɪənt] adj (dress) vistoso; (person) extravagante

**flame** [fleɪm] n llama

**flamingo** [flə'mɪŋgəʊ] n flamenco

**flammable** ['flæməbl] adj inflamable

**flan** [flæn] (BRIT) n tarta

❚ Be careful not to translate **flan** by the Spanish word flan.

**flank** [flæŋk] n (of animal) ijar m; (of army) flanco ▷ vt flanquear

**flannel** ['flænl] n (BRIT: also: **face ~**) manopla; (fabric) franela

**flap** [flæp] n (of pocket, envelope) solapa ▷ vt (wings, arms) agitar ▷ vi (sail, flag) ondear

**flare** [fleə*] n llamarada; (Mil) bengala; (in skirt etc) vuelo; **flares** npl (trousers) pantalones mpl de campana; **flare up** vi encenderse; (fig: person) encolerizarse; (: revolt) estallar

**flash** [flæʃ] n relámpago; (also: **news ~**) noticias fpl de última hora; (Phot) flash m ▷ vt (light, headlights) lanzar un destello; (news, message) transmitir; (smile) lanzar ▷ vi brillar; (hazard light etc) lanzar destellos; **in a ~** en un instante; **he ~ed by or past** pasó como un rayo; **flashback** n (Cinema) flashback m; **flashbulb** n bombilla fusible; **flashlight** n linterna

**flask** [flɑːsk] n frasco; (also: **vacuum ~**) termo

**flat** [flæt] adj llano; (smooth) liso; (tyre) desinflado; (battery) descargado; (beer) muerto; (refusal etc) rotundo; (Mus) desafinado; (rate) fijo ▷ n (BRIT: apartment) piso (SP), departamento (LAM), apartamento; (Aut) pinchazo; (Mus) bemol m; **to work ~ out** trabajar a toda mecha; **flatten** vt (also: **flatten out**) allanar; (smooth out) alisar; (building, plants) arrasar

**flatter** ['flætə*] vt adular, halagar; **flattering** adj halagüeño; (dress) que favorece

**flaunt** [flɔːnt] vt ostentar, lucir

**flavour** etc ['fleɪvə*] (US **flavor** etc) n sabor m, gusto ▷ vt sazonar, condimentar; **strawberry-flavoured** con sabor a fresa; **flavouring** n (in product) aromatizante m

**flaw** [flɔː] n defecto; **flawless** adj impecable

**flea** [fliː] n pulga; **flea market** n rastro, mercadillo

**flee** [fliː] (pt, pp **fled**) vt huir de ▷ vi huir, fugarse

**fleece** [fliːs] n vellón m; (wool) lana; (top) forro polar ▷ vt (inf) desplumar

**fleet** [fliːt] n flota; (of lorries etc) escuadra

**fleeting** ['fliːtɪŋ] adj fugaz

**Flemish** ['flemɪʃ] adj flamenco

**flesh** [fleʃ] n carne f; (skin) piel f; (of fruit) pulpa

**flew** [fluː] pt of **fly**

**flex** [fleks] n cordón m ▷ vt (muscles)

tensar; **flexibility** n flexibilidad f; **flexible**
adj flexible; **flexitime** (us **flextime**) n
horario flexible

**flick** [flɪk] n capirotazo; chasquido ▷vt
(with hand) dar un capirotazo a; (whip etc)
chasquear; (switch) accionar; **flick through**
vt fus hojear

**flicker** ['flɪkə*] vi (light) parpadear; (flame)
vacilar

**flies** [flaɪz] npl of **fly**

**flight** [flaɪt] n vuelo; (escape) huida, fuga;
(also: ~ **of steps**) tramo (de escaleras); **flight
attendant** n auxiliar mf de vuelo

**flimsy** ['flɪmzɪ] adj (thin) muy ligero;
(building) endeble; (excuse) flojo

**flinch** [flɪntʃ] vi encogerse; **to ~ from**
retroceder ante

**fling** [flɪŋ] (pt, pp **flung**) vt arrojar

**flint** [flɪnt] n pedernal m; (in lighter) piedra

**flip** [flɪp] vt dar la vuelta a; (switch: turn
on) encender; (turn) apagar; (coin) echar a
cara o cruz

**flip-flops** ['flɪpflɒps] npl (esp BRIT)
chancletas fpl

**flipper** ['flɪpə*] n aleta

**flirt** [flə:t] vi coquetear, flirtear ▷n
coqueta

**float** [fləut] n flotador m; (in procession)
carroza; (money) reserva ▷vi flotar;
(swimmer) hacer la plancha

**flock** [flɒk] n (of sheep) rebaño; (of birds)
bandada ▷vi: **to ~ to** acudir en tropel a

**flood** [flʌd] n inundación f; (of letters,
imports etc) avalancha ▷vt inundar ▷vi
(place) inundarse; (people): **to ~ into** inundar;
**flooding** n inundaciones fpl; **floodlight**
n foco

**floor** [flɔ:*] n suelo; (storey) piso; (of sea)
fondo ▷vt (question) dejar sin respuesta;
(: blow) derribar; **ground ~, first ~** (us)
planta baja; **first ~, second ~** (us) primer
piso; **floorboard** n tabla; **flooring** n suelo;
(material) solería; **floor show** n cabaret m

**flop** [flɒp] n fracaso ▷vi (fail) fracasar;
(fall) derrumbarse; **floppy** adj flojo ▷n
(Comput: also: **floppy disk**) floppy m

**flora** ['flɔ:rə] n flora

**floral** ['flɔ:rl] adj (pattern) floreado

**florist** ['flɒrɪst] n florista mf; **florist's
(shop)** n floristería

**flotation** [fləu'teɪʃən] n (of shares)
emisión f; (of company) lanzamiento

**flour** ['flauə*] n harina

**flourish** ['flʌrɪʃ] vi florecer ▷n ademán m,
movimiento (ostentoso)

**flow** [fləu] n (movement) flujo; (of traffic)
circulación f; (tide) corriente f ▷vi (river,
blood) fluir; (traffic) circular

**flower** ['flauə*] n flor f ▷vi florecer;
**flower bed** n macizo; **flowerpot** n tiesto

**flown** [fləun] pp of **fly**

**fl. oz.** abbr (= fluid ounce)

**flu** [flu:] n: **to have ~** tener la gripe

**fluctuate** ['flʌktjueɪt] vi fluctuar

**fluent** ['flu:ənt] adj (linguist) que habla
perfectamente; (speech) elocuente; **he
speaks ~ French, he's ~ in French** domina
el francés

**fluff** [flʌf] n pelusa; **fluffy** adj de pelo
suave

**fluid** ['flu:ɪd] adj (movement) fluido, líquido;
(situation) inestable ▷n fluido, líquido;
**fluid ounce** n onza f líquida

**fluke** [flu:k] (inf) n chiripa

**flung** [flʌŋ] pt, pp of **fling**

**fluorescent** [fluə'rɛsnt] adj fluorescente

**fluoride** ['fluəraɪd] n fluoruro

**flurry** ['flʌrɪ] n (of snow) temporal m; **~ of
activity** frenesí m de actividad

**flush** [flʌʃ] n rubor m; (fig: of youth etc)
resplandor m ▷vt limpiar con agua ▷vi
ruborizarse ▷adj: **~ with** a ras de; **to ~ the
toilet** hacer funcionar la cisterna

**flute** [flu:t] n flauta

**flutter** ['flʌtə*] n (of wings) revoloteo,
aleteo; (fig): **a ~ of panic/excitement**
una oleada de pánico/excitación ▷vi
revolotear

**fly** [flaɪ] (pt **flew**, pp **flown**) n mosca;
(on trousers: also: **flies**) bragueta ▷vt
(plane) pilot(e)ar; (cargo) transportar (en
avión); (distances) recorrer (en avión) ▷vi
volar; (passengers) ir en avión; (escape)
evadirse; (flag) ondear; **fly away, fly off** vi
emprender el vuelo; **fly-drive** n: **fly-drive
holiday** vacaciones que incluyen vuelo y alquiler
de coche; **flying** n (activity) (el) volar; (action)
vuelo ▷adj: **flying visit** visita relámpago;
**with flying colours** con lucimiento; **flying
saucer** n platillo volante; **flyover** (BRIT) n
paso a desnivel or superior

**FM** abbr (Radio) (= frequency modulation) FM

**foal** [fəul] n potro

**foam** [fəum] n espuma ▷vi hacer espuma

**focus** ['fəukəs] (pl **~es**) n foco; (centre)
centro ▷vt (field glasses etc) enfocar ▷vi: **to
~ (on)** enfocar (a); (issue etc) centrarse en;
**in/out of ~** enfocado/desenfocado

**foetus** ['fi:təs] (us **fetus**) n feto

**fog** [fɒg] n niebla; **foggy** adj: **it's foggy**
hay niebla, está brumoso; **fog lamp** (us **fog
light**) n (Aut) faro de niebla

**foil** [fɔɪl] vt frustrar ▷n hoja; (kitchen
foil) papel m (de) aluminio; (complement)
complemento; (Fencing) florete m

**fold** [fəuld] n (bend, crease) pliegue m; (Agr)

redil m ▷ vt doblar; (arms) cruzar; **fold up**
vi plegarse, doblarse; (business) quebrar
▷ vt (map etc) plegar; **folder** n (for papers)
carpeta; (Comput) directorio; **folding** adj
(chair, bed) plegable
**foliage** ['fəulɪɪdʒ] n follaje m
**folk** [fəuk] npl gente f ▷ adj popular,
folklórico; **folks** npl (family) familia sg,
parientes mpl; **folklore** ['fəuklɔ:*] n
folklore m; **folk music** n música folk; **folk
song** n canción f popular
**follow** ['fɒləu] vt seguir ▷ vi seguir;
(result) resultar; **to ~ suit** hacer lo mismo;
**follow up** vt (letter, offer) responder a; (case)
investigar; **follower** n (of person, belief)
partidario/a; **following** adj siguiente
▷ n afición f, partidarios mpl; **follow-up** n
continuación f
**fond** [fɒnd] adj (memory, smile etc) cariñoso;
(hopes) ilusorio; **to be ~ of** tener cariño a;
(pastime, food) ser aficionado a
**food** [fu:d] n comida; **food mixer** n
batidora; **food poisoning** n intoxicación
f alimenticia; **food processor** n robot m
de cocina; **food stamp** (us) n vale m para
comida
**fool** [fu:l] n tonto/a; (Culin) puré m de
frutas con nata ▷ vt engañar ▷ vi (gen)
bromear; **fool about, fool around** vi
hacer el tonto; **foolish** adj tonto; (careless)
imprudente; **foolproof** adj (plan etc)
infalible
**foot** [fut] (pl feet) n pie m; (measure) pie m
(=304 mm); (of animal) pata ▷ vt (bill) pagar;
**on ~ a** pie; **footage** n (Cinema) imágenes
fpl; **foot-and-mouth (disease)**
[futənd'mauθ-] n fiebre f aftosa; **football**
n balón m; (game: BRIT) fútbol m; (: US) fútbol
m americano; **footballer** n (BRIT) = **football
player**; **football match** n partido de
fútbol; **football player** n (BRIT) futbolista
mf; (us) jugador m de fútbol americano;
**footbridge** n puente m para peatones;
**foothills** npl estribaciones fpl; **foothold**
n pie m firme; **footing** n (fig) posición f; **to
lose one's footing** perder el pie; **footnote**
n nota (al pie de la página); **footpath**
n sendero; **footprint** n huella, pisada;
**footstep** n paso; **footwear** n calzado

**for** [fɔ:*] prep 1(indicating destination,
intention) para; **the train for London** el
tren con destino a or de Londres; **he left for
Rome** marchó para Roma; **he went for the
paper** fue por el periódico; **is this for me?**
¿es esto para mí?; **it's time for lunch** es la

hora de comer
2 (indicating purpose) para; **what('s it) for?**
¿para qué (es)?; **to pray for peace** rezar
por la paz
3 (on behalf of, representing): **the MP for Hove**
el diputado por Hove; **he works for the
government/a local firm** trabaja para el
gobierno/en una empresa local; **I'll ask him
for you** se
lo pediré por ti; **G for George** G de Gerona
4 (because of) por esta razón; **for fear of
being criticized** por temor a ser criticado
5 (with regard to) para; **it's cold for July** hace
frío para julio; **he has a gift for languages**
tiene don de lenguas
6 (in exchange for) por; **I sold it for £5** lo vendí
por £5; **to pay 50 pence for a ticket** pagar
50 peniques por un billete
7 (in favour of): **are you for or against us?**
¿estás con nosotros o contra nosotros?; **I'm
all for it** estoy totalmente a favor; **vote for
X** vote (a) X
8 (referring to distance): **there are roadworks
for 5 km** hay obras en 5 km; **we walked for
miles** caminamos kilómetros y kilómetros
9 (referring to time): **he was away for two
years** estuvo fuera (durante) dos años; **it
hasn't rained for 3 weeks** no ha llovido
durante or en 3 semanas; **I have known her
for years** la conozco desde hace años; **can
you do it for tomorrow?** ¿lo podrás hacer
para mañana?
10 (with infinitive clauses): **it is not for me to
decide** la decisión no es cosa mía; **it would
be best for you to leave** sería mejor que
te fueras; **there is still time for you to do
it** todavía te queda tiempo para hacerlo;
**for this to be possible ...** para que esto sea
posible ...
11 (in spite of) a pesar de; **for all his
complaints** a pesar de sus quejas ▷ conj
(since, as: rather formal) puesto que

**forbid** [fə'bɪd] (pt **forbad(e)**, pp **forbidden**)
vt prohibir; **to ~ sb to do sth** prohibir a algn
hacer algo; **forbidden** pt of **forbid** ▷ adj
(food, area) prohibido; (word, subject) tabú
**force** [fɔ:s] n fuerza ▷ vt forzar; (push)
meter a la fuerza; **to ~ o.s. to do** hacer un
esfuerzo por hacer; **forced** adj forzado;
**forceful** adj enérgico
**ford** [fɔ:d] n vado
**fore** [fɔ:*] n: **to come to the ~** empezar
a destacar; **forearm** n antebrazo;
**forecast** (pt, pp **forecast**) n pronóstico
▷ vt pronosticar; **forecourt** n patio;
**forefinger** n (dedo) índice m; **forefront**
n: **in the forefront of** en la vanguardia de;

**foreground** n primer plano; **forehead** ['forɪd] n frente f
**foreign** ['forɪn] adj extranjero; (trade) exterior; (object) extraño; **foreign currency** n divisas fpl; **foreigner** n extranjero/a; **foreign exchange** n divisas fpl; **Foreign Office** (BRIT) n Ministerio de Asuntos Exteriores; **Foreign Secretary** (BRIT) n Ministro de Asuntos Exteriores
**fore: foreman** (irreg) n capataz m; (in construction) maestro de obras; **foremost** adj principal ▷ adv: **first and foremost** ante todo; **forename** n nombre m (de pila)
**forensic** [fə'rɛnsɪk] adj forense
**foresee** [fɔː'siː] (pt **foresaw**, pp **foreseen**) vt prever; **foreseeable** adj previsible
**forest** ['forɪst] n bosque m; **forestry** n silvicultura
**forever** [fə'rɛvə*] adv para siempre; (endlessly) constantemente
**foreword** ['fɔːwəːd] n prefacio
**forfeit** ['fɔːfɪt] vt perder
**forgave** [fə'geɪv] pt of **forgive**
**forge** [fɔːdʒ] n herrería ▷ vt (signature, money) falsificar; (metal) forjar; **forger** n falsificador(a) m/f; **forgery** n falsificación f
**forget** [fə'gɛt] (pt **forgot**, pp **forgotten**) vt olvidar ▷ vi olvidarse; **forgetful** adj despistado
**forgive** [fə'gɪv] (pt **forgave**, pp **forgiven**) vt perdonar; **to ~ sb for sth** perdonar algo a algn
**forgot** [fə'gɔt] pt of **forget**
**forgotten** [fə'gɔtn] pp of **forget**
**fork** [fɔːk] n (for eating) tenedor m; (for gardening) horca; (of roads) bifurcación f ▷ vi (road) bifurcarse
**forlorn** [fə'lɔːn] adj (person) triste, melancólico; (place) abandonado; (attempt, hope) desesperado
**form** [fɔːm] n forma; (BRIT Scol) clase f; (document) formulario ▷ vt formar; (idea) concebir; (habit) adquirir; **in top ~** en plena forma; **to ~ a queue** hacer cola
**formal** ['fɔːməl] adj (offer, receipt) por escrito; (person etc) correcto; (occasion, dinner) de etiqueta; (dress) correcto; (garden) (de estilo) clásico; **formality** [-'mælɪtɪ] n (procedure) trámite m; corrección f; etiqueta
**format** ['fɔːmæt] n formato ▷ vt (Comput) formatear
**formation** [fɔː'meɪʃən] n formación f
**former** ['fɔːmə*] adj anterior; (earlier) antiguo; (ex) ex; **the ~ ... the latter ...** aquél ... éste ...; **formerly** adv antes
**formidable** ['fɔːmɪdəbl] adj formidable
**formula** ['fɔːmjulə] n fórmula
**fort** [fɔːt] n fuerte m

**forthcoming** [fɔː'θkʌmɪŋ] adj próximo, venidero; (help, information) disponible; (character) comunicativo
**fortieth** ['fɔːtɪɪθ] adj cuadragésimo
**fortify** ['fɔːtɪfaɪ] vt (city) fortificar; (person) fortalecer
**fortnight** ['fɔːtnaɪt] (BRIT) n quince días mpl; quincena; **fortnightly** adj de cada quince días, quincenal ▷ adv cada quince días, quincenalmente
**fortress** ['fɔːtrɪs] n fortaleza
**fortunate** ['fɔːtʃənɪt] adj afortunado; **it is ~ that ...** (es una) suerte que ...; **fortunately** adv afortunadamente
**fortune** ['fɔːtʃən] n suerte f; (wealth) fortuna; **fortune-teller** n adivino/a
**forty** ['fɔːtɪ] num cuarenta
**forum** ['fɔːrəm] n foro
**forward** ['fɔːwəd] adj (movement, position) avanzado; (front) delantero; (in time) adelantado; (not shy) atrevido ▷ n (Sport) delantero ▷ vt (letter) remitir; (career) promocionar; **to move ~** avanzar; **forwarding address** n destinatario; **forward(s)** adv (hacia) adelante; **forward slash** n barra diagonal
**fossil** ['fɔsl] n fósil m
**foster** ['fɔstə*] vt (child) acoger en una familia; fomentar; **foster child** n hijo/a adoptivo/a; **foster mother** n madre f adoptiva
**fought** [fɔːt] pt, pp of **fight**
**foul** [faul] adj sucio, puerco; (weather, smell etc) asqueroso; (language) grosero; (temper) malísimo ▷ n (Sport) falta ▷ vt (dirty) ensuciar; **foul play** n (Law) muerte f violenta
**found** [faund] pt, pp of **find** ▷ vt fundar; **foundation** [-'deɪʃən] n (act) fundación f; (basis) base f; (also: **foundation cream**) crema base; **foundations** npl (of building) cimientos mpl
**founder** ['faundə*] n fundador(a) m/f ▷ vi hundirse
**fountain** ['fauntɪn] n fuente f; **fountain pen** n (pluma) estilográfica (SP), pluma-fuente f (LAM)
**four** [fɔː*] num cuatro; **on all ~s** a gatas; **four-letter word** n taco; **four-poster** n (also: **four-poster bed**) cama de columnas; **fourteen** num catorce; **fourteenth** adj decimocuarto; **fourth** num cuarto; **four-wheel drive** n tracción f a las cuatro ruedas
**fowl** [faul] n ave f (de corral)
**fox** [fɔks] n zorro ▷ vt confundir
**foyer** ['fɔɪeɪ] n vestíbulo
**fraction** ['frækʃən] n fracción f
**fracture** ['fræktʃə*] n fractura

**fragile** ['frædʒaɪl] adj frágil
**fragment** ['frægmənt] n fragmento
**fragrance** ['freɪgrəns] n fragancia
**frail** [freɪl] adj frágil; (person) débil
**frame** [freɪm] n (Tech) armazón m; (of person) cuerpo; (of picture, door etc) marco; (of spectacles: also: **~s**) montura ▷ vt enmarcar; **framework** n marco
**France** [frɑːns] n Francia
**franchise** ['fræntʃaɪz] n (Pol) derecho de votar, sufragio; (Comm) licencia, concesión f
**frank** [fræŋk] adj franco ▷ vt (letter) franquear; **frankly** adv francamente
**frantic** ['fræntɪk] adj (distraught) desesperado; (hectic) frenético
**fraud** [frɔːd] n fraude m; (person) impostor(a) m/f
**fraught** [frɔːt] adj: **~ with** lleno de
**fray** [freɪ] vi deshilacharse
**freak** [friːk] n (person) fenómeno; (event) suceso anormal
**freckle** ['frɛkl] n peca
**free** [friː] adj libre; (gratis) gratuito ▷ vt (prisoner etc) poner en libertad; (jammed object) soltar; **~ (of charge), for ~** gratis; **freedom** n libertad f; **Freefone®** n número gratuito; **free gift** n prima; **free kick** n tiro libre; **freelance** adj independiente ▷ adv por cuenta propia; **freely** adv libremente; (liberally) generosamente; **Freepost®** n porte m pagado; **free-range** adj (hen, eggs) de granja; **freeway** (US) n autopista; **free will** n libre albedrío; **of one's own free will** por su propia voluntad
**freeze** [friːz] (pt **froze**, pp **frozen**) vi (weather) helar; (liquid, pipe, person) helarse, congelarse ▷ vt helar; (food, prices, salaries) congelar ▷ n helada; (on arms, wages) congelación f; **freezer** n congelador m, freezer m (sc)
**freezing** ['friːzɪŋ] adj helado; **three degrees below ~** tres grados bajo cero; **freezing point** n punto de congelación
**freight** [freɪt] n (goods) carga; (money charged) flete m; **freight train** (US) n tren m de mercancías
**French** [frɛntʃ] adj francés/esa ▷ n (Ling) francés m; **the French** npl los franceses; **French bean** n judía verde; **French bread** n pan m francés; **French dressing** n (Culin) vinagreta; **French fried potatoes**, **French fries** (US) npl patatas fpl (SP) or papas fpl (LAM) fritas; **Frenchman** (irreg) n francés m; **Frenchwoman** (irreg) n francesa; **French stick** n barra de pan; **French window** n puerta de cristal
**frenzy** ['frɛnzɪ] n frenesí m

**frequency** ['friːkwənsɪ] n frecuencia
**frequent** [adj 'friːkwənt, vb frɪ'kwɛnt] adj frecuente ▷ vt frecuentar; **frequently** [-əntlɪ] adv frecuentemente, a menudo
**fresh** [frɛʃ] adj fresco; (bread) tierno; (new) nuevo; **freshen** vi (wind, air) soplar más recio; **freshen up** vi (person) arreglarse, lavarse; **fresher** (BRIT: inf) n (Univ) estudiante mf de primer año; **freshly** adv (made, painted etc) recién; **freshman** (US: irreg) n =**fresher**; **freshwater** adj (fish) de agua dulce
**fret** [frɛt] vi inquietarse
**Fri** abbr (=Friday) vier
**friction** ['frɪkʃən] n fricción f
**Friday** ['fraɪdɪ] n viernes m inv
**fridge** [frɪdʒ] (BRIT) n frigorífico (SP), nevera (SP), refrigerador m (LAM), heladera (RPL)
**fried** [fraɪd] adj frito
**friend** [frɛnd] n amigo/a; **friendly** adj simpático; (government) amigo; (place) acogedor(a); (match) amistoso; **friendship** n amistad f
**fries** [fraɪz] (esp US) npl =**French fried potatoes**
**frigate** ['frɪgɪt] n fragata
**fright** [fraɪt] n (terror) terror m; (scare) susto; **to take ~** asustarse; **frighten** vt asustar; **frightened** adj asustado; **frightening** adj espantoso; **frightful** adj espantoso, horrible
**frill** [frɪl] n volante m
**fringe** [frɪndʒ] n (BRIT: of hair) flequillo; (on lampshade etc) flecos mpl; (of forest etc) borde m, margen m
**Frisbee®** ['frɪzbɪ] n frisbee® m
**fritter** ['frɪtə*] n buñuelo
**frivolous** ['frɪvələs] adj frívolo
**fro** [frəu] see **to**
**frock** [frɔk] n vestido
**frog** [frɔg] n rana; **frogman** (irreg) n hombre-rana m

○ **KEYWORD**

**from** [frɔm] prep **1** (indicating starting place) de, desde; **where do you come from?** ¿de dónde eres?; **from London to Glasgow** de Londres a Glasgow; **to escape from sth/sb** escaparse de algo/algn
**2** (indicating origin etc) de; **a letter/ telephone call from my sister** una carta/ llamada de mi hermana; **tell him from me that ...** dígale de mi parte que ...
**3** (indicating time): **from one o'clock to** or **until** or **till two** de(sde) la una a or hasta las dos; **from January (on)** a partir de enero

**4** (*indicating distance*) de; **the hotel is 1 km from the beach** el hotel está a 1 km de la playa
**5** (*indicating price, number etc*) de; **prices range from £10 to £50** los precios van desde £10 a or hasta £50; **the interest rate was increased from 9% to 10%** el tipo de interés fue incrementado de un 9% a un 10%
**6** (*indicating difference*) de; **he can't tell red from green** no sabe distinguir el rojo del verde; **to be different from sb/sth** ser diferente a algn/algo
**7** (*because of, on the basis of*): **from what he says** por lo que dice; **weak from hunger** debilitado por el hambre

**front** [frʌnt] n (*foremost part*) parte f delantera; (*of house*) fachada; (*of dress*) delantero; (*promenade: also:* **sea ~**) paseo marítimo; (*Mil, Pol, Meteorology*) frente m; (*fig: appearances*) apariencias fpl ▷ adj (*wheel, leg*) delantero; (*row, line*) primero; **in ~ (of)** delante (de); **front door** n puerta principal; **frontier** ['frʌntɪə*] n frontera; **front page** n primera plana; **front-wheel drive** n tracción f delantera
**frost** [frost] n helada; (*also:* **hoar~**) escarcha; **frostbite** n congelación f; **frosting** n (*esp us: icing*) glaseado; **frosty** adj (*weather*) de helada; (*welcome etc*) glacial
**froth** [frɔθ] n espuma
**frown** [fraun] vi fruncir el ceño
**froze** [frəuz] pt of **freeze**
**frozen** ['frəuzn] pp of **freeze**
**fruit** [fruːt] n inv fruta; fruto; (*fig*) fruto; resultados mpl; **fruit juice** n zumo (SP) or jugo (LAM) de fruta; **fruit machine** (BRIT) n máquina f tragaperras; **fruit salad** n macedonia (SP) or ensalada (LAM) de frutas
**frustrate** [frʌs'treɪt] vt frustrar; **frustrated** adj frustrado
**fry** [fraɪ] (*pt, pp* **fried**) vt freír; **small ~** gente f menuda; **frying pan** n sartén f
**ft.** abbr = **foot; feet**
**fudge** [fʌdʒ] n (*Culin*) caramelo blando
**fuel** [fjuəl] n (*for heating*) combustible m; (*coal*) carbón m; (*wood*) leña; (*for engine*) carburante m; **fuel tank** n depósito (de combustible)
**fulfil** [ful'fɪl] vt (*function*) cumplir con; (*condition*) satisfacer; (*wish, desire*) realizar
**full** [ful] adj lleno; (*fig*) pleno; (*complete*) completo; (*maximum*) máximo; (*information*) detallado; (*price*) íntegro; (*skirt*) amplio ▷ adv: **to know ~ well that** saber perfectamente que; **I'm ~ (up)** no puedo más; **~ employment** pleno empleo; **a ~ two hours** dos horas completas; **at ~ speed** a

máxima velocidad; **in ~** (*reproduce, quote*) íntegramente; **full-length** adj (*novel etc*) entero; (*coat*) largo; (*portrait*) de cuerpo entero; **full moon** n luna llena; **full-scale** adj (*attack, war*) en gran escala; (*model*) de tamaño natural; **full stop** n punto; **full-time** adj (*work*) de tiempo completo ▷ adv: **to work full-time** trabajar a tiempo completo; **fully** adv completamente; (*at least*) por lo menos
**fumble** ['fʌmbl] vi: **to ~ with** manejar torpemente
**fume** [fjuːm] vi (*rage*) estar furioso; **fumes** npl humo, gases mpl
**fun** [fʌn] n (*amusement*) diversión f; **to have ~** divertirse; **for ~** en broma; **to make ~ of** burlarse de
**function** ['fʌŋkʃən] n función f ▷ vi funcionar
**fund** [fʌnd] n fondo; (*reserve*) reserva; **funds** npl (*money*) fondos mpl
**fundamental** [fʌndə'mɛntl] adj fundamental
**funeral** ['fjuːnərəl] n (*burial*) entierro; (*ceremony*) funerales mpl; **funeral director** n director(a) m/f de pompas fúnebres; **funeral parlour** (BRIT) n funeraria
**funfair** ['fʌnfɛə*] (BRIT) n parque m de atracciones
**fungus** ['fʌŋɡəs] (*pl* **fungi**) n hongo; (*mould*) moho
**funnel** ['fʌnl] n embudo; (*of ship*) chimenea
**funny** ['fʌnɪ] adj gracioso, divertido; (*strange*) curioso, raro
**fur** [fəː*] n piel f; (BRIT: *in kettle etc*) sarro; **fur coat** n abrigo de pieles
**furious** ['fjuərɪəs] adj furioso; (*effort*) violento
**furnish** ['fəːnɪʃ] vt amueblar; (*supply*) suministrar; (*information*) facilitar; **furnishings** npl muebles mpl
**furniture** ['fəːnɪtʃə*] n muebles mpl; **piece of ~** mueble m
**furry** ['fəːrɪ] adj peludo
**further** ['fəːðə*] adj (*new*) nuevo, adicional ▷ adv más lejos; (*more*) más; (*moreover*) además ▷ vt promover, adelantar; **further education** n educación f superior; **furthermore** adv además
**furthest** ['fəːðɪst] superlative of **far**
**fury** ['fjuərɪ] n furia
**fuse** [fjuːz] (us **fuze**) n fusible m; (*for bomb etc*) mecha ▷ vt (*metal*) fundir; (*fig*) fusionar ▷ vi fundirse; fusionarse; (BRIT Elec): **to ~ the lights** fundir los plomos; **fuse box** n caja de fusibles
**fusion** ['fjuːʒən] n fusión f

**fuss** [fʌs] n (excitement) conmoción f; (trouble) alboroto; **to make a ~** armar un lío or jaleo; **to make a ~ of sb** mimar a algn; **fussy** adj (person) exigente; (too ornate) recargado

**future** ['fjuːtʃə*] adj futuro; (coming) venidero ▷ n futuro; (prospects) porvenir m; **in ~** de ahora en adelante; **futures** npl (Comm) operaciones fpl a término, futuros mpl

**fuze** [fjuːz] (US) = **fuse**

**fuzzy** ['fʌzɪ] adj (Phot) borroso; (hair) muy rizado

**G** [dʒiː] n (Mus) sol m

**g.** abbr (= gram(s)) gr.

**gadget** ['gædʒɪt] n aparato

**Gaelic** ['geɪlɪk] adj, n (Ling) gaélico

**gag** [gæg] n (on mouth) mordaza; (joke) chiste m ▷ vt amordazar

**gain** [geɪn] n: **~ (in)** aumento (de); (profit) ganancia ▷ vt ganar ▷ vi (watch) adelantarse; **to ~ from/by sth** sacar provecho de algo; **to ~ on sb** ganar terreno a algn; **to ~ 3 lbs (in weight)** engordar 3 libras

**gal.** abbr = **gallon**

**gala** ['gɑːlə] n fiesta

**galaxy** ['gæləksɪ] n galaxia

**gale** [geɪl] n (wind) vendaval m

**gall bladder** ['gɔːl-] n vesícula biliar

**gallery** ['gælərɪ] n (also: **art ~**: public) pinacoteca; (: private) galería de arte; (for spectators) tribuna

**gallon** ['gæln] n galón m (BRIT = 4,546 litros, US = 3,785 litros)

**gallop** ['gæləp] n galope m ▷ vi galopar

**gallstone** ['gɔːlstəʊn] n cálculo biliario

**gamble** ['gæmbl] n (risk) riesgo ▷ vt jugar, apostar ▷ vi (take a risk) jugárselas; (bet) apostar; **to ~ on** apostar a; (success etc) contar con; **gambler** n jugador(a) m/f; **gambling** n juego

**game** [geɪm] n juego; (match) partido; (of cards) partida; (Hunting) caza ▷ adj (willing): **to be ~ for anything** atreverse a todo; **big ~** caza mayor (contest) juegos; (BRIT: Scol) deportes mpl; **games console** [geɪmz-] n consola de juegos; **game show** n programa m concurso m, concurso

**gammon** ['gæmən] n (bacon) tocino ahumado; (ham) jamón m ahumado

**gang** [gæŋ] n (of criminals) pandilla; (of friends etc) grupo; (of workmen) brigada

**gangster** ['gæŋstə*] n gángster m

**gap** [gæp] n vacío (SP), hueco (LAM);

(*in trees, traffic*) claro; (*in time*) intervalo; (*difference*): **~ (between)** diferencia (entre)

**gape** [geɪp] *vi* mirar boquiabierto; (*shirt etc*) abrirse (completamente)

**gap year** *n* año sabático (antes de empezar a estudiar en la universidad)

**garage** [ˈgærɑ:ʒ] *n* garaje *m*; (*for repairs*) taller *m*; **garage sale** *n* venta de objetos usados (*en el jardín de una casa particular*)

**garbage** [ˈgɑ:bɪdʒ] (*us*) *n* basura; (*inf: nonsense*) tonterías *fpl*; **garbage can** *n* cubo *or* bote *m* (*MEX*) *or* tacho (*SC*) de la basura; **garbage collector** (*US*) *n* basurero/a

**garden** [ˈgɑ:dn] *n* jardín *m*; **gardens** *npl* (*park*) parque *m*; **garden centre** (*BRIT*) *n* centro de jardinería; **gardener** *n* jardinero/a; **gardening** *n* jardinería

**garlic** [ˈgɑ:lɪk] *n* ajo

**garment** [ˈgɑ:mənt] *n* prenda (de vestir)

**garnish** [ˈgɑ:nɪʃ] *vt* (*Culin*) aderezar

**garrison** [ˈgærɪsn] *n* guarnición *f*

**gas** [gæs] *n* gas *m*; (*fuel*) combustible *m*; (*US: gasoline*) gasolina ▷ *vt* asfixiar con gas; **gas cooker** (*BRIT*) *n* cocina de gas; **gas cylinder** *n* bombona de gas; **gas fire** *n* estufa de gas

**gasket** [ˈgæskɪt] *n* (*Aut*) junta de culata

**gasoline** [ˈgæsəli:n] (*US*) *n* gasolina

**gasp** [gɑ:sp] *n* boqueada; (*of shock etc*) grito sofocado ▷ *vi* (*pant*) jadear

**gas: gas pedal** *n* (*esp US*) acelerador *m*; **gas station** (*US*) *n* gasolinera; **gas tank** (*US*) *n* (*Aut*) depósito (de gasolina)

**gate** [geɪt] *n* puerta; (*iron gate*) verja

**gateau** [ˈgætəʊ] (*pl* **~x**) *n* tarta

**gatecrash** [ˈgeɪtkræʃ] (*BRIT*) *vt* colarse en

**gateway** [ˈgeɪtweɪ] *n* puerta

**gather** [ˈgæðə*] *vt* (*flowers, fruit*) coger (*SP*), recoger; (*assemble*) reunir; (*pick up*) recoger; (*Sewing*) fruncir; (*understand*) entender ▷ *vi* (*assemble*) reunirse; **to ~ speed** ganar velocidad; **gathering** *n* reunión *f*, asamblea

**gauge** [geɪdʒ] *n* (*instrument*) indicador *m* ▷ *vt* medir; (*fig*) juzgar

**gave** [geɪv] *pt of* **give**

**gay** [geɪ] *adj* (*homosexual*) gay; (*joyful*) alegre; (*colour*) vivo

**gaze** [geɪz] *n* mirada fija ▷ *vi*: **to ~ at sth** mirar algo fijamente

**GB** *abbr* = **Great Britain**

**GCSE** (*BRIT*) *n abbr* (= *General Certificate of Secondary Education*) examen de reválida que se hace a los 16 años

**gear** [gɪə*] *n* equipo, herramientas *fpl*; (*Tech*) engranaje *m*; (*Aut*) velocidad *f*, marcha ▷ *vt* (*fig: adapt*): **to ~ sth to** adaptar

*or* ajustar algo a; **top** *or* **high** (*US*)/**low ~** cuarta/primera velocidad; **in ~** en marcha; **gear up** *vi* prepararse; **gear box** *n* caja de cambios; **gear lever** *n* palanca de cambio; **gear shift** (*US*) *n* = **gear lever**; **gear stick** *n* (*BRIT*) palanca de cambios

**geese** [gi:s] *npl of* **goose**

**gel** [dʒel] *n* gel *m*

**gem** [dʒem] *n* piedra preciosa

**Gemini** [ˈdʒemɪnaɪ] *n* Géminis *m*, Gemelos *mpl*

**gender** [ˈdʒendə*] *n* género

**gene** [dʒi:n] *n* gen(e) *m*

**general** [ˈdʒenərl] *n* general *m* ▷ *adj* general; **in ~** en general; **general anaesthetic** (*US* **general anesthetic**) *n* anestesia general; **general election** *n* elecciones *fpl* generales; **generalize** *vi* generalizar; **generally** *adv* generalmente, en general; **general practitioner** *n* médico general; **general store** *n* tienda (*que vende de todo*) (*LAM, SP*), almacén *m* (*SC, SP*)

**generate** [ˈdʒenəreɪt] *vt* (*Elec*) generar; (*jobs, profits*) producir

**generation** [dʒenəˈreɪʃən] *n* generación *f*

**generator** [ˈdʒenəreɪtə*] *n* generador *m*

**generosity** [dʒenəˈrɔsɪtɪ] *n* generosidad *f*

**generous** [ˈdʒenərəs] *adj* generoso

**genetic** [dʒɪˈnetɪk] *adj*: **~ engineering** ingeniería genética; **~ fingerprinting** identificación *f* genética; **genetically modified** *adj* transgénico; **genetics** *n* genética

**genitals** [ˈdʒenɪtlz] *npl* (órganos *mpl*) genitales *mpl*

**genius** [ˈdʒi:nɪəs] *n* genio

**genome** [ˈgi:nəʊm] *n* genoma *m*

**gent** [dʒent] *n abbr* (*BRIT inf*) = **gentleman**

**gentle** [ˈdʒentl] *adj* apacible, dulce; (*animal*) manso; (*breeze, curve etc*) suave

   ▌ Be careful not to translate **gentle** by the Spanish word *gentil*.

**gentleman** [ˈdʒentlmən] (*irreg*) *n* señor *m*; (*well-bred man*) caballero

**gently** [ˈdʒentlɪ] *adv* dulcemente; suavemente

**gents** [dʒents] *n* aseos *mpl* (de caballeros)

**genuine** [ˈdʒenjuɪn] *adj* auténtico; (*person*) sincero; **genuinely** *adv* sinceramente

**geographic(al)** [dʒɪəˈgræfɪk(l)] *adj* geográfico

**geography** [dʒɪˈɔgrəfɪ] *n* geografía

**geology** [dʒɪˈɔlədʒɪ] *n* geología

**geometry** [dʒɪˈɔmətrɪ] *n* geometría

**geranium** [dʒɪˈreɪnjəm] *n* geranio

**geriatric** [dʒerɪˈætrɪk] *adj, n* geriátrico/a *m/f*

**germ** [dʒə:m] n (*microbe*) microbio, bacteria; (*seed*, *fig*) germen m

**German** ['dʒə:mən] adj alemán/ana ▷ n alemán/ana m/f; (*Ling*) alemán m; **German measles** n rubéola

**Germany** ['dʒə:mənɪ] n Alemania

**gesture** ['dʒestʃə*] n gesto; (*symbol*) muestra

○ **KEYWORD**

**get** [gɛt] (pt, pp **got**, pp **gotten** (US)) vi
1 (*become*, *be*) ponerse, volverse; **to get old/tired** envejecer/cansarse; **to get drunk** emborracharse; **to get dirty** ensuciarse; **to get married** casarse; **when do I get paid?** ¿cuándo me pagan or se me paga?; **it's getting late** se está haciendo tarde
2 (*go*): **to get to/from** llegar a/de; **to get home** llegar a casa
3 (*begin*) empezar a; **to get to know sb** (llegar a) conocer a algn; **I'm getting to like him** me está empezando a gustar; **let's get going** or **started** ¡vamos (a empezar)!
4 (*modal aux vb*): **you've got to do it** tienes que hacerlo
▷ vt 1: **to get sth done** (*finish*) terminar algo; (*have done*) mandar hacer algo; **to get one's hair cut** cortarse el pelo; **to get the car going** or **to go** arrancar el coche; **to get sb to do sth** conseguir or hacer que algn haga algo; **to get sth/sb ready** preparar algo/a algn
2 (*obtain*: *money*, *permission*, *results*) conseguir; (*find*: *job*, *flat*) encontrar; (*fetch*: *person*, *doctor*) buscar; (*object*) ir a buscar, traer; **to get sth for sb** conseguir algo para algn; **get me Mr Jones, please** (*Tel*) póngame (SP) or comuníqueme (LAM) con el Sr. Jones, por favor; **can I get you a drink?** ¿quieres algo de beber?
3 (*receive*: *present*, *letter*) recibir; (*acquire*: *reputation*) alcanzar; (: *prize*) ganar; **what did you get for your birthday?** ¿qué te regalaron tu cumpleaños?; **how much did you get for the painting?** ¿cuánto sacaste por el cuadro?
4 (*catch*) coger (SP), agarrar (LAM); (*hit*: *target etc*) dar en; **to get sb by the arm/throat** coger or agarrar a algn por el brazo/cuello; **get him!** ¡cógelo! (SP), ¡atrápalo! (LAM); **the bullet got him in the leg** la bala le dio en la pierna
5 (*take*, *move*) llevar; **to get sth to sb** hacer llegar algo a algn; **do you think we'll get it through the door?** ¿crees que lo podremos meter por la puerta?
6 (*catch*, *take*: *plane*, *bus etc*) coger (SP),

tomar (LAM); **where do I get the train for Birmingham?** ¿dónde se coge or se toma el tren para Birmingham?
7 (*understand*) entender; (*hear*) oír; **I've got it!** ¡ya lo tengo!, ¡eureka!; **I don't get your meaning** no te entiendo; **I'm sorry, I didn't get your name** lo siento, no cogí tu nombre
8 (*have*, *possess*): **to have got** tener

**get away** vi marcharse; (*escape*) escaparse
**get away with** vt fus hacer impunemente
**get back** vi (*return*) volver ▷ vt recobrar
**get in** vi entrar; (*train*) llegar; (*arrive home*) volver a casa, regresar
**get into** vt fus entrar en; (*vehicle*) subir a; **to get into a rage** enfadarse
**get off** vi (*from train etc*) bajar; (*depart*: *person*, *car*) marcharse ▷ vt (*remove*) quitar ▷ vt fus (*train*, *bus*) bajar de
**get on** vi (*at exam etc*): **how are you getting on?** ¿cómo te va?; (*agree*): **to get on (with)** llevarse bien (con) ▷ vt fus subir a
**get out** vi salir; (*of vehicle*) bajar ▷ vt sacar
**get out of** vt fus salir de; (*duty etc*) escaparse de
**get over** vt fus (*illness*) recobrarse de
**get through** vi (*Tel*) (lograr) comunicarse
**get up** vi (*rise*) levantarse ▷ vt fus subir

**getaway** ['gɛtəweɪ] n fuga
**Ghana** ['gɑːnə] n Ghana
**ghastly** ['gɑːstlɪ] adj horrible
**ghetto** ['gɛtəu] n gueto
**ghost** [gəust] n fantasma m
**giant** ['dʒaɪənt] n gigante mf ▷ adj gigantesco, gigante
**gift** [gɪft] n regalo; (*ability*) talento; **gifted** adj dotado; **gift shop** (US **gift store**) n tienda de regalos; **gift token**, **gift voucher** n vale m canjeable por un regalo
**gig** [gɪg] n (*inf: concert*) actuación f
**gigabyte** ['dʒɪgəbaɪt] n gigabyte m
**gigantic** [dʒaɪˈgæntɪk] adj gigantesco
**giggle** ['gɪgl] vi reírse tontamente
**gills** [gɪlz] npl (*of fish*) branquias fpl, agallas fpl
**gilt** [gɪlt] adj, n dorado
**gimmick** ['gɪmɪk] n truco
**gin** [dʒɪn] n ginebra
**ginger** ['dʒɪndʒə*] n jengibre m
**gipsy** ['dʒɪpsɪ] n = **gypsy**
**giraffe** [dʒɪˈrɑːf] n jirafa
**girl** [gə:l] n (*small*) niña; (*young woman*) chica, joven f, muchacha; (*daughter*) hija; **an English ~** una (chica) inglesa; **girl band** n girl band m (*grupo musical de chicas*); **girlfriend** n (*of girl*) amiga; (*of boy*) novia; **Girl Scout** (US) n = **Girl Guide**
**gist** [dʒɪst] n lo esencial

**give** [gɪv] (pt **gave**, pp **given**) vt dar;
(deliver) entregar; (as gift) regalar ▷ vi (break)
romperse; (stretch: fabric) dar de sí; **to ~ sb
sth, ~ sth to sb** dar algo a algn; **give away**
vt (give free) regalar; (betray) traicionar;
(disclose) revelar; **give back** vt devolver;
**give in** vi ceder ▷ vt entregar; **give out**
vt distribuir; **give up** vi rendirse, darse
por vencido ▷ vt renunciar a; **to give up
smoking** dejar de fumar; **to give o.s. up**
entregarse

**given** ['gɪvn] pp of **give** ▷ adj (fixed: time,
amount) determinado ▷ conj: **~ (that) ...**
dado (que) ...; **~ the circumstances ...**
dadas las circunstancias ...

**glacier** ['glæsɪə*] n glaciar m

**glad** [glæd] adj contento; **gladly** ['-lɪ] adv
con mucho gusto

**glamour** ['glæmər] (US **glamor**) n
encanto, atractivo; **glamorous** adj
encantador(a), atractivo

**glance** [glɑːns] n ojeada, mirada ▷ vi: **to ~
at** echar una ojeada a

**gland** [glænd] n glándula

**glare** [glɛə*] n (of anger) mirada feroz; (of
light) deslumbramiento, brillo; **to be in
the ~ of publicity** ser el foco de la atención
pública ▷ vi deslumbrar; **to ~ at** mirar con
odio a; **glaring** adj (mistake) manifiesto

**glass** [glɑːs] n vidrio, cristal m; (for
drinking) vaso; (: with stem) copa; **glasses** npl
(spectacles) gafas fpl

**glaze** [gleɪz] vt (window) poner cristales a;
(pottery) vidriar ▷ n vidriado

**gleam** [gliːm] vi brillar

**glen** [glɛn] n cañada

**glide** [glaɪd] vi deslizarse; (Aviat: birds)
planear; **glider** n (Aviat) planeador m

**glimmer** ['glɪmə*] n luz f tenue; (of
interest) muestra; (of hope) rayo

**glimpse** [glɪmps] n vislumbre m ▷ vt
vislumbrar, entrever

**glint** [glɪnt] vi centellear

**glisten** ['glɪsn] vi relucir, brillar

**glitter** ['glɪtə*] vi relucir, brillar

**global** ['gləubl] adj mundial;
**globalization** n globalización f; **global
warming** n (re)calentamiento global or
de la tierra

**globe** [gləub] n globo; (model) globo
terráqueo

**gloom** [gluːm] n oscuridad f; (sadness)
tristeza; **gloomy** adj (dark) oscuro; (sad)
triste; (pessimistic) pesimista

**glorious** ['glɔːrɪəs] adj glorioso; (weather
etc) magnífico

**glory** ['glɔːrɪ] n gloria

**gloss** [glɔs] n (shine) brillo; (paint) pintura
de aceite

**glossary** ['glɔsərɪ] n glosario

**glossy** ['glɔsɪ] adj lustroso; (magazine)
de lujo

**glove** [glʌv] n guante m; **glove
compartment** n (Aut) guantera

**glow** [gləu] vi brillar

**glucose** ['gluːkəus] n glucosa

**glue** [gluː] n goma (de pegar), cemento
▷ vt pegar

**GM** adj abbr (= genetically modified)
transgénico

**gm** abbr (= gram) g

**GMO** n abbr (= genetically modified organism)
organismo transgénico

**GMT** abbr (= Greenwich Mean Time) GMT

**gnaw** [nɔː] vt roer

**go** [gəu] (pt **went**, pp **gone**, pl **~es**) vi ir;
(travel) viajar; (depart) irse, marcharse; (work)
funcionar, marchar; (be sold) venderse;
(time) pasar; (fit, suit): **to ~ with** hacer
juego con; (become) ponerse; (break etc)
estropearse, romperse ▷ n: **to have a ~
(at)** probar suerte (con); **to be on the ~** no
parar; **whose ~ is it?** ¿a quién le toca?; **he's
~ing to do it** va a hacerlo; **to ~ for a walk**
ir de paseo; **to ~ dancing** ir a bailar; **how
did it ~?** ¿qué tal salió or resultó?, ¿cómo ha
ido?; **to ~ round the back** pasar por detrás;
**go ahead** vi seguir adelante; **go away**
vi irse, marcharse; **go back** vi volver; **go
by** vi (time) pasar ▷ vt fus guiarse por;
**go down** vi bajar; (ship) hundirse; (sun)
ponerse ▷ vt fus bajar; **go for** vt fus (fetch)
ir por; (like) gustar; (attack) atacar; **go in** vi
entrar; **go into** vt fus entrar en; (investigate)
investigar; (embark on) dedicarse a; **go off**
vi irse, marcharse; (food) pasarse; (explode)
estallar; (event) realizarse ▷ vt fus dejar
de gustar; **I'm going off him/the idea**
ya no me gusta tanto él/la idea; **go on** vi
(continue) seguir, continuar; (happen) pasar,
ocurrir; **to go on doing sth** seguir haciendo
algo; **go out** vi salir; (fire, light) apagarse;
**go over** vi (ship) zozobrar ▷ vt fus (check)
revisar; **go past** vi, vt fus pasar; (go round)
vi (circulate: news, rumour) correr; (suffice)
alcanzar, bastar; (revolve) girar, dar vueltas;
(visit): **to go round (to sb's)** pasar a ver (a
algn); **to go round (by)** (make a detour) dar
la vuelta (por); **go through** vt fus (town etc)
atravesar; **go up** vi, vt fus subir; **go with**
vt fus (accompany) ir con, acompañar a; **go
without** vt fus pasarse sin

**go-ahead** ['gəuəhɛd] adj (person)
dinámico; (firm) innovador(a) ▷ n luz f
verde

**goal** [gəul] n meta; (score) gol m;

**goalkeeper** n portero; **goal-post** n poste m (de la portería)

**goat** [gəʊt] n cabra

**gobble** ['gɒbl] vt (also: **~ down, ~ up**) tragarse, engullir

**God** [gɒd] n Dios m; **godchild** n ahijado/a; **goddaughter** n ahijada; **goddess** n diosa; **godfather** n padrino; **godmother** n madrina; **godson** n ahijado

**goggles** ['gɒglz] npl gafas fpl

**going** ['gəʊɪŋ] n (conditions) estado del terreno ▷ adj: **the ~ rate** la tarifa corriente or en vigor

**gold** [gəʊld] n oro ▷ adj de oro; **golden** adj (made of gold) de oro; (gold in colour) dorado; **goldfish** n pez m de colores; **goldmine** n (also fig) mina de oro; **gold-plated** adj chapado en oro

**golf** [gɒlf] n golf m; **golf ball** n (for game) pelota de golf; (on typewriter) esfera; **golf club** n club m de golf; (stick) palo (de golf); **golf course** n campo de golf; **golfer** n golfista mf

**gone** [gɒn] pp of **go**

**gong** [gɒŋ] n gong m

**good** [gʊd] adj bueno; (pleasant) agradable; (kind) bueno, amable; (well-behaved) educado ▷ n bien m, provecho; **goods** npl (Comm) mercancías fpl; **~!** ¡qué bien!; **to be ~ at** tener aptitud para; **to be ~ for** servir para; **it's ~ for you** te hace bien; **would you be ~ enough to ...?** ¿podría hacerme el favor de ...?, ¿sería tan amable de ...?; **a ~ deal (of)** mucho; **a ~ many** muchos; **to make ~** reparar; **it's no ~ complaining** no vale la pena (de) quejarse; **for ~** para siempre, definitivamente; **~ morning/afternoon!** ¡buenos días/buenas tardes!; **~ evening!** ¡buenas noches!; **~ night!** ¡buenas noches!

**goodbye** [gʊd'baɪ] excl ¡adiós!; **to say ~ (to)** (person) despedirse (de)

**good: Good Friday** n Viernes m Santo; **good-looking** adj guapo; **good-natured** adj amable, simpático; **goodness** n (of person) bondad f; **for goodness sake!** ¡por Dios!; **goodness gracious!** ¡Dios mío!; **goods train** (BRIT) n tren m de mercancías; **goodwill** n buena voluntad f

**Google®** ['guːgəl] n Google ® m ▷ vi hacer búsquedas en Internet ▷ vt buscar información en Internet sobre

**goose** [guːs] (pl **geese**) n ganso, oca

**gooseberry** ['gʊzbərɪ] n grosella espinosa; **to play ~** hacer de carabina

**goose bumps, goose pimples** npl carne f de gallina

**gorge** [gɔːdʒ] n barranco ▷ vr: **to ~ o.s. (on)** atracarse (de)

**gorgeous** ['gɔːdʒəs] adj (thing) precioso; (weather) espléndido; (person) guapísimo

**gorilla** [gə'rɪlə] n gorila m

**gosh** [gɒʃ] (inf) excl ¡cielos!

**gospel** ['gɒspl] n evangelio

**gossip** ['gɒsɪp] n (scandal) cotilleo, chismes mpl; (chat) charla; (scandalmonger) cotilla m/f, chismoso/a ▷ vi cotillear; **gossip column** n ecos mpl de sociedad

**got** [gɒt] pt, pp of **get**

**gotten** (US) ['gɒtn] pp of **get**

**gourmet** ['gʊəmeɪ] n gastrónomo/a m/f

**govern** ['gʌvən] vt gobernar; (influence) dominar; **government** n gobierno; **governor** n gobernador(a) m/f; (of school etc) miembro del consejo; (of jail) director(a) m/f

**gown** [gaʊn] n traje m; (of teacher, BRIT: of judge) toga

**G.P.** n abbr = **general practitioner**

**grab** [græb] vt coger (SP), agarrar (LAM), arrebatar ▷ vi: **to ~ at** intentar agarrar

**grace** [greɪs] n gracia ▷ vt honrar; (adorn) adornar; **5 days' ~** un plazo de 5 días; **graceful** adj grácil, ágil; (style, shape) elegante, gracioso; **gracious** ['greɪʃəs] adj amable

**grade** [greɪd] n (quality) clase f, calidad f; (in hierarchy) grado; (Scol: mark) nota; (US: school class) curso ▷ vt clasificar; **grade crossing** (US) n paso a nivel; **grade school** (US) n escuela primaria

**gradient** ['greɪdɪənt] n pendiente f

**gradual** ['grædjʊəl] adj paulatino; **gradually** adv paulatinamente

**graduate** [n 'grædjuːɪt, vb 'grædjueɪt] n (US: of high school) graduado/a; (of university) licenciado/a ▷ vi graduarse; licenciarse; **graduation** [-'eɪʃən] n (ceremony) entrega del título

**graffiti** [grə'fiːtɪ] n pintadas fpl

**graft** [grɑːft] n (Agr, Med) injerto; (BRIT: inf) trabajo duro; (bribery) corrupción f ▷ vt injertar

**grain** [greɪn] n (single particle) grano; (corn) granos mpl, cereales mpl; (of wood) fibra

**gram** [græm] n gramo

**grammar** ['græmə*] n gramática; **grammar school** (BRIT) n ≈ instituto de segunda enseñanza, liceo (SP)

**gramme** [græm] n = **gram**

**gran** [græn] (inf) n (BRIT) abuelita

**grand** [grænd] adj magnífico, imponente; (wonderful) estupendo; (gesture etc) grandioso; **grandad** (inf) n = **granddad**; **grandchild** (pl **grandchildren**) n nieto/a m/f; **granddad** (inf) n yayo, abuelito;

**granddaughter** n nieta; **grandfather** n abuelo; **grandma** (inf) n yaya, abuelita; **grandmother** n abuela; **grandpa** (inf) n = **granddad**; **grandparents** npl abuelos mpl; **grand piano** n piano de cola; **Grand Prix** ['grɑ̃:'pri:] n (Aut) gran premio, Grand Prix m; **grandson** n nieto

**granite** ['grænɪt] n granito

**granny** ['grænɪ] (inf) n abuelita, yaya

**grant** [grɑ:nt] vt (concede) conceder; (admit) reconocer ▷ n (Scol) beca; (Admin) subvención f; **to take sth/sb for ~ed** dar algo por sentado/no hacer ningún caso a algn

**grape** [greɪp] n uva

**grapefruit** ['greɪpfru:t] n pomelo (SP, SC), toronja (LAM)

**graph** [grɑ:f] n gráfica; **graphic** ['græfɪk] adj gráfico; **graphics** n artes fpl gráficas ▷ npl (drawings) dibujos mpl

**grasp** [grɑ:sp] vt agarrar, asir; (understand) comprender ▷ n (grip) asimiento; (understanding) comprensión f

**grass** [grɑ:s] n hierba; (lawn) césped m; **grasshopper** n saltamontes m inv

**grate** [greɪt] n parrilla de chimenea ▷ vi: **to ~ (on)** chirriar (sobre) ▷ vt (Culin) rallar

**grateful** ['greɪtful] adj agradecido

**grater** ['greɪtə*] n rallador m

**gratitude** ['grætɪtju:d] n agradecimiento

**grave** [greɪv] n tumba ▷ adj serio, grave

**gravel** ['grævl] n grava

**gravestone** ['greɪvstəun] n lápida

**graveyard** ['greɪvjɑ:d] n cementerio

**gravity** ['grævɪtɪ] n gravedad f

**gravy** ['greɪvɪ] n salsa de carne

**gray** [greɪ] adj = **grey**

**graze** [greɪz] vi pacer ▷ vt (touch lightly) rozar; (scrape) raspar ▷ n (Med) abrasión f

**grease** [gri:s] n (fat) grasa; (lubricant) lubricante m ▷ vt engrasar; lubrificar; **greasy** adj grasiento

**great** [greɪt] adj grande; (inf) magnífico, estupendo; **Great Britain** n Gran Bretaña; **great-grandfather** n bisabuelo; **great-grandmother** n bisabuela; **greatly** adv muy; (with verb) mucho

**Greece** [gri:s] n Grecia

**greed** [gri:d] n (also: **~iness**) codicia, avaricia; (for food) gula; (for power etc) avidez f; **greedy** adj avaro; (for food) glotón/ona

**Greek** [gri:k] adj griego ▷ n griego/a; (Ling) griego

**green** [gri:n] adj (also Pol) verde; (inexperienced) novato ▷ n verde m; (stretch of grass) césped m; (Golf) green; m **greens** npl (vegetables) verduras fpl; **green card**

n (Aut) carta verde; (US: work permit) permiso de trabajo para los extranjeros en EE. UU.; **greengage** n (ciruela) claudia; **greengrocer** (BRIT) n verdulero/a; **greenhouse** n invernadero; **greenhouse effect** n efecto invernadero

**Greenland** ['gri:nlənd] n Groenlandia

**green salad** n ensalada f (de lechuga, pepino, pimiento verde, etc)

**greet** [gri:t] vt (welcome) dar la bienvenida a; (receive: news) recibir; **greeting** n (welcome) bienvenida; **greeting(s) card** n tarjeta de felicitación

**grew** [gru:] pt of **grow**

**grey** [greɪ] (US **gray**) adj gris; (weather) sombrío; **grey-haired** adj canoso; **greyhound** n galgo

**grid** [grɪd] n reja; (Elec) red f; **gridlock** n (traffic jam) retención f

**grief** [gri:f] n dolor m, pena

**grievance** ['gri:vəns] n motivo de queja, agravio

**grieve** [gri:v] vi afligirse, acongojarse ▷ vt dar pena a; **to ~ for** llorar por

**grill** [grɪl] n (on cooker) parrilla; (also: **mixed ~**) parrillada ▷ vt (BRIT) asar a la parrilla; (inf: question) interrogar

**grille** [grɪl] n reja; (Aut) rejilla

**grim** [grɪm] adj (place) sombrío; (situation) triste; (person) ceñudo

**grime** [graɪm] n mugre f, suciedad f

**grin** [grɪn] n sonrisa abierta ▷ vi sonreír abiertamente

**grind** [graɪnd] (pt, pp ground) vt (coffee, pepper etc) moler; (US: meat) picar; (make sharp) afilar ▷ n (work) rutina

**grip** [grɪp] n (hold) asimiento; (control) control m, dominio; (of tyre etc) **to have a good/bad ~** agarrarse bien/mal; (handle) asidero; (holdall) maletín m ▷ vt agarrar; (viewer, reader) fascinar; **to get to ~s with** enfrentarse con; **gripping** adj absorbente

**grit** [grɪt] n gravilla; (courage) valor m ▷ vt (road) poner gravilla en; **to ~ one's teeth** apretar los dientes

**grits** [grɪts] (US) npl maíz msg a medio moler

**groan** [grəun] n gemido; quejido ▷ vi gemir; quejarse

**grocer** ['grəusə*] n tendero (de ultramarinos (SP)); **groceries** npl comestibles mpl; **grocer's (shop)** n tienda de comestibles or (MEX, CAM) abarrotes, almacén (SC); **grocery** n (shop) tienda de ultramarinos

**groin** [grɔɪn] n ingle f

**groom** [gru:m] n mozo/a de cuadra; (also: **bride~**) novio ▷ vt (horse) almohazar;

(*fig*): **to ~ sb for** preparar a algn para; **well-~ed** de buena presencia

**groove** [gruːv] n ranura, surco

**grope** [grəʊp] vi: **to ~ for** buscar a tientas

**gross** [grəʊs] adj (*neglect, injustice*) grave; (*vulgar: behaviour*) grosero; (*: appearance*) de mal gusto; (*Comm*) bruto; **grossly** adv (*greatly*) enormemente

**grotesque** [grə'tɛsk] adj grotesco

**ground** [graʊnd] pt, pp of **grind** ▷ n suelo, tierra; (*Sport*) campo, terreno; (*reason: gen pl*) causa, razón f; (*US: also:* **~ wire**) (*plane*) mantener en tierra; (*US Elec*) conectar con tierra; **grounds** npl (*of coffee etc*) poso; (*gardens etc*) jardines mpl, parque m; **on the ~** en el suelo; **to the ~** al suelo; **to gain/lose ~** ganar/perder terreno; **ground floor** (*BRIT*) planta baja; **groundsheet** (*BRIT*) n tela impermeable; suelo; **groundwork** n preparación f

**group** [gruːp] n grupo; (*musical*) conjunto ▷ vt (*also:* **~ together**) agrupar ▷ vi (*also:* **~ together**) agruparse

**grouse** [graʊs] n inv (*bird*) urogallo ▷ vi (*complain*) quejarse

**grovel** ['grɔvl] vi (*fig*): **to ~ before** humillarse ante

**grow** [grəʊ] (*pt* **grew**, *pp* **grown**) vi crecer; (*increase*) aumentar; (*expand*) desarrollarse; (*become*) volverse; **to ~ rich/weak** enriquecerse/debilitarse ▷ vt cultivar; (*hair, beard*) dejar crecer; **grow on** vt fus: **that painting is growing on me** ese cuadro me gusta cada vez más; **grow up** vi crecer, hacerse hombre/mujer

**growl** [graʊl] vi gruñir

**grown** [grəʊn] pp of **grow**; **grown-up** n adulto/a, mayor mf

**growth** [grəʊθ] n crecimiento, desarrollo; (*what has grown*) brote m; (*Med*) tumor m

**grub** [grʌb] n larva, gusano; (*inf: food*) comida

**grubby** ['grʌbɪ] adj sucio, mugriento

**grudge** [grʌdʒ] n (motivo de) rencor m ▷ vt: **to ~ sb sth** dar algo a algn de mala gana; **to bear sb a ~** guardar rencor a algn

**gruelling** ['gruəlɪŋ] (*US* **grueling**) adj penoso, duro

**gruesome** ['gruːsəm] adj horrible

**grumble** ['grʌmbl] vi refunfuñar, quejarse

**grumpy** ['grʌmpɪ] adj gruñón/ona

**grunt** [grʌnt] vi gruñir

**guarantee** [gærən'tiː] n garantía ▷ vt garantizar

**guard** [gɑːd] n (*squad*) guardia; (*one man*) guardia mf; (*BRIT Rail*) jefe m de tren; (*on machine*) dispositivo de seguridad; (*also:* **fire~**) rejilla de protección ▷ vt guardar;

(*prisoner*) vigilar; **to be on one's ~** estar alerta; **guardian** n guardián/ana m/f; (*of minor*) tutor(a) m/f

**guerrilla** [gə'rɪlə] n guerrillero/a

**guess** [gɛs] vi adivinar; (*US*) suponer ▷ vt adivinar; suponer ▷ n suposición f, conjetura; **to take** *or* **have a ~** tratar de adivinar

**guest** [gɛst] n invitado/a; (*in hotel*) huésped mf; **guest house** n casa de huéspedes, pensión f; **guest room** n cuarto de huéspedes

**guidance** ['gaɪdəns] n (*advice*) consejos mpl

**guide** [gaɪd] n (*person*) guía mf; (*book, fig*) guía; (*also:* **Girl ~**) guía ▷ vt (*round museum etc*) guiar; (*lead*) conducir; (*direct*) orientar; **guidebook** n guía; **guide dog** n perro m guía; **guided tour** n visita f con guía; **guidelines** npl (*advice*) directrices fpl

**guild** [gɪld] n gremio

**guilt** [gɪlt] n culpabilidad f; **guilty** adj culpable

**guinea pig** ['gɪnɪ-] n cobaya; (*fig*) conejillo de Indias

**guitar** [gɪ'tɑː*] n guitarra; **guitarist** n guitarrista m/f

**gulf** [gʌlf] n golfo; (*abyss*) abismo

**gull** [gʌl] n gaviota

**gulp** [gʌlp] vi tragar saliva ▷ vt (*also:* **~ down**) tragarse

**gum** [gʌm] n (*Anat*) encía; (*glue*) goma, cemento; (*sweet*) caramelo de goma; (*also:* **chewing-~**) chicle m ▷ vt pegar con goma

**gun** [gʌn] n (*small*) pistola, revólver m; (*shotgun*) escopeta; (*rifle*) fusil m; (*cannon*) cañón m; **gunfire** n disparos mpl; **gunman** (*irreg*) n pistolero; **gunpoint** n: **at gunpoint** a mano armada; **gunpowder** n pólvora; **gunshot** n escopetazo

**gush** [gʌʃ] vi salir a raudales; (*person*) deshacerse en efusiones

**gust** [gʌst] n (*of wind*) ráfaga

**gut** [gʌt] n intestino; **guts** npl (*Anat*) tripas fpl; (*courage*) valor m

**gutter** ['gʌtə*] n (*of roof*) canalón m; (*in street*) cuneta

**guy** [gaɪ] n (*also:* **~rope**) cuerda; (*inf: man*) tío (*SP*), tipo; (*figure*) monigote m

**Guy Fawkes' Night** [gaɪ'fɔːks-] n ver abajo

> **GUY FAWKES' NIGHT**
>
> La noche del cinco de noviembre, **Guy Fawkes' Night**, se celebra en el Reino Unido el fracaso de la conspiración de la pólvora ("Gunpowder Plot"), un

intento fallido de volar el parlamento de Jaime I en 1605. Esa noche se lanzan fuegos artificiales y se hacen hogueras en las que se queman unos muñecos de trapo que representan a **Guy Fawkes**, uno de los cabecillas de la revuelta. Días antes, los niños tienen por costumbre pedir a los transeúntes "a penny for the guy", dinero que emplean en comprar cohetes y petardos.

**gym** [dʒɪm] *n* gimnasio; **gymnasium** *n* gimnasio *mf*; **gymnast** *n* gimnasta *mf*; **gymnastics** *n* gimnasia; **gym shoes** *npl* zapatillas *fpl* (de deporte)
**gynaecologist** [gaɪnɪ'kɔlədʒɪst] (*US* **gynecologist**) *n* ginecólogo/a
**gypsy** ['dʒɪpsɪ] *n* gitano/a

**haberdashery** [hæbə'dæʃərɪ] (*BRIT*) *n* mercería
**habit** ['hæbɪt] *n* hábito, costumbre *f*; (*drug habit*) adicción *f*; (*costume*) hábito
**habitat** ['hæbɪtæt] *n* hábitat *m*
**hack** [hæk] *vt* (*cut*) cortar; (*slice*) tajar ▷ *n* (*pej: writer*) escritor(a) *m/f* a sueldo; **hacker** *n* (*Comput*) pirata *mf* informático/a
**had** [hæd] *pt, pp of* **have**
**haddock** ['hædək] (*pl ~ or ~s*) *n* especie de merluza
**hadn't** ['hædnt] = **had not**
**haemorrhage** ['hɛmərɪdʒ] (*US* **hemorrhage**) *n* hemorragia
**haemorrhoids** ['hɛmərɔɪdz] (*US* **hemorrhoids**) *npl* hemorroides *fpl*
**haggle** ['hægl] *vi* regatear
**Hague** [heɪg] *n*: **The ~** La Haya
**hail** [heɪl] *n* granizo; (*fig*) lluvia ▷ *vt* saludar; (*taxi*) llamar a; (*acclaim*) aclamar ▷ *vi* granizar; **hailstone** *n* (piedra de) granizo
**hair** [hɛə*] *n* pelo, cabellos *mpl*; (*one hair*) pelo, cabello; (*on legs etc*) vello; **to do one's ~** arreglarse el pelo; **to have grey ~** tener canas *fpl*; **hairband** *n* cinta; **hairbrush** *n* cepillo (para el pelo); **haircut** *n* corte *m* (de pelo); **hairdo** *n* peinado; **hairdresser** *n* peluquero/a; **hairdresser's** *n* peluquería; **hair dryer** *n* secador *m* de pelo; **hair gel** *n* fijador; **hair spray** *n* laca; **hairstyle** *n* peinado; **hairy** *adj* peludo; velludo; (*inf: frightening*) espeluznante
**hake** [heɪk] (*pl ~ or ~s*) *n* merluza
**half** [hɑːf] (*pl* **halves**) *n* mitad *f*; (*of beer*) ≈ caña (*SP*), media pinta; (*Rail, Bus*) billete *m* de niño ▷ *adj* medio ▷ *adv* medio, a medias; **two and a ~** dos y media; **~ a dozen** media docena; **~ a pound** media libra; **to cut sth in ~** cortar algo por la mitad; **half board** *n* (*BRIT: in hotel*) media pensión; **half-**

brother n hermanastro; **half day** n medio día m, media jornada; **half fare** n medio pasaje m; **half-hearted** adj indiferente, poco entusiasta; **half-hour** n media hora; **half-price** adj, adv a mitad de precio; **half term** n (Scol) vacaciones de mediados del trimestre; **half-time** n descanso; **halfway** adv a medio camino; **halfway through** a mitad de

**hall** [hɔːl] n (for concerts) sala; (entrance way) hall m; vestíbulo

**hallmark** ['hɔːlmɑːk] n sello

**hallo** [hə'ləʊ] excl = **hello**

**hall of residence** (BRIT) n residencia

**Hallowe'en** [hæləʊ'iːn] n víspera de Todos los Santos

**hallucination** [həluːsɪ'neɪʃən] n alucinación f

**hallway** ['hɔːlweɪ] n vestíbulo

**halo** ['heɪləʊ] n (of saint) halo, aureola

**halt** [hɔːlt] n (stop) alto, parada ▷ vt parar; interrumpir ▷ vi pararse

**halve** [hɑːv] vt partir por la mitad

**halves** [hɑːvz] npl of **half**

**ham** [hæm] n jamón m (cocido)

**hamburger** ['hæmbɜːgə*] n hamburguesa

**hamlet** ['hæmlɪt] n aldea

**hammer** ['hæmə*] n martillo ▷ vt (nail) clavar; (force): **to ~ an idea into sb/a message home** meter una idea en la cabeza a algn/machacar una idea ▷ vi dar golpes

**hammock** ['hæmək] n hamaca

**hamper** ['hæmpə*] vt estorbar ▷ n cesto

**hamster** ['hæmstə*] n hámster m

**hamstring** ['hæmstrɪŋ] n (Anat) tendón m de la corva

**hand** [hænd] n mano f; (of clock) aguja; (writing) letra; (worker) obrero ▷ vt dar, pasar; **to give** or **lend sb a ~** echar una mano a algn, ayudar a algn; **at ~** a mano; **in ~** (time) libre; (job etc) entre manos; **on ~** (person, services) a mano, al alcance; **to ~** (information

etc) a mano; **on the one ~ ..., on the other ~ ...** por una parte ... por otra (parte) ...; **hand down** vt pasar, bajar; (tradition) transmitir; (heirloom) dejar en herencia; (us: sentence, verdict) imponer; **hand in** vt entregar; **hand out** vt distribuir; **hand over** vt (deliver) entregar; **handbag** n bolso (SP), cartera (LAM), bolsa (MEX); **hand baggage** n = **hand luggage**; **handbook** n manual m; **handbrake** n freno de mano; **handcuffs** npl esposas fpl; **handful** n puñado

**handicap** ['hændɪkæp] n minusvalía; (disadvantage) desventaja; (Sport) handicap m ▷ vt estorbar; **to be mentally ~ped** ser mentalmente m/f discapacitado; **to be physically ~ped** ser minusválido/a

**handkerchief** ['hæŋkətʃɪf] n pañuelo

**handle** ['hændl] n (of door etc) tirador m; (of cup etc) asa; (of knife etc) mango; (for winding) manivela ▷ vt (touch) tocar; (deal with) encargarse de; (treat: people) manejar; **"~ with care"** "(manéjese) con cuidado"; **to fly off the ~** perder los estribos; **handlebar(s)** n(pl) manillar m

**hand luggage** n equipaje m de mano; **handmade** adj hecho a mano; **handout** n (money etc) limosna; (leaflet) folleto; **hands-free** adj (phone) manos libres inv; **hands-free kit** n manos libres m inv

**handsome** ['hænsəm] adj guapo; (building) bello; (fig: profit) considerable

**handwriting** ['hændraɪtɪŋ] n letra

**handy** ['hændɪ] adj (close at hand) a la mano; (tool etc) práctico; (skilful) hábil, diestro

**hang** [hæŋ] (pt, pp hung) vt colgar; (criminal: pt, pp hanged) ahorcar ▷ vi (painting, coat etc) colgar; (hair, drapery) caer; **to get the ~ of sth** (inf) lograr dominar algo; **hang about** or **around** vi haraganear; **hang down** vi colgar, pender; **hang on** vi (wait) esperar; **hang out** vt (washing) tender, colgar ▷ vi (inf: live) vivir; (spend time) pasar el rato; **to hang out of sth** colgar fuera de algo; **hang round** vi = **hang around**; **hang up** vi (Tel) colgar ▷ vt colgar

**hanger** ['hæŋə*] n percha

**hang-gliding** ['-glaɪdɪŋ] n vuelo libre

**hangover** ['hæŋəʊvə*] n (after drinking) resaca

**hankie, hanky** ['hæŋkɪ] n abbr = **handkerchief**

**happen** ['hæpən] vi suceder, ocurrir; (chance): **he ~ed to hear/see** dió la casualidad de que oyó/vió; **as it ~s** da la casualidad de que

**happily** ['hæpɪlɪ] adv (luckily)

afortunadamente; (*cheerfully*) alegremente

**happiness** ['hæpɪnɪs] n felicidad f; (*cheerfulness*) alegría

**happy** ['hæpɪ] adj feliz; (*cheerful*) alegre; **to be ~ (with)** estar contento (con); **to be ~ to do** estar encantado de hacer; **~ birthday!** ¡feliz cumpleaños!

**harass** ['hærəs] vt acosar, hostigar; **harassment** n persecución f

**harbour** ['hɑːbə*] (us **harbor**) n puerto ▷ vt (*fugitive*) dar abrigo a; (*hope etc*) abrigar

**hard** [hɑːd] adj duro; (*difficult*) difícil; (*work*) arduo; (*person*) severo; (*fact*) innegable ▷ adv (*work*) mucho, duro; (*think*) profundamente; **to look ~ at** clavar los ojos en; **to try ~** esforzarse; **no ~ feelings!** ¡sin rencor(es)!; **to be ~ of hearing** ser duro de oído; **to be ~ done by** ser tratado injustamente; **hardback** n libro en cartoné; **hardboard** n aglomerado m (*de madera*); **hard disk** n (*Comput*) disco duro or rígido; **harden** vt endurecer; (*fig*) curtir ▷ vi endurecerse; curtirse

**hardly** ['hɑːdlɪ] adv apenas; **~ ever** casi nunca

**hard: hardship** n privación f; **hard shoulder** n (*BRIT*) (Aut) arcén m; **hard-up** (*inf*) adj sin un duro (*SP*), pelado, sin un centavo (*MEX*), pato (*SC*); **hardware** n ferretería; (*Comput*) hardware m; (*Mil*) armamento; **hardware shop** (us **hardware store**) ferretería; **hard-working** adj trabajador(a)

**hardy** ['hɑːdɪ] adj fuerte; (*plant*) resistente

**hare** [hɛə*] n liebre f

**harm** [hɑːm] n daño, mal m ▷ vt (*person*) hacer daño a; (*health, interests*) perjudicar; (*thing*) dañar; **out of ~'s way** a salvo; **harmful** adj dañino; **harmless** adj (*person*) inofensivo; (*joke etc*) inocente

**harmony** ['hɑːmənɪ] n armonía

**harness** ['hɑːnɪs] n arreos mpl; (*for child*) arnés m; (*safety harness*) arneses mpl ▷ vt (*horse*) enjaezar; (*resources*) aprovechar

**harp** [hɑːp] n arpa ▷ vi: **to ~ on (about)** machacar (con)

**harsh** [hɑːʃ] adj (*cruel*) duro, cruel; (*severe*) severo; (*sound*) áspero; (*light*) deslumbrador(a)

**harvest** ['hɑːvɪst] n (*harvest time*) siega; (*of cereals etc*) cosecha; (*of grapes*) vendimia ▷ vt cosechar

**has** [hæz] vb see **have**

**hasn't** ['hæznt] = **has not**

**hassle** ['hæsl] (*inf*) n lata

**haste** [heɪst] n prisa; **hasten** ['heɪsn] vt acelerar ▷ vi darse prisa; **hastily** adv de prisa; precipitadamente; **hasty** adj

apresurado; (*rash*) precipitado

**hat** [hæt] n sombrero

**hatch** [hætʃ] n (*Naut: also:* **~way**) escotilla; (*also:* **service ~**) ventanilla ▷ vi (*bird*) salir del cascarón ▷ vt incubar; (*plot*) tramar; **5 eggs have ~ed** han salido 5 pollos

**hatchback** ['hætʃbæk] n (*Aut*) tres or cinco puertas m

**hate** [heɪt] vt odiar, aborrecer ▷ n odio; **hatred** ['heɪtrɪd] n odio

**haul** [hɔːl] vt tirar ▷ n (*of fish*) redada; (*of stolen goods etc*) botín m

**haunt** [hɔːnt] vt (*ghost*) aparecerse en; (*obsess*) obsesionar ▷ n guarida; **haunted** adj (*castle etc*) embrujado; (*look*) de angustia

○ KEYWORD

**have** [hæv] (*pt, pp* **had**) aux vb 1 (*gen*) haber; **to have arrived/eaten** haber llegado/comido; **having finished** or **when he had finished, he left** cuando hubo acabado, se fue

2 (*in tag questions*): **you've done it, haven't you?** lo has hecho, ¿verdad? or ¿no?

3 (*in short answers and questions*): **I haven't** no; **so I have** pues, es verdad; **we haven't paid – yes we have!** no hemos pagado – ¡sí que hemos pagado!; **I've been there before, have you?** he estado allí antes, ¿y tú?

▷ modal aux vb (*be obliged*): **to have (got) to do sth** tener que hacer algo; **you haven't to tell her** no hay que or no debes decírselo

▷ vt 1 (*possess*): **he has (got) blue eyes/ dark hair** tiene los ojos azules/el pelo negro

2 (*referring to meals etc*): **to have breakfast/ lunch/dinner** desayunar/comer/cenar; **to have a drink/a cigarette** tomar algo/ fumar un cigarrillo

3 (*receive*) recibir; (*obtain*) obtener; **may I have your address?** ¿puedes darme tu dirección?; **you can have it for £5** te lo puedes quedar por £5; **I must have it by tomorrow** lo necesito para mañana; **to have a baby** tener un niño or bebé

4 (*maintain, allow*): **I won't have it/this nonsense!** ¡no lo permitiré!/¡no permitiré estas tonterías!; **we can't have that** no podemos permitir eso

5 **to have sth done** hacer or mandar hacer algo; **to have one's hair cut** cortarse el pelo; **to have sb do sth** hacer que algn haga algo

6 (*experience, suffer*): **to have a cold/flu** tener un resfriado/la gripe; **she had her bag stolen/her arm broken** le robaron el bolso/se rompió un brazo; **to have an**

**operation** operarse
**7** (+ noun): **to have a swim/walk/bath/rest** nadar/dar un paseo/darse un baño/ descansar; **let's have a look** vamos a ver; **to have a meeting/party** celebrar una reunión/una fiesta; **let me have a try** déjame intentarlo

**haven** ['heɪvn] n puerto; (fig) refugio
**haven't** ['hævnt] = **have not**
**havoc** ['hævək] n estragos mpl
**Hawaii** [hə'waɪi:] n (Islas fpl) Hawai fpl
**hawk** [hɔ:k] n halcón m
**hawthorn** ['hɔ:θɔ:n] n espino
**hay** [heɪ] n heno; **hay fever** n fiebre f del heno; **haystack** n almiar m
**hazard** ['hæzəd] n peligro ▷ vt aventurar; **hazardous** adj peligroso; **hazard warning lights** npl (Aut) señales fpl de emergencia
**haze** [heɪz] n neblina
**hazel** ['heɪzl] n (tree) avellano ▷ adj (eyes) color m de avellano; **hazelnut** n avellana
**hazy** ['heɪzɪ] adj brumoso; (idea) vago
**he** [hi:] pron él; **~ who ...** él que ..., quien ...
**head** [hɛd] n cabeza; (leader) jefe a m/f; (of school) director(a) m/f ▷ vt (list) encabezar; (group) capitanear; (company) dirigir; **~s (or tails)** cara (o cruz); **~ first** de cabeza; **~ over heels** (in love) perdidamente; **to ~ the ball** cabecear (la pelota); **head for** vt fus dirigirse a; (disaster) ir camino de; **head off** vt (threat, danger) evitar; **headache** n dolor m de cabeza; **heading** n título; **headlamp** (BRIT) n = **headlight**; **headlight** n faro; **headline** n titular m; **head office** n oficina central, central f; **headphones** npl auriculares mpl; **headquarters** npl sede f central; (Mil) cuartel m general; **headroom** n (in car) altura interior; (under bridge) (límite m de) altura; **headscarf** n pañuelo; **headset** n cascos mpl; **headteacher** n director(a)(a); **head waiter** n maître m
**heal** [hi:l] vt curar ▷ vi cicatrizarse
**health** [hɛlθ] n salud f; **health care** n asistencia sanitaria; **health centre** (BRIT) n ambulatorio, centro médico; **health food** n alimentos mpl orgánicos; **Health Service** (BRIT) n el servicio de salud pública, ≈ el Insalud (SP); **healthy** adj sano, saludable
**heap** [hi:p] n montón m ▷ vt: **to ~ (up)** amontonar; **to ~ sth with** llenar algo hasta arriba de; **~s of** un montón de
**hear** [hɪə*] (pt, pp **~d**) vt (also Law) oír; (news) saber ▷ vi oír; **to ~ about** oír hablar de; **to ~ from sb** tener noticias de algn
**heard** [hɜ:d] pt, pp of **hear**
**hearing** [ˈhɪərɪŋ] n (sense) oído; (Law) vista;

**hearing aid** n audífono
**hearse** [hɜ:s] n coche m fúnebre
**heart** [hɑ:t] n corazón m; (fig) valor m; (of lettuce) cogollo; **hearts** npl (Cards) corazones mpl; **to lose/take ~** descorazonarse/cobrar ánimo; **at ~** en el fondo; **by ~** (learn, know) de memoria; **heart attack** n infarto (de miocardio); **heartbeat** n latido (del corazón); **heartbroken** adj: **she was heartbroken about it** esto le partió el corazón; **heartburn** n acedía; **heart disease** n enfermedad f cardíaca
**hearth** [hɑ:θ] n (fireplace) chimenea
**heartless** ['hɑ:tlɪs] adj despiadado
**hearty** ['hɑ:tɪ] adj (person) campechano; (laugh) sano; (dislike, support) absoluto
**heat** [hi:t] n calor m; (Sport: also: **qualifying ~**) prueba eliminatoria ▷ vt calentar; **heat up** vi calentarse ▷ vt calentar; **heated** adj caliente; (fig) acalorado; **heater** n estufa; (in car) calefacción f
**heather** ['hɛðə*] n brezo
**heating** ['hi:tɪŋ] n calefacción f
**heatwave** ['hi:tweɪv] n ola de calor
**heaven** ['hɛvn] n cielo; (fig) una maravilla; **heavenly** adj celestial; (fig) maravilloso
**heavily** ['hɛvɪlɪ] adv pesadamente; (drink, smoke) con exceso; (sleep, sigh) profundamente; (depend) mucho
**heavy** ['hɛvɪ] adj pesado; (work, blow) duro; (sea, rain, meal) fuerte; (drinker, smoker) grande; (responsibility) grave; (schedule) ocupado; (weather) bochornoso
**Hebrew** ['hi:bru:] adj, n (Ling) hebreo
**hectare** ['hɛktɑ:*] n (BRIT) hectárea
**hectic** ['hɛktɪk] adj agitado
**he'd** [hi:d] = **he would; he had**
**hedge** [hɛdʒ] n seto ▷ vi contestar con evasivas; **to ~ one's bets** cubrirse
**hedgehog** ['hɛdʒhɔg] n erizo
**heed** [hi:d] vt (also: **take ~**: pay attention to) hacer caso de
**heel** [hi:l] n talón m; (of shoe) tacón m ▷ vt (shoe) poner tacón a
**hefty** ['hɛftɪ] adj (person) fornido; (parcel, profit) gordo
**height** [haɪt] n (of person) estatura; (of building) altura; (high ground) cerro; (altitude) altitud f; (fig: of season): **at the ~ of summer** en los días más calurosos del verano; (: of power etc) cúspide f; (: of stupidity etc) colmo; **heighten** vt elevar; (fig) aumentar
**heir** [ɛə*] n heredero; **heiress** n heredera
**held** [hɛld] pt, pp of **hold**
**helicopter** ['hɛlɪkɔptə*] n helicóptero
**hell** [hɛl] n infierno; **~!** (inf) ¡demonios!

**he'll** [hi:l] = **he will; he shall**

**hello** [hə'ləu] *excl* ¡hola!; *(to attract attention)* ¡oiga!; *(surprise)* ¡caramba!

**helmet** ['hɛlmɪt] *n* casco

**help** [hɛlp] *n* ayuda; *(cleaner etc)* criada, asistenta ▷ *vt* ayudar; **~!** ¡socorro!; **~ yourself** sírvete; **he can't ~ it** no es culpa suya; **help out** *vi* ayudar, echar una mano ▷ *vt*: **to help sb out** ayudar a algn, echar una mano a algn; **helper** *n* ayudante *mf*; **helpful** *adj* útil; *(person)* servicial; *(advice)* útil; **helping** *n* ración *f*; **helpless** *adj* *(incapable)* incapaz; *(defenceless)* indefenso; **helpline** *n* teléfono de asistencia al público

**hem** [hɛm] *n* dobladillo ▷ *vt* poner or coser el dobladillo de

**hemisphere** ['hɛmɪsfɪə*] *n* hemisferio

**hemorrhage** ['hɛmərɪdʒ] *(US)* *n* = **haemorrhage**

**hemorrhoids** ['hɛmərɔɪdz] *(US)* *npl* = **haemorrhoids**

**hen** [hɛn] *n* gallina; *(female bird)* hembra

**hence** [hɛns] *adv* *(therefore)* por lo tanto; **2 years ~** de aquí a 2 años

**hen night, hen party** *n* *(inf)* despedida de soltera

**hepatitis** [hɛpə'taɪtɪs] *n* hepatitis *f*

**her** [hə:*] *pron* *(direct)* la; *(indirect)* le; *(stressed, after prep)* ella ▷ *adj* su; *see also* **me; my**

**herb** [hə:b] *n* hierba; **herbal** *adj* de hierbas; **herbal tea** *n* infusión *f* de hierbas

**herd** [hə:d] *n* rebaño

**here** [hɪə*] *adv* aquí; *(at this point)* en este punto; **~!** *(present)* ¡presente!; **~ is/are** aquí está/están; **~ she is** aquí está

**hereditary** [hɪ'rɛdɪtrɪ] *adj* hereditario

**heritage** ['hɛrɪtɪdʒ] *n* patrimonio

**hernia** ['hə:nɪə] *n* hernia

**hero** ['hɪərəu] *(pl ~es)* *n* héroe *m*; *(in book, film)* protagonista *m*; **heroic** [hɪ'rəuɪk] *adj* heroico

**heroin** ['hɛrəuɪn] *n* heroína

**heroine** ['hɛrəuɪn] *n* heroína; *(in book, film)* protagonista

**heron** ['hɛrən] *n* garza

**herring** ['hɛrɪŋ] *n* arenque *m*

**hers** [hə:z] *pron* (el) suyo/(la) suya) *etc*; *see also* **mine¹**

**herself** [hə:'sɛlf] *pron* *(reflexive)* se; *(emphatic)* ella misma; *(after prep)* sí (misma); *see also* **oneself**

**he's** [hi:z] = **he is; he has**

**hesitant** ['hɛzɪtənt] *adj* vacilante

**hesitate** ['hɛzɪteɪt] *vi* vacilar; *(in speech)* titubear; *(be unwilling)* resistirse a; **hesitation** ['-teɪʃən] *n* indecisión *f*; titubeo; dudas *fpl*

**heterosexual** [hɛtərəu'sɛksjuəl] *adj* heterosexual

**hexagon** ['hɛksəgən] *n* hexágono

**hey** [heɪ] *excl* ¡oye!, ¡oiga!

**heyday** ['heɪdeɪ] *n*: **the ~ of** el apogeo de

**HGV** *n abbr* (= *heavy goods vehicle*) vehículo pesado

**hi** [haɪ] *excl* ¡hola!; *(to attract attention)* ¡oiga!

**hibernate** ['haɪbəneɪt] *vi* invernar

**hiccough** ['hɪkʌp] = **hiccup**

**hiccup** ['hɪkʌp] *vi* hipar

**hid** [hɪd] *pt of* **hide**

**hidden** ['hɪdn] *pp of* **hide** ▷ *adj*: **~ agenda** plan *m* encubierto

**hide** [haɪd] *(pt hid, pp hidden)* *n* *(skin)* piel *f* ▷ *vt* esconder, ocultar ▷ *vi*: **to ~ (from sb)** esconderse or ocultarse (de algn)

**hideous** ['hɪdɪəs] *adj* horrible

**hiding** ['haɪdɪŋ] *n* *(beating)* paliza; **to be in ~** *(concealed)* estar escondido

**hi-fi** ['haɪfaɪ] *n* estéreo, hifi *m* ▷ *adj* de alta fidelidad

**high** [haɪ] *adj* alto; *(speed, number)* grande; *(price)* elevado; *(wind)* fuerte; *(voice)* agudo ▷ *adv* alto, a gran altura; **it is 20 m ~** tiene 20 m de altura; **~ in the air** en las alturas; **highchair** *n* silla alta; **high-class** *adj* *(hotel)* de lujo; *(person)* distinguido, de categoría; *(food)* de alta categoría; **higher education** *n* educación *f* or enseñanza superior; **high heels** *npl* *(heels)* tacones *mpl* altos; *(shoes)* zapatos *mpl* de tacón; **high jump** *n* *(Sport)* salto de altura; **highlands** ['haɪləndz] *npl* tierras *fpl* altas; **the Highlands** *(in Scotland)* las Tierras Altas de Escocia; **highlight** *n* *(fig: of event)* punto culminante ▷ *vt* subrayar; **highlights** *npl* *(in hair)* reflejos *mpl*; **highlighter** *n* rotulador; **highly** *adv* *(paid)* muy bien; *(critical, confidential)* sumamente; *(a lot)*: **to speak/think highly of** hablar muy bien de/tener en mucho a; **highness** *n* altura; **Her/His Highness** Su Alteza; **high-rise** *n* *(also:* **high-rise block, high-rise building***)* torre *f* de pisos; **high school** *n* ≈ Instituto Nacional de Bachillerato *(SP)*; **high season** *(BRIT)* *n* temporada alta; **high street** *(BRIT)* *n* calle *f* mayor; **high-tech** *(inf)* *adj* al-tec *(inf)*, de alta tecnología; **highway** *n* carretera; *(US)* carretera nacional; autopista; **Highway Code** *(BRIT)* *n* código de la circulación

**hijack** ['haɪdʒæk] *vt* secuestrar; **hijacker** *n* secuestrador(a) *m/f*

**hike** [haɪk] *vi* *(go walking)* ir de excursión (a pie) ▷ *n* caminata; **hiker** *n* excursionista *mf*; **hiking** *n* senderismo

**hilarious** [hɪ'lɛərɪəs] *adj* divertidísimo

**hill** [hɪl] *n* colina; *(high)* montaña; *(slope)* cuesta; **hillside** *n* ladera; **hill walking** *n* senderismo (de montaña); **hilly** *adj* montañoso

**him** [hɪm] *pron (direct)* le, lo; *(indirect)* le; *(stressed, after prep)* él; *see also* **me**; **himself** *pron (reflexive)* se; *(emphatic)* él mismo; *(after prep)* sí (mismo); *see also* **oneself**

**hind** [haɪnd] *adj* posterior

**hinder** ['hɪndə*] *vt* estorbar, impedir

**hindsight** ['haɪndsaɪt] *n:* **with ~** en retrospectiva

**Hindu** ['hɪnduː] *n* hindú *mf*; **Hinduism** *n (Rel)* hinduismo

**hinge** [hɪndʒ] *n* bisagra, gozne *m* ▷ *vi (fig):* **to ~ on** depender de

**hint** [hɪnt] *n* indirecta; *(advice)* consejo; *(sign)* dejo ▷ *vt:* **to ~ that** insinuar que ▷ *vi:* **to ~ at** hacer alusión a

**hip** [hɪp] *n* cadera

**hippie** ['hɪpɪ] *n* hippie *m/f*, jipi *m/f*

**hippo** ['hɪpəʊ] *(pl* **~s)** *n* hipopótamo

**hippopotamus** [hɪpə'pɒtəməs] *(pl* **~es** *or* **hippopotami)** *n* hipopótamo

**hippy** ['hɪpɪ] *n* = **hippie**

**hire** ['haɪə*] *vt (BRIT: car, equipment)* alquilar; *(worker)* contratar ▷ *n* alquiler *m*; **for ~** se alquila; *(taxi)* libre; **hire(d) car** *(BRIT) n* coche *m* de alquiler; **hire purchase** *(BRIT) n* compra a plazos

**his** [hɪz] *pron* (el) suyo/(la) suya) *etc* ▷ *adj* su; *see also* **mine¹**; **my**

**Hispanic** [hɪs'pænɪk] *adj* hispánico

**hiss** [hɪs] *vi* silbar

**historian** [hɪ'stɔːrɪən] *n* historiador(a) *m/f*

**historic(al)** [hɪ'stɔrɪk(l)] *adj* histórico

**history** ['hɪstərɪ] *n* historia

**hit** [hɪt] *(pt, pp* **~)** *vt (strike)* golpear, pegar; *(reach: target)* alcanzar; *(collide with: car)* chocar contra; *(fig: affect)* afectar ▷ *n* golpe *m*; *(success)* éxito; *(on website)* visita; *(in web search)* correspondencia; **to ~ it off with sb** llevarse bien con algn; **hit back** *vi* defenderse; *(fig)* devolver golpe por golpe

**hitch** [hɪtʃ] *vt (fasten)* atar, amarrar; *(also: ~ up)* remangar ▷ *n (difficulty)* dificultad *f*; **to ~ a lift** hacer autostop

**hitch-hike** ['hɪtʃhaɪk] *vi* hacer autostop; **hitch-hiker** *n* autostopista *m/f*; **hitch-hiking** *n* autostop *m*

**hi-tech** [haɪ'tɛk] *adj* de alta tecnología

**hitman** ['hɪtmæn] *(irreg) n* asesino a sueldo

**HIV** *n abbr* (= *human immunodeficiency virus*) VIH *m*; **~-negative/positive** VIH negativo/positivo

**hive** [haɪv] *n* colmena

**hoard** [hɔːd] *n (treasure)* tesoro; *(stockpile)* provisión *f* ▷ *vt* acumular; *(goods in short supply)* acaparar

**hoarse** [hɔːs] *adj* ronco

**hoax** [həʊks] *n* trampa

**hob** [hɒb] *n* quemador *m*

**hobble** ['hɒbl] *vi* cojear

**hobby** ['hɒbɪ] *n* pasatiempo, afición *f*

**hobo** ['həʊbəʊ] *(US) n* vagabundo

**hockey** ['hɒkɪ] *n* hockey *m*; **hockey stick** *n* palo *m* de hockey

**hog** [hɒg] *n* cerdo, puerco ▷ *vt (fig)* acaparar; **to go the whole ~** poner toda la carne en el asador

**Hogmanay** [hɒgmə'neɪ] *n ver abajo*

**hoist** [hɔɪst] *n (crane)* grúa ▷ *vt* levantar, alzar; *(flag, sail)* izar

**hold** [həʊld] *(pt, pp* **held)** *vt* sostener; *(contain)* contener; *(have: power, qualification)* tener; *(keep back)* retener; *(believe)* sostener; *(consider)* considerar; *(keep in position):* **to ~ one's head up** mantener la cabeza alta; *(meeting)* celebrar ▷ *vi (withstand pressure)* resistir; *(be valid)* valer ▷ *n (grasp)* asimiento; *(fig)* dominio; **~ the line!** *(Tel)* ¡no cuelgue!; **to ~ one's own** *(fig)* defenderse; **to catch** *or* **get (a) ~ of** agarrarse *or* asirse de; **hold back** *vt* retener; *(secret)* ocultar; **hold on** *vi* agarrarse bien; *(wait)* esperar; **hold on!** *(Tel)* ¡(espere) un momento!; **hold out** *vt* ofrecer ▷ *vi (resist)* resistir; **hold up** *vt (raise)* levantar; *(support)* apoyar; *(delay)* retrasar; *(rob)* asaltar; **holdall** *(BRIT) n* bolsa; **holder** *n (container)* receptáculo; *(of ticket, record)* poseedor(a) *m/f*; *(of office, title etc)* titular *mf*

**hole** [həʊl] *n* agujero

**holiday** ['hɒlədɪ] *n* vacaciones *fpl*; *(public holiday)* (día *m* de) fiesta, día *m* feriado; **on ~** de vacaciones; **holiday camp** *n (BRIT: also:* **holiday centre)** centro de vacaciones; **holiday job** *n (BRIT)* trabajillo extra para las vacaciones; **holiday-maker** (BRIT) n turista mf; **holiday resort** n centro turístico

**Holland** ['hɔlənd] n Holanda

**hollow** ['hɔləʊ] adj hueco; (claim) vacío; (eyes) hundido; (sound) sordo ▷ n hueco; (in ground) hoyo ▷ vt: **to ~ out** excavar

**holly** ['hɔlɪ] n acebo

**Hollywood** ['hɔlɪwʊd] n Hollywood m

**holocaust** ['hɔləkɔːst] n holocausto

**holy** ['həʊlɪ] adj santo, sagrado; (water) bendito

**home** [həʊm] n casa; (country) patria; (institution) asilo ▷ cpd (domestic) casero, de casa; (Econ, Pol) nacional ▷ adv (direction) a casa; (right in: nail etc) a fondo; **at ~** en casa; (in country) en el país; (fig) como pez en el agua; **to go/come ~** ir/volver a casa; **make yourself at ~** ¡estás en tu casa!; **home address** n domicilio; **homeland** n tierra natal; **homeless** adj sin hogar, sin casa; **homely** adj (simple) sencillo; **home-made** adj casero; **home match** n partido en casa; **Home Office** (BRIT) n Ministerio del Interior; **home owner** n propietario/a m/f de una casa; **home page** n página de inicio; **Home Secretary** (BRIT) n Ministro del Interior; **homesick** adj: **to be homesick** tener morriña, sentir nostalgia; **home town** n ciudad f natal; **homework** n deberes mpl

**homicide** ['hɔmɪsaɪd] (US) n homicidio

**homoeopathic** [həʊmɪə'pæθɪk] (US **homeopathic**) adj homeopático

**homoeopathy** [həʊmɪ'ɔpəθɪ] (US **homeopathy**) n homeopatía

**homosexual** [hɔməʊ'sɛksjʊəl] adj, n homosexual mf

**honest** ['ɔnɪst] adj honrado; (sincere) franco, sincero; **honestly** adv honradamente; francamente; **honesty** n honradez f

**honey** ['hʌnɪ] n miel f; **honeymoon** n luna de miel; **honeysuckle** n madreselva

**Hong Kong** ['hɔŋ'kɔŋ] n Hong-Kong m

**honorary** ['ɔnərərɪ] adj (member, president) de honor; (title) honorífico; **~ degree** doctorado honoris causa

**honour** ['ɔnə*] (US **honor**) vt honrar; (commitment, promise) cumplir con ▷ n honor m, honra; **to graduate with ~s** ≈ licenciarse con matrícula (de honor); **honourable** (US **honorable**) adj honorable; **honours degree** n (Scol) título de licenciado con calificación alta

**hood** [hʊd] n capucha; (BRIT Aut) capota; (US Aut) capó m; (of cooker) campana de humos; **hoodie** n (top) jersey m con capucha

**hoof** [huːf] (pl **hooves**) n pezuña

**hook** [hʊk] n gancho; (on dress) corchete m, broche m; (for fishing) anzuelo ▷ vt enganchar; (fish) pescar

**hooligan** ['huːlɪgən] n gamberro

**hoop** [huːp] n aro

**hooray** [huː'reɪ] excl = **hurray**

**hoot** [huːt] (BRIT) vi (Aut) tocar el pito, pitar; (siren) (hacer) sonar; (owl) ulular

**Hoover®** ['huːvə*] (BRIT) n aspiradora ▷ vt: **to hoover** pasar la aspiradora por

**hooves** [huːvz] npl of **hoof**

**hop** [hɔp] vi saltar, brincar; (on one foot) saltar con un pie

**hope** [həʊp] vt, vi esperar ▷ n esperanza; **I ~ so/not** espero que sí/no; **hopeful** adj (person) optimista; (situation) prometedor(a); **hopefully** adv con esperanza; (one hopes): **hopefully he will recover** esperamos que se recupere; **hopeless** adj desesperado; (person): **to be hopeless** ser un desastre

**hops** [hɔps] npl lúpulo

**horizon** [hə'raɪzn] n horizonte m; **horizontal** [hɔrɪ'zɔntl] adj horizontal

**hormone** ['hɔːməʊn] n hormona

**horn** [hɔːn] n cuerno; (Mus: also: **French ~**) trompa; (Aut) pito, claxon m

**horoscope** ['hɔrəskəʊp] n horóscopo

**horrendous** [hə'rɛndəs] adj horrendo

**horrible** ['hɔrɪbl] adj horrible

**horrid** ['hɔrɪd] adj horrible, horroroso

**horrific** [hə'rɪfɪk] adj (accident) horroroso; (film) horripilante

**horrifying** ['hɔrɪfaɪɪŋ] adj horroroso

**horror** ['hɔrə*] n horror m; **horror film** n película de horror

**hors d'œuvre** [ɔː'dəːvrə] n entremeses mpl

**horse** [hɔːs] n caballo; **horseback** n: **on horseback** a caballo; **horse chestnut** n (tree) castaño de Indias; (nut) castaña de Indias; **horsepower** n caballo (de fuerza); **horse-racing** n carreras fpl de caballos; **horseradish** n rábano picante; **horse riding** n (BRIT) equitación f

**hose** [həʊz] n manguera; **hosepipe** n manguera

**hospital** ['hɔspɪtl] n hospital m

**hospitality** [hɔspɪ'tælɪtɪ] n hospitalidad f

**host** [həʊst] n anfitrión m; (TV, Radio) presentador m; (Rel) hostia; (large number): **a ~ of** multitud de

**hostage** ['hɔstɪdʒ] n rehén m

**hostel** ['hɔstl] n hostal m; **(youth) ~** albergue m juvenil

**hostess** ['həʊstɪs] n anfitriona; (BRIT: air hostess) azafata; (TV, Radio) presentadora

**hostile** ['hɔstaɪl] *adj* hostil
**hostility** [hɔ'stɪlɪtɪ] *n* hostilidad *f*
**hot** [hɔt] *adj* caliente; (*weather*) caluroso, de calor; (*as opposed to warm*) muy caliente; (*spicy*) picante; **to be ~** (*person*) tener calor; (*object*) estar caliente; (*weather*) hacer calor; **hot dog** *n* perro caliente
**hotel** [həʊ'tɛl] *n* hotel *m*
**hot-water bottle** [hɔt'wɔ:tə\*-] *n* bolsa de agua caliente
**hound** [haʊnd] *vt* acosar ▷ *n* perro (de caza)
**hour** ['aʊə\*] *n* hora; **hourly** *adj* (de) cada hora
**house** [*n* haʊs, *pl* 'haʊzɪz, *vb* haʊz] *n* (*gen, firm*) casa; (*Pol*) cámara; (*Theatre*) sala ▷ *vt* (*person*) alojar; (*collection*) albergar; **on the ~** (*fig*) la casa invita; **household** *n* familia; (*home*) casa; **householder** *n* propietario/a; (*head of house*) cabeza de familia; **housekeeper** *n* ama de llaves; **housekeeping** *n* (*work*) trabajos *mpl* domésticos; **housewife** (*irreg*) *n* ama de casa; **house wine** *n* vino *m* de la casa; **housework** *n* faenas *fpl* (de la casa)
**housing** ['haʊzɪŋ] *n* (*act*) alojamiento; (*houses*) viviendas *fpl*; **housing development, housing estate** (BRIT) *n* urbanización *f*
**hover** ['hɔvə\*] *vi* flotar (en el aire); **hovercraft** *n* aerodeslizador *m*
**how** [haʊ] *adv* (*in what way*) cómo; **~ are you?** ¿cómo estás?; **~ much milk/many people?** ¿cuánta leche/gente?; **~ much does it cost?** ¿cuánto cuesta?; **~ long have you been here?** ¿cuánto hace que estás aquí?; **~ old are you?** ¿cuántos años tienes?; **~ tall is he?** ¿cómo es de alto?; **~ is school?** ¿cómo (te) va (en) la escuela?; **~ was the film?** ¿qué tal la película?; **~ lovely/awful!** ¡qué bonito/horror!
**however** [haʊ'ɛvə\*] *adv*: **~ I do it** lo haga como lo haga; **~ cold it is** por mucho frío que haga; **~ fast he runs** por muy rápido que corra; **~ did you do it?** ¿cómo lo hiciste? ▷ *conj* sin embargo, no obstante
**howl** [haʊl] *n* aullido ▷ *vi* aullar; (*person*) dar alaridos; (*wind*) ulular
**H.P.** *n abbr* = **hire purchase**
**h.p.** *abbr* = **horsepower**
**HQ** *n abbr* = **headquarters**
**hr(s)** *abbr* (= *hour(s)*) h
**HTML** *n abbr* (= *hypertext markup language*) lenguaje *m* de hipertexto
**hubcap** ['hʌbkæp] *n* tapacubos *m inv*
**huddle** ['hʌdl] *vi*: **to ~ together** acurrucarse
**huff** [hʌf] *n*: **in a ~** enojado

**hug** [hʌg] *vt* abrazar; (*thing*) apretar con los brazos
**huge** [hju:dʒ] *adj* enorme
**hull** [hʌl] *n* (*of ship*) casco
**hum** [hʌm] *vt* tararear, canturrear ▷ *vi* tararear, canturrear; (*insect*) zumbar
**human** ['hju:mən] *adj, n* humano
**humane** [hju:'meɪn] *adj* humano, humanitario
**humanitarian** [hju:mænɪ'teərɪən] *adj* humanitario
**humanity** [hju:'mænɪtɪ] *n* humanidad *f*
**human rights** *npl* derechos *mpl* humanos
**humble** ['hʌmbl] *adj* humilde
**humid** ['hju:mɪd] *adj* húmedo; **humidity** [-'mɪdɪtɪ] *n* humedad *f*
**humiliate** [hju:'mɪlɪeɪt] *vt* humillar
**humiliating** [hju:'mɪlɪeɪtɪŋ] *adj* humillante, vergonzoso
**humiliation** [hju:mɪlɪ'eɪʃən] *n* humillación *f*
**hummus** ['huməs] *n* paté de garbanzos
**humorous** ['hju:mərəs] *adj* gracioso, divertido
**humour** ['hju:mə\*] (US **humor**) *n* humorismo, sentido del humor; (*mood*) humor *m* ▷ *vt* complacer
**hump** [hʌmp] *n* (*in ground*) montículo; (*camel's*) giba
**hunch** [hʌntʃ] *n* (*premonition*) presentimiento
**hundred** ['hʌndrəd] *num* ciento; (*before n*) cien; **~s of** centenares de; **hundredth** [-ɪdθ] *adj* centésimo
**hung** [hʌŋ] *pt, pp of* **hang**
**Hungarian** [hʌŋ'gɛərɪən] *adj, n* húngaro/a *m/f*
**Hungary** ['hʌŋgərɪ] *n* Hungría
**hunger** ['hʌŋgə\*] *n* hambre *f* ▷ *vi*: **to ~ for** (*fig*) tener hambre de, anhelar
**hungry** ['hʌŋgrɪ] *adj*: **~ (for)** hambriento (de); **to be ~** tener hambre
**hunt** [hʌnt] *vt* (*seek*) buscar; (*Sport*) cazar ▷ *vi* (*search*): **to ~ (for)** buscar; (*Sport*) cazar ▷ *n* búsqueda; caza, cacería; **hunter** *n* cazador(a) *m/f*; **hunting** *n* caza
**hurdle** ['hə:dl] *n* (*Sport*) valla; (*fig*) obstáculo
**hurl** [hə:l] *vt* lanzar, arrojar
**hurrah** [hu'rɑ:] *excl* = **hurray**
**hurray** [hu'reɪ] *excl* ¡viva!
**hurricane** ['hʌrɪkən] *n* huracán *m*
**hurry** ['hʌrɪ] *n* prisa ▷ *vt* (*also*: **~ up**: *person*) dar prisa a; (: *work*) apresurar, hacer de prisa; **to be in a ~** tener prisa; **hurry up** *vi* darse prisa, apurarse (LAM)
**hurt** [hə:t] (*pt, pp* **~**) *vt* hacer daño a ▷ *vi* doler ▷ *adj* lastimado

**husband** ['hʌzbənd] *n* marido

**hush** [hʌʃ] *n* silencio ▷ *vt* hacer callar; **~!** ¡chitón!, ¡cállate!

**husky** ['hʌski] *adj* ronco ▷ *n* perro esquimal

**hut** [hʌt] *n* cabaña; (*shed*) cobertizo

**hyacinth** ['haɪəsɪnθ] *n* jacinto

**hydrangea** [haɪ'dreɪnʒə] *n* hortensia

**hydrofoil** ['haɪdrəfɔɪl] *n* aerodeslizador *m*

**hydrogen** ['haɪdrədʒən] *n* hidrógeno

**hygiene** ['haɪdʒiːn] *n* higiene *f*; **hygienic** [-'dʒiːnɪk] *adj* higiénico

**hymn** [hɪm] *n* himno

**hype** [haɪp] (*inf*) *n* bombardeo publicitario

**hyphen** ['haɪfn] *n* guión *m*

**hypnotize** ['hɪpnətaɪz] *vt* hipnotizar

**hypocrite** ['hɪpəkrɪt] *n* hipócrita *mf*

**hypocritical** [hɪpə'krɪtɪkl] *adj* hipócrita

**hypothesis** [haɪ'pɔθɪsɪs] (*pl* **hypotheses**) *n* hipótesis *f inv*

**hysterical** [hɪ'sterɪkl] *adj* histérico; (*funny*) para morirse de risa

**hysterics** [hɪ'sterɪks] *npl* histeria; **to be in ~** (*fig*) morirse de risa

---

**I** [aɪ] *pron* yo

**ice** [aɪs] *n* hielo; (*ice cream*) helado ▷ *vt* (*cake*) alcorzar ▷ *vi* (*also:* **~ over, ~ up**) helarse; **iceberg** *n* iceberg *m*; **ice cream** *n* helado; **ice cube** *n* cubito de hielo; **ice hockey** *n* hockey *m* sobre hielo

**Iceland** ['aɪslənd] *n* Islandia; **Icelander** *n* islandés/esa *m/f*; **Icelandic** [aɪs'lændɪk] *adj* islandés/esa ▷ *n* (*Ling*) islandés *m*

**ice: ice lolly** (*BRIT*) *n* polo; **ice rink** *n* pista de hielo; **ice skating** *n* patinaje *m* sobre hielo

**icing** ['aɪsɪŋ] *n* (*Culin*) alcorza; **icing sugar** (*BRIT*) *n* azúcar *m* glas(eado)

**icon** ['aɪkɔn] *n* icono

**ICT** (*BRIT: Scol*) *n abbr* (= *information and communications technology*) informática

**icy** ['aɪsɪ] *adj* helado

**I'd** [aɪd] = **I would; I had**

**ID card** *n* (*identity card*) DNI *m*

**idea** [aɪ'dɪə] *n* idea

**ideal** [aɪ'dɪəl] *n* ideal *m* ▷ *adj* ideal; **ideally** [-dɪəlɪ] *adv* idealmente; **they're ideally suited** hacen una pareja ideal

**identical** [aɪ'dentɪkl] *adj* idéntico

**identification** [aɪdentɪfɪ'keɪʃən] *n* identificación *f*; **(means of) ~** documentos *mpl* personales

**identify** [aɪ'dentɪfaɪ] *vt* identificar

**identity** [aɪ'dentɪtɪ] *n* identidad *f*; **identity card** *n* carnet *m* de identidad; **identity theft** *n* robo de identidad

**ideology** [aɪdɪ'ɔlədʒɪ] *n* ideología

**idiom** ['ɪdɪəm] *n* modismo; (*style of speaking*) lenguaje *m*

> Be careful not to translate **idiom** by the Spanish word *idioma*.

**idiot** ['ɪdɪət] *n* idiota *mf*

**idle** ['aɪdl] *adj* (*inactive*) ocioso; (*lazy*) holgazán/ana; (*unemployed*) parado, desocupado; (*machinery etc*) parado; (*talk etc*) frívolo ▷ vi *(machine)* marchar en vacío

**idol** ['aɪdl] n ídolo

**idyllic** [ɪ'dɪlɪk] adj idílico

**i.e.** abbr *(= that is)* esto es

**if** [ɪf] conj si; **~ necessary** si fuera necesario, si hiciese falta; **~ I were you** yo en tu lugar; **~ so/not** de ser así/si no; **~ only I could!** ¡ojalá pudiera!; *see also* **as; even**

**ignite** [ɪg'naɪt] vt *(set fire to)* encender ▷ vi encenderse

**ignition** [ɪg'nɪʃən] n *(Aut: process)* ignición f; *(: mechanism)* encendido; **to switch on/off the ~** arrancar/apagar el motor

**ignorance** ['ɪgnərəns] n ignorancia

**ignorant** ['ɪgnərənt] adj ignorante; **to be ~ of** ignorar

**ignore** [ɪg'nɔː*] vt *(person, advice)* no hacer caso de; *(fact)* pasar por alto

**I'll** [aɪl] = **I will; I shall**

**ill** [ɪl] adj enfermo, malo ▷ n mal m ▷ adv mal; **to be taken ~** ponerse enfermo

**illegal** [ɪ'liːgl] adj ilegal

**illegible** [ɪ'ledʒɪbl] adj ilegible

**illegitimate** [ɪlɪ'dʒɪtɪmət] adj ilegítimo

**ill health** n mala salud f; **to be in ~** estar mal de salud

**illiterate** [ɪ'lɪtərət] adj analfabeto

**illness** ['ɪlnɪs] n enfermedad f

**illuminate** [ɪ'luːmɪneɪt] vt *(room, street)* iluminar, alumbrar

**illusion** [ɪ'luːʒən] n ilusión f; *(trick)* truco

**illustrate** ['ɪləstreɪt] vt ilustrar

**illustration** [ɪlə'streɪʃən] n *(act of illustrating)* ilustración f; *(example)* ejemplo, ilustración f; *(in book)* lámina

**I'm** [aɪm] = **I am**

**image** ['ɪmɪdʒ] n imagen f

**imaginary** [ɪ'mædʒɪnərɪ] adj imaginario

**imagination** [ɪmædʒɪ'neɪʃən] n imaginación f; *(inventiveness)* inventiva

**imaginative** [ɪ'mædʒɪnətɪv] adj imaginativo

**imagine** [ɪ'mædʒɪn] vt imaginarse

**imbalance** [ɪm'bæləns] n desequilibrio

**imitate** ['ɪmɪteɪt] vt imitar; **imitation** [ɪmɪ'teɪʃən] n imitación f; *(copy)* copia

**immaculate** [ɪ'mækjulət] adj inmaculado

**immature** [ɪmə'tjuə*] adj *(person)* inmaduro

**immediate** [ɪ'miːdɪət] adj inmediato; *(pressing)* urgente, apremiante; *(nearest: family)* próximo; *(: neighbourhood)* inmediato; **immediately** adv *(at once)* en seguida; *(directly)* inmediatamente; **immediately next to** muy junto a

**immense** [ɪ'mɛns] adj inmenso, enorme; *(importance)* enorme; **immensely** adv enormemente

**immerse** [ɪ'mɜːs] vt *(submerge)* sumergir; **to be ~d in** *(fig)* estar absorto en

**immigrant** ['ɪmɪgrənt] n inmigrante mf; **immigration** [ɪmɪ'greɪʃən] n inmigración f

**imminent** ['ɪmɪnənt] adj inminente

**immoral** [ɪ'mɔrl] adj inmoral

**immortal** [ɪ'mɔːtl] adj inmortal

**immune** [ɪ'mjuːn] adj: **~ (to)** inmune (a); **immune system** n sistema m inmunitario

**immunize** ['ɪmjunaɪz] vt inmunizar

**impact** ['ɪmpækt] n impacto

**impair** [ɪm'pɛə*] vt perjudicar

**impartial** [ɪm'pɑːʃl] adj imparcial

**impatience** [ɪm'peɪʃəns] n impaciencia

**impatient** [ɪm'peɪʃənt] adj impaciente; **to get** or **grow ~** impacientarse

**impeccable** [ɪm'pɛkəbl] adj impecable

**impending** [ɪm'pɛndɪŋ] adj inminente

**imperative** [ɪm'pɛrətɪv] adj *(tone)* imperioso; *(need)* imprescindible

**imperfect** [ɪm'pəːfɪkt] adj *(goods etc)* defectuoso ▷ n *(Ling: also: ~ tense)* imperfecto

**imperial** [ɪm'pɪərɪəl] adj imperial

**impersonal** [ɪm'pəːsənl] adj impersonal

**impersonate** [ɪm'pəːsəneɪt] vt hacerse pasar por; *(Theatre)* imitar

**impetus** ['ɪmpətəs] n ímpetu m; *(fig)* impulso

**implant** [ɪm'plɑːnt] vt *(Med)* injertar, implantar; *(fig: idea, principle)* inculcar

**implement** [n 'ɪmplɪmənt, vb 'ɪmplɪmɛnt] n herramienta; *(for cooking)* utensilio ▷ vt *(regulation)* hacer efectivo; *(plan)* realizar

**implicate** ['ɪmplɪkeɪt] vt *(compromise)* comprometer; **to ~ sb in sth** comprometer a algn en algo

**implication** [ɪmplɪ'keɪʃən] n consecuencia; **by ~** indirectamente

**implicit** [ɪm'plɪsɪt] adj implícito; *(belief, trust)* absoluto

**imply** [ɪm'plaɪ] vt *(involve)* suponer; *(hint)* dar a entender que

**impolite** [ɪmpə'laɪt] adj mal educado

**import** [vb ɪm'pɔːt, n 'ɪmpɔːt] vt importar ▷ n *(Comm)* importación f; *(article)* producto importado; *(meaning)* significado, sentido

**importance** [ɪm'pɔːtəns] n importancia

**important** [ɪm'pɔːtənt] adj importante; **it's not ~** no importa, no tiene importancia

**importer** [ɪm'pɔːtə*] n importador(a) m/f

**impose** [ɪm'pəuz] vt imponer ▷ vi: **to ~ on sb** abusar de algn; **imposing** adj imponente, impresionante

**impossible** [ɪm'pɔsɪbl] adj imposible;

(*person*) insoportable

**impotent** ['ɪmpətənt] *adj* impotente

**impoverished** [ɪm'pɒvərɪʃt] *adj* necesitado

**impractical** [ɪm'præktɪkl] *adj* (*person, plan*) poco práctico

**impress** [ɪm'prɛs] *vt* impresionar; (*mark*) estampar; **to ~ sth on sb** hacer entender algo a algn

**impression** [ɪm'prɛʃən] *n* impresión *f*; (*imitation*) imitación *f*; **to be under the ~ that** tener la impresión de que

**impressive** [ɪm'prɛsɪv] *adj* impresionante

**imprison** [ɪm'prɪzn] *vt* encarcelar; **imprisonment** *n* encarcelamiento; (*term of imprisonment*) cárcel *f*

**improbable** [ɪm'prɒbəbl] *adj* improbable, inverosímil

**improper** [ɪm'prɒpə*] *adj* (*unsuitable: conduct etc*) incorrecto; (*: activities*) deshonesto

**improve** [ɪm'pruːv] *vt* mejorar; (*foreign language*) perfeccionar ▷ *vi* mejorarse; **improvement** *n* mejoramiento; perfección *f*; progreso

**improvise** ['ɪmprəvaɪz] *vt, vi* improvisar

**impulse** ['ɪmpʌls] *n* impulso; **to act on ~** obrar sin reflexión; **impulsive** [ɪm'pʌlsɪv] *adj* irreflexivo

○ **KEYWORD**

**in** [ɪn] *prep* 1 (*indicating place, position, with place names*) en; **in the house/garden** en (la) casa/el jardín; **in here/there** aquí/ahí or allí dentro; **in London/England** en Londres/Inglaterra

2 (*indicating time*) en; **in spring** en (la) primavera; **in the afternoon** por la tarde; **at 4 o'clock in the afternoon** a las 4 de la tarde; **I did it in 3 hours/days** lo hice en 3 horas/días; **I'll see you in 2 weeks** or **in 2 weeks' time** te veré dentro de 2 semanas

3 (*indicating manner etc*) en; **in a loud/soft voice** en voz alta/baja; **in pencil/ink** a lápiz/bolígrafo; **the boy in the blue shirt** el chico de la camisa azul

4 (*indicating circumstances*): **in the sun/shade/rain** al sol/a la sombra/bajo la lluvia; **a change in policy** un cambio de política

5 (*indicating mood, state*): **in tears** en lágrimas, llorando; **in anger/despair** enfadado/desesperado; **to live in luxury** vivir lujosamente

6 (*with ratios, numbers*): **1 in 10 households, 1 household in 10** una de cada 10 familias;

**20 pence in the pound** 20 peniques por libra; **they lined up in twos** se alinearon de dos en dos

7 (*referring to people, works*) en; entre; **the disease is common in children** la enfermedad es común entre los niños; **in (the works of) Dickens** en (las obras de) Dickens

8 (*indicating profession etc*): **to be in teaching** estar en la enseñanza

9 (*after superlative*) de; **the best pupil in the class** el(la) mejor alumno/a de la clase

10 (*with present participle*): **in saying this** al decir esto

▷ *adv*: **to be in** (*person: at home*) estar en casa; (*at work*) estar; (*train, ship, plane*) haber llegado; (*in fashion*) estar de moda; **she'll be in later today** llegará más tarde hoy; **to ask sb in** hacer pasar a algn; **to run/limp etc in** entrar corriendo/cojeando *etc*

▷ *n*: **the ins and outs** (*of proposal, situation etc*) los detalles

**inability** [ɪnə'bɪlɪtɪ] *n*: **~ (to do)** incapacidad *f* (de hacer)

**inaccurate** [ɪn'ækjurət] *adj* inexacto, incorrecto

**inadequate** [ɪn'ædɪkwət] *adj* (*income, reply etc*) insuficiente; (*person*) incapaz

**inadvertently** [ɪnəd'vəːtntlɪ] *adv* por descuido

**inappropriate** [ɪnə'prəʊprɪət] *adj* inadecuado; (*improper*) poco oportuno

**inaugurate** [ɪ'nɔːgjureɪt] *vt* inaugurar; (*president, official*) investir

**Inc.** (*us*) *abbr* (= *incorporated*) S.A.

**incapable** [ɪn'keɪpəbl] *adj* incapaz

**incense** [*n* 'ɪnsɛns, *vb* ɪn'sɛns] *n* incienso ▷ *vt* (*anger*) indignar, encolerizar

**incentive** [ɪn'sɛntɪv] *n* incentivo, estímulo

**inch** [ɪntʃ] *n* pulgada; **to be within an ~ of** estar a dos dedos de; **he didn't give an ~** no dio concesión alguna

**incidence** ['ɪnsɪdns] *n* (*of crime, disease*) incidencia

**incident** ['ɪnsɪdnt] *n* incidente *m*

**incidentally** [ɪnsɪ'dɛntəlɪ] *adv* (*by the way*) a propósito

**inclination** [ɪnklɪ'neɪʃən] *n* (*tendency*) tendencia, inclinación *f*; (*desire*) deseo; (*disposition*) propensión *f*

**incline** [*n* 'ɪnklaɪn, *vb* ɪn'klaɪn] *n* pendiente *m*, cuesta ▷ *vt* (*head*) poner de lado ▷ *vi* inclinarse; **to be ~d to** (*tend*) tener tendencia a hacer algo

**include** [ɪn'kluːd] *vt* (*incorporate*) incluir; (*in letter*) adjuntar; **including** *prep* incluso, inclusive

**inclusion** [ɪn'kluːʒən] n inclusión f

**inclusive** [ɪn'kluːsɪv] adj inclusivo; **~ of tax** incluidos los impuestos

**income** ['ɪŋkʌm] n (earned) ingresos mpl; (from property etc) renta; (from investment etc) rédito; **income support** n (BRIT) ≈ ayuda familiar; **income tax** n impuesto sobre la renta

**incoming** ['ɪnkʌmɪŋ] adj (flight, government etc) entrante

**incompatible** [ɪnkəm'pætɪbl] adj incompatible

**incompetence** [ɪn'kɔmpɪtəns] n incompetencia

**incompetent** [ɪn'kɔmpɪtənt] adj incompetente

**incomplete** [ɪnkəm'pliːt] adj (partial: achievement etc) incompleto; (unfinished: painting etc) inacabado

**inconsistent** [ɪnkən'sɪstənt] adj inconsecuente; (contradictory) incongruente; **~ with** (que) no concuerda con

**inconvenience** [ɪnkən'viːnjəns] n inconvenientes mpl; (trouble) molestia, incomodidad f ▷ vt incomodar

**inconvenient** [ɪnkən'viːnjənt] adj incómodo, poco práctico; (time, place, visitor) inoportuno

**incorporate** [ɪn'kɔːpəreɪt] vt incorporar; (contain) comprender; (add) agregar

**incorrect** [ɪnkə'rɛkt] adj incorrecto

**increase** [n 'ɪnkriːs, vb ɪn'kriːs] n aumento ▷ vi aumentar; (grow) crecer; (price) subir ▷ vt aumentar; (price) subir; **increasingly** adv cada vez más, más y más

**incredible** [ɪn'krɛdɪbl] adj increíble; **incredibly** adv increíblemente

**incur** [ɪn'kəː*] vt (expenditure) incurrir; (loss) sufrir; (anger, disapproval) provocar

**indecent** [ɪn'diːsnt] adj indecente

**indeed** [ɪn'diːd] adv efectivamente, en realidad; (in fact) en efecto; (furthermore) es más; **yes ~!** ¡claro que sí!

**indefinitely** [ɪn'dɛfɪnɪtlɪ] adv (wait) indefinidamente

**independence** [ɪndɪ'pɛndns] n independencia; **Independence Day** (US) n Día m de la Independencia

○ En ella se proclamaba la independencia
○ total de Gran Bretaña de las trece
○ colonias americanas que serían el origen
○ de los Estados Unidos de América.

**independent** [ɪndɪ'pɛndənt] adj independiente; **independent school** n (BRIT) escuela f privada, colegio m privado

**index** ['ɪndɛks] (pl **~es**) n (in book) índice m; (: in library etc) catálogo; (pl **indices**: ratio, sign) exponente m

**India** ['ɪndɪə] n la India; **Indian** adj, n indio/a; **Red Indian** piel roja mf

**indicate** ['ɪndɪkeɪt] vt indicar; **indication** [-'keɪʃən] n indicio, señal f; **indicative** [ɪn'dɪkətɪv] adj: **to be indicative of** indicar; **indicator** n indicador m; (Aut) intermitente m

**indices** ['ɪndɪsiːz] npl of **index**

**indict** [ɪn'daɪt] vt acusar; **indictment** n acusación f

**indifference** [ɪn'dɪfrəns] n indiferencia

**indifferent** [ɪn'dɪfrənt] adj indiferente; (mediocre) regular

**indigenous** [ɪn'dɪdʒɪnəs] adj indígena

**indigestion** [ɪndɪ'dʒɛstʃən] n indigestión f

**indignant** [ɪn'dɪgnənt] adj: **to be ~ at sth/ with sb** indignarse por algo/con algn

**indirect** [ɪndɪ'rɛkt] adj indirecto

**indispensable** [ɪndɪ'spɛnsəbl] adj indispensable, imprescindible

**individual** [ɪndɪ'vɪdjuəl] n individuo ▷ adj individual; (personal) personal; (particular) particular; **individually** adv (singly) individualmente

**Indonesia** [ɪndə'niːzɪə] n Indonesia

**indoor** ['ɪndɔː*] adj (swimming pool) cubierto; (plant) de interior; (sport) bajo cubierta; **indoors** [ɪn'dɔːz] adv dentro

**induce** [ɪn'djuːs] vt inducir, persuadir; (bring about) producir; (labour) provocar

**indulge** [ɪn'dʌldʒ] vt (whim) satisfacer; (person) complacer; (child) mimar ▷ vi: **to ~ in** darse el gusto de; **indulgent** adj indulgente

**industrial** [ɪn'dʌstrɪəl] adj industrial; **industrial estate** (BRIT) n polígono (SP) or zona (LAM) industrial; **industrialist** n industrial mf; **industrial park** (US) n = **industrial estate**

**industry** ['ɪndəstrɪ] n industria; (diligence) aplicación f

**inefficient** [ɪnɪ'fɪʃənt] adj ineficaz, ineficiente

**inequality** [ɪnɪ'kwɔlɪtɪ] n desigualdad f

**inevitable** [ɪn'ɛvɪtəbl] adj inevitable; **inevitably** adv inevitablemente

**inexpensive** [ɪnɪk'spɛnsɪv] adj económico

**inexperienced** [ɪnɪk'spɪərɪənst] adj inexperto

**inexplicable** [ɪnɪk'splɪkəbl] adj inexplicable

**infamous** ['ɪnfəməs] adj infame

**infant** ['ɪnfənt] n niño/a; (baby) niño/a pequeño/a, bebé mf; (pej) aniñado

**infantry** ['ɪnfəntrɪ] n infantería

**infant school** (BRIT) n parvulario

**infect** [ɪn'fɛkt] vt (wound) infectar; (food) contaminar; (person, animal) contagiar; **infection** [ɪn'fɛkʃən] n infección f; (fig) contagio; **infectious** [ɪn'fɛkʃəs] adj (also fig) contagioso

**infer** [ɪn'fə:*] vt deducir, inferir

**inferior** [ɪn'fɪərɪə*] adj, n inferior mf

**infertile** [ɪn'fə:taɪl] adj estéril; (person) infecundo

**infertility** [ɪnfə:'tɪlɪtɪ] n esterilidad f; infecundidad f

**infested** [ɪn'fɛstɪd] adj: **~ with** plagado de

**infinite** ['ɪnfɪnɪt] adj infinito; **infinitely** adv infinitamente

**infirmary** [ɪn'fə:mərɪ] n hospital m

**inflamed** [ɪn'fleɪmd] adj: **to become ~** inflamarse

**inflammation** [ɪnflə'meɪʃən] n inflamación f

**inflatable** [ɪn'fleɪtəbl] adj (ball, boat) inflable

**inflate** [ɪn'fleɪt] vt (tyre, price etc) inflar; (fig) hinchar; **inflation** [ɪn'fleɪʃən] n (Econ) inflación f

**inflexible** [ɪn'flɛksəbl] adj (rule) rígido; (person) inflexible

**inflict** [ɪn'flɪkt] vt: **to ~ sth on sb** infligir algo en algn

**influence** ['ɪnfluəns] n influencia ▷ vt influir en, influenciar; **under the ~ of alcohol** en estado de embriaguez; **influential** [-'ɛnʃl] adj influyente

**influx** ['ɪnflʌks] n afluencia

**info** (inf) ['ɪnfəʊ] n = **information**

**inform** [ɪn'fɔ:m] vt: **to ~ sb of sth** informar a algn sobre or de algo ▷ vi: **to ~ on sb** delatar a algn

**informal** [ɪn'fɔ:məl] adj (manner, tone) familiar; (dress, interview, occasion) informal; (visit, meeting) extraoficial

**information** [ɪnfə'meɪʃən] n información f; (knowledge) conocimientos mpl; **a piece of ~** un dato; **information office** n información f; **information technology** n informática

**informative** [ɪn'fɔ:mətɪv] adj informativo

**infra-red** [ɪnfrə'rɛd] adj infrarrojo

**infrastructure** ['ɪnfrəstrʌktʃə*] n (of system etc) infraestructura

**infrequent** [ɪn'fri:kwənt] adj infrecuente

**infuriate** [ɪn'fjʊərɪeɪt] vt: **to become ~d** ponerse furioso

**infuriating** [ɪn'fjʊərɪeɪtɪŋ] adj (habit, noise) enloquecedor(a)

**ingenious** [ɪn'dʒi:njəs] adj ingenioso

**ingredient** [ɪn'gri:dɪənt] n ingrediente m

**inhabit** [ɪn'hæbɪt] vt vivir en; **inhabitant** n habitante mf

**inhale** [ɪn'heɪl] vt inhalar ▷ vi (breathe in) aspirar; (in smoking) tragar; **inhaler** n inhalador m

**inherent** [ɪn'hɪərənt] adj: **~ in** or **to** inherente a

**inherit** [ɪn'hɛrɪt] vt heredar; **inheritance** n herencia; (fig) patrimonio

**inhibit** [ɪn'hɪbɪt] vt inhibir, impedir; **inhibition** [-'bɪʃən] n cohibición f

**initial** [ɪ'nɪʃl] adj primero ▷ n inicial f ▷ vt firmar con las iniciales; **initials** npl (as signature) iniciales fpl; (abbreviation) siglas fpl; **initially** adv al principio

**initiate** [ɪ'nɪʃɪeɪt] vt iniciar; **to ~ proceedings against sb** (Law) entablar proceso contra algn

**initiative** [ɪ'nɪʃətɪv] n iniciativa

**inject** [ɪn'dʒɛkt] vt inyectar; **to ~ sb with sth** inyectar algo a algn; **injection** [ɪn'dʒɛkʃən] n inyección f

**injure** ['ɪndʒə*] vt (hurt) herir, lastimar; (fig: reputation etc) perjudicar; **injured** adj (person, arm) herido, lastimado; **injury** n herida, lesión f; (wrong) perjuicio, daño

▌ Be careful not to translate **injury** by the Spanish word injuria.

**injustice** [ɪn'dʒʌstɪs] n injusticia

**ink** [ɪŋk] n tinta; **ink-jet printer** ['ɪŋkdʒɛt-] n impresora de chorro de tinta

**inland** [adj 'ɪnlənd, adv ɪn'lænd] adj (waterway, port etc) interior ▷ adv tierra adentro; **Inland Revenue** (BRIT) n departamento de impuestos ≈ Hacienda (SP)

**in-laws** ['ɪnlɔ:z] npl suegros mpl

**inmate** ['ɪnmeɪt] n (in prison) preso/a, presidiario/a; (in asylum) internado/a

**inn** [ɪn] n posada, mesón m

**inner** ['ɪnə*] adj (courtyard, calm) interior; (feelings) íntimo; **inner-city** adj (schools, problems) de las zonas céntricas pobres, de los barrios céntricos pobres

**inning** ['ɪnɪŋ] n (us: Baseball) inning m, entrada; **~s** (Cricket) entrada, turno

**innocence** ['ɪnəsns] n inocencia

**innocent** ['ɪnəsnt] adj inocente

**innovation** [ɪnəu'veɪʃən] n novedad f
**innovative** ['ɪnəu'veɪtɪv] adj innovador
**in-patient** ['ɪnpeɪʃənt] n paciente m/f interno/a
**input** ['ɪnput] n entrada; (of resources) inversión f; (Comput) entrada de datos
**inquest** ['ɪnkwɛst] n (coroner's) encuesta judicial
**inquire** [ɪn'kwaɪə*] vi preguntar ▷ vt: **to ~ whether** preguntar si; **to ~ about** (person) preguntar por; (fact) informarse de; **inquiry** n pregunta; (investigation) investigación f, pesquisa; **"Inquiries"** "Información"
**ins.** abbr = **inches**
**insane** [ɪn'seɪn] adj loco; (Med) demente
**insanity** [ɪn'sænɪtɪ] n demencia, locura
**insect** ['ɪnsɛkt] n insecto; **insect repellent** n loción f contra insectos
**insecure** [ɪnsɪ'kjuə*] adj inseguro
**insecurity** [ɪnsɪ'kjuərɪtɪ] n inseguridad f
**insensitive** [ɪn'sɛnsɪtɪv] adj insensible
**insert** [vb ɪn'sə:t, n 'ɪnsə:t] vt (into sth) introducir ▷ n encarte m
**inside** ['ɪn'saɪd] n interior m ▷ adj interior, interno ▷ adv (be) (por) dentro; (go) hacia dentro ▷ prep dentro de; (of time): **~ 10 minutes** en menos de 10 minutos; **inside lane** n (Aut: in Britain) carril m izquierdo; (: in US, Europe etc) carril m derecho; **inside out** adv (turn) al revés; (know) a fondo
**insight** ['ɪnsaɪt] n perspicacia
**insignificant** [ɪnsɪg'nɪfɪknt] adj insignificante
**insincere** [ɪnsɪn'sɪə*] adj poco sincero
**insist** [ɪn'sɪst] vi insistir; **to ~ on** insistir en; **to ~ that** insistir en que; (claim) exigir que; **insistent** adj insistente; (noise, action) persistente
**insomnia** [ɪn'sɔmnɪə] n insomnio
**inspect** [ɪn'spɛkt] vt inspeccionar, examinar; (troops) pasar revista a; **inspection** [ɪn'spɛkʃən] n inspección f, examen m; (of troops) revista; **inspector** n inspector(a) m/f; (BRIT: on buses, trains) revisor(a) m/f
**inspiration** [ɪnspə'reɪʃən] n inspiración f; **inspire** [ɪn'spaɪə*] vt inspirar; **inspiring** adj inspirador(a)
**instability** [ɪnstə'bɪlɪtɪ] n inestabilidad f
**install** [ɪn'stɔ:l] (US **instal**) vt instalar; (official) nombrar; **installation** [ɪnstə'leɪʃən] n instalación f
**installment** [ɪn'stɔ:lmənt] (US **installment**) n plazo; (of story) entrega; (of TV serial etc) capítulo; **in ~s** (pay, receive) a plazos
**instance** ['ɪnstəns] n ejemplo, caso; **for ~** por ejemplo; **in the first ~** en primer lugar

**instant** ['ɪnstənt] n instante m, momento ▷ adj inmediato; (coffee etc) instantáneo; **instantly** adv en seguida; **instant messaging** n mensajería instantánea
**instead** [ɪn'stɛd] adv en cambio; **~ of** en lugar de, en vez de
**instinct** ['ɪnstɪŋkt] n instinto; **instinctive** adj instintivo
**institute** ['ɪnstɪtju:t] n instituto; (professional body) colegio ▷ vt (begin) iniciar, empezar; (proceedings) entablar; (system, rule) establecer
**institution** [ɪnstɪ'tju:ʃən] n institución f; (Med: home) asilo; (: asylum) manicomio; (of system etc) establecimiento; (of custom) iniciación f
**instruct** [ɪn'strʌkt] vt: **to ~ sb in sth** instruir a algn en or sobre algo; **to ~ sb to do sth** dar instrucciones a algn de hacer algo; **instruction** [ɪn'strʌkʃən] n (teaching) instrucción f; **instructions** npl (orders) órdenes fpl; **instructions (for use)** modo de empleo; **instructor** n instructor(a) m/f
**instrument** ['ɪnstrəmənt] n instrumento; **instrumental** [-'mɛntl] adj (Mus) instrumental; **to be instrumental in** ser (el) artífice de
**insufficient** [ɪnsə'fɪʃənt] adj insuficiente
**insulate** ['ɪnsjuleɪt] vt aislar; **insulation** [-'leɪʃən] n aislamiento
**insulin** ['ɪnsjulɪn] n insulina
**insult** [n 'ɪnsʌlt, vb ɪn'sʌlt] n insulto ▷ vt insultar; **insulting** adj insultante
**insurance** [ɪn'ʃuərəns] n seguro; **fire/life ~** seguro contra incendios/sobre la vida; **insurance company** n compañía f de seguros; **insurance policy** n póliza (de seguros)
**insure** [ɪn'ʃuə*] vt asegurar
**intact** [ɪn'tækt] adj íntegro; (unharmed) intacto
**intake** ['ɪnteɪk] n (of food) ingestión f; (of air) consumo; (BRIT Scol): **an ~ of 200 a year** 200 matriculados al año
**integral** ['ɪntɪgrəl] adj (whole) íntegro; (part) integrante
**integrate** ['ɪntɪgreɪt] vt integrar ▷ vi integrarse
**integrity** [ɪn'tɛgrɪtɪ] n honradez f, rectitud f
**intellect** ['ɪntəlɛkt] n intelecto; **intellectual** [-'lɛktjuəl] adj, n intelectual mf
**intelligence** [ɪn'tɛlɪdʒəns] n inteligencia
**intelligent** [ɪn'tɛlɪdʒənt] adj inteligente
**intend** [ɪn'tɛnd] vt (gift etc): **to ~ sth for** destinar algo a; **to ~ to do sth** tener intención de or pensar hacer algo

**intense** [ɪnˈtɛns] adj intenso
**intensify** [ɪnˈtɛnsɪfaɪ] vt intensificar; (increase) aumentar
**intensity** [ɪnˈtɛnsɪtɪ] n (gen) intensidad f
**intensive** [ɪnˈtɛnsɪv] adj intensivo; **intensive care** n: **to be in intensive care** estar bajo cuidados intensivos; **intensive care unit** n unidad f de vigilancia intensiva
**intent** [ɪnˈtɛnt] n propósito; (Law) premeditación f ▷ adj (absorbed) absorto; (attentive) atento: **to all ~s and purposes** prácticamente: **to be ~ on doing sth** estar resuelto a hacer algo
**intention** [ɪnˈtɛnʃən] n intención f, propósito; **intentional** adj deliberado
**interact** [ɪntərˈækt] vi influirse mutuamente; **interaction** [ɪntərˈækʃən] n interacción f, acción f recíproca; **interactive** adj (Comput) interactivo
**intercept** [ɪntəˈsɛpt] vt interceptar; (stop) detener
**interchange** [ˈɪntətʃeɪndʒ] n intercambio; (on motorway) intersección f
**intercourse** [ˈɪntəkɔːs] n (sexual) relaciones fpl sexuales
**interest** [ˈɪntrɪst] n (also Comm) interés m ▷ vt interesar; **interested** adj interesado; **to be interested in** interesarse por; **interesting** adj interesante; **interest rate** n tipo or tasa de interés
**interface** [ˈɪntəfeɪs] n (Comput) junción f
**interfere** [ɪntəˈfɪə*] vi: **to ~ in** entrometerse en; **to ~ with** (hinder) estorbar; (damage) estropear
**interference** [ɪntəˈfɪərəns] n intromisión f; (Radio, TV) interferencia
**interim** [ˈɪntərɪm] n: **in the ~** en el ínterin ▷ adj provisional
**interior** [ɪnˈtɪərɪə*] n interior m ▷ adj interior; **interior design** n interiorismo, decoración f de interiores
**intermediate** [ɪntəˈmiːdɪət] adj intermedio
**intermission** [ɪntəˈmɪʃən] n intermisión f; (Theatre) descanso
**intern** [vb ɪnˈtəːn, n ˈɪntəːn] (us) vt internar ▷ n interno/a
**internal** [ɪnˈtəːnl] adj (layout, pipes, security) interior; (injury, structure, memo) internal; **Internal Revenue Service** (us) n departamento de impuestos, ≈ Hacienda (sp)
**international** [ɪntəˈnæʃənl] adj internacional ▷ n (brit: match) partido internacional
**Internet** [ˈɪntənɛt] n: **the ~** Internet m or f; **Internet café** n cibercafé m; **Internet Service Provider** n proveedor m de (acceso

a) Internet; **Internet user** n internauta mf
**interpret** [ɪnˈtəːprɪt] vt interpretar; (translate) traducir; (understand) entender ▷ vi hacer de intérprete; **interpretation** [ɪntəːprɪˈteɪʃən] n interpretación f; traducción f; **interpreter** n intérprete mf
**interrogate** [ɪnˈtɛrəugeɪt] vt interrogar; **interrogation** [-ˈgeɪʃən] n interrogatorio
**interrogative** [ɪntəˈrɔgətɪv] adj interrogativo
**interrupt** [ɪntəˈrʌpt] vt, vi interrumpir; **interruption** [-ˈrʌpʃən] n interrupción f
**intersection** [ɪntəˈsɛkʃən] n (of roads) cruce m
**interstate** [ˈɪntərsteɪt] (us) n carretera interestatal
**interval** [ˈɪntəvl] n intervalo; (brit Theatre, Sport) descanso; (Scol) recreo; **at ~s** a ratos, de vez en cuando
**intervene** [ɪntəˈviːn] vi intervenir; (event) interponerse; (time) transcurrir
**interview** [ˈɪntəvjuː] n entrevista ▷ vt entrevistarse con; **interviewer** n entrevistador(a) m/f
**intimate** [adj ˈɪntɪmət, vb ˈɪntɪmeɪt] adj íntimo; (friendship) estrecho; (knowledge) profundo ▷ vt dar a entender
**intimidate** [ɪnˈtɪmɪdeɪt] vt intimidar, amedrentar
**intimidating** [ɪnˈtɪmɪdeɪtɪŋ] adj amedrentador, intimidante
**into** [ˈɪntuː] prep en; (towards) a; (inside) hacia el interior de; **~ 3 pieces/French** en 3 pedazos/al francés
**intolerant** [ɪnˈtɔlərənt] adj: **~ (of)** intolerante (con or para)
**intranet** [ˈɪntrənɛt] n intranet f
**intransitive** [ɪnˈtrænsɪtɪv] adj intransitivo
**intricate** [ˈɪntrɪkət] adj (design, pattern) intrincado
**intrigue** [ɪnˈtriːg] n intriga ▷ vt fascinar; **intriguing** adj fascinante
**introduce** [ɪntrəˈdjuːs] vt introducir, meter; (speaker, TV show etc) presentar; **to ~ sb (to sb)** presentar a algn (a algn); **to ~ sb to** (pastime, technique) introducir a algn a; **introduction** [-ˈdʌkʃən] n introducción f; (of person) presentación f; **introductory** [-ˈdʌktərɪ] adj introductorio; (lesson, offer) de introducción
**intrude** [ɪnˈtruːd] vi (person) entrometerse; **to ~ on** estorbar; **intruder** n intruso/a
**intuition** [ɪntjuːˈɪʃən] n intuición f
**inundate** [ˈɪnʌndeɪt] vt: **to ~ with** inundar de
**invade** [ɪnˈveɪd] vt invadir

**invalid** [n 'ɪnvəlɪd, adj ɪn'vælɪd] n (Med) minusválido/a ▷ adj (not valid) inválido, nulo

**invaluable** [ɪn'væljuəbl] adj inestimable

**invariably** [ɪn'vɛərɪəblɪ] adv sin excepción, siempre; **she is ~ late** siempre llega tarde

**invasion** [ɪn'veɪʒən] n invasión f

**invent** [ɪn'vɛnt] vt inventar; **invention** [ɪn'vɛnʃən] n invento; (lie) ficción f, mentira; **inventor** n inventor(a) m/f

**inventory** ['ɪnvəntrɪ] n inventario

**inverted commas** [ɪn'vɜːtɪd-] (BRIT) npl comillas fpl

**invest** [ɪn'vɛst] vt invertir ▷ vi: **to ~ in** (company etc) invertir dinero en; (fig: sth useful) comprar

**investigate** [ɪn'vɛstɪgeɪt] vt investigar; **investigation** [-'geɪʃən] n investigación f, pesquisa

**investigator** [ɪn'vɛstɪgeɪtə*] n investigador(a) m/f; **private ~** investigador/a m/f privado/a

**investment** [ɪn'vɛstmənt] n inversión f

**investor** [ɪn'vɛstə*] n inversionista mf

**invisible** [ɪn'vɪzɪbl] adj invisible

**invitation** [ɪnvɪ'teɪʃən] n invitación f

**invite** [ɪn'vaɪt] vt invitar; (opinions etc) solicitar, pedir; **inviting** adj atractivo; (food) apetitoso

**invoice** ['ɪnvɔɪs] n factura ▷ vt facturar

**involve** [ɪn'vɔlv] vt suponer, implicar; tener que ver con; (concern, affect) corresponder; **to ~ sb (in sth)** comprometer a algn (con algo); **involved** adj complicado; **to be involved in** (take part) tomar parte en; (be engrossed) estar muy metido en; **involvement** n participación f; dedicación f

**inward** ['ɪnwəd] adj (movement) interior, interno; (thought, feeling) íntimo; **inward(s)** adv hacia dentro

**iPod** ® ['aɪpɔd] n iPod ® m

**IQ** n abbr (= intelligence quotient) cociente m intelectual

**IRA** n abbr (= Irish Republican Army) IRA m

**Iran** [ɪ'rɑːn] n Irán m; **Iranian** [ɪ'reɪnɪən] adj, n iraní mf

**Iraq** [ɪ'rɑːk] n Iraq; **Iraqi** adj, n iraquí mf

**Ireland** ['aɪələnd] n Irlanda

**iris** ['aɪrɪs] (pl ~es) n (Anat) iris m; (Bot) lirio

**Irish** ['aɪrɪʃ] adj irlandés/esa ▷ npl: **the ~** los irlandeses; **Irishman** (irreg) n irlandés m; **Irishwoman** (irreg) n irlandésa

**iron** ['aɪən] n hierro; (for clothes) plancha ▷ cpd de hierro ▷ vt (clothes) planchar

**ironic(al)** [aɪ'rɔnɪk(l)] adj irónico; **ironically** adv irónicamente

**ironing** ['aɪənɪŋ] n (activity) planchado; (clothes: ironed) ropa planchada; (: to be ironed) ropa por planchar; **ironing board** n tabla de planchar

**irony** ['aɪrənɪ] n ironía

**irrational** [ɪ'ræʃənl] adj irracional

**irregular** [ɪ'rɛgjulə*] adj irregular; (surface) desigual; (action, event) anómalo; (behaviour) poco ortodoxo

**irrelevant** [ɪ'rɛləvənt] adj fuera de lugar, inoportuno

**irresistible** [ɪrɪ'zɪstɪbl] adj irresistible

**irresponsible** [ɪrɪ'spɔnsɪbl] adj (act) irresponsable; (person) poco serio

**irrigation** [ɪrɪ'geɪʃən] n riego

**irritable** ['ɪrɪtəbl] adj (person) de mal humor

**irritate** ['ɪrɪteɪt] vt fastidiar; (Med) picar; **irritating** adj fastidioso; **irritation** [-'teɪʃən] n fastidio; enfado; picazón f

**IRS** (US) n abbr = **Internal Revenue Service**

**is** [ɪz] vb see **be**

**ISDN** n abbr (= Integrated Services Digital Network) RDSI f

**Islam** ['ɪzlɑːm] n Islam m; **Islamic** [ɪz'læmɪk] adj islámico

**island** ['aɪlənd] n isla; **islander** n isleño/a

**isle** [aɪl] n isla

**isn't** ['ɪznt] = **is not**

**isolated** ['aɪsəleɪtɪd] adj aislado

**isolation** [aɪsə'leɪʃən] n aislamiento

**ISP** n abbr = **Internet Service Provider**

**Israel** ['ɪzreɪl] n Israel m; **Israeli** [ɪz'reɪlɪ] adj, n israelí mf

**issue** ['ɪsjuː] n (problem, subject) cuestión f; (outcome) resultado; (of banknotes etc) emisión f; (of newspaper etc) edición f ▷ vt (rations, equipment) distribuir, repartir; (orders) dar; (certificate, passport) expedir; (decree) promulgar; (magazine) publicar; (cheques) extender; (banknotes, stamps) emitir; **at ~** en cuestión; **to take ~ with sb (over)** estar en desacuerdo con algn (sobre); **to make an ~ of sth** hacer una cuestión de algo

**IT** n abbr = **information technology**

○ KEYWORD

**it** [ɪt] pron **1** (specific subject: not generally translated) él (ella); (: direct object) lo, la; (: indirect object) le; (after prep) él (ella); (abstract concept) ello; **it's on the table** está en la mesa; **I can't find it** no lo (or la) encuentro; **give it to me** dámelo (or dámela); **I spoke to him about it** le hablé del asunto; **what did you learn from it?** ¿qué aprendiste de él (or ella)?; **did you go**

**to it?** (party, concert etc) ¿fuiste?
**2** (impersonal): **it's raining** llueve, está
lloviendo; **it's 6 o'clock/the 10th of**
**August** son las 6/es el 10 de agosto; **how far**
**is it? – it's 10 miles/2 hours on the train** ¿a
qué distancia está? – a 10 millas/2 horas en
tren; **who is it? – it's me** ¿quién es? – soy yo

**Italian** [ɪ'tæljən] adj italiano ▷ n
italiano/a; (Ling) italiano
**italics** [ɪ'tælɪks] npl cursiva
**Italy** ['ɪtəlɪ] n Italia
**itch** [ɪtʃ] n picazón f ▷ vi (part of body)
picar; **to ~ to do sth** rabiar por hacer algo;
**itchy** adj: **my hand is itchy** me pica la
mano
**it'd** ['ɪtd] = **it would; it had**
**item** ['aɪtəm] n artículo; (on agenda)
asunto (a tratar); (also: **news ~**) noticia
**itinerary** [aɪ'tɪnərərɪ] n itinerario
**it'll** ['ɪtl] = **it will; it shall**
**its** [ɪts] adj su; sus pl
**it's** [ɪts] = **it is; it has**
**itself** [ɪt'sɛlf] pron (reflexive) sí mismo/a;
(emphatic) él mismo(ella misma)
**ITV** n abbr (BRIT: = Independent Television)
cadena de televisión comercial independiente
del Estado
**I've** [aɪv] = **I have**
**ivory** ['aɪvərɪ] n marfil m
**ivy** ['aɪvɪ] n (Bot) hiedra

**jab** [dʒæb] vt: **to ~ sth into sth** clavar algo
en algo ▷ n (inf: Med) pinchazo
**jack** [dʒæk] n (Aut) gato; (Cards) sota
**jacket** ['dʒækɪt] n chaqueta, americana
(SP), saco (LAM); (of book) sobrecubierta;
**jacket potato** n patata asada (con piel)
**jackpot** ['dʒækpɔt] n premio gordo
**Jacuzzi®** [dʒə'ku:zɪ] n jacuzzi® m
**jagged** ['dʒægɪd] adj dentado
**jail** [dʒeɪl] n cárcel f ▷ vt encarcelar; **jail**
**sentence** n pena f de cárcel
**jam** [dʒæm] n mermelada; (also: **traffic ~**)
embotellamiento; (inf: difficulty) apuro ▷ vt
(passage etc) obstruir; (mechanism, drawer etc)
atascar; (Radio) interferir ▷ vi atascarse,
trabarse; **to ~ sth into sth** meter algo a la
fuerza en algo
**Jamaica** [dʒə'meɪkə] n Jamaica
**jammed** [dʒæmd] adj atascado
**Jan** abbr (= January) ene
**janitor** ['dʒænɪtə*] n (caretaker) portero,
conserje m
**January** ['dʒænjuərɪ] n enero
**Japan** [dʒə'pæn] n (el) Japón; **Japanese**
[dʒæpə'ni:z] adj japonés/esa ▷ n inv
japonés/esa m/f; (Ling) japonés m
**jar** [dʒɑː*] n tarro, bote m ▷ vi (sound)
chirriar; (colours) desentonar
**jargon** ['dʒɑːgən] n jerga
**javelin** ['dʒævlɪn] n jabalina
**jaw** [dʒɔː] n mandíbula
**jazz** [dʒæz] n jazz m
**jealous** ['dʒɛləs] adj celoso; (envious)
envidioso; **jealousy** n celos mpl; envidia
**jeans** [dʒiːnz] npl vaqueros mpl, tejanos mpl
**Jello®** ['dʒɛləu] (US) n gelatina
**jelly** ['dʒɛlɪ] n (jam) jalea; (dessert etc)
gelatina; **jellyfish** n inv medusa, aguaviva
(RPL)
**jeopardize** ['dʒɛpədaɪz] vt arriesgar,
poner en peligro

**jerk** [dʒəːk] n (jolt) sacudida; (wrench) tirón m; (inf) imbécil mf ▷ vt tirar bruscamente de ▷ vi (vehicle) traquetear

**Jersey** ['dʒəːzɪ] n Jersey m

**jersey** ['dʒəːzɪ] n jersey m; (fabric) (tejido de) punto

**Jesus** ['dʒiːzəs] n Jesús m

**jet** [dʒɛt] n (of gas, liquid) chorro; (Aviat) avión m a reacción; **jet lag** n desorientación f después de un largo vuelo; **jet-ski** vi practicar el motociclismo acuático

**jetty** ['dʒɛtɪ] n muelle m, embarcadero

**Jew** [dʒuː] n judío/a

**jewel** ['dʒuːəl] n joya; (in watch) rubí m; **jeweller** (us **jeweler**) n joyero/a; **jeweller's (shop)** (us **jewelry store**) n joyería; **jewellery** (us **jewelry**) n joyas fpl, alhajas fpl

**Jewish** ['dʒuːɪʃ] adj judío

**jigsaw** ['dʒɪgsɔː] n (also: ~ **puzzle**) rompecabezas m inv, puzle m

**job** [dʒɔb] n (task) tarea; (post) empleo; **it's not my** ~ no me incumbe a mí; **it's a good ~ that ...** menos mal que ...; **just the** ~! ¡estupendo!; **job centre** (BRIT) n oficina estatal de colocaciones; **jobless** adj sin trabajo

**jockey** ['dʒɔkɪ] n jockey mf ▷ vi: **to ~ for position** maniobrar para conseguir una posición

**jog** [dʒɔg] vt empujar (ligeramente) ▷ vi (run) hacer footing; **to ~ sb's memory** refrescar la memoria a algn; **jogging** n footing m

**join** [dʒɔɪn] vt (things) juntar, unir; (club) hacerse socio de; (Pol: party) afiliarse a; (queue) ponerse en; (meet: people) reunirse con ▷ vi (roads) juntarse; (rivers) confluir ▷ n juntura; **join in** vi tomar parte, participar ▷ vt fus tomar parte o participar en; **join up** vi reunirse; (Mil) alistarse

**joiner** ['dʒɔɪnə*] (BRIT) n carpintero/a

**joint** [dʒɔɪnt] n (Tech) junta, unión f; (Anat) articulación f; (Brit Culin) pieza de carne (para asar); (inf: place) tugurio; (: of cannabis) porro ▷ adj (common) común; (combined) combinado; **joint account** n (with bank etc) cuenta común; **jointly** adv (gen) en común; (together) conjuntamente

**joke** [dʒəuk] n chiste m; (also: **practical ~**) broma ▷ vi bromear; **to play a ~ on** gastar una broma a; **joker** n (Cards) comodín m

**jolly** ['dʒɔlɪ] adj (merry) alegre; (enjoyable) divertido ▷ adv (BRIT: inf) muy, terriblemente

**jolt** [dʒəult] n (jerk) sacudida; (shock) susto ▷ vt (physically) sacudir; (emotionally) asustar

**Jordan** ['dʒɔːdən] n (country) Jordania; (river) Jordán m

**journal** ['dʒəːnl] n (magazine) revista; (diary) periódico, diario; **journalism** n periodismo; **journalist** n periodista mf, reportero/a

**journey** ['dʒəːnɪ] n viaje m; (distance covered) trayecto

**joy** [dʒɔɪ] n alegría; **joyrider** n gamberro que roba un coche para dar una vuelta y luego abandonarlo; **joy stick** n (Aviat) palanca de mando; (Comput) palanca de control

**Jr** abbr = **junior**

**judge** [dʒʌdʒ] n juez mf; (fig: expert) perito ▷ vt juzgar; (consider) considerar

**judo** ['dʒuːdəu] n judo

**jug** [dʒʌg] n jarra

**juggle** ['dʒʌgl] vi hacer juegos malabares; **juggler** n malabarista mf

**juice** [dʒuːs] n zumo (SP), jugo (LAM); **juicy** adj jugoso

**Jul** abbr (= July) jul

**July** [dʒuː'laɪ] n julio

**jumble** ['dʒʌmbl] n revoltijo ▷ vt (also: ~ **up**) revolver; **jumble sale** (BRIT) n venta de objetos usados con fines benéficos

○ **JUMBLE SALE**
○
○ Los **jumble sales** son unos mercadillos
○ que se organizan con fines benéficos
○ en los locales de un colegio, iglesia u
○ otro centro público. En ellos puede
○ comprarse todo tipo de artículos
○ baratos de segunda mano, sobre
○ todo ropa, juguetes, libros, vajillas o
○ muebles.

**jumbo** ['dʒʌmbəu] n (also: ~ **jet**) jumbo

**jump** [dʒʌmp] vi saltar, dar saltos; (with fear etc) pegar un bote; (increase) aumentar ▷ vt saltar ▷ n salto; aumento; **to ~ the queue** (BRIT) colarse

**jumper** ['dʒʌmpə*] n (BRIT: pullover) suéter m, jersey m; (us: dress) mandil m

**jumper cables** (us) npl = **jump leads**

**jump leads** (BRIT) npl cables mpl puente de batería

**Jun.** abbr = **junior**

**junction** ['dʒʌŋkʃən] n (BRIT: of roads) cruce m; (Rail) empalme m

**June** [dʒuːn] n junio

**jungle** ['dʒʌŋgl] n selva, jungla

**junior** ['dʒuːnɪə*] adj (in age) menor, más joven; (brother/sister etc): **seven years her ~** siete años menor que ella; (position) subalterno ▷ n menor mf, joven mf; **junior high school** (us) n centro de educación secundaria; *see also* **high school**; **junior school** (*BRIT*) *n* escuela primaria

**junk** [dʒʌŋk] *n* (*cheap goods*) baratijas *fpl*; (*rubbish*) basura; **junk food** *n* alimentos preparados y envasados de escaso valor nutritivo

**junkie** ['dʒʌŋkɪ] (*inf*) *n* drogadicto/a, yonqui *mf*

**junk mail** *n* propaganda de buzón

**Jupiter** ['dʒu:pɪtə*] *n* (*Mythology, Astrology*) Júpiter *m*

**jurisdiction** [dʒuərɪs'dɪkʃən] *n* jurisdicción *f*; **it falls** *or* **comes within/ outside our ~** es/no es de nuestra competencia

**jury** ['dʒuərɪ] *n* jurado

**just** [dʒʌst] *adj* justo ▷ *adv* (*exactly*) exactamente; (*only*) sólo, solamente; **he's ~ done it/left** acaba de hacerlo/irse; **~ right** perfecto; **~ two o'clock** las dos en punto; **she's ~ as clever as you** (ella) es tan lista como tú; **~ as well that ...** menos mal que ...; **~ as he was leaving** en el momento en que se marchaba; **~ before/enough** justo antes/lo suficiente; **~ here** aquí mismo; **he ~ missed** ha fallado por poco; **~ listen to this** escucha esto un momento

**justice** ['dʒʌstɪs] *n* justicia; (*us: judge*) juez *mf*; **to do ~ to** (*fig*) hacer justicia a

**justification** [dʒʌstɪfɪ'keɪʃən] *n* justificación *f*

**justify** ['dʒʌstɪfaɪ] *vt* justificar; (*text*) alinear

**jut** [dʒʌt] *vi* (*also: ~ out*) sobresalir

**juvenile** ['dʒu:vənaɪl] *adj* (*court*) de menores; (*humour, mentality*) infantil ▷ *n* menor *m* de edad

# K

**K** *abbr* (= *one thousand*) mil; (= *kilobyte*) kilobyte *m*, kilooecteto

**kangaroo** [kæŋgə'ru:] *n* canguro

**karaoke** [kɑːrə'əʊkɪ] *n* karaoke

**karate** [kə'rɑːtɪ] *n* karate *m*

**kebab** [kə'bæb] *n* pincho moruno

**keel** [kiːl] *n* quilla; **on an even ~** (*fig*) en equilibrio

**keen** [kiːn] *adj* (*interest, desire*) grande, vivo; (*eye, intelligence*) agudo; (*competition*) reñido; (*edge*) afilado; (*eager*) entusiasta; **to be ~ to do** *or* **on doing sth** tener muchas ganas de hacer algo; **to be ~ on sth/sb** interesarse por algo/algn

**keep** [kiːp] (*pt, pp* **kept**) *vt* (*preserve, store*) guardar; (*hold back*) quedarse con; (*maintain*) mantener; (*detain*) detener; (*shop*) ser propietario de; (*feed: family etc*) mantener; (*promise*) cumplir; (*chickens, bees etc*) criar; (*accounts*) llevar; (*diary*) escribir; (*prevent*): **to ~ sb from doing sth** impedir a algn hacer algo ▷ *vi* (*food*) conservarse; (*remain*) seguir, continuar ▷ *n* (*of castle*) torreón *m*; (*food etc*) comida, subsistencia; (*inf*): **for ~s** para siempre; **to ~ doing sth** seguir haciendo algo; **to ~ sb happy** tener a algn contento; **to ~ a place tidy** mantener un lugar limpio; **to ~ sth to o.s.** guardar algo para sí mismo; **to ~ sth (back) from sb** ocultar algo a algn; **to ~ time** (*clock*) mantener la hora exacta; **keep away** *vt*: **to keep sth/sb away from sb** mantener algo/a algn apartado de algn ▷ *vi*: **to keep away (from)** mantenerse apartado (de); **keep back** *vt* (*crowd, tears*) contener; (*money*) quedarse con; (*conceal: inf ormation*): **to keep sth back from sb** ocultar algo a algn ▷ *vi* hacerse a un lado; **keep off** *vt* (*dog, person*) mantener a distancia ▷ *vi*: **if the rain keeps off** so no lleuve; **keep your hands off!** ¡no toques!; **"keep off the grass"** "prohibido pisar el césped"; **keep**

**on** vi: **to keep on doing** seguir or continuar haciendo; **to keep on (about sth)** no parar de hablar (de algo); **keep out** vi (stay out) permanecer fuera; **"keep out"** "prohibida la entrada"; **keep up** vt mantener, conservar ▷ vi no retrasarse; **to keep up with** (pace) ir al paso de; (level) mantenerse a la altura de; **keeper** n guardián/ana m/f; **keeping** n (care) cuidado; **in keeping with** de acuerdo con

**kennel** ['kɛnl] n perrera; **kennels** npl residencia canina

**Kenya** ['kɛnjə] n Kenia

**kept** [kɛpt] pt, pp of **keep**

**kerb** [kə:b] (BRIT) n bordillo

**kerosene** ['kɛrəsi:n] n keroseno

**ketchup** ['kɛtʃəp] n salsa de tomate, catsup m

**kettle** ['kɛtl] n hervidor m de agua

**key** [ki:] n llave f; (Mus) tono; (of piano, typewriter) tecla ▷ adj (issue etc) clave inv ▷ vt (also: **~ in**) teclear; **keyboard** n teclado; **keyhole** n ojo (de la cerradura); **keyring** n llavero

**kg** abbr (= kilogram) kg

**khaki** ['kɑ:kɪ] n caqui

**kick** [kɪk] vt dar una patada or un puntapié a; (inf: habit) quitarse de ▷ vi (horse) dar coces ▷ n patada; puntapié m; (of animal) coz f; (thrill): **he does it for ~s** lo hace por pura diversión; **kick off** vi (Sport) hacer el saque inicial; **kick-off** n saque inicial; **the kick-off is at 10 o'clock** el partido empieza a las diez

**kid** [kɪd] n (inf: child) chiquillo/a; (animal) cabrito; (leather) cabritilla ▷ vi (inf) bromear

**kidnap** ['kɪdnæp] vt secuestrar; **kidnapping** n secuestro

**kidney** ['kɪdnɪ] n riñón m; **kidney bean** n judía, alubia

**kill** [kɪl] vt matar; (murder) asesinar ▷ n matanza; **to ~ time** matar el tiempo; **killer** n asesino/a; **killing** n (one) asesinato; (several) matanza; **to make a killing** (fig) hacer su agosto

**kiln** [kɪln] n horno

**kilo** ['ki:ləu] n kilo; **kilobyte** n (Comput) kilobyte m, kilocteto; **kilogram(me)** n kilo, kilogramo; **kilometre** ['kɪləmi:tə*] (us **kilometer**) n kilómetro; **kilowatt** n kilovatio

**kilt** [kɪlt] n falda escocesa

**kin** [kɪn] n see **next-of-kin**

**kind** [kaɪnd] adj amable, atento ▷ n clase f, especie f; (species) género; **in ~** (Comm) en especie; **a ~ of** una especie de; **to be two of a ~** ser tal para cual

**kindergarten** ['kɪndəgɑ:tn] n jardín m de la infancia

**kindly** ['kaɪndlɪ] adj bondadoso; cariñoso ▷ adv bondadosamente, amablemente; **will you ~ ...** sea usted tan amable de ...

**kindness** ['kaɪndnɪs] n (quality) bondad f, amabilidad f; (act) favor m

**king** [kɪŋ] n rey m; **kingdom** n reino; **kingfisher** n martín m pescador; **king-size(d) bed** n cama de matrimonio extragrande

**kiosk** ['ki:ɔsk] n quiosco; (BRIT Tel) cabina

**kipper** ['kɪpə*] n arenque m ahumado

**kiss** [kɪs] n beso ▷ vt besar; **to ~ (each other)** besarse; **kiss of life** n respiración f boca a boca

**kit** [kɪt] n (equipment) equipo; (tools etc) (caja de) herramientas fpl; (assembly kit) juego de armar

**kitchen** ['kɪtʃɪn] n cocina

**kite** [kaɪt] n (toy) cometa

**kitten** ['kɪtn] n gatito/a

**kiwi** ['ki:wi:-] n (also: **~ fruit**) kiwi m

**km** abbr (= kilometre) km

**km/h** abbr (= kilometres per hour) km/h

**knack** [næk] n: **to have the ~ of doing sth** tener el don de hacer algo

**knee** [ni:] n rodilla; **kneecap** n rótula

**kneel** [ni:l] (pt, pp **knelt**) vi (also: **~ down**) arrodillarse

**knelt** [nɛlt] pt, pp of **kneel**

**knew** [nju:] pt of **know**

**knickers** ['nɪkəz] (BRIT) npl bragas fpl

**knife** [naɪf] (pl **knives**) n cuchillo ▷ vt acuchillar

**knight** [naɪt] n caballero; (Chess) caballo

**knit** [nɪt] vt tejer, tricotar ▷ vi hacer punto, tricotar; (bones) soldarse; **to ~ one's brows** fruncir el ceño; **knitting** n labor f de punto; **knitting needle** n aguja de hacer punto; **knitwear** n prendas fpl de punto

**knives** [naɪvz] npl of **knife**

**knob** [nɔb] n (of door) tirador m; (of stick) puño; (on radio, TV) botón m

**knock** [nɔk] vt (strike) golpear; (bump into) chocar contra; (inf) criticar ▷ vi (at door etc): **to ~ at/on** llamar a ▷ n golpe m; (on door) llamada; **knock down** vt atropellar; **knock off** (inf) vi (finish) salir del trabajo ▷ vt (from price) descontar; (inf: steal) birlar; **knock out** vt dejar sin sentido; (Boxing) poner fuera de combate, dejar K.O.; (in competition) eliminar; **knock over** vt (object) tirar; (person) atropellar; **knockout** n (Boxing) K.O. m, knockout m ▷ cpd (competition etc) eliminatorio

**knot** [nɔt] n nudo ▷ vt anudar

**know** [nəʊ] (pt **knew**, pp **known**) vt (facts) saber; (be acquainted with) conocer;

(recognize) reconocer, conocer; **to ~ how to swim** saber nadar; **to ~ about** or **of sb/sth** saber de algn/algo; **know-all** n sabelotodo mf; **know-how** n conocimientos mpl; **knowing** adj (look) de complicidad; **knowingly** adv (purposely) adrede; (smile, look) con complicidad; **know-it-all**(US) n = **know-all**

**knowledge** ['nɔlɪdʒ] n conocimiento; (learning) saber m, conocimientos mpl; **knowledgeable** adj entendido

**known** [nəʊn] pp of **know** ▷ adj (thief, facts) conocido; (expert) reconocido

**knuckle** ['nʌkl] n nudillo

**koala** [kəʊ'ɑːlə] n (also: ~ **bear**) koala m

**Koran** [kɔ'rɑːn] n Corán m

**Korea** [kə'rɪə] n Corea; **Korean** adj, n coreano/a m/f

**kosher** ['kəʊʃə*] adj autorizado por la ley judía

**Kosovar** ['kɔsəvɑ*], **Kosovan** ['kɔːsəvən] adj kosovar

**Kosovo** ['kɔsəvəʊ] n Kosovo

**Kremlin** ['kremlɪn] n: **the ~** el Kremlin

**Kuwait** [ku'weɪt] n Kuwait m

**L** (BRIT) abbr = **learner driver**

**l.** abbr (=litre) l

**lab** [læb] n abbr = **laboratory**

**label** ['leɪbl] n etiqueta ▷ vt poner etiqueta a

**labor** etc ['leɪbə*] (US) = **labour** etc

**laboratory** [lə'bɔrətərɪ] n laboratorio

**Labor Day** (US) n día m de los trabajadores (primer lunes de septiembre)

**labor union** (US) n sindicato

**labour** ['leɪbə*] (US **labor**) n (hard work) trabajo; (labour force) mano f de obra; (Med): **to be in ~** estar de parto ▷ vi: **to ~ (at sth)** trabajar (en algo) ▷ vt: **to ~ a point** insistir en un punto; **L~, the L~ party** (BRIT) el partido laborista, los laboristas mpl; **labourer** n peón m; **farm labourer** peón m; (day labourer) jornalero

**lace** [leɪs] n encaje m; (of shoe etc) cordón m ▷ vt (shoes: also: ~ **up**) atarse (los zapatos)

**lack** [læk] n (absence) falta ▷ vt faltarle a algn, carecer de; **through** or **for ~ of** por falta de; **to be ~ing** faltar, no haber; **to be ~ing in sth** faltarle a algn algo

**lacquer** ['lækə*] n laca

**lacy** ['leɪsɪ] adj (of lace) de encaje; (like lace) como de encaje

**lad** [læd] n muchacho, chico

**ladder** ['lædə*] n escalera (de mano); (BRIT: in tights) carrera

**ladle** ['leɪdl] n cucharón m

**lady** ['leɪdɪ] n señora; (dignified, graceful) dama; **"ladies and gentlemen ..."** "señoras y caballeros ..."; **young ~** señorita; **the ladies' (room)** los servicios de señoras; **ladybird** (US **ladybug**) n mariquita

**lag** [læg] n retraso ▷ vi (also: ~ **behind**) retrasarse, quedarse atrás ▷ vt (pipes) revestir

**lager** ['lɑːgə*] n cerveza (rubia)

**lagoon** [lə'guːn] n laguna

**laid** [leɪd] *pt, pp of* **lay**; **laid back** (*inf*) *adj* relajado

**lain** [leɪn] *pp of* **lie**

**lake** [leɪk] *n* lago

**lamb** [læm] *n* cordero; (*meat*) (carne *f* de) cordero

**lame** [leɪm] *adj* cojo; (*excuse*) poco convincente

**lament** [lə'mɛnt] *n* quejo ▷ *vt* lamentarse de

**lamp** [læmp] *n* lámpara; **lamppost** (*BRIT*) *n* (poste *m* de) farol *m*; **lampshade** *n* pantalla

**land** [lænd] *n* tierra; (*country*) país *m*; (*piece of land*) terreno; (*estate*) tierras *fpl*, finca ▷ *vi* (*from ship*) desembarcar; (*Aviat*) aterrizar; (*fig: fall*) caer, terminar ▷ *vt* (*passengers, goods*) desembarcar; **to ~ sb with sth** (*inf*) hacer cargar a algn con algo; **landing** *n* aterrizaje *m*; (*of staircase*) rellano; **landing card** *n* tarjeta de desembarque; **landlady** *n* (*of rented house, pub etc*) dueña; **landlord** *n* propietario; (*of pub etc*) patrón *m*; **landmark** *n* lugar *m* conocido; **to be a landmark** (*fig*) marcar un hito histórico; **landowner** *n* terrateniente *mf*; **landscape** *n* paisaje *m*; **landslide** *n* (*Geo*) corrimiento de tierras; (*fig: Pol*) victoria arrolladora

**lane** [leɪn] *n* (*in country*) camino; (*Aut*) carril *m*; (*in race*) calle *f*

**language** ['læŋgwɪdʒ] *n* lenguaje *m*; (*national tongue*) idioma *m*, lengua; **bad ~** palabrotas *fpl*; **language laboratory** *n* laboratorio de idiomas; **language school** *n* academia de idiomas

**lantern** ['læntn] *n* linterna, farol *m*

**lap** [læp] *n* (*of track*) vuelta; (*of body*) regazo ▷ *vt* (*also: ~ up*) beber a lengüetadas ▷ *vi* (*waves*) chapotear; **to sit on sb's ~** sentarse en las rodillas de algn

**lapel** [lə'pɛl] *n* solapa

**lapse** [læps] *n* fallo; (*moral*) desliz *m*; (*of time*) intervalo ▷ *vi* (*expire*) caducar; (*time*) pasar, transcurrir; **to ~ into bad habits** caer en malos hábitos

**laptop (computer)** ['læptɔp-] *n* (ordenador *m*) portátil *m*

**lard** [lɑːd] *n* manteca (de cerdo)

**larder** ['lɑːdə*] *n* despensa

**large** [lɑːdʒ] *adj* grande; **at ~** (*free*) en libertad; (*generally*) en general

▌Be careful not to translate **large** by the Spanish word *largo*.

**largely** *adv* (*mostly*) en su mayor parte; (*introducing reason*) en gran parte; **large-scale** *adj* (*map*) en gran escala; (*fig*) importante

**lark** [lɑːk] *n* (*bird*) alondra; (*joke*) broma

**laryngitis** [lærɪn'dʒaɪtɪs] *n* laringitis *f*

**lasagne** [lə'zænjə] *n* lasaña

**laser** ['leɪzə*] *n* láser *m*; **laser printer** *n* impresora (por) láser

**lash** [læʃ] *n* latigazo; (*also:* **eye~**) pestaña ▷ *vt* azotar; (*tie*): **to ~ to/together** atar a/atar; **lash out** *vi*: **to lash out (at sb)** (*hit*) arremeter (contra algn); **to lash out against sb** lanzar invectivas contra algn

**lass** [læs] (*BRIT*) *n* chica

**last** [lɑːst] *adj* último; (*end: of series etc*) final ▷ *adv* (*most recently*) la última vez; (*finally*) por último ▷ *vi* durar; (*continue*) continuar, seguir; **~ night** anoche; **~ week** la semana pasada; **at ~** por fin; **~ but one** penúltimo; **lastly** *adv* por último, finalmente; **last-minute** *adj* de última hora

**latch** [lætʃ] *n* pestillo; **latch onto** *vt fus* (*person, group*) pegarse a; (*idea*) agarrarse a

**late** [leɪt] *adj* (*far on: in time, process etc*) al final de; (*not on time*) tarde, atrasado; (*dead*) fallecido ▷ *adv* tarde; (*behind time, schedule*) con retraso; **of ~** últimamente; **~ at night** a última hora de la noche; **in ~ May** hacia fines de mayo; **the ~ Mr X** el difunto Sr X; **latecomer** *n* recién llegado/a; **lately** *adv* últimamente; **later** *adj* (*date etc*) posterior; (*version etc*) más reciente ▷ *adv* más tarde, después; **latest** ['leɪtɪst] *adj* último; **at the latest** a más tardar

**lather** ['lɑːðə*] *n* espuma (de jabón) ▷ *vt* enjabonar

**Latin** ['lætɪn] *n* latín *m* ▷ *adj* latino; **Latin America** *n* América latina; **Latin American** *adj, n* latinoamericano/a *m/f*

**latitude** ['lætɪtjuːd] *n* latitud *f*; (*fig*) libertad *f*

**latter** ['lætə*] *adj* último; (*of two*) segundo ▷ *n*: **the ~** el último, éste

**laugh** [lɑːf] *n* risa ▷ *vi* reír(se); **(to do sth) for a ~** (hacer algo) en broma; **laugh at** *vt fus* reírse de; **laughter** *n* risa

**launch** [lɔːntʃ] *n* lanzamiento; (*boat*) lancha ▷ *vt* (*ship*) botar; (*rocket etc*) lanzar; (*fig*) comenzar; **launch into** *vt fus* lanzarse a

**launder** ['lɔːndə*] *vt* lavar

**Launderette®** [lɔːn'drɛt] (*BRIT*) *n* lavandería (automática)

**Laundromat®** ['lɔːndrəmæt] (*US*) *n* = **Launderette**

**laundry** ['lɔːndrɪ] *n* (*dirty*) ropa sucia; (*clean*) colada; (*room*) lavadero

**lava** ['lɑːvə] *n* lava

**lavatory** ['lævətərɪ] *n* wáter *m*

**lavender** ['lævəndə*] *n* lavanda

**lavish** ['lævɪʃ] *adj* (*amount*) abundante;

(*person*): **~ with** pródigo en ▷ *vt*: **to ~ sth on sb** colmar a algn de algo

**law** [lɔː] *n* ley *f*; (*Scol*) derecho; (*a rule*) regla; (*professions connected with law*) jurisprudencia; **lawful** *adj* legítimo, lícito; **lawless** *adj* (*action*) criminal

**lawn** [lɔːn] *n* césped *m*; **lawnmower** *n* cortacésped *m*

**lawsuit** [ˈlɔːsuːt] *n* pleito

**lawyer** [ˈlɔːjə*] *n* abogado/a; (*for sales, wills etc*) notario/a

**lax** [læks] *adj* laxo

**laxative** [ˈlæksətɪv] *n* laxante *m*

**lay** [leɪ] (*pt, pp* **laid**) *pt of* **lie** ▷ *adj* laico; (*not expert*) lego ▷ *vt* (*place*) colocar; (*eggs, table*) poner; (*cable*) tender; (*carpet*) extender; **lay down** *vt* (*pen etc*) dejar; (*rules etc*) establecer; **to lay down the law** (*pej*) imponer las normas; **lay off** *vt* (*workers*) despedir; **lay on** *vt* (*meal, facilities*) proveer; **lay out** *vt* (*spread out*) disponer, exponer; **lay-by** *n* (*BRIT Aut*) área de aparcamiento

**layer** [ˈleɪə*] *n* capa

**layman** [ˈleɪmən] (*irreg*) *n* lego

**layout** [ˈleɪaut] *n* (*design*) plan *m*, trazado; (*Press*) composición *f*

**lazy** [ˈleɪzɪ] *adj* perezoso, vago; (*movement*) lento

**lb.** *abbr* = **pound** (*weight*)

**lead¹** [liːd] (*pt, pp* **led**) *n* (*front position*) delantera; (*clue*) pista; (*Elec*) cable *m*; (*for dog*) correa; (*Theatre*) papel *m* principal ▷ *vt* (*walk etc in front*) ir a la cabeza de; (*guide*): **to ~ sb somewhere** conducir a algn a algún sitio; (*be leader*) dirigir; (*start, guide: activity*) protagonizar ▷ *vi* (*road, pipe etc*) conducir a; (*Sport*) ir primero; **to be in the ~** (*Sport*) llevar la delantera; (*fig*) ir a la cabeza; **to ~ the way** llevar la delantera; **lead up to** *vt fus* (*events*) conducir a; (*in conversation*) preparar el terreno para

**lead²** [lɛd] *n* (*metal*) plomo; (*in pencil*) mina

**leader** [ˈliːdə*] *n* jefe/a *m/f*, líder *mf*; (*Sport*) líder *mf*; **leadership** *n* dirección *f*; (*position*) mando; (*quality*) iniciativa

**lead-free** [ˈlɛdfriː] *adj* sin plomo

**leading** [ˈliːdɪŋ] *adj* (*main*) principal; (*first*) primero; (*front*) delantero

**lead singer** [liːd-] *n* cantante *mf*

**leaf** [liːf] (*pl* **leaves**) *n* hoja ▷ *vi*: **to ~ through** hojear; **to turn over a new ~** reformarse

**leaflet** [ˈliːflɪt] *n* folleto

**league** [liːɡ] *n* sociedad *f*; (*Football*) liga; **to be in ~ with** haberse confabulado con

**leak** [liːk] *n* (*of liquid, gas*) escape *m*, fuga; (*in pipe*) agujero; (*in roof*) gotera; (*in security*) filtración *f* ▷ *vi* (*shoes, ship*) hacer agua;

(*pipe*) tener (un) escape; (*roof*) gotear; (*liquid, gas*) escaparse, fugarse; (*fig*) divulgarse ▷ *vt* (*fig*) filtrar

**lean** [liːn] (*pt, pp* **~ed** *or* **~t**) *adj* (*thin*) flaco; (*meat*) magro ▷ *vt*: **to ~ sth on sth** apoyar algo en algo ▷ *vi* (*slope*) inclinarse; **to ~ against** apoyarse contra; **to ~ on** apoyarse en; **lean forward** *vi* inclinarse hacia adelante; **lean over** *vi* inclinarse; **leaning** *n*: **leaning (towards)** inclinación *f* (hacia)

**leant** [lɛnt] *pt, pp of* **lean**

**leap** [liːp] (*pt, pp* **~ed** *or* **~t**) *n* salto ▷ *vi* saltar

**leapt** [lɛpt] *pt, pp of* **leap**

**leap year** *n* año bisiesto

**learn** [lɜːn] (*pt, pp* **~ed** *or* **~t**) *vt* aprender ▷ *vi* aprender; **to ~ about sth** enterarse de algo; **to ~ to do sth** aprender a hacer algo; **learner** *n* (*BRIT: also*: **learner driver**) principiante *mf*; **learning** *n* el saber *m*, conocimientos *mpl*

**learnt** [lɜːnt] *pp of* **learn**

**lease** [liːs] *n* arriendo ▷ *vt* arrendar

**leash** [liːʃ] *n* correa

**least** [liːst] *adj*: **the ~** (*slightest*) el menor, el más pequeño; (*smallest amount of*) mínimo ▷ *adv* (+ *vb*) menos; (+ *adj*): **the ~ expensive** el (la) menos costoso/a; **the ~ possible effort** el menor esfuerzo posible; **at ~** por lo menos, al menos; **you could at ~ have written** por lo menos podías haber escrito; **not in the ~** en absoluto

**leather** [ˈlɛðə*] *n* cuero

**leave** [liːv] (*pt, pp* **left**) *vt* dejar; (*go away from*) abandonar; (*place etc: permanently*) salir de ▷ *vi* irse; (*train etc*) salir ▷ *n* permiso; **to ~ sth to sb** (*money etc*) legar algo a algn; (*responsibility etc*) encargar a algn de algo; **to be left** quedar, sobrar; **there's some milk left over** sobra *or* queda algo de leche; **on ~** de permiso; **leave behind** *vt* (*on purpose*) dejar; (*accidentally*) dejarse; **leave out** *vt* omitir

**leaves** [liːvz] *npl of* **leaf**

**Lebanon** [ˈlɛbənən] *n*: **the ~** el Líbano

**lecture** [ˈlɛktʃə*] *n* conferencia; (*Scol*) clase *f* ▷ *vi* dar una clase ▷ *vt* (*scold*): **to ~ sb on** *or* **about sth** echar una reprimenda a algn por algo; **to give a ~ on** dar una conferencia sobre; **lecture hall** *n* sala de conferencias; (*Univ*) aula; **lecturer** *n* conferenciante *mf*; (*BRIT: at university*) profesor(a) *m/f*; **lecture theatre** *n* = **lecture hall**

**led** [lɛd] *pt, pp of* **lead¹**

**ledge** [lɛdʒ] *n* repisa; (*of window*) alféizar *m*; (*of mountain*) saliente *m*

**leek** [liːk] *n* puerro

**left** [lɛft] *pt, pp of* **leave** ▷ *adj* izquierdo;

(remaining): **there are two ~** quedan dos ▷ *n* izquierda ▷ *adv* a la izquierda; **on** or **to the ~** a la izquierda; **the L~** (*Pol*) la izquierda; **left-hand** *adj*: **the left-hand side** la izquierda; **left-hand drive** *adj*: **a left-hand drive car** un coche con el volante a la izquierda; **left-handed** *adj* zurdo; **left-luggage locker** *n* (*BRIT*) consigna *f* automática; **left-luggage (office)** (*BRIT*) *n* consigna; **left-overs** *npl* sobras *fpl*; **left-wing** *adj* (*Pol*) de izquierdas, izquierdista

**leg** [lɛg] *n* pierna; (*of animal, chair*) pata; (*trouser leg*) pernera; (*Culin: of lamb*) pierna; (: *of chicken*) pata; (*of journey*) etapa

**legacy** ['lɛgəsɪ] *n* herencia

**legal** ['li:gl] *adj* (*permitted by law*) lícito; (*of law*) legal; **legal holiday** (*US*) *n* fiesta oficial; **legalize** *vt* legalizar; **legally** *adv* legalmente

**legend** ['lɛdʒənd] *n* (*also fig: person*) leyenda; **legendary** [-ərɪ] *adj* legendario

**leggings** ['lɛgɪŋz] *npl* mallas *fpl*, leggins *mpl*

**legible** ['lɛdʒəbl] *adj* legible

**legislation** [lɛdʒɪs'leɪʃən] *n* legislación *f*

**legislative** ['lɛdʒɪslətɪv] *adj* legislativo

**legitimate** [lɪ'dʒɪtɪmət] *adj* legítimo

**leisure** ['lɛʒə*] *n* ocio, tiempo libre; **at ~** con tranquilidad; **leisure centre** (*BRIT*) *n* centro de recreo; **leisurely** *adj* sin prisa; lento

**lemon** ['lɛmən] *n* limón *m*; **lemonade** *n* (*fizzy*) gaseosa; **lemon tea** *n* té *m* con limón

**lend** [lɛnd] (*pt, pp* **lent**) *vt*: **to ~ sth to sb** prestar algo a algn

**length** [lɛŋθ] *n* (*size*) largo, longitud *f*; (*distance*): **the ~ of** todo lo largo de; (*of swimming pool, cloth*) largo; (*of wood, string*) trozo; (*amount of time*) duración *f*; **at ~** (*at last*) por fin, finalmente; (*lengthily*) largamente; **lengthen** *vt* alargar ▷ *vi* alargarse; **lengthways** *adv* a lo largo; **lengthy** *adj* largo, extenso

**lens** [lɛnz] *n* (*of spectacles*) lente *f*; (*of camera*) objetivo

**Lent** [lɛnt] *n* Cuaresma

**lent** [lɛnt] *pt, pp of* **lend**

**lentil** ['lɛntl] *n* lenteja

**Leo** ['li:əu] *n* Leo

**leopard** ['lɛpəd] *n* leopardo

**leotard** ['li:ətɑ:d] *n* mallas *fpl*

**leprosy** ['lɛprəsɪ] *n* lepra

**lesbian** ['lɛzbɪən] *n* lesbiana

**less** [lɛs] *adj* (*in size, degree etc*) menor; (*in quality*) menos ▷ *pron, adv* menos ▷ *prep*: ~ **tax/10% discount** menos impuestos/el 10 por ciento de descuento; **~ than half** menos de la mitad; **~ than ever** menos que

nunca; **~ and ~** cada vez menos; **the ~ he works ...** cuanto menos trabaja ...; **lessen** *vi* disminuir, reducirse ▷ *vt* disminuir, reducir; **lesser** ['lɛsə*] *adj* menor; **to a lesser extent** en menor grado

**lesson** ['lɛsn] *n* clase *f*; (*warning*) lección *f*

**let** [lɛt] (*pt, pp ~*) *vt* (*allow*) dejar, permitir; (*BRIT: lease*) alquilar; **to ~ sb do sth** dejar que algn haga algo; **to ~ sb know sth** comunicar algo a algn; **~'s go** ¡vamos!; **~ him come** que venga; **"to ~"** "se alquila"; **let down** *vt* (*tyre*) desinflar; (*disappoint*) defraudar; **let in** *vt* dejar entrar; (*visitor etc*) hacer pasar; **let off** *vt* (*culprit*) dejar escapar; (*gun*) disparar; (*bomb*) accionar; (*firework*) hacer estallar; **let out** *vt* dejar salir; (*sound*) soltar

**lethal** ['li:θl] *adj* (*weapon*) mortífero; (*poison, wound*) mortal

**letter** ['lɛtə*] *n* (*of alphabet*) letra; (*correspondence*) carta; **letterbox** (*BRIT*) *n* buzón *m*

**lettuce** ['lɛtɪs] *n* lechuga

**leukaemia** [lu:'ki:mɪə] (*US* **leukemia**) *n* leucemia

**level** ['lɛvl] *adj* (*flat*) llano ▷ *adv*: **to draw ~ with** llegar a la altura de ▷ *n* nivel *m*; (*height*) altura ▷ *vt* nivelar; allanar; (*destroy: building*) derribar; (: *forest*) arrasar; **to be ~ with** estar a nivel de; **A ~s** (*BRIT*) ≈ exámenes *mpl* de bachillerato superior, B.U.P., E.S.O.; **AS ~** (*BRIT*) asignatura aprobada entre los "GCSEs" y los "A levels"; **on the ~** (*fig: honest*) serio; **level crossing** (*BRIT*) *n* paso a nivel

**lever** ['li:və*] *n* (*also fig*) palanca ▷ *vt*: **to ~ up** levantar con palanca; **leverage** *n* (*using bar etc*) apalancamiento; (*fig: influence*) influencia

**levy** ['lɛvɪ] *n* impuesto ▷ *vt* exigir, recaudar

**liability** [laɪə'bɪlətɪ] *n* (*pej: person, thing*) estorbo, lastre *m*; (*Jur: responsibility*) responsabilidad *f*

**liable** ['laɪəbl] *adj* (*subject*): **~ to** sujeto a; (*responsible*): **~ for** responsable de; (*likely*): **~ to do** propenso a hacer

**liaise** [lɪ'eɪz] *vi*: **to ~ with** enlazar con

**liar** ['laɪə*] *n* mentiroso/a

**liberal** ['lɪbərəl] *adj* liberal; (*offer, amount etc*) generoso; **Liberal Democrat** *n* (*BRIT*) demócrata *m/f* liberal

**liberate** ['lɪbəreɪt] *vt* (*people: from poverty etc*) librar; (*prisoner*) libertar; (*country*) liberar

**liberation** [lɪbə'reɪʃən] *n* liberación *f*

**liberty** ['lɪbətɪ] *n* libertad *f*; **to be at ~** (*criminal*) estar en libertad; **to be at ~ to do** estar libre para hacer; **to take the ~ of doing sth** tomarse la libertad de hacer algo

**Libra** ['li:brə] *n* Libra

**librarian** [laɪˈbrɛərɪən] n bibliotecario/a
**library** [ˈlaɪbrərɪ] n biblioteca

> Be careful not to translate **library** by the Spanish word **librería**.

**Libya** [ˈlɪbɪə] n Libia
**lice** [laɪs] npl of **louse**
**licence** [ˈlaɪsəns] (US **license**) n licencia;
(permit) permiso; (also: **driving ~**) carnet m
de conducir (SP), licencia de manejo (LAM)
**license** [ˈlaɪsəns] n (US) = **licence** ▷ vt
autorizar, dar permiso a; **licensed** adj (for
alcohol) autorizado para vender bebidas
alcohólicas; (car) matriculado; **license
plate** (US) n placa (de matrícula); **licensing
hours** (BRIT) npl horas durante las cuales se
permite la venta y consumo de alcohol (en un
bar etc)
**lick** [lɪk] vt lamer; (inf: defeat) dar una paliza
a; **to ~ one's lips** relamerse
**lid** [lɪd] n (of box, case) tapa; (of pan)
tapadera
**lie** [laɪ] (pt **lay**, pp **lain**) vi (rest) estar
echado, estar acostado; (of object: be
situated) estar, encontrarse; (tell lies: pt, pp
**lied**) mentir ▷ n mentira; **to ~ low** (fig)
mantenerse a escondidas; **lie about** or
**around** vi (things) estar tirado; (BRIT: people)
estar tumbado; **lie down** vi echarse,
tumbarse
**Liechtenstein** [ˈlɪktənstaɪn] n
Liechtenstein m
**lie-in** [ˈlaɪɪn] (BRIT) n: **to have a ~** quedarse
en la cama
**lieutenant** [lɛfˈtenənt, US luːˈtenənt] n
(Mil) teniente mf
**life** [laɪf] (pl **lives**) n vida; **to come to ~**
animarse; **life assurance** (BRIT) n seguro
de vida; **lifeboat** n lancha de socorro;
**lifeguard** n vigilante mf, socorrista mf;
**life insurance** n = **life assurance**; **life
jacket** n chaleco salvavidas; **lifelike**
adj (model etc) que parece vivo; (realistic)
realista; **life preserver** (US) n cinturón
m/chaleco salvavidas; **life sentence** n
cadena perpetua; **lifestyle** n estilo de vida;
**lifetime** n (of person) vida; (of thing) período
de vida
**lift** [lɪft] vt levantar; (end: ban, rule)
levantar, suprimir ▷ vi (fog) disiparse ▷ n
(BRIT: machine) ascensor m; **to give sb a ~**
(BRIT) llevar a algn en el coche; **lift up** vt
levantar; **lift-off** n despegue m
**light** [laɪt] (pt, pp **~ed** or **lit**) n luz f; (lamp)
luz f, lámpara; (Aut) faro; (for cigarette
etc): **have you got a ~?** ¿tienes fuego? ▷ vt
(candle, cigarette, fire) encender (SP), prender
(LAM); (room) alumbrar ▷ adj (colour) claro;
(not heavy, also fig) ligero; (room) con mucha
luz; (gentle, graceful) ágil; **lights** npl (traffic
lights) semáforos mpl; **to come to ~** salir a
luz; **in the ~ of** (new evidence etc) a la luz de;
**light up** vi (smoke) encender un cigarrillo;
(face) iluminarse ▷ vt (illuminate) iluminar,
alumbrar; (set fire to) encender; **light bulb**
n bombilla (SP), foco (MEX), bujía (CAM),
bombita (RPL); **lighten** vt (make less heavy)
aligerar; **lighter** n (also: **cigarette lighter**)
encendedor m, mechero; **light-hearted**
adj (person) alegre; (remark etc) divertido;
**lighthouse** n faro; **lighting** n (system)
alumbrado; **lightly** adv ligeramente; (not
seriously) con poca seriedad; **to get off
lightly** ser castigado con poca severidad
**lightning** [ˈlaɪtnɪŋ] n relámpago, rayo
**lightweight** [ˈlaɪtweɪt] adj (suit) ligero
▷ n (Boxing) peso ligero
**like** [laɪk] vt gustarle a algn ▷ prep como
▷ adj parecido, semejante ▷ n: **and the
~ y** otros por el estilo; **his ~s and dislikes**
sus gustos y aversiones; **I would ~, I'd ~**
me gustaría; (for purchase) quisiera; **would
you ~ a coffee?** ¿te apetece un café?; **I ~
swimming** me gusta nadar; **she ~s apples**
le gustan las manzanas; **to be** or **look ~
sb/sth** parecerse a algn/algo; **what does it
look/taste/sound ~?** ¿cómo es/a qué sabe/
cómo suena?; **that's just ~ him** es muy de
él, es característico de él; **do it ~ this** hazlo
así; **it is nothing ~ ...** no tiene parecido
alguno con ...; **likeable** adj simpático,
agradable
**likelihood** [ˈlaɪklɪhud] n probabilidad f
**likely** [ˈlaɪklɪ] adj probable; **he's ~ to leave**
es probable que se vaya; **not ~!** ¡ni hablar!
**likewise** [ˈlaɪkwaɪz] adv igualmente; **to
do ~** hacer lo mismo
**liking** [ˈlaɪkɪŋ] n: **~ (for)** (person) cariño
(a); (thing) afición (a); **to be to sb's ~** ser del
gusto de algn
**lilac** [ˈlaɪlək] n (tree) lilo; (flower) lila
**Lilo®** [ˈlaɪləu] n colchoneta inflable
**lily** [ˈlɪlɪ] n lirio, azucena; **~ of the valley**
lirio de los valles
**limb** [lɪm] n miembro
**limbo** [ˈlɪmbəu] n: **to be in ~** (fig) quedar a
la expectativa
**lime** [laɪm] n (tree) limero; (fruit) lima;
(Geo) cal f
**limelight** [ˈlaɪmlaɪt] n: **to be in the ~** (fig)
ser el centro de atención
**limestone** [ˈlaɪmstəun] n piedra caliza
**limit** [ˈlɪmɪt] n límite m ▷ vt limitar;
**limited** adj limitado; **to be limited to**
limitarse a
**limousine** [ˈlɪməziːn] n limusina
**limp** [lɪmp] n: **to have a ~** tener cojera ▷ vi

cojear ▷ adj flojo; (material) fláccido
**line** [laɪn] n línea; (rope) cuerda; (for fishing) sedal m; (wire) hilo; (row, series) fila, hilera; (of writing) renglón m, línea; (of song) verso; (of face) arruga; (Rail) vía ▷ vt (road etc) llenar; (Sewing) forrar; **to ~ the streets** llenar las aceras; **in ~ with** alineado con; (according to) de acuerdo con; **line up** vi hacer cola ▷ vt alinear; (prepare) preparar; organizar
**linear** ['lɪnɪə*] adj lineal
**linen** ['lɪnɪn] n ropa blanca; (cloth) lino
**liner** ['laɪnə*] n vapor m de línea, transatlántico; (for bin) bolsa (de basura)
**line-up** ['laɪnʌp] n (us: queue) cola; (Sport) alineación f
**linger** ['lɪŋgə*] vi retrasarse, tardar en marcharse; (smell, tradition) persistir
**lingerie** ['lænʒəriː] n lencería
**linguist** ['lɪŋgwɪst] n lingüista mf; **linguistic** adj lingüístico
**lining** ['laɪnɪŋ] n forro; (Anat) (membrana) mucosa
**link** [lɪŋk] n (of a chain) eslabón m; (relationship) relación f, vínculo; (Internet) link m, enlace m ▷ vt vincular, unir; (associate): **to ~ with** or **to** relacionar con; **links** npl (Golf) campo de golf; **link up** vt acoplar ▷ vi unirse
**lion** ['laɪən] n león m; **lioness** n leona
**lip** [lɪp] n labio; **lipread** vi leer los labios; **lip salve** n crema protectora para labios; **lipstick** n lápiz m de labios, carmín m
**liqueur** [lɪ'kjuə*] n licor m
**liquid** ['lɪkwɪd] adj, n líquido; **liquidizer** [-aɪzə*] n licuadora
**liquor** ['lɪkə*] n licor m, bebidas fpl alcohólicas; **liquor store** (us) n bodega, tienda de vinos y bebidas alcohólicas
**Lisbon** ['lɪzbən] n Lisboa
**lisp** [lɪsp] n ceceo ▷ vi cecear
**list** [lɪst] n lista ▷ vt (mention) enumerar; (put on a list) poner en una lista
**listen** ['lɪsn] vi escuchar, oír; **to ~ to sb/sth** escuchar a algn/algo; **listener** n oyente mf; (Radio) radioyente mf
**lit** [lɪt] pt, pp of **light**
**liter** ['liːtə*] (us) n = **litre**
**literacy** ['lɪtərəsɪ] n capacidad f de leer y escribir
**literal** ['lɪtərl] adj literal; **literally** adv literalmente
**literary** ['lɪtərərɪ] adj literario
**literate** ['lɪtərət] adj que sabe leer y escribir; (educated) culto
**literature** ['lɪtərɪtʃə*] n literatura; (brochures etc) folletos mpl
**litre** ['liːtə*] (us **liter**) n litro
**litter** ['lɪtə*] n (rubbish) basura; (young

animals) camada, cría; **litter bin** (BRIT) n papelera; **littered** adj: **littered with** (scattered) lleno de
**little** ['lɪtl] adj (small) pequeño; (not much) poco ▷ adv poco; **a ~** un poco (de); **~ house/bird** casita/pajarito; **a ~ bit** un poquito; **~ by ~** poco a poco; **little finger** n dedo meñique
**live¹** [laɪv] adj (animal) vivo; (wire) conectado; (broadcast) en directo; (shell) cargado
**live²** [lɪv] vi vivir; **live together** vi vivir juntos; **live up to** vt fus (fulfil) cumplir con
**livelihood** ['laɪvlɪhud] n sustento
**lively** ['laɪvlɪ] adj vivo; (interesting: place, book etc) animado
**liven up** ['laɪvn-] vt animar ▷ vi animarse
**liver** ['lɪvə*] n hígado
**lives** [laɪvz] npl of **life**
**livestock** ['laɪvstɔk] n ganado
**living** ['lɪvɪŋ] adj (alive) vivo ▷ n: **to earn** or **make a ~** ganarse la vida; **living room** n sala (de estar)
**lizard** ['lɪzəd] n lagarto; (small) lagartija
**load** [ləud] n carga; (weight) peso ▷ vt (Comput) cargar; (also: **~ up**): **to ~ (with)** cargar (con or de); **a ~ of rubbish** (inf) tonterías fpl; **a ~ of, ~s of** (fig) (gran) cantidad de, montones de; **loaded** adj (vehicle): **to be loaded with** estar cargado de
**loaf** [ləuf] (pl **loaves**) n (barra de) pan m
**loan** [ləun] n préstamo ▷ vt prestar; **on ~** prestado
**loathe** [ləuð] vt aborrecer; (person) odiar
**loaves** [ləuvz] npl of **loaf**
**lobby** ['lɔbɪ] n vestíbulo, sala de espera; (Pol: pressure group) grupo de presión ▷ vt presionar
**lobster** ['lɔbstə*] n langosta
**local** ['ləukl] adj local ▷ n (pub) bar m; **the locals** npl los vecinos, los del lugar; **local anaesthetic** n (Med) anestesia local; **local authority** n municipio, ayuntamiento (SP); **local government** n gobierno municipal; **locally** [-kəlɪ] adv en la vecindad; por aquí
**locate** [ləu'keɪt] vt (find) localizar; (situate): **to be ~d in** estar situado en
**location** [ləu'keɪʃən] n situación f; **on ~** (Cinema) en exteriores
**loch** [lɔx] n lago
**lock** [lɔk] n (of door, box) cerradura; (of canal) esclusa; (of hair) mechón m ▷ vt (with key) cerrar (con llave) ▷ vi (door etc) cerrarse (con llave); (wheels) trabarse; **lock in** vt encerrar; **lock out** vt (person) cerrar la puerta a; **lock up** vt (criminal) meter en la cárcel; (mental patient) encerrar; (house)

cerrar (con llave) ▷ vi echar la llave

**locker** ['lɔkə*] n casillero; **locker-room** (US) n (Sport) vestuario

**locksmith** ['lɔksmɪθ] n cerrajero/a

**locomotive** [ləukə'məutɪv] n locomotora

**lodge** [lɔdʒ] n casita (del guarda) ▷ vi (person): **to ~ (with)** alojarse (en casa de); (bullet, bone) incrustarse ▷ vt presentar; **lodger** n huésped mf

**lodging** ['lɔdʒɪŋ] n alojamiento, hospedaje m

**loft** [lɔft] n desván m

**log** [lɔg] n (of wood) leño, tronco; (written account) diario ▷ vt anotar; **log in, log on** vi (Comput) entrar en el sistema; **log off, log out** vi (Comput) salir del sistema

**logic** ['lɔdʒɪk] n lógica; **logical** adj lógico

**logo** ['ləugəu] n logotipo

**lollipop** ['lɔlɪpɔp] n pirulí m; **lollipop man/lady** (BRIT: irreg) n persona encargada de ayudar a los niños a cruzar la calle

**lolly** ['lɔlɪ] n (inf: ice cream) polo; (: lollipop) piruleta; (: money) guita

**London** ['lʌndən] n Londres; **Londoner** n londinense mf

**lone** [ləun] adj solitario

**loneliness** ['ləunlɪnɪs] n soledad f; aislamiento

**lonely** ['ləunlɪ] adj (situation) solitario; (person) solo; (place) aislado

**long** [lɔŋ] adj largo ▷ adv mucho tiempo, largamente ▷ vi: **to ~ for sth** anhelar algo; **so** or **as ~ as** mientras, con tal que; **don't be ~!** ¡no tardes!, ¡vuelve pronto!; **how ~ is the street?** ¿cuánto tiene la calle de largo?; **how ~ is the lesson?** ¿cuánto dura la clase?; **6 metres ~** que mide 6 metros, de 6 metros de largo; **6 months ~** que dura 6 meses, de 6 meses de duración; **all night ~** toda la noche; **he no ~er comes** ya no viene; **I can't stand it any ~er** ya no lo aguanto más; **~ before** mucho antes; **before ~** (+ future) dentro de poco; (+ past) poco tiempo después; **at ~ last** al fin, por fin; **long-distance** adj (race) de larga distancia; (call) interurbano; **long-haul** adj (flight) de larga distancia; **longing** n anhelo, ansia; (nostalgia) nostalgia ▷ adj anhelante

**longitude** ['lɔŋgɪtjuːd] n longitud f

**long: long jump** n salto de longitud; **long-life** adj (batteries) de larga duración; (milk) uperizado; **long-sighted** (BRIT) adj présbita; **long-standing** adj de mucho tiempo; **long-term** adj a largo plazo

**loo** [luː] (BRIT: inf) n wáter m

**look** [luk] vi mirar; (seem) parecer; (building etc): **to ~ south/on to the sea** dar al sur/al mar ▷ n (gen): **to have a ~** mirar; (glance) mirada; (appearance) aire m, aspecto; **looks** npl (good looks) belleza; **~ (here)!** (expressing annoyance etc) ¡oye!; **~!** (expressing surprise) ¡mira!; **look after** vt fus (care for) cuidar a; (deal with) encargarse de; **look around** vi echar una mirada alrededor; **look at** vt fus mirar; (read quickly) echar un vistazo a; **look back** vi mirar hacia atrás; **look down on** vt fus (fig) despreciar, mirar con desprecio; **look for** vt fus buscar; **look forward to** vt fus esperar con ilusión; (in letters): **we look forward to hearing from you** quedamos a la espera de sus gratas noticias; **look into** vt investigar; **look out** vi (beware): **to look out (for)** tener cuidado (de); **look out for** vt fus (seek) buscar; (await) esperar; **look round** vi volver la cabeza; **look through** vt fus (examine) examinar; **look up** vi mirar hacia arriba; (improve) mejorar ▷ vt (word) buscar; **look up to** vt fus admirar; **lookout** n (tower etc) puesto de observación; (person) vigía mf; **to be on the lookout for sth** estar al acecho de algo

**loom** [luːm] vi: **~ (up)** (threaten) surgir, amenazar; (event: approach) aproximarse

**loony** ['luːnɪ] (inf) n, adj loco/a m/f

**loop** [luːp] n lazo ▷ vt: **to ~ sth round sth** pasar algo alrededor de algo; **loophole** n escapatoria

**loose** [luːs] adj suelto; (clothes) ancho; (morals, discipline) relajado; **to be on the ~** estar en libertad; **to be at a ~ end** or **at ~ ends** (US) no saber qué hacer; **loosely** adv libremente, aproximadamente; **loosen** vt aflojar

**loot** [luːt] n botín m ▷ vt saquear

**lop-sided** ['lɔp'saɪdɪd] adj torcido

**lord** [lɔːd] n señor m; **L~ Smith** Lord Smith; **the L~** el Señor; **my ~** (to bishop) Ilustrísima; (to noble etc) Señor; **good L~!** ¡Dios mío!; **Lords** npl (BRIT: Pol): **the (House of) Lords** la Cámara de los Lores

**lorry** ['lɔrɪ] (BRIT) n camión m; **lorry driver** (BRIT) n camionero/a

**lose** [luːz] (pt, pp **lost**) vt perder ▷ vi perder, ser vencido; **to ~ (time)** (clock) atrasarse; **lose out** vi salir perdiendo; **loser** n perdedor(a) m/f

**loss** [lɔs] n pérdida; **heavy ~es** (Mil) grandes pérdidas; **to be at a ~** no saber qué hacer; **to make a ~** sufrir pérdidas

**lost** [lɔst] pt, pp of **lose** ▷ adj perdido; **lost property** (US **lost and found**) n objetos mpl perdidos

**lot** [lɔt] n (group: of things) grupo; (at auctions) lote m; **the ~** el todo, todos; **a ~ (large number: of books etc)** muchos; (a great deal) mucho, bastante; **a ~ of, ~s**

**of** mucho(s) (pl); **I read a ~** leo bastante;
**to draw ~s (for sth)** echar suertes (para
decidir algo)
**lotion** ['ləʊʃən] n loción f
**lottery** ['lɒtərɪ] n lotería
**loud** [laʊd] adj (voice, sound) fuerte;
(laugh, shout) estrepitoso; (condemnation
etc) enérgico; (gaudy) chillón/ona ▷ adv
(speak etc) fuerte; **out ~** en voz alta;**loudly**
adv (noisily) fuerte; (aloud) en voz alta;
**loudspeaker** n altavoz m
**lounge** [laʊndʒ] n salón m, sala (de estar);
(at airport etc) sala; (BRIT: also: **~-bar**) salón-
bar m ▷ vi (also: **~ about** or **around**) reposar,
holgazanear
**louse** [laʊs] (pl **lice**) n piojo
**lousy** ['laʊzɪ] (inf) adj (bad quality)
malísimo, asqueroso; (ill) fatal
**love** [lʌv] n (romantic, sexual) amor m; (kind,
caring) cariño ▷ vt amar, querer; (thing,
activity) encantarle a algn; **"~ from Anne"**
(on letter) "un abrazo (de) Anne"; **to ~ to do**
encantarle a algn hacer; **to be/fall in ~ with**
estar enamorado/enamorarse de; **to make
~** hacer el amor; **for the ~ of** por amor de;
**"15 ~"** (Tennis) "15 a cero"; **I ~ you** te quiero;
**I ~ paella** me encanta la paella;**love affair**
n aventura sentimental;**love life** n vida
sentimental
**lovely** ['lʌvlɪ] adj (delightful)
encantador(a); (beautiful) precioso
**lover** ['lʌvə*] n amante mf; (person in
love) enamorado; (amateur): **a ~ of** un(a)
aficionado/a or un(a) amante de
**loving** ['lʌvɪŋ] adj amoroso, cariñoso;
(action) tierno
**low** [ləʊ] adj, adv bajo ▷ n (Meteorology)
área de baja presión; **to be ~ on** (supplies etc)
andar mal de; **to feel ~** sentirse deprimido;
**to turn (down) ~** bajar;**low-alcohol** adj de
bajo contenido en alcohol;**low-calorie** adj
bajo en calorías
**lower** ['ləʊə*] adj más bajo; (less important)
menos importante ▷ vt bajar; (reduce)
reducir ▷ vr: **to ~ o.s. to** (fig) rebajarse a
**low-fat** adj (milk, yoghurt) desnatado; (diet)
bajo en calorías
**loyal** ['lɔɪəl] adj leal;**loyalty** n lealtad f;
**loyalty card** n tarjeta cliente
**L.P.** n abbr (= long-playing record) elepé m
**L-plates** ['ɛl-] (BRIT) npl placas fpl de
aprendiz de conductor

**Lt** abbr (= lieutenant) Tte.
**Ltd** abbr (= limited company) S.A.
**luck** [lʌk] n suerte f; **bad ~** mala suerte;
**good ~!** ¡que tengas suerte!, ¡suerte!; **bad**
or **hard** or **tough ~!** ¡qué pena!;**luckily** adv
afortunadamente;**lucky** adj afortunado;
(at cards etc) con suerte; (object) que trae
suerte
**lucrative** ['lu:krətɪv] adj lucrativo
**ludicrous** ['lu:dɪkrəs] adj absurdo
**luggage** ['lʌgɪdʒ] n equipaje m;**luggage
rack** n (on car) baca, portaequipajes m inv
**lukewarm** ['lu:kwɔ:m] adj tibio
**lull** [lʌl] n tregua ▷ vt: **to ~ sb to sleep**
arrullar a algn; **to ~ sb into a false sense of
security** dar a algn una falsa sensación de
seguridad
**lullaby** ['lʌləbaɪ] n nana
**lumber** ['lʌmbə*] n (junk) trastos mpl
viejos; (wood) maderos mpl
**luminous** ['lu:mɪnəs] adj luminoso
**lump** [lʌmp] n terrón m; (fragment) trozo;
(swelling) bulto ▷ vt (also: **~ together**)
juntar;**lump sum** n suma global;**lumpy**
adj (sauce) lleno de grumos; (mattress) lleno
de bultos
**lunatic** ['lu:nətɪk] adj loco
**lunch** [lʌntʃ] n almuerzo, comida ▷ vi
almorzar;**lunch break, lunch hour** n hora
del almuerzo;**lunch time** n hora de comer
**lung** [lʌŋ] n pulmón m
**lure** [luə*] n (attraction) atracción f ▷ vt
tentar
**lurk** [lə:k] vi (person, animal) estar al
acecho; (fig) acechar
**lush** [lʌʃ] adj exuberante
**lust** [lʌst] n lujuria; (greed) codicia
**Luxembourg** ['lʌksəmbə:g] n
Luxemburgo
**luxurious** [lʌg'zjʊərɪəs] adj lujoso
**luxury** ['lʌkʃərɪ] n lujo ▷ cpd de lujo
**Lycra**® ['laɪkrə] n licra®
**lying** ['laɪɪŋ] n mentiras fpl ▷ adj
mentiroso
**lyrics** ['lɪrɪks] npl (of song) letra

**m.** *abbr* = **metre; mile; million**

**M.A.** *abbr* = **Master of Arts**

**ma** (*inf*) [mɑː] *n* mamá

**mac** [mæk] (*BRIT*) *n* impermeable *m*

**macaroni** [mækəˈrəʊnɪ] *n* macarrones *mpl*

**Macedonia** [mæsɪˈdəʊnɪə] *n* Macedonia; **Macedonian** [-ˈdəʊnɪən] *adj* macedonio ▷*n* macedonio/a; (*Ling*) macedonio

**machine** [məˈʃiːn] *n* máquina ▷*vt* (*dress etc*) coser a máquina; (*Tech*) hacer a máquina; **machine gun** *n* ametralladora; **machinery** *n* maquinaria; (*fig*) mecanismo; **machine washable** *adj* lavable a máquina

**macho** [ˈmætʃəʊ] *adj* machista

**mackerel** [ˈmækrl] *n inv* caballa

**mackintosh** [ˈmækɪntɒʃ] (*BRIT*) *n* impermeable *m*

**mad** [mæd] *adj* loco; (*idea*) disparatado; (*angry*) furioso; (*keen*): **to be ~ about sth** volverle loco a algn algo

**Madagascar** [mædəˈgæskəʳ] *n* Madagascar *m*

**madam** [ˈmædəm] *n* señora

**mad cow disease** *n* encefalopatía espongiforme bovina

**made** [meɪd] *pt, pp* of **make; made-to-measure** (*BRIT*) *adj* hecho a la medida; **made-up** [ˈmeɪdʌp] *adj* (*story*) ficticio

**madly** [ˈmædlɪ] *adv* locamente

**madman** [ˈmædmən] (*irreg*) *n* loco

**madness** [ˈmædnɪs] *n* locura

**Madrid** [məˈdrɪd] *n* Madrid

**Mafia** [ˈmæfɪə] *n* Mafia

**mag** [mæg] *n abbr* (*BRIT inf*) = **magazine**

**magazine** [mægəˈziːn] *n* revista; (*Radio, TV*) programa *m* magazina

**maggot** [ˈmægət] *n* gusano

**magic** [ˈmædʒɪk] *n* magia ▷*adj* mágico; **magical** *adj* mágico; **magician** [məˈdʒɪʃən] *n* mago/a; (*conjurer*) prestidigitador(a) *m/f*

**magistrate** [ˈmædʒɪstreɪt] *n* juez *mf* (municipal)

**magnet** [ˈmægnɪt] *n* imán *m*; **magnetic** [-ˈnɛtɪk] *adj* magnético; (*personality*) atrayente

**magnificent** [mægˈnɪfɪsənt] *adj* magnífico

**magnify** [ˈmægnɪfaɪ] *vt* (*object*) ampliar; (*sound*) aumentar; **magnifying glass** *n* lupa

**magpie** [ˈmægpaɪ] *n* urraca

**mahogany** [məˈhɒgənɪ] *n* caoba

**maid** [meɪd] *n* criada; **old ~** (*pej*) solterona

**maiden name** *n* nombre *m* de soltera

**mail** [meɪl] *n* correo; (*letters*) cartas *fpl* ▷*vt* echar al correo; **mailbox**(*us*) *n* buzón *m*; **mailing list** *n* lista de direcciones; **mailman**(*us: irreg*) *n* cartero; **mail-order** *n* pedido postal

**main** [meɪn] *adj* principal, mayor ▷*n* (*pipe*) cañería maestra; (*us*) red *f* eléctrica ▷ **the ~s** *npl* (*BRIT Elec*) la red eléctrica; **in the ~** en general; **main course** *n* (*Culin*) plato principal; **mainland** *n* tierra firme; **mainly** *adv* principalmente; **main road** *n* carretera; **mainstream** *n* corriente *f* principal; **main street** *n* calle *f* mayor

**maintain** [meɪnˈteɪn] *vt* mantener; **maintenance** [ˈmeɪntənəns] *n* mantenimiento; (*Law*) manutención *f*

**maisonette** [meɪzəˈnɛt] *n* dúplex *m*

**maize** [meɪz] (*BRIT*) *n* maíz *m*, choclo (*sc*)

**majesty** [ˈmædʒɪstɪ] *n* majestad *f*; (*title*): **Your M~** Su Majestad

**major** [ˈmeɪdʒəʳ] *n* (*Mil*) comandante *mf* ▷*adj* principal; (*Mus*) mayor

**Majorca** [məˈjɔːkə] *n* Mallorca

**majority** [məˈdʒɒrɪtɪ] *n* mayoría

**make** [meɪk] (*pt, pp* **made**) *vt* hacer; (*manufacture*) fabricar; (*mistake*) cometer; (*speech*) pronunciar; (*cause to be*): **to ~ sb sad** poner triste a algn; (*force*): **to ~ sb do sth** obligar a algn a hacer algo; (*earn*) ganar; (*equal*): **2 and 2 ~ 4** 2 y 2 son 4 ▷*n* marca; **to ~ the bed** hacer la cama; **to ~ a fool of sb** poner a algn en ridículo; **to ~ a profit/loss** obtener ganancias/sufrir pérdidas; **to ~ it** (*arrive*) llegar; (*achieve sth*) tener éxito; **what time do you ~ it?** ¿qué hora tienes?; **to ~ do with** contentarse con; **make off** *vi* largarse; **make out** *vt* (*decipher*) descifrar; (*understand*) entender; (*see*) distinguir; (*cheque*) extender; **make up** *vt* (*invent*) inventar; (*prepare*) hacer; (*constitute*) constituir ▷*vi* reconciliarse; (*with cosmetics*) maquillarse; **make up for** *vt*

*fus* compensar; **makeover** ['meɪkəʊvə*]
*n* (*by beautician*) sesión *f* de maquillaje y
peluquería; (*change of image*) lavado de cara;
**maker** *n* fabricante *mf*; (*of film, programme*)
autor(a) *m/f*; **makeshift** *adj* improvisado;
**make-up** *n* maquillaje *m*

**making** ['meɪkɪŋ] *n* (*fig*): **in the ~** en vías
de formación; **to have the ~s of** (*person*)
tener madera de

**malaria** [mə'leərɪə] *n* malaria

**Malaysia** [mə'leɪzɪə] *n* Malasia, Malaysia

**male** [meɪl] *n* (*Biol*) macho ▷ *adj* (*sex,
attitude*) masculino; (*child etc*) varón

**malicious** [mə'lɪʃəs] *adj* malicioso;
rencoroso

**malignant** [mə'lɪgnənt] *adj* (*Med*)
maligno

**mall** [mɔːl] (*US*) *n* (*also*: **shopping ~**) centro
comercial

**mallet** ['mælɪt] *n* mazo

**malnutrition** [mælnjuː'trɪʃən] *n*
desnutrición *f*

**malpractice** [mæl'præktɪs] *n*
negligencia profesional

**malt** [mɔːlt] *n* malta; (*whisky*) whisky *m*
de malta

**Malta** ['mɔːltə] *n* Malta; **Maltese** [-'tiːz]
*adj, n inv* maltés/esa *m/f*

**mammal** ['mæml] *n* mamífero

**mammoth** ['mæməθ] *n* mamut *m* ▷ *adj*
gigantesco

**man** [mæn] (*pl* **men**) *n* hombre *m*;
(*mankind*) el hombre ▷ *vt* (*Naut*) tripular;
(*Mil*) guarnecer; (*operate: machine*) manejar;
**an old ~** un viejo; **~ and wife** marido y
mujer

**manage** ['mænɪdʒ] *vi* arreglárselas,
ir tirando ▷ *vt* (*be in charge of*) dirigir;
(*control: person*) manejar; (*: ship*)
gobernar; **manageable** *adj* manejable;
**management** *n* dirección *f*; **manager** *n*
director(a) *m/f*; (*of pop star*) mánager *mf*;
(*Sport*) entrenador(a) *m/f*; **manageress**
*n* directora; entrenadora; **managerial**
[-ə'dʒɪərɪəl] *adj* directivo; **managing
director** *n* director(a) *m/f* general

**mandarin** ['mændərɪn] *n* (*also*: **~ orange**)
mandarina; (*person*) mandarín *m*

**mandate** ['mændeɪt] *n* mandato

**mandatory** ['mændətərɪ] *adj* obligatorio

**mane** [meɪn] *n* (*of horse*) crin *f*; (*of lion*)
melena

**maneuver** [mə'nuːvə*] (*US*) = **manoeuvre**

**mangetout** [mɔnʒ'tuː] *n* tirabeque *m*

**mango** ['mæŋgəʊ] (*pl* **~es**) *n* mango

**man:** **manhole** *n* agujero de acceso;
**manhood** *n* edad *f* viril; (*state*) virilidad *f*

**mania** ['meɪnɪə] *n* manía; **maniac** *n*
['meɪnɪæk] *n* maníaco/a; (*fig*) maniático

**manic** ['mænɪk] *adj* frenético

**manicure** ['mænɪkjʊə*] *n* manicura

**manifest** ['mænɪfest] *vt* manifestar,
mostrar ▷ *adj* manifiesto

**manifesto** [mænɪ'festəu] *n* manifiesto

**manipulate** [mə'nɪpjuleɪt] *vt* manipular

**man: mankind** [mæn'kaɪnd] *n*
humanidad *f*, género humano; **manly** *adj*
varonil; **man-made** *adj* artificial

**manner** ['mænə*] *n* manera, modo;
(*behaviour*) conducta, manera de ser;
(*type*): **all ~ of things** toda clase de cosas;
**manners** *npl* (*behaviour*) modales *mpl*; **bad
~s** mala educación

**manoeuvre** [mə'nuːvə*] (*US* **maneuver**)
*vt, vi* maniobrar ▷ *n* maniobra

**manpower** ['mænpauə*] *n* mano *f* de
obra

**mansion** ['mænʃən] *n* palacio, casa
grande

**manslaughter** ['mænslɔːtə*] *n*
homicidio no premeditado

**mantelpiece** ['mæntlpiːs] *n* repisa,
chimenea

**manual** ['mænjuəl] *adj* manual ▷ *n*
manual *m*

**manufacture** [mænju'fæktʃə*] *vt*
fabricar ▷ *n* fabricación *f*; **manufacturer** *n*
fabricante *mf*

**manure** [mə'njuə*] *n* estiércol *m*

**manuscript** ['mænjuskrɪpt] *n*
manuscrito

**many** ['menɪ] *adj, pron* muchos/as; **a
great ~** muchísimos, un buen número de; **~
a time** muchas veces

**map** [mæp] *n* mapa *m* ▷ **to ~ out** *vt*
proyectar

**maple** ['meɪpl] *n* arce *m*, maple *m* (*LAM*)

**Mar** *abbr* (= *March*) mar

**mar** [mɑː*] *vt* estropear

**marathon** ['mærəθən] *n* maratón *m*

**marble** ['mɑːbl] *n* mármol *m*; (*toy*) canica

**March** [mɑːtʃ] *n* marzo

**march** [mɑːtʃ] *vi* (*Mil*) marchar;
(*demonstrators*) manifestarse ▷ *n* marcha;
(*demonstration*) manifestación *f*

**mare** [meə*] *n* yegua

**margarine** [mɑːdʒə'riːn] *n* margarina

**margin** ['mɑːdʒɪn] *n* margen *m*;
(*Comm: profit margin*) margen *m* de
beneficios; **marginal** *adj* marginal;
**marginally** *adv* ligeramente

**marigold** ['mærɪgəʊld] *n* caléndula

**marijuana** [mærɪ'wɑːnə] *n* marijuana

**marina** [mə'riːnə] *n* puerto deportivo

**marinade** [mærɪ'neɪd] *n* adobo

**marinate** ['mærɪneɪt] *vt* marinar

**marine** [mə'ri:n] *adj* marino ▷ *n* soldado de marina

**marital** ['mærɪtl] *adj* matrimonial; **marital status** *n* estado *m* civil

**maritime** ['mærɪtaɪm] *adj* marítimo

**marjoram** ['mɑ:dʒərəm] *n* mejorana

**mark** [mɑ:k] *n* marca, señal *f*; (*in snow, mud etc*) huella; (*stain*) mancha; (*BRIT Scol*) nota ▷ *vt* marcar; manchar; (*damage: furniture*) rayar; (*indicate: place etc*) señalar; (*BRIT Scol*) calificar, corregir; **to ~ time** marcar el paso; (*fig*) marcar(se) un ritmo; **marked** *adj* (*obvious*) marcado, acusado; **marker** *n* (*sign*) marcador *m*; (*bookmark*) señal *f* (de libro)

**market** ['mɑ:kɪt] *n* mercado ▷ *vt* (*Comm*) comercializar; **marketing** *n* márketing *m*; **marketplace** *n* mercado; **market research** *n* análisis *m inv* de mercados

**marmalade** ['mɑ:məleɪd] *n* mermelada de naranja

**maroon** [mə'ru:n] *vt*: **to be ~ed** quedar aislado; (*fig*) quedar abandonado ▷ *n* (*colour*) granate *m*

**marquee** [mɑ:'ki:] *n* entoldado

**marriage** ['mærɪdʒ] *n* (*relationship, institution*) matrimonio; (*wedding*) boda; (*act*) casamiento; **marriage certificate** *n* partida de casamiento

**married** ['mærɪd] *adj* casado; (*life, love*) conyugal

**marrow** ['mærəu] *n* médula; (*vegetable*) calabacín *m*

**marry** ['mærɪ] *vt* casarse con; (*father, priest etc*) casar ▷ *vi* (*also*: **get married**) casarse

**Mars** [mɑ:z] *n* Marte *m*

**marsh** [mɑ:ʃ] *n* pantano; (*salt marsh*) marisma

**marshal** ['mɑ:ʃl] *n* (*Mil*) mariscal *m*; (*at sports meeting etc*) oficial *m*; (*us: of police, fire department*) jefe/a *m/f* ▷ *vt* (*thoughts etc*) ordenar; (*soldiers*) formar

**martyr** ['mɑ:tə*] *n* mártir *mf*

**marvel** ['mɑ:vl] *n* maravilla, prodigio ▷ *vi*: **to ~ (at)** maravillarse (de); **marvellous** (*us* **marvelous**) *adj* maravilloso

**Marxism** ['mɑ:ksɪzəm] *n* marxismo

**Marxist** ['mɑ:ksɪst] *adj, n* marxista *mf*

**marzipan** ['mɑ:zɪpæn] *n* mazapán *m*

**mascara** [mæs'kɑ:rə] *n* rímel *m*

**mascot** ['mæskət] *n* mascota

**masculine** ['mæskjulɪn] *adj* masculino

**mash** [mæʃ] *vt* machacar; **mashed potato(es)** *n(pl)* puré *m* de patatas (*sp*) or papas (*LAM*)

**mask** [mɑ:sk] *n* máscara ▷ *vt* (*cover*): **to ~ one's face** ocultarse la cara; (*hide: feelings*) esconder

**mason** ['meɪsn] *n* (*also*: **stone~**) albañil *m*; (*also*: **free~**) masón *m*; **masonry** *n* (*in building*) mampostería

**mass** [mæs] *n* (*people*) muchedumbre *f*; (*of air, liquid etc*) masa; (*of detail, hair etc*) gran cantidad *f*; (*Rel*) misa ▷ *cpd* masivo ▷ *vi* reunirse; concentrarse; **the masses** *npl* las masas; **~es of** (*inf*) montones de

**massacre** ['mæsəkə*] *n* masacre *f*

**massage** ['mæsɑ:ʒ] *n* masaje *m* ▷ *vt* dar masaje en

**massive** ['mæsɪv] *adj* enorme; (*support, changes*) masivo

**mass media** *npl* medios *mpl* de comunicación

**mass-produce** ['mæsprə'dju:s] *vt* fabricar en serie

**mast** [mɑ:st] *n* (*Naut*) mástil *m*; (*Radio etc*) torre *f*

**master** ['mɑ:stə*] *n* (*of servant*) amo; (*of situation*) dueño, maestro; (*in primary school*) maestro; (*in secondary school*) profesor *m*; (*title for boys*): **M~ X** Señorito X ▷ *vt* dominar; **mastermind** *n* inteligencia superior ▷ *vt* dirigir, planear; **Master of Arts/Science** *n* licenciatura superior en Letras/Ciencias; **masterpiece** *n* obra maestra

**masturbate** ['mæstəbeɪt] *vi* masturbarse

**mat** [mæt] *n* estera; (*also*: **door~**) felpudo; (*also*: **table ~**) salvamanteles *m inv*, posavasos *m inv* ▷ *adj* = **matt**

**match** [mætʃ] *n* cerilla, fósforo; (*game*) partido; (*equal*) igual *m/f* ▷ *vt* (*go well with*) hacer juego con; (*equal*) igualar; (*correspond to*) corresponderse con; (*pair: also*: **~ up**) casar con ▷ *vi* hacer juego; **to be a good ~** hacer juego; **matchbox** *n* caja de cerillas; **matching** *adj* que hace juego

**mate** [meɪt] *n* (*workmate*) colega *mf*; (*inf: friend*) amigo/a; (*animal*) macho/hembra; (*in merchant navy*) segundo de a bordo ▷ *vi* acoplarse, aparearse ▷ *vt* aparear

**material** [mə'tɪərɪəl] *n* (*substance*) materia; (*information*) material *m*; (*cloth*) tela, tejido ▷ *adj* material; (*important*) esencial; **materials** *npl* materiales *mpl*

**materialize** [mə'tɪərɪəlaɪz] *vi* materializarse

**maternal** [mə'tə:nl] *adj* maternal

**maternity** [mə'tə:nɪtɪ] *n* maternidad *f*; **maternity hospital** *n* hospital *m* de maternidad; **maternity leave** *n* baja por maternidad

**math** [mæθ] (*us*) *n* = **mathematics**

**mathematical** [mæθə'mætɪkl] *adj* matemático

**mathematician** [mæθəmə'tɪʃən] *n*
matemático/a
**mathematics** [mæθə'mætɪks] *n*
matemáticas *fpl*
**maths** [mæθs] (BRIT) *n* = **mathematics**
**matinée** ['mætɪneɪ] *n* sesión *f* de tarde
**matron** ['meɪtrən] *n* enfermera *f* jefe; (*in
school*) ama de llaves
**matt** [mæt] *adj* mate
**matter** ['mætə*] *n* cuestión *f*, asunto;
(*Physics*) sustancia, materia; (*reading matter*)
material *m*; (*Med: pus*) pus *m* ▷ *vi* importar;
**matters** *npl* (*affairs*) asuntos *mpl*, temas
*mpl*; **it doesn't ~** no importa; **what's the
~?** ¿qué pasa?; **no ~ what** pase lo que pase;
**as a ~ of course** por rutina; **as a ~ of fact**
de hecho
**mattress** ['mætrɪs] *n* colchón *m*
**mature** [mə'tjuə*] *adj* maduro ▷ *vi*
madurar; **mature student** *n* estudiante *de
más de 21 años*; **maturity** *n* madurez *f*
**maul** [mɔːl] *vt* magullar
**mauve** [məʊv] *adj* de color malva (SP) or
guinda (LAM)
**max** *abbr* = **maximum**
**maximize** ['mæksɪmaɪz] *vt* (*profits etc*)
llevar al máximo; (*chances*) maximizar
**maximum** ['mæksɪməm] (*pl* **maxima**) *adj*
máximo ▷ *n* máximo
**May** [meɪ] *n* mayo
**may** [meɪ] (*conditional* **might**) *vi* (*indicating
possibility*): **he ~ come** puede que venga;
(*be allowed to*): **~ I smoke?** ¿puedo fumar?;
(*wishes*): **~ God bless you!** ¡que Dios le
bendiga!; **you ~ as well go** bien puedes irte
**maybe** ['meɪbiː] *adv* quizá(s)
**May Day** *n* el primero de Mayo
**mayhem** ['meɪhɛm] *n* caos *m* total
**mayonnaise** [meɪə'neɪz] *n* mayonesa
**mayor** [mɛə*] *n* alcalde *m*; **mayoress** *n*
alcaldesa
**maze** [meɪz] *n* laberinto
**MD** *n abbr* = **managing director**
**me** [miː] *pron* (*direct*) me; (*stressed, after
pron*) mí; **can you hear ~?** ¿me oyes?; **he
heard ME** ¡me oyó a mí!; **it's ~** soy yo; **give
them to ~** dámelos/las; **with/without ~**
conmigo/sin mí
**meadow** ['mɛdəʊ] *n* prado, pradera
**meagre** ['miːgə*] (US **meager**) *adj* escaso,
pobre
**meal** [miːl] *n* comida; (*flour*) harina;
**mealtime** *n* hora de comer
**mean** [miːn] (*pt, pp* **~t**) *adj* (*with money*)
tacaño; (*unkind*) mezquino, malo; (*shabby*)
humilde; (*average*) medio ▷ *vt* (*signify*)
querer decir, significar; (*refer to*) referirse
a; (*intend*): **to ~ to do sth** pensar or

pretender hacer algo ▷ *n* medio, término
medio; **means** *npl* (*way*) medio, manera;
(*money*) recursos *mpl*, medios *mpl*; **by ~s
of** mediante, por medio de; **by all ~s!**
¡naturalmente!, ¡claro que sí!; **do you ~ it?**
¿lo dices en serio?; **what do you ~?** ¿qué
quiere decir?; **to be ~t for sb/sth** ser para
algn/algo
**meaning** ['miːnɪŋ] *n* significado, sentido;
(*purpose*) sentido, propósito; **meaningful**
*adj* significativo; **meaningless** *adj* sin
sentido
**meant** [mɛnt] *pt, pp of* **mean**
**meantime** ['miːntaɪm] *adv* (*also:* **in the ~**)
mientras tanto
**meanwhile** ['miːnwaɪl] *adv* = **meantime**
**measles** ['miːzlz] *n* sarampión *m*
**measure** ['mɛʒə*] *vt, vi* medir ▷ *n*
medida; (*ruler*) regla; **measurement**
['mɛʒəmənt] *n* (*measure*) medida; (*act*)
medición *f*; **to take sb's measurements**
tomar las medidas a algn
**meat** [miːt] *n* carne *f*; **cold ~** fiambre *m*;
**meatball** *n* albóndiga
**Mecca** ['mɛkə] *n* La Meca
**mechanic** [mɪ'kænɪk] *n* mecánico/a;
**mechanical** *adj* mecánico
**mechanism** ['mɛkənɪzəm] *n* mecanismo
**medal** ['mɛdl] *n* medalla; **medallist** (US
**medalist**) *n* (*Sport*) medallista *mf*
**meddle** ['mɛdl] *vi*: **to ~ in** entrometerse en;
**to ~ with sth** manosear algo
**media** ['miːdɪə] *npl* medios *mpl* de
comunicación ▷ *npl of* **medium**
**mediaeval** [mɛdɪ'iːvl] *adj* = **medieval**
**mediate** ['miːdɪeɪt] *vi* mediar
**medical** ['mɛdɪkl] *adj* médico ▷ *n*
reconocimiento médico; **medical
certificate** *n* certificado *m* médico
**medicated** ['mɛdɪkeɪtɪd] *adj* medicinal
**medication** [mɛdrɪ'keɪʃən] *n* medicación *f*
**medicine** ['mɛdsɪn] *n* medicina; (*drug*)
medicamento
**medieval** [mɛdr'iːvl] *adj* medieval
**mediocre** [miːdr'əʊkə*] *adj* mediocre
**meditate** ['mɛdɪteɪt] *vi* meditar
**meditation** [mɛdr'teɪʃən] *n* meditación *f*
**Mediterranean** [mɛdɪtə'reɪnɪən]
*adj* mediterráneo; **the ~ (Sea)** el (Mar)
Mediterráneo
**medium** ['miːdɪəm] (*pl* **media**) *adj*
mediano, regular ▷ *n* (*means*) medio; (*pl
mediums: person*) médium *mf*; **medium-
sized** *adj* de tamaño mediano; (*clothes*) de
(la) talla mediana; **medium wave** *n* onda
media
**meek** [miːk] *adj* manso, sumiso
**meet** [miːt] (*pt, pp* **met**) *vt* encontrar;

(*accidentally*) encontrarse con, tropezar con; (*by arrangement*) reunirse con; (*for the first time*) conocer; (*go and fetch*) ir a buscar; (*opponent*) enfrentarse con; (*obligations*) cumplir; (*encounter: problem*) hacer frente a; (*need*) satisfacer ▷ *vi* encontrarse; (*in session*) reunirse; (*join: objects*) unirse; (*for the first time*) conocerse; **meet up** *vi*: **to meet up with sb** reunirse con algn; **meet with** *vt fus* (*difficulty*) tropezar con; **to meet with success** tener éxito; **meeting** *n* encuentro; (*arranged*) cita, compromiso; (*business meeting*) reunión *f*; (*Pol*) mítin *m*; **meeting place** *n* lugar *m* de reunión *or* encuentro

**megabyte** ['mɛɡəbaɪt] *n* (*Comput*) megabyte *m*, megaocteto

**megaphone** ['mɛɡəfəʊn] *n* megáfono

**megapixel** ['mɛɡəpɪksl] *n* megapíxel *m*

**melancholy** ['mɛlənkəlɪ] *n* melancolía ▷ *adj* melancólico

**melody** ['mɛlədɪ] *n* melodía

**melon** ['mɛlən] *n* melón *m*

**melt** [mɛlt] *vi* (*metal*) fundirse; (*snow*) derretirse ▷ *vt* fundir

**member** ['mɛmbə*] *n* (*gen, Anat*) miembro; (*of club*) socio/a; **Member of Congress** (*US*) *n* miembro *mf* del Congreso; **Member of Parliament** *n* (*BRIT*) diputado/a *m/f*, parlamentario/a *m/f*; **Member of the European Parliament** *n* diputado/a *m/f* del Parlamento Europeo, eurodiputado/a *m/f*; **Member of the Scottish Parliament** (*BRIT*) diputado/a del Parlamento escocés; **membership** *n* (*members*) número de miembros; (*state*) filiación *f*; **membership card** *n* carnet *m* de socio

**memento** [mə'mɛntəʊ] *n* recuerdo

**memo** ['mɛməʊ] *n* apunte *m*, nota

**memorable** ['mɛmərəbl] *adj* memorable

**memorandum** [mɛmə'rændəm] (*pl* **memoranda**) *n* apunte *m*, nota; (*official note*) acta

**memorial** [mɪ'mɔːrɪəl] *n* monumento conmemorativo ▷ *adj* conmemorativo

**memorize** ['mɛməraɪz] *vt* aprender de memoria

**memory** ['mɛmərɪ] *n* (*also: Comput*) memoria; (*instance*) recuerdo; (*of dead person*): **in ~ of** a la memoria de; **memory card** *n* (*for digital camera*) tarjeta de memoria

**men** [mɛn] *npl of* **man**

**menace** ['mɛnəs] *n* amenaza ▷ *vt* amenazar

**mend** [mɛnd] *vt* reparar, arreglar; (*darn*) zurcir ▷ *vi* reponerse ▷ *n* arreglo, reparación *f* zurcido ▷ *n*: **to be on the ~** ir mejorando; **to ~ one's ways** enmendarse

**meningitis** [mɛnɪn'dʒaɪtɪs] *n* meningitis *f*

**menopause** ['mɛnəupɔːz] *n* menopausia

**men's room** (*US*) *n*: **the ~** el servicio de caballeros

**menstruation** [mɛnstru'eɪʃən] *n* menstruación *f*

**menswear** ['mɛnzwɛə*] *n* confección *f* de caballero

**mental** ['mɛntl] *adj* mental; **mental hospital** *n* (*hospital m*) psiquiátrico;

**mentality** [mɛn'tælɪtɪ] *n* mentalidad *f*;

**mentally** *adv*: **to be mentally ill** tener una enfermedad mental

**menthol** ['mɛnθɔl] *n* mentol *m*

**mention** ['mɛnʃən] *n* mención *f* ▷ *vt* mencionar; (*speak*) hablar de; **don't ~ it!** ¡de nada!

**menu** ['mɛnjuː] *n* (*set menu*) menú *m*; (*printed*) carta; (*Comput*) menú *m*

**MEP** *n abbr* = **Member of the European Parliament**

**mercenary** ['məːsɪnərɪ] *adj*, *n* mercenario/a

**merchandise** ['məːtʃəndaɪz] *n* mercancías *fpl*

**merchant** ['məːtʃənt] *n* comerciante *mf*; **merchant navy** (*US*), **merchant marine** *n* marina mercante

**merciless** ['məːsɪlɪs] *adj* despiadado

**mercury** ['məːkjurɪ] *n* mercurio

**mercy** ['məːsɪ] *n* compasión *f*; (*Rel*) misericordia; **at the ~ of** a la merced de

**mere** [mɪə*] *adj* simple, mero; **merely** *adv* simplemente, sólo

**merge** [məːdʒ] *vt* (*join*) unir ▷ *vi* unirse; (*Comm*) fusionarse; (*colours etc*) fundirse; **merger** *n* (*Comm*) fusión *f*

**meringue** [mə'ræŋ] *n* merengue *m*

**merit** ['mɛrɪt] *n* mérito ▷ *vt* merecer

**mermaid** ['məːmeɪd] *n* sirena

**merry** ['mɛrɪ] *adj* alegre; **M~ Christmas!** ¡Felices Pascuas!; **merry-go-round** *n* tiovivo

**mesh** [mɛʃ] *n* malla

**mess** [mɛs] *n* (*muddle: of situation*) confusión *f*; (: *of room*) revoltijo; (*dirt*) porquería; (*Mil*) comedor *m*; **mess about** *or* **around** (*inf*) *vi* perder el tiempo; (*pass the time*) entretenerse; **mess up** *vt* (*spoil*) estropear; (*dirty*) ensuciar; **mess with** (*inf*) *vt fus* (*challenge, confront*) meterse con (*inf*); (*interfere with*) interferir con

**message** ['mɛsɪdʒ] *n* recado, mensaje *m*

**messenger** ['mɛsɪndʒə*] *n* mensajero/a

**Messrs** *abbr* (*on letters*) (= *Messieurs*) Sres

**messy** ['mɛsɪ] *adj* (*dirty*) sucio; (*untidy*) desordenado

**met** [mɛt] *pt, pp of* **meet**
**metabolism** [mɛ'tæbəlɪzəm] *n*
metabolismo
**metal** ['mɛtl] *n* metal *m*; **metallic** [-'tælɪk]
*adj* metálico
**metaphor** ['mɛtəfə*] *n* metáfora
**meteor** ['miːtɪə*] *n* meteoro; **meteorite**
[-aɪt] *n* meteorito
**meteorology** [miːtɪə'rɒlədʒɪ] *n*
meteorología
**meter** ['miːtə*] *n* (*instrument*) contador *m*;
(*us: unit*) = **metre** ▷ *vt* (*us Post*) franquear
**method** ['mɛθəd] *n* método; **methodical**
[mɪ'θɒdɪkl] *adj* metódico
**meths** [mɛθs] *n* (BRIT) alcohol *m* metilado
or desnaturalizado
**meticulous** [mɛ'tɪkjuləs] *adj* meticuloso
**metre** ['miːtə*] (US **meter**) *n* metro
**metric** ['mɛtrɪk] *adj* métrico
**metro** ['mɛtrəu] *n* metro
**metropolitan** [mɛtrə'pɒlɪtən] *adj*
metropolitano; **the M~ Police** (BRIT) la
policía londinense
**Mexican** ['mɛksɪkən] *adj, n* mexicano/a
, mejicano/a
**Mexico** ['mɛksɪkəu] *n* México, Méjico (SP)
**mg** *abbr* (= *milligram*) mg
**mice** [maɪs] *npl of* **mouse**
**micro...** [maɪkrəu] *prefix* micro...;
**microchip** *n* microplaqueta; **microphone**
*n* micrófono; **microscope** *n* microscopio;
**microwave** *n* (*also:* **microwave oven**)
horno microondas
**mid** [mɪd] *adj:* **in ~ May** a mediados de
mayo; **in ~ afternoon** a media tarde; **in ~ air**
en el aire; **midday** *n* mediodía *m*
**middle** ['mɪdl] *n* centro; (*half-way point*)
medio; (*waist*) cintura ▷ *adj* de en medio;
(*course, way*) intermedio; **in the ~ of the
night** en plena noche; **middle-aged** *adj*
de mediana edad; **Middle Ages** *npl:* **the
Middle Ages** la Edad Media; **middle-class**
*adj* de clase media; **the middle class(es)**
la clase media; **Middle East** *n* Oriente *m*
Medio; **middle name** *n* segundo nombre;
**middle school** *n* (US) colegio para niños de
doce a catorce años; (BRIT) colegio para niños de
ocho o nueve a doce o trece años
**midge** [mɪdʒ] *n* mosquito
**midget** ['mɪdʒɪt] *n* enano/a
**midnight** ['mɪdnaɪt] *n* medianoche *f*
**midst** [mɪdst] *n:* **in the ~ of** (*crowd*) en
medio de; (*situation, action*) en mitad de
**midsummer** [mɪd'sʌmə*] *n:* **in ~** en pleno
verano
**midway** [mɪd'weɪ] *adj, adv:* **~ (between)**
a medio camino (entre); **~ through** a la
mitad (de)

**midweek** [mɪd'wiːk] *adv* entre semana
**midwife** ['mɪdwaɪf] (*irreg*) *n* comadrona,
partera
**midwinter** [mɪd'wɪntə*] *n:* **in ~** en pleno
invierno
**might** [maɪt] *vb see* **may** ▷ *n* fuerza, poder
*m;* **mighty** *adj* fuerte, poderoso
**migraine** ['miːgreɪn] *n* jaqueca
**migrant** ['maɪgrənt] *n, adj* (*bird*)
migratorio; (*worker*) emigrante
**migrate** [maɪ'greɪt] *vi* emigrar
**migration** [maɪ'greɪʃən] *n* emigración *f*
**mike** [maɪk] *n abbr* (= *microphone*) micro
**mild** [maɪld] *adj* (*person*) apacible; (*climate*)
templado; (*slight*) ligero; (*taste*) suave;
(*illness*) leve; **mildly** ['-lɪ] *adv* ligeramente;
suavemente; **to put it mildly** para no decir
más
**mile** [maɪl] *n* milla; **mileage** *n* número
de millas ≈ kilometraje *m;* **mileometer**
[maɪ'lɒmɪtə] *n* ≈ cuentakilómetros *m inv;*
**milestone** *n* mojón *m*
**military** ['mɪlɪtərɪ] *adj* militar
**militia** [mɪ'lɪʃə] *n* milicia
**milk** [mɪlk] *n* leche *f* ▷ *vt* (*cow*) ordeñar;
(*fig*) chupar; **milk chocolate** *n* chocolate *m*
con leche; **milkman** (*irreg*) *n* lechero; **milky**
*adj* lechoso
**mill** [mɪl] *n* (*windmill etc*) molino; (*coffee
mill*) molinillo; (*factory*) fábrica ▷ *vt* moler
▷ *vi* (*also:* **~ about**) arremolinarse
**millennium** [mɪ'lɛnɪəm] (*pl* **~s** *or*
**millennia**) *n* milenio, milenario
**milli...** ['mɪlɪ] *prefix:* **milligram(me)** *n*
miligramo; **millilitre** (US **milliliter**)
['mɪlɪliːtə*] *n* mililitro; **millimetre** (US
**millimeter**) *n* milímetro
**million** ['mɪljən] *n* millón *m;* **a ~ times**
un millón de veces; **millionaire** [-jə'nɛə*]
*n* millonario/a; **millionth** [-θ] *adj*
millonésimo
**milometer** [maɪ'lɒmɪtə*] (BRIT) *n* =
**mileometer**
**mime** [maɪm] *n* mímica; (*actor*) mimo/a
▷ *vt* remedar ▷ *vi* actuar de mimo
**mimic** ['mɪmɪk] *n* imitador(a) *m/f* ▷ *adj*
mímico ▷ *vt* remedar, imitar
**min.** *abbr* = **minimum; minute(s)**
**mince** [mɪns] *vt* picar ▷ *n* (BRIT Culin)
carne *f* picada; **mincemeat** *n* conserva de
fruta picada; (US: *meat*) carne *f* picada; **mince
pie** *n* empanadilla rellena de fruta picada
**mind** [maɪnd] *n* mente *f;* (*intellect*)
intelecto; (*contrasted with matter*) espíritu
*m* ▷ *vt* (*attend to, look after*) ocuparse de,
cuidar; (*be careful*) tener cuidado con; (*object
to*): **I don't ~ the noise** no me molesta el
ruido; **it is on my ~** me preocupa; **to bear**

**sth in** ~ tomar or tener algo en cuenta; **to make up one's** ~ decidirse; **I don't** ~ me es igual; **~ you ...** te advierto que ...; **never ~!** ¡es igual!, ¡no importa!; (*don't worry*) ¡no te preocupes!; **"~ the step"** "cuidado con el escalón"; **mindless** *adj* (*crime*) sin motivo; (*work*) de autómata

**mine¹** [maɪn] *pron* el mío/la mía etc; **a friend of** ~ un(a) amigo/a mío/mía ▷ *adj*: **this book is** ~ este libro es mío

**mine²** [maɪn] *n* mina ▷ *vt* (*coal*) extraer; (*bomb: beach etc*) minar; **minefield** *n* campo de minas; **miner** *n* minero/a

**mineral** ['mɪnərəl] *adj* mineral ▷ *n* mineral *m*; **mineral water** *n* agua mineral

**mingle** ['mɪŋgl] *vi*: **to ~ with** mezclarse con

**miniature** ['mɪnətʃə*] *adj* (en) miniatura ▷ *n* miniatura

**minibar** ['mɪnɪbɑː*] *n* minibar *m*

**minibus** ['mɪnɪbʌs] *n* microbús *m*

**minicab** ['mɪnɪkæb] *n* taxi *m* (*que sólo puede pedirse por teléfono*)

**minimal** ['mɪnɪml] *adj* mínimo

**minimize** ['mɪnɪmaɪz] *vt* minimizar; (*play down*) empequeñecer

**minimum** ['mɪnɪməm] (*pl* **minima**) *n*, *adj* mínimo

**mining** ['maɪnɪŋ] *n* explotación *f* minera

**miniskirt** ['mɪnɪskəːt] *n* minifalda

**minister** ['mɪnɪstə*] *n* (*BRIT Pol*) ministro/a (*SP*), secretario/a (*LAM*); (*Rel*) pastor *m* ▷ *vi*: **to ~ to** atender a

**ministry** ['mɪnɪstrɪ] *n* (*BRIT Pol*) ministerio, secretaría (*MEX*); (*Rel*) sacerdocio

**minor** ['maɪnə*] *adj* (*repairs, injuries*) leve; (*poet, planet*) menor; (*Mus*) menor ▷ *n* (*Law*) menor *m* de edad

**Minorca** [mɪ'nɔːkə] *n* Menorca

**minority** [maɪ'nɔrɪtɪ] *n* minoría

**mint** [mɪnt] *n* (*plant*) menta, hierbabuena; (*sweet*) caramelo de menta ▷ *vt* (*coins*) acuñar; **the (Royal) M~, the (US) M~** la Casa de la Moneda; **in ~ condition** en perfecto estado

**minus** ['maɪnəs] *n* (*also: ~ **sign***) signo de menos ▷ *prep* menos; **12 ~ 6 equals 6** 12 menos 6 son 6; **~ 24 °C** menos 24 grados

**minute¹** ['mɪnɪt] *n* minuto; (*fig*) momento; **minutes** *npl* (*of meeting*) actas *fpl*; **at the last ~** a última hora

**minute²** [maɪ'njuːt] *adj* diminuto; (*search*) minucioso

**miracle** ['mɪrəkl] *n* milagro

**miraculous** [mɪ'rækjuləs] *adj* milagroso

**mirage** ['mɪrɑːʒ] *n* espejismo

**mirror** ['mɪrə*] *n* espejo; (*in car*) retrovisor *m*

**misbehave** [mɪsbɪ'heɪv] *vi* portarse mal

**misc.** *abbr* = **miscellaneous**

**miscarriage** ['mɪskærɪdʒ] *n* (*Med*) aborto; **~ of justice** error *m* judicial

**miscellaneous** [mɪsɪ'leɪnɪəs] *adj* varios/as, diversos/as

**mischief** ['mɪstʃɪf] *n* travesuras *fpl*, diabluras *fpl*; (*maliciousness*) malicia; **mischievous** [-ʃɪvəs] *adj* travieso

**misconception** [mɪskən'sɛpʃən] *n* idea equivocada; equivocación *f*

**misconduct** [mɪs'kɔndʌkt] *n* mala conducta; **professional ~** falta profesional

**miser** ['maɪzə*] *n* avaro/a

**miserable** ['mɪzərəbl] *adj* (*unhappy*) triste, desgraciado; (*unpleasant, contemptible*) miserable

**misery** ['mɪzərɪ] *n* tristeza; (*wretchedness*) miseria, desdicha

**misfortune** [mɪs'fɔːtʃən] *n* desgracia

**misgiving** [mɪs'gɪvɪŋ] *n* (*apprehension*) presentimiento; **to have ~s about sth** tener dudas acerca de algo

**misguided** [mɪs'gaɪdɪd] *adj* equivocado

**mishap** ['mɪshæp] *n* desgracia, contratiempo

**misinterpret** [mɪsɪn'təːprɪt] *vt* interpretar mal

**misjudge** [mɪs'dʒʌdʒ] *vt* juzgar mal

**mislay** [mɪs'leɪ] *vt* extraviar, perder

**mislead** [mɪs'liːd] *vt* llevar a conclusiones erróneas; **misleading** *adj* engañoso

**misplace** [mɪs'pleɪs] *vt* extraviar

**misprint** ['mɪsprɪnt] *n* errata, error *m* de imprenta

**misrepresent** [mɪsrɛprɪ'zɛnt] *vt* falsificar

**Miss** [mɪs] *n* Señorita

**miss** [mɪs] *vt* (*train etc*) perder; (*fail to hit: target*) errar; (*regret the absence of*): **I ~ him** (yo) le echo de menos or a faltar; (*fail to see*): **you can't ~ it** no tiene pérdida ▷ *vi* fallar ▷ *n* (*shot*) tiro fallido or perdido; **miss out** (*BRIT*) *vt* omitir; **miss out on** *vt fus* (*fun, party, opportunity*) perderse

**missile** ['mɪsaɪl] *n* (*Aviat*) mísil *m*; (*object thrown*) proyectil *m*

**missing** ['mɪsɪŋ] *adj* (*pupil*) ausente; (*thing*) perdido; (*Mil*): **~ in action** desaparecido en combate

**mission** ['mɪʃən] *n* misión *f*; (*official representation*) delegación *f*; **missionary** *n* misionero/a

**misspell** [mɪs'spɛl] (*pt, pp* **misspelt** (*BRIT*) *or* **~ed**) *vt* escribir mal

**mist** [mɪst] *n* (*light*) neblina; (*heavy*) niebla; (*at sea*) bruma ▷ *vi* (*eyes: also:* **~ over, ~ up**) llenarse de lágrimas; (*BRIT: windows: also:* **~**

over, ~ up) empañarse

**mistake** [mɪs'teɪk] (vt: irreg) n error m
▷ vt entender mal; **by ~** por equivocación;
**to make a ~** equivocarse; **to ~ A for B**
confundir A con B; **mistaken** pp of **mistake**
▷ adj equivocado; **to be mistaken**
equivocarse, engañarse

**mister** ['mɪstə*] (inf) n señor m; see **Mr**

**mistletoe** ['mɪsltəu] n muérdago

**mistook** [mɪs'tuk] pt of **mistake**

**mistress** ['mɪstrɪs] n (lover) amante
f; (of house) señora (de la casa); (BRIT: in
primary school) maestra; (in secondary school)
profesora; (of situation) dueña

**mistrust** [mɪs'trʌst] vt desconfiar de

**misty** ['mɪstɪ] adj (day) de niebla; (glasses
etc) empañado

**misunderstand** [mɪsʌndə'stænd] (irreg)
vt, vi entender mal; **misunderstanding** n
malentendido

**misunderstood** [mɪsʌndə'stud] pt,
pp of **misunderstand** ▷ adj (person)
incomprendido

**misuse** [n mɪs'juːs, vb mɪs'juːz] n mal uso;
(of power) abuso; (of funds) malversación f
▷ vt abusar de; malversar

**mitt(en)** ['mɪt(n)] n manopla

**mix** [mɪks] vt mezclar; (combine) unir ▷ vi
mezclarse; (people) llevarse bien ▷ n mezcla;
**mix up** vt mezclar; (confuse) confundir;
**mixed** adj mixto; **mixed grill** n (BRIT)
parrillada mixta; **mixed salad** n ensalada mixta; **mixed-up**
adj (confused) confuso, revuelto; **mixer** n
(for food) licuadora; (for drinks) coctelera;
(person): **he's a good mixer** tiene don de
gentes; **mixture** n mezcla; (also: **cough
mixture**) jarabe m; **mix-up** n confusión f

**ml** abbr (= millilitre(s)) ml

**mm** abbr (= millimetre) mm

**moan** [məun] n gemido ▷ vi gemir;
(inf: complain): **to ~ (about)** quejarse (de)

**moat** [məut] n foso

**mob** [mɔb] n multitud f ▷ vt acosar

**mobile** ['məubaɪl] adj móvil ▷ n móvil m;
**mobile home** n caravana; **mobile phone** n
teléfono móvil

**mobility** [məu'bɪlɪtɪ] n movilidad f

**mobilize** ['məubɪlaɪz] vt movilizar

**mock** [mɔk] vt (ridicule) ridiculizar; (laugh
at) burlarse de ▷ adj fingido; **~ exam**
examen preparatorio antes de los exámenes
oficiales° (BRIT: Scol: inf) exámenes mpl de
prueba; **mockery** n burla

**mod cons** ['mɔd'kɔnz] npl abbr (= modern
conveniences) see **convenience**

**mode** [məud] n modo

**model** ['mɔdl] n modelo; (fashion model,

artist's model) modelo mf ▷ adj modelo ▷ vt
(with clay etc) modelar; (copy): **to ~ o.s. on**
tomar como modelo a ▷ vi ser modelo; **to ~
clothes** pasar modelos, ser modelo

**modem** ['məudəm] n modem m

**moderate** [adj 'mɔdərət, vb 'mɔdəreɪt]
adj moderado/a ▷ vi moderarse, calmarse
▷ vt moderar

**moderation** [mɔdə'reɪʃən] n moderación
f; **in ~** con moderación

**modern** ['mɔdən] adj moderno;
**modernize** vt modernizar; **modern
languages** npl lenguas fpl modernas

**modest** ['mɔdɪst] adj modesto; (small)
módico; **modesty** n modestia

**modification** [mɔdɪfɪ'keɪʃən] n
modificación f

**modify** ['mɔdɪfaɪ] vt modificar

**module** ['mɔdjuːl] n (unit, component,
Space) módulo

**mohair** ['məuhɛə*] n mohair m

**Mohammed** [mə'hæmɛd] n Mahoma m

**moist** [mɔɪst] adj húmedo; **moisture**
['mɔɪstʃə*] n humedad f; **moisturizer**
['mɔɪstʃəraɪzə*] n crema hidratante

**mold** etc [məuld] (US) = **mould** etc

**mole** [məul] n (animal, spy) topo; (spot)
lunar m

**molecule** ['mɔlɪkjuːl] n molécula

**molest** [məu'lɛst] vt importunar; (assault
sexually) abusar sexualmente de

> Be careful not to translate **molest** by the
> Spanish word molestar.

**molten** ['məultən] adj fundido; (lava)
líquido

**mom** [mɔm] (US) n = **mum**

**moment** ['məumənt] n momento; **at the
~** de momento, por ahora; **momentarily**
adv momentáneamente; (US: very soon)
de un momento a otro; **momentary** adj
momentáneo; **momentous** [-'mɛntəs] adj
trascendental, importante

**momentum** [məu'mɛntəm] n momento;
(fig) ímpetu m; **to gather ~** cobrar
velocidad; (fig) ganar fuerza

**mommy** ['mɔmɪ] (US) n = **mummy**

**Mon** abbr (= Monday) lun

**Monaco** ['mɔnəkəu] n Mónaco

**monarch** ['mɔnək] n monarca mf;
**monarchy** n monarquía

**monastery** ['mɔnəstərɪ] n monasterio

**Monday** ['mʌndɪ] n lunes m inv

**monetary** ['mʌnɪtərɪ] adj monetario

**money** ['mʌnɪ] n dinero; (currency)
moneda; **to make ~** ganar dinero; **money
belt** n riñonera; **money order** n giro

**mongrel** ['mʌŋgrəl] n (dog) perro mestizo

**monitor** ['mɔnɪtə*] n (Scol) monitor m;

(*also*: **television ~**) receptor *m* de control; (*of computer*) monitor *m* ▷ *vt* controlar

**monk** [mʌŋk] *n* monje *m*

**monkey** ['mʌŋkɪ] *n* mono

**monologue** ['mɔnəlɔg] *n* monólogo

**monopoly** [mə'nɔpəlɪ] *n* monopolio

**monosodium glutamate** [mɔnə'səʊdɪəm'gluːtəmeɪt] *n* glutamato monosódico

**monotonous** [mə'nɔtənəs] *adj* monótono

**monsoon** [mɔn'suːn] *n* monzón *m*

**monster** ['mɔnstə*] *n* monstruo

**month** [mʌnθ] *n* mes *m*; **monthly** *adj* mensual ▷ *adv* mensualmente

**monument** ['mɔnjumənt] *n* monumento

**mood** [muːd] *n* humor *m*; (*of crowd, group*) clima *m*; **to be in a good/bad ~** estar de buen/mal humor; **moody** *adj* (*changeable*) de humor variable; (*sullen*) malhumorado

**moon** [muːn] *n* luna; **moonlight** *n* luz *f* de la luna

**moor** [mʊə*] *n* páramo ▷ *vt* amarrar ▷ *vi* echar las amarras

**moose** [muːs] *n inv* alce *m*

**mop** [mɔp] *n* fregona; (*of hair*) greña, melena ▷ *vt* fregar; **mop up** *vt* limpiar

**mope** [məʊp] *vi* estar *or* andar deprimido

**moped** ['məʊpɛd] *n* ciclomotor *m*

**moral** ['mɔrl] *adj* moral ▷ *n* moraleja; **morals** *npl* moralidad *f*, moral *f*

**morale** [mɔ'rɑːl] *n* moral *f*

**morality** [mə'rælɪtɪ] *n* moralidad *f*

**morbid** ['mɔːbɪd] *adj* (*interest*) morboso; (*Med*) mórbido

○ **KEYWORD**

**more** [mɔː*] *adj* **1** (*greater in number etc*) más; **more people/work than before** más gente/trabajo que antes

**2** (*additional*) más; **do you want (some) more tea?** ¿quieres más té?; **is there any more wine?** ¿queda vino?; **it'll take a few more weeks** tardará unas semanas más; **it's 2 kms more to the house** faltan 2 kms para la casa; **more time/letters than we expected** más tiempo del que/más cartas de las que esperábamos

▷ *pron* (*greater amount, additional amount*) más; **more than 10** más de 10; **it cost more than the other one/than we expected** costó más que el otro/más de lo que esperábamos; **is there any more?** ¿hay más?; **many/much more** muchos(as)/mucho(a) más

▷ *adv* más; **more dangerous/easily (than)** más peligroso/fácilmente (que); **more and more expensive** cada vez más caro; **more or less** más o menos; **more than ever** más que nunca

**moreover** [mɔː'rəʊvə*] *adv* además, por otra parte

**morgue** [mɔːg] *n* depósito de cadáveres

**morning** ['mɔːnɪŋ] *n* mañana; (*early morning*) madrugada ▷ *cpd* matutino, de la mañana; **in the ~** por la mañana; **7 o'clock in the ~** las 7 de la mañana; **morning sickness** *n* náuseas *fpl* matutinas

**Moroccan** [mə'rɔkən] *adj, n* marroquí *m/f*

**Morocco** [mə'rɔkəʊ] *n* Marruecos *m*

**moron** ['mɔːrɔn] (*inf*) *n* imbécil *mf*

**morphine** ['mɔːfiːn] *n* morfina

**Morse** [mɔːs] *n* (*also*: **~ code**) (código) Morse

**mortal** ['mɔːtl] *adj, n* mortal *m*

**mortar** ['mɔːtə*] *n* argamasa

**mortgage** ['mɔːgɪdʒ] *n* hipoteca ▷ *vt* hipotecar

**mortician** [mɔː'tɪʃən] (*us*) *n* director/a *m/f* de pompas fúnebres

**mortified** ['mɔːtɪfaɪd] *adj*: **I was ~** me dio muchísima vergüenza

**mortuary** ['mɔːtjuərɪ] *n* depósito de cadáveres

**mosaic** [məʊ'zeɪɪk] *n* mosaico

**Moslem** ['mɔzləm] *adj, n* = **Muslim**

**mosque** [mɔsk] *n* mezquita

**mosquito** [mɔs'kiːtəʊ] (*pl* **~es**) *n* mosquito (*SP*), zancudo (*LAM*)

**moss** [mɔs] *n* musgo

**most** [məʊst] *adj* la mayor parte de, la mayoría de ▷ *pron* la mayor parte, la mayoría ▷ *adv* el más; (*very*) muy; **the ~** (*also*: **+ adj**) el más; **~ of them** la mayor parte de ellos; **I saw the ~** yo vi el que más; **at the (very) ~** a lo sumo, todo lo más; **to make the ~ of** aprovechar (al máximo); **a ~ interesting book** un libro interesantísimo; **mostly** *adv* en su mayor parte, principalmente

**MOT** (*BRIT*) *n abbr* = **Ministry of Transport**; **the ~ (test)** inspección (*anual*) *obligatoria de coches y camiones*

**motel** [məʊ'tɛl] *n* motel *m*

**moth** [mɔθ] *n* mariposa nocturna; (*clothes moth*) polilla

**mother** ['mʌðə*] *n* madre *f* ▷ *adj* materno ▷ *vt* (*care for*) cuidar (como una madre); **motherhood** *n* maternidad *f*; **mother-in-law** *n* suegra; **mother-of-pearl** *n* nácar *m*; **Mother's Day** *n* Día *m* de la Madre; **mother-to-be** *n* futura madre *f*; **mother tongue** *n* lengua materna

**motif** [məuˈtiːf] n motivo
**motion** [ˈməuʃən] n movimiento; (gesture) ademán m, señal f; (at meeting) moción f ▷ vt, vi: **to ~ (to) sb to do sth** hacer señas a algn para que haga algo; **motionless** adj inmóvil; **motion picture** n película
**motivate** [ˈməutiveit] vt motivar
**motivation** [məutiˈveiʃən] n motivación f
**motive** [ˈməutiv] n motivo
**motor** [ˈməutə*] n motor m; (BRIT: inf: vehicle) coche m (SP), carro (LAM), automóvil m ▷ adj motor (f: motora or motriz); **motorbike** n moto f; **motorboat** n lancha motora; **motorcar** (BRIT) n coche m, carro, automóvil m; **motorcycle** n motocicleta; **motorcyclist** n motociclista mf; **motoring** (BRIT) n automovilismo; **motorist** n conductor(a) m/f, automovilista mf; **motor racing** (BRIT) n carreras fpl de coches, automovilismo; **motorway** (BRIT) n autopista
**motto** [ˈmɔtəu] (pl ~es) n lema m; (watchword) consigna
**mould** [məuld] (US **mold**) n molde m; (mildew) moho ▷ vt moldear; (fig) formar; **mouldy** adj enmohecido
**mound** [maund] n montón m, montículo
**mount** [maunt] n monte m ▷ vt montar, subir a; (jewel) engarzar; (picture) enmarcar; (exhibition etc) organizar ▷ vi (increase) aumentar; **mount up** vi aumentar
**mountain** [ˈmauntin] n montaña ▷ cpd de montaña; **mountain bike** n bicicleta de montaña; **mountaineer** n alpinista mf (SP, MEX), andinista mf (LAM); **mountaineering** n alpinismo (SP, MEX), andinismo (LAM); **mountainous** adj montañoso; **mountain range** n sierra
**mourn** [mɔːn] vt llorar, lamentar ▷ vi: **to ~ for** llorar la muerte de; **mourner** n doliente mf; dolorido/a; **mourning** n luto; **in mourning** de luto
**mouse** [maus] (pl **mice**) n (Zool, Comput) ratón m; **mouse mat** n (Comput) alfombrilla
**moussaka** [muˈsɑːkə] n musaca
**mousse** [muːs] n (Culin) crema batida; (for hair) espuma (moldeadora)
**moustache** [məsˈtɑːʃ] (US **mustache**) n bigote m
**mouth** [mauθ, pl mauðz] n boca; (of river) desembocadura; **mouthful** n bocado; **mouth organ** n armónica; **mouthpiece** n (of musical instrument) boquilla; (spokesman) portavoz mf; **mouthwash** n enjuague m
**move** [muːv] n (movement) movimiento; (in game) jugada; (: turn to play) turno; (change: of house) mudanza; (: of job) cambio

de trabajo ▷ vt mover; (emotionally) conmover; (Pol: resolution etc) proponer ▷ vi moverse; (traffic) circular; (also: ~ **house**) trasladarse, mudarse; **to ~ sb to do sth** mover a algn a hacer algo; **to get a ~ on** darse prisa; **move back** vi retroceder; **move in** vi (to a house) instalarse; (police, soldiers) intervenir; **move off** vi ponerse en camino; **move on** vi ponerse en camino; **move out** vi (of house) mudarse; **move over** vi apartarse, hacer sitio; **move up** vi (employee) ser ascendido; **movement** n movimiento
**movie** [ˈmuːvi] n película; **to go to the ~s** ir al cine; **movie theater** (US) n cine m
**moving** [ˈmuːvɪŋ] adj (emotional) conmovedor(a); (that moves) móvil
**mow** [məu] (pt ~**ed**, pp **mowed** or **mown**) vt (grass, corn) cortar, segar; **mower** n (also: **lawnmower**) cortacéspedes m inv
**Mozambique** [məuzæmˈbiːk] n Mozambique m
**MP** n abbr = **Member of Parliament**
**MP3** n MP3; **MP3 player** n reproductor m (de) MP3
**mpg** n abbr = **miles per gallon**
**m.p.h.** abbr = **miles per hour** (60 m.p.h. = 96 k.p.h.)
**Mr** [ˈmistə*] (US **Mr.**) n: ~ **Smith** (el) Sr. Smith
**Mrs** [ˈmisiz] (US **Mrs.**) n: ~ **Smith** (la) Sra. Smith
**Ms** [miz] (US **Ms.**) n = **Miss** or **Mrs**; ~ **Smith** (la) Sr(t)a. Smith
**MSP** n abbr = **Member of the Scottish Parliament**
**Mt** abbr (Geo) (= mount) m
**much** [mʌtʃ] adj mucho ▷ pron mucho; (before pp) muy ▷ n or pron mucho; **how ~ is it?** ¿cuánto es?, ¿cuánto cuesta?; **too ~** demasiado; **it's not ~** no es mucho; **as ~ as** tanto como; **however ~ he tries** por mucho que se esfuerce
**muck** [mʌk] n suciedad f; **muck up** (inf) vt arruinar, estropear; **mucky** adj (dirty) sucio
**mucus** [ˈmjuːkəs] n mucosidad f, moco
**mud** [mʌd] n barro, lodo
**muddle** [ˈmʌdl] n desorden m, confusión f; (mix-up) embrollo, lío ▷ vt (also: ~ **up**) embrollar, confundir
**muddy** [ˈmʌdi] adj fangoso, cubierto de lodo
**mudguard** [ˈmʌdgɑːd] n guardabarros m inv
**muesli** [ˈmjuːzli] n muesli m
**muffin** [ˈmʌfin] n panecillo dulce
**muffled** [ˈmʌfld] adj (noise etc) amortiguado, apagado

**muffler** (US) ['mʌflə*] n (Aut) silenciador m

**mug** [mʌg] n taza grande (sin platillo); (for beer) jarra; (inf: face) jeta ▷ vt (assault) asaltar; **mugger** ['mʌgə*] n atracador(a) m/f; **mugging** n asalto

**muggy** ['mʌgɪ] adj bochornoso

**mule** [mju:l] n mula

**multicoloured** ['mʌltɪkʌləd] (US), **multicolored** adj multicolor

**multimedia** ['mʌltɪ'mi:dɪə] adj multimedia

**multinational** [mʌltɪ'næfənl] n multinacional f ▷ adj multinacional

**multiple** ['mʌltɪpl] adj múltiple ▷ n múltiplo; **multiple choice (test)** n examen m de tipo test; **multiple sclerosis** n esclerosis f múltiple

**multiplex cinema** ['mʌltɪplɛks-] n multicines mpl

**multiplication** [mʌltɪplɪ'keɪʃən] n multiplicación f

**multiply** ['mʌltɪplaɪ] vt multiplicar ▷ vi multiplicarse

**multistorey** [mʌltɪ'stɔ:rɪ] (BRIT) adj de muchos pisos

**mum** [mʌm] (BRIT: inf) n mamá ▷ adj: **to keep ~** mantener la boca cerrada

**mumble** ['mʌmbl] vt, vi hablar entre dientes, refunfuñar

**mummy** ['mʌmɪ] n (BRIT: mother) mamá; (embalmed) momia

**mumps** [mʌmps] n paperas fpl

**munch** [mʌntʃ] vt, vi mascar

**municipal** [mju:'nɪsɪpl] adj municipal

**mural** ['mjuərl] n (pintura) mural m

**murder** ['mə:də*] n asesinato; (in law) homicidio ▷ vt asesinar, matar; **murderer** n asesino

**murky** ['mə:kɪ] adj (water) turbio; (street, night) lóbrego

**murmur** ['mə:mə*] n murmullo ▷ vt, vi murmurar

**muscle** ['mʌsl] n músculo; (fig: strength) garra, fuerza; **muscular** ['mʌskjulə*] adj muscular; (person) musculoso

**museum** [mju:'zɪəm] n museo

**mushroom** ['mʌʃrum] n seta, hongo; (Culin) champiñón m ▷ vi crecer de la noche a la mañana

**music** ['mju:zɪk] n música; **musical** adj musical; (sound) melodioso; (person) con talento musical ▷ n (show) comedia musical; **musical instrument** n instrumento musical; **musician** [-'zɪʃən] n músico/a

**Muslim** ['mʌzlɪm] adj, n musulmán/ana m/f

**muslin** ['mʌzlɪn] n muselina

**mussel** ['mʌsl] n mejillón m

**must** [mʌst] aux vb (obligation): **I ~ do it** debo hacerlo, tengo que hacerlo; (probability): **he ~ be there by now** ya debe (de) estar allí ▷ n: **it's a ~** es imprescindible

**mustache** ['mʌstæʃ] (US) = **moustache**

**mustard** ['mʌstəd] n mostaza

**mustn't** ['mʌsnt] = **must not**

**mute** [mju:t] adj, n mudo/a m/f

**mutilate** ['mju:tɪleɪt] vt mutilar

**mutiny** ['mju:tɪnɪ] n motín m ▷ vi amotinarse

**mutter** ['mʌtə*] vt, vi murmurar

**mutton** ['mʌtn] n carne f de cordero

**mutual** ['mju:tʃuəl] adj mutuo; (interest) común

**muzzle** ['mʌzl] n hocico; (for dog) bozal m; (of gun) boca ▷ vt (dog) poner un bozal a

**my** [maɪ] adj mi(s); **~ house/brother/ sisters** mi casa/mi hermano/mis hermanas; **I've washed ~ hair/cut ~ finger** me he lavado el pelo/cortado un dedo; **is this ~ pen or yours?** ¿es este bolígrafo mío o tuyo?

**myself** [maɪ'sɛlf] pron (reflexive) me; (emphatic) yo mismo; (after prep) mí (mismo); see also **oneself**

**mysterious** [mɪs'tɪərɪəs] adj misterioso

**mystery** ['mɪstərɪ] n misterio

**mystical** ['mɪstɪkl] adj místico

**mystify** ['mɪstɪfaɪ] vt (perplex) dejar perplejo

**myth** [mɪθ] n mito; **mythology** [mɪ'θɔlədʒɪ] n mitología

**n**

**n/a** *abbr* (= *not applicable*) no interesa
**nag** [næg] *vt* (*scold*) regañar
**nail** [neɪl] *n* (*human*) uña; (*metal*) clavo ▷ *vt*
clavar; **to ~ sth to sth** clavar algo en algo;
**to ~ sb down to doing sth** comprometer a
algn a que haga algo; **nailbrush** *n* cepillo
para las uñas; **nailfile** *n* lima para las uñas;
**nail polish** *n* esmalte *m or* laca para las
uñas; **nail polish remover** *n* quitaesmalte
*m*; **nail scissors** *npl* tijeras *fpl* para las uñas;
**nail varnish** (BRIT) *n* = **nail polish**
**naïve** [naɪˈiːv] *adj* ingenuo
**naked** [ˈneɪkɪd] *adj* (*nude*) desnudo; (*flame*)
expuesto al aire
**name** [neɪm] *n* nombre *m*; (*surname*)
apellido; (*reputation*) fama, renombre *m* ▷ *vt*
(*child*) poner nombre a; (*criminal*) identificar;
(*price, date etc*) fijar; **what's your ~?** ¿cómo
se llama?; **by ~** de nombre; **in the ~ of** en
nombre de; **to give one's ~ and address** dar
sus señas; **namely** *adv* a saber
**nanny** [ˈnænɪ] *n* niñera
**nap** [næp] *n* (*sleep*) sueñecito, siesta
**napkin** [ˈnæpkɪn] *n* (*also:* **table ~**)
servilleta
**nappy** [ˈnæpɪ] (BRIT) *n* pañal *m*
**narcotics** *npl* (*illegal drugs*)
estupefacientes *mpl*, narcóticos *mpl*
**narrative** [ˈnærətɪv] *n* narrativa ▷ *adj*
narrativo
**narrator** [nəˈreɪtə*] *n* narrador(a) *m/f*
**narrow** [ˈnærəu] *adj* estrecho, angosto;
(*fig: majority etc*) corto; (: *ideas etc*) estrecho
▷ *vi* (*road*) estrecharse; (*diminish*) reducirse;
**to have a ~ escape** escaparse por los pelos;
**narrow down** *vt* (*search, investigation,
possibilities*) restringir, limitar; (*list*) reducir;
**narrowly** *adv* (*miss*) por poco; **narrow-
minded** *adj* de miras estrechas
**nasal** [ˈneɪzl] *adj* nasal
**nasty** [ˈnɑːstɪ] *adj* (*remark*) feo; (*person*)

antipático; (*revolting: taste, smell*) asqueroso;
(*wound, disease etc*) peligroso, grave
**nation** [ˈneɪʃən] *n* nación *f*
**national** [ˈnæʃənl] *adj, n* nacional
*m/f*; **national anthem** *n* himno nacional;
**national dress** *n* vestido nacional;
**National Health Service** (BRIT) *n* servicio
nacional de salud pública = Insalud *m* (SP);
**National Insurance** (BRIT) *n* seguro social
nacional; **nationalist** *adj, n* nacionalista
*mf*; **nationality** [-ˈnælɪtɪ] *n* nacionalidad *f*;
**nationalize** *vt* nacionalizar; **national park**
(BRIT) *n* parque *m* nacional; **National Trust**
*n* (BRIT) *organización encargada de preservar el
patrimonio histórico británico*
**nationwide** [ˈneɪʃənwaɪd] *adj* en escala or
a nivel nacional
**native** [ˈneɪtɪv] *n* (*local inhabitant*) natural
*mf*, nacional *mf* ▷ *adj* (*indigenous*) indígena;
(*country*) natal; (*innate*) natural, innato; **a ~
of Russia** un(a) natural *mf* de Rusia; **Native
American** *adj, n* americano/a indígena,
amerindio/a; **native speaker** *n* hablante
*mf* nativo/a
**NATO** [ˈneɪtəu] *n abbr* (= *North Atlantic
Treaty Organization*) OTAN *f*
**natural** [ˈnætʃrəl] *adj* natural; **natural
gas** *n* gas *m* natural; **natural history** *n*
historia natural; **naturally** *adv* (*speak etc*)
naturalmente; (*of course*) desde luego, por
supuesto; **natural resources** *npl* recursos
*mpl* naturales
**nature** [ˈneɪtʃə*] *n* (*also:* **N~**) naturaleza;
(*group, sort*) género, clase *f*; (*character*)
carácter *m*, genio; **by ~** por or de naturaleza;
**nature reserve** *n* reserva natural
**naughty** [ˈnɔːtɪ] *adj* (*child*) travieso
**nausea** [ˈnɔːsɪə] *n* náuseas *fpl*
**naval** [ˈneɪvl] *adj* naval, de marina
**navel** [ˈneɪvl] *n* ombligo
**navigate** [ˈnævɪgeɪt] *vt* gobernar ▷ *vi*
navegar; (*Aut*) ir de copiloto; **navigation**
[-ˈgeɪʃən] *n* (*action*) navegación *f*; (*science*)
náutica
**navy** [ˈneɪvɪ] *n* marina de guerra; (*ships*)
armada, flota
**Nazi** [ˈnɑːtsɪ] *n* nazi *mf*
**NB** *abbr* (= *nota bene*) nótese
**near** [nɪə*] *adj* (*place, relation*) cercano;
(*time*) próximo ▷ *adv* cerca ▷ *prep* (*also:* **~
to:** *space*) cerca de, junto a; (: *time*) cerca de
▷ *vt* acercarse a, aproximarse a; **nearby**
[nɪəˈbaɪ] *adj* cercano, próximo ▷ *adv* cerca;
**nearly** *adv* casi, por poco; **I nearly fell** por
poco me caigo; **near-sighted** *adj* miope,
corto de vista
**neat** [niːt] *adj* (*place*) ordenado, bien
cuidado; (*person*) pulcro; (*plan*) ingenioso;

(spirits) solo; **neatly** adv (tidily) con esmero; (skilfully) ingeniosamente

**necessarily** ['nɛsɪsrɪlɪ] adv necesariamente

**necessary** ['nɛsɪsrɪ] adj necesario, preciso

**necessity** [nɪ'sɛsɪtɪ] n necesidad f

**neck** [nɛk] n (of person, garment, bottle) cuello; (of animal) pescuezo ▷ vi (inf) besuquearse; **~ and ~** parejos; **necklace** ['nɛklɪs] n collar m; **necktie** ['nɛktaɪ] n corbata

**nectarine** ['nɛktərɪn] n nectarina

**need** [niːd] n (lack) escasez f, falta; (necessity) necesidad f ▷ vt (require) necesitar; **I ~ to do it** tengo que or debo hacerlo; **you don't ~ to go** no hace falta que (te) vayas

**needle** ['niːdl] n aguja ▷ vt (fig: inf) picar, fastidiar

**needless** ['niːdlɪs] adj innecesario; **~ to say** huelga decir que

**needlework** ['niːdlwəːk] n (activity) costura, labor f de aguja

**needn't** ['niːdnt] = **need not**

**needy** ['niːdɪ] adj necesitado

**negative** ['nɛgətɪv] n (Phot) negativo; (Ling) negación f ▷ adj negativo

**neglect** [nɪ'glɛkt] vt (one's duty) faltar a, no cumplir con; (child) descuidar, desatender ▷ n (of house, garden etc) abandono; (of child) desatención f; (of duty) incumplimiento

**negotiate** [nɪ'gəʊʃɪeɪt] vt (treaty, loan) negociar; (obstacle) franquear; (bend in road) tomar ▷ vi: **to ~ (with)** negociar (con)

**negotiations** [nɪgəʊʃɪ'eɪʃənz] pl n negociaciones

**negotiator** [nɪ'gəʊʃɪeɪtə*] n negociador(a) m/f

**neighbour** ['neɪbə*] (US **neighbor** etc) n vecino/a; **neighbourhood** n (place) vecindad f, barrio; (people) vecindario; **neighbouring** adj vecino

**neither** ['naɪðə*] adj ni ▷ conj: **I didn't move and ~ did John** no me he movido, ni Juan tampoco ▷ pron ninguno ▷ adv: **~ good nor bad** ni bueno ni malo; **~ is true** ninguno/a de los(las) dos es cierto/a

**neon** ['niːɔn] n neón m

**Nepal** [nɪ'pɔːl] n Nepal m

**nephew** ['nɛvjuː] n sobrino

**nerve** [nəːv] n (Anat) nervio; (courage) valor m; (impudence) descaro, frescura (nervousness) nerviosismo msg, nervios mpl; **a fit of ~s** un ataque de nervios

**nervous** ['nəːvəs] adj (anxious, Anat) nervioso; (timid) tímido, miedoso; **nervous breakdown** n crisis f nerviosa

**nest** [nɛst] n (of bird) nido; (wasps' nest) avispero ▷ vi anidar

**net** [nɛt] n (gen) red f; (fabric) tul m ▷ adj (Comm) neto, líquido ▷ vt coger (SP) or agarrar (LAM) con red; (Sport) marcar; **netball** n básquet m

**Netherlands** ['nɛðələndz] npl: **the ~** los Países Bajos

**nett** [nɛt] adj = **net**

**nettle** ['nɛtl] n ortiga

**network** ['nɛtwəːk] n red f

**neurotic** [njuə'rɔtɪk] adj neurótico/a

**neuter** ['njuːtə*] adj (Ling) neutro ▷ vt castrar, capar

**neutral** ['njuːtrəl] adj (person) neutral; (colour etc, Elec) neutro ▷ n (Aut) punto muerto

**never** ['nɛvə*] adv nunca, jamás; **I ~ went** no fui nunca; **~ in my life** jamás en la vida; see also **mind**; **never-ending** adj interminable, sin fin; **nevertheless** [nɛvəðə'lɛs] adv sin embargo, no obstante

**new** [njuː] adj nuevo; (brand new) a estrenar; (recent) reciente; **New Age** n Nueva Era; **newborn** adj recién nacido; **newcomer** ['njuːkʌmə*] n recién venido/a or llegado/a; **newly** adv nuevamente, recién

**news** [njuːz] n noticias fpl; **a piece of ~** una noticia; **the ~** (Radio, TV) las noticias fpl; **news agency** n agencia de noticias; **newsagent** (BRIT) n vendedor(a) m/f de periódicos; **newscaster** n presentador(a) m/f, locutor(a) m/f; **news dealer** (US) n = **newsagent**; **newsletter** n hoja informativa, boletín m; **newspaper** n periódico, diario; **newsreader** n = **newscaster**

**newt** [njuːt] n tritón m

**New Year** n Año Nuevo; **New Year's Day** n Día m de Año Nuevo; **New Year's Eve** n Nochevieja

**New Zealand** [njuː'ziːlənd] n Nueva Zelanda; **New Zealander** n neozelandés/ esa m/f

**next** [nɛkst] adj (house, room) vecino; (bus stop, meeting) próximo; (following: page etc) siguiente ▷ adv después; **the ~ day** el día siguiente; **~ time** la próxima vez; **~ year** el año próximo or que viene; **~ to** junto a, al lado de; **~ to nothing** casi nada; **~ please!** ¡el siguiente!; **next door** adv en la casa de al lado ▷ adj vecino, de al lado; **next-of-kin** n pariente m más cercano

**NHS** n abbr = **National Health Service**

**nibble** ['nɪbl] vt mordisquear, mordiscar

**nice** [naɪs] adj (likeable) simpático; (kind) amable; (pleasant) agradable;

(*attractive*) bonito, lindo (*LAM*); **nicely** *adv* amablemente; bien

**niche** [niːʃ] *n* (*Arch*) nicho, hornacina

**nick** [nɪk] *n* (*wound*) rasguño; (*cut, indentation*) mella, muesca ▷ *vt* (*inf*) birlar, robar; **in the ~ of time** justo a tiempo

**nickel** ['nɪkl] *n* níquel *m*; (*US*) moneda de 5 centavos

**nickname** ['nɪkneɪm] *n* apodo, mote *m* ▷ *vt* apodar

**nicotine** ['nɪkətiːn] *n* nicotina

**niece** [niːs] *n* sobrina

**night** [naɪt] *n* noche *f*; (*evening*) tarde *f*; **the ~ before last** anteanoche; **at ~, by ~** de noche, por la noche; **night club** *n* cabaret *m*; **nightdress**(*BRIT*) *n* camisón *m*; **nightie** ['naɪtɪ] *n* =**nightdress**; **nightlife** *n* vida nocturna; **nightly** *adj* de todas las noches ▷ *adv* todas las noches, cada noche; **nightmare** *n* pesadilla; **night school** *n* clase(s) *f(pl)* nocturna(s); **night shift** *n* turno nocturno or de noche; **night-time** *n* noche *f*

**nil** [nɪl] (*BRIT*) *n* (*Sport*) cero, nada

**nine** [naɪn] *num* nueve; **nineteen** *num* diecinueve, diez y nueve; **nineteenth** [naɪn'tiːnθ] *adj* decimonoveno, decimonono; **ninetieth** ['naɪntɪɪθ] *adj* nonagésimo; **ninety** *num* noventa

**ninth** [naɪnθ] *adj* noveno

**nip** [nɪp] *vt* (*pinch*) pellizcar; (*bite*) morder

**nipple** ['nɪpl] *n* (*Anat*) pezón *m*

**nitrogen** ['naɪtrədʒən] *n* nitrógeno

○ **KEYWORD**

**no** [nəu] (*pl* **noes**) *adv* (*opposite of "yes"*) no; **are you coming? – no (I'm not)** ¿vienes? – no; **would you like some more? – no thank you** ¿quieres más? – no gracias ▷ *adj* (*not any*): **I have no money/time/books** no tengo dinero/tiempo/libros; **no other man would have done it** ningún otro lo hubiera hecho; **"no entry"** "prohibido el paso"; **"no smoking"** "prohibido fumar" ▷ *n* no *m*

**nobility** [nəu'bɪlɪtɪ] *n* nobleza

**noble** ['nəubl] *adj* noble

**nobody** ['nəubədɪ] *pron* nadie

**nod** [nɔd] *vi* saludar con la cabeza; (*in agreement*) decir que sí con la cabeza; (*doze*) dar cabezadas ▷ *vt*: **to ~ one's head** inclinar la cabeza ▷ *n* inclinación *f* de cabeza; **nod off** *vi* dar cabezadas

**noise** [nɔɪz] *n* ruido; (*din*) escándalo, estrépito; **noisy** *adj* ruidoso; (*child*) escandaloso

**nominal** ['nɔmɪnl] *adj* nominal

**nominate** ['nɔmɪneɪt] *vt* (*propose*) proponer; (*appoint*) nombrar; **nomination** [nɔmɪ'neɪʃən] *n* propuesta; nombramiento; **nominee** [-'niː] *n* candidato/a

**none** [nʌn] *pron* ninguno/a ▷ *adv* de ninguna manera; **~ of you** ninguno de vosotros; **I've ~ left** no me queda ninguno/a; **he's ~ the worse for it** no le ha hecho ningún mal

**nonetheless** [nʌnðə'lɛs] *adv* sin embargo, no obstante

**non-fiction** [nɔn'fɪkʃən] *n* literatura no novelesca

**nonsense** ['nɔnsəns] *n* tonterías *fpl*, disparates *fpl*; **~!** ¡qué tonterías!

**non: non-smoker** *n* no fumador(a) *m/f*; **non-smoking** *adj* (de) no fumador; **non-stick** *adj* (*pan, surface*) antiadherente

**noodles** ['nuːdlz] *npl* tallarines *mpl*

**noon** [nuːn] *n* mediodía *m*

**no-one** ['nəuwʌn] *pron* =**nobody**

**nor** [nɔː*] *conj* =**neither** ▷ *adv see* **neither**

**norm** [nɔːm] *n* norma

**normal** ['nɔːml] *adj* normal; **normally** *adv* normalmente

**north** [nɔːθ] *n* norte *m* ▷ *adj* del norte, norteño ▷ *adv* al or hacia el norte; **North America** *n* América del Norte; **North American** *adj, n* norteamericano/a *m/f*; **northbound** ['nɔːθbaund] *adj* (*traffic*) que se dirige al norte; (*carriageway*) de dirección norte; **north-east** *n* nor(d)este *m*; **northeastern** *adj* nor(d)este, del nor(d)este; **northern** ['nɔːðən] *adj* norteño, del norte; **Northern Ireland** *n* Irlanda del Norte; **North Korea** *n* Corea del Norte; **North Pole** *n* Polo Norte; **North Sea** *n* Mar *m* del Norte; **north-west** *n* nor(d)oeste *m*; **northwestern** ['nɔːθ'westən] *adj* noroeste, del noroeste

**Norway** ['nɔːweɪ] *n* Noruega; **Norwegian** [-'wiːdʒən] *adj* noruego/a ▷ *n* noruego/a; (*Ling*) noruego

**nose** [nəuz] *n* (*Anat*) nariz *f*; (*Zool*) hocico; (*sense of smell*) olfato ▷ *vi*: **to ~ about** curiosear; **nosebleed** *n* hemorragia nasal; **nosey**(*inf*) *adj* curioso, fisgón/ona

**nostalgia** [nɔs'tældʒɪə] *n* nostalgia

**nostalgic** [nɔs'tældʒɪk] *adj* nostálgico

**nostril** ['nɔstrɪl] *n* ventana de la nariz

**nosy** ['nəuzɪ] (*inf*) *adj* =**nosey**

**not** [nɔt] *adv* no; **~ that ...** no es que ...; **it's too late, isn't it?** es demasiado tarde, ¿verdad or no?; **~ yet/now** todavía/ahora no; **why ~?** ¿por qué no?; *see also* **all; only**

**notable** ['nəutəbl] *adj* notable; **notably**
*adv* especialmente

**notch** [nɔtʃ] *n* muesca, corte *m*

**note** [nəut] *n* (*Mus, record, letter*) nota;
(*banknote*) billete *m*; (*tone*) tono ▷ *vt*
(*observe*) notar, observar; (*write down*)
apuntar, anotar; **notebook** *n* libreta,
cuaderno; **noted** ['nəutɪd] *adj* célebre,
conocido; **notepad** *n* bloc *m*; **notepaper** *n*
papel *m* para cartas

**nothing** ['nʌθɪŋ] *n* nada; (*zero*) cero; **he
does ~** no hace nada; **~ new** nada nuevo; **~
much** no mucho; **for ~** (*free*) gratis, sin pago;
(*in vain*) en balde

**notice** ['nəutɪs] *n* (*announcement*) anuncio;
(*warning*) aviso; (*dismissal*) despido;
(*resignation*) dimisión *f*; (*period of time*) plazo
▷ *vt* (*observe*) notar, observar; **to bring sth
to sb's ~** (*attention*) llamar la atención de
algn sobre algo; **to take ~ of** tomar nota
de, prestar atención a; **at short ~** con poca
anticipación; **until further ~** hasta nuevo
aviso; **to hand in one's ~** dimitir

⬛ Be careful not to translate **notice** by the
Spanish word *noticia*.

**noticeable** *adj* evidente, obvio

**notify** ['nəutɪfaɪ] *vt*: **to ~ sb (of sth)**
comunicar (algo) a algn

**notion** ['nəuʃən] *n* idea; (*opinion*) opinión
*f*; **notions** *npl* (*us*) mercería

**notorious** [nəu'tɔ:rɪəs] *adj* notorio

**notwithstanding** [nɔtwɪθ'stændɪŋ] *adv*
no obstante, sin embargo; **~ this** a pesar
de esto

**nought** [nɔ:t] *n* cero

**noun** [naun] *n* nombre *m*, sustantivo

**nourish** ['nʌrɪʃ] *vt* nutrir; (*fig*) alimentar;
**nourishment** *n* alimento, sustento

**Nov.** *abbr* (= *November*) nov

**novel** ['nɔvl] *n* novela ▷ *adj* (*new*) nuevo,
original; (*unexpected*) insólito; **novelist** *n*
novelista *mf*; **novelty** *n* novedad *f*

**November** [nəu'vɛmbə*] *n* noviembre *m*

**novice** ['nɔvɪs] *n* (*Rel*) novicio/a

**now** [nau] *adv* (*at the present time*) ahora;
(*these days*) actualmente, hoy día ▷ *conj*: **~
(that)** ya que, ahora que; **right ~** ahora
mismo; **by ~** ya; **just ~** ahora mismo; **~
and then, ~ and again** de vez en cuando;
**from ~ on** de ahora en adelante; **nowadays**
['nauədeɪz] *adv* hoy (en) día, actualmente

**nowhere** ['nəuwɛə*] *adv* (*direction*) a
ninguna parte; (*location*) en ninguna parte

**nozzle** ['nɔzl] *n* boquilla

**nr** *abbr* (*BRIT*) = **near**

**nuclear** ['nju:klɪə*] *adj* nuclear

**nucleus** ['nju:klɪəs] (*pl* **nuclei**) *n* núcleo

**nude** [nju:d] *adj, n* desnudo/a *m/f*; **in the
~ desnudo**

**nudge** [nʌdʒ] *vt* dar un codazo a

**nudist** ['nju:dɪst] *n* nudista *mf*

**nudity** ['nju:dɪtɪ] *n* desnudez *f*

**nuisance** ['nju:sns] *n* molestia, fastidio;
(*person*) pesado, latoso; **what a ~!** ¡qué lata!

**numb** [nʌm] *adj*: **~ with cold/fear**
entumecido por el frío/paralizado de miedo

**number** ['nʌmbə*] *n* número; (*quantity*)
cantidad *f* ▷ *vt* (*pages etc*) numerar, poner
número a; (*amount to*) sumar, ascender a; **to
be ~ed among** figurar entre; **a ~ of** varios,
algunos; **they were ten in ~** eran diez;
**number plate** (*BRIT*) *n* matrícula, placa;
**Number Ten** (*BRIT*: 10 *Downing Street*)
*residencia del primer ministro*

**numerical** [nju:'mɛrɪkl] *adj* numérico

**numerous** ['nju:mərəs] *adj* numeroso

**nun** [nʌn] *n* monja, religiosa

**nurse** [nə:s] *n* enfermero/a; (*also:* **~maid**)
niñera ▷ *vt* (*patient*) cuidar, atender

**nursery** ['nə:sərɪ] *n* (*institution*) guardería
infantil; (*room*) cuarto de los niños; (*for
plants*) criadero, semillero; **nursery
rhyme** *n* canción *f* infantil; **nursery
school** *n* parvulario, escuela de párvulos;
**nursery slope** (*BRIT*) *n* (*Ski*) cuesta para
principiantes

**nursing** ['nə:sɪŋ] *n* (*profession*) profesión
*f* de enfermera; (*care*) asistencia, cuidado;
**nursing home** *n* clínica de reposo

**nurture** ['nə:tʃə*] *vt* (*child, plant*)
alimentar, nutrir

**nut** [nʌt] *n* (*Tech*) tuerca; (*Bot*) nuez *f*

**nutmeg** ['nʌtmeg] *n* nuez *f* moscada

**nutrient** ['nju:trɪənt] *adj* nutritivo ▷ *n*
elemento nutritivo

**nutrition** [nju:'trɪʃən] *n* nutrición *f*,
alimentación *f*

**nutritious** [nju:'trɪʃəs] *adj* nutritivo,
alimenticio

**nuts** [nʌts] (*inf*) *adj* loco

**NVQ** *n abbr* (*BRIT*) = **National Vocational
Qualification**

**nylon** ['naɪlɔn] *n* nilón *m* ▷ *adj* de nilón

# O

**oath** [əυθ] *n* juramento; (*swear word*) palabrota; **on** (*BRIT*) or **under ~** bajo juramento

**oak** [əυk] *n* roble *m* ▷ *adj* de roble

**O.A.P.** (*BRIT*) *n, abbr* = **old-age pensioner**

**oar** [ɔ:*] *n* remo

**oasis** [əυ'eɪsɪs] (*pl* **oases**) *n* oasis *m inv*

**oath** [əυθ] *n* juramento; (*swear word*) palabrota; **on** (*BRIT*) or **under ~** bajo juramento

**oatmeal** ['əυtmi:l] *n* harina de avena

**oats** [əυts] *npl* avena

**obedience** [ə'bi:dɪəns] *n* obediencia

**obedient** [ə'bi:dɪənt] *adj* obediente

**obese** [əυ'bi:s] *adj* obeso

**obesity** [əυ'bi:sɪtɪ] *n* obesidad *f*

**obey** [ə'beɪ] *vt* obedecer; (*instructions, regulations*) cumplir

**obituary** [ə'bɪtjuərɪ] *n* necrología

**object** [*n* 'ɔbdʒɪkt, *vb* əb'dʒɛkt] *n* objeto; (*purpose*) objeto, propósito; (*Ling*) complemento ▷ *vi*: **to ~ to** estar en contra de; (*proposal*) oponerse a; **to ~ that** objetar que; **expense is no ~** no importa cuánto cuesta; **I ~!** ¡yo protesto!; **objection** [əb'dʒɛkʃən] *n* protesta; **I have no objection to ...** no tengo inconveniente en que ...; **objective** *adj, n* objetivo

**obligation** [ɔblɪ'geɪʃən] *n* obligación *f*; (*debt*) deber *m*; **without ~** sin compromiso

**obligatory** [ə'blɪgətərɪ] *adj* obligatorio

**oblige** [ə'blaɪdʒ] *vt* (*do a favour for*) complacer, hacer un favor a; **to ~ sb to do sth** forzar or obligar a algn a hacer algo; **to be ~d to sb for sth** estarle agradecido a algn por algo

**oblique** [ə'bli:k] *adj* oblicuo; (*allusion*) indirecto

**obliterate** [ə'blɪtəreɪt] *vt* borrar

**oblivious** [ə'blɪvɪəs] *adj*: **~ of** inconsciente de

**oblong** ['ɔblɔŋ] *adj* rectangular ▷ *n* rectángulo

**obnoxious** [əb'nɔkʃəs] *adj* odioso, detestable; (*smell*) nauseabundo

**oboe** ['əυbəυ] *n* oboe *m*

**obscene** [əb'si:n] *adj* obsceno

**obscure** [əb'skjυə*] *adj* oscuro ▷ *vt* oscurecer; (*hide: sun*) esconder

**observant** [əb'zə:vnt] *adj* observador(a)

**observation** [ɔbzə'veɪʃən] *n* observación *f*; (*Med*) examen *m*

**observatory** [əb'zə:vətrɪ] *n* observatorio

**observe** [əb'zə:v] *vt* observar; (*rule*) cumplir; **observer** *n* observador(a) *m/f*

**obsess** [əb'sɛs] *vt* obsesionar; **obsession** [əb'sɛʃən] *n* obsesión *f*; **obsessive** *adj* obsesivo; obsesionante

**obsolete** ['ɔbsəli:t] *adj*: **to be ~** estar en desuso

**obstacle** ['ɔbstəkl] *n* obstáculo; (*nuisance*) estorbo

**obstinate** ['ɔbstɪnɪt] *adj* terco, porfiado; (*determined*) obstinado

**obstruct** [əb'strʌkt] *vt* obstruir; (*hinder*) estorbar, obstaculizar; **obstruction** [əb'strʌkʃən] *n* (*action*) obstrucción *f*; (*object*) estorbo, obstáculo

**obtain** [əb'teɪn] *vt* obtener; (*achieve*) conseguir

**obvious** ['ɔbvɪəs] *adj* obvio, evidente; **obviously** *adv* evidentemente, naturalmente; **obviously not** por supuesto que no

**occasion** [ə'keɪʒən] *n* oportunidad *f*, ocasión *f*; (*event*) acontecimiento; **occasional** *adj* poco frecuente, ocasional; **occasionally** *adv* de vez en cuando

**occult** [ɔ'kʌlt] *adj* (*gen*) oculto

**occupant** ['ɔkjupənt] *n* (*of house*) inquilino/a; (*of car*) ocupante *mf*

**occupation** [ɔkju'peɪʃən] *n* ocupación *f*; (*job*) trabajo; ocupaciones *fpl*

**occupy** ['ɔkjupaɪ] *vt* (*seat, post, time*) ocupar; (*house*) habitar; **to ~ o.s. in doing** pasar el tiempo haciendo

**occur** [ə'kə:*] *vi* pasar, suceder; **to ~ to sb** ocurrírsele a algn; **occurrence** [ə'kʌrəns] *n* acontecimiento; (*existence*) existencia

**ocean** ['əυʃən] *n* océano

**o'clock** [ə'klɔk] *adv*: **it is 5 ~** son las 5

**Oct.** *abbr* (= *October*) oct

**October** [ɔk'təυbə*] *n* octubre *m*

**octopus** ['ɔktəpəs] *n* pulpo

**odd** [ɔd] *adj* extraño, raro; (*number*) impar; (*sock, shoe etc*) suelto; **60-~** 60 y pico; **at ~ times** de vez en cuando; **to be the ~ one out** estar de más; **oddly** *adv* curiosamente, extrañamente; *see also* **enough**; **odds** *npl* (*in betting*) puntos *mpl* de ventaja; **it makes no odds** da lo mismo; **at odds** reñidos/as; **odds and ends** minucias *fpl*

**odometer** [ɔˈdɔmɪtə*] (*US*) *n* cuentakilómetros *m inv*

**odour** [ˈəudə*] (*US* **odor**) *n* olor *m*; (*unpleasant*) hedor *m*

○ KEYWORD

**of** [ɔv, əv] *prep* **1** (*gen*) de; **a friend of ours** un amigo nuestro; **a boy of 10** un chico de 10 años; **that was kind of you** eso fue muy amable por *or* de tu parte
**2** (*expressing quantity, amount, dates etc*) de; **a kilo of flour** un kilo de harina; **there were three of them** había tres; **three of us went** tres de nosotros fuimos; **the 5th of July** el 5 de julio
**3** (*from, out of*) de; **made of wood** (hecho) de madera

**off** [ɔf] *adj, adv* (*engine*) desconectado *or* (*light*) apagado; (*tap*) cerrado; (*BRIT: food: bad*) pasado, malo; (: *milk*) cortado; (*cancelled*) cancelado ▷ *prep* de; **to be ~** (*to leave*) irse, marcharse; **to be ~ sick** estar enfermo *or* de baja; **a day ~** un día libre *or* sin trabajar; **to have an ~ day** tener un día malo; **he had his coat ~** se había quitado el abrigo; **10% ~** (*Comm*) (con el) 10% de descuento; **5 km ~ (the road)** a 5 km (de la carretera); **~ the coast** frente a la costa; **I'm ~ meat** (*no longer eat/like it*) paso de la carne; **on the ~ chance** por si acaso; **~ and on** de vez en cuando

**offence** [əˈfɛns] (*US* **offense**) *n* (*crime*) delito; **to take ~ at** ofenderse por

**offend** [əˈfɛnd] *vt* (*person*) ofender; **offender** *n* delincuente *mf*

**offense** [əˈfɛns] (*US*) *n* = **offence**

**offensive** [əˈfɛnsɪv] *adj* ofensivo; (*smell etc*) repugnante ▷ *n* (*Mil*) ofensiva

**offer** [ˈɔfə*] *n* oferta, ofrecimiento; (*proposal*) propuesta ▷ *vt* ofrecer; (*opportunity*) facilitar; **"on ~"** (*Comm*) "en oferta"

**offhand** [ɔfˈhænd] *adj* informal ▷ *adv* de improviso

**office** [ˈɔfɪs] *n* (*place*) oficina; (*room*) despacho; (*position*) carga, oficio; **doctor's ~** (*US*) consultorio; **to take ~** entrar en funciones; **office block** (*US*)**, office building** *n* bloque *m* de oficinas; **office hours** *npl* horas *fpl* de oficina; (*US Med*) horas *fpl* de consulta

**officer** [ˈɔfɪsə*] *n* (*Mil etc*) oficial *mf*; (*also*: **police ~**) agente *mf* de policía; (*of organization*) director(a) *m/f*

**office worker** *n* oficinista *mf*

**official** [əˈfɪʃl] *adj* oficial, autorizado ▷ *n* funcionario/a, oficial *mf*

**off:** **off-licence** (*BRIT*) *n* (*shop*) bodega *tienda de vinos y bebidas alcohólicas*; **off-line** *adj, adv* (*Comput*) fuera de línea; **off-peak** *adj* (*electricity*) de banda económica; (*ticket*) billete de precio reducido por viajar fuera de las horas punta; **off-putting** (*BRIT*) *adj* (*person*) asqueroso; (*remark*) desalentador(a); **off-season** *adj, adv* fuera de temporada

◉ OFF-LICENCE

En el Reino Unido la venta de bebidas alcohólicas está estrictamente regulada y se necesita una licencia especial, con la que cuentan los bares, restaurantes y los establecimientos de **off-licence**, los únicos lugares en donde se pueden adquirir bebidas alcohólicas para su consumo fuera del local, de donde viene su nombre. También venden bebidas no alcohólicas, tabaco, chocolatinas, patatas fritas, etc. y a menudo forman parte de una cadena nacional.

**offset** [ˈɔfsɛt] *vt* contrarrestar, compensar

**offshore** [ɔfˈʃɔ:*] *adj* (*breeze, island*) costera; (*fishing*) de bajura

**offside** [ˈɔfsaɪd] *adj* (*Sport*) fuera de juego; (*Aut: in UK*) del lado derecho; (: *in US, Europe etc*) del lado izquierdo

**offspring** [ˈɔfsprɪŋ] *n inv* descendencia

**often** [ˈɔfn] *adv* a menudo, con frecuencia; **how ~ do you go?** ¿cada cuánto vas?

**oh** [əu] *excl* ¡ah!

**oil** [ɔɪl] *n* aceite *m*; (*petroleum*) petróleo; (*for heating*) aceite *m* combustible ▷ *vt* engrasar; **oil filter** *n* (*Aut*) filtro de aceite; **oil painting** *n* pintura al óleo; **oil refinery** *n* refinería de petróleo; **oil rig** *n* torre *f* de perforación; **oil slick** *n* marea negra; **oil tanker** *n* petrolero; (*truck*) camión *m* cisterna; **oil well** *n* pozo (de petróleo); **oily** *adj* aceitoso; (*food*) grasiento

**ointment** [ˈɔɪntmənt] *n* ungüento

**O.K., okay** [ˈəuˈkeɪ] *excl* ¡O.K.!, ¡está bien!, ¡vale! (*SP*) ▷ *adj* bien ▷ *vt* dar el visto bueno a

**old** [əuld] *adj* viejo; (*former*) antiguo; **how ~ are you?** ¿cuántos años tienes?, ¿qué edad tienes?; **he's 10 years ~** tiene 10 años; **~er brother** hermano mayor; **old age** *n* vejez *f*; **old-age pension** *n* (*BRIT*) jubilación *f*, pensión *f*; **old-age pensioner** (*BRIT*) *n* jubilado/a; **old-fashioned** *adj* anticuado, pasado de moda; **old people's home** n (*esp* BRIT) residencia f de ancianos

**olive** ['ɔlɪv] n (*fruit*) aceituna; (*tree*) olivo ▷ adj (*also*: **~-green**) verde oliva; **olive oil** n aceite m de oliva

**Olympic** [əu'lɪmpɪk] adj olímpico; **the ~ Games, the ~s** las Olimpiadas

**omelet(te)** ['ɔmlɪt] n tortilla francesa (*SP*), omelette f (*LAM*)

**omen** ['əumən] n presagio

**ominous** ['ɔmɪnəs] adj de mal agüero, amenazador(a)

**omit** [əu'mɪt] vt omitir

○ **KEYWORD**

**on** [ɔn] prep **1** (*indicating position*) en; sobre; **on the wall** en la pared; **it's on the table** está sobre or en la mesa; **on the left** a la izquierda

**2** (*indicating means, method, condition etc*): **on foot** a pie; **on the train/plane** (*go*) en tren/avión; (*be*) en el tren/el avión; **on the radio/television/telephone** por or en la radio/televisión/al teléfono; **to be on drugs** drogarse; (*Med*) estar a tratamiento; **to be on holiday/business** estar de vacaciones/en viaje de negocios

**3** (*referring to time*): **on Friday** el viernes; **on Fridays** los viernes; **on June 20th** el 20 de junio; **a week on Friday** del viernes en una semana; **on arrival** al llegar; **on seeing this** al ver esto

**4** (*about, concerning*) sobre, acerca de; **a book on physics** un libro de or sobre física ▷ adv **1** (*referring to dress*): **to have one's coat on** tener or llevar el abrigo puesto; **she put her gloves on** se puso los guantes

**2** (*referring to covering*): **"screw the lid on tightly"** "cerrar bien la tapa"

**3** (*further, continuously*): **to walk** *etc* **on** seguir caminando *etc* ▷ adj **1** (*functioning, in operation: machine, radio, TV, light*) encendido/a (*SP*), prendido/a (*LAM*); (: *tap*) abierto/a; (: *brakes*) echado/a, puesto/a; **is the meeting still on?** (*in progress*) ¿todavía continúa la reunión?; (*not cancelled*) ¿va a haber reunión al fin?; **there's a good film on at the cinema** ponen una buena película en el cine

**2** **that's not on!** (*inf: not possible*) ¡eso ni hablar!; (: *not acceptable*) ¡eso no se hace!

**once** [wʌns] adv una vez; (*formerly*) antiguamente ▷ conj una vez que; **~ he had left/it was done** una vez que se había marchado/se hizo; **at ~** en seguida, inmediatamente; (*simultaneously*) a la vez;

**~ a week** una vez por semana; **~ more** otra vez; **~ and for all** de una vez por todas; **~ upon a time** érase una vez

**oncoming** ['ɔnkʌmɪŋ] adj (*traffic*) que viene de frente

○ **KEYWORD**

**one** [wʌn] num un(o)/una; **one hundred and fifty** ciento cincuenta; **one by one** uno a uno ▷ adj **1** (*sole*) único; **the one book which** el único libro que; **the one man who** el único que

**2** (*same*) mismo/a; **they came in the one car** vinieron en un solo coche ▷ pron **1** **this one** éste(ésta); **that one** ése(ésa); (*more remote*) aquél(aquella); **I've already got (a red) one** ya tengo uno/a rojo/a; **one by one** uno/a por uno/a

**2** **one another** os (*SP*), se (+ *el uno al otro, unos a otros etc*); **do you two ever see one another?** ¿vosotros dos os veis alguna vez? (*SP*), ¿se ven ustedes dos alguna vez?; **the boys didn't dare look at one another** los chicos no se atrevieron a mirarse (el uno al otro); **they all kissed one another** se besaron unos a otros

**3** (*impers*): **one never knows** nunca se sabe; **to cut one's finger** cortarse el dedo; **one needs to eat** hay que comer

**one-off** (*BRIT: inf*) n (*event*) acontecimiento único

**oneself** [wʌn'sɛlf] pron (*reflexive*) se; (*after prep*) sí; (*emphatic*) uno/a mismo/a; **to hurt ~** hacerse daño; **to keep sth for ~** guardarse algo; **to talk to ~** hablar solo

**one: one-shot** [wʌn'ʃɔt] (*US*) n = **one-off**; **one-sided** adj (*argument*) parcial; **one-to-one** adj (*relationship*) de dos; **one-way** adj (*street*) de sentido único

**ongoing** ['ɔngəuɪŋ] adj continuo

**onion** ['ʌnjən] n cebolla

**on-line** ['ɔnlaɪn] adj, adv (*Comput*) en línea

**onlooker** ['ɔnlukə*] n espectador(a) m/f

**only** ['əunlɪ] adv solamente, sólo ▷ adj único, solo ▷ conj solamente que, pero; **an ~ child** un hijo único; **not ~ ... but also ...** no sólo ... sino también ...

**on-screen** [ɔn'skri:n] adj (*Comput etc*) en pantalla; (*romance, kiss*) cinematográfico

**onset** ['ɔnsɛt] n comienzo

**onto** ['ɔntu] prep = **on to**

**onward(s)** ['ɔnwəd(z)] adv (*move*) (hacia) adelante; **from that time ~** desde entonces en adelante

**oops** [ups] excl (*also*: **~-a-daisy!**) ¡huy!

**ooze** [uːz] *vi* rezumar

**opaque** [əuˈpeɪk] *adj* opaco

**open** [ˈəupn] *adj* abierto; (*car*) descubierto; (*road, view*) despejado; (*meeting*) público; (*admiration*) manifiesto ▷ *vt* abrir ▷ *vi* abrirse; (*book etc: commence*) comenzar; **in the ~ (air)** al aire libre; **open up** *vt* abrir; (*blocked road*) despejar ▷ *vi* abrirse, empezar; **open-air** *adj* al aire libre; **opening** *n* abertura; (*start*) comienzo; (*opportunity*) oportunidad *f*; **opening hours** *npl* horario de apertura; **open learning** *n* enseñanza flexible a tiempo parcial; **openly** *adv* abiertamente; **open-minded** *adj* imparcial; **open-necked** *adj* (*shirt*) desabrochado, sin corbata; **open-plan** *adj*: **open-plan office** gran oficina sin particiones; **Open University** *n* (BRIT) ≈ Universidad *f* Nacional de Enseñanza a Distancia, UNED *f*

○ OPEN UNIVERSITY

○ La **Open University**, fundada en
○ 1969, está especializada en impartir
○ cursos a distancia que no exigen una
○ dedicación exclusiva. Cuenta con sus
○ propios materiales de apoyo, entre
○ ellos programas de radio y televisión
○ emitidos por la **BBC** y para conseguir los
○ créditos de la licenciatura es necesaria
○ la presentación de unos trabajos y la
○ asistencia a los cursos de verano.

**opera** [ˈɔpərə] *n* ópera; **opera house** *n* teatro de la ópera; **opera singer** *n* cantante *m/f* de ópera

**operate** [ˈɔpəreɪt] *vt* (*machine*) hacer funcionar; (*company*) dirigir ▷ *vi* funcionar; **to ~ on sb** (*Med*) operar a algn

**operating room** [ˈɔpəreɪtɪŋ-] (US) *n* quirófano, sala de operaciones

**operating theatre** (BRIT) *n* sala de operaciones

**operation** [ɔpəˈreɪʃən] *n* operación *f*; (*of machine*) funcionamiento; **to be in ~** estar funcionando *or* en funcionamiento; **to have an ~** (*Med*) ser operado; **operational** *adj* operacional, en buen estado

**operative** [ˈɔpərətɪv] *adj* en vigor

**operator** [ˈɔpəreɪtə*] *n* (*of machine*) maquinista *mf*, operario/a; (*Tel*) operador(a) *m/f*, telefonista *mf*

**opinion** [əˈpɪnɪən] *n* opinión *f*; **in my ~** en mi opinión, a mi juicio; **opinion poll** *n* encuesta, sondeo

**opponent** [əˈpəunənt] *n* adversario/a, contrincante *mf*

**opportunity** [ɔpəˈtjuːnɪtɪ] *n* oportunidad *f*; **to take the ~ of doing** aprovechar la ocasión para hacer

**oppose** [əˈpəuz] *vt* oponerse a; **to be ~d to sth** oponerse a algo; **as ~d to** a diferencia de

**opposite** [ˈɔpəzɪt] *adj* opuesto, contrario a; (*house etc*) de enfrente ▷ *adv* en frente ▷ *prep* en frente de, frente a ▷ *n* lo contrario

**opposition** [ɔpəˈzɪʃən] *n* oposición *f*

**oppress** [əˈprɛs] *vt* oprimir

**opt** [ɔpt] *vi*: **to ~ for** optar por; **to ~ to do** optar por hacer; **opt out** *vi*: **to opt out of** optar por no hacer

**optician** [ɔpˈtɪʃən] *n* óptico *m/f*

**optimism** [ˈɔptɪmɪzəm] *n* optimismo

**optimist** [ˈɔptɪmɪst] *n* optimista *mf*; **optimistic** [-ˈmɪstɪk] *adj* optimista

**optimum** [ˈɔptɪməm] *adj* óptimo

**option** [ˈɔpʃən] *n* opción *f*; **optional** *adj* facultativo, discrecional

**or** [ɔː*] *conj* o; (*before o, ho*) u; (*with negative*): **he hasn't seen ~ heard anything** no ha visto ni oído nada; **~ else** si no

**oral** [ˈɔːrəl] *adj* oral ▷ *n* examen *m* oral

**orange** [ˈɔrɪndʒ] *n* (*fruit*) naranja ▷ *adj* color naranja; **orange juice** *n* jugo *m* de naranja, zumo *m* de naranja (SP); **orange squash** *n* naranjada

**orbit** [ˈɔːbɪt] *n* órbita ▷ *vt*, *vi* orbitar

**orchard** [ˈɔːtʃəd] *n* huerto

**orchestra** [ˈɔːkɪstrə] *n* orquesta; (*US: seating*) platea

**orchid** [ˈɔːkɪd] *n* orquídea

**ordeal** [ɔːˈdiːl] *n* experiencia horrorosa

**order** [ˈɔːdə*] *n* orden *m*; (*command*) orden *f*; (*good order*) buen estado; (*Comm*) pedido ▷ *vt* (*also*: **put in ~**) arreglar, poner en orden; (*Comm*) pedir; (*command*) mandar, ordenar; **in ~** en orden; (*of document*) en regla; **in (working) ~** en funcionamiento; **in ~ to do/that** para hacer/que; **on ~** (*Comm*) pedido; **to be out of ~** estar desordenado; (*not working*) no funcionar; **to ~ sb to do sth** mandar a algn hacer algo; **order form** *n* hoja de pedido; **orderly** *n* (*Mil*) ordenanza *m*; (*Med*) enfermero/a (auxiliar) ▷ *adj* ordenado

**ordinary** [ˈɔːdnrɪ] *adj* corriente, normal; (*pej*) común y corriente; **out of the ~** fuera de lo común

**ore** [ɔː*] *n* mineral *m*

**oregano** [ɔrɪˈgɑːnəu] *n* orégano

**organ** [ˈɔːgən] *n* órgano; **organic** [ɔːˈgænɪk] *adj* orgánico; **organism** *n* organismo

**organization** [ɔːgənaɪˈzeɪʃən] *n* organización *f*

**organize** [ˈɔːgənaɪz] *vt* organizar;

**organized** ['ɔːgənaizd] adj organizado;
**organizer** n organizador(a) m/f
**orgasm** ['ɔːgæzəm] n orgasmo
**orgy** ['ɔːdʒi] n orgía
**oriental** [ɔːri'entl] adj oriental
**orientation** [ɔːrien'teiʃən] n orientación f
**origin** ['ɔridʒin] n origen m
**original** [ə'ridʒinl] adj original; (first)
primero; (earlier) primitivo ▷ n original m;
**originally** adv al principio
**originate** [ə'ridʒineit] vi: **to ~ from, to ~
in** surgir de, tener su origen en
**Orkneys** ['ɔːkniz] npl: **the ~** (also: **the
Orkney Islands**) las Orcadas
**ornament** ['ɔːnəmənt] n adorno; (trinket)
chuchería; **ornamental** [-'mentl] adj
decorativo, de adorno
**ornate** [ɔː'neit] adj muy ornado, vistoso
**orphan** ['ɔːfn] n huérfano/a
**orthodox** ['ɔːθədɔks] adj ortodoxo
**orthopaedic** [ɔːθə'piːdik] (us **orthopedic**)
adj ortopédico
**osteopath** ['ɔstiəpæθ] n osteópata mf
**ostrich** ['ɔstritʃ] n avestruz m
**other** ['ʌðə*] adj otro ▷ pron: **the ~** (one)
el(la) otro/a ▷ adv: **~ than** aparte de;
**otherwise** adv de otra manera ▷ conj (if
not) si no
**otter** ['ɔtə*] n nutria
**ouch** [autʃ] excl ¡ay!
**ought** [ɔːt] (pt ~) aux vb: **I ~ to do it** debería
hacerlo; **this ~ to have been corrected**
esto debiera haberse corregido; **he ~ to win**
(probability) debe or debiera ganar
**ounce** [auns] n onza (28.35g)
**our** ['auə*] adj nuestro; see also **my**; **ours**
pron (el) nuestro/(la) nuestra etc; see also
**mine¹**; **ourselves** pron pl (reflexive, after
prep) nosotros etc; (emphatic) nosotros mismos;
see also **oneself**
**oust** [aust] vt desalojar
**out** [aut] adv fuera, afuera; (not at home)
fuera (de casa); (light, fire) apagado; **~ there**
allí (fuera); **he's ~** (absent) no está, ha salido;
**to be ~ in one's calculations** equivocarse
(en sus cálculos); **to run ~** salir corriendo;
**~ loud** en alta voz; **~ of** (outside) fuera
de; (because of: anger etc) por; **~ of petrol**
sin gasolina; **"~ of order"** "no funciona";
**outback** n interior m; **outbound** adj
(flight) de salida; (flight: not return) de ida;
**outbreak** n (of war) comienzo; (of disease)
epidemia; (of violence etc) ola; **outburst** n
explosión f, arranque m; **outcast** n paria
mf; **outcome** n resultado; **outcry** n
protestas fpl; **outdated** adj anticuado,
fuera de moda; **outdoor** adj exterior, de
aire libre; (clothes) de calle; **outdoors** adv

al aire libre
**outer** ['autə*] adj exterior, externo; **outer
space** n espacio exterior
**outfit** ['autfit] n (clothes) conjunto
**out: outgoing** adj (character) extrovertido;
(retiring: president etc) saliente; **outgoings**
(BRIT) npl gastos mpl; **outhouse** n
dependencia
**outing** ['autiŋ] n excursión f, paseo
**out: outlaw** n proscrito ▷ vt proscribir;
**outlay** n inversión f; **outlet** n salida;
(of pipe) desagüe m; (US Elec) toma de
corriente; (also: **retail outlet**) punto de
venta; **outline** n (shape) contorno, perfil m;
(sketch, plan) esbozo ▷ vt (plan etc) esbozar;
**in outline** (fig) a grandes rasgos; **outlook** n
(fig: prospects) perspectivas fpl; (: for weather)
pronóstico; **outnumber** vt superar
en número; **out-of-date** adj (passport)
caducado; (clothes) pasado de moda; **out-of-
doors** adv al aire libre; **out-of-the-way** adj
apartado; **out-of-town** adj (shopping centre
etc) en las afueras; **outpatient** n paciente
mf externo/a; **outpost** n puesto avanzado;
**output** n (volumen m de) producción m,
rendimiento; (Comput) salida
**outrage** ['autreidʒ] n escándalo; (atrocity)
atrocidad f ▷ vt ultrajar; **outrageous**
[-'reidʒəs] adj monstruoso
**outright** [adv aut'rait, adj 'autrait]
adv (ask, deny) francamente; (refuse)
rotundamente; (win) de manera absoluta;
(be killed) en el acto ▷ adj franco; rotundo
**outset** ['autset] n principio
**outside** [aut'said] n exterior m ▷ adj
exterior, externo ▷ adv fuera ▷ prep fuera
de; (beyond) más allá de; **at the ~** (fig) a lo
sumo; **outside lane** n (Aut: in Britain) carril
m de la derecha; (: in US, Europe etc) carril m
de la izquierda; **outside line** n (Tel) línea
(exterior); **outsider** n (stranger) extraño,
forastero
**out: outsize** adj (clothes) de talla grande;
**outskirts** npl alrededores mpl, afueras fpl;
**outspoken** adj muy franco; **outstanding**
adj excepcional, destacado; (remaining)
pendiente
**outward** ['autwəd] adj externo; (journey)
de ida; **outweigh** vt (esp BRIT) = **outward**
**outweigh** [aut'wei] vt pesar más que
**oval** ['əuvl] adj ovalado ▷ n óvalo
**ovary** ['əuvəri] n ovario
**oven** ['ʌvn] n horno; **oven glove** n
guante m para el horno, manopla para el
horno; **ovenproof** adj resistente al horno;
**oven-ready** adj listo para el horno
**over** ['əuvə*] adv encima, por encima
▷ adj or adv (finished) terminado; (surplus)

de sobra ▷ *prep* (por) encima de; *(above)*
sobre; *(on the other side of)* al otro lado de;
*(more than)* más de; *(during)* durante; **~
here** (por) aquí; **~ there** (por) allí *or* allá;
**all ~** *(everywhere)* por todas partes; **~ and ~
(again)** una y otra vez; **~ and above** además
de; **to ask sb ~** invitar a algn a casa; **to bend
~** inclinarse

**overall** [*adj, n* 'əuvərɔ:l, *adv* əuvər'ɔ:l]
*adj (length etc)* total; *(study)* de conjunto
▷ *adv* en conjunto ▷ *n* (BRIT) guardapolvo;
**overalls** *npl (boiler suit)* mono (SP) *or* overol
*m* (LAM) (de trabajo)

**overboard** *adv* (Naut) por la borda
**overcame** [əuvə'keɪm] *pt of* **overcome**
**overcast** ['əuvəkɑ:st] *adj* encapotado
**overcharge** [əuvə'tʃɑ:dʒ] *vt:* **to ~ sb** cobrar
un precio excesivo a algn
**overcoat** ['əuvəkəut] *n* abrigo, sobretodo
**overcome** [əuvə'kʌm] *vt* vencer;
*(difficulty)* superar
**over: overcrowded** *adj* atestado de gente;
*(city, country)* superpoblado; **overdo** *(irreg)*
*vt* exagerar; *(overcook)* cocer demasiado; **to
overdo it** *(work etc)* pasarse; **overdone**
[əuvə'dʌn] *adj (vegetables)* recocido; *(steak)*
demasiado hecho; **overdose** *n* sobredosis
*f inv;* **overdraft** *n* saldo deudor; **overdrawn**
*adj (account)* en descubierto; **overdue** *adj*
retrasado; **overestimate** *vt* sobreestimar
**overflow** [*vb* əuvə'fləu, *n* 'əuvəfləu] *vi*
desbordarse ▷ *n (also:* **~ pipe**) (cañería de)
desagüe *m*
**overgrown** [əuvə'grəun] *adj (garden)*
invadido por la vegetación
**overhaul** [*vb* əuvə'hɔ:l, *n* 'əuvəhɔ:l] *vt*
revisar, repasar ▷ *n* revisión *f*
**overhead** [*adv* əuvə'hɛd, *adj, n* 'əuvəhɛd]
*adv* por arriba *or* encima ▷ *adj (cable)* aéreo
▷ *n* (US) = **overheads**; **overhead projector**
*n* retroproyector; **overheads** *npl (expenses)*
gastos *mpl* generales
**over: overhear** *(irreg) vt* oír por casualidad;
**overheat** *vi (engine)* recalentarse; **overland**
*adj, adv* por tierra; **overlap**
[əuvə'læp] *vi* traslaparse; **overleaf** *adv* al
dorso; **overload** *vt* sobrecargar; **overlook**
*vt (have view of)* dar a, tener vistas a; *(miss: by
mistake)* pasar por alto; *(excuse)* perdonar
**overnight** [əuvə'naɪt] *adv* durante la
noche; *(fig)* de la noche a la mañana ▷ *adj* de
noche; **to stay ~** pasar la noche; **overnight
bag** *n* fin *m* de semana, neceser *m* de viaje
**overpass** (US) ['əuvəpɑ:s] *n* paso superior
**overpower** [əuvə'pauə*] *vt* dominar;
*(fig)* embargar; **overpowering** *adj (heat)*
agobiante; *(smell)* penetrante
**over: overreact** [əuvərɪ'ækt] *vi* reaccionar

de manera exagerada; **overrule** *vt*
*(decision)* anular; *(claim)* denegar; **overrun**
*(irreg) vt (country)* invadir; *(time limit)*
rebasar, exceder
**overseas** [əuvə'si:z] *adv (abroad: live)* en el
extranjero; *(travel)* al extranjero ▷ *adj (trade)*
exterior; *(visitor)* extranjero
**oversee** [əuvə'si:] *(irreg) vt* supervisar
**overshadow** [əuvə'ʃædəu] *vt:* **to be ~ed
by** estar a la sombra de
**oversight** ['əuvəsaɪt] *n* descuido
**oversleep** [əuvə'sli:p] *(irreg) vi* quedarse
dormido
**overspend** [əuvə'spɛnd] *(irreg) vi* gastar
más de la cuenta; **we have overspent by
5 pounds** hemos excedido el presupuesto
en 5 libras
**overt** [əu'vɜ:t] *adj* abierto
**overtake** [əuvə'teɪk] *(irreg) vt* sobrepasar;
*(BRIT Aut)* adelantar
**over: overthrow** *(irreg) vt (government)*
derrocar; **overtime** *n* horas *fpl*
extraordinarias
**overtook** [əuvə'tuk] *pt of* **overtake**
**over: overturn** *vt* volcar; *(fig: plan)*
desbaratar; *(: government)* derrocar ▷ *vi*
volcar; **overweight** *adj* demasiado gordo *or*
pesado; **overwhelm** *vt* aplastar; *(emotion)*
sobrecoger; **overwhelming** *adj (victory,
defeat)* arrollador(a); *(feeling)* irresistible
**ow** [au] *excl* ¡ay!
**owe** [əu] *vt:* **to ~ sb sth, to ~ sth to sb**
deber algo a algn; **owing to** *prep* debido a,
por causa de
**owl** [aul] *n* búho, lechuza
**own** [əun] *vt* tener, poseer ▷ *adj* propio; **a
room of my ~** una habitación propia; **to get
one's ~ back** tomar revancha; **on one's ~**
solo, a solas; **own up** *vi* confesar; **owner** *n*
dueño/a; **ownership** *n* posesión *f*
**ox** [ɔks] *(pl* **~en**) *n* buey *m*
**Oxbridge** ['ɔksbrɪdʒ] *n* universidades de
Oxford y Cambridge
**oxen** ['ɔksən] *npl of* **ox**
**oxygen** ['ɔksɪdʒən] *n* oxígeno
**oyster** ['ɔɪstə*] *n* ostra
**oz.** *abbr* = **ounce(s)**
**ozone** ['əuzəun] *n* ozono; **ozone friendly**
*adj* que no daña la capa de ozono; **ozone
layer** *n* capa *f* de ozono

# p

**p** [piː] *abbr* = **penny; pence**

**P.A.** *n abbr* = **personal assistant; public address system**

**p.a.** *abbr* = **per annum**

**pace** [peɪs] *n* paso ▷ *vi*: **to ~ up and down** pasearse de un lado a otro; **to keep ~ with** llevar el mismo paso que; **pacemaker** *n* (Med) regulador *m* cardíaco, marcapasos *m inv*; (Sport: also: **pacesetter**) liebre *f*

**Pacific** [pəˈsɪfɪk] *n*: **the ~ (Ocean)** el (Océano) Pacífico

**pacifier** [ˈpæsɪfaɪə*] (US) *n* (dummy) chupete *m*

**pack** [pæk] *n* (packet) paquete *m*; (of hounds) jauría; (of people) manada, bando; (of cards) baraja; (bundle) fardo; (US: of cigarettes) paquete *m*; (back pack) mochila ▷ *vt* (fill) llenar; (in suitcase etc) meter, poner; (cram) llenar, atestar; **to ~ (one's bags)** hacerse la maleta; **to ~ sb off** despachar a algn; **pack in** *vi* (watch, car) estropearse ▷ *vt* (inf) dejar; **pack it in!** ¡para!, ¡basta ya!; **pack up** *vi* (inf: machine) estropearse; (person) irse ▷ *vt* (belongings, clothes) recoger; (goods, presents) empaquetar, envolver

**package** [ˈpækɪdʒ] *n* paquete *m*; (bulky) bulto; (also: **~ deal**) acuerdo global; **package holiday** *n* vacaciones *fpl* organizadas; **package tour** *n* viaje *m* organizado

**packaging** [ˈpækɪdʒɪŋ] *n* envase *m*

**packed** [pækt] *adj* abarrotado; **packed lunch** *n* almuerzo frío

**packet** [ˈpækɪt] *n* paquete *m*

**packing** [ˈpækɪŋ] *n* embalaje *m*

**pact** [pækt] *n* pacto

**pad** [pæd] *n* (of paper) bloc *m*; (cushion) cojinete *m*; (inf: home) casa ▷ *vt* rellenar; **padded** *adj* (jacket) acolchado; (bra) reforzado

**paddle** [ˈpædl] *n* (oar) canalete *m*; (US: for table tennis) paleta ▷ *vt* impulsar con canalete ▷ *vi* (with feet) chapotear; **paddling pool** (BRIT) *n* estanque *m* de juegos

**paddock** [ˈpædək] *n* corral *m*

**padlock** [ˈpædlɔk] *n* candado

**paedophile** [ˈpiːdəufaɪl] (US **pedophile**) *adj* de pedófilos ▷ *n* pedófilo/a

**page** [peɪdʒ] *n* (of book) página; (of newspaper) plana; (also: **~ boy**) paje *m* ▷ *vt* (in hotel etc) llamar por altavoz a

**pager** [ˈpeɪdʒə*] *n* (Tel) busca *m*

**paid** [peɪd] *pt, pp of* **pay** ▷ *adj* (work) remunerado; (holiday) pagado; (official etc) a sueldo; **to put ~ to** (BRIT) acabar con

**pain** [peɪn] *n* dolor *m*; **to be in ~** sufrir; **to take ~s to do sth** tomarse grandes molestias en hacer algo; **painful** *adj* doloroso; (difficult) penoso; (disagreeable) desagradable; **painkiller** *n* analgésico; **painstaking** [ˈpeɪnzteɪkɪŋ] *adj* (person) concienzudo, esmerado

**paint** [peɪnt] *n* pintura ▷ *vt* pintar; **to ~ the door blue** pintar la puerta de azul; **paintbrush** *n* (of artist) pincel *m*; (of decorator) brocha; **painter** *n* pintor(a) *m/f*; **painting** *n* pintura

**pair** [peə*] *n* (of shoes, gloves etc) par *m*; (of people) pareja; **a ~ of scissors** unas tijeras; **a ~ of trousers** unos pantalones, un pantalón

**pajamas** [pəˈdʒɑːməz] (US) *npl* pijama *m*

**Pakistan** [pɑːkɪˈstɑːn] *n* Paquistán *m*; **Pakistani** *adj, n* paquistaní *mf*

**pal** [pæl] (inf) *n* compinche *mf*, compañero/a

**palace** [ˈpæləs] *n* palacio

**pale** [peɪl] *adj* (gen) pálido; (colour) claro ▷ *n*: **to be beyond the ~** pasarse de la raya

**Palestine** [ˈpælɪstaɪn] *n* Palestina; **Palestinian** [-ˈtɪnɪən] *adj, n* palestino/a *m/f*

**palm** [pɑːm] *n* (Anat) palma; (also: **~ tree**) palmera, palma ▷ *vt*: **to ~ sth off on sb** (inf) encajar algo a algn

**pamper** [ˈpæmpə*] *vt* mimar

**pamphlet** [ˈpæmflət] *n* folleto

**pan** [pæn] *n* (also: **sauce~**) cacerola, cazuela, olla; (also: **frying ~**) sartén *f*

**pancake** [ˈpænkeɪk] *n* crepe *f*

**panda** [ˈpændə] *n* panda *m*

**pane** [peɪn] *n* cristal *m*

**panel** [ˈpænl] *n* (of wood etc) panel *m*; (Radio, TV) panel *m* de invitados

**panhandler** [ˈpænhændlə*] (US) *n* (inf) mendigo/a

**panic** [ˈpænɪk] *n* terror *m* pánico ▷ *vi* dejarse llevar por el pánico

**panorama** [pænəˈrɑːmə] *n* panorama *m*

**pansy** [ˈpænzɪ] *n* (Bot) pensamiento; (inf,

*pej*) maricón *m*

**pant** [pænt] *vi* jadear

**panther** ['pænθə*] *n* pantera

**panties** ['pæntɪz] *npl* bragas *fpl*, pantis *mpl*

**pantomime** ['pæntəmaɪm] (BRIT) *n* revista musical representada en Navidad, basada en cuentos de hadas

● **PANTOMIME**
●
● En época navideña se ponen en escena
● en los teatros británicos las llamadas
● **pantomimes**, que son versiones libres
● de cuentos tradicionales como Aladino
● o El gato con botas. En ella nunca faltan
● personajes como la dama ("dame"),
● papel que siempre interpreta un actor,
● el protagonista joven ("principal boy"),
● normalmente interpretado por una
● actriz, y el malvado ("villain"). Es un
● espectáculo familiar en el que se anima
● al público a participar y aunque va
● dirigido principalmente a los niños,
● cuenta con grandes dosis de humor para
● adultos.

**pants** [pænts] *n* (BRIT: *underwear*: *woman's*) bragas *fpl*; (: *man's*) calzoncillos *mpl*; (US: *trousers*) pantalones *mpl*

**paper** ['peɪpə*] *n* papel *m*; (*also*: **news~**) periódico, diario; (*academic essay*) ensayo; (*exam*) examen *m* ▷ *adj* de papel ▷ *vt* empapelar, tapizar (MEX); **papers** *npl* (*also*: **identity ~s**) papeles *mpl*, documentos *mpl*; **paperback** *n* libro en rústica; **paper bag** *n* bolsa de papel; **paper clip** *n* clip *m*; **paper shop** (BRIT) *n* tienda de periódicos; **paperwork** *n* trabajo administrativo

**paprika** ['pæprɪkə] *n* pimentón *m*

**par** [pɑ:*] *n* par *f*; (*Golf*) par *m*; **to be on a ~ with** estar a la par con

**paracetamol** [pærə'si:təmɔl] (BRIT) *n* paracetamol *m*

**parachute** ['pærəʃu:t] *n* paracaídas *m inv*

**parade** [pə'reɪd] *n* desfile *m* ▷ *vt* (*show*) hacer alarde de ▷ *vi* desfilar; (*Mil*) pasar revista

**paradise** ['pærədaɪs] *n* paraíso

**paradox** ['pærədɔks] *n* paradoja

**paraffin** ['pærəfɪn] (BRIT) *n* (*also*: **~ oil**) parafina

**paragraph** ['pærəgrɑ:f] *n* párrafo

**parallel** ['pærəlɛl] *adj* en paralelo; (*fig*) semejante ▷ *n* (*line*) paralela; (*fig, Geo*) paralelo

**paralysed** ['pærəlaɪzd] *adj* paralizado

**paralysis** [pə'rælɪsɪs] *n* parálisis *f inv*

**paramedic** [pærə'mɛdɪk] *n* auxiliar *m/f*

sanitario/a

**paranoid** ['pærənɔɪd] *adj* (*person, feeling*) paranoico

**parasite** ['pærəsaɪt] *n* parásito/a

**parcel** ['pɑ:sl] *n* paquete *m* ▷ *vt* (*also*: **~ up**) empaquetar, embalar

**pardon** ['pɑ:dn] *n* (*Law*) indulto ▷ *vt* perdonar; **~ me!, I beg your ~!** (*I'm sorry!*) ¡perdone usted!; **(I beg your) ~?, ~ me?** (US: *what did you say?*) ¿cómo?

**parent** ['pɛərənt] *n* (*mother*) madre *f*; (*father*) padre *m*; **parents** *npl* padres *mpl*

▌ Be careful not to translate **parent** by the Spanish word *pariente*.

**parental** [pə'rɛntl] *adj* paternal/maternal

**Paris** ['pærɪs] *n* París

**parish** ['pærɪʃ] *n* parroquia

**Parisian** [pə'rɪzɪən] *adj, n* parisiense *mf*

**park** [pɑ:k] *n* parque *m* ▷ *vt* aparcar, estacionar ▷ *vi* aparcar, estacionarse

**parking** ['pɑ:kɪŋ] *n* aparcamiento, estacionamiento; **"no ~"** "prohibido estacionarse"; **parking lot** (US) *n* parking *m*; **parking meter** *n* parquímetro; **parking ticket** *n* multa de aparcamiento

**parkway** ['pɑ:kweɪ] (US) *n* alameda

**parliament** ['pɑ:ləmənt] *n* parlamento; (*Spanish*) Cortes *fpl*; **parliamentary** [-'mɛntərɪ] *adj* parlamentario

● **PARLIAMENT**
●
● El Parlamento británico (**Parliament**)
● tiene como sede el palacio de
● Westminster, también llamado "Houses
● of Parliament" y consta de dos cámaras.
● La Cámara de los Comunes ("House
● of Commons"), compuesta por 650
● diputados (**Members of Parliament**)
● elegidos por sufragio universal en su
● respectiva circunscripción electoral
● (**constituency**), se reúne 175 días al año
● y sus sesiones son moderadas por el
● Presidente de la Cámara (**Speaker**). La
● cámara alta es la Cámara de los Lores
● ("House of Lords") y está formada por
● miembros que han sido nombrados
● por el monarca o que han heredado su
● escaño. Su poder es limitado, aunque
● actúa como tribunal supremo de
● apelación, excepto en Escocia.

**Parmesan** [pɑ:mɪ'zæn] *n* (*also*: **~ cheese**) queso parmesano

**parole** [pə'rəul] *n*: **on ~** libre bajo palabra

**parrot** ['pærət] *n* loro, papagayo

**parsley** ['pɑ:slɪ] *n* perejil *m*

**parsnip** ['pɑ:snɪp] *n* chirivía

**parson** ['pɑːsn] n cura m
**part** [pɑːt] n (gen, Mus) parte f; (bit) trozo; (of machine) pieza; (Theatre etc) papel m; (of serial) entrega; (US: in hair) raya ▷ adv = **partly** ▷ vt separar ▷ vi (people) separarse; (crowd) apartarse; **to take ~ in** tomar parte or participar en; **to take sth in good ~** tomar algo en buena parte; **to take sb's ~** defender a algn; **for my ~** por mi parte; **for the most ~** en su mayor parte; **to ~ one's hair** hacerse la raya; **part with** vt fus ceder, entregar; (money) pagar; **part of speech** n parte f de la oración, categoría f gramatical
**partial** ['pɑːʃl] adj parcial; **to be ~ to** ser aficionado a
**participant** [pɑːˈtɪsɪpənt] n (in competition) concursante mf; (in campaign etc) participante mf
**participate** [pɑːˈtɪsɪpeɪt] vi: **to ~ in** participar en
**particle** ['pɑːtɪkl] n partícula; (of dust) grano
**particular** [pəˈtɪkjʊlə*] adj (special) particular; (concrete) concreto; (given) determinado; (fussy) quisquilloso; (demanding) exigente; **in ~** en particular; **particularly** adv (in particular) sobre todo; (difficult, good etc) especialmente; **particulars** npl (information) datos mpl; (details) pormenores mpl
**parting** ['pɑːtɪŋ] n (act) separación f; (farewell) despedida; (BRIT: in hair) raya ▷ adj de despedida
**partition** [pɑːˈtɪʃən] n (Pol) división f; (wall) tabique m
**partly** ['pɑːtlɪ] adv en parte
**partner** ['pɑːtnə*] n (Comm) socio/a; (Sport, at dance) pareja; (spouse) cónyuge mf; (lover) compañero/a; **partnership** n asociación f; (Comm) sociedad f
**partridge** ['pɑːtrɪdʒ] n perdiz f
**part-time** ['pɑːt'taɪm] adj, adv a tiempo parcial
**party** ['pɑːtɪ] n (Pol) partido; (celebration) fiesta; (group) grupo; (Law) parte f interesada ▷ cpd (Pol) de partido
**pass** [pɑːs] vt (time, object) pasar; (place) pasar por; (overtake) rebasar; (exam) aprobar; (approve) aprobar ▷ vi pasar; (Scol) aprobar, ser aprobado ▷ n (permit) permiso; (membership card) carnet m; (in mountains) puerto, desfiladero; (Sport) pase m; (Scol: also: ~ **mark**): **to get a ~ in** aprobar en; **to ~ sth through sth** pasar algo por algo; **to make a ~ at sb** (inf) hacer proposiciones a algn; **pass away** vi fallecer; **pass by** vi pasar ▷ vt (ignore) pasar por alto; **pass on** vt transmitir; **pass out** vi desmayarse;

**pass over** vi, vt omitir, pasar por alto; **pass up** vt (opportunity) renunciar a; **passable** adj (road) transitable; (tolerable) pasable
**passage** ['pæsɪdʒ] n (also: ~**way**) pasillo; (act of passing) tránsito; (fare, in book) pasaje m; (by boat) travesía; (Anat) tubo
**passenger** ['pæsɪndʒə*] n pasajero/a, viajero/a
**passer-by** [pɑːsə'baɪ] n transeúnte mf
**passing place** n (Aut) apartadero
**passion** ['pæʃən] n pasión f; **passionate** adj apasionado; **passion fruit** n fruta de la pasión, granadilla
**passive** ['pæsɪv] adj (gen, also Ling) pasivo
**passport** ['pɑːspɔːt] n pasaporte m; **passport control** n control m de pasaporte; **passport office** n oficina de pasaportes
**password** ['pɑːswəːd] n contraseña
**past** [pɑːst] prep (in front of) por delante de; (further than) más allá de; (later than) después de ▷ adj pasado; (president etc) antiguo ▷ n (time) pasado; (of person) antecedentes mpl; **he's ~ forty** tiene más de cuarenta años; **ten/quarter ~ eight** las ocho y diez/cuarto; **for the ~ few/3 days** durante los últimos días/últimos 3 días; **to run ~ sb** pasar a algn corriendo
**pasta** ['pæstə] n pasta
**paste** [peɪst] n pasta; (glue) engrudo ▷ vt pegar
**pastel** ['pæstl] adj pastel; (painting) al pastel
**pasteurized** ['pæstəraɪzd] adj pasteurizado
**pastime** ['pɑːstaɪm] n pasatiempo
**pastor** ['pɑːstə*] n pastor m
**past participle** [-'pɑːtɪsɪpl] n (Ling) participio m (de) pasado or (Ling) pretérito or pasivo
**pastry** ['peɪstrɪ] n (dough) pasta; (cake) pastel m
**pasture** ['pɑːstʃə*] n pasto
**pasty¹** ['pæstɪ] n empanada
**pasty²** ['peɪstɪ] adj (complexion) pálido
**pat** [pæt] vt dar una palmadita a; (dog etc) acariciar
**patch** [pætʃ] n (of material.: eye patch) parche m; (mended part) remiendo; (of land) terreno ▷ vt remendar; **(to go through) a bad ~** (pasar por) una mala racha; **patchy** adj desigual
**pâté** ['pæteɪ] n paté m
**patent** ['peɪtnt] n patente f ▷ vt patentar ▷ adj patente, evidente
**paternal** [pə'təːnl] adj paternal; (relation) paterno
**paternity leave** [pə'təːnɪtɪ-] n permiso m

por paternidad, licencia por paternidad

**path** [pɑːθ] n camino, sendero; (trail, track) pista; (of missile) trayectoria

**pathetic** [pə'θetɪk] adj patético, lastimoso; (very bad) malísimo

**pathway** ['pɑːθweɪ] n sendero, vereda

**patience** ['peɪʃns] n paciencia; (BRIT Cards) solitario

**patient** ['peɪʃnt] n paciente mf ▷ adj paciente, sufrido

**patio** ['pætɪəu] n patio

**patriotic** [pætrɪ'ɔtɪk] adj patriótico

**patrol** [pə'trəul] n patrulla ▷ vt patrullar por; **patrol car** n coche m patrulla

**patron** ['peɪtrən] n (in shop) cliente mf; (of charity) patrocinador(a) m/f; **~ of the arts** mecenas m

**patronizing** ['pætrənaɪzɪŋ] adj condescendiente

**pattern** ['pætən] n (Sewing) patrón m; (design) dibujo; **patterned** adj (material) estampado

**pause** [pɔːz] n pausa ▷ vi hacer una pausa

**pave** [peɪv] vt pavimentar; **to ~ the way for** preparar el terreno para

**pavement** ['peɪvmənt] (BRIT) n acera, banqueta (MEX), andén m (CAM), vereda (SC)

**pavilion** [pə'vɪlɪən] n (Sport) caseta

**paving** ['peɪvɪŋ] n pavimento, enlosado

**paw** [pɔː] n pata

**pawn** [pɔːn] n (Chess) peón m; (fig) instrumento ▷ vt empeñar; **pawn broker** n prestamista mf

**pay** [peɪ] (pt, pp **paid**) n (wage etc) sueldo, salario ▷ vt pagar ▷ vi (be profitable) rendir; **to ~ attention (to)** prestar atención (a); **to ~ sb a visit** hacer una visita a algn; **to ~ one's respects to sb** presentar sus respetos a algn; **pay back** vt (money) reembolsar; (person) pagar; **pay for** vt fus pagar; **pay in** vt ingresar; **pay off** vt saldar ▷ vi (scheme, decision) dar resultado; **pay out** vt (money) gastar, desembolsar; **pay up** vt pagar (de mala gana); **payable** adj: **payable to** pagadero a; **pay day** n día m de paga; **pay envelope** (US) n = **pay packet**; **payment** n pago; **monthly payment** mensualidad f; **payout** n (pt, pp competition) premio en metálico; **pay packet** (BRIT) n sobre m (de paga); **pay phone** n teléfono público; **payroll** n nómina; **pay slip** n recibo de sueldo; **pay television** n televisión f de pago

**PC** n abbr = **personal computer**; (BRIT) (= police constable) policía mf ▷ adv abbr = **politically correct**

**p.c.** abbr = **per cent**

**PDA** n abbr (= personal digital assistant)

agenda electrónica

**PE** n abbr (= physical education) ed. física

**pea** [piː] n guisante m (SP), arveja (LAM), chícharo (MEX, CAM)

**peace** [piːs] n paz f; (calm) paz f, tranquilidad f; **peaceful** adj (gentle) pacífico; (calm) tranquilo, sosegado

**peach** [piːtʃ] n melocotón m (SP), durazno (LAM)

**peacock** ['piːkɔk] n pavo real

**peak** [piːk] n (of mountain) cumbre f, cima; (of cap) visera; (fig) cumbre f; **peak hours** npl horas fpl punta

**peanut** ['piːnʌt] n cacahuete m (SP), maní m (LAM), cacahuate m (MEX); **peanut butter** n manteca de cacahuete or maní

**pear** [pɛə*] n pera

**pearl** [pɜːl] n perla

**peasant** ['pɛznt] n campesino/a

**peat** [piːt] n turba

**pebble** ['pɛbl] n guijarro

**peck** [pɛk] vt (also: ~ at) picotear ▷ n picotazo; (kiss) besito; **peckish** (BRIT: inf) adj: **I feel peckish** tengo ganas de picar algo

**peculiar** [pɪ'kjuːlɪə*] adj (odd) extraño, raro; (typical) propio, característico; **~ to** propio de

**pedal** ['pɛdl] n pedal m ▷ vi pedalear

**pedalo** ['pɛdələu] n patín m a pedal

**pedestal** ['pɛdəstl] n pedestal m

**pedestrian** [pɪ'dɛstrɪən] n peatón/ona m/f ▷ adj pedestre; **pedestrian crossing** (BRIT) n paso de peatones; **pedestrianized** adj: **a pedestrianized street** una calle peatonal; **pedestrian precinct** (US **pedestrian zone**) n zona peatonal

**pedigree** ['pɛdɪgriː] n genealogía; (of animal) raza, pedigrí n ▷ cpd (animal) de raza, de casta

**pedophile** ['piːdəufaɪl] (US) n = **paedophile**

**pee** [piː] (inf) vi mear

**peek** [piːk] vi mirar a hurtadillas

**peel** [piːl] n piel f; (of orange, lemon) cáscara; (: removed) peladuras fpl ▷ vt pelar ▷ vi (paint etc) desconcharse; (wallpaper) despegarse, desprenderse; (skin) pelar

**peep** [piːp] n (BRIT: look) mirada furtiva; (sound) pío ▷ vi (BRIT: look) mirar furtivamente

**peer** [pɪə*] vi: **to ~ at** esudriñar ▷ n (noble) par m; (equal) igual m; (contemporary) contemporáneo/a

**peg** [pɛg] n (for coat etc) gancho, colgadero; (BRIT: also: **clothes ~**) pinza

**pelican** ['pɛlɪkən] n pelícano; **pelican crossing** (BRIT) n (Aut) paso de peatones señalizado

**pelt** [pɛlt] vt: **to ~ sb with sth** arrojarle algo a algn ▷ vi (rain) llover a cántaros; (inf: run) correr ▷ n pellejo

**pelvis** ['pɛlvɪs] n pelvis f

**pen** [pɛn] n (fountain pen) pluma; (ballpoint pen) bolígrafo; (for sheep) redil m

**penalty** ['pɛnltɪ] n (gen) pena; (fine) multa

**pence** [pɛns] npl of **penny**

**pencil** ['pɛnsl] n lápiz m; **pencil in** vt (appointment) apuntar con carácter provisional; **pencil case** n estuche m; **pencil sharpener** n sacapuntas m inv

**pendant** ['pɛndnt] n pendiente m

**pending** ['pɛndɪŋ] prep antes de ▷ adj pendiente

**penetrate** ['pɛnɪtreɪt] vt penetrar

**penfriend** ['pɛnfrɛnd] (BRIT) n amigo/a por carta

**penguin** ['pɛŋgwɪn] n pingüino

**penicillin** [pɛnɪ'sɪlɪn] n penicilina

**peninsula** [pə'nɪnsjulə] n península

**penis** ['piːnɪs] n pene m

**penitentiary** [pɛnɪ'tɛnʃərɪ] (US) n cárcel f, presidio

**penknife** ['pɛnnaɪf] n navaja

**penniless** ['pɛnɪlɪs] adj sin dinero

**penny** ['pɛnɪ] (pl **pennies** or **pence**) (BRIT) n penique m; (US) centavo

**penpal** ['pɛnpæl] n amigo/a por carta

**pension** ['pɛnʃən] n (state benefit) jubilación f; **pensioner** (BRIT) n jubilado/a

**pentagon** ['pɛntəgən] (US) n: **the P~** (Pol) el Pentágono

**penthouse** ['pɛnthaus] n ático de lujo

**penultimate** [pɛ'nʌltɪmət] adj penúltimo

**people** ['piːpl] npl gente f; (citizens) pueblo, ciudadanos mpl; (Pol): **the ~** el pueblo ▷ n (nation, race) pueblo, nación f; **several ~ came** vinieron varias personas; **~ say that ...** dice la gente que ...

**pepper** ['pɛpə*] n (spice) pimienta; (vegetable) pimiento ▷ vt: **to ~ with** (fig) salpicar de; **peppermint** n (sweet) pastilla de menta

**per** [pə:*] prep por; **~ day/~son** por día/ persona; **~ annum** al año

**perceive** [pə'siːv] vt percibir; (realize) darse cuenta de

**per cent** n por ciento

**percentage** [pə'sɛntɪdʒ] n porcentaje m

**perception** [pə'sɛpʃən] n percepción f; (insight) perspicacia; (opinion etc) opinión f

**perch** [pə:tʃ] n (fish) perca; (for bird) percha ▷ vi: **to ~ (on)** (bird) posarse (en); (person) encaramarse (en)

**percussion** [pə'kʌʃən] n percusión f

**perfect** [adj, n 'pə:fɪkt, vb pə'fɛkt] adj perfecto ▷ n (also: **~ tense**) perfecto ▷ vt perfeccionar; **perfection** [pə'fɛkʃən] n perfección f; **perfectly** ['pə:fɪktlɪ] adv perfectamente

**perform** [pə'fɔ:m] vt (carry out) realizar, llevar a cabo; (Theatre) representar; (piece of music) interpretar ▷ vi (well, badly) funcionar; **performance** n (of a play) representación f; (of actor, athlete etc) actuación f; (of car, engine, company) rendimiento; (of economy) resultados mpl; **performer** n (actor) actor m, actriz f

**perfume** ['pə:fju:m] n perfume m

**perhaps** [pə'hæps] adv quizá(s), tal vez

**perimeter** [pə'rɪmɪtə*] n perímetro

**period** ['pɪərɪəd] n período; (Scol) clase f; (full stop) punto; (Med) regla ▷ adj (costume, furniture) de época; **periodical** [pɪərɪ'ɔdɪkl] n periódico; **periodically** adv de vez en cuando, cada cierto tiempo

**perish** ['pɛrɪʃ] vi perecer; (decay) echarse a perder

**perjury** ['pə:dʒərɪ] n (Law) perjurio

**perk** [pə:k] n extra m

**perm** [pə:m] n permanente f

**permanent** ['pə:mənənt] adj permanente; **permanently** adv (lastingly) para siempre, de modo definitivo; (all the time) permanentemente

**permission** [pə'mɪʃən] n permiso

**permit** [n 'pə:mɪt, vt pə'mɪt] n permiso, licencia ▷ vt permitir

**perplex** [pə'plɛks] vt dejar perplejo

**persecute** ['pə:sɪkju:t] vt perseguir

**persecution** [pə:sɪ'kju:ʃən] n persecución f

**persevere** [pə:sɪ'vɪə*] vi persistir

**Persian** ['pə:ʃən] adj, n persa mf: **the ~ Gulf** el Golfo Pérsico

**persist** [pə'sɪst] vi: **to ~ (in doing sth)** persistir (en hacer algo); **persistent** adj persistente; (determined) porfiado

**person** ['pə:sn] n persona; **in ~** en persona; **personal** adj personal; individual; (visit) en persona; **personal assistant** n ayudante mf personal; **personal computer** n ordenador m personal; **personality**

[-'næliti] n personalidad f; **personally** adv personalmente; (in person) en persona; **to take sth personally** tomarse algo a mal; **personal organizer** n agenda; **personal stereo** n Walkman® m

**personnel** [pə:sə'nɛl] n personal m

**perspective** [pə'spɛktɪv] n perspectiva

**perspiration** [pə:spɪ'reɪʃən] n transpiración f

**persuade** [pə'sweɪd] vt: **to ~ sb to do sth** persuadir a algn para que haga algo

**persuasion** [pə'sweɪʒən] n persuasión f; (persuasiveness) persuasiva

**persuasive** [pə'sweɪsɪv] adj persuasivo

**perverse** [pə'və:s] adj perverso; (wayward) travieso

**pervert** [n 'pə:və:t, vb pə'və:t] n pervertido/a ▷ vt pervertir; (truth, sb's words) tergiversar

**pessimism** ['pɛsɪmɪzəm] n pesimismo

**pessimist** ['pɛsɪmɪst] n pesimista mf; **pessimistic** [-'mɪstɪk] adj pesimista

**pest** [pɛst] n (insect) insecto nocivo; (fig) lata, molestia

**pester** ['pɛstə*] vt molestar, acosar

**pesticide** ['pɛstɪsaɪd] n pesticida m

**pet** [pɛt] n animal m doméstico ▷ cpd favorito ▷ vt acariciar; **teacher's ~** favorito/a (del profesor); **~ hate** manía

**petal** ['pɛtl] n pétalo

**petite** [pə'ti:t] adj chiquita

**petition** [pə'tɪʃən] n petición f

**petrified** ['pɛtrɪfaɪd] adj horrorizado

**petrol** ['pɛtrəl] (BRIT) n gasolina

**petroleum** [pə'trəuliəm] n petróleo

**petrol: petrol pump** (BRIT) n (in garage) surtidor m de gasolina; **petrol station** (BRIT) n gasolinera; **petrol tank** (BRIT) n depósito (de gasolina)

**petticoat** ['pɛtɪkəut] n enaguas fpl

**petty** ['pɛtɪ] adj (mean) mezquino; (unimportant) insignificante

**pew** [pju:] n banco

**pewter** ['pju:tə*] n peltre m

**phantom** ['fæntəm] n fantasma m

**pharmacist** ['fɑ:məsɪst] n farmacéutico/a

**pharmacy** ['fɑ:məsɪ] n farmacia

**phase** [feɪz] n fase f; **phase in** vt introducir progresivamente; **phase out** vt (machinery, product) retirar progresivamente; (job, subsidy) eliminar por etapas

**Ph.D.** abbr = **Doctor of Philosophy**

**pheasant** ['fɛznt] n faisán m

**phenomena** [fə'nɔmɪnə] npl of **phenomenon**

**phenomenal** [fɪ'nɔmɪnl] adj fenomenal, extraordinario

**phenomenon** [fə'nɔmɪnən] (pl **phenomena**) n fenómeno

**Philippines** ['fɪlɪpi:nz] npl: **the ~** las Filipinas

**philosopher** [fɪ'lɔsəfə*] n filósofo/a

**philosophical** [fɪlə'sɔfɪkl] adj filosófico

**philosophy** [fɪ'lɔsəfɪ] n filosofía

**phlegm** [flɛm] n flema

**phobia** ['fəubjə] n fobia

**phone** [fəun] n teléfono ▷ vt telefonear, llamar por teléfono; **to be on the ~** tener teléfono; (be calling) estar hablando por teléfono; **phone back** vt, vi volver a llamar; **phone up** vt, vi llamar por teléfono; **phone book** n guía telefónica; **phone booth** n cabina telefónica; **phone box** (BRIT) n = **phone booth**; **phone call** n llamada (telefónica); **phonecard** n teletarjeta; **phone number** n número de teléfono

**phonetics** [fə'nɛtɪks] n fonética

**phoney** ['fəunɪ] adj falso

**photo** ['fəutəu] n foto f; **photo album** n álbum m de fotos; **photocopier** n fotocopiadora; **photocopy** n fotocopia ▷ vt fotocopiar

**photograph** ['fəutəgrɑ:f] n fotografía ▷ vt fotografiar; **photographer** [fə'tɔgrəfə*] n fotógrafo; **photography** [fə'tɔgrəfɪ] n fotografía

**phrase** [freɪz] n frase f ▷ vt expresar; **phrase book** n libro de frases

**physical** ['fɪzɪkl] adj físico; **physical education** n educación f física; **physically** adv físicamente

**physician** [fɪ'zɪʃən] n médico/a

**physicist** ['fɪzɪsɪst] n físico/a

**physics** ['fɪzɪks] n física

**physiotherapist** [fɪziəu'θɛrəpɪst] n fisioterapeuta

**physiotherapy** [fɪziəu'θɛrəpɪ] n fisioterapia

**physique** [fɪ'zi:k] n físico

**pianist** ['pi:ənɪst] n pianista mf

**piano** [pɪ'ænəu] n piano

**pick** [pɪk] n (tool: also: **~-axe**) pico, piqueta ▷ vt (select) elegir, escoger; (gather) coger (SP), recoger; (remove, take out) sacar, quitar; (lock) abrir con ganzúa; **take your ~** escoja lo que quiera; **the ~ of** lo mejor de; **to ~ one's nose/teeth** hurgarse las narices/limpiarse los dientes; **to ~ a quarrel with sb** meterse con algn; **pick on** vt fus (person) meterse con; **pick out** vt escoger; (distinguish) identificar; **pick up** vi (improve: sales) ir mejor; (: patient) reponerse; (Finance) recobrarse ▷ vt recoger; (learn) aprender; (Police: arrest) detener; (person: for sex) ligar; (Radio) captar; **to pick up speed**

acelerarse; **to pick o.s. up** levantarse

**pickle** ['pɪkl] n (also: **~s**: as condiment)
escabeche m; (fig: mess) apuro ▷ vt encurtir

**pickpocket** ['pɪkpɔkɪt] n carterista mf

**pick-up** ['pɪkʌp] n (also: **~ truck**)
furgoneta, camioneta

**picnic** ['pɪknɪk] n merienda ▷ vi ir de
merienda; **picnic area** n zona de picnic;
(Aut) área de descanso

**picture** ['pɪktʃə*] n cuadro; (painting)
pintura; (photograph) fotografía; (TV)
imagen f; (film) película; (fig: description)
descripción f; (: situation) situación f ▷ vt
(imagine) imaginar; **pictures** npl: **the ~s**
(BRIT) el cine; **picture frame** n marco;
**picture messaging** n (envío de) mensajes
con imágenes

**picturesque** [pɪktʃə'rɛsk] adj pintoresco

**pie** [paɪ] n pastel m; (open) tarta; (small: of
meat) empanada

**piece** [piːs] n pedazo, trozo; (of cake) trozo;
(item): **a ~ of clothing/furniture/advice**
una prenda (de vestir)/un mueble/un
consejo ▷ vt: **to ~ together** juntar; (Tech)
armar; **to take to ~s** desmontar

**pie chart** n gráfico de sectores or tarta

**pier** [pɪə*] n muelle m, embarcadero

**pierce** [pɪəs] vt perforar; **pierced** adj: **I've
got pierced ears** tengo los agujeros hechos
en las orejas

**pig** [pɪg] n cerdo, chancho (LAM);
(pej: unkind person) asqueroso; (: greedy
person) glotón/ona m/f

**pigeon** ['pɪdʒən] n paloma; (as food)
pichón m

**piggy bank** ['pɪgɪ-] n hucha (en forma de
cerdito)

**pigsty** ['pɪgstaɪ] n pocilga

**pigtail** n (girl's) trenza

**pike** [paɪk] n (fish) lucio

**pilchard** ['pɪltʃəd] n sardina

**pile** [paɪl] n montón m; (of carpet, cloth)
pelo; **pile up** vi +adv (accumulate: work)
amontonarse, acumularse ▷ vt +adv (put
in a heap: books, clothes) apilar, amontonar;
(accumulate) acumular; **piles** npl (Med)
almorranas fpl, hemorroides mpl; **pile-up** n
(Aut) accidente m múltiple

**pilgrimage** ['pɪlgrɪmɪdʒ] n peregrinación
f, romería

**pill** [pɪl] n píldora; **the ~** la píldora

**pillar** ['pɪlə*] n pilar m

**pillow** ['pɪləʊ] n almohada; **pillowcase**
n funda

**pilot** ['paɪlət] n piloto ▷ cpd (scheme etc)
piloto ▷ vt pilotar; **pilot light** n piloto

**pimple** ['pɪmpl] n grano

**PIN** n abbr (= personal identification number)
número personal

**pin** [pɪn] n alfiler m ▷ vt prender (con
alfiler); **~s and needles** hormigueo; **to ~
sb down** (fig) hacer que algn concrete; **to ~
sth on sb** (fig) colgarle a algn el sambenito
de algo

**pinafore** ['pɪnəfɔː*] n delantal m

**pinch** [pɪntʃ] n (of salt etc) pizca ▷ vt
pellizcar; (inf: steal) birlar; **at a ~** en caso
de apuro

**pine** [paɪn] n (also: **~ tree**) pino ▷ vi: **to ~
for** suspirar por

**pineapple** ['paɪnæpl] n piña, ananás m

**ping** [pɪŋ] n (noise) sonido agudo; **ping-
pong®** n pingpong® m

**pink** [pɪŋk] adj rosado, (color de) rosa ▷ n
(colour) rosa; (Bot) clavel m, clavellina

**pinpoint** ['pɪnpɔɪnt] vt precisar

**pint** [paɪnt] n pinta (BRIT = 568cc, US =
473cc); (BRIT: inf: of beer) pinta de cerveza ≈
jarra (SP)

**pioneer** [paɪə'nɪə*] n pionero/a

**pious** ['paɪəs] adj piadoso, devoto

**pip** [pɪp] n (seed) pepita; **the ~s** (BRIT) la
señal

**pipe** [paɪp] n tubo, caño; (for smoking) pipa
▷ vt conducir en cañerías; **pipeline** n (for
oil) oleoducto; (for gas) gasoducto; **piper** n
gaitero/a

**pirate** ['paɪərət] n pirata mf ▷ vt (cassette,
book) piratear

**Pisces** ['paɪsiːz] n Piscis m

**piss** [pɪs] (inf!) vi mear; **pissed** (inf!) adj
(drunk) borracho

**pistol** ['pɪstl] n pistola

**piston** ['pɪstən] n pistón m, émbolo

**pit** [pɪt] n hoyo; (also: **coal ~**) mina; (in
garage) foso de inspección; (also: **orchestra
~**) platea ▷ vt: **to ~ one's wits against sb**
medir fuerzas con algn

**pitch** [pɪtʃ] n (Mus) tono; (BRIT Sport)
campo, terreno; (fig) punto; (tar) brea ▷ vt
(throw) arrojar, lanzar ▷ vi (fall) caer(se); **to
~ a tent** montar una tienda (de campaña);
**pitch-black** adj negro como boca de lobo

**pitfall** ['pɪtfɔːl] n riesgo

**pith** [pɪθ] n (of orange) médula

**pitiful** ['pɪtɪfʊl] adj (touching) lastimoso,
cònmovedor(a)

**pity** ['pɪtɪ] n compasión f, piedad f ▷ vt
compadecer(se de); **what a ~!** ¡qué pena!

**pizza** ['piːtsə] n pizza

**placard** ['plækɑːd] n letrero; (in march etc)
pancarta

**place** [pleɪs] n lugar m, sitio; (seat) plaza,
asiento; (post) puesto; (home): **at/to his ~**
en/a su casa; (role: in society etc) papel m ▷ vt
(object) poner, colocar; (identify) reconocer;

**to take ~** tener lugar; **to be ~d** (in race, exam) colocarse; **to be ~d** (not suitable) fuera de lugar; **in the first ~** en primer lugar; **to change ~s with sb** cambiarse de sitio con algn; **~ of birth** lugar m de nacimiento; **place mat** n (wooden etc) salvamanteles m inv; (linen etc) mantel m individual; **placement** n (positioning) colocación f; (at work) emplazamiento

**placid** ['plæsɪd] adj apacible

**plague** [pleɪg] n plaga; (Med) peste f ▷ vt (fig) acosar, atormentar

**plaice** [pleɪs] n inv platija

**plain** [pleɪn] adj (unpatterned) liso; (clear) claro, evidente; (simple) sencillo; (not handsome) poco atractivo ▷ adv claramente ▷ n llano, llanura; **plain chocolate** n chocolate m amargo; **plainly** adv claramente

**plaintiff** ['pleɪntɪf] n demandante mf

**plait** [plæt] n trenza

**plan** [plæn] n (drawing) plano; (scheme) plan m, proyecto ▷ vt proyectar, planificar ▷ vi hacer proyectos; **to ~ to do** pensar hacer

**plane** [pleɪn] n (Aviat) avión m; (Math, fig) plano; (also: ~ tree) plátano; (tool) cepillo

**planet** ['plænɪt] n planeta m

**plank** [plæŋk] n tabla

**planning** ['plænɪŋ] n planificación f; **family ~** planificación familiar

**plant** [plɑːnt] n planta; (machinery) maquinaria; (factory) fábrica ▷ vt plantar; (field) sembrar; (bomb) colocar

**plantation** [plæn'teɪʃən] n plantación f; (estate) hacienda

**plaque** [plæk] n placa

**plaster** ['plɑːstə*] n (for walls) yeso; (also: ~ of Paris) yeso mate, escayola (SP); (BRIT: also: **sticking ~**) tirita (SP), curita (LAM) ▷ vt enyesar; (cover): **to ~ with** llenar or cubrir de; **plaster cast** n (Med) escayola; (model, statue) vaciado de yeso

**plastic** ['plæstɪk] n plástico ▷ adj de plástico; **plastic bag** n bolsa de plástico; **plastic surgery** n cirujía plástica

**plate** [pleɪt] n (dish) plato; (metal, in book) lámina; (dental plate) placa de dentadura postiza

**plateau** ['plætəʊ] (pl ~s or ~x) n meseta, altiplanicie f

**platform** ['plætfɔːm] n (Rail) andén m; (stage, BRIT: on bus) plataforma; (at meeting) tribuna; (Pol) programa m (electoral)

**platinum** ['plætɪnəm] adj, n platino

**platoon** [plə'tuːn] n pelotón m

**platter** ['plætə*] n fuente f

**plausible** ['plɔːzɪbl] adj verosímil; (person) convincente

**play** [pleɪ] n (Theatre) obra, comedia ▷ vt (game) jugar; (compete against) jugar contra; (instrument) tocar; (part: in play etc) hacer el papel de; (tape, record) poner ▷ vi jugar; (band) tocar; (tape, record) sonar; **to ~ safe** ir a lo seguro; **play back** vt (tape) poner; **play up** vi (cause trouble to) dar guerra; **player** n jugador(a) m/f; (Theatre) actor(actriz) m/f; (Mus) músico/a; **playful** adj juguetón/ona; **playground** n (in school) patio de recreo; (in park) parque m infantil; **playgroup** n jardín m de niños; **playing card** n naipe m, carta; **playing field** n campo de deportes; **playschool** n = **playgroup**; **playtime** n (Scol) recreo; **playwright** n dramaturgo/a

**plc** abbr (= public limited company) ≈ S.A.

**plea** [pliː] n súplica, petición f; (Law) alegato, defensa

**plead** [pliːd] vt (Law): **to ~ sb's case** defender a algn; (give as excuse) poner como pretexto ▷ vi (Law) declararse; (beg): **to ~ with sb** suplicar or rogar a algn

**pleasant** ['plɛznt] adj agradable

**please** [pliːz] excl ¡por favor! ▷ vt (give pleasure to) dar gusto a, agradar ▷ vi (think fit): **do as you ~** haz lo que quieras; **~ yourself!** (inf) ¡haz lo que quieras!, ¡como quieras!; **pleased** adj (happy) alegre, contento; **pleased (with)** satisfecho (de); **pleased to meet you** ¡encantado!, ¡tanto gusto!

**pleasure** ['plɛʒə*] n placer m, gusto; **"it's a ~"** "el gusto es mío"

**pleat** [pliːt] n pliegue m

**pledge** [plɛdʒ] n (promise) promesa, voto ▷ vt prometer

**plentiful** ['plɛntɪful] adj copioso, abundante

**plenty** ['plɛntɪ] n: **~ of** mucho(s)/a(s)

**pliers** ['plaɪəz] npl alicates mpl, tenazas fpl

**plight** [plaɪt] n situación f difícil

**plod** [plɒd] vi caminar con paso pesado; (fig) trabajar laboriosamente

**plonk** [plɒŋk] (inf) n (BRIT: wine) vino peleón ▷ vt: **to ~ sth down** dejar caer algo

**plot** [plɒt] n (scheme) complot m, conjura; (of story, play) argumento; (of land) terreno ▷ vt (mark out) trazar; (conspire) tramar, urdir ▷ vi conspirar

**plough** [plaʊ] (us **plow**) n arado ▷ vt (earth) arar; **to ~ money into** invertir dinero en; **ploughman's lunch** (BRIT) n almuerzo de pub a base de pan, queso y encurtidos

**plow** [plaʊ] (us) = **plough**

**ploy** [plɔɪ] n truco, estratagema

**pluck** [plʌk] vt (fruit) coger (SP), recoger (LAM); (musical instrument) puntear; (bird) desplumar; (*eyebrows*) depilar; **to ~ up courage** hacer de tripas corazón

**plug** [plʌg] *n* tapón *m*; (*Elec*) enchufe *m*, clavija; (*Aut: also:* **spark(ing) ~**) bujía ▷ *vt* (*hole*) tapar; (*inf: advertise*) dar publicidad a; **plug in** *vt* (*Elec*) enchufar; **plughole** *n* desagüe *m*

**plum** [plʌm] *n* (*fruit*) ciruela

**plumber** ['plʌmə*] *n* fontanero/a (*SP*, *CAM*), plomero/a (*LAM*)

**plumbing** ['plʌmɪŋ] *n* (*trade*) fontanería, plomería; (*piping*) cañería

**plummet** ['plʌmɪt] *vi*: **to ~ (down)** caer a plomo

**plump** [plʌmp] *adj* rechoncho, rollizo ▷ *vi*: **to ~ for** (*inf: choose*) optar por

**plunge** [plʌndʒ] *n* zambullida ▷ *vt* sumergir, hundir ▷ *vi* (*fall*) caer; (*dive*) saltar; (*person*) arrojarse; **to take the ~** lanzarse

**plural** ['pluərl] *adj* plural ▷ *n* plural *m*

**plus** [plʌs] *n* (*also:* **~ sign**) signo más ▷ *prep* más, y, además de; **ten/twenty ~** más de diez/veinte

**ply** [plaɪ] *vt* (*a trade*) ejercer ▷ *vi* (*ship*) ir y venir ▷ *n* (*of wool, rope*) cabo; **to ~ sb with drink** insistir en ofrecer a algn muchas copas; **plywood** *n* madera contrachapada

**P.M.** *n abbr* = **Prime Minister**

**p.m.** *adv abbr* (= *post meridiem*) de la tarde or noche

**PMS** *n abbr* (= *premenstrual syndrome*) SPM *m*

**PMT** *n abbr* (= *premenstrual tension*) SPM *m*

**pneumatic drill** [njuːˈmætɪk-] *n* martillo neumático

**pneumonia** [njuːˈməʊnɪə] *n* pulmonía

**poach** [pəʊtʃ] *vt* (*cook*) escalfar; (*steal*) cazar (or pescar) en vedado ▷ *vi* cazar (or pescar) en vedado; **poached** *adj* escalfado

**P.O. Box** *n abbr* (= *Post Office Box*) apdo., aptdo.

**pocket** ['pɒkɪt] *n* bolsillo; (*fig: small area*) bolsa ▷ *vt* meter en el bolsillo; (*steal*) embolsar; **to be out of ~** (*BRIT*) salir perdiendo; **pocketbook** (*us*) *n* cartera; **pocket money** *n* asignación *f*

**pod** [pɒd] *n* vaina

**podiatrist** [pɒˈdiːətrɪst] (*us*) *n* pedicuro/a

**podium** ['pəʊdɪəm] *n* podio

**poem** ['pəʊɪm] *n* poema *m*

**poet** ['pəʊɪt] *n* poeta *m/f*; **poetic** [-ˈɛtɪk] *adj* poético; **poetry** *n* poesía

**poignant** ['pɔɪnjənt] *adj* conmovedor(a)

**point** [pɔɪnt] *n* punto; (*tip*) punta; (*purpose*) fin *m*, propósito; (*use*) utilidad *f*; (*significant part*) lo significativo; (*moment*) momento; (*Elec*) toma (de corriente); (*also:* **decimal ~**): **2 ~ 3 (2.3)** dos coma tres (2,3) ▷ *vt* señalar; (*gun etc*): **to ~ sth at sb** apuntar

algo a algn ▷ *vi*: **to ~ at** señalar; **points** *npl* (*Aut*) contactos *mpl*; (*Rail*) agujas *fpl*; **to be on the ~ of doing sth** estar a punto de hacer algo; **to make a ~ of** poner empeño en; **to get/miss the ~** comprender/no comprender; **to come to the ~** ir al meollo; **there's no ~ (in doing)** no tiene sentido (hacer); **point out** *vt* señalar; **point-blank** *adv* (*say, refuse*) sin más hablar; (*also:* **at point-blank range**) a quemarropa; **pointed** *adj* (*shape*) puntiagudo, afilado; (*remark*) intencionado; **pointer** *n* (*needle*) aguja, indicador *m*; **pointless** *adj* sin sentido; **point of view** *n* punto de vista

**poison** ['pɔɪzn] *n* veneno ▷ *vt* envenenar; **poisonous** *adj* venenoso; (*fumes etc*) tóxico

**poke** [pəʊk] *vt* (*jab with finger, stick etc*) empujar; (*put*): **to ~ sth in(to)** introducir algo en; **poke about or around** *vi* fisgonear; **poke out** *vi* (*stick out*) salir

**poker** ['pəʊkə*] *n* atizador *m*; (*Cards*) póker *m*

**Poland** ['pəʊlənd] *n* Polonia

**polar** ['pəʊlə*] *adj* polar; **polar bear** *n* oso polar

**Pole** [pəʊl] *n* polaco/a

**pole** [pəʊl] *n* palo; (*fixed*) poste *m*; (*Geo*) polo; **pole bean** (*us*) *n* = judía verde; **pole vault** *n* salto con pértiga

**police** [pəˈliːs] *n* policía ▷ *vt* vigilar; **police car** *n* coche-patrulla *m*; **police constable** (*BRIT*) *n* guardia *m*, policía *m*; **police force** *n* cuerpo de policía; **policeman** (*irreg*) *n* policía *m*, guardia *m*; **police officer** *n* guardia *m*, policía *m*; **police station** *n* comisaría; **policewoman** (*irreg*) *n* mujer *f* policía

**policy** ['pɒlɪsɪ] *n* política; (*also:* **insurance ~**) póliza

**polio** ['pəʊlɪəʊ] *n* polio *f*

**Polish** ['pəʊlɪʃ] *adj* polaco ▷ *n* (*Ling*) polaco

**polish** ['pɒlɪʃ] *n* (*for shoes*) betún *m*; (*for floor*) cera (de lustrar); (*shine*) brillo, lustre *m*; (*fig: refinement*) educación *f* ▷ *vt* (*shoes*) limpiar; (*make shiny*) pulir, sacar brillo a; **polish off** *vt* (*food*) despachar; **polished** *adj* (*fig: person*) elegante

**polite** [pəˈlaɪt] *adj* cortés, atento; **politeness** *n* cortesía

**political** [pəˈlɪtɪkl] *adj* político; **politically** *adv* políticamente; **politically correct** políticamente correcto

**politician** [pɒlɪˈtɪʃən] *n* político/a

**politics** ['pɒlɪtɪks] *n* política

**poll** [pəʊl] *n* (*election*) votación *f*; (*also:* **opinion ~**) sondeo, encuesta ▷ *vt* encuestar; (*votes*) obtener

**pollen** ['pɒlən] n polen m
**polling station** ['pəulɪŋ-] n centro electoral
**pollute** [pə'luːt] vt contaminar
**pollution** [pə'luːʃən] n polución f, contaminación f del medio ambiente
**polo** ['pəuləu] n (sport) polo; **polo-neck** adj de cuello vuelto ▷ n (sweater) suéter m de cuello vuelto; **polo shirt** n polo, niqui m
**polyester** [pɒlɪ'estə*] n poliéster m
**polystyrene** [pɒlɪ'staɪriːn] n poliestireno
**polythene** ['pɒlɪθiːn] (BRIT) n politeno; **polythene bag** n bolsa de plástico
**pomegranate** ['pɒmɪgrænɪt] n granada
**pompous** ['pɒmpəs] adj pomposo
**pond** [pɒnd] n (natural) charca; (artificial) estanque m
**ponder** ['pɒndə*] vt meditar
**pony** ['pəunɪ] n poni m; **ponytail** n coleta; **pony trekking** (BRIT) n excursión f a caballo
**poodle** ['puːdl] n caniche m
**pool** [puːl] n (natural) charca; (also: **swimming ~**) pop m; (inf: father) papá m; (drink) gaseosa ▷ vt juntar; **pools** npl quinielas fpl
**poor** [puə*] adj pobre; (bad) de mala calidad ▷ npl: **the ~** los pobres; **poorly** adj mal, enfermo ▷ adv mal
**pop** [pɒp] n (sound) ruido seco; (Mus) (música) pop m; (inf: father) papá m; (drink) gaseosa ▷ vt (put quickly) meter (de prisa) ▷ vi reventar; (cork) saltar; **pop in** vi entrar un momento; **pop out** vi salir un momento; **popcorn** n palomitas fpl
**poplar** ['pɒplə*] n álamo
**popper** ['pɒpə*] (BRIT) n automático
**poppy** ['pɒpɪ] n amapola
**Popsicle®** ['pɒpsɪkl] (US) n polo
**pop star** n estrella del pop
**popular** ['pɒpjulə*] adj popular; **popularity** [pɒpju'lærɪtɪ] n popularidad f
**population** [pɒpju'leɪʃən] n población f
**pop-up** ['pɒpʌp] (Comput) adj (menu, window) emergente ▷ n ventana emergente, (ventana f) pop-up f
**porcelain** ['pɔːslɪn] n porcelana
**porch** [pɔːtʃ] n pórtico, entrada; (US) veranda
**pore** [pɔː*] n poro ▷ vi: **to ~ over** engolfarse en
**pork** [pɔːk] n carne f de cerdo or (LAM) chancho; **pork chop** n chuleta de cerdo; **pork pie** n (BRIT: Culin) empanada de carne de cerdo
**porn** [pɔːn] adj (inf) porno inv ▷ n porno; **pornographic** [pɔːnə'græfɪk] adj pornográfico; **pornography** [pɔː'nɒgrəfɪ] n pornografía

**porridge** ['pɒrɪdʒ] n gachas fpl de avena
**port** [pɔːt] n puerto; (Naut: left side) babor m; (wine) vino de Oporto; **~ of call** puerto de escala
**portable** ['pɔːtəbl] adj portátil
**porter** ['pɔːtə*] n (for luggage) maletero; (doorkeeper) portero/a, conserje m/f
**portfolio** [pɔːt'fəuliəu] n cartera
**portion** ['pɔːʃən] n porción f; (of food) ración f
**portrait** ['pɔːtreɪt] n retrato
**portray** [pɔː'treɪ] vt retratar; (actor) representar
**Portugal** ['pɔːtjugl] n Portugal m
**Portuguese** [pɔːtju'giːz] adj portugués/ esa ▷ n inv portugués/esa m/f; (Ling) portugués m
**pose** [pəuz] n postura, actitud f ▷ vi (pretend): **to ~ as** hacerse pasar por ▷ vt (question) plantear; **to ~ for** posar para
**posh** [pɒʃ] (inf) adj elegante, de lujo
**position** [pə'zɪʃən] n posición f; (job) puesto; (situation) situación f ▷ vt colocar
**positive** ['pɒzɪtɪv] adj positivo; (certain) seguro; (definite) definitivo; **positively** adv (affirmatively, enthusiastically) de forma positiva; (inf: really) absolutamente
**possess** [pə'zes] vt poseer; **possession** [pə'zeʃən] n posesión f; **possessions** npl (belongings) pertenencias fpl; **possessive** adj posesivo
**possibility** [pɒsɪ'bɪlɪtɪ] n posibilidad f
**possible** ['pɒsɪbl] adj posible; **as big as ~** lo más grande posible; **possibly** adv posiblemente; **I cannot possibly come** me es imposible venir
**post** [pəust] n (BRIT: system) correos mpl; (BRIT: letters, delivery) correo; (job, situation) puesto; (pole) poste m ▷ vt (BRIT: send by post) echar al correo; (BRIT: appoint): **to ~ to** enviar a; **postage** n porte m, franqueo; **postal** adj postal, de correos; **postal order** n giro postal; **postbox** (BRIT) n buzón m; **postcard** n tarjeta postal; **postcode** (BRIT) n código postal
**poster** ['pəustə*] n cartel m
**postgraduate** ['pəust'grædjuət] n posgraduado/a
**postman** ['pəustmən] (BRIT: irreg) n cartero
**postmark** ['pəustmɑːk] n matasellos m inv
**post-mortem** [-'mɔːtəm] n autopsia
**post office** n (building) (oficina de) correos m; (organization): **the Post Office** Correos m inv (SP), Dirección f General de Correos (LAM)
**postpone** [pəs'pəun] vt aplazar

**posture** ['pɔstʃə*] n postura, actitud f

**postwoman** ['pəustwumən] (BRIT: irreg) n cartera

**pot** [pɔt] n (for cooking) olla; (teapot) tetera; (coffeepot) cafetera; (for flowers) maceta; (for jam) tarro, pote m; (inf: marijuana) chocolate m ⊳ vt (plant) poner en tiesto; **to go to ~** (inf) irse al traste

**potato** [pə'teɪtəu] (pl **-es**) n patata (SP), papa (LAM); **potato peeler** n pelapatatas m inv

**potent** ['pəutnt] adj potente, poderoso; (drink) fuerte

**potential** [pə'tɛnʃl] adj potencial, posible ⊳ n potencial m

**pothole** ['pɔthəul] n (in road) bache m; (BRIT: underground) gruta

**pot plant** ['pɔtplɑ:nt] n planta de interior

**potter** ['pɔtə*] n alfarero/a ⊳ vi: **to ~ around** or **about** (BRIT) hacer trabajitos; **pottery** n cerámica; (factory) alfarería

**potty** ['pɔtɪ] n orinal m de niño

**pouch** [pautʃ] n (Zool) bolsa; (for tobacco) petaca

**poultry** ['pəultrɪ] n aves fpl de corral; (meat) pollo

**pounce** [pauns] vi: **to ~ on** precipitarse sobre

**pound** [paund] n libra (weight = 453g or 16oz; money = 100 pence) ⊳ vt (beat) golpear; (crush) machacar ⊳ vi (heart) latir; **pound sterling** n libra esterlina

**pour** [pɔ:*] vt echar; (tea etc) servir ⊳ vi correr, fluir; **to ~ sb a drink** servirle a algn una copa; **pour in** vi (people) entrar en tropel; **pour out** vi salir en tropel ⊳ vt (drink) echar, servir; (fig): **to pour out one's feelings** desahogarse; **pouring** adj: **pouring rain** lluvia torrencial

**pout** [paut] vi hacer pucheros

**poverty** ['pɔvətɪ] n pobreza, miseria

**powder** ['paudə*] n polvo; (also: **face ~**) polvos mpl ⊳ vt polvorear; **to ~ one's face** empolvarse la cara; **powdered milk** n leche f en polvo

**power** ['pauə*] n poder m; (strength) fuerza; (nation, Tech) potencia; (drive) empuje m; (Elec) fuerza, energía ⊳ vt impulsar; **to be in ~** (Pol) estar en el poder; **power cut** (BRIT) n apagón m; **power failure** n = **power cut; powerful** adj poderoso; (engine) potente; (speech etc) convincente; **powerless** adj: **powerless (to do)** incapaz (de hacer); **power point** (BRIT) n enchufe m; **power station** n central f eléctrica

**p.p.** abbr (= per procurationem); **p.p. J. Smith** p.p. (por poder de) J. Smith; (= pages) págs

**PR** n abbr = **public relations**

**practical** ['præktɪkl] adj práctico; **practical joke** n broma pesada; **practically** adv (almost) casi

**practice** ['præktɪs] n (habit) costumbre f; (exercise) práctica, ejercicio; (training) adiestramiento; (Med: of profession) práctica, ejercicio; (Med, Law: business) consulta ⊳ vt, vi (US) = **practise; in ~** (in reality) en la práctica; **out of ~** desentrenado

**practise** ['præktɪs] (US **practice**) vt (carry out) practicar; (profession) ejercer; (train at) practicar ⊳ vi ejercer; (train) practicar; **practising** adj (Christian etc) practicante; (lawyer) en ejercicio

**practitioner** [præk'tɪʃənə*] n (Med) médico/a

**pragmatic** [præg'mætɪk] adj pragmático

**prairie** ['prɛərɪ] n pampa

**praise** [preɪz] n alabanza(s) f(pl), elogio(s) m(pl) ⊳ vt alabar, elogiar

**pram** [præm] (BRIT) n cochecito de niño

**prank** [præŋk] n travesura

**prawn** [prɔ:n] n gamba; **prawn cocktail** n cóctel m de gambas

**pray** [preɪ] vi rezar; **prayer** [prɛə*] n oración f, rezo; (entreaty) ruego, súplica

**preach** [pri:tʃ] vi predicar; **preacher** n predicador(a) m/f

**precarious** [prɪ'kɛərɪəs] adj precario

**precaution** [prɪ'kɔ:ʃən] n precaución f

**precede** [prɪ'si:d] vt, vi preceder; **precedent** ['prɛsɪdənt] n precedente m; **preceding** [prɪ'si:dɪŋ] adj anterior

**precinct** ['pri:sɪŋkt] n recinto

**precious** ['prɛʃəs] adj precioso

**precise** [prɪ'saɪs] adj preciso, exacto; **precisely** adv precisamente, exactamente; **precision** [prɪ'sɪʒən] n precisión f

**predator** ['prɛdətə*] n depredador m

**predecessor** ['pri:dɪsɛsə*] n antecesor(a) m/f

**predicament** [prɪ'dɪkəmənt] n apuro

**predict** [prɪ'dɪkt] vt pronosticar; **predictable** adj previsible; **prediction** [-'dɪkʃən] n predicción f

**predominantly** [prɪ'dɔmɪnəntlɪ] adv en su mayoría

**preface** ['prɛfəs] n prefacio

**prefect** ['pri:fɛkt] (BRIT) n (in school) monitor(a) m/f

**prefer** [prɪ'fə:*] vt preferir; **to ~ doing** or **to do** preferir hacer; **preferable** ['prɛfrəbl] adj preferible; **preferably** ['prɛfrəblɪ] adv de preferencia; **preference** ['prɛfrəns] n preferencia; (priority) prioridad f

**prefix** ['pri:fɪks] n prefijo

**pregnancy** ['prɛgnənsɪ] n (of woman) embarazo; (of animal) preñez f

**pregnant** ['prɛgnənt] *adj* (*woman*) embarazada; (*animal*) preñada
**prehistoric** ['pri:hɪs'tɔrɪk] *adj* prehistórico
**prejudice** ['prɛdʒudɪs] *n* prejuicio; **prejudiced** *adj* (*person*) predispuesto
**preliminary** [prɪ'lɪmɪnərɪ] *adj* preliminar
**prelude** ['prɛljuːd] *n* preludio
**premature** ['prɛmətʃuə*] *adj* prematuro
**premier** ['prɛmɪə*] *adj* primero, principal ▷ *n* (*Pol*) primer(a) ministro/a
**première** ['prɛmɪɛə*] *n* estreno
**Premier League** [prɛmɪə'liːg] *n* primera división
**premises** ['prɛmɪsɪz] *npl* (*of business etc*) local *m*; **on the ~** en el lugar mismo
**premium** ['priːmɪəm] *n* premio; (*insurance*) prima; **to be at a ~** ser muy solicitado
**premonition** [prɛmə'nɪʃən] *n* presentimiento
**preoccupied** [prɪː'ɔkjupaɪd] *adj* ensimismado
**prepaid** [priː'peɪd] *adj* porte pagado
**preparation** [prɛpə'reɪʃən] *n* preparación *f*; **preparations** *npl* preparativos *mpl*
**preparatory school** [prɪ'pærətərɪ-] *n* escuela preparatoria
**prepare** [prɪ'pɛə*] *vt* preparar, disponer; (*Culin*) preparar ▷ *vi*: **to ~ for** (*action*) prepararse *or* disponerse para; (*event*) hacer preparativos para; **~d to** dispuesto a; **~d for** listo para
**preposition** [prɛpə'zɪʃən] *n* preposición *f*
**prep school** [prɛp-] *n* = **preparatory school**
**prerequisite** [priː'rɛkwɪzɪt] *n* requisito
**preschool** ['priː'skuːl] *adj* preescolar
**prescribe** [prɪ'skraɪb] *vt* (*Med*) recetar
**prescription** [prɪ'skrɪpʃən] *n* (*Med*) receta
**presence** ['prɛzns] *n* presencia; **in sb's ~** en presencia de algn; **~ of mind** aplomo
**present** [*adj, n* 'prɛznt, *vb* prɪ'zɛnt] *adj* (*in attendance*) presente; (*current*) actual ▷ *n* (*gift*) regalo; (*actuality*): **the ~** la actualidad, el presente ▷ *vt* (*introduce, describe*) presentar; (*expound*) exponer; (*give*) presentar, dar, ofrecer; (*Theatre*) representar; **to give sb a ~** regalar algo a algn; **at ~** actualmente; **presentable** [prɪ'zɛntəbl] *adj*: **to make o.s. presentable** arreglarse; **presentation** [-'teɪʃən] *n* presentación *f*; (*of report etc*) exposición *f*; (*formal ceremony*) entrega de un regalo; **present-day** *adj* actual; **presenter** [prɪ'zɛntə*] *n* (*Radio, TV*) locutor(a) *m/f*; **presently** *adv* (*soon*) dentro de poco; (*now*) ahora; **present participle** *n* participio (de) presente

**preservation** [prɛzə'veɪʃən] *n* conservación *f*
**preservative** [prɪ'zəːvətɪv] *n* conservante *m*
**preserve** [prɪ'zəːv] *vt* (*keep safe*) preservar, proteger; (*maintain*) mantener; (*food*) conservar ▷ *n* (*for game*) coto, vedado; (*often pl: jam*) conserva, confitura
**preside** [prɪ'zaɪd] *vi* presidir
**president** ['prɛzɪdənt] *n* presidente *m/f*; **presidential** [-'dɛnʃl] *adj* presidencial
**press** [prɛs] *n* (*newspapers*): **the P~** la prensa; (*printer's*) imprenta; (*of button*) pulsación *f* ▷ *vt* empujar; (*button etc*) apretar; (*clothes: iron*) planchar; (*put pressure on: person*) presionar; (*insist*): **to ~ sth on sb** insistir en que algn acepte algo ▷ *vi* (*squeeze*) apretar; (*pressurize*): **to ~ for** presionar por; **we are ~ed for time/money** estamos apurados de tiempo/dinero; **press conference** *n* rueda de prensa; **pressing** *adj* apremiante; **press stud** (*BRIT*) *n* botón *m* de presión; **press-up** (*BRIT*) *n* plancha
**pressure** ['prɛʃə*] *n* presión *f*; **to put ~ on sb** presionar a algn; **pressure cooker** *n* olla a presión; **pressure group** *n* grupo de presión
**prestige** [prɛs'tiːʒ] *n* prestigio
**prestigious** [prɛs'tɪdʒəs] *adj* prestigioso
**presumably** [prɪ'zjuːməblɪ] *adv* es de suponer que, cabe presumir que
**presume** [prɪ'zjuːm] *vt*: **to ~ (that)** presumir (que), suponer (que)
**pretence** [prɪ'tɛns] (*us* **pretense**) *n* fingimiento; **under false ~s** con engaños
**pretend** [prɪ'tɛnd] *vt, vi* (*feign*) fingir
▌ Be careful not to translate **pretend** by the Spanish word *pretender*.
**pretense** [prɪ'tɛns] (*us*) *n* = **pretence**
**pretentious** [prɪ'tɛnʃəs] *adj* presumido; (*ostentatious*) ostentoso, aparatoso
**pretext** ['priːtɛkst] *n* pretexto
**pretty** ['prɪtɪ] *adj* bonito, lindo (*LAM*) ▷ *adv* bastante
**prevail** [prɪ'veɪl] *vi* (*gain mastery*) prevalecer; (*be current*) predominar; **prevailing** *adj* (*dominant*) predominante
**prevalent** ['prɛvələnt] *adj* (*widespread*) extendido
**prevent** [prɪ'vɛnt] *vt*: **to ~ sb from doing sth** impedir a algn hacer algo; **to ~ sth from happening** evitar que ocurra algo; **prevention** [prɪ'vɛnʃən] *n* prevención *f*; **preventive** *adj* preventivo
**preview** ['priːvjuː] *n* (*of film*) preestreno
**previous** ['priːvɪəs] *adj* previo, anterior; **previously** *adv* antes
**prey** [preɪ] *n* presa ▷ *vi*: **to ~ on** (*feed on*)

alimentarse de; **it was ~ing on his mind** le preocupaba, le obsesionaba

**price** [praɪs] n precio ▷ vt (goods) fijar el precio de; **priceless** adj que no tiene precio; **price list** n tarifa

**prick** [prɪk] n (sting) picadura ▷ vt pinchar; (hurt) picar; **to ~ up one's ears** aguzar el oído

**prickly** ['prɪklɪ] adj espinoso; (fig: person) enojadizo

**pride** [praɪd] n orgullo; (pej) soberbia ▷ vt: **to ~ o.s. on** enorgullecerse de

**priest** [priːst] n sacerdote m

**primarily** ['praɪmərɪlɪ] adv ante todo

**primary** ['praɪmərɪ] adj (first in importance) principal ▷ n (us Pol) elección f primaria; **primary school** (BRIT) n escuela primaria

**prime** [praɪm] adj primero, principal; (excellent) selecto, de primera clase ▷ n: **in the ~ of life** en la flor de la vida ▷ vt (wood; fig) preparar; **~ example** ejemplo típico; **Prime Minister** n primer(a) ministro/a

**primitive** ['prɪmɪtɪv] adj primitivo; (crude) rudimentario

**primrose** ['prɪmrəuz] n primavera, prímula

**prince** [prɪns] n príncipe m

**princess** [prɪn'sɛs] n princesa

**principal** ['prɪnsɪpl] adj principal, mayor ▷ n director(a) m/f; **principally** adv principalmente

**principle** ['prɪnsɪpl] n principio; **in ~** en principio; **on ~** por principio

**print** [prɪnt] n (footprint) huella; (fingerprint) huella dactilar; (letters) letra de molde; (fabric) estampado; (Art) grabado; (Phot) impresión f ▷ vt imprimir; (cloth) estampar; (write in capitals) escribir en letras de molde; **out of ~** agotado; **print out** vt (Comput) imprimir; **printer** n (person) impresor(a) m/f; (machine) impresora; **printout** n (Comput) impresión f

**prior** ['praɪə*] adj anterior, previo; (more important) más importante; **~ to** antes de

**priority** [praɪ'ɔrɪtɪ] n prioridad f; **to have ~ (over)** tener prioridad (sobre)

**prison** ['prɪzn] n cárcel f, prisión f ▷ cpd carcelario; **prisoner** n (in prison) preso/a; (captured person) prisionero; **prisoner-of-war** n prisionero de guerra

**pristine** ['prɪstiːn] adj pristino

**privacy** ['prɪvəsɪ] n intimidad f

**private** ['praɪvɪt] adj (personal) particular; (property, industry, discussion etc) privado; (person) reservado; (place) tranquilo ▷ n soldado raso; "**~**" (on envelope) "confidencial"; (on door) "prohibido el paso";

**in ~** en privado; **privately** adv en privado; (in o.s.) en secreto; **private property** n propiedad f privada; **private school** n colegio particular

**privatize** ['praɪvɪtaɪz] vt privatizar

**privilege** ['prɪvɪlɪdʒ] n privilegio; (prerogative) prerrogativa

**prize** [praɪz] n premio ▷ adj de primera clase ▷ vt apreciar, estimar; **prize-giving** n distribución f de premios; **prizewinner** n premiado/a

**pro** [prəu] n (Sport) profesional mf ▷ prep a favor de; **the ~s and cons** los pros y los contras

**probability** [prɔbə'bɪlɪtɪ] n probabilidad f; **in all ~** con toda probabilidad

**probable** ['prɔbəbl] adj probable

**probably** ['prɔbəblɪ] adv probablemente

**probation** [prə'beɪʃən] n: **on ~** (employee) a prueba; (Law) en libertad condicional

**probe** [prəub] n (Med, Space) sonda; (enquiry) encuesta, investigación f ▷ vt sondar; (investigate) investigar

**problem** ['prɔbləm] n problema m

**procedure** [prə'siːdʒə*] n procedimiento; (bureaucratic) trámites mpl

**proceed** [prə'siːd] vi (do afterwards): **to ~ to do sth** proceder a hacer algo; (continue): **to ~ (with)** continuar or seguir (con); **proceedings** npl acto(s) (pl); (Law) proceso; **proceeds** ['prəusiːdz] npl (money) ganancias fpl, ingresos mpl

**process** ['prəusɛs] n proceso ▷ vt tratar, elaborar

**procession** [prə'sɛʃən] n desfile m; **funeral ~** cortejo fúnebre

**proclaim** [prə'kleɪm] vt (announce) anunciar

**prod** [prɔd] vt empujar ▷ n empujón m

**produce** [n 'prɔdjuːs, vt prə'djuːs] n (Agr) productos mpl agrícolas ▷ vt producir; (play, film, programme) presentar; **producer** n productor(a) m/f; (of film, programme) director(a) m/f; (of record) productor(a) m/f

**product** ['prɔdʌkt] n producto; **production** [prə'dʌkʃən] n producción f; (Theatre) presentación f; **productive** [prə'dʌktɪv] adj productivo; **productivity** [prɔdʌk'tɪvɪtɪ] n productividad f

**Prof.** [prɔf] abbr (= professor) Prof

**profession** [prə'fɛʃən] n profesión f; **professional** adj profesional ▷ n profesional mf; (skilled person) perito

**professor** [prə'fɛsə*] n (BRIT) catedrático/a; (US, CANADA) profesor(a) m/f

**profile** ['prəufaɪl] n perfil m

**profit** ['prɔfɪt] n (Comm) ganancia ▷ vi: **to ~ by** or **from** aprovechar or sacar provecho

de; **profitable** adj (Econ) rentable
**profound** [prə'faund] adj profundo
**programme** ['prəugræm] (us **program**) n
programa m ▷ vt programar; **programmer**
(us **programer**) n programador(a)
m/f; **programming** (us **programing**) n
programación f

**progress** [n 'prəugres, vi prə'gres] n
progreso; (development) desarrollo
▷ vi progresar, avanzar; **in ~** en curso;
**progressive** [-'gresɪv] adj progresivo;
(person) progresista

**prohibit** [prə'hɪbɪt] vt prohibir; **to ~ sb
from doing sth** prohibir a algn hacer algo
**project** [n 'prɔdʒekt, vb prə'dʒekt] n
proyecto ▷ vt proyectar ▷ vi (stick out) salir,
sobresalir; **projection** [prə'dʒekʃən]
n proyección f; (overhang) saliente m;
**projector** [prə'dʒektə*] n proyector m
**prolific** [prə'lɪfɪk] adj prolífico
**prolong** [prə'lɔŋ] vt prolongar, extender
**prom** [prɔm] n abbr = **promenade** (us: ball)
baile m de gala; **the P~s** ver abajo

● **PROM**
●
● El ciclo de conciertos de música clásica
● más conocido de Londres es el llamado
● **the Proms** (promenade concerts),
● que se celebra anualmente en el Royal
● Albert Hall. Su nombre se debe a que
● originalmente el público paseaba
● durante las actuaciones, costumbre que
● en la actualidad se mantiene de forma
● simbólica, permitiendo que parte de
● los asistentes permanezcan de pie. En
● Estados Unidos se llama **prom** a un
● baile de gala en un centro de educación
● secundaria o universitaria.

**promenade** [prɔmə'nɑːd] n (by sea) paseo
marítimo
**prominent** ['prɔmɪnənt] adj (standing out)
saliente; (important) eminente, importante
**promiscuous** [prə'mɪskjuəs] adj
(sexually) promiscuo
**promise** ['prɔmɪs] n promesa ▷ vt, vi
prometer; **promising** adj prometedor(a)
**promote** [prə'məut] vt (employee)
ascender; (product, pop star) hacer
propaganda por; (ideas) fomentar;
**promotion** [-'məuʃən] n (advertising
campaign) campaña f de promoción; (in rank)
ascenso
**prompt** [prɔmpt] adj rápido ▷ adv: **at 6
o'clock ~** a las seis en punto ▷ n (Comput)
aviso ▷ vt (urge) mover, incitar; (when
talking) instar; (Theatre) apuntar; **to ~ sb to**

**do sth** instar a algn a hacer algo; **promptly**
adv rápidamente; (exactly) puntualmente
**prone** [prəun] adj (lying) postrado; **~ to**
propenso a
**prong** [prɔŋ] n diente m, punta
**pronoun** ['prəunaun] n pronombre m
**pronounce** [prə'nauns] vt pronunciar
**pronunciation** [prənʌnsɪ'eɪʃən] n
pronunciación f
**proof** [pruːf] n prueba ▷ adj: **~ against** a
prueba de
**prop** [prɔp] n apoyo; (fig) sostén m
accesorios mpl, at(t)rezzo msg; **prop up**
vt (roof, structure) apuntalar; (economy)
respaldar
**propaganda** [prɔpə'gændə] n
propaganda
**propeller** [prə'pelə*] n hélice f
**proper** ['prɔpə*] adj (suited, right) propio;
(exact) justo; (seemly) correcto, decente;
(authentic) verdadero; (referring to place): **the
village ~** el pueblo mismo; **properly** adv
(adequately) correctamente; (decently)
decentemente; **proper noun** n nombre
m propio
**property** ['prɔpətɪ] n propiedad f;
(personal) bienes mpl muebles
**prophecy** ['prɔfɪsɪ] n profecía
**prophet** ['prɔfɪt] n profeta m
**proportion** [prə'pɔːʃən] n proporción
f; (share) parte f; **proportions** npl
(size) dimensiones fpl; **proportional**
adj: **proportional (to)** en proporción (con)
**proposal** [prə'pəuzl] n (offer of marriage)
oferta de matrimonio; (plan) proyecto
**propose** [prə'pəuz] vt proponer ▷ vi
declararse; **to ~ to do** tener intención de
hacer
**proposition** [prɔpə'zɪʃən] n propuesta
**proprietor** [prə'praɪətə*] n propietario/a,
dueño/a
**prose** [prəuz] n prosa
**prosecute** ['prɔsɪkjuːt] vt (Law) procesar;
**prosecution** [-'kjuːʃən] n proceso, causa;
(accusing side) acusación f; **prosecutor** n
acusador(a) m/f; (also: **public prosecutor**)
fiscal mf
**prospect** [n 'prɔspekt, vb prə'spekt]
n (possibility) posibilidad f; (outlook)
perspectiva ▷ vi: **to ~ for** buscar; **prospects**
npl (for work etc) perspectivas fpl;
**prospective** [prə'spektɪv] adj futuro
**prospectus** [prə'spektəs] n prospecto
**prosper** ['prɔspə*] vi prosperar;
**prosperity** [-'sperɪtɪ] n prosperidad f;
**prosperous** adj próspero
**prostitute** ['prɔstɪtjuːt] n prostituta;
(male) hombre que se dedica a la prostitución

**protect** [prəˈtɛkt] vt proteger; **protection** [-ˈtɛkʃən] n protección f; **protective** adj protector(a)

**protein** [ˈprəʊtiːn] n proteína

**protest** [n ˈprəʊtɛst, vb prəˈtɛst] n protesta ▷ vi: **to ~ about** or **at/against** protestar de/contra ▷ vt (insist): **to ~ (that)** insistir en (que)

**Protestant** [ˈprɒtɪstənt] adj, n protestante mf

**protester** [prəˈtɛstə*] n manifestante mf

**protractor** [prəˈtræktə*] n (Geom) transportador m

**proud** [praud] adj orgulloso; (pej) soberbio, altanero

**prove** [pruːv] vt probar; (show) demostrar ▷ vi: **to ~ (to be) correct** resultar correcto; **to ~ o.s.** probar su valía

**proverb** [ˈprɒvəːb] n refrán m

**provide** [prəˈvaɪd] vt proporcionar, dar; **to ~ sb with sth** proveer a algn de algo; **provide for** vt fus (person) mantener a; (problem etc) tener en cuenta; **provided** conj: **provided (that)** con tal de que, a condición de que; **providing** [prəˈvaɪdɪŋ] conj: **providing (that)** a condición de que, con tal de que

**province** [ˈprɒvɪns] n provincia; (fig) esfera; **provincial** [prəˈvɪnʃəl] adj provincial; (pej) provinciano

**provision** [prəˈvɪʒən] n (supplying) suministro, abastecimiento; (of contract etc) disposición f; **provisions** npl (food) comestibles mpl; **provisional** adj provisional

**provocative** [prəˈvɒkətɪv] adj provocativo

**provoke** [prəˈvəʊk] vt (cause) provocar, incitar; (anger) enojar

**prowl** [praul] vi (also: **~ about, ~ around**) merodear ▷ n: **on the ~** de merodeo

**proximity** [prɒkˈsɪmɪtɪ] n proximidad f

**proxy** [ˈprɒksɪ] n: **by ~** por poderes

**prudent** [ˈpruːdənt] adj prudente

**prune** [pruːn] n ciruela pasa ▷ vt podar

**pry** [praɪ] vi: **to ~ (into)** entrometerse (en)

**PS** n abbr (= postscript) P.D.

**pseudonym** [ˈsjuːdəʊnɪm] n seudónimo

**PSHE** (BRIT: Scol) n abbr (= personal, social and health education) formación social y sanitaria

**psychiatric** [saɪkɪˈætrɪk] adj psiquiátrico

**psychiatrist** [saɪˈkaɪətrɪst] n psiquiatra mf

**psychic** [ˈsaɪkɪk] adj (also: **~al**) psíquico

**psychoanalysis** [saɪkəʊəˈnælɪsɪs] n psicoanálisis m inv

**psychological** [saɪkəˈlɒdʒɪkl] adj psicológico

**psychologist** [saɪˈkɒlədʒɪst] n psicólogo/a

**psychology** [saɪˈkɒlədʒɪ] n psicología

**psychotherapy** [saɪkəʊˈθɛrəpɪ] n psicoterapia

**pt** abbr = **pint(s); point(s)**

**PTO** abbr (= please turn over) sigue

**pub** [pʌb] n abbr (= public house) pub m, bar m

**puberty** [ˈpjuːbətɪ] n pubertad f

**public** [ˈpʌblɪk] adj público ▷ n: **the ~** el público; **in ~** en público; **to make ~** hacer público

**publication** [pʌblɪˈkeɪʃən] n publicación f

**public: public company** n sociedad f anónima; **public convenience** (BRIT) n aseos mpl públicos (SP), sanitarios mpl (LAM); **public holiday** n (día m de) fiesta (SP), (día m) feriado (LAM); **public house** (BRIT) n bar m, pub m

**publicity** [pʌbˈlɪsɪtɪ] n publicidad f

**publicize** [ˈpʌblɪsaɪz] vt publicitar

**public: public limited company** n sociedad f anónima (S.A.); **publicly** adv públicamente, en público; **public opinion** n opinión f pública; **public relations** n relaciones fpl públicas; **public school** n (BRIT) escuela privada; (US) instituto; **public transport** n transporte m público

**publish** [ˈpʌblɪʃ] vt publicar; **publisher** n (person) editor(a) m/f; (firm) editorial f; **publishing** n (industry) industria del libro

**pub lunch** n almuerzo que se sirve en un pub; **to go for a ~** almorzar o comer en un pub

**pudding** [ˈpudɪŋ] n pudín m; (BRIT: dessert) postre m; **black ~** morcilla

**puddle** [ˈpʌdl] n charco

**Puerto Rico** [ˈpwɛːtəʊˈriːkəʊ] n Puerto Rico

**puff** [pʌf] n soplo; (of smoke, air) bocanada; (of breathing) resoplido ▷ vt: **to ~ one's pipe** chupar la pipa ▷ vi (pant) jadear; **puff pastry** n hojaldre m

**pull** [pul] n (tug): **to give sth a ~** dar un tirón a algo ▷ vt tirar de; (press: trigger) apretar; (haul) tirar, arrastrar; (close: curtain) echar ▷ vi tirar; **to ~ to pieces** hacer pedazos; **not to ~ one's punches** no andarse con bromas; **to ~ one's weight** hacer su parte; **to ~ o.s. together** sobreponerse; **to ~ sb's leg** tomar el pelo a algn; **pull apart** vt (break) romper; **pull away** vi (vehicle: move off) salir, arrancar; (draw back) apartarse bruscamente; **pull back** vt (lever etc) tirar hacia sí; (curtains) descorrer ▷ vi (refrain) contenerse; (Mil: withdraw) retirarse; **pull down** vt

(building) derribar; **pull in** vi (car etc) parar
(junto a la acera); (train) llegar a la estación;
**pull off** vt (deal etc) cerrar; **pull out** vi (car,
train etc) salir ▷ vt sacar, arrancar; **pull over**
vi (Aut) hacerse a un lado; **pull up** vi (stop)
parar ▷ vt (raise) levantar; (uproot) arrancar,
desarraigar

**pulley** ['pulɪ] n polea

**pullover** ['puləuvə*] n jersey m, suéter m

**pulp** [pʌlp] n (of fruit) pulpa

**pulpit** ['pulpɪt] n púlpito

**pulse** [pʌls] n (Anat) pulso; (rhythm)
pulsación f; (Bot) legumbre f; **pulses** pl n
legumbres

**puma** ['pju:mə] n puma m

**pump** [pʌmp] n bomba; (shoe) zapatilla
▷ vt sacar con una bomba; **pump up** vt
inflar

**pumpkin** ['pʌmpkɪn] n calabaza

**pun** [pʌn] n juego de palabras

**punch** [pʌntʃ] n (blow) golpe m, puñetazo;
(tool) punzón m; (drink) ponche m ▷ vt
(hit): **to ~ sb/sth** dar un puñetazo or golpear
a algn/algo; **punch-up** (BRIT: inf) n riña

**punctual** ['pʌŋktjuəl] adj puntual

**punctuation** [pʌŋktju'eɪʃən] n
puntuación f

**puncture** ['pʌŋktʃə*] (BRIT) n pinchazo
▷ vt pinchar

**punish** ['pʌnɪʃ] vt castigar; **punishment**
n castigo

**punk** [pʌŋk] n (also: ~ rocker) punki mf;
(also: ~ rock) música punk; (US: inf: hoodlum)
rufián m

**pup** [pʌp] n cachorro

**pupil** ['pju:pl] n alumno/a; (of eye) pupila

**puppet** ['pʌpɪt] n títere m

**puppy** ['pʌpɪ] n cachorro, perrito

**purchase** ['pə:tʃɪs] n compra ▷ vt
comprar

**pure** [pjuə*] adj puro; **purely** adv
puramente

**purify** ['pjuərɪfaɪ] vt purificar, depurar

**purity** ['pjuərɪtɪ] n pureza

**purple** ['pə:pl] adj purpúreo; morado

**purpose** ['pə:pəs] n propósito; **on ~** a
propósito, adrede

**purr** [pə:*] vi ronronear

**purse** [pə:s] n monedero; (US: handbag)
bolso (SP), cartera (LAM), bolsa (MEX) ▷ vt
fruncir

**pursue** [pə'sju:] vt seguir

**pursuit** [pə'sju:t] n (chase) caza;
(occupation) actividad f

**pus** [pʌs] n pus m

**push** [puʃ] n empuje m, empujón m;
(of button) presión f; (drive) empuje m
▷ vt empujar; (button) apretar; (promote)
promover ▷ vi empujar; (demand): **to ~ for**
luchar por; **push in** vi colarse; **push off** (inf)
vi largarse; **push on** vi seguir adelante;
**push over** vt (cause to fall) hacer caer,
derribar; (knock over) volcar; **push through**
vi (crowd) abrirse paso a empujones ▷ vt
(measure) despachar; **pushchair** (BRIT) n
sillita de ruedas; **pusher** n (drug pusher)
traficante mf de drogas; **push-up** (US) n
plancha

**pussy(-cat)** ['pusɪ-] (inf) n minino (inf)

**put** [put] (pt, pp ~) vt (place) poner, colocar;
(put into) meter; (say) expresar; (a question)
hacer; (estimate) estimar; **put aside** vt (lay
down: book etc) dejar or poner a un lado;
(save) ahorrar; (in shop) guardar; **put away**
vt (store) guardar; **put back** vt (replace)
devolver a su lugar; (postpone) aplazar; **put
by** vt (money) guardar; **put down** vt (on
ground) poner en el suelo; (animal) sacrificar;
(in writing) apuntar; (revolt etc) sofocar;
(attribute): **to put sth down to** atribuir
algo a; **put forward** vt (ideas) presentar,
proponer; **put in** vt (complaint) presentar;
(time) dedicar; **put off** vt (postpone) aplazar;
(discourage) desanimar; **put on** vt ponerse;
(light etc) encender; (play etc) presentar;
(gain): **to put on weight** engordar; (brake)
echar; (record, kettle etc) poner; (assume)
adoptar; **put out** vt (fire, light) apagar;
(rubbish etc) sacar; (cat etc) echar; (one's hand)
alargar; (inf: person): **to be put out** alterarse;
**put through** vt (Tel) poner; (plan etc) hacer
aprobar; **put together** vt unir, reunir;
(assemble: furniture) armar, montar; (meal)
preparar; **put up** vt (raise) levantar, alzar;
(hang) colgar; (build) construir; (increase)
aumentar; (accommodate) alojar; **put up
with** vt fus aguantar

**putt** [pʌt] n putt m, golpe m corto; **putting
green** n green m; minigolf m

**puzzle** ['pʌzl] n rompecabezas m inv;
(also: **crossword ~**) crucigrama m; (mystery)
misterio ▷ vi: **to ~ over sth** devanarse los sesos con
algo; **puzzled** adj perplejo; **puzzling** adj
misterioso, extraño

**pyjamas** [pɪ'dʒɑ:məz] (BRIT) npl pijama m

**pylon** ['paɪlən] n torre f de conducción
eléctrica

**pyramid** ['pɪrəmɪd] n pirámide f

# q

**quack** [kwæk] n graznido; (pej: doctor) curandero/a
**quadruple** [kwɔ'drupl] vt, vi cuadruplicar
**quail** [kweɪl] n codorniz f ▷ vi: **to ~ at** or **before** amedrentarse ante
**quaint** [kweɪnt] adj extraño; (picturesque) pintoresco
**quake** [kweɪk] vi temblar ▷ n abbr = **earthquake**
**qualification** [kwɔlɪfɪ'keɪʃən] n (ability) capacidad f; (often pl: diploma etc) título; (reservation) salvedad f
**qualified** ['kwɔlɪfaɪd] adj capacitado; (professionally) titulado; (limited) limitado
**qualify** ['kwɔlɪfaɪ] vt (make competent) capacitar; (modify) modificar ▷ vi (in competition): **to ~ (for)** calificarse (para); (pass examination(s): **to ~ (as)** calificarse (de), graduarse (en); (be eligible): **to ~ (for)** reunir los requisitos (para)
**quality** ['kwɔlɪtɪ] n calidad f; (of person) cualidad f
**qualm** [kwɑːm] n escrúpulo
**quantify** ['kwɔntɪfaɪ] vt cuantificar
**quantity** ['kwɔntɪtɪ] n cantidad f; **in ~** en grandes cantidades
**quarantine** ['kwɔrəntiːn] n cuarentena
**quarrel** ['kwɔrl] n riña, pelea ▷ vi reñir, pelearse
**quarry** ['kwɔrɪ] n cantera
**quart** [kwɔːt] n ≈ litro
**quarter** ['kwɔːtə*] n cuarto, cuarta parte f; (us: coin) moneda de 25 centavos; (of year) trimestre m; (district) barrio ▷ vt dividir en cuartos; (Mil: lodge) alojar; **quarters** npl (barracks) cuartel m; (living quarters) alojamiento; **a ~ of an hour** un cuarto de hora; **quarter final** n cuarto de final; **quarterly** adj trimestral ▷ adv cada 3 meses, trimestralmente
**quartet(te)** [kwɔː'tɛt] n cuarteto

**quartz** [kwɔːts] n cuarzo
**quay** [kiː] n (also: **~side**) muelle m
**queasy** ['kwiːzɪ] adj: **to feel ~** tener náuseas
**queen** [kwiːn] n reina; (Cards etc) dama
**queer** [kwɪə*] adj raro, extraño ▷ n (inf: highly offensive) maricón m
**quench** [kwɛntʃ] vt: **to ~ one's thirst** apagar la sed
**query** ['kwɪərɪ] n (question) pregunta ▷ vt dudar de
**quest** [kwɛst] n busca, búsqueda
**question** ['kwɛstʃən] n pregunta; (doubt) duda; (matter) asunto, cuestión f ▷ vt (doubt) dudar de; (interrogate) interrogar, hacer preguntas a; **beyond ~** fuera de toda duda; **out of the ~** imposible; ni hablar; **questionable** adj dudoso; **question mark** n punto de interrogación; **questionnaire** [-'nɛə*] n cuestionario
**queue** [kjuː] (BRIT) n cola ▷ vi (also: **~ up**) hacer cola
**quiche** [kiːʃ] n quiche m
**quick** [kwɪk] adj rápido; (agile) ágil; (mind) listo ▷ n: **cut to the ~** (fig) herido en lo vivo; **be ~!** ¡date prisa!; **quickly** adv rápidamente, de prisa
**quid** [kwɪd] (BRIT: inf) n inv libra
**quiet** ['kwaɪət] adj (voice, music etc) bajo; (person, place) tranquilo; (ceremony) íntimo ▷ n silencio; (calm) tranquilidad f ▷ vt, vi (US) = **quieten**

⊓ Be careful not to translate **quiet** by the Spanish word *quieto*.

**quietly** adv tranquilamente; (silently) silenciosamente
**quilt** [kwɪlt] n edredón m
**quirky** ['kwɜːkɪ] adj raro, estrafalario
**quit** [kwɪt] (pt, pp = **~** or **~ted**) vt dejar, abandonar; (premises) desocupar ▷ vi (give up) renunciar; (resign) dimitir
**quite** [kwaɪt] adv (rather) bastante; (entirely) completamente; **that's not ~ big enough** no acaba de ser lo bastante grande; **~ a few of them** un buen número de ellos; **~ (so)!** ¡así es!, ¡exactamente!
**quits** [kwɪts] adj: **~ (with)** en paz (con); **let's call it ~** dejémoslo en tablas
**quiver** ['kwɪvə*] vi estremecerse
**quiz** [kwɪz] n concurso ▷ vt interrogar
**quota** ['kwəutə] n cuota
**quotation** [kwəu'teɪʃən] n cita; (estimate) presupuesto; **quotation marks** npl comillas fpl
**quote** [kwəut] n cita; (estimate) presupuesto ▷ vt citar; (price) cotizar ▷ vi: **to ~ from** citar de; **quotes** npl (inverted commas) comillas fpl

# r

**rabbi** ['ræbaɪ] n rabino
**rabbit** ['ræbɪt] n conejo
**rabies** ['reɪbiːz] n rabia
**RAC** (BRIT) n abbr (= Royal Automobile Club) ≈ RACE m
**rac(c)oon** [rə'kuːn] n mapache m
**race** [reɪs] n carrera; (species) raza ▷ vt (horse) hacer correr; (engine) acelerar ▷ vi (compete) competir; (run) correr; (pulse) latir a ritmo acelerado; **race car** (US) n = **racing car**; **racecourse** n hipódromo; **racehorse** n caballo de carreras; **racetrack** n pista; (for cars) autódromo
**racial** ['reɪʃl] adj racial
**racing** ['reɪsɪŋ] n carreras fpl; **racing car** (BRIT) n coche m de carreras; **racing driver** (BRIT) n piloto mf de carreras
**racism** ['reɪsɪzəm] n racismo; **racist** [-sɪst] adj, n racista mf
**rack** [ræk] n (also: **luggage ~**) rejilla; (shelf) estante m; (also: **roof ~**) baca, portaequipajes m inv; (dish rack) escurreplatos m inv; (clothes rack) percha ▷ vt atormentar; **to ~ one's brains** devanarse los sesos
**racket** ['rækɪt] n (for tennis) raqueta; (noise) ruido, estrépito; (swindle) estafa, timo
**racquet** ['rækɪt] n raqueta
**radar** ['reɪdɑ:*] n radar m
**radiation** [reɪdɪ'eɪʃən] n radiación f
**radiator** ['reɪdɪeɪtə*] n radiador m
**radical** ['rædɪkl] adj radical
**radio** ['reɪdɪəu] n radio f; **on the ~** por radio; **radioactive** adj radioactivo; **radio station** n emisora
**radish** ['rædɪʃ] n rábano
**RAF** n abbr (= Royal Air Force) las Fuerzas Aéreas Británicas
**raffle** ['ræfl] n rifa, sorteo
**raft** [rɑːft] n balsa; (also: **life ~**) balsa salvavidas

**rag** [ræg] n (piece of cloth) trapo; (torn cloth) harapo; (pej: newspaper) periodicucho; (for charity) actividades estudiantiles benéficas; **rags** npl (torn clothes) harapos mpl
**rage** [reɪdʒ] n rabia, furor m ▷ vi (person) rabiar, estar furioso; (storm) bramar; **it's all the ~** (very fashionable) está muy de moda
**ragged** ['rægɪd] adj (edge) desigual, mellado; (appearance) andrajoso, harapiento
**raid** [reɪd] n (Mil) incursión f; (criminal) asalto; (by police) redada ▷ vt invadir, atacar; asaltar
**rail** [reɪl] n (on stair) barandilla, pasamanos m inv; (on bridge, balcony) pretil m; (of ship) barandilla; (also: **towel ~**) toallero; **railcard** n (BRIT) tarjeta para obtener descuentos en el tren; **railing(s)** n(pl) vallado; **railroad** (US) n = **railway**; **railway** (BRIT) n ferrocarril m, vía férrea; **railway line** (BRIT) n línea (de ferrocarril); **railway station** (BRIT) n estación f de ferrocarril
**rain** [reɪn] n lluvia ▷ vi llover; **in the ~** bajo la lluvia; **it's ~ing** llueve, está lloviendo; **rainbow** n arco iris; **raincoat** n impermeable m; **raindrop** n gota de lluvia; **rainfall** n lluvia; **rainforest** n selvas fpl tropicales; **rainy** adj lluvioso
**raise** [reɪz] n aumento ▷ vt levantar; (increase) aumentar; (improve: morale) subir; (: standards) mejorar; (doubts) suscitar; (a question) plantear; (cattle, family) criar; (crop) cultivar; (army) reclutar; (loan) obtener; **to ~ one's voice** alzar la voz
**raisin** ['reɪzn] n pasa de Corinto
**rake** [reɪk] n (tool) rastrillo; (person) libertino ▷ vt (garden) rastrillar
**rally** ['rælɪ] n (Pol etc) reunión f, mitin m; (Aut) rallye m; (Tennis) peloteo ▷ vt reunir ▷ vi recuperarse
**RAM** [ræm] n abbr (= random access memory) RAM f
**ram** [ræm] n carnero; (also: **battering ~**) ariete m ▷ vt (crash into) dar contra, chocar con; (push: fist etc) empujar con fuerza
**Ramadan** [ræmə'dæn] n ramadán m
**ramble** ['ræmbl] n caminata, excursión f en el campo ▷ vi (pej: also: **~ on**) divagar; **rambler** n excursionista mf; (Bot) trepadora; **rambling** adj (speech) inconexo; (house) laberíntico; (Bot) trepador(a)
**ramp** [ræmp] n rampa; **on/off ~** (US Aut) vía de acceso/salida
**rampage** [ræm'peɪdʒ] n: **to be on the ~** desmandarse ▷ vi: **they went rampaging through the town** recorrieron la ciudad armando alboroto
**ran** [ræn] pt of **run**
**ranch** [rɑːntʃ] n hacienda, estancia

**random** ['rændəm] adj fortuito, sin orden; (Comput, Math) aleatorio ▷ n: **at ~** al azar

**rang** [ræŋ] pt of **ring**

**range** [reɪndʒ] n (of mountains) cadena de montañas, cordillera; (of missile) alcance m; (of voice) registro; (series) serie f; (of products) surtido; (Mil: also: **shooting ~**) campo de tiro; (also: **kitchen ~**) fogón m ▷ vt (place) colocar; (arrange) arreglar ▷ vi: **to ~ over** (extend) extenderse por; **to ~ from ... to ...** oscilar entre ... y ...

**ranger** [reɪndʒə*] n guardabosques mf inv

**rank** [ræŋk] n (row) fila; (Mil) rango; (status) categoría; (BRIT: also: **taxi ~**) parada de taxis ▷ vi: **to ~ among** figurar entre ▷ adj fétido, rancio; **the ~ and file** (fig) la base

**ransom** ['rænsəm] n rescate m; **to hold to ~** (fig) hacer chantaje a

**rant** [rænt] vi divagar, desvariar

**rap** [ræp] vt golpear, dar un golpecito en ▷ n (music) rap m

**rape** [reɪp] n violación f; (Bot) colza ▷ vt violar

**rapid** ['ræpɪd] adj rápido; **rapidly** adv rápidamente; **rapids** npl (Geo) rápidos mpl

**rapist** ['reɪpɪst] n violador m

**rapport** [ræ'pɔ:*] n simpatía

**rare** [rɛə*] adj raro, poco común; (Culin: steak) poco hecho; **rarely** adv pocas veces

**rash** [ræʃ] adj imprudente, precipitado ▷ n (Med) sarpullido, erupción f (cutánea); (of events) serie f

**rasher** ['ræʃə*] n lonja

**raspberry** ['rɑ:zbərɪ] n frambuesa

**rat** [ræt] n rata

**rate** [reɪt] n (ratio) razón f; (price) precio; (: of hotel etc) tarifa; (of interest) tipo; (speed) velocidad f ▷ vt (value) tasar; (estimate) estimar; **rates** npl (BRIT: property tax) impuesto municipal; (fees) tarifa; **to ~ sth/sb as** considerar algo/a algn como

**rather** ['rɑ:ðə*] adv: **it's ~ expensive** es algo caro; (too much) es demasiado caro; (to some extent) más bien; **there's ~ a lot** hay bastante; **I would** or **I'd ~ go** preferiría ir; **or ~ mejor dicho

**rating** ['reɪtɪŋ] n tasación f; (score) índice m; (of ship) clase f; **ratings** npl (Radio, TV) niveles mpl de audiencia

**ratio** ['reɪʃɪəu] n razón f; **in the ~ of 100 to 1** a razón de 100 a 1

**ration** ['ræʃən] n ración f ▷ vt racionar; **rations** npl víveres mpl

**rational** ['ræʃənl] adj (solution, reasoning) lógico, razonable; (person) cuerdo, sensato

**rattle** ['rætl] n golpeteo; (of train etc)

traqueteo; (for baby) sonaja, sonajero ▷ vi castañetear; (car, bus): **to ~ along** traquetear ▷ vt hacer sonar agitando

**rave** [reɪv] vi (in anger) encolerizarse; (with enthusiasm) entusiasmarse; (Med) delirar, desvariar ▷ n (inf: party) rave m

**raven** ['reɪvən] n cuervo

**ravine** [rə'vi:n] n barranco

**raw** [rɔ:] adj crudo; (not processed) bruto; (sore) vivo; (inexperienced) novato, inexperto; **~ materials** materias primas

**ray** [reɪ] n rayo; **~ of hope** (rayo de) esperanza

**razor** ['reɪzə*] n (open) navaja; (safety razor) máquina de afeitar; (electric razor) máquina (eléctrica) de afeitar; **razor blade** n hoja de afeitar

**Rd** abbr = **road**

**RE** n abbr (BRIT) = **religious education**

**re** [ri:] prep con referencia a

**reach** [ri:tʃ] n alcance m; (of river etc) extensión f entre dos recodos ▷ vt alcanzar, llegar a; (achieve) lograr ▷ vi extenderse; **within ~** al alcance (de la mano); **out of ~** fuera del alcance; **reach out** vt (hand) tender ▷ vi: **to reach out for sth** alargar or tender la mano para tomar algo

**react** [ri:'ækt] vi reaccionar; **reaction** [-'ækʃən] n reacción f; **reactor** [ri:'æktə*] n (also: **nuclear reactor**) reactor m (nuclear)

**read** [ri:d, pt, pp red] (pt, pp ~) vi leer ▷ vt leer; (understand) entender; (study) estudiar; **read out** vt leer en alta voz; **reader** n lector(a) m/f; (BRIT: at university) profesor(a) m/f adjunto/a

**readily** ['redɪlɪ] adv (willingly) de buena gana; (easily) fácilmente; (quickly) en seguida

**reading** ['ri:dɪŋ] n lectura; (on instrument) indicación f

**ready** ['redɪ] adj listo, preparado; (willing) dispuesto; (available) disponible ▷ adv: **~-cooked** listo para comer ▷ n: **at the ~** (Mil) listo para tirar ▷ **to get ~** vi prepararse ▷ **to get ~** vt preparar; **ready-made** adj confeccionado

**real** [rɪəl] adj verdadero, auténtico; **in ~ terms** en términos reales; **real ale** n cerveza elaborada tradicionalmente; **real estate** n bienes mpl raíces; **realistic** [-'lɪstɪk] adj realista; **reality** [ri:'ælɪtɪ] n realidad f; **reality TV** n telerrealidad f

**realization** [rɪəlaɪ'zeɪʃən] n comprensión f; (fulfilment, Comm) realización f

**realize** ['rɪəlaɪz] vt (understand) darse cuenta de

**really** ['rɪəlɪ] adv realmente; (for emphasis) verdaderamente; (actually): **what ~ happened** lo que pasó en realidad; **~?** ¿de

veras?; **~!** (*annoyance*) ¡vamos!, ¡por favor!
**realm** [rɛlm] *n* reino; (*fig*) esfera
**realtor** ['rɪəltɔ:*] (*us*) *n* agente *mf*
inmobiliario/a
**reappear** [ri:ə'pɪə*] *vi* reaparecer
**rear** [rɪə*] *adj* trasero ▷ *n* parte *f* trasera
▷ *vt* (*cattle, family*) criar ▷ *vi* (*also:* **~
up:** *animal*) encabritarse
**rearrange** [ri:ə'reɪndʒ] *vt* ordenar *or*
arreglar de nuevo
**rear: rear-view mirror** *n* (*Aut*) (espejo)
retrovisor *m*; **rear-wheel drive** *n* tracción
*f* trasera
**reason** ['ri:zn] *n* razón *f* ▷ *vi*: **to ~ with sb**
tratar de que algn entre en razón; **it stands
to ~ that ...** es lógico que ...; **reasonable** *adj*
razonable; (*sensible*) sensato; **reasonably**
*adv* razonablemente; **reasoning** *n*
razonamiento, argumentos *mpl*
**reassurance** [ri:ə'ʃuərəns] *n* consuelo
**reassure** [ri:ə'ʃuə*] *vt* tranquilizar,
alentar; **to ~ sb that ...** tranquilizar a algn
asegurando que ...
**rebate** ['ri:beɪt] *n* (*on tax etc*) desgravación
*f*
**rebel** [*n* 'rɛbl, *vi* rɪ'bɛl] *n* rebelde *mf* ▷ *vi*
rebelarse, sublevarse; **rebellion** [rɪ'bɛljən]
*n* rebelión *f*, sublevación *f*; **rebellious**
[rɪ'bɛljəs] *adj* rebelde; (*child*) revoltoso
**rebuild** [ri:'bɪld] *vt* reconstruir
**recall** [*vb* rɪ'kɔ:l, *n* 'ri:kɔl] *vt* (*remember*)
recordar; (*ambassador etc*) retirar ▷ *n*
recuerdo; retirada
**rec'd** *abbr* (= *received*) rbdo
**receipt** [rɪ'si:t] *n* (*document*) recibo; (*for
parcel etc*) acuse *m* de recibo; (*act of receiving*)
recepción *f*; **receipts** *npl* (*Comm*) ingresos
*mpl*

⬛ Be careful not to translate **receipt** by the
Spanish word *receta*.

**receive** [rɪ'si:v] *vt* recibir; (*guest*) acoger;
(*wound*) sufrir; **receiver** *n* (*Tel*) auricular *m*;
(*Radio*) receptor *m*; (*of stolen goods*) perista
*mf*; (*Comm*) administrador *m* jurídico
**recent** ['ri:snt] *adj* reciente; **recently** *adv*
recientemente; **recently arrived** recién
llegado
**reception** [rɪ'sɛpʃən] *n* recepción *f*;
(*welcome*) acogida; **reception desk** *n*
recepción *f*; **receptionist** *n* recepcionista
*mf*
**recession** [rɪ'sɛʃən] *n* recesión *f*
**recharge** [ri:'tʃɑ:dʒ] *vt* (*battery*) recargar
**recipe** ['rɛsɪpɪ] *n* receta; (*for disaster,
success*) fórmula
**recipient** [rɪ'sɪpɪənt] *n* recibidor(a) *m/f*;
(*of letter*) destinatario/a
**recital** [rɪ'saɪtl] *n* recital *m*

**recite** [rɪ'saɪt] *vt* (*poem*) recitar
**reckless** ['rɛkləs] *adj* temerario,
imprudente; (*driving, driver*) peligroso
**reckon** ['rɛkən] *vt* calcular; (*consider*)
considerar; (*think*): **I ~ that ...** me parece
que ...
**reclaim** [rɪ'kleɪm] *vt* (*land, waste*)
recuperar; (*land: from sea*) rescatar; (*demand
back*) reclamar
**recline** [rɪ'klaɪn] *vi* reclinarse
**recognition** [rɛkəg'nɪʃən] *n*
reconocimiento; **transformed beyond ~**
irreconocible
**recognize** ['rɛkəgnaɪz] *vt*: **to ~ (by/as)**
reconocer (por/como)
**recollection** [rɛkə'lɛkʃən] *n* recuerdo
**recommend** [rɛkə'mɛnd] *vt* recomendar;
**recommendation** [rɛkəmɛn'deɪʃən] *n*
recomendación *f*
**reconcile** ['rɛkənsaɪl] *vt* (*two people*)
reconciliar; (*two facts*) compaginar; **to ~ o.s.
to sth** conformarse a algo
**reconsider** [ri:kən'sɪdə*] *vt* repensar
**reconstruct** [ri:kən'strʌkt] *vt* reconstruir
**record** [*n, adj* 'rɛkɔ:d, *vt* rɪ'kɔ:d] *n* (*Mus*)
disco; (*of meeting etc*) acta; (*register*) registro,
partida; (*file*) archivo; (*also:* **criminal ~**)
antecedentes *mpl*; (*written*) expediente
*m*; (*Sport, Comput*) récord *m* ▷ *adj* récord,
sin precedentes ▷ *vt* registrar; (*Mus: song
etc*) grabar; **in ~ time** en un tiempo
récord; **off the ~** *adj* no oficial ▷ *adv*
confidencialmente; **recorded delivery**
(*BRIT*) *n* (*Post*) entrega con acuse de recibo;
**recorder** *n* (*Mus*) flauta de pico; **recording**
*n* (*Mus*) grabación *f*; **record player** *n*
tocadiscos *m inv*
**recount** [rɪ'kaunt] *vt* contar
**recover** [rɪ'kʌvə*] *vt* recuperar ▷ *vi* (*from
illness, shock*) recuperarse; **recovery** *n*
recuperación *f*
**recreate** [ri:krɪ'eɪt] *vt* recrear
**recreation** [rɛkrɪ'eɪʃən] *n* recreo;
**recreational vehicle** (*us*) *n* caravana *or*
rulota pequeña; **recreational drug** droga
recreativa
**recruit** [rɪ'kru:t] *n* recluta *mf* ▷ *vt*
reclutar; (*staff*) contratar; **recruitment** *n*
reclutamiento
**rectangle** ['rɛktæŋgl] *n* rectángulo;
**rectangular** [-'tæŋgjulə*] *adj* rectangular
**rectify** ['rɛktɪfaɪ] *vt* rectificar
**rector** ['rɛktə*] *n* (*Rel*) párroco
**recur** [rɪ'kə:*] *vi* repetirse; (*pain, illness*)
producirse de nuevo; **recurring** *adj*
(*problem*) repetido, constante
**recyclable** [ri:'saɪkləbl] *adj* reciclable
**recycle** [ri:'saɪkl] *vt* reciclar

**recycling** [ri:'saɪklɪŋ] n reciclaje
**red** [rɛd] n rojo ▷ adj rojo; (hair) pelirrojo; (wine) tinto; **to be in the ~** (account) estar en números rojos; (business) tener un saldo negativo; **to give sb the ~ carpet treatment** recibir a algn con todos los honores; **Red Cross** n Cruz f Roja; **redcurrant** n grosella roja
**redeem** [rɪ'di:m] vt redimir; (promises) cumplir; (sth in pawn) desempeñar; (fig. also Rel) rescatar
**red: red-haired** adj pelirrojo; **redhead** n pelirrojo/a; **red-hot** adj candente; **red light** n: **to go through a red light** (Aut) pasar la luz roja; **red-light district** n barrio chino
**red meat** n carne f roja
**reduce** [rɪ'dju:s] vt reducir; **to ~ sb to tears** hacer llorar a algn; **"~ speed now"** (Aut) "reduzca la velocidad"; **reduced** adj (decreased) reducido, rebajado; **at a reduced price** con rebaja or descuento; **"greatly reduced prices"** "grandes rebajas"; **reduction** [rɪ'dʌkʃən] n reducción f; (of price) rebaja; (discount) descuento; (smaller-scale copy) copia reducida
**redundancy** [rɪ'dʌndənsɪ] n (dismissal) despido; (unemployment) desempleo
**redundant** [rɪ'dʌndnt] adj (BRIT: worker) parado, sin trabajo; (detail, object) superfluo; **to be made ~** quedar(se) sin trabajo
**reed** [ri:d] n (Bot) junco, caña; (Mus) lengüeta
**reef** [ri:f] n (at sea) arrecife m
**reel** [ri:l] n carrete m, bobina; (of film) rollo; (dance) baile escocés ▷ vt (also: ~ up) devanar; (also: ~ in) sacar ▷ vi (sway) tambalear(se)
**ref** [rɛf] (inf) n abbr = **referee**
**refectory** [rɪ'fɛktərɪ] n comedor m
**refer** [rɪ'fə:*] vt (send: patient) referir; (: matter) remitir ▷ vi: **to ~ to** (allude to) referirse a, aludir a; (apply to) relacionarse con; (consult) consultar
**referee** [rɛfə'ri:] n árbitro; (BRIT: for job application): **to be a ~ for sb** proporcionar referencias a algn ▷ vt (match) arbitrar en
**reference** ['rɛfrəns] n referencia; (for job application: letter) carta de recomendación; **with ~ to** (Comm: in letter) me remito a; **reference number** n número de referencia
**refill** [vt ri:'fɪl, n 'ri:fɪl] vt rellenar ▷ n repuesto, recambio
**refine** [rɪ'faɪn] vt refinar; **refined** adj (person) fino; **refinery** n refinería
**reflect** [rɪ'flɛkt] vt reflejar ▷ vi (think): **it ~s badly/well on him** le perjudica/le hace honor; **reflection** [-'flɛkʃən] n (act) reflexión f; (image) reflejo;

(criticism) crítica; **on reflection** pensándolo bien
**reflex** ['ri:flɛks] adj, n reflejo
**reform** [rɪ'fɔ:m] n reforma ▷ vt reformar
**refrain** [rɪ'freɪn] vi: **to ~ from doing** abstenerse de hacer ▷ n estribillo
**refresh** [rɪ'frɛʃ] vt refrescar; **refreshing** adj refrescante; **refreshments** npl refrescos mpl
**refrigerator** [rɪ'frɪdʒəreɪtə*] n frigorífico (SP), nevera (SP), refrigerador m (LAM), heladera (RPL)
**refuel** [ri:'fjuəl] vi repostar (combustible)
**refuge** ['rɛfju:dʒ] n refugio, asilo; **to take ~ in** refugiarse en; **refugee** [rɛfju'dʒi:] n refugiado/a
**refund** [n 'ri:fʌnd, vb ri'fʌnd] n reembolso ▷ vt devolver, reembolsar
**refurbish** [ri:'fə:bɪʃ] vt restaurar, renovar
**refusal** [rɪ'fju:zəl] n negativa; **to have first ~ on** tener la primera opción a
**refuse**[1] ['rɛfju:s] n basura
**refuse**[2] [rɪ'fju:z] vt rechazar; (invitation) declinar; (permission) denegar ▷ vi: **to ~ to do sth** negarse a hacer algo; (horse) rehusar
**regain** [rɪ'geɪn] vt recobrar, recuperar
**regard** [rɪ'gɑ:d] n mirada; (esteem) respeto; (attention) consideración f ▷ vt (consider) considerar; **to give one's ~s to** saludar de su parte a; **"with kindest ~s"** "con muchos recuerdos"; **as ~s, with ~ to** con respecto a, en cuanto a; **regarding** prep con respecto a, en cuanto a; **regardless** adv a pesar de todo; **regardless of** sin reparar en
**regenerate** [rɪ'dʒɛnəreɪt] vt regenerar
**reggae** ['rɛgeɪ] n reggae m
**regiment** ['rɛdʒɪmənt] n regimiento
**region** ['ri:dʒən] n región f; **in the ~ of** (fig) alrededor de; **regional** adj regional
**register** ['rɛdʒɪstə*] n registro ▷ vt registrar; (birth) declarar; (car) matricular; (letter) certificar; (instrument) marcar, indicar ▷ vi (at hotel) registrarse; (as student) matricularse; (make impression) producir impresión; **registered** adj (letter, parcel) certificado
**registrar** ['rɛdʒɪstrɑ:*] n secretario/a (del registro civil)
**registration** [rɛdʒɪs'treɪʃən] n (act) declaración f; (Aut: also: ~ number) matrícula
**registry office** ['rɛdʒɪstrɪ-] (BRIT) n registro civil; **to get married in a ~** casarse por lo civil
**regret** [rɪ'grɛt] n sentimiento, pesar m ▷ vt sentir, lamentar; **regrettable** adj lamentable
**regular** ['rɛgjulə*] adj regular; (soldier)

profesional; (*usual*) habitual; (: *doctor*) de cabecera ▷ n (*client etc*) cliente/a m/f habitual; **regularly** adv con regularidad; (*often*) repetidas veces

**regulate** ['regjuleıt] vt controlar; **regulation** [-'leıʃən] n (*rule*) regla, reglamento

**rehabilitation** ['ri:əbılı'teıʃən] n rehabilitación f

**rehearsal** [rı'hə:səl] n ensayo

**rehearse** [rı'hə:s] vt ensayar

**reign** [reın] n reinado; (*fig*) predominio ▷ vi reinar; (*fig*) imperar

**reimburse** [ri:ım'bə:s] vt reembolsar

**rein** [reın] n (*for horse*) rienda

**reincarnation** [ri:ınkɑ:'neıʃən] n reencarnación f

**reindeer** ['reındıə*] n inv reno

**reinforce** [ri:ın'fɔ:s] vt reforzar; **reinforcements** npl (*Mil*) refuerzos mpl

**reinstate** [ri:ın'steıt] vt reintegrar; (*tax, law*) reinstaurar

**reject** [n 'ri:dʒɛkt, vb rı'dʒɛkt] n (*thing*) desecho ▷ vt rechazar; (*suggestion*) descartar; (*coin*) expulsar; **rejection** [rı'dʒɛkʃən] n rechazo

**rejoice** [rı'dʒɔıs] vi: to ~ at or over regocijarse or alegrarse de

**relate** [rı'leıt] vt (*tell*) contar, relatar; (*connect*) relacionar ▷ vi relacionarse; **related** adj afín; (*person*) emparentado; **related to** (*subject*) relacionado con; **relating to** prep referente a

**relation** [rı'leıʃən] n (*person*) familiar mf, pariente mf; (*link*) relación f; **relations** npl (*relatives*) familiares mpl: **relationship** n relación f; (*personal*) relaciones fpl; (*also*: **family relationship**) parentesco

**relative** ['relətıv] n pariente mf, familiar mf ▷ adj relativo; **relatively** adv (*comparatively*) relativamente

**relax** [rı'læks] vi descansar; (*unwind*) relajarse ▷ vt (*one's grip*) soltar, aflojar; (*control*) relajar; (*mind, person*) descansar; **relaxation** [ri:læk'seıʃən] n descanso; (*of rule, control*) relajamiento; (*entertainment*) diversión f; **relaxed** adj relajado; (*tranquil*) tranquilo; **relaxing** adj relajante

**relay** ['ri:leı] n (*race*) carrera de relevos ▷ vt (*Radio, TV*) retransmitir

**release** [rı'li:s] n (*liberation*) liberación f; (*from prison*) puesta en libertad; (*of gas etc*) escape m; (*of film etc*) estreno; (*of record*) lanzamiento ▷ vt (*prisoner*) poner en libertad; (*gas*) despedir, arrojar; (*from wreckage*) soltar; (*catch, spring etc*) desenganchar; (*film*) estrenar; (*book*) publicar; (*news*) difundir

**relegate** ['reləgeıt] vt relegar; (*BRIT Sport*): to be ~d to bajar a

**relent** [rı'lent] vi ablandarse; **relentless** adj implacable

**relevant** ['reləvənt] adj (*fact*) pertinente; ~ to relacionado con

**reliable** [rı'laıəbl] adj (*person, firm*) de confianza, de fiar; (*method, machine*) seguro; (*source*) fidedigno

**relic** ['relık] n (*Rel*) reliquia; (*of the past*) vestigio

**relief** [rı'li:f] n (*from pain, anxiety*) alivio; (*help, supplies*) socorro, ayuda; (*Art, Geo*) relieve m

**relieve** [rı'li:v] vt (*pain*) aliviar; (*bring help to*) ayudar, socorrer; (*take over from*) sustituir; (: *guard*) relevar; to ~ sb of sth quitar algo a algn; to ~ o.s. hacer sus necesidades; **relieved** adj: to be relieved sentir un gran alivio

**religion** [rı'lıdʒən] n religión f

**religious** [rı'lıdʒəs] adj religioso; **religious education** n educación f religiosa

**relish** ['relıʃ] n (*Culin*) salsa; (*enjoyment*) entusiasmo ▷ vt (*food etc*) saborear; (*enjoy*): to ~ sth hacerle mucha ilusión a algn algo

**relocate** [ri:ləu'keıt] vt cambiar de lugar, mudar ▷ vi mudarse

**reluctance** [rı'lʌktəns] n renuencia

**reluctant** [rı'lʌktənt] adj renuente; **reluctantly** adv de mala gana

**rely on** [rı'laı-] vt fus depender de; (*trust*) contar con

**remain** [rı'meın] vi (*survive*) quedar; (*be left*) sobrar; (*continue*) quedar(se), permanecer; **remainder** n resto; **remaining** adj que queda(n); (*surviving*) restante(s); **remains** npl restos mpl

**remand** [rı'mɑ:nd] n: on ~ detenido (bajo custodia) ▷ vt: to be ~ed in custody quedar detenido bajo custodia

**remark** [rı'mɑ:k] n comentario ▷ vt comentar; **remarkable** adj (*outstanding*) extraordinario

**remarry** [ri:'mærı] vi volver a casarse

**remedy** ['remədı] n remedio ▷ vt remediar, curar

**remember** [rı'membə*] vt recordar, acordarse de; (*bear in mind*) tener presente; (*send greetings to*): ~ me to him dale recuerdos de mi parte; **Remembrance Day** n ≈ día en el que se recuerda a los caídos en las dos guerras mundiales

● **REMEMBRANCE DAY**

● En el Reino Unido el domingo más

próximo al 11 de noviembre se conoce como **Remembrance Sunday** o **Remembrance Day**, aniversario de la firma del armisticio de 1918 que puso fin a la Primera Guerra Mundial. Ese día, a las once de la mañana (hora en que se firmó el armisticio), se recuerda a los que murieron en las dos guerras mundiales con dos minutos de silencio ante los monumentos a los caídos. Allí se colocan coronas de amapolas, flor que también se suele llevar prendida en el pecho tras pagar un donativo destinado a los inválidos de guerra.

**remind** [rɪˈmaɪnd] vt: **to ~ sb to do sth** recordar a algn que haga algo; **to ~ sb of sth** (of fact) recordar algo a algn; **she ~s me of her mother** me recuerda a su madre; **reminder** n notificación f; (memento) recuerdo

**reminiscent** [rɛmɪˈnɪsnt] adj: **to be ~ of sth** recordar algo

**remnant** [ˈrɛmnənt] n resto; (of cloth) retal m

**remorse** [rɪˈmɔːs] n remordimientos mpl

**remote** [rɪˈməut] adj (distant) lejano; (person) distante; **remote control** n telecontrol m; **remotely** adv remotamente; (slightly) levemente

**removal** [rɪˈmuːvəl] n (taking away) el quitar; (BRIT: from house) mudanza; (from office: dismissal) destitución f; (Med) extirpación f; **removal man** (irreg) n (BRIT) mozo de mudanzas; **removal van** (BRIT) n camión m de mudanzas

**remove** [rɪˈmuːv] vt quitar; (employee) destituir; (name: from list) tachar, borrar; (doubt) disipar; (abuse) suprimir, acabar con; (Med) extirpar

**Renaissance** [rɪˈneɪsɑ̃s] n: **the ~** el Renacimiento

**rename** [riːˈneɪm] vt poner nuevo nombre a

**render** [ˈrɛndə*] vt (thanks) dar; (aid) proporcionar, prestar; (make): **to ~ sth useless** hacer algo inútil

**rendezvous** [ˈrɒndɪvuː] n cita

**renew** [rɪˈnjuː] vt renovar; (resume) reanudar; (loan etc) prorrogar

**renovate** [ˈrɛnəveɪt] vt renovar

**renowned** [rɪˈnaund] adj renombrado

**rent** [rɛnt] n (for house) arriendo, renta ▷ vt alquilar; **rental** n (for television, car) alquiler m

**reorganize** [riːˈɔːgənaɪz] vt reorganizar

**rep** [rɛp] n abbr = **representative**

**repair** [rɪˈpɛə*] n reparación f, compostura ▷ vt reparar, componer; (shoes) remendar; **in good/bad ~** en buen/mal estado; **repair kit** n caja de herramientas

**repay** [riːˈpeɪ] vt (money) devolver, reembolsar; (person) pagar; (debt) liquidar; (sb's efforts) devolver, corresponder a; **repayment** n reembolso, devolución f; (sum of money) recompensa

**repeat** [rɪˈpiːt] n (Radio, TV) reposición f ▷ vt repetir ▷ vi repetirse; **repeatedly** adv repetidas veces; **repeat prescription** n (BRIT) receta renovada

**repellent** [rɪˈpɛlənt] adj repugnante ▷ n: **insect ~** crema or loción f anti-insectos

**repercussions** [riːpəˈkʌʃənz] npl consecuencias fpl

**repetition** [rɛpɪˈtɪʃən] n repetición f

**repetitive** [rɪˈpɛtɪtɪv] adj repetitivo

**replace** [rɪˈpleɪs] vt (put back) devolver a su sitio; (take the place) reemplazar, sustituir; **replacement** n (act) reposición f; (thing) recambio; (person) suplente mf

**replay** [ˈriːpleɪ] n (Sport) desempate m; (of tape, film) repetición f

**replica** [ˈrɛplɪkə] n copia, reproducción f (exacta)

**reply** [rɪˈplaɪ] n respuesta, contestación f ▷ vi contestar, responder

**report** [rɪˈpɔːt] n informe m; (Press etc) reportaje m; (BRIT: also: **school ~**) boletín m escolar; (of gun) estallido ▷ vt informar de; (Press etc) hacer un reportaje sobre; (notify: accident, culprit) denunciar ▷ vi (make a report) presentar un informe; (present o.s.): **to ~ (to sb)** presentarse (ante algn); **report card** n (US, SCOTTISH) cartilla escolar; **reportedly** adv según se dice; **reporter** n periodista mf

**represent** [rɛprɪˈzɛnt] vt representar; (Comm) ser agente de; (describe): **to ~ sth as** describir algo como; **representation** [-ˈteɪʃən] n representación f; **representative** n representante mf; (US Pol) diputado/a m/f ▷ adj representativo

**repress** [rɪˈprɛs] vt reprimir; **repression** [-ˈprɛʃən] n represión f

**reprimand** [ˈrɛprɪmɑːnd] n reprimenda ▷ vt reprender

**reproduce** [riːprəˈdjuːs] vt reproducir ▷ vi reproducirse; **reproduction** [-ˈdʌkʃən] n reproducción f

**reptile** [ˈrɛptaɪl] n reptil m

**republic** [rɪˈpʌblɪk] n república; **republican** adj, n republicano/a m/f

**reputable** [ˈrɛpjutəbl] adj (make etc) de renombre

**reputation** [rɛpjuˈteɪʃən] n reputación f

**request** [rɪˈkwɛst] n petición f; (formal)

solicitud f ▷ vt: **to ~ sth of** or **from sb** solicitar algo a algn; **request stop** (BRIT) n parada discrecional

**require** [rɪ'kwaɪə*] vt (need: person) necesitar, tener necesidad de; (: thing, situation) exigir; (want) pedir; **to ~ sb to do sth** pedir a algn que haga algo; **requirement** n requisito; (need) necesidad f

**resat** [ri:'sæt] pt, pp of **resit**

**rescue** ['rɛskjuː] n rescate m ▷ vt rescatar

**research** [rɪ'sɜːtʃ] n investigaciones fpl ▷ vt investigar

**resemblance** [rɪ'zɛmbləns] n parecido

**resemble** [rɪ'zɛmbl] vt parecerse a

**resent** [rɪ'zɛnt] vt tomar a mal; **resentful** adj resentido; **resentment** n resentimiento

**reservation** [rɛzə'veɪʃən] n reserva; **reservation desk** (US) n (in hotel) recepción f

**reserve** [rɪ'zɜːv] n reserva; (Sport) suplente mf ▷ vt (seats etc) reservar; **reserved** adj reservado

**reservoir** ['rɛzəvwɑː*] n (artificial lake) embalse m, tank; (small) depósito

**residence** ['rɛzɪdəns] n (formal: home) domicilio; (length of stay) permanencia; **residence permit** (BRIT) n permiso de permanencia

**resident** ['rɛzɪdənt] n (of area) vecino/a; (in hotel) huésped mf ▷ adj (population) permanente; (doctor) residente; **residential** [-'dɛnʃəl] adj residencial

**residue** ['rɛzɪdjuː] n resto

**resign** [rɪ'zaɪn] vt renunciar a ▷ vi dimitir; **to ~ o.s. to** (situation) resignarse a; **resignation** [rɛzɪg'neɪʃən] n dimisión f; (state of mind) resignación f

**resin** ['rɛzɪn] n resina

**resist** [rɪ'zɪst] vt resistir, oponerse a; **resistance** n resistencia

**resit** ['riːsɪt] (BRIT) (pt, pp **resat**) vt (exam) volver a presentarse a; (subject) recuperar, volver a examinarse de (SP)

**resolution** [rɛzə'luːʃən] n resolución f

**resolve** [rɪ'zɔlv] n resolución f ▷ vt resolver ▷ vi: **to ~ to do** resolver hacer

**resort** [rɪ'zɔːt] n (town) centro turístico; (recourse) recurso ▷ vi: **to ~ to** recurrir a; **in the last ~** como último recurso

**resource** [rɪ'sɔːs] n recurso; **resourceful** adj despabilado, ingenioso

**respect** [rɪs'pɛkt] n respeto ▷ vt respetar; **respectable** adj respetable; (large: amount) apreciable; (passable) tolerable; **respectful** adj respetuoso; **respective** adj respectivo; **respectively** adv respectivamente

**respite** ['rɛspaɪt] n respiro

**respond** [rɪs'pɔnd] vi responder; (react) reaccionar; **response** [-'pɔns] n respuesta; reacción f

**responsibility** [rɪspɔnsɪ'bɪlɪtɪ] n responsabilidad f

**responsible** [rɪs'pɔnsɪbl] adj (character) serio, formal; (job) de confianza; (liable): **~ (for)** responsable (de); **responsibly** adv con seriedad

**responsive** [rɪs'pɔnsɪv] adj sensible

**rest** [rɛst] n descanso, reposo; (Mus. pause) pausa, silencio; (support) apoyo; (remainder) resto ▷ vi descansar; (be supported): **to ~ on** descansar sobre ▷ vt: **to ~ sth on/against** apoyar algo en or sobre/contra; **the ~ of them** (people, objects) los demás; **it ~s with him to ...** depende de él el que ...

**restaurant** ['rɛstərɔŋ] n restaurante m; **restaurant car** (BRIT) n (Rail) coche-comedor m

**restless** ['rɛstlɪs] adj inquieto

**restoration** [rɛstə'reɪʃən] n restauración f; devolución f

**restore** [rɪ'stɔː*] vt (building) restaurar; (sth stolen) devolver; (health) restablecer; (to power) volver a poner a

**restrain** [rɪs'treɪn] vt (feeling) contener, refrenar; (person): **to ~ (from doing)** disuadir (de hacer); **restraint** n (restriction) restricción f; (moderation) moderación f; (of manner) reserva

**restrict** [rɪs'trɪkt] vt restringir, limitar; **restriction** [-kʃən] n restricción f, limitación f

**rest room** (US) n aseos mpl

**restructure** [riː'strʌktʃə*] vt reestructurar

**result** [rɪ'zʌlt] n resultado ▷ vi: **to ~ in** terminar en, tener por resultado; **as a ~ of** a consecuencia de

**resume** [rɪ'zjuːm] vt reanudar ▷ vi comenzar de nuevo

> ▌ Be careful not to translate **resume** by the Spanish word *resumir*.

**résumé** ['reɪzjuːmeɪ] n resumen m; (US) currículum m

**resuscitate** [rɪ'sʌsɪteɪt] vt (Med) resucitar

**retail** ['riːteɪl] adj, adv al por menor; **retailer** n detallista mf

**retain** [rɪ'teɪn] vt (keep) retener, conservar

**retaliation** [rɪtælɪ'eɪʃən] n represalias fpl

**retarded** [rɪ'tɑːdɪd] adj retrasado

**retire** [rɪ'taɪə*] vi (give up work) jubilarse; (withdraw) retirarse; (go to bed) acostarse; **retired** adj (person) jubilado; **retirement** n (giving up work: state) retiro; (: act) jubilación f

**retort** [rɪ'tɔ:t] vi contestar
**retreat** [rɪ'tri:t] n (place) retiro; (Mil) retirada ▷ vi retirarse
**retrieve** [rɪ'tri:v] vt recobrar; (situation, honour) salvar; (Comput) recuperar; (error) reparar
**retrospect** ['retrəspekt] n: **in ~** retrospectivamente; **retrospective** [-'spektɪv] adj retrospectivo; (law) retroactivo
**return** [rɪ'tə:n] n (going or coming back) vuelta, regreso; (of sth stolen etc) devolución f; (Finance: from land, shares) ganancia, ingresos mpl ▷ cpd (journey) de regreso; (BRIT: ticket) de ida y vuelta; (match) de vuelta ▷ vi (person etc: come or go back) volver, regresar; (symptoms etc) reaparecer; (regain): **to ~ to** recuperar ▷ vt devolver; (favour, love etc) corresponder a; (verdict) pronunciar; (Pol: candidate) elegir; **returns** npl (Comm) ingresos mpl; **in ~ (for)** a cambio (de); **by ~ of post** a vuelta de correo; **many happy ~s (of the day)!** ¡feliz cumpleaños!; **return ticket** n (esp BRIT) billete m (SP) or boleto m (LAM) de ida y vuelta, billete m redondo (MEX)
**reunion** [ri:'ju:nɪən] n (of family) reunión f; (of two people, school) reencuentro
**reunite** [ri:ju:'naɪt] vt reunir; (reconcile) reconciliar
**revamp** [ri:'væmp] vt renovar
**reveal** [rɪ'vi:l] vt revelar; **revealing** adj revelador(a)
**revel** ['revl] vi: **to ~ in sth/in doing sth** gozar de algo/con hacer algo
**revelation** [revə'leɪʃən] n revelación f
**revenge** [rɪ'vendʒ] n venganza; **to take ~ on** vengarse de
**revenue** ['revənju:] n ingresos mpl, rentas fpl
**Reverend** ['revərənd] adj (in titles): **the ~ John Smith** (Anglican) el Reverendo John Smith; (Catholic) el Padre John Smith; (Protestant) el Pastor John Smith
**reversal** [rɪ'və:sl] n (of order) inversión f; (of direction, policy) cambio; (of decision) revocación f
**reverse** [rɪ'və:s] n (opposite) contrario; (back: of cloth) revés m; (: of coin) reverso; (: of paper) dorso; (Aut: also: **~ gear**) marcha atrás, revés m ▷ adj (order) inverso; (direction) contrario; (process) opuesto ▷ vt (decision, Aut) dar marcha atrás a; (position, function) invertir ▷ vi (BRIT Aut) dar marcha atrás; **reverse-charge call** (BRIT) n llamada a cobro revertido; **reversing lights** (BRIT) npl (Aut) luces fpl de retroceso
**revert** [rɪ'və:t] vi: **to ~ to** volver a

**review** [rɪ'vju:] n (magazine, Mil) revista; (of book, film) reseña; (US: examination) repaso, examen m ▷ vt repasar, examinar; (Mil) pasar revista a; (book, film) reseñar
**revise** [rɪ'vaɪz] vt (manuscript) corregir; (opinion) modificar; (price, procedure) revisar ▷ vi (study) repasar; **revision** [rɪ'vɪʒən] n corrección f; modificación f; (for exam) repaso
**revival** [rɪ'vaɪvəl] n (recovery) reanimación f; (of interest) renacimiento; (Theatre) reestreno; (of faith) despertar m
**revive** [rɪ'vaɪv] vt resucitar; (custom) restablecer; (hope) despertar; (play) reestrenar ▷ vi (person) volver en sí; (business) reactivarse
**revolt** [rɪ'vəult] n rebelión f ▷ vi rebelarse, sublevarse ▷ vt dar asco a, repugnar; **revolting** adj asqueroso, repugnante
**revolution** [revə'lu:ʃən] n revolución f; **revolutionary** adj, n revolucionario/a m/f
**revolve** [rɪ'vɔlv] vi dar vueltas, girar; (life, discussion): **to ~ (a)round** girar en torno a
**revolver** [rɪ'vɔlvə*] n revólver m
**reward** [rɪ'wɔ:d] n premio, recompensa ▷ vt: **to ~ (for)** recompensar or premiar (por); **rewarding** adj (fig) valioso
**rewind** [ri:'waɪnd] vt rebobinar
**rewritable** [ri:'raɪtəbl] adj (CD, DVD) reescribible
**rewrite** [ri:'raɪt] (pt **rewrote**, pp **rewritten**) vt reescribir
**rheumatism** ['ru:mətɪzəm] n reumatismo, reúma m
**rhinoceros** [raɪ'nɔsərəs] n rinoceronte m
**rhubarb** ['ru:ba:b] n ruibarbo
**rhyme** [raɪm] n rima; (verse) poesía
**rhythm** ['rɪðm] n ritmo
**rib** [rɪb] n (Anat) costilla ▷ vt (mock) tomar el pelo a
**ribbon** ['rɪbən] n cinta; **in ~s** (torn) hecho trizas
**rice** [raɪs] n arroz m; **rice pudding** n arroz m con leche
**rich** [rɪtʃ] adj rico; (soil) fértil; (food) pesado; (: sweet) empalagoso; (abundant): **~ in** (minerals etc) rico en
**rid** [rɪd] (pt, pp **~**) vt: **to ~ sb of sth** librar a algn de algo; **to get ~ of** deshacerse or desembarazarse de
**riddle** ['rɪdl] n (puzzle) acertijo; (mystery) enigma m, misterio ▷ vt: **to be ~d with** ser lleno or plagado de
**ride** [raɪd] (pt **rode**, pp **ridden**) n paseo; (distance covered) viaje m, recorrido ▷ vi (as sport) montar; (go somewhere: on horse, bicycle) dar un paseo, pasearse; (travel: on bicycle, motorcycle, bus) viajar ▷ vt (a horse)

montar a; (a bicycle, motorcycle) andar en; (distance) recorrer; **to take sb for a ~** (fig) engañar a algn; **rider** n (on horse) jinete mf; (on bicycle) ciclista mf; (on motorcycle) motociclista mf

**ridge** [rɪdʒ] n (of hill) cresta; (of roof) caballete m; (wrinkle) arruga

**ridicule** ['rɪdɪkjuːl] n irrisión f, burla ▷ vt poner en ridículo, burlarse de; **ridiculous** [-'dɪkjuləs] adj ridículo

**riding** ['raɪdɪŋ] n equitación f; **I like ~** me gusta montar a caballo; **riding school** n escuela de equitación

**rife** [raɪf] adj: **to be ~** ser muy común; **to be ~ with** abundar en

**rifle** ['raɪfl] n rifle m, fusil m ▷ vt saquear

**rift** [rɪft] n (in clouds) claro; (fig: disagreement) desavenencia

**rig** [rɪg] n (also: **oil ~**: at sea) plataforma petrolera ▷ vt (election etc) amañar

**right** [raɪt] adj (correct) correcto, exacto; (suitable) indicado, debido; (proper) apropiado; (just) justo; (morally good) bueno; (not left) derecho ▷ n bueno; (title, claim) derecho; (not left) derecha ▷ adv bien, correctamente; (not left) a la derecha; (exactly): **~ now** ahora mismo ▷ vt enderezar; (correct) corregir ▷ excl ¡bueno!, ¡está bien!; **to be ~** (person) tener razón; (answer) ser correcto; **is that the ~ time?** (of clock) ¿es esa la hora buena?; **by ~s** en justicia; **on the ~** a la derecha; **to be in the ~** tener razón; **~ away** en seguida; **~ in the middle** exactamente en el centro; **right angle** n ángulo recto; **rightful** adj legítimo; **right-hand** adj: **right-hand drive** conducción f por la derecha; **the right-hand side** derecha; **right-handed** adj diestro; **rightly** adv correctamente, debidamente; (with reason) con razón; **right of way** n (on path etc) derecho de paso; (Aut) prioridad f; **right-wing** adj (Pol) derechista

**rigid** ['rɪdʒɪd] adj rígido; (person, ideas) inflexible

**rigorous** ['rɪgərəs] adj riguroso

**rim** [rɪm] n borde m; (of spectacles) aro; (of wheel) llanta

**rind** [raɪnd] n (of bacon) corteza; (of lemon etc) cáscara; (of cheese) costra

**ring** [rɪŋ] (pt **rang**, pp **rung**) n (of metal) aro; (on finger) anillo; (of people) corro; (of objects) círculo; (gang) banda; (for boxing) cuadrilátero; (of circus) pista; (bull ring) ruedo, plaza; (sound of bell) toque m ▷ vi (on telephone) llamar por teléfono; (bell) repicar; (doorbell, phone) sonar; (also: **~ out**) sonar; (ears) zumbar ▷ vt (BRIT Tel) llamar, telefonear; (bell etc) hacer sonar; (doorbell)

tocar; **to give sb a ~** (BRIT Tel) llamar or telefonear a algn; **ring back** (BRIT) vt, vi (Tel) devolver la llamada; **ring off** (BRIT) vi (Tel) colgar, cortar la comunicación; **ring up** (BRIT) vt (Tel) llamar, telefonear; **ringing tone** n (Tel) tono de llamada; **ringleader** n (of gang) cabecilla m; **ring road** (BRIT) n carretera periférica or de circunvalación; **ringtone** n (on mobile) tono de llamada

**rink** [rɪŋk] n (also: **ice ~**) pista de hielo

**rinse** [rɪns] n aclarado; (dye) tinte m ▷ vt aclarar; (mouth) enjuagar

**riot** ['raɪət] n motín m, disturbio ▷ vi amotinarse; **to run ~** desmandarse

**rip** [rɪp] n rasgón m, rasgadura ▷ vt rasgar, desgarrar ▷ vi rasgarse, desgarrarse; **rip off** vt (inf: cheat) estafar; **rip up** vt hacer pedazos

**ripe** [raɪp] adj maduro

**rip-off** ['rɪpɔf] n (inf): **it's a ~!** ¡es una estafa!, ¡es un timo!

**ripple** ['rɪpl] n onda, rizo; (sound) murmullo ▷ vi rizarse

**rise** [raɪz] (pt **rose**, pp **risen**) n (slope) cuesta, pendiente f; (hill) altura; (BRIT: in wages) aumento; (in prices, temperature) subida; (fig: to power etc) ascenso ▷ vi subir; (waters) crecer; (sun, moon) salir; (person: from bed etc) levantarse; (also: **~ up**: rebel) sublevarse; (in rank) ascender; **to give ~ to** dar lugar or origen a; **to ~ to the occasion** ponerse a la altura de las circunstancias; **risen** ['rɪzn] pp of **rise**; **rising** adj (increasing: number) creciente; (: prices) en aumento or alza; (tide) creciente; (sun, moon) naciente

**risk** [rɪsk] n riesgo, peligro ▷ vt arriesgar; (run the risk of) exponerse a; **to take** or **run the ~ of doing** correr el riesgo de hacer; **at ~** en peligro; **at one's own ~** bajo su propia responsabilidad; **risky** adj arriesgado, peligroso

**rite** [raɪt] n rito; **last ~s** exequias fpl

**ritual** ['rɪtjuəl] adj ritual ▷ n ritual m, rito

**rival** ['raɪvl] n rival mf; (in business) competidor(a) m/f ▷ adj rival, opuesto ▷ vt competir con; **rivalry** n competencia

**river** ['rɪvə*] n río ▷ cpd (port) de río; (traffic) fluvial; **up/down ~** río arriba/abajo; **riverbank** n orilla (del río)

**rivet** ['rɪvɪt] n roblón m, remache m ▷ vt (fig) captar

**road** [rəud] n camino; (motorway etc) carretera; (in town) calle f ▷ cpd (accident) de tráfico; **major/minor ~** carretera principal/ secundaria; **roadblock** n barricada; **road map** n mapa m de carreteras; **road rage** n agresividad en la carretera; **road safety** n seguridad *f* vial; **roadside** *n* borde *m* (del camino); **roadsign** *n* señal *f* de tráfico; **road tax** *n* (BRIT) impuesto de rodaje; **roadworks** *npl* obras *fpl*

**roam** [rəum] *vi* vagar

**roar** [rɔː*] *n* rugido; (*of vehicle, storm*) estruendo; (*of laughter*) carcajada ▷ *vi* rugir; hacer estruendo; **to ~ with laughter** reírse a carcajadas; **to do a ~ing trade** hacer buen negocio

**roast** [rəust] *n* carne *f* asada, asado ▷ *vt* asar; (*coffee*) tostar; **roast beef** *n* rosbif *m*

**rob** [rɔb] *vt* robar; **to ~ sb of sth** robar algo a algn; (*fig: deprive*) quitar algo a algn; **robber** *n* ladrón/ona *m/f*; **robbery** *n* robo

**robe** [rəub] *n* (*for ceremony etc*) toga; (*also:* **bath~**) albornoz *m*

**robin** ['rɔbɪn] *n* petirrojo

**robot** ['rəubɔt] *n* robot *m*

**robust** [rəu'bʌst] *adj* robusto, fuerte

**rock** [rɔk] *n* roca; (*boulder*) peña, peñasco; (*us: small stone*) piedrecita; (BRIT: *sweet*) ≈ pirulí ▷ *vt* (*swing gently: cradle*) balancear, mecer; (: *child*) arrullar; (*shake*) sacudir ▷ *vi* mecerse, balancearse; sacudirse; **on the ~s** (*drink*) con hielo; (*marriage etc*) en ruinas; **rock and roll** *n* rocanrol *m*; **rock climbing** *n* (*Sport*) escalada

**rocket** ['rɔkɪt] *n* cohete *m*; **rocking chair** ['rɔkɪŋ-] *n* mecedora

**rocky** ['rɔkɪ] *adj* rocoso

**rod** [rɔd] *n* vara, varilla; (*also:* **fishing ~**) caña

**rode** [rəud] *pt of* **ride**

**rodent** ['rəudnt] *n* roedor *m*

**rogue** [rəug] *n* pícaro, pillo

**role** [rəul] *n* papel *m*; **role-model** *n* modelo a imitar

**roll** [rəul] *n* rollo; (*of bank notes*) fajo; (*also:* **bread ~**) panecillo; (*register, list*) lista, nómina; (*sound of drums etc*) redoble *m* ▷ *vt* hacer rodar; (*also:* **~ up:** *string*) enrollar; (*cigarette*) liar; (*also:* **~ out:** *pastry*) aplanar; (*flatten: road, lawn*) apisonar ▷ *vi* rodar; (*drum*) redoblar; (*ship*) balancearse; **roll over** *vi* dar una vuelta; **roll up** *vi* (*inf: arrive*) aparecer ▷ *vt* (*carpet*) arrollar; (: *sleeves*) arremangar; **roller** *n* rodillo; (*wheel*) rueda; (*for road*) apisonadora; (*for hair*) rulo; **Rollerblades®** *npl* patines *mpl* en línea; **roller coaster** *n* montaña rusa; **roller skates** *npl* patines *mpl* de rueda; **roller-skating** *n* patinaje sobre ruedas; **to go roller-skating** ir a patinar (*sobre ruedas*); **rolling pin** *n* rodillo (de cocina)

**ROM** [rɔm] *n abbr* (*Comput: = read only memory*) ROM *f*

**Roman** ['rəumən] (*irreg*) *adj* romano/a;

**Roman Catholic** (*irreg*) *adj, n* católico/a *m/f* (romano/a)

**romance** [rə'mæns] *n* (*love affair*) amor *m*; (*charm*) lo romántico; (*novel*) novela de amor

**Romania** *etc* [ruː'meɪnɪə] *n* = **Rumania** *etc*

**Roman numeral** *n* número romano

**romantic** [rə'mæntɪk] *adj* romántico

**Rome** [rəum] *n* Roma

**roof** [ruːf] (*pl* **~s**) *n* techo; (*of house*) techo, tejado ▷ *vt* techar, poner techo a; **the ~ of the mouth** el paladar; **roof rack** *n* (Aut) baca, portaequipajes *m inv*

**rook** [ruk] *n* (*bird*) graja; (*Chess*) torre *f*

**room** [ruːm] *n* cuarto, habitación *f*; (*also:* **bed~**) dormitorio, recámara (MEX), pieza (sc); (*in school etc*) sala; (*space, scope*) sitio, cabida; **roommate** *n* compañero/a de cuarto; **room service** *n* servicio de habitaciones; **roomy** *adj* espacioso; (*garment*) amplio

**rooster** ['ruːstə*] *n* gallo

**root** [ruːt] *n* raíz *f* ▷ *vi* arraigarse

**rope** [rəup] *n* cuerda; (*Naut*) cable *m* ▷ *vt* (*tie*) atar or amarrar con (una) cuerda; (*climbers: also:* **~ together**) encordarse; (*an area: also:* **~ off**) acordonar; **to know the ~s** (*fig*) conocer los trucos (del oficio)

**rose** [rəuz] *pt of* **rise** ▷ *n* (*shrub*) rosal *m*; (*on watering can*) roseta

**rosé** ['rəuzeɪ] *n* vino rosado

**rosemary** ['rəuzmərɪ] *n* romero

**rosy** ['rəuzɪ] *adj* rosado, sonrosado; **a ~ future** un futuro prometedor

**rot** [rɔt] *n* podredumbre *f*; (*fig: pej*) tonterías *fpl* ▷ *vt* pudrir ▷ *vi* pudrirse

**rota** ['rəutə] *n* (*sistema m de*) turnos *m*

**rotate** [rəu'teɪt] *vt* (*revolve*) hacer girar, dar vueltas a; (*jobs*) alternar ▷ *vi* girar, dar vueltas

**rotten** ['rɔtn] *adj* podrido; (*dishonest*) corrompido; (*inf: bad*) pocho; **to feel ~** (*ill*) sentirse fatal

**rough** [rʌf] *adj* (*skin, surface*) áspero; (*terrain*) quebrado; (*road*) desigual; (*voice*) bronco; (*person, manner*) tosco, grosero; (*weather*) borrascoso; (*treatment*) brutal; (*sea*) picado; (*town, area*) peligroso; (*cloth*) basto; (*plan*) preliminar; (*guess*) aproximado ▷ *n* (*Golf*): **in the ~** en las hierbas altas; **to ~ it** vivir sin comodidades; **to sleep ~** (BRIT) pasar la noche al raso; **roughly** *adv* (*handle*) torpemente; (*make*) toscamente; (*speak*) groseramente; (*approximately*) aproximadamente

**roulette** [ruː'let] *n* ruleta

**round** [raund] *adj* redondo ▷ *n* círculo; (BRIT: *of toast*) rebanada; (*of policeman*) ronda; (*of milkman*) recorrido; (*of doctor*)

visitas *fpl*; (*game: of cards, in competition*)
partida; (*of ammunition*) cartucho; (*Boxing*)
asalto; (*of talks*) ronda ▷ *vt* (*corner*) doblar
▷ *prep* alrededor de; (*surrounding*): **~ his
neck/the table** en su cuello/alrededor de
la mesa; (*in a circular movement*): **to move ~
the room/sail ~ the world** dar una vuelta a
la habitación/circunnavegar el mundo; (*in
various directions*): **to move ~ a room/house**
moverse por toda la habitación/casa;
(*approximately*): **all (the) year ~** durante
todo el año; **it's just ~ the corner** (*fig*) está
a la vuelta de la esquina; **~ the clock** *adv* las
24 horas; **to go ~ to sb's (house)** ir a casa
de algn; **to go ~ the back** pasar por atrás;
**enough to go ~** bastante (para todos); **a ~
of applause** una salva de aplausos; **a ~ of
drinks/sandwiches** una ronda de bebidas/
bocadillos; **round off** *vt* (*speech etc*) acabar,
poner término a; **round up** *vt* (*cattle*)
acorralar; (*people*) reunir; (*price*) redondear;
**roundabout** (*BRIT*) *n* (*Aut*) isleta; (*at fair*)
tiovivo ▷ *adj* (*route, means*) indirecto; **round
trip** *n* viaje *m* de ida y vuelta; **roundup**
*n* rodeo; (*of criminals*) redada; (*of news*)
resumen *m*

**rouse** [rauz] *vt* (*wake up*) despertar; (*stir
up*) suscitar

**route** [ru:t] *n* ruta, camino; (*of bus*)
recorrido; (*of shipping*) derrota

**routine** [ru:'ti:n] *adj* rutinario ▷ *n* rutina;
(*Theatre*) número

**row¹** [rəu] *n* (*line*) fila, hilera; (*Knitting*)
pasada ▷ *vi* (*in boat*) remar ▷ *vt* conducir
remando; **4 days in a ~** 4 días seguidos

**row²** [rau] *n* (*racket*) escándalo; (*dispute*)
bronca, pelea; (*scolding*) regaño ▷ *vi*
pelear(se)

**rowboat** ['rəubəut] (*US*) = **rowing boat**

**rowing** ['rəuɪŋ] *n* remo; **rowing boat**
(*BRIT*) *n* bote *m* de remos

**royal** ['rɔɪəl] *adj* real; **royalty** *n* (*royal
persons*) familia real; (*payment to author*)
derechos *mpl* de autor

**rpm** *abbr* (= *revs per minute*) r.p.m.

**R.S.V.P.** *abbr* (= *répondez s'il vous plaît*) SRC

**Rt. Hon.** *abbr* (*BRIT*) (= *Right Honourable*)
título honorífico de diputado

**rub** [rʌb] *vt* frotar; (*scrub*) restregar ▷ *n*: **to
give sth a ~** frotar algo; **to ~ sb up** *or* **~ sb**
(*US*) **the wrong way** entrañar a algn por mal
ojo; **rub in** *vt* (*ointment*) aplicar frotando;
**rub off** *vi* desteñirse; **rub out** *vt* borrar

**rubber** ['rʌbə*] *n* caucho, goma;
(*BRIT: eraser*) goma de borrar; **rubber band** *n*
goma, gomita; **rubber gloves** *npl* guantes
*mpl* de goma

**rubbish** ['rʌbɪʃ] (*BRIT*) *n* basura; (*waste*)
desperdicios *mpl*; (*fig: pej*) tonterías *fpl*; (*junk*)
pacotilla; **rubbish bin** (*BRIT*) *n* cubo o bote
*m* (*MEX*) *or* tacho (*SC*) de la basura; **rubbish
dump** (*BRIT*) *n* vertedero, basurero

**rubble** ['rʌbl] *n* escombros *mpl*

**ruby** ['ru:bɪ] *n* rubí *m*

**rucksack** ['rʌksæk] *n* mochila

**rudder** ['rʌdə*] *n* timón *m*

**rude** [ru:d] *adj* (*impolite: person*) mal
educado; (*: word, manners*) grosero; (*crude*)
crudo; (*indecent*) indecente

**ruffle** ['rʌfl] *vt* (*hair*) despeinar; (*clothes*)
arrugar; **to get ~d** (*fig: person*) alterarse

**rug** [rʌg] *n* alfombra; (*BRIT: blanket*) manta

**rugby** ['rʌgbɪ] *n* rugby *m*

**rugged** ['rʌgɪd] *adj* (*landscape*)
accidentado; (*features*) robusto

**ruin** ['ru:ɪn] *n* ruina ▷ *vt* arruinar; (*spoil*)
estropear; **ruins** *npl* ruinas *fpl*, restos *mpl*

**rule** [ru:l] *n* (*norm*) norma, costumbre
*f*; (*regulation, ruler*) regla; (*government*)
dominio ▷ *vt* (*country, person*) gobernar
▷ *vi* gobernar; (*Law*) fallar; **as a ~** por
regla general; **rule out** *vt* excluir; **ruler** *n*
(*sovereign*) soberano; (*for measuring*) regla;
**ruling** *adj* (*party*) gobernante; (*class*)
dirigente ▷ *n* (*Law*) fallo, decisión *f*

**rum** [rʌm] *n* ron *m*

**Rumania** [ru:'meɪnɪə] *n* Rumanía;
**Rumanian** *adj* rumano/a ▷ *n* rumano/a
*m/f*; (*Ling*) rumano

**rumble** ['rʌmbl] *n* (*noise*) ruido sordo ▷ *vi*
retumbar, hacer un ruido sordo; (*stomach,
pipe*) sonar

**rumour** ['ru:mə*] (*US* **rumor**) *n* rumor *m*
▷ *vt*: **it is ~ed that ...** se rumorea que ...

**rump steak** *n* filete *m* de lomo

**run** [rʌn] (*pt* **ran**, *pp* **run**) *n* (*fast pace*): **at
a ~** corriendo; (*Sport, in tights*) carrera;
(*outing*) paseo, excursión *f*; (*distance travelled*)
trayecto; (*series*) serie *f*; (*Theatre*) temporada;
(*Ski*) pista ▷ *vt* correr; (*operate: business*)
dirigir; (*: competition, course*) organizar;
(*: hotel, house*) administrar, llevar; (*Comput*)
ejecutar; (*pass: hand*) pasar; (*Press: feature*)
publicar ▷ *vi* correr; (*work: machine*)
funcionar, marchar; (*bus, train: operate*)
circular, ir; (*: travel*) ir; (*continue: play*)
seguir; (*contract*) ser válido; (*flow: river*) fluir;
(*colours, washing*) desteñirse; (*in election*)
ser candidato; **there was a ~ on** (*meat,
tickets*) hubo mucha demanda de; **in the
long ~** a la larga; **on the ~** en fuga; **I'll ~ you
to the station** te llevaré a la estación (en
coche); **to ~ a risk** correr un riesgo; **to ~ a
bath** llenar la bañera; **run after** *vt fus* (*to*

*catch up*) correr tras; (*chase*) perseguir; **run away** *vi* huir; **run down** *vt* (*production*) ir reduciendo; (*factory*) ir restringiendo la producción en; (*car*) atropellar; (*criticize*) criticar; **to be run down** (*person: tired*) estar debilitado; **run into** *vt fus* (*meet: person, trouble*) tropezar con; (*collide with*) chocar con; **run off** *vt* (*water*) dejar correr; (*copies*) sacar ▷ *vi* huir corriendo; **run out** *vi* (*person*) salir corriendo; (*liquid*) irse; (*lease*) caducar, vencer; (*money etc*) acabarse; **run out of** *vt fus* quedar sin; **run over** *vt* (*Aut*) atropellar ▷ *vt fus* (*revise*) repasar; **run through** *vt fus* (*instructions*) repasar; **run up** *vt* (*debt*) contraer; **to run up against** (*difficulties*) tropezar con; **runaway** *adj* (*horse*) desbocado; (*truck*) sin frenos; (*child*) escapado de casa

**rung** [rʌŋ] *pp of* **ring** ▷ *n* (*of ladder*) escalón *m*, peldaño

**runner** ['rʌnə*] *n* (*in race: person*) corredor(a) *m/f*; (*: horse*) caballo; (*on sledge*) patín *m*; **runner bean** (BRIT) *n* ≈ judía verde; **runner-up** *n* subcampeón/ona *m/f*

**running** ['rʌnɪŋ] *n* (*sport*) atletismo; (*of business*) administración *f* ▷ *adj* (*water, costs*) corriente; (*commentary*) continuo; **to be in/out of the ~ for sth** tener/no tener posibilidades de ganar algo; **6 days ~** 6 días seguidos

**runny** ['rʌnɪ] *adj* fluido; (*nose, eyes*) gastante

**run-up** ['rʌnʌp] *n*: **~ to** (*election etc*) período previo a

**runway** ['rʌnweɪ] *n* (*Aviat*) pista de aterrizaje

**rupture** ['rʌptʃə*] *n* (*Med*) hernia ▷ *vt*: **to ~ o.s** causarse una hernia

**rural** ['ruərl] *adj* rural

**rush** [rʌʃ] *n* ímpetu *m*; (*hurry*) prisa; (*Comm*) demanda repentina; (*current*) corriente *f* fuerte; (*of feeling*) torrente *m*; (*Bot*) junco ▷ *vt* apresurar; (*work*) hacer de prisa ▷ *vi* correr, precipitarse; **rush hour** *n* horas *fpl* punta

**Russia** ['rʌʃə] *n* Rusia; **Russian** *adj* ruso/a ▷ *n* ruso/a *m/f*; (*Ling*) ruso

**rust** [rʌst] *n* herrumbre *f*, moho ▷ *vi* oxidarse

**rusty** ['rʌstɪ] *adj* oxidado

**ruthless** ['ruːθlɪs] *adj* despiadado

**RV** (*us*) *n abbr* = **recreational vehicle**

**rye** [raɪ] *n* centeno

# S

**Sabbath** ['sæbəθ] *n* domingo; (*Jewish*) sábado

**sabotage** ['sæbətɑːʒ] *n* sabotaje *m* ▷ *vt* sabotear

**saccharin(e)** ['sækərɪn] *n* sacarina

**sachet** ['sæʃeɪ] *n* sobrecito

**sack** [sæk] *n* (*bag*) saco, costal *m* ▷ *vt* (*dismiss*) despedir; (*plunder*) saquear; **to get the ~** ser despedido

**sacred** ['seɪkrɪd] *adj* sagrado, santo

**sacrifice** ['sækrɪfaɪs] *n* sacrificio ▷ *vt* sacrificar

**sad** [sæd] *adj* (*unhappy*) triste; (*deplorable*) lamentable

**saddle** ['sædl] *n* silla (de montar); (*of cycle*) sillín *m* ▷ *vt* (*horse*) ensillar; **to be ~d with sth** (*inf*) quedar cargado con algo

**sadistic** [sə'dɪstɪk] *adj* sádico

**sadly** ['sædlɪ] *adv* lamentablemente; **to be ~ lacking in** estar por desgracia carente de

**sadness** ['sædnɪs] *n* tristeza

**s.a.e.** *abbr* (= *stamped addressed envelope*) sobre con las propias señas de uno y con sello

**safari** [sə'fɑːrɪ] *n* safari *m*

**safe** [seɪf] *adj* (*out of danger*) fuera de peligro; (*not dangerous, sure*) seguro; (*unharmed*) ileso ▷ *n* caja de caudales, caja fuerte; **~ and sound** sano y salvo; **(just) to be on the ~ side** para mayor seguridad; **safely** *adv* seguramente, con seguridad; **to arrive safely** llegar bien; **safe sex** *n* sexo seguro *or* sin riesgo

**safety** ['seɪftɪ] *n* seguridad *f*; **safety belt** *n* cinturón *m* (de seguridad); **safety pin** *n* imperdible *m*, seguro (MEX), alfiler *m* de gancho (SC)

**saffron** ['sæfrən] *n* azafrán *m*

**sag** [sæg] *vi* aflojarse

**sage** [seɪdʒ] *n* (*herb*) salvia; (*man*) sabio

**Sagittarius** [sædʒɪ'tɛərɪəs] *n* Sagitario

**Sahara** [sə'hɑːrə] *n*: **the ~ (Desert)** el

(desierto del) Sáhara

**said** [sɛd] *pt, pp of* **say**

**sail** [seɪl] *n* (*on boat*) vela; (*trip*): **to go for a ~** dar un paseo en barco ▷ *vt* (*boat*) gobernar ▷ *vi* (*travel: ship*) navegar; (*Sport*) hacer vela; (*begin voyage*) salir; **they ~ed into Copenhagen** arribaron a Copenhague; **sailboat** (*US*) *n* = **sailing boat**; **sailing** *n* (*Sport*) vela; **to go sailing** hacer vela; **sailing boat** *n* barco de vela; **sailor** *n* marinero, marino

**saint** [seɪnt] *n* santo

**sake** [seɪk] *n*: **for the ~ of** por

**salad** [ˈsæləd] *n* ensalada; **salad cream** (BRIT) *n* (especie *f* de) mayonesa; **salad dressing** *n* aliño

**salami** [səˈlɑːmɪ] *n* salami *m*, salchichón *m*

**salary** [ˈsælərɪ] *n* sueldo

**sale** [seɪl] *n* venta; (*at reduced prices*) liquidación *f*, saldo; (*auction*) subasta; **sales** *npl* (*total amount sold*) ventas *fpl*, facturación *f*; **"for ~"** "se vende"; **on ~** en venta; **on ~ or return** (*goods*) venta por reposición; **sales assistant** (*US*), **sales clerk** *n* dependiente/a *m/f*; **salesman/woman** (*irreg*) *n* (*in shop*) dependiente/a *m/f*; **salesperson** (*irreg*) *n* vendedor(a) *m/f*, dependiente/a *m/f*; **sales rep** *n* representante *mf*, agente *mf* comercial

**saline** [ˈseɪlaɪn] *adj* salino

**saliva** [səˈlaɪvə] *n* saliva

**salmon** [ˈsæmən] *n inv* salmón *m*

**salon** [ˈsælɔn] *n* (*hairdressing salon*) peluquería; (*beauty salon*) salón *m* de belleza

**saloon** [səˈluːn] *n* (*US*) bar *m*, taberna; (BRIT Aut) coche *m* (de) turismo; (*ship's lounge*) cámara, salón *m*

**salt** [sɔlt] *n* sal *f* ▷ *vt* salar; (*put salt on*) poner sal en; **saltwater** *adj* de agua salada; **salty** *adj* salado

**salute** [səˈluːt] *n* saludo; (*of guns*) salva ▷ *vt* saludar

**salvage** [ˈsælvɪdʒ] *n* (*saving*) salvamento, recuperación *f*; (*things saved*) objetos *mpl* salvados ▷ *vt* salvar

**Salvation Army** [sælˈveɪʃən-] *n* Ejército de Salvación

**same** [seɪm] *adj* mismo ▷ *pron*: **the ~** el(la) mismo/a, los(las) mismos/as; **the ~ book as** el mismo libro que; **at the ~ time** (*at the same moment*) al mismo tiempo; (*yet*) sin embargo; **all** *or* **just the ~** sin embargo, aun así; **to do the ~ (as sb)** hacer lo mismo (que algn); **the ~ to you!** ¡igualmente!

**sample** [ˈsɑːmpl] *n* muestra ▷ *vt* (*food*) probar; (*wine*) catar

**sanction** [ˈsæŋkʃən] *n* aprobación *f* ▷ *vt* sancionar; aprobar; **sanctions** *npl* (*Pol*)

sanciones *fpl*

**sanctuary** [ˈsæŋktjuərɪ] *n* santuario; (*refuge*) asilo, refugio; (*for wildlife*) reserva

**sand** [sænd] *n* arena; (*beach*) playa ▷ *vt* (*also*: **~ down**) lijar

**sandal** [ˈsændl] *n* sandalia

**sand**: **sandbox** (*US*) *n* = **sandpit**; **sandcastle** *n* castillo de arena; **sand dune** *n* duna; **sandpaper** *n* papel *m* de lija; **sandpit** *n* (*for children*) cajón *m* de arena; **sands** *npl* playa *sg* de arena; **sandstone** [ˈsændstəun] *n* piedra arenisca

**sandwich** [ˈsændwɪtʃ] *n* sandwich *m* ▷ *vt* intercalar; **~ed between** apretujado entre; **cheese/ham ~** sandwich de queso/jamón

**sandy** [ˈsændɪ] *adj* arenoso; (*colour*) rojizo

**sane** [seɪn] *adj* cuerdo; (*sensible*) sensato

> ▌ Be careful not to translate **sane** by the Spanish word *sano*.

**sang** [sæŋ] *pt of* **sing**

**sanitary towel** (*US* **sanitary napkin**) *n* paño higiénico, compresa

**sanity** [ˈsænɪtɪ] *n* cordura; (*of judgment*) sensatez *f*

**sank** [sæŋk] *pt of* **sink**

**Santa Claus** [sæntəˈklɔːz] *n* San Nicolás, Papá Noel

**sap** [sæp] *n* (*of plants*) savia ▷ *vt* (*strength*) minar, agotar

**sapphire** [ˈsæfaɪə*] *n* zafiro

**sarcasm** [ˈsɑːkæzm] *n* sarcasmo

**sarcastic** [sɑːˈkæstɪk] *adj* sarcástico

**sardine** [sɑːˈdiːn] *n* sardina

**SASE** (*US*) *n abbr* (= *self-addressed stamped envelope*) sobre con las propias señas de uno y con sello

**Sat.** *abbr* (= *Saturday*) sáb

**sat** [sæt] *pt, pp of* **sit**

**satchel** [ˈsætʃl] *n* (*child's*) mochila, cartera (SP)

**satellite** [ˈsætəlaɪt] *n* satélite *m*; **satellite dish** *n* antena de televisión por satélite; **satellite television** *n* televisión *f* vía satélite

**satin** [ˈsætɪn] *n* raso ▷ *adj* de raso

**satire** [ˈsætaɪə*] *n* sátira

**satisfaction** [sætɪsˈfækʃən] *n* satisfacción *f*

**satisfactory** [sætɪsˈfæktərɪ] *adj* satisfactorio

**satisfied** [ˈsætɪsfaɪd] *adj* satisfecho; **to be ~ (with sth)** estar satisfecho (de algo)

**satisfy** [ˈsætɪsfaɪ] *vt* satisfacer; (*convince*) convencer

**Saturday** [ˈsætədɪ] *n* sábado

**sauce** [sɔːs] *n* salsa; (*sweet*) crema; jarabe *m*; **saucepan** *n* cacerola, olla

**saucer** [ˈsɔːsə*] *n* platillo; **Saudi Arabia** *n*

Arabia Saudí or Saudita

**sauna** ['sɔːnə] n sauna

**sausage** ['sɒsɪdʒ] n salchicha; **sausage roll** n empanadita de salchicha

**sautéed** ['səuteɪd] adj salteado

**savage** ['sævɪdʒ] adj (cruel, fierce) feroz, furioso; (primitive) salvaje ▷ n salvaje mf ▷ vt (attack) embestir

**save** [seɪv] vt (rescue) salvar, rescatar; (money, time) ahorrar; (put by, keep: seat) guardar; (Comput) salvar (y guardar); (avoid: trouble) evitar; (Sport) parar ▷ vi (also: ~ up) ahorrar ▷ n (Sport) parada ▷ prep salvo, excepto

**savings** ['seɪvɪŋz] npl ahorros mpl; **savings account** n cuenta de ahorros; **savings and loan association** (us) n sociedad f de ahorro y préstamo

**savoury** ['seɪvərɪ] (us **savory**) adj sabroso; (dish: not sweet) salado

**saw** [sɔː] (pt **-ed**, pp **-ed** or **~n**) pt of **see** ▷ n (tool) sierra ▷ vt serrar; **sawdust** n (a)serrín m

**sawn** [sɔːn] pp of **saw**

**saxophone** ['sæksəfəun] n saxófono

**say** [seɪ] (pt, pp **said**) n: **to have one's ~** expresar su opinión ▷ vt decir; **to have a** or **some ~ in sth** tener voz or tener que ver en algo; **to ~ yes/no** decir que sí/no; **could you ~ that again?** ¿podría repetir eso?; **that is to ~** es decir; **that goes without ~ing** ni que decir tiene; **saying** n dicho, refrán m

**scab** [skæb] n costra; (pej) esquirol m

**scaffolding** ['skæfəldɪŋ] n andamio, andamiaje m

**scald** [skɔːld] n escaldadura ▷ vt escaldar

**scale** [skeɪl] n (gen, Mus) escala; (of fish) escama; (of salaries, fees etc) escalafón m ▷ vt (mountain) escalar; (tree) trepar; **scales** npl (for weighing: small) balanza; (: large) báscula; **on a large ~** en gran escala; **~ of charges** tarifa, lista de precios

**scallion** ['skæljən] (us) n cebolleta

**scallop** ['skɒləp] n (Zool) venera; (Sewing) festón m

**scalp** [skælp] n cabellera ▷ vt escalpar

**scalpel** ['skælpl] n bisturí m

**scam** [skæm] n (inf) estafa, timo

**scampi** ['skæmpɪ] npl gambas fpl

**scan** [skæn] vt (examine) escudriñar; (glance at quickly) dar un vistazo a; (TV, Radar) explorar, registrar ▷ n (Med): **to have a ~** pasar por el escáner

**scandal** ['skændl] n escándalo; (gossip) chismes mpl

**Scandinavia** [skændɪ'neɪvɪə] n Escandinavia; **Scandinavian** adj, n escandinavo/a m/f

**scanner** ['skænə*] n (Radar, Med) escáner m

**scapegoat** ['skeɪpgəut] n cabeza de turco, chivo expiatorio

**scar** [skɑː] n cicatriz f; (fig) señal f ▷ vt dejar señales en

**scarce** [skɛəs] adj escaso; **to make o.s. ~** (inf) esfumarse; **scarcely** adv apenas

**scare** [skɛə*] n susto, sobresalto; (panic) pánico ▷ vt asustar, espantar; **to ~ sb stiff** dar a algn un susto de muerte; **bomb ~** amenaza de bomba; **scarecrow** n espantapájaros m inv; **scared** adj: **to be scared** estar asustado

**scarf** [skɑːf] (pl **-s** or **scarves**) n (long) bufanda; (square) pañuelo

**scarlet** ['skɑːlɪt] adj escarlata

**scarves** [skɑːvz] npl of **scarf**

**scary** ['skɛərɪ] (inf) adj espeluznante

**scatter** ['skætə*] vt (spread) esparcir, desparramar; (put to flight) dispersar ▷ vi desparramarse; dispersarse

**scenario** [sɪ'nɑːrɪəu] n (Theatre) argumento; (Cinema) guión m; (fig) escenario

**scene** [siːn] n (Theatre, fig etc) escena; (of crime etc) escenario; (view) panorama m; (fuss) escándalo; **scenery** (Theatre) decorado; (landscape) paisaje m

> ▎Be careful not to translate **scenery** by the Spanish word escenario.

**scenic** adj pintoresco

**scent** [sɛnt] n perfume m, olor m; (fig: track) rastro, pista

**sceptical** ['skɛptɪkl] adj escéptico

**schedule** ['ʃɛdjuːl] (us) ['skɛdjuːl] n (timetable) horario; (of events) programa m; (list) lista ▷ vt (visit) fijar la hora de; **to arrive on ~** llegar a la hora debida; **to be ahead of/behind ~** estar adelantado/en retraso; **scheduled flight** n vuelo regular

**scheme** [skiːm] n (plan) plan m, proyecto; (plot) intriga; (arrangement) disposición f; (pension scheme etc) sistema m ▷ vi (intrigue) intrigar

**schizophrenic** [skɪtzə'frɛnɪk] adj esquizofrénico

**scholar** ['skɒlə*] n (pupil) alumno/a; (learned person) sabio/a, erudito/a; **scholarship** n erudición f; (grant) beca

**school** [skuːl] n escuela, colegio; (in university) facultad f ▷ cpd escolar; **schoolbook** n libro de texto; **schoolboy** n alumno; **school children** npl alumnos mpl; **schoolgirl** n alumna; **schooling** n enseñanza; **schoolteacher** n (primary) maestro/a; (secondary) profesor(a) m/f

**science** ['saɪəns] n ciencia; **science**

**fiction** n ciencia-ficción f; **scientific** [-'tɪfɪk] adj científico; **scientist** n científico/a

**sci-fi** ['saɪfaɪ] n abbr (inf) = **science fiction**

**scissors** ['sɪzəz] npl tijeras fpl; **a pair of ~** unas tijeras

**scold** [skəʊld] vt regañar

**scone** [skɒn] n pastel de pan

**scoop** [sku:p] n (for flour etc) pala; (Press) exclusiva

**scooter** ['sku:tə*] n moto f; (toy) patinete m

**scope** [skəʊp] n (of plan) ámbito; (of person) competencia; (opportunity) libertad f (de acción)

**scorching** ['skɔ:tʃɪŋ] adj (heat, sun) abrasador(a)

**score** [skɔ:*] n (points etc) puntuación f; (Mus) partitura; (twenty) veintena ▷ vt (goal, point) ganar; (mark) rayar; (achieve: success) conseguir ▷ vi marcar un tanto; (Football) marcar (un) gol; (keep score) llevar el tanteo; **~s of** (lots of) decenas de; **on that ~** en lo que se refiere a eso; **to ~ 6 out of 10** obtener una puntuación de 6 sobre 10; **score out** vt tachar; **scoreboard** n marcador m; **scorer** n marcador m; (keeping score) encargado/a del marcador

**scorn** [skɔ:n] n desprecio

**Scorpio** ['skɔ:pɪəʊ] n Escorpión m

**scorpion** ['skɔ:pɪən] n alacrán m

**Scot** [skɒt] n escocés/esa m/f

**Scotch tape®** (us) n cinta adhesiva, celo, scotch® m

**Scotland** ['skɒtlənd] n Escocia

**Scots** [skɒts] adj escocés/esa; **Scotsman** (irreg) n escocés; **Scotswoman** (irreg) n escocesa; **Scottish** ['skɒtɪʃ] adj escocés/esa; **Scottish Parliament** n Parlamento escocés

**scout** [skaʊt] n (Mil: also: **boy ~**) explorador m; **girl ~** = (us) niña exploradora

**scowl** [skaʊl] vi fruncir el ceño; **to ~ at sb** mirar con ceño a algn

**scramble** ['skræmbl] n (climb) subida (difícil); (struggle) pelea ▷ vi: **to ~ through/ out** abrirse paso/salir con dificultad; **to ~ for** pelear por; **scrambled eggs** npl huevos mpl revueltos

**scrap** [skræp] n (bit) pedacito; (fig) pizca; (fight) riña, bronca; (also: **~ iron**) chatarra, hierro viejo ▷ vt (discard) desechar, descartar ▷ vi reñir, armar una bronca; **scraps** npl (waste) sobras fpl, desperdicios mpl; **scrapbook** n álbum m de recortes

**scrape** [skreɪp] n: **to get into a ~** meterse en un lío ▷ vt raspar; (skin etc) rasguñar; (scrape against) rozar ▷ vi: **to ~ through**

(exam) aprobar por los pelos; **scrap paper** n pedazos mpl de papel

**scratch** [skrætʃ] n rasguño; (from claw) arañazo ▷ vt (paint, car) rayar; (with claw, nail) rasguñar, arañar; (rub: nose etc) rascarse ▷ vi rascarse; **to start from ~** partir de cero; **to be up to ~** cumplir con los requisitos; **scratch card** n (BRIT) tarjeta f de "rasque y gane"

**scream** [skri:m] n chillido ▷ vi chillar

**screen** [skri:n] n (Cinema, TV) pantalla; (movable barrier) biombo ▷ vt (conceal) tapar; (from the wind etc) proteger; (film) proyectar; (candidates etc) investigar a; **screening** n (Med) investigación f médica; **screenplay** n guión m; **screen saver** n (Comput) protector m de pantalla

**screw** [skru:] n tornillo ▷ vt (also: **~ in**) atornillar; **screw up** vt (paper etc) arrugar; **to screw up one's eyes** arrugar el entrecejo; **screwdriver** n destornillador m

**scribble** ['skrɪbl] n garabatos mpl ▷ vt, vi garabatear

**script** [skrɪpt] n (Cinema etc) guión m; (writing) escritura, letra

**scroll** [skrəʊl] n rollo

**scrub** [skrʌb] n (land) maleza ▷ vt fregar, restregar; (inf: reject) cancelar, anular

**scruffy** ['skrʌfɪ] adj desaliñado, piojoso

**scrum(mage)** ['skrʌm(mɪdʒ)] n (Rugby) melée f

**scrutiny** ['skru:tɪnɪ] n escrutinio, examen m

**scuba diving** ['sku:bə'daɪvɪŋ] n submarinismo

**sculptor** ['skʌlptə*] n escultor(a) m/f

**sculpture** ['skʌlptʃə*] n escultura

**scum** [skʌm] n (on liquid) espuma; (pej: people) escoria

**scurry** ['skʌrɪ] vi correr; **to ~ off** escabullirse

**sea** [si:] n mar m ▷ cpd de mar, marítimo; **by ~** (travel) en barco; **on the ~** (boat) en el mar; (town) junto al mar; **to be all at ~** (fig) estar despistado; **out to ~, at ~** en alta mar; **seafood** n mariscos mpl; **sea front** n paseo marítimo; **seagull** n gaviota

**seal** [si:l] n (animal) foca; (stamp) sello ▷ vt (close) cerrar; **seal off** vt (area) acordonar

**sea level** n nivel m del mar

**seam** [si:m] n costura; (of metal) juntura; (of coal) veta, filón m

**search** [sə:tʃ] n (for person, thing) busca, búsqueda; (Comput) búsqueda; (inspection: of sb's home) registro ▷ vt (look in) buscar en; (examine) examinar; (person, place) registrar ▷ vi: **to ~ for** buscar; **in ~ of** en busca de; **search engine** n (Comput) buscador m;

**search party** n pelotón m de salvamento
**sea: seashore** n playa, orilla del mar;
**seasick** adj mareado; **seaside** n playa,
orilla del mar; **seaside resort** n centro
turístico costero

**season** ['si:zn] n (of year) estación f;
(sporting etc) temporada; (of films etc)
ciclo ▷ vt (food) sazonar; **in/out of ~** en
sazón/fuera de temporada; **seasonal** adj
estacional; **seasoning** n condimento,
aderezo; **season ticket** n abono

**seat** [si:t] n (in bus, train) asiento; (chair)
silla; (Parliament) escaño; (buttocks) culo,
trasero; (of trousers) culera ▷ vt sentar;
(have room for) tener cabida para; **to be
~ed** sentarse; **seat belt** n cinturón m de
seguridad; **seating** n asientos mpl

**sea: sea water** n agua del mar; **seaweed** n
alga marina

**sec.** abbr = **second(s)**
**secluded** [sɪ'klu:dɪd] adj retirado

**second** ['sɛkənd] adj segundo ▷ adv en
segundo lugar ▷ n segundo; (Aut: also:
**~ gear**) segunda; (Comm) artículo con
algún desperfecto; (BRIT Scol: degree) título
de licenciado con calificación de notable
▷ vt (motion) apoyar; **secondary** adj
secundario; **secondary school** n escuela
secundaria; **second-class** adj de segunda
clase ▷ adv (Rail) en segunda; **secondhand**
adj de segunda mano, usado; **secondly**
adv en segundo lugar; **second-rate** adj de
segunda categoría; **second thoughts: to
have second thoughts** cambiar de
opinión; **on second thoughts** or **thought**
(US) pensándolo bien

**secrecy** ['si:krəsɪ] n secreto
**secret** ['si:krɪt] adj, n secreto; **in ~** en
secreto

**secretary** ['sɛkrətərɪ] n secretario/a; **S~
of State (for)** (BRIT Pol) Ministro (de)

**secretive** ['si:krətɪv] adj reservado,
sigiloso

**secret service** n servicio secreto
**sect** [sɛkt] n secta

**section** ['sɛkʃən] n sección f; (part) parte f;
(of document) artículo; (of opinion) sector m;
(cross-section) corte m transversal

**sector** ['sɛktə*] n sector m
**secular** ['sɛkjulə*] adj secular, seglar
**secure** [sɪ'kjuə*] adj seguro; (firmly fixed)
firme, fijo ▷ vt (fix) asegurar, afianzar; (get)
conseguir

**security** [sɪ'kjuərɪtɪ] n seguridad f; (for
loan) fianza; (: object) prenda; **securities** npl
(Comm) valores mpl, títulos mpl; **security
guard** n guardia m/f de seguridad

**sedan** [sɪ'dæn] (US) n (Aut) sedán m

**sedate** [sɪ'deɪt] adj tranquilo ▷ vt tratar
con sedantes

**sedative** ['sɛdɪtɪv] n sedante m, sedativo
**seduce** [sɪ'dju:s] vt seducir; **seductive**
[-'dʌktɪv] adj seductor(a)

**see** [si:] (pt **saw**, pp **seen**) vt ver;
(accompany): **to ~ sb to the door** acompañar
a algn a la puerta; (understand) ver,
comprender ▷ vi ver ▷ n (arz)obispado; **to
~ that** (ensure) asegurar que; **~ you soon!**
¡hasta pronto!; **see off** vt despedir; **see
out** vt (take to the door) acompañar hasta la
puerta; **see through** vt fus (plan) calar ▷ vt
(plan) llevar a cabo; **see to** vt fus atender a,
encargarse de

**seed** [si:d] n semilla; (in fruit) pepita;
(fig: gen pl) germen m; (Tennis etc)
preseleccionado/a; **to go to ~** (plant)
granar; (fig) descuidarse

**seeing** ['si:ɪŋ] conj: **~ (that)** visto que, en
vista de que

**seek** [si:k] (pt, pp **sought**) vt buscar; (post)
solicitar

**seem** [si:m] vi parecer; **there ~s to
be ...** parece que hay ...; **seemingly** adv
aparentemente, según parece

**seen** [si:n] pp of **see**
**seesaw** ['si:sɔ:] n subibaja
**segment** ['sɛgmənt] n (part) sección f; (of
orange) gajo

**segregate** ['sɛgrɪgeɪt] vt segregar
**seize** [si:z] vt (grasp) agarrar, asir;
(take possession of) secuestrar; (: territory)
apoderarse de; (opportunity) aprovecharse de

**seizure** ['si:ʒə*] n (Med) ataque m; (Law, of
power) incautación f

**seldom** ['sɛldəm] adv rara vez
**select** [sɪ'lɛkt] adj selecto, escogido
▷ vt escoger, elegir; (Sport) seleccionar;
**selection** n selección f, elección f; (Comm)
surtido; **selective** adj selectivo

**self** [sɛlf] (pl **selves**) n uno mismo; **the
~** el yo ▷ prefix auto...; **self-assured** adj
seguro de sí mismo; **self-catering** (BRIT)
adj (flat etc) con cocina; **self-centred** (US
**self-centered**) adj egocéntrico; **self-
confidence** n confianza en sí mismo;
**self-confident** adj seguro de sí (mismo),
lleno de confianza en sí mismo; **self-
conscious** adj cohibido; **self-contained**
(BRIT) adj (flat) con entrada particular;
**self-control** n autodominio; **self-defence**
(US **self-defense**) n defensa propia; **self-
drive** adj (BRIT) sin chofer or (SP) chófer;
**self-employed** adj que trabaja por cuenta
propia; **self-esteem** n amor m propio;
**self-indulgent** adj autocomplaciente;
**self-interest** n egoísmo; **selfish** adj

egoísta; **self-pity** n lástima de sí mismo; **self-raising** [sɛlfˈreɪzɪŋ] (US **self-rising**) adj: **self-raising flour** harina con levadura; **self-respect** n amor m propio; **self-service** adj de autoservicio

**sell** [sɛl] (pt, pp **sold**) vt vender ▷ vi venderse; **to ~ at** or **for £10** venderse a 10 libras; **sell off** vt liquidar; **sell out** vi: **to sell out of tickets/milk** vender todas las entradas/toda la leche; **sell-by date** n fecha de caducidad; **seller** n vendedor(a) m/f

**Sellotape®** [ˈsɛləʊteɪp] (BRIT) n celo (SP), cinta Scotch® (LAM) or Dúrex® (MEX, ARG)

**selves** [sɛlvz] npl of **self**

**semester** [sɪˈmɛstə*] (US) n semestre m

**semi...** [ˈsɛmɪ] prefix semi..., medio...; **semicircle** n semicírculo; **semidetached (house)** n (casa) semiseparada; **semi-final** n semi-final m

**seminar** [ˈsɛmɪnɑ:*] n seminario

**semi-skimmed** [sɛmɪˈskɪmd] adj semidesnatado; **semi-skimmed (milk)** n leche semidesnatada

**senate** [ˈsɛnɪt] n senado; **the S~** (US) el Senado; **senator** n senador(a) m/f

**send** [sɛnd] (pt, pp **sent**) vt mandar, enviar; (signal) transmitir; **send back** vt devolver; **send for** vt fus mandar traer; **send in** vt (report, application, resignation) mandar; **send off** vt (goods) despachar; (BRIT Sport: player) expulsar; **send on** vt (letter, luggage) remitir; (person) mandar; **send out** vt (invitation) mandar; (signal) emitir; **send up** vt (person, price) hacer subir; (BRIT: parody) parodiar; **sender** n remitente mf; **send-off** n: **a good send-off** una buena despedida

**senile** [ˈsiːnaɪl] adj senil

**senior** [ˈsiːnɪə*] adj (older) mayor, más viejo; (: on staff) de más antigüedad; (of higher rank) superior; **senior citizen** n persona de la tercera edad; **senior high school** (US) n ≈ instituto de enseñanza media; see also **high school**

**sensation** [sɛnˈseɪʃən] n sensación f; **sensational** adj sensacional

**sense** [sɛns] n (faculty, meaning) sentido; (feeling) sensación f; (good sense) sentido común, juicio ▷ vt sentir, percibir; **it makes ~** tiene sentido; **senseless** adj estúpido, insensato; (unconscious) sin conocimiento; **sense of humour** (BRIT) n sentido del humor

**sensible** [ˈsɛnsɪbl] adj sensato; (reasonable) razonable, lógico

▌Be careful not to translate **sensible** by the Spanish word *sensible*.

**sensitive** [ˈsɛnsɪtɪv] adj sensible; (touchy) susceptible

**sensual** [ˈsɛnsjʊəl] adj sensual

**sensuous** [ˈsɛnsjʊəs] adj sensual

**sent** [sɛnt] pt, pp of **send**

**sentence** [ˈsɛntns] n (Ling) oración f; (Law) sentencia, fallo ▷ vt: **to ~ sb to death/to 5 years (in prison)** condenar a algn a muerte/a 5 años de cárcel

**sentiment** [ˈsɛntɪmənt] n sentimiento; (opinion) opinión f; **sentimental** [-ˈmɛntl] adj sentimental

**Sep.** abbr (= September) sep., set.

**separate** [adj ˈsɛprɪt, vb ˈsɛpəreɪt] adj separado; (distinct) distinto ▷ vt separar; (part) dividir ▷ vi separarse; **separately** adv por separado; **separates** npl (clothes) coordinados mpl; **separation** [-ˈreɪʃən] n separación f

**September** [sɛpˈtɛmbə*] n se(p)tiembre m

**septic** [ˈsɛptɪk] adj séptico; **septic tank** n fosa séptica

**sequel** [ˈsiːkwl] n consecuencia, resultado; (of story) continuación f

**sequence** [ˈsiːkwəns] n sucesión f, serie f; (Cinema) secuencia

**sequin** [ˈsiːkwɪn] n lentejuela

**Serb** [sə:b] adj, n = **Serbian**

**Serbian** [ˈsə:bɪən] adj serbio ▷ n serbio/a; (Ling) serbio

**sergeant** [ˈsɑ:dʒənt] n sargento

**serial** [ˈsɪərɪəl] n (TV) telenovela, serie f televisiva; (Book) serie f; **serial killer** n asesino/a múltiple; **serial number** n número de serie

**series** [ˈsɪərɪ:s] n inv serie f

**serious** [ˈsɪərɪəs] adj serio; (grave) grave; **seriously** adv en serio; (ill, wounded etc) gravemente

**sermon** [ˈsə:mən] n sermón m

**servant** [ˈsə:vənt] n servidor(a) m/f; (house servant) criado/a

**serve** [sə:v] vt servir; (customer) atender; (train) pasar por; (apprenticeship) hacer; (prison term) cumplir ▷ vi (at table) servir; (Tennis) sacar; **to ~ as/for/to do** servir de/para/para hacer ▷ n (Tennis) saque m; **it ~s him right** se lo tiene merecido; **server** n (Comput) servidor m

**service** [ˈsə:vɪs] n servicio; (Rel) misa; (Aut) mantenimiento; (dishes etc) juego ▷ vt (car etc) revisar; (: repair) reparar; **to be of ~ to sb** ser útil a algn; **~ included/not included** servicio incluido/no incluido (Econ: tertiary sector) sector m terciario or (de) servicios; (BRIT: on motorway) área de servicio; (Mil): **the S~s** las fuerzas armadas; **service area** n (on motorway) área de servicio; **service charge** (BRIT) n servicio; **serviceman** (irreg) n militar m; **service station** n estación f de servicio

**serviette** [sə:vɪ'ɛt] (BRIT) n servilleta

**session** ['sɛʃən] n sesión f; **to be in ~** estar en sesión

**set** [sɛt] (pt, pp ~) n juego; (Radio) aparato; (TV) televisor m; (of utensils) batería; (of cutlery) cubierto; (of books) colección f; (Tennis) set m; (group of people) grupo; (Cinema) plató m; (Theatre) decorado; (Hairdressing) marcado ▷ adj (fixed) fijo; (ready) listo ▷ vt (place) poner, colocar; (fix) fijar; (adjust) ajustar, arreglar; (decide: rules etc) establecer, decidir ▷ vi (sun) ponerse; (jam, jelly) cuajarse; (concrete) fraguar; (bone) componerse; **to be ~ on doing sth** estar empeñado en hacer algo; **to ~ to music** poner música a; **to ~ on fire** incendiar, poner fuego a; **to ~ free** poner en libertad; **to ~ sth going** poner algo en marcha; **to ~ sail** zarpar, hacerse a la vela; **set aside** vt poner aparte, dejar de lado; (money, time) reservar; **set down** vt (bus, train) dejar; **set in** vi (infection) declararse; (complications) comenzar; **the rain has set in for the day** parece que va a llover todo el día; **set off** vi partir ▷ vt (bomb) hacer estallar; (events) poner en marcha; (show up well) hacer resaltar; **set out** vi partir ▷ vt (arrange) disponer; (state) exponer; **to set out to do sth** proponerse hacer algo; **set up** vt establecer; **setback** n revés m, contratiempo; **set menu** n menú m

**settee** [sɛ'ti:] n sofá m

**setting** ['sɛtɪŋ] n (scenery) marco; (position) disposición f; (of sun) puesta; (of jewel) engaste m, montadura

**settle** ['sɛtl] vt (argument) resolver; (accounts) ajustar, liquidar; (Med: calm) calmar, sosegar ▷ vi (dust etc) depositarse; (weather) serenarse; **to ~ for sth** convenir en aceptar algo; **to ~ on sth** decidirse por algo; **settle down** vi (get comfortable) ponerse cómodo, acomodarse; (calm down) calmarse, tranquilizarse; (live quietly) echar raíces; **settle in** vi instalarse; **settle up** vi: **to settle up with sb** ajustar cuentas con algn; **settlement** n (payment) liquidación f; (agreement) acuerdo, convenio; (village etc) pueblo

**setup** ['sɛtʌp] n sistema m; (situation) situación f

**seven** ['sɛvn] num siete; **seventeen** num diez y siete, diecisiete; **seventeenth** [sevn'ti:nθ] adj decimoséptimo; **seventh** num séptimo; **seventieth** ['sɛvntɪɪθ] adj septuagésimo; **seventy** num setenta

**sever** ['sɛvə*] vt cortar; (relations) romper

**several** ['sɛvərl] adj, pron varios/as m/f pl, algunos/as m/f pl; **~ of us** varios de nosotros

**severe** [sɪ'vɪə*] adj severo; (serious) grave; (hard) duro; (pain) intenso

**sew** [səu] (pt ~ed, pp ~n) vt, vi coser

**sewage** ['su:ɪdʒ] n aguas f pl residuales

**sewer** ['su:ə*] n alcantarilla, cloaca

**sewing** ['səuɪŋ] n costura; **sewing machine** n máquina de coser

**sewn** [səun] pp of **sew**

**sex** [sɛks] n sexo; (lovemaking): **to have ~** hacer el amor; **sexism** ['sɛksɪzəm] n sexismo; **sexist** adj, n sexista mf; **sexual** ['sɛksjuəl] adj sexual; **sexual intercourse** n relaciones f pl sexuales; **sexuality** [sɛksju'ælɪtɪ] n sexualidad f; **sexy** adj sexy

**shabby** ['ʃæbɪ] adj (person) desharrapado; (clothes) raído, gastado; (behaviour) ruin inv

**shack** [ʃæk] n choza, chabola

**shade** [ʃeɪd] n sombra; (for lamp) pantalla; (for eyes) visera; (of colour) matiz m, tonalidad f; (small quantity): **a ~ (too big/more)** un poquitín (grande/más) ▷ vt dar sombra a; (eyes) proteger del sol; **in the ~** en la sombra; **shades** npl (sunglasses) gafas f pl de sol

**shadow** ['ʃædəu] n sombra ▷ vt (follow) seguir y vigilar; **shadow cabinet** n (BRIT) (Pol) gabinete paralelo formado por el partido de oposición

**shady** ['ʃeɪdɪ] adj sombreado; (fig: dishonest) sospechoso; (: deal) turbio

**shaft** [ʃɑ:ft] n (of arrow, spear) astil m; (Aut, Tech) eje m, árbol m; (of mine) pozo; (of lift) hueco, caja; (of light) rayo

**shake** [ʃeɪk] (pt shook, pp shaken) vt sacudir; (building) hacer temblar; (bottle, cocktail) agitar ▷ vi (tremble) temblar; **to ~ one's head** (in refusal) negar con la cabeza; (in dismay) mover or menear la cabeza, incrédulo; **to ~ hands with sb** estrechar la mano a algn; **shake off** vt sacudirse; (fig) deshacerse de; **shake up** vt agitar; (fig) reorganizar; **shaky** adj (hand, voice) trémulo; (building) inestable

**shall** [ʃæl] aux vb: **~ I help you?** ¿quieres que te ayude?; **I'll buy three, ~ I?** compro tres, ¿no te parece?

**shallow** ['ʃæləu] adj poco profundo; (fig) superficial

**sham** [ʃæm] n fraude m, engaño

**shambles** ['ʃæmblz] n confusión f

**shame** [ʃeɪm] n vergüenza ▷ vt avergonzar; **it is a ~ that/to do** es una lástima que/hacer; **what a ~!** ¡qué lástima!; **shameful** adj vergonzoso; **shameless** adj desvergonzado

**shampoo** [ʃæm'pu:] n champú m ▷ vt

lavar con champú

**shandy** ['ʃændɪ] *n* mezcla de cerveza con gaseosa

**shan't** [ʃɑːnt] = **shall not**

**shape** [ʃeɪp] *n* forma ▷*vt* formar, dar forma a; (*sb's ideas*) formar; (*sb's life*) determinar; **to take ~** tomar forma

**share** [ʃɛə*] *n* (*part*) parte *f*, porción *f*; (*contribution*) cuota; (*Comm*) acción *f* ▷*vt* dividir; (*have in common*) compartir; **to ~ out (among** *or* **between)** repartir (entre); **shareholder** (BRIT) *n* accionista *mf*

**shark** [ʃɑːk] *n* tiburón *m*

**sharp** [ʃɑːp] *adj* (*blade, nose*) afilado; (*point*) puntiagudo; (*outline*) definido; (*pain*) intenso; (*Mus*) desafinado; (*contrast*) marcado; (*voice*) agudo; (*person: quick-witted*) astuto; (: *dishonest*) poco escrupuloso ▷*n* (*Mus*) sostenido ▷*adv*: **at 2 o'clock ~** a las 2 en punto; **sharpen** *vt* afilar; (*pencil*) sacar punta a; (*fig*) aguidizar; **sharpener** *n* (*also*: **pencil sharpener**) sacapuntas *m inv*; **sharply** *adv* (*turn, stop*) bruscamente; (*stand out, contrast*) claramente; (*criticize, retort*) severamente

**shatter** ['ʃætə*] *vt* hacer añicos *or* pedazos; (*fig: ruin*) destruir, acabar con ▷*vi* hacerse añicos; **shattered** *adj* (*grief-stricken*) destrozado, deshecho; (*exhausted*) agotado, hecho polvo

**shave** [ʃeɪv] *vt* afeitar, rasurar ▷*vi* afeitarse, rasurarse ▷*n*: **to have a ~** afeitarse; **shaver** *n* (*also*: **electric shaver**) máquina de afeitar (eléctrica)

**shavings** ['ʃeɪvɪŋz] *npl* (*of wood etc*) virutas *fpl*

**shaving cream** ['ʃeɪvɪŋ-] *n* crema de afeitar

**shaving foam** *n* espuma de afeitar

**shawl** [ʃɔːl] *n* chal *m*

**she** [ʃiː] *pron* ella

**sheath** [ʃiːθ] *n* vaina; (*contraceptive*) preservativo

**shed** [ʃed] (*pt, pp ~*) *n* cobertizo ▷*vt* (*skin*) mudar; (*tears, blood*) derramar; (*load*) derramar; (*workers*) despedir

**she'd** [ʃiːd] = **she had; she would**

**sheep** [ʃiːp] *n inv* oveja; **sheepdog** *n* perro pastor; **sheepskin** *n* piel *f* de carnero

**sheer** [ʃɪə*] *adj* (*utter*) puro, completo; (*steep*) escarpado; (*material*) diáfano ▷*adv* verticalmente

**sheet** [ʃiːt] *n* (*on bed*) sábana; (*of paper*) hoja; (*of glass, metal*) lámina; (*of ice*) capa

**sheik(h)** [ʃeɪk] *n* jeque *m*

**shelf** [ʃelf] (*pl* **shelves**) *n* estante *m*

**shell** [ʃel] *n* (*on beach*) concha; (*of egg, nut etc*) cáscara; (*explosive*) proyectil *m*,

obús *m*; (*of building*) armazón *f* ▷*vt* (*peas*) desenvainar; (*Mil*) bombardear

**she'll** [ʃiːl] = **she will; she shall**

**shellfish** ['ʃelfɪʃ] *n inv* crustáceo; (*as food*) mariscos *mpl*

**shelter** ['ʃeltə*] *n* abrigo, refugio ▷*vt* (*aid*) amparar, proteger; (*give lodging to*) abrigar ▷*vi* abrigarse, refugiarse; **sheltered** *adj* (*life*) protegido; (*spot*) abrigado

**shelves** [ʃelvz] *npl of* **shelf**

**shelving** ['ʃelvɪŋ] *n* estantería

**shepherd** ['ʃepəd] *n* pastor *m* ▷*vt* (*guide*) guiar, conducir; **shepherd's pie** (BRIT) *n* pastel de carne y patatas

**sheriff** ['ʃerɪf] (US) *n* sheriff *m*

**sherry** ['ʃerɪ] *n* jerez *m*

**she's** [ʃiːz] = **she is; she has**

**Shetland** ['ʃetlənd] *n* (*also*: **the ~s, the ~ Isles**) las Islas de Zetlandia

**shield** [ʃiːld] *n* escudo; (*protection*) blindaje *m* ▷*vt*: **to ~ (from)** proteger (de)

**shift** [ʃɪft] *n* (*change*) cambio; (*at work*) turno ▷*vt* trasladar; (*remove*) quitar ▷*vi* moverse

**shin** [ʃɪn] *n* espinilla

**shine** [ʃaɪn] (*pt, pp* **shone**) *n* brillo, lustre *m* ▷*vi* brillar, relucir ▷*vt* (*shoes*) lustrar, sacar brillo a; **to ~ a torch on sth** dirigir una linterna hacia algo

**shingles** ['ʃɪŋglz] *n* (*Med*) herpes *mpl or fpl*

**shiny** ['ʃaɪnɪ] *adj* brillante, lustroso

**ship** [ʃɪp] *n* buque *m*, barco ▷*vt* (*goods*) embarcar; (*send*) transportar *or* enviar por vía marítima; **shipment** *n* (*goods*) envío; **shipping** *n* (*act*) embarque *m*; (*traffic*) buques *mpl*; **shipwreck** *n* naufragio ▷*vt*: **to be shipwrecked** naufragar; **shipyard** *n* astillero

**shirt** [ʃəːt] *n* camisa; **in (one's) ~ sleeves** en mangas de camisa

**shit** [ʃɪt] (*inf!*) *excl* ¡mierda! (!)

**shiver** ['ʃɪvə*] *n* escalofrío ▷*vi* temblar, estremecerse; (*with cold*) tiritar

**shock** [ʃɔk] *n* (*impact*) choque *m*; (*Elec*) descarga (eléctrica); (*emotional*) conmoción *f*; (*start*) sobresalto, susto; (*Med*) postración *f* nerviosa ▷*vt* dar un susto a; (*offend*) escandalizar; **shocking** *adj* (*awful*) espantoso; (*outrageous*) escandaloso

**shoe** [ʃuː] (*pt, pp* **shod**) *n* zapato; (*for horse*) herradura ▷*vt* (*horse*) herrar; **shoelace** *n* cordón *m*; **shoe polish** *n* betún *m*; **shoeshop** *n* zapatería

**shone** [ʃɔn] *pt, pp of* **shine**

**shook** [ʃuk] *pt of* **shake**

**shoot** [ʃuːt] (*pt, pp* **shot**) *n* (*on branch, seedling*) retoño, vástago ▷*vt* disparar; (*kill*) matar a tiros; (*wound*) pegar un tiro; (*execute*) fusilar; (film) rodar, filmar ⊳vi (Football) chutar; **shoot down** vt (plane) derribar; **shoot up** vi (prices) dispararse; **shooting** n (shots) tiros mpl; (Hunting) caza con escopeta

**shop** [ʃɔp] n tienda; (workshop) taller m ⊳vi (also: **go ~ping**) ir de compras; **shop assistant** (BRIT) n dependiente/a m/f; **shopkeeper** n tendero/a; **shoplifting** n mechería; **shopping** n (goods) compras fpl; **shopping bag** n bolsa (de compras); **shopping centre** (US **shopping center**) n centro comercial; **shopping mall** n centro comercial; **shopping trolley** n (BRIT) carrito de la compra; **shop window** n escaparate m (SP), vidriera (LAM)

**shore** [ʃɔː*] n orilla ⊳vt: **to ~ (up)** reforzar; **on ~** en tierra

**short** [ʃɔːt] adj corto; (in time) breve, de corta duración; (person) bajo; (curt) brusco, seco; (insufficient) insuficiente; **(a pair of) ~s** (unos) pantalones mpl cortos; **to be ~ of sth** estar falto de algo; **in ~** en pocas palabras; **~ of doing ...** fuera de hacer ...; **it is ~ for** es la forma abreviada de; **to cut ~** (speech, visit) interrumpir, terminar inesperadamente; **everything ~ of ...** todo menos ...; **to fall ~ of** no alcanzar; **to run ~ of** quedarle a algn poco; **to stop ~** parar en seco; **to stop ~ of** detenerse antes de; **shortage** n: **a shortage of** una falta de; **shortbread** n especie de mantecada; **shortcoming** n defecto, deficiencia; **short(crust) pastry** (BRIT) n pasta quebradiza; **shortcut** n atajo; **shorten** vt acortar; (visit) interrumpir; **shortfall** n déficit m; **shorthand** (BRIT) n taquigrafía; **short-lived** adj efímero; **shortly** adv en breve, dentro de poco; **shorts** npl pantalones mpl cortos; (US) calzoncillos mpl; **short-sighted** (BRIT) adj miope; (fig) imprudente; **short-sleeved** adj de manga corta; **short story** n cuento; **short-tempered** adj enojadizo; **short-term** adj (effect) a corto plazo

**shot** [ʃɔt] pt, pp of **shoot** ⊳n (sound) tiro, disparo; (try) tentativa; (injection) inyección f; (Phot) toma, fotografía; **to be a good/ poor ~** (person) tener buena/mala puntería; **like a ~** (without any delay) como un rayo; **shotgun** n escopeta

**should** [ʃud] aux vb: **I ~ go now** debo irme ahora; **he ~ be there now** debe de haber llegado (ya); **I ~ go if I were you** yo en tu lugar me iría; **I ~ like to** me gustaría

**shoulder** [ʃauldə*] n hombro ⊳vt (fig) cargar con; **shoulder blade** n omóplato

**shouldn't** [ʃudnt] = **should not**

**shout** [ʃaut] n grito ⊳vt gritar ⊳vi gritar, dar voces

**shove** [ʃʌv] n empujón m ⊳vt empujar; (inf: put): **to ~ sth in** meter algo a empellones

**shovel** [ʃʌvl] n pala; (mechanical) excavadora ⊳vt mover con pala

**show** [ʃəu] (pt **~ed**, pp **~n**) n (of emotion) demostración f; (semblance) apariencia; (exhibition) exposición f; (Theatre) función f, espectáculo; (TV) show m ⊳vt mostrar, enseñar; (courage etc) mostrar, manifestar; (exhibit) exponer; (film) proyectar ⊳vi mostrarse; (appear) aparecer; **for ~** para impresionar; **on ~** (exhibits etc) expuesto; **show in** vt (person) hacer pasar; **show off** (pej) vi presumir ⊳vt (display) lucir; **show out** vt: **to show sb out** acompañar a algn a la puerta; **show up** vi (stand out) destacar; (inf: turn up) aparecer ⊳vt (unmask) desenmascarar; **show business** n mundo del espectáculo

**shower** [ʃauə*] n (rain) chaparrón m, chubasco; (of stones etc) lluvia; (for bathing) ducha, regadera (MEX) ⊳vi llover ⊳vt (fig): **to ~ sb with sth** colmar a algn de algo; **to have a ~** ducharse; **shower cap** n gorro de baño; **shower gel** n gel m de ducha

**showing** [ʃəuɪŋ] n (of film) proyección f

**show jumping** n hípica

**shown** [ʃəun] pp of **show**

**show-off** (inf) n (person) presumido/a; **showroom** n sala de muestras

**shrank** [ʃræŋk] pt of **shrink**

**shred** [ʃred] n (gen pl) triza, jirón m ⊳vt hacer trizas; (Culin) desmenuzar

**shrewd** [ʃruːd] adj astuto

**shriek** [ʃriːk] n chillido ⊳vi chillar

**shrimp** [ʃrɪmp] n camarón m

**shrine** [ʃraɪn] n santuario, sepulcro

**shrink** [ʃrɪŋk] (pt **shrank**, pp **shrunk**) vi encogerse; (be reduced) reducirse; (also: **~ away**) retroceder ⊳vt encoger ⊳n (inf, pej) loquero/a; **to ~ from (doing) sth** no atreverse a hacer algo

**shrivel** [ʃrɪvl] (also: **~ up**) vt (dry) secar ⊳vi secarse

**shroud** [ʃraud] n sudario ⊳vt: **~ed in mystery** envuelto en el misterio

**Shrove Tuesday** [ʃrəuv-] n martes m de carnaval

**shrub** [ʃrʌb] n arbusto

**shrug** [ʃrʌg] n encogimiento de hombros ⊳vt, vi: **to ~ (one's shoulders)** encogerse de hombros; **shrug off** vt negar importancia a

**shrunk** [ʃrʌŋk] pp of **shrink**

**shudder** [ʃʌdə*] n estremecimiento, escalofrío ⊳vi estremecerse

**shuffle** [ʃʌfl] vt (cards) barajar ⊳vi: **to ~**

**(one's feet)** arrastrar los pies
**shun** [ʃʌn] vt rehuir, esquivar
**shut** [ʃʌt] (pt, pp **~**) vt cerrar ▷ vi
cerrarse; **shut down** vt, vi cerrar; **shut
up** vi (inf: keep quiet) callarse ▷ vt (close)
cerrar; (silence) hacer callar; **shutter** n
contraventana; (Phot) obturador m
**shuttle** ['ʃʌtl] n lanzadera; (also: **~ service**)
servicio rápido y continuo entre dos puntos;
(Aviat) puente m aéreo; **shuttlecock** n
volante m
**shy** [ʃaɪ] adj tímido
**sibling** ['sɪblɪŋ] n (formal) hermano/a
**Sicily** ['sɪsɪlɪ] n Sicilia
**sick** [sɪk] adj (ill) enfermo; (nauseated)
mareado; (humour) negro; (vomiting): **to be
~** (BRIT) vomitar; **to feel ~** tener náuseas;
**to be ~ of** (fig) estar harto de; **sickening**
adj (fig) asqueroso; **sick leave** n baja por
enfermedad; **sickly** adj enfermizo; (smell)
nauseabundo; **sickness** n enfermedad f,
mal m; (vomiting) náuseas fpl
**side** [saɪd] n (gen) lado; (of body) costado;
(of lake) orilla; (of hill) ladera; (team) equipo
▷ adj (door, entrance) lateral ▷ vi: **to ~ with
sb** tomar el partido de algn; **by the ~ of** al
lado de; **~ by ~** juntos/as; **from ~ to ~** de un
lado para otro; **from all ~s** de todos lados;
**to take ~s (with)** tomar partido (con);
**sideboard** n aparador m; **sideboards**
(BRIT) npl = **sideburns**; **sideburns** npl
patillas fpl; **sidelight** n (Aut) luz f lateral;
**sideline** n (Sport) línea de banda; (fig)
empleo suplementario; **side order** n plato
de acompañamiento; **side road** n (BRIT)
calle f lateral; **side street** n calle f lateral;
**sidetrack** vt (fig) desviar (de su propósito);
**sidewalk** (US) n acera; **sideways** adv de
lado
**siege** [siːdʒ] n cerco, sitio
**sieve** [sɪv] n colador m ▷ vt cribar
**sift** [sɪft] vt cribar; (fig: information)
escudriñar
**sigh** [saɪ] n suspiro ▷ vi suspirar
**sight** [saɪt] n (faculty) vista; (spectacle)
espectáculo; (on gun) mira, alza ▷ vt divisar;
**in ~** a la vista; **out of ~** fuera de (la) vista;
**on ~** (shoot) sin previo aviso; **sightseeing**
n excursionismo, turismo; **to go sightseeing**
hacer turismo
**sign** [saɪn] n (with hand) señal f, seña;
(trace) huella, rastro; (notice) letrero; (written)
signo ▷ vt firmar; (Sport) fichar; **to ~ sth
over to sb** firmar el traspaso de algo a algn;
**sign for** vt fus (item) firmar el recibo de;
**sign in** vi firmar el registro (al entrar); **sign
on** vi (BRIT: as unemployed) registrarse como
desempleado; (for course) inscribirse ▷ vt

(Mil) alistar; (employee) contratar; **sign up**
vi (Mil) alistarse; (for course) inscribirse ▷ vt
(player) fichar
**signal** ['sɪɡnl] n señal f ▷ vi señalizar ▷ vt
(person) hacer señas a; (message) comunicar
por señales
**signature** ['sɪɡnətʃə*] n firma
**significance** [sɪɡ'nɪfɪkəns] n (importance)
trascendencia
**significant** [sɪɡ'nɪfɪkənt] adj
significativo; (important) trascendente
**signify** ['sɪɡnɪfaɪ] vt significar
**sign language** n lenguaje m para
sordomudos
**signpost** ['saɪnpəust] n indicador m
**Sikh** [siːk] adj, n sij mf
**silence** ['saɪləns] n silencio ▷ vt acallar;
(guns) reducir al silencio
**silent** ['saɪlnt] adj silencioso; (not speaking)
callado; (film) mudo; **to remain ~** guardar
silencio
**silhouette** [sɪluːˈɛt] n silueta
**silicon chip** ['sɪlɪkən-] n plaqueta de
silicio
**silk** [sɪlk] n seda ▷ adj de seda
**silly** ['sɪlɪ] adj (person) tonto; (idea) absurdo
**silver** ['sɪlvə*] n plata; (money) moneda
suelta ▷ adj de plata; (colour) plateado;
**silver-plated** adj plateado
**similar** ['sɪmɪlə*] adj: **~ (to)** parecido
or semejante (a); **similarity** [-'lærɪtɪ] n
semejanza; **similarly** adv del mismo modo
**simmer** ['sɪmə*] vi hervir a fuego lento
**simple** ['sɪmpl] adj (easy) sencillo;
(foolish, Comm: interest) simple; **simplicity**
[-'plɪsɪtɪ] n sencillez f; **simplify** ['sɪmplɪfaɪ]
vt simplificar; **simply** adv (live, talk)
sencillamente; (just, merely) sólo
**simulate** ['sɪmjuːleɪt] vt fingir, simular
**simultaneous** [sɪməl'teɪnɪəs] adj
simultáneo; **simultaneously** adv
simultáneamente
**sin** [sɪn] n pecado ▷ vi pecar
**since** [sɪns] adv desde entonces, después
▷ prep desde ▷ conj (time) desde que;
(because) ya que, puesto que; **~ then, ever ~**
desde entonces
**sincere** [sɪnˈsɪə*] adj sincero; **sincerely**
adv: **yours sincerely** (in letters) le saluda
atentamente
**sing** [sɪŋ] (pt **sang**, pp **sung**) vt, vi cantar
**Singapore** [sɪŋəˈpɔː*] n Singapur m
**singer** ['sɪŋə*] n cantante mf
**singing** ['sɪŋɪŋ] n canto
**single** ['sɪŋɡl] adj único, solo; (unmarried)
soltero; (not double) simple, sencillo ▷ n
(BRIT: also: **~ ticket**) billete m sencillo;
(record) sencillo, single m; **singles** npl

(*Tennis*) individual *m*; **single out** *vt* (*choose*) escoger; **single bed** *n* cama individual; **single file** *n*: **in single file** en fila de uno; **single-handed** *adv* sin ayuda; **single-minded** *adj* resuelto, firme; **single parent** *n* padre *m* soltero, madre *f* soltera (*o divorciado etc*); **single parent family** familia monoparental; **single room** *n* cuarto individual

**singular** ['sɪŋgjulə*] *adj* (*odd*) raro, extraño; (*outstanding*) excepcional ▷ *n* (*Ling*) singular *m*

**sinister** ['sɪnɪstə*] *adj* siniestro

**sink** [sɪŋk] (*pt* **sank**, *pp* **sunk**) *n* fregadero ▷ *vt* (*ship*) hundir, echar a pique; (*foundations*) excavar ▷ *vi* hundirse; **to ~ sth into** hundir algo en; **sink in** *vi* (*fig*) penetrar, calar

**sinus** ['saɪnəs] *n* (*Anat*) seno

**sip** [sɪp] *n* sorbo ▷ *vt* sorber, beber a sorbitos

**sir** [sə*] *n* señor *m*; **S~ John Smith** Sir John Smith; **yes ~** sí, señor

**siren** ['saɪərn] *n* sirena

**sirloin** ['sə:lɔɪn] *n* (*also*: **~ steak**) solomillo

**sister** ['sɪstə*] *n* hermana; (*BRIT*: *nurse*) enfermera jefe; **sister-in-law** *n* cuñada

**sit** [sɪt] (*pt*, *pp* **sat**) *vi* sentarse; (*be sitting*) estar sentado; (*assembly*) reunirse; (*for painter*) posar ▷ *vt* (*exam*) presentarse a; **sit back** *vi* (*in seat*) recostarse; **sit down** *vi* sentarse; **sit on** *vt fus* (*jury*, *committee*) ser miembro de, formar parte de; **sit up** *vi* incorporarse; (*not go to bed*) velar

**sitcom** ['sɪtkɔm] *n abbr* (= *situation comedy*) comedia de situación

**site** [saɪt] *n* sitio; (*also*: **building ~**) solar *m* ▷ *vt* situar

**sitting** ['sɪtɪŋ] *n* (*of assembly etc*) sesión *f*; (*in canteen*) turno; **sitting room** *n* sala de estar

**situated** ['sɪtjueɪtɪd] *adj* situado

**situation** [sɪtju'eɪʃən] *n* situación *f*; **"~s vacant"** (*BRIT*) "ofrecen trabajo"

**six** [sɪks] *num* seis; **sixteen** *num* dieciséis; **sixteenth** [sɪks'tiːnθ] *adj* decimosexto; **sixth** [sɪksθ] *num* sexto; **sixth form** *n* (*BRIT*) clase *f* de alumnos del sexto año (*de 16 a 18 años de edad*); **sixth-form college** *n* instituto *m* para alumnos de 16 a 18 años; **sixtieth** ['sɪkstɪɪθ] *adj* sexagésimo; **sixty** *num* sesenta

**size** [saɪz] *n* tamaño; (*extent*) extensión *f*; (*of clothing*) talla; (*of shoes*) número; **sizeable** *adj* importante, considerable

**sizzle** ['sɪzl] *vi* crepitar

**skate** [skeɪt] *n* patín *m*; (*fish: pl inv*) raya ▷ *vi* patinar; **skateboard** *n* monopatín *m*;

**skateboarding** *n* monopatín *m*; **skater** *n* patinador(a) *m/f*; **skating** *n* patinaje *m*; **skating rink** *n* pista de patinaje

**skeleton** ['skelɪtn] *n* esqueleto; (*Tech*) armazón *f*; (*outline*) esquema *m*

**skeptical** ['skeptɪkl] (*us*) = **sceptical**

**sketch** [sketʃ] *n* (*drawing*) dibujo; (*outline*) esbozo, bosquejo; (*Theatre*) sketch *m* ▷ *vt* dibujar; (*plan etc*: *also*: **~ out**) esbozar

**skewer** ['skjuːə*] *n* broqueta

**ski:** [skiː] *n* esquí *m* ▷ *vi* esquiar; **ski boot** *n* bota de esquí

**skid** [skɪd] *n* patinazo ▷ *vi* patinar

**ski: skier** *n* esquiador(a) *m/f*; **skiing** *n* esquí *m*

**skilful** ['skɪlful] (*us* **skillful**) *adj* diestro, experto

**ski lift** *n* telesilla *m*, telesquí *m*

**skill** [skɪl] *n* destreza, pericia; técnica; **skilled** *adj* hábil, diestro; (*worker*) cualificado

**skim** [skɪm] *vt* (*milk*) desnatar; (*glide over*) rozar, rasar ▷ *vi*: **to ~ through** (*book*) hojear; **skimmed milk** (*us* **skim milk**) *n* leche *f* desnatada

**skin** [skɪn] *n* piel *f*; (*complexion*) cutis *m* ▷ *vt* (*fruit etc*) pelar; (*animal*) despellejar; **skinhead** *n* cabeza *m/f* rapada, skin(head) *m/f*; **skinny** *adj* flaco

**skip** [skɪp] *n* brinco, salto; (*BRIT*: *container*) contenedor *m* ▷ *vi* brincar; (*with rope*) saltar a la comba ▷ *vt* saltarse

**ski: ski pass** *n* forfait *m* (de esquí); **ski pole** *n* bastón *m* de esquiar

**skipper** ['skɪpə*] *n* (*Naut*, *Sport*) capitán *m*

**skipping rope** ['skɪpɪŋ-] (*us* **skip rope**) *n* comba

**skirt** [skə:t] *n* falda, pollera (*sc*) ▷ *vt* (*go round*) ladear

**skirting board** ['skə:tɪŋ-] (*BRIT*) *n* rodapié *m*

**ski slope** *n* pista de esquí

**ski suit** *n* traje *m* de esquiar

**skull** [skʌl] *n* calavera; (*Anat*) cráneo

**skunk** [skʌŋk] *n* mofeta

**sky** [skaɪ] *n* cielo; **skyscraper** *n* rascacielos *m inv*

**slab** [slæb] *n* (*stone*) bloque *m*; (*flat*) losa; (*of cake*) trozo

**slack** [slæk] *adj* (*loose*) flojo; (*slow*) de poca actividad; (*careless*) descuidado; **slacks** *npl* pantalones *mpl*

**slain** [sleɪn] *pp* of **slay**

**slam** [slæm] *vt* (*throw*) arrojar (violentamente); (*criticize*) criticar duramente ▷ *vi* (*door*) cerrarse de golpe; **to ~ the door** dar un portazo

**slander** ['slɑːndə*] *n* calumnia,

difamación f

**slang** [slæŋ] n argot m; (jargon) jerga

**slant** [slɑːnt] n sesgo, inclinación f; (fig) interpretación f

**slap** [slæp] n palmada; (in face) bofetada ▷vt dar una palmada o bofetada a; (paint etc): **to ~ sth on sth** embadurnar algo con algo ▷adv (directly) exactamente, directamente

**slash** [slæʃ] vt acuchillar; (fig: prices) fulminar

**slate** [sleɪt] n pizarra ▷vt (fig: criticize) criticar duramente

**slaughter** ['slɔːtə*] n (of animals) matanza; (of people) carnicería ▷vt matar; **slaughterhouse** n matadero

**Slav** [slɑːv] adj eslavo

**slave** [sleɪv] n esclavo/a ▷vi (also: ~ **away**) sudar tinta; **slavery** n esclavitud f

**slay** [sleɪ] (pt **slew**, pp **slain**) vt matar

**sleazy** ['sliːzɪ] adj de mala fama

**sled** [slɛd] (US) = **sledge**

**sledge** [slɛdʒ] n trineo

**sleek** [sliːk] adj (shiny) lustroso; (car etc) elegante

**sleep** [sliːp] (pt, pp **slept**) n sueño ▷vi dormir; **to go to ~** quedarse dormido; **sleep in** vi (oversleep) quedarse dormido; **sleep together** vi (have sex) acostarse juntos; **sleeper** n (person) durmiente mf; (BRIT Rail: on track) traviesa; (: train) coche-cama m; **sleeping bag** n saco de dormir; **sleeping car** n coche-cama m; **sleeping pill** n somnífero; **sleepover** n: **we're having a sleepover at Jo's** nos vamos a quedar a dormir en casa de Jo; **sleepwalk** vi caminar dormido; (habitually) ser sonámbulo; **sleepy** adj soñoliento; (place) soporífero

**sleet** [sliːt] n aguanieve f

**sleeve** [sliːv] n manga; (Tech) manguito; (of record) portada; **sleeveless** adj sin mangas

**sleigh** [sleɪ] n trineo

**slender** ['slɛndə*] adj delgado; (means) escaso

**slept** [slɛpt] pt, pp of **sleep**

**slew** [sluː] pt of **slay** ▷vi (BRIT: veer) torcerse

**slice** [slaɪs] n (of meat) tajada; (of bread) rebanada; (of lemon) rodaja; (utensil) pala ▷vt cortar (en tajos), rebanar

**slick** [slɪk] adj (skilful) hábil, diestro; (clever) astuto ▷n (also: **oil ~**) marea negra

**slide** [slaɪd] (pt, pp **slid**) n (movement) descenso, desprendimiento; (in playground) tobogán m; (Phot) diapositiva; (BRIT: also: **hair ~**) pasador m ▷vt correr, deslizar ▷vi

(slip) resbalarse; (glide) deslizarse; **sliding** adj (door) corredizo

**slight** [slaɪt] adj (slim) delgado; (frail) delicado; (pain etc) leve; (trivial) insignificante; (small) pequeño ▷n desaire m ▷vt (insult) ofender, desairar; **not in the ~est** en absoluto; **slightly** adv ligeramente un poco

**slim** [slɪm] adj delgado, esbelto; (fig: chance) remoto ▷vi adelgazar; **slimming** n adelgazamiento

**slimy** ['slaɪmɪ] adj cenagoso

**sling** [slɪŋ] (pt, pp **slung**) n (Med) cabestrillo; (weapon) honda ▷vt tirar, arrojar

**slip** [slɪp] n (slide) resbalón m; (mistake) descuido; (underskirt) combinación f; (of paper) papelito ▷vt (slide) deslizar ▷vi deslizarse; (stumble) resbalar(se); (decline) decaer; (move smoothly): **to ~ into/out of** (room etc) introducirse en/salirse de; **to give sb the ~** eludir a algn; **a ~ of the tongue** un lapsus; **to ~ sth on/off** ponerse/quitarse algo; **slip up** vi (make mistake) equivocarse; meter la pata

**slipper** ['slɪpə*] n zapatilla, pantufla

**slippery** ['slɪpərɪ] adj resbaladizo; **slip road** (BRIT) n carretera de acceso

**slit** [slɪt] (pt, pp **~**) n raja; (cut) corte m ▷vt rajar; cortar

**slog** [slɒg] (BRIT) vi sudar tinta; **it was a ~** costó trabajo (hacerlo)

**slogan** ['sləugən] n eslogan m, lema m

**slope** [sləup] n (up) cuesta, pendiente f; (down) declive m; (side of mountain) falda, vertiente m ▷vi: **to ~ down** estar en declive; **to ~ up** inclinarse; **sloping** adj en pendiente; (writing) inclinado

**sloppy** ['slɒpɪ] adj (work) descuidado; (appearance) desaliñado

**slot** [slɒt] n ranura ▷vt: **to ~ into** encajar en; **slot machine** n (BRIT: vending machine) distribuidor m automático; (for gambling) tragaperras m inv

**Slovakia** [sləu'vækɪə] n Eslovaquia

**Slovene** [sləu'viːn] adj esloveno ▷n esloveno/a; (Ling) esloveno; **Slovenia** [sləu'viːnɪə] n Eslovenia; **Slovenian** adj, n = **Slovene**

**slow** [sləu] adj lento; (not clever) lerdo; (watch): **to be ~** atrasar ▷adv lentamente, despacio ▷vt, vi retardar; **"~"** (road sign) "disminuir velocidad"; **slow down** vi reducir la marcha; **slowly** adv lentamente, despacio; **slow motion** n: **in slow motion** a cámara lenta

**slug** [slʌg] n babosa; (bullet) posta; **sluggish** adj lento; (person) perezoso

**slum** [slʌm] n casucha
**slump** [slʌmp] n (economic) depresión f
▷ vi hundirse; (prices) caer en picado
**slung** [slʌŋ] pt, pp of **sling**
**slur** [slə:*] n: **to cast a ~ on** insultar ▷ vt
(speech) pronunciar mal
**sly** [slaɪ] adj astuto; (smile) taimado
**smack** [smæk] n bofetada ▷ vt dar con la
mano a; (child, on face) abofetear ▷ vi: **to ~ of**
saber a, oler a
**small** [smɔ:l] adj pequeño; **small ads**
(BRIT) npl anuncios mpl por palabras; **small
change** n suelto, cambio
**smart** [sma:t] adj elegante; (clever) listo,
inteligente; (quick) rápido, vivo ▷ vi escocer,
picar; **smartcard** n tarjeta inteligente
**smash** [smæʃ] n (also: **~-up**) choque m;
(Mus) exitazo ▷ vt (break) hacer pedazos;
(car etc) estrellar; (Sport: record) batir
▷ vi hacerse pedazos; (against wall etc)
estrellarse; **smashing** (inf) adj estupendo
**smear** [smɪə*] n mancha; (Med) frotis m inv
▷ vt untar; **smear test** n (Med) citología,
frotis m inv (cervical)
**smell** [smɛl] (pt, pp **smelt** or **~ed**) n olor
m; (sense) olfato ▷ vt, vi oler; **smelly** adj
maloliente
**smelt** [smɛlt] pt, pp of **smell**
**smile** [smaɪl] n sonrisa ▷ vi sonreír
**smirk** [smə:k] n sonrisa falsa or afectada
**smog** [smɔg] n esmog m
**smoke** [sməuk] n humo ▷ vi fumar;
(chimney) echar humo ▷ vt (cigarettes)
fumar; **smoke alarm** n detector m de
humo, alarma contra incendios; **smoked**
adj (bacon, glass) ahumado; **smoker** n
fumador(a) m/f; (Rail) coche m fumador;
**smoking** n: **"no smoking"** prohibido
fumar"

> ▌Be careful not to translate **smoking** by
> the Spanish word smoking.

**smoky** adj (room) lleno de humo; (taste)
ahumado
**smooth** [smu:ð] adj liso; (sea) tranquilo;
(flavour, movement) suave; (sauce) fino;
(person: pej) meloso ▷ vt (also: **~ out**) alisar;
(creases, difficulties) allanar
**smother** ['smʌðə*] vt sofocar; (repress)
contener
**SMS** n abbr (= short message service) (servicio)
SMS; **SMS message** n (mensaje m) SMS
**smudge** [smʌdʒ] n mancha ▷ vt manchar
**smug** [smʌg] adj presumido; orondo
**smuggle** ['smʌgl] vt pasar de
contrabando; **smuggling** n contrabando
**snack** [snæk] n bocado; **snack bar** n
cafetería
**snag** [snæg] n problema m

**snail** [sneɪl] n caracol m
**snake** [sneɪk] n serpiente f
**snap** [snæp] n (sound) chasquido;
(photograph) foto f ▷ adj (decision)
instantáneo ▷ vt (break) quebrar; (fingers)
castañetear ▷ vi quebrarse; (fig: speak
sharply) contestar bruscamente; **to ~ shut**
cerrarse de golpe; **snap at** vt fus (dog)
intentar morder; **snap up** vt agarrar;
**snapshot** n foto f (instantánea)
**snarl** [sna:l] vi gruñir
**snatch** [snætʃ] n (small piece) fragmento
▷ vt (snatch away) arrebatar; (fig) agarrar; **to
~ some sleep** encontrar tiempo para dormir
**sneak** [sni:k] (pt (US) **snuck**) vi: **to ~
in/out** entrar/salir a hurtadillas ▷ n (inf)
soplón/ona m/f; **to ~ up on sb** aparecérsele
de improviso a algn; **sneakers** npl zapatos
mpl de lona
**sneer** [snɪə*] vi reír con sarcasmo;
(mock): **to ~ at** burlarse de
**sneeze** [sni:z] vi estornudar
**sniff** [snɪf] vi sollozar ▷ vt husmear, oler;
(drugs) esnifar
**snigger** ['snɪgə*] vi reírse con disimulo
**snip** [snɪp] n tijeretazo; (BRIT: inf: bargain)
ganga ▷ vt tijeretear
**sniper** ['snaɪpə*] n francotirador(a) m/f
**snob** [snɔb] n (e)snob mf
**snooker** ['snu:kə*] n especie de billar
**snoop** [snu:p] vi: **to ~ about** fisgonear
**snooze** [snu:z] n siesta ▷ vi echar una
siesta
**snore** [snɔ:*] vi ronquido ▷ vi roncar
**snorkel** ['snɔ:kl] n (tubo) respirador m
**snort** [snɔ:t] n bufido ▷ vi bufar
**snow** [snəu] n nieve f ▷ vi nevar;
**snowball** n bola de nieve ▷ vi (fig)
agrandirse, ampliarse; **snowstorm** n
nevada, nevasca
**snub** [snʌb] vt (person) desairar ▷ n
desaire m, repulsa
**snug** [snʌg] adj (cosy) cómodo; (fitted)
ajustado

○ **KEYWORD**

**so** [səu] adv **1** (thus, likewise) así, de este
modo; **if so** de ser así; **I like swimming – so
do I** a mí me gusta nadar – a mí también;
**I've got work to do – so has Paul** tengo
trabajo que hacer – Paul también; **it's 5
o'clock – so it is!** son las cinco – ¡pues es
verdad!; **I hope/think so** espero/creo que
sí; **so far** hasta ahora; (in past) hasta este
momento
**2** (in comparisons etc: to such a degree) tan;
**so quickly (that)** tan rápido (que); **so big**

**(that)** tan grande (que); **she's not so clever as her brother** no es tan lista como su hermano; **we were so worried** estábamos preocupadísimos

**3**: **so much** adj, adv tanto; **so many** tantos/as

**4** (phrases): **10 or so** unos 10, 10 o así; **so long!** (inf: goodbye) ¡hasta luego!
▷ conj **1** (expressing purpose): **so as to do** para hacer; **so (that)** para que +subjun
**2** (expressing result) así que; **so you see, I could have gone** así que ya ves, (yo) podría haber ido

**soak** [səuk] vt (drench) empapar; (steep in water) remojar ▷ vi remojarse, estar a remojo; **soak up** vt absorber; **soaking** adj (also: **soaking wet**) calado or empapado (hasta los huesos or el tuétano)
**so-and-so** ['səuənsəu] n (somebody) fulano/a de tal
**soap** [səup] n jabón m; **soap opera** n telenovela; **soap powder** n jabón m en polvo
**soar** [sɔ:*] vi (on wings) remontarse; (rocket: prices) dispararse; (building etc) elevarse
**sob** [sɔb] n sollozo ▷ vi sollozar
**sober** ['səubə*] adj (serious) serio; (not drunk) sobrio; (colour, style) discreto; **sober up** vt quitar la borrachera
**so-called** ['səu'kɔ:ld] adj así llamado
**soccer** ['sɔkə*] n fútbol m
**sociable** ['səuʃəbl] adj sociable
**social** ['səuʃl] adj social ▷ n velada, fiesta; **socialism** n socialismo; **socialist** adj, n socialista mf; **socialize** vi: **to socialize (with)** alternar (con); **social life** n vida social; **socially** adv socialmente; **social security** n seguridad f social; **social services** npl servicios mpl sociales; **social work** n asistencia social; **social worker** n asistente/a m/f social
**society** [sə'saɪətɪ] n sociedad f; (club) asociación f; (also: **high ~**) alta sociedad
**sociology** [səusɪ'ɔlədʒi] n sociología
**sock** [sɔk] n calcetín m
**socket** ['sɔkɪt] n cavidad f; (BRIT Elec) enchufe m
**soda** ['səudə] n (Chem) sosa; (also: **~ water**) soda; (US: also: **~ pop**) gaseosa
**sodium** ['səudiəm] n sodio
**sofa** ['səufə] n sofá m; **sofa bed** n sofá-cama m
**soft** [sɔft] adj (lenient, not hard) blando; (gentle, not bright) suave; **soft drink** n bebida no alcohólica; **soft drugs** npl drogas fpl blandas; **soften** ['sɔfn] vt

ablandar; suavizar; (effect) amortiguar
▷ vi ablandarse; suavizarse; **softly** adv suavemente; (gently) delicadamente, con delicadeza; **software** n (Comput) software m
**soggy** ['sɔgɪ] adj empapado
**soil** [sɔɪl] n (earth) tierra, suelo ▷ vt ensuciar
**solar** ['səulə*] adj solar; **solar power** n energía solar; **solar system** n sistema m solar
**sold** [səuld] pt, pp of **sell**
**soldier** ['səuldʒə*] n soldado; (army man) militar m
**sold out** adj (Comm) agotado
**sole** [səul] n (of foot) planta; (of shoe) suela; (fish: pl inv) lenguado ▷ adj único; **solely** adv únicamente, sólo, solamente; **I will hold you solely responsible** le consideraré el único responsable
**solemn** ['sɔləm] adj solemne
**solicitor** [sə'lɪsɪtə*] (BRIT) n (for wills etc) ≈ notario/a; (in court) ≈ abogado/a
**solid** ['sɔlɪd] adj sólido; (gold etc) macizo ▷ n sólido
**solitary** ['sɔlɪtərɪ] adj solitario, solo
**solitude** ['sɔlɪtju:d] n soledad f
**solo** ['səuləu] n solo ▷ adv (fly) en solitario; **soloist** n solista m/f
**soluble** ['sɔljʊbl] adj soluble
**solution** [sə'lu:ʃən] n solución f
**solve** [sɔlv] vt resolver, solucionar
**solvent** ['sɔlvənt] adj (Comm) solvente ▷ n (Chem) solvente m
**sombre** ['sɔmbə*] (US **somber**) adj sombrío

○ **KEYWORD**

**some** [sʌm] adj **1** (a certain amount or number): **some tea/water/biscuits** té/agua/(unas) galletas; **there's some milk in the fridge** hay leche en el frigo; **there were some people outside** había algunas personas fuera; **I've got some money, but not much** tengo algo de dinero, pero no mucho
**2** (certain: in contrasts) algunos/as; **some people say that ...** hay quien dice que ...; **some films were excellent, but most were mediocre** hubo películas excelentes, pero la mayoría fueron mediocres
**3** (unspecified): **some woman was asking for you** una mujer estuvo preguntando por ti; **he was asking for some book (or other)** pedía un libro; **some day** algún día; **some day next week** un día de la semana que viene

▷ *pron* **1** (*a certain number*): **I've got some** (*books etc*) tengo algunos/as **2** (*a certain amount*) algo; **I've got some** (*money, milk*) tengo algo; **could I have some of that cheese?** ¿me puede dar un poco de ese queso?; **I've read some of the book** he leído parte del libro

▷ *adv*: **some 10 people** unas 10 personas, una decena de personas

**some: somebody** ['sʌmbədɪ] *pron* = **someone; somehow** *adv* de alguna manera; (*for some reason*) por una u otra razón; **someone** *pron* alguien; **someplace** (*us*) *adv* = **somewhere; something** *pron* algo; **would you like something to eat/drink?** ¿te gustaría cenar/tomar algo?; **sometime** *adv* (*in future*) algún día, en algún momento; (*in past*): **sometime last month** durante el mes pasado; **sometimes** *adv* a veces; **somewhat** *adv* algo; **somewhere** *adv* (*be*) en alguna parte; (*go*) a alguna parte; **somewhere else** (*be*) en otra parte; (*go*) a otra parte

**son** [sʌn] *n* hijo

**song** [sɔŋ] *n* canción *f*

**son-in-law** ['sʌnɪnlɔː] *n* yerno

**soon** [suːn] *adv* pronto, dentro de poco; **~ afterwards** poco después; *see also* **as; sooner** *adv* (*time*) antes, más temprano; (*preference: rather*): **I would sooner do that** preferiría hacer eso; **sooner or later** tarde o temprano

**soothe** [suːð] *vt* tranquilizar; (*pain*) aliviar

**sophisticated** [sə'fɪstɪkeɪtɪd] *adj* sofisticado

**sophomore** ['sɔfəmɔː*] (*us*) *n* estudiante *mf* de segundo año

**soprano** [sə'prɑːnəu] *n* soprano *f*

**sorbet** ['sɔːbeɪ] *n* sorbete *m*

**sordid** ['sɔːdɪd] *adj* (*place etc*) sórdido; (*motive etc*) mezquino

**sore** [sɔː*] *adj* (*painful*) doloroso, que duele ▷ *n* llaga

**sorrow** ['sɔrəu] *n* pena, dolor *m*

**sorry** ['sɔrɪ] *adj* (*regretful*) arrepentido; (*condition, excuse*) lastimoso; **~!** ¡perdón!, ¡perdone!; **~?** ¿cómo?; **to feel ~ for sb** tener lástima a algn; **I feel ~ for him** me da lástima

**sort** [sɔːt] *n* clase *f*, género, tipo; **sort out** *vt* (*papers*) clasificar; (*organize*) ordenar, organizar; (*resolve: problem, situation etc*) arreglar, solucionar

**SOS** *n* SOS *m*

**so-so** ['səusəu] *adv* regular, así así

**sought** [sɔːt] *pt, pp of* **seek**

**soul** [səul] *n* alma

**sound** [saund] *n* (*noise*) sonido, ruido; (*volume: on TV etc*) volumen *m*; (*Geo*) estrecho ▷ *adj* (*healthy*) sano; (*safe, not damaged*) en buen estado; (*reliable: person*) digno de confianza; (*sensible*) sensato, razonable; (*secure: investment*) seguro ▷ *adv*: **~ asleep** profundamente dormido ▷ *vt* (*alarm*) sonar ▷ *vi* sonar, resonar; (*fig: seem*) parecer; **to ~ like** sonar a; **soundtrack** *n* (*of film*) banda sonora

**soup** [suːp] *n* (*thick*) sopa; (*thin*) caldo

**sour** ['sauə*] *adj* agrio; (*milk*) cortado; **it's ~ grapes** (*fig*) están verdes

**source** [sɔːs] *n* fuente *f*

**south** [sauθ] *n* sur *m* ▷ *adj* del sur, sureño ▷ *adv* al sur, hacia el sur; **South Africa** *n* África del Sur; **South African** *adj, n* sudafricano/a *m/f*; **South America** *n* América del Sur, Sudamérica; **South American** *adj, n* sudamericano/a *m/f*; **southbound** *adj* (con) rumbo al sur; **southeastern** [sauθ'iːstən] *adj* sureste, del sureste; **southern** ['sʌðən] *adj* del sur, meridional; **South Korea** *n* Corea del Sur; **South Pole** *n* Polo Sur; **southward(s)** *adv* hacia el sur; **south-west** *n* suroeste *m*; **southwestern** [sauθ'westən] *adj* suroeste

**souvenir** [suːvə'nɪə*] *n* recuerdo

**sovereign** ['sɔvrɪn] *adj, n* soberano/a *m/f*

**sow¹** [səu] (*pt ~ed, pp sown*) *vt* sembrar

**sow²** [sau] *n* cerda, puerca

**soya** ['sɔɪə] (*BRIT*) *n* soja

**spa** [spɑː] *n* balneario

**space** [speɪs] *n* espacio; (*room*) sitio ▷ *cpd* espacial ▷ *vt* (*also: ~ out*) espaciar; **spacecraft** *n* nave *f* espacial; **spaceship** *n* = **spacecraft**

**spacious** ['speɪʃəs] *adj* amplio

**spade** [speɪd] *n* (*tool*) pala, laya; **spades** *npl* (*Cards: British*) picas *fpl*; (: *Spanish*) espadas *fpl*

**spaghetti** [spə'getɪ] *n* espaguetis *mpl*, fideos *mpl*

**Spain** [speɪn] *n* España

**spam** [spæm] *n* (*junk e-mail*) spam *m*

**span** [spæn] *n* (*of bird, plane*) envergadura; (*of arch*) luz *f*; (*in time*) lapso ▷ *vt* extenderse sobre, cruzar; (*fig*) abarcar

**Spaniard** ['spænjəd] *n* español(a) *m/f*

**Spanish** ['spænɪʃ] *adj* español(a) ▷ *n* (*Ling*) español *m*, castellano; **the Spanish** *npl* los españoles

**spank** [spæŋk] *vt* zurrar

**spanner** ['spænə*] (*BRIT*) *n* llave *f* (inglesa)

**spare** [speə*] *adj* de reserva; (*surplus*) sobrante, de más ▷ *n* = **spare part** ▷ *vt* (*do without*) pasarse sin; (*refrain from hurting*) perdonar; **to ~** (*surplus*) sobrante, de sobra; **spare part** *n* pieza de repuesto; **spare**

**room** n cuarto de los invitados; **spare time** n tiempo libre; **spare tyre** (US **spare tire**) n (Aut) neumático or llanta (LAM) de recambio; **spare wheel** n (Aut) rueda de recambio

**spark** [spɑːk] n chispa; (fig) chispazo; **spark(ing) plug** n bujía

**sparkle** ['spɑːkl] n centelleo, destello ▷ vi (shine) relucir, brillar

**sparrow** ['spærəu] n gorrión m

**sparse** [spɑːs] adj esparcido, escaso

**spasm** ['spæzəm] n (Med) espasmo

**spat** [spæt] pt, pp of **spit**

**spate** [speit] n (fig): **a ~ of** un torrente de

**spatula** ['spætjulə] n espátula

**speak** [spiːk] (pt **spoke**, pp **spoken**) vt (language) hablar; (truth) decir ▷ vi hablar; (make a speech) intervenir; **to ~ to sb/of** or **about sth** hablar con algn/de or sobre algo; **~ up!** ¡habla fuerte!; **speaker** n (in public) orador(a) m/f; (also: **loudspeaker**) altavoz m; (for stereo etc) bafle m; (Pol): **the Speaker** (BRIT) el Presidente de la Cámara de los Comunes; (US) el Presidente del Congreso

**spear** [spiə*] n lanza ▷ vt alancear

**special** ['spɛʃl] adj especial; (edition etc) extraordinario; (delivery) urgente; **special delivery** n (Post): **by special delivery** por entrega urgente; **special effects** npl (Cine) efectos mpl especiales; **specialist** n especialista mf; **speciality** [spɛʃɪ'ælɪtɪ] (BRIT) n especialidad f; **specialize** vi: **to specialize (in)** especializarse (en); **specially** adv sobre todo, en particular; **special needs** npl (BRIT): **children with special needs** niños que requieren una atención diferenciada; **special offer** n (Comm) oferta especial; **special school** n (BRIT) colegio m de educación especial; **specialty** (US) n = **speciality**

**species** ['spiːʃiːz] n inv especie f

**specific** [spə'sɪfɪk] adj específico; **specifically** adv específicamente

**specify** ['spɛsɪfaɪ] vt, vi especificar, precisar

**specimen** ['spɛsɪmən] n ejemplar m; (Med: of urine) espécimen m; (: of blood) muestra

**speck** [spɛk] n grano, mota

**spectacle** ['spɛktəkl] n espectáculo; **spectacles** npl (BRIT: glasses) gafas fpl (SP), anteojos mpl; **spectacular** [-'tækjulə*] adj espectacular; (success) impresionante

**spectator** [spɛk'teɪtə*] n espectador(a) m/f

**spectrum** ['spɛktrəm] (pl **spectra**) n espectro

**speculate** ['spɛkjuleɪt] vi: **to ~ (on)** especular (en)

**sped** [spɛd] pt, pp of **speed**

**speech** [spiːtʃ] n (faculty) habla; (formal talk) discurso; (spoken language) lenguaje m; **speechless** adj mudo, estupefacto

**speed** [spiːd] n velocidad f; (haste) prisa; (promptness) rapidez f; **at full** or **top ~** a máxima velocidad; **speed up** vi acelerarse ▷ vt acelerar; **speedboat** n lancha motora; **speeding** n (Aut) exceso de velocidad; **speed limit** n límite m de velocidad, velocidad f máxima; **speedometer** [spɪ'dɔmɪtə*] n velocímetro; **speedy** adj (fast) veloz, rápido; (prompt) pronto

**spell** [spɛl] (pt, pp **spelt** (BRIT) or **~ed**) n (also: **magic ~**) encanto, hechizo; (period of time) rato, período ▷ vt deletrear; (fig) anunciar, presagiar; **to cast a ~ on sb** hechizar a algn; **he can't ~** pone faltas de ortografía; **spell out** vt (explain): **to spell sth out for sb** explicar algo a algn en detalle; **spellchecker** ['spɛltʃɛkə*] n corrector m ortográfico; **spelling** n ortografía

**spelt** [spɛlt] pt, pp of **spell**

**spend** [spɛnd] (pt, pp **spent**) vt (money) gastar; (time) pasar; (life) dedicar; **spending** n: **government spending** gastos mpl del gobierno

**spent** [spɛnt] pt, pp of **spend** ▷ adj (cartridge, bullets, match) usado

**sperm** [spəːm] n esperma

**sphere** [sfɪə*] n esfera

**spice** [spaɪs] n especia ▷ vt condimentar

**spicy** ['spaɪsɪ] adj picante

**spider** ['spaɪdə*] n araña

**spike** [spaɪk] n (point) punta; (Bot) espiga

**spill** [spɪl] (pt, pp **spilt** or **~ed**) vt derramar, verter ▷ vi derramarse; **to ~ over** desbordarse

**spin** [spɪn] (pt, pp **spun**) n (Aviat) barrena; (trip in car) paseo (en coche); (on ball) efecto ▷ vt (wool etc) hilar; (ball etc) hacer girar ▷ vi girar, dar vueltas

**spinach** ['spɪnɪtʃ] n espinaca; (as food) espinacas fpl

**spinal** ['spaɪnl] adj espinal

**spin doctor** n informador(a) parcial al servicio de un partido político etc

**spin-dryer** (BRIT) n secador m centrífugo

**spine** [spaɪn] n espinazo, columna vertebral; (thorn) espina

**spiral** ['spaɪərl] n espiral f ▷ vi (fig: prices) subir desorbitadamente

**spire** ['spaɪə*] n aguja, chapitel m

**spirit** ['spɪrɪt] n (soul) alma; (ghost) fantasma m; (attitude, sense) espíritu m; (courage) valor m, ánimo; **spirits** npl (drink) licor(es) m(pl); **in good ~s** alegre, de buen

ánimo
**spiritual** ['spɪrɪtjuəl] *adj* espiritual ▷ *n*
espiritual *m*
**spit** [spɪt] (*pt, pp* **spat**) *n* (*for roasting*)
asador *m*, espetón *m*; (*saliva*) saliva ▷ *vi*
escupir; (*sound*) chisporrotear; (*rain*)
lloviznar
**spite** [spaɪt] *n* rencor *m*, ojeriza ▷ *vt*
causar pena a, mortificar; **in ~ of** a pesar de,
pese a; **spiteful** *adj* rencoroso, malévolo
**splash** [splæʃ] *n* (*sound*) chapoteo; (*of
colour*) mancha ▷ *vt* salpicar ▷ *vi* (*also:* **~
about**) chapotear; **splash out** (*inf*) *vi* (*BRIT*)
derrochar dinero
**splendid** ['splɛndɪd] *adj* espléndido
**splinter** ['splɪntə*] *n* (*of wood etc*) astilla;
(*in finger*) espigón *m* ▷ *vi* astillarse, hacer
astillas
**split** [splɪt] (*pt, pp* **~**) *n* hendedura, raja;
(*fig*) división *f*; (*Pol*) escisión *f* ▷ *vt* partir,
rajar; (*party*) dividir; (*share*) repartir ▷ *vi*
dividirse, escindirse; **split up** *vi* (*couple*)
separarse; (*meeting*) acabarse
**spoil** [spɔɪl] (*pt, pp* **~t** *or* **~ed**) *vt* (*damage*)
dañar; (*mar*) estropear; (*child*) mimar,
consentir
**spoilt** [spɔɪlt] *pt, pp of* **spoil** ▷ *adj* (*child*)
mimado, consentido; (*ballot paper*)
invalidado
**spoke** [spəʊk] *pt of* **speak** ▷ *n* rayo, radio
**spoken** ['spəʊkn] *pp of* **speak**
**spokesman** ['spəʊksmən] (*irreg*) *n*
portavoz *m*
**spokesperson** ['spəʊkspə:sn] (*irreg*) *n*
portavoz *m/f*, vocero/a (*LAM*)
**spokeswoman** ['spəʊkswumən] (*irreg*)
*n* portavoz *f*
**sponge** [spʌndʒ] *n* esponja; (*also:* **~ cake**)
bizcocho ▷ *vt* (*wash*) lavar con esponja
▷ *vi*: **to ~ off** *or* **on sb** vivir a costa de algn;
**sponge bag** (*BRIT*) *n* esponjera
**sponsor** ['spɒnsə*] *n* patrocinador(a)
*m/f* ▷ *vt* (*applicant, proposal etc*) proponer;
**sponsorship** *n* patrocinio
**spontaneous** [spɒn'teɪnɪəs] *adj*
espontáneo
**spooky** ['spu:kɪ] (*inf*) *adj* espeluznante,
horripilante
**spoon** [spu:n] *n* cuchara; **spoonful** *n*
cucharada
**sport** [spɔ:t] *n* deporte *m*; (*person*): **to be
a good ~** ser muy majo ▷ *vt* (*wear*) lucir,
ostentar; **sport jacket** (*US*) *n* = **sports
jacket**; **sports car** *n* coche *m* deportivo;
**sports centre** (*BRIT*) *n* polideportivo;
**sports jacket** (*BRIT*) *n* chaqueta deportiva;
**sportsman** (*irreg*) *n* deportista *m*; **sports
utility vehicle** *n* todoterreno *m inv*;

**sportswear** *n* trajes *mpl* de deporte *or*
sport; **sportswoman** (*irreg*) *n* deportista;
**sporty** *adj* deportista
**spot** [spɒt] *n* sitio, lugar *m*; (*dot: on pattern*)
punto, mancha; (*pimple*) grano; (*Radio*)
cuña publicitaria; (*TV*) espacio publicitario;
(*small amount*): **a ~ of** un poquito de ▷ *vt*
(*notice*) notar, observar; **on the ~** allí mismo;
**spotless** *adj* perfectamente limpio;
**spotlight** *n* foco, reflector *m*; (*Aut*) faro
auxiliar
**spouse** [spauz] *n* cónyuge *mf*
**sprain** [spreɪn] *n* torcedura ▷ *vt*: **to ~
one's ankle/wrist** torcerse el tobillo/la
muñeca
**sprang** [spræŋ] *pt of* **spring**
**sprawl** [sprɔ:l] *vi* tumbarse
**spray** [spreɪ] *n* rociada; (*of sea*) espuma;
(*container*) atomizador *m*; (*for paint etc*)
pistola rociadora; (*of flowers*) ramita ▷ *vt*
rociar; (*crops*) regar
**spread** [sprɛd] (*pt, pp* **~**) *n* extensión *f*;
(*for bread etc*) pasta para untar; (*inf: food*)
comilona ▷ *vt* extender; (*butter*) untar;
(*wings, sails*) desplegar; (*work, wealth*)
repartir; (*scatter*) esparcir ▷ *vi* (*also:* **~
out**: *stain*) extenderse; (*news*) diseminarse;
**spread out** *vi* (*move apart*) separarse;
**spreadsheet** *n* hoja electrónica *or* de
cálculo
**spree** [spri:] *n*: **to go on a ~** ir de juerga
**spring** [sprɪŋ] (*pt* **sprang**, *pp* **sprung**) *n*
(*season*) primavera; (*leap*) salto, brinco;
(*coiled metal*) resorte *m*; (*of water*) fuente *f*,
manantial *m* ▷ *vi* saltar, brincar; **spring up**
*vi* (*thing: appear*) aparecer; (*problem*) surgir;
**spring onion** *n* cebolleta
**sprinkle** ['sprɪŋkl] *vt* (*pour: liquid*) rociar;
(*: salt, sugar*) espolvorear; **to ~ water** *etc*
**on,** **~ with water** *etc* rociar *or* salpicar de
agua *etc*
**sprint** [sprɪnt] *n* esprint *m* ▷ *vi* esprintar
**sprung** [sprʌŋ] *pp of* **spring**
**spun** [spʌn] *pt, pp of* **spin**
**spur** [spə:*] *n* espuela; (*fig*) estímulo,
aguijón *m* ▷ *vt* (*also:* **~ on**) estimular,
incitar; **on the ~ of the moment** de
improviso
**spurt** [spə:t] *n* chorro; (*of energy*) arrebato
▷ *vi* chorrear
**spy** [spaɪ] *n* espía *mf* ▷ *vi*: **to ~ on** espiar a
▷ *vt* (*see*) divisar, lograr ver
**sq.** *abbr* = **square**
**squabble** ['skwɒbl] *vi* reñir, pelear
**squad** [skwɒd] *n* (*Mil*) pelotón *m*; (*Police*)
brigada; (*Sport*) equipo
**squadron** ['skwɒdrn] *n* (*Mil*) escuadrón *m*;
(*Aviat, Naut*) escuadra

**squander** ['skwɔndə*] vt (money) derrochar, despilfarrar; (chances) desperdiciar

**square** [skwεə*] n cuadro; (in town) plaza; (inf: person) carca m/f ▷ adj cuadrado; (inf: ideas, tastes) trasnochado ▷ vt (arrange) arreglar; (Math) cuadrar; (reconcile) compaginar; **all ~** igual(es); **to have a ~ meal** comer caliente; **2 metres ~** 2 metros en cuadro; **2 ~ metres** 2 metros cuadrados; **square root** n raíz f cuadrada

**squash** [skwɔʃ] n (BRIT: drink): **lemon/orange ~** zumo (SP) or jugo (LAM) de limón/naranja; (US Bot) calabacín m; (Sport) squash m ▷ vt aplastar

**squat** [skwɔt] adj achaparrado ▷ vi (also: **~ down**) agacharse, sentarse en cuclillas; **squatter** n okupa mf(SP)

**squeak** [skwi:k] vi (hinge) chirriar, rechinar; (mouse) chillar

**squeal** [skwi:l] vi chillar, dar gritos agudos

**squeeze** [skwi:z] n presión f; (of hand) apretón m; (Comm) restricción f ▷ vt (hand, arm) apretar

**squid** [skwɪd] n inv calamar m; (Culin) calamares mpl

**squint** [skwɪnt] vi bizquear, ser bizco ▷ n (Med) estrabismo

**squirm** [skwə:m] vi retorcerse, revolverse

**squirrel** ['skwɪrəl] n ardilla

**squirt** [skwə:t] vi salir a chorros ▷ vt chiscar

**Sr** abbr = **senior**

**Sri Lanka** [srɪ'læŋkə] n Sri Lanka m

**St** abbr = **saint; street**

**stab** [stæb] n (with knife) puñalada; (of pain) pinchazo; (inf: try): **to have a ~ at (doing) sth** intentar (hacer) algo ▷ vt apuñalar

**stability** [stə'bɪlɪtɪ] n estabilidad f

**stable** ['steɪbl] adj estable ▷ n cuadra, caballeriza

**stack** [stæk] n montón m, pila ▷ vt amontonar, apilar

**stadium** ['steɪdɪəm] n estadio

**staff** [stɑ:f] n (work force) personal m, plantilla; (BRIT Scol) cuerpo docente ▷ vt proveer de personal

**stag** [stæg] n ciervo, venado

**stage** [steɪdʒ] n escena; (point) etapa; (platform) plataforma; (profession): **the ~** el teatro ▷ vt (play) poner en escena, representar; (organize) montar, organizar; **in ~s** por etapas

**stagger** ['stægə*] vi tambalearse ▷ vt (amaze) asombrar; (hours, holidays) escalonar; **staggering** adj asombroso

**stagnant** ['stægnənt] adj estancado

**stag night, stag party** n despedida de soltero

**stain** [steɪn] n mancha; (colouring) tintura ▷ vt manchar; (wood) teñir; **stained glass** n vidrio m de color; **stainless steel** n acero inoxidable

**staircase** ['stεəkeɪs] n = **stairway**

**stairs** [stεəz] npl escaleras fpl

**stairway** ['stεəweɪ] n escalera

**stake** [steɪk] n estaca, poste m; (Comm) interés m; (Betting) apuesta ▷ vt (money) apostar; (life) arriesgar; (reputation) poner en juego; (claim) presentar una reclamación; **to be at ~** estar en juego

**stale** [steɪl] adj (bread) duro; (food) pasado; (smell) rancio; (beer) agrio

**stalk** [stɔ:k] n tallo, caña ▷ vt acechar, cazar al acecho

**stall** [stɔ:l] n (in market) puesto; (in stable) casilla (de establo) ▷ vt (Aut) calar; (fig) dar largas a ▷ vi (Aut) calarse; (fig) andarse con rodeos

**stamina** ['stæmɪnə] n resistencia

**stammer** ['stæmə*] n tartamudeo ▷ vi tartamudear

**stamp** [stæmp] n sello (SP), estampilla (LAM), timbre m (MEX); (mark) marca, huella; (on document) timbre m ▷ vi (also: **~ one's foot**) patear ▷ vt (mark) marcar; (letter) franquear; (with rubber stamp) sellar; **stamp out** vt (fire) apagar con el pie; (crime, opposition) acabar con; **stamped addressed envelope** n (BRIT) sobre m sellado con las señas propias

**stampede** [stæm'pi:d] n estampida

**stance** [stæns] n postura

**stand** [stænd] n (pt, pp **stood**) n (position) posición f, postura; (for taxis) parada; (hall stand) perchero; (music stand) atril m; (Sport) tribuna; (at exhibition) stand m ▷ vi (be) estar, encontrarse; (be on foot) estar de pie; (rise) levantarse; (remain) quedar en pie; (in election) presentar candidatura ▷ vt (place) poner, colocar; (withstand) aguantar, soportar; (invite to) invitar; **to make a ~** (fig) mantener una postura firme; **to ~ for parliament** (BRIT) presentarse (como candidato) a las elecciones; **stand back** vi retirarse; **stand by** vi (be ready) estar listo ▷ vt fus (opinion) aferrarse a; (person) apoyar; **stand down** vi (withdraw) ceder el puesto; **stand for** vt fus (signify) significar; (tolerate) aguantar, permitir; **stand in for** vt fus suplir a; **stand out** vi destacarse; **stand up** vi levantarse, ponerse de pie; **stand up for** vt fus defender; **stand up to** vt fus hacer frente a

**standard** ['stændəd] n patrón m, norma; (level) nivel m; (flag) estandarte m ▷ adj

(size etc) normal, corriente; (text) básico;
**standards** npl (morals) valores mpl morales;
**standard of living** n nivel m de vida
**standing** ['stændɪŋ] adj (on foot) de
pie, en pie; (permanent) permanente ▷ n
reputación f; **of many years' ~** que lleva
muchos años; **standing order** (BRIT) n (at
bank) orden f de pago permanente
**stand: standpoint** n punto de vista;
**standstill** n: **at a standstill** (industry, traffic)
paralizado; (car) parado; **to come to a**
**standstill** quedar paralizado; pararse
**stank** [stæŋk] pt of **stink**
**staple** ['steɪpl] n (for papers) grapa ▷ adj
(food etc) básico ▷ vt grapar
**star** [stɑ:*] n estrella; (celebrity) estrella,
astro ▷ vt (Theatre, Cinema) ser el/la
protagonista de; **the stars** npl (Astrology)
el horóscopo
**starboard** ['stɑ:bəd] n estribor m
**starch** [stɑ:tʃ] n almidón m
**stardom** ['stɑ:dəm] n estrellato
**stare** [stɛə*] n mirada fija ▷ vi: **to ~ at**
mirar fijo
**stark** [stɑ:k] adj (bleak) severo, escueto
▷ adv: **~ naked** en cueros
**start** [stɑ:t] n principio, comienzo;
(departure) salida; (sudden movement)
salto, sobresalto; (advantage) ventaja ▷ vt
empezar, comenzar; (cause) causar; (found)
fundar; (engine) poner en marcha ▷ vi
comenzar, empezar; (with fright) asustarse,
sobresaltarse; (train etc) salir; **to ~ doing** or
**to do sth** empezar a hacer algo; **start off**
vi empezar, comenzar; (leave) salir, ponerse
en camino; **start out** vi (begin) empezar;
(set out) partir, salir; **start up** vi comenzar;
(car) ponerse en marcha ▷ vt comenzar;
poner en marcha; **starter** n (Aut) botón m
de arranque; (Sport: official) juez mf de salida;
(BRIT Culin) entrante m; **starting point** n
punto de partida
**startle** ['stɑ:tl] vt asustar, sobrecoger;
**startling** adj alarmante
**starvation** [stɑ:'veɪʃən] n hambre f
**starve** [stɑ:v] vi tener mucha hambre; (to
death) morir de hambre ▷ vt hacer pasar
hambre
**state** [steɪt] n estado ▷ vt (say, declare)
afirmar; **the S~s** los Estados Unidos; **to**
**be in a ~** estar agitado; **statement** n
afirmación f; **state school** n escuela
or colegio estatal; **statesman** (irreg) n
estadista m
**static** ['stætɪk] n (Radio) parásitos mpl
▷ adj estático
**station** ['steɪʃən] n estación f; (Radio)
emisora; (rank) posición f social ▷ vt

colocar, situar; (Mil) apostar
**stationary** ['steɪʃnərɪ] adj estacionario,
fijo
**stationer's (shop)** (BRIT) n papelería
**stationery** [-nərɪ] n papel m de escribir,
artículos mpl de escritorio
**station wagon** (US) n ranchera
**statistic** [stə'tɪstɪk] n estadística;
**statistics** n (science) estadística
**statue** ['stætju:] n estatua
**stature** ['stætʃə*] n estatura; (fig) talla
**status** ['steɪtəs] n estado; (reputation)
estatus m; **status quo** n (e)statu quo m
**statutory** ['stætjutrɪ] adj estatutario
**staunch** [stɔ:ntʃ] adj leal, incondicional
**stay** [steɪ] n estancia ▷ vi quedar(se);
(as guest) hospedarse; **to ~ put** seguir en el
mismo sitio; **to ~ the night/5 days** pasar
la noche/estar 5 días; **stay away** vi (from
person, building) no acercarse; (from event)
no acudir; **stay behind** vi quedar atrás;
**stay in** vi quedarse en casa; **stay on** vi
quedarse; **stay out** vi (of house) no volver a
casa; (on strike) permanecer en huelga; **stay**
**up** vi (at night) velar, no acostarse
**steadily** ['stedɪlɪ] adv constantemente;
(firmly) firmemente; (work, walk) sin parar;
(gaze) fijamente
**steady** ['stedɪ] adj (firm) firme; (regular)
regular; (person, character) sensato, juicioso;
(boyfriend) formal; (look, voice) tranquilo ▷ vt
(stabilize) estabilizar; (nerves) calmar
**steak** [steɪk] n filete m; (beef) bistec m
**steal** [sti:l] (pt **stole**, pp **stolen**) vt robar
▷ vi robar; (move secretly) andar a hurtadillas
**steam** [sti:m] n vapor m; (mist) vaho,
humo ▷ vt (Culin) cocer al vapor ▷ vi echar
vapor; **steam up** vi (window) empañarse;
**to get steamed up about sth** (fig) ponerse
negro por algo; **steamy** adj (room) lleno
de vapor; (window) empañado; (heat,
atmosphere) bochornoso
**steel** [sti:l] n acero ▷ adj de acero
**steep** [sti:p] adj escarpado, abrupto; (stair)
empinado; (price) exorbitante, excesivo ▷ vt
empapar, remojar
**steeple** ['sti:pl] n aguja
**steer** [stɪə*] vt (car) conducir (SP), manejar
(LAM); (person) dirigir ▷ vi conducir,
manejar; **steering** n (Aut) dirección f;
**steering wheel** n volante m
**stem** [stem] n (of plant) tallo; (of glass) pie
m ▷ vt detener; (blood) restañar
**step** [step] n paso; (on stair) peldaño,
escalón m ▷ vi: **to ~ forward/back** dar
un paso adelante/hacia atrás; **steps** npl
(BRIT) = **stepladder**; **in/out of ~ (with)**
acorde/en disonancia (con); **step down**

stereo | 398

vi (fig) retirarse; **step in** vi entrar; (fig) intervenir; **step up** vt (increase) aumentar; **stepbrother** n hermanastro; **stepchild** (pl **stepchildren**) n hijastro/a m/f; **stepdaughter** n hijastra; **stepfather** n padrastro; **stepladder** n escalera doble or de tijera; **stepmother** n madrastra; **stepsister** n hermanastra; **stepson** n hijastro

**stereo** ['stɛrɪəu] n estéreo ▷ adj (also: **~phonic**) estéreo, estereofónico

**stereotype** ['stɪərɪətaɪp] n estereotipo ▷ vt estereotipar

**sterile** ['stɛraɪl] adj estéril; **sterilize** ['stɛrɪlaɪz] vt esterilizar

**sterling** ['stə:lɪŋ] adj (silver) de ley ▷ n (Econ) libras fpl esterlinas fpl; **one pound ~** una libra esterlina

**stern** [stə:n] adj severo, austero ▷ n (Naut) popa

**steroid** ['stɪərɔɪd] n esteroide m

**stew** [stju:] n estofado, guiso ▷ vt estofar, guisar; (fruit) cocer

**steward** ['stju:əd] n camarero; **stewardess** n (esp on plane) azafata

**stick** [stɪk] (pt, pp **stuck**) n palo; (of dynamite) barreno; (as weapon) porra; (also: **walking ~**) bastón m ▷ vt (glue) pegar; (inf: put) meter; (: tolerate) aguantar, soportar; (thrust): **to ~ sth into** clavar or hincar algo en ▷ vi pegarse; (be unmoveable) quedarse parado; (in mind) quedarse grabado; **stick out** vi sobresalir; **stick up** vi sobresalir; **stick up for** vt fus defender; **sticker** n (label) etiqueta engomada; (with slogan) pegatina; **sticking plaster** n esparadrapo; **stick shift** (US) n (Aut) palanca de cambios

**sticky** ['stɪkɪ] adj pegajoso; (label) engomado; (fig) difícil

**stiff** [stɪf] adj rígido, tieso; (hard) duro; (manner) estirado; (difficult) difícil; (person) inflexible; (price) exorbitante ▷ adv: **scared/bored ~** muerto de miedo/aburrimiento

**stifling** ['staɪflɪŋ] adj (heat) sofocante, bochornoso

**stigma** ['stɪgmə] n (fig) estigma m

**stiletto** [stɪ'lɛtəu] (BRIT) n (also: **~ heel**) tacón m de aguja

**still** [stɪl] adj inmóvil, quieto ▷ adv todavía; (even) aun; (nonetheless) sin embargo, aun así

**stimulate** ['stɪmjuleɪt] vt estimular

**stimulus** ['stɪmjuləs] (pl **stimuli**) n estímulo, incentivo

**sting** [stɪŋ] (pt, pp **stung**) n picadura; (pain) escozor m, picazón f; (organ) aguijón m ▷ vt, vi picar

**stink** [stɪŋk] (pt **stank**, pp **stunk**) n hedor m, tufo ▷ vi heder, apestar

**stir** [stə:*] n (fig: agitation) conmoción f ▷ vt (tea etc) remover; (fig: emotions) provocar ▷ vi moverse; **stir up** vt (trouble) fomentar; **stir-fry** vt sofreír removiendo ▷ n plato preparado sofriendo y removiendo los ingredientes

**stitch** [stɪtʃ] n (Sewing) puntada; (Knitting) punto; (Med) punto (de sutura); (pain) punzada ▷ vt coser; (Med) suturar

**stock** [stɔk] n (Comm: reserves) existencias fpl, stock m; (: selection) surtido; (Agr) ganado, ganadería; (Culin) caldo; (descent) raza, estirpe f; (Finance) capital m ▷ adj (fig: reply etc) clásico ▷ vt (have in stock) tener existencias de; **~s and shares** acciones y valores; **in ~** en existencia or almacén; **out of ~** agotado; **to take ~ of** (fig) asesorar, examinar; **stockbroker** ['stɔkbrəukə*] n agente mf or corredor mf de bolsa(s); **stock cube** (BRIT) n pastilla de caldo; **stock exchange** n bolsa; **stockholder** ['stɔkhəuldə*] (US) n accionista m/f

**stocking** ['stɔkɪŋ] n media

**stock market** n bolsa (de valores)

**stole** [stəul] pt of **steal** ▷ n estola

**stolen** ['stəuln] pp of **steal**

**stomach** ['stʌmək] n (Anat) estómago; (belly) vientre m ▷ vt tragar, aguantar; **stomachache** n dolor m de estómago

**stone** [stəun] n piedra; (in fruit) hueso (= 6.348 kg; 14 libras) ▷ adj de piedra ▷ vt apedrear; (fruit) deshuesar

**stood** [stud] pt, pp of **stand**

**stool** [stu:l] n taburete m

**stoop** [stu:p] vi (also: **~ down**) doblarse, agacharse; (also: **have a ~**) ser cargado de espaldas

**stop** [stɔp] n parada; (in punctuation) punto ▷ vt parar, detener; (break) suspender; (block: pay) suspender; (: cheque) invalidar; (also: **put a ~ to**) poner término a ▷ vi pararse, detenerse; (end) acabarse; **to ~ doing sth** dejar de hacer algo; **stop by** vi pasar por; **stop off** vi interrumpir el viaje; **stopover** n parada; (Aviat) escala; **stoppage** n (strike) paro; (blockage) obstrucción f

**storage** ['stɔ:rɪdʒ] n almacenaje m

**store** [stɔ:*] n (stock) provisión f; (depot) (BRIT: large shop) almacén m; (US) tienda; (reserve) reserva, repuesto ▷ vt almacenar; **stores** npl víveres mpl; **to be in ~ for sb** (fig) esperarle a algn; **storekeeper** (US) n tendero/a

**storey** ['stɔ:rɪ] (US **story**) n piso

**storm** [stɔ:m] n tormenta; (fig: of

*applause*) salva; (: *of criticism*) nube f ▷ vi (*fig*) rabiar ▷ vt tomar por asalto; **stormy** *adj* tempestuoso

**story** ['stɔ:rɪ] *n* historia; (*lie*) mentira; (*us*) = **storey**

**stout** [staut] *adj* (*strong*) sólido; (*fat*) gordo, corpulento; (*resolute*) resuelto ▷ *n* cerveza negra

**stove** [stəuv] *n* (*for cooking*) cocina; (*for heating*) estufa

**straight** [streit] *adj* recto, derecho; (*frank*) franco, directo; (*simple*) sencillo ▷ *adv* derecho, directamente; (*drink*) sin mezcla; **to put** or **get sth** ~ dejar algo en claro; ~ **away**, ~ **off** en seguida; **straighten** *vt* (*also:* **straighten out**) enderezar, poner derecho ▷ vi (*also:* **straighten up**) enderezarse, ponerse derecho; **straightforward** *adj* (*simple*) sencillo; (*honest*) honrado, franco

**strain** [streɪn] *n* tensión f; (*Tech*) presión f; (*Med*) torcedura; (*breed*) tipo, variedad f ▷ *vt* (*back etc*) torcerse; (*resources*) agotar; (*stretch*) estirar; (*food, tea*) colar; **strained** *adj* (*muscle*) torcido; (*laugh*) forzado; (*relations*) tenso; **strainer** *n* colador *m*

**strait** [streit] *n* (*Geo*) estrecho (*fig*): **to be in dire ~s** estar en un gran apuro

**strand** [strænd] *n* (*of thread*) hebra; (*of hair*) trenza; (*of rope*) ramal *m*; **stranded** *adj* (*person: without money*) desamparado; (: *without transport*) colgado

**strange** [streɪndʒ] *adj* (*not known*) desconocido; (*odd*) extraño, raro; **strangely** *adv* de un modo raro; **stranger** *n* desconocido/a; (*from another area*) forastero/a

> Be careful not to translate **stranger** by the Spanish word *extranjero*.

**strangle** ['stræŋgl] *vt* estrangular

**strap** [stræp] *n* correa; (*of slip, dress*) tirante *m*

**strategic** [strə'tiːdʒɪk] *adj* estratégico

**strategy** ['strætɪdʒɪ] *n* estrategia

**straw** [strɔ:] *n* paja; (*drinking straw*) caña, pajita; **that's the last ~!** ¡eso es el colmo!

**strawberry** ['strɔ:bərɪ] *n* fresa, frutilla (*sc*)

**stray** [streɪ] *adj* (*animal*) extraviado; (*bullet*) perdido; (*scattered*) disperso ▷ vi extraviarse, perderse

**streak** [stri:k] *n* raya; (*in hair*) raya ▷ vt rayar ▷ vi: **to ~ past** pasar como un rayo

**stream** [stri:m] *n* riachuelo, arroyo; (*of people, vehicles*) riada, caravana; (*of smoke, insults etc*) chorro ▷ vt (*Scol*) dividir en grupos por habilidad ▷ vi correr, fluir; **to ~ in/out** (*people*) entrar/salir en tropel

**street** [stri:t] *n* calle f; **streetcar** (*us*) *n* tranvía m; **street light** *n* farol *m* (LAM), farola (*sp*); **street map** *n* plano (de la ciudad); **street plan** *n* plano

**strength** [strɛŋθ] *n* fuerza; (*of girder, knot etc*) resistencia; (*fig: power*) poder m; **strengthen** *vt* fortalecer, reforzar

**strenuous** ['strɛnjuəs] *adj* (*energetic, determined*) enérgico

**stress** [strɛs] *n* presión f; (*mental strain*) estrés m; (*accent*) acento ▷ vt subrayar, recalcar; (*syllable*) acentuar; **stressed** *adj* (*tense*) estresado, agobiado; (*syllable*) acentuado; **stressful** *adj* (*job*) estresante

**stretch** [strɛtʃ] *n* (*of sand etc*) trecho ▷ vi estirarse; (*extend*): **to ~ to** or **as far as** extenderse hasta ▷ vt extender, estirar; (*make demands*) exigir el máximo esfuerzo a; **stretch out** vi tenderse ▷ vt (*arm etc*) extender; (*spread*) estirar

**stretcher** ['strɛtʃə*] *n* camilla

**strict** [strɪkt] *adj* severo; (*exact*) estricto; **strictly** *adv* severamente; estrictamente

**stride** [straɪd] (*pt* **strode**, *pp* **stridden**) *n* zancada, tranco ▷ vi dar zancadas, andar a trancos

**strike** [straɪk] (*pt*, *pp* **struck**) *n* huelga; (*of oil etc*) descubrimiento; (*attack*) ataque *m* ▷ vt golpear, pegar; (*oil etc*) descubrir; (*bargain, deal*) cerrar ▷ vi declarar la huelga; (*attack*) atacar; (*clock*) dar la hora; **on ~** (*workers*) en huelga; **to ~ a match** encender un fósforo; **striker** *n* huelguista mf; (*Sport*) delantero; **striking** *adj* llamativo

**string** [strɪŋ] (*pt*, *pp* **strung**) *n* cuerda; (*row*) hilera ▷ vt: **to ~ together** ensartar; **to ~ out** extenderse; **the strings** *npl* (*Mus*) los instrumentos de cuerda; **to pull ~s** (*fig*) mover palancas

**strip** [strɪp] *n* tira; (*of land*) franja; (*of metal*) cinta, lámina ▷ vt desnudar; (*paint*) quitar; (*also:* ~ **down**: *machine*) desmontar ▷ vi desnudarse; **strip off** vt (*paint etc*) quitar ▷ vi (*person*) desnudarse

**stripe** [straip] *n* raya; (*Mil*) galón m; **striped** *adj* a rayas, rayado

**stripper** ['strɪpə*] *n* artista mf de striptease

**strip-search** ['strɪpsə:tʃ] *vt*: **to ~ sb** desnudar y registrar a algn

**strive** [straɪv] (*pt* **strove**, *pp* **striven**) *vi*: **to ~ for sth/to do sth** luchar por conseguir/ hacer algo

**strode** [strəud] *pt of* **stride**

**stroke** [strəuk] *n* (*blow*) golpe m; (*Swimming*) brazada; (*Med*) apoplejía; (*of paintbrush*) toque m ▷ vt acariciar; **at a ~** de un solo golpe

**stroll** [strəul] n paseo, vuelta ▷ vi dar un paseo or una vuelta; **stroller** (US) n (for child) sillita de ruedas

**strong** [strɔŋ] adj fuerte; **they are 50 ~** son 50; **stronghold** n fortaleza; (fig) baluarte m; **strongly** adv fuertemente, con fuerza; (believe) firmemente

**strove** [strəuv] pt of **strive**

**struck** [strʌk] pt, pp of **strike**

**structure** ['strʌktʃə*] n estructura; (building) construcción f

**struggle** ['strʌgl] n lucha ▷ vi luchar

**strung** [strʌŋ] pt, pp of **string**

**stub** [stʌb] n (of ticket etc) talón m; (of cigarette) colilla; **to ~ one's toe on sth** dar con el dedo (del pie) contra algo; **stub out** vt apagar

**stubble** ['stʌbl] n rastrojo; (on chin) barba (incipiente)

**stubborn** ['stʌbən] adj terco, testarudo

**stuck** [stʌk] pt, pp of **stick** ▷ adj (jammed) atascado

**stud** [stʌd] n (shirt stud) corchete m; (of boot) taco; (earring) pendiente m (de bolita); (also: ~ **farm**) caballeriza; (also: ~ **horse**) caballo semental ▷ vt (fig): **~ded with** salpicado de

**student** ['stju:dənt] n estudiante mf ▷ adj estudiantil; **student driver** (US) n conductor(a) mf en prácticas; **students' union** n (building) centro de estudiantes; (BRIT: association) federación f de estudiantes

**studio** ['stju:dɪəu] n estudio; (artist's) taller m; **studio flat** n estudio

**study** ['stʌdɪ] n estudio ▷ vt estudiar; (examine) examinar, investigar ▷ vi estudiar

**stuff** [stʌf] n materia; (substance) material m, sustancia; (things) cosas fpl ▷ vt llenar; (Culin) rellenar; (animals) disecar; (inf: push) meter; **stuffing** n relleno; **stuffy** adj (room) mal ventilado; (person) de miras estrechas

**stumble** ['stʌmbl] vi tropezar, dar un traspié; **to ~ across, ~ on** (fig) tropezar con

**stump** [stʌmp] n (of tree) tocón m; (of limb) muñón m ▷ vt: **to be ~ed for an answer** no saber qué contestar

**stun** [stʌn] vt dejar sin sentido

**stung** [stʌŋ] pt, pp of **sting**

**stunk** [stʌŋk] pp of **stink**

**stunned** [stʌnd] adj (dazed) aturdido, atontado; (amazed) pasmado; (shocked) anonadado

**stunning** ['stʌnɪŋ] adj (fig: news) pasmoso; (: outfit etc) sensacional

**stunt** [stʌnt] n (in film) escena peligrosa; (publicity stunt) truco publicitario

**stupid** ['stju:pɪd] adj estúpido, tonto; **stupidity** [-'pɪdɪtɪ] n estupidez f

**sturdy** ['stə:dɪ] adj robusto, fuerte

**stutter** ['stʌtə*] n tartamudeo ▷ vi tartamudear

**style** [staɪl] n estilo; **stylish** adj elegante, a la moda; **stylist** n (hair stylist) peluquero/a

**sub...** [sʌb] prefix sub...; **subconscious** adj subconsciente

**subdued** [səb'dju:d] adj (light) tenue; (person) sumiso, manso

**subject** [n 'sʌbdʒɪkt, vb səb'dʒɛkt] n súbdito; (Scol) asignatura; (matter) tema m; (Grammar) sujeto ▷ vt: **to ~ sb to sth** someter a algn a algo; **to be ~ to** (law) estar sujeto a; (person) ser propenso a; **subjective** [-'dʒɛktɪv] adj subjetivo; **subject matter** n (content) contenido

**subjunctive** [səb'dʒʌŋktɪv] adj, n subjuntivo

**submarine** [sʌbmə'ri:n] n submarino

**submission** [səb'mɪʃən] n sumisión f

**submit** [səb'mɪt] vt someter ▷ vi: **to ~ to sth** someterse a algo

**subordinate** [sə'bɔ:dɪnət] adj, n subordinado/a m/f

**subscribe** [səb'skraɪb] vi suscribir; **to ~ to** (opinion, fund) suscribir, aprobar; (newspaper) suscribirse a

**subscription** [səb'skrɪpʃən] n abono; (to magazine) subscripción f

**subsequent** ['sʌbsɪkwənt] adj subsiguiente, posterior; **subsequently** adv posteriormente, más tarde

**subside** [səb'saɪd] vi hundirse; (flood) bajar; (wind) amainar

**subsidiary** [səb'sɪdɪərɪ] adj secundario ▷ n sucursal f, filial f

**subsidize** ['sʌbsɪdaɪz] vt subvencionar

**subsidy** ['sʌbsɪdɪ] n subvención f

**substance** ['sʌbstəns] n sustancia

**substantial** [səb'stænʃl] adj sustancial, sustancioso; (fig) importante

**substitute** ['sʌbstɪtju:t] n (person) suplente mf; (thing) sustituto ▷ vt: **to ~ A for B** sustituir A por B, reemplazar B por A; **substitution** n sustitución f

**subtle** ['sʌtl] adj sutil

**subtract** [səb'trækt] vt restar, sustraer

**suburb** ['sʌbə:b] n barrio residencial; **the ~s** las afueras (de la ciudad); **suburban** [sə'bə:bən] adj suburbano; (train etc) de cercanías

**subway** ['sʌbweɪ] n (BRIT) paso subterráneo or inferior; (US) metro

**succeed** [sək'si:d] vi (person) tener éxito; (plan) salir bien ▷ vt suceder a; **to ~ in**

**doing** lograr hacer
**success** [sək'sɛs] n éxito

> Be careful not to translate **success** by the Spanish word *suceso*.

**successful** adj exitoso; (business) próspero; **to be successful (in doing)** lograr (hacer); **successfully** adv con éxito
**succession** [sək'sɛʃən] n sucesión f, serie f
**successive** [sək'sɛsɪv] adj sucesivo, consecutivo
**successor** [sək'sɛsə*] n sucesor(a) m/f
**succumb** [sə'kʌm] vi sucumbir
**such** [sʌtʃ] adj tal, semejante; (of that kind): **~ a book** tal libro; (so much): **~ courage** tanto valor ▷ adv tan; **~ a long trip** un viaje tan largo; **~ a lot of** tanto(s)/a(s); **~ as** (like) tal como; **as ~** como tal; **such-and-such** adj tal o cual
**suck** [sʌk] vt chupar; (bottle) sorber; (breast) mamar
**Sudan** [su'dæn] n Sudán m
**sudden** ['sʌdn] adj (rapid) repentino, súbito; (unexpected) imprevisto; **all of a ~** de repente; **suddenly** adv de repente
**sue** [su:] vt demandar
**suede** [sweɪd] n ante m, gamuza
**suffer** ['sʌfə*] vt sufrir, padecer; (tolerate) aguantar, soportar ▷ vi sufrir; **to ~ from** (illness etc) padecer; **suffering** n sufrimiento
**suffice** [sə'faɪs] vi bastar, ser suficiente
**sufficient** [sə'fɪʃənt] adj suficiente, bastante
**suffocate** ['sʌfəkeɪt] vi ahogarse, asfixiarse
**sugar** ['ʃʊɡə*] n azúcar m ▷ vt echar azúcar a, azucarar
**suggest** [sə'dʒɛst] vt sugerir; **suggestion** [-'dʒɛstʃən] n sugerencia
**suicide** ['sʊɪsaɪd] n suicidio; (person) suicida m/f; see also **commit**; **suicide attack** n atentado suicida; **suicide bomber** n terrorista m/f suicida; **suicide bombing** n atentado suicida
**suit** [su:t] n (man's) traje m; (woman's) conjunto; (Law) pleito; (Cards) palo ▷ vt convenir; (clothes) sentar a, ir bien a; (adapt): **to ~ sth to** adaptar or ajustar algo a; **well ~ed** (well matched: couple) hecho el uno para el otro; **suitable** adj conveniente; (apt) indicado; **suitcase** n maleta, valija (RPL)
**suite** [swi:t] n (of rooms, Mus) suite f; (furniture): **bedroom/dining room ~** (juego de) dormitorio/comedor; see also **three-piece suite**
**sulfur** ['sʌlfə*] (US) n = **sulphur**
**sulk** [sʌlk] vi estar de mal humor
**sulphur** ['sʌlfə*] (US **sulfur**) n azufre m

**sultana** [sʌl'tɑːnə] n (fruit) pasa de Esmirna
**sum** [sʌm] n suma; (total) total m; **sum up** vt resumir ▷ vi hacer un resumen
**summarize** ['sʌməraɪz] vt resumir
**summary** ['sʌmərɪ] n resumen m ▷ adj (justice) sumario
**summer** ['sʌmə*] n verano ▷ cpd de verano; **in ~** en verano; **summer holidays** npl vacaciones fpl de verano; **summertime** n (season) verano
**summit** ['sʌmɪt] n cima, cumbre f; (also: **~ conference, ~ meeting**) (conferencia) cumbre f
**summon** ['sʌmən] vt (person) llamar; (meeting) convocar; (Law) citar
**Sun.** abbr (= Sunday) dom
**sun** [sʌn] n sol m; **sunbathe** vi tomar el sol; **sunbed** n cama solar; **sunblock** n filtro solar; **sunburn** n (painful) quemadura; (tan) bronceado; **sunburned, sunburnt** adj (painfully) quemado por el sol; (tanned) bronceado
**Sunday** ['sʌndɪ] n domingo
**sunflower** ['sʌnflaʊə*] n girasol m
**sung** [sʌŋ] pp of **sing**
**sunglasses** ['sʌnɡlɑːsɪz] npl gafas fpl (SP) or anteojos fpl (LAM) de sol
**sunk** [sʌŋk] pp of **sink**
**sun:** **sunlight** n luz f del sol; **sun lounger** n tumbona, perezosa (LAM); **sunny** adj soleado; (day) de sol; (fig) alegre; **sunrise** n salida del sol; **sun roof** n (Aut) techo corredizo; **sunscreen** n protector m solar; **sunset** n puesta del sol; **sunshade** n (over table) sombrilla; **sunshine** n sol m; **sunstroke** n insolación f; **suntan** n bronceado; **suntan lotion** n bronceador m; **suntan oil** n aceite m bronceador
**super** ['su:pə*] (inf) adj genial
**superb** [su:'pə:b] adj magnífico, espléndido
**superficial** [su:pə'fɪʃəl] adj superficial
**superintendent** [su:pərɪn'tɛndənt] n director(a) m/f; (Police) subjefe/a m/f
**superior** [su:'pɪərɪə*] adj superior; (smug) desdeñoso ▷ n superior m
**superlative** [su:'pə:lətɪv] n superlativo
**supermarket** ['su:pəmɑ:kɪt] n supermercado
**supernatural** [su:pə'nætʃərəl] adj sobrenatural ▷ n: **the ~** lo sobrenatural
**superpower** ['su:pəpaʊə*] n (Pol) superpotencia
**superstition** [su:pə'stɪʃən] n superstición f
**superstitious** [su:pə'stɪʃəs] adj supersticioso

**superstore** ['su:pəstɔ:*] n (BRIT)
hipermercado
**supervise** ['su:pəvaɪz] vt supervisar;
**supervision** [-'vɪʒən] n supervisión f;
**supervisor** n supervisor(a) m/f
**supper** ['sʌpə*] n cena
**supple** ['sʌpl] adj flexible
**supplement** [n 'sʌplɪmənt, vb sʌplɪ'mɛnt]
n suplemento ▷ vt suplir
**supplier** [sə'plaɪə*] n (Comm)
distribuidor(a) m/f
**supply** [sə'plaɪ] vt (provide) suministrar;
(equip): **to ~ (with)** proveer (de) ▷ n
provisión f; (of gas, water etc) suministro;
**supplies** npl (food) víveres mpl; (Mil)
pertrechos mpl
**support** [sə'pɔ:t] n apoyo; (Tech) soporte
m ▷ vt apoyar; (financially) mantener;
(uphold, Tech) sostener

> Be careful not to translate **support** by
> the Spanish word soportar.

**supporter** n (Pol etc) partidario/a; (Sport)
aficionado/a
**suppose** [sə'pəuz] vt suponer; (imagine)
imaginarse; (duty): **to be ~d to do sth** deber
hacer algo; **supposedly** [sə'pəuzɪdlɪ] adv
según cabe suponer; **supposing** conj en
caso de que
**suppress** [sə'prɛs] vt suprimir; (yawn)
ahogar
**supreme** [su'pri:m] adj supremo
**surcharge** ['sə:tʃɑ:dʒ] n sobretasa,
recargo
**sure** [ʃuə*] adj seguro; (definite, convinced)
cierto; **to make ~ of sth/that** asegurarse
de algo/asegurar que; **~!** (of course) ¡claro!,
¡por supuesto!; **~ enough** efectivamente;
**surely** adv (certainly) seguramente
**surf** [sə:f] n olas fpl ▷ vt: **to ~ the Net**
navegar por Internet
**surface** ['sə:fɪs] n superficie f ▷ vt (road)
revestir ▷ vi salir a la superficie; **by ~ mail**
por vía terrestre
**surfboard** ['sə:fbɔ:d] n tabla (de surf)
**surfer** ['sə:fə*] n (in sea) surfista mf; **web or
net ~** internauta mf
**surfing** ['sə:fɪŋ] n surf m
**surge** [sə:dʒ] n oleada, oleaje m ▷ vi (wave)
romper; (people) avanzar en tropel
**surgeon** ['sə:dʒən] n cirujano/a
**surgery** ['sə:dʒərɪ] n cirugía; (BRIT: room)
consultorio
**surname** ['sə:neɪm] n apellido
**surpass** [sə:'pɑ:s] vt superar, exceder
**surplus** ['sə:pləs] n excedente m; (Comm)
superávit m ▷ adj excedente, sobrante
**surprise** [sə'praɪz] n sorpresa ▷ vt
sorprender; **surprised** adj (look, smile) de

sorpresa; **to be surprised** sorprenderse;
**surprising** adj sorprendente; **surprisingly**
adv: **it was surprisingly easy** me etc
sorprendió lo fácil que fue
**surrender** [sə'rɛndə*] n rendición f,
entrega ▷ vi rendirse, entregarse
**surround** [sə'raund] vt rodear,
circundar; (Mil etc) cercar; **surrounding**
adj circundante; **surroundings** npl
alrededores mpl, cercanías fpl
**surveillance** [sə:'veɪləns] n vigilancia
**survey** [n 'sə:veɪ, vb sə:'veɪ] n inspección
f, reconocimiento; (inquiry) encuesta ▷ vt
examinar, inspeccionar; (look at) mirar,
contemplar; **surveyor** n agrimensor(a) m/f
**survival** [sə'vaɪvl] n supervivencia
**survive** [sə'vaɪv] vi sobrevivir; (custom
etc) perdurar ▷ vt sobrevivir a; **survivor** n
superviviente mf
**suspect** [adj, n 'sʌspɛkt, vb səs'pɛkt] adj, n
sospechoso/a m/f ▷ vt (person) sospechar
de; (think) sospechar
**suspend** [səs'pɛnd] vt suspender;
**suspended sentence** n (Law) libertad f
condicional; **suspenders** npl (BRIT) ligas
fpl; (US) tirantes mpl
**suspense** [səs'pɛns] n incertidumbre f,
duda; (in film etc) suspense m; **to keep sb in
~** mantener a algn en suspense
**suspension** [səs'pɛnʃən] n (gen, Aut)
suspensión f; (of driving licence) privación f;
**suspension bridge** n puente m colgante
**suspicion** [səs'pɪʃən] n sospecha; (distrust)
recelo; **suspicious** adj receloso; (causing
suspicion) sospechoso
**sustain** [səs'teɪn] vt sostener, apoyar;
(suffer) sufrir, padecer
**SUV** (esp US) n abbr (= sports utility vehicle)
todoterreno m inv, 4x4 m
**swallow** ['swɔləu] n (bird) golondrina ▷ vt
tragar; (fig.: pride) tragarse
**swam** [swæm] pt of **swim**
**swamp** [swɔmp] n pantano, ciénaga
▷ vt (with water etc) inundar; (fig) abrumar,
agobiar
**swan** [swɔn] n cisne m
**swap** [swɔp] n canje m, intercambio
▷ vt: **to ~ (for)** cambiar (por)
**swarm** [swɔ:m] n (of bees) enjambre
m; (fig) multitud f ▷ vi (bees) formar un
enjambre; (people) pulular; **to be ~ing with**
ser un hervidero de
**sway** [sweɪ] vi mecerse, balancearse ▷ vt
(influence) mover, influir en
**swear** [swɛə*] (pt **swore**, pp **sworn**) vi
(curse) maldecir; (promise) jurar ▷ vt jurar;
**swear in** vt: **to be sworn in** prestar
juramento; **swearword** n taco, palabrota

**sweat** [swɛt] n sudor m ▷ vi sudar
**sweater** ['swɛtə*] n suéter m
**sweatshirt** ['swɛtʃəːt] n suéter m
**sweaty** ['swɛtɪ] adj sudoroso
**Swede** [swiːd] n sueco/a
**swede** [swiːd] (BRIT) n nabo
**Sweden** ['swiːdn] n Suecia; **Swedish**
['swiːdɪʃ] adj sueco ▷ n (Ling) sueco
**sweep** [swiːp] (pt, pp **swept**) n (act)
barrido; (also: **chimney ~**) deshollinador(a)
m/f ▷ vt barrer; (with arm) empujar; (current)
arrastrar ▷ vi barrer; (arm etc) moverse
rápidamente; (wind) soplar con violencia
**sweet** [swiːt] n (candy) dulce m, caramelo;
(BRIT: pudding) postre m ▷ adj dulce;
(fig: kind) dulce, amable; (: attractive) mono;
**sweetcorn** n maíz m; **sweetener**
['swiːtnə*] n (Culin) edulcorante m;
**sweetheart** n novio/a; **sweetshop** n
(BRIT) confitería, bombonería
**swell** [swɛl] (pt **~ed**, pp **swollen** or
**~ed**) n (of sea) marejada, oleaje m ▷ adj
(US: inf: excellent) estupendo, fenomenal ▷ vt
hinchar, inflar ▷ vi (also: **~ up**) hincharse;
(numbers) aumentar; (sound, feeling) ir
aumentando; **swelling** n (Med) hinchazón f
**swept** [swɛpt] pt, pp of **sweep**
**swerve** [swəːv] vi desviarse bruscamente
**swift** [swɪft] n (bird) vencejo ▷ adj rápido,
veloz
**swim** [swɪm] (pt **swam**, pp **swum**) n: **to go**
**for a ~** ir a nadar or a bañarse ▷ vi nadar;
(head, room) dar vueltas ▷ vt nadar; (the
Channel etc) cruzar a nado; **swimmer** n
nadador(a) m/f; **swimming** n natación f;
**swimming costume** (BRIT) n bañador m,
traje m de baño; **swimming pool** n piscina,
alberca (MEX), pileta (RPL); **swimming**
**trunks** npl bañador m (de hombre);
**swimsuit** n = **swimming costume**
**swing** [swɪŋ] (pt, pp **swung**) n (in
playground) columpio; (movement) balanceo,
vaivén m; (change of direction) viraje m;
(rhythm) ritmo ▷ vt balancear; (also: **~**
**round**) voltear, girar ▷ vi balancearse,
columpiarse; (also: **~ round**) dar media
vuelta; **to be in full ~** estar en plena marcha
**swipe card** [swaɪp-] n tarjeta magnética
deslizante, tarjeta swipe
**swirl** [swəːl] vi arremolinarse
**Swiss** [swɪs] adj, n inv suizo/a m/f
**switch** [swɪtʃ] n (for light etc) interruptor
m; (change) cambio ▷ vt (change) cambiar
de; **switch off** vt apagar; (engine) parar;
**switch on** vt encender (SP), prender (LAM);
(engine, machine) arrancar; **switchboard** n
(Tel) centralita (SP), conmutador m (LAM)
**Switzerland** ['swɪtsələnd] n Suiza

**swivel** ['swɪvl] vi (also: **~ round**) girar
**swollen** ['swəʊlən] pp of **swell**
**swoop** [swuːp] n (by police etc) redada ▷ vi
(also: **~ down**) calarse
**swop** [swɔp] = **swap**
**sword** [sɔːd] n espada; **swordfish** n pez
m espada
**swore** [swɔː*] pt of **swear**
**sworn** [swɔːn] pp of **swear** ▷ adj
(statement) bajo juramento; (enemy)
implacable
**swum** [swʌm] pp of **swim**
**swung** [swʌŋ] pt, pp of **swing**
**syllable** ['sɪləbl] n sílaba
**syllabus** ['sɪləbəs] n programa m de
estudios
**symbol** ['sɪmbl] n símbolo; **symbolic(al)**
[sɪm'bɔlɪk(l)] adj simbólico; **to be**
**symbolic(al) of sth** simbolizar algo
**symmetrical** [sɪ'mɛtrɪkl] adj simétrico
**symmetry** ['sɪmɪtrɪ] n simetría
**sympathetic** [sɪmpə'θɛtɪk] adj
(understanding) comprensivo; (showing
support): **~ to(wards)** bien dispuesto hacia

▌ Be careful not to translate **sympathetic**
by the Spanish word simpático.

**sympathize** ['sɪmpəθaɪz] vi: **to ~ with**
(person) compadecerse de; (feelings)
comprender; (cause) apoyar
**sympathy** ['sɪmpəθɪ] n (pity) compasión f
**symphony** ['sɪmfənɪ] n sinfonía
**symptom** ['sɪmptəm] n síntoma m,
indicio
**synagogue** ['sɪnəgɔg] n sinagoga
**syndicate** ['sɪndɪkɪt] n sindicato; (of
newspapers) agencia (de noticias)
**syndrome** ['sɪndrəʊm] n síndrome m
**synonym** ['sɪnənɪm] n sinónimo
**synthetic** [sɪn'θɛtɪk] adj sintético
**Syria** ['sɪrɪə] n Siria
**syringe** [sɪ'rɪndʒ] n jeringa
**syrup** ['sɪrəp] n jarabe m; (also: **golden ~**)
almíbar m
**system** ['sɪstəm] n sistema m; (Anat)
organismo; **systematic** [-'mætɪk] adj
sistemático, metódico; **systems analyst** n
analista m/f de sistemas

**t**

**ta** [tɑː] (BRIT: inf) excl ¡gracias!
**tab** [tæb] n lengüeta; (label) etiqueta; **to keep ~s on** (fig) vigilar
**table** ['teɪbl] n mesa; (of statistics etc) cuadro, tabla ▷ vt (BRIT: motion etc) presentar; **to lay** or **set the ~** poner la mesa; **tablecloth** n mantel m; **table d'hôte** [tɑː'bl'dəʊt] adj del menú; **table lamp** n lámpara de mesa; **tablemat** n (for plate) posaplatos m inv; (for hot dish) salvamantel m; **tablespoon** n cuchara de servir; (also: **tablespoonful**: as measurement) cucharada
**tablet** ['tæblɪt] n (Med) pastilla, comprimido; (of stone) lápida
**table tennis** n ping-pong m, tenis m de mesa
**tabloid** ['tæblɔɪd] n periódico popular sensacionalista

**taboo** [tə'buː] adj, n tabú m
**tack** [tæk] n (nail) tachuela; (fig) rumbo ▷ vt (nail) clavar con tachuelas; (stitch) hilvanar ▷ vi virar
**tackle** ['tækl] n (fishing tackle) aparejo (de pescar); (for lifting) aparejo ▷ vt (difficulty) enfrentarse con; (challenge: person) hacer frente a; (grapple with) agarrar; (Football) cargar; (Rugby) placar
**tacky** ['tækɪ] adj pegajoso; (pej) cutre
**tact** [tækt] n tacto, discreción f; **tactful** adj discreto, diplomático
**tactics** ['tæktɪks] npl táctica
**tactless** ['tæktlɪs] adj indiscreto
**tadpole** ['tædpəʊl] n renacuajo
**taffy** ['tæfɪ] (US) n melcocha
**tag** [tæg] n (label) etiqueta
**tail** [teɪl] n cola; (of shirt, coat) faldón m ▷ vt (follow) vigilar a; **tails** npl (formal suit) levita
**tailor** ['teɪlə'] n sastre m
**Taiwan** [taɪ'wɑːn] n Taiwán m; **Taiwanese** [taɪwə'niːz] adj, n taiwanés/esa m/f
**take** [teɪk] (pt **took**, pp **taken**) vt tomar; (grab) coger (SP), agarrar (LAM); (gain: prize) ganar; (require: effort, courage) exigir; (tolerate: pain etc) aguantar; (hold: passengers etc) tener cabida para; (accompany, bring, carry) llevar; (exam) presentarse a; **to ~ sth from** (drawer etc) sacar algo de; (person) quitar algo a; **I ~ it that ...** supongo que ...; **take after** vt fus parecerse a; **take apart** vt desmontar; **take away** vt (remove) quitar; (carry) llevar; (Math) restar; **take back** vt (return) devolver; (one's words) retractarse de; **take down** vt (building) derribar; (letter etc) apuntar; **take in** vt (deceive) engañar; (understand) entender; (include) abarcar; (lodger) acoger, recibir; **take off** vi (Aviat) despegar ▷ vt (remove) quitar; **take on** vt (work) aceptar; (employee) contratar; (opponent) desafiar; **take out** vt sacar; **take over** vt (business) tomar posesión de; (country) tomar el poder ▷ vi: **to take over from sb** reemplazar a algn; **take up** vt (a dress) acortar; (occupy: time, space) ocupar; (engage in: hobby etc) dedicarse a; (accept): **to take sb up on** aceptar algo de algn; **takeaway** (BRIT) adj (food) para llevar ▷ n tienda or restaurante m de comida para llevar; **taken** pp of **take**; **takeoff** n (Aviat) despegue m; **takeout** (US) n = **takeaway**; **takeover** n (Comm) absorción f; **takings** npl (Comm) ingresos mpl
**talc** [tælk] n (also: **~um powder**) (polvos de) talco
**tale** [teɪl] n (story) cuento; (account) relación f; **to tell ~s** (fig) chivarse
**talent** ['tælnt] n talento; **talented** adj de talento
**talk** [tɔːk] n charla; (conversation) conversación f; (gossip) habladurías fpl, chismes mpl ▷ vi hablar; **talks** npl (Pol etc) conversaciones fpl; **to ~ about** hablar de; **to ~ sb into doing sth** convencer a algn para que haga algo; **to ~ sb out of doing sth**

disuadir a algn de que haga algo; **to ~ shop** hablar del trabajo; **talk over** vt discutir; **talk show** n programa m de entrevistas

**tall** [tɔ:l] adj alto; (object) grande; **to be 6 feet ~** (person) ≈ medir 1 metro 80

**tambourine** [tæmbə'ri:n] n pandereta

**tame** [teɪm] adj domesticado; (fig) mediocre

**tamper** ['tæmpə*] vi: **to ~ with** tocar, andar con

**tampon** ['tæmpən] n tampón m

**tan** [tæn] n (also: **sun~**) bronceado ▷ vi ponerse moreno ▷ adj (colour) marrón

**tandem** ['tændəm] n tándem m

**tangerine** [tændʒə'ri:n] n mandarina

**tangle** ['tæŋgl] n enredo; **to get in(to) a ~** enredarse

**tank** [tæŋk] n (water tank) depósito, tanque m; (for fish) acuario; (Mil) tanque m

**tanker** ['tæŋkə*] n (ship) buque m, cisterna; (truck) camión m cisterna

**tanned** [tænd] adj (skin) moreno

**tantrum** ['tæntrəm] n rabieta

**Tanzania** [tænzə'nɪə] n Tanzania

**tap** [tæp] n (BRIT: on sink etc) grifo (SP), llave f, canilla (RPL); (gas tap) llave f; (gentle blow) golpecito ▷ vt (hit gently) dar golpecitos en; (resources) utilizar, explotar; (telephone) intervenir; **on ~** (fig: resources) a mano; **tap dancing** n claqué m

**tape** [teɪp] n (also: **magnetic ~**) cinta magnética; (cassette) cassette f, cinta; (sticky tape) cinta adhesiva; (for tying) cinta ▷ vt (record) grabar (en cinta); (stick with tape) pegar con cinta adhesiva; **tape measure** n cinta métrica, metro; **tape recorder** n grabadora

**tapestry** ['tæpɪstrɪ] n (object) tapiz m; (art) tapicería

**tar** [tɑ:] n alquitrán m, brea

**target** ['tɑ:gɪt] n blanco

**tariff** ['tærɪf] n (on goods) arancel m; (BRIT: in hotels etc) tarifa

**tarmac** ['tɑ:mæk] n (BRIT: on road) asfaltado; (Aviat) pista (de aterrizaje)

**tarpaulin** [tɑ:'pɔ:lɪn] n lona impermeabilizada

**tarragon** ['tærəgən] n estragón m

**tart** [tɑ:t] n (Culin) tarta; (BRIT: inf: prostitute) puta ▷ adj agrio, ácido

**tartan** ['tɑ:tn] n tejido escocés m

**tartar(e) sauce** ['tɑ:tə-] n salsa tártara

**task** [tɑ:sk] n tarea; **to take to ~** reprender

**taste** [teɪst] n (sense) gusto; (flavour) sabor m; (sample) **have a ~!** ¡prueba un poquito!; (fig) muestra, idea ▷ vt probar ▷ vi: **to ~ of** or **like** (fish, garlic etc) saber a; **you can ~ the garlic (in it)** se nota el sabor a ajo; **in**

**good/bad ~** de buen/mal gusto; **tasteful** adj de buen gusto; **tasteless** adj (food) soso; (remark etc) de mal gusto; **tasty** adj sabroso, rico

**tatters** ['tætəz] npl: **in ~** hecho jirones

**tattoo** [tə'tu:] n tatuaje m; (spectacle) espectáculo militar ▷ vt tatuar

**taught** [tɔ:t] pt, pp of **teach**

**taunt** [tɔ:nt] n burla ▷ vt burlarse de

**Taurus** ['tɔ:rəs] n Tauro

**taut** [tɔ:t] adj tirante, tenso

**tax** [tæks] n impuesto ▷ vt gravar (con un impuesto); (fig: memory) poner a prueba; (: patience) agotar; **tax-free** adj libre de impuestos

**taxi** ['tæksɪ] n taxi m ▷ vi (Aviat) rodar por la pista; **taxi driver** n taxista mf; **taxi rank** (BRIT) n = **taxi stand; taxi stand** n parada de taxis

**tax payer** n contribuyente mf

**TB** n abbr = **tuberculosis**

**tea** [ti:] n té m; (BRIT: meal) ≈ merienda (SP); cena; **high ~** (BRIT) merienda-cena (SP); **tea bag** n bolsita de té; **tea break** (BRIT) n descanso para el té

**teach** [ti:tʃ] (pt, pp **taught**) vt: **to ~ sb sth, ~ sth to sb** enseñar algo a algn ▷ vi (be a teacher) ser profesor(a), enseñar; **teacher** n (in secondary school) profesor(a) m/f; (in primary school) maestro/a, profesor(a) de EGB; **teaching** n enseñanza

**tea: tea cloth** n (BRIT) paño de cocina, trapo de cocina (LAM); **teacup** n taza para el té

**tea leaves** npl hojas de té

**team** [ti:m] n equipo; (of horses) tiro; **team up** vi asociarse

**teapot** ['ti:pɔt] n tetera

**tear¹** [tɪə*] n lágrima; **in ~s** llorando

**tear²** [tɛə*] (pt **tore**, pp **torn**) n rasgón m, desgarrón m ▷ vt romper, rasgar ▷ vi rasgarse; **tear apart** vt (also fig) hacer pedazos; **tear down** vt +adv (building, statue) derribar; (poster, flag) arrancar; **tear off** vt (sheet of paper etc) arrancar; (one's clothes) quitarse a tirones; **tear up** vt (sheet of paper etc) romper

**tearful** ['tɪəful] adj lloroso

**tear gas** ['tɪə-] n gas m lacrimógeno

**tearoom** ['tɪru:m] n salón m de té

**tease** [ti:z] vt tomar el pelo a

**tea: teaspoon** n cucharita; (also: **teaspoonful**: as measurement) cucharadita; **teatime** n hora del té; **tea towel** (BRIT) n paño de cocina

**technical** ['tɛknɪkl] adj técnico

**technician** [tɛk'nɪʃn] n técnico/a

**technique** [tɛk'ni:k] n técnica

**technology** [tɛk'nɔlədʒɪ] n tecnología

**teddy (bear)** ['tɛdɪ-] n osito de felpa
**tedious** ['tiːdɪəs] adj pesado, aburrido
**tee** [tiː] n (Golf) tee m
**teen** [tiːn] adj =**teenage** ▷ n (US) =
**teenager**
**teenage** ['tiːneɪdʒ] adj (fashions etc)
juvenil; (children) quinceañero; **teenager** n
adolescente mf
**teens** [tiːnz] npl: **to be in one's ~** ser
adolescente
**teeth** [tiːθ] npl of **tooth**
**teetotal** ['tiːtəʊtl] adj abstemio
**telecommunications**
[tɛlɪkəmjuːnɪˈkeɪʃənz] n
telecomunicaciones fpl
**telegram** ['tɛlɪgræm] n telegrama m
**telegraph pole** ['tɛlɪgrɑːf-] n poste m
telegráfico
**telephone** ['tɛlɪfəʊn] n teléfono ▷ vt
llamar por teléfono, telefonear; (message)
dar por teléfono; **to be on the ~** (talking)
hablar por teléfono; (possessing telephone)
tener teléfono; **telephone book** n guía f
telefónica; **telephone booth, telephone
box** (BRIT) n cabina telefónica; **telephone
call** n llamada (telefónica); **telephone
directory** n guía (telefónica); **telephone
number** n número de teléfono
**telesales** ['tɛlɪseɪlz] npl televenta(s) f(pl)
**telescope** ['tɛlɪskəʊp] n telescopio
**televise** ['tɛlɪvaɪz] vt televisar
**television** ['tɛlɪvɪʒən] n televisión f; **on ~**
en la televisión; **television programme** n
programa m de televisión
**tell** [tɛl] (pt, pp **told**) vt decir; (relate: story)
contar; (distinguish): **to ~ sth from**
distinguir algo de ▷ vi (talk): **to ~ (of)**
contar; (have effect) tener efecto; **to ~ sb to
do sth** mandar a algn hacer algo; **tell off**
vt: **to tell sb off** regañar a algn; **teller** n (in
bank) cajero/a
**telly** ['tɛlɪ] (BRIT: inf) n abbr (= television)
tele f
**temp** [tɛmp] n abbr (BRIT) (= temporary)
temporero/a
**temper** ['tɛmpə*] n (nature) carácter m;
(mood) humor m; (bad temper) (mal) genio;
(fit of anger) acceso de ira ▷ vt (moderate)
moderar; **to be in a ~** estar furioso; **to lose
one's ~** enfadarse, enojarse
**temperament** ['tɛmprəmənt] n
(nature) temperamento; **temperamental**
[tɛmprəˈmɛntl] adj temperamental
**temperature** ['tɛmprətʃə*] n
temperatura; **to have** or **run a ~** tener fiebre
**temple** ['tɛmpl] n (building) templo; (Anat)
sien f
**temporary** ['tɛmpərərɪ] adj provisional;

(passing) transitorio; (worker) temporero;
(job) temporal
**tempt** [tɛmpt] vt tentar; **to ~ sb into
doing sth** tentar or inducir a algn a hacer
algo; **temptation** n tentación f; **tempting**
adj tentador(a); (food) apetitoso/a
**ten** [tɛn] num diez
**tenant** ['tɛnənt] n inquilino/a
**tend** [tɛnd] vt cuidar ▷ vi: **to ~ to do sth**
tener tendencia a hacer algo; **tendency**
['tɛndənsɪ] n tendencia
**tender** ['tɛndə*] adj (person, care) tierno,
cariñoso; (meat) tierno; (sore) sensible ▷ n
(Comm: offer) oferta; (money): **legal ~** moneda
de curso legal ▷ vt ofrecer
**tendon** ['tɛndən] n tendón m
**tenner** ['tɛnə*] n (inf) (billete m de) diez
libras m
**tennis** ['tɛnɪs] n tenis m; **tennis ball** n
pelota de tenis; **tennis court** n cancha de
tenis; **tennis match** n partido de tenis;
**tennis player** n tenista mf; **tennis racket**
n raqueta de tenis
**tenor** ['tɛnə*] n (Mus) tenor m
**tenpin bowling** ['tɛnpɪn-] n (juego de
los) bolos
**tense** [tɛns] adj (person) nervioso; (moment,
atmosphere) tenso; (muscle) tenso, en tensión
▷ n (Ling) tiempo
**tension** ['tɛnʃən] n tensión f
**tent** [tɛnt] n tienda (de campaña) (SP),
carpa (LAM)
**tentative** ['tɛntətɪv] adj (person, smile)
indeciso; (conclusion, plans) provisional
**tenth** [tɛnθ] num décimo
**tent: tent peg** n clavija, estaca; **tent pole**
n mástil m
**tepid** ['tɛpɪd] adj tibio
**term** [tɜːm] n (word) término; (period)
período; (Scol) trimestre m ▷ vt llamar;
**terms** npl (conditions, Comm) condiciones
fpl; **in the short/long ~** a corto/largo plazo;
**to be on good ~s with sb** llevarse bien con
algn; **to come to ~s with** (problem) aceptar
**terminal** ['tɜːmɪnl] adj (disease) mortal;
(patient) terminal ▷ n (Elec) borne m;
(Comput) terminal m; (also: **air ~**) terminal f;
(BRIT: also: **coach ~**) estación f terminal f
**terminate** ['tɜːmɪneɪt] vt terminar
**termini** ['tɜːmɪnaɪ] npl of **terminus**
**terminology** [tɜːmɪˈnɔlədʒɪ] n
terminología
**terminus** ['tɜːmɪnəs] (pl **termini**) n
término, (estación f) terminal f
**terrace** ['tɛrəs] n terraza; (BRIT: row of
houses) hilera de casas adosadas; **the ~s**
(BRIT Sport) las gradas fpl; **terraced** adj
(garden) en terrazas; (house) adosado

**terrain** [tɛˈreɪn] n terreno
**terrestrial** [tɪˈrestrɪəl] adj (life) terrestre; (BRIT: channel) de transmisión (por) vía terrestre
**terrible** ['terɪbl] adj terrible, horrible; (inf) atroz; **terribly** adv terriblemente; (very badly) malísimamente
**terrier** ['terɪə*] n terrier m
**terrific** [təˈrɪfɪk] adj (very great) tremendo; (wonderful) fantástico, fenomenal
**terrified** ['terɪfaɪd] adj aterrorizado
**terrify** ['terɪfaɪ] vt aterrorizar; **terrifying** adj aterrador(a)
**territorial** [terɪˈtɔːrɪəl] adj territorial
**territory** ['terɪtərɪ] n territorio
**terror** ['terə*] n terror m; **terrorism** n terrorismo; **terrorist** n terrorista mf; **terrorist attack** n atentado (terrorista)
**test** [test] n (gen, Chem) prueba; (Med) examen m; (Scol) examen m, test m; (also: **driving ~**) examen m de conducir ▷ vt probar, poner a prueba; (Med, Scol) examinar
**testicle** ['testɪkl] n testículo
**testify** ['testɪfaɪ] vi (Law) prestar declaración; **to ~ to sth** atestiguar algo
**testimony** ['testɪmənɪ] n (Law) testimonio
**test: test match** n (Cricket, Rugby) partido internacional; **test tube** n probeta
**tetanus** ['tetənəs] n tétano
**text** [tekst] n texto; (on mobile phone) mensaje m de texto ▷ vt: **to ~ sb** (inf) enviar un mensaje (de texto) or un SMS a algn; **textbook** n libro de texto
**textile** ['tekstaɪl] n textil m, tejido
**text message** n mensaje m de texto
**text messaging** [-ˈmesɪdʒɪŋ] n (envío de) mensajes mpl de texto
**texture** ['tekstʃə*] n textura
**Thai** [taɪ] adj, n tailandés/esa m/f
**Thailand** ['taɪlænd] n Tailandia
**than** [ðæn] conj (in comparisons): **more ~ 10/once** más de 10/una vez; **I have more/ less ~ you/Paul** tengo más/menos que tú/Paul; **she is older ~ you think** es mayor de lo que piensas
**thank** [θæŋk] vt dar las gracias a, agradecer; **~ you (very much)** muchas gracias; **~ God!** ¡gracias a Dios! ▷ excl (also: **many ~s, ~s a lot**) ¡gracias! ▷ **~s to** prep gracias a; **thanks** npl gracias fpl; **thankfully** adv (fortunately) afortunadamente; **Thanksgiving (Day)** n día m de Acción de Gracias

⬤ **THANKSGIVING (DAY)**
⬤
⬤ En Estados Unidos el cuarto jueves
⬤ de noviembre es **Thanksgiving Day**,
⬤ fiesta oficial en la que se recuerda la
⬤ celebración que hicieron los primeros
⬤ colonos norteamericanos ("Pilgrims"
⬤ o "Pilgrim Fathers") tras la estupenda
⬤ cosecha de 1621, por la que se dan gracias
⬤ a Dios. En Canadá se celebra una fiesta
⬤ semejante el segundo lunes de octubre,
⬤ aunque no está relacionada con dicha
⬤ fecha histórica.

○ **KEYWORD**

**that** [ðæt] (pl **those**) adj (demonstrative) ese/a; (pl) esos/as; (more remote) aquel(aquella); (pl) aquellos/as; **leave those books on the table** deja esos libros sobre la mesa; **that one** ése(ésa); (more remote) aquél(aquélla); **that one over there** ése(ésa) de ahí; aquél(aquélla) de allí
▷ pron **1** (demonstrative) ése/a; (pl) ésos/as; (neuter) eso; (more remote) aquél(aquélla); (pl) aquéllos/as; (neuter) aquello; **what's that?** ¿qué es eso (or aquello)?; **who's that?** ¿quién es ése/a (or aquél (aquella))?; **is that you?** ¿eres tú?; **will you eat all that?** ¿vas a comer todo eso?; **that's my house** ésa es mi casa; **that's what he said** eso es lo que dijo; **that is (to say)** es decir
**2** (relative: subject, object) que; (with preposition) (el (la)) que etc, el(la) cual etc; **the book (that) I read** el libro que leí; **the books that are in the library** los libros que están en la biblioteca; **all (that) I have** todo lo que tengo; **the box (that) I put it in** la caja en la que or donde lo puse; **the people (that) I spoke to** la gente con la que hablé
**3** (relative: of time) que; **the day (that) he came** el día (en) que vino
▷ conj que; **he thought that I was ill** creyó que yo estaba enfermo
▷ adv (demonstrative): **I can't work that much** no puedo trabajar tanto; **I didn't realise it was that bad** no creí que fuera tan malo; **that high** así de alto

**thatched** [θætʃt] adj (roof) de paja; (cottage) con tejado de paja
**thaw** [θɔː] n deshielo ▷ vi (ice) derretirse; (food) descongelarse ▷ vt (food) descongelar

○ **KEYWORD**

**the** [ðiː, ðə] def art **1** (gen) el m, la f, los mpl, las (NB 'el' immediately before f n beginning with stressed (h)a; a + el = al; de + el = del); **the boy/ girl** el chico/la chica; **the books/flowers**

los libros/las flores; **to the postman/from the drawer** al cartero/del cajón; **I haven't the time/money** no tengo tiempo/dinero **2** (+adj to form n) los; lo; **the rich and the poor** los ricos y los pobres; **to attempt the impossible** intentar lo imposible **3** (in titles): **Elizabeth the First** Isabel primera; **Peter the Great** Pedro el Grande **4** (in comparisons): **the more he works the more he earns** cuanto más trabaja más gana

**theatre** ['θɪətə*] (us **theater**) n teatro; (also: **lecture ~**) aula; (Med: also: **operating ~**) quirófano

**theft** [θeft] n robo

**their** [ðeə*] adj su; **theirs** pron (el) suyo/(la) suya etc); see also **my; mine¹**

**them** [ðɛm, ðəm] pron (direct) los/las; (indirect) les; (stressed, after prep) ellos(ellas); see also **me**

**theme** [θi:m] n tema m; **theme park** n parque de atracciones (en torno a un tema central)

**themselves** [ðəm'sɛlvz] pl pron (subject) ellos mismos(ellas mismas); (complement) se; (after prep) sí (mismos(as)); see also **oneself**

**then** [ðɛn] adv (at that time) entonces; (next) después; (later) luego, después; (and also) además ▷ conj (therefore) en ese caso, entonces ▷ adj: **the ~ president** el entonces presidente; **by ~** para entonces; **from ~ on** desde entonces

**theology** [θɪ'ɔlədʒɪ] n teología

**theory** ['θɪərɪ] n teoría

**therapist** ['θɛrəpɪst] n terapeuta mf

**therapy** ['θɛrəpɪ] n terapia

○ KEYWORD

**there** ['ðeə*] adv **1 there is, there are** hay; **there is no-one here/no bread left** no hay nadie aquí/no queda pan; **there has been an accident** ha habido un accidente **2** (referring to place) ahí; (distant) allí; **it's there** está ahí; **put it in/on/up/down there** ponlo ahí dentro/encima/arriba/abajo; **I want that book there** quiero ese libro de ahí; **there he is!** ¡ahí está! **3 there, there** (esp to child) ea, ea

**there: thereabouts** adv por ahí; **thereafter** adv después; **thereby** adv así, de ese modo; **therefore** adv por lo tanto; **there's = there is; there has**

**thermal** ['θə:ml] adj termal; (paper) térmico

**thermometer** [θə'mɔmɪtə*] n termómetro

**thermostat** ['θə:məustæt] n termostato

**these** [ði:z] pl adj estos/as ▷ pl pron éstos/as

**thesis** ['θi:sɪs] (pl **theses**) n tesis f inv

**they** [ðeɪ] pl pron ellos(ellas); (stressed) ellos (mismos)(ellas (mismas)); **~ say that ...** (it is said that) se dice que ...; **they'd = they had; they would; they'll = they shall; they will; they're = they are; they've = they have**

**thick** [θɪk] adj (in consistency) espeso; (in size) grueso; (stupid) torpe ▷ n: **in the ~ of the battle** en lo más reñido de la batalla; **it's 20 cm =** tiene 20 cm de espesor; **thicken** vi espesarse ▷ vt (sauce etc) espesar; **thickness** n espesor m; grueso

**thief** [θi:f] (pl **thieves**) n ladrón/ona m/f

**thigh** [θaɪ] n muslo

**thin** [θɪn] adj (person, animal) flaco; (in size) delgado; (in consistency) poco espeso; (hair, crowd) escaso ▷ vt: **to ~ (down)** diluir

**thing** [θɪŋ] n cosa; (object) objeto, artículo; (matter) asunto; (mania): **to have a ~ about sb/sth** estar obsesionado con algn/algo; **things** npl (belongings) efectos mpl (personales); **the best ~ would be to ...** lo mejor sería ...; **how are ~s?** ¿qué tal?

**think** [θɪŋk] (pt, pp **thought**) vi pensar ▷ vt pensar, creer; **what did you ~ of them?** ¿qué te parecieron?; **to ~ about sth/sb** pensar en algo/algn; **I'll ~ about it** lo pensaré; **to ~ of doing sth** pensar en hacer algo; **I ~ so/not** creo que sí/no; **to ~ well of sb** tener buen concepto de algn; **think over** vt reflexionar sobre, meditar; **think up** vt (plan etc) idear

**third** [θə:d] adj (before n) tercer(a); (following n) tercero/a ▷ n tercero/a; (fraction) tercio; (BRIT Scol: degree) título de licenciado con calificación de aprobado; **thirdly** adv en tercer lugar; **third party insurance** (BRIT) n seguro contra terceros; **Third World** n Tercer Mundo

**thirst** [θə:st] n sed f; **thirsty** adj (person, animal) sediento; (work) que da sed; **to be thirsty** tener sed

**thirteen** ['θə:'ti:n] num trece; **thirteenth** [-'ti:nθ] adj decimotercero

**thirtieth** ['θə:tɪəθ] adj trigésimo

**thirty** ['θə:tɪ] num treinta

○ KEYWORD

**this** [ðɪs] (pl **these**) adj (demonstrative) este/a pl; estos/as; (neuter) esto; **this man/woman** este hombre(esta mujer); **these children/flowers** estos chicos/estas flores;

**this one (here)** éste/a, esto (de aquí)
▷ pron (*demonstrative*) éste/a pl, éstos/as;
(*neuter*) esto; **who is this?** ¿quién es
éste/ésta?; **what is this?** ¿qué es esto?; **this
is where I live** aquí vivo; **this is what he
said** esto es lo que dijo; **this is Mr Brown**
(*in introductions*) le presento al Sr. Brown;
(*photo*) éste es el Sr. Brown; (*on telephone*)
habla el Sr. Brown
▷ adv (*demonstrative*): **this high/long** etc así
de alto/largo etc; **this far** hasta aquí

**thistle** ['θɪsl] n cardo
**thorn** [θɔːn] n espina
**thorough** ['θʌrə] adj (*search*) minucioso;
(*wash*) a fondo; (*knowledge, research*)
profundo; (*person*) meticuloso; **thoroughly**
adv (*search*) minuciosamente; (*study*)
profundamente; (*wash*) a fondo; (*utterly: bad,
wet* etc) completamente, totalmente
**those** [ðəuz] pl adj esos(esas); (*more
remote*) aquellos/as
**though** [ðəu] conj aunque ▷ adv sin
embargo
**thought** [θɔːt] pt, pp of **think** ▷ n
pensamiento; (*opinion*) opinión f;
**thoughtful** adj pensativo; (*serious*) serio;
(*considerate*) atento; **thoughtless** adj
desconsiderado
**thousand** ['θauzənd] num mil; **two ~**
dos mil; **~s of** miles de; **thousandth** num
milésimo
**thrash** [θræʃ] vt azotar; (*defeat*) derrotar
**thread** [θrɛd] n hilo; (*of screw*) rosca ▷ vt
(*needle*) enhebrar
**threat** [θrɛt] n amenaza; **threaten** vi
amenazar ▷ vt: **to threaten sb with/to
do** amenazar a algn con/con hacer;
**threatening** adj amenazador(a),
amenazante
**three** [θriː] num tres; **three-dimensional**
adj tridimensional; **three-piece suite** n
tresillo; **three-quarters** npl tres cuartas
partes; **three-quarters full** tres cuartas
partes lleno
**threshold** ['θrɛʃhəuld] n umbral m
**threw** [θruː] pt of **throw**
**thrill** [θrɪl] n (*excitement*) emoción f;
(*shudder*) estremecimiento ▷ vt emocionar;
**to be ~ed** (*with gift* etc) estar encantado;
**thrilled** adj: **I was thrilled** Estaba
emocionada; **thriller** n novela (*or obra
or película*) de suspense; **thrilling** adj
emocionante
**thriving** ['θraɪvɪŋ] adj próspero
**throat** [θrəut] n garganta; **to have a sore
~** tener dolor de garganta
**throb** [θrɒb] vi latir; dar punzadas; vibrar

**throne** [θrəun] n trono
**through** [θruː] prep por, a través de;
(*time*) durante; (*by means of*) por medio de,
mediante; (*owing to*) gracias a ▷ adj (*ticket,
train*) directo ▷ adv completamente, de
parte a parte; de principio a fin; **to put sb ~
to sb** (*Tel*) poner or pasar a algn con algn; **to
be ~** (*Tel*) tener comunicación; (*have finished*)
haber terminado; **"no - road"** (*BRIT*) "calle
sin salida"; **throughout** prep (*place*) por
todas partes de, por todo; (*time*) durante
todo ▷ adv por or en todas partes
**throw** [θrəu] n (pt **threw**, pp **thrown**) n tiro;
(*Sport*) lanzamiento ▷ vt tirar, echar; (*Sport*)
lanzar; (*rider*) derribar; (*fig*) desconcertar;
**to ~ a party** dar una fiesta; **throw away**
vt tirar; (*money*) derrochar; **throw in** vt
(*Sport: ball*) sacar; (*include*) incluir; **throw
off** vt deshacerse de; **throw out** vt tirar;
(*person*) echar; expulsar; **throw up** vi
vomitar
**thru** [θruː] (*US*) = **through**
**thrush** [θrʌʃ] n zorzal m, tordo
**thrust** [θrʌst] (pt, pp **~**) vt empujar con
fuerza
**thud** [θʌd] n golpe m sordo
**thug** [θʌg] n gamberro/a
**thumb** [θʌm] n (*Anat*) pulgar m; **to ~ a
lift** hacer autostop; **thumbtack** (*US*) n
chincheta (*SP*)
**thump** [θʌmp] n golpe m; (*sound*) ruido
seco or sordo ▷ vt golpear ▷ vi (*heart* etc)
palpitar
**thunder** ['θʌndə*] n trueno ▷ vi tronar;
(*train* etc): **to ~ past** pasar como un trueno;
**thunderstorm** n tormenta
**Thur(s).** abbr (= *Thursday*) juev
**Thursday** ['θɜːzdɪ] n jueves m inv
**thus** [ðʌs] adv así, de este modo
**thwart** [θwɔːt] vt frustrar
**thyme** [taɪm] n tomillo
**Tibet** [tɪ'bɛt] n el Tibet
**tick** [tɪk] n (*sound: of clock*) tictac m; (*mark*)
palomita; (*Zool*) garrapata; (*BRIT: inf*): **in
a ~** en un instante ▷ vi hacer tictac ▷ vt
marcar; **tick off** vt marcar; (*person*) reñir
**ticket** ['tɪkɪt] n billete m (*SP*), boleto
(*LAM*); (*for cinema* etc) entrada; (*in shop: on
goods*) etiqueta; (*for raffle*) papeleta; (*for
library*) tarjeta; (*parking ticket*) multa de
aparcamiento (*SP*) or por estacionamiento
(*indebido*) (*LAM*); **ticket barrier** n
(*BRIT: Rail*) barrera más allá de la cual se
necesita billete/boleto; **ticket collector**
n revisor(a) m/f; **ticket inspector** n
revisor(a) m/f, inspector(a) m/f de boletos
(*LAM*); **ticket machine** n máquina de
billetes (*SP*) or boletos (*LAM*); **ticket office** n

*(Theatre)* taquilla (sp), boletería (LAM); *(Rail)* mostrador *m* de billetes (sp) or boletos (LAM)

**tickle** ['tɪkl] *vt* hacer cosquillas a ▷ *vi* hacer cosquillas; **ticklish** *adj (person)* cosquilloso; *(problem)* delicado

**tide** [taɪd] *n* marea; *(fig: of events etc)* curso, marcha

**tidy** ['taɪdɪ] *adj (room etc)* ordenado; *(dress, work)* limpio; *(person)* (bien) arreglado ▷ *vt (also: ~ up)* poner en orden

**tie** [taɪ] *n (string etc)* atadura; *(BRIT: also: **neck~**)* corbata; *(fig: link)* vínculo, lazo; *(Sport etc: draw)* empate *m* ▷ *vt* atar ▷ *vi (Sport etc)* empatar; **to ~ in a bow** atar con un lazo; **to ~ a knot in sth** hacer un nudo en algo; **tie down** *vt (fig: person: restrict)* atar; (: to price, date etc) obligar a; **tie up** *vt (dog, person)* atar; *(arrangements)* concluir; **to be tied up** *(busy)* estar ocupado

**tier** [tɪə*] *n* grada; *(of cake)* piso

**tiger** ['taɪgə*] *n* tigre *m*

**tight** [taɪt] *adj (rope)* tirante; *(money)* escaso; *(clothes)* ajustado; *(bend)* cerrado; *(shoes, schedule)* apretado; *(budget)* ajustado; *(security)* estricto; *(inf: drunk)* borracho ▷ *adv (squeeze)* muy fuerte; *(shut)* bien; **tighten** *vt (rope)* estirar; *(screw, grip)* apretar; *(security)* reforzar ▷ *vi* estirarse; apretarse; **tightly** *adv (grasp)* muy fuerte; **tights** (BRIT) *npl* panti *mpl*

**tile** [taɪl] *n (on roof)* teja; *(on floor)* baldosa; *(on wall)* azulejo

**till** [tɪl] *n* caja (registradora) ▷ *vt (land)* cultivar ▷ *prep, conj* = **until**

**tilt** [tɪlt] *vt* inclinar ▷ *vi* inclinarse

**timber** ['tɪmbə*] *n (material)* madera

**time** [taɪm] *n* tiempo; *(epoch: often pl)* época; *(by clock)* hora; *(moment)* momento; *(occasion)* vez *f*; *(Mus)* compás *m* ▷ *vt* calcular or medir el tiempo de; *(race)* cronometrar; *(remark, visit etc)* elegir el momento para; **a long ~** mucho tiempo; **4 at a ~** de 4 en 4; 4 a la vez; **for the ~ being** de momento, por ahora; **from ~ to ~** de vez en cuando; **at ~s** a veces; **in ~** *(soon enough)* a tiempo; *(after some time)* con el tiempo; *(Mus)* al compás; **in a week's ~** dentro de una semana; **in no ~** en un abrir y cerrar de ojos; **any ~** cuando sea; **on ~** a la hora; **5 ~s 5** 5 por 5; **what ~ is it?** ¿qué hora es?; **to have a good ~** pasarlo bien, divertirse; **time limit** *n* plazo; **timely** *adj* oportuno; **timer** *n (in kitchen etc)* programador *m* horario; **timeshare** *n* apartamento (or casa) a tiempo compartido; **timetable** *n* horario; **time zone** *n* huso horario

**timid** ['tɪmɪd] *adj* tímido

**timing** ['taɪmɪŋ] *n (Sport)* cronometraje *m*;

**the ~ of his resignation** el momento que eligió para dimitir

**tin** [tɪn] *n* estaño; *(also: ~ **plate**)* hojalata; *(BRIT: can)* lata; **tinfoil** *n* papel *m* de estaño

**tingle** ['tɪŋgl] *vi (person)*: **to ~ (with)** estremecerse (de); *(hands etc)* hormiguear

**tinker** ['tɪŋkə*]: **~ with** *vt fus* jugar con, tocar

**tinned** [tɪnd] (BRIT) *adj (food)* en lata, en conserva

**tin opener** [-əupnə*] (BRIT) *n* abrelatas *m inv*

**tint** [tɪnt] *n* matiz *m*; *(for hair)* tinte *m*; **tinted** *adj (hair)* teñido; *(glass, spectacles)* ahumado

**tiny** ['taɪnɪ] *adj* minúsculo, pequeñito

**tip** [tɪp] *n (end)* punta; *(gratuity)* propina; *(BRIT: for rubbish)* vertedero; *(advice)* consejo ▷ *vt (waiter)* dar una propina a; *(tilt)* inclinar; *(empty: also: ~ **out**)* vaciar, echar; *(overturn: also: ~ **over**)* volcar; **tip off** *vt* avisar, poner sobreaviso a

**tiptoe** ['tɪptəu] *n*: **on ~** de puntillas

**tire** ['taɪə*] *n* (us) = **tyre** ▷ *vt* cansar ▷ *vi* cansarse; *(become bored)* aburrirse; **tired** *adj* cansado; **to be tired of sth** estar harto de algo; **tire pressure** (us) = **tyre pressure**; **tiring** *adj* cansado

**tissue** ['tɪʃu:] *n* tejido; *(paper handkerchief)* pañuelo de papel, kleenex® *m*; **tissue paper** *n* papel *m* de seda

**tit** [tɪt] *n (bird)* herrerillo común; **to give ~ for tat** dar ojo por ojo

**title** ['taɪtl] *n* título

**T-junction** ['ti:dʒʌŋkʃən] *n* cruce *m* en T

**TM** *abbr* = **trademark**

○ **KEYWORD**

**to** [tu:, tə] *prep* **1** *(direction)* a; **to go to France/London/school/the station** ir a Francia/Londres/al colegio/a la estación; **to go to Claude's/the doctor's** ir a casa de Claude/al médico; **the road to Edinburgh** la carretera de Edimburgo

**2** *(as far as)* hasta, a; **from here to London** de aquí a or hasta Londres; **to count to 10** contar hasta 10; **from 40 to 50 people** entre 40 y 50 personas

**3** *(with expressions of time)*: **a quarter/ twenty to 5** las 5 menos cuarto/veinte

**4** *(for, of)*: **the key to the front door** la llave de la puerta principal; **she is secretary to the director** es la secretaria del director; **a letter to his wife** una carta a or para su mujer

**5** *(expressing indirect object)* a; **to give sth to sb** darle algo a algn; **to talk to sb** hablar con algn; **to be a danger to sb** ser un peligro para algn; **to carry out repairs to sth** hacer reparaciones en algo

**6** (*in relation to*): **3 goals to 2** 3 goles a 2; **30 miles to the gallon** ≈ 94 litros a los cien (kms)

**7** (*purpose, result*): **to come to sb's aid** venir en auxilio *or* ayuda de algn; **to sentence sb to death** condenar a algn a muerte; **to my great surprise** con gran sorpresa mía ▷ *with vb* **1** (*simple infin*): **to go/eat** ir/comer **2** (*following another vb*): **to want/try/start to do** querer/intentar/empezar a hacer **3** (*with vb omitted*): **I don't want to** no quiero **4** (*purpose, result*) para; **I did it to help you** lo hice para ayudarte; **he came to see you** vino a verte

**5** (*equivalent to relative clause*): **I have things to do** tengo cosas que hacer; **the main thing is to try** lo principal es intentarlo

**6** (*after adj etc*): **ready to go** listo para irse; **too old to ...** demasiado viejo (como) para ...

▷ *adv*: **pull/push the door to** tirar de/ empujar la puerta

**toad** [təʊd] *n* sapo; **toadstool** *n* hongo venenoso

**toast** [təʊst] *n* (*Culin*) tostada; (*drink, speech*) brindis *m* ▷ *vt* (*Culin*) tostar; (*drink to*) brindar por; **toaster** *n* tostador *m*

**tobacco** [təˈbækəʊ] *n* tabaco

**toboggan** [təˈbɒgən] *n* tobogán *m*

**today** [təˈdeɪ] *adv, n* (*also fig*) hoy *m*

**toddler** [ˈtɒdlə*] *n* niño/a (que empieza a andar)

**toe** [təʊ] *n* dedo (del pie); (*of shoe*) punta; **to ~ the line** (*fig*) conformarse; **toenail** *n* uña del pie

**toffee** [ˈtɒfɪ] *n* toffee *m*

**together** [təˈgeðə*] *adv* juntos; (*at same time*) al mismo tiempo, a la vez; **~ with** junto con

**toilet** [ˈtɔɪlət] *n* inodoro; (*BRIT: room*) (cuarto de) baño, servicio ▷ *cpd* (*soap etc*) de aseo; **toilet bag** *n* neceser *m*, bolsa de aseo; **toilet paper** *n* papel *m* higiénico; **toiletries** *npl* artículos *mpl* de tocador; **toilet roll** *n* rollo de papel higiénico

**token** [ˈtəʊkən] *n* (*sign*) señal *f*, muestra; (*souvenir*) recuerdo; (*disc*) ficha ▷ *adj* (*strike, payment etc*) simbólico; **book/record ~** (*BRIT*) vale *m* para comprar libros/discos; **gift ~** (*BRIT*) vale-regalo

**Tokyo** [ˈtəʊkjəʊ] *n* Tokio, Tókio

**told** [təʊld] *pt, pp of* **tell**

**tolerant** [ˈtɒlərnt] *adj*: **~ of** tolerante con

**tolerate** [ˈtɒləreɪt] *vt* tolerar

**toll** [təʊl] *n* (*of casualties*) número de víctimas; (*tax, charge*) peaje *m* ▷ *vi* (*bell*) doblar; **toll call** *n* (*US Tel*) conferencia, llamada interurbana; **toll-free** (*US*) *adj, adv* gratis

**tomato** [təˈmɑːtəʊ] (*pl ~es*) *n* tomate *m*; **tomato sauce** *n* salsa de tomate

**tomb** [tuːm] *n* tumba; **tombstone** *n* lápida

**tomorrow** [təˈmɒrəʊ] *adv, n* (*also: fig*) mañana; **the day after ~** pasado mañana; **~ morning** mañana por la mañana

**ton** [tʌn] *n* tonelada (*BRIT* = 1016 *kg*; *US* = 907 *kg*); (*metric ton*) tonelada métrica; **~s of** (*inf*) montones de

**tone** [təʊn] *n* tono ▷ *vi* (*also: ~ in*) armonizar; **tone down** *vt* (*criticism*) suavizar; (*colour*) atenuar

**tongs** [tɒŋz] *npl* (*for coal*) tenazas *fpl*; (*curling tongs*) tenacillas *fpl*

**tongue** [tʌŋ] *n* lengua; **~ in cheek** irónicamente

**tonic** [ˈtɒnɪk] *n* (*Med*) tónico; (*also: ~ water*) (agua) tónica

**tonight** [təˈnaɪt] *adv, n* esta noche; esta tarde

**tonne** [tʌn] *n* tonelada (métrica) (1.000*kg*)

**tonsil** [ˈtɒnsl] *n* amígdala; **tonsillitis** [-ˈlaɪtɪs] *n* amigdalitis *f*

**too** [tuː] *adv* (*excessively*) demasiado; (*also*) también; **~ much** demasiado; **~ many** demasiados/as

**took** [tʊk] *pt of* **take**

**tool** [tuːl] *n* herramienta; **tool box** *n* caja de herramientas; **tool kit** *n* juego de herramientas

**tooth** [tuːθ] (*pl teeth*) *n* (*Anat, Tech*) diente *m*; (*molar*) muela; **toothache** *n* dolor *m* de muelas; **toothbrush** *n* cepillo de dientes; **toothpaste** *n* pasta de dientes; **toothpick** *n* palillo

**top** [tɒp] *n* (*of mountain*) cumbre *f*, cima; (*of tree*) copa; (*of head*) coronilla; (*of ladder, page*) lo alto; (*of table*) superficie *f*; (*of cupboard*) parte *f* de arriba; (*lid: of box*) tapa; (: *of bottle, jar*) tapón *m*; (*of list etc*) cabeza; (*toy*) peonza; (*garment*) blusa; camiseta ▷ *adj* de arriba; (*in rank*) principal, primero; (*best*) mejor ▷ *vt* (*exceed*) exceder; (*be first in*) encabezar; **on ~ of** (*above*) sobre, encima de; (*in addition to*) además de; **from ~ to bottom** de pies a cabeza; **top up** *vt* llenar; (*mobile phone*) recargar (el saldo de); **top floor** *n* último piso; **top hat** *n* sombrero de copa

**topic** [ˈtɒpɪk] *n* tema *m*; **topical** *adj* actual

**topless** [ˈtɒplɪs] *adj* (*bather, bikini*) topless *inv*

**topping** [ˈtɒpɪŋ] *n* (*Culin*): **with a ~ of**

**cream** con nata por encima

**topple** ['tɔpl] vt derribar ▷ vi caerse

**top-up card** n (for mobile phone) tarjeta prepago

**torch** [tɔːtʃ] n antorcha; (BRIT: electric) linterna

**tore** [tɔː*] pt of **tear²**

**torment** [n 'tɔːmɛnt, vt tɔː'mɛnt] n tormento ▷ vt atormentar; (fig: annoy) fastidiar

**torn** [tɔːn] pp of **tear²**

**tornado** [tɔː'neɪdəu] (pl **~es**) n tornado

**torpedo** [tɔː'piːdəu] (pl **~es**) n torpedo

**torrent** ['tɔrnt] n torrente m; **torrential** [tɔ'rɛnʃl] adj torrencial

**tortoise** ['tɔːtəs] n tortuga

**torture** ['tɔːtʃə*] n tortura ▷ vt torturar; (fig) atormentar

**Tory** ['tɔːrɪ] (BRIT) adj, n (Pol) conservador(a) m/f

**toss** [tɔs] vt tirar, echar; (one's head) sacudir; **to ~ a coin** echar a cara o cruz; **to ~ up for sth** jugar a cara o cruz algo; **to ~ and turn** (in bed) dar vueltas

**total** ['təutl] adj total, entero; (emphatic: failure etc) completo, total ▷ n total m, suma ▷ vt (add up) sumar; (amount to) ascender a

**totalitarian** [təutælɪ'tɛərɪən] adj totalitario

**totally** ['təutəlɪ] adv totalmente

**touch** [tʌtʃ] n tacto; (contact) contacto ▷ vt tocar; (emotionally) conmover; **a ~ of** (fig) un poquito de; **to get in ~ with sb** ponerse en contacto con algn; **to lose ~** (friends) perder contacto; **touch down** vi (on land) aterrizar; **touchdown** n aterrizaje m; (on sea) amerizaje m; (us Football) ensayo m; **touched** adj (moved) conmovido; **touching** adj (moving) conmovedor(a); **touchline** n (Sport) línea de banda; **touch-sensitive** adj sensible al tacto

**tough** [tʌf] adj (material) resistente; (meat) duro; (problem etc) difícil; (policy, stance) inflexible; (person) fuerte

**tour** ['tuə*] n viaje m, vuelta; (also: **package ~**) viaje m todo comprendido; (of town, museum) visita; (by band etc) gira ▷ vt recorrer, visitar; **tour guide** n guía mf turístico/a

**tourism** ['tuərɪzm] n turismo

**tourist** ['tuərɪst] n turista mf ▷ cpd turístico; **tourist office** n oficina de turismo

**tournament** ['tuənəmənt] n torneo

**tour operator** n touroperador(a) m/f, operador(a) m/f turístico/a

**tow** [təu] vt remolcar; **"on** or **in** (us) **~"**

(Aut) "a remolque"; **tow away** vt llevarse a remolque

**toward(s)** [tə'wɔːd(z)] prep hacia; (attitude) respecto a, con; (purpose) para

**towel** ['tauəl] n toalla; **towelling** n (fabric) felpa

**tower** ['tauə*] n torre f; **tower block** (BRIT) n torre f (de pisos)

**town** [taun] n ciudad f; **to go to ~** ir a la ciudad; (fig) echar la casa por la ventana; **town centre** (BRIT) n centro de la ciudad; **town hall** n ayuntamiento

**tow truck** (us) n camión m grúa

**toxic** ['tɔksɪk] adj tóxico

**toy** [tɔɪ] n juguete m; **toy with** vt fus jugar con; (idea) acariciar; **toyshop** n juguetería

**trace** [treɪs] n rastro ▷ vt (draw) trazar, delinear; (locate) encontrar; (follow) seguir la pista de

**track** [træk] n (mark) huella, pista; (path: gen) camino, senda; (: of bullet etc) trayectoria; (: of suspect, animal) pista, rastro; (Rail) vía; (Sport) pista; (on tape, record) canción f ▷ vt seguir la pista de; **to keep ~ of** mantenerse al tanto de, seguir; **track down** vt (prey) seguir el rastro de; (sth lost) encontrar; **tracksuit** n chandal m

**tractor** ['træktə*] n tractor m

**trade** [treɪd] n comercio; (skill, job) oficio ▷ vi negociar, comerciar ▷ vt (exchange): **to ~ sth (for sth)** cambiar algo (por algo); **trade in** vt (old car etc) ofrecer como parte del pago; **trademark** n marca de fábrica; **trader** n comerciante m/f; **tradesman** (irreg) n (shopkeeper) tendero; **trade union** n sindicato

**trading** ['treɪdɪŋ] n comercio

**tradition** [trə'dɪʃən] n tradición f; **traditional** adj tradicional

**traffic** ['træfɪk] n (gen, Aut) tráfico, circulación f ▷ vi: **to ~ in** (pej: liquor, drugs) traficar en; **traffic circle** (us) n isleta; **traffic island** n refugio, isleta; **traffic jam** n embotellamiento; **traffic lights** npl semáforo; **traffic warden** n guardia mf de tráfico

**tragedy** ['trædʒədɪ] n tragedia

**tragic** ['trædʒɪk] adj trágico

**trail** [treɪl] n (tracks) rastro, pista; (path) camino, sendero; (dust, smoke) estela ▷ vt (drag) arrastrar; (follow) seguir la pista de ▷ vi arrastrar; (in contest etc) ir perdiendo; **trailer** n (Aut) remolque m; (caravan) caravana; (Cinema) trailer m, avance m

**train** [treɪn] n tren m; (of dress) cola; (series) serie f ▷ vt (educate, teach skills to) formar; (sportsman) entrenar; (dog) adiestrar; (point: gun etc): **to ~ on** apuntar a ▷ vi (Sport) entrenarse; (learn a skill): **to ~ as a teacher** etc estudiar para profesor etc; **one's ~ of thought** el razonamiento de algn; **trainee** [treɪ'niː] n aprendiz(a) m/f; **trainer** n (Sport: coach) entrenador(a) m/f; (of animals) domador(a) m/f; **trainers** npl (shoes) zapatillas fpl (de deporte); **training** n formación f; entrenamiento; **to be in training** (Sport) estar entrenando; **training course** n curso de formación; **training shoes** npl zapatillas fpl (de deporte)

**trait** [treɪt] n rasgo

**traitor** ['treɪtə*] n traidor(a) m/f

**tram** [træm] (BRIT) n (also: **~car**) tranvía m

**tramp** [træmp] n (person) vagabundo/a; (inf: pej: woman) puta

**trample** ['træmpl] vt: **to ~ (underfoot)** pisotear

**trampoline** ['træmpəliːn] n trampolín m

**tranquil** ['træŋkwɪl] adj tranquilo; **tranquillizer** (US **tranquilizer**) n (Med) tranquilizante m

**transaction** [træn'zækʃən] n transacción f, operación f

**transatlantic** ['trænzət'læntɪk] adj transatlántico

**transcript** ['trænskrɪpt] n copia

**transfer** [n 'trænsfə:*, vb træns'fə:*] n (of employees) traslado; (of money, power) transferencia; (Sport) traspaso; (picture, design) calcomanía ▷ vt trasladar; transferir; **to ~ the charges** (BRIT Tel) llamar a cobro revertido

**transform** [træns'fɔ:m] vt transformar; **transformation** n transformación f

**transfusion** [træns'fjuːʒən] n transfusión f

**transit** ['trænzɪt] n: **in ~** en tránsito

**transition** [træn'zɪʃən] n transición f

**transitive** ['trænzɪtɪv] adj (Ling) transitivo

**translate** [trænz'leɪt] vt traducir; **translation** [-'leɪʃən] n traducción f; **translator** n traductor(a) m/f

**transmission** [trænz'mɪʃən] n transmisión f

**transmit** [trænz'mɪt] vt transmitir; **transmitter** n transmisor m

**transparent** [træns'pærnt] adj transparente

**transplant** ['trænsplɑːnt] n (Med) transplante m

**transport** [n 'trænspɔːt, vt træns'pɔːt] n transporte m; (car) coche m (SP), carro (LAM), automóvil m ▷ vt transportar; **transportation** [-'teɪʃən] n transporte m

**transvestite** [trænz'vɛstaɪt] n travestí mf

**trap** [træp] n (snare, trick) trampa; (carriage) cabriolé m ▷ vt coger (SP) or agarrar (LAM) (en una trampa); (trick) engañar; (confine) atrapar

**trash** [træʃ] n (rubbish) basura; (nonsense) tonterías fpl; (pej): **the book/film is ~** el libro/la película no vale nada; **trash can** (US) n cubo or bote m (MEX) or tacho (SC) de la basura

**trauma** ['trɔːmə] n trauma m; **traumatic** [trɔː'mætɪk] adj traumático

**travel** ['trævl] n el viajar ▷ vi viajar ▷ vt (distance) recorrer; **travel agency** n agencia de viajes; **travel agent** n agente mf de viajes; **travel insurance** n seguro de viaje; **traveller** (US **traveler**) n viajero/a; **traveller's cheque** (US **traveler's check**) n cheque m de viajero; **travelling** (US **traveling**) n los viajes, el viajar; **travel-sick** adj: **to get travel-sick** marearse al viajar; **travel sickness** n mareo

**tray** [treɪ] n (on desk) cajón m

**treacherous** ['trɛtʃərəs] adj traidor, traicionero; (dangerous) peligroso

**treacle** ['triːkl] (BRIT) n melaza

**tread** [trɛd] (pt **trod**, pp **trodden**) n (step) paso, pisada; (sound) ruido de pasos; (of stair) escalón m; (of tyre) banda de rodadura ▷ vi pisar; **tread on** vt fus pisar

**treasure** ['trɛʒə*] n tesoro ▷ vt (value: object, friendship) apreciar; (: memory) guardar; **treasurer** n tesorero/a

**treasury** ['trɛʒərɪ] n: **the T~** el Ministerio de Hacienda

**treat** [triːt] n (present) regalo ▷ vt tratar; **to ~ sb to sth** invitar a algn a algo; **treatment** n tratamiento

**treaty** ['triːtɪ] n tratado

**treble** ['trɛbl] adj triple ▷ vt triplicar ▷ vi triplicarse

**tree** [triː] n árbol m; **~ trunk** tronco (de árbol)

**trek** [trɛk] n (long journey) viaje m largo y difícil; (tiring walk) caminata

**tremble** ['trɛmbl] vi temblar

**tremendous** [trɪ'mɛndəs] adj tremendo, enorme; (excellent) estupendo

**trench** [trɛntʃ] n zanja

**trend** [trɛnd] n (tendency) tendencia; (of events) curso; (fashion) moda; **trendy** adj de moda

**trespass** ['trɛspəs] vi: **to ~ on** entrar sin permiso en; **"no ~ing"** "prohibido el paso"

**trial** ['traɪəl] n (Law) juicio, proceso; (test: of machine etc) prueba; **trial period** n periodo de prueba

**triangle** ['traɪæŋgl] n (Math, Mus) triángulo

**triangular** [traɪˈæŋgjulə*] *adj* triangular
**tribe** [traɪb] *n* tribu *f*
**tribunal** [traɪˈbjuːnl] *n* tribunal *m*
**tribute** [ˈtrɪbjuːt] *n* homenaje *m*, tributo; **to pay ~ to** rendir homenaje a
**trick** [trɪk] *n* (*skill, knack*) tino, truco; (*conjuring trick*) truco; (*joke*) broma; (*Cards*) baza ▷ *vt* engañar; **to play a ~ on sb** gastar una broma a algn; **that should do the ~** a ver si funciona así
**trickle** [ˈtrɪkl] *n* (*of water etc*) goteo ▷ *vi* gotear
**tricky** [ˈtrɪkɪ] *adj* difícil; delicado
**tricycle** [ˈtraɪsɪkl] *n* triciclo
**trifle** [ˈtraɪfl] *n* bagatela; (*Culin*) dulce de bizcocho borracho, gelatina, fruta y natillas ▷ *adv*: **a ~ long** un poquito largo
**trigger** [ˈtrɪgə*] *n* (*of gun*) gatillo
**trim** [trɪm] *adj* (*house, garden*) en buen estado; (*person, figure*) esbelto ▷ *n* (*haircut etc*) recorte *m*; (*on car*) guarnición *f* ▷ *vt* (*neaten*) arreglar; (*cut*) recortar; (*decorate*) adornar; (*Naut: a sail*) orientar
**trio** [ˈtriːəu] *n* trío
**trip** [trɪp] *n* viaje *m*; (*excursion*) excursión *f*; (*stumble*) traspié *m* ▷ *vi* (*stumble*) tropezar; (*go lightly*) andar a paso ligero; **on a ~** de viaje; **trip up** *vi* tropezar, caerse ▷ *vt* hacer tropezar *or* caer
**triple** [ˈtrɪpl] *adj* triple
**triplets** [ˈtrɪplɪts] *npl* trillizos/as *mpl/fpl*
**tripod** [ˈtraɪpɔd] *n* trípode *m*
**triumph** [ˈtraɪʌmf] *n* triunfo ▷ *vi*: **to ~ (over)** vencer; **triumphant** [traɪˈʌmfənt] *adj* (*team etc*) vencedor(a); (*wave, return*) triunfal
**trivial** [ˈtrɪvɪəl] *adj* insignificante; (*commonplace*) banal
**trod** [trɔd] *pt of* **tread**
**trodden** [ˈtrɔdn] *pp of* **tread**
**trolley** [ˈtrɔlɪ] *n* carrito; (*also*: **~ bus**) trolebús *m*
**trombone** [trɔmˈbəun] *n* trombón *m*
**troop** [truːp] *n* grupo, banda; **troops** *npl* (*Mil*) tropas *fpl*
**trophy** [ˈtrəufɪ] *n* trofeo
**tropical** [ˈtrɔpɪkl] *adj* tropical
**trot** [trɔt] *n* trote *m* ▷ *vi* trotar; **on the ~** (*Brit: fig*) seguidos/as
**trouble** [ˈtrʌbl] *n* problema *m*, dificultad *f*; (*worry*) preocupación *f*; (*bother, effort*) molestia, esfuerzo; (*unrest*) inquietud *f*; (*Med*): **stomach** *etc* **~** problemas *mpl* gástricos *etc* ▷ *vt* (*disturb*) molestar; (*worry*) preocupar, inquietar ▷ *vi*: **to ~ to do sth** molestarse en hacer algo; **troubles** *npl* (*Pol etc*) conflictos *mpl*; (*personal*) problemas *mpl*; **to be in ~** estar en un apuro; **it's no ~!** ¡no

es molestia (ninguna)!; **what's the ~?** (*with broken TV etc*) ¿cuál es el problema?; (*doctor to patient*) ¿qué pasa?; **troubled** *adj* (*person*) preocupado; (*country, epoch, life*) agitado; **troublemaker** *n* agitador(a) *m/f*; (*child*) alborotador *m*; **troublesome** *adj* molesto
**trough** [trɔf] *n* (*also*: **drinking ~**) abrevadero; (*also*: **feeding ~**) comedero; (*depression*) depresión *f*
**trousers** [ˈtrauzəz] *npl* pantalones *mpl*; **short ~** pantalones *mpl* cortos
**trout** [traut] *n inv* trucha
**trowel** [ˈtrauəl] *n* (*of gardener*) palita; (*of builder*) paleta
**truant** [ˈtruənt] *n*: **to play ~** (*Brit*) hacer novillos
**truce** [truːs] *n* tregua
**truck** [trʌk] *n* (*lorry*) camión *m*; (*Rail*) vagón *m*; **truck driver** *n* camionero
**true** [truː] *adj* verdadero; (*accurate*) exacto; (*genuine*) auténtico; (*faithful*) fiel; **to come ~** realizarse
**truly** [ˈtruːlɪ] *adv* (*really*) realmente; (*truthfully*) verdaderamente; (*faithfully*): **yours ~** (*in letter*) le saluda atentamente
**trumpet** [ˈtrʌmpɪt] *n* trompeta
**trunk** [trʌŋk] *n* (*of tree, person*) tronco; (*of elephant*) trompa; (*case*) baúl *m*; (*us Aut*) maletero; **trunks** *npl* (*also*: **swimming ~s**) bañador *m* (*de hombre*)
**trust** [trʌst] *n* confianza; (*responsibility*) responsabilidad *f*; (*Law*) fideicomiso ▷ *vt* (*rely on*) tener confianza en; (*hope*) esperar; (*entrust*): **to ~ sth to sb** confiar algo a algn; **to take sth on ~** fiarse de algo; **trusted** *adj* de confianza; **trustworthy** *adj* digno de confianza
**truth** [truːθ, *pl* truːðz] *n* verdad *f*; **truthful** *adj* veraz
**try** [traɪ] *n* tentativa, intento; (*Rugby*) ensayo ▷ *vt* (*attempt*) intentar; (*test: also*: **~ out**) probar, someter a prueba; (*Law*) juzgar, procesar; (*strain: patience*) hacer perder ▷ *vi* probar; **to have a ~** probar suerte; **to ~ to do sth** intentar hacer algo; **~ again!** ¡vuelve a probar!; **~ harder!** ¡esfuérzate más!; **well, I tried** al menos lo intenté; **try on** *vt* (*clothes*) probarse; **trying** *adj* (*experience*) cansado; (*person*) pesado
**T-shirt** [ˈtiːʃəːt] *n* camiseta
**tub** [tʌb] *n* cubo (*sp*), cubeta (*sp, mex*), balde *m* (*lam*); (*bath*) bañera (*sp*), tina (*lam*), bañadera (*rpl*)
**tube** [tjuːb] *n* tubo; (*Brit: underground*) metro; (*for tyre*) cámara de aire
**tuberculosis** [tjubəːkjuˈləusɪs] *n* tuberculosis *f inv*

**tube station** (BRIT) n estación f de metro
**tuck** [tʌk] vt (put) poner; **tuck away** vt (money) guardar; (building): **to be tucked away** esconderse, ocultarse; **tuck in** vt meter dentro; (child) arropar ▷ vi (eat) comer con apetito; **tuck shop** n (Scol) tienda ≈ bar m (del colegio) (SP)
**Tue(s).** abbr (= Tuesday) mart
**Tuesday** ['tju:zdɪ] n martes m inv
**tug** [tʌg] n (ship) remolcador m ▷ vt tirar de
**tuition** [tju:'ɪʃən] n (BRIT) enseñanza; (: private tuition) clases fpl particulares; (US: school fees) matrícula
**tulip** ['tju:lɪp] n tulipán m
**tumble** ['tʌmbl] n (fall) caída ▷ vi caer; **to ~ to sth** (inf) caer en la cuenta de algo; **tumble dryer** (BRIT) n secadora
**tumbler** ['tʌmblə*] n (glass) vaso
**tummy** ['tʌmɪ] (inf) n barriga, tripa
**tumour** ['tju:mə*] (US **tumor**) n tumor m
**tuna** ['tju:nə] n inv (also: **~ fish**) atún m
**tune** [tju:n] n melodía ▷ vt (Mus) afinar; (Radio, TV, Aut) sintonizar; **to be in/out of ~** (instrument) estar afinado/desafinado; (singer) cantar afinadamente/desafinar; **to be in/out of ~ with** (fig) estar de acuerdo/en desacuerdo con; **tune in** vi: **to tune in (to)** (Radio, TV) sintonizar (con); **tune up** vi (musician) afinar (su instrumento)
**tunic** ['tju:nɪk] n túnica
**Tunisia** [tju:'nɪzɪə] n Túnez m
**tunnel** ['tʌnl] n túnel m; (in mine) galería ▷ vi construir un túnel/una galería
**turbulence** ['tə:bjuləns] n (Aviat) turbulencia
**turf** [tə:f] n césped m; (clod) tepe m ▷ vt cubrir con césped
**Turk** [tə:k] n turco/a
**Turkey** ['tə:kɪ] n Turquía
**turkey** ['tə:kɪ] n pavo
**Turkish** ['tə:kɪʃ] adj, n turco; (Ling) turco
**turmoil** ['tə:mɔɪl] n: **in ~** revuelto
**turn** [tə:n] n turno; (in road) curva; (of mind, events) rumbo; (Theatre) número; (Med) ataque m ▷ vt girar, volver; (collar, steak) dar la vuelta a; (page) pasar; (change): **to ~ sth into** convertir algo en ▷ vi volver; (person: look back) volverse; (reverse direction) dar la vuelta; (milk) cortarse; (become): **to ~ nasty/forty** ponerse feo/cumplir los cuarenta; **a good ~** un favor; **it gave me quite a ~** me dio un susto; **"no left ~"** (Aut) "prohibido girar a la izquierda"; **it's your ~** te toca a ti; **in ~** por turnos; **to take ~s (at)** turnarse (en); **turn around** vi (person) volverse, darse la vuelta ▷ vt (object) dar la vuelta a, voltear (LAM); **turn away** vi

apartar la vista ▷ vi rechazar; **turn back** vi volverse atrás ▷ vt hacer retroceder; (clock) retrasar; **turn down** vt (refuse) rechazar; (reduce) bajar; (fold) doblar; **turn in** vi (inf: go to bed) acostarse ▷ vt (fold) doblar hacia dentro; **turn off** vi (from road) desviarse ▷ vt (light, radio etc) apagar; (tap) cerrar; (engine) parar; **turn on** vt (light, radio etc) encender (SP), prender (LAM); (tap) abrir; (engine) poner en marcha; **turn out** vt (light, gas) apagar; (produce) producir ▷ vi (voters) concurrir; **to turn out to be ...** resultar ser ...; **turn over** vi (person) volverse ▷ vt (object) dar la vuelta a; (page) volver; **turn round** vi volverse; (rotate) girar; **turn to** vt fus: **to turn to sb** acudir a algn; **turn up** vi (person) llegar, presentarse; (lost object) aparecer ▷ vt (gen) subir; **turning** n (in road) vuelta; **turning point** n (fig) momento decisivo
**turnip** ['tə:nɪp] n nabo
**turn: turnout** n concurrencia; **turnover** n (Comm: amount of money) volumen m de ventas; (: of goods) movimiento; **turnstile** n torniquete m; **turn-up** (BRIT) n (on trousers) vuelta
**turquoise** ['tə:kwɔɪz] n (stone) turquesa ▷ adj color turquesa
**turtle** ['tə:tl] n galápago; **turtleneck (sweater)** n jersey m de cuello vuelto
**tusk** [tʌsk] n colmillo
**tutor** ['tju:tə*] n profesor(a) m/f; **tutorial** [-'tɔ:rɪəl] n (Scol) seminario
**tuxedo** [tʌk'si:dəu] (US) n smóking m, esmoquin m
**TV** [ti:'vi:] n abbr (= television) tele f
**tweed** [twi:d] n tweed m
**tweezers** ['twi:zəz] npl pinzas fpl (de depilar)
**twelfth** [twelfθ] num duodécimo
**twelve** [twelv] num doce; **at ~ o'clock** (midday) a mediodía; (midnight) a medianoche
**twentieth** ['twentɪɪθ] adj vigésimo
**twenty** ['twentɪ] num veinte
**twice** [twaɪs] adv dos veces; **~ as much** dos veces más
**twig** [twɪg] n ramita
**twilight** ['twaɪlaɪt] n crepúsculo
**twin** [twɪn] adj, n gemelo/a m/f ▷ vt hermanar; **twin(-bedded) room** n habitación f doble; **twin beds** npl camas fpl gemelas
**twinkle** ['twɪŋkl] vi centellear; (eyes) brillar
**twist** [twɪst] n (action) torsión f; (in road, coil) vuelta; (in wire, flex) doblez f; (in story) giro ▷ vt torcer; (weave) trenzar; (roll around) enrollar; (fig) deformar ▷ vi serpentear

**twit** [twɪt] (inf) n tonto

**twitch** [twɪtʃ] n (pull) tirón m; (nervous) tic m ▷ vi crisparse

**two** [tu:] num dos; **to put ~ and ~ together** (fig) atar cabos

**type** [taɪp] n (category) tipo, género; (model) tipo; (Typ) tipo, letra ▷ vt (letter etc) escribir a máquina; **typewriter** n máquina de escribir

**typhoid** ['taɪfɔɪd] n tifoidea

**typhoon** [taɪ'fu:n] n tifón m

**typical** ['tɪpɪkl] adj típico; **typically** adv típicamente

**typing** ['taɪpɪŋ] n mecanografía

**typist** ['taɪpɪst] n mecanógrafo/a

**tyre** ['taɪə*] (us **tire**) n neumático, llanta (LAM); **tyre pressure** (BRIT) n presión f de los neumáticos

**UFO** ['ju:fəu] n abbr (= unidentified flying object) OVNI m

**Uganda** [ju:'gændə] n Uganda

**ugly** ['ʌglɪ] adj feo; (dangerous) peligroso

**UHT** abbr (= UHT milk) leche f UHT, leche f uperizada

**UK** n abbr = **United Kingdom**

**ulcer** ['ʌlsə*] n úlcera; (mouth ulcer) llaga

**ultimate** ['ʌltɪmət] adj último, final; (greatest) máximo; **ultimately** adv (in the end) por último, al final; (fundamentally) a or en fin de cuentas

**ultimatum** [ʌltɪ'meɪtəm] (pl **~s** or **ultimata**) n ultimátum m

**ultrasound** ['ʌltrəsaund] n (Med) ultrasonido

**ultraviolet** ['ʌltrə'vaɪəlɪt] adj ultravioleta

**umbrella** [ʌm'brɛlə] n paraguas m inv; (for sun) sombrilla

**umpire** ['ʌmpaɪə*] n árbitro

**UN** n abbr (= United Nations) NN. UU.

**unable** [ʌn'eɪbl] adj: **to be ~ to do sth** no poder hacer algo

**unacceptable** [ʌnək'sɛptəbl] adj (proposal, behaviour, price) inaceptable; **it's ~ that** no se puede aceptar que

**unanimous** [ju:'nænɪməs] adj unánime

**unarmed** [ʌn'ɑ:md] adj (defenceless) inerme; (without weapon) desarmado

**unattended** [ʌnə'tɛndɪd] adj desatendido

**unattractive** [ʌnə'træktɪv] adj poco atractivo

**unavailable** [ʌnə'veɪləbl] adj (article, room, book) no disponible; (person) ocupado

**unavoidable** [ʌnə'vɔɪdəbl] adj inevitable

**unaware** [ʌnə'wɛə*] adj: **to be ~ of** ignorar; **unawares** adv: **to catch sb unawares** pillar a algn desprevenido

**unbearable** [ʌn'bɛərəbl] adj insoportable

**unbeatable** [ʌn'bi:təbl] adj (team)

invencible; (price) inmejorable; (quality) insuperable

**unbelievable** [ʌnbɪ'liːvəbl] adj increíble

**unborn** [ʌn'bɔːn] adj que va a nacer

**unbutton** [ʌn'bʌtn] vt desabrochar

**uncalled-for** [ʌn'kɔːldfɔː*] adj gratuito, inmerecido

**uncanny** [ʌn'kænɪ] adj extraño

**uncertain** [ʌn'səːtn] adj incierto; (indecisive) indeciso; **uncertainty** n incertidumbre f

**unchanged** [ʌn'tʃeɪndʒd] adj igual, sin cambios

**uncle** ['ʌŋkl] n tío

**unclear** [ʌn'klɪə*] adj poco claro; **I'm still ~ about what I'm supposed to do** todavía no tengo muy claro lo que tengo que hacer

**uncomfortable** [ʌn'kʌmfətəbl] adj incómodo; (uneasy) inquieto

**uncommon** [ʌn'kɔmən] adj poco común, raro

**unconditional** [ʌnkən'dɪʃənl] adj incondicional

**unconscious** [ʌn'kɔnʃəs] adj sin sentido; (unaware): **to be ~ of** no darse cuenta de ▷ n: **the ~** el inconsciente

**uncontrollable** [ʌnkən'trəuləbl] adj (child etc) incontrolable; (temper) indomable; (laughter) incontenible

**unconventional** [ʌnkən'vɛnʃənl] adj poco convencional

**uncover** [ʌn'kʌvə*] vt descubrir; (take lid off) destapar

**undecided** [ʌndɪ'saɪdɪd] adj (character) indeciso; (question) no resuelto

**undeniable** [ʌndɪ'naɪəbl] adj innegable

**under** ['ʌndə*] prep debajo de; (less than) menos de; (according to) según, de acuerdo con; (sb's leadership) bajo ▷ adv debajo, abajo; **~ there** allí abajo; **~ repair** en reparación; **undercover** adj clandestino; **underdone** adj (Culin) poco hecho; **underestimate** vt subestimar; **undergo** (irreg) vt sufrir; (treatment) recibir; **undergraduate** n estudiante mf; **underground** n (BRIT: railway) metro; (Pol) movimiento clandestino ▷ adj (car park) subterráneo ▷ adv (work) en la clandestinidad; **undergrowth** n maleza; **underline** vt subrayar; **undermine** vt socavar, minar; **underneath** [ʌndə'niːθ] adv debajo ▷ prep debajo de, bajo; **underpants** npl calzoncillos mpl; **underpass** (BRIT) n paso subterráneo; **underprivileged** adj desposeído; **underscore** vt subrayar; **undershirt** (US) n camiseta; **underskirt** (BRIT) n enaguas fpl

**understand** [ʌndə'stænd] vt, vi entender, comprender; (assume) tener entendido; **understandable** adj comprensible; **understanding** adj comprensivo ▷ n comprensión f, entendimiento; (agreement) acuerdo

**understatement** ['ʌndəsteɪtmənt] n modestia (excesiva); **that's an ~!** ¡eso es decir poco!

**understood** [ʌndə'stud] pt, pp of **understand** ▷ adj (agreed) acordado; (implied): **it is ~ that** se sobreentiende que

**undertake** [ʌndə'teɪk] (irreg) vt emprender; **to ~ to do sth** comprometerse a hacer algo

**undertaker** ['ʌndəteɪkə*] n director(a) m/f de pompas fúnebres

**undertaking** ['ʌndəteɪkɪŋ] n empresa; (promise) promesa

**under: underwater** adv bajo el agua ▷ adj submarino; **underway** adj: **to be ~** (meeting) estar en marcha; (investigation) estar llevándose a cabo; **underwear** n ropa interior; **underwent** vb see **undergo**; **underworld** n (of crime) hampa, inframundo

**undesirable** [ʌndɪ'zaɪrəbl] adj (person) indeseable; (thing) poco aconsejable

**undisputed** [ʌndɪ'spjuːtɪd] adj incontestable

**undo** [ʌn'duː] (irreg) vt (laces) desatar; (button etc) desabrochar; (spoil) deshacer

**undone** [ʌn'dʌn] pp of **undo** ▷ adj: **to come ~** (clothes) desabrocharse; (parcel) desatarse

**undoubtedly** [ʌn'dautɪdlɪ] adv indudablemente, sin duda

**undress** [ʌn'drɛs] vi desnudarse

**unearth** [ʌn'əːθ] vt desenterrar

**uneasy** [ʌn'iːzɪ] adj intranquilo, preocupado; (feeling) desagradable; (peace) inseguro

**unemployed** [ʌnɪm'plɔɪd] adj parado, sin trabajo ▷ npl: **the ~** los parados

**unemployment** [ʌnɪm'plɔɪmənt] n paro, desempleo; **unemployment benefit** n (BRIT) subsidio de desempleo or paro

**unequal** [ʌn'iːkwəl] adj (unfair) desigual; (size, length) distinto

**uneven** [ʌn'iːvn] adj desigual; (road etc) lleno de baches

**unexpected** [ʌnɪk'spɛktɪd] adj inesperado; **unexpectedly** adv inesperadamente

**unfair** [ʌn'fɛə*] adj: **~ (to sb)** injusto (con algn)

**unfaithful** [ʌn'feɪθful] adj infiel

**unfamiliar** [ʌnfə'mɪlɪə*] adj extraño, desconocido; **to be ~ with** desconocer

**unfashionable** [ʌn'fæʃnəbl] *adj* pasado
or fuera de moda
**unfasten** [ʌn'fɑːsn] *vt* (*knot*) desatar;
(*dress*) desabrochar; (*open*) abrir
**unfavourable** [ʌn'feivərəbl] (*us*
**unfavorable**) *adj* desfavorable
**unfinished** [ʌn'fɪnɪʃt] *adj* inacabado, sin
terminar
**unfit** [ʌn'fɪt] *adj* bajo de forma;
(*incompetent*): **~ (for)** incapaz (de); **~ for
work** no apto para trabajar
**unfold** [ʌn'fəuld] *vt* desdoblar ⊳ *vi* abrirse
**unforgettable** [ʌnfə'getəbl] *adj*
inolvidable
**unfortunate** [ʌn'fɔːtʃnət] *adj*
desgraciado; (*event, remark*) inoportuno;
**unfortunately** *adv* desgraciadamente
**unfriendly** [ʌn'frendlɪ] *adj* antipático;
(*behaviour, remark*) hostil, poco amigable
**unfurnished** [ʌn'fəːnɪʃt] *adj* sin amueblar
**unhappiness** [ʌn'hæpɪnɪs] *n* tristeza,
desdicha
**unhappy** [ʌn'hæpɪ] *adj* (*sad*) triste;
(*unfortunate*) desgraciado; (*childhood*) infeliz;
**~ about/with** (*arrangements etc*) poco
contento con, descontento de
**unhealthy** [ʌn'hɛlθɪ] *adj* (*place*) malsano;
(*person*) enfermizo; (*fig: interest*) morboso
**unheard-of** [ʌn'həːdɔv] *adj* inaudito, sin
precedente
**unhelpful** [ʌn'hɛlpful] *adj* (*person*) poco
servicial; (*advice*) inútil
**unhurt** [ʌn'həːt] *adj* ileso
**unidentified** [ʌnaɪ'dentɪfaɪd] *adj* no
identificado, sin identificar; *see also* **UFO**
**uniform** ['juːnɪfɔːm] *n* uniforme *m* ⊳ *adj*
uniforme
**unify** ['juːnɪfaɪ] *vt* unificar, unir
**unimportant** [ʌnɪm'pɔːtənt] *adj* sin
importancia
**uninhabited** [ʌnɪn'hæbɪtɪd] *adj* desierto
**unintentional** [ʌnɪn'tenʃənəl] *adj*
involuntario
**union** ['juːnjən] *n* unión *f*; (*also*: **trade
~**) sindicato ⊳ *cpd* sindical; **Union Jack** *n*
bandera del Reino Unido
**unique** [juː'niːk] *adj* único
**unisex** ['juːnɪseks] *adj* unisex
**unit** ['juːnɪt] *n* unidad *f*; (*section: of furniture
etc*) elemento; (*team*) grupo; **kitchen ~**
módulo de cocina
**unite** [juː'naɪt] *vt* unir ⊳ *vi* unirse;
**united** *adj* unido; (*effort*) conjunto; **United
Kingdom** *n* Reino Unido; **United Nations
(Organization)** *n* Naciones *fpl* Unidas;
**United States (of America)** *n* Estados
*mpl* Unidos
**unity** ['juːnɪtɪ] *n* unidad *f*

**universal** [juːnɪ'vəːsl] *adj* universal
**universe** ['juːnɪvəːs] *n* universo
**university** [juːnɪ'vəːsɪtɪ] *n* universidad *f*
**unjust** [ʌn'dʒʌst] *adj* injusto
**unkind** [ʌn'kaɪnd] *adj* poco amable;
(*behaviour, comment*) cruel
**unknown** [ʌn'nəun] *adj* desconocido
**unlawful** [ʌn'lɔːful] *adj* ilegal, ilícito
**unleaded** [ʌn'ledɪd] *adj* (*petrol, fuel*) sin
plombo
**unleash** [ʌn'liːʃ] *vt* desatar
**unless** [ʌn'lɛs] *conj* a menos que; **~ he
comes** a menos que venga; **~ otherwise
stated** salvo indicación contraria
**unlike** [ʌn'laɪk] *adj* (*not alike*) distinto
de or a; (*not like*) poco propio de ⊳ *prep* a
diferencia de
**unlikely** [ʌn'laɪklɪ] *adj* improbable;
(*unexpected*) inverosímil
**unlimited** [ʌn'lɪmɪtɪd] *adj* ilimitado
**unlisted** [ʌn'lɪstɪd] (*us*) *adj* (*Tel*) que no
consta en la guía
**unload** [ʌn'ləud] *vt* descargar
**unlock** [ʌn'lɔk] *vt* abrir (con llave)
**unlucky** [ʌn'lʌkɪ] *adj* desgraciado; (*object,
number*) que da mala suerte; **to be ~** tener
mala suerte
**unmarried** [ʌn'mærɪd] *adj* soltero
**unmistak(e)able** [ʌnmɪs'teɪkəbl] *adj*
inconfundible
**unnatural** [ʌn'nætʃrəl] *adj* (*gen*)
antinatural; (*manner*) afectado; (*habit*)
perverso
**unnecessary** [ʌn'nɛsəsərɪ] *adj*
innecesario, inútil
**UNO** ['juːnəu] *n abbr* (= *United Nations
Organization*) ONU *f*
**unofficial** [ʌnə'fɪʃl] *adj* no oficial; (*news*)
sin confirmar
**unpack** [ʌn'pæk] *vi* deshacer las maletas
⊳ *vt* deshacer
**unpaid** [ʌn'peɪd] *adj* (*bill, debt*) sin pagar,
impagado; (*Comm*) pendiente; (*holiday*) sin
sueldo; (*work*) sin pago, voluntario
**unpleasant** [ʌn'plɛznt] *adj* (*disagreeable*)
desagradable; (*person, manner*) antipático
**unplug** [ʌn'plʌg] *vt* desenchufar,
desconectar
**unpopular** [ʌn'pɔpjulə*] *adj* impopular,
poco popular
**unprecedented** [ʌn'prɛsɪdəntɪd] *adj* sin
precedentes
**unpredictable** [ʌnprɪ'dɪktəbl] *adj*
imprevisible
**unprotected** ['ʌnprə'tɛktɪd] *adj* (*sex*) sin
protección
**unqualified** [ʌn'kwɔlɪfaɪd] *adj* sin título,
no cualificado; (*success*) total

**unravel** [ʌnˈrævl] vt desenmarañar
**unreal** [ʌnˈrɪəl] adj irreal; (extraordinary) increíble
**unrealistic** [ʌnrɪəˈlɪstɪk] adj poco realista
**unreasonable** [ʌnˈriːznəbl] adj irrazonable; (demand) excesivo
**unrelated** [ʌnrɪˈleɪtɪd] adj sin relación; (family) no emparentado
**unreliable** [ʌnrɪˈlaɪəbl] adj (person) informal; (machine) poco fiable
**unrest** [ʌnˈrɛst] n inquietud f, malestar m; (Pol) disturbios mpl
**unroll** [ʌnˈrəʊl] vt desenrollar
**unruly** [ʌnˈruːlɪ] adj indisciplinado
**unsafe** [ʌnˈseɪf] adj peligroso
**unsatisfactory** [ˈʌnsætɪsˈfæktərɪ] adj poco satisfactorio
**unscrew** [ʌnˈskruː] vt destornillar
**unsettled** [ʌnˈsɛtld] adj inquieto, intranquilo; (weather) variable
**unsettling** [ʌnˈsɛtlɪŋ] adj perturbador(a), inquietante
**unsightly** [ʌnˈsaɪtlɪ] adj feo
**unskilled** [ʌnˈskɪld] adj (work) no especializado; (worker) no cualificado
**unspoiled** [ˈʌnˈspɔɪld], **unspoilt** [ˈʌnˈspɔɪlt] adj (place) que no ha perdido su belleza natural
**unstable** [ʌnˈsteɪbl] adj inestable
**unsteady** [ʌnˈstɛdɪ] adj inestable
**unsuccessful** [ʌnsəkˈsɛsful] adj (attempt) infructuoso; (writer, proposal) sin éxito; to be ~ (in attempting sth) no tener éxito, fracasar
**unsuitable** [ʌnˈsuːtəbl] adj inapropiado; (time) inoportuno
**unsure** [ʌnˈʃuə*] adj inseguro, poco seguro
**untidy** [ʌnˈtaɪdɪ] adj (room) desordenado; (appearance) desaliñado
**untie** [ʌnˈtaɪ] vt desatar
**until** [ənˈtɪl] prep hasta ▷ conj hasta que; ~ he comes hasta que venga; ~ now hasta ahora; ~ then hasta entonces
**untrue** [ʌnˈtruː] adj (statement) falso
**unused** [ʌnˈjuːzd] adj sin usar
**unusual** [ʌnˈjuːʒuəl] adj insólito, poco común; (exceptional) inusitado; **unusually** adv (exceptionally) excepcionalmente; **he arrived unusually early** llegó más temprano que de costumbre
**unveil** [ʌnˈveɪl] vt (statue) descubrir
**unwanted** [ʌnˈwɒntɪd] adj (clothing) viejo; (pregnancy) no deseado
**unwell** [ʌnˈwɛl] adj: **to be/feel ~** estar indispuesto/sentirse mal
**unwilling** [ʌnˈwɪlɪŋ] adj: **to be ~ to do sth** estar poco dispuesto a hacer algo
**unwind** [ʌnˈwaɪnd] (irreg) vt desenvolver ▷ vi (relax) relajarse

**unwise** [ʌnˈwaɪz] adj imprudente
**unwittingly** [ʌnˈwɪtɪŋlɪ] adv inconscientemente, sin darse cuenta
**unwrap** [ʌnˈræp] vt desenvolver
**unzip** [ʌnˈzɪp] vt abrir la cremallera de; (Comput) descomprimir

○ **KEYWORD**

**up** [ʌp] prep: **to go/be up sth** subir/estar subido en algo; **he went up the stairs/the hill** subió las escaleras/la colina; **we walked/climbed up the hill** subimos la colina; **they live further up the street** viven más arriba en la calle; **go up that road and turn left** sigue por esa calle y gira a la izquierda
▷ adv **1** (upwards, higher) más arriba; **up in the mountains** en lo alto (de la montaña); **put it a bit higher up** ponlo un poco más arriba or alto; **up there** ahí or allí arriba; **up above** en lo alto, por encima, arriba
**2**: **to be up** (out of bed) estar levantado; (prices, level) haber subido
**3**: **up to** (as far as) hasta; **up to now** hasta ahora or la fecha
**4**: **to be up to: it's up to you** (depending on) depende de ti; **he's not up to it** (job, task etc) no es capaz de hacerlo; **his work is not up to the required standard** su trabajo no da la talla; (inf: be doing): **what is he up to?** ¿que estará tramando?
▷ n: **ups and downs** altibajos mpl

**up-and-coming** [ʌpəndˈkʌmɪŋ] adj prometedor(a)
**upbringing** [ˈʌpbrɪŋɪŋ] n educación f
**update** [ʌpˈdeɪt] vt poner al día
**upfront** [ʌpˈfrʌnt] adj claro, directo ▷ adv a las claras; (pay) por adelantado; **to be ~ about sth** admitir algo claramente
**upgrade** [ʌpˈɡreɪd] vt (house) modernizar; (employee) ascender
**upheaval** [ʌpˈhiːvl] n trastornos mpl; (Pol) agitación f
**uphill** [ʌpˈhɪl] adj cuesta arriba; (fig: task) penoso, difícil ▷ adv: **to go ~** ir cuesta arriba
**upholstery** [ʌpˈhəʊlstərɪ] n tapicería
**upmarket** [ʌpˈmɑːkɪt] adj (product) de categoría
**upon** [əˈpɒn] prep sobre
**upper** [ˈʌpə*] adj superior, de arriba ▷ n (of shoe: also: ~s) empeine m; **upper-class** adj de clase alta
**upright** [ˈʌpraɪt] adj derecho; (vertical) vertical; (fig) honrado
**uprising** [ˈʌpraɪzɪŋ] n sublevación f
**uproar** [ˈʌprɔː*] n escándalo

**upset** [n 'ʌpsɛt, vb, adj ʌp'sɛt] n (to plan etc) revés m, contratiempo; (Med) trastorno ▷ vt irreg (glass etc) volcar; (plan) alterar; (person) molestar, disgustar ▷ adj molesto, disgustado; (stomach) revuelto

**upside-down** [ʌpsaɪd'daun] adv al revés; **to turn a place ~** (fig) revolverlo todo

**upstairs** [ʌp'stɛəz] adv arriba ▷ adj (room) de arriba ▷ n el piso superior

**up-to-date** ['ʌptə'deɪt] adj al día

**uptown** ['ʌptaun] (US) adv hacia las afueras ▷ adj exterior, de las afueras

**upward** ['ʌpwəd] adj ascendente; **upward(s)** adv hacia arriba; (more than): **upward(s) of** más de

**uranium** [juə'reɪnɪəm] n uranio

**Uranus** [juə'reɪnəs] n Urano

**urban** ['ə:bən] adj urbano

**urge** [ə:dʒ] n (desire) deseo ▷ vt: **to ~ sb to do sth** animar a algn a hacer algo

**urgency** ['ə:dʒənsɪ] n urgencia

**urgent** ['ə:dʒənt] adj urgente; (voice) perentorio

**urinal** ['juərɪnl] n (building) urinario; (vessel) orinal m

**urinate** ['juərɪneɪt] vi orinar

**urine** ['juərɪn] n orina, orines mpl

**US** n abbr (= United States) EE. UU.

**us** [ʌs] pron nos; (after prep) nosotros/as; see also **me**

**USA** n abbr (= United States (of America)) EE.UU.

**use** [n ju:s, vb ju:z] n uso, empleo; (usefulness) utilidad f ▷ vt usar, emplear; **she ~d to do it** (ella) solía or acostumbraba hacerlo; **in ~** en uso; **out of ~** en desuso; **to be of ~** servir; **it's no ~** (pointless) es inútil; (not useful) no sirve; **to be ~d to** estar acostumbrado a, acostumbrar; **use up** vt (food) consumir; (money) gastar; **used** [ju:zd] adj (car) usado; **useful** adj útil; **useless** adj (unusable) inservible; (pointless) inútil; (person) inepto; **user** n usuario/a; **user-friendly** adj (computer) amistoso

**usual** ['ju:ʒuəl] adj normal, corriente; **as ~** como de costumbre; **usually** adv normalmente

**utensil** [ju:'tɛnsl] n utensilio; **kitchen ~s** batería de cocina

**utility** [ju:'tɪlɪtɪ] n utilidad f; (public utility) (empresa de) servicio público

**utilize** ['ju:tɪlaɪz] vt utilizar

**utmost** ['ʌtməust] adj mayor ▷ n: **to do one's ~** hacer todo lo posible

**utter** ['ʌtə*] adj total, completo ▷ vt pronunciar, proferir; **utterly** adv completamente, totalmente

**U-turn** ['ju:'tə:n] n viraje m en redondo

# V

**v.** abbr = **verse; versus;** (= volt) v; (= vide) véase

**vacancy** ['veɪkənsɪ] n (BRIT: job) vacante f; (room) habitación f libre; **"no vacancies"** "completo"

**vacant** ['veɪkənt] adj desocupado, libre; (expression) distraído

**vacate** [və'keɪt] vt (house, room) desocupar; (job) dejar (vacante)

**vacation** [və'keɪʃən] n vacaciones fpl; **vacationer** (US **vacationist**) n turista m/f

**vaccination** [væksɪ'neɪʃən] n vacunación f

**vaccine** ['væksi:n] n vacuna

**vacuum** ['vækjum] n vacío; **vacuum cleaner** n aspiradora

**vagina** [və'dʒaɪnə] n vagina

**vague** [veɪg] adj vago; (memory) borroso; (ambiguous) impreciso; (person: absent-minded) distraído; (: evasive): **to be ~** no decir las cosas claramente

**vain** [veɪn] adj (conceited) presumido; (useless) vano, inútil; **in ~** en vano

**Valentine's Day** ['væləntaɪnzdeɪ] n día de los enamorados

**valid** ['vælɪd] adj válido; (ticket) valedero; (law) vigente

**valley** ['vælɪ] n valle m

**valuable** ['væljuəbl] adj (jewel) de valor; (time) valioso; **valuables** npl objetos mpl de valor

**value** ['vælju:] n valor m; (importance) importancia ▷ vt (fix price of) tasar, valorar; (esteem) apreciar; **values** npl (principles) principios mpl

**valve** [vælv] n válvula

**vampire** ['væmpaɪə*] n vampiro

**van** [væn] n (Aut) furgoneta, camioneta

**vandal** ['vændl] n vándalo/a; **vandalism** n vandalismo; **vandalize** vt dañar, destruir

**vanilla** [və'nɪlə] n vainilla

**vanish** ['vænɪʃ] vi desaparecer
**vanity** ['vænɪtɪ] n vanidad f
**vapour** ['veɪpə*] (us **vapor**) n vapor m; (on breath, window) vaho
**variable** ['vɛərɪəbl] adj variable
**variant** ['vɛərɪənt] n variante f
**variation** [vɛərɪ'eɪʃən] n variación f
**varied** ['vɛərɪd] adj variado
**variety** [və'raɪətɪ] n (diversity) diversidad f; (type) variedad f
**various** ['vɛərɪəs] adj (several: people) varios/as; (reasons) diversos/as
**varnish** ['vɑ:nɪʃ] n barniz m; (nail varnish) esmalte m ▷ vt barnizar; (nails) pintar (con esmalte)
**vary** ['vɛərɪ] vt variar; (change) cambiar ▷ vi variar
**vase** [vɑ:z] n jarrón m
▌ Be careful not to translate **vase** by the Spanish word vaso.
**Vaseline®** ['væsɪli:n] n vaselina®
**vast** [vɑ:st] adj enorme
**VAT** [væt] (BRIT) n abbr (= value added tax) IVA m
**vault** [vɔ:lt] n (of roof) bóveda; (tomb) panteón m; (in bank) cámara acorazada ▷ vt (also: ~ **over**) saltar (por encima de)
**VCR** n abbr = **video cassette recorder**
**VDU** n abbr (= visual display unit) UPV f
**veal** [vi:l] n ternera
**veer** [vɪə*] vi (vehicle) virar; (wind) girar
**vegan** ['vi:gən] n vegetariano/a estricto/a, vegetaliano/a
**vegetable** ['vɛdʒtəbl] n (Bot) vegetal m; (edible plant) legumbre f, hortaliza ▷ adj vegetal
**vegetarian** [vɛdʒɪ'tɛərɪən] adj, n vegetariano/a m/f
**vegetation** [vɛdʒɪ'teɪʃən] n vegetación f
**vehicle** ['vi:ɪkl] n vehículo; (fig) medio
**veil** [veɪl] n velo ▷ vt velar
**vein** [veɪn] n vena; (of ore etc) veta
**Velcro®** ['vɛlkrəu] n velcro® m
**velvet** ['vɛlvɪt] n terciopelo
**vending machine** ['vɛndɪŋ-] n distribuidor m automático
**vendor** ['vɛndə*] n vendedor(a) m/f; **street ~** vendedor(a) m/f callejero/a
**vengeance** ['vɛndʒəns] n venganza; **with a ~** (fig) con creces
**venison** ['vɛnɪsn] n carne f de venado
**venom** ['vɛnəm] n veneno; (bitterness) odio
**vent** [vɛnt] n (in jacket) respiradero; (in wall) rejilla (de ventilación) ▷ vt (fig: feelings) desahogar
**ventilation** [vɛntɪ'leɪʃən] n ventilación f
**venture** ['vɛntʃə*] n empresa ▷ vt

(opinion) ofrecer ▷ vi arriesgarse, lanzarse; **business ~** empresa comercial
**venue** ['vɛnju:] n lugar m
**Venus** ['vi:nəs] n Venus m
**verb** [və:b] n verbo; **verbal** adj verbal
**verdict** ['və:dɪkt] n veredicto, fallo; (fig) opinión f, juicio
**verge** [və:dʒ] (BRIT) n borde m; **"soft ~s"** (Aut) "arcén m no asfaltado"; **to be on the ~ of doing sth** estar a punto de hacer algo
**verify** ['vɛrɪfaɪ] vt comprobar, verificar
**versatile** ['və:sətaɪl] adj (person) polifacético; (machine, tool etc) versátil
**verse** [və:s] n poesía; (stanza) estrofa; (in bible) versículo
**version** ['və:ʃən] n versión f
**versus** ['və:səs] prep contra
**vertical** ['və:tɪkl] adj vertical
**very** ['vɛrɪ] adv muy ▷ adj: **the ~ book which** el mismo libro que; **the ~ last** el último de todos; **at the ~ least** al menos; **~ much** muchísimo
**vessel** ['vɛsl] n (ship) barco; (container) vasija; see **blood**
**vest** [vɛst] n (BRIT) camiseta; (us: waistcoat) chaleco
**vet** [vɛt] vt (candidate) investigar ▷ n abbr (BRIT) = **veterinary surgeon**
**veteran** ['vɛtərn] n excombatiente m/f, veterano/a
**veterinary surgeon** ['vɛtrɪnərɪ-] (us **veterinarian**) n veterinario/a m/f
**veto** ['vi:təu] (pl **~es**) n veto ▷ vt prohibir, poner el veto a
**via** ['vaɪə] prep por, por medio de
**viable** ['vaɪəbl] adj viable
**vibrate** [vaɪ'breɪt] vi vibrar
**vibration** [vaɪ'breɪʃən] n vibración f
**vicar** ['vɪkə*] n párroco (de la Iglesia Anglicana)
**vice** [vaɪs] n (evil) vicio; (Tech) torno de banco; **vice-chairman** (irreg) n vicepresidente m
**vice versa** ['vaɪsɪ'və:sə] adv viceversa
**vicinity** [vɪ'sɪnɪtɪ] n: **in the ~ (of)** cercano(a)
**vicious** ['vɪʃəs] adj (attack) violento; (words) cruel; (horse, dog) resabido
**victim** ['vɪktɪm] n víctima
**victor** ['vɪktə*] n vencedor(a) m/f
**Victorian** [vɪk'tɔ:rɪən] adj victoriano
**victorious** [vɪk'tɔ:rɪəs] adj vencedor(a)
**victory** ['vɪktərɪ] n victoria
**video** ['vɪdɪəu] n vídeo (SP), video (LAM); **video call** n videollamada; **video camera** n videocámara, cámara de vídeo; **video (cassette) recorder** n vídeo (SP), video (LAM); **video game** n videojuego;

**videophone** n videoteléfono; **video shop** n videoclub m; **video tape** n cinta de vídeo
**vie** [vaɪ] vi: **to ~ (with sb for sth)** competir (con algn por algo)
**Vienna** [vɪˈɛnə] n Viena
**Vietnam** [vjɛtˈnæm] n Vietnam m; **Vietnamese** [-nəˈmiːz] n inv, adj vietnamita mf
**view** [vjuː] n vista; (outlook) perspectiva; (opinion) opinión f, criterio ▷ vt (look at) mirar; (fig) considerar; **on ~** (in museum etc) expuesto; **in full ~ (of)** en plena vista (de); **in ~ of the weather/the fact that** en vista del tiempo/del hecho de que; **in my ~** en mi opinión; **viewer** n espectador(a) m/f; (TV) telespectador(a) m/f; **viewpoint** n (attitude) punto de vista; (place) mirador m
**vigilant** [ˈvɪdʒɪlənt] adj vigilante
**vigorous** [ˈvɪgərəs] adj enérgico, vigoroso
**vile** [vaɪl] adj vil, infame; (smell) asqueroso; (temper) endemoniado
**villa** [ˈvɪlə] n (country house) casa de campo; (suburban house) chalet m
**village** [ˈvɪlɪdʒ] n aldea; **villager** n aldeano/a
**villain** [ˈvɪlən] n (scoundrel) malvado/a; (in novel) malo; (BRIT: criminal) maleante mf
**vinaigrette** [vɪneɪˈgrɛt] n vinagreta
**vine** [vaɪn] n vid f
**vinegar** [ˈvɪnɪgə*] n vinagre m
**vineyard** [ˈvɪnjɑːd] n viña, viñedo
**vintage** [ˈvɪntɪdʒ] n (year) vendimia, cosecha ▷ cpd de época
**vinyl** [ˈvaɪnl] n vinilo
**viola** [vɪˈəʊlə] n (Mus) viola
**violate** [ˈvaɪəleɪt] vt violar
**violation** [vaɪəˈleɪʃən] n violación f; **in ~ of sth** en violación de algo
**violence** [ˈvaɪələns] n violencia
**violent** [ˈvaɪələnt] adj violento; (intense) intenso
**violet** [ˈvaɪələt] adj violado, violeta ▷ n (plant) violeta
**violin** [vaɪəˈlɪn] n violín m
**VIP** n abbr (= very important person) VIP m
**virgin** [ˈvəːdʒɪn] n virgen f
**Virgo** [ˈvəːgəʊ] n Virgo m
**virtual** [ˈvəːtjʊəl] adj virtual; **virtually** adv prácticamente; **virtual reality** n (Comput) mundo or realidad f virtual
**virtue** [ˈvəːtjuː] n virtud f; (advantage) ventaja; **by ~ of** en virtud de
**virus** [ˈvaɪərəs] n (also Comput) virus m inv
**visa** [ˈviːzə] n (also Comput) visado (SP), visa (LAM)
**vise** [vaɪs] (US) n (Tech) = **vice**
**visibility** [vɪzɪˈbɪlɪtɪ] n visibilidad f
**visible** [ˈvɪzəbl] adj visible
**vision** [ˈvɪʒən] n (sight) vista; (foresight, dream) visión f

**visit** [ˈvɪzɪt] n visita ▷ vt (person (US: also: ~ **with**)) visitar, hacer una visita a; (place) ir a, (ir a) conocer; **visiting hours** npl (in hospital etc) horas fpl de visita; **visitor** n (in museum) visitante mf; (invited to house) visita; (tourist) turista mf; **visitor centre** (US **visitor center**) n centro m de información
**visual** [ˈvɪzjʊəl] adj visual; **visualize** vt imaginarse
**vital** [ˈvaɪtl] adj (essential) esencial; (dynamic) dinámico; (organ) vital
**vitality** [vaɪˈtælɪtɪ] n energía, vitalidad f
**vitamin** [ˈvɪtəmɪn] n vitamina
**vivid** [ˈvɪvɪd] adj (account) gráfico; (light) intenso; (imagination, memory) vivo
**V-neck** [ˈviːnɛk] n cuello de pico
**vocabulary** [vəʊˈkæbjʊlərɪ] n vocabulario
**vocal** [ˈvəʊkl] adj vocal; (articulate) elocuente
**vocational** [vəʊˈkeɪʃənl] adj profesional
**vodka** [ˈvɔdkə] n vodka m
**vogue** [vəʊg] n: **in ~** en boga
**voice** [vɔɪs] n voz f ▷ vt expresar; **voice mail** n fonobuzón m
**void** [vɔɪd] n vacío; (hole) hueco ▷ adj (invalid) nulo, inválido; (empty): **~ of** carente or desprovisto de
**volatile** [ˈvɔlətaɪl] adj (situation) inestable; (person) voluble; (liquid) volátil
**volcano** [vɔlˈkeɪnəʊ] (pl **~es**) n volcán m
**volleyball** [ˈvɔlɪbɔːl] n vol(e)ibol m
**volt** [vəʊlt] n voltio; **voltage** n voltaje m
**volume** [ˈvɔljuːm] n (gen) volumen m; (book) tomo
**voluntarily** [ˈvɔləntrɪlɪ] adv libremente, voluntariamente
**voluntary** [ˈvɔləntərɪ] adj voluntario
**volunteer** [vɔlənˈtɪə*] n voluntario/a ▷ vt (information) ofrecer ▷ vi ofrecerse (de voluntario); **to ~ to do** ofrecerse a hacer
**vomit** [ˈvɔmɪt] n vómito ▷ vt, vi vomitar
**vote** [vəʊt] n voto; (votes cast) votación f; (right to vote) derecho de votar; (franchise) sufragio ▷ vt (chairman) elegir; (propose): **to ~ that** proponer que ▷ vi votar, ir a votar; **~ of thanks** voto de gracias; **voter** n votante mf; **voting** n votación f
**voucher** [ˈvaʊtʃə*] n (for meal etc) vale m
**vow** [vaʊ] n voto ▷ vt: **to ~ to do/that** jurar hacer/que
**vowel** [ˈvaʊəl] n vocal f
**voyage** [ˈvɔɪɪdʒ] n viaje m
**vulgar** [ˈvʌlgə*] adj (rude) ordinario, grosero; (in bad taste) de mal gusto
**vulnerable** [ˈvʌlnərəbl] adj vulnerable
**vulture** [ˈvʌltʃə*] n buitre m

**W**

**waddle** ['wɔdl] vi anadear
**wade** [weɪd] vi: **to ~ through** (water) vadear; (fig: book) leer con dificultad
**wafer** ['weɪfə*] n galleta, barquillo
**waffle** ['wɔfl] n (Culin) gofre m ⊳ vi dar el rollo
**wag** [wæg] vt menear, agitar ⊳ vi moverse, menearse
**wage** [weɪdʒ] n (also: **~s**) sueldo, salario ⊳ vt: **to ~ war** hacer la guerra
**wag(g)on** ['wægən] n (horse-drawn) carro; (BRIT Rail) vagón m
**wail** [weɪl] n gemido ⊳ vi gemir
**waist** [weɪst] n cintura, talle m; **waistcoat** (BRIT) n chaleco
**wait** [weɪt] n (interval) pausa ⊳ vi esperar; **to lie in ~ for** acechar a; **I can't ~ to** (fig) estoy deseando; **to ~ for** esperar (a); **wait on** vt fus servir a; **waiter** n camarero; **waiting list** n lista de espera; **waiting room** n sala de espera; **waitress** ['weɪtrɪs] n camarera
**waive** [weɪv] vt suspender
**wake** [weɪk] (pt **woke** or **~d**, pp **woken** or **~d**) vt (also: **~ up**) despertar ⊳ vi (also: **~ up**) despertarse ⊳ n (for dead person) vela, velatorio; (Naut) estela
**Wales** [weɪlz] n País m de Gales; **the Prince of ~** el príncipe de Gales
**walk** [wɔːk] n (stroll) paseo; (hike) excursión f a pie, caminata; (gait) paso, andar m; (in park etc) paseo, alameda ⊳ vi andar, caminar; (for pleasure, exercise) pasear ⊳ vt (distance) recorrer a pie, andar; (dog) pasear; **10 minutes' ~ from here** a 10 minutos de aquí andando; **people from all ~s of life** gente de todas las esferas; **walk out** vi (audience) salir; (workers) declararse en huelga; **walker** n (person) paseante mf, caminante mf; **walkie-talkie** ['wɔːkɪ'tɔːkɪ] n walkie-talkie m; **walking**

n el andar; **walking shoes** npl zapatos mpl para andar; **walking stick** n bastón m; **Walkman®** n Walkman® m; **walkway** n paseo
**wall** [wɔːl] n pared f; (exterior) muro; (city wall etc) muralla
**wallet** ['wɔlɪt] n cartera, billetera
**wallpaper** ['wɔːlpeɪpə*] n papel m pintado ⊳ vt empapelar
**walnut** ['wɔːlnʌt] n nuez f; (tree) nogal m
**walrus** ['wɔːlrəs] (pl **~** or **~es**) n morsa
**waltz** [wɔːlts] n vals m ⊳ vi bailar el vals
**wand** [wɔnd] n (also: **magic ~**) varita (mágica)
**wander** ['wɔndə*] vi (person) vagar; deambular; (thoughts) divagar ⊳ vt recorrer, vagar por
**want** [wɔnt] vt querer, desear; (need) necesitar ⊳ n: **for ~ of** por falta de; **wanted** adj (criminal) buscado; **"wanted"** (in advertisements) "se busca"
**war** [wɔː*] n guerra; **to make ~ (on)** declarar la guerra (a)
**ward** [wɔːd] n (in hospital) sala; (Pol) distrito electoral; (Law: child: also: **~ of court**) pupilo/a
**warden** ['wɔːdn] n (BRIT: of institution) director(a) m/f; (of park, game reserve) guardián/ana m/f; (BRIT: also: **traffic ~**) guardia mf
**wardrobe** ['wɔːdrəub] n armario, ropero; (clothes) vestuario
**warehouse** ['wɛəhaus] n almacén m, depósito
**warfare** ['wɔːfɛə*] n guerra
**warhead** ['wɔːhɛd] n cabeza armada
**warm** [wɔːm] adj caliente; (thanks) efusivo; (clothes etc) abrigado; (welcome, day) caluroso; **it's ~** hace calor; **I'm ~** tengo calor; **warm up** vi (room) calentarse; (person) entrar en calor; (athlete) hacer ejercicios de calentamiento ⊳ vt calentar; **warmly** adv afectuosamente; **warmth** n calor m
**warn** [wɔːn] vt avisar, advertir; **warning** n aviso, advertencia; **warning light** n luz f de advertencia
**warrant** ['wɔrnt] n autorización f; (Law: to arrest) orden f de detención; (: to search) mandamiento de registro
**warranty** ['wɔrəntɪ] n garantía
**warrior** ['wɔrɪə*] n guerrero/a
**Warsaw** ['wɔːsɔː] n Varsovia
**warship** ['wɔːʃɪp] n buque m or barco de guerra
**wart** [wɔːt] n verruga
**wartime** ['wɔːtaɪm] n: **in ~** en tiempos de guerra, en la guerra
**wary** ['wɛərɪ] adj cauteloso

**was** [wɔz] *pt of* **be**

**wash** [wɔʃ] *vt* lavar ▷ *vi* lavarse; (*sea etc*): **to ~ against/over sth** llegar hasta/cubrir algo ▷ *n* (*clothes etc*) lavado; (*of ship*) estela; **to have a ~** lavarse; **wash up** *vi* (*BRIT*) fregar los platos; (*US*) lavarse; **washbasin** (*US*) *n* lavabo; **wash cloth** (*US*) *n* manopla; **washer** *n* (*Tech*) arandela; **washing** *n* (*dirty*) ropa sucia; (*clean*) colada; **washing line** *n* cuerda de (colgar) la ropa; **washing machine** *n* lavadora; **washing powder** (*BRIT*) *n* detergente *m* (en polvo) **Washington** ['wɔʃɪŋtən] *n* Washington *m* **wash: washing-up** (*BRIT*) *n* fregado, platos *mpl* (para fregar); **washing-up liquid** (*BRIT*) *n* líquido lavavajillas; **washroom** (*US*) *n* servicios *mpl*

**wasn't** ['wɔznt] = **was not**

**wasp** [wɔsp] *n* avispa

**waste** [weɪst] *n* derroche *m*, despilfarro; (*of time*) pérdida; (*food*) sobras *fpl*; (*rubbish*) basura, desperdicios *mpl* ▷ *adj* (*material*) de desecho; (*left over*) sobrante; (*land*) baldío, descampado ▷ *vt* malgastar, derrochar; (*time*) perder; (*opportunity*) desperdiciar; **waste ground** (*BRIT*) *n* terreno baldío; **wastepaper basket** *n* papelera

**watch** [wɔtʃ] *n* (*also*: **wrist ~**) reloj *m*; (*Mil: group of guards*) centinela *m*; (*act*) vigilancia; (*Naut: spell of duty*) guardia ▷ *vt* (*look at*) mirar, observar; (: *match, programme*) ver; (*spy on, guard*) vigilar; (*be careful of*) cuidarse de, tener cuidado de ▷ *vi* ver, mirar; (*keep guard*) montar guardia; **watch out** *vi* cuidarse, tener cuidado; **watchdog** *n* perro guardián; (*fig*) persona u organismo encargado de asegurarse de que las empresasactúan dentro de la legalidad; **watch strap** *n* pulsera (de reloj)

**water** ['wɔːtə*] *n* agua ▷ *vt* (*plant*) regar ▷ *vi* (*eyes*) llorar; (*mouth*) hacerse la boca agua; **water down** *vt* (*milk etc*) aguar; (*fig: story*) dulcificar, diluir; **watercolour** (*US* **watercolor**) *n* acuarela; **watercress** *n* berro; **waterfall** *n* cascada, salto de agua; **watering can** *n* regadera; **watermelon** *n* sandía; **waterproof** *adj* impermeable; **water-skiing** *n* esquí *m* acuático

**watt** [wɔt] *n* vatio

**wave** [weɪv] *n* (*of hand*) señal *f* con la mano; (*on water*) ola; (*Radio, in hair*) onda; (*fig*) oleada ▷ *vi* agitar la mano; (*flag etc*) ondear ▷ *vt* (*handkerchief, gun*) agitar; **wavelength** *n* longitud *f* de onda

**waver** ['weɪvə*] *vi* (*voice, love etc*) flaquear; (*person*) vacilar

**wavy** ['weɪvɪ] *adj* ondulado

**wax** [wæks] *n* cera ▷ *vt* encerar ▷ *vi* (*moon*) crecer

**way** [weɪ] *n* camino; (*distance*) trayecto, recorrido; (*direction*) dirección *f*, sentido; (*manner*) modo, manera; (*habit*) costumbre *f*; **which ~? – this ~** ¿por dónde? or ¿en qué dirección? – por aquí; **on the ~** en (el) camino; **to be on one's ~** estar en camino; **to be in the ~** bloquear el camino; (*fig*) estorbar; **to go out of one's ~ to do sth** desvivirse por hacer algo; **under ~** en marcha; **to lose one's ~** extraviarse; **in a ~** en cierto modo *or* sentido; **no ~!** (*inf*) ¡de eso nada!; **by the ~ ...** a propósito ...; **"~ in"** (*BRIT*) "entrada"; **"~ out"** (*BRIT*) "salida"; **the ~ back** el camino de vuelta; **"give ~"** (*BRIT Aut*) "ceda el paso"

**W.C.** *n* (*BRIT*) wáter *m*

**we** [wiː] *pl pron* nosotros/as

**weak** [wiːk] *adj* débil, flojo; (*tea etc*) claro; **weaken** *vi* debilitarse; (*give way*) ceder ▷ *vt* debilitar; **weakness** *n* debilidad *f*; (*fault*) punto débil; **to have a weakness for** tener debilidad por

**wealth** [wɛlθ] *n* riqueza; (*of details*) abundancia; **wealthy** *adj* rico

**weapon** ['wɛpən] *n* arma; **~s of mass destruction** armas de destrucción masiva

**wear** [wɛə*] (*pt* **wore**, *pp* **worn**) *n* (*use*) uso; (*deterioration through use*) desgaste *m* ▷ *vt* (*clothes*) llevar; (*shoes*) calzar; (*damage: through use*) gastar, usar ▷ *vi* (*last*) durar; (*rub through etc*) desgastarse; **evening ~** ropa de etiqueta; **sports~/baby~** ropa de deportes/de niños; **wear off** *vi* (*pain etc*) pasar, desaparecer; **wear out** *vt* desgastar; (*person, strength*) agotar

**weary** ['wɪərɪ] *adj* cansado; (*dispirited*) abatido ▷ *vi*: **to ~ of** cansarse de

**weasel** ['wiːzl] *n* (*Zool*) comadreja

**weather** ['wɛðə*] *n* tiempo ▷ *vt* (*storm, crisis*) hacer frente a; **under the ~** (*fig: ill*) indispuesto, pachucho; **weather forecast** *n* boletín *m* meteorológico

**weave** [wiːv] (*pt* **wove**, *pp* **woven**) *vt* (*cloth*) tejer; (*fig*) entretejer

**web** [wɛb] *n* (*of spider*) telaraña; (*on duck's foot*) membrana; (*network*) red *f*; **the (World Wide) W~** la Red; **web address** *n* dirección *f* de Internet; **webcam** *n* webcam *f*; **web page** *n* (página) web *m* or *f*; **website** *n* sitio web

**Wed.** *abbr* (= *Wednesday*) miérc.

**wed** [wɛd] (*pt*, *pp* **~ded**) *vt* casar ▷ *vi* casarse

**we'd** [wiːd] = **we had; we would**

**wedding** ['wɛdɪŋ] *n* boda, casamiento; **silver/golden ~ (anniversary)** bodas *fpl* de plata/de oro; **wedding anniversary** *n* aniversario de boda;**wedding day** n día m de la boda;**wedding dress** n traje m de novia;**wedding ring** n alianza

**wedge** [wedʒ] n (of wood etc) cuña; (of cake) trozo ▷ vt acuñar; (push) apretar

**Wednesday** ['wednzdɪ] n miércoles m inv

**wee** [wi:] (SCOTTISH) adj pequeñito

**weed** [wi:d] n mala hierba, maleza ▷ vt escardar, desherbar;**weedkiller** n herbicida m

**week** [wi:k] n semana; **a ~ today/on Friday** de hoy/del viernes en ocho días;**weekday** n día m laborable; **weekend** n fin m de semana;**weekly** adv semanalmente, cada semana ▷ adj semanal ▷ n semanario

**weep** [wi:p] (pt, pp **wept**) vi, vt llorar

**weigh** [weɪ] vt, vi pesar; **to ~ anchor** levar anclas;**weigh up** vt sopesar

**weight** [weɪt] n peso; (metal weight) pesa; **to lose/put on ~** adelgazar/engordar; **weightlifting** n levantamiento de pesas

**weir** [wɪə*] n presa

**weird** [wɪəd] adj raro, extraño

**welcome** ['welkəm] adj bienvenido ▷ n bienvenida ▷ vt dar la bienvenida a; (be glad of) alegrarse de; **thank you – you're ~** gracias – de nada

**weld** [weld] n soldadura ▷ vt soldar

**welfare** ['welfeə*] n bienestar m; (social aid) asistencia social;**welfare state** n estado del bienestar

**well** [wel] n fuente f, pozo ▷ adv bien ▷ adj: **to be ~** estar bien (de salud) ▷ excl ¡vaya!, ¡bueno!; **as ~** también; **as ~ as** además de; **~ done!** ¡bien hecho!; **get ~ soon!** ¡que te mejores pronto!; **to do ~** (business) ir bien; (person) tener éxito

**we'll** [wi:l] = **we will; we shall**

**well: well-behaved** adj bueno;**well-built** adj (person) fornido;**well-dressed** adj bien vestido

**wellies** ['welɪz] (inf) npl (BRIT) botas de goma

**well: well-known** adj (person) conocido; **well-off** adj acomodado;**well-paid** [wel'peɪd] adj bien pagado, bien retribuido

**Welsh** [welʃ] adj galés/esa ▷ n (Ling) galés m;**Welshman** (irreg) n galés m; **Welshwoman** (irreg) n galesa

**went** [went] pt of **go**

**wept** [wept] pt, pp of **weep**

**were** [wə:*] pt of **be**

**we're** [wɪə*] = **we are**

**weren't** [wə:nt] = **were not**

**west** [west] n oeste m ▷ adj occidental, del oeste ▷ adv al or hacia el oeste; **the W~** el Oeste, el Occidente;**westbound**

['westbaund] adj (traffic, carriageway) con rumbo al oeste;**western** adj occidental ▷ n (Cinema) película del oeste;**West Indian** adj, n antillano/a m/f

**wet** [wet] adj (damp) húmedo; (soaked): **~ through** mojado; (rainy) lluvioso ▷ n (BRIT: Pol) conservador(a) m/f moderado/ a; **to get ~** mojarse; **"~ paint"** "recién pintado";**wetsuit** n traje m térmico

**we've** [wi:v] = **we have**

**whack** [wæk] vt dar un buen golpe a

**whale** [weɪl] n (Zool) ballena

**wharf** [wɔ:f] (pl **wharves**) n muelle m

○ KEYWORD

**what** [wɔt] adj 1 (in direct/indirect questions) qué; **what size is he?** ¿qué talla usa?; **what colour/shape is it?** ¿de qué color/forma es?
2 (in exclamations): **what a mess!** ¡qué desastre!; **what a fool I am!** ¡qué tonto soy!
▷ pron 1 (interrogative) qué; **what are you doing?** ¿qué haces or estás haciendo?; **what is happening?** ¿qué pasa or está pasando?; **what is it called?** ¿cómo se llama?; **what about me?** ¿y yo qué?; **what about doing ...?** ¿qué tal si hacemos ...?
2 (relative) lo que; **I saw what you did/was on the table** vi lo que hiciste/había en la mesa
▷ excl (disbelieving) ¡cómo!; **what, no coffee!** ¡que no hay café!

**whatever** [wɔt'evə*] adj: **~ book you choose** cualquier libro que elijas ▷ pron: **do ~ is necessary** haga lo que sea necesario; **~ happens** pase lo que pase; **no reason ~ or whatsoever** ninguna razón sea la que sea; **nothing ~** nada en absoluto

**whatsoever** [wɔtsəu'evə*] adj see **whatever**

**wheat** [wi:t] n trigo

**wheel** [wi:l] n rueda; (Aut: also: **steering ~**) volante m; (Naut) timón m ▷ vt (pram etc) empujar ▷ vi (also: **~ round**) dar la vuelta, girar;**wheelbarrow** n carretilla; **wheelchair** n silla de ruedas;**wheel clamp** n (Aut) cepo

**wheeze** [wi:z] vi resollar

○ KEYWORD

**when** [wen] adv cuando; **when did it happen?** ¿cuándo ocurrió?; **I know when it happened** sé cuándo ocurrió
▷ conj 1 (at, during, after the time that) cuando; **be careful when you cross the road** ten cuidado al cruzar la calle; **that**

was when I needed you fue entonces que
te necesité
2(*on, at which*): on the day when I met him
el día en qué le conocí
3(*whereas*) cuando

**whenever** [wɛn'ɛvə*] *conj* cuando; (*every
time that*) cada vez que ▷ *adv* cuando sea
**where** [wɛə*] *adv* dónde ▷ *conj* donde;
this is ~ aquí es donde; **whereabouts**
*adv* dónde ▷ *n*: **nobody knows his
whereabouts** nadie conoce su paradero;
**whereas** *conj* visto que, mientras;
**whereby** *pron* por lo cual; **wherever** *conj*
dondequiera que; (*interrogative*) dónde
**whether** ['wɛðə*] *conj* si; **I don't know ~
to accept or not** no sé si aceptar o no; **~ you
go or not** vayas o no vayas

○ **KEYWORD**

**which** [wɪtʃ] *adj* 1(*interrogative: direct,
indirect*) qué; **which picture(s) do you
want?** ¿qué cuadro(s) quieres?; **which one?**
¿cuál?
2 **in which case** en cuyo caso; **we got
there at 8 pm, by which time the cinema
was full** llegamos allí a las 8, cuando el cine
estaba lleno
▷ *pron* 1(*interrogative*) cuál; **I don't mind
which** el/la que sea
2(*relative: replacing noun*) que; (: *replacing
clause*) lo que; (: *after preposition*) (el(la)) que
etc el/la cual etc; **the apple which you
ate/which is on the table** la manzana que
comiste/que está en la mesa; **the chair on
which you are sitting** la silla en la que estás
sentado; **he said he knew, which is true/I
feared** dijo que lo sabía, lo cual or lo que es
cierto/me temía

**whichever** [wɪtʃ'ɛvə*] *adj*: **take ~ book
you prefer** coja (*sp*) el libro que prefiera; **~
book you take** cualquier libro que coja
**while** [waɪl] *n* rato, momento ▷ *conj*
mientras; (*although*) aunque; **for a ~** durante
algún tiempo
**whilst** [waɪlst] *conj* =**while**
**whim** [wɪm] *n* capricho
**whine** [waɪn] *n* (*of pain*) gemido; (*of engine*)
zumbido; (*of siren*) aullido ▷ *vi* gemir;
zumbar; (*fig: complain*) gimotear
**whip** [wɪp] *n* látigo; (*Pol: person*) encargado
de la disciplina partidaria en el parlamento
▷ *vt* azotar; (*Culin*) batir; (*move quickly*): **to ~
sth out/off** sacar/quitar algo de un tirón;
**whipped cream** *n* nata or crema montada
**whirl** [wə:l] *vt* hacer girar, dar vueltas

a ▷ *vi* girar, dar vueltas; (*leaves etc*)
arremolinarse
**whisk** [wɪsk] *n* (*Culin*) batidor *m* ▷ *vt*
(*Culin*) batir; **to ~ sb away or off** llevar
volando a algn
**whiskers** ['wɪskəz] *npl* (*of animal*) bigotes
*mpl*; (*of man*) patillas *fpl*
**whiskey** ['wɪskɪ] (*US, IRELAND*) *n* =**whisky**
**whisky** ['wɪskɪ] *n* whisky *m*
**whisper** ['wɪspə*] *n* susurro ▷ *vi*, *vt*
susurrar
**whistle** ['wɪsl] *n* (*sound*) silbido; (*object*)
silbato ▷ *vi* silbar
**white** [waɪt] *adj* blanco; (*pale*) pálido ▷ *n*
blanco; (*of egg*) clara; **whiteboard** *n* pizarra
blanca; **interactive whiteboard** pizarra
interactiva; **White House**(*us*) *n* Casa
Blanca; **whitewash** *n* (*paint*) jalbegue *m*,
cal *f* ▷ *vt* blanquear
**whiting** ['waɪtɪŋ] *n inv* (*fish*) pescadilla
**Whitsun** ['wɪtsn] *n* pentecostés *m*
**whittle** ['wɪtl] *vt*: **to ~ away, ~ down** ir
reduciendo
**whizz** [wɪz] *vi*: **to ~ past or by** pasar a toda
velocidad

○ **KEYWORD**

**who** [hu:] *pron* 1(*interrogative*) quién; **who
is it?, who's there?** ¿quién es?; **who are
you looking for?** ¿a quién buscas?; **I told
her who I was** le dije quién era yo
2(*relative*) que; **the man/woman who
spoke to me** el hombre/la mujer que habló
conmigo; **those who can swim** los que
saben or sepan nadar

**whoever** [hu:'ɛvə*] *pron*: **~ finds it**
cualquiera or quienquiera que lo encuentre;
**ask ~ you like** pregunta a quien quieras; **~
he marries** no importa con quién se case
**whole** [həul] *adj* (*entire*) todo, entero;
(*not broken*) intacto ▷ *n* todo; (*all*): **the
~ of the town** toda la ciudad, la ciudad
entera ▷ *n* (*total*) total *m*; (*sum*) conjunto;
**on the ~, as a ~** en general; **wholefood(s)**
*n*(*pl*) alimento(s) *m*(*pl*) integral(es);
**wholeheartedly** [həul'hɑ:tɪdlɪ] *adv* con
entusiasmo; **wholemeal** *adj* integral;
**wholesale** *n* venta al por mayor ▷ *adj* al
por mayor; (*fig: destruction*) sistemático;
**wholewheat** *adj* =**wholemeal**; **wholly**
*adv* totalmente, enteramente

○ **KEYWORD**

**whom** [hu:m] *pron* 1(*interrogative*):
**whom did you see?** ¿a quién viste?; **to**

**whom did you give it?** ¿a quién se lo diste?; **tell me from whom you received it** dígame de quién lo recibió
**2** (*relative*) que; **to whom** a quien(es); **of whom** de quien(es), del/de la que *etc*; **the man whom I saw/to whom I wrote** el hombre que vi/a quien escribí; **the lady about/with whom I was talking** la señora de (la) que/con quien *or* (la) que hablaba

**whore** [hɔː*] (*inf, pej*) *n* puta

○ **KEYWORD**

**whose** [huːz] *adj* **1** (*possessive: interrogative*) : **whose book is this?, whose is this book?** ¿de quién es este libro?; **whose pencil have you taken?** ¿de quién es el lápiz que has cogido?; **whose daughter are you?** ¿de quién eres hija?
**2** (*possessive: relative*) cuyo/a, *pl* cuyos/as; **the man whose son you rescued** el hombre cuyo hijo rescataste; **those whose passports I have** aquellas personas cuyos pasaportes tengo; **the woman whose car was stolen** la mujer a quien le robaron el coche ▷ *pron* de quién; **whose is this?** ¿de quién es esto?; **I know whose it is** sé de quién es

○ **KEYWORD**

**why** [waɪ] *adv* por qué; **why not?** ¿por qué no?; **why not do it now?** ¿por qué no lo haces (*or* hacemos *etc*) ahora? ▷ *conj*: **I wonder why he said that** me pregunto por qué dijo eso; **that's not why I'm here** no es por eso (por lo) que estoy aquí; **the reason why** la razón por la que
▷ *excl* (*expressing surprise, shock, annoyance*) ¡hombre!, ¡vaya!; (*explaining*): **why, it's you!** ¡hombre, eres tú!; **why, that's impossible** ¡pero sí eso es imposible!

**wicked** ['wɪkɪd] *adj* malvado, cruel
**wicket** ['wɪkɪt] *n* (*Cricket: stumps*) palos *mpl*; (: *grass area*) terreno de juego
**wide** [waɪd] *adj* ancho; (*area, knowledge*) vasto, grande; (*choice*) amplio ▷ *adv*: **to open ~** abrir de par en par; **to shoot ~** errar el tiro; **widely** *adv* (*travelled*) mucho; (*spaced*) muy; **it is widely believed/known that ...** mucha gente piensa/sabe que ...; **widen** *vt* ensanchar; (*experience*) ampliar ▷ *vi* ensancharse; **wide open** *adj* abierto de par en par; **widespread** *adj* extendido, general

**widow** ['wɪdəu] *n* viuda; **widower** *n* viudo
**width** [wɪdθ] *n* anchura; (*of cloth*) ancho
**wield** [wiːld] *vt* (*sword*) blandir; (*power*) ejercer
**wife** [waɪf] (*pl* **wives**) *n* mujer *f*, esposa
**wig** [wɪg] *n* peluca
**wild** [waɪld] *adj* (*animal*) salvaje; (*plant*) silvestre; (*person*) furioso, violento; (*idea*) descabellado; (*rough: sea*) bravo; (: *land*) agreste; (: *weather*) muy revuelto; **wilderness** ['wɪldənɪs] *n* desierto; **wildlife** *n* fauna; **wildly** *adv* (*behave*) locamente; (*lash out*) a diestro y siniestro; (*guess*) a lo loco; (*happy*) a más no poder

○ **KEYWORD**

**will** [wɪl] *aux vb* **1** (*forming future tense*): **I will finish it tomorrow** lo terminaré *or* voy a terminar mañana; **I will have finished it by tomorrow** lo habré terminado para mañana; **will you do it? – yes I will/no I won't** ¿lo harás? – sí/no
**2** (*in conjectures, predictions*): **he will** *or* **he'll be there by now** ya habrá *or* debe (de) haber llegado; **that will be the postman** será *or* debe ser el cartero
**3** (*in commands, requests, offers*): **will you be quiet!** ¿quieres callarte?; **will you help me?** ¿quieres ayudarme?; **will you have a cup of tea?** ¿te apetece un té?; **I won't put up with it!** ¡no lo soporto! ▷ *vt* (*pt, pp* **willed**): **to will sb to do sth** desear que algn haga algo; **he willed himself to go on** con gran fuerza de voluntad, continuó
▷ *n* voluntad *f*; (*testament*) testamento

**willing** ['wɪlɪŋ] *adj* (*with goodwill*) de buena voluntad; (*enthusiastic*) entusiasta; **he's ~ to do it** está dispuesto a hacerlo; **willingly** *adv* con mucho gusto
**willow** ['wɪləu] *n* sauce *m*
**willpower** ['wɪlpauə*] *n* fuerza de voluntad
**wilt** [wɪlt] *vi* marchitarse
**win** [wɪn] (*pt, pp* **won**) *n* victoria, triunfo ▷ *vt* ganar; (*obtain*) conseguir, lograr ▷ *vi* ganar; **win over** *vt* convencer a
**wince** [wɪns] *vi* encogerse
**wind¹** [wɪnd] *n* viento; (*Med*) gases *mpl* ▷ *vt* (*take breath away from*) dejar sin aliento a
**wind²** [waɪnd] (*pt, pp* **wound**) *vt* enrollar; (*wrap*) envolver; (*clock, toy*) dar cuerda a ▷ *vi* (*road, river*) serpentear; **wind down** *vt* (*car window*) bajar; (*fig: production, business*) disminuir; **wind up** *vt* (*clock*) dar cuerda a; (*debate, meeting*) concluir, terminar

**windfall** ['wɪndfɔːl] n golpe m de
suerte

**winding** ['waɪndɪŋ] adj (road) tortuoso;
(staircase) de caracol

**windmill** ['wɪndmɪl] n molino de viento

**window** ['wɪndəu] n ventana; (in car, train)
ventanilla; (in shop etc) escaparate m (SP),
vidriera (LAM); **window box** n jardinera
de ventana; **window cleaner** n (person)
limpiacristales mf inv; **window pane** n
cristal m; **window seat** n asiento junto a la
ventana; **windowsill** n alféizar m, repisa

**windscreen** ['wɪndskriːn] (US **windshield**)
n parabrisas m inv; **windscreen wiper** (US
**windshield wiper**) n limpiaparabrisas
m inv

**windsurfing** ['wɪndsəːfɪŋ] n windsurf m

**windy** ['wɪndɪ] adj de mucho viento; **it's**
**~** hace viento

**wine** [waɪn] n vino; **wine bar** n enoteca;
**wine glass** n copa (para vino); **wine list** n
lista de vinos; **wine tasting** n degustación
f de vinos

**wing** [wɪŋ] n ala; (Aut) aleta; **wing mirror**
n (espejo) retrovisor m

**wink** [wɪŋk] n guiño, pestañeo ▷ vi
guiñar, pestañear

**winner** ['wɪnə*] n ganador(a) m/f

**winning** ['wɪnɪŋ] adj (team) ganador(a);
(goal) decisivo; (smile) encantador(a)

**winter** ['wɪntə*] n invierno ▷ vi invernar;
**winter sports** npl deportes mpl de
invierno; **wintertime** n invierno

**wipe** [waɪp] n: **to give sth a ~** pasar un
trapo sobre algo ▷ vt limpiar; (tape) borrar;
**wipe out** vt (debt) liquidar; (memory) borrar;
(destroy) destruir; **wipe up** vt limpiar

**wire** ['waɪə*] n alambre m; (Elec) cable m
(eléctrico); (Tel) telegrama m ▷ vt (house)
poner la instalación eléctrica en;
(also: **~ up**) conectar; (person: telegram)
telegrafiar

**wiring** ['waɪərɪŋ] n instalación f
eléctrica

**wisdom** ['wɪzdəm] n sabiduría, saber
m; (good sense) cordura; **wisdom tooth** n
muela del juicio

**wise** [waɪz] adj sabio; (sensible) juicioso

**wish** [wɪʃ] n deseo ▷ vt querer; **best ~es**
(on birthday etc) felicidades fpl; **with best**
**~es** (in letter) saludos mpl, recuerdos mpl; **to**
**~ sb goodbye** despedirse de algn; **he ~ed**
**me well** me deseó mucha suerte; **to ~ to**
**do/sb to do sth** querer hacer/que algn haga
algo; **to ~ for** desear

**wistful** ['wɪstful] adj pensativo

**wit** [wɪt] n ingenio, gracia; (also: **~s**)
inteligencia; (person) chistoso/a

**witch** [wɪtʃ] n bruja

○ **KEYWORD**

**with** [wɪð, wɪθ] prep **1** (accompanying, in
the company of) con (con +mí, ti, sí = conmigo,
contigo, consigo); **I was with him** estaba con
él; **we stayed with friends** nos quedamos
en casa de unos amigos; **I'm (not) with you**
(don't understand) (no) te entiendo; **to be**
**with it** (inf: person: up-to-date) estar al tanto;
(: alert) ser despabilado
**2** (descriptive, indicating manner etc) con; de;
**a room with a view** una habitación con
vistas; **the man with blue eyes** el hombre
de los ojos azules; **red with anger** rojo de
ira; **to shake with fear** temblar de miedo;
**to fill sth with water** llenar algo de agua

**withdraw** [wɪθ'drɔː] vt retirar, sacar ▷ vi
retirarse; **to ~ money (from the bank)**
retirar fondos (del banco); **withdrawal** n
retirada; (of money) reintegro; **withdrawn**
pp of **withdraw** ▷ adj (person) reservado,
introvertido

**withdrew** [wɪθ'druː] pt of **withdraw**

**wither** ['wɪðə*] vi marchitarse

**withhold** [wɪθ'həuld] vt (money) retener;
(decision) aplazar; (permission) negar;
(information) ocultar

**within** [wɪð'ɪn] prep dentro de ▷ adv
dentro; **~ reach (of)** al alcance (de); **~ sight**
**(of)** a la vista (de); **~ the week** antes de
acabar la semana; **~ a mile (of)** a menos de
una milla (de)

**without** [wɪð'aut] prep sin; **to go ~ sth**
pasar sin algo

**withstand** [wɪθ'stænd] vt resistir a

**witness** ['wɪtnɪs] n testigo mf ▷ vt
(event) presenciar; (document) atestiguar
la veracidad de; **to bear ~ to** (fig) ser
testimonio de

**witty** ['wɪtɪ] adj ingenioso

**wives** [waɪvz] npl of **wife**

**wizard** ['wɪzəd] n hechicero

**wk** abbr = **week**

**wobble** ['wɔbl] vi temblar; (chair) cojear

**woe** [wəu] n desgracia

**woke** [wəuk] pt of **wake**

**woken** ['wəukən] pp of **wake**

**wolf** [wulf] n lobo

**woman** ['wumən] (pl **women**) n mujer f

**womb** [wuːm] n matriz f, útero

**won** [wʌn] pt, pp of **win**

**wonder** ['wʌndə*] n maravilla, prodigio;
(feeling) asombro ▷ vi: **to ~ whether/why**
preguntarse si/por qué; **to ~ at** asombrarse
de; **to ~ about** pensar sobre or en; **it's no**

**~ (that)** no es de extrañarse (que +*subjun*);
**wonderful** *adj* maravilloso
**won't** [wəʊnt] = **will not**
**wood** [wʊd] *n* (*timber*) madera; (*forest*)
bosque *m*; **wooden** *adj* de madera;
**woodwind** *n* (*Mus*) instrumentos *mpl*
de viento de madera; **woodwork** *n*
carpintería
**wool** [wʊl] *n* lana; **to pull the ~ over sb's
eyes** (*fig*) engatusar a algn; **woollen** (*us*
**woolen**) *adj* de lana; **woolly** (*us* **wooly**) *adj*
lanudo, de lana; (*fig*: *ideas*) confuso
**word** [wəːd] *n* palabra; (*news*) noticia;
(*promise*) palabra (de honor) ▷ *vt* redactar;
**in other ~s** en otras palabras; **to break/
keep one's ~** faltar a la palabra/cumplir la
promesa; **to have ~s with sb** reñir con algn;
**word processing** *n* proceso de textos;
**word processor** *n* procesador *m* de textos
**wore** [wɔː*] *pt of* **wear**
**work** [wəːk] *n* trabajo; (*job*) empleo,
trabajo; (*Art, Literature*) obra ▷ *vi* trabajar;
(*mechanism*) funcionar, marchar; (*medicine*)
ser eficaz, surtir efecto ▷ *vt* (*shape*)
trabajar; (*stone etc*) tallar; (*mine etc*) explotar;
(*machine*) manejar, hacer funcionar ▷ *npl*
(*of clock, machine*) mecanismo; **to be out
of ~** estar parado, no tener trabajo; **to ~
loose** (*part*) desprenderse; (*knot*) aflojarse;
**works** *n* (*BRIT: factory*) fábrica; **work out**
*vi* (*plans etc*) salir bien, funcionar; **works**
*vt* (*problem*) resolver; (*plan*) elaborar;
**it works out at £100** suma 100 libras;
**worker** *n* trabajador(a) *m/f*, obrero/a;
**work experience** *n*: **I'm going to do my
work experience in a factory** voy a hacer
las prácticas en una fábrica; **workforce**
*n* mano de obra; **working class** *n* clase
f obrera ▷ *adj*: **working-class** obrero;
**working week** *n* semana laboral;
**workman** (*irreg*) *n* obrero; **work of art** *n*
obra de arte; **workout** *n* (*Sport*) sesión f
de ejercicios; **work permit** *n* permiso de
trabajo; **workplace** *n* lugar *m* de trabajo;
**worksheet** *n* (*Scol*) hoja de ejercicios;
**workshop** *n* taller *m*; **work station** *n*
puesto *or* estación f de trabajo; **work
surface** *n* encimera; **worktop** *n* encimera
**world** [wəːld] *n* mundo ▷ *cpd* (*champion*)
del mundo; (*power, war*) mundial; **to think
the ~ of sb** (*fig*) tener un concepto muy alto
de algn; **World Cup** *n* (*Football*): **the World
Cup** el Mundial, los Mundiales; **world-wide**
*adj* mundial, universal; **World-Wide Web**
*n*: **the World-Wide Web** el World Wide Web
**worm** [wəːm] *n* (*also*: **earth ~**) lombriz f
**worn** [wɔːn] *pp of* **wear** ▷ *adj* usado;
**worn-out** *adj* (*object*) gastado; (*person*)

rendido, agotado
**worried** ['wʌrɪd] *adj* preocupado
**worry** ['wʌrɪ] *n* preocupación f ▷ *vt*
preocupar, inquietar ▷ *vi* preocuparse;
**worrying** *adj* inquietante
**worse** [wəːs] *adj, adv* peor ▷ *n* lo peor;
**a change for the ~** un empeoramiento;
**worsen** *vt, vi* empeorar; **worse off** *adj*
(*financially*): **to be worse off** tener menos
dinero; (*fig*): **you'll be worse off this way**
de esta forma estarás peor que nunca
**worship** ['wəːʃɪp] *n* adoración f ▷ *vt*
adorar; **Your W~** (*BRIT: to mayor*) señor
alcalde; (: *to judge*) señor juez
**worst** [wəːst] *adj, adv* peor ▷ *n* lo peor; **at
~** en lo peor de los casos
**worth** [wəːθ] *n* valor *m* ▷ *adj*: **to be ~**
valer; **it's ~ it** vale *or* merece la pena; **to be ~
one's while (to do)** merecer la pena (hacer);
**worthless** *adj* sin valor; (*useless*) inútil;
**worthwhile** *adj* (*activity*) que merece la
pena; (*cause*) loable
**worthy** ['wəːði] *adj* respetable; (*motive*)
honesto; **~ of** digno de

○ **KEYWORD**

**would** [wʊd] *aux vb* **1** (*conditional tense*): **if
you asked him he would do it** si se lo
pidieras, lo haría; **if you had asked him
he would have done it** si se lo hubieras
pedido, lo habría *or* hubiera hecho
**2** (*in offers, invitations, requests*): **would you
like a biscuit?** ¿quieres una galleta?; (*formal*)
¿querría una galleta?; **would you ask him
to come in?** ¿quiere hacerle pasar?; **would
you open the window please?** ¿quiere *or*
podría abrir la ventana, por favor?
**3** (*in indirect speech*): **I said I would do it** dije
que lo haría
**4** (*emphatic*): **it would have to snow today!**
¡tenía que nevar precisamente hoy!
**5** (*insistence*): **she wouldn't behave** no
quiso comportarse bien
**6** (*conjecture*): **it would have been midnight**
sería medianoche; **it would seem so** parece
ser que sí
**7** (*indicating habit*): **he would go there on
Mondays** iba allí los lunes

**wouldn't** ['wʊdnt] = **would not**
**wound¹** [wuːnd] *n* herida ▷ *vt* herir
**wound²** [waʊnd] *pt, pp of* **wind²**
**wove** [wəʊv] *pt of* **weave**
**woven** ['wəʊvən] *pp of* **weave**
**wrap** [ræp] *vt* (*also*: **~ up**) envolver;
(*gift*) envolver, abrigar ▷ *vi* (*dress warmly*)
abrigarse; **wrapper** *n* (*on chocolate*) papel

m; (BRIT: of book) sobrecubierta; **wrapping**
n envoltura, envase m; **wrapping paper**
n papel m de envolver; (fancy) papel m de
regalo

**wreath** [ri:ð, pl ri:ðz] n (funeral wreath)
corona

**wreck** [rɛk] n (ship: destruction) naufragio;
(: remains) restos mpl del barco; (pej: person)
ruina ▷ vt (car etc) destrozar; (chances)
arruinar; **wreckage** n restos mpl; (of
building) escombros mpl

**wren** [rɛn] n (Zool) reyezuelo

**wrench** [rɛntʃ] n (Tech) llave f inglesa; (tug)
tirón m; (fig) dolor m ▷ vt arrancar; **to ~
sth from sb** arrebatar algo violentamente
a algn

**wrestle** ['rɛsl] vi: **to ~ (with sb)** luchar (con
or contra algn); **wrestler** n luchador(a) m/f
(de lucha libre); **wrestling** n lucha libre

**wretched** ['rɛtʃɪd] adj miserable

**wriggle** ['rɪgl] vi (also: ~ **about**) menearse,
retorcerse

**wring** [rɪŋ] (pt, pp **wrung**) vt retorcer;
(wet clothes) escurrir; (fig): **to ~ sth out of sb**
sacar algo por la fuerza a algn

**wrinkle** ['rɪŋkl] n arruga ▷ vt arrugar ▷ vi
arrugarse

**wrist** [rɪst] n muñeca

**writable** ['raɪtəbl] adj (CD, DVD) escribible

**write** [raɪt] (pt **wrote**, pp **written**) vt
escribir; (cheque) extender ▷ vi escribir;
**write down** vt escribir; (note) apuntar;
**write off** vt (debt) borrar (como
incobrable); (fig) desechar por inútil; **write
out** vt escribir; **write-off** n siniestro total;
**writer** n escritor(a) m/f

**writing** ['raɪtɪŋ] n escritura; (hand-writing)
letra; (of author) obras fpl; **in ~** por escrito;
**writing paper** n papel m de escribir

**written** ['rɪtn] pp of **write**

**wrong** [rɔŋ] adj (wicked) malo; (unfair)
injusto; (incorrect) equivocado, incorrecto;
(not suitable) inoportuno, inconveniente;
(reverse) del revés ▷ adv equivocadamente
▷ n injusticia ▷ vt ser injusto con; **you
are ~ to do it** haces mal en hacerlo; **you
are ~ about that, you've got it ~** en eso
estás equivocado; **to be in the ~** no tener
razón, tener la culpa; **what's ~?** ¿qué pasa?;
**to go ~** (person) equivocarse; (plan) salir
mal; (machine) estropearse; **wrongly** adv
mal, incorrectamente; (by mistake) por
error; **wrong number** n (Tel): **you've got
the wrong number** se ha equivocado de
número

**wrote** [rəʊt] pt of **write**

**wrung** [rʌŋ] pt, pp of **wring**

**WWW** n abbr (= World Wide Web) WWW m

**XL** abbr = **extra large**

**Xmas** ['ɛksməs] n abbr = **Christmas**

**X-ray** ['ɛksreɪ] n radiografía ▷ vt
radiografiar, sacar radiografías de

**xylophone** ['zaɪləfəʊn] n xilófono

# Y

**yacht** [jɔt] n yate m; **yachting** n (sport) balandrismo

**yard** [jɑːd] n patio; (measure) yarda; **yard sale** (US) n venta de objetos usados (en el jardín de una casa particular)

**yarn** [jɑːn] n hilo; (tale) cuento, historia

**yawn** [jɔːn] n bostezo ▷ vi bostezar

**yd.** abbr (= yard) yda

**yeah** [jɛə] (inf) adv sí

**year** [jɪə*] n año; **to be 8 ~s old** tener 8 años; **an eight-~-old child** un niño de ocho años (de edad); **yearly** adj anual ▷ adv anualmente, cada año

**yearn** [jəːn] vi: **to ~ for sth** añorar algo, suspirar por algo

**yeast** [jiːst] n levadura

**yell** [jɛl] n grito, alarido ▷ vi gritar

**yellow** ['jɛləu] adj amarillo; **Yellow Pages®** npl páginas fpl amarillas

**yes** [jɛs] adv sí ▷ n sí m; **to say/answer ~** decir/contestar que sí

**yesterday** ['jɛstədɪ] adv ayer ▷ n ayer m; **~ morning/evening** ayer por la mañana/tarde; **all day ~** todo el día de ayer

**yet** [jɛt] adv ya; (negative) todavía ▷ conj sin embargo, a pesar de todo; **it is not finished ~** todavía no está acabado; **the best ~** el/la mejor hasta ahora; **as ~** hasta ahora, todavía

**yew** [juː] n tejo

**Yiddish** ['jɪdɪʃ] n yiddish m

**yield** [jiːld] n (Agr) cosecha; (Comm) rendimiento ▷ vt ceder; (results) producir, dar; (profit) rendir ▷ vi rendirse, ceder; (US Aut) ceder el paso

**yob(bo)** ['jɔb(bəu)] n (BRIT inf) gamberro

**yoga** ['jəugə] n yoga m

**yog(h)ourt** ['jəugət] n yogur m

**yog(h)urt** ['jəugət] n = **yog(h)ourt**

**yolk** [jəuk] n yema (de huevo)

○ **KEYWORD**

**you** [juː] pron **1** (subject: familiar) tú; (pl) vosotros/as (SP), ustedes (LAM); (polite) usted; (pl) ustedes; **you are very kind** eres/es etc muy amable; **you Spanish enjoy your food** a vosotros (or ustedes) los españoles os (or les) gusta la comida; **you and I will go** iremos tú y yo

**2** (object: direct: familiar) te; (pl) os (SP), les (LAM); (polite) le; (pl) les; (f) la; (pl) las; **I know you** te/le etc conozco

**3** (object: indirect: familiar) te; (pl) os (SP), les (LAM); (polite) le; (pl) les; **I gave the letter to you yesterday** te/os etc di la carta ayer

**4** (stressed): **I told you to do it** te dije a ti que lo hicieras, es a ti a quien dije que lo hicieras; see also **3; 5**

**5** (after prep: NB: con +ti = contigo: familiar) ti; (pl) vosotros/as (SP), ustedes (LAM); (: polite) usted; (pl) ustedes; **it's for you** es para ti/vosotros etc

**6** (comparisons: familiar) tú; (pl) vosotros/as (SP), ustedes (LAM); (: polite) usted; (pl) ustedes; **she's younger than you** es más joven que tú/vosotros etc

**7** (impersonal one): **fresh air does you good** el aire puro (te) hace bien; **you never know** nunca se sabe; **you can't do that!** ¡eso no se hace!

**you'd** [juːd] = **you had; you would**

**you'll** [juːl] = **you will; you shall**

**young** [jʌŋ] adj joven ▷ npl (of animal) cría; (people): **the ~** los jóvenes, la juventud; **youngster** n joven mf

**your** [jɔː*] adj tu; (pl) vuestro; (formal) su; see also **my**

**you're** [juə*] = **you are**

**yours** [jɔːz] pron tuyo (pl), vuestro; (formal) suyo; see also **faithfully; mine¹** see also **sincerely**

**yourself** [jɔːˈsɛlf] pron tú mismo; (complement) te; (after prep) ti (mismo); (formal) usted mismo; (: complement) se; (: after prep) sí (mismo); **yourselves** pl pron vosotros mismos; (after prep) vosotros (mismos); (formal) ustedes (mismos); (: complement) se; (: after prep) sí mismos; see also **oneself**

**youth** [pl juːðz n juventud f; (young man) joven m; **youth club** n club m juvenil; **youthful** adj juvenil; **youth hostel** n albergue m de juventud

**you've** [juːv] = **you have**

# Z

**zeal** [ziːl] *n* celo, entusiasmo
**zebra** ['ziːbrə] *n* cebra; **zebra crossing** (*BRIT*) *n* paso de peatones
**zero** ['zɪərəu] *n* cero
**zest** [zɛst] *n* ánimo, vivacidad *f*; (*of orange*) piel *f*
**zigzag** ['zɪgzæg] *n* zigzag *m* ▷ *vi* zigzaguear, hacer eses
**Zimbabwe** [zɪm'bɑːbwɪ] *n* Zimbabwe *m*
**zinc** [zɪŋk] *n* cinc *m*, zinc *m*
**zip** [zip] *n* (*also:* **~ fastener,** (*US*) **~per**) cremallera (*SP*), cierre (*AM*), zíper *m* (*MEX, CAM*) ▷ *vt* (*also:* **~ up**) cerrar la cremallera de; (*file*) comprimir; **zip code** (*US*) *n* código postal; **zip file** *n* (*Comput*) archivo comprimido; **zipper** (*US*) *n* cremallera
**zit** [zɪt] *n* grano
**zodiac** ['zəudiæk] *n* zodíaco
**zone** [zəun] *n* zona
**zoo** [zuː] *n* (jardín *m*) zoo *m*
**zoology** [zuˈɔlədʒɪ] *n* zoología
**zoom** [zuːm] *vi:* **to ~ past** pasar zumbando; **zoom lens** *n* zoom *m*
**zucchini** [zuːˈkiːnɪ] (*US*) *n(pl)* calabacín(ines) *m(pl)*